North Carolina in the American Revolution:

A Source Guide for Genealogists and Historians

by

Eric G. Grundset

for
The National Society
Daughters of the American Revolution

DAR Source Guides on the American Revolution Series
No. 7

TABLE OF CONTENTS

Acknowledgments

The unnamed catalogers of the major North Carolina and Tennessee research centers and of other institutions as well, for their helpful cataloging descriptions of innumerable manuscript collections and publications. Many of these descriptions have been quoted and incorporated into this source guide as the best descriptions of materials available.

Pamela Baster, Publications Assistant, DAR Library, for excellent assistance with locating sources for inclusion and for fact-checking, proofreading, and indexing. She has produced an exceptional amount of superb content for this publication, all of it of high quality and informative.

Adam F. Yacovissi, Reference Assistant, DAR Library, for assistance with locating sources for inclusion and for fact-checking, proofreading, and indexing.

Forest C. Crosley, Assistant Director for Supplementals, Office of the Registrar General, National Society Daughters of the American Revolution, for continual advice, reminders, and assistance with details during the process of preparing this publication.

Penelope L. Secord, Staff Genealogist, Office of the Registrar General, National Society Daughters of the American Revolution, for contribution of the chronology and analysis concerning North Carolina Land Grants in Tennessee.

Elizabeth M. Hopkins, Genealogical Records Committee Assistant, DAR Library; Dennis L. Simpson, Research Assistant, DAR Library, for proofreading and indexing.

Marilyn Gabriel Mills, Staff Genealogist/Supplemental Team Leader, Genealogy Office, Office of the Registrar General, National Society Daughters of the American Revolution, for assistance the interpretation and use of certain North Carolina records.

Bevin J. Creel and Austin Spencer, Staff Genealogists, Office of the Registrar General, National Society Daughters of the American Revolution, for assistance with fact checking, for providing obscure details about the use of some records, and for indexing.

Henry B. Hoff, Editor, *New England Historical and Genealogical Register*, for help with research and indexing.

Donna Rhyne, Lineage Research Chairman, North Carolina Daughters of the American Revolution, for assistance in locating finding aids and other materials.

Edith Rianzares, Printing and Publications Manager, NSDAR, has been of inestimable assistance and support in the preparation of this publication and associated materials including the cover design.

Finally, to my Wilmington-born granddaughter, Hollis Anabelle Pike, grandpa loves you down there in North Carolina!

Cover map:
John Bew and John Lodge. *A New and Correct Map of North Carolina and Part of South Carolina with the Field of Battle between Earl Cornwallis and General Greene*. London: J. Bew, Paternoster Row, 1780. [in *The Political Magazine*, 1 (November 1780), opposite page 731.] Geography and Map Division, Library of Congress, Washington, D. C.

Introduction

This guide's purpose is to provide information on numerous subjects relating to North Carolina during the period of the American Revolution to assist genealogical and historical researchers in locating widely scattered and often hidden materials. There surely are more that have not come to the surface in footnotes of books and articles, in online catalogs, and in Google searches, but the contents of this guide offer researchers a wealth of information arranged by subjects and geographical areas gathered from listings of the institutions that own them.

Using the NSDAR's 2005 publication *Is That Service Right?* as a *very* basic starting point, this study presents in far greater detail the sources for research that are available for North Carolina for the period of the American Revolution. It highlights those that are considered to be of proven acceptable for use as documentation in support of membership applications and supplemental applications for the National Society Daughters of the American Revolution and perhaps for other lineage societies as well. This guide is not, however, limited to lineage purposes only.

North Carolina has a rich history of involvement in the American Revolution, and despite some loss of historical sources over the centuries, it also has a substantial documentary record from those years. Historical and genealogical studies for these states are extensive. This source guide presents a substantial majority of those sources in bibliographic form arranged by subjects to aid researchers in locating published and manuscript materials available in many respositories both within and outside the Tarheel State.

One of the major inspirations for this publication was the fact that research materials relating to the period of the American Revolution in North Carolina are scattered in numerous research centers, libraries, archives, and local historical centers. This book brings together into this one guide references to as many of these sources as possible to give researchers a starting place for their studies.

During the period of the American Revolution, North Carolina was considered to be one of Britain's poorest colonies in North America. It was overwhelmingly agricultural Tennessee until 1796.

The most important intention of this publication is to provide as many sources of information in either manuscript or printed form to help researchers in the geographical areas in which they are interested. Resources are rarely centralized, but in North Carolina a great deal is in the major research repositories in Raleigh, Chapel Hill, and Durham, with much around the state in facilities large and small. Likewise for Tennessee, there are centralized research centers in Nashville and Knoxville, but much else is available in other facilities around the state. Providing a guide to this wealth of material is this book's purpose. It cannot possibly cover every article, document, or book that relates to some subject for the period of concentration, but it does include the vast majority of them.

An important feature of this source guide that all users should remember at all times is that the approach to the placement of information is very geographical with the concept of North Carolina of the last third of the eighteenth century directing all considerations relating to arrangement. In those chapters that cover broad topics, one will find in one place references to materials and studies from all of the geographical areas contained within North Carolina. For example, articles or books about agriculture will all appear as entries in the section of Chapter Five, "Agricultural Conditions in North Carolina during the Revolution." Remember, there was no independent Tennessee during the period covered by this guide. All was North Carolina, and as such, all content is focused with that in mind.

A great many of the published materials that appear in this guide can be found in major libraries or in regional public library systems and research facilities. Publications from before the mid-1920s may also have been digitized and may be found online having passed out of copyright. Even some newer publications have been posted online. Not all of the sources listed are in research centers within North Carolina itself, illustrating the need for researchers to cast their nets widely when seeking information.

Many historical records remain in their original forms and have not been microfilmed or digitized, especially those that reside in small libraries, local historical societies, and other repositories. Such reformatting is always costly. Many others, however, have been microfilmed, and this is particularly the case with significant collections held

Raleigh and Nashville. Some of these microfilmed materials are also available for borrowing through the LDS Family History Centers (visit www.familysearch.org for film availability and the locations of church and affiliate libraries that participate in the microfilm lending system.)

As part of the DAR Library's ongoing series of source guides for all of the original states, *North Carolina in the American Revolution* is the seventh. It really is not finished despite being printed and produced. As soon as the final word has been entered, new materials will begin to appear in journals and as books. Original sources exist in courthouses and research centers that have not been investigated. This is why this publication is a guide rather than an encyclopedia – it could never cover everything, but it should help lead others to a great deal of information.

Eric G. Grundset
Library Director
DAR Library
Washington, D. C.

April 22, 2016

Chapter One:
Developing a North Carolina and Tennessee Research Strategy

General Background[1]

The First Provincial Congress that met in August 1774 at New Bern recommended that each county elect a Committee of Safety, and in April 1775, the Second Provincial Congress met. In May 1775, the Mecklenburg Resolves were adopted at a public meeting at Charlotte declaring null and void all commissions granted by the King and making provisions for a new government. At New Bern, the Committee of Safety called for a union of all colonies and pledged support for the Continental Congress. Governor Martin fled the state; royal rule ended.

On 12 April 1776, the Fourth Provincial Congress met at Halifax, unanimously adopting a resolution to Continental Congress known as the Halifax Resolves. This resolution gave the delegates of North Carolina the power to concur with delegates of other colonies to declare independence.

In addition to the Continental forces, North Carolina organized Military Districts – Edenton, Halifax, Hillsborough, New Bern, Wilmington, Salisbury and eventually Morgan. Three areas of North Carolina had heavy concentrations of Loyalists; the Cape Fear Region with its wealthy merchants and plantation owners; the Piedmont whose Scottish highlanders had received land in exchange for an oath of loyalty to the King; and the western counties whose German and Quaker populations did not sympathize with the war.

Because of the shortage of money in all of the colonies, various types of "notes of credit" were devised. In North Carolina, those who provided goods or services were given slips of paper, official forms, or handwritten scraps of paper. These slips were to be redeemed for cash with interest. In 1780, these vouchers were recalled and new notes were issued, cut from its stub in a curved manner called "indented" for later identification. Not all vouchers were records of Revolutionary War military service. Only forty to fifty thousand of the vouchers have been saved. These vouchers were registered in the Revolutionary Army Account books. An explanation of the types of records contained in each volume in which the researcher is interested should be consulted.

A designation of patriotic service is given to any person who entered a land claim for a land grant between 1 January 1778 and 26 November 1783 (the date of the law and the latest date accepted by NSDAR for any service). The law states (State Records of North Carolina, vol. 24, p. 44) "That every person . . .before he shall enter a claim for any of the lands aforesaid, shall take and subscribe the Oath or Affirmation of Allegiance and Abjuration prescribed by the law of this state." Many of the entries for vacant land in individual counties have been abstracted and published by A. B. Pruitt, Weynette Parks Haun, and others.

During the revolution, the area now known as Tennessee was claimed and loosely administered by North Carolina. The settlers in southeastern Tennessee, in the area around the Watauga River, drew up a compact of government called the Watauga Association. This association petitioned the North Carolina Legislature in August 1776 requesting annexation to North Carolina. In May 1780, persons from a settlement on the Cumberland River in Middle Tennessee drafted the Cumberland Compact. Signers of both of these documents are considered to have patriotic service as a signer of a petition. Men from the area that is now Tennessee served in North Carolina units.

North Carolina gave military bounty warrants to its continental line soldiers. The Military Land District, where these grants were to be located was in Middle Tennessee mainly in the area of then Davidson and Sumner Counties. No military bounty land was given within the present boundaries of North Carolina. These military warrants could be sold or assigned so the person receiving the grant was not necessarily the person who performed the military service. Not all land grants in Tennessee at this time period were given for military service. The North Carolina Archives may be able to help in determining the person to whom a revolutionary military bounty land warrant was awarded.

---

[1] This text of the first six paragraphs in this chapter comes from the current edition of the Office of the Registrar General's compilation, *Genealogy Guidelines* (Washington, D. C.: National Society Daughters of the American Revolution, 2014), 94-95.

Each state offers research challenges to those studying its history and records during the American Revolution. North Carolina is no exception. Record loses from numerous causes, original lack of record-keeping, and other situations have affected the documentary record over the centuries. Stories, traditions, and myths also color the way people view historical sources and events. Researchers must develop a research strategy to account for these variations and challenges. This source guide is designed to provide them with as many possible avenues of investigation as have been identified after extensive study and searching all in one publication.

Naturally, an understanding of available archives, historical societies, libraries, etc., is essential to anyone's research. Chapter Two, "Major Research Centers in North Carolina and Tennessee and Elsewhere with Revolutionary War Collections," provides a list of the major facilities in the two states. It does not include all such repositories, and many smaller places own valuable materials.

The geography of a state, region, county, or community affects its history. The use of maps, atlases, gazetteers, and related sources is crucial to successful research. Listings of these for North Carolina appear in Chapter Three, "Geographical Factors Affecting Research in North Carolina." The formation of counties and other subdivisions of a state and knowledge of boundary disputes (with resulting records) are basic topics of study for genealogists and historians and are often confusing until fully understood. Many published studies exist to assist readers in gaining this awareness and are listed in a subsection of this chapter. Visiting locations of interest is another aspect of research, and this chapter includes a subsection "Travel to Revolutionary War Sites in North Carolina."

The overall history of the events in North Carolina leading up to the American Revolution and during the struggle for independence is introduced through the bibliographic listings in Chapter Four, "Pre-Revolutionary Events in the Province of North Carolina and Chapter Five, "General Histories of the American Revolution in North Carolina." These focus on titles specific to the Old North State, but an untold quantity of information on the state's history during the Revolution also appears in general histories of the period that cover the entire country. In addition, such topics as economic and business history, agricultural history, education, publishing, books, art, fine art, music, and culture in general serve as back topics for the more familiar military history. They are important in their own right as areas of study as revealed in the many listings in this chapter. Similarly, the subjects of servitude and apprenticeship are important in social history and genealogical studies, particularly when examining records of individuals from the period. Finally, archaeological studies can reveal much information on a period that is not evident in the printed or written record, and is an area of growing interest and success not always considered by genealogists.

Documents and other sources from beyond the boundaries of North Carolina are, of course, among the most basic of materials for study of the Revolution and the people involved in it. Chapter Six, "General Revolutionary War Sources," presents the most important of these materials such as the holdings of the National Archives and Records Administration. It is not, however, the purpose of this source guide to offer in-depth coverage of non-North Carolina sources, because many other publications cover these already and in far greater detail than would be possible here.

The government of each state directed the war effort and created a new governing system based on some earlier practices and on new thinking in ways unique to itself. Records are the primary surviving evidence for the myriad ways that North Carolina's government dealt with war emergencies, interacted with its citizens, and created the structure of the new state. An understanding of the numerous records of all levels of government in North Carolina that have survived is absolutely essential to the study of individuals, families, groups, and broad topics during the Revolutionary period. These extensive resources are presented in Chapter Seven, "The Government of North Carolina as a Colony and a State in the Revolutionary Period." Featured here are gubernatorial and legislative records, laws and legislation, committees, justices of the peace/magistrates, the constitutions, elections and suffrage, oaths of allegiance, and the centralized court and probate systems of the state during the period.

Paying for a war is never a cheap proposition, and North Carolina's need to do so during the Revolution has generated records and historical studies. These sources are highlighted in Chapter Eight, "North Carolina Finances and Taxation during the Revolutionary Era." While not the most exciting of records, financial and tax records are crucial sources for understanding an individual or a family's economic standing and other factors important in research.

The acquisition, maintenance, and transfer of land are fundamental aspects of the history of every state, and fortunately for modern researchers, North Carolina offers an abundance of material for study. Chapter Nine, "North

Carolina Land and Land Records," points readers to the many original and transcribed, abstracted, and published forms of this information. The Revolution had a major impact on the distribution of vacant land in the modern State of Tennessee, the western offspring of North Carolina, and the resulting records offer much information to researchers.

Military records for North Carolina troops and officers are plentiful and many have been transcribed and published, sometimes multiple times. Others remain in their original form in archives, libraries, and historical societies. Chapter Ten, "Military Records," and Chapter Twelve, "Naval and Maritime Records," provide listings of these. Information on espionage and spies in North Carolina during the war appears in Chapter Eleven. One basic fact of war is that prisoners are taken and must be held somewhere. The numerous sources and studies on this topic in North Carolina appear in Chapter Thirteen, "Prisoners of War, Prisons, and Prison Ships."

Numerous references to Revolutionary War service appear in documents created after the conflict ended, sometimes decades later. Such sources can come in many forms and are located in numerous research repositories. See Chapter Fourteen, "Records and Sources Relating to Veterans of the American Revolution in North Carolina," for references to materials such as pension records, claims, newspapers, obituaries or death notices, studies on individual veterans, and grave records. This chapter also includes information on "Commemorations of the American Revolution in North Carolina" throughout the many decades since the end of the conflict.

North Carolina's local government structure in the colonial and Revolutionary periods is familiar to residents of most states, but researchers must have a good understanding of it to search for records and to understand those that they find. Historical and genealogical publications of the nineteenth to twenty-first centuries provide insights and interpretations of Revolutionary events in North Carolina's localities. See Chapter Fifteen, "Regions, Counties, Towns, Districts, and Localities in North Carolina and Tennessee during the American Revolution," for details on these jurisdictions and their Revolutionary history and records. This chapter incorporates material for the modern state of Tennessee during the Revolutionary period because it Washington County, North Carolina for most of the Revolution, and remained a portion of the parent state until obtaining statehood in 1796. North Carolina created several counties in early Tennessee from the original Washington County before the states separated.

Every state has distinctive groups of people that have flavored its history in varied and interesting ways. In North Carolina the roles of these groups in the history of the Revolutionary period have been the subject of numerous studies by many historians and genealogists. African-American, English, Jewish, Native-American, Loyalist, French, Moravians, Germans, Irish, Scots, Melungeons, and other residents created a complex social mixture and a fascinating history for North Carolina. Other groups such as Freemasons played their own part in the state's history. Religious groups across the state reacted to the Revolution in different ways, and their histories developed in various courses during the conflict. North Carolina's female residents at all levels of society and of all ages were intimately involved in the events of the Revolution and have received considerable study over the years. Readers will find references to all of these distinctive groups in Chapter Sixteen. In addition, the major lineage societies associated with the Revolutionary War have gathered major collections of research materials that are essential for anyone's research in this period. The listings for ways to access this information appear in Chapter Seventeen.

Some are interested in the prominent figures of the Revolutionary period in North Carolina history. Chapter Eighteen, "Prominent North Carolinians and Tennesseans and Others Active in the State during the American Revolution," gives listings of studies and manuscript collections relating to many of these individuals. Even if one is not related to one of these prominent individuals or clearly connected to them in some fashion, the thorough researcher of a family living near a prominent person or a topic closely associated with that person's life will consult the surviving papers and subsequent studies on the famous man, woman, or family in hopes of gleaning therein details on their own research subject or family.

The index is another essential tool for finding information hidden in entries throughout this publication.

North Carolina and Tennessee Research Guides

Alderson, William T. *A Guide to the Study and Reading of Tennessee History*. Nashville: Tennessee Historical Commission, 1959.

Bamman, Gale Williams. *Research in Tennessee*. Arlington, Va.: National Genealogical Society, 1993; 2nd ed.: Barbara Vines Little, ed.; revised and updated by Charles A. Sherrill. Arlington, Va.: National Genealogical Society, 2009.

Crabtree, Beth Gilbert, and Ruth Clow Langston, eds. *North Carolina Historical Review: Fifty-Year Index, 1924-1973*. Raleigh: Division of Archives and History, North Carolina Department of Cultural Resources, 1984.

Draughton, Wallace R. "Tips for Genealogists Searching in North Carolina Records." *World Conference on Records and Genealogical Seminar*. Salt Lake City: Genealogical Society of the Church of Jesus Christ of Latter Day Saints, 1969.

Fulcher, Richard Carlton. *A Guide to County Records and Genealogical Resources in Tennessee*. Brentwood, Tenn.: R. C. Fulcher Company, 1979.

Franklin, Ann York. *Clues for Tennessee Revolutionary Patriots from Birth to Burial*. [Louisville,Ky.]: John Marshall Chapter, NSDAR, 2011.

Franklin, Ann York. *Clues for the Carolinas and Georgia Revolutionary Patriots: From Birth to Burial*. [Louisville, Ky.]: John Marshall Chapter, NSDAR, 2014. [A note states that the book is only an index.]

Haines, Jeffrey L. *Research in North Carolina*. Arlington, Va.: National Genealogical Society, 2008.

Haller, Charles R. "Finding Your Revolutionary War Ancestor." *A Lot of Bunkum*, 30:4 (November 2009), 5-6.

Hofmann, Margaret M. *Intermediate Short, Short Course in the Use of Some North Carolina Records in Genealogical Research*. Rocky Mount: Copy-It Printing, 1990.

Hofmann, Margaret M. *Short, Short Course in the Use of North Carolina's Early County-Level Records in Genealogical Research*. Ahoskie: Atlantic Printers, 1998.

Hehir, Donald M. *Carolina Families: A Bibliography of Books about North and South Carolina Families*. Bowie, Md.: Heritage Books, Inc., 1994.

Kelly, Norma. *Tennessee History: Resources for Teaching and Learning*. Nashville: Tennessee Department of Education, 1970.

Langston, Ruth Clow, ed. *North Carolina Historical Review: Supplement to Fifty-Year Index, 1974-1983*. Raleigh: Division of Archives and History, North Carolina Department of Cultural Resources, 1989.

Leary, Helen F. M. and Maurice R. Stirewalt, ed. *North Carolina Research: Genealogy and Local History*. Raleigh: North Carolina Genealogical Society, 1980; 2nd ed.: Helen F. M. Leary, ed., Raleigh: North Carolina Genealogical Society, 1996.

Leary, Helen F. M. "A Master Plan for North Carolina Research." *National Genealogical Society Quarterly*, 75:1 (March 1987), 15-36.

Moore, Terry. "Finding Your North Carolina Revolutionary War Soldier or Patriot, Part 1: [Continental Line]." *NCGS News: The Newsletter of the North Carolina Genealogical Society*, 38:2 (March 2014), 10-11; online: http://www.ncgenealogy.org/articles_tools/Finding_Your_Rev_War_Soldier.pdf.

Moore, Terry. "Finding Your North Carolina Revolutionary War Soldier or Patriot, Part 2: [Continental Line and Militia]." *NCGS News: The Newsletter of the North Carolina Genealogical Society*, 38:3 (May 2014), 10-11; online: http://www.ncgenealogy.org/articles_tools/Finding_Your_Rev_War_Soldier.pdf.

Moore, Terry. "Finding Your North Carolina Revolutionary War Soldier or Patriot, Part 3: Pensions." *NCGS News: The Newsletter of the North Carolina Genealogical Society*, 38:4 (July 2014), 10-11; online: http://www.ncgenealogy.org/articles_tools/Finding_Your_Rev_War_Soldier.pdf.

Moore, Terry. "Finding Your North Carolina Revolutionary War Soldier or Patriot, Part 4: NC Revolutionary War Bounty Land Grants." *NCGS News: The Newsletter of the North Carolina Genealogical Society*, 38:5 (September 2014), 10-11; online: http://www.ncgenealogy.org/articles_tools/Finding_Your_Rev_War_Soldier.pdf.

Munn, Robert F. *The Southern Appalachians: A Bibliography and Guide to Studies*. Morgantown, W. Va.: West Virginia University Library, 1961.

Schweitzer, George Keene. *North Carolina Genealogical Research*. Knoxville: G. K. Schweitzer, 1984.

Schweitzer, George Keene. *Tennessee Genealogical Research*. Knoxville: G. K. Schweitzer, 1986

Schweitzer, George Keene. *Revolutionary War Genealogy*. Knoxville: G. K. Schweitzer, 1982; reprinted: Knoxville, Tenn.: G. K. Schweitzer, 1984, 1987, 1997. [This book provides a short history of the Revolutionary War. It then broadly discusses the overall resources available at national and state archival repositories, state historical societies, the American Military History Institute, and other local level holdings. The book discusses locating military rosters, rolls, pension records, bounty land and other claim records, prison records, listings of clergy, French and Irish soldiers, and Loyalist and German lists. State publications and resources are listed. Approaches to locating local records are mentioned. The author also suggests researching other histories, such as: personal, regimental, battle, state, and group histories. Various resources are listed for each. Museums and historical sites are also mentioned as resources for research.]

Stevenson, George. *North Carolina Revolutionary War Records of Primary Interest to Genealogists*. (Archives Information Circular no. 13). Raleigh: North Carolina Department of Archives and History, 1975; updated, 1980.

Stevenson, George. "The Revolutionary War, 1776-1783." In Helen F. M. Leary, ed. *North Carolina Research: Genealogy and Local History*. 2nd ed. (Raleigh: North Carolina Genealogical Society, 1996), Chapter 33: "Military Records," 367-401. Contains subheadings: "Records," with sections:

- Pay Vouchers [Description; Issuing Authorities; Fiscal Districts and Auditors (Edenton, Halifax, Hillsborough, Morgan, New Bern, Salisbury (before and after 1782), and Wilmington]
- Army Account Books, with sections:
  - Account Books: First Series (Description of Volumes I-XII.
  - Account Books: Second Series (with sections:
    - Account Book A and Account Book C;
    - Account Book B; Account Books D, H, J, and K (at Kinston)
    - Account Books E-G
    - Account Books 1-6
    - Journal A (Public Accounts) 1775-1776
    - The Snow Campaign
    - Great Bridge
    - Moores Creek Bridge
    - Account Books W-1 and W-2
  - Account Books: Third & Fourth Series
    - Account Books 1-6
    - Account Books 19, 28, and 30
    - Abstract of the Army Accounts of the North Carolina Line, 1782-1792 [Published in 1792 as pages in *Pierce's Register*, certificate numbers 89501-91938. See also: North Carolina Daughters of the American Revolution; foreword by Gertrude Sloan Hay (Mrs. R. Duke). *Roster of Soldiers from North Carolina in the American Revolution with an Appendix Containing a Collection of Miscellaneous Records* Durham: North Carolina Daughters of the American Revolution, 1932: reprinted: Baltimore: Genealogical Publishing Company, 1977), 3-24.]
  - Final Settlements
    - The Revolutionary Army Account Books
    - Unbound Original Papers
  - *Register of the North Carolina Continental Line*
  - Bounty Land Warrents
  - Troop Returns, 1775-1783
  - Secretary of State Military Papers
  - General Assembly Records
  - State Pensions to Invalid Veterans and Widows
  - Records of Loyalists and Confiscated Lands
    - Loyalty Oaths
    - Property Confiscations
    - Confiscation Act, 1782
    - Loyalist Claims
      - English Records Series
      - British Records Series [See Murtie June Clark's *Loyalists in the Southern Campaign of the Revolutionary War* (Baltimore: Genealogical Publishing Company, 1981), vol. 2; and B. Ransom McBride "Claims by British Merchants after the Revolutionary War." *North Carolina Genealogical Society Journal*, 4:3 (August 1978), 152-161; 5:1 (February 1979), 4-13; 5:3 (August 1979), 177-183; 6:1 (February 1980), 17-26; 6:2 (May 1980), 110-118; 6:3 (August 1980), 195-200; 7:3 (August 1981), 155-159; 8:1 (February 1982) 18-23; 9:3 (August 1983), 155-164; 11:1 (February 1985), 25-32; 11:4 (November 1985), 243-251.
  - Trials for Treason

Cemetery Records, Cemetery Art, and Gravestone Carving and Carvers of North Carolina

There are cemetery transcriptions published for every county and city in North Carolina and Tennessee, in both book form and in articles in periodicals. A great many others can also be found online at various sites such as "Find a Grave." Many of these include the burials of individuals living during the Revolutionary Era. They are too numerous to list in the publication, but they can be found easily in the online catalogs of the DAR Library, the major research libraries in the two modern states, university and college libraries, and local public libraries throughout the North Carolina and Tennessee. Numerous transcriptions of cemetery records appear in the North Carolina and Tennessee DARs' digitized *Genealogical Records Committee Reports* at the DAR Library, Washington, D. C.

Ehinger, Autumn R. "Gravestones as Artifacts of the Upper Cape Fear: Identity, Economy, and Mortality in North Carolina's Cumberland and Harnett Counties, 1770-1900." Honor's Essay, Department of Anthropology, University of North Carolina at Chapel Hill, 2006.

Jabbour, Alan, and Karen Singer Jabour. *Decoration Day in the Mountains: Traditions of Cemetery Decoration in the Southern Appalachians*. Chapel Hill: University of North Carolina Press, 2010. [Publisher's description: "Decoration Day is a late spring or summer tradition that involves cleaning a community cemetery, decorating it with flowers, holding a religious service in the cemetery, and having dinner on the ground. These commemorations seem to predate the post-Civil War celebrations that ultimately gave us our national Memorial Day. Little has been written about this tradition, but it is still observed widely throughout the Upland South, from North Carolina to the Ozarks."]

King, Kenry. *Tar Heel Tombstones and the Tales They Tell*. Asheboro: Down Home Press, 1990.

Little, M. Ruth. "Sticks and Stones: A Profile of North Carolina Gravemarkers through Three Centuries." Ph. D. dissertation, University of North Carolina at Chapel Hill, 1984; published as: *Sticks and Stones: Three Centuries of North Carolina Gravemarkers*. Chapel Hill: University of North Carolina Press, 2014. [Publisher's description: "An old graveyard, writes Ruth Little, is a cultural encyclopedia – an invaluable source of insight and information about the families, traditions, and cultural connections that shape a community. But although graveyards and gravemarkers have long been recognized as vital elements of the material culture of New England, they have not received the same attention in the South. *Sticks and Stones* is the first book to consider the full spectrum of gravemarkers, both plain and fancy, in a southeastern state. From gravehouses to cedar boards to seashell mounds to tomb-tables to pierced soapstones to homemade concrete headstones, an incredibly rich collection of gravemarker types populates North Carolina's graveyards. Exploring the cultural, economic, and material differences that gave rise to such variation, Little traces three major parallel developments: a tradition of headstones crafted of native materials by country artisans; a series of marble monuments created by metropolitan stonecutters; and a largely twentieth-century legacy of wood and concrete markers made within the African American community."]

McEachern, Leora H. "Private Records: Cemetery Records." In Helen F. M. Leary, ed. *North Carolina Research: Genealogy and Local History*. 2nd ed. (Raleigh: North Carolina Genealogical Society, 1996), Chapter 38, 483-490.

Moore, Terry. "Cemetery Research in North Carolina." *NCGS News: The Newsletter of the North Carolina Genealogical Society*, 37:1 (January 2013), 10-11; online: http://www.ncgenealogy.org/articles_tools/Cemetery_Research_in_NC.pdf.

Patterson, Daniel W. *The True Image: Gravestone Art and the Culture of Scotch Irish Settlers in the Pennsylvania and Carolina Backcountry*. Chapel Hill: University of North Carolina Press, 2012.

Stewart, Judy. "Death and Burial in the Mountains: Superstitions, Customs, Practices." *Appalachian Heritage*, 1:3 (Summer 1973), 8-19; 1:4 (Fall 1973), 22-24; 2:1 (Winter 1974), 57-61.

Marriage, Divorce and Vital Records in North Carolina

Albright, Lee, and Helen F. M. Leary. "Strategy for Marriage Records." In Helen F. M. Leary, ed. *North Carolina Research: Genealogy and Local History*. 2nd ed. (Raleigh: North Carolina Genealogical Society, 1996), Chapter Two: "Designing Research Strategies," 39-42.

Albright, Lee, and Helen F. M. Leary. "Strategy for Vital Records." In Helen F. M. Leary, ed. *North Carolina Research: Genealogy and Local History*. 2nd ed. (Raleigh: North Carolina Genealogical Society, 1996), Chapter Two: "Designing Research Strategies," 24.

Bamman, Gale Williams, and Debbie W. Spero. *Tennessee Divorces, 1797-1858, Taken from 750 Legislative Petitions and Acts*. Nashville: G. W. Bamman, 1985.

McBride, Ransom. *Divorces and Separations from Petitions in the North Carolina General Assembly, 1779-1826*. Raleigh: North Carolina Genealogical Society, 2009.

McBride, Ransom, and Janet McBride. "Divorces and Separations from Petitions to the North Carolina General Assembly from 1779." *North Carolina Genealogical Society Journal*, 17:4 (November 1991), 201-208; 18:2 (May 1992), 101-110; 18:4 (November 1992), 228-235. [Online description from "North Carolina Periodicals Index," East Carolina University: "McBride discusses divorce and separation in North Carolina during the period following the Revolutionary War."]

Moore, Terry. "Vital Records: The Screws in Genealogical Research, Part 2: Marriage Records." *NCGS News: The Newsletter of the North Carolina Genealogical Society*, 36:6 (November 2012), 10-11; online: http://www.ncgenealogy.org/articles_tools/Vital_Records.pdf.

Sell, Laura E. "The Hazard of Intimacy or a Heaven of Bliss?: Eighteenth-Century North Carolinians on Love and Marriage." M. A. thesis, University of North Carolina at Chapel Hill, 1997. ["Researched from the papers of Henry E. McCulloh, James Iredell, Thomas Burke and John Steele."]

Stevenson, George. "State Records: Marriage and Divorce Records." In Helen F. M. Leary, ed. *North Carolina Research: Genealogy and Local History*. 2nd ed. (Raleigh: North Carolina Genealogical Society, 1996), Chapter 29, 303-306.

Winslow, Raymond S., Jr. "County Records: Marriage, Divorce and Vital Records." In Helen F. M. Leary, ed. *North Carolina Research: Genealogy and Local History*. 2nd ed. (Raleigh: North Carolina Genealogical Society, 1996), Chapter 10, 151-172.

Children, Youth, Minors

Brewer, Holly. *By Birth or Consent: Children, Laws, and the Anglo-American Revolution in Authority*. Chapel Hill: University of North Carolina Press for the Omonhundro Institute of Early American History and Culture, 2005.

Watson, Alan D. "Orphanage in Colonial North Carolina: Edgecombe County as a Case Study." *North Carolina Historical Review*, 52:2 (April 1975), 105-119.

Probate Records

Albright, Lee, and Helen F. M. Leary. "Strategy for Estates Records." In Helen F. M. Leary, ed. *North Carolina Research: Genealogy and Local History*. 2nd ed. (Raleigh: North Carolina Genealogical Society, 1996), Chapter Two: "Designing Research Strategies," 31-39.

Albright, Lee, and Helen F. M. Leary. "Strategy for Wills." In Helen F. M. Leary, ed. *North Carolina Research: Genealogy and Local History*. 2nd ed. (Raleigh: North Carolina Genealogical Society, 1996), Chapter Two: "Designing Research Strategies," 27-31.

Grimes, J. Bryan. *Abstract of North Carolina Wills Compiled from Original and Recorded Wills in the Office of the Secretary of State*. Raleigh: E. M. Uzzell & Company, 1910.

Grimes, J. Bryan. *North Carolina Wills and Inventories Copied from Original and Recorded Wills and Inventories in the Office of the Secretary of State*. Raleigh: Edwards & Broughton, 1912; reprinted: Baltimore, Genealogical Pub. Co., 1967.

Johnson, William Perry, comp. and ed. *Index to North Carolina Wills, 1663-1900*. Raleigh, N.C.: Johnson, 1963-1972.

McGalliard, Harry W. "The Widow's Mite." *Popular Government*, 3:6 (March 1936), 12-13. . [Online description from "North Carolina Periodicals Index," East Carolina University: "Mr. McGalliard reviews legislation concerning a widow's dower should her husband die owning land. A wife's rights regarding inheritance of her husband's property remained antiquated in 1936 North Carolina, and similar policies had been abolished in other states."]

Mitchell, Thornton W. *North Carolina Wills: A Testator Index, 1665-1900*. Raleigh, N.C.: Mitchell, 1987; corrected and revised ed.: Baltimore: Genealogical Publishing Company, 1992.

Olds, Fred A. *Abstract of North Carolina Wills from About 1760 to About 1800, Supplementing Grimes' Abstract of North Carolina Wills, 1663-1760*. Baltimore: Genealogical Publishing Company, 1968.

Orth, John V. "After the Revolution, 'Reform' of the Law of Inheritance." *Law & History Review*, 10:1 (Spring 1992), 33-44.

Stevenson, George. "State Records: Wills and Estates Records." In Helen F. M. Leary, ed. *North Carolina Research: Genealogy and Local History*. 2nd ed. (Raleigh: North Carolina Genealogical Society, 1996), Chapter 30, 307-312.

"Wills and Other Documents from Burned Counties as Found in Supreme Court Records, Part 1." *North Carolina Genealogical Society Journal*, 29:4 (November 2003), 363-462.

Winslow, Raymond A., Jr. "County Records: Estates Records." In Helen F. M. Leary, ed. *North Carolina Research: Genealogy and Local History*. 2nd ed. (Raleigh: North Carolina Genealogical Society, 1996), Chapter 12, 185-208.

Winslow, Raymond A., Jr. "County Records: Wills." In Helen F. M. Leary, ed. *North Carolina Research: Genealogy and Local History*. 2nd ed. (Raleigh: North Carolina Genealogical Society, 1996), Chapter 11, 173-184.

Migrations to, within, and from North Carolina and Tennessee

Barnhart, John D. "Sources of Southern Migration into the Old Northwest." *Mississippi Valley Historical Review*, 22:1 (June 1935), 49-62.

Beckerdite, Luke. "The Development of Regional Style in the Catawba River Valley: A Further Look." *Journal of Early Southern Decorative Arts*, 7:2 (November 1981), 31-48; online: https://archive.org/details/journalofearlyso721981muse. [Online description from "North Carolina Periodicals Index," East Carolina University: "This article examines the development of regional furniture styles in the Catawaba Valley of the North Carolina Piedmont through an anonymous group of furniture called the 'fluted pilaster group.' The Catawaba Valley style of furniture is heavily influenced by Delaware Valley settlers who moved to Catawaba Valley during the last half of the 18th century."]

Corbitt, D. L. "People Leaving North Carolina and Virginia for Mississippi." *North Carolina Historical Review*, 4:1 (January 1927), 106-107.

De Ville, Winston. "Some Post-Revolutionary North Carolinians in Latin Louisiana: 1783." *North Carolina Genealogical Society Journal*, 18:1 (February 1992), 11-12.

Eno, Clara B. "Revolutionary Soldiers Buried in Arkansas." *Arkansas Historical Quarterly*, 1:1 (March 1942), 53-62.

McBride, Ransom. "Migration as Shown in Powers of Attorney." *The North Carolina Genealogical Society Journal*, 7:2 (May 1981), 89-95.

Monaghan, Jay. "North Carolinians in Illinois History." *North Carolina Historical Review*, 22:4 (October 1945), 418-459.

Morton, Jennie C. "Boone's Memory is Honored: Monument Now Shows Spot Where Pioneer Entered Kentucky with North Carolinians: Four States Pay Tribute to Heroes of Early Days." *Register of the Kentucky Historical Society*, 13:39 (September 1915), 45, 47-52.

Newsome, A. R. "Records of Emigrants from England and Scotland to North Carolina, 1774-1775." *North Carolina Historical Review*, 11:1 (January 1934), 39-54; 11:2 (April 1934), 129-143.

Pauley, James Harrison. "Early North Carolina Migrations into Tennesse Country, 1768-1782: A Study in Historical Demography." M. A. thesis, Middle Tennessee State University, Murfreesboro, 1969.

Rogers, Adolph. "North Carolina and Indiana: A Tie That Binds." *Indiana Quarterly Magazine of History*, 5:2 (June 1909), 49-56.

Silver, James Wesley. "North Carolinians in Mississippi History." *North Carolina Historical Review*, 22:1 (January 1945), 43-57; online: http://digital.ncdcr.gov/cdm/ref/collection/p16062coll9/id/4207. [Online description from "North Carolina Periodicals Index," East Carolina University: "This article looks at the shared history of North Carolina and Mississippi. Some attention is given to overland travel routes between the two states used after 1783, the settlement of the Mississippi territory, the influence of extant North Carolina on developing Gulf cotton states, and some biographical information on prominent Mississippians who came from North Carolina."]

Language: Pronunciations, Vocabularies, and Names

Baker, Bruce E. "Why North Carolinians Are Tar Heels: A New Explanation." *Southern Cultures*, 21:4 (Winter 2015), 81-94.

Bender, Margaret. *Linguistic Diversity in the South*. Athens: University of Georgia Press, 2004.

Bishop, Stephen. "Tracing Back a Tar Heel." *North Carolina Folklore Journal*, 58:2 (Fall/Winter 2011), 37-44; online: http://paws.wcu.edu/ncfj/NCFJ582.pdf. [Online description from "North Carolina Periodicals Index," East Carolina University: "No one, including historians, is quite sure when and how North Carolina became dubbed the Tar Heel State, but Bishop elaborates on the legend in terms of the production of tar and turpentine in the state and traces the history of that production through time."]

Brown, Patrick Cavan. "Saving Cherokee." *Our State: Down Home in North Carolina*, 82:12 (May 2015), 53-54; online: https://www.ourstate.com/cheerokee-language-atse-kituwah-academy/. [Online description from "North Carolina Periodicals Index," East Carolina University: "The Cherokee language is slowly dying out as the younger generations are taught English rather than Cherokee. An immersion program at the Atse Kituwah Academy in Cherokee, North Carolina teaches students the language to avoid its extinction."]

Carter, Gazelia. "Lumbee English." Online at LearnNC: http://www.learnnc.org/lp/editions/nc-american-indians/5569.

Cobb, Collier. "Early English Survivals on Hatteras Island." *North Carolina Booklet*, 14:2 (October 1914), 91-99; online: http://digital.ncdcr.gov/cdm/ref/collection/p249901coll37/id/14180. [Online description from "North Carolina Periodicals Index," East Carolina University: "The isolated situation and culture of Hatteras Island, North Carolina has contributed to the preservation of speech patterns characteristic of the early English and Scottish inhabitants of the island."]

Devany, Ed. "Paul Green, Documentarian." *North Carolina Literary Review*, 1:2 (1994), 47-55. [Online description from "North Carolina Periodicals Index," East Carolina University: "Pulitzer prize-winner Paul Green is best known for his nearly 100 plays for stage and screen, most notably The Lost Colony about the lost English colony on Roanoke Island, North Carolina. While not what he is mostly known for, Green was also a documentarian who collected mounds of data on the life history of the people of the Cape Fear Valley and documented language usage as early as World War I. Green's estate posthumously published Paul Green's *Wordbook,* a two-volume, 1,245 page tome which included decades of his research on the Cape Fear Valley."]

Eliason, Norman E. *Tarheel Talk: An Historical Study of the English Language in North Carolina*. Chapel Hill: University of North Carolina Press, 1956.

Goerch, Carl. "Land of Hoigh Toides." *The State: A Weekly Survey of North Carolina*, 7:43 (March 1940), 1-3, 20, 26; online: http://digital.ncdcr.gov/cdm/ref/collection/p16062coll18/id/5282. [Online description from "North Carolina Periodicals Index," East Carolina University: "In another of his travel articles to various places in the state, Goerch visits Ocracoke Island, part of the Outer Banks."]

Grizzle, Ralph. "Vanishing Bits of North Carolina." *Our State: Down Home in North Carolina*, 66:6 (November 1998), 47-51; online: http://digital.ncdcr.gov/cdm/ref/collection/p16062coll18/id/70505. [Online description from "North Carolina Periodicals Index," East Carolina University: "People, places, and things we grew up with give us a sense of place in time. Across the state many of these things, including service station attendants, clotheslines, downtown movie houses, soda fountains in drugstores, and dialects, are slowly disappearing from the scene."]

Hunt, Marvin w. "The Carolinians of Cherokee Sounds: Cultural and Linguistic Connections between North Carolina and the Bahamas." *North Carolina Literary Review*, 7 (1998), 82-95. [Online description from "North Carolina Periodicals Index," East Carolina University: "Following the American Revolution, defeated Loyalists fled to the remote corner of Abaco in The Bahamas. Since then, the descendants of those Loyalists have maintained a population that is racially, culturally, and politically distinct from the other twenty-nine populated islands that make up The Bahamas. The Abaco population more closely resembles isolated communities on Ocracoke and Harkers Island, where the population still speaks with a brogue, resembling the tongue spoken by the earliest Scots-Irish settlers."]

Leary, Helen F. M. "Bridal Names and Other 'Inconsequential' Details: A Statistical Glimpse of Legal Laxity in North Carolina." 81:3 (September 1993), 213-215. [1779-1808 materials reflecting oddities in North Carolina marriage records and other documents.]

Mallinson, Christine, and Becky Childs. "The Intersection of Regional and Ethnic Identity: African American English in Appalachia." *Journal of Applachian Studies*, 129-142.

Montgomery, Michael B., and Joseph S. Hall. *Dictionary of Smoky Mountain English*. Knoxville:University of Tennessee Press, 2004.

Moore, Terry. "Understanding the Lingo." *NCGS News: The Newsletter of the North Carolina Genealogical Society*, 37:2 (March 2013), 10-11; 37:3 (May 2013), 10-11; online: http://www.ncgenealogy.org/articles_tools/Understanding_the_Lingo.pdf. [Covers nicknames, abbreviations, titles, the calendar, relationships, and legal terms.]

Owen, Guy. "The Pleasures of Tar Heel Speech." *The State: Down Home in North Carolina*, 51:8 (January 1984), 5-6; online: http://digital.ncdcr.gov/cdm/ref/collection/p16062coll18/id/60612. [Online description from "North Carolina Periodicals Index," East Carolina University: "North Carolinians speak a peculiar mix of southern and folk. The Tar Heel language, a reflection of a rural past, is dying under the growth of the New South. Guy Owen, however, is working to record the Tar Heel language through his writing. An author of several books, Owen sets his stories in rural North Carolina and includes old-time folk sayings. The Duke University Press is also preserving North Carolina's linguistic heritage in its Frank C. Brown Collection of North Carolina Folklore. Included in the article are many of the typical Tar Heel folk sayings."]

Reid, William W. "The Agricultural Idiom of the North Carolina Coastal Plain." *North Carolina Folklore Journal*, 17:1 (May 1969), 9-11. [Online description from "North Carolina Periodicals Index," East Carolina University: "Farmers of the coastal plain section of North Carolina can be completely understood by each other and almost incomprehensible to others. Shades of meaning of some phrases or terms depend much on locale, and dissimilar terms sometimes describe an identical activity. Additionally, the passage of time and the advent of new agricultural technology yields a changing and newer dialect."]

Peters, Sarah Friday. "Coastal Dialects: Queen's English or a Language of Their Own?" *Coastwatch*, (September/October 1993), 12-17. [Online description from "North Carolina Periodicals Index," East Carolina University: "A survey of the various dialects heard along the Outer Banks, this article addresses both the unique language patterns and the settlement pattern of the North Carolina coast."]

Sanders, John L. "Guide to Pronouncing County Names." *Popular Government*. 63:3 (Spring 1998), 38. [Online description from "North Carolina Periodicals Index," East Carolina University: "There are one hundred counties in North Carolina and probably several hundred pronunciations of their names. Recognizing that there are local variations in the way the name is said, Sanders offers a list to provide a ready guide to customary county name pronunciation."]

Tager, Miles. "The Life of Language in Appalachia." *WNC Magazine*, 2:1 (January/February 2008), 92-99. [Online description from "North Carolina Periodicals Index," East Carolina University: "Tager discusses the history of Appalachian dialects, how they changed over the years, and how some academics have recorded and studied the dialects."]

Tomlin, Jimmy. "A Matter of Speaking." *Our State: Down Home in North Carolina*, 71:8 (January 2004), 99-100; online: http://digital.ncdcr.gov/cdm/ref/collection/p16062coll18/id/78730. [Online description from "North Carolina Periodicals Index," East Carolina University: "Tomlin discusses the work of linguist Walt Wolfram, William C. Friday Distinguished Professor in North Carolina State University's English Department. Wolfram is director of the university's North Carolina Language and Life Project. The mission of the program is '…to describe and celebrate the state's linguistic diversity, and to raise awareness of how language is a part of our cultural heritage.' The project has about twenty research sites stretching from the mountains to the coast."]

Walser, Richard. "That Word 'Tar Heel' Again." *North Carolina Folklore Journal*, 5:1 (July 1957), 3-4. [Online descrip-tion from "North Carolina Periodicals Index," East Carolina University: "The legends revolving around the origin of the word 'Tar Heel' are numerous. The two most frequently cited yarns come from explanations in Clark's *North Carolina Regiments* (1901) and in Creecy's *Grandfather's Tales Of North Carolina History* (1901)."]

Walser, Richard. "Why North Carolinians are Called Tar Heels." *The State: Down Home in North Carolina*, 26:5 (August 1958), 97; online: http://digital.ncdcr.gov/cdm/ref/collection/p16062coll18/id/51628. [Online description from "North Carolina Periodicals Index," East Carolina University: "The legends revolving around the origin of the word 'Tar Heel' are numerous and confusing. The two most frequently cited yarns come from explanations in Clark's *North Carolina Regiments* (1901), and Creecy's *Grandfather's Tales of North Carolina History* (1901). Both versions were written long after the supposed events, and refer to the Civil War era, when the North Carolina soldiers were presumably noted for not retreating from advanced positions that they gained a reputation of having tar on their heels, incapacitating their flight in the heat of battle."]

Weslager, C. A. "Place Names on Ocracoke Island." *North Carolina Historical Review*, 31:1 (January 1954), 41-49; online: http://digital.ncdcr.gov/cdm/ref/collection/p16062coll9/id/4207. [Online description from "North Carolina Periodicals Index," East Carolina University: "Until recently, the fishing community of Ocracoke Island had little direct contact with the outside world. The present population speaks a language unlike anything else heard in Virginia or the Carolinas, maintaining early English influence in idioms and place names."]

West, John Foster. "Dialect of the Southern Mountains." *North Carolina Folklore Journal*, 14:2 (November 1966), 31-34. [Online description from "North Carolina Periodicals Index," East Carolina University: "West presents examples of the unique dialect encountered in the Southern Appalachians Mountains."]

Williams, Cratis. "Appalachian Speech." *North Carolina Historical Review*, 55:2 (April 1978), 174-179. [Online description from "North Carolina Periodicals Index," East Carolina University: "The Appalachian region of the United States, including the western mountains of North Carolina, has a unique dialect formed by the Scotch-Irish settlement of the region before and after the Revolutionary War. Isolated by the rugged terrain of the Appalachian region, communities still speak in a manner that has not changed much when compared to other regions of the country."]

Wolfram, Walt, and Jeffrey Reaser. "Language Tells North Carolina History." *Tar Heel Junior Historian*, 54:2 (Spring 2006); online: http://ncpedia.org/culture/stories/nc-history.

Wolfram, Walt, and Jeffrey Reaser. *Talkin' Tar Heel: How Our Voices Tell the Story of North Carolina.* Chapel Hill: University of North Carolina Press, 2014. [Publisher's description: "Drawing on over two decades of research and 3,000 recorded interviews from every corner of the state, Walt Wolfram and Jeffrey Reaser's lively book introduces readers to the unique regional, social, and ethnic dialects of North Carolina, as well as its major languages, including American Indian languages and Spanish. Considering how we speak as a reflection of our past and present, Wolfram and Reaser show how languages and dialects are a fascinating way to understand our state's rich and diverse cultural heritage. The book is enhanced by maps and illustrations and augmented by more than 100 audio and video recordings, which can be found online at talkintarheel.com."]

Wolfram, Walt, and Natalie Schilling-Estes. *Hoi Toide on the Outer Banks: The Story of the Oracoke Brogue.* Chapel Hill: University of North Carolina Press, 1997. [Publisher's description: "As many visitors to Ocracoke will attest, the island's vibrant dialect is one of its most distinctive cultural features. In *Hoi Toide on the Outer Banks*, Walt Wolfram and Natalie Schilling-Estes present a fascinating account of the Ocracoke brogue. They trace its development, identify the elements of pronunciation, vocabulary, and syntax that make it unique, and even provide a glossary and quiz to enhance the reader's knowledge of 'Ocracokisms.' In the process, they offer an intriguing look at the role language plays in a culture's efforts to define and maintain itself. But *Hoi Toide on the Outer Banks* is more than a linguistic study. Based on extensive interviews with more than seventy Ocracoke residents of all ages and illustrated with captivating photographs by Ann Ehringhaus and Herman Lankford, the book offers valuable insight on what makes Ocracoke special. In short, by tracing the history of island speech, the authors succeed in opening a window on the history of the islanders themselves."]

Woodard, Clement Manly. *A Word-List from Virginia and North Carolina.* (Publications of the American Dialect Society, no. 6). Greensboro, N. C.: American Dialect Society, 1946.

National Society Daughters of the American Revolution Source Advice for Applicants and Researchers

DAR ADVICE NOTE: The NSDAR does not prejudge the acceptability of specific documentation regarding lineage or Revolutionary War service before an individual application for membership arrives for consideration in the Office of the Registrar General. Please note that for the NSDAR, procedures and policies on the acceptability of any source as proof of service reside with the Office of the Registrar General, NSDAR, 1776 D St., N. W., Washington, D. C. 20006-5303. For other lineage societies, similar responsibility exists within their own structure. Entries in this source guide that contain the reference to this "advice note" are ones that the NSDAR considers as *likely* sources for acceptable Revolutionary War service within the overall context of an application and its documentation.

Points to Consider When Verifying Revolutionary War Service

The following sections provide advice on various aspects of completing a membership application or a supplemental application for the National Society Daughters of the American Revolution. They may also be useful for applications to other lineage societies related to the Revolutionary War.[2] These are recommendations, not hard and fast rules.

Dates: Acceptable Revolutionary service must fall between April 19, 1775 (the Battle of Lexington) and November 26, 1783 (Evacuation Day when the British sailed from New York City).

Types of Service:

Military/Naval: Those persons who served in a military capacity with the Continental Army, Navy, Marines, state and local militias, state navies, the French army and navy, and privateers. The Continental Line was the "national army" formed at the outset of the Revolutionary War and commanded by General George Washington. The term of enlistment in the Continental Line varied, but is oftentimes seen in enlistments lasting six months, one year, three years, or the duration of the war, while service with the militia might be only a day or so. Due to the difference in periods of enlistment, it is logical that the Continental Line was comprised primarily of younger men, while the ages of militia troops varied greatly.

---

[2] Several genealogists in the Office of the Registrar General have worked to provide this advice. The author of this book has drawn these from several documents and made very minor changes.

The militia was a longstanding English tradition that existed in the thirteen colonies long before the Revolution. Although various states had slightly different militia regulations, generally speaking, in most states all able-bodied white males between the ages of 16 and 50 were obligated to serve time in the militia, unless excused for physical disabilities or other reasons. Occasionally documentation is found excusing these men. Men serving in the militia from a particular town or county are very likely to have been residents of that town or county. When British troops were active in a specific area, local militia units were often incorporated into service alongside Continental Line regiments. However, as militia troops lacked the military training, discipline, and battle experience of Continental Line veterans, militia units were often untrustworthy in the heat of battle. There were notable exceptions however, such as King's Mountain and Cowpens, where the militia units performed admirably.

Patriotic Service: Those persons who by an act or series of actions demonstrated unfailing loyalty to the cause of independence from England.

Civil Service: Those persons who conducted public business under the authority of the new state governments. Individuals would have been at least 21 years of age to hold a civil office, and oftentimes middle-age or elderly men held these positions. They would have taken a state oath of allegiance in order to service.

Signers of the Declaration of Independence

Age: Establishing Age for Militia Service and other Military or Naval Service[3]

Albright, Lee, and Helen F. M. Leary. "Strategy for Estimating Birth Date." In Helen F. M. Leary, ed. *North Carolina Research: Genealogy and Local History*. 2nd ed. (Raleigh: North Carolina Genealogical Society, 1996), Chapter Two: "Designing Research Strategies," 61-62.

The militia is the most basic of all of North Carolina's military forces and dates from the very beginning of the colony. Technically, all men between the ages of 16 and 50 were eligible for militia service automatically throughout much of North Carolina history. An example of this is:

> From legislation passed by governing bodies in the various states it becomes clear that while most states agreed that able-bodied males in the basic age range between 16 and 50 years old were subject to military service, there were some minor variations between states. There is one interesting study of the age of soldiers at time of enlistment in the *Pennsylvania* Line that gives us insight into the vast difference in age between the youngest and oldest soldiers. The total number of men in the study came to 1,068. The youngest soldiers were 10 years old (a total of four), and one individual in the study was 73 years old. Following the practice of the British Army, the positions of fifers and drummers tended to be reserved for boys. In this study it becomes clear that the vast majority of men who served in the Pennsylvania Line were between the ages of 16 and 33. After age 33 the numbers of men in each age group declined steadily.[4]

Some considerations to remember when attempting to establish the age of an individual in a record are the following prepared by the Genealogy Section, Office of the Registrar General, Daughters of the American Revolution, Washington, D. C.:

1. Is the patriot's age appropriate for the type of service assigned to that individual? Are they too young or too old? Most men who served militarily were between the ages of 16-50. Teenagers were rarely officers! Is the individual asserted to be the patriot old enough to have any type of Revolutionary War service? For example, a William Singleton, born c. 1717 had a son also named William who was born c. 1760, and mentioned in his father's 1781 will that was probated in 1782. In 1777 a man named William Singleton enlisted for three years in the Continental Line. Is it likely to be William the father or son? In 1781 a William Singleton furnished supplies to the military. Is this likely to be the father or son?
2. There are various sources that can be used to find or estimate the birthdate of the patriot ancestor. Sometimes exact dates can be found in town vital records, church records, parish records, cemetery records, pension

---

[3] Office of the Registrar General, Genealogy Office, National Society Daughters of the American Revolution, Washington, D. C. [internal notes]

[4] John B. B. Trussell, Jr., *The Pennsylvania Line: Regimental Organization and Operations, 1776-1783* (Harrisburg: Pennsylvania Historical and Museum Commission, 1977), 244-247. [Emphasis added.]

records, or Bibles. Birthdates can be estimated using sources such as buying or selling land, acting as a witness to a will, deed, or some other legal document, tax lists, tithes lists, processioning records, birth of children, etc.

3. Sometimes marriages can be used to help establish an estimated birthdate. For estimation of the year a patriot was born, one can use the ages of a man marrying at age 21 and a woman at 18. (These are only extremely for the sake of discussion.) There are, however, certain other considerations at times. For example, if the patriot attained the rank of colonel during the Revolution, and one has a documented marriage date of 1782 for him, it is very possible that he was older and that this was not his first marriage; a man about 21 years old was unlikely to have attained this high rank. If the exact year of marriage cannot be documented, it is best to leave it blank rather than to estimate the marriage based upon a child's birth. This can cause problems in the future if someone joins on a different, older child, and a genealogist questions whether they share the same mother. Also, the wife named in a patriot's will dated in the 1820s or 1830s may not have been the same woman who was the mother of his children born in the eighteenth century. However, if the patriot were married during the Revolution and the location can be documented, this can be used to establish residence if no other information is available.

Economic Status:

It was a sacrifice for most people to support the cause of American independence. Because they stood to lose the most, many of America's wealthiest individuals were pro-British. The contributions made often depended upon the economic status of the person involved. Studying the economic status of men of the same name in a locality can sometimes help to determine their Revolutionary service. Individuals who were reasonably affluent were more likely to be older, wield greater clout in their communities, and serve as military officers, civil officials, or members of patriotic committees and governmental bodies.

Religious Affiliation:

If any of the supporting documentation for the patriot indicates that they may have belonged to a group such as the Quakers, Mennonites, or Moravians, one must do more research. These groups all preached pacifism, and as such most did not actively serve in the military. Quakers who served militarily, or openly supported the war, e.g. by swearing the oath of allegiance or paying taxes to finance the Revolution, risked being disowned by their meeting. Check to see whether there is church documentation to show they were disowned and the reasons for such actions taken against them.[5] During the Revolution, however, some Quaker monthly meeting-houses took a more conservative stand than others, and an action that might have resulted in someone being disowned in one monthly meeting might have been dealt with differently in another meeting house. Certain states passed legislation exempting pacifist groups from militia service, but there were often stipulations and variations from state to state.

These various groups did not believe in "swearing" to an oath of allegiance, as they did not believe in allegiance to earthly government. As states recognized these religious beliefs, however, they allowed these individuals to "affirm" the oath. If an individual "affirmed" the oath, this is patriotic service.

Other types of service one should check for if someone belonged to any one of these faiths (or something similar) include paying the supply tax (1783) or furnished supplies/provided material aid (see Publick Service Claims).

Residence:

Establishing Residence for Militia (and other Military and Naval) Service[6]

While the Revolutionary War pension records are among the easiest and most complete records to use in regards to documenting both Revolutionary War service and residence, there are other contemporaneous records that merit inclusion for use in regards to both service and residence. The validation for using these records is based upon various criteria. Certain military records explicitly state "residence", "abode", or "enlisted". Some patriotic petitions

---

[5] William Wade Hinshaw. *Encyclopedia of American Quaker Genealogy: Vol. X, North Carolina Yearly Meetings*. Ann Arbor, Mich.: Edwards Brothers, Inc., 1950.

[6] Office of the Registrar General, Genealogy Office, National Society Daughters of the American Revolution, Washington, D. C. [internal notes].

and lists of those who took the oath of allegiance state "We the residents/inhabitants of town/county…" Other residences can be established by closely reviewing the wording of legislation that created types of service. The following service sources given here that also document residence are some of the clearest examples, but are not intended to be a list of the only acceptable sources.

The connections between service and residence must be considered in context of the lineage. If there appears to be a possible error in lineage indicating that the patriot ancestor may have resided in a locale different than the service performed, or that a life event such as a marriage or birth of a child occurred in a location different from the service, or if there is a major question regarding service that needs to be resolved, then a review of the available records at hand is in order. However, when we are not questioning service, and the source for service either explicitly states the residence or is indicated by legislation, such as the examples given here, it is unnecessary to search for alternate sources of residence.

Examples of Sources of Revolutionary Service That Provide Locations of Residence:

- Revolutionary War Pension Records
- State Pension Records
- Continental Line Size Rolls, Muster Rolls, or similar lists that mention the county in which they were raised. Created by Continental Line officers to document the physical description and residences of troops in various units to help track them down if they deserted. Unfortunately, these records are rare and scattered among various sources.

Some considerations to remember when attempting to establish the residence of an individual in a record are the following prepared by the Genealogy Section, Office of the Registrar General, Daughters of the American Revolution, Washington, D. C.:

1. Was there more than one person in this town or county by the same name that the service might belong to? If so, one will have to try and sort out these individuals.
2. Court records, tax records, census records, deeds, vital records, church records, etc., may all help to document where the ancestor lived during the Revolution.
3. Military companies were raised on a local level (town/county), while regiments were composed of varying numbers of companies often from multiple towns or counties within a given state. Therefore, if you can determine the residence of the captain of the company in which a patriot served you can often begin to get a clue as to his residence as well. However, determining the residence of a soldier in the Continental Line can be more difficult than a local militiaman. As the Continental Line marched through various areas along the eastern seaboard, it picked up troops along the way. At times Continental Line recruiters traveled outside their state boundaries to find fresh troops. The Georgia Continental Line is an excellent example. Of the four Continental Line battalions (used interchangeably with the word regiment) that served from Georgia, only the 1st Georgia Battalion was actually recruited in Georgia. The 2nd Georgia Battalion was recruited primarily in Virginia, the 3rd Georgia Battalion was recruited primarily in North Carolina, and the 4th Georgia Battalion was recruited primarily in Pennsylvania. Also, in border areas between two states sometimes men would travel from their state of residence to the neighboring state to join the military if offered better enlistment bonuses.[7] This was particularly true in the New England states because of the short distances between them and the rather "thickly settled" nature of the region – colonial/state boundaries did not prevent a man from joining up in another jurisdiction.
4. Is the type of service compatible with the place of residence? For example, someone who lived in a mountainous region on the western frontier was unlikely to have served in the navy, but it is not impossible. Conversely, a middle-aged man who resided on the Cape Fear River was more likely to be a ship's captain than a guide on the frontier in Tryon County. Look for service near where the patriot ancestor lived.
5. If the patriot ancestor were too young to have owned property, prove the residence of the parent and also prove the relationship between parent and child.
6. If the patriot ancestor were born and died in the same town/county, that location can be assigned to them as their Revolutionary residence.

---

[7] (Robert K. Wright, Jr. *The Continental Army* (Harrisburg: Pennsylvania Historical and Museum Commission, 1977), 313-314.

7. All designations of residence should be historically correct and accurate to the time period. For example, one would not list the place of residence of an individual in a modern county that had not been formed by the time of or during the American Revolution, for example: *not* Transylvania County, N. C., *but* Tryon County or Rutherford County, N. C., or, *not* Robeson County *but* Bladen County. These references must be specific to the time period and not reflective of post-1783 boundary changes. Please note, however, that in this source guide, entries are arranged mostly by modern jurisdictions because of the complexity of trying to sort out all of the material available into the governmental arrangement at the time of the Revolution. In addition, so much has been published using the modern names that sorting into counties from the Revolutionary era would be very confusing to everyone.

Residence Documented in Service Sources[8]

While the Revolutionary War pension records are among the easiest and most complete records to use in regards to documenting both Revolutionary War service and residence, there are other contemporaneous records that merit inclusion for use in regards to both service and residence. The validation for using these records is based upon various criteria. Certain military records explicitly state "Residence," "Abode," or "Enlisted." Some patriotic petitions and lists of those who took the oath of allegiance state "We the residents/inhabitants of town/county…" Other residences can be established by closely reviewing the wording of legislation that created types of service. The following service sources given here that also document residence are some of the clearest examples, but are not intended to be a list of the only acceptable sources.

The connections between service and residence must be considered in context of the lineage. If there appears to be a possible error in lineage indicating that the patriot ancestor may have resided in a locale different than the service performed, or that a life event such as a marriage or birth of a child occurred in a location different from the service, or if there is a major question regarding service that needs to be resolved, then a review of the available records at hand is in order. However, when DAR is not questioning service, and the source for service either explicitly states the residence or is indicated by legislation, such as the examples given here, it is unnecessary to search for alternate sources of residence.

Examples of Proof of Residence Determined by Legislation:

- ***Militia Acts of Various States***
  A review of the examples of legislation in states such as North Carolina, South Carolina, and Virginia regarding the militia all reflect very similar regulations: able-bodied white males, ages 16 to between 50 and 60 (varies from state to state) **were to enroll in the county in which they resided** (*Backgrounds of Selective Service: Military Obligation: The American Tradition, Special Monograph No. 1, Vol. II, Part 10, North Carolina Enactments,* pp. 52-128; *Part 13, South Carolina Enactments,* pp. 61-77; *Part 14, Virginia Enactments,* pp. 321-328). As militia service was a local obligation, this practice of enrolling in their home-counties can be said to extend to all states.

Potential Difficulties Faced With Using Tax Lists to Prove the Residence of Troops With Continental Line Service
[See also, Chapter Eight, particularly the section titled: "Select Tax Sources for North Carolina or Tennessee Revolutionary War Residence," 198-205.]

> Robert K. Wright, Jr.'s, well-documented *The Continental Army* (p. 184) states "The long-term Continentals tended to come from the poorer, rootless elements of American society to whom the Army, despite its problems, offered greater opportunity than did civilian life. Enlisted men were young (over half were under twenty-two when they enlisted) **and mostly common laborers so poor as to be virtually tax-exempt**. A sizable minority were hired substitutes or not native to the place where they had enlisted." This

[8] Terry Davis Ward and Forrest C. Crosley. "[Internal Memorandum on Considerations for Determining a Man's Place of Residence during the American Revolution and Sources and Concerns Useful for this Research]." Genealogy Office, Office of the Registrar General, National Society Daughters of the American Revolution, Washington, D. C., 2006. [Note: Most of the text of this m1emorandum is reproduced here.]

combination of youth and the high probability that many troops came from the financially disadvantaged lower-classes in society would seem to indicate that tax lists are probably one of the least likely sources of residence for enlisted men in the Continental Line. Also, in May 1779, the Virginia General Assembly enacted legislation exempting all active duty officers, soldiers, sailors, and marines in the Virginia Continental Line from taxation (*Hening's Statutes at Large,* Vol. X, p. 24).

Traditional Sources to Use Where Residence Is Not Stated or Implied by Legislation:

- Patriot was born & died in the same town/county. Or if there is documentation showing he/she lived in a given location prior to the Revolution and died there, it can be assumed they resided there during the war.
- Legal and court records, such as buying or selling land, witnessing a deed or will, etc. **It is acceptable to use a court record for both Revolutionary service and residence.**
- Tax & tithes lists.
- State "censuses", sometimes compiled from Revolutionary period tax lists rather than actual state enumerations.
- Particularly in cases of militia service, do we know where the officers (especially the captain) resided? In Continental Line service, knowing where the captain was from may be of limited value unless your patriot enlisted about the time the regiment was first organizing in its home state.
- Proof of location where a patriot was married and or had children during the Revolution. This category also includes the death of a spouse or minor child.
- Church records, such as membership rolls, baptism records, parish & vestry records.
  If the patriot was too young to have owned property during the war, but we know who his/her parents are, we can assume the patriot resided in the same location as the parents.

Chapter Two:
Major Research Centers in North Carolina and Elsewhere with Pertinent Revolutionary War Collections

This chapter provides basic information on major research facilities in the area once covered by North Carolina and Tennessee. It is not in any way comprehensive, and hundreds of libraries, historical societies, genealogical societies, and other facilities across these two states contain an abundance of research materials to keep a researcher busy for several lifetimes.

Important Websites for North Carolina Research

Lewis, J. D. "The American Revolution in North Carolina." Online: http://www.carolana.com/NC/Revolution/home.html. [The information provided on the website is valuable for any researcher interested in North Carolina during the Revolutionary War.]

"Southern Campaigns of the American Revolution." Online: http://www.southerncampaign.org/.

Major North Carolina Research Centers and Societies

State Archives of North Carolina

Office of Archives and History
Street Address: 109 Jones Street, Raleigh, NC 27601
Mailing address: State Archives of North Carolina, 4614 Mail Service Center, Raleigh, NC 27699-4614
Phone: 919-807-7310
Fax: 919-733-1354
Website: http://archives.ncdcr.gov/.

NOTE: Many of the documents cited in this source guide come from the State Archives of North Carolina. Researchers should consult the Archive's online catalog before visiting the agency in downtown Raleigh to be sure that the materials of interest are available onsite or if they need to be ordered in advance of a visit. Should there be any question of the location of specific items, one should contact the State Archives prior to travelling to Raleigh.

Andersen, William L. "'To Rescue the Fair Fame and Good Name of North Carolina:' A History of the Colonial Records of North Carolina." Ph. D. dissertation, University of North Carolina at Chapel Hill, 2010; online: http://dc.lib.unc.edu/cdm/ref/collection/s_papers/id/1812.

Bassett, John Spencer. "Report on the Public Archives of North Carolina." In "First Report of the Public Archives Commission." In *Annual Report of the American Historical Association for the Year 1900* (Washington, D. C.: The Association, 1901), 2:261-266.

Bennett, William Doub, ed. *North Carolina State Archives State Agency Finding Aids of Interest to Genealogists: Volume I: Colonial Higher Courts, District Superior Courts, North Carolina Supreme Court, Treasurers & Comptrollers Papers, State Auditors Papers*. Raleigh: W. D. Bennett, 1997. [While superseded by the Archive's MARS online catalog, this guide still provides useful information to help search in that tool. The sections on court records help provide a structure for the arrangement of these extensive materials, and the section on the Treasurer's and Comptroller's Papers does the same. Many of the latter's collections and documents are listed in this guide. Especially useful is the section on the "Military Papers [Collection]" that lists the contents of boxes then (1997) used to store the materials (pages 88-97). A section titled "War of the Revolution" includes a listing of "State Pensions to Invalids and Widows" (with a list of names). "Miscellanous Group (1735-1909)" contains a few Revolutionary War materials, as does the section titled "Ports" (pages 99-101). This is followed by "An Explanation of the 'Revolutionary Army Accounts' in the North Carolina Department of Archives & History" (pages 101-144).]

Bennett, William Doub, ed. *North Carolina State Archives State Agency Finding Aids of Interest to Genealogists: Volume II: Military Collection, Adjutant General's Papers*. Raleigh: W. D. Bennett, 1998. [While superseded by the Archive's MARS online catalog, this guide still provides useful information to help search in that tool. Contents include:

"Frontier Scouting and Indian Wars (1758-1788)" containing a few Revolutionary War documents.
"Troop Returns, 1747-1859," by Kenrick N. Simpson and containing a list of colonial and Revolutionary War lists and muster rolls of militia from many counties and in different years from 1775 to 1783. Post-war lists also appear.]
The "War of the Revolution" section (pages 26-32). Listings in this section are: Board of War, 1780-1781; Commissary Correspondence, 1779-1781; Commissary Correspondence, 1783-1783; British and Loyalist Papers; Miscellaneous Papers (with a list of documents from 1776 to 1789); Miscellaneous Papers focusing on "An Original Orderly Book of a Portion of the American Army, during the War of the Revolution…[1777]; and Declaration of Service to Accompany U. S. Pension Applications (with a list of applicants produced by Betty Camin that covers pages 27-32; Loyalist Records; State Pensions to Invalids and Widows (with a page long list of the names of those receiving such pensions on pages 32-33.).]

Blake, Debra A. "Private Collections in the North Carolina State Archives." *Wake Treasures: Journal of the Wake County Genealogical Society*, 20:1 (Winter/Spring 2010), 1-4. [Includes: "Private Collections and the Revolutionary War."]

Brown, Douglas. "A Preliminary Slave Name Database for the North Carolina State Archives." *NCGS News: The Newsletter of the North Carolina Genealogical Society*, 28:1 (Winter 2004), 8-11.

Christopher. "Digital Duplication of Microfilm: Improving Access to the State Archives' Collection." Online: https://ncarchives.wordpress.com/2015/11/01/digital-duplication-of-microfilm-improving-access-to-the-state-archives-collections-2/.

Clark, Walter. "How Can Interest Be Aroused in the Study of the History of North Carolina? *North Carolina Booklet*, 11 (October 1911), 82-98.

Coker, Charles Frederick William, and George Stevenson, eds. *Records Relating to Tennessee in the North Carolina State Archives* (Archives Information Circular no. 3). Raleigh: North Carolina Department of Archives and History, 1980.

Connor, R. D. W.; Michael Hill, ed. "Old Leaves: Present at the Creation: R. D. W. Connor Reminisces, 1948." *Carolina Comments: Published Quarterly by the North Carolina Office of Archives and History*, 51:2 (April 2003), 51-62.

Connor, R. D. W. "A State Library Building and Department of Archives and Records." *North Carolina Booklet*, 6:3 (January 1907), 159-176; online: http://digital.ncdcr.gov/cdm/ref/collection/p249901coll37/id/14180. [Online description from "North Carolina Periodicals Index," East Carolina University: "This article consists of an assessment of the current {1907} condition of historical records in North Carolina in general and a call to action for every resident of the state to assist in the collection, preservation, storage, and utilization of these records about the history of North Carolina for the betterment of the state."]

Corbitt, D. L., ed. *Calendars of Manuscript Collections, Volume 1, Prepared from Original Mansucripts in the Collections of the North Carolina Historical Commission by D. L. Corbitt, Calendar Clerk.* Raleigh: Edwards & Broughton Company [for the North Carolina Historical Commission], 1926. [This publication contains a few index references to Revolutionary War materials, some of which appear in this source guide.]

Corey, John. "He Keeps Books on Our History." *The State: Down Home in North Carolina*, 29:24 (April 1962), 9, 23. [Online description from "North Carolina Periodicals Index," East Carolina University: "State Archivist H. G. Jones, a 37-year-old Caswell native, heads the largest department of archives in the nation. Guardian of documents for the entire family of four million North Carolinians, Jones is responsible for more than 7,000 cubic feet of records in the State Archives in Raleigh. Documents in Jones' charge include the 1663 Carolina Charter, county records, historical maps, and other valuable records of North Carolina's past."]

Crowell, Michael. "Access to Court Records in North Carolina and Judicial Privilege." *Administration of Justice Bulletin*, 1 (June 2012), 1-13. [Online description from "North Carolina Periodicals Index," East Carolina University: "This bulletin reviews the constitutional and statutory law on public access to court records in North Carolina and also discusses whether North Carolina courts might recognize a judicial privilege for judges' notes and drafts."]

Ellis, John Willis. "[A Signed Letter by John Willis Ellis, Executive Office, Raleigh, to {David L.} Swain {Chapel Hill}, February 24, 1859]." Manuscript (MARS ID: 340; record group) (presumably) in: North Carolina. Office of the Governor. "Governor's Papers – Office of the Governor. "Governor's Papers – John Willis Ellis (23

November 1820—7 July 1861), 1859-1861," State Archives of North Carolina, Raleigh. [In the letter, Ellis states that he "has found in Capitol many Revolutionary Papers."][9]

Elliston, Jon. "Historic Homecoming." *WNC Magazine*, 6:6 (August 2012), 24. [Online description from "North Carolina Periodicals Index," East Carolina University: "For years many collections of Western NC's historical records have been stored in the State Archives in Raleigh. However, as of August 10, 2014, Western NC will have its own official archive dedicated to the region. Its collections will be housed in a former Veterans' Administration nurses' dormitory in Asheville."]

Graham, Will[iam] A[lexander]. "[A Signed Letter by Graham to {David L.} Swain, {Chapel Hill}, August 26, 1845.]" Manuscript [presumably] in: North Carolina. Office of the Governor. "Governor's Papers – William Alexander Graham (5 September 1804—11 August 1875)." Manuscript (MARS ID: 335; record group), State Archives of North Carolina, Raleigh. [Concerns "public documents of the Revolution" and other matters.][10]

Guide to Private Manuscripts Collections in the North Carolina State Archives. Raleigh: North Carolina Office of Archives and History, 2002.

Guide to Research Materials in the North Carolina State Archives: County Records. Raleigh: Department of Cultural Resources, Division of Archives and History, Archives and Records Section, 1997.

Guide to Research Materials in the North Carolina State Archives: State Agency Records. Raleigh: Department of Cultural Resources, Division of Archives and History, Archives and Records Section, 1995. [See index references for "American Revolution."]

Jones, H. G. "Up from a Cultural Wasteland." *The State: Down Home in North Carolina*, 43:4 (September 1975), 9-12; online: http://digital.ncdcr.gov/cdm/ref/collection/p16062coll18/id/9593. [Online description from "North Carolina Periodicals Index," East Carolina University: "On September 18, 1900, a group of men and women met to form 'an organization to stimulate literary and historical activity in North Carolina.' In 1903, the association created the North Carolina Historical Commission, which was the forerunner of the North Carolina State Department of Archives and History. Jones discusses important events in the department's seventy-five-year history."]

Lewis, McDaniel. "A New History Building for North Carolina." *North Carolina Historical Review*, 40:2 (April 1963), 200-205.

McCree, Mary Lynn. "C. F. W. Coker." *American Archivist,* 47:3 (Summer 1984), 335-337. [obituary]

McMahon, John Alexander. "Photographing and Disposing of County Records." *Popular Government*, 18:6 (February 1952), 7-14. [Online description from "North Carolina Periodicals Index," East Carolina University: "McMahon discusses the modernization of record keeping for counties in North Carolina, including ways to preserve records for further use."]

North Carolina Revolutionary War Records of Primary Interest to Genealogists. (North Carolina State Archives Information Circular no. 13) Raleigh: Department of Cultural Resources, Division of Archives and History, 1975; revised (March 2002), online: http://archives.ncdar.gov/ FindingAids/Circulars/AIC13.pdf.

North Carolina. Department of Archives and History. "Finding Aid for Records in the Archives [1973]." Online at the State Archives of North Carolina's website: http://archives.ncdcr.gov/Portals/3/PDF/findingaids/search_room_scans/state/Archives_and_History.pdf.

North Carolina (State). General Assembly. "[Document dated:] April 16, 1778: Bill to Impower the County Court of Each County to Take into Their Possession the Records Belonging to Each Respective County (Rejected)." Manuscript; General Assembly Record Group; Session Records, April-May 1778, Senate Bills, House Bills, House Resolutions (April 27-May 1, 1778), Box 2 (MARS ID: 66.8.13.14; folder), State Archives of North Carolina, Raleigh.

North Carolina (State). General Assembly. "[Document dated:] April 25, 1783: House Bill to Preserve County Records (Rejected)." Manuscript: General Assembly Record Group; Session Records, April-May 1783; Unidentified Amendements; Senate Bills, House Bills, Box 2 (MARS ID: 66.8.30.48; folder), State Archives of North Carolina, Raleigh. [Online catalog description: "Bill requires all county records to be maintained in a suitable repository and kept until required by the Clerk of the County Courts."]

"Office of Archives and History Celebrates Its Centennial." *Carolina Comments: Published Quarterly by the North Carolina Office of Archives and History*, 51:2 (April 2003), 1.

Price, William S., Jr. "Plowing Virgin Fields: State Support for Southern Archives, Particularly in North Carolina."

---

[9]North Carolina Historical Commission. *Calendars of Manuscript Collections, Volume 1, Prepared from Original Mansucripts in the Collections of the North Carolina Historical Commission by D. L. Corbitt, Calendar Clerk* (Raleigh: Edwards & Broughton Company [for the North Carolina Historical Commission], 1926), 195.

[10] Ibid., 153.

Carolina Comments, 29:2 (March 1981), 41-47.

Saunders, William Laurence. *Prefatory Notes to the Colonial Records of North Carolina, Vols. 1 to 10*. Raleigh: J. Daniels, 1887.

Spindel, Donna. *Introductory Guide to Indian-Related Records, to 1876, in the North Carolina State Archives*. Raleigh: Division of Archives and History, Department of Archives and History, 1977, 1979.

Stroupe, Henry S. "The North Carolina Department of Archives and History – The First Half Century." *North Carolina Historical Review*, 31:2 (April 1954), 184-200; online: http://digital.ncdcr.gov/cdm/ref/collection/p16062coll9/id/4207. [Online description from "North Carolina Periodicals Index," East Carolina University: "Stroupe recounts the development of the North Carolina Department of Archives and History from the work of the North Carolina Historical Commission and William Joseph Peele."]

Swain, David L. *Report of Hon. David L. Swain on the Historical Agency for Procuring Documentary Evidence of the History of North Carolina*. Raleigh: Holden & Wilson, State Printers, 1857.

Tracy-Walls, Fran. "Private Manuscripts and Business Account Books: State Archives of North Carolina." *NCGS News: The Newsletter of the North Carolina Genealogical Society*, 35:3 (Summer 2011), 6.

State Archives of North Carolina – Outer Banks History Center

1 Festival Park Boulevard
Manteo, NC 27954
Phone: 252-473-2655
Fax: 252-473-1483
Email: obhc@ncdcr.gov
Website: http://archives.ncdcr.gov/Public/Outer-Banks-History-Center/Collections

Description from website: "The Outer Banks History Center is a regional archives and research library in Manteo, N. C. on historic Roanoke Island administered by the Special Collections Section of the State Archives of North Carolina. Its holdings document the history and culture of the North Carolina coast and adjacent areas."

Hart, Kay. "A Place in History: The Outer Banks History Center." *Coastwatch*, (January/February 1995), 16-18. [Online description from "North Carolina Periodicals Index," East Carolina University: "Built in 1988 to house the personal library and papers of historian and author David Stick, the growing Outer Banks History Center in Manteo is now the state's third largest collection of North Caroliniana."]

Parks, Stuart, III. "Preserving the Sights and Sounds of Outer Banks History." *Carolina Comments*, 61:3 (January 2013); online: http://www.ncpublications.com/comments/ccJan2013.pdf.

Pittard, Janet C. "Keep of Banks Lore." *Our State: Down Home in North Carolina*, 76:1 (June 2008), 116-118, 120-122, 124; online: http://digital.ncdcr.gov/cdm/ref/collection/p16062coll18/id/99562. [Online description from "North Carolina Periodicals Index," East Carolina University: "Pittard discusses the life and work of David Stick, who is the leading authority on the people and events that shaped the Outer Banks over the last four hundred years. The author of a dozen books and numerous articles, Stick donated his personal library and archives to the North Carolina Office of Archives and History in 1986, to be maintained as a public research center. Located in Manteo, the Outer Banks History Center opened to the public in 1989."]

Sharpe, Bill. "Outer Banks History Center Officially Opened at Manteo." *Carolina Comments*, 37:4 (July 1989), 93-95. [Online description from "North Carolina Periodicals Index," East Carolina University: "The Outer Banks History Center officially opened May 7, 1989. The collection, which includes 25,000 items donated by author/historian David Stick, is the country's largest holding of North Carolina coastal history."]

State Archives of North Carolina – Western Regional Archives

176 Riceville Rd.
Asheville, NC 28805
Phone: 828-296-7230, ext. 240
Fax: 828-296-4551
Email: wrachrives@ncdcr.gov
Website: http://archives.ncdcr.gov/Public/Visit-Us/Visit-Us-Western-Regional-Archives

Description from website: "The Western Regional Archives (WRA) collects, preserves, and makes available for public use historical and evidential materials relating to western North Carolina. The WRA is administered by the State Archives of North Carolina and operates under North Carolina General Statutes 121 and 132 in carrying out its archival mission and programs. The holdings consist primarily of private collections and some microfilmed county records."

Elliston, Jon. "Historic Homecoming." *WNC Magazine*, 6:6 (August 2012), 24. [Online description from "North Carolina Periodicals Index," East Carolina University: "For years many collections of Western NC's historical records have been stored in the State Archives in Raleigh. However, as of August 10, 2014, Western NC will have its own official archive dedicated to the region. Its collections will be housed in a former Veterans' Administration nurses' dormitory in Asheville."]
"New Western Office Building Opens." *Carolina Comments,* 59:2 (April 2011), 6-7.

State Library of North Carolina

Street Address: 109 Jones Street, Raleigh, NC 27601
Mailing Address: 4640 Mail Service Center, Raleigh, NC 27699-4600
Phone: 919-807-7450
Website: http://statelibrary.ncdcr.gov/.

"North Carolina Family Bible Records Online Collection Makes Finding Your Ancestors One Step Easier." *NCGS News: The Newsletter of the North Carolina Genealogical Society*, 33:3 (Summer 2009), 8.
York, Maurice C. *A History of the North Carolina State Library, 1812-1888*. Chapel Hill, [s. n.], 1978.
York, Maurice C. "Zeb Vance and the Library." *The State: Down Home in North Carolina*, 48:7 (December 1980), 10-12, 32; online: http://digital.ncdcr.gov/cdm/ref/collection/p16062coll18/id/59408. [Online description from "North Carolina Periodicals Index," East Carolina University: "In 1877, Governor Zeb Vance began his third term, deeply concerned about the state of the North Carolina State Library. He enlisted the help of Cornelia Phillips Spencer from Chapel Hill to re-catalogue the entire collection. Once the catalogue was complete, the collection had to be reorganized by State Librarian Sherwood Haywood. Spencer's catalogue, if published, did not survive."]

David M. Rubenstein Rare Book & Manuscript Library

Duke University
411 Chapel Drive
Durham, NC 27708
Phone: 919-660-5822
http://library.duke.edu/rubenstein

Davis, Richard C., and Linda Angle Miller, eds. *Guide to the Cataloged Collections in the Manuscript Department of the William R. Perkins Library, Duke University.* Santa Barbara, Calif.: Clio Books, 1980. [This guide is dated, but it still contains useful information, most of which is also in the Duke libraries' online catalog.]
Dunn, E. "The American Revolution, an Overview of the Manuscript Sources in the Rare Book, Manuscript, and Special Collections Library Duke University." http://library.duke.edu/rubenstein/scriptorium/pathfinders/american-revolution/

Louis Round Wilson Special Collections Library

University of North Carolina at Chapel Hill
Chapel Hill, NC 27515-8890

Hewitt, Joe A. "Louis Round Wilson Library: An Enduring Monument to Learning." The Louis Round Wilson Special Collections Library; online: http://library.unc.edu/wilson/about/wilsonhistory/.
Johnson, Lucia Porcher. "A Study of the Printed North Carolina Revolutionary Source Materials in the Wilson Library of the University of North Carolina." M. S. L. S. thesis, University of North Carolina at Chapel Hill, 1957.

Louis Round Wilson Special Collections Library – North Carolina Collection

CB# 3926, Louis Round Wilson Special Collections Library
University of North Carolina at Chapel Hill
Chapel Hill, NC 27515-8890
Phone: 919-962-1172

Website: http://library.unc.edu/wilson/ncc/.

Wilson, Louis Round. "The Acquisition of the Stephen B. Weeks Collection of Caroliniana." *North Carolina Historical Review*, 42:4 (October 1965), 424-429.

Yanchisin, D. A. "For Carolina's Sake – A Case History in Special Librarianship." *Journal of Library History (1966-1972)*, 6:1 (January 1971), 41-71. [Mary Lindsay Thornton and William Stevens Powell at the North Carolina Collection, Louis Round Wilson Library, University of North Carolina at Chapel Hill.]

Louis Round Wilson Special Collections Library – Southern Historical Collection

CB# 3926, Louis Round Wilson Special Collections Library
University of North Carolina at Chapel Hill
Chapel Hill, NC 27515-8890
Phone: 919-962-1345
FAX: 919-962-4452
Website: http://www2.lib.unc.edu/mss/shc/

Arthur, Billy. "The Stuff Southern History is Made of." *The State: Down Home in North Carolina*, 55:3 (August 1987), 8-10; online: http://digital.ncdcr.gov/cdm/ref/collection/p16062coll18/id/62583. [Online description from "North Carolina Periodicals Index," East Carolina University: "The dream of its first director, J. G. de Roulhac Hamilton, the Southern Historical Collection at the University of North Carolina at Chapel Hill is the largest repository of manuscript material pertaining to the South." Joseph Grégoire de Roulhac Hamilton (1878-1961).]

Blosser, Susan Sokol, and Clyde Norman Wilson. *The Southern Historical Collection: A Guide to Manuscripts*. 2 vols. Chapel Hill: University of North Carolina, 1970, 1975. [This guide is dated, but it can still provide useful information on the SHC's holdings.]

Norris, Jeannie Faris. "Southern Historical Collection Celebrates 75 Years." *Metro Magazine*, 6:2 (February 2005), 14-15; online: http://www.metronc.com/article/?id=434. [Online description from "North Carolina Periodicals Index," East Carolina University: "The University of North Carolina at Chapel Hill's Southern Historical Collection, the world's largest collection of manuscript material documenting the American South, is celebrating its seventy-fifth anniversary. Although manuscript collecting at the university had started in 1844, it was not until 1915, when Dr. J. G. de Roulhac Hamilton proposed the collection, that work began in earnest. The collection was officially established in 1930 with Dr. Hamilton as its first director."]

North Carolina Genealogical Society

P. O. Box 30815
Raleigh, NC 27622-0815
Website: http://www.ncgenealogy.org/

Linn, Jo White; revised by Elizabeth E. Ross. "North Carolina Genealogical Society: A Brief History, 1973-1995." *NCGS News: The Newsletter of the North Carolina Genealogical Society*, 34:1 (Winter 2010), 10-12.

Moore, Terry. "Getting the Most from the Archived *NCGS Journal Articles*." *NCGS News: The Newsletter of the North Carolina Genealogical Society*, 39:3 (May 2015), 10-11; online: http://www.ncgenealogy.org/articles_tools/Getting_the_Most_from_Archived_NCGS_Journal.pdf.

Selected Additional Research Centers for North Carolina

North Carolina Societies, Libraries, and Archives

"Societies/Libraries/Archives." Online guide at the North Carolina Genealogical Society's website: http://www.ncgenealogy.org/menu-resources/societies-libraries-archives.

Edith M. Clark History Room

Rowan Public Library
201 W. Fisher Street
Salisburg, NC 28144
Phone: 704-216-8253
Website: http://edithclark.omeka.net/.

Comer, Susan L. "Black Sheep & Kissing Cousins: Charting Your N. C. History." *Our State: Down Home in North Carolina*, 67:12 (May 2000), 88-92; online: http://digital.ncdcr.gov/cdm/ref/collection/p16062coll18/id/71146. [Online description from "North Carolina Periodicals Index," East Carolina University: "Rowan County in the 1700s was a junction of two major roads: the Great Pennsylvania Wagon Road and the Warrior's Trading Path. Records of who passed through, who settled, then moved on, were stored in the courthouse at Salisbury. Through the single-handed efforts of Mary Elizabeth Gaskill McCubbins, who amassed over 150,000 pieces of genealogical information, the records were made more accessible to the public. Today the Rowan Public Library's genealogical section, with 4,000 microfilms, 20,000 books, and the McCubbins' Collection, is one of the nation's top genealogical research libraries."]

Gertrude S. Carraway Research Library

Tryon Palace
529 South Front Street
New Bern, NC 28562
Phone: 252-639-3537; toll free: 1-800-767-1560
"Research Library." Online: http://www.tryonpalace.org/research-library.
Hawley, Nancy. "The Gertrude Carraway Research Library." *The Palace*, 4:4 (Summer 2004), 4-5. [Online description from "North Carolina Periodicals Index," East Carolina University: "Named after the first director of Tryon Palace Restoration, the Gertrude Carraway Research Library has helped educate the staff and public at the historic site."]

Kellenberger Room

New Bern-Craven County Public Library
400 Johnson Street
New Bern, NC 28560-4048
Phone: 252.638.7800
Fax: 252-638-7817
Website: http://newbern.cpclib.org/research/
Genealogical Holdings in the Kellenberger Room of the New Bern-Craven County Public Library, Vol. 1: North Carolina Histories and North Carolina Records. 3rd ed. Online: http://newbern.cpclib.org/research/pdf/GenBooks2010Mar10.pdf.

Museum of Early Southern Decorative Arts

Anne P. and Thomas A. Gray Library and MESDA Research Center
Frank L. Horton Museum Center
924 South Main Street
Winston-Salem, NC 27101
Phone: 336-721-7360
Website: http://www.mesda.org/
Email: Library@oldsalem.org
Online description: "Old Salem Museums & Gardens' Anne P. and Thomas A. Gray Library houses materials on southern decorative arts and material culture, the social history of the antebellum South, and Moravian history. The library contains over 20,000 cataloged volumes, including books, periodicals, rare books and manuscripts, and microforms. Of particular note is The Thomas A. Gray Rare Book Collection, including rare books and manuscripts dating from 1590 to 1865, that focuses on early North Carolina material, as well as Tennessee, Kentucky, South Carolina, Maryland, Virginia, and Georgia."]
African Impact on the Material Culture of the Americas: A Conference Presented at Diggs Gallery at Winston-Salem State University, Old Salem, the Museum of Early Southern Decorative Arts, May 30-June 2, 1996. Winston-Salem: Museum of Early Southern Decorative Arts, 1998. [Contents include: "Tools of the Spirit: Reflections on the Enduring Meaning of African American Culture"; "African Influences on the Decorative Arts of Tidewater Virginia and Maryland, and the Carolinas before 1800"; "African American Material Culture in North Carolina."]
Fox, Janet. "At Home in the 18th Century." *The State: Down Home in North Carolina*, 55:10 (March 1988), 8-11; online: http://digital.ncdcr.gov/cdm/ref/collection/p16062coll18/id/62890. [Online description from "North Carolina Periodicals Index," East Carolina University: "Founded in 1965, the Museum of Early Southern

Decorative Arts (MEDSA) in Winston-Salem houses reconstruction's of actual rooms from historic houses located across the South."]

"MESDA Craftsman Database." Online: http://www.mesda.org/research_sprite/mesda_craftsman_database.html. [This database is essential for research in North Carolina and neighboring states during the eighteenth and nineteenth centuries. Online description: "The MESDA Craftsman Database is a collection of primary source information on nearly 85,000 artisans and artists practicing 127 trades in the early South."]

Museum of Early Southern Decorative Arts. "MESDA Craftsman Database." Online: http://www.mesda.org/research_sprite/mesda_craftsman_database.html. [Online description from "North Carolina Periodicals Index," East Carolina University: "The MESDA Craftsman Database is a collection of primary source information on nearly 85,000 artisans and artists practicing 127 trades in the early South."]

North Carolina Collection

Pack Memorial Library
67 Haywood Street
Asheville, NC 28801
Phone: 828-250.-4740
Email: http://packlibraryncroom.wordpress.com
Website: https://ncroom.buncombecounty.org/Presto/home/home.aspx

North Carolina Room

New Hanover County Public Library
201 Chestnut Street
Wilmington, NC 28401
Phone: 910-798-6305
Website: http://libguides.nhclibrary.org/friendly.php?s=wilmhistory

Seldon, Lynn. "Genealogical Genies." *Our State: Down Home in North Carolina*, 73:10 (March 2006), 112-114, 116, 118; online: http://digital.ncdcr.gov/cdm/ref/collection/p16062coll18/id/85697. [Online description from "North Carolina Periodicals Index," East Carolina University: "The New Hanover County Public Library's North Carolina Room was created in 1910. Since then, library personnel have collected material relating to the history of the area, the state, and the families that live there. The collection includes over 10,000 state and local history books, over 5,000 photographs pertaining to the region, 1,500 postcards, major Wilmington newspapers published since 1792, vertical files, and census records. The library's North Carolina Room is considered the most comprehensive collection of genealogical research materials for southeastern North Carolina."]

Robinson-Spangler Carolina Room

Charlotte Mecklenburg Library
Main Library
310 N. Tryon Street
Charlotte, NC. 28202
Phone: 704-416-0150
Website: https://www.cmlibrary.org/services/genealogy-history-services

Wachovia Historical Society

P. O. Box 20803
Winston-Salem, NC 27120-0803
Phone: 336-624-0803
Website: http://www.wachoviahistoricalsociety.org/

Bauschenberg, Bradford L. *The Wachovia Historical Society, 1895-1995*. Winston-Salem: The Society, 1995.

Western Carolina University

Special Collections, Hunter Library
Cullowhee, NC 28723
Phone: 828-227-7211
Website: http://www.wcu.edu/hunter-library/collections/special-collections/

Western Carolina University – Mountain Heritage Center

Hunter Library
176 Central Drive #240
Western Carolina University
Cullowhee, NC 28723
Phone: 828-227-7129
Website: http://www.wcu.edu/engage/community-resources/mountain-heritage-center/

Conway, Bob. "They Guard Our Mountain Heritage." *The State: Down Home in North Carolina*, 55:2 (July 1987), 8-9, 36; online: http://digital.ncdcr.gov/cdm/ref/collection/p16062coll18/id/62538. [Online description from "North Carolina Periodicals Index," East Carolina University: "The Mountain Heritage Center at Western Carolina University in Cullowhee contains over 10,000 items pertaining to folk songs and dance, handicrafts, and oral traditions of the Southern Appalachian region."]

Major Tennessee Research Centers

Tennessee Archives Directory

Online: http://tnsos.net/TSLA/archives/index.php

Tennessee State Library and Archives

403 7th Avenue North
Nashville, TN 37243
Phone: 615-741-2764
Website: http://sos.tn.gov/tsla

Owsley, Harriet C., ed. Tennessee Historical Society. *Guide to the Processed Manuscripts of the Tennessee Historical Society.* Nashville: Tennessee Historical Commission, 1969.

Tennessee State Library and Archives. *Guide to the Microfilmed Manuscript Holdings of the Tennessee State Library and Archives.* Nashville: Tennessee State Library and Archives, 1983; updated, online version: http://sos.tn.gov/products/tsla/guide-manuscript-materials-microfilm.

Tennessee State Library and Archives. *Tennessee Diaries, Memoirs and Church Records in the Tennessee State Library and Archives*. Nashville: Tennessee State Library and Archives, 1965.

Wingfield, Marshall. "The Preservation of History in Tennessee." *West Tennessee Historical Society Papers*, 23 (1969), 129-133; online: http://register.shelby.tn.us/wths/?acc=Y.

East Tennessee Historical Society

Calvin M. McClung Historical Collection
East Tennessee History Center
601 South Gay Street
Knoxville, TN 37902
Phone: 865-215-8801
Websites: http://www.easttnhistory.org/calvin-m-mcclung-historical-collection and http://www.knoxlib.org/local-family-history/calvin-m-mcclung-historical-collection

Description from website: "One of the premier research libraries in the Southeast, the Calvin M. McClung Historical Collection provides a wealth of materials for East Tennessee research. While the collection is regional in focus, visitors will find a wide range of materials for all of Tennessee and for most other states. These include the First Families of Tennessee files, which are the largest collection of resource information for Tennessee pioneer settlers, a large manuscript collection, photographs, books, thousands of surname and subject files, published and unpublished family histories, military records, materials for Cherokee and African American research, published and microfilmed Tennessee county records, and much, much more. Established in 1921, the McClung Historical Collection is the genealogy and history research branch of the Knox County Public Library."]

Lawson McGhee Library (Knoxville). *Calvin Morgan McClung Historical Collection of Books, Pamphlets, Manuscripts, Pictures and Maps Relating to Early Western Travel and the History and Genealogy of Tennessee and Other Southern States*. Knoxville: Knoxville Lithographing Company, 1921.

Posey, Linda Langdon. "A Guide to the Manuscript Collections of the Calvin M. McClung Historical Collection." M. A. thesis, University of Tennessee Knoxville, 1974.

Archives of Appalachia
Sherrod Library
East Tennessee State University
Room 422; P. O. Box 70295
344 J. L. Seehorn Rd.
Johnson City, TN 37614
Phone: 423-439-4337
Website: http://www.etsu.edu/cas/cass/archives/

Memphis Public Library
History Department
Benjamin L. Hooks Central Library
3030 Poplar Avenue
Memphis, TN 38111
Phone: 901-415-2742
Website: http://www.memphislibrary.org/research/topics/genealogy/
West Tennessee Historical Society. *West Tennessee Historical Society Guide to Archives and Collections*. Memphis: Mississippi Valley Collection, 1979.

Tennessee Genealogical Society
7779 Poplar Pike
Germantown, TN 38138
Office phone: 901-954-4300
Library phone: 901-767-8480; Germantown Regional History and Genealogy Center Library
Website: http://www.tngs.org/

Major Research Centers Outside of North Carolina and Tennessee with Pertinent Revolutionary War Materials

DAR Library
1776 D St., NW
Washington, DC 20006-5303
Phone: 202-879-3229
Website: www.dar.org/library
Publications:

Grundset, Eric G. and Stephen B. Rhodes. *American Genealogical Research at the DAR, Washington, D. C.* (2007). [Out of print in 2016; available in many libraries nationwide.]

Grundset, Eric G., Briana L. Diaz, Hollis L. Gentry, and Jean D. Strahan. *Forgotten Patriots: African American and American Indian Patriots in the Revolutionary War* (2008). Free online at: http://www.dar.org/library/fp.cfm.

Grundset, Eric G., Briana L. Diaz, and Hollis L. Gentry. *America's Women in the Revolutionary Era: A History through Bibliography*. 3 vols. Washington, D. C.: National Society Daughters of the American Revolution, 2011. [Out of print in 2016; available in many libraries nationwide.]

David Library of the American Revolution
1201 River Rd ,
Washington Crossing, PA 18977
Phone: 215-493-6776
Website: http://www.dlar.org/. [This will take you to the library's online catalog.]

The David Library contains many manuscript and other sources on the American Revolution. See the online catalog and the published guide to its manuscript collection for details of holdings: David J. Fowler. *Guide to the Sol Feinstone Collection of the David Library of the American Revolution*. Washington Crossing, Pa.: The Library, 1994.

Family History Library
35 North West Temple Street
Salt Lake City, Utah, 84150
Phone: 1.866.406-1830
Website: www.familysearch.org

Library of Congress
101 Independence Ave, SE
Washington, DC 20540
Phone: 202-727-5000
Website: http://www.loc.gov

National Archives and Records Administration
700 Pennsylvania Avenue, NW
Washington, DC 20408-0001
Phone: 1-866-272-6272
Website: http://www.archives.gov/

McConnell, Roland C. "Records in the National Archives Pertaining to the History of North Carolina, 1775-1943." *North Carolina Historical Review,* 25:3 (July 1948), 318-340.

Wehmann, Howard H.; revised by Benjamin L. DeWhitt. *A Guide to Pre-Federal Records in the National Archives*. Washington, D. C.: National Archives and Records Administration, 1989.

SAR Genealogical Research Library
809 West Main Street
Louisville, KY 40209
Phone: 502-589-1776
Website: http://library.sar.org/

Society of the Cincinnati Library
2118 Massachusetts Avenue, NW
Washington, DC. 20008
Phone: 202-785-2040
Website: http://societyofthecincinnati.org/collections/library/about

Chapter Three: Geographical Factors Affecting Research in North Carolina and Tennessee

The area covered by North Carolina during the American Revolution was quite large and included the modern State of Tennessee with undefined boundaries to the north and east. The geographical and topographical features of this expanse were exceptionally varied and offered many challenges and benefits to the population of the state. The entries that follow help illustrate this variety and point to areas for further study for researchers to have a better understanding of the physical background against which North Carolina and Tennessee lives unfolded. A knowledge of these factors is essential to grasping the complexities of life in both states during this period.

Merrens, Harry Roy. *Colonial North Carolina in the Eighteenth Century: A Study in Historical Geography*. Chapel Hill: University of North Carolina Press, 1964.

Geographical Tools: Atlases, Maps, and Gazetteers

"1770 John Collet Map of North Carolina for George III." Manuscript, N.52.7.20-21, Photographic Collections, State Archives of North Carolina, Raleigh. [Online catalog description: "John Abraham Collett was a Swiss military engineer, map maker and captain in the British army. He also was military governor of Fort Johnston, N.C. (near the Cape Fear River). His map of colonial North Carolina was regarded as one of the best of the provincial maps." This is a Reprograph by Jim Mercer.]

Cappon, Lester J., editor-in-chief; Barbara Bartz Petchenik, cartographic editor; John Hamilton Long, assistant editor; William B. Bedford, *et al.*, research associates; Nancy K. Morbeck, cartographic assistant; Gretchen M. Oberfranc, editorial assistant. *Atlas of Early American History: The Revolutionary Era, 1760-1790*. Princeton: Published for the Newberry Library and the Institute of Early American History and Culture by Princeton University Press, 1976.

Cherry, Kevin. "Dotting the Map with the *North Carolina Gazetteer*." *Tar Heel Junior Historian*, 44:2 (Spring 2005), 4-5. [Online description from "North Carolina Periodicals Index," East Carolina University: "Because of the work of Dr. William S. Powell, professor of history at UNC-CH, and local historians, North Carolina possesses one of the most comprehensive gazetteers of any state in the nation. Titled *The North Carolina Gazetteer: A Dictionary of Tar Heel Places*, the reference book records when the state's places were founded, when their names were first used, and how the place-names came into existence."]

Corbitt, David Leroy. *The Formation of the North Carolina Counties, 1663-1943*. Raleigh: Division of Archives and History, North Carolina Department of Cultural Resources, 1969. [Besides the useful information found throughout this publication on its main topic, there are maps following page 282 showing the development of county boundaries as of 1700,1740, 1760, 1775, 1780, Tennessee at the Beginning of 1790, 1800, 1840, 1850, 1870, 1900 and 1912, along with a chart of county formations. For a video showing the progression of county formation for the above years, see: http://www.learnnc.org/lp/editions/nchist-colonial/2040.]

Creekmore, Pollyanna. *Maps of Tennessee and Other Southern States for Genealogical Searching*. Knoxville: Clinchdale Press, 1965. [Contents: Map 1. Southern section of the United States, by John Melish, 1816; Map 2. Aboriginal map of Tennessee. Nashville, {Tenn.}, Goodspeed Pub. Co., 1886; Map 3. Map of Cumberland and Franklin. As refered [*sic*] to by Ramsey's *Annals of Tennessee*. Engraved by W. Keenan, Charleston, S. C. For Ramsey's *Annals of Tennessee*, 1853; Map 4. State of Tennessee, 1795 [1814?]; Map 5. Map of Tennessee, constructed from the surveys of the late John Strother and others. Documented by John Melish. Philadelphia, John Melish and Saml. Harrison, 1818; Map 6. Geographical, statistical and historical map of Tennessee. Drawn by F. Lucas, Jr., 1824; Map 7. Tennessee, 1824. Anthony Finley; Map 8. Tennessee, 1838. Philadelphia, T. G. Bradford; Map 9. A new map of Tennessee, with its roads and distances ... along the stage and steam boat routes. Published by Augustus Mitchell, 1850; Map 10. State of North Carolina from the best authorities. New York, published by John Reid, c1795; Map 11. Map of the state of Kentucky with the adjoining territories, by John Russell. London, H.D. Symonds, 1794; Map 12. Map of the state of Kentucky, from actual survey, by Elihu Barker. London, J. Debrett, 1795; Map 13. Alabama. Constructed from the surveys in the General Land Office and other documents. Philadelphia, John Melish, 1818.]

Cumming, William P. "Mapping the Southeast: The First Two Centuries." *Southeastern Geographer*, 6 (1966), 3-19.

Cumming, William P. *North Carolina in Maps.* Raleigh: State Department of Archives and History, 1966.

Cumming, William P. *The Southeast in Early Maps, with an Annotated Check List of Printed and Manuscript Regional and Local Maps of Southeastern North America during the Colonial Period.* Chapel Hill: University of North Carolina Press, 1958; 2nd edition, 1962; 3rd edition revised and enlarged by Louis De Vorsey, Jr., 1998.

Davenport, John Scott; cartography by Garland P. Stout. *Cornwallis' Invasion of North Carolina in 1781, Involving the Piedmont and the Dunker Congregations therein, with Notation of Tory Uprisings in 1780 Counter to His Lordship's Strategy (Not Including Skirmishes, Pyle's Massacre, or Fanning's Activities).* Charlotte: Carolina Maps by Mail, 2004.

Davis, George B., Leslie J. Perry, and Joseph W., Kirkley; compiled by Calvin D. Cowles; introduction by Richard J. Sommers. *Atlas to Accompany the Official Records of the Union and Confederate Armies.* Washington: Government Printing Office, 1891; reprinted with the title: *The Official Military Atlas of the Civil War.* New York: Arno Press, 1978; New York: The Fairfax Press, 1983. [Despite the fact that this atlas is for the period of the Civil War, the extensive mapping of the Southern States by Union cartographers provides a mid-nineteenth century overview of the landscape with many long-time historic details and place names that have vanished from more recent maps.]

DenBoer, Gordon. *North Carolina Atlas of Historical County Boundaries.* New York: Charles Scribner's Sons for the Newberry Library, 1998.

Eldridge, Carrie. *An Atlas of Appalachian Trails to the Ohio River.* Huntington, W. Va.: C. Eldridge, 1998.

Eldridge, Carrie. *An Atlas of Settlement between the Appalachian Mountains and the Mississippi-Missouri Valleys, 1760-1880.* Chesapeake, Ohio: C. Eldridge, 2006.

Eldridge, Carrie. *An Atlas of Southern Trails to the Mississippi.* Huntington, W. Va.: C. Eldridge, 1999.

Ellis, C. T. "Counties That Have Vanished." *The State: A Weekly Survey of North Carolina*, 10:51 (May 1943), 7, 14; online: http://digital.ncdcr.gov/cdm/ref/collection/p16062coll18/id/17263. [Online description from "North Carolina Periodicals Index," East Carolina University: "You will look in vain on the North Carolina map for Tryon, Bute, Glasgow, and Dobbs Counties, but many years ago they were a part of the State."]

Flowers, Paul. "Place Names in Tennessee." *West Tennessee Historical Society Papers*, 14 (1960), 114-123; online: http://register.shelby.tn.us/wths/?acc=Y.

Friis, Herman R. "Highlights of the Geographical and Cartographical Activities of the Federal Government in the Southeastern United States: 1776-1865." *Southeastern Geographer*, 6 (1966), 41-57.

Goree, John Arlin. "Price and Strother, Joshua Potts, and the Evolution of 'A Map of Cape Fear River and Its Vicinity." *North Carolina Historical Review*, 76:4 (October 1999), 391-409. [Online description from "North Carolina Periodicals Index," East Carolina University: "A look at the work of surveyors and cartographers Jonathan Price, John Strother, and Joshua Potts. Price and Strother published the first actual survey and map of North Carolina in 1798, and Potts' first map came in 1801. All three significantly advanced the cartography of the state during their careers and their work formed the basis for subsequent maps and plans for fortification of Wilmington and the Cape Fear River."]

Harley, J. B.; Barbara Bartz Petchenik; and Lawrence W. Towner. *Mapping the American Revolutionary War: The Kenneth Nebenzahl, Jr., Lectures in the History of Cartography at the Newberry Library.* Chicago: University of Chicago Press, 1978.

Hedgepeth, G. C. "After All, What's in a Name?" *The State: A Weekly Survey of North Carolina*, 16:1 (June 1948), 28-29; online: http://digital.ncdcr.gov/cdm/ref/collection/p16062coll18/id/22420. [Online description from "North Carolina Periodicals Index," East Carolina University: "The article serves as a brief introduction into historic North Carolina town names and how their names changed. Commonly, town names were chosen for an influential individual in North Carolina culture or a city's industry. For example, Wilmington, a shipping town, had its name transformed from New Liverpool, New Town, Newton, and finally Wilmington."]

Hill, Michael. "NC Places Named for Governors." *Tar Heel Junior Historian*, (Spring 2005); online: http://ncpedia.org/geography/places-named-for-governors.

Hunter, Priscilla Speed. "It's Beginning to Look at Lot Like Christmas." *The Palace*, 2:1 (Fall 2001), 4-5. [Online description from "North Carolina Periodicals Index," East Carolina University: "Tryon Palace's Christmas celebration encompasses two hundred years of North Carolina Christmas traditions including the African American Jonkonnu parade, historic greenery designs, and candle light tours of a Civil War Encampment."]

Lemert, Ben Franklin. "Geographic Influences in the History of North Carolina." *North Carolina Historical Review*, 12:4 (October 1935), 297-319; online: http://digital.ncdcr.gov/cdm/ref/collection/p16062coll9/id/4207. [Online description from "North Carolina Periodicals Index," East Carolina University: "This article looks at the impact of North Carolina's geography on the settlement, industry, and agricultural development of the state. The article is divided into sections that look at settlement, human activities, environmental influenced and the revolution, conflicting environmental influences between 1790 and 1860, the civil war, and the results of better adaptation to environmental influences."]

Lewis, J. D. "The American Revolution in North Carolina: Maps of Revolutionary War Battles/Skirmishes in North Carolina." Online: http://www.carolana.com/NC/Revolution/home.html.

Lewis, J. D. "The American Revolution in North Carolina: [Map:] Roads and Trails as of 1775 [North Carolina Transportation and Commerce, 1775, map.]; online: http://www.carolana.com/NC/Revolution/roads_and_indian_trails_1775.html. [Map caption: "At the outbreak of the American Revolution, there was already a growing network of roads and trails all across North Carolina. As new counties were created during the Revolutionary War, the citizens of North Carolina continued to improve their roads and trails, both internally and to/from the neighboring states of Virginia and South Carolina."]

Lewis, J. D. "North Carolina on the Maps after 1729." Online: http://www.carolana.com/NC/Maps/home.html.

Lonsdale, Richard E., ed. *Atlas of North Carolina.* Chapel Hill: University of North Carolina Press, 1967. [Includes a section, "The Revolutionary War," with a map of the major campaigns and battles.]

"Maps of Revolutionary War Battles/Skirmishes in North Carolina." Online: http://www.carolana.com/NC/Revolution/home.html. [Modern maps of events in many North Carolina counties during the war.]

Marshall, Douglas W., and Howard H. Peckham. *Campaigns of the American Revolution: An Atlas of Manuscript Maps*. Ann Arbor: University of Michigan Press, 1976. Miller, Larry L. *Tennessee Place Names*. Bloomington: Indiana University Press, 2001.

Mouzon, Henry. "Mouzon Map of 1775." *The State: Down Home in North Carolina*, 22:3 (July 1954), 37; online: http://digital.ncdcr.gov/cdm/ref/collection/p16062coll18/id/3219623:3 (July 1955), 11; online: http://digital.ncdcr.gov/cdm/ref/collection/p16062coll18/id/81662 [northeastern North Carolina and the Albemarle Sound region]; 23:4 (July 1955), 21; online: http://digital.ncdcr.gov/cdm/ref/collection/p16062coll18/id/81707 [Online description from "North Carolina Periodicals Index," East Carolina University: "The map was drawn up for use by the British Military but was used on by both sides of the Revolution. It designates landholdings, inns, ferries, bridges, and other prominent features."]; 23:6 (August 1955), 14; online: http://digital.ncdcr.gov/cdm/ref/collection/p16062coll18/id/81821. [Pamlico Sound region; Carteret County]; 23:7 (August 1955), 13; online: http://digital.ncdcr.gov/cdm/ref/collection/p16062coll18/id/81866; 23:8 (September 1955), 17; online: http://digital.ncdcr.gov/cdm/ref/collection/p16062coll18/id/81911 [focuses on Brunwick County and the lower Cape Fear River]; 23:10 (October 1955), 17; online: http://digital.ncdcr.gov/cdm/ref/collection/p16062coll18/id/82009 [Centers on the area of Salem, Salisbury, and Hillsborough and shows the Trading Path and other features]; 23:11 (October 1955), 19; online: http://digital.ncdcr.gov/ cdm/ref/collection/p16062coll 18/id/82062 [shows the area long the border with South Carolina]; 23:13 (November 1955), 15; online: http://digital.ncdcr.gov/cdm/ref/collection/p16062coll18/id/82160 [the far southwestern portion of North Carolina bordering South Carolina and Georgia].

Nebenzahl, Kenneth. *A Bibliography of Printed Battle Plans of the American Revolution, 1775-1795*. Chicago: Published for the Hermon Dunlap Smith Center for the History of Cartography at the Newberry Library [by] the University of Chicago Press, 1975.

Nebenzahl, Kenneth, and Don Higgenbotham. *Atlas of the American Revolution*. Chicago: Rand McNally, 1974.

Norris, Jeannie Faris. "How They Obtained Their Names." *The State: A Weekly Survey of North Carolina*, 17:5 (September 1949), 6-7, 20; online: http://digital.ncdcr.gov/cdm/ref/collection/p16062coll18/id/24382. [Online description from "North Carolina Periodicals Index," East Carolina University: "Here is a partial list of cities, towns and villages in North Carolina, together with a brief account of how they were given their present names."]

"North Carolina Revolutionary War Forts – 1775 to 1783." Online: http://www.carolana.com/NC/Revolution/nc_revolution_forts.html.

O'Reilly, Noel S., David C. Bosse, and Robert W. Karrow, Jr. (Occasional Publication of the Herman Dunlap Smith Center for the History of Cartography, no. 1) *Civil War Maps: A Graphic Index to the Atlas to Accompany the Union and Confederate Armies*. Chicago: Newberry Library, 1987. [Despite the fact that the atlas that serves as the basis for this index is for the period of the Civil War, the extensive mapping of the Southern States by Union cartographers provides a mid-nineteenth century overview of the landscape with many long-time historic details and place names that have vanished from more recent maps. Despite the passage of time between the Revolution and the Civil War, this atlas can still be useful for eighteenth-century research.]

Orr, Douglas M., Jr., and Aldred W. Stuart, eds. *The North Carolina Atlas: Portrait of a Changing Southern State*. Chapel Hill: University of North Carolina Press, 2000. [Publisher's description: "As North Carolina enters a new century, perhaps no southern state faces a more intriguing combination of challenges and opportunities. Changes in the state's economy, shifts in its population, and a widening breach between urban and rural areas are just some of the forces that are reshaping North Carolina at this pivotal time in its history. *The North Carolina Atlas* will be an invaluable aid in any effort to better comprehend the past, present, and future of our changing state. Using text and more than three hundred maps, charts, and photographs, the book offers an in-depth yet accessible look at the state's physical environment, history, population, and economy as well as such other aspects of life as government, politics, education, health, culture, and outdoor recreation. Tracing the shifts and patterns that have made North Carolina what it is today, the book also forecasts where these and other trends are taking us in this new century."]

Paysour, Conrad. "The Man Who Puts N. C. History on the Maps." *The State: Down Home in North Carolina*, 51:1 (June 1983), 15, 33, 34; online: http://digital.ncdcr.gov/cdm/ref/collection/p16062coll18/id/12300. [Online description from "North Carolina Periodicals Index," East Carolina University: "Garland Stout, a retired engineer, began making maps after researching his wife's Randolph County ancestors. Since then, Stout has drawn over 3,000 maps that include drawings of all 100 North Carolina counties. Stout's maps include old family residences, old churches, deserted towns with the dates they were incorporated, and abandoned roads. Stout is also a highly respected genealogist and is considered an expert in North Carolina post office history. Stout is currently trying to locate, by present county boundaries, the locations of original North Carolina land patents and land grants. He has completed sixty percent of the project to date."]

Poteat, RaeLana. "The Colony of Carolina." *Tar Heel Junior Historian*, 44:2 (Spring 2005), 8-13; online with the title: "Naming Places in Early Carolina:" http://ncpedia.org/history/colonial/place-names. [Online description from "North Carolina Periodicals Index," East Carolina University: "King Charles II of England in 1663 granted land in America to eight noblemen who had helped him regain the throne. The land was later named Carolina. Poteat discusses how the arriving colonists chose names for the places they encountered. For example, sometimes the Native American place-names were retained; towns and counties were named after a well-known persons associated with the colony; and often the name of the local Native American tribes was used."]

Powell, William S. *The North Carolina Gazetteer: A Dictionary of Tar Heel Places and Their History*. Chapel Hill: University of North Carolina Press, 1976; 2nd ed.: Chapel Hill: University of North Carolina Press, 2010. [Publisher's description: "The *North Carolina Gazetteer* first appeared to wide acclaim in 1968 and has remained an essential reference for anyone with a serious interest in the Tar Heel State, from historians to journalists, from creative writers to urban planners, from backpackers to armchair travelers. This revised and expanded edition adds approximately 1,200 new entries, bringing to nearly 21,000 the number of North Carolina cities, towns, crossroads, waterways, mountains, and other places identified here. The stories attached to place names are at the core of the book and the reason why it has stood the test of time. Some recall faraway places: Bombay, Shanghai, Moscow, Berlin. Others paint the locality as a little piece of heaven on earth: Bliss, Splendor, Sweet Home. In many cases the name derivations are unusual, sometimes wildly so: Cat Square, Huggins Hell, Tater Hill, Whynot. Telling us much about our own history in these snapshot histories of particular locales, *The North Carolina Gazetteer* provides an engaging, authoritative, and fully updated reference to place names from all corners of the Tar Heel State."]

Pruitt, Albert Bruce. *Creeks and Rivers in Tennessee, 1824*. Whitakers: A. B. Pruitt, 1996.

Pruitt, Albert Bruce. *North Carolina County Maps (1800)*. Whitakers: A. B. Pruitt, 2004. [Shows the locations of watercourses in every county, as they were bounded in 1800. Maps of the former Bute and Dobbs Counties are included. The table of contents shows the parents of counties formed since 1800.]

Revolutionary War: Carolina's Backcountry Revolutionary War Trail. Raleigh: North Carolina Division of Tourism, Film, and Sports Development, 2008. [map]

Revolutionary War: Carolina's Revolutionary War Trail: The Road to Victory. Raleigh: North Carolina Division of Tourism, Film, and Sports Development, 2004. [map]

The Revolutionary War in North Carolina. Raleigh: Office of Archives and History, [2008]. [map]

Richards, Nancy. "Mapping North Carolina." *The Palace*, 7:3 (Spring 2007), 6-7; 7:4 (Summer 2007), 4-7. [Online description from "North Carolina Periodicals Index," East Carolina University: "North Carolina has been mapped from the documentation of America to the present. Tryon Palace houses an important collection of maps recording the Carolinas and the Colonial history of the state."]

Robertson, John A., et al. "Global Gazetteer of the American Revolution." Online: http://gaz.jrshelby.com/a.htm. [This amazing website provides details on the location of events during the Revolution all over the world and often includes sources, maps, and other documentation for each entry.]

Ross, Thomas E.; Wesley D. Taukchiray; and Nathan Phillipi. "Map Errors and Indians of the Carolinas." *North Carolina Geographer*, 17 (2009), 54-59.

Sellers, John R., and Patricia Molen Van Ee. *Maps and Charts of North America and the West Indies, 1750-1789: A Guide to the Collections of the Library of Congress*. Washington, D. C.: Library of Congress, 1981; online: http://catalog.hathitrust.org/Record/000184071.

Sharpe, Bill. *A New Geography of North Carolina*. 4 vols. Raleigh: Sharpe Publishing Company, 1954-1965.

Shellans, Herbert. "Tarheel Place Names." *North Carolina Folklife Journal*, 4:2 (December 1956), 28-32. [Online description from "North Carolina Periodicals Index," East Carolina University: "Local legends and place-names constitute a part of popular history. Although they usually contain more fancy than fact, they possess a charm that appeals to all. This article is a sampling of what North Carolina has to offer in the way of local lore and legend concerning place names."]

Simpson, Bland, and Michael McFee. "North Carolina Place Names." Online: http://library.unc.edu/wilson/ncc/talk-like-a-tar-heel/.

Tenney, Brooks. "From Hatteras to Hiawassee." *Wildlife in North Carolina*, 57:12 (December 1993), 24-27. [Online description from "North Carolina Periodicals Index," East Carolina University: "All across North Carolina, native Americans have left a permanent legacy in the names of many towns, rivers, and other places."]

Trimble, Susan M. *Index to the Collet Map of North Carolina, 1770.* Raleigh: North Carolina Colonial Records Project, 1990.

Trimble, Susan M. *Index to the Mouzon Map of North and South Carolina, 1775*. Raleigh: North Carolina Colonial Records Project, 1990.

Westbrook, Kathy Grant. "Seeing Double in North Carolina." *Our State: Down Home in North Carolina*, 67:4 (September 1999), 52-54, 58; online: http://digital.ncdcr.gov/cdm/ref/collection/p16062coll18/id/68228. [Online description from "North Carolina Periodicals Index," East Carolina University: "Travelers might be confused by the many towns throughout the state that bear the same names. For example, there are seven Bethels and two former Bethels in North Carolina. A number of these communities including Bethels, Town Creeks, Concords, and Piney Greens, are profiled."]

Wiley, Mary Callum. "Changes on the Map." *The State: A Weekly Survey of North Carolina*, 12:4 (June 1944), 9, 24, 26; online: http://digital.ncdcr.gov/cdm/ref/collection/p16062coll18/id/19194. [Online description from "North Carolina Periodicals Index," East Carolina University: "Many names, once representing important towns, have entirely disappeared from state maps, while in other instances names have been changed not only once but several times. The first seat of government, Tower Hill, existed only on paper and there were changes at Hillsboro, Martinsville, and old Bloomsbury."]

North Carolina's Boundaries (generally)

Cuyler, Telamon Cruger Smith. "Telamon Cuyler Historical Manuscripts, 1754-1905." Manuscript MS1170, Richard B. Russell Building Special Collections Libraries, University of Georgia Libraries, Athens. [Description on ArchiveGrId: "The series consists of historical manuscripts relating to Georgia history collected by Telamon Cuyler covering the period 1754-1905. The series includes correspondence; bonds; county records, particularly for Jones County (Ga.); court records; indentures; inventories; land grants; newspaper clippings; and official Georgia government records for the office of the Adjutant General, Comptroller General, Governor, and Treasurer from 1754-1905 (with gaps). Topics documented within the collection include the Georgia militia; the Revolutionary War; Indian affairs in Georgia during the 1830s (particularly treaties); shipping (1770s-1780s); and boundary disputes between Georgia and Alabama, Florida, North Carolina, South Carolina, and Tennessee."]

North Carolina (State). Office of Secretary of State. "Boundary Papers, 1749-1841." Manuscript (MARS ID: 12.110; series), State Archives of North Carolina, Raleigh. ["Copies of originals located at the Archives and the Southern Historical Collection at Chapel Hill, relating to boundary issues between North Carolina and the states of Georgia, South Carolina, Tennessee, and Virginia."]

North Carolina's Boundary Dispute with Georgia

Battle, Charlton E. "The Georgia-Tennessee Boundary Dispute." *Georgia State Bar Journal,* 19 (1902).

Coulter, E. Merton. "The Georgia-Tennessee Boundary Line." *Georgia Historical Quarterly*, 35:4 (December 1951), 269-306.

Davis, Robert Scott, Jr. "The Settlement of the Head of the French Broad River, or the Bizarre Story of the First Walton County, Georgia." *North Carolina Genealogical Society Journal*, 7:2 (May 1981), 62-75. [Walton County existed from 1802-1812 and is now mostly the area of modern Transylvania County, North Carolina. Its existence is confusing for researchers, hence its inclusion in this publication.]

Georgia (State). Surveyor General. "General Administrative Records – State Boundary Records, 1783-1972." Manuscript RG 3/1/72, Georgia Archives, Morrow. [Online catalog description: "This series contains material related to Georgia's boundaries with the adjoining states of Alabama, Florida, North Carolina, South Carolina, and Tennessee. The documents include correspondence, journals, surveyor's field notes, plats, and secondary source material."]

Goodloe, Daniel Reaves. "The North Carolina and Georgia Boundary." *North Carolina Booklet*, 3:12 (April 1904), 5-22; online: http://digital.ncdcr.gov/cdm/ref/collection/p249901coll37/id/14180. [Online description from "North Carolina Periodicals Index," East Carolina University: "An examination of the dispute between Georgia and North Carolina over lands that fell within the boundary of Georgia, and the subsequent appeals to Congress by Georgia to establish a decided border at the 35 degree North latitude. Congressional records as well as state records from Georgia and North Carolina serve as source material."]

Gudger, Owen. "The Georgia Dispute." *The State: Down Home in North Carolina*, 10:36 (February 1943), 5; online: http://digital.ncdcr.gov/cdm/ref/collection/p16062coll18/id/16740. [Online description from "North Carolina Periodicals Index," East Carolina University: "North Carolina and Georgia had quite a time settling their boundary dispute. Both claimed an area which Georgia had named Walton County. They argued for five years while the area became a lawless no man's land. Gudger recounts the steps taken to settle the dispute in 1807 and return the land to North Carolina."]

Harper, Dave C. "How the N. C.-Ga. Line Was Finally Settled." *The State: Down Home in North Carolina*, 51:11 (April 1984), 10-12; online: http://digital.ncdcr.gov/cdm/ref/collection/p16062coll18/id/60729. [Online description from "North Carolina Periodicals Index," East Carolina University: "The boundary between North Carolina, South Carolina, and Georgia was disputed in the early 1800s. While South Carolina and Georgia settled their boundary along the Tugaloo River in 1802, North Carolina and Georgia did not settle their boundary until 1807. Both sides claimed rights to an area called Walton County, and for five years the area became a lawless no-man's land where no state had the power to enforce laws. Both states sent representatives to a meeting in 1807, where the current boundaries were established. North Carolina successfully claimed the Walton County region."]

Hood, Jack B. "Georgia's Northern Boundary." *Georgia State Bar Journal,* 8 (1971-1972), 192-203.

Jackson, L. A. "The Walton War." *Our State: Down Home in North Carolina*, 73:5 (October 2005), 98-100, 102-103; online: http://digital.ncdcr.gov/cdm/ref/collection/p16062coll18/id/84540. [Online description from "North Carolina Periodicals Index," East Carolina University: "A twelve-mile tract of land in the western part of the state, often called the 'Orphan Strip,' was claimed in the early 1800s by North Carolina, South Carolina, and Georgia. Georgia called it Walton County. South Carolina said their settlers were there in 1786. North Carolina said their state was formed before Georgia. Jackson traces the claims and counter-claims among the states. The issue was finally settled at MaGaha Branch in January 1811, in what is called the Walton War. After 200 North Carolina militiamen fought an unorganized band of Georgians, the property became the sole possession of North Carolina."]

"[North Carolina/Georgia Boundary]." Reference Vertical File, State Library of North Carolina, Raleigh.

Skaggs, Marvin L. *North Carolina's Boundary Disputes Involving Her Southern Line.* Chapel Hill: University of North Carolina Press, 1941.

Wright, Harry R. "Georgia's Northern Boundary is Marked." *Georgia Magazine*, 14:8 (1971), 19-21.

Wright, Harry R. "The History of Ellicott's Rock." *The State: Down Home in North Carolina*, 27:22 (April 1970), 9-10; online: http://digital.ncdcr.gov/cdm/ref/collection/p16062coll18/id/42266. [Online description from "North Carolina Periodicals Index," East Carolina University: "North Carolina, South Carolina, and Georgia claimed a twelve-mile tract of land in the western part of the state, often called the 'Orphan Strip,' in the early 1800s. Unable to settle the riotous border dispute, the Georgia-North Carolina commissioners engaged Major Andrew Ellicott, a noted surveyor, to locate the 35th parallel and set the boundary between North Carolina and Georgia."]

North Carolina's Boundary Dispute with Georgia – Extinct Old Walton County

[Note: The county only existed from 1802 to 1812 and was part of the boundary dispute between Georgia and North Carolina.]

Davis, Robert Scott, Jr. *A Researcher's Library of Georgia History, Genealogy, and Records Sources.* Easley, S. C.: Southern Historical Press, 1987.
This publication includes:
Chapter XIX: "The Walton War (Transylvania County, North Carolina)."
Chapter XX: "The Walton War – A Supplement."

Davis, Robert Scott, Jr. "The Settlement of the Head of the French Broad River, or the Bizarre Story of the First Walton County, Georgia." *North Carolina Genealogical Society Journal*, 7:2 (May 1981), 62-75. [Walton County existed from 1802-1812 and is now mostly the area of modern Transylvania County, North Carolina. Its existence is confusing for researchers, hence its inclusion in this publication.]

Hood, Jack B. "Georgia's Northern Boundary." *Georgia State Bar Journal,* 8 (1971-1972), 192-203.

Jackson, L. A. "The Walton War." *Our State: Down Home in North Carolina*, 73:5 (October 2005), 98-100, 102-103; online: http://digital.ncdcr.gov/cdm/ref/collection/p16062coll18/id/84540. [Online description from "North Carolina Periodicals Index," East Carolina University: "A twelve-mile tract of land in the western part of the state, often called the 'Orphan Strip,' was claimed in the early 1800s by North Carolina, South Carolina, and Georgia. Georgia called it Walton County. South Carolina said their settlers were there in 1786. North Carolina said their state was formed before Georgia. Jackson traces the claims and counter-claims among the states. The issue was finally settled at MaGaha Branch in January 1811, in what is called the Walton War. After 200 North Carolina militiamen fought an unorganized band of Georgians, the property became the sole possession of North Carolina."]

"[Map Showing Walton County and Surrounding Areas of Georgia, South Carolina, North Carolina, and Tennessee.]" [S. l.: s. n., ca. 1804] Genealogy Map Case, State Library of North Carolina, Raleigh; online: http://worldcat.org/oclc/320258141/viewonline. [Online catalog description: "Map shows the boundaries of now-defunct Walton County in what is presently Transylvania County, N.C. Ownership of the county was disputed by Georgia and North Carolina in the early 1800s, resulting in the 'Walton War' between the two state's militias. The map also shows Wofford's Settlement in what is now Georgia; at the time of settlement and surveying, it fell within Cherokee Indian lands. Map also shows surrounding areas of Tennessee, North Carolina, and South Carolina, including now-obsolete Pendleton 'County'(actually Pendleton District) in S. C."]

North Carolina's Boundary Dispute with South Carolina

[Note: The State Archives of North Carolina owns a considerable number of documents relating the colonial and state relations with South Carolina. A search of the term "South Carolina" in the MARS catalog yields 29 pages of results for the years 1775-1783, too many to include in this source guide. Such topics as military affairs, refugees, British troops, Loyalists, the Royal North Carolina Militia units from various counties (Anson, Bladen, Cumberland, and a few others), payments to British troops in the Army or the Royal Militia, prisoner exchanges, His Majesty's Hospital at Charleston, His Majesty's Hospital at Wilmington, Royal Navy ships in Charleston harbor, and maps. Most of the documents come from British headquarters in Charleston, S. C., and are copies of items in the National Archives of the United Kingdom, Kew, London.]

During its existence (1768/1769-1779), Tryon County, North Carolina straddled the modern North Carolina-South Carolina border and included the territory of Burke, Cleveland, Gaston, Henderson, Lincoln, McDowell, and Rutherford Counties, North Carolina, and claimed the territory of all or parts of modern Cherokee, Chester, Greenville, Lancaster, Laurens, Spartanburg, Union, and York Counties, and the Catawba Indian Reservation, South Carolina. Consequently, any studies of people and events in the northern part of South Carolina in the Revolutionary period must involve Tryon County sources.

Ball, Billy. "A Sad State of Affairs." *Indy Week*, 30:19 (April 2013), 19. [Online description from "North Carolina Periodicals Index," East Carolina University: "Property owners in the southwest corner of the state are affected by an unsettled boundary dispute between North and South Carolina which stems from a 278 year old mapping error. A 15-year dispute between 125 affected property owners and both states may soon reach a resolution with a new Joint Boundary Commission formed to resolve the problem."]

Bulletin of the Genealogical Society of Old Tryon County, North Carolina. Forest City, N. C., vol. 1 (1973)-present (2013). [This journal contains many articles on the history and records of Tryon County. See: "Topical Guide to Volumes 1-29," in the *Bulletin*, 30:1 (February 2002), 2-24 for an overview of the contents.]

Corbitt, D. L. "Boundary Line between North and South Carolina: Proclamations of Governor Martin." *North Carolina Historical Review*, 4:1 (January 1927), 104-105.

Davis, Charles S. "The Journal of William Moultrie While a Commissioner on the North and South Carolina Boundary Survey, 1772." *Journal of Southern History*, 8:4 (November 1942), 549-555.

Garrett, William Robertson. *History of the South Carolina Cession, and the Northern Boundary of* [i. e., with] *Tennessee*. (Tennessee Historical Society Papers, 1884) Nashville: Southern Methodist Publishing House, 1884. [Description from the Library of Virginia's online catalog: "Two papers read before the Tennessee historical society, Nov. 8, 1881, and March 18, 1884. The South Carolina cession was a strip of land 12 miles wide and more than 400 miles long, south of the southern boundary of the present state of Tennessee. It was claimed by both South Carolina and Georgia and, pending the settlement of the controversy, was ceded to the United States by the former state in 1787. In 1802 the portion of the strip north of Georgia was granted to that state, and in 1804 the remainder became a part of Mississippi territory, now forming northern portions of Mississippi and Alabama."]

Griffin, Clarence W. *History of Old Tryon and Rutherford Counties, North Carolina, 1730-1936*. Ashville, N. C.: Miller Printing Company, 1937.

Harper, Dave C. "How Our Line Got the Notch." *The State: Down Home in North Carolina*, 47:5 (October 1979), 10-12. [Online description from "North Carolina Periodicals Index," East Carolina University: "A land survey ending in 1737 established a boundary between North and South Carolina. In 1750, both states colonized towns in the same region, but it was not until 1762 that the British Board of Trade asked for the boundary to be resurveyed. Finally, in 1813, the boundary line dispute was concluded to the satisfaction of both states."]

Harper, Dave C. "They Put the Line Where It Belongs." *The State: Down Home in North Carolina*, 46:11 (April 1979), 10-13; online: http://digital.ncdcr.gov/cdm/ref/collection/p16062coll18/id/58402. [Online description from "North Carolina Periodicals Index," East Carolina University: "The original boundary line between North and South Carolina was established in 1735. Because of confusion between the states about the exact location of the line, it was re-drawn in 1928 by George Syme of North Carolina and Monroe Johnson of South Carolina. Using evidence found near the boundary, the two were able to recover the original line. Eight-inch granite posts serve as markers along the boundary, set at two mile intervals."]

Holcomb, Brent H. *Anson County, North Carolina Deed Abstracts, 1749-1766; Abstracts of Wills & Estates, 1749-1795*. Baltimore: Genealogical Publishing Company, 1980.

Holcomb, Brent H. *Deed Abstracts of Tryon, Lincoln and Rutherford, Counties, North Carolina, 1769-1786; Tryon County Wills and Estates*. Easley, S. C.: Southern Historical Press, 1977.

Holcomb, Brent H. *Mecklenburg County, North Carolina, Abstracts of Early Wills, 1763-1790 (1749-1790)*. Greenville: A Press, 1980.

Holcomb, Brent H. *North Carolina Land Grants in South Carolina*. Baltimore: Genealogical Publishing Company, 1980.

Holcomb, Brent H. *Tryon County, North Carolina, Minutes of the Court of Pleas and Quarter Sessions, 1769-1779*. Columbia: SCMAR, 1994.

Holcomb, Brent H. and Elmer O. Parker. *Mecklenburg County, North Carolina, Deed Abstracts, 1763-1779*. Easley, S. C.: Southern Historical Press, 1979.

Huhta, James K. "Tennessee and the American Revolution Bicentennial." *Tennessee Historical Quarterly*, 31:4 (Winter 1972), 303-315.

Jackson, L. A. "The Walton War." *Our State: Down Home in North Carolina*, 73:5 (October 2005), 98-100, 102-103; online: http://digital.ncdcr.gov/cdm/ref/collection/p16062coll18/id/84540. [Online description from "North Carolina Periodicals Index," East Carolina University: "A twelve-mile tract of land in the western part of the state, often called the 'Orphan Strip,' was claimed in the early 1800s by North Carolina, South Carolina, and Georgia. Georgia called it Walton County. South Carolina said their settlers were there in 1786. North Carolina said their state was formed before Georgia. Jackson traces the claims and counter-claims among the states. The issue was finally settled at MaGaha Branch in January 1811, in what is called the Walton War. After 200 North Carolina militiamen fought an unorganized band of Georgians, the property became the sole possession of North Carolina."]

Landrum, John Belton O'Neall. *Colonial and Revolutionary History of Upper South Carolina; Embracing for the Most Part the Primitive and Colonial History of the Territory Comprising the Original County of Spartanburg; with a General Review of the Entire Military Operations in the Upper Portion of South Carolina and Portions of North Carolina*. Greenville, S. C.: Shannon & Co., Printers, 1897; reprinted: (South Carolina Heritage Series, no. 1) Spartanburg: The Reprint Company, 1959; reprinted 1962, 1977.

Lefler, Hugh Talmadge. "The 100-Year Boundary Dispute." *The State: A Weekly Survey of North Carolina*, 20:34 (January 1953), 3-4, 19; online: http://digital.ncdcr.gov/cdm/ref/collection/p16062coll18/id/29847. [Online description from "North Carolina Periodicals Index," East Carolina University: "An issue since 1712, the boundary lines between North and South Carolina have caused numerous disputes spanning three centuries. This article discusses the history of this disagreement as well the use of Native Americans as pawns and the property mix-ups that started the controversy."]

Menzies, R. M. "How N. C. – S. C. Line Was Made." *The State: A Weekly Survey of North Carolina*, 5:7 (July 1937), 3, 18, 23; online: http://digital.ncdcr.gov/cdm/ref/collection/p16062coll18/id/103257. [Online description from "North Carolina Periodicals Index," East Carolina University: "North Carolina and South Carolina argued for eighty-five years – from 1730 to 1815 – over the placing of the boundary line between them. Menzies discusses the disagreement and its settlement."]

Moore, Louis T. "Boundary Line Dispute is Settled by a Tree." *The State: A Weekly Survey of North Carolina*, 12:50 (May 1945), 16-17; online: http://digital.ncdcr.gov/cdm/ref/collection/p16062coll18/id/13151. [Online description from "North Carolina Periodicals Index," East Carolina University: "The original boundary line between North and South Carolina, established more than two centuries ago, was clearly proved in recent years by a stately pine tree whose age is found to exceed 350 years. And if it weren't for this tree, chances are the states would still be squabbling over the location of the state line."]

Parker, Elmer Oris. "Site of Old Tryon County, North Carolina, Courthouse." *Bulletin of the Chester County Genealogical Society*, 3:3 (September 1980), 47-48. [with map of the site in present York County; 1769-1771]

"Petitioners from 'South Carolina,' Formerly Tryon County, 1775." *Bulletin of the Genealogical Society of Old Tryon County*, 38:2 (Mary 2010), 82-99.

Pettus, Louise. "Old North Corner." Online: http://www.rootsweb.ancestry.com/~sclancas/history/history_oldnorthcorner.htm.

Pettus, Louise. "North Carolina – South Carolina Boundary Line." (2001). Online: http://www.rootsweb.ancestry.com/~sclancas/history/boundary.htm.

Pettus, Louise. "Tryon (N. C.) Courthouse in York County." *The Charlotte* Observer, (May 30, 1986); reprinted: *Quarterly: A Publication of the York County Genealogical and Historical Society*, 5:3 (December 1993), 26.

Philbeck, Miles S. *Tryon County, North Carolina, Index to Land Surveys*. Chapel Hill: M. S. Philbeck, 1987. [from the beginning of the index: "Although usually considered to have been formed in 1769 and to have been abolished in 1779 in favor of Rutherford and Lincoln Counties, Tryon County land grants begin in 1768 and continued into 1784 with one being granted as late as 1789."]

Philbeck, Miles S. *Tryon County, North Carolina Land Warrants, 1768-1774*. Chapel Hill: M. S. Philbeck, 1987. [from the introduction: "These records are in the Secretary of State collection with current stack numbers S.S. 946, S.S. 946.3, and S.S. 588 and consist of lists of the warrants by number, name, acreage, and brief description."]

"Pioneer Families of Old Tryon County." *Broad River Notebook: A Publication of the Broad River Basin Historical Society*, 3:4 (December 1994), 85-87.

Pleasant, Paul. "No Man's Land." *The State: Down Home in North Carolina*, 29:9 (September 1961), 16-17, 29. [Online description from "North Carolina Periodicals Index," East Carolina University: "The boundary dispute in the 1740s between North and South Carolina found Anson County caught in the middle. Continued confusion over land rights resulted in forced land seizures, and land holders refusing to pay taxes to North or South Carolina. The dispute and confusion continued until after the Revolutionary War."]

Pruitt, A. B. [Albert Bruce]. *Abstracts of Land Entrys, Tryon and Lincoln Counties, North Carolina, 1778-1780; Lincoln County, North Carolina, 1780 and 1783-1834; and Lincolnton, North Carolina, 1785-1868*. 4 vols. [Whitakers, N. C.]: A. B. Pruitt, 1987. [Contents: Vol. 1: Tryon and Lincoln Counties, 1778-1780; Vol. 2: Lincoln County, 1783-1795; Vol. 3: Lincoln County, 1798-1825; Vol. 4: Abstracts of Lincoln County, North Carolina: Land Entries 1780 and 1795-1797; Land Processions 1789-1834; and Lincolnton, North Carolina, Deeds 1785-1868.]

Salley, A. S. "The Boundary Line between North and South Carolina." *South Carolina Historical Commission Bulletin 10*. Columbia: The State Company, 1929.

Skaggs, Marvin Lucian. "The First Boundary Survey between the Carolinas." *North Carolina Historical Review*, 12:3 (July 1935), 213-232; online: http://digital.ncdcr.gov/cdm/ref/collection/p16062coll9/id/4207. [Online description from "North Carolina Periodicals Index," East Carolina University: "This article examines the disputes between North and South Carolina over the establishment of the boundary lines between the two states dating back to the establishment of both colonies and concluding with the process of conducting the first boundary survey."]

Skaggs, Marvin Lucian. *North Carolina Boundary Disputes Involving Her Southern Line*. Chapel Hill: University of North Carolina Press, 1941.

Skaggs, Marvin Lucian. "Progress in the North Carolina-South Carolina Boundary Dispute." *North Carolina Historical Review*, 15:4 (October 1938), 341-353. [Online description from "North Carolina Periodicals Index," East Carolina University: "North and South Carolina's border dispute began in 1735 when survey work on the northwestern portion of the line was pushed forward by Governor Johnston in spite of South Carolina dissension. The article looks at the history of this dispute between colonies and the various proposals for boundary lines through a period between 1735 and the start of the Seven Years War. At the time of war, the line remained incomplete and further work was halted until conflicts end."]

Sullivan, Kathy Gunter. *Tryon County Documents, 1769-1779: A North Carolina County*. Forest City: The Genealogical Society of Old Tryon County, 2000.

Temple, Robert D. "Troublesome Boundaries: Royal Proclamations, Indian Treaties, Lawsuits, Political Deals, and Other Errors Defining Our Strange State Lines." *Carologue: A Bulletin of South Carolina History*, 27:1 (Summer 2011), 12-19; online: http://www.southcarolinahistoricalsociety.org/wp-content/uploads/2013/03/troublesome-boundaries.pdf.

Tryon County, North Carolina. *Tryon County, North Carolina Crown Docket, July 1769-April 1776; Tryon County, North Carolina, State Docket, October 1777-January 1779; Lincoln County, North Carolina, State Docket, April 1779-April 1780*. Forest City, N. C.: The Genealogical Society of Old Tryon County, 19[??].

Tryon County, North Carolina. Inferior Court of Pleas and Quarter Sessions. "Court Minutes of Tryon and Lincoln Counties, North Carolina, 1769-1782." Manuscript, State Archives of North Carolina, Raleigh; also available on LDS Family History Library microfilm 833297.

Tryon County, North Carolina. Inferior Court of Pleas and Quarter Sessions. Tryon County; Virginia Greene DePriest and Lucille Hendrick Gardner, [eds]. *Minutes of the Inferior Court of Please and Quarter Sessions for Tryon County, North Carolina*. Shelby: V. G. DePriest and L. H. Gardner, 1985. [Vol. 1: 1769-1772; Vol. 2: 1773-1779]

Wallace, Robert E. "The North-South Carolina Lines and Counties, 1669-1897." *The Quarterly: A Publication of the York County Genealogical and Historical Society*, 5:2 (September 1993), 12-14.

"The Whiskey Wagon and the State Line." *Bulletin of the Chester District Genealogical Society*, 11:2 (June 1988), 38-39.

Whiteside, Don. *Whiteside(s) Names Abstracted from 1) Tryon County, North Carolina, Court Minutes, 1772-1779; 2) Rutherford County, North Carolina, Court Minutes, 1779-1799*. Ottawa, Ont.: D. Whiteside, 1983.

Wright, Harry R. "The History of Ellicott's Rock." *The State: Down Home in North Carolina*, 27:22 (April 1970), 9-10; online: http://digital.ncdcr.gov/cdm/ref/collection/p16062coll18/id/42266. [Online description from "North Carolina Periodicals Index," East Carolina University: "North Carolina, South Carolina, and Georgia claimed a twelve-mile tract of land in the western part of the state, often called the 'Orphan Strip,' in the early 1800s. Unable to settle the riotous border dispute, the Georgia-North Carolina commissioners engaged Major Andrew Ellicott, a noted surveyor, to locate the 35th parallel and set the boundary between North Carolina and Georgia."]

North Carolina's Boundary Dispute with Tennessee (after 1796)

Hairr, John. "Along the Tennessee 1799 Border." *Wildlife in North Carolina*, 64:5 (May 2000), 22-27. [Online description from "North Carolina Periodicals Index," East Carolina University: "In 1789, North Carolina gave its western lands, which eventually became the state of Tennessee, to the federal government to settle debts. Starting in April 1799, a survey party struggled through this wilderness area for five weeks to mark the boundary between the two states. The surveyors, John Strother and Robert Henry, left notebooks that give a picture of what this area was like two hundred years ago."]

Strother, John. "The Boundary Diary." *The State: Down Home in North Carolina*, 33:24 (May 1966), 12-14; online: http://digital.ncdcr.gov/cdm/ref/collection/p16062coll18/id/49089. [Online description from "North Carolina Periodicals Index," East Carolina University: "In this second and concluding installment of his diary, John Strother describes the survey of the North Carolina-Tennessee line in 1799, from Pond Mountain to Painted Rock on the French Broad River."]

Strother, John. "John Strother's Survey Diary." *The State: Down Home in North Carolina*, 33:23 (May 1966), 10-11, 14; online: http://digital.ncdcr.gov/cdm/ref/collection/p16062coll18/id/49036. [Online description from "North Carolina Periodicals Index," East Carolina University: "In 1799, part of the boundary between North Carolina and Tennessee was established by surveyor John Strother, who kept a field book and diary of his wilderness trip. As far as *The State* magazine can determine, the diary has never before been published in its entirety."]

North Carolina's Boundary Dispute with Virginia

[Note: Both the Library of Virginia and the State Archives of North Carolina hold numerous documents relating to the boundary disputes between the two states over the centuries.]

[Note: The State Archives of North Carolina owns a considerable number of documents relating the colonial and state relations with Virginia. A search of the term "South Carolina" in the MARS catalog yields 10 pages of results for the years 1775-1783, too many to include in this source guide. Such topics as events in Norfolk, politics, the Cherokee, the Royal Navy and its ships, British mercantile claims against Virginians and North Carolinians, correspondence between the governors of the two states, maps, and boundary line between the states."]

Barnes, Arthur G. "The Virginia-North Carolina Frontier in 1776: William Preston, William Christian and the Military Expedition against the Overhill Cherokee Towns." M. A. thesis, The College of William and Mary, 1969.

Hardesty, C. H. "The Kentucky-Tennessee Boundary Line." M. A. thesis, University of Louisville, 1918.

Hohmann, Jack. "We Finally Draw the Line." *The State: Down Home in North Carolina*, 46:4 (September 1978), 10-11, 36; online: http://digital.ncdcr.gov/cdm/ref/collection/p16062coll18/id/58065. [Online description from "North Carolina Periodicals Index," East Carolina University: "In 1728, the dividing line between Virginia and North Carolina was drawn. The most famous member of the commission to establish the line was Colonel William Byrd of Virginia. Byrd, who was a self-proclaimed ladies man, wrote two books about the expeditions leading to the line's drawing. The books were frank and caustic, often admonishing settlers in both Virginia and North Carolina. Byrd died in 1744."]

Johnston, J. Stoddard. "Kentucky-Tennessee Boundary Line: History of the 36:30, the Boundary Line between Virginia and North Carolina and between Kentucky and Tennessee Virginia and North Carolina and between Kentucky and Tennessee." *Register of the Kentucky State Historical Society*, 6:whole no. 18 (September 1908), 23, 25-35.

"Legislative History of the Southern Boundary of Virginia." *Old Dominion*, 4 (1870), 380-392.

McCullar, Albert L. "The Kentucky-Tennessee Boundary Dispute." M. A. thesis, University of Kentucky, 1933.

North Carolina (State). General Assembly. "[Document dated:] January 28, 1779: Bill for Extending the Boundary Line between This State and the Commonwealth of Virginia." Manuscript; General Assembly Session Records; Session of January-February, 1779; Miscellaneous Bills, Senate Bills, House Bills, Box 2 (MARS ID: 66.8.16.9; folder), State Archives of North Carolina, Raleigh. [Online catalog description: "The bill appoints and grants specific powers to boundary commissioners to work with commissioners from Virginia to extend the boundary between the two states."]

North Carolina (State). General Assembly. "[Document dated:] October 25, 1779: Bill for Securing the Right of Such Persons in the County of Washington as Lie between the River Holstein and the Line Lately Run by Commissioners of North Carolina and Virginia." Manuscript; General Assembly Session Records; Session of October-November 1779; Unidentified Amendments, Senate Bills, House Bills; Senate Bills, Box 2 (MARS ID: 66.8.19.8; folder), State Archives of North Carolina, Raleigh. [Online catalog description: "The bill also divides Washington County into the counties of Washington and Sullivan, appoints commissioners to oversee the establishment of the new county, sets up its basic court regulations, and levies taxes for various purposes."]

North Carolina (State). General Assembly. "[Document dated:] May 2, 1780: Re[specting] Boundary with Virginia and Petition from Inhabitants of Roanoke, North Banks, Cape Hatteras, and Ocacock Island." Manuscript; General Assembly Session Records; Session of April-May 1780; Joint Papers, Committee Papers, Resolutions; Joint Papers (April-May, 1780); Joint Select Committee Reports and Papers, Box 1 (MARS ID: 66.8.20.8.19; item), State Archives of North Carolina, Raleigh. [Online catalog description: "The committee to which was referred the resolutions, dispatches, etc. from the Continental Congress report that the boundary commissioners have had a misunderstanding. The committee recommends that the governor confer with the governor of Virginia to find replacements and that the governor obtain the approval of the Assembly for any plan he may devise concerning the boundary. After investigating the petition, the committee also recommends that the inhabitants therein mentioned be exempted from the draft and that they organize into companies to defend the inlets. The Assembly concurs."]

North Carolina (State). General Assembly. "[Document dated:] May 6, 1780: Bill for vesting in Hannah Reed, widow of Reverend James Reed, his estate [and for suspending law concerning land grants near Virginia]." Manuscript; General Assembly Session Records; Session of April-May 1780; Miscellaneous Bills, Senate Bills, House Bills; Senate Bills, Box 2 (MARS ID: 66.8.21.19; folder), State Archives of North Carolina, Raleigh. [Online catalog description: "The bill also suspends the operation of the intestate law until the next session in the region recently discovered to be in the state due to the extension of the boundary line with Virginia. Also includes a draft of the bill."]

North Carolina (State). General Assembly. "[Document dated:] September 8, 1780: House Bills: Bill for Quieting Persons Who May Suffer by Extension of Boundary between Virginia and North Carolina." Manuscript;

General Assembly Session Records; Session of August-September 1780; Joint Papers, Committee Papers, Resolutions, Senate Bills, House Bills, Box 1 (MARS ID: 66.8.22.26; folder), State Archives of North Carolina, Raleigh. [Online catalog description: "The bill suspends until the next session of the Assembly all entries in the region affected by the extension of the boundary line. Includes two versions of the bill."]

North Carolina (State). General Assembly. "[Document dated:] February 1, 1781: Senate Bills: Bill to continue act for quieting such persons as may suffer in titles by extension of boundary with Virginia." Manuscript; General Assembly Session Records; Session of January-February 1781; Senate Bills, House Bills, Box 2 (MARS ID: 66.8.24.3; folder), State Archives of North Carolina, Raleigh. [Online catalog description: "The bill extends the named act, which was passed at the previous session. Includes statement from the clerk of the Virginia house of delegates on delays in furnishing attested copies of records."]

North Carolina (State). General Assembly. "[Document dated:] February 3, 1781: Resolution that the Assembly at next session hear claims of patentees and settlers under the State of Virginia." Manuscript; General Assembly Session Records; Session of January-February 1781; Joint Papers, Committee Papers, Resolutions; House Joint Resolutions: February 3-4, 1781, Box 1 (MARS ID: 66.8.23.16.2; item), State Archives of North Carolina, Raleigh.

North Carolina (State). General Assembly. "[Document dated:] April 29, 1783: Petition of Arthur Campbell of Virginia Requesting Land Title." Manuscript; General Assembly Session Records; Session of April-May 1783; Joint Papers, Committee Papers, Resolutions; Joint Select Committees, Reports and Papers: April 19-May 2, 1783, Box 1 (MARS ID: 66.8.29.8.10, State Archives of North Carolina, Raleigh. [Online catalog description: "Petition requests land along the Cumberland River that falls to the south of the Virginia/North Carolina border; land formerly thought to be in Virginia."]

"Northern Boundary of Tennessee." *American Historical Magazine*, 6:1 (January 1901), 18-39.

Sames, James W., III. *Four Steps West: A Documentary History Concerning the First Dividing Line in America, and Its Three Extensions, between Virginia and North Carolina, Kentucky, and Tennessee*. Versailles, Ky.: Published by the author, 1971. [Reprints Daniel Smith's journal of August 1779-July 1780], 26-40.

Sioussat, St. George L. "The Journal of Daniel Smith, One of the Commissioners to Extend the Boundary Line between the Commonwealths of Virginia and North Carolina, August, 1779, to July 1780." *Tennessee Historical Magazine*, 1:1 (March 1915), 40-65.

Smith, Daniel, 1778-1818; introduction and notes by St. George L. Sioussat. "The Journal of Daniel Smith." *Tennessee Historical Magazine*, 1:1 (March 1915), 41-66. [Description: "The journal of General Daniel Smith, one of the commissioners to extend the boundary line between ... Virginia and North Carolina, August, 1779, to July, 1780."]

Tyler, Walter Eugene. "A History of the Boundary Line between the Colonies of Virginia and North Carolina." Typescript Mss7:3 F229 T9:1, Virginia Historical Society, Richmond.

Virginia. Auditor of Public Accounts (1776-1928). "Boundary Line Surveys: 1781-1803. Accounts, Orders, and Vouchers." Manuscript, Auditor of Public Accounts Inventory entry no. 157, State Government Records Collection, Library of Virginia, Richmond. [Online catalog description: "Series contains accounts, orders, and vouchers from the Council of State for payment of survey expenses. Boundaries surveyed include those between Virginia and Kentucky, North Carolina, Pennsylvania, and Tennessee. These records cover the following dates: 1781, 1784-1786, 1799, 1802-1803, and n. d. The accounts contain the names of persons to whom payments were made, the amounts, and the dates paid. The orders authorize payments to surveyors, and the vouchers include the names of persons to whom money was owed, the amounts, and the dates the vouchers were submitted. Alphabetical by boundary."]

Virginia. Commission on Boundary Lines (1870-1874). "The Report of the Commissioners on Boundary Lines between the State of Virginia, and the States of Maryland, North Carolina, and Tennessee, Read in the Senate, Jan. 17, 1872." *Virginia Senate Documents, 1871-1872*. Richmond: [s. n.], 1872.

Virginia. General Assembly. "Representation, General Assembly of Virginia to Legislature of North Carolina, June 12, 1781." Manuscript, Library of Virginia, Richmond; online: http://image.lva.virginia.gov/GLR/01441/. [Online catalog description: "Part of a collection of letters and other documents received in the Governor's Office during the period June 29, 1776-Nov. 30, 1784. Re{garding} title to lands now thought to be in N. C."]

Virginia. General Assembly. House of Delegates. Speaker. "Papers, 1793 Oct. 21." Manuscript 36912, misc. reel 5379, Library of Virginia, Richmond. [Online catalog description shows that this material includes: "Enclosure #3 contains a letter from Thomas Jefferson enclosing an act of Congress passed 18 January 1793 for determining the northern boundary of the territory ceded to the United States by the State of North Carolina. Also included is a letter from Richard Dobbs Spaight, Governor of North Carolina, enclosing two acts passed by the General Assembly regarding the navigation of the Roanoke River and the canal from North Carolina to Virginia."]

Virginia. Plaintiff. *Boundary Line between Virginia and Tennessee. Bill and Exhibits in Chancery*. [Washington, D. C.: s. n., 1886?] [case in the United States Supreme Court: *In the Supreme Court of the United States, the state of Virginia vs. the state of Tennessee. Original no.--Bill in chancery*.]

Virginia State Library. "Virginia-North Carolina Boundary research materials, 1965-1966." Manuscript accession no. 30222, State Government Records Collection, Library of Virginia, Richmond. [Online catalog record: "Contains photocopies of printed and manuscript materials used to research the history of the boundary between Virginia and North Carolina. Dates of items photocopies range from 1715 to 1966 and include printed materials, original documents and copies of legislation."]

Wellford, Harry W. "Dr. Thomas Walker, his Uncelebrated Impact on Early Tennessee." *Tennessee Historical Quarterly*, 34:2 (Summer 1975), 130-144.

Wellford, Harry W. "The Virginia-Tennessee Boundary: The Walker Line?" *Tennessee Historical Quarterly*, 62:2 (Summer 2003), 110-129.

Transportation and Roads

Alford, Michael B. "The Ferry from Trent: Researching Colonial River Ferries." *Tributaries*, 1:1 (October 1991), 10-16. [Online description from "North Carolina Periodicals Index," East Carolina University: "Discovery in 1989 of a flatboat in a Trent River meander near New Bern gave insight into the building and use of an important transportation mode, the ferry in colonial North Carolina."]

Allhands, William A. "Historic Mountain Trails." *The State: A Weekly Survey of North Carolina*, 13:27 (December 1945), 26-27; online: [Online description from "North Carolina Periodicals Index," East Carolina University: "Originally there were the buffalo trails in western North Carolina. Then came the paths made by Indians, and finally the rough roads built by early settlers."]

Autry, Randall Franklin. "An Account of the Old Negro Head Point Road and the Part It Played in the Early Days of the American Revolution." Typscript (1978), North Carolina Collection, Louis Round Wilson Special Collections Library, University of North Carolina at Chapel Hill. [Varying title: "Scotch Highlanders Passed This Way, February 20-26, 1776." New Hanover, Sampson, and Pender Counties]

Brannon, Barbara. *The Ferries of North Carolina: Traveling the State's Nautical Highways*. Wilmington: Winoca Press, 2007. [Includes a history of ferries in the state.]

Clonts, F. W. "Travel and Transportation in Colonial North Carolina." *North Carolina Historical Review*, 3:1 (January 1926), 16-35; online: http://digital.ncdcr.gov/cdm/ref/collection/p16062coll9/id/4207. [Online description from "North Carolina Periodicals Index," East Carolina University: "Early colonists attempted to establish roads and highways in eastern North Carolina but inhabitants of the Albemarle region depended largely on the area's natural waterways for transportation. Documentation of colonial transportation avenues is limited but the article outlines the history of travel throughout the region during the early colonial phase. The article expounds on early types of watercraft and the difficulties of travel over land."]

Crittenden, Charles Christopher. "Inland Navigation in North Carolina, 1763-1789." *North Carolina Historical Review*, 8:2 (April 1931), 145-154; online: http://digital.ncdcr.gov/cdm/ref/collection/p16062coll9/id/4207. [Online description from "North Carolina Periodicals Index," East Carolina University: "The numerous sounds, rivers and creeks of North Carolina's coastal plain, although shallow and dangerous for large ocean-going vessels, were well suited for small craft and were great channels of commerce and trade before the installation of railroads. This article looks at changes in the inland waterways during this period as well as use for waterways, the kinds of vessels found on the waterways and difficulties in navigation."]

Crittenden, Charles Christopher. "Means of Communication in North Carolina, 1763-1789." *North Carolina Historical Review,* 8:4 (October 1931), 373-384; online: http://digital.ncdcr.gov/cdm/ref/collection/p16062coll9/id/4207. [Online description from "North Carolina Periodicals Index," East Carolina University: "This article looks at the limited means for communication in North Carolina during the revolutionary period. The piece focuses on challenges to timely communication centered on the slow development of a proper postal system in the state, including an examination of messenger services, poor facilities and roads, and prohibitive costs as well as the consequences of unreliable communication methods."]

Crittenden, Charles C. "Overland Travel and Transportation in North Carolina, 1763-1789." *North Carolina Historical Review,* 8:3 (July 1931), 239-257; online: http://digital.ncdcr.gov/cdm/ref/collection/p16062coll9/id/4207. [Online description from "North Carolina Periodicals Index," East Carolina University: "This article looks at the conditions of various overland travel routes and methods of transportation from 1763-1789 using period accounts. This includes descriptions of road conditions, river and stream crossings, east-west travel routes, ferry crossings, bridges, woodland trails, lodgings, ordinaries, inns, taverns, travel on horseback, travel by wagon, travel by carriage, travel on foot, and travel during the Revolutionary War."]

Dunaway, Stewart E. *Bute County, North Carolina, County Records: Road, Bridge, Ferry (1765-1779)* Hillsborough: North Carolina Historical Books, 2009. [Note: While not specifically concerning the Revolution, these sources can be used in tandem with land records and other documents to help locate places of residence, occupations, geographical features, and place names.]

Dunaway, Stewart E. *Carteret County Road Records (1774-1905), Bridge Record (1888), Ferry Record (1813).* Hillsborough: North Carolina Historical Books, 2013. [Note: While not specifically concerning the Revolution, these sources can be used in tandem with land records and other documents to help locate places of residence, occupations, geographical features, and place names.]

Dunaway, Stewart E. *Chatham County, North Carolina, Road and Bridge Records, Vol. 1 (1781-1899).* Hillsborough: North Carolina Historical Books, 2008. [Note: While not specifically concerning the Revolution, these sources can be used in tandem with land records and other documents to help locate places of residence, occupations, geographical features, and place names.]

Dunaway, Stewart E. *Chowan County, North Carolina, Mill Records (1731-1813) and Ferry Records.* Hillsborough: North Carolina Historical Books, 2010. [Note: While not specifically concerning the Revolution, these sources can be used in tandem with land records and other documents to help locate places of residence, occupations, geographical features, and place names.]

Dunaway, Stewart E. *Chowan County, North Carolina, Road Records (1717-1819) and Bridge Records (1744-1900.* Hillsborough: North Carolina Historical Books, 2013. [Note: While not specifically concerning the Revolution, these sources can be used in tandem with land records and other documents to help locate places of residence, occupations, geographical features, and place names.]

Dunaway, Stewart E. *Craven County, North Carolina, Mill Records (1766-1885) & Ferry Petitions (1784-1883).* Hillsborough: North Carolina Historical Books, 2012. [Note: While not specifically concerning the Revolution, these sources can be used in tandem with land records and other documents to help locate places of residence, occupations, geographical features, and place names.]

Dunaway, Stewart E. *Craven County, North Carolina, Road Records (1767-1839).* Hillsborough: North Carolina Historical Books, 2012. [Note: While not specifically concerning the Revolution, these sources can be used in tandem with land records and other documents to help locate places of residence, occupations, geographical features, and place names.]

Dunaway, Stewart E. *Edgecombe County, North Carolina, Road Records (1761-1849).* Hillsborough: North Carolina Historical Books, 2011. [Note: While not specifically concerning the Revolution, these sources can be used in tandem with land records and other documents to help locate places of residence, occupations, geographical features, and place names.]

Dunaway, Stewart E. *Gates County Road (1779-1849) and Bridge Records (1786-1900).* Hillsborough: North Carolina Historical Books, 2013. [Note: While not specifically concerning the Revolution, these sources can be used in tandem with land records and other documents to help locate places of residence, occupations, geographical features, and place names.]

Dunaway, Stewart E. *Granville County, North Carolina, Bridge Records, 1748-1868.* Hillsborough: North Carolina Historical Books, 2009. [Note: While not specifically concerning the Revolution, these sources can be used in tandem with land records and other documents to help locate places of residence, occupations, geographical features, and place names.]

Dunaway, Stewart E. *Granville County, North Carolina, Road Records, Vol. 1 (1747-1799).* Hillsborough: North Carolina Historical Books, 2009. [Note: While not specifically concerning the Revolution, these sources can be used in tandem with land records and other documents to help locate places of residence, occupations, geographical features, and place names.]

Dunaway, Stewart E. *Hyde County, North Carolina, Bridge Records (1748-1890), Road Records (1742-1859)* Hillsborough: North Carolina Historical Books, 2012. [Note: While not specifically concerning the Revolution, these sources can be used in tandem with land records and other documents to help locate places of residence, occupations, geographical features, and place names.]

Dunaway, Stewart E. *Lincoln County Road Records (1781-1822), Bridge Records (1813-1868).* Hillsborough: North Carolina Historical Books, 2015. [Note: While not specifically concerning the Revolution, these sources can be used in tandem with land records and other documents to help locate places of residence, occupations, geographical features, and place names.]

Dunaway, Stewart E. *Mecklenburg County, North Carolina, Road, Bridge, and Ferry Records, 1783-1921.* Hillsborough: North Carolina Historical Books, 2009. [Note: While not specifically concerning the Revolution, these sources can be used in tandem with land records and other documents to help locate places of residence, occupations, geographical features, and place names.]

Dunaway, Stewart E. *Miscellaneous North Carolina Road, Bridge, and Mill CRX Records: Brunswick Co. (1928, 1937), Burke Co. (1777-1786), Bute Co. (1767-1778), Cumberland Co. (1865-1868); Randolph Co. (1800-1845), Warren Co. (1780-1937).* Hillsborough: North Carolina Historical Books, 2015. [Note: While not specifically concerning the Revolution, these sources can be used in tandem with land records and other documents to help locate places of residence, occupations, geographical features, and place names.]

Dunaway, Stewart E. *Nash County, North Carolina, Bridge Records (1779-1834).* Hillsborough: North Carolina Historical Books, 2011. [Note: While not specifically concerning the Revolution, these sources can be used in tandem with land records and other documents to help locate places of residence, occupations, geographical features, and place names.]

Dunaway, Stewart E. *Nash County, North Carolina, Road Records (1768-1833).* Hillsborough: North Carolina Historical Books, 2013. [Note: While not specifically concerning the Revolution, these sources can be used in tandem with land records and other documents to help locate places of residence, occupations, geographical features, and place names.]

Dunaway, Stewart E. *North Carolina Ferry Records: A Historical Overview, 1739-1909: Including county records from: Bertie, Brunswick, Carteret, Chowan, Craven, Davidson, Davie, Montgomery, Northampton, Onslow, Orange, Pasquotank, Perquimans, Richmond, Rowan.* Hillsborough: North Carolina Historical Books, 2013.

Dunaway, Stewart E. *Onslow County Road Records (1775-1889), Bridge Records (1779-1875).* Hillsborough: North Carolina Historical Books, 2013. [Note: While not specifically concerning the Revolution, these sources can be used in tandem with land records and other documents to help locate places of residence, occupations, geographical features, and place names.]

Dunaway, Stewart E. *Pasquotank County, North Carolina, Mill Records (1731-1813) and Goat Island Ferry Records.* Hillsborough: North Carolina Historical Books, 2009. [Note: While not specifically concerning the Revolution, these sources can be used in tandem with land records and other documents to help locate places of residence, occupations, geographical features, and place names.]

Dunaway, Stewart E. *Pasquotank County, North Carolina, Road Records (1734-1799).* Hillsborough: North Carolina Historical Books, 2010. [Note: While not specifically concerning the Revolution, these sources can be used in tandem with land records and other documents to help locate places of residence, occupations, geographical features, and place names.]

Dunaway, Stewart E. *Perquimans County, North Carolina, Mill Records (1744-1885) & Ferry Petitions (1740-1866).* Hillsborough: North Carolina Historical Books, 2009. [Note: While not specifically concerning the Revolution, these sources can be used in tandem with land records and other documents to help locate places of residence, occupations, geographical features, and place names.]

Dunaway, Stewart E. *Perquimans County, North Carolina, Road and Bridge Records, Vol. 1: 1711-1799.* Hillsborough: North Carolina Historical Books, 2009. [Note: While not specifically concerning the Revolution, these sources can be used in tandem with land records and other documents to help locate places of residence, occupations, geographical features, and place names.]

Dunaway, Stewart E. *Randolph County, North Carolina, Bridge Records (1803-1864) and Mill Records, (1782-1879).* Hillsborough: North Carolina Historical Books, 2009.

Dunaway, Stewart E. *Richmond County Road Records (1778-1826), Bridge Records (1790-1897), Ferry Records, 1784-1857), Mill Records (1790-1875).* Hillsborough: North Carolina Historical Books, 2013.

Dunaway, Stewart E. *Road, Bridge and Ferry History of North Carolina: An 18th and Early 19th Century Review.* Hillsborough: North Carolina Historical Books, 2011. [Note: While not specifically concerning the Revolution, these sources can be used in tandem with land records and other documents to help locate places of residence, occupations, geographical features, and place names.]

Dunaway, Stewart E. *Rowan County, North Carolina, Ferry Records (1793-1848), Mill Records (1769-1895).* Hillsborough: North Carolina Historical Books, 2010. [Note: While not specifically concerning the Revolution, these sources can be used in tandem with land records and other documents to help locate places of residence, occupations, geographical features, and place names.]

Dunaway, Stewart E. *Rowan County, North Carolina, Road and Bridge Records (1758-1882).* Hillsborough: North Carolina Historical Books, 2010. [Note: While not specifically concerning the Revolution, these sources can be used in tandem with land records and other documents to help locate places of residence, occupations, geographical features, and place names.]

Dunaway, Stewart E. *Surry County, North Carolina, County Records: Road, Bridge, Ferry, Mill Petitions and Tavern Bonds (1772-1839).* Hillsborough: North Carolina Historical Books, 2011. [Contents: County records;

Ordinary record: Surry County, 1774; Road records, 1772-1799 (broken series); Bridge repair records, 1777-1839 (broken series); Bridge records, 1822; Mill records, 1823; Ordinary bond, 1774; Reference maps.] [Note: While not specifically concerning the Revolution, these sources can be used in tandem with land records and other documents to help locate places of residence, occupations, geographical features, and place names.]

Dunaway, Stewart E. *Wilkes County Road Records (1776-1853)*. Hillsborough: North Carolina Historical Books, 2013. [Note: While not specifically concerning the Revolution, these sources can be used in tandem with land records and other documents to help locate places of residence, occupations, geographical features, and place names.]

Fecher, Rebecca Taft. "The Trading Path and North Carolina." *Journal of Backcountry Studies*. 3:2 (Fall 2008); online: https://libjournal.uncg.edu/index.php/jbc/article/viewFile/26/15.

Hartley, Michael O., and Martha B. Hartley. "The Great Philadelphia Wagon Road." *Tar Heel Junior Historian*, 45:2 (Spring 2006), 8-11; online: http://ncpedia.org/history/colonial/philadelphia-wagon-road. [Online description from "North Carolina Periodicals Index," East Carolina University: "This road is known by several names. In North Carolina it is called the Great Philadelphia Wagon Road, or just Great Wagon Road. In Virginia it is called the Carolina Road because it led down into North Carolina. This road from Pennsylvania to the backcountry of North Carolina followed early Indian trails. It brought settlers for a number of reasons: fertile land at good prices, new opportunities, and religious freedom. The authors describe a trip on the road and some of the groups that traveled it."]

Hoffman, Paul Taylor, and Carroll Van West. "The Old West Passage: Exploring the First Road into Middle Tennessee." M. A. thesis, Middle Tennessee State University, 2012.

Hosking, Katherine. "From Buffaloes to Buses." *The State: A Weekly Survey of North Carolina*, 13:40 (February 1946), 10-111, 24-25; online: http://digital.ncdcr.gov/cdm/ref/collection/p16062coll18/id/15168. [Online description from "North Carolina Periodicals Index," East Carolina University: "Many of the roads North Carolinians drive on today started centuries before the coming of the colonists. Centuries ago woodlands and meadowlands were thick with deer, buffalo, and other smaller animals that made trails from one feeding ground to another. Later Native Americans would follow these trails. As the colonists began to arrive, these trails gradually widened. Usually they were dirt and in rainy periods could be almost impassable. Plank roads followed some in the mid-1800s, but it would be around 1900 before North Carolina began to take a serious interest in road improvement."]

James, Hunter. "Let's Retrace the Great Wagon Road." *The State: Down Home in North Carolina*, 52:1 (June 1984), 17-19; online: http://digital.ncdcr.gov/cdm/ref/collection/p16062coll18/id/60843. [Online description from "North Carolina Periodicals Index," East Carolina University: "The Great Philadelphia Wagon Road served as a main north-south thoroughfare in Colonial America. Prior to English settlement, Iroquois tribes used the road as a trading route. A portion of the Wagon Road can still be found on William H. McGee's farm in Stokes County. As Stokes County Historical Council president, McGee is directing a project to retrace the Great Philadelphia Wagon Road through North Carolina. This project is sponsored by the North Carolina Quadricentennial Anniversary Committee. Along with other projects, such as the building of the Elizabeth II and the excavation of the Lost Colony on Roanoke Island, the North Carolina Quadricentennial Anniversary Committee is attempting to call attention to the first English settlements in America."]

Larson, John Lauritz. "East against West: The Fight over Internal Improvements." *Tar Heel Junior Historian*, 36 (Fall 1996), 5-9; online with the title: "Improvements in Transportation: Post-Revolution to the Civil War," http://ncpedia.org/internal-improvements.

Lewis, J. D. "Carolina – The Indian Trails: Indian Trails Became Trading Paths, Which Later Became Roads." (map of western North Carolina and neighboring states showing early paths) Online: http://www.carolana.com/Carolina/Settlement/indian_trails.html.

Lewis, J. D. "The American Revolution in North Carolina." (map of Indian trails in the state in 1775). Online: http://www.carolana.com/NC/Revolution/roads_and_indian_trails_1775.html.

Lewis, J. D. "The Royal Colony of North Carolina: Internal Roads as of 1775." (map of North Carolina roads as of 1775). Online: http://www.carolana.com/NC/Royal_Colony/nc_internal_roads_1775.html.

Magnuson, Tom. "Marks on the Land We Can See: Routes of Carolina's Earliest Explorers." *Tar Heel Junior Historian*, 47:1 (Fall 2007), 9-11. [Online description from "North Carolina Periodicals Index," East Carolina University: "The earliest system of trails was developed by Native Americans connecting various settlements throughout the territory. Later, European settlers followed these same paths and developed a system of roads based on these and often enlarging them to permit wagons to pass. Traces of these are still visible, like The Carolina Trail between Crooked Creek in Stokes County and South Mayo River in Patrick County, Virginia."]

Morgan, J. Allen. "State Aid to Transportation in North Carolina." *North Carolina Booklet*, 10:3 (January 1911),

122-154. [Online description from "North Carolina Periodicals Index," East Carolina University: "Various policies and types of state aid were used to create and repair the transportation networks in early North Carolina."]

"North Carolina Transportation and Commerce, 1775." Online map: http://www.carolana.com/NC/Revolution/roads_and_indian_trails_1775.html.

Rights, Douglas L. "The Trading Path to the Indians." *North Carolina Historical Review*, 8:4 (October 1931), 403-426. [Online description from "North Carolina Periodicals Index," East Carolina University: "This article looks at the colonial roots of the Trading Path, an extremely popular travel and trade route through North Carolina that would later become the route for a system of 20th century highways. The article utilizes period accounts of exploration and travel along the path as well as descriptions of encounters with various Indian tribes with a particular focus on the travels of surveyor John Lawson, traders James Needham and Gabriel Arthur, and explorer John Lederer."]

Rouse, Parke. *The Great Wagon Road from Philadelphia to the North Carolina Piedmont*. New York: McGraw Hill, 1973.

Rouse, Parke, Jr. "The Great Wagon Road." *The State: Down Home in North Carolina,* 40:1 (June 1972), 6-8; online: http://digital.ncdcr.gov/cdm/ref/collection/p16062coll18/id/55232. [Online description from "North Carolina Periodicals Index," East Carolina University: "The Great Philadelphia Wagon Road, which cut diagonally through North Carolina's Piedmont, was the primary southbound route for English, Scotch-Irish, and Germanic immigrants who began arriving in Pennsylvania in the 1720s. By 1760, it had become the most heavily traveled road in America, fostering the establishment of new towns throughout the south, including Salisbury, Charlotte, and the Moravian settlements of Bethania and Salem in North Carolina. Revolutionary War battles fought along the Wagon Road include Camden, Cowpens, King's Mountain, and Guilford Courthouse."]

Rouse, Parke, Jr. "Traveling the Roads and Waterways of Early Virginia." *The Ironworker*, 37:1 (Winter 1973), 2-11. [Includes information on North Carolina.]

Watson, Alan D. "The Ferry in Colonial North Carolina: A Vital Link in Transportation." *North Carolina Historical Review*, 51:3 (July 1974), 247-260. [Online description from "North Carolina Periodicals Index," East Carolina University: "Starting with one ferry in 1700, the ferry service has expanded since North Carolina's settlement to facilitate travel for various purposes. During the colonial period, ferries made it easier for colonists to go to court, church, taking livestock to market, traveling for muster and for quicker delivery of mail through the postal service."]

Watson, Alan D. "The King's Highway." *The State: Down Home in North Carolina*, 41:7 (December 1973), 9-11; online: http://digital.ncdcr.gov/cdm/ref/collection/p16062coll18/id/56324. [Online description from "North Carolina Periodicals Index," East Carolina University: "The first intercolonial roadway through North Carolina completed in 1727, roughly paralleled U. S. 17. Most of the principal towns and tourist goals which attract north-south travelers along the Coastal Highway today were already stopping places in pre-Revolutionary times."]

Watson, Alan D. "North Carolina and Internal Improvements, 1783-1861: The Case of Inland Navigation." *North Carolina Historical Review*, 74:1 (January 1997), 37-73. [Online description from "North Carolina Periodicals Index," East Carolina University: "This article concentrates on the efforts made to improve the navigability of watercourses - rivers and streams - within the state in the years between the American Revolution and the Civil War. Additional attention is given to the role of government, particularly that of the state of North Carolina, as a political force that energized improvements for the benefit of the people first through the 'quasi-public corporation' system of encouraging private corporations to undertake navigation improvements, and then eventually moving to direct investment in corporate enterprises while assuming responsibility for supervising the more important navigation projects."]

Watson, Alan D. "Regulation and Administration of Roads and Brides in Colonial Eastern North Carolina." *North Carolina Historical Review*, 45:4 (October 1968), 399-417. [Online description from "North Carolina Periodicals Index," East Carolina University: "During the colonial period, eastern North Carolina possessed an inadequate and underdeveloped system of roads. To better road conditions, the colony tried appointing road commissioners, building bridges at public expense and putting up signposts and mile markers. Though they tried to improve the road network, the failure to enforce laws, the physical obstacles of the state's geography and shortages in the labor pool kept road conditions poor."]

Watson, Alan D. "Travel Conditions in Colonial North Carolina: The Case of the Lower Cape Fear." *Lower Cape Fear Historical Society Bulletin*, 41:2 (February 1997), 1-8. [Online description from "North Carolina Periodicals Index," East Carolina University: "Colonial travel in the lower Cape Fear region was by water and often slow and hazardous. As the population spread inland, a system of roads, bridges, ferries, and taverns developed. Since counties provided the upkeep, some routes were better than others."]

Waynick, Capus and John Harden. *North Carolina Roads and Their Builders*. 2 Vol. Raleigh: Superior Stone Company, 1952.

Travel to Revolutionary War Sites in North Carolina and Tennessee and Travel to the State during the Revolution

Alderman, Derek H. "'History by the Spoonful:' The Textual Politics of State Highway Historical Markers." *Southeastern Geographer*, 52:4 (Winter 2012), 355-373.

Arthur, Billy. "A Trip to Remember." *The State: Down Home in North Carolina*, 62:2 (July 1994), 14-15; online: http://digital.ncdcr.gov/cdm/ref/collection/p16062coll18/id/66840. [Online description from "North Carolina Periodicals Index," East Carolina University: "Spanish captain Francisco de Miranda recorded in his diary his 47-day trip to North Carolina in 1783. His writings give insight into the infant North Carolina communities of the time."]

Bartram, William. "Bartram's Travels VI." *The State: Down Home in North Carolina*, 27:3 (November 1959), 10, 16; online: http://digital.ncdcr.gov/cdm/ref/collection/p16062coll18/id/37151. [Online description from "North Carolina Periodicals Index," East Carolina University: "The visit of William Bartram in 1776 to western North Carolina was recorded in his book, Travels. In the sixth installment of his diary offered by The State, Bartram discusses his encounter with Little Carpenter, emperor or grand chief of the Cherokees."]

Boatner, Mark Mayo, III; introduction by Barnet Schecter. *Landmarks of the American Revolution: Library of Military History*. Harrisburg, Penn.: Stackpole Books, 1973; rev. ed.: Detroit: Charles Scribner's Sons, 2006. [Publisher's description: "Zooming in on key locations connected to the American Revolution, this expanded and completely revised edition of Col. Mark M. Boatner III's *Landmarks of the American Revolution* goes beyond U.S. borders when profiling historical sites and landmarks significant to the war. The original state-by-state guide now also includes coverage of the war in the West Indies and an expanded treatment of Canada. Bringing history to life through travel, this informative and practical approach anchors the American Revolution to the present, providing real-life context readers can relate to and even locate. Contact information on individual historical sites is provided. All entries, maps, photographs and contacts have been updated."]

Bradford, Samuel S. *Liberty's Road: A Guide to Revolutionary War Sites*. 2 vols. New York: McGraw-Hill, 1976. [See vol. 2:42-59 for North Carolina.]

Hill, Michael, ed. *Guide to North Carolina Highway Historical Markers*. 9th ed. Raleigh: Office of Archives and History, 2001.

Kapp, Chancy. "State Battlegrounds." *We the People of North Carolina*, 40:5 (May 1982), 20-22, 47-48. [Online description from "North Carolina Periodicals Index," East Carolina University: "Visitors are now welcomed on battlefields in the state where muskets once rattled and cannon roared during Revolutionary and Civil War battles. Kapp describes what visitors will find during a tour."]

La Vere, David. "The Royal Tour." *Our State: Down Home in North Carolina*, 68:10 (March 2001), 40-43; online: http://digital.ncdcr.gov/cdm/ref/collection/p16062coll18/id/72796. [Online description from "North Carolina Periodicals Index," East Carolina University: "La Vere describes a tour of Revolutionary War sites, with stops at Tryon Palace in New Bern, Moore Creek National Battlefield, the Battle of Guilford Courthouse, and Kings Mountain."]

Mitchell, Tucker. "Virtual Revolutionary Reality." *The State: Down Home in North Carolina*, 62:12 (May 1995), 24-27; online: http://digital.ncdcr.gov/cdm/ref/collection/p16062coll18/id/14495. [Online description from "North Carolina Periodicals Index," East Carolina University: "The half-dozen Revolutionary War battlefields in North Carolina are mostly in the Piedmont and mountains. A few, such as Guilford Courthouse, are large, but most represent small encounters between Whigs and Tories at bridges and crossroads."]

Moss, Patricia B., Jeffrey J. Crow, ed. *A Guidebook to Revolutionary Sites in North Carolina*. (Bicentennial Pamphlet Series, No. 3). Raleigh: North Carolina Department of Cultural Resources, Division of Archives and History, 1975.

"North Carolina State Historical Markers." Online: ncmarkers.com.

Patton, James W. "Glimpses of North Carolina in the Writings of Northern and Foreign Travelers, 1738-1860." *North Carolina Historical Review*, 45:3 (July 1968), 298-323.

Peixotto, Ernest Clifford. *A Revolutionary Pilgrimage; Being an Account of a Series of Visits to Battlegrounds & Other Places Made Memorable by the War of the Revolution*. New York: C. Scribner's Sons, 1917; online: http://hdl.loc.gov/loc.gdc/scd0001.00117121598.

Rippy, J. Fred. "A View of the Carolinas in 1783." *North Carolina Historical Review*, 6:4 (October 1929), 362-270; online: http://digital.ncdcr.gov/cdm/ref/collection/p16062coll9/id/4207. [Online description from "North Carolina Periodicals Index," East Carolina University: "A summary of descriptions and accounts of visits to several towns in North and South Carolina in 1783 culled from the diary of Francisco de Miranda, known best as a leader and proponent of the independence movement in the Spanish-American Colonies. Includes details of the Ocracroke Inlet area, New Bern, Beaufort, and Wilmington."]

Sarles, Frank B., Jr., and Charles E. Shedd; John Porter Bloom and Robert M. Utley, eds. *Colonials and Patriots: Historic Places Commemorating Our Forebears, 1700-1783*. Washington, D. C.: National Park Service, United States Department of the Interior, 1964.

Setzer, Lynn. *Tar Heel History on Foot*. Chapel Hill: University of North Carolina Press, 2013. [Publisher's description: "This lively collection of 34 of the best history walks in North Carolina highlights the richness and diversity of the state's history, from the time of its first settlement to the present. Veteran guidebook author Lynn Setzer leads readers on short walks in state parks and natural areas, state historic sites, charming small towns from the mountains to the sea, and the state's largest cities. Along the way, she brings to life some of our state's most momentous events, most accomplished and notorious characters, and most famous firsts.

Shively, Julie. *The Ideals Guide to Places of the American Revolution*. Nashville, Tenn.: Ideals Publications, 2001. [Publisher's description: "The Ideals Guide to Places of the American Revolution captures a significant period in American History. This book features expert research and writing that guide both the casual reader and the Revolutionary War enthusiast to hundreds of sites found throughout the Eastern United States. Major battles are outlined with Colonial and British commanders, quotes given by the commanders, strength of forces and number of casualties listed. Battlegrounds, cemeteries, museums, homes, taverns, monuments, and town halls are visited, and each has a listing of address, days of operation, admission fees and a short description of the site."]

Smyth, J. F. D. "Corn." *The State: Down Home in North Carolina*, 23:1 (June 1955), 11-12; online: http://digital.ncdcr.gov/cdm/ref/collection/p16062coll18/id/81572. [Online description from "North Carolina Periodicals Index," East Carolina University: "How would you describe corn to a person who has never seen or heard of its appearance, use, or production? Smyth, an Englishman who visited the colonies in 1773, and published in 1784, an account of his travels in which he describes North Carolina corn. His narrative centers on his travels just north of the Dan River along the Smith River near the present Rockingham County."]

Stewart, Matilda H. comp. *Markers Placed by the North Carolina Daughters of the American Revolution, 1900-1940*. Raleigh: Edwards & Broughton Press, [1940?].

Turner, Michael. "History on a Stick." *Our State: Down Home in North Carolina*, 82:10 (March 2015), 37-38, 40, 42; online: https://www.ourstate.com/highway-historical-marker-program/. [Online description from "North Carolina Periodicals Index," East Carolina University: "Along the state roads of North Carolina over 1,500 historical markers commemorate important people, places and events in the state's history. The author investigates the origins of the N. C. Highway Historical Marker Program, the Program's procedures, and the stories behind some of the state's markers."]

Carolina Bays, Pocosins, and Swamps

Beane, Jeff. "God's Ponds." *Wildlife in North Carolina*, 62:4 (April 1998), 12-17. [Online description from "North Carolina Periodicals Index," East Carolina University: "Carolina bays are oval-shaped depressions found in the Coastal Plain that are dependent on rainwater and are less than six feet deep. Dry in some seasons, wetland-like in others, they provide habitats for rare and not- so-rare plants and animals."]

Brooks, Mark J.; Barbara E. Taylor; and Andrew H. Iveser. "Carolina Bays:Time Capsules of Culture and Climate Change." *Southeastern Archaeology*, 29:1 (Summer 2010), 146-163.

Cooke, C. W. "Discussion of the Origin of the Supposed Meteorite Scars of South Carolina." *Journal of Geology*, 42 (1934), 88-96.

Davis, Alison. "A Trek through the Alligator River Refuge." *Coastwatch*, (November/December 1993), 3-7. [Online description from "North Carolina Periodicals Index," East Carolina University: "Dare County's Alligator River National Wildlife Refuge is one of the last large pocosin tracts in North Carolina and home to several U. S. Fish and Wildlife Service projects, such as the re-introduction of the red wolf."]

Early, Lawrence S. "Two Days in John Green's Swamp." *Wildlife in North Carolina*, 47:6 (June 1983), 14-21. [Online description from "North Carolina Periodicals Index," East Carolina University: "Brunswick County's Green Swamp is a 140-square-mile haven for plants and wildlife. All fourteen of the state's carnivorous plants live there. The area lay untouched for centuries until 1907 when the Waccamaw Lumber Company began logging operations. In 1974, the Department of the Interior designated 24,800 acres as a National Natural Landmark."]

Green, Ann. "Insect-Eating Plants Thrive in Green Swamp." *Coastwatch*, (Spring 2001), 26-28. [Online description from "North Carolina Periodicals Index," East Carolina University: "Fourteen varieties of carnivorous plants live in Brunswick County's Green Swamp. Some are small aquatic ones, while others rise to three feet. Species growing there include the Venus flytrap, pitcher plant, and sundew."]

Hairr, John. "Our Great Lakes." *Our State: Down Home in North Carolina*, 76:4 (September 2008), 44-46, 48-50; online: http://digital.ncdcr.gov/cdm/ref/collection/p16062coll18/id/100179. [Online description from "North Carolina Periodicals Index," East Carolina University: "Some of the most interesting lakes in the eastern United States lie in North Carolina's Coastal Plain and include Lake Mattamuskeet, Lake Phelps, and the mysterious Carolina Bays."]

Johnson, Douglas Wilson. *The Origin of the Carolina Bays*. New York: Columba University Press, 1942

Justus, L. "Swamps That Puzzle Everyone." *Atlanta Journal and Constitution Magazine*, (November 10, 1974), 10-21.

Krochmal, Connie. "Swamp on a Hill." *The State: Down Home in North Carolina*, 50:12 (May 1983), 16-18; online: http://digital.ncdcr.gov/cdm/ref/collection/p16062coll18/id/12257. [Online description from "North Carolina Periodicals Index," East Carolina University: "A large pocosin, or raised swamp formed some 9000 years ago, is located in the Croatan National Forest. Pocosins are shrub-tree communities, with trees only about five feet in height."]

Lide, Robert F. "When Is a Depression Wetland a Carolina Bay?" *Southeastern Geographer*, 37:1 (May 1997), 90-98.

Morris, Glenn. "The Great Lakes." *The State: Down Home in North Carolina*, 63:12 (May 1996), 25-27; online: http://digital.ncdcr.gov/cdm/ref/collection/p16062coll18/id/33931. [Online description from "North Carolina Periodicals Index," East Carolina University: "Carolina bay lakes are a unique natural wonder in that they are no deeper than six feet, elliptical, and dependent on rainwater. Among the best known are Lake Phelps, Lake Mattamuskeet, and White Lake."]

Otte, Lee J. "Origin, Development, and Maintenance of the Pocosin Wetlands of North Carolina: Report Submitted to North Carolina Natural Heritage Program and the Nature Conservancy." Kent, Ohio: Kent State University, 1981.

Norris, Jeannie Faris. "How Come Bladen's Big Bays? *The State: Down Home in North Carolina*, 28:2 (June 1960), 9, 22; online: http://digital.ncdcr.gov/cdm/ref/collection/p16062coll18/id/42584. [Online description from "North Carolina Periodicals Index," East Carolina University: "In an attempt to figure out the cause of the formation of the at least 1,200 pocosins, or bays, spreading over an area of some 25,000 miles, through North Carolina, South Carolina, and Georgia, scientists have formulated 29 hypotheses to explain the phenomenon. Discovered through the use of aerial photography, the pocosins or bays appear as large, dark, regular-shaped elliptical ovals. All but seven of the pocosins have since dried up or were filled in. White, Black, Salters, Suggs, and Singletary Lakes are examples of the remaining mysteries."]

Payne, Pegg. "Our Mysterious Carolina Bays." *Wildlife in North Carolina*, 42:11 (November 1978), 2-6. [Online description from "North Carolina Periodicals Index," East Carolina University: "Stretching across the Atlantic Coastal Plain from Florida to New Jersey are around 500,000 elliptical depressions known as Carolina Bays. Over half of them are found in eastern Carolina, and they are a land feature that exists nowhere else in the world. No one knows how they were formed."]

Raynor, Jerry. "Exploring the Magical Swamps." *The State: Down Home in North Carolina*, 52:11 (April 1985), 12-13; online: http://digital.ncdcr.gov/cdm/ref/collection/p16062coll18/id/61267. [Online description from "North Carolina Periodicals Index," East Carolina University: "Eastern North Carolina is home to many swamps ranging in size from small wet strips to the magnificent spread of the Great Dismal Swamp. When exploring North Carolina's swamps, one can find a wide variety of plant and animal life. Many swamps contain plant life unique to their areas, but almost all of North Carolina's swamps are home to the majestic cypress tree. Swamp visitors must always take safety precautions from such things as poisonous snakes and plants. With proper precautions, a swamp expedition provides a fascinating adventure."]

Roberts, Liza. "Did a Comet Cause the Carolina Bays?" *Metro Magazine*, 10:1 (January 2009), 16-19; online: http://www.metronc.com/article/?id=1806.

Ross, Thomas E. "Bays That Aren't Bays." *The State: Down Home in North Carolina*, 68:6 (November 2000), 82-84, 86. [Online description from "North Carolina Periodicals Index," East Carolina University: "Stretching across the Atlantic Coastal Plain from Florida to New Jersey are around 500,000 elliptical depressions known as Carolina bays. Over half of them are found in eastern Carolina. The bays are a land feature that exist nowhere else in the world. No one knows how they were formed. Some have water; others are dry. Lake Waccamaw is the largest of the bays, being about five miles long."]

Ross, Thomas E. "The Mysteries of the 'Carolina Bays'." *Carolina Country*, 30:9 (September 1998), 22-25. [Online description from "North Carolina Periodicals Index," East Carolina University: "Thousands of oval-shaped depressions, called 'Carolina Bays,' stretch across the Coastal Plain. Some of the larger ones have served humans from 10,000 years ago to the present. White Lake is an example. Their origins have been attributed to meteorites, fish wallows, and beaver dams."]

Ross, Thomas E. "Pocosins and Carolina Bays Compared." *North Carolina Geographer*, 11 (2003), 22-32; online: http://core.ecu.edu/crawfordt/ncgs/ncg/ncg_2003/2003_ross.pdf. [Online description from "North Carolina Periodicals Index," East Carolina University: "Carolina bays and pocosins are two distinct physiographic features found on the Atlantic Coastal Plain of the southeastern United States. Confusion frequently still exists pertaining to the definitions of both as they are often incorrectly assumed to be synonymous. This article defines each term and illustrates how bays and pocosins differ."]

Sasser, Janna. "Carolina Bays: Another Man's Treasure." *Coastwatch*, 4 (Autumn 2015), 24-29. [Online description from "North Carolina Periodicals Index," East Carolina University: "The Carolina bays, which include places like Lake Waccamaw and White Lake, are natural wonders of North Carolina. The author discusses the prevailing theories of these bays' origins, as well as the array of wildlife and vegetation found there."]

Savage, Henry, Jr. *The Mysterious Carolina Bays*. Columbia: University of South Carolina Press, 1982.

Sharpe, Bill. "Savanna and Pocosin." *Wildlife in North Carolina*, 59:3 (March 1995), 16-17. [Online description from "North Carolina Periodicals Index," East Carolina University: "Pocosins, vast, densely vegetated areas, and savannas, grassy flat areas, exist only in the state's Coastal Plain. Savannas are important because of their diverse plant and animal life, while pocosins absorb excess rainwater."]

Simpson, Bland. "Swamps." *Our State: Down Home in North Carolina*, 81:3 (August 2013), 134-136, 138, 140, 142-143; online: https://www.ourstate.com/swamps/. [Online description from "North Carolina Periodicals Index," East Carolina University: "Swamps lie in various regions of North Carolina, bringing unique environmental and cultural aspects to the state."]

Venters, Vic. "A New Look at Our Newest Refuge." *Wildlife in North Carolina*, 55:8 (August 1991), 8-13. [Online description from "North Carolina Periodicals Index," East Carolina University: "Formed from Tyrrell, Washington, and Hyde Counties, the 110,000-acre Pocosin Lakes National Wildlife Refuge is the state's newest refuge. Venters describes the area which, in addition to preserving valuable wetlands, provides an excellent habitat for wintering waterfowl, including tundra swans."]

Inlets of North Carolina

Angley, Wilson. "New Topsail Inlet: A Brief History." *Tributaries*, 5 (October 1995), 15-21. [Online description from "North Carolina Periodicals Index," East Carolina University: "Since people began settling near it in the early 1700s, New Topsail Inlet has witnessed commerce passing, ships sinking, wars, and now extensive recreational development."]

Dean, Earl. "Changes in Our Inlets." *The State: A Weekly Survey of North Carolina*, 18:28 (December 1950), 11, 17; online: http://digital.ncdcr.gov/cdm/ref/collection/p16062coll18/id/26294. [Online description from "North Carolina Periodicals Index," East Carolina University: "Storm tides and shifting sands have often changed the coastline of North Carolina with many of the inlets here today and gone tomorrow."]

Leutze, Jim. "Coastal Shoaling at Danger Point." *Metro Magazine*, 8:6 (June 2007), 27; online: http://www.metronc.com/article/?id=1345. [Online description from "North Carolina Periodicals Index," East Carolina University: "Leutze discusses the dangers of coastal shoaling at sites such as Carolina Beach Inlet, where coastal changes make navigation difficult and dangerous for boats."]

Mosher, Katie. "Dynamic Inlets: The Changing Shape of North Carolina's Coastline." *Coastwatch*, (Holiday 1999), 24-25. [Online description from "North Carolina Periodicals Index," East Carolina University: "Between the state's barrier islands are twenty- two inlets, stretching from Oregon Inlet in the northern Outer Banks to Mad Inlet near the South Carolina border. Inlets are more than just openings where the ocean flows in and out. They are dynamic places were the tidal currents try to deepen the channel while ocean waves carry sand to fill it up. Whichever force is dominant determines whether the inlet widens or closes up."]

Islands of North Carolina

Simpson, Bland. *The Inner Islands: A Carolinian's Sound Country Chronicle*. Chapel Hill: University of North Carolina Press, 2006. [Publisher's description: "Blending history, oral history, autobiography, and travel narrative, Bland Simpson explores the islands that lie in the sounds, rivers, and swamps of North Carolina's inner coast. In each of the fifteen chapters in the book, Simpson covers a single island or group of islands, many of which, were it not for the buffering Outer Banks, would be lost to the ebbs and flows of the Atlantic. Instead they are home to unique plant and animal species and well-established hardwood forests, and many retain vestiges of an earlier human history."]

Major Rivers of North Carolina

Early, Lawrence S. "Monster Fish." *Wildlife in North Carolina*, 54:3 (March 1990), 2-3. [Online description from "North Carolina Periodicals Index," East Carolina University: "About twenty-five species of sturgeon are distributed throughout the northern hemisphere and nowhere else in the world. The Atlantic sturgeon which inhabits North Carolina's waterways is among two groups of fish that migrate between salt and freshwater systems. It is the state's largest inland fish and can reach twelve feet in length and weigh over 500 pounds. This fish mates between late March and May and prefers rivers like the Cape Fear, Tar, Roanoke, and Chowan. Until 1900, the Atlantic sturgeon was one of the state's chief commercial fisheries. Overfishing caused its numbers to plummet, and the sturgeon population remains small into the twenty-first century."]

Jones, Doward N. "Tide Me Over." *Our State: Down Home in North Carolina*, 73:6 (November 2005), 200-202, 204; online: http://digital.ncdcr.gov/cdm/ref/collection/p16062coll18/id/84831. [Jones recounts the history of the Sans Souci ferry, a small two-car cable ferry that carries traffic across Cashie River in Bertie County. In 1722, a man named Tomlinson applied for and received permission to build a ferry. Since then a ferry has operated at that crossing. Artist Francis Speight's famous painting of the idyllic ferry crossing brought the scene to wider audience beyond the state."]

Jones, Morgan. "Dinosaurs in the Rivers?" *Coastwatch*, 2 (Spring 2013), 31-33; online: https://ncseagrant.ncsu.edu/. [Online description from "North Carolina Periodicals Index," East Carolina University: "North Carolina is home to a prehistoric species that was a common menu item along the east coast in the 19th century: Atlantic sturgeon. Although the extensive estuary system of North Carolina has allowed the Atlantic sturgeon to thrive, it has recently been placed on the endangered species list."]

Lewis, J. D. "North Carolina Watersheds." (map) Online: http://www.carolana.com/NC/Transportation/nc_watersheds.html.

Simpson, Bland. *Little Rivers and Waterway Tales: A Carolinians Eastern Streams.* Chapel Hill: University of North Carolina Press, 2015. [Publisher's description: "Bland Simpson regales us with new tales of coastal North Carolina's 'water-loving land,' revealing how its creeks, streams, and rivers shape the region's geography as well as its culture. Drawing on deep family ties and coastal travels, Simpson and wife and collaborator Ann Cary Simpson tell the stories of those who have lived and worked in this country, chronicling both a distinct environment and a way of life. Whether rhapsodizing about learning to sail on the Pasquotank River or eating oysters on Ocracoke, he introduces readers to the people and communities along the watery web of myriad "little rivers" that define North Carolina's sound country as it meets the Atlantic. With nearly sixty of Ann Simpson's photographs, *Little Rivers* joins the Simpsons' two previous works, *Into the Sound Country* and *The Inner Islands*, in offering a rich narrative and visual document of eastern North Carolina's particular beauty. Urging readers to take note of the poetry in 'every rivulet and rill, every creek, crick, branch, run, stream, prong, fork, river, pocosin, swamp, basin, estuary, cove, bay, and sound,' the Simpsons show how the coastal plain's river systems are in many ways the region's heart and soul."]

Alligator River

Davis, Alison. "A Trek through the Alligator River Refuge." *Coastwatch*, (November/December 1993), 3-7. [Online description from "North Carolina Periodicals Index," East Carolina University: "Dare County's Alligator River National Wildlife Refuge is one of the last large pocosin tracts in North Carolina and home to several U. S. Fish and Wildlife Service projects, such as the re-introduction of the red wolf."]

Dean, Jim. "A Piece of the Wild." *Wildlife in North Carolina*, 48:7 (July 1984), 14-15. [Online description from "North Carolina Periodicals Index," East Carolina University: "On March 26, 1984, the Prudential Insurance Company gave to the federal government 120,000 acres in Tyrrell and Dare Counties. The property is worth $50 million and will become part of the Alligator River National Wildlife Refuge."]

Luthy, Corrine. "A River and Refuge." *Greenville Times/Pitt's Past*, 28:2 (January 20, 2010), 12-13. [Online description from "North Carolina Periodicals Index," East Carolina University: "The Alligator River, which divides Tyrrell and Dare counties, is part of the Intercoastal Waterway and is important for its ecosystem and wildlife."]

Wilkins, Cherry. "Lotus of the Pungees." *The State: A Weekly Survey of North Carolina*, 7:5 (July 1939), 11, 20; online: http://digital.ncdcr.gov/cdm/ref/collection/p16062coll18/id/35176. [Online description from "North Carolina Periodicals Index," East Carolina University: "There is a Pungee Indian legend that tells why the Lotus, the lovely, exotic flower of the water lily family blooms so profusely on the Alligator River near the Albemarle Sound in eastern North Carolina. Although this flower of thick, waxen petals is a thing of beauty, deep in the center lies a seed so poisonous that it is fatal to those who eat it. This seed was once the cruel and callous heart of Lotus, a lovely but wanton Indian maid."]

Black River

Burgess, Carla B. "Walking to the River." *Coastwatch*, 2 (March/April 1994), 2-9. [Online description from "North Carolina Periodicals Index," East Carolina University: "The Black River contains clean water and cypress trees thought to be up to 2,000 years old. Friends of the river hope to protect its pristine condition."]

Burgin, William G. "Black River." *The State: Down Home in North Carolina*, 60:3 (August 1992), 26-29; online: http://digital.ncdcr.gov/cdm/ref/collection/p16062coll18/id/65595. [Online description from "North Carolina Periodicals Index," East Carolina University: "It is not very deep or wide, but this unique southeastern North Carolina tributary is in a class by itself."]

Earley, Lawrence S. "Exploring the Black River." *Wildlife in North Carolina*, 50:9 (September 1986), 4-11. [Online description from "North Carolina Periodicals Index," East Carolina University: "The Black River begins in Sampson County and flows sixty-six miles before emptying into the Cape Fear River fourteen miles above Wilmington. The water is black because unlike the Neuse and Cape Fear rivers, the Black River does not have sediment deposits, and its water is more acidic. Earley traveled two months on the river discovering its history and exploring the natural surroundings. Once a commercial thoroughfare, the river has again returned to its ancient ways. The steamboats and naval stores industry are gone. Some of the towns have fallen into ruin. No industries pollute it; no dams interrupt it; and no reservoirs disturb its flooding patterns."]

Hart, Kathy. "The Legend of Black River." *Coastwatch*, (March/April 1994), 10-15. [Online description from "North Carolina Periodicals Index," East Carolina University: "The Black River was a commercial highway from the colonial period until the late 19th-century. Truck and rail transportation ended this activity, which may have saved the river from environmental degradation."]

Peterson, Dwight L. "Black River: Journey to the Ocean." *Wildlife in North Carolina*, 37:8 (August 1973), 4-6. [Online description from "North Carolina Periodicals Index," East Carolina University: "Near Ingold in Sampson County, the Coharie and Six Runs Creeks join to form the Black River, which flows 66 miles before emptying into the Cape Fear River 14 miles above Wilmington. The Black River was a commercial highway from the colonial period until the late 19-century. Peterson describes a journey down the river in which he discovers its history and explores its natural surroundings."]

Brunswick River

Reaves, William M. *Notes on the Brunswick River and Its Environs*. Wilmington: W. M. Reaves, 1988.

Tidewater Atlantic Research, Inc. *An Historical and Archaelogical Assessment of the Submerged Cultural Resource Potential of the Brunswick River, Brunswick County, North Carolina.* [S. l.: TAR, Inc., [198?].

Cape Fear River

Ashe, Samuel A'Court "The Stamp Act on the Cape Fear." In *Addresses Delivered under the Auspices of the North Carolina Society of the Colonial Dames of American, 1900-1926.* [S. l.]: Jackson & Bell, [1927?].

Battle, Kemp P. *Letters and Documents Relating to the Early History of the Lower Cape Fear* (James Sprunt Historical Monograph, no. 4) Chapel Hill: University of North Carolina, 1903.

Blair, John J. "Colonial Governors of the Cape Fear." In Addresses Delivered under the Auspices of the North Carolina Society of the Colonial Dames of American, 1900-1926. [S. l.]: Jackson & Bell, [1927?].

Blethen, H. Tyler, and Curtis W. Wood, Jr. "Scotch-Irish Frontier Society in Southwestern North Carolina, 1780-1840." In H. Tyler Blethen and Curtis W. Wood, Jr., ed., *Ulster and North America: Transatlantic Perspectives on the Scotch-Irish* (Tuscaloosa: University of Alabama Press, 1997), 213-226.

Clifton, James M. "Golden Grains of White Rice: Planting on the Lower Cape Fear." *North Carolina Historical Review*, 50:4 (October 1973), 365-393. [Online description from "North Carolina Periodicals Index," East Carolina University: "Wealthy planters from the St. James Goose Creek Parish, 20 miles north of Charleston, established a permanent settlement in the Lower Cape Fear in the 1720s and introduced rice as a new agricultural staple in North Carolina."]

Connor, H. B. "Lower Cape Fear Leaders in the Struggle for Freedom." In *Addresses Delivered under the Auspices of the North Carolina Society of the Colonial Dames of America, 1900-1926*. [S. l.]: Jackson & Bell, [1927?].

Connor, R. D. W. "The Settlement of the Cape Fear." *South Atlantic Quarterly*, 6:3 (July 1907), 272-287.

Conser, Walter H., Jr. *A Coat of Many Colors: Religion and Society along the Cape Fear River of North Carolina*. Lexington: The University Press of Kentucky, 2006. [Publisher's description: "While religious diversity is often considered a recent phenomenon in America, the Cape Fear region of southeastern North Carolina has been a diverse community since the area was first settled. Early on, the region and the port city of Wilmington were more urban than the rest of the state and thus provided people with opportunities seldom found in other parts of North Carolina. This area drew residents from many ethnic backgrounds, and the men and women who settled there became an integral part of the region's culture. Set against the backdrop of national and southern religious experience, *A Coat of Many Colors* examines issues of religious diversity and regional identity in the Cape Fear area. Author Walter H. Conser Jr. draws on a broad range of sources, including congregational records, sermon texts, liturgy, newspaper accounts, family memoirs, and technological developments to explore the evolution of religious life in this area. Beginning with the story of prehistoric Native Americans and continuing through an examination of life at the end of twentieth century, Conser tracks the development of the various religions, denominations, and ethnic groups that call the Cape Fear region home. From early Native American traditions to the establishment of the first churches, cathedrals, synagogues, mosques, and temples, *A Coat of Many Colors* offers a comprehensive view of the religious and ethnic diversity that have characterized Cape Fear throughout its history. Through the lens of regional history, Conser explores how this area's rich religious and racial diversity can be seen as a microcosm for the South, and he examines the ways in which religion can affect such diverse aspects of life as architecture and race relations."]

Dosher, Randall. "The Old Middle Cape Fear in the Colonial and Antebellum Eras: Manuscript: An Introduction." *Footnotes: Occasional Publication of the Research Committee of the Duplin County Historical Society*, no. 46 (1992), 42 pages.

Dowd, Connor. *Deep River: The Story of a Man and His Family during the American Revolution*. Durham: Moore Publishing Company, 1977. [Connor Dowd, a Loyalist]

Earley, Lawrence S. "The Wall on the Cape Fear." *Wildlife in North Carolina*, 74:11 (November 2010), 26-31. [Online description from "North Carolina Periodicals Index," East Carolina University: "The wall in the title refers to the area in North Carolina where the soft sedimentary rock of the Coastal Plain meets the hard crystalline rock of the Piedmont. Such a meeting causes river rapids, such as Smiley's Falls in the Cape Fear River. For merchants and farmers living upstream in the 19th-century, the rapids blocked commercial traffic and goods from getting to market. Earley describes North Carolina's effort to overcome the rapids and open the river to traffic."]

Foard, John; compiled by Claude V. Jackson. *Stories of the Cape Fear Region: A Collection of Articles*. Carolina Beach: Federal Point Historic Preservation Society, 2000.

Foushee, Rodney. "Cape Fear Gold." *Wildlife in North Carolina*, 65:1 (January 2001), 4-11. [Online description from "North Carolina Periodicals Index," East Carolina University: "Once almost 30 rice plantations producing millions of pounds of rice annually lined the lower Cape Fear River and its tributaries. Rice grew there from the 18th-century till the last harvest in 1931. Today the land is a refuge for wildlife. The North Carolina Coastal Land Trust has conserved 4,000 acres of this land and seeks to save more before developers can move in."]

Fracaro, Angela. "A Fast Start at Looking Back." *The State: Down Home in North Carolina*, 57:1 (June 1989), 24-27; online: http://digital.ncdcr.gov/cdm/ref/collection/p16062coll18/id/63663. [Online description from "North Carolina Periodicals Index," East Carolina University: "The Museum of the Cape Fear in Fayetteville, which opened in 1988, is the third branch of the N. C. Museum of History. The opening assures that all citizens are no further than 100 miles from a state-affiliated museum."]

Gerard, Philip. *Down the Wild Cape Fear: A River Journey through the Heart of North Carolina*. Chapel Hill: University of North Carolina Press, 2013. [Publisher's description: "In Down the Wild Cape Fear, novelist and nonfiction writer Philip Gerard invites readers onto the fabled waters of the Cape Fear River and guides them on the 200-mile voyage from the confluence of the Deep and Haw Rivers at Mermaid Point all the way to the Cape of Fear on Bald Head Island. Accompanying the author by canoe and powerboat are a cadre of people passionate about the river, among them a river guide, a photographer, a biologist, a river keeper, and a boat captain. Historical voices also lend their wisdom to our understanding of this river, which has been a main artery of commerce, culture, settlement, and war for the entire region since it was first discovered by Verrazzano in 1524."]

Graham, Charles P. *A Glimpse of Carolina Medicine and the Lower Cape Fear Area: From Colonial Times to 1860.* Wilmington: Wilmington-New Hanover County American Revolution Bicentennial Association, 1975.

Great Britain. Admiralty. "Whitehall [London]. Copy of Lord George Germain, [Secretary of State,] to Lord [Charles] Cornwallis. 6 Dec. 1775." Copy of a manuscript in the National Archives of the United Kingdom (formerly the Public Records Office), Kew, Richmond, Surrey, England; (MARS Id: 21.114.208.46; folder), "British Records Collection," State Archives of North Carolina, Raleigh. [Online catalog description: "Plan of operations for expedition to Cape Fear. Encl{osed} in Germain to Admiralty, 6 Dec. 1775. {See 21.114.209.1.45}."]

Hairr, John. *Bizarre Tales of the Cape Fear Country.* Fuquay-Varina: Research Triangle Publishing, 1995.

Hairr, John. *Ghost Towns on the Upper Cape Fear.* Erwin: Averasboro Press, 1996.

Hall, Lewis Philip. Land of the Golden River: Historical Events and Stories of Southeastern North Carolina and the Lower Cape Fear. 3 vols. [Wilmington?: L. P. Hall, 1975-1980; and, William M. Reaves. Index to Land of the Golden River. 2 vols. Wilmington: W. M. Reaves, 1981. [A copy is located in the North Carolina Room, Main Library, New Hanover County Public Library, Wilmington.]

Hayden, Harry. *Rah! Rah! Carolina, and Three Confluent Rivers.* [S. l.: H. Hayden, 1966?]; and, William M. Reaves. *Index to Rah! Rah! Carolina...* [A copy is located in the North Carolina Room, Main Library, New Hanover County Public Library, Wilmington.]

Hirchak, John. *Legends of Old Wilmington & Cape Fear.* Charleston: History Press, 2014.

Jackson, Claude V., III. *Cape Fear-Northeast Cape Fear Rivers Comprehensive Study, a Maritime History and Survey of the Cape Fear and Northeast Cape Fear Rivers, Wilmington Harbor, North Carolina, Volume 1: Maritime History.* [Raleigh and Wilmington?]: Underwater Archaeology Unit, State Historic Preservation Office, Division of Archives and History; U. S. Army Corps of Engineers, Wilmington District, 1996; and, William M. Reaves. *Index to ....* Wilmington: W. M. Reaves, 1998. [A copy is located in the North Carolina Room, Main Library, New Hanover County Public Library, Wilmington.]

Lathan, Hannis Taylor, III. "Running Log Rafts on the Upper Cape Fear River." *North Carolina Folklore Journal*, 11:1 (July 1963), 6-13. [Online description from "North Carolina Periodicals Index," East Carolina University: "The Cape Fear River is formed by the confluence of the Deep and Haw Rivers. It flows in a general southeasterly direction and empties into the Atlantic Ocean. The river is navigable as far north as Fayetteville. From Fayetteville down, the quiet waters of the Cape Fear offered quick and inexpensive transportation of logs to the sawmills and lumber yards of the eastern seaport."]

Lee, Enoch Lawrence. "The History of the Lower Cape Fear: The Colonial Period." Ph. D. dissertation, University of North Carolina at Chapel Hill, 1955; published as: *The Lower Cape Fear in Colonial Days.* Chapel Hill: University of North Carolina Press, 1965.

McEachern, Leora H., and Isabel M. Williams, for the Wilmington-New Hanover County American Revolution Bicentennial Committee. *Lower Cape Fear Revolutionary War Events, 1765-1774.* [Wilmington: The Committee, 197?].

McEachern, Leora H., and Isabel M. Williams, for the Wilmington-New Hanover County American Revolution Bicentennial Association. *Lower Cape Fear Revolutionary War Events, 1776.* Wilmington: The Association, [1976?].

McEachern, Leora H., and William M. Reaves. *History of St. James Parish, 1729-1979.* [Wilmington?: s. n.], 1982. ["From the original manuscript 'Chronological History of St. James Parish, 1729-1979'." A copy is located in the North Carolina Room, Main Library, New Hanover County Public Library, Wilmington.]

McGeachy, John A. "Revolutionary Reminiscences from the *Cape Fear Sketches*." Typescript, North Carolina Room, New Hanover County Public Library, Wilmington. [Online catalog description: "Paper for History 590 at North Carolina State University, December 12, 2001, slightly revised January 21, 2002."]

McGeachy, John A. "Revolutionary Reminiscences from *The Cape Fear Sketches*." *Argyll Colony Plus*, 20:2 (July 2006), 10-23; 20:3 (Fall/Winter 2006), 58-70.

McKoy, W. B. "Incidents of the Early and Permanent Settlement of the Cape Fear." *North Carolina Booklet*, 7:3 (January 1908), 210-235; online: http://digital.ncdcr.gov/cdm/ref/collection/p249901coll37/id/14180. [Online description from "North Carolina Periodicals Index," East Carolina University: "An account of the exploration and settlement of the lands around the Cape Fear River, including details of settlements, land charters, laws, and citizens."]

Moore, Louis Toomer. *Stories Old and New of the Cape Fear Region.* Wilmington: Broadfoot Publishing Company, 1956; 1999.

Nickens, T. Edward. "Cape Fear: River of Water, River of Time." *Coastwatch*, 4 (High Season 1999), 6-13. [Online description from "North Carolina Periodicals Index," East Carolina University: "The Cape Fear River is a history-filled waterway, having seen early European explorers, including English, French, and Spanish ply its waters; bustling commerce, especially naval stores from 1720 to the Civil War; and warfare, including Spanish harassment during the 18th-century and the Union's blockade during the Civil War. Today it is a quiet stream, inviting travelers back through time."]

North Carolina. "Miscellaneous Papers, 1689-1912." Manuscript PC.21 (MARS ID: 530; record group), State Archives of North Carolina, Raleigh. [Online catalog description shows that this collection includes: "…Photocopies are chiefly material relating to…; expeditions against the British at Cape Fear; …"]

North Carolina (State). General Assembly. "[Document dated:] July 14, [1781]: Presenting Letter from Colonel Emmit, Cumberland County Militia." Manuscript; General Assembly Record Group; Session Records, June-July 1781; Joint Papers, Committee Papers, Resolutions, Senate Bills, House Bills, Box 1 (MARS ID: 66.8.25.4.9), State Archives of North Carolina, Raleigh. [Online catalog description: "Burke explains that the letter contains intelligence indicating British activity near the Cape Fear River and notes the lack of arms and ammunition."]

Rankin, Richard. "Musquetoe Bites: Caricatures of Lower Cape Fear Whigs and Tories on the Eve of the American Revolution." *North Carolina Historical Review*, 65:2 (April 1988), 173-207. [Online description from "North Carolina Periodicals Index," East Carolina University: "Leading up to the American Revolution, a document authored by the anonymous 'Musquetoe' was released that caricatured and satirized the leading Whigs and Tories of the Lower Cape Fear River Valley in North Carolina. The document exposed how the region exhibited many of the same strains found in other regions of the colony that had already escalated into open conflict. A large conflict was between the merchant class who had recently attained gentry status and therefore remained in the Loyalist camp, and the planters who resented the rise of merchants and were more often Whigs."]

Reaves, William M.; Dan Cobb, ed. "Cape Fear: American Revolution Bicentennial 1776-1976." *Sunday Star News* [Wilmington], 1975-1976; six volumes bound as one: NC 975.62 R, "Bill Reaves Collection Finding Aid and Index," North Carolina Room, Main Library, New Hanover County Public Library, Wilmington.

Rehder, Barbara Beeland. "Development of Libraries in the Lower Cape Fear." *Lower Cape Fear Historical Society Bulletin,* 7:2 (February 1964), 3-7. [Online description from "North Carolina Periodicals Index," East Carolina University: "Rehder divides her discussion of early North Carolina libraries into three types. First to be established were parochial-public libraries. These were books that were sent to ministers by England's Society for the Propagation of the Gospel. Eventually these books met the needs of the whole community and became public property. Second were private libraries of individual citizens. Wills, inventories, existing collections, and a few books in the hands of descendants help to identify the books' original owners. Third was the Cape Fear Library. A group of area gentlemen donated a fee each year for the purchase of books, newspapers, and periodicals, and the acquisition of a reading room to hold them. This library lasted until 1781, when British soldiers and North Carolina Militia soldiers stole much of the material."]

"Revolutionary War: Lower Cape Fear – American Revolutionary War." North Carolina Vertical Files Revol, Special Collections, New Hanover County Public Library, Wilmington.

Robeson, Susan Stroud. "The Cape Fear Section during the Revolution." *American Monthly Magazine* [DAR], 11:4 (October 1897), 371-381.

Robeson, Susan Stroud, and Caroline Franciscus Stroud. *An Historical and Genealogical Account of Andrew Robeson, of Scotland, New Jersey and Pennsylvania, and of His Descendants from 1653 to 1916.* Philadelphia: J. B. Lippincott Company, 1916. [Contains a chapter titled: "The Battle of Elizabethtown and the Cape Fear Section during the Revolution," 71-83.]

Ross, John Ray. "The Cape Fear River and Internal Improvements in North Carolina." M. A. thesis, Duke University, 1966.

Ross, Malcolm. *The Cape Fear*. (Rivers of America series). New York: Holt, Rinehart and Winston, 1965.

Ross, Malcolm. "Malcolm Ross Papers, 1961-1965." Manuscript 3729, Southern Historical Collection, Louis Round Wilson Special Collections Library, University of North Carolina at Chapel Hill. [Online catalog description: "Correspondence and notes of Malcolm Harrison Ross and, after his death, of his wife, related to his *The Cape Fear* (Rivers of America Series, 1965), including a manuscript of the book, and to related research projects, especially concerning Scottish immigrants to North Carolina. Correspondents include Jean Crawford, Paul Green, Inglis Fletcher, William S. Powell, Camille (Mrs. Malcolm) Ross, Lawrence Sprunt, Archibald Donald McDonald Strange, and Roy Wilder, Jr."]

Russell, David Lee. *Victory on Sullivan's Island: The British Cape Fear/Charles Town Expedition of 1776.* Haverford, Pa.: Infinity Publishing.com, 2002.

Sprunt, James. "Anecdotes of the Cape Fear." *The State: Down Home in North Carolina*, 28:17 (January 1961), 13-15. [Online description from "North Carolina Periodicals Index," East Carolina University: "Seventy-five years ago, James Sprunt, author of Chronicles of the Cape Fear, made a boat trip down the river from Wilmington, recording information for his book, Tales of the Cape Fear. Contained in the article are excerpts from this book, describing points of interest as they appeared during that period."]

Sprunt, James. *Chronicles of the Cape Fear River, 1660-1916*. Raleigh: Edwards & Broughton, 1914; 2nd ed., 1916; reprinted: Wilmington: Broadfoot Publishing Company, 1992.

Sprunt, James. *Tales and Traditions of the Lower Cape Fear, 1661-1896*. Wilmington: LeGwin Brothers, 1896; reprinted: Spartanburg, S. C.: Reprint Company, 1973; 1896 edition available online through the HathiTrust.

Sprunt, James; Jack E. Fryar, Jr., ed. *A James Sprunt Reader: Two Complete Classic Books by the Cape Fear's Greatest Historian: Tales and Traditions of the Lower Cape Fear; Tales of the Cape Fear Blockade; Newly Illustrated and with an Additional Short Short* [*sic*]; *A Colonial Apparition, Plus the Essay, "Stories of the Old Plantations, by Dr. John Hampton Hill.* Wilmington: Dram Tree Books, 2009.

Waddell, Alfred Moore. "Historic Homes in the Cape Fear Country." *North Carolina Booklet*, 2:9 (January 1903), 16-22; online: http://digital.ncdcr.gov/cdm/ref/collection/p249901coll37/id/14180. [Online description from "North Carolina Periodicals Index," East Carolina University: "This article examines the lack of historic homes preserved by North Carolina residents and discusses the few remaining historic homes in the Cape Fear region such as the adjoining Orton and Kendall plantations."]

Waddell, Alfred Moore. *A History of New Hanover County and the Lower Cape Fear Region*. Wilmington: [s. n.], 1909; reprinted: Salem, Mass.: Higginson Book Company, 1998.

Waddell, Alfred Moore. "The Stamp Act on the Cape Fear." *North Carolina Booklet*, 1:3 (July 1901), 3-22.

Warren, Harry. "When Waterways Were Highways: The Cape Fear River as a Transportation Link." *Tar Heel Junior Historian*, 28:2 (Spring 1989), 16-19. [Online description from "North Carolina Periodicals Index," East Carolina University: "Cape Fear River connected communities in eastern Carolina's coastal plain. Transportation transformed from sail and rowboats to steamboats in the 19th-century. River traffic again evolved in the early 19th-century when motorized boat traffic replaced steamboats. Regardless of propulsion, river traffic promoted growth of two of the river's largest cities, Fayetteville and Wilmington."]

Williams, Isabel M. *History of the Lower Cape Fear: Exploration, Colonization, Growth, 1524-1900*. Wilmington: Greater Wilmington Chamber of Commerce, 1980.

Wood, Bradford J. "The Formation of a Region in Colonial North Carolina: The Lower Cape Fear, 1725-1775." Ph. D. dissertation, Johns Hopkins University, 1999.

Wood, Bradford J. "Politics and Authority in Colonial North Carolina: A Regional Perspective." *North Carolina Historical Review*, 81:1 (January 2004), 1-37. [Online description from "North Carolina Periodicals Index," East Carolina University: "This article examines the political landscape of the Lower Cape Fear region of colonial North Carolina, comparing it to the rest of the colony. The Lower Cape Fear region developed quite distinctly from nearby regions as it contained a stable and wealthy ruling class and a large, unruly slave population. The differences between the Lower Cape Fear region and the rest of the colony emphasize the problem with generalizing North Carolina's political environment."]

Wood, Bradford J. *This Remote Part of the World: Regional Formation in Lower Cape Fear, North Carolina, 1725-1775*. Columbia: University of South Carolina Press, 2004.

Catawba River

Abernethy, Edgar. "Taming the Catawba." *The State: A Weekly Survey of North Carolina*, 12:3 (June 1944), 4-5, 21; online: http://digital.ncdcr.gov/cdm/ref/collection/p16062coll18/id/19161. [Online description from "North Carolina Periodicals Index," East Carolina University: "The various dams, such as the Mountain Island Waterpower Station, along the course of the Catawba River were built primarily for the purpose of generating power, but they also have been of tremendous aid in helping control the floods in that area from the often heavy rains."]

Beckerdite, Luke. "The Development of Regional Style in the Catawba River Valley: A Further Look." *Journal of Early Southern Decorative Arts*, 7:2 (November 1981), 31-48; online: https://archive.org/details/journalofearlyso721981muse. [Online description from "North Carolina Periodicals Index," East Carolina University: "This article examines the development of regional furniture styles in the Catawaba Valley of the North Carolina Piedmont through an anonymous group of furniture called the 'fluted pilaster group.' The Catawaba Valley style of furniture is heavily influenced by Delaware Valley settlers who moved to Catawaba Valley during the last half of the 18th century."]

"Catawba River Expedition, August 30, 1780." In Paul W. Gregory, *Early Settlers of Reddies River* (Wilkes Co.: Wilkes Genealogical Society, 1976), 48.

Chattooga/Chatooga/Chatuga/Chautaga/Chatthooga/Guinekelokee River

Clay, Butch. *Chattooga River Southcebook: A Comprehensive Guide to the River and Its Natural and Human History* [S. l.]: Chattooga River Publishing, 1995; 2nd edition with the title: *A Guide to the Chattooga River: A Comprehensive Guide to the River and Its Natural and Human History.* Birmingham, Ala.: Menahsa Ridge Press for the Chattooga River Community and Conservation Fund, 2012.

Mellinger, Marie B. "The Real Chattooga." *The State: Down Home in North Carolina*, 46:1 (June 1978), 24-25. [Online description from "North Carolina Periodicals Index," East Carolina University: "The Chattooga River was important for the 'Under the Hill' Cherokees. William Bartram wrote about the river in 1776 as did botanist Arthur Devernon Huger much later. The river changes with the seasons, and the banks are lined with ancient pines and hemlocks as well as sapling maples and basswoods."]

Siler, Leon M. "To Guard the Wild Chatthooga." *The State: Down Home in North Carolina*, 37:15 (January 1970), 8-9; online: http://digital.ncdcr.gov/cdm/ref/collection/p16062coll18/id/53168. [Online description from "North Carolina Periodicals Index," East Carolina University: "The Chattahooga River, which runs through western portion of our state, is apt to become much more familiar to North Carolinians through its projected inclusion by Congress in a system of National Wild and Scenic Rivers. The system will be modeled on the current network of national parks and national historic monuments with which many North Carolinians are familiar. Governors of the four states through which the river runs have given their public support for the river's inclusion, as have representatives from many outdoorsmen's organizations."]

Tetra Tech EC, Inc. *Chattooga River History Project, Literature Review, and Interview Summary.* Atlanta, Ga.: Tetra Tech EC, Inc., for the United States Department of Agriculture, Forest Service, Francis Marion and Sumter National Forests, 2006.

Chowan River

"The Chowan River." Online: http://aeaontheweb.org/chowrivtxt.htm.

"Chowan River Basin." Online: http://www.eenorthcarolina.org/Documents/RiverBasin_pdfs/final_web_chowan.pdf.

Jenkins, Jay. "Chowan." *Greenville Times/Pitt's Past*, 28:2 (January 20, 2010), 20-22. [Online description from "North Carolina Periodicals Index," East Carolina University: "The Chowan River begins in Franklin, VA and is one of the major freshwater contributors to the Albemarle Sound."]

Johnson, F. Roy. *Tales from Old Carolina: Traditional and Historical Sketches of the Area between and about the Chowan River and Great Dismal Swamp.* Murfreesboro: Johnson Publishing Company, 1965.

Dan River

Butler, Lindley S. "The Forgotten Boatman: Navigation on the Dan River, 1792-1892." *Tributaries*, 3:1 (October 1993), 11-16. [Online description from "North Carolina Periodicals Index," East Carolina University: "River navigation was invaluable during the 18th- and 19th-century throughout the state and remains an understudied aspect of maritime culture. The Dan River serves as a case study to demonstrate the range of riverine activities from canals, to fish dams, and the movement of goods and people. Dan River is a tributary of the larger Roanoke and opened a rich agricultural area for commerce."]

Ingram, Bruce. "The Many Faces of the Dan River, Part 2." *Wildlife in North Carolina*, 74:8 (August 2010), 22-29. [Online description from "North Carolina Periodicals Index," East Carolina University: "Part 1 of this two-part series on the Dan River discussed the stream from its Virginia headwaters along the Blue Ridge Parkway to Hanging Rock State Park in Stokes County. Part 2 follows the river from the park to Kerr Lake."]

Eno River

Anderson, Jean Bradley. *The History of Few's Ford.* Durham: Association for the Preservation of the Eno River Valley, 1989.

Ellis, Marshall. "The Faraway Nearby." *Our State: Down Home in North Carolina*, 67:9 (February 2000), 50-54; online: http://digital.ncdcr.gov/cdm/ref/collection/p16062coll18/id/70751. [Online description from "North Carolina Periodicals Index," East Carolina University: "Rising in Orange County, the Eno River flows thirty miles before merging with the Flat and Little rivers to form the Neuse. Yet this small river has been fought over by developers who wanted to exploit it and environmentalists who wanted to preserve it. In 1965, Margaret Nygard helped organize the Association for the Preservation of the Eno River, a group that defeated every attempt to spoil the river. Today the Eno River State Park stands as a monument to their perseverance."]

Engstrom, Mary Claire. *Early Quakers in the Eno River Valley, ca: 1750-1847*. Durham: Association for the Preservation of the Eno River, 1989.

Schurmann, Marguerite. "The Living Eno." *The State: Down Home in North Carolina*, 45:1 (June 1977), 18-20; online: http://digital.ncdcr.gov/cdm/compoundobject/collection/p16062coll18/id/57306. [Online description from "North Carolina Periodicals Index," East Carolina University: "The Eno is a small but unusually clean free-flowing recreation river in the Piedmont region of North Carolina. It has inspired many locals to work for its preservation and protection from pollution. This article highlights the importance of the river to the area."]

French Broad River

Burnett, Edmund Cody. "Hog Raising and Hog Driving in the Region o f the French Broad River." *Agricultural History*, 20:2 (April 1946), 86-103.

Dykeman, Wilma. *The French Broad*. New York: Rinehart, 1955; reprinted: Knoxville: University of Tennessee Press, 1965.

Murphy, Jim. "The Story of the French Broad River." *Laurel of Asheville*, 9:3 (March 2012), 56. [Online description from "North Carolina Periodicals Index," East Carolina University: "The author discusses the French Broad River's name origins and the various myths surrounding its nomenclature."]

Smathers, George H. *The History of Land Titles in Western North Carolina. A History of the Cherokee Land Laws Affecting the Title to Land Lying West of the Meigs and Freemand Line, and Laws Affecting the Title of Land Lying East of the Meigs and Freeman Line Back to the Top of the Blue Ridge, Including all the Land on the Waters of the French Broad River in What Was Formerly Buncombe County as Created by the Act of 1792*. Asheville: Miller Printing Company, 1938.

Green River

Hensley, Julia. *A Pictorial Visit to Green River Plantation*. Rutherfordton: Hilltop Publications, 1993.

Lattimore, Robin Spencer; Julia Hensley, ed. *Across Two Centuries: The Lost World of Green River Plantation*. Rutherfordton: Hilltop Publications, 2003.

Manual John. "Green River Extravaganza." *Wildlife in North Carolina*, 62:5 (May 1998), 22-27. [Online description from "North Carolina Periodicals Index," East Carolina University: "The state-owned Green River Preserve, located in Henderson, Polk, and Rutherford counties, is 20,000 acres of diverse flora and fauna. It is also a managed game preserve providing hunters a place to hunt."]

Painter, An. "Do You Know the Green River?" *Wildlife in North Carolina*, 40:10 (October 1976), 17-19; 40:11 (November 1976), 20-22, 27; 40:12 (December 1976), 21-25. [Online description from "North Carolina Periodicals Index," East Carolina University: "The Green River, which is actually green when road sediment and other erosion aren't being washed in, flows through Polk and Henderson Counties. The river is narrow and swift in some places and dammed in others. The river has many faces, but fast water with many falls and cataracts provide one of its claims to fame. In this first of three articles on the river, Painter describes the land and the general aspects of the entire river."]

Painter, An. "The Green River as a Resource." *Wildlife in North Carolina*, 40:12 (December 1976), 21-25. [Online description from "North Carolina Periodicals Index," East Carolina University: "In this concluding article of a three-part series on the Green River, Painter discusses its use, management, and vulnerability."]

Williams, Sadie A. "Many Moods of the Wild Green River." *The State: Down Home in North Carolina*, 47:2 (July 1979), 8-10, 32; online: http://digital.ncdcr.gov/cdm/ref/collection/p16062coll18/id/58575. [Online description from "North Carolina Periodicals Index," East Carolina University: "The Green River provided a barrier to the early settlers of Henderson County. The river is a rushing stream in some places and not more than a creek in others. Currently, the river is being considered as a potential State Natural and Scenic River, but the final decision still has to be voted on by citizens of Henderson and Polk counties."]

Horsepasture River

Early, Lawrence S., and Jay Davies. "Saving the Horsepasture." *Wildlife in North Carolina*, 49:2 (February 1985), 23-27. [Online description from "North Carolina Periodicals Index," East Carolina University: "The wild, free-running Horsepasture River flows through Jackson and Transylvania Counties and drops 2,000 feet in 14.8 miles. Plans to build a controversial power plant on it have been delayed for three years while the federal government considers it for inclusion in the Wild and Scenic River Program. Water diverted to the plant along a 2.5 mile stretch would diminish the water flow in five scenic waterfalls. No other state river has so many waterfalls in so short a stretch."]

Linville River

Abernethy, George. "Linville Gorge." *The State: A Weekly Survey of North Carolina*, 13:24 (November 1945), 3-5; online: http://digital.ncdcr.gov/cdm/ref/collection/p16062coll18/id/13955. [Online description from "North Carolina Periodicals Index," East Carolina University: "Linville Gorge lies in Burke County. Beginning at Linville Falls, it is some fifteen or twenty miles in length and the mountains along the sides rise from 1500 to 2000 feet above the Linville River."]

Lumber River

Simpson, Bland. "Sweetheart Stream." *Wildlife in North Carolina*, 54:9 (September 1990), 10-15. [Online description from "North Carolina Periodicals Index," East Carolina University: "In 1907, John McNeill called the Lumbee (Lumber) River 'a tortuous, delicious flirt,' a description that still fits today."]

McLean, Hamilton; John Edwin Purcell; John Edwin Purcell [2nd]; Archibald Gilchrist Singletary. *The Lumber River Scots and Their Descendants: The McLeans, the Torreys, the Purcells, the McIntyres, the Gilchrists.* Richmond: William Byrd Press, 1942; reprinted: 1986.

Neuse River

Duff, Jim. "Prehistory Preserved." *The State: Down Home in North Carolina*, 59:9 (February 1992), 27-29; online: http://digital.ncdcr.gov/cdm/ref/collection/p16062coll18/id/65281. [Online description from "North Carolina Periodicals Index," East Carolina University: "A 90-foot-high rock formation at Cliffs of the Neuse State Park near Goldsboro contains the strata of 180 million years of geological history."]

Historic and Architectural Resources of the Tar-Neuse Basin. 6 vols. Raleigh: Survey and Planning Branch, Historic Preservation Section, Division of Archives and History, North Carolina Dept. of Cultural Resources, 1977.

North Carolina (State). General Assembly. "[Document dated:] October 25, 1779: House to Prevent Persons from Stopping the Passage of Fish Up Tar and Dan Rivers." Manuscript; General Assembly Session Records; Session of October-November 1779; Unidentified Amendments, Senate Bills, House Bills, Box 2 (MARS ID: 66.8.19.35; folder), State Archives of North Carolina, Raleigh.

North Carolina (State). General Assembly. "[Document dated:] April 23, 1783: Senate Bill to Amend Act to Prevent Persons from Stopping the Passage of Fish Up Tar and Dan Rivers." Manuscript; General Assembly Session Records; Session of April-May 1783; Unidentified Amendments, Senate Bills, House Bills, Box 2 (MARS ID: 66.8.30.3; folder), State Archives of North Carolina, Raleigh. [Online catalog description: "The amendment would keep the Tar River open to Potter's Mill and defines punishment for anyone who defies this law."]

New River [in Western North Carolina]

Adams, Noah. *Far Appalachia: Following the New River North*. New York: Delacorte Press, 2001.

Albert, Ralph. "The New River." *Journal of the New River Historical Society*, 8:1 (1995), 17-18.

Anderson-Green, Paula Hathaway. "The New River Frontier Settlement on the Virginia-North Carolina Border, 1760-1820." *Virginia Magazine of History and Biography*, 86:4 (October 1978), 413-431.

Bennet, William D. "Early Settlement along the New River (NC and VA) Basin." *Proceedings of the New River Symposium, 1984*; online: http://www.nps.gov/parkhistory/online_books/symposia/newriver-84/sec3.htm

Collins, Robert L. "Rip." "Pleasures of the Ancient New." *The State: Down Home in North Carolina*, 42:2 (July 1974), 11-14. [Online description from "North Carolina Periodicals Index," East Carolina University: "South Fork of the New River is a part of the oldest river system in North America. The gentle mountain river remains one of North Carolina's best-kept travel secrets providing the perfect setting for leisurely canoeists and nature and wildlife enthusiasts. The river is in danger from both ends due to rapid development around Blowing Rock and Boone, and from efforts of the Appalachian Power Company of Virginia seeking to permit damming."]

Cooper, Leland R., and Mary Lee Cooper. *The People of the New River: Oral Histories from Ashe, Alleghany, and Watauga Counties, North Carolina.* Jefferson: McFarland & Company, 2001. [Publisher's description: "Said to be one of the oldest rivers in the world, the New River begins at two locations in Watauga County in northwest North Carolina. From there the North and South Forks meander north through Ashe County until they meet near the Virginia border and continue through a corner of Alleghany County before turning north again into Virginia and West Virginia and on to the Ohio. Settlers came to the fertile bottom lands along the New River during the 18th and 19th centuries and many of their descendants still live there today. In this collection of oral histories, 33 people in Ashe, Alleghany, and Watauga counties – most of whom are in their 70s, 80s, and 90s – share memories of their lives and work on the New River and their hopes for its future. They tell of floods, snows, sickness, the Great Depression, education, religion, quilting, weaving and other crafts, and the fight against a large power company that planned to flood thousands of acres of land. They also recall how the river has been central to their lives in providing food, transportation and recreation."]

Crawford, B. Scott. "Economic Interdependence along a Colonial Frontier: Capitalism in the New River Valley, 1745-1789." M. A. thesis, Old Dominion University, 1996.

Cross, Jerry L. "A Historical Overview of the New River Valley with Particular Emphasis on the Early Settlement of Ashe, Alleghany and Watauga Counties." *Historical Research Reports,* series 1, no. 45, State Archives of North Carolina, Raleigh; also on microfilm at the North Carolina Collection, Louis Round Wilson Special Collections Library, University of North Carolina at Chapel Hill.

"Expedition to New River, November 22, 1780." In Paul W. Gregory, *Early Settlers of Reddies River* (Wilkes Co.: Wilkes Genealogical Society, 1976), 46.

Knapp, Emerson. "The Kanawha/New River on Mid-Eighteenth-Century Maps." *Journal of the History Museum and Historical Society of Western Virginia*, 15:2 (2003).

Morgan, John T., and Michael W. Mayfield. "Research Note: The Second Oldest River in the World? *Southeastern Geographer*, 34:2 (November 1994), 138-144. [Abstract from entry in Project MUSE online: "The New River is widely accepted as the oldest river in North America and the second oldest river in the world, although there is no conclusive evidence that it is even the oldest river in the Appalachian highlands through which it flows. Promotion of the stream as the 'oldest river' dates to the 1970s when politicians and preservationists used the antiquity of the river as a battle cry to block proposed damming of the stream. Recreation and tourism agencies and both scholarly and popular books and magazines have served to reinforce acceptance of the superlative age of New River."]

Rudden, Bernard. *The New River: A Legal History*. Oxford: Clarendon Press; New York: Oxford University Press, 1985.

Schoenbaum, Thomas J. *The New River Controversy*. Jefferson: McFarland & Company, 2007.

Sturgill, David Andrew. "The Ride of Martin Gambill." *Proceedings of the New River Symposium* Online: http://www.nps.gov/parkhistory/online_books/symposia/newriver-84/sec23.htm. [Martin Gambill (1750-by 1834)

Tise, Larry E. "Treasures of the New River Valley." *The State: Down Home in North Carolina*, 44:4 (September 1976), 18-21, 35; online: http://digital.ncdcr.gov/cdm/ref/collection/p16062coll18/id/11881.

Williams, Cratis. "The New River Valley (N. C.) in Settlement Days." Typscript Cp971.05 W72n, North Carolina Collection, Louis Round Wilson Special Collections Library, University of North Carolina at Chapel Hill. [Note on cover: "Presented at Banquet of the New River Symposium in the Center for Continuing Education at Applachian State University, April 13, 1984."]

Northeast Cape Fear River

Angley, Wilson. "Colonial Phantom on the Northeast Cape Fear: A Brief History of the Exeter Site." *Tributaries*, 3 (October 1993), 26-31. [Online description from "North Carolina Periodicals Index," East Carolina University: "Exeter, a proposed town in colonial North Carolina's New Hanover County, never developed as its promoters had hoped. Two centuries later little is known of the Northeast Cape Fear River settlement or its ultimate fate."]

Angley, Wilson. "An Historical Overview of the Northeast Cape Fear River." Typescript, "Historical Research Reports," series 1, no. 48, State Archives of North Carolina; microfilm also available at the Southern Historical Collection, Louis Round Wilson Special Collections Library, State Archives of North Carolina, Raleigh.

Hall, Wes. "An Underwater Archaeological Survey of Heron's Colonial Bridge Crossing Site over the Northeast Cape Fear River near Castle Hayne, North Carolina." M. A. thesis, East Carolina University, 1992.

Jackson, Claude V., III. *The Cape Fear-Northeast Cape Fear Rivers Comprehensive Study: A Maritime History and Survey of the Cape Fear and Northeast Cape Fear Rivers, Wilmington Harbor, North Carolina: Vol. 1: Maritime History*. Raleigh: North Carolina Department of Archives and History and United States Army Corps of Engineers, 1996; republished: Jack E. Fryar, Jr., ed. *The Big Book of the Cape Fear*. Wilmington: Dram Tree Books, 2008. [Publisher's description: "In 1993-1994, the North Carolina Department of Cultural Resources' Underwater Archaeology Unit teamed with the U.S. Army Corps of Engineers to conduct a comprehensive survey of Cape Fear River. The volume has been enhanced with more than 250 photos, illustrations, and maps."]

"Revolutionary War Raids & Skirmishes in 1781: January 30, at Heron Bridge, North Carolina." Online: http://www.myrevolutionarywar.com/battles/1781-skirmish/.

Watts, Gordon P.; and Wesley K. Hall. *An Investigation of Blossom's Ferry on the Northeast Cape Fear River* (East Carolina University Research Reports, no. 1) Greenville: ECU, 1986.

Occonaluftee River

Wilburn, H. C. "A River and a Name: Both Beautiful." *The State: A Weekly Survey of North Carolina*, 19:43 (March 1952), 8; online: http://digital.ncdcr.gov/cdm/ref/collection/p16062coll18/id/28357. [Online description from "North Carolina Periodicals Index," East Carolina University: "Oconaluftee was the original name of a village destroyed by Colonel Moore on the banks of the river also named Oconaluftee."]

Pamlico River

Bellis, Vince. "Where Fresh and Salt Water Meet – The Upper Pamlico River Estuary." *Currents*, 20:1 (Winter 2001), 1, 8. [Online description from "North Carolina Periodicals Index," East Carolina University: "Bellis discusses how the land surfaces of the North Carolina Coastal Plain were shaped over the eons by the flow of water and why Goose Creek State Park is an excellent place to view the transition zone between brackish marsh and coastal forest."]

Harrell, Melinda. "Beaufort County's Lifeline." *Greenville Times/Pitt's Past*, 28:2 (January 20, 2010), 28-30. [Online description from "North Carolina Periodicals Index," East Carolina University: "The Pamlico River has always been an economic hub in eastern North Carolina and boasts a colorful history that includes war, trade, and development."]

Humphries, Tara L. "New N. C. Estuarium in Washington Celebrates Life in and on the Water." *Southern City*, 48:1 (January 1998), 6-7. [Online description from "North Carolina Periodicals Index," East Carolina University: "Opening in January, 1998, the N.C. Estuarium in Washington portrays the estuarine system created by the Pamlico River and Pamlico Sound. Exhibits pertain to fish and wildlife, ecosystems, human interaction with the estuary, and history."]

Pee Dee River

Freeman, Douglas Southall. "Douglas Southall Freeman Papers, 1632-1953." Manuscript accession no. 23682, Library of Virginia, Richmond. [This collection includes "…maps of the Pee Dee region of North Carolina during the Revolution;…"]

Gregg, Alexander. *History of the Old Cheraws: Containing an Account of the Aborigines of the Pedee, the First White Settlements, Their Subsequent Progress, Civil Changes, the Struggle of the Revolution, and Growth of the Country Afterward, Extending from about A. D. 1730 to 1810, with Notices of Families and Sketches of Individuals*. New York: Richardson & Co., 1867; reprinted: Greenville, S. C.: Southern Historical Press, 1991.

Hurley, Suzanne Cameron Linder. "A River in Time: A Cultural Study of the Yadkin/Pee Dee River System to 1825." Ph. D. dissertation, University of South Carolina, 1993.

Johnson, George Lloyd. *The Frontier in the Colonial South: South Carolina Backcountry, 1736-1800*. Westport, Conn.: Greenwood Press, 1997.

Spivey, Michael. *Native Americans in the Carolina Borderlands: A Critical Ethnography*. Southern Pines: Carolinas Press, 2000.

Roanoke River

Bivins, John, Jr. "Furniture of the North Carolina Roanoke River Basin in the Collection of Historic Hope Foundation." *Journal of Early Southern Decorative Arts*, 22:1 (Summer 1996), 1-90.

Friedman, Adam D. *The Legal Choice in a Cultural Landscape: An Explanatory Model of the Roanoke River, North Carolina*. Greenville: Program in Maritime Studies, East Carolina University, 2008.

Ginther, Herman. *Captain Staunton's River*. Richmond: Dietz Press, 1968.

Johnson, Rufus, and Jerry Dickerson. *Treasures of the Roanoke Valley: Historical and Interesting Sites in Halifax and Northampton Counties*. Gaston: J. Dickerson; Roanoke Rapids: Printed by River Stone Graphics, 2000.

Looking Back: Roanoke Valley, the Early Years. Vancouver, Wash.: Pediment Publishing, 2005.

Manning, Louise. "River of Ruin and Promise." *The State: A Weekly Survey of North Carolina*, 19:39 (February 1952), 6-7; online: http://digital.ncdcr.gov/cdm/ref/collection/p16062coll18/id/28233. [Online description from "North Carolina Periodicals Index," East Carolina University: "The Roanoke is a capricious stream which has brought wealth-making silt and deadly floods to the northern coastal plains."]

Peele, Wendell. "Return to the River." *The State: Down Home in North Carolina*, 35:1 (June 1967), 8-9; online: http://digital.ncdcr.gov/cdm/ref/collection/p16062coll18/id/50206. [Online description from "North Carolina Periodicals Index," East Carolina University: "The history of the Roanoke River in Martin County dates back to the time of Sir Walter Raleigh. Crews of men from Raleigh's expedition oared their way up the Roanoke to the present day site of the Williamston bridge before being attacked and driven back to their boats by Tuscarora Indian warriors. Since that time, the Roanoke has served Martin County as a fishery, as a means of transportation, as a resource for manufacturing plants, and even as a military conduit during the Civil War. Because of this long-term interconnectivity, many Martin County residents feel that the river, despite flowing through two states and many counties, is their own."]

Rice, Phillip M. "The Early Development of the Roanoke Waterway – A Study in Interstate Relations." *North Carolina Historical Review*, 31:1 (January 1954), 50-74; online: http://digital.ncdcr.gov/cdm/ref/collection/p16062coll9/id/4207. [Online description from "North Carolina Periodicals Index," East Carolina University: "In the period following the American Revolution, commercial rivalry between states resulted in attempts to establish cooperation between state governments. Once such project was the Roanoke Waterway, one of the first efforts by states to institute cooperative undertakings in internal improvements."]

Shannon, Renee Walcott. "The Fate of a Fishery – Shad and River Herring at the Turn of the 21st Century." *Coastwatch*, (Spring 2000), 6-13. [Online description from "North Carolina Periodicals Index," East Carolina University: "Shad and herring fisheries on coastal rivers have fed generations of eastern Carolinians. However, technological innovations, pollution, and overfishing have decreased the size of the annual harvest. Shannon describes the fisheries at Lock and Dam No. 1, Cape Fear River; Contentnea Creek, in Grifton; and the Roanoke River at Jamesville; and their prospects in the twenty-first century."]

Shields, Carol. "Exploring the Bountiful Roanoke." *Greenville Times/Pitt's Past*, 28:2 (January 20, 2010), 34-38. [Online description from "North Carolina Periodicals Index," East Carolina University: "The lower Roanoke River provides locals and visitors with all sorts of outdoor activities. The historical river has supported farmers, provided cover for slaves and moonshiners, and served as a means for transport of goods."]

Wilborn, Elizabeth W.; Boyd Cathey; Jerry Lee Cross. *The Roanoke Valley: A Report for the Historic Halifax State Historic Site*. Raleigh: Historic Sites and Museums Section, Division of Archives and History, 1974.

South River

Carraway, Dollie C. *South River: A Local History from Turnagain Bay to Adams Creek*. Fayetteville: M&L Designs, 1994.

Tar River

Harrell, Melinda. "The 'Mighty' River Named Tar." *Greenville Times/Pitt's Past*, 28:2 (January 20, 2010), 50-52. [Online description from "North Carolina Periodicals Index," East Carolina University: "The Tar River, which originates in Person County North Carolina, is a historical river that has connected southeastern towns for years."]

Historic and Architectural Resources of the Tar-Neuse Basin. 6 vols. Raleigh: Survey and Planning Branch, Historic Preservation Section, Division of Archives and History, North Carolina Dept. of Cultural Resources, 1977.

Kammerer, Roger. "Bridges over the Tar." *Greenville Times/Pitt's Past*, 31:7 (July 3-August 7, 2013), 3. [Online description from "North Carolina Periodicals Index," East Carolina University: "With the increase in travel and transportation in Pitt County since the 18th century, the Tar River has been an important feature of the area. Several bridges have been built over the Tar River throughout Pitt County's settlement history."]

Kammerer, Roger. "The Grimesland Bridge." *Greenville Times/Pitt's Past*, 31:1 (January 2-February 6, 2013), 6. [Online description from "North Carolina Periodicals Index," East Carolina University: "The new bridge that now spans the Tar River at Grimesland crosses one of the most historic spots on the River. This spot is one of the earliest settled places on the Tar River, settled by the English in 1714."]

North Carolina (State). General Assembly. "[Document dated:] October 25, 1779: House to Prevent Persons from Stopping the Passage of Fish Up Tar and Dan Rivers." Manuscript; General Assembly Session Records; Session of October-November 1779; Unidentified Amendments, Senate Bills, House Bills, Box 2 (MARS ID: 66.8.19.35; folder), State Archives of North Carolina, Raleigh.

North Carolina (State). General Assembly. "[Document dated:] April 23, 1783: Senate Bill to Amend Act to Prevent Persons from Stopping the Passage of Fish Up Tar and Dan Rivers." Manuscript; General Assembly Session Records; Session of April-May 1783; Unidentified Amendments, Senate Bills, House Bills, Box 2 (MARS ID: 66.8.30.3; folder), State Archives of North Carolina, Raleigh. [Online catalog description: "The amendment would keep the Tar River open to Potter's Mill and defines punishment for anyone who defies this law."]

Toe River

Bailey, Lloyd Richard, Sr., ed. *The Heritage of the Toe River Valley*. 12 vols. Durham: L. R. Bailey, 1994-2007.

Deyton, Jason Basil. "The Toe River Valley to 1865." *North Carolina Historical Review*, 24:4 (October 1947), 423-466.

Sharpe, Bill. "Valley on the Roof of North Carolina." *The State: A Weekly Survey of North Carolina*, 20:2 (June 1952), 3-5, 21-25; online: http://digital.ncdcr.gov/cdm/compoundobject/collection/p16062coll18/id/28765. [Online description from "North Carolina Periodicals Index," East Carolina University: "The author presents the history and appeal of the Toe River Valley, which is a valley by virtue of its drainage system and the high mountain ranges, such as the Black Mountains, Blue Ridge, and Unakas, that hem it in. The article highlights some of the popular tourist attractions in the area."]

Uwharrie River

Ingram, Bruce. "No Worries on the Uwharrie." *Wildlife in North Carolina*, 74:5 (May 2010), 26-31. [Online description from "North Carolina Periodicals Index," East Carolina University: "The Uwharrie River which winds through the Piedmont in Uwharrie National Forest, is becoming popular for its enticing fishing, especially bass."]

Waccamaw River

Earley, Lawrence S. "Mysteries of the Waccamaw." *Wildlife in North Carolina*, 54:7 (July 1990), 8-14. [Online description from "North Carolina Periodicals Index," East Carolina University: "Traveling the Waccamaw River, explorers may encounter hundreds of wildlife species."]

Manuel, John. *The Natural Traveler along the North Carolina Coast*. Winston-Salem: John F. Blair, 2003.

White Oak River

Manuel, John. *The Natural Traveler along the North Carolina Coast*. Winston-Salem: John F. Blair, 2003.

North Carolina (State). General Assembly. "[Document Dated]: February 13, 1781: That Militia Company Be Reaised for Defense of Sea Coast of Onslow County." Manuscript; General Assembly Record Group; Session Records, January-February 1781; Joint Papers, Committee Papers, Resolutions, House Joint Resolutions: February 12-14, Box 1 (MARS ID: 66.8.23.19.11; item), State Archives of North Carolina, Raleigh. [Online catalog description: "The resolution directs that the company be stationed at the mouth of the White Oak River."]

Powers, Julia Ann. "The White Oak River: An Overlooked Jewel." *Coastwatch*, (Early Summer 2003), 12-15. [Online description from "North Carolina Periodicals Index," East Carolina University: "The White Oak River, comprising one of North Carolina's smallest river basins, flows fifty miles, passing through several coastal counties on its journey to the sea. Powers discusses this natural treasure and the people who are working to keep it that way."]

Yadkin River

Brown, Roger F. *Wheels and Deals in the Yadkin Valley: A Chronicle of Transportation in the Yadkin Valley of North Carolina*. Boone: Parkway Publishers, 2005.

Hurley, Suzanne Cameron Linder. "A River in Time: A Cultural Study of the Yadkin/Pee Dee River System to 1825." Ph. D. dissertation, University of South Carolina, 1993.

Polk, Thomas, 1732-1793. "[Letter] 1780 Oct. 11, Camp Yadkin River [to] the Board of War." Manuscript VCC970.33 P76, North Carolina Collection Cotton, Louis Round Wilson Special Collections Library, University of North Carolina at Chapel Hill. [Online catalog description: "Letter informing of the demise of Col. Ferguson in the battle at King's Mountain."]

Rogers, Rhea J. "A Re-Examination of the Concept of the Tribe: A Case Study from the Upper Yadkin Valley, North Carolina." Ph. D. dissertation, University of North Carolina at Chapel Hill, 1993.

Rouse, Jordan K. *From Blowing Rock to Georgetown*. Kannapolis: J. K. Rouse, [1975?]

Trading Ford: Ten Thousand Years of Piedmont North Carolina History. Salisbury: Trading Ford Historic District Preservation Association, [2003?].

Waugh, Betty Linney. "The Upper Yadkin Valley in the American Revolution: Benjamin Cleveland, Symbol of Continuity." Ph. D. dissertation, University of New Mexico, 1971; published: *The Upper Yadkin Valley in the American Revolution: Benjamin Cleveland, Symbol of Continuity*. Wilkesboro: Wilkes Community College, 1971.

Major Rivers of Tennessee

Cumberland River

Arnow, Harriette Louisa Simpson. *Flowering of the Cumberland.* New York: Macmillian, 1963; reprinted: Lexington: University Press of Kentucky, 1984; East Lansing: Michigan State University Press, 2013.

Arnow, Harriette Louisa Simpson. *Seedtime on the Cumberland.* New York: Macmillan, 1960; reprinted: Lexington: University Press of Kentucky, 1983; Lincoln: University of Nebraska Press, 1995.

Birdwell, Michael E. *People of the Upper Cumberland: Achievements and Contradictions.* Knoxville: University of Tennessee Press, 2015.

Crutchfield, James A. *Early Times in the Cumberland Valley: From Its Beginnings to 1800.* Nashville: First American National Bank, 1976.

Dickinson, W. Calvin. *Lend an Ear: Heritage of the Tennessee Upper Cumberland.* Lanham, Md.: University Press of America, 1983.

Jillson, Willard R. *A Bibliography of the Cumberland River Valley in Kentucky and Tennessee: Citations of Printed and Manuscript Sources Touching upon its History, Geology, Cartography, Coal, Iron, Salt, Fluorspar, Phosphate, Clays, Oil and Gas, with Annotations.* Frankfort, Ky.: Perry Publishing Company, 1960.

McCague, James. *The Cumberland.* (Rivers of American series). New York: Holt, Rinehart and Winston, 1973.

United States. Army. Corps of Engineers. Nashville District. *The Tennessee-Cumberland Rivers Navigation System.* Nashvile: The Corps, [1995?].

French Broad River

Burnett, Edmund Cody. "Hog Raising and Hog Driving in the Region o f the French Broad River." *Agricultural History*, 20:2 (April 1946), 86-103.

Dykeman, Wilma. *The French Broad.* New York: Rinehart, 1955; reprinted: Knoxville: University of Tennessee Press, 1965.

Murphy, Jim. "The Story of the French Broad River." *Laurel of Asheville*, 9:3 (March 2012), 56. [Online description from "North Carolina Periodicals Index," East Carolina University: "The author discusses the French Broad River's name origins and the various myths surrounding its nomenclature."]

Smathers, George H. *The History of Land Titles in Western North Carolina. A History of the Cherokee Land Laws Affecting the Title to Land Lying West of the Meigs and Freemand Line, and Laws Affecting the Title of Land Lying East of the Meigs and Freeman Line Back to the Top of the Blue Ridge, Including all the Land on the Waters of the French Broad River in What Was Formerly Buncombe County as Created by the Act of 1792.* Asheville: Miller Printing Company, 1938.

Hiwassee River

Kidd, Gary. *A Survey of Historical Development Potential of the Lower Hiwassee Valley: A Resource Intern Report.* [S. l.]: Hiwassee River Watershed Development Association.; Tennessee Valley Authority. Office of Tributary Area Development, Tennessee Valley Authority, 1971.

Holston River and the Treaty of Long Island of the Holston (1777)

Henderson, Archibald, ed. "The Treaty of Long Island of Holston: July 1777." *North Carolina Historical Review*, 8:1 (January 1931), 55-116.

King, Duane H. "Long Island of the Holston: Sacred Cherokee Ground." *Journal of Cherokee Studies*, 1:2 (Fall 1976), 113-127.

Preston, Thomas Wilson. *Historical Sketches of the Holston Valleys.* (Holston Historical Library series) Kingsport: Kinsport Press, 1926.

Spoden, Muriel M. *The Long Island of the Holston: Sacred Island of the Cherokee Nation.* Nashville: Tennessee American Revolution Bicentennial Commission, 1977.

White, Alfred H. "Account of a Battle Ax Taken from an Indian at the Battle of Long Island Flats in 1776." Manuscript tl019, Special Collections Library, University of Tennessee, Knoxville; and at the Tennessee State Library and Archives, Nashville. [Online description: "...description of a Tomahawk rendered to the Historical Society of Tennessee by Alfred H. White. According to White's story, which was related to him by Mr. George W. Netherland, the tomahawk was believed to have belonged to a Cherokee known as 'Big Indian' on account of his stature and status. During this East Tennessee Revolutionary battle, an American soldier by the name of

Moore came in contact with 'Big Indian' during a charge. The two engaged in a one-on-one conflict, which eventually resulted in Moore defeating and killing the Cherokee. The referred to tomahawk was found near where the action took place and was further believed to have belonged to the 'Big Indian' because of its large size. The document was received by the Historical Society of Tennessee on January 6, 1860."]

Tennessee River

Crane, Verner W. "The Tennessee River as the Road to Carolina: The Beginnings of Explorations and Trade." *Mississippi Valley Historical Review*, 3:1 (June 1916), 18 p.

Davidson, Donald, and Theresa Julienna Sherrer Davidson. *The Tennessee*. 2 vols. New York: Rinehart, 1946-1948.

Holmes, Tony. "Early Cherokee Ferry Crossings of the Eastern Tennessee River Basin." *Journal of East Tennessee History*, 62 (1992), 54-79.

Larsen, Torben Huus. "The River of Conquest: Three Stories of the Tennessee River." *American Studies in Scandinavia,* 38:2 (2006), 149-161; online: http://ej.lib.cbs.dk/index.php/assc/article/view/4535/4970. [Includes the story of Donelson's expedition down the river in the winter of 1779.]

McFarland, Robert E[rnest]. "Of Time and the River: Economy, People, and Environment in the Tennessee Valley, 1500-1990." Ph. D. thesis, University of Alabama, 1997.

United States. Army. Corps of Engineers. Nashville District. *The Tennessee-Cumberland Rivers Navigation System*. Nashvile: The Corps, [1995?].

Williams, Samuel Cole. *Dawn of Tennessee Valley and Tennessee History*. Johnson City: Watauga Press, 1937.

The Gulf Stream

Bailey, Josiah W. "The Gulf Stream." *The State: A Weekly Survey of North Carolina*, 7:13 (August 1939), 2-3; online: http://digital.ncdcr.gov/cdm/ref/collection/p16062coll18/id/35436. [Online description from "North Carolina Periodicals Index," East Carolina University: "The grand and mighty Gulf Stream flows quite near to the coast of North Carolina and is in fact somewhat nearer to the North Carolina coast than to the other coast of any other state except Florida. The water of the Gulf Stream is warmer that the water on either side of the flow, and while the sea water off the North Carolina shore is green, the water of the Gulf Stream is indigo blue."]

Lee, David S.; foreword by J. Christopher Haney. *Gulf Stream Chronicles: A Naturalist Explores Life in an Ocean River*. Chapel Hill: University of North Carolina Press, 2015. [Publisher's description: "Off the shore of Hatteras Island, where the inner edge of the Gulf Stream flows northward over the outer continental shelf, the marine life is unlike that of any other area in the Atlantic. Here the powerful ocean river helps foster an extraordinarily rich diversity of life, including Sargassum mats concealing strange creatures and exotic sea beans, whales and sea turtles, sunfish and flying fish, and shearwaters and Bermuda petrels. During his long career as a research scientist, David S. Lee made more than 300 visits to this area off the North Carolina coast, documenting its extraordinary biodiversity. In this collection of twenty linked essays, Lee draws on his personal observations and knowledge of the North Atlantic marine environment to introduce us to the natural wonders of an offshore treasure. Lee guides readers on adventures miles offshore and leagues under the sea, blending personal anecdotes with richly detailed natural history, local culture, and seafaring lore. These journeys provide entertaining and informative connections between the land and the diverse organisms that live in the Gulf Stream off the coast of North Carolina. Lee also reminds us that ocean environments are fragile and vulnerable to threats such as pollution, offshore energy development, and climate change, challenging those of us on land to consider carefully the costs of ignoring sea life that thrives just beyond our view."]

Ulanski, Stan. *The Gulf Stream: Tiny Plankton, Giant Bluefin, and the Amazing Story of the Powerful River in the Atlantic*. Chapel Hill: University of North Carolina Press, 2010. [Publisher's description: "Coursing through the Atlantic Ocean is a powerful current with a force 300 times that of the mighty Amazon. Ulanski explores the fascinating science and history of this sea highway known as the Gulf Stream, a watery wilderness that stretches from the Caribbean to the North Atlantic. Spanning both distance and time, Ulanski's investigation reveals how the Gulf Stream affects and is affected by every living thing that encounters it--from tiny planktonic organisms to giant bluefin tuna, from ancient mariners to big-game anglers. He examines the scientific discovery of ocean circulation, the role of ocean currents in the settlement of the New World, and the biological life teeming in the stream."]

Sandhills of North Carolina

Norris, Jeannie Faris. "The North Carolina Sandhills." *We the People of North Carolina*, 5:6 (October 1947), 12-13. [Online description from "North Carolina Periodicals Index," East Carolina University: "Located in the south-central portion of North Carolina, the Sandhills is one of the country's finest fruit producing sections and hunting areas. It is also known as the winter golf capital of the nation with its two famous resorts – Pinehurst and Southern Pines."]

Sorrie, Bruce A. "A Hidden Treasure." *Wildlife in North Carolina*, 65:5 (May 2001), 4-9. [Online description from "North Carolina Periodicals Index," East Carolina University: "Lying between the southern Piedmont and the Coastal Plain is an area known as the Sandhills. Two million years ago it was the shore of the ocean. Today the North Carolina Wildlife Commission manages 60,000 acres, the Sandhills Game Land, which covers parts of Moore, Richmond, and Scotland Counties. This area is home to a rich diversity of plants and wildlife--some found nowhere else."]

Turner, William Newton. "The North Carolina Sandhills." Ph. D. dissertation, University of North Carolina at Chapel Hill, 1949.

Mountains of North Carolina and Tennessee

Abernethy, Edgar. "The Brushies." *The State: A Weekly Survey of North Carolina*, 9:50 (May 1942), 8-9, 16. [Online description from "North Carolina Periodicals Index," East Carolina University: "The Brushy Mountains are not as high as some of the peaks in western North Carolina, but they offer viewers beautiful and interesting scenery. They extend from Lenoir some 65 miles northeast to Pilot Mountain and include parts of Caldwell, Alexander, Wilkes, Yadkin and Surry counties. Abernethy's article covers the mountainous area between Lenoir and the Yadkin County line, about 35 miles distant."]

Abernethy, Edgar. "Hawksbill Mtn." *The State: A Weekly Survey of North Carolina*, 9:29 (December 1941), 10-11; online: http://digital.ncdcr.gov/cdm/ref/collection/p16062coll18/id/40626. [Online description from "North Carolina Periodicals Index," East Carolina University: "Hawksbill Mountain in Burke County takes its name from its peak where overhanging rocks project the striking likeness of a hawk's beak. At 4,000 feet the mountain is one of the few locations in the state's mountains where you can get a completely unobstructed view in every direction. Abernethy relates some of the interesting things visitors will find there."]

Abernethy, Edgar. "In the Uwharries." *The State: A Weekly Survey of North Carolina*, 13:4 (June 1945), 4-5, 22; online: http://digital.ncdcr.gov/cdm/ref/collection/p16062coll18/id/13329. [Online description from "North Carolina Periodicals Index," East Carolina University: "The Uwharries Mountains are located mainly in Stanly, Montgomery, and Randolph Counties. These little mountains aren't very high, but all the same, there's a quiet loveliness about their gently rounded contours which gives them a charm all their own."]

Allhands, William A. "Historic Mountain Trails." *The State: A Weekly Survey of North Carolina*, 13:27 (December 1945), 26-27; online: [Online description from "North Carolina Periodicals Index," East Carolina University: "Originally there were the buffalo trails in western North Carolina. Then came the paths made by Indians, and finally the rough roads built by early settlers."]

Bridges, Anne; Russell Clement; and Ken Wise. *Terra Incognita: An Annotated Bibliography of the Great Smoky Mountains, 1544-1934*. Knoxville: University of Tennessee Press, 2014.

Brown, Margaret Lynn. *The Wild East: A Biography of the Great Smoky Mountains*. Gainesville: University Press of Florida, 2000.

Chapman, Ashton. "What Makes the Blue Ridge Blue?" *The State: Down Home in North Carolina*, 35:7 (September 1967), 9-10; online: http://digital.ncdcr.gov/cdm/ref/collection/p16062coll18/id/50490. [Online description from "North Carolina Periodicals Index," East Carolina University: "A theory advanced some time ago by Dr. F. W. Went, Director of the Missouri Botanical Gardens in St. Louis, offers the explanation that the blue haze commonly seen over the Blue Ridge Mountains is due to the presence of organic matter which drifts into the atmosphere from trees and plants growing on the mountains."]

Colton, Henry E. *Mountain Scenery: The Scenery of the Mountains of Western North Carolina and Northwestern South Carolina*. Raleigh: W. L. Pomeroy; Philadelphia: Hayes & Zell, 1859; online: http://docsouth.unc.edu/nc/colton/colton.html.

Earley, Lawrence S. "Islands in the Sky." *Wildlife in North Carolina*, 51:4 (April 1987), 8-12. [Online description from "North Carolina Periodicals Index," East Carolina University: "The North Carolina mountain peaks are unique places. Rising to great heights and containing the tallest mountain east of the Mississippi River, they are separated from each other by warmer valleys. The peaks, isolated by altitude and climate, have developed their own unique plants and animals."]

Earley, Lawrence S. "Wetlands in the Highlands." *Wildlife in North Carolina*, 53:10 (October 1989), 10-14. [Online description from "North Carolina Periodicals Index," East Carolina University: "Small, scattered and disappearing, mountain bogs are some of our rarest habitats and contain some of the least common plants and animals. Yet we know almost nothing about these tiny, isolated worlds."]

Ellis, Harry. "Garden in the Sky." *Wildlife in North Carolina*, 56:5 (May 1992), 4-12. [Online description from "North Carolina Periodicals Index," East Carolina University: "Long admired for its dazzling display of rhododendron, Roan Mountain is also a magnificent garden of rare plants left over from the last Ice Age."]

Ellis, Harry. "Lowlands in the Highlands." *Wildlife in North Carolina*, 60:6 (June 1996), 4-9. [Online description from "North Carolina Periodicals Index," East Carolina University: "Although usually less than six acres in size, mountain bogs support an uncommon collection of plants, including lady slippers and cinnamon ferns, and animals like wood frogs and crab spiders."]

Eubanks, Georgann. *Literary Trails of the North Carolina Mountains.* Chapel Hill: University of North Carolina Press, 2007.

Frick-Ruppoert, Jennifer. *Mountain Nature: A Seasonal Natural History of the Southern Appalachians*. Chapel Hill: University of North Carolina Press, 2010. [Publisher's description: "The Southern Appalachians are home to a breathtakingly diverse array of living things--from delicate orchids to carnivorous pitcher plants, from migrating butterflies to flying squirrels, and from brawny black bears to more species of salamander than anywhere else in the world. *Mountain Nature* is a lively and engaging account of the ecology of this remarkable region. It explores the animals and plants of the Southern Appalachians and the webs of interdependence that connect them."]

Huffman, Steve. "A Secret Unveiled." *The State: Down Home in North Carolina*, 63:10 (March 1996), 27-28; online: http://digital.ncdcr.gov/cdm/ref/collection/p16062coll18/id/33833. [Online description from "North Carolina Periodicals Index," East Carolina University: "Located in the southern Piedmont, the Uwharrie Lake Region covers parts of seven counties and contains the nation's oldest mountains. Largely overlooked by tourists, the region is now being promoted to attract them."]

Johnson, Randy. *Grandfather Mountain: The History and Guide to an Appalachian Icon.* Chapel Hill: University of North Carolina Press, 2016. [Publisher's description: "With its prominent profile recognizable for miles around and featuring vistas among the most beloved in the Appalachians, North Carolina's Grandfather Mountain is many things to many people: an easily recognized landmark along the Blue Ridge Parkway, a popular tourist destination, a site of annual Highland Games, and an internationally recognized nature preserve. In this definitive book on Grandfather, Randy Johnson guides readers on a journey through the mountain's history, from its geological beginnings millennia ago and the early days of exploration to its role in regional development and eventual establishment as a North Carolina state park. Along the way, he shows how Grandfather has changed, and has been changed by, the people of western North Carolina and beyond."]

Morley, Margaret W. *The Carolina Mountains*. Boston: Houghton Mifflin, 1913.

Newfont, Kathryn. *Blue Ridge Commons: Environmental Activism and Forest History in Western North Carolina.* Athens: University of Georgia Press, 2012.

Norris, Jeannie Faris. "Children of the Volcanoes." *The State: Down Home in North Carolina*, 24:4 (July 1956), 10-11; online: http://digital.ncdcr.gov/cdm/ref/collection/p16062coll18/id/7326. [Online description from "North Carolina Periodicals Index," East Carolina University: "Located in Randolph County, in the Huronian Crystalline Belt, lies the Uwharries. Dwarfed mountains or hills that do not exceed 1,050 feet in elevation, the Uwharries are characterized by heavy mineralization, unusual drainage, and thick woodlands."]

Norris, Jeannie Faris. "The Great Smokies." *The State: A Weekly Survey of North Carolina*, 20:52 (May 1953), 24-26; online: http://digital.ncdcr.gov/cdm/ref/collection/p16062coll18/id/30409. [Online description from "North Carolina Periodicals Index," East Carolina University: "The largest land mass in the eastern United States, the Great Smoky Mountains encompass 500,000 acres and rise to an elevation of 6,642 feet. Containing 16 peaks exceeding 6,000 feet, the Great Smoky Mountains are mostly contained within a National Park that borders North Carolina and Tennessee."]

Norris, Jeannie Faris. "The Unakas Die in the Unicois." *The State: Down Home in North Carolina*, 20:52 (May 1953), 27-28; online: http://digital.ncdcr.gov/cdm/ref/collection/p16062coll18/id/30409. [Online description from "North Carolina Periodicals Index," East Carolina University: "The least known and least visited of the mountain ranges in North Carolina; the Unicois Mountains are located along the southwestern border of North Carolina and Tennessee. The highest peak within the Unicois Range is Huckleberry Knob, rising 5,580 feet in altitude."]

Perry, Sarah, and Emily Chaplin. "An American Wilderness." *Our State: Down Home in North Carolina*, 81:6 (November 2013), 68-87. [Online description from "North Carolina Periodicals Index," East Carolina University: "During the Great Depression, the federal government purchased unused farmland in the Piedmont region. In 1961, President John F. Kennedy named this land the Uwharrie National Forest. It occupies parts of

Montgomery, Randolph, and Davidson counties, and it is one of the nation's smallest national forest. It contains a mountain range older than the Rockies or Appalachians and lakes. Perry describes the forest and the people who live in and around it."]

Ray, Don M. "Our Other Mountains." *Tar Heel*, 8:7 (September 1980), 44-45. [Online description from "North Carolina Periodicals Index," East Carolina University: "Ray discusses the creation and history of the Uwharrie Mountains, which are the oldest mountains on the North American continent. Located in the Piedmont, the mountains' attractions include the Uwharrie National Forest, which covers 46,000 acres; Morrow Mountain State Park, Town Creek Indian Mound; and the Uwharrie Trail, a forty-five mile hiking route."]

Reardon, Melissa; Michael Oppenheim, photographer. "The Vanishing Point." *WNC Magazine*, 7:3 (May/June 2013), 54-61. [Online description from "North Carolina Periodicals Index," East Carolina University: "Bogs are among the most imperiled habitats in the mountains. In Western North Carolina, conservationists hope to bring these ecosystems back from the brink of extinction through the creation of a wildlife refuge."]

Sharpe, Bill. "Mountain Bog." *Wildlife in North Carolina*, 59:3 (March 1995), 10-11. [Online description from "North Carolina Periodicals Index," East Carolina University: "Although usually less than five acres in size, mountain bogs have important environmental functions: helping to control flooding, filtering water supplies of pollutants, and providing plant and animal habitats."]

Sharpe, Bill. "The Mountains of North Carolina." *The State: Down Home in North Carolina*, 51:8 (January 1984), 26-28. [Online description from "North Carolina Periodicals Index," East Carolina University: "North Carolina's mountains are some of the oldest ranges in the world. The state's mountain ranges create a ladder running north and south. The Unaka Mountains and the Blue Ridge make up the ladder's two sides. Between the sides are smaller ranges that run east and west. North Carolina's mountains contain both igneous and sedimentary rock. They also are home to a wide variety of plant species that range from sub-arctic to sub-tropic."]

Sharpe, Bill. "Our Mountains." *The State: A Weekly Survey of North Carolina*, 19:49 (May 1952), 3-5, 27-28. [Online description from "North Carolina Periodicals Index," East Carolina University: "This article is about the unique nature of the Blue Ridge mountains."]

Silver, Timothy. *Mount Mitchell and the Black Mountains: An Environmental History of the Highest Peaks in Eastern America*. Chapel Hill: University of North Carolina Press, 2003.

Straw, Richard A., and H. Tyler Blethen. *High Mountains Rising: Appalachia in Time and Place*. Urbana: University of Illinois Press, 2004.

Thornborough, Laura [pseud.]. *The Great Smoky Mountains*. New York: Thomas Y. Crowell Company, 1937; 1942; 1946; revised and enlarged: Knoxville: University of Tennessee Press, 1967.

Wilburn, H. C. "Standing in a Row." *The State: A Weekly Survey of North Carolina*, 19:39 (February 1952), 7; online: http://digital.ncdcr.gov/cdm/ref/collection/p16062coll18/id/28233. [Online description from "North Carolina Periodicals Index," East Carolina University: "The Cherokees named a famous valley in the Great Smokies, Catalochee, from the way the ridges rose."]

Ziegler, Wilbur, and Ben S. Grosscup. "Our First Mountaineers." *The State: Down Home in North Carolina*, 23:25 (May 1956), 19-20; online: http://digital.ncdcr.gov/cdm/ref/collection/p16062coll18/id/7031. [Online description from "North Carolina Periodicals Index," East Carolina University: "This article is taken from the 1881 travel book. This excerpt details the background of the Alleghany Mountains from the view of the Indian population."]

Chapter Four:
Pre-Revolutionary Events in the Province of North Carolina

The following sampling of studies and documents that relate to the coming of the American Revolution in North Carolina and Tennessee only scratches the surface of what is available for the Colonial Period. A search of the online catalog of any major library will yield many more publications.

General Bibliography

Arthur, Billy. "Doers of a Daring Deed." *The State: Down Home in North Carolina*, 63:12 (May 1996), 16-17; online: http://digital.ncdcr.gov/cdm/ref/collection/p16062coll18/id/33931. [Online description from "North Carolina Periodicals Index," East Carolina University: "The first rebellious act against British rule in the state may have been carried out by nine patriots, known to history as the 'Black Boys of Cabarrus.' They destroyed Governor William Tryon's munitions train on May 2, 1771, near Concord."]

Boyd, William K. "Some N. C. Tracts of the Eighteenth Century." *North Carolina Historical Review*:

2:1 (January 1925), 30-82; online: http://digital.ncdcr.gov/cdm/ref/collection/p16062coll9/id/4207. [Online description from "North Carolina Periodicals Index," East Carolina University: "The first article in the series, 'Some North Carolina Tracts of the Eighteenth Century,' includes a re-printing of the ca. 1740 pamphlet, *A True and Faithful Narrative of the Proceedings of the House of Burgesses of North Carolina*, describing an attempt to impeach the colony's Chief Justice William Smith in 1739."] [Part I]

2:2 (April 1925), 188-234; online: http://digital.ncdcr.gov/cdm/ref/collection/p16062coll9/id/4207. [Online description from "North Carolina Periodicals Index," East Carolina University: "William Borden was a shipbuilder from Rhode Island who relocated to Carteret County where he established a shipbuilding business on the Newport River. His 'Address to the Inhabitants of North Carolina,' addresses issues of commercial conditions and trade and monetary policies in the colony. It includes a plan for sound currency and a criticism of the Assembly of 1744."]

2:3 (July 1925), 351-386; online: http://digital.ncdcr.gov/cdm/ref/collection/p16062coll9/id/4207. [Online description from "North Carolina Periodicals Index," East Carolina University: "The third installment of 'Some North Carolina Tracts of the Eighteenth Century,' by William K. Boyd. John Rutherfurd (1724-1782) was born in Scotland and migrated to North Carolina sometime prior to 1735, settling in Wilmington. He was twice elected town commissioner of Wilmington, appointed by Governor Johnston as a member of the Council and Receiver General of Quit Rents in 1751, and was appointed Lieutenant General of the expedition against the Regulators by Governor Tryon prior to 1768. He wrote 'The Importance of the Colonies to Great Britain, etc.,' reproduced here in full, in 1761 while in England. The piece examines themes of traditional mercantilism such as the balance of trade between England and the colonies and the future of that balance."] [Part II]

2:4 (October 1925), 475-501; online: http://digital.ncdcr.gov/cdm/ref/collection/p16062coll9/id/4207. [Online description from "North Carolina Periodicals Index," East Carolina University: "Henry McCullough, author of 'Miscellaneous Representations Relative to Our Concerns in America,' 1761, was a holder of vast tracts of land in North Carolina and was once a special agent of His Majesty's Government in the Carolinas. He was the individual behind the policy of Prime Minister George Grenville's Stamp Act. Maurice Moore Jr. belonged to a prominent political family in North Carolina who settled in the colony near the lower Cape Fear River. Moore Jr. was a lawyer who represented the borough of Brunswick in the Assembly and was appointed Associate Justice of the Province until his participation in resistance to the Stamp Act. His pamphlet 'Justice and Policy of Taxing the American Colonies in England,' 1765 centers on the idea that Parliament has no right to tax the colonies and criticizes the claim of virtual representation in Parliament."] [Part III]

3:1 (January 1926), 52-118; online: http://digital.ncdcr.gov/cdm/ref/collection/p16062coll9/id/4207. [Online description from "North Carolina Periodicals Index," East Carolina University: "Part IV and V in this series, presents three documents – 'The Petition of Reuben Searcy and Others' (1759), George Sim's 'Address to the People of Granville,' and Hermon Husband's 'Remarks on Religion.' Both historic documents record incidents of property taxation in the Granville District. The first document is a complaint lodged against Robert Jones Jr., Attorney General of the state, for over taxation and the latter a public speech addressed to Granville County Residents to join together and overthrow local government. The third document is a reprint of Husband's 1761 pamphlet concerning his personal opinions about the connection between religion and politics. [Parts IV and V]

3:1 (January 1926), "Parts VI & VII: Husbands, Hermon, 1724-1795. "Some Remarks on Religion." Searcy, Reuben, active 1759. Petition of Reuben Searcy and others, March 23, 1759. Sims, George, active 1765. Address to the people of Granville County. Online: http://archive.org/stream/northcarolinahis1926nort#page/52/mode/2up.

3:2 (April 1926), 223-362; online: http://digital.ncdcr.gov/cdm/ref/collection/p16062coll9/id/4207. [Online description from "North Carolina Periodicals Index," East Carolina University: "The eighth and ninth installment in this series presents a reprint of Hermon Husband's 'An Impartial Relation of the First Rise and Cause of the Recent Differences in Public Affairs' (1770) and 'Fan for Fanning and a Touchstone for Tryon' (1771). Both offer an account of complaints of many Regulators during the Colonial Period. [Parts VIII and IX]

3:3 (July 1926), 457-476; online: http://digital.ncdcr.gov/cdm/ref/collection/p16062coll9/id/4207. [Online description from "North Carolina Periodicals Index," East Carolina University: "Dr. George Micklejohn's 'Sermon to Tryon's Militia' (1768) and a 'Table of North Carolina Taxes, 1748-1770' are the subjects of this article. Micklejohn's sermon denounces Regulators Governor Tryon's aggression and reaffirms his loyalty to the Crown. The Table of Taxes was the third report in a series by John Burgwyn, Clerk of the Court of Chancery and Secretary of the Council that addressed investigations any fraudulent or excessive taxation." [Parts X and XI]

4:1 (January 1927), 50-94; online: http://digital.ncdcr.gov/cdm/ref/collection/p16062coll9/id/4207. [Online description from "North Carolina Periodicals Index," East Carolina University: Parts XII and XIII. "From the close of the American Revolution to the ratification of the United States Constitution there was a deep and increasing conviction among a considerable portion of North Carolinians that certain fundamental rights, based on the law of nature and guaranteed by various charters and statutes of England, were violated and jeopardized. This is the subject of the pamphlet anonymously published in the summer of 1787 under the title, *The Independent Citizen*."]

Butler, Lindley S. "The Coming of the Revolution in North Carolina, 1763-1776." Ph. D. dissertation, University of North Carolina at Chapel Hill, 1971; published: Raleigh: North Carolina Department of Cultural Resources, 1976.

Butler, Lindley S. *North Carolina and the Coming of the Revolution, 1763-1776*. (North Carolina Bicentennial Pamphlet Series, no. 6) Raleigh: North Carolina Dept. of Cultural Resources, Division of Archives and History, 1976. [Traces the development of the Revolution from the initial resistance to the outbreak of violence. Excellent bibliographic essay is included in the back.]

Corbitt, D. L. "Resistance to the Stamp Act." *North Carolina Historial Review*, 2:3 (July 1925), 387-388.

Davidson, Philip G. "Sons of Liberty and Stamp Men." *North Carolina Historical Review,* 9:1 (January 1932), 38-56.

Donnell, James H., III. "The South on the Eve of the Revolution." In W. Robert Higgins, ed. *The Revolutionary War in the South: Power, Conflict, and Leadership: Essays in Honor of John Richard Allen* (Durham: Duke University Press, 1979), 64-78.

Ekirch, A[rthur] Roger. "'Poor Carolina:' Society and Politics in North Carolina, 1729-1771." Ph. D. dissertation, Johns Hopkins University, 1979; published: *"Poor Carolina;" Politics and Society in Colonial North Carolina, 1729-1776*. Chapel Hill: The University of North Carolina Press, 1981. ["This book attempts to describe North Carolina's embroiled politics and, in doing so, to analyze the social determinants of political instability..." Includes bibliographic essay and useful appendix.]

Fowler, Malcolm. "Rebellion in Carolina." The State: A Weekly Survey of North Carolina, 7:51 (May 1940), 1, 23, 26; online: http://digital.ncdcr.gov/cdm/ref/collection/p16062coll18/id/5554. [Online description from "North Carolina Periodicals Index," East Carolina University: " Boston still brags about its Tea Party, but one hundred years before they started throwing out tea in Boston, North Carolina was throwing out governors in this state. In protest of the tax on tobacco, open rebellion began in 1677. In 1766, many North Carolina towns were also up in arms about the Stamp Act, and the people of Wilmington had their own tea party while under the leadership of Ashe, Harnett, and others. Inhabitants marched on Governor Tyron's house and demanded the surrender of the official in charge of the stamps."]

Girten, John C. "Pre-Revolutionary North Carolina, 1760-1775: A Case Study in the Anatomy of Revolution." M. A. thesis, Middle Tennessee State University, Murfreesboro.

Guasco, Michael. "The Very Curious Case of Colonial North Carolina." *Tar Heel Junior Historian,* 51:2 (Spring 2012), 1-3. [Online description from "North Carolina Periodicals Index," East Carolina University: "It may seem strange today, but North Carolina often got ignored during the colonial period. But once North Carolina got really going, it became an impressive place for development."]

Haywood, C. Robert. "The Mind of the North Carolina Opponents of the Stamp Act." *North Carolina Historical Review*, 29 (1952), 317-343; online: http://digital.ncdcr.gov/cdm/ref/collection/p16062coll9/id/4207. [Online description from "North Carolina Periodicals Index," East Carolina University: "Colonial North Carolinians demanded a great deal of autonomy from the suppressing English government. Governors of the colony found it difficult to collect taxes without adequate support from the crown and if collected revenue was not used locally it was impossible to get taxes from the populace. North Carolinians' independent spirit was further inflamed with the introduction of the Stamp Act of 1765. The author looks at the colonist's opposition to this act which primarily came from the aristocratic plantation owning sect of the population."]

High, James. "Henry McCulloh: Progenitor of the Stamp Act." *North Carolina Historical Review,* 29:1 (January 1952), 24-38; online: http://digital.ncdcr.gov/cdm/ref/collection/p16062coll9/id/4207. [Online description from "North Carolina Periodicals Index," East Carolina University: "Henry McCullo[g]h wrote The Stamp Act of 1765 which he first drafted and submitted to Earl of Bute in 1761. Besides being a clerk for the British Government, McCullo[g]h was also a speculator after being granted 1,200,000 acres in North Carolina. The article examines manuscripts to understand how McCullo[g]h administered the million plus acres in the state and how this gave him new insight for drafting The Stamp Act of 1765."]

Husbands, Hermon, 1724-1795. *An Impartial Relation of the First Rise and Cause of the Recent Difference in Publick Affairs: in the Province of North-Carolina, and the Past Tumults and Riots that Lately Happened in the Province: Containing Most of the True and Genuine Copies of Letters, Messages and Remonstrances between the Parties Contending…* [North Carolina?]: Printed for the Compiler, 1770.

Hutchins, Zachary McLeod, ed. *Community without Consent: New Perspectives on the Stamp Act*. Hanover, N. H.: University Press of New England, 2016.

Kay, M. L. M. "An Analysis of a British Colony in Late Eighteenth Century America in the Light of Current American Historiographical Controversy." *Australian Journal of Politics & History*, 11:2 (1965), 170-84. [North Carolina]

Lawrence, R. C. "Ahead of the Revolution." *The State: A Weekly Survey of North Carolina*, 13:6 (July 1945), 9, 14; online: http://digital.ncdcr.gov/cdm/ref/collection/p16062coll18/id/13387. [Online description from "North Carolina Periodicals Index," East Carolina University: "Histories of the United States give prominent place to the Boston Tea Party, and to the patriots who boarded the British ships and dumped tea into the bay. But the national histories are silent concerning much earlier demonstrations against royal misrule that occurred in North Carolina."]

Lee, Lawrence. "Days of Defiance: Resistance to the Stamp Act in the Lower Cape Fear." *North Carolina Historical Review*, 43:2 (April 1966), 186-202.

Lee, Lawrence. "Resistance to the Stamp Act in North Carolina." *Tar Heel Junior Historian*, 14:3 (February 1975), 5-6. [Online description from "North Carolina Periodicals Index," East Carolina University: "Retaliating against the English Stamp Act, 1,000 Wilmington men organized against local English official Captain Lobb. The men demanded that the captain cease enforcing the act in the Port of Brunswick, just south of Wilmington."]

Maas, John R. "'All This Poor Province Could Do:' North Carolina and the Seven Years' War." *North Carolina Historical Review*, 79:1 (January 2002), 50-89.

Martin, James Kirby. *Men in Rebellion: Higher Governmental Leaders and Coming of the American Revolution*. New Brunswick, N. J.: Rutgers University Press, 1973.

McKown, Harry. "November 1765: The Stamp Act Crisis in North Carolina." Online: www.lib.unc.edu/ncc/ref/nchistory/nov2006/.

Norris, David A. "Resolves, Prerevolutionary." In William S. Powell, ed.; Jay Mazzocchi, assoc. ed., *Encyclopedia of North Carolina* (Chapel Hill: University of North Carolina Press in association with the University of North Carolina Library, 2006), 965-966.

Norris, Jeannie Faris. "North Carolina on the Eve of the Revolution." *Tar Heel Junior Historian*, 15:1 (Fall 1975), 2-5. [Online description from "North Carolina Periodicals Index," East Carolina University: "By 1776, Carolina was one of the larger colonies with a system of roads, schools, and newspapers. The makeup of the colony is statistically broken down into the following categories: population, nationalities, boundaries, towns, counties, roads, newspapers, education, religion, and economy."]

Norris, Jeannie Faris. "Up in Arms." *Tar Heel Junior Historian*, 9:4 (May 1971), 6-11. [Online description from "North Carolina Periodicals Index," East Carolina University: "Lack of currency in the colony promoted a system of bartering amongst the colonists. By the mid-1700s, exasperated colonist rebelled against the oppressive English Stamp Act. Further taxation led to both organized and disorganized riots by the state's early citizens."]

Price, William S., Jr. "Reasons behind the Revolutionary War." *Tar Heel Junior Historian*, (Fall 1992); online: http://ncpedia.org/history/usrevolution/reasons.

Price, William Solomon, Jr. *Not a Conquered People: Two Carolinians View Parliamentary Taxation*. (Bicentennial Pamphlet series, no. 2). Raleigh: Department of Cultural Resources, Division of Archives and History, North Carolina Bicentennial Committee, 1975. [The article includes: Howard Martin, ca. 1730-1781. "Letter from a Gentleman at Halifax to His Friend in Rhode-Island;" and, Maurice Moore, 1735-1777. "Justice and Policy of Taxing the American Colonies, in Great Britain, Considered."]

Prince, William S., Jr. "Sowing the Seeds of War." *Tar Heel Junior Historian,* 14:3 (February 1975), 2-3. [Online description from "North Carolina Periodicals Index," East Carolina University: "In 1763, English authorities attempted to raise revenue after costly wars and stem illegal smuggling in New England by passing more regulatory customs demands. These regulations were realized in legislature like The Sugar Act and The Stamp Act, which displeased the residents in the American colonies. Further restrictive acts would push disgruntled colonists into war with England and lead to the American Revolution."]

North Carolina (State). General Assembly. "[Document dated:] Apr. 29, 1784: Joint Papers, Committee Papers, Resolutions, Senate Bills, House Bills, Report on Petition of Robert Rowan and Others (Rejected)." Manuscript; General Assembly Record Group; Session Records, April-June, 1784, Box 2 (MARS ID: 66.8.32.1.6), State Archives of North Carolina, Raleigh. [Online catalog description: "Memorials are all from officers or heirs of officers who served with the late Col. Hugh Waddell in the provincial army and were promised land for their service from George the Third by proclamation. Memorialists hope to claim this land which is now vested in the state of North Carolina. Committee awards land to officers who served, but asks the consideration of the House in regards to the memorials of the heirs." Note that this relates to pre-Revolutionary War service under the colonial government.]

Spindel, Donna J. "Law and Disorder: The North Carolina Stamp Act Crisis." *North Carolina Historical Review*, 57:1 (January 1980), 1-16. [Online description from "North Carolina Periodicals Index," East Carolina University: "In 1766, opposition to the Stamp Act in North Carolina was met with weak police action in stamping out anti-British activity. Governor William Tryon was unable to effectively enforce the Stamp Act in the Wilmington area due to several acts of civil disobedience. Police often supported these conflicts or did not have the means to suppress them"]

Taylor, H. Braughn. "The Foreign Attachment Law and the Coming of the Revolution in North Carolina." *North Carolina Historical Review*, 52:1 (January 1975), 20-36.

Thompson, Ray. *Before Liberty: Their New World Made the North Carolinians Different.* Winston-Salem: Piedmont Publishing Company, 1976.

Vaughan, John H. "The Downfall of Royal Government in North Carolina." M. A. thesis, University of North Carolina at Chapel Hill, 1905.

Waddell, Alfred Moore. *A Colonial Officer and His Times, 1754-1773 : A Biographical Sketch of Gen. Hugh Waddell, of North Carolina: with Notices of the French and Indian War in the Southern Colonies, the Resistance to the Stamp Act in North Carolina, ... the Regulators' War, and an Historical Sketch of the Former Town of Brunswick, on the Cape Fear River*. Raleigh: Edwards & Broughton, 1890; online through the HathiTrust.

Waddell, Alfred M[oore]. "The Stamp Act on the Cape Fear." *North Carolina Booklet*, 1:3 (July 1901), 3-22; online: http://digital.ncdcr.gov/cdm/ref/collection/p249901coll37/id/14180. [Online description from "North Carolina Periodicals Index," East Carolina University: "A look at the Stamp Act and its enforcement in colonial North Carolina."]

Wood, Bradford J. "Becoming North Carolina." *Tar Heel Junior Historian*, 51:2 (Spring 2012), 4-7. [Online description from "North Carolina Periodicals Index," East Carolina University: "Wood discusses how North Carolina developed from a fledgling spot on the British Empire map to a powerful colonial state."]

The Regulator Movement/War of the Regulation and the Battle of Alamance Creek (1771)

[Note: The National Society Daughters of the American Revolution does not consider participation in the Regulator Movement as service in the American Revolution because it pre-dates the start of the latter on April 19, 1775.]

Adams, George R. "The Carolina Regulators: A Note on Changing Interpretations." *North Carolina Historical Review*, 49:4 (October 1972), 345-352.

"Alamance Battleground: Where the War of the Regulation Came to an End." Manuscript F7 11:A3/2 1997, North Carolina Collection, State Documents Collection, Davis Library, University of North Carolina, Chapel Hill. [Raleigh]: North Carolina Historic Sites, Division of Archives and History, Dept. of Cultural Resources, [1997?]

"Alamance Battleground Research Project Concludes Extensive Work." *Carolina Comments,* 59:1 (January 2011), 5-8.

Anson County. "Anson County Miscellaneous Records, 1759-1960: Deposition of William Pickett Concerning the Regulators." Manuscript C.R.05.928.1, State Archives of North Carolina, Raleigh.

Arnett, Ethel Stephens. *David Caldwell.* Greensboro: Media, Inc., 1976. [Leader in the Regulator movement]

Bailey, W. H. Sr. "The Regulators of North Carolina." *American Historical Register*, 3:15 (November 1895), 313-334; 3:15 (December 1895), 464-471; 3:17 (January 1896), 554-567.

Bassett, John S. "The Regulators of North Carolina, 1765-1771." *Annual Report of the American Historical Association for the Year 1893* (Washington, D. C.: The Association, 1894), 200-205.

Bassett, John Spencer. "The Regulators of North Carolina (1765-1771)." *Annual Report of the American Historical Association*, (1895), 141-212.

Blower, Daniel Frederick. "The Orange County and Mecklenburg County Instructions: The Development of Political Individualism in Backcountry North Carolina, 1740-1776." Ph. D. dissertation, University of Michigan, 1984. [Online abstract: "State constitutions written in 1776 were heavily indebted to the dominant Whig theories of politics. Though they enlarged the role of 'the people,' the new constitutions assumed an organic, hierarchical society and attempted to incorporate the social values of the different layers into government. The ideals of deferential politics remained powerful. In North Carolina, the two backcountry counties of Orange and Mecklenburg called for a new system of government. The government designed by the two counties was democratic, limited, and instrumental. It was democratic in that all citizens were politically equal and the government was operated by a majority of them; limited in that it was invested only with certain powers by the sovereign citizenry and those were few; instrumental in that it was a neutral mechanism for the use of majorities, with representatives acting as agents for their constituents. This essay explains how the two counties came to embrace the new ideas by examining the history of settlement in the piedmont and the development of the community there. Numerous social, political, and economic factors undermined the legitimacy of the colonial government and broke the social bonds that undergirt it. The pace and pattern of settlement in the West led to strains on existing political and governmental institutions. Local government repeatedly failed in its fundamental obligations to provide stability and security. Corruption and abuses by government officials proliferated and the institutions of government were unable to restrain them. Other circumstances combined to erode the government's claims to allegiance. The settlers of the backcountry responded to a series of these failures by associating to solve particular problems themselves. The pattern of problems and ad hoc associations to meet them climaxed in the Regulation, which featured a massive failure of government and widespread organized resistance to it. The inappropriateness of existing institutions was acknowledged and alternatives explored. The political ideas of the backcountry emerged from the concrete struggles of a dispersed, socially isolated population to solve specific political problems."]

Bolden, Don. "Alamance Battleground Revisited." *The State: Down Home in North Carolina*, 38:21 (April 1971), 11-12; online: http://digital.ncdcr.gov/cdm/ref/collection/p16062coll18/id/54244. [Online description from "North Carolina Periodicals Index," East Carolina University: "On May 16, 1771, the Regulators met the forces of Royal Governor William Tryon in the Battle of Alamance, climaxing an expedition by Tryon to suppress the uprising known as the War of Regulation. The site of the battle has been designated a state historical site, and many relics from the battlefield are displayed in the museum. In May of this year, there will be a week of events sponsored by the Alamance County Historical Association to commemorate the 200th anniversary of the battle."]

Broomall, James Joseph. "'Making a Considerable Tumult in the Streets': People, Papers, and Perspectives in the North Carolina Regulation." M. A. thesis, University of North Carolina at Greensboro, 2006.

Broomall, James Joseph. "'Making a Considerable Tumult in the Streets': Protest and Place in the North Carolina Regulation." *Journal of Backcountry Studies,* 3:1 (Spring 2008); online: http://libjournal.uncg.edu/jbc/article/view/32/21.

Burns, Jason S. "Few People were More Industrious than We: An Interpretation of the North Carolina Regulator Movement." M. A. thesis, University of North Carolina at Chapel Hill, 1996.

Butler, William. "Regulator Papers, 1766-1781." Manuscript 626-z, Southern Historical Collection, Louis Round Wilson Special Collections Library, University of North Carolina, Chapel Hill; online finding aid available at http://www2.lib.unc.edu/mss/inv/r/Regulator_Papers.html. [Online finding aid description: "The Regulator movement in colonial North Carolina was a rebellion initiated by residents of the colony's inland region who believed that royal government officials were charging them excessive fees, falsifying records, and engaging in other mistreatments. The collection contains miscellaneous letters and other papers (in part photocopies and typed transcriptions) pertaining to the Regulator movement in North Carolina and its aftermath, chiefly papers of William Butler, a leader."]

Butterfield, Roger. "The First Battle for American Freedom." *Saturday Evening Post*, 223:47 (May 19, 1951), 36-37, 127, 129, 131-132, 134-136.

Cabarrus Black Boys, a Short Historical Sketch of a Daring Deed. Concord: Times Presses, 1909.

Cameron, Annie Sutton. *Hillsborough and the Regulators*. Hillsborough: Orange County Historical Museum, 1964.

Caruthers, Eli Washington. *A Sketch of the Life and Character of the Rev. David Caldwell, D. D.: Near Sixty Years Pastor of the Churches of Buffalo and Alamance: Including Two of His Sermons, Some Account of the Regulation, Together with the Revolutionary... Incidents in Which He was Concerned, and a Very Brief Notice of the Ecclesiastical and Moral Condition of North Carolina while in its Colonial State.* Greensborough: Swaim and Sherwood, 1842.

"Collaborative Research Program Reexamines Battle of Alamance." *Carolina Comments,* 57:4 (October 2009), 97, 99-100.

Compton, Stephen C. "'James Pugh,' Regulator Sharpshooter: A Conundrum Unfolded." *North Carolina Historical Review*, 90:2 (April 2013), 173-196.

Connor, R. W. D. "A Sermon by Rev. George Micklejohn." *North Carolina Booklet,* 8:1 (July 1908), 57-78; online: http://digital.ncdcr.gov/cdm/ref/collection/p249901coll37/id/14180. [Online description from "North Carolina Periodicals Index," East Carolina University: "This article recites the sermon given by Reverend George Micklejohn to Governor Tryon's army at Hillsborough, North Carolina on September 25, 1768. This force had been convened by Governor Tryon to quell insurrection by Regulators in the countryside."]

Corbitt, D. L. "A Grievance of the Regulators." *North Carolina Historical Review,* 4:2 (April 1927), 210-211.

Corbitt, D. L. "Historical Notes." *North Carolina Historical Review*, 3:3 (July 1926), 477-505; online: http://digital.ncdcr.gov/cdm/ref/collection/p16062coll9/id/4207. [Online description from "North Carolina Periodicals Index," East Carolina University: "A series of newspaper articles are presented concerning Governor Tryon's reputation after he lost the Battle of Alamance on May 16, 1771 and was appointed Governor of New York. These select letters submitted to various newspapers demonstrate North Carolinians dogged loyalty to Governor Tryon despite criticism from others who viewed him as a dictator."]

Denson, Andrew C. "Diversity, Religion, and the North Carolina Regulators." *North Carolina Historical Review*, 72:1 (January 1995), 30-53. [Online description from "North Carolina Periodicals Index," East Carolina University: "This article looks at religious life in the North Carolina interior and suggests how religion influenced the North Carolina Regulator Movement, a loosely organized protest movement of settlers in the North Carolina backcountry during the 1760s and early 1770s that began as a peaceful expression of the settlers' discontent over political and economic conditions and developed into a series of increasingly violent mob actions that ended with a pitched battle between the Regulators and militia led by the colonial governor."]

Edward, Brother C. "The Regulators North Carolina Taxpayers Take Arms Against the Governing Elite." *American History Illustrated*, 18:2 (April 1983), 42-48.

Ekirch, A. Roger. "The North Carolina Regulators on Liberty and Corruption, 1766-1771." *Perspectives in American History*, 11 (1977-1978), 197-256.

"Extraordinary Conduct of the Regulators in the Back Settlements of North Carolina. [London?: J. Dodsley?, 1770]. *The Chronicle: Annual Register [for the year 1770],* 13 (October 5, 1770), 230.

Fitch, William Edward. *Some Neglected History of North Carolina, Being an Account of the Revolution of the Regulators and the Battle of Alamance, the First Battle of the American Revolution*. New York: Neale Publishing Co., 1895; Reprinted: 1905; 2nd ed. New York: W. E. Fitch, 1914.

Fitch, William Edward. "The Battle of Alamance: The First Battle of the American Revolution." *Burlington Times-News* [n. d.]; reprinted: Burlington: Burlington, North Carolina, Alamance Battle Ground Commission, 1939. [Battle of Alamance, 1771. Contains information on the Regulator Movement, the Watauga Association, and the proposed State of Franklin.]

Gammons, P. Keith. "Revivalist Rhetoric and the North Carolina Regulator Rebellion." Ph. D. dissertation, University of North Carolina at Greensboro, 2001.

Graham, Christopher. "Historiographical Notes: Reading the Regulators." *Journal of Backcountry Studies,* 3:1 (Spring 2008); online: http://libjournal.uncg.edu/jbc/article/view/35/24.

Great Britain. Colonial Office. "Various Documents Relating to the Battle of Alamance, 1770-1771." Copy of a manuscript in the National Archives of the United Kingdom (formerly the Public Records Office), Kew,

Richmond, Surrey, England; (MARS Id: 21.1.23.11; folder), "British Records Collection," State Archives of North Carolina, Raleigh. [Online catalog description: "Return of casualties; plan of camp and battle; orders from Gov. Tryon to N. C. provincials; letters Tryon to Richard from Henderson, Alexander McCulloch, Thomas McGwire, colonels of militia regiments, Capt. Robert Howe, Col. John Simpson, Col. Richard Caswell, Col. John Hinton, Col. James Sampson, Col. Joseph Leach, Col. Edmund Fanning, Col. John Frohock, Col. John Ashe, Col. William Cray, Col. William Thomson, Christopher Neal, Francis Nash, Col. Bryan, Maurice Moore, various sheriffs, Thomas Hart, Col. John Harvey, Col. Moses Alexander, Col. James Moore, Col. Robert Schaw, Col. James Rutherfurd, Col. William Haywood, John Burgwin, Col. Needham Bryan, Alexander Martin, Col. Edward Buncombe, Col. Farquhard Campbell, Richard Blackledge, Jacob Mitchell, Gen. Waddell, Marmaduke Jones, Col. Martin Armstrong, Lt. Col. Lanier, Capt. Simon Bright, Robert Hogg, Archibald Maclaine, William Hooper."]

Hamilton, Jon Jay. "Herman Husband: Penman of the Regulation." Graduate thesis. Wake Forest University, 1969. ["Rejecting interpretations of Husband as a mere agitator with an inflexible plan, Husband's influence is discussed in the light of his diverse actions during the various stages of the movement."]

Haywood, Marshall De Lancey. *Governor William Tryon and His Administration in the Province of North Carolina, 1765-1771: Services in a Civil Capacity and Military Career as Commander-in-Chief of Colonial Forces which Suppressed the Insurrection of the Regulators*. Raleigh: Reproduced by Edwards & Broughton Co., 1958.

Helmbold, F. Wilbur. *Religious Aspects of the Regulator Movement in North Carolina (1765-1771).* [S. l., s. n.]: 1953. [Copy available in the North Carolina Collection, University of North Carolina at Chapel Hill.]

Henderson, Archibald. "The Origin of the Regulation in North Carolina." *American Historical Review*, 21:2 (January 1916), 171-186. [Online description from "North Carolina Periodicals Index," East Carolina University: "The early stages of the Regulator Movement in Eastern North Carolina may have had its roots in the division of power between the royal governor and Lord Granville's agents. George Sims first summed up the grievances of the Regulator movement; his family roots in Granville County constitute an addendum to add detail to the little that is known of Sims' life and association."]

Henderson, Archibald. "Hermon Husband's Continuation of the Impartial Relation." *Administration of Justice Bulletin*, 18:1 (January 1941), 48-81. [Online description from "North Carolina Periodicals Index," East Carolina University: "This is a reprint of *The Continuation of the Impartial Relation of the First Rise and Cause of the Recent Differences in Publik* [*sic*] *Affairs in the Province of North Carolina, Second Part*, by Hermon Husband and printed in 1770. The Introduction establishes the document as being produced by Husband, a leading champion of the Regulators during the period of popular uprising in North Carolina between 1765 and 1771, and suggests that it is the primary source of knowledge of the Regulator's side in the conflict between Regulators and Royalists. Background information on the document and its author are also included in the introduction."]

Holt, Arthur. "A Barren Battlefield." *The State: Down Home in North Carolina*, 38:21 (April 1971), 19; online: http://digital.ncdcr.gov/cdm/ref/collection/p16062coll18/id/30327. [Online description from "North Carolina Periodicals Index," East Carolina University: "On 16 May 1771, 2,000 Regulators fought against 1,200 Militia led by Royal Governor Tryon in the battle of Alamance Creek. Holt discusses the men and circumstances of this famous North Carolina battle fought in Alamance County."]

Horne, Virginia. "The War of the Regulation: the First American Revolution." *Daughters of the American Revolution Magazine*, 86:3 (March 1952), 279-282, 310.

Hudson, Arthur Palmer. "Songs of the North Carolina Regulators." *William and Mary Quarterly*, 3rd series, 4:4 (October 1947), 470-485.

Husband, Herman. "A Fan for Fanning and a Touchstone for Tryon, Containing an Impartial Account of the Rise and Progress of the So Much Talked about Regulation in North Carolina." In William K. Boyd, ed., *Some Eighteenth Century Tracts Concerning North Carolina.* (Spartanburg, S. C.: The Reprint Company, 1973), 350-352.

Johnson, Elmer D. "The War of the Regulation: Its Place in History." M. A. thesis, University of North Carolina at Chapel Hill, 1942.

Jones, Mark Haddon. "Herman Husband: Millenarian, Carolina Regulator, and Whiskey Rebel (North Carolina)." Ph. D. dissertation, Northern Illinois University, 1983.

Kars, Marjoleine. "'Breaking Loose Together': Religion and Rebellion in the North Carolina Piedmont, 1730-1790." Ph. D. dissertation, Duke University, 1994; published: *Breaking Loose Together: The Regulator Rebellion in Pre-Revolutionary North Carolina.* Chapel Hill: University of North Carolina Press, 2002. [Online abstract: "Because the North Carolina Piedmont was the center of the Great Awakening in the South, the site of the largest uprising among colonial farmers before 1776, and the theater of intense partisan warfare during the

Revolution, it provides an ideal site to investigate how religion, economics, and politics interacted to shape rural life in the eighteenth century. In the first part of the work, I use land and court records, and loyalty claims to sketch the changing economy of the Piedmont from the beginning of settlement in the 1740s to the 1770s. I argue that local elites tried as much as possible to manipulate the chaotic land market to their own advantage. While growing integration into the Atlantic economy created opportunities for some Piedmont inhabitants, many others fell into debt. A scarcity of currency and the collusion of creditors and court officials created great hardships for farmers trying to pay off debts and taxes. The majority of Piedmont settlers came from northern colonies and brought with them much of the radical ferment of the Great Awakening. Using church records and the diaries of itinerant ministers, I argue in part two that denominational divisions among Piedmont inhabitants have been exaggerated and that the religious enthusiasm of the unchurched has been overlooked. In fact, many backcountry immigrants, whether they officially belonged to a church or not, were deeply influenced by the radical religious climate unleashed by the Great Awakening. As people grew increasingly exasperated with the corruption of their officials, they fused radical Protestant ideas about the importance of individual conscience with radical Whig ideas about the right to resist unjust government to fuel and justify their rebellion. In the third and last part of the dissertation, I examine the Regulation and its relationship to the American Revolution. I use petitions, participants' papers, and government sources to discuss the rebellion in terms of the enfolding revolutionary conflict at home and in the larger context of agrarian conflict and popular resistance elsewhere in the world. I argue that the Regulation foreshadowed many of the social struggles which accompanied the conflict with Britain."]

Kay, Marvin L. Michael. "The North Carolina Regulation, 1766-1776: A Class Conflict." In Alfred F. Young, ed., *American Revolution: Explorations in the History of American Radicalism* (DeKalb: Northern Illinois University Press, 1976), 71-123.

Kay, Marvin Lawrence Michael. "The Institutional Background to the Regulation in Colonial North America." Ph. D. dissertation, University of Minnesota, 1962.

Lawrence, R. C. "Herman Husbands, Regulator." *The State: A Weekly Survey of North Carolina*, 17:24 (November 1949), 11, 17; online: http://digital.ncdcr.gov/cdm/ref/collection/p16062coll18/id/24643. [Online description from "North Carolina Periodicals Index," East Carolina University: "Herman Husband was a leader of the Regulators during the pre-Revolutionary era. He was a man of education and had a talent for public leadership with an inborn hatred of oppression. He represented Orange County in the Colonial Assembly and would have been acclaimed as a patriot had the Regulators been successful at the battle on Great Alamance Creek."]

Lawrence, R. C. "The Rout of the Regulators." *The State: A Weekly Survey of North Carolina*, 12:18 (September 1944), 5, 18; online: http://digital.ncdcr.gov/cdm/ref/collection/p16062coll18/id/19620. [Online description from "North Carolina Periodicals Index," East Carolina University: "The Regulators were vigorous in their protest against unjust tax collections. They offered armed resistance long before the Revolution, but they finally were defeated at Hillsboro."]

Leach, Richard Michael. "Regulation to Revolution Continuity of Political Control in North Carolina." M. A. thesis, University of Wisconsin, Madison, 1971.

Lindsay, Charles. *The Regulation Movement in North Carolina with Special Reference to its Relation to the Settlement of Eastern Tennessee.* [S. l., s. n.]: 1928. [Copy available at the University of North Carolina at Chapel Hill, North Carolina Collection.]

London, Lawrence Foushee. "Sectionalism in the Colony of North Carolina." M. A. thesis, University of North Carolina at Chapel Hill, 1933. [Covers the Regulator Movement]

McCorkle, Lutie Andrews. "Was Alamance the First Battle of the Revolution?" *North Carolina Booklet*, 3:7 (November 1903), 4-26; online: http://digital.ncdcr.gov/cdm/ref/collection/p249901coll37/id/14180. [Online description from "North Carolina Periodicals Index," East Carolina University: "A reexamination of the revolutionary War Battle of Alamance to determine if it was the first battle of the Revolutionary war, as some historians had claimed, or if the article 'Regulators in a New Light' published in the *Charlotte Observer* in January of 1903 correctly dispels that notion."]

Menius Arthur C., III. "The Regulators of North Carolina and the Colonial Press: A Collection of Documents." History Honors Essay, University of North Carolina at Chapel Hill, 1977.

Merrill, William Ernest. *Captain Benjamin Merrill and the Merrill Family of North Carolina*. [Penrose: Merrill, 1935]. [Fought in the Battle of Alamance, but died before the Revolution]

Micklejohn, George. *On the Important Duty of Subjection to the Civil Powers. A Sermon Preached Before... William Tryon... Governor... of the Province of North-Carolina, and the Troops Raised to Quell the Late Insurrection at Hillsborough... September 25, 1768*. Newbern: Printed by James Davis, 1768.

Middleton, Lamar. "The War of the Regulators." In *Revolt, U. S. A.* (New York: Stackpole Sons, 1938), 85-122.

"Military Collection. III. War of the Regulation, 1768-1779." Manuscript, State Archives of North Carolina, Raleigh. Online: http://www.archives.ncdcr.gov/Portals/ 3/PDF/findingaids/pdf/MilColl_WarofRegulation.pdf.

Mitchell, Memory F., ed. *North Carolina Documents, 1584-1868*. Raleigh: State Department of Archives and History, 1967. [Revolutionary War-era contents: Petition of the Regulators, 1769; Minutes of Committee of Safety, Tryon County, 1775-1776; Halifax Resolves, Apr. 12, 1776; Constitution of 1776.]

Morehead, Joseph Motley. *Address of Joseph M. Morehead, Esq., of Guilford, on the Life and Times of Hames Hunter, "General" of the Regulators at Guilford Battle Ground... July 3, 1897.* 2nd cor. And enl. Ed. Greensboro: C. F. Thomas, Printer, 1898.

Nash, Francis. *Hillsboro, Colonial and Revolutionary*. Raleigh: Edwards & Broughton, 1903; reprinted: Chapel Hill: Orange Printshop, 1953.

Norris, Jeanne Faris. "Alamance Battleground Research Project Concludes Extensive Work." *Carolina Comments*, 59:1 (January 2011), 5-8; online: http://www.ncpublications.com/comments/Jan11.pdf. [Online description from "North Carolina Periodicals Index," East Carolina University: "Alamance Battleground Research Project focused on compiling new archaeological data and reviewing historic documents to elucidate the events of May 16, 1771. On that date Regulators met the state's militia in the cumulative battle of the War of Regulation, which ended in defeat of the uprising farmers. The project drew on help from professionals and over two hundred volunteers."]

Norris, Jeanne Faris. The Boggan-Hammond House in Wadesboro." *The State: Down Home in North Carolina*, 38:11 (November 1970), 14-16, 29; online: http://digital.ncdcr.gov/cdm/ref/collection/p16062coll18/id/53874. [Online description from "North Carolina Periodicals Index," East Carolina University: "The Anson County Historical Society, under the leadership of Linn D. Garibaldi, took possession of the oldest and most historically significant house in Wadesboro from Major L. P. McLendon, prominent Greensboro lawyer, state civic leader, and descendant of Capt. Patrick Boggan, the original builder of the house. The historical society's efforts to preserve the home for a museum and for educational purposes was aided by a 1969 General Assembly grant of $20,000 and a Richardson Foundation grant of $3,000. Capt. Boggan was one of the Anson Regulators who stormed the county courthouse on April 28, 1768 demanding relief from the injustices of Royal Local Magistrates. The Regulators nominated their own Assembly representative, Charles Robinson, making them possibly the first citizens group in America to make a political nomination and certainly among the first to forcibly demand justice from local officers."]

Norris, Jeanne Faris. "Collaborative Research Program Reexamines Battle of Alamance." *Carolina Comments*, 57:4 (October 2009), 97-100; online: http://www.ncpublications.com/comments/Oct09.pdf. [Online description from "North Carolina Periodicals Index," East Carolina University: The Office of Archives and History oversees the Alamance Battleground, site of the climatic conflict between rogue farmers and Governor William Tryons colonial militia in the War of Regulation on May 16, 1771. A collaborative effort between the Office of State Archaeology, Research Branch of the Office of Archives and History, and the Division of State Historic Sites and Properties will pursue a multi-disciplinary project reviewing the archaeological and historical record."]

North Carolina (Colony). "War of the Regulation." Manuscript (MARS ID: 5863; record group), State Archives of North Carolina, Raleigh.

North Carolina (State). General Assembly. "[Document dated:] May 8, 1780: In Favor of Isaac Reed (Messages and Petition Only." Manuscript; General Assembly Record Group; Session Records, April-May 1780: Joint Papers, Committee Papers, Resolutions; House Joint Resolutions, Box 1 (MARS ID: 66.8.20.17.11; item), State Archives of North Carolina, Raleigh. [Online catalog description: "Reed, of Craven County, informs the Assembly that the pension he received after his injury in the Battle of Alamance is no longer sufficient to meet his family's needs."]

North Carolina (State). Office of State Treasurer. Office of Comptroller. "Military Papers – General Records, 1747-1909." Manuscript Box 1-Box 12, Box 74, Box 89, Box 93-Box 98, Box 120, Box 121-A (MARS ID: 13.26), State Archive of North Carolina, Raleigh. [Online catalog description: "Records relating to the financing of military activities in North Carolina, including accounts, certificates, claims against the state, receipts, returns, inventories, promissory notes, payrolls, contracts, officials' bonds and oaths, correspondence, petitions, affidavits, testimony, powers of attorney, resolutions and committee reports of the General Assembly, governors' messages to the assembly and memorials to Congress, insurance policies, and railroad passes. Records from the colonial and Revolutionary periods concern scouting on the frontier; the purchase, impressment, seizure, and issuance of provisions, supplies, arms, ammunition, accoutrements, horses, cattle, and tobacco; pay, clothing, and ration allowances for Continental Line and militia units, guards of public property, and the governors' escort; the development of public salt works, lead mines, fisheries, and gun factories; work on fortifications by slaves; capture and imprisonment of Loyalists, deserters, felons, and fugitive slaves; county commissioners of the specific tax; lost certificates; expenses of the commissioners of army accounts, the Board of Trade, and the Board of War; instructions to surveyors of the bounty land tract; accounts with the federal government; and postwar sales of public property. In the antebellum period the records concern settlement of outstanding claims for Revolutionary War service; surveying bounty lands; {end of Revolutionary War contents}."] There are online finding aids for this collection.

Pittard, Janet. "Let Freedom Ring." *Our State: Down Home in North Carolina*, 72:10 (March 2005), 68-70, 72-73; online: http://digital.ncdcr.gov/cdm/ref/collection/p16062coll18/id/82887. [Online description from "North Carolina Periodicals Index," East Carolina University: "Before America declared for independence, a group of Piedmont farmers challenged the royal government which was led by Governor William Tryon. The group was not seeking independence from England but reform of existing local governments. Among the complaints against local governments were excessive taxes, illegal fees, corrupt officials, and appointment by the Crown of local officials. Pittard discusses the Regulator Revolt, which culminated in a battle on May 14, 1771, on Alamance Creek between Royal forces and the Regulators and the subsequent hanging of six of the Regulators."]

Powell, William S. *The War of the Regulation and the Battle of Alamance, May 16, 1771*. Raleigh: Division of Archives and History, N. C. Dept. of Cultural Resources, 1976.

Powell, William S., James K. Huhta, and Thomas J. Farnham, ed. *The Regulators in North Carolina: A Documentary History, 1759-1776*. Raleigh: State Dept. of Archives and History, 1971. [Collection of primary sources concerning the Regulator Insurrection including minutes of meetings, legislation, personal accounts, etc.]

"Revolutionary North Carolina, 1763-1790: A Digital Textbook." Online at the LearnNC website: http://www.learnnc.org/lp/editions/nchist-revolution/cover.

Sadler, Sarah. "Prelude to the American Revolution? The War of Regulation: A Revolutionary Reaction for Reform." *History Teacher,* 46:1 (November 2012), 97-126.

Seawell, Joseph Lacy. *The First Lynching was the First Overt Act for American Liberty*. [North Carolina?: J. L. Seawell?], 1927.

Stevenson, George. "The War of the Regulation, 1768-1771: Records." In Helen F. M. Leary, ed. *North Carolina Research: Genealogy and Local History*. 2nd ed. (Raleigh: North Carolina Genealogical Society, 1996), Chapter 33: "Military Records," 361-362.

Troxler, Carole Watterson. *Farming Dissenters: The Regulator Movement in Piedmont North Carolina*. Raleigh: Office of Archives and History, North Carolina Department of Cultural Resources, 2011. [Contents: The Regulators and Alamance; Land Speculation and a Geographic Imbalance of Power; Orderly Outbursts of Backcountry Resentment; A Century's Legacy: Dissenter Religious Culture as a Carrier of Political Expectations; Herman Husband, Crystallizer; The Sandy Creek Network and Its Allies in the Regulator Movement; The Gentlemen's Agreement in Mecklenburg; Petitions, Court Proceedings, and Rioting in Hillsborough and Salisbury; Tryon's Militia, Regulator Confrontation, and the Battle of Alamance; Regulators as Victims: Repercussions of the Militia Attack; Politics at Work before the Revolution; Land Ownership and Local Power; Religious Divergence and Growing Support for Revolution; Appendix 1. An Incomplete Compilation of Names in a Regulator Context; Appendix 2. Bibliographic Essay: The Historians and the Regulators.]

Tune, Richard G. "Collective Violence in American History: The Revolutionary Era, 1763-1794." M. A. thesis, Middle Tennessee State University, Murfreesboro.

Turner, Justin G. "The Regulators." *Autograph Collector's Journal*, 3:3 (April 1951), 23-31.

Waddell, Alfred M. *A Colonial Officer and His Times, 1754-1773: A Biographical Sketch of General Hugh Waddell of North Carolina; with Notices of the French and Indian War in the Southern Colonies, the Resistance to the Stamp Act in North Carolina... The Regulators War, and an Historical Sketch of the Former Town of Brunswick, on the Cape Fear River.* Raleigh: Edwards & Broughton, 1890.

Walker, James Loy. The Regulator Movement: Sectional Controversy in North Carolina, 1765-1771. Graduate thesis. Louisiana State University, 1962. ["Addresses the issue of who joined the Regulator Movement and the idea that 'the Regulation was not directly related to the Revolution."]

Watson, Alan D. "The Origin of the Regulation in North Carolina." *Mississippi Quarterly*, 47:4 (Fall 1994), 567-598.

Whittenburg, James P. "Planters, Merchants, and Lawyers: Social Change and the Origins of the North Carolina Regulation." *William and Mary Quarterly*, 3rd series, 3:34 (April 1977), 215-238.

Whittenburg, James Penn. "Backwoods Revolutionaries: Social Context and Constitutional Theories of the North Carolina Regulators, 1765-1771." Graduate thesis. University of Georgia, 1974. ["Close examination of 'the complexity of social forces that prompted the insurrection' and 'the constitutional principles of the rebels'."]

Woodcock, John Bryan. "From Friction to Freedom: The Political Attitudes of the North Carolina Regulators, 1771-6." History Honors Essay, University of North Carolina at Chapel Hill, 2005.

The Edenton Tea Party of 1774 and Penelope Barker (1728-1796)

[See also the section in Chapter Fifteen on Chowan County and Edenton. This was a Pre-Revolutionary War Event.]

"51 Women Stage Edenton Tea Party." *Colonial Heritage*, 6:3 (April 1975), 1, 6.

Arthur, Billy. "Edenton's Tea Party." *The State: Down Home in North Carolina*, 62:5 (October 1994), 13-14; online: http://digital.ncdcr.gov/cdm/ref/collection/p16062coll18/id/66995. [Online description from "North Carolina Periodicals Index," East Carolina University: "Although considered a significant event in North Carolina's Revolutionary period, many questions still surround Edenton's Tea Party of October 25, 1774. Arthur describes the event and addresses questions concerning its authenticity."]

Ashe, Samuel A'Court. *History of North Carolina.* Greensboro: Charles L. Van Noppen, 1908. [Edenton Tea Party, 427-429]

"Association Signed by Ladies of Edenton, October 25, 1774." [with list of names] from "Extract of a letter from North Carolina, October 27." *Morning Chronicle and London Advertiser*, January 16, 1775.

Barnard, Ella Kent. *Dorothy Payne, Quakeress.* Philadelphia: Ferris & Leach Co., 1909; micropublished in *History of Women.* (New Haven: Research Publications, Inc., 1975), reel 705, no. 5650. [Dorothy Payne became "Dolly" Madison, wife of James Madison.]

Barnes, Lottie. "Edenton Tea Party." *College Message* [Greensboro Female College], 11 (January 1903), 109-119.

Bell, Thelma Harrington. "Edenton, North Carolina's Cradle of Liberty." *Ford Times*, 49 (April 1957), 25-29.

Cheeseman, Bruce S. "The Survival of the Cupola House: A Venerable Old Mansion." *North Carolina Historical Review*, 63:1 (January 1986), 40-73.

Colihan, Jane. "At Home in Edenton: A Colonial Capital Remembered for its Women." *American Heritage,* 55:1 (February/March 2004), 33-35. [Topic: Edenton "Tea Party" of 1774.]

Copeland, David A. *Debating the Issues in Colonial Newspapers: Primary Documents on Events of the Period.* Westport, Conn.: Greenwood Publishing Group, 2000. [Chapter 26: "The Edenton Tea Party and Perceptions of Women, 1774," 316-328.]

Coxe, Vivian Barbee; illustrations by Vivian Barbee Coxe and Jacqueline Breckling. *Eliza and the Edenton Tea Party*. Raleigh: Martini Print Media, 1997. [a novel about the Edenton Tea Party of 1774]

Creecy, Richard Benbury "The Edenton Tea Party." In Richard Benbury Creecy. *Grandfather's Tales* (Raleigh: Edwards & Broughton, 1901), 35-39. [Tale of the tea party held by patriotic women in to protest against the tax on tea; includes a tale relating to the recovery of a painting on glass of the Edenton Tea Party and its exhibition in Pasquotank County during the 1820's.]

Cumming, Inez Parker. "The Edenton Ladies' Tea Party." *Georgia Review*, 8:4 (Winter 1954), 389-395.

Cummins, Joseph. *Ten Tea Parties: Patriotic Protests That History Forgot*. Philadelphia: Quirk Books, 2012.

Davis, Curtis Carroll. "Another Echo of the Tea Party." *The State*, (March 1982), 16-18; online: http://digital.ncdcr.gov/cdm/ref/collection/p16062coll18/id/59551. [Traces the discovery of a painting on glass dated London 1775, a representation of a print titled "A Society of Ladies at Edenton, in North Carolina," that was discovered on the island of Minorca in 1826. Online description from "North Carolina Periodicals Index," East Carolina University: "A satirical mezzotint depicting the Edenton Tea Party of 1774 was found at a shoemaker's shop in Ciudadela in 1826. In 1774, a group of fifty-one Edenton women gathered and signed a resolution against drinking tea. News of their tea party spread to London where the mezzotint was made, probably by artist Philip Dawe. Over the years, the mezzotint was shattered and only two-thirds of it has been successfully restored. It once again disappeared, but, years later, it was rediscovered by William Easterling in his bank in Edenton."]

Dean, Earl. "That Celebrated Tea Party." *The State: A Weekly Survey of North Carolina*, 17:20 (October 1949), 11, 22; online: http://digital.ncdcr.gov/cdm/ref/collection/p16062coll18/id/24527. [Online description from "North Carolina Periodicals Index," East Carolina University: "October marks the 175th anniversary of the historic Edenton Tea Party which took place on the afternoon of October 25, 1774 at the home of Mrs. Elizabeth King, where 51 patriotic ladies met and signed a spirited resolution."]

DePriest, Virginia Greene. "The Edenton Tea Party." *Eswau Huppeday (Broad River Genealogical Society)*, 3:4 (November 1983), 104-106.

Dillard, Richard. "Historic Tea-Party of Edenton, October 25th 1774." *North Carolina Booklet,* 1:4 (10 August 1901), 3-16.

Dillard, Richard. "Historic Tea-Party of Edenton: An Incident in North Carolina Connected with Taxation." *Magazine of American History*, 28:2 (August 1892), 81-88.

Dillard, Richard. "Historic Tea-Party of Edenton: An Incident in North Carolina Connected with British Taxation." *North Carolina Booklet,* 23 (1926), 3-14; online: http://digital.ncdcr.gov/cdm/ref/collection/p249901coll37/id/14180. [Online description from "North Carolina Periodicals Index," East Carolina University: "An account of the events that came to be known as the 'Edenton Tea-Party,' the resolution of protest against tax on tea drafted by fifty-one ladies of Edenton. Particular attention is given correcting misinformation and myth that the author feels permeated the popular account of the events at the time."]

Dillard, Richard. *The Historic Tea-Party of Edenton, October 25th, 1774; an Incident in North Carolina Connected with British Taxation.* Edenton: [s. n.], 1898; reprinted: Raleigh: Capital Printing Company, 1901.

"The Edenton Tea Party." In Doris Weatherford, gen. ed. *A History of Women in the United States: State-by-State Reference* (Danbury, Conn.: Grolier Academic Reference, An Imprint of Scholastic Library Publishing, Inc., 2004), 3:157.

"The Edenton Tea Party." *Journal of the Genealogical Society of Rowan County, North Carolina*, 21:4 (December 2007), 133-134.

Great Britain. Colonial Office. "Beacon Island Road [Wallace Channel, N. C.]. Extract of Andrew Little to Joseph Barter, a Merchant in Poole, [Eng.]. 8 Oct., 1775." Copy of a manuscript in the National Archives of the United Kingdom (formerly the Public Records Office), Kew, Richmond, Surrey, England; 71.187.1-2 (MARS ID: 21.20.115.4; folder), State Archives of North Carolina, Raleigh. [Online catalog description: "Recruitment of soldiers and minutemen in N. C.; 200 minutemen stationed in Edenton; dismay at large numbers of 'countrymen' joining the rebels."]

Griffin, Mary Rose. "Edenton's Tempest over Tea." *New East*, 4:3 (June 1976), 24-27. [Online description from "North Carolina Periodicals Index," East Carolina University: "On October 25, 1774, Penelope Barker organized fifty women to participate in the Edenton Tea Party, in order to tell the government in England what North Carolina women were prepared to do to resist repressive laws. Griffin discusses the event, which was 'the earliest instance of political activity on the part of women in the American colonies.'"]

Hampton, Jeffrey. "Caring for Cupola." *Our State: Down Home in North Carolina*, 79:4 (September 2011), 188-190, 192, 194, 196; online: http://digital.ncdcr.gov/cdm/ref/collection/p16062coll18/id/97517. [Online description from "North Carolina Periodicals Index," East Carolina University: "The Cupola House, built in Edenton in 1758, is one of the state's most historic buildings. The gardens that surround the house follow the design laid out in a detailed 1769 map, and they are maintained by a group of volunteer Edenton citizens."]

Hardy, Doris E. "The Edenton Tea Party." *Daughters of the American Revolution Magazine*, 93:4 (April 1959), 406.

Hathaway, J. R. B. "The Edenton Tea Party." *Carolina Trees & Branches*, 1:7 (July 1992), 68.

Hathaway, J. R. B. "The Edenton Tea Party." *North Carolina Historical and Genealogical Register*, 2:1 (January 1901), 120-124; 2:2 (April 1901), 163-170; 2:3 (July 1901), 458-464; 2:4 (October 1901), 602-607; 3:1 (January 1903), 116-124; 3:2 (April 1903), 300-304. [The journal ceased publication before this series was completed.]

Hinton, Mary Hilliard. "Unveiling and Dedication of the Edenton Tea Party Memorial Tablet." *North Carolina Bulletin*, 8 (April 1909), 265-298; online: http://digital.ncdcr.gov/cdm/ref/collection/p249901coll37/id/14180. [Online description from "North Carolina Periodicals Index," East Carolina University: "The unveiling of the Memorial to the Edenton Tea Party involved steps taken by both local and national organizations to raise funds for the erection of the monument."]

Huso, Deborah R. "Tea, Anyone?" *Our State: Down Home in North Carolina*, 68:10 (March 2001), 48-50; online: http://digital.ncdcr.gov/cdm/ref/collection/p16062coll18/id/72796. [Online description from "North Carolina Periodicals Index," East Carolina University: "Edenton was a hotbed of revolutionary fervor when the American nation was coming into being. Among its contributions were a signer of the Declaration of Independence, a signer of the U. S. Constitution, and the Edenton Tea Party. Huso describes the patriots, protestors, and politicians who peopled these momentous times in Edenton."]

Kickler, Troy. "Edenton Tea Party: Inspired Defense of Liberty." *Patriots of the American Revolution*, 2:1 (Summer 2009), 32.

Kierner, Cynthia A. "The Edenton Ladies: Women, Tea, and Politics in Revolutionary North Carolina." In Michele Gillespie and Sally G. McMillen, eds. *North Carolina Women: Their Lives and Times.* 2 vols. (Athens: University of Georgia Press, 2014), 1:12-33.

Luten, William. "[Ledger, 1764-1787]." Manuscript AB.214 [Transferred to P.C.1712] (MARS ID: 3114; record group), State Archives of North Carolina, Raleigh. [1 vol. Edenton, Chowan County]

Martin, Michael G., Jr. "Penelope Barker (1728-96)." In William Stevens Powell, ed., *Dictionary of North Carolina Biography, vol. 1: A-C* (Chapel Hill: University of North Carolina Press, 1979), 95-96. [Barker was involved in the Edenton Tea Party.]

Martin, Michael G., Jr. "Rejecting a Pernicious Custom." Jack Claiborne and William Price, eds., *Discovering North Carolina: A Tar Heel Reader* (Chapel Hill: University of North Carolina Press, 1991), 115-117. [Discusses Penelope Barker.]

McCormick, Katherine Raynolds. *Tea, Its Part in Peace and in War.* Baltimore: McCormick & Company, 1917.

Muse, Wilma. "Edenton Tea Party." *A Lot of Bunkum,* 22:1 (February 2001), 110.

Muniz, Maria L. "From Teapot to Tempest: The Beverage That Sparked a Revolution." *The Palace*, 11:6 (Spring 2012), 16-30. [Online description from "North Carolina Periodicals Index," East Carolina University: "First used as a medicinal drink in Asian, tea became a commodity that fueled the British Empire and sparked revolution in the American colonies. In North Carolina, it would prove to be a catalyst for the first political actions by women in the state's history."]

Nash, Jaquelin Drane. "Edenton Tea Party." In William S. Powell, ed.; Jay Mazzocchi, assoc. ed., *Encyclopedia of North Carolina* (Chapel Hill: University of North Carolina Press in association with the University of North Carolina Library, 2006), 372.

Norris, Jeannie Faris. "Tea Party." *The State: Down Home in North Carolina*, 25:20 (February 1958), 15; online: http://digital.ncdcr.gov/cdm/ref/collection/p16062coll18/id/50936. [Online description from "North Carolina Periodicals Index," East Carolina University: "On October 25th, 1774, fifty-one women in Edenton met at the home of Mrs. Elizabeth King, signing a resolution not to drink tea until the taxes placed upon the commodity had been removed."]

North Carolina Society, Daughters of the American Revolution. *Programme of the Unveiling and Dedication of the Tablet in Memory of the Fifty-One Signers of the Edenton Tea Party Resolves in the Capitol, Raleigh, North Carolina, Erected by the North Carolina Society of the Daughters of the American Revolution, October the Twenth-Four, Nineteen Hundred and Eight, Eleven-Thirty. A. M.* Raleigh: The Society, 1908.

Oldham, Thomas. "[Ledger, 1771-1775]." Manuscript AB.326 (MARS ID: 3226; record group), State Archives of North Carolina, Raleigh. [Edenton, Chowan County]

Olds, Fred A. [Frederick Augustus] "Revolutionary Heroines of North Carolina; Important Part Played by Edenton Women in American Independence." *Orphan's Friend* [no date shown]. Typescript in the "Women in the American Revolution Collection," DAR Library, Washington, D. C., [no date shown; 193?].

Olds, Fred A. [Frederick Augustus] "The Celebrated Edenton, North Carolina Tea Party." *Daughters of the American Revolution Magazine*, 56:6 (June 1922), 327-333.

"Penelope Barker (1728-1796), Edenton, N. C., ca. 1775." Manuscript, 55.11.33, Photographic Collection, State Archives of North Carolina, Raleigh. [Online catalog description: "Portrait of Penelope Barker (1728- 1796); Revolutionary Patriot and Leader of the Edenton Tea Party, 25 October 1774; Wife of Thomas Barker (1713-1789), London Agent for the North Carolina Colony; Portrait circa 1775, and Photographed circa 1905 by Sylvester Hough of Winston Salem, North Carolina."]

"Programme of the Unveiling and Dedication of the Tablet in Memory of the Fifty-One Signers of the Edenton Tea Party Resolves in the Capitol, Raleigh, North Carolina." *North Carolina Booklet*, 8:4 (April 1909), 268-298. [Online description from "North Carolina Periodicals Index," East Carolina University: "This article reviews the program for the 1908 dedication of a memorial tablet commemorating the signers of the 1774 Edenton Tea Party Resolve. Also noted were the Tea Party descendants in attendance, dedication participants and selected speeches from the dedication ceremony."]

Ravi, Jennifer. *Notable North Carolina Women.* Winston-Salem: Bandit Books, 1992. [Includes Penelope Barker (1728-1796) of Edenton .]

Righton, William. "[Commission Merchant's Ledger, 1776-1790]." Manuscript AB.221 (MARS ID: 3121; record group), State Archives of North Carolina, Raleigh. [Edenton, Chowan County]

Rogers, Lou. "Penelope Barker, President of Our Famous Tea Party." *We the People of North Carolina*, 2:2 (July 1944), 15-17. [Online description from "North Carolina Periodicals Index," East Carolina University: "Penelope Barker had had an eventful life even before the famous Edenton Tea Party. She had three husbands and lost two to death; the third died in 1787. She bore six children, mothered three of her first husband's, and saw eight of her children die. The Edenton Tea party took place on October 25, 1774 and is the first recorded women's political rally in America. Barker organized fifty women to participate in order to send the English government a message of what women in North Carolina were prepared to do to resist repressive laws."]

Rogers, Lou. *Tar Heel Women*. Raleigh: Warren Publishing Company, 1949. [Includes Penelope Barker, 21.]

[Shannonhouse, Edna M.] "The Edenton Tea Party." In Edna M. Shannonhouse, ed., *Year Book, Pasquotank Historical Society, Elizabeth City, North Carolina* (Baltimore: Gateway Press, Inc., 1983), 53-55. [Provides a brief account of the Edenton Tea Party of 1774 and a list of the names of fifty-six ladies who participated in the event; J. R. B. Hathaway was the compiler of the list included in this article.]

Shelton, Eliza Love. "The Edenton Tea Party, 25 October 1774: A Patriotic Female Community in Revolutionary North Carolina." M. A. thesis, East Tennessee State University, 2012.

Smith, Donna Campbell. "The Rebel Was a Lady." *Our State: Down Home in North Carolina*, 68:10 (March 2001), 52-54; online: http://digital.ncdcr.gov/cdm/ref/collection/p16062coll18/id/72796. [Online description from "North Carolina Periodicals Index," East Carolina University: "The first recorded women's political rally in America took place when Penelope Barker organized fifty women to participate in the Edenton Tea Party on October 25, 1774, in order to send the English government a message of what women in North Carolina were prepared to do to resist repressive laws. Smith recounts the life of this revolutionary woman."]

Staples, Mary Dawes. "The Edenton Tea Party." *American Monthly Magazine* [DAR], 31:2 (August 1907), 355-361.

"The Unveiling and Dedication of the Edenton Tea Party Memorial Tablet." *The North Carolina Booklet*, 8:4 (April 1909), 265-297. [Includes photographs.]

Webb and Bateman. "[Commission Merchants' Daybooks and Ledgers, 1781-1786." Manuscript AB.211 (MARS ID: 3111; record group), State Archives of North Carolina, Raleigh. [6 vols. Edenton, Chowan County]

Webb, Bryer, and Company. "[Commission Merchants' Ledger, Invoice Book, and Tobacco Book, 1781-1786." Manuscript AB.212 (MARS ID: 3112; record group), State Archives of North Carolina, Raleigh. [3 vols. Edenton, Chowan County]

"Wit, Mirth & Spleen." *Colonial Williamsburg*, 28:2 (Spring 2006), 90. ["Ladies of Edenton" – the famous satirical print of the Edenton Tea Party of 1774]

The Mecklenburg Declaration of Independence, May 10, 1775

Bancroft, George. "Letter, 1856 June 13, New York, [N. Y.], to [Hugh Blair Grigsby, Charlotte County, Va.]." Manuscript Mss2 B2215 a 1, Virginia Historical Society, Richmond. [Online catalog description: "Concerns the authenticity of the Mecklenburg Declaration of Independence, 20 May 1775."]

Charlotte Chamber of Commerce. "The Mecklenburg Declaration of Independence." *Daughters of the American Revolution Magazine*, 86:3 (March 1952), 286-284.

Clark, Walter. "In Commemoration of the Famous 20th of May, 1775." In Addresses Delivered under the Auspices of the North Carolina Society of the Colonial Dames of America, 1900-1926. [S. l.]: Jackson & Bell, [1927?].

Connor, Robert Digges Wimberly. "North Carolina's Priority in the Demand for a Declaration of Independence: The Resolution of the Congress at Halifax, April 12, 1776, and Its Influence on the Sentiment for Independence in the United Colonies." *South Atlantic Quarterly*, 8:3 (July 1904), 3-23.

Craven, Bruce. "The Mecklenburg Declaration of Independence." *North Carolina Booklet*, 8:3 (January 1909), 203-248.

Craven, Bruce. "The Significance of the Mecklenburg Declaration of Independence." *North Carolina Booklet*, 8:2 (October 1908), 141-148; online: http://digital.ncdcr.gov/cdm/ref/collection/p249901coll37/id/14180. [Online description from "North Carolina Periodicals Index," East Carolina University: "The article details the Mecklenburg Declaration of Independence, created by Mecklenburg County residents on May 20, 1775 to declare their separation from the British government. It also highlights the freedom loving nature of Mecklenburg County's original settlers from the mid-17th [*sic*; i. e., 18th] century and the county's resistance to British over reach throughout its history."]

Current, Richard N. "That Other Declaration: May 20, 1775-May 20, 1975." *North Carolina Historical Review*, 54:2 (April 1977), 169-191. [Online description from "North Carolina Periodicals Index," East Carolina University: "This article examines research into the history of the Mecklenburg Declaration, the purported first American official document declaring a desire to be independent from Great Britain. A history of how the story of the document surfaced, as well as how it was used, celebrated, and remembered throughout history both in and outside of North Carolina is included."]

Current, Richard Nelson. "An Imaginary Declaration of Independence, 1775-1975." In Richard Nelson Current, *Arguing with Historians: Essays on the Historical and the Unhistorical* (Middletown, Conn.: Wesleyan University Press, 1988), 9-30.

Current, Richard Nelson. *Arguing With Historians: Essays on the Historical and the Unhistorical*. Middletown, Conn,: Wesleyan University Press, 1988, 1987. [Chapter One: "An Imaginary Declaration of Independence,

1775-1975,"provides an excellent discussion of both the historical and modern debate over the authenticity of the Mecklenburg Declaration.]

Davidson, Chalmers G. "Celebrating May 20 for 200 Years." *The State: Down Home in North Carolina*, 42:11 (April 1975), 9-12; 36-37; online: http://digital.ncdcr.gov/cdm/ref/collection/p16062coll18/id/9338. [Online description from "North Carolina Periodicals Index," East Carolina University: "On May 20, 1975 Mecklenburg's bicentennial celebration marked the anniversary of the signing of the Mecklenburg Declaration of Independence, one of history's lost artifacts claimed to be earliest overt act of independence in the thirteen colonies by a legally constituted body. The article includes a copy of the Mecklenburg Declaration of Independence."]

Declaration of Independence by the Citizens of Mecklenburg County, on May 20, 1775. [Knoxville: Heiskell & Brown, Printers, 1826]. [Broadside. A copy is located in Special Collections (E215.9.M42 1826; oversize, Map Case 2, drawer 1), J. Murrey Atkins Library, University of North Carolina at Charlotte.]

The Declaration of Independence by the Citizens of Mecklenburg County, on the Twentieth Day of May, 1775: With Accompanying Documents, and the Proceedings of the Cumberland Association. Published by the Governor, under the Authority And Direction of the General Assembly of the State of North Carolina. Raleigh: Lawrence & Lemay, printers to the state, 1831.

"Died – Col. William Polk, at His Residence in Raleigh, N. C. on Jan. 14, 1834, in his 76th Year. He Was One of Those Who Declared Independence at Mecklenburg on May 20, 1775, and Served during the Revolution." *American Beacon and Virginia and North-Carolina Gazette*, (Thursday, January 23, 1834), 2:col. 5.

Faulkner, Ronnie W. "Mecklenburg Declaration of Independence." In William S. Powell, ed.; Jay Mazzocchi, assoc. ed., *Encyclopedia of North Carolina* (Chapel Hill: University of North Carolina Press in association with the University of North Carolina Library, 2006), 725-726.

"Footprints of the Mecklenburg Declaration," *American Monthly Magazine* [Daughters of the American Revolution], 13:4 (October 1898), 329-337.

Force, Peter, and William Q. Force. "Peter Force and William Q. Force Collection, 1775-1875." Manuscript 2967 and microfilm negative M-2967, Southern Historical Collection, Louis Round Wilson Special Collections Library, University of North Carolina at Chapel Hill. [Online catalog description: "Papers acquired by Peter Force, collector and historical editor of Washington, D. C., and his son, William Q. Force, concerning the dispute over the authenticity of the Mecklenburg County, N. C., declaration of independence of 1775, including correspondence of the Forces and other persons, copies of pertinent materials, and a scrapbook of clippings."]

Fries, Adelaide Lisetta. *The Mecklenburg Declaration of Independence as Mentioned in Records of Wachovia.* Raleigh: Edwards & Broughton Printing Co., 1907.

Goode, Minnie May. "The Mecklenberg Declaration of Independence." *Daughters of the American Revolution Magazine*, 53:9 (September 1919), 558-559.

Goodloe, Daniel R[eaves]. "[An Essay on the Mecklenburg Declaration of Independence." Manuscript 278, Southern Historical Collection, Louis Round Wilson Special Collections Library, University of North Carolina at Chapel Hill.

Graham, George Washington. *The Mecklenburg Declaration of Independence, May 20, 1775, and Lives of Its Signers*. New York: Neale Publishing Co., 1905.

Graham, George Washington. *Why North Carolinians Believe in the Mecklenburg Declaration of Independence of May 20th, 1775.* 2d ed., rev. and enl.: Charlotte: Queen City Printing and Paper Co., 1895.

Graham, Joseph. "Celebration of the Anniversary of May 20, 1775." *North Carolina Booklet*, 5:3 (January 1906), 209-216; online: http://digital.ncdcr.gov/cdm/ref/collection/p249901coll37/id/14180. [Online description from "North Carolina Periodicals Index," East Carolina University: "A reprint of an address given by Revolutionary War General Joseph Graham on the first anniversary of the Mecklenburg Declaration of Independence at celebrations in Charlotte, North Carolina on May 20, 1835."]

Graham, William Alexander. *The Address on the Mecklenburg Declaration of Independence of the 20th of May, 1775: Delivered in Charlotte, on the 4th Day of Feb'y, 1875, by Request of the Citizens of Mecklenburg County; with Accompanying Documents*. New York: E. J. Hale & Son, 1875.

Harris, William S. *Historical Sketch of Poplar Tent Church*. S. l.: s. n., 1873; reprinted under the auspices of the Cabarrus Black Boys Chapter, North Carolina Daughters of the American Revolution Concord: The Times Book and Job Presses, 1924. [Contents: W. Hampton Eubank. "Introduction;" Wm. S. Harris. "Historical Sketch of Popular Tent Church;" W. Hampton Eubank. "Brief Resume of the History of Poplar Tent Church, from 1873 to 1923;" W. Hampton Eubank. "Poplar Tent Church and Cemetery and Tomb of Rev. Hezekiah James Balch, Author of the *Mecklenburg Declaration of Independence, May 20, 1775*; "Cabarrus Black Boys Chapter, Concord, N. C."]

Henderson, Archibald. "The Mecklenburg Declaration of Independence." *Mississippi Valley Historical Review*, 5:2 (September 1918), 207-215.

Hoyt, William Henry. *The Mecklenburg Declaration of Independence: A Study of Evidence Showing That the Alleged Declaration of Mecklenburg County, North Carolina, on May 20th, 1775, is Spurious*. New York: G. P. Putnam's Sons, 1907.

Hoyt, William Henry. "William Henry Hoyt Papers, 1769-1957." Manuscript 3410 and microfilm 1-4485 (3410) (47 rolls), Southern Historical Collection, Louis Round Wilson Special Collections Library, University of North Carolina, Chapel Hill; online finding aid available at http://www2.lib.unc.edu/mss/inv/h/Hoyt,William_Henry.html. [Online finding aid description: "Lawyer, of New York, N.Y., and amateur historian. Hoyt's papers include correspondence and notes, pictures, and copies of documents from repositories in France, Italy, Great Britain, and the United States, all related to his research into the legend of Peter Stewart Ney, a 19th-century North Carolina schoolmaster alleged to be Michel Ney (1765-1815), marshal of France; and concerning the declaration of independence signed in Mecklenburg County, N.C., 20 May 1775. In 1907, Hoyt published a book on the Mecklenburg declaration."]

Hunter, Elizabeth Pettit. "Mecklenburg County, North Carolina in the Revolutionary War." *American Monthly Magazine* [DAR], 31:4 (October 1907), 626-629.

Jack, Gerald Ignatius. "Just Who Was Captain Jack? Unveiling the Obscurity of the 'Mecklenburg Declaration'." *Drumbeat with Flintlock & Powderhorn: News of the Sons of the Revolution,* 27:3 (Fall 2009), 11-12.

"John Davidson: A Notable Signer of the Mecklenburg Declaration of Independence." *Olde Mecklenburg Genealogical Society Quarterly*, 11:4 (1993), 14-18.

Johnson, Alden B. "Hezekiah James Balch: Signer of the Mecklenburg Declaration of Independence." *Olde Mecklenburg Genealogical Society Quarterly*, 11:3 (1993), 3-9.

King, Victor C. *Lives and Times of the 27 Signers of the Mecklenburg Declaration of Independence of May 20, 1775.* Charlotte: Anderson Press, 1956.

McNitt, V.V. *Chain of Error and the Mecklenburg Declarations of Independence*. Charlotte: Mecklenburg Historical Association, 1996. [Modern account of the historical evidence and arguments proving the authenticity of the Mecklenburg Declaration.]

Mecklenburg Declaration of Independence, May 20, 1775. Charlotte: [s. n., 1954]. [Pamphlet "[d]one on the occasion of the visit of President Dwight David Eisenhower on Freedom Celebration Day, Charlotte, North Carolina."]

"The Mecklenburg Declaration, May 20, 1775." William L. Saunders, ed., *The Colonial Records of North Carolina, Volume IX, 1771-1775* (Raleigh: Josephus Daniels, 1890; reprinted: Wilmington: Broadfoot Publishing Company, 1993), 1263-1265.

"Mecklenburg Declaration Papers, 1775-1982 (bulk 1775-1853)." Manuscript 501, Southern Historical Collection, Louis Round Wilson Special Collections Library, University of North Carolina, Chapel Hill; online finding aid available at http://www2.lib.unc.edu/mss/inv/m/Mecklenburg_Declaration.html. [Online finding aid description: "The collection contains papers, chiefly 1775-1853, accumulated by Joseph McKnitt Alexander and others relating to the Mecklenburg Declaration and Resolves of May 1775, and the controversy over them, including later testimony of witnesses and copies of documents, papers of North Carolina officials concerning the publication of a pamphlet on the subject in 1831, and later letters related to aspects of the controversy."]

"The Mecklenburg Declaration of Independence and Andrew Jackson's Birthplace." *Mississippi Valley Historical Review*, 29:1 (January 1942), 79-90.

Miller, S. Millington. "The True Cradle of American Liberty: Independence Bell Rang a Year Earlier in Charlotte Than in Philadelphia." *Collier's*, (July 1, 1905), 19, 21.

Misenheimer, John E., Jr. "The Mecklenburg Declaration of Independence, May 20th, 1775." *The Golden Nugget (Cabarrus Genealogical Society)*, 13:2 (Summer 2005), 56.

Moore, James Hall. *Defence of the Mecklenburg Declaration of Independence*. Raleigh: Edwards & Broughton Printing Co., 1908.

Murphey, Archibald D; William Henry Hoyt, ed. *The Papers of Archibald D. Murphey*. Raleigh: E. M. Uzzell & Co., State Printers, 1914. [Contents: v. 1. William A. Graham. Chronological List of the Murphey Papers Here Printed. Memoir of Murphey; Correspondence 1801-1832; v. 2. *Public Papers. Historical, Biographical, and Literary Papers. Papers on the North Carolina-Tennessee Land Controversy. Petition of Rev. John Debow to the General Assembly, 1777*. Appendix. Also: *General Joseph Graham's Narrative of the Revolutionary War in North Carolina, in 1780 and 1781*, 443-444.]

Nash, Frederick; John H. Wheeler (attrib.) "Memorial of the Mecklenburg Monumental Association." In North Carolina. General Assembly. *Executive Documents*. [S. l.]: Printed for the General Assembly of North Carolina, 1842-1843.

Noël Hume, Ivor. "Mecklenburg's Declaration of Independence." *Colonial Williamsburg: The Journal of the Colonial Williamsburg Foundation*, 34:2 (Summer 2012), 56-61. [Description: "Analysis of the 1775 Mecklenburg (North Carolina) Declaration of Independence absolving allegiance to the British Crown; positions taken by Jefferson and Adams re its validity and the ensuing dispute between VA & NC re its precedence over Jefferson's 1776 document; conclusion that document was carried to Philadelphia though never formally laid before the Congress."]

"North Carolina Independence." *American Historical Record and Repertory of Notes and Queries Concerning the History and Antiquities of America and Biography of Americans*, 2:23 (November 1873), 510. ["Before me is a Sheriff's warrant, which closes as follows: 'Witness, Reuben Sanders, Clerk of said court, the 4th day of November in the XXXth year of the Independence of the said State, Anno Domini 1805'." "This shows that the North Carolinians were in the habit of dating their official documents from the date of the Mecklenburgh Declaration of Independence in May, 1775, instead of from the date of the National Declaration in July, 1776. When did this state sovereignty habit cease? or has it ceased?"]. For a response to this question see: Frank M. Etting. "North Carolina Independence." *American Historical Record and Repertory of Notes and Queries Concerning the History and Antiquities of America and Biography of Americans*, 3:25 (January 1874), 35. [Etting states that this earlier article was in error, and that North Carolinians had always used the 1776 date.]

Phillips, Charles. *May 1775: Article on the Alleged Mecklenburg Declaration of Independence, and His Subsequent Letters in Regard to the Matter*. Greensboro: Thomas, Reece & Company, Power book and Job Printers, 1887.

Plumer, Richard P. *Charlotte and the American Revolution: Reverend Alexander Craighead, the Mecklenburg Declaration and the Foothills Fight for Independence*. Charleston, S. C.: History Press, 2014. [Contents: Mecklenburg's Fiery Preacher; Reverend Craighead's Ferocious Parishioners; The War of Sugar Creek; Reverend Alexander Craighead's Death; Rebellion in Mecklenburg County and the Foothills of North Carolina; The First Battle of the Revolutionary War; The Mecklenburg Declaration of Independence and Resolves; Mecklenburg's Role in the Revolutionary War; Appendix: List of Mecklenburg County Revolutionary War Soldiers. Publisher's description: "Charlotte was a hotbed of Revolutionary activity well before the fervency of revolt reached its boiling point in New England. Considered a wild frontier region at the time, Mecklenburg County welcomed the Reverend Alexander Craighead with ready hands for battle. Craighead's fiery rhetoric inspired the people of the region to action. What resulted was the creation of the Mecklenburg Declaration of Independence, the first such document in the nation, and although the county had less than 3 percent of the colony's population, its Patriots accounted for over one-quarter of North Carolina's Revolutionary troops. Join author Richard P. Plumer as he reveals how the Queen City played an integral role in the formation of a proud and free America."]

Ray, Worth S. *The Mecklenburg Signers and Their Neighbors*. Baltimore: Genealogical Publishing Co., 1962. Study of the people of Mecklenburg County in the colonial and Revolutionary periods. Some of the material is more relevant for genealogy but there are also many maps and lists of Mecklenburg County inhabitants that may help in finding of primary source material.

Salley, A. S., Jr. "The Mecklenburg Declaration of Independence." *The North Carolina Booklet*, 8:3 (January 1909), 155-202; online: http://digital.ncdcr.gov/cdm/ref/collection/p249901coll37/id/14180. [Online description from "North Carolina Periodicals Index," East Carolina University: "This article discusses the Mecklenburg Declaration of Independence, which is commonly believed to be the first public declaration of independence from the Crown, in the colonies. It includes a reprinting of the original declaration as well as correspondence between several colonial leaders regarding the declaration and the political climate in North Carolina."]

Swain, Bob. "The Mecklenburg Declaration of Independence: Who Signed the Document." *Olde Mecklenburg Genealogical Society Quarterly*, 11:1 (January-March 1993), 3-6; plus: "Neighbors of the Signers of the Mecklenburg Declaration of Independence," 7.

Smyth, Thomas. *The True Origin and Source of the Mecklenburg and National Declaration of Independence...* Columbia, S. C.: I. C. Morgan, 1847. [Online description from "North Carolina Periodicals Index," East Carolina University: "This article discusses the Mecklenburg Declaration of Independence, which is commonly believed to be the first public declaration of independence from the Crown, in the colonies. It includes a reprinting of the original declaration as well as correspondence between several colonial leaders regarding the declaration and the political climate in North Carolina."]

Syfert, Scott. *The First American Declaration of Independence?: The Disputed History of the Mecklenburg Declaration of May 20, 1775*. Jefferson: McFarland & Co., 2014.

Timblin, Carol. "Hoax or History?" *Our State: Down Home in North Carolina*, 73:5 (October 2005), 104-106, 108, 110-111; online: http://digital.ncdcr.gov/cdm/compoundobject/collection/p16062coll18/id/84540. [Online description from "North Carolina Periodicals Index," East Carolina University: "Fourteen months before the Declaration of Independence was signed in Philadelphia, a group of leaders in Mecklenburg County met on May 20, 1775, to sign the Mecklenburg Declaration of Independence. Was this the first document declaring freedom for the American colonies, or was it just a fanciful story? Mecklenburg has celebrated and commemorated the document for 180, but the controversy over its origination challenges its legitimacy. Timblin examines this dispute over legitimacy, beginning in 1819 down to the present-day."]

Van Noppen, Charles Leonard. *Mecklenburg Declaration of Independence Written in 1800*. Lynchburg, Va.: Brown-Morrison Company, [s. d.].

Weeks, Stephen Beauregard. *Truth and Justice for the History of North Carolina: The Mecklenburg Resolves of May 31, 1775 vs. the Mecklenburg Declaration of May 20, 1775*. Greensboro: C. L. Van Noppen, 1908?

Wheeler, John Hill. *The Lives and Characters of the Signers of the Mecklenburg Declaration of Independence, of the 20th of May, 1775; Delivered at Charlotte, N. C., on the 24th of May, 1875, at the Request of the Mecklenburg Historical Society*. Charlotte: Observer Book and Job Power Press Print, 1875.

Yandle, Lois M. "General Robert Irwin, Signer of the Mecklenburg Declaration of Independence." *Olde Mecklenburg Genealogical Society Quarterly*, 10:2 (April-June 1992), 13-15.

Chapter Five:
General Histories of the American Revolution in North Carolina

The following listings are for most of the basic studies on the history of North Carolina and Tennessee during the American Revolution. Some others may have been unintentionally missed, and so this cannot be considered a complete bibliography.

General Bibliography

Alden, John R. *The American Revolution, 1775-1783*. New York: Harper & Row, 1954; reprinted: New York: Alfred A. Knopf, Inc., 1969.

Alden, John Richard. *The First South*. (Walter Lynwood Fleming Lectures in Southern History series) Gloucester, Mass.: P. Smith, 1968.

Alden, John Richard. *The South in the American Revolution, 1763-1789*. (*A History of the South*, vol. 3) Baton Rouge: Louisiana State University Press, 1957.

Alderman, J. T. "Some Overlooked North Carolina History." *North Carolina Booklet*, 6:4 (April 1907), 238-242; online: http://digital.ncdcr.gov/cdm/ref/collection/p249901coll37/id/14180. [Online description from "North Carolina Periodicals Index," East Carolina University: "This article discusses North Carolina history relating to the Revolutionary War that the author feels has been overlooked by historians, including Governor Burke's orders to mobilize the North Carolina militia to preemptively cut off the escape route of General Cornwallis from Yorktown and the efforts and deeds of the North Carolina militia in military engagements throughout the North Carolina and South Carolina."]

Alexander, Lamar. *The Tennesseans: A People and Their Land.* Nashville: Thomas Nelson, 1981.

Alexander, Suzanne. "Sketches of the Revolutionary War in North Carolina." *The Carolinas Genealogical Society Bulletin*. 9:3 (Winter 1972), 52-63. [See also: "*National Intelligencer* Revolutionary Legends." *The Carolinas Genealogical Society Bulletin*, 9:4 (Spring 1973), 77-82, for comments on Suzanne Alexander's reminiscences.]

Allen, William Cicero. *North Carolina History Stories.* Richmond: B. F. Johnson Publishing Co., 1901.

Angiel, Lucien. *The Late Affair Almost Broke My Heart: The American Revolution in the South, 1780-1781.* Riverside, Conn.: The Chatham Press, Inc., 1972.

Ashe, Samuel A'Court, ed. *Biographical History of North Carolina*. 8 vols. Greensboro: Charles L. Van Noppen, 1905-1917.

Ashe, Samuel A'Court. *History of North Carolina*. 2 vols. Greensboro: Charles L. Van Noppen, 1908; reprinted: Greensboro: C.L. Van Noppen, 1925; reprinted: Spartanburg, S.C.: Reprint Co., 1971.

Bancroft, George. "Letters, 1845-1885." Manuscript Sec. A Box 7 items 1-22, David M. Rubenstein Rare Book & Manuscript Library, Duke University, Durham. [Online catalog description: "Fifteen letters to David L. Swain, president of the University of North Carolina, relating to the history of the state. Topics include the Regulators, Loyalists, Mecklenburg Declaration, Governors William Tryon and Alexander Martin, and Hermon Husbands and Edmund Fanning. Original items include a letter to C. C. Jones on the employment of women and children in Germany and a note, 1885, of thanks for Jones's article on Richard H. Wilde; a letter from H. C. Van Schaack regarding the publication of his pamphlet on Henry Cruger; and notes relating to appointments by Bancroft as Secretary of the Navy, and to payment from publishers."]

Berry, A. L. "The Carolinas in the American Revolution: A Paper Read before the Kiwanis Club of Tryon, N. C." *The Polk County News* (Tryon, N. C.), (June 7, 1928), 8. [Copies are at the North Carolina Collection, Louis Round Wilson Special Collections Library, University of North Carolina at Chapel Hill, and at the State Library of North Carolina, Raleigh.]

Blackburn, Charles, Jr. "The Dean of North Carolina History." *Our State: Down Home in North Carolina*, 76:1 (June 2008), 106-108, 110, 112-114; online: http://digital.ncdcr.gov/cdm/ref/collection/p16062coll18/id/99562. [Online description from "North Carolina Periodicals Index," East Carolina University: "William S. Powell is professor emeritus of history at the University of North Carolina at Chapel Hill. After World War II, Powell began his life's work in 1948, as a research historian at the North Carolina Office of Archives and History and later spent the bulk of his career at UNC. A leading authority on the people and events that have shaped North Carolina over the last four hundred years, he has written many books on the state's history and geography."]

Blackmon, Richard D. *Dark and Bloody Ground: The American Revolution along the Southern Frontier*. Yardley, Pa.: Westholme Publishing, 2012. [Publisher's description: "The Battles along the Rivers, Mountains, and in the Deep Woods of the South that Changed the Fate of Nations. The American Revolution marked a dramatic change in the struggle for land along the southern frontier. In the colonial era, American Indian leaders and British officials attempted to accommodate the westward expansion of Anglo-Americans through land cessions designed to have the least impact on Indian societies. The region remained generally peaceful, but with the onset of the Revolution, the British no longer exercised sole authority to curb the settlements appearing within territory claimed by the Creeks, Shawnee, and most importantly, the Cherokee. Whether it was to escape the economic uncertainty of the east, the rigors of the conflict, or the depredations of troops and militias on both sides, settlers flooded west. Under these conditions, the war in the south took on a savage character as Indians, Loyalists, and Whigs all desperately fought to defend their communities and maintain control of their own destinies. Taking advantage of the political turmoil in the east, the Cherokee Nation launched a coordinated offensive in 1776 against illegal frontier settlements. The Whigs responded with a series of expeditions from each of the Southern colonies that razed Cherokee towns and their food supplies. All the while, both British and Whig leaders walked a fine line: If the Indians attacked settlers without distinguishing between Loyalists and Whigs, those groups could unite and thwart both British and Indian interests; if the Indians attacked the western frontier with Loyalist and British support, the Whigs would face a two-front war – an event that ended up happening. Blackmon uses a wealth of primary source material to recount the conflict between American Indians and Anglo-Americans in the colonial South during one of the most turbulent periods of North American history. He explains the complex points of contact in Georgia, Kentucky, North Carolina, South Carolina, Tennessee, and Virginia between native groups and settlers, while revealing the political gamesmanship between rival British and Whig traders and officials to secure Indian loyalty. The author also explains the critical role of the southern frontier to the American victory, a victory achieved long after the decision at Yorktown. Before the war, clashes between Cherokee and Shawnee hunters in Kentucky had become so commonplace that it was known as a 'dark and bloody ground.' With the rise in Anglo-American settlements there, led by Daniel Boone and others, the dark and bloody ground became a metaphor for the entire struggle for the Southern frontier."]

Boyd, William Kenneth. *The American Revolution and Reform in the South: Presidential Address before the Twenty-Second Annual Session of the State Literary and Historical Association of North Carolina, at Raleigh, December 7, 8, 1922*. Raleigh: Bynum Printing Company, State Printers, 1923.

Boyd, William Kenneth. "North Carolina, 1775-1861." In: *The South in the Building of the Nation* (1909), 1:462-482.

Boyd, William Kenneth. *History of North Carolina*. Chicago and New York: Lewis Publishing Company, 1919.

Buchanan, John. *The Road to Guilford Courthouse: The American Revolution in the Carolinas*. New York: Wiley, 1997. [Contents: 1. The Battle of Sullivan's Island; 2. The Rice Kings; 3. Southern Strategy; 4. The Approach March; 5. Charleston Besieged; 6. The Rise of Banastre Tarleton; 7. Into the Back Country; 8. Hearts and Minds; 9. Trouble in the Back Country; 10. More Trouble in the Back Country; 11. A Hero Takes Charge; 12. The Battle of Camden; 13. The Partisans Fight On; 14. The Rise of Patrick Ferguson; 15. To Catch Ferguson; 16. King's Mountain; 17. Retreat and Turmoil; 18. A General from Rhode Island; 19. The Stage is Set; 20. Tarleton Pursues Morgan; 21. Cowpens; 22. Bayonets and Zeal; 23. Patience and Finesse; 24. Guilford Courthouse: "Long, Obstinate, and Bloody".]

Burnett, Edmund Cody. "Southern Statesmen and the Confederation." *North Carolina Historical Review*, 14:4 (October 1937), 343-360.

Burnett, Fred M. "A Sketch of the Ancestors, Life and War Experiences of Marcus Lafayette Burnett, 1929." Manuscript (00107-z), Southern Historical Collection, The Louis Round Wilson Special Collections Library, University of North Carolina at Chapel Hill. [Online catalog description: "The collection consists of a typescript copy of an account of the life and Confederate service of Marcus LaFayette Burnett (b. 1845), describing his family history, his grandfather's emigration to Old Fort, N.C., in 1770; pioneer life; hunting; Revolutionary War battles in North Carolina and South Carolina…"]

Bussell, E[verett] Wayne. *Matthew Bussell and the American Revolution: Sailor and Soldier*. Lexington, Ky.: E. W. Bussell, 2012. [Virginia State Navy; ship *Dragon*; 1st Continental Artillery, Captain Anthony Singleton's Artillery Company; Military Campaigns in South Carolina, North Carolina, and Virginia]

Calhoon, Robert M. *Revolutionary America: An Interpretative Overview*. New York: Harcourt Brace Jovanovich, 1976.

Caruthers, E[li] W[ashington]. *Interesting Revolutionary Incidents; and Sketches of Character, Chiefly in the "Old North State."* Philadelphia: Hayes & Zell, 1854; 2nd series: 1856.

Cashin, Edward. *William Bartram and the American Revolution on the Southern Frontier*. Columbia: University of South Carolina Press, 2000. [Contents: The Georgia Coast; The Ceded Lands; East Florida; The Cherokee Country; The Creek County; The Military Engagements; Philadelphia. Relates to Bartram's *Travels through*

North & South Carolina, Georgia, East & West Florida, the Cherokee Country, the Extensive Territories of the Muscogulges, or Creek Confederacy, and the Country of the Chactaws]

Chesney, Charles Cornwallis. *Essays in Military Biography*. New York: Henry Holt and Co., 1874. [Includes essays titled: "Cornwallis and the Indian Services" and "A Carolina Loyalist in the Revolutionary War."]

Chidsey, Donald Barr. *The War in the South: The Carolinas and Georgia in the American Revolution: An Informal History*. New York: Crown Publishers, Inc., 1969.

Clark, Walter. "Negro Soldiers." *North Carolina Booklet*, 18:1 (July 1918), 57-62.

Clark, Walter. (Walker Clark (1846-1924) Papers, 1783-1924." Manuscript PC.8 (MARS ID: 517; record group), State Archives of North Carolina, Raleigh. [Online catalog description: "'Collection also includes many papers of David L. Swain (Clark was executor of Mrs. Swain's estate), including: …; on Cherokee fighting (1776), Tories, and settlers in Surry Co. and southern Virginia;…'."]

Clarkson, Heriot. "The Hornet's Nest: Sketch of Revolutionary War at Charlotte and Vicinity." *North Carolina Booklet*, 1:6 (October 10, 1901), 3-24; online: http://digital.ncdcr.gov/cdm/ref/collection/p249901coll37/id/14180. [Online des-cription from "North Carolina Periodicals Index," East Carolina University: "An essay on events in colonial and revolutionary North Carolina with a particular focus on Mecklenburg County and recurring religious and political themes."]

Clinton, Henry, Sir; William B. Willcox, ed. *The American Rebellion: Sir Henry Clinton's Narrative of His Campaigns, 1775-1782, with an Appendix of Original Documents*. New Haven: Yale University Press, 1954.

Clitherall, James. "James Clitherall Diary, 1776." Manuscript 159-z, Southern Historical Collection, Louis Round Wilson Special Collections Library, University of North Carolina, Chapel Hill; online finding aid available at http://www2.lib.unc.edu/mss/inv/c/Clitherall,James.html. [Online finding aid description: " James Clitherall travelled as an escort to Mary Izard Middleton (Mrs. Arthur) and Henrietta Middleton Rutledge (Mrs. Edward), wives of two members of the Continental Congress, from Charleston, S. C., to Philadelphia, Pa., in April-July 1776. The collection contains transcripts of the diary kept by Clitherall on this trip. Clitherall described land fertility, road conditions, tavern accommodations and entertainment, and leisure-time gatherings of local society on a trip through Camden, S. C.; Charlotte, N. C., Salisbury, N. C., and Guilford Court House, N. C.; Charlotte Court House and Orange Court House, Va.; and Lancaster, Pa. The volume includes the words of two songs, *New Song for Liberty* and *Liberty Song*, which the travelers heard at Charlotte, N. C."]

Connor, R. D. W. *History of North Carolina: The Colonial and Revolutionary Periods (1584-1783).* Chicago and New York: Lewis Publishing Company, 1919.

Connor, R. D. W. *North Carolina: Rebuilding an Ancient Commonwealth*. 4 vols. Chicago and New York: The American Historical Society, 1929.

Connor, R. D. W. "Postwar Planning in North Carolina." *Popular Government*, 10:5 (August 1944), 4-6, 13-14, 17. [Online description from "North Carolina Periodicals Index," East Carolina University: "Connor discusses the history of postwar planning after the Revolutionary War, the American Civil War, and World War I for the state of North Carolina."]

Cross, Jerry L. *A Chronicle of North Carolina during the American Revolution, 1763-1789.* (North Carolina Bicentennial Pamphlet Series, no. 1) Raleigh: Department of Cultural Resources, Division of Archives and History, 1975.

Crow, Jeffrey J., and Larry E. Tise. *The Southern Experience in the American Revolution*. Chapel Hill: University of North Carolina Press, 1978. [Description: "Based on lectures given at the University of North Carolina at Chapel Hill, Duke University, and North Carolina State University, in the fall of 1975, and sponsored by the North Carolina Bicentennial Committee ... {et al.}"]

Cumming, William P., and Hugh F. Rankin. *The Fate of a Nation: The American Revolution through Contemporary Eyes*. London: Phaidon; New York: distributed in the United States of American by Praeger, 1975.

Davidson, Chalmers G. "Three Hundred Years of Carolina History." *North Carolina Historial Review*, 40:2 (April 1963), 213-220.

Davidson, Jan. *Rise and Fight Again.* Greensboro: Grassroots Productions Limited, 1890. [drama]

Davie, Preston. "Preston Davie Collection, 1560-1903." Collection Number 03406, Southern Historical Collection, Louis Round Wilson Special Collections Library, University of North Carolina, Chapel Hill; online finding aid and some digital surrogates available at http://www2.lib.unc.edu/mss/inv/d/Davie,Preston.html. [Online finding aid description: "A significant portion of the collection relates to the American Revolutionary War in the South, 1775-1883, particularly the Carolinas, Georgia, and Virginia. These include letters and other documents of military and civic leaders regarding administrative details, troop movements, supplies, and prisoners. A series of letters, 1774-1779, from John Pringle (1753-1843) of South Carolina discusses American Revolutionary diplomacy from Europe, and British attitudes toward the war (folders 59 and 104). Another series of letters relates to the siege and capture of Charleston, S. C., 1780. Three of these letters from Sir Henry Clinton to General Benjamin Lincoln regarding the terms of surrender are believed to have been written by Major John André, acting as aide to Clinton (folders 129-138). Other important letters include one from General Horatio Gates to General Nathanael Greene, 4 December 1780, written two days after he had been replaced by Greene, asking Greene for a court-martial to pass upon Gate's conduct at the Battle of Camden (folder 147); and a letter from William Smallwood, 6 December 1780, to General Greene, relating to Colonel William Washington's victory in the 'Quaker Gun' battle with Colonel Ridgely and 112 Tory officers and men (folder 148)." The online catalog description of this collection shows that it contains: "historical manuscripts and books chiefly relating to the history of the American South during the colonial, Revolutionary, and early national periods. Papers are scattered, largely unrelated items, some of interest chiefly as autographs, others containing significant information on political and military affairs. The greatest number of items relates to the Revolutionary War in the South, particularly the Carolinas, but also Virginia and Georgia. These include letters and other documents of many military and civic leaders. There are papers related … the siege of Charleston, S.C., 1780; and letters, 1774-1779, from John Pringle (1753-1843) of South Carolina discussing American Revolutionary diplomacy from Europe. A separate series consists of documents pertaining to lands in North and South Carolina acquired by the Kershaw and Chesnut families of South Carolina. Persons represented in the collection include: John Ashe (1720?- 1781), Theodore Broughton, William Bull (1710-1791), Thomas Burke (ca. 1747-1783), Richard Caswell (1729-1789), Gaspard de Coligny (1519-1572), Christopher Gadsden (1724-1805), Horatio Gates (1728-1806), Alexander Gillon (1741-1794), James Glen (1701-1777), Nathanael Greene (1742-1786), Wade Hampton (1754-1835), Cornelius Harnett (1723-1781), William Howe (1732-1786), Allen Jones (1729-1793), Henry Laurens (1724-1792), John Laurens (1754-1782), John Alexander Lillington (1725-1786), Francis Marion (1732-1795), Alexander Martin (1740-1807), Abner Nash (1740-1786), Thomas Pinckney (1750-1828), Griffith Rutherford (1721-1805), John Rutledge (1739- 1800), Jethro Sumner (1733-1785), Nicholas Trott (1663-1740), and William Tryon (1729-1788)."]

Davis, Chester. "What's Different about Tar Heels." *The State: A Weekly Survey of North Carolina*, 21:30 (December 1953), 3-5, 12-13; online: http://digital.ncdcr.gov/cdm/ref/collection/p16062coll18/id/31352. [Online description from "North Carolina Periodicals Index," East Carolina University: "Davis recounts the numerous reasons why North Carolina is unique."]

Davis, Sallie Joyner. "North Carolina's Part in the Revolution." *South Atlantic Quarterly*, 2:4 (October 1903), 314-324; 3:1 (January 1904), 27-38; 3:2 (April 1904), 154-165.

De Roulhac Hamilton, J. G. "The Preservation of North Carolina History." *North Carolina Historical Review*, 4:1 (January 1927), 3-21. [Online description from "North Carolina Periodicals Index," East Carolina University: "An examination of the development of North Carolina's policy in respect to the preservation of historical material shows an uninterrupted movement which reached a climax in the creation of the Historical Commission."]

Dickson, William. "A Picture of the Last Days of the Revolutionary War in North Carolina." *North Carolina Booklet*, 21 (1922), 59-67.

Donnell, James H., III. "The South on the Eve of the Revolution." In W. Robert Higgins, ed. *The Revolutionary War in the South: Power, Conflict, and Leadership: Essays in Honor of John Richard Allen* (Durham: Duke University Press, 1979), 64-78.

Douglass, Elisha P. *Rebels and Democrats: The Struggle for Equal Political Rights and Majority Rule during the American Revolution*. Chapel Hill: University of North Carolina Press, 1955.

Drayton, John. *Memoirs of the American Revolution: From Its Commencement to the Year 1776, Inclusive, as Relating to the State of South Carolina and Occasionally Refering* [*sic*] *to the States of North-Carolina and Georgia.* Charleston, S. C.: Miller, 1821.

Dunaway, Wilma A. *The First American Frontier: Transition to Capitalism in Southern Appalachia, 1700-1860.* Chapel Hill: University of North Carolina Press, 1996.

Duncan, W. "North Carolina, Part 1." *Debow's Review*, 11:1 (July 1851), 30-40; online at Memory of America, University of Michigan, website.

Edgar, Walter. *Partisans and Redcoats: The Southern Conflict That Turned the Tide of the American Revolution.* New York: Harper Collins, 2001.

Edwards, Laura F. *The People and Their Peace: Legal Culture and the Transformation of Inequality in the Post-Revolutionary South.* Chapel Hill: University of North Carolina Press, 2009. [Description: "This study discusses changes in the legal logic of slavery, race, and gender. Drawing on extensive archival research in North and South Carolina, Laura F. Edwards illuminates those changes by revealing the importance of localized legal practice." Contents: All Was Chaos in Our Legal World: Excavating Localized Law from Beneath the Layers of

Southern History; Keeping the Peace: People's Proximity to Law; Bread from Chaff: Defining Offenses against the Peace; Possession and the Personality of Property: The Material Basis of Authority; Wasted Substance: The Operation and Regulation of Patriarchy; Subjects vs. Rights-Holding Individuals; New States: Freemen as Consistent Units of Measure.]

Eldridge, James W. *Historic Minutes*. [Greensboro?: WFMY-TV?, 1976] [A copy is at the State Library of North Carolina, Raleigh. The online catalog descriptions shows that this consists of "Scripts of the 315 one minute programs presented on WFMY-TV, Greensboro, N. C., Monday through Saturday, at 5:59 p.m., the year ending July 4, 1976."]

Ellis, John Wills; Noble J. Tolbert, ed. *Papers*. 2 vols. Raleigh: North Carolina State Department of Archives and History, 1964. [Contains source material on the history of the state during the American Revolution.]

Emmet, Thomas Addison. "Thomas Addison Emmet Collection, 1757-1847." Manuscript PC.38 (MARS ID: 547; record group), State Archives of North Carolina, Raleigh. [Online catalog description: "Bound typed copies of 128 letters and papers relating to North Carolina in the Emmet Manuscripts, {Manuscripts and Archives Division}, New York Public Library, including deeds, estate papers, petitions, a resolution of the Second Provincial Congress with 67 signatures approving the nonimportation association (1775), and Thomas Burke's notes on the debates of the Continental Congress (Feb.-Mar., 1777). Early letters are from Gov. Arthur Dobbs (1757), from the Committee of Correspondence (1774), from John Williams in Kentucky (1775), and from Joseph Hewes, William Hooper, Thomas Burke, John Penn, Cornelius Harnett, and Willie Jones as congressional delegates in Philadelphia. There are messages from Gov. Richard Caswell to the General Assembly (1777), items concerning loyalists, and letters about schools in Granville Co. (1778) and Mecklenburg Co. (1779). Reports on the British in Georgia (1778-1779) are from Joseph Lane, John Ashe, John Rutledge and others and include a description of the surrender of Ft. Morris and a list of prisoners. Also a British letter about a Creek raid on the rebels, 1782. Relating to military action and defenses in the Carolinas, 1779-1781, are letters from Joseph Hewes, John Baptista Ashe, Nathanael Greene, Gov. Abner Nash to Governor-elect Thomas Burke on details of the government, William Hooper on the capture of his family and property by the British, Waightstill Avery, Richard Caswell, Allen Jones, Jethro Sumner, Horatio Gates, W. R. Davie, Alexander Lillington, Willie Jones, and others. Several papers relate to Norfolk in 1776, Virginia troops in North Carolina, and Virginia's responsibility for defense (Gov. Thomas Jefferson, 1780). Postwar letters include Josiah Martin (1784) on a loyalist claim; William Hooper to James Iredell (1785-1786) on the courts; two letters about ratification of the U. S. Constitution; Richard Dobbs Spaight to the governor of North Carolina (1794) about the enticement of slaves and to Jacob Reed on French depredations (1797); Benjamin Hawkins on the Tennessee Indians (1797); William Polk on the Mecklenburg Declaration (1819); and D. L. Swain on North Carolina records (1847). Other correspondents include John Butler, William Davidson, Patrick Henry, Samuel Johnston, Nathaniel Macon, Griffith Rutherford, John Steele, and Hugh Williamson."] [Note: A calendar of part of this collection for the years 1757 to 1847 was published in 1926.][11]

Fenn, Elizabeth A.; Peter H. Wood; Harry L. Watson; Thomas H. Clayton; Sydney Nathans; Thomas C. Parramore; and Jean B. Anderson; maps by Mark Anderson Moore; Joe A. Mobley, ed. *The Way We Lived in North Carolina*. Chapel Hill: University of North Carolina Press, 2003. [Publisher's description: "Weaving research and interpretation around dozens of historic sites and the lives of ordinary people who lived and worked nearby, The Way We Lived in North Carolina explores the social history of the Tar Heel State from the precolonial period to the present. First published in 1983 as a five-volume series, this comprehensive state history is now available in a revised and up-to-date single volume with more than 250 photographs and over two dozen maps. Based on the premise that the past can be most fully understood through the combined experience of reading history and visiting historic places, *The Way We Lived* serves as a travel guide to North Carolina's history, enhancing the reader's appreciation and understanding of historic preservation. Discussion of recently designated historic sites has been added to this edition, as have twenty-eight detailed maps newly prepared by Mark Anderson Moore. A new appendix provides an extensive list of over thirty historic sites to visit. This volume provides an entertaining and informative guide to North Carolina history for students and professionals, teens and seniors, natives and newcomers."]

Ferguson, Clyde R. "Carolina and Georgia Patriots and Loyalist Militia in Action, 1778-1783." In Jeffrey J. Crow and Larry E. Tise, eds., *The Southern Experience in the American Revolution, 1778-1783* (Chapel Hill: University of North Carolina Press, 1978), 174-199.

---

[11] See: D. L. Corbitt, ed., *Calendar of Manuscript Collections, Vol. 1* (Raleigh: Edwards & Broughton, 1926), 102-134.

Ferguson, Clyde R. "Functions of the Partisan-Militia in the South during the American Revolution: An Interpretation." In W. Robert Higgins, ed., *The Revolutionary War in the South: Power, Conflict, and Leadership: Essays in Honor of John Richard Allen* (Durham: Duke University Press, 1979), 239-258.

Ferling, John. *Almost a Miracle: The American Victory in the War of Independence*. New York: Oxford University Press, 2007.

Foote, William Henry. *Sketches of North Carolina, Historical and Biographical, Illustrative of the Principles of a Portion of Her Early Settlers*. New York: Robert Carter, 1846; online: http://docsouth.unc.edu/nc/foote/menu.html.

Fremont-Barnes, Gregory, and Richard Alan Ryerson, eds. *The Encyclopedia of the American Revolutionary War: A Political, Social and Military History*. Santa Barbara, Calif.: ABC Clio, 2006. [Many aspects of the Revolution in North Carolina appear in this encyclopedia. Check the indexes in each volume for details.]

Ganyard, Robert Loyal. "North Carolina during the American Revolution: The First Phase, 1774-1777." Ph. D. Dissertation, Duke University, 1963.

Garden, Alexander. *Anecdotes of the American Revolution: Illustrative of the Talents and Virtues of the Heroes and Patriots, Who Acted the Most Conspicuous Parts Therein.* Second series. Charleston, S. C.: Printed by A. E. Miller, 1828. [240 pages] reprinted as volume 3 of a three volume set: Thomas Warren Field, ed; in 3 vols.: vols. 1-2 (paged continuously), 1st series; v. 3, 2nd series: Brooklyn, N. Y.: Union Press, 1865.

Garden, Alexander. *Anecdotes of the American Revolution: Illustrative of the Talents and Virtues of the Heroes and Patriots, Who Acted the Most Conspicuous Parts Therein*. 3 vols. Thomas Warren Field, ed.; Brooklyn, N. Y.: Union Press, 1865 [vols. 1-2 (paged continuously), 1st series; vol. 3, 2nd series]; micropublished (microfiche) (Louisville, Ky.: Lost Cause Press, 1972); micropub-lished in American Culture series (Ann Arbor, Mich.: University Microfilms, [s. d.]), reel 427.4; reprinted: Spartanburg, S. C.: Reprint Company, 1972; micropublished (microfiche): (Series: Selected Americana from Sabin's Dictionary of Books Relating to America, from Its Discovery to the Present Time; Sabin 26599) (Woodbridge, Conn.: Primary Source Microfilm, 2004), fiche 46913-46931. [1865 edition, vol. 1 and 2 includes many of the same entries as in the 1828 editions but with different pagination.]

Garden, Alexander. *Anecdotes of the Revolutionary War, with Sketches of Character of Persons the Most Distinguished, in the Southern States*. [Became the first series when the second series was published in 1828 with the title Anecdotes of the American Revolution.] Charleston, S. C.: Printed for the author by A. E. Miller, 1822; reprinted as volume 1 of a three volume set: Thomas Warren Field, ed.; Brooklyn, N. Y.: Union Press, 1865 [vols. 1-2 (paged continuously), 1st series]; reprinted: Spartanburg, S. C.: The Reprint Company, 1972. [The 1822 edition of 459 pages is online and comprises the first series in one volume.]

Garrison, Webb. *Great Stories of the American Revolution.* Nashville: Rutledge Hill Press, 1990.

Gephart, Ronald M. *Revolutionary America: A Bibliography.* 2 vols. Washington, D. C.: Library of Congress, 1984.

Goodloe, Daniel R[eaves]. *The Birth of the Republic: Compiled from the National and Colonial Histories and Historical Collections, from American Archives and from Memoirs, and from the Journals and Proceedings of the British Parliament.* Chicago and New York: Belford, Clarke, 1889; online: http://babel.hathitrust.org/cgi/pt?id=loc.ark:/ 3960/t55d9680b.

Goodspeed's History of Tennessee, from the Earliest Time to the Present; Together with an Historical and Biographical Sketch of from Twenty-Five to Thirty Counties of East Tennesee, Besides a Valuable Fund of Notes, Original Observations, Reminiscences, etc., etc.; Containing Historical and Biographical Sketches of Thirty East Tennessee Counties: Anderson, Blount, Bradley, Campbell, Carter, Claiborne, Cocke, Grainger, Greene, Hamblen, Hamilton, Hancock, Hawkins, James, Jefferson, Johnson, Knox, Loudon, McMinn, Meigs, Monroe, Morgan, Polk, Rhea, Roane, Sevier, Sullivan, Unicoi, Union, Washington. Chicago and Nashville: Goodspeed Publishing Company, 1887; reprinted: Nashville: Charles and Randy Elder Booksellers, 1972; Salem: Higginson Books, 1984; and: McNamara, Billie R[uth]. *Index to Goodspeed's History of Tennessee [1887 Edition]*. Easley, S. C.: Southern Historical Press, 1980; Knoxville: B. R. McNamara, 1995.

Graham, Joseph. "Closing Scenes of the Revolution in North Carolina from an Unpublished Manuscript." *North Carolina University Magazine*, 1:5 (June 1852), 182-194; online: http://babel.hathitrust.org/cgi/pt?id=wu.89072958770;.

Graham, Joseph. "Joseph Graham Papers, 1769-1864." Manuscript 284-z, Southern Historical Collection, Louis Round Wilson Special Collections Library, University of North Carolina, Chapel Hill; online finding aid available at http://www2.lib.unc.edu/mss/inv/g/Graham,Joseph.html. [Online finding aid description: "Joseph Graham fought with American troops in North Carolina in the Revolutionary War; was a North Carolina state senator, 1788-1793; fought against the Creek Indians in 1814; and became wealthy producing iron. The collection includes a handwritten manuscript of 'Historical notices or suplement [*sic*] to the *History of the*

Revolutionary War in the Western Part of No. Carolina' (16 pages) by Joseph Graham; a letter from Archibald De Bow Murphey to Charles Conner and two letters from Murphey to Graham about this manuscript; a letter from Graham to Conner discussing the Revolutionary War in North Carolina; part of a volume, 1769-1864, containing lists of slaves belonging to Graham and his son-in-law, Robert Hall Morrison (1798-1889); and *The National Intelligencer and Revolutionary War Legends* by William A. Graham."]

Graham, Mary Owen. "Beginnings of the Revolution in North Carolina." Manuscript ("Miscellaneous Papers," #517.55), Southern Historical Collection, University of North Carolina at Chapel Hill.

Graham, William A. "William A. Graham Papers, 1750-1940." Manuscript 285, Southern Historical Collection, Louis Round Wilson Special Collections Library, University of North Carolina, Chapel Hill; online finding aid available at http://www2.lib.unc.edu/mss/inv/g/Graham,William_A.html. [Online finding aid description: "William Alexander Graham of Hillsborough, N. C., was a lawyer, legislator, United States senator, Secretary of the Navy, Whig vice-presidential candidate in 1852, Confederate senator, trustee of the Peabody Fund, and member of the board of arbitration for the Maryland and Virginia boundary dispute. The collection includes William A. Graham's correspondence with prominent persons about state and national politics... Also included is material relating to legal business; the Graham family; iron foundry; plantations, slavery, and overseers in North Carolina and South Carolina; affairs at the University of North Carolina, the Revolutionary War history of North Carolina, and letters from sons serving as soldiers in the Confederate army."]

Graham, William A[lexander]. "British Invasion of North Carolina, in 1780, and 1781: A Lecture Delivered before the New-York Historical Society, in Jan., 1853." *North Carolina University Magazine*, 2:3 (April 1853), 97-126.

[Gray, Robert]. "Colonel Robert Gray's Observations on the War in the Carolinas. *South Carolina Historical and Genealogical Magazine*, 11:3 (July 1910), 139-159.

Great Britain. Colonial Office. "Edenton, [N. C.]. Extract of James Iredell to Henry Eustace McCulloch. 1 Nov., 1775." Copy of a manuscript in the National Archives of the United Kingdom (formerly the Public Records Office), Kew, Richmond, Surrey, England; 71.184.1-5 (MARS ID: 21.20.115.1; folder), "British Records Collection," State Archives of North Carolina, Raleigh. [Online catalog description: "General topics: the Third Provincial Congress (Hillsborough); proposed funding to recruit, train, and maintain two provincial regiments and numerous local companies of minutemen; defeated 'scheme' for immediate independence; N. C. Gov. Josiah Martin in residence on a ship at Cape Fear."]

Great Britain. Colonial Office. "Halifax, N. C. Extract of Robert Nelson, [Merchant], to Henry Nelson, Merchant in Messrs. Atkinson and Nelson. 20 Oct., 1775." Copy of a manuscript in the National Archives of the United Kingdom (formerly the Public Records Office), Kew, Richmond, Surrey, England; 71.198.1-2 (MARS ID: 21.20.115.15; folder), "British Records Collection," State Archives of North Carolina, Raleigh. [Online catalog description: "General topics: third Provincial Congress (Hillsborough) orders recruitment of 1,000 regulars (soldiers) and 5,000 minutemen; tar and feathering to be the punishment for anyone who expresses pro-British loyalties."]

Great Britain. Colonial Office. "*HMS Rainbow* [Ship of the Line], off Portsmouth, Virginia. [Sir] Geo[rge] Collier [Naval Commander in Chief, North America] to [Lord George] Germain [Sec. of State]. 22 May, 1779." Copy of a manuscript in the National Archives of the United Kingdom (formerly the Public Records Office), Kew, Richmond, Surrey, England; Z.5.19N (MARS ID: 21.20.67.20), "British Records Collection," State Archives of North Carolina, Raleigh. [Online catalog description: "Letter has detailed account of the capture of Portsmouth and 'the Remains' of Norfolk; possible advantageous consequences of the event, including cutting of communications between the Carolinas and the head of the Elk River."]

Hall, John W. "*Petite Guerre* in Retreat." *Patriots of the American Revolution*, 4:5 (September/October 2011), 14-19. [the Southern Campaigns, Nathanael Greene, and the path to Yorktown]

Hathaway, J. R. B. *North Carolina Historical and Genealogical Register: With Genealogical Notes and Annotations*. Edenton: Hathaway, 1900; and Worth S. Ray. *Ray's Index and Digest to Hathaway's North Carolina Historical and Genealogical Register*. Austin, Tex.: Worth S. Ray, 1945; reprinted: Baltimore: Southern Book Company, 1956; Batimore: Genealogical Publishing Company, 1979.

Hawks, Francis L.; David L. Swain; and William A. Graham. *Revolutionary History of North Carolina: In Three Lectures, by Rev. Francis L. Hawks. Hon. David L. Swain, LL. D., and Hon. Wm. A. Graham, LL. D. To Which Is Prefixed a Preliminary Sketch of the Battle of the Alamance. Comp. by William D. Cooke*. Raleigh: W. D. Cooke, 1853. [Contents: Hawks, F. L. "Battle of the Alamance and War of the Regulation;" Hawks, F. L. "The Mecklenburg Declaration of Independence: A Lecture Delivered before the New York Historical Society, Dec. 16, 1852;" Swain, D. L. "British Invasion of North Carolina, in 1776: A Lecture Delivered before the Historical Society of the University of North Carolina, Apr. 1, 1853. Appendix."]

Hardee, Lewis J., Jr. "Lewis J. Hardee, Jr., Family Papers." Manuscript MS249, Archives and Special Collections, William M. Randall Library, University of North Carolina Wilmington; online finding aId: http://randall3.uncw.edu/ascod/index.php?p=collections/findingaid&id=97&q=+revolution+. [The collection includes: research material on Capt. John Hardee, 1742-1803 {of Pitt County; Box 4, folders 5-11}, research material on North Carolina's Revolutionary War Navy {Box 4, folder 11}; "The Town Fathers of Beaufort, Carteret County, NC, 1723-1988 {Box 7, folder 12}; "Carteret County NC Taxpayers, 1701-1786 {Box 8, folder 3}; "Carteret County Court Minutes, 1723-1747 and 1778-1789" {Box 8, folder 3}; "One Dozen Pre-Revolutionary War Families of Eastern North Carolina & Some of Their Descendants" {Box 13, folder 13}.]

Hibbert, Christopher. *Redcoats and Rebels: The War for America 1770-1781*. Barnsley, South Yorkshire, England: Pen & Sword Books, 2008.

Higgonbotham, Don. *Revolution in America: Considerations & Comparisons*. Charlottesville: University of Virginia Press, 2005. [Contents: Washington's Remarkable Generation; Virginia's Trinity of Immortals; George Washington and Three Women; War and State Formation in Revolutionary America; The Federalized Militia Debate; Military Education before West Point; The Martial Spirit in the Antebellum South; Fomenters of Revolution.]

Higginbotham, Don. "Some Reflections on the South in the American Revolution." *Journal of Southern History*, 73:3 (August 2007), 659-670.

Higginbotham, Don. *The War of American Independence: Military Attitudes, Policies, and Practice, 1763-1789*. New York: Macmillan, 1971; reprinted: Boston: Northeastern University Press, 1983.

Higgins, W. Robert, ed. *The Revolutionary War in the South — Power, Conflict and Leadship*. Durham, N. C.: Duke University Press, 1979.

Hindle, Brooke. *The Pursuit of Science in Revolutionary America, 1735-1789*. Chapel Hill: University of North Carolina Press for the Institute of Early American History and Culture, Williamsburg, Va. 1956.

Hinton, Mary Hilliard. "The Spirit of the Revolution." *North Carolina Booklet*, 20:2-4 (October 1920-April 1921), 207-212.

"Historical Society of Pennsylvania Papers, 1760-1888." Manuscript, PC.244, State Archives of North Carolina, Raleigh. [Online catalog description: "Photocopies of letters, resolutions, commissions, and other papers relating to North Carolina in the Society's archives in Philadelphia. Revolutionary War papers are chiefly letters from John Armstrong, Waightstill Avery, Thomas Burke, Robert Burton, William L. Davidson, Robert Howe, Samuel Johnston, Allen Jones, Stephen Moore, John Sevier, and William Sharpe. Subjects include conduct of the war, prisoners at Charleston, Cherokees, and Continental Congress. A number of these letters (1777-1780, 1785-1786) are addressed to Gov. Richard Caswell, as are letters from Benjamin Hawkins and Congressman James White about the Cherokee treaty of 1785."]

"History of North Carolina during the Revolutionary War." 2 Reference Vertical Files, State Library of North Carolina, Raleigh.

Hodge, Alan. "Patriot Games." *Our State: Down Home in North Carolina*, 68:10 (March 2001), 68-71; online: http://digital.ncdcr.gov/cdm/ref/collection/p16062coll18/id/72796. [Online description from "North Carolina Periodicals Index," East Carolina University: "A number of North Carolina citizens participate in recreating the Revolutionary War period with historical accuracy in dress and battle. Reenacting can be expensive, with uniforms and accessories costing thousands of dollars. Revolutionary War reenactments, having between 300 and 500 participants, are smaller than Civil War ones, which can have thousands."]

Holland, J. Ron. "The Tory-Patriot War." *Tar Heel Junior Historian*, 11:2 (December 1971), 10-11; online: http://digital.ncdcr.gov/cdm/ref/collection/p16062coll9/id/4207. [Online description from "North Carolina Periodicals Index," East Carolina University: "Guilford Court-house was the state's only major battle of the American Revolution but smaller skirmishes broke out between the state's citizen loyal to the crown and those demanding independence. The most notorious Tory loyal was David Fanning who, for two years between 1781 and 1782, rampaged between Deep River and the Pee Dee."]

Hooper, William, and Joseph Hewes. *To the Committees of the Several Towns and Counties of the Province of North-Carolina: Appointed for the Purpose of Carrying into Execution the Resolves of the Continental Congress*. [New Bern, N. C.?: Printed by James Davis?], 1775. [William Hooper, 1742-1790; Joseph Hewes, 1730-1779; Richard Caswell, 1729-1789. Description from the online Hollis Catalog, Harvard University: "Circular letter, exhorting the people of North Carolina to awake to their present danger, and to train and equip a militia; signed and dated on p. {2}: William Hooper, Joseph Hewes, Richard Caswell. Philadelphia, June 19, 1775. Hooper, Hewes and Caswell were the delegates to the Continental Congress from North Carolina."]

House, R. B. "A Picture of the Last Days of the Revolutionary War in North Carolina." *North Carolina Booklet*, 21:1-4 (July 1921-April 1922), 59-67.

Johnson, Joseph. *Traditions and Reminiscences Chiefly of the American Revolution in the South: Including Biographical Sketches, Incidents and Anecdotes, Few of Which Have Been Published, Particularly of Residents in the Upper Country*. Charleston, S. C.: Walker & James, 1851; reprinted with a shortened title: *Traditions and Reminiscences of the American Revolution in the South.* Spartanburg, S. C.: The Reprint Co., 1972. Online: http://hdl.loc.gov/loc.gdc/scd0001.00118 015423.

Johnston, Peter R. *Poorest of the Thirteen: North Carolina and the Southern Department in the American Revolution*. Haverford, Pa.: Infinity Publishing, 2001.

Jones, H. G. *For History's Sake: The Preservation and Publication of North Carolina History, 1663-1903.* Chapel Hill: University of North Carolina Press, 1966.

Jones, Joseph Seawell. *A Defense of the Revolutionary History of the State of North Carolina from the Aspersions of Mr. Jefferson.* Boston and Raleigh: C. Bowen and Turner and Hughes, 1834.

Kirke, Edmund [pseud.] (James R. Gilmore). *The Rear-Guard of the Revolution*. New York: D. Appleton & Co., 1886; reprinted 1891; Spartanburg, S. C.: The Reprint Company, 1974.

Koesy, Sheldon F. "Continuity and Change in North Carolina, 1775-1789." Ph. D. dissertation, Duke University, 1963.

Lamm, Alan K. "American Revolution." In William S. Powell, ed.; Jay Mazzocchi, assoc. ed., *Encyclopedia of North Carolina* (Chapel Hill: University of North Carolina Press in association with the University of North Carolina Library, 2006), 40-45.

Lee, Henry; Robert E. Lee, ed. *The American Revolution in the South* (originally published as *Memoirs of the War in the Southern Department*) New York: University Pub. Co., 1869; reprinted: New York: Arno Press, 1969; printed: New York: Arno Press, 1969.

Lee, Henry, Jr. *The Campaign of 1781 in the Carolinas: with Remarks Historical and Critical on Johnson's Life of Greene; to Which is Added an Appendix of Original Documents, Relating to the History of the Revolution.* Philadelphia: E. Little, 1824; reprinted: Chicago: Quadrangle Books, 1962; Spartanburg, S. C.: The Reprint Co., 1975; Cranbury, N. J.: Scholar's Bookshelf, 2006.

Lefler, Hugh T. *History of North Carolina.* 4 vols. New York: Lewis Historical Publishing Company, [1956].

Lefler, Hugh T. *North Carolina: History, Geography, Government*. New York: Harcourt, Brace & World, 19966.

Lefler, Hugh T., and Albert Ray Newsome. *North Carolina: The History of a Southern State.* [3rd ed.] Chapel Hill: University of North Carolina Press, 1973.

Lefler, Hugh T., and William S. Powell. *Colonial North Carolina: A History*. New York: Charles Scribner's Sons, 1973.

Lefler, Hugh Talmadge. *North Carolina History Told by Contemporaries*. 4th ed., rev. and enl. Chapel Hill: University of North Carolina Press, 1965.

Lennon, Donald R. "The Graveyard of the American Commanders: The Continental Army's Southern Department, 1776-1778." *North Carolina Historical Review*, 67:2 (April 1990), 133-158. [Online description from "North Carolina Periodicals Index," East Carolina University: "During the Revolutionary War, commanders of the Continental Army faced many difficulties in the southern states due the numerous self-contradictory restrictions coming from the Continental Congress and local civil authorities. While military commanders were under direct orders from Congress, they were at the mercy of state governments for troops, supplies, and weaponry. Southern political divisions constantly challenged the authority of Congress, making a strong defense of the southern colonies very difficult."]

Lewis, J. D. "The American Revolution in North Carolina: Timeline of Key Events, 1774-1783." Online: http://www.carolana.com/NC/Revolution/nc_revolution_key_events.html.

Lewis, J. D. "North Carolina – From Statehood to 1800: Overview of Early Statehood to 1800." Online: http://www.carolana.com/NC/Early_Statehood/nc_statehood_1800_overview.html.

Lewis, Taylor Biggs, photographer; Joanne Young, text. *Spirit up the People: North Carolina, the First Two Hundred Years*. Birmingham, Ala.: Oxmoor House, 1975.

Lodge, Henry Cabot. "The Story of the Revolution: Green's Campaign in the South." *Scribner's Magazine*, September 1898, 333-348.

Lossing, Benson J. *Benson J. Lossing's Pictorial Fieldbook of the Revolution in Virginia and Maryland (Including West Virginia, Washington, D. C., and the Albemarle of North Carolina.* [Lossing's original publication: 2 vols.: New York: Harper & Brothers, 1851-1852; reprinted [Extracts from the original publication] Wilmington, N. C.: Dram Tree Books, 2008.

Lossing, Benson J. *The Pictorial Field Book of the Revolution, or, Illustrations, by Pen and Pencil, of the History, Biography, Relics, and Traditions of the War for Independence, with Eleven Hundred Engravings on Wood by Lossing and Barritt, Chiefly from Original Sketches by the Author.* 2 vols. New York: Harper & Brothers, 1851-

1852; 1855; 1859-1860; Spartanburg, S. C.: The Reprint Company, 1969; Freeport, N. Y.: Books for Libraries Press, 1969; New Rochelle, N. Y.: Caratzas Brothers, 1976.

Lossing, Benson J.; Jack E. Fryar, Jr., ed. *The Pictorial Field Book of the Revolution in the Carolinas & Georgia*. Wilmington: Dram Tree Books, 2004.

Lumpkin, Henry. *From Savannah to Yorktown: The American Revolution in the South*. Columbia: University of South Carolina Press, 1981.

Lumpkin, Henry. "Why the British Lost the War in the South." Typescript, Oct. 1, 1984, Manuscripts I&O) (Forum Club), Manuscripts Division, South Caroliniana Library, University of South Carolina, Columbia.

Maass, John R. "A Complicated Scene of Difficulties: North Carolina and the Revolutionary Settlement, 1776-1789." Ph. D. dissertation, Ohio State University, 2007; online: https://etd.ohiolink.edu/!etd.send_file?accession=osu1185482848&disposition=inline.

Martin, Georgia Worth. "North Carolina after the Revolution." *North Carolina Booklet*, 12:4 (April 1913), 216-223.

Mathes, Mildred Spotswood. "Romances and Incidents on This Side of the Mountains." *American Monthly Magazine*, 2:5 (May 1893), 478-498.

McLean, Angus Wilton. *North Carolina in the War of Independence: Address by Angus Wilton McLean, Governor of North Carolina, Valley Forge, June 17, 1926*. [S. l.: s. n., 1926?]

Merrens, Harry Roy. *Colonial North Carolina in the Eighteenth Century: A Study in Historical Geography*. Chapel Hill: University of North Carolina Press, 1964.

Miles, Edwin A. "Benson J. Lossing and North Carolina Revolutionary History." *North Carolina Historical Review*, 35:1 (January 1958), 11-19; online: http://digital.ncdcr.gov/cdm/ref/collection/p16062coll9/id/4207. [Online description from "North Carolina Periodicals Index," East Carolina University: "In the mid-19th century, Benson J. Lossing traveled to North Carolina to create a series of engravings that detailed the Revolutionary War in the state."]

Moore, Mary R. Ludley. "Some Scraps from Revolutionary History in North Carolina." *American Monthly Magazine* [DAR], 9:5 (November 1897), 457-462.

Morgan, Gwenda. "Community and Authority in the Eighteenth-Century South: Tidewater, Southside, and Backcountry." *Journal of American Studies*, 20:3 (December 1986), 435-448.

Morrill, Dan L. *Southern Campaigns in the American Revolution*. Baltimore: The Nautical and Aviation Publishing Company of America, 1993.

Moultrie, William. *Memoir of the American Revolution, So Far as It Related to the States of North and South Carolina, and Georgia*. 2 vols. New York: Printed by D. Longworth, 1802.

Nevins, Allan. *American States during and after the Revolution, 1775-1789*. New York: Macmillan, 1924.

North Carolina. American Revolution Bicentennial Commission. *North Carolina Bicentennial Gazette*, 1:1 (January 1971)-3:2 (April 1973).

North Carolina. "Frontier Scouting and Indian Wars, 1754-1777." Manuscript (MARS ID: 5862; record group), State Archives of North Carolina, Raleigh.

North Carolina. "Miscellaneous Papers, 1689-1912." Manuscript PC.21 (MARS ID: 530; record group), State Archives of North Carolina, Raleigh. [Online catalog description shows that this collection includes: "Revolutionary War letters discuss the Battle of Moores Creek Bridge and southern campaigns, loyalists, privateers, condition of soldiers, parole of Governor Burke, and surrender of Cornwallis at Yorktown. There are also letters from Benjamin Hawkins in Philadelphia (1781) and as Creek Indian agent (1811)."]

North Carolina. "War of the Revolution, 1776-1789." Manuscript (MARS ID: 5865; record group), State Archives of North Carolina, Raleigh. [Online catalog description: "'The War of the Revolution' related papers include correspondence, declarations of service, depositions, lists of veterans, state pension papers to widows and invalids, and miscellaneous papers, including inquiries, courts martial, and prisoners of war. There is also a listing of collections, both military and other, which indicates where information on Loyalists can be found."]

North Carolina Bicentennial Commission, Department of Cultural Resources. *North Carolina in the American Revolution* (North Carolina Bicentennial Pamphlet Series). Raleigh: The Commission, [1976?] [Online catalog description: "1 folded sheet (6 pages). Includes annotated bibliography of v. 1-8 and a list of v. 9-16 in the North Carolina bicentennial pamphlet series."]

North Carolina Bicentennial Foundation. *North Carolina Bicentennial Newsletter*, 1-3 (1973-1977?). [Copies are located at the State Library of North Carolina, Raleigh.]

O'Kelley, Patrick. *Nothing but Blood and Slaughter: The Revolutionary War in the Carolinas: Volume 1, 1771-1779*. Bangor, Me.: Booklocker.com, Inc., 2004.

O'Kelley, Patrick. *Nothing but Blood and Slaughter: The Revolutionary War in the Carolinas: Volume 2, Military Operations and Order of Battle of the Revolutionary War in South Carolina: Volume Two: 1780*. Bangor, Me.: Booklocker.com, Inc., 2004.

O'Kelley, Patrick. *Nothing but Blood and Slaughter: The Revolutionary War in the Carolinas: Volume Three, 1781*. Lillington, N. C.: Blue House Tavern Press, 2005.

O'Kelley, Patrick. *Nothing but Blood and Slaughter: The Revolutionary War in the Carolinas: Volume Four, 1782*. Lillington, N. C.: Blue House Tavern Press, 2005.

O'Neall, John Belton, ed. *Random Recollections of Revolutionary Characters and Incidents*. Charleston: Printed by J. S. Burges, 1838.

Olds, Fred A. "Colonial and Revolutionary Relics in the Hall of History." North Carolina Booklet, 6:2 (October 1906), 123-145; online: http://digital.ncdcr.gov/cdm/ref/collection/p249901coll37/id/14180. [Online description from "North Carolina Periodicals Index," East Carolina University: "This article discusses the Colonial and Revolutionary Period artifacts and documents housed in the Hall of History at the Agricultural Building in Raleigh {in 1906}. The items found in the Hall pertain to North Carolina's history and culture."]

Pancake, John S. *This Destructive War: The British Campaign in the Carolinas, 1780-1782*. Tuscaloosa, AL: The University of Alabama Press, 1985. [Includes an excellent bibliographic essay.]

Parkinson, Robert G. "An Astonishing Account of Civil War in North Carolina." *Journalism History*, 32:4 (Winter 2007), 223-230.

Parramore, Thomas C., and Barbara M. Parramore. *A Resource Study Unit on North Carolina in the Revolutionary War*. Raleigh: North Carolina Department of Public Instruction, Division of Social Studies Education, and the North Carolina Bicentennial Commission, 1974; online: https://archive.org/details/resourcestudyuni00parr. [Includes various short articles on North Carolina topics during the Revolution along with lesson plans.]

Parramore, Thomas C.; Barbara M. Parramore; and Barbara Parramore. *Did the American Revolution Begin in North Carolina?: A History Lesson*. Raleigh: Office of Publications, School of Education, North Carolina State University, 1973. [a book for young readers]

Peckham, Howard H. *Sources of American Independence: Selected Manuscripts from the Collections of the William L. Clements Library*. 2 vols. Chicago: University of Chicago Press, 1978.

Peixotto, Ernest Clifford. *A Revolutionary Pilgrimage; Being an Account of a Series of Visits to Battlegrounds & Other Places Made Memorable by the War of the Revolution*. New York: C. Scribner's Sons, 1917; online: http://hdl.loc.gov/ loc.gdc/scd0001.00117 121598.

Powell, William S. *A Chronolog of the American Revolution in North Carolina*. Raleigh: North Carolina Department of Cultural Resources, Division of Archives and History, 1975-1976; online: https://archive.org/details/chronologofameri00powe.

Powell, William S. *North Carolina: A History*. Chapel Hill: University of North Carolina Press, 1977. [Publisher's description: "A leading authority on the people and events that have shaped North Carolina over four centuries, Powell here provides a sharply drawn overall history of the state for general readers. In twelve chapters this volume traces North Carolina's history from England's initial efforts to found a colony in America in the sixteenth century to uncertain and often-turbulent times as the final quarter of the twentieth century approached."]

Powell, William S. *North Carolina: A Student's Guide to Localized History*. New York: Bureau of Publications, Teachers College, Columbia University, 1965.

Powell, William S. *North Carolina through Four Centuries*. Chapel Hill: University of North Carolina Press, 1989. [Publisher's description: "This successor to the classic Lefler-Newsome North Carolina: The History of a Southern State, published in 1954, presents a fresh survey history that includes the contemporary scene. Drawing upon recent scholarship, the advice of specialists, and his own knowledge, Powell has created a splendid narrative that makes North Carolina history accessible to both students and general readers. For years to come, this will be the standard college text and an essential reference for home and office."]

Powell, William S.; Jay Mazzocchi, assoc. ed. *Encyclopedia of North Carolina*. Chapel Hill: University of North Carolina Press, 2006; online: http://ncpedia.org/.

Ramsay, David, 1749-1815. *A Chronological Table of the Principal Events Which Have Taken Place in the English Colonies, Now the United States, from 1607, till 1810, Explanatory of and Supplementary to Dr. Ramsay's Map Historical and Biographical Chart of the United States, and Noticing the Progress of Improvement in the Same*. Charleston: From the Press of J. Hoff, 1811.

Ramsay, David, 1749-1815. *The History of the American Revolution*. Trenton: Isaac Collins, 1785; Philadelphia: R. Aitken & Son, 1789; London: J. Johnson, etc., 1791; London: J. Stockdale, 1793; Dublin, Ire.: W. Jones, 1795; Trenton: James J. Wilson, 1811; Lexington, Ky.: Downing and Phillips, 1815; Philadelphia: J. Maxwell, 1815;

Philadelphia: M. Carey and Son, 1816-1817, 1818; New York: Russell and Russell, 1968; reprinted: edited by Lester H. Cohen. Indianapolis: Liberty Classics, 1990.

Rankin, Hugh F. *North Carolina in the American Revolution*. Raleigh: State Department of Archives and History, 1959; reprinted (6th) 1996.

Ray, Worth S. Comp. and ed. *Ray's Index and Digest to Hathaway's North Carolina Historical and Genealogical Register: With Genealogical Notes and Annotations*. Baltimore: Genealogical Publishing Co., 1971.

Raynor, George. *Patriots and Tories in Piedmont Carolina*. Salisbury, N. C.: The Salisbury Post, 1990.

Ready, Milton. *The Tar Heel State: A History of North Carolina*. Columbia: University of South Carolina Press, 2005. [Chapters include: Slavery and Servitude in Early North Carolina; Resistance, Regulators, and the Rhetoric of Rebellion in North Carolina, 1729-1771; Beginning of the Revolution in North Carolina; Cautious Revolutionaries: North Carolina in the American Revolution, 1776-1780; Country Dance: Cornwallis's March through North Carolina; Jeffersonian State.]

"Revolutionary North Carolina, 1763-1790: A Digital Textbook." Online at the LearnNC website: http://www.learnnc.org/lp/editions/nchist-revolution/cover.

"Revolutionary War Papers." Manuscript (2194-z), Southern Historical Collection, The Louis Round Wilson Special Collections Library, University of North Carolina at Chapel Hill. [Online catalog description: "The collection contains miscellaneous Revolutionary War papers, chiefly relating to North Carolina, South Carolina, and Georgia, 1781-1782. The collection includes letters, reports, invoices, and other papers of the North Carolina General Assembly and of Governor Richard Caswell concerning military activities and supplies, records of local proceedings, and other items."]

Ripley, Richard M. "The American Revolution in the South." *Recall*, 3:2 (October 1997), 1-5. [Online description from "North Carolina Periodicals Index," East Carolina University: "British forces made two attempts to control North and South Carolina during the first two years of the American Revolution. Both failed. From 1775 to 1778, the northern colonies bore the brunt of most of the major fighting. With fighting in the north stalemated late in 1778, British commanders again looked southward. Ripley recounts the fighting in the South up to 1781, much of which was a bitter, violent civil war between Tories and American militia, with little participation by British soldiers."]

Robson, Eric. "The Expedition to the Southern Colonies, 1775-1776." *English Historical Review*, 116 (1951), 535-560.

Roller, David C., and Robert W. Tyman. *The Encyclopedia of Southern History*. Baton Rouge: Louisiana State University Press, 1979.

Rubin, Benjamin H. "The Rhetoric of Revenge: Atrocity and Identity in the Revolutionary Carolinas." M. A. Thesis, Western Carolina University, 2010.

Russell, David Lee. *The American Revolution in the Southern Colonies*. Jefferson: McFarland & Company, 2000. [Publisher's description: "While the American Revolution is often associated with New England and names like Boston, Concord, and Lexington, the Southern Colonies and names like Kings Mountain, Cowpens, and Charleston were also crucial to the war that established the United States of America. This analysis of the role of the Southern Colonies in the Revolution covers the origin of these five colonies – Maryland, Virginia, North Carolina, South Carolina, and Georgia – and their participation in the cause of American independence. Crucial Southern battles, from the coast to the mountains, are examined in detail, with attention to the larger context of the war and its significance, as well as to the role of the ordinary Southerner, both patriot and Tory."]

Russell, Phillips. *North Carolina in the Revolutionary War*. Charlotte: Heritage Printers, Inc. 1965.

Sarson, Steven. "Similarities and Continuities: Free Society in the Tobacco South before and after the American Revolution." In Eliga H. Gould and Peter S. Onuf, eds., *Empire and Nation: the American Revolution in the Atlantic World* (Anglo-America in the Transatlantic World) (Baltimore: Johns Hopkins University Press, 2005), 136-158.

Scheer, George F. and Hugh Rankin, eds. *Rebels and Redcoats: The American Revolution through the Eyes of Those Who Fought and Lived It*. Cleveland, Ohio: World Publishing, 1957.

Schulz, Emily L. *North Carolina in the American Revolution: An Exhibition by the Society of the Cincinnati: Anderson House, Washington, D. C., October 14, 2006-April 25, 2007*. Washington, D. C.: Society of the Cincinnati, 2006. ["Based on the exhibition 'Liberty or Death: Rebels and Loyalists in the Southern Piedmont,' Presented at the Museum of York County, June 2005-Dec. 2007."]

Scoggins, Michael C. *Relentless Fury: The Revolutionary War in the Southern Piedmont*. Rock Hill, S. C.: Culture & Heritage Museums, 2006. [Description: "Based on the exhibition 'Liberty or Death: Rebels and Loyalists in the Southern Piedmont,' presented at the Museum of York County, June 2005-Dec. 2007."]

Selesky, Larry E., chief ed., *Encyclopedia of the American Revolution.* 2nd ed. (Library of Military History) (Detroit: Thomson Gale, 2006. [Many aspects of the Revolution in North Carolina and many battles, skirmishes, individuals, etc., appear in this encyclopedia. Check the indexes in each volume for details.]

Sellers, C. G., Jr. "The American Revolution: Southern Founders of a National Tradition." In Arthur S. Link and Rembert W. Patrick, eds., *Writing Southern History: Essays in Historiography in Honor of Fletcher M. Green* (Baton Rouge: Louisiana State University Press, 1965), 38-66.

Seymour, William. "A Journal of the Southern Expedition." *Pennsylvania Magazine of History and Biography*, 7:3 (1883), 286-298.

Seymour, William. *A Journal of the Southern Expedition, 1780-1783, by William Seymour, Sergeant-Major of the Delaware Regiment.* (Papers of the Historical Society of Delaware, 15) Wilmington: Historical Society of Delaware, 1896.

Shinoda, Yasuko Ichihashi. "Nōsu Karoraina ni okeru dokuritsu kakumei: naibu kakumeisei no igi to genkai." *Shien* [Tokyo], 19:2 (December 1958), 107-130. [The title partially translates as "Revolution in North Carolina." A copy is in the North Carolina Collection, Louis Round Wilson Special Collections Library, University of North Carolina at Chapel Hill.]

Sikes, Enoch Walter. *Transition of North Carolina from Colony to Commonwealth.* (Johns Hopkins Studies in Historical and Political Science, Series 16, nos. 10/11) Baltimore: Johns Hopkins University Press, 1898.

Smith, Thomas Marshall. *Legends of the War of Independence, and of the Earlier Settlements in the West.* Louisville, Ky.: J. F. Brennan, 1855; reprinted: Nashville: L. D. McClanahan, 1992.

Snapp, J. Russell. *John Stuart and the Struggle for Empire on the Southern Frontier: A Study of Indian Relations, War, Trade, and Land Problems in the Southern Wilderness, 1754-1775.* Baton Rouge: Louisiana State University Press, 1996. [John Stuart died 1779.]

Southern, Ed., ed. *Voices of the American Revolution in the Carolinas.* (Real Voices, Real History series) Winston-Salem: John F. Blair, 2009. [Contents: "Times began to be troublesome," 1775-1776. "The Meck Dec;" from the *Southern Literary Messenger*; "Persuading the Back Country," by William Henry Drayton and William Tennent; "The Making of a Tory Partisan:" from *The Narrative of Colonel David Fanning*; "Account of the Attack on Fort Moultrie:" from the *South Carolina and American General Gazette* of August 2, 1776; "Cornwallis Comes to Carolina, January-August 1780." "The Siege of Charleston:" from *Memoirs of the American Revolution,* by William Moultrie; "Buford's Quarter:" from *A History of the Campaigns of 1780 and 1781 in the Southern Provinces* of North America, by Banastre Tarleton; "Moffitt's Minute Men:" from *Autobiography of a Revolutionary Soldier*, by James Collins; "The Battle of Ramsour's Mill:" from *The Revolutionary War sketches of William R. Davie*; "The Battle at Stallions:" from *The Memoir of Major Thomas Young*; "Huck's Defeat:" from Colonel William Hill's *Memoirs of the Revolution*; "The Gamecock:" from Colonel William Hill's *Memoirs of the Revolution*; "A Narrative of the Battle of Camden:" from *A Narrative of the Campaign of 1780*, by Otho Holland Williams; "The Partisans Rise, September-October 1780;" "The Swamp Fox:" from *The Life of General Francis Marion*, by Peter Horry and Mason Locke Weems; "The Hornet's Nest:" from *The Revolutionary War Sketches of William R. Davie* and from *A History of the Campaigns of 1780 and 1781 in the Southern Provinces of North America*, by Banastre Tarleton; "Aunt Susie and Andy Jackson," by John R. Gibbon, in a letter to the *National Intelligencer*, August 29, 1845; Fanning's "Rules and Regulations:" from *The Narrative of Colonel David Fanning*; "Lay Waste with Fire and Sword," October 1780-January 1781. Kings Mountain:" from a pamphlet by Isaac Shelby, from *Autobiography of a Revolutionary Soldier* by James Collins, and from *The Memoir of Major Thomas Young*; "The Battle of the Cowpens:" *from General Daniel Morgan's Report to Nathanael Greene* and from *The Memoir of Major Thomas Young*; "'Then He Is Ours,' February-March 1781: The Battle of Cowan's Ford:" from *Narrative of the Battle of Cowan's Ford*, by Robert Henry; "The Race to the Dan: from *Memoirs of the War in the Southern Department of the United States*, by Henry "Light Horse Harry" Lee; "The Battle of Guilford Courthouse:" from *Memoirs of the War in the Southern Department of the United States,* by Henry "Light Horse Harry" Lee; "Endgame, September 1781-December 1782. The Battle of Eutaw Springs," by Nathanael Greene, in a letter to Congress; "A Loyalist Seeks Refuge:" from *The Narrative of Colonel David Fanning*.]

Southern Campaigns of the American Revolution, 1-7 (September 2004-2011), online: www.southerncampaign.org. [Contains many articles and news accounts of Revolutionary War events, personages, etc., and modern Revolutionary War activities, commemorations, seminars, etc., including: "Southern Campaign Revolutionary War Pension Statements & Rosters."]

Steelman, Joseph F. *Of Tar Heel Towns, Shipbuilders, Reconstructionists and Alliancemen: Papers in North Carolina History.* (East Carolina University Publications in History, v. 5) Greenville: East Carolina University, Department of History, 1981.

Stephenson, Wendell Holmes. *Southern History in the Making: Pioneer Historians of the South*. Baton Rouge: Louisiana State University Press, 1964.

Strong, Robert C. "North Carolina's Attitude to the Revolution." *North Carolina Booklet*, 6:4 (April 1907), 217-226; online: http://digital.ncdcr.gov/cdm/ref/collection/p249901coll37/id/14180. [Online description: "This article discusses the cultural and political climate of North Carolina just before and during the American Revolution. The article highlights the effects of the War of Regulation before 1775, the opposition of the Cumberland district during the Revolutionary War, and the opposition of some political leaders to independence."]

Swain, David L. *British Invasion of North Carolina, in 1776: A Lecture, Delivered before the Historical Society of the University of North Carolina, Friday, April 1st, 1853*. [Chapel Hill?: s. n.], 1853.

Swain, David L. "Historical Sketch of the Indian War of 1776." *North Carolina University Magazine*, 1:4 (May 1852), 132-136.

Tindall, George Brown. *The Pursuit of Southern History: Presidential Addresses of the Southern Historical Association, 1935-1963*. Baton Rouge: Louisiana State University Press, 1964.

Troxler, George W. "The Home Front in Revolutionary North Carolina." Ph. D. dissertation, University of North Carolina at Chapel Hill, 1970.

Turner, Oscar, and Vivian Simpson. *The Spirit of '76: Our Heritage Too*. Raleigh: North Carolina Internship Office, [1976?].

United States. Federal Works Agency. Works Progress Administration. Federal Writers' Project. *North Carolina: The Guide to the Old North State*. Columbia: University of South Carolina Press, 1988.

Ward, Christopher; John Richard Alden, ed. *The War of the Revolution.* 2 vols. New York: Macmillan, 1952.

Ward, George Atkinson. "The Civil Warfare in the Carolinas and Georgia during the Revolution." *Southern Literary Messenger*, no. 382 (July 12, 1847), 385-400.

Watson, Alan D. "Revolutionary North Carolina, 1765-1789." In Jeffrey J. Crow and Larry E. Tise, eds., *Writing North Carolina History* (Chapel Hill: University of North Carolina Press, 1979), 36-75.

Wheeler, John H. *Historical Sketches of North Carolina from 1581 to 1851*. 2 Vol. Philadelphia: Lippincott, Grambo, and Company, 1851; reprinted: New York: Frederick H. Hitchcock, 1925.

Weir, Robert M. *"The Last of American Freemen": Studies in Political Culture of the Colonial and Revolutionary South.* Macon, Ga.: Mercer University Press, 1986.

Weir, Robert M. "Rebelliousness: Personality Development and the American Revolution in the Southern Colonies." In Jeffrey J. Crow and Larry E. Tise, eds., *The Southern Experience in the American Revolution* (Chapel Hill: University of North Carolina Press, 1978), 25-54.

Weir, Robert M. "Who Shall Rule at Home: The American Revolution as a Crisis of Legitimacy for the Colonial Elite." *Journal of Interdisciplinary History*, 6:4 (Spring 1976), 679-700.

Whitfield, John. *The Early History of Tennessee: From Frontier to State*. Paducah, Ky.: Turner Publishing Company, 1999.

Wiley, Mary C. "Forgotten Bits of North Carolina's Past." *The State: A Weekly Survey of North Carolina*, 21:13 (August 1953), 12-13; online: http://digital.ncdcr.gov/cdm/ref/collection/p16062coll18/id/30856. [Online description from "North Carolina Periodicals Index," East Carolina University: "A list of all the North Carolina counties and the origin of their names is listed alphabetically in this article. From Alamance County to Yancey, the dates and inspiration for these names hold a long history of the state."]

Williams, Maxville Burt. *First for Freedom: Story of the First Official Act for American Independence*. Murfreesboro: Johnson Publishing Company, 1972. [a drama]

Williamson, Hugh. *The History of North Carolina*. 2 vols. Philadelphia: Thomas Dobson, 1812.

Wyatt-Brown, Bertram. *The Shaping of Southern Culture: Honor, Grace, and War, 1760s-1890s*. Chapel Hill: University of North Carolina Press, 2001.

Young, Joanne; photographs by Taylor Biggs Lewis. *Spirit of the People: The First Two Hundred Years*. Birmingham, Ala.: Oxmoor House, 1975.

General North Carolina Records of the Revolutionary Era

Jenkins, William Sumner, ed. *Records of the States of the United States of America: A Microfilm Compilation.* 1,871 microfilm reels. Washington, D. C.: Library of Congress Photoduplication Service, 1949. [General contents: A. Legislative records; B. Statutory records; C. Constitutional records; D. Administrative records; E. Executive records; F. Court records; F.X. Special records; L. Local records, county and city; M. Records of American Indian nations; N. Newspapers; R. Rudimentary states and courts; X. Miscellany.] And: Lillian A. Hamrick. *A*

Guide to the Microfilm Collection of Early State Records, Prepared by the Library of Congress in Association with the University of North Carolina: Collected and Compiled under the Direction of William Sumner Jenkins. Washington, D. C.: Library of Congress, Photoduplication Service, 1950. Also see: William Sumner Jenkins, ed. *Records of the States: Supplementary Microfilms.* Washington, D. C.: Library of Congress, Photoduplication Service, 1955.

Jenkins, William Sumner. "State Document Microfilms as Research Sources for Law Libraries." *Law Library Journal,* 41:2 (1948), 77-87; offprint: New York: [s. n.], 1948.

Jenkins, William Sumner. *Collected Public Documents of the States: A Check List.* Boston: [s. n.], 1947.

Jenkins, William Sumner. *Collecting and Using the Records of the States of the United States: Twenty-Five Years in Retrospection.* Chapel Hill: The University of North Carolina, Bureau of Public Records Collection and Research, 1960[?].

"Miscellaneous Papers, 1755-1912." Manuscripts at the North Carolina Historical Commission in 1926. [Most likely these have all been cataloged individually and appear as such in the State Archives of North Carolina's online MARS catalog. Consultation of the published list will give researchers a place to start searching in the online catalog.][12]

"North Carolina Papers." Manuscript, Historical Society of Pennsylvania, Philadelphia. [Online catalog description: "Also included are: manuscript map of the dividing line between Virginia and Carolina, 1728; printed copy of the amendment to the Constitution of North Carolina and of the Declaration of Rights, 1788; 'Orderly Book, North Carolina Line,' 1777; muster roll of British troops in Charleston, S. C., 1782. The participation of North Carolina troops in the Revolution is described in letters of General Robert Howe, Stephen Moore, R. Rutherford, Allen Jones, John Armstrong, Thomas Burke, William Davidson, Richard Caswell, John Penn, and others, 1777-1783; and in orders of the Assembly, 1777. The letters discuss the resolutions of the Assembly concerning the ratification of the Constitution, 1787-1788; the question of imposts by North Carolina, 1788; paper currency, 1785; treaties and sales of Indian lands, 1827; slavery, laws, finances, freemasonry, religion, local affairs, political and military appointments."]

North Carolina (Colony); William L. Saunders, ed. *The Colonial Records of North Carolina.* 10 vols. Raleigh: P. M. Hale, [etc.], State Printer, for the Trustees of the Public Libaries and by Order of the General Assembly, 1886-1890; reprinted: Wilmington, N. C.: Broadfoot Publishing Company, 1993 [Contents: Contents: I. 1662-1712; II. 1713-1728; III. 1728-1734; IV. 1734-1752; V. 1752-1759; VI. 1759-1765; VII. 1765-1768; VIII. 1769-1771; IX. 1771-1775; X. 1775-1776.] Online: "Documenting the Colonial South: Colonial and State Records of North Carolina," http://docsouth.unc.edu/csr/.

North Carolina (State); Walter Clark, ed. *The State Records of North Carolina.* 26 vols. Goldsboro: Nash Brothers, Printers, 1886-1907. [Contents: XI. 1777, supplement, 1730-1776; XII. 1777-1778; XIII. 1778-1779; XIV. 1779-1780; XV. 1780-1781; XVI. 1782-1783; XVII. 1781-1785; XVIII. 1786, with supplement, 1779; XIX. 1782-1784, with supplement, 1771-1782; XX. 1785-1788; XXI. 1788-1790; XXII. Miscellaneous; XXIII. Laws, 1715-1776; XXIV. Laws, 1777-1788; XXV. Laws, 1789-1790, supplement 1669-1771, index to vols. 23-25 [prepared by S.B. Weeks]; XXVI. Census, 1790, names, heads of families with index; XXVII. Index to A to E; XXVIII. Index F to L; XXIX. Index M to R; XXX. Index S to Z, with historical review.] Online: "Documenting the Colonial South: Colonial and State Records of North Carolina," http://docsouth.unc.edu/csr/.

Saunders, William Laurence. *Lessons from Our North Carolina Records: An Address Read before the Faculty and Students of Trinity College, November 27th, 1888.* Raleigh: E. M. Uzzell, Printer and Binder, 1888.

Saunders, William Laurence. *Prefatory Notes to the Colonial Records of North Carolina: Vols. 1 to 10.* Raleigh: J. Daniels, 1887.

Swain, David L. "David L. Swain Manuscripts, 1772-1869." Manuscript collection owned by the North Carolina Historical Commission in 1926. [Presumably these documents have been cataloged individually. They were calendared and published in 1926. This calendar is useful for searching for the individual documents in the State Archives of North Carolina's online MARS catalog.][13]

Weeks, Stephen B. "Historical Review of the Colonial and State Records of North Carolina." In Stephen B. Weeks, ed., *Index to the Colonial and State Records of North Carolina, Covering Volumes I-XXV* (Raleigh: State of North Carolina, 1909-1914), 1-169.

Weeks, Stephen Beauregard. *Historical Review of the Colonial and State Records of North Carolina.* Raleigh: E. M. Uzzell & Company, State Printers, 1914. [Description: "The attempts, public and private, to gather and publish

---

[12] See: D. L. Corbitt, ed., *Calendar of Manuscript Collections, Vol. 1* (Raleigh: Edwards & Broughton, 1926), 28-101.

[13] Ibid., 135-222.

the colonial and state records of North Carolina; The colonial and state records; Sources still uncollected." Taken from vol. 4 of the *Index to the Colonial and State Papers of North Carolina.*]

Agricultural and Forestry Conditions in North Carolina and Tennessee

Angley, Wilson. "Swine, Corn, and Timber: Colonial North Carolina." *Tar Heel Junior Historian*, 27:1 (Fall 1987), 4-5. [Online description from "North Carolina Periodicals Index," East Carolina University: "In colonial North Carolina over 90 percent of the colonists got their livelihoods from the land. However, they faced problems modern farmers do not. Colonists had no heavy machinery for plowing and clearing the land. There were no fertilizers and pesticides. Wild animals devoured crops. There were no weather forecasters. Still they persevered, raising enough crops and animals to feed themselves and others and producing enough farm and timber products for export to England and the West Indies."]

Ashe, William Willard. *The Forests, Forest Lands, and Forest Products of Eastern North Carolina*. Raleigh: Josephus Daniels, State Printer and Binder, 1894.

Carter, Mason C.; Robert C. Kellison; and R. Scott Wallinger. *Forestry in the U. S. South: A History*. Baton Rouge: Louisiana State University Press, 2015.

Cathey, Cornelius O. *Agricultural Developments in North Carolina, 1783-1860*. Chapel Hill: University of North Carolina Press, 1956.

Clifton, James M. "Golden Grains of White Rice: Planting on the Lower Cape Fear." *North Carolina Historical Review*, 50:4 (October 1973), 365-393. [Online description from "North Carolina Periodicals Index," East Carolina University: "Wealthy planters from the St. James Goose Creek Parish, 20 miles north of Charleston, established a permanent settlement in the Lower Cape Fear in the 1720s and introduced rice as a new agricultural staple in North Carolina."]

Cobb, Collier. "The Forests of North Carolina." *North Carolina Booklet*, 12:2 (1912), 136-157.

Foushee, Rodney. "Cape Fear Gold." *Wildlife in North Carolina*, 65:1 (January 2001), 4-11. [Online description from "North Carolina Periodicals Index," East Carolina University: "Once almost 30 rice plantations producing millions of pounds of rice annually lined the lower Cape Fear River and its tributaries. Rice grew there from the 18th-century till the last harvest in 1931. Today the land is a refuge for wildlife. The North Carolina Coastal Land Trust has conserved 4,000 acres of this land and seeks to save more before developers can move in."]

Franklin, W. Neil. "Agriculture in Colonial North Carolina." *North Carolina Historical Review*, 3:4 (October 1926), 539-574; online: http://digital.ncdcr.gov/cdm/ref/collection/p16062coll9/id/4207. [Online description from "North Carolina Periodicals Index," East Carolina University: "This article is divided into two parts concerning agriculture in colonial North Carolina. The first part reviews foreign perceptions regarding the quality of the land and its potential for great agricultural endeavors. The second part reviews the specific crops planted and profits made from each."]

Gray, Lewis C[ecil]. *History of Agriculture in the Southern United States to 1860*. 2 vols. Washington, D. C.: Carnegie Institution of Washington, 1933; reprinted: Gloucester, Mass.: Peter Smith, 1958.

Herndon, G. Melvin. "Indian Agriculture in the Southern Colonies." *North Carolina Historical Review*, 44:3 (July 1967), 283-297; online: http://digital.ncdcr.gov/cdm/ref/collection/p16062coll9/id/4207. [Online description from "North Carolina Periodicals Index," East Carolina University: "This article examines Native American agriculture during the colonial period in the South. Article details are provided from colonial records and accounts as well as more recent scholarship."]

McCullen, J. T., Jr. "The Tobacco Controversy, 1571-1961." *North Carolina Folklore Journal*, 10:1 (July 1962), 30-35. [Online description from "North Carolina Periodicals Index," East Carolina University: "Although most are aware of current anxiety aroused by the question as to tobacco and health, many may not know that the controversy over the effects of tobacco has flared up periodically during the past four hundred years. Physicians, kings, preachers, laymen, and even popes have taken their stand on the subject. All of them have spoken, pro or con, on the score of what tobacco does for or against the consumer."]

McPherson, James R., and G. R. Roberts. "300 Years of the Golden Weed." *The State: Down Home in North Carolina*, 43:11 (April 1976), 12-21; online: http://digital.ncdcr.gov/cdm/compoundobject/collection/p16062coll18/id/11608. [Online description from "North Carolina Periodicals Index," East Carolina University: "This article discusses the Living Tobacco Museum and how it will preserve North Carolina's tobacco industry and heritage. It is located at the Duke Homestead State Historic Site in Durham."]

Moore, Louis T. "The Culture of Indigo." *The State: A Weekly Survey of North Carolina*, 13:7 (July 1945), 3, 17; online: http://digital.ncdcr.gov/cdm/ref/collection/p16062coll18/id/13416. [Online description from "North Carolina Periodicals Index," East Carolina University: "At one time indigo represented the leading money crop for plantation owners along the coast. This article presents the interesting story of the indigo's beginning in colonial Carolina."]

Norris, Jeannie Faris. "187-Year-Old Tobacco Shop Joins Old Salem Restoration." *We the People of North Carolina*, 18:2 (June 1960), 6-7. [Online description from "North Carolina Periodicals Index," East Carolina University: "In 1771, Johann Matthew Miksch opened a tobacco shop in the Moravian village of Salem along with a log-cabin tobacco manufactory. Both buildings have now been restored and authentically furnished as part of the Old Salem Restoration project. To date, eight village buildings have been restored to their original appearance."]

North Carolina (State). General Assembly. "[Document dated]: February 8, 1781: Resolution Directing District Auditors Re[specting] Allowance for Corn Supplied the Army (Rejected)." Manuscript; General Assembly Record Group; Session Records, January-February 1781; Joint Papers, Committee Papers, Resolutions; Senate Joint Resolutions: February 8-9, 1781, Box 1 (MARS ID: 66.8.23.13.3; item), State Archives of North Carolina, Raleigh. [Online catalog description: "The resolution would have changed the price allowed for corn supplied by certain counties."]

Otto, John Solomon. *The Southern Frontiers, 1607-1860: The Agricultural Evolution of the Colonial and Antebellum South*. (Contributions in American History, no. 133) New York: Greenwood Press, 1989.

Sharpe, Bill. "Indigo." *The State: Down Home in North Carolina*, 34:15 (January 1967), 11, 13; online: http://digital.ncdcr.gov/cdm/ref/collection/p16062coll18/id/49802.

Sharpless, Rebecca. "Southern Women and the Land." *Agricultural History*, 67:2 (Spring 1993), 30-42. [Online description from "North Carolina Periodicals Index," East Carolina University: "Indigo was the second highest grossing crop in the colonial Carolinas. Found in India, this crop was transported to the colonies by the English in the mid-18th-century. The plant prospered after Eliza Lucas, the daughter of wealthy Antiguan plantation owner, planted the crop in Charleston, South Carolina and then Wilmington, North Carolina. The high demand for Indigo in Europe was such that the product was shipped with cotton and rice en masse every year and garnered vast wealth for the local elite planters."]

Street, Louis T. "Blue Gold." *The State: Down Home in North Carolina*, 43:12 (May 1976), 18-19, 27; online: http://digital.ncdcr.gov/cdm/compoundobject/collection/p16062coll18/id/11657. [Online description from "North Carolina Periodicals Index," East Carolina University: "Early in the settlement of North Carolina, indigo was an exciting and valuable crop for colonists. This article discusses the history and importance of the crop and methods of production."]

Sweet, Julia M. "Golden Harvest from the Swamp." *The State: Down Home in North Carolina*, 14-16, 39; online: http://digital.ncdcr.gov/cdm/ref/collection/p16062coll18/id/12016. [Online description from "North Carolina Periodicals Index," East Carolina University: "By the 1720s, rice was becoming a staple crop in North Carolina. In 1860, the rice yield from the Lower Cape Fear region reached eight million pounds. Swamp land had to be cleared to plant rice and slaves were used to cultivate and harvest the crop. Although rice continued to be grown after the Civil War, rice-growing in North Carolina came to a cessation in the 1890s."]

Three Centuries of Tobacco. Online: http://repository.lib.ncsu.edu/collections/bitstream/1840.6/597/5/0005_Threecenturiesoftobacco.pdf.

Agricultural and Forestry Conditions in North Carolina and Tennessee in the Revolutionary Era – Mills and Milling, Windmills, Gristmills, etc.

Barnes, Jay. "Carolina Wind." *Our State: Down Home in North Carolina*, 77:3 (August 2009), 32-34, 36; online: http://digital.ncdcr.gov/cdm/ref/collection/p16062coll18/id/92382. [Online description from "North Carolina Periodicals Index," East Carolina University: "North Carolina has a long history of windmills dating back to the 18-century. Carteret County had the most with over 65 of the total of 155 documented ones found along the coast. Today, with emphasis on clean energy, new wind projects are under consideration along the mountain ridges and the coastal areas."]

Downing, Sarah. *Hidden History of the Outer Banks* Charleston, S. C.: History Press, 2013. [Includes a section titled: "Windmills Once Dotted the Coast," 30-32.]

Dunaway, Stewart E. *A Beginner's Guide to Grist Mills of North Carolina: A Historical Review Using Original Count Records*. Hillsborough: North Carolina Historical Books, 2013. [Contents: Introduction; Mills; Mills Components; General Grist Mill Design; Mill Economics; Grist Mill, Beginning Days; Grist Mill, Ending Days; County Records; Appendix A. Examples of Mill Documents; Appendix B. Examples of Mill Stones.

Dunaway, Stewart E. *Bertie County, North Carolina, Mill Records (1736-1827) and Ferry Records (1747-1842)*. Hillsborough: North Carolina Historical Books, 2010. [Note: While not specifically concerning the Revolution, these sources can be used in tandem with land records and other documents to help locate places of residence, occupations, geographical features, and place names.]

Dunaway, Stewart E. *Craven County, North Carolina, Mill Records (1766-1885) & Ferry Petitions (1784-1883).* Hillsborough: North Carolina Historical Books, 2012. [Note: While not specifically concerning the Revolution, these sources can be used in tandem with land records and other documents to help locate places of residence, occupations, geographical features, and place names.]

Dunaway, Stewart E. *Edgecombe County, North Carolina, Mill Records (1760-1868), Bridge Records (1787-1890).* Hillsborough: North Carolina Historical Books, 2010. [Note: While not specifically concerning the Revolution, these sources can be used in tandem with land records and other documents to help locate places of residence, occupations, geographical features, and place names.]

Dunaway, Stewart E. *Gates County, North Carolina, Mill Records (1754-1890).* Hillsborough: North Carolina Historical Books, 2010. [Note: While not specifically concerning the Revolution, these sources can be used in tandem with land records and other documents to help locate places of residence, occupations, geographical features, and place names.]

Dunaway, Stewart E. *Grist Mills of North Carolina: A Historical Review Using County Records.* 6 vols. Hillsborough: North Carolina Historical Books, 2010-2015. [Contents: v. 1. Introduction; Mills; Mill components; General grist mill design; Mill economics; Grist mill: beginning days; Grist mill: ending days; County records; County mill petitions; Alexander County; Anson County; Ashe County; Bertie County; Brunswick County; Bute County; Caldwell County; Caswell County; Chowan County; Cumberland County; Davidson County; Edgecombe County (Pt. 1). v. 2. Edgecombe County (Pt. 2) ; Franklin County; Gates County; Jones County; Lenoir County; Lincoln County; Montgomery County; Moore County; Nash County. v. 3. Northampton County; Onslow County; Orange County; Pasquotank County. v. 4. Perquimans County; Person County; Randolph County; Robeson County; Stokes County; Surry County; Tryon County; Tyrrell County; Wake County. v. 5. Warren County; Wayne County; Wilkes County; Wilson County; Cleveland County; Gaston County; Pitt County; Rowan County; v. 6. Cleveland; Gaston; McDowell; Pitt; Rowan; Also CRX records for Burke, Bute, and Warren Co.]

Dunaway, Stewart E. *Miscellaneous North Carolina Road, Bridge, and Mill CRX Records: Brunswick Co. (1928, 1937), Burke Co. (1777-1786), Bute Co. (1767-1778), Cumberland Co. (1865-1868); Randolph Co. (1800-1845), Warren Co. (1780-1937).* Hillsborough: North Carolina Historical Books, 2015. [Note: While not specifically concerning the Revolution, these sources can be used in tandem with land records and other documents to help locate places of residence, occupations, geographical features, and place names.]

Dunaway, Stewart E. *Nash County, North Carolina, Mill Records (1782-1875).* Hillsborough: North Carolina Historical Books, 2010. [Note: While not specifically concerning the Revolution, these sources can be used in tandem with land records and other documents to help locate places of residence, occupations, geographical features, and place names.]

Dunaway, Stewart E. *Onslow County, North Carolina, Mill Records (1765-1861), Ferry Records (1774-1906).* Hillsborough: North Carolina Historical Books, 2010. [Note: While not specifically concerning the Revolution, these sources can be used in tandem with land records and other documents to help locate places of residence, occupations, geographical features, and place names.]

Dunaway, Stewart E. *Orange County, North Carolina, Mill Records (1782-1859).* Hillsborough: North Carolina Historical Books, 2010. [Note: While not specifically concerning the Revolution, these sources can be used in tandem with land records and other documents to help locate places of residence, occupations, geographical features, and place names.]

Dunaway, Stewart E. *Perquimans County, North Carolina, Mill Records (1744-1885) & Ferry Petitions (1740-1866).* Hillsborough: North Carolina Historical Books, 2009. [Note: While not specifically concerning the Revolution, these sources can be used in tandem with land records and other documents to help locate places of residence, occupations, geographical features, and place names.]

Dunaway, Stewart E. *Randolph County, North Carolina, Bridge Records (1803-1864) and Mill Records, (1782-1879).* Hillsborough: North Carolina Historical Books, 2009.

Dunaway, Stewart E. *Richmond County Road Records (1778-1826), Bridge Records (1790-1897), Ferry Records, 1784-1857), Mill Records (1790-1875).* Hillsborough: North Carolina Historical Books, 2013.

Dunaway, Stewart E. *Summers Mill: A Historical Overview.* Hillsborough: North Carolina Historical Books, 2010. [Originally known as Weitzell's Mill. Reedy Fork, Guilford County, North Carolina.]

Dunaway, Stewart E. *Surry County, North Carolina, County Records: Road, Bridge, Ferry, Mill Petitions and Tavern Bonds (1772-1839).* Hillsborough: North Carolina Historical Books, 2011. [Contents: County records; Ordinary record: Surry County, 1774; Road records, 1772-1799 (broken series); Bridge repair records, 1777-

1839 (broken series); Bridge records, 1822; Mill records, 1823; Ordinary bond, 1774; Reference maps.] [Note: While not specifically concerning the Revolution, these sources can be used in tandem with land records and other documents to help locate places of residence, occupations, geographical features, and place names.]

Dunaway, Stewart E. *Wake County, North Carolina, Mill Records, 1772-1872.* Hillsborough: North Carolina Historical Books, 2009. [Note: While not specifically concerning the Revolution, these sources can be used in tandem with land records and other documents to help locate places of residence, occupations, geographical features, and place names.]

Littleton, Tucker R. "When Windmills Whirled on the Tar Heel Coast." *The State: Down Home in North Carolina*, 51:8 (January 1984), 7-8; online: http://digital.ncdcr.gov/cdm/ref/collection/p16062coll18/id/60612. [Online description from "North Carolina Periodicals Index," East Carolina University: "The coastal region of North Carolina was home to over 155 windmills during the 18th- and 19th-centuries. The windmills incorporated a post-mill design better suited for the region than tower-mills. Post-mills were effective because they allowed the windmill to be turned into the wind, were cheaper to construct, and were made with materials available in eastern North Carolina. Coastal mills were built for grinding grain or pumping water. Researcher Tucker Littleton found that in North Carolina, mills built above the Onslow County-Pender County line tended to be grist mills while those built below the line tended to be water mills. Littleton also discovered that Carteret County contained the largest number of windmills. Few North Carolinians remember the role windmills played in the state's past. Lynanne Westcott is trying to change this as she has built an exact replica of a 19th-century windmill in Manteo."]

Littleton, Tucker R. "Wind Plus Water Equaled Salt." *The State: Down Home in North Carolina*, 49:9 (February 1982), 16-18, 28; online: http://digital.ncdcr.gov/cdm/ref/collection/p16062coll18/id/59506. [Online description from "North Carolina Periodicals Index," East Carolina University: "During the blockades of the Revolution, the War of 1812, and the Civil War, it became necessary for North Carolina to convert its gristmills to saltworks. Windmills were used to pump sea water into the plant, where it was then either boiled or evaporated, leaving only salt residue. Toward the end of the Civil War, several saltworks were destroyed by Yankee forces. So far, only thirteen saltworks that used windmills in production have been identified. They are in New Hanover, Carteret, and Brunswick counties."]

"Outer Banks Windmills." Online: http://beaufortartist.blogspot.com/2008/03/outer-banks-windmills.html.

Stick, David. "Windmills." Online: http://ncpedia.org/windmills.

"This Windmill Doesn't Need Space Age Technology." *Carolina Country*, 11:9 (September 1979), 14-15. [Online description from "North Carolina Periodicals Index," East Carolina University: "The world's largest windmill stands atop Howard's Knob in Watauga County, ready to generate electricity. On Roanoke Sound at Nags Head, Lynanne Wescott of Manteo is building a windmill based on a 19th-century design. The 35-foot windmill is authentic down to the hand-forged metal work and wooden parts that were cut with the old style tools. Handcut wooden nails join pieces of the structure together. Total cost for the project is $250,000. Wescott hopes the windmill will be a tourist attraction and a moneymaker. The windmill will be used to grind grain, and visitors will be able to view the entire process. Windmills of this type were part of North Carolina's coastal life in the early 1700s, but fell into disuse by the end of the 19th-century."]

Yocum, Thomas. "Windmill History on the Outer Banks." Online: http://www.coastalguide.com/windmill-history-outer-banks.html.

Animals and Birds of North Carolina and Tennessee (generally)

Abernethy, Mrs. Max. "The New State Bird." *The State: A Weekly Survey of North Carolina*, 10:43 (March 1943), 7, 17; online: http://digital.ncdcr.gov/cdm/ref/collection/p16062coll18/id/16987. [Online description from "North Carolina Periodicals Index," East Carolina University: "Since the Great Seal was authorized by the State Constitution, North Carolina has been slow to add other official emblems. The flag was not adopted until 1885, the state motto until 1893, the state song in 1927, and the state flower in 1941. The Carolina chickadee became the state bird in 1931 by an act of the General Assembly, but the act was repealed seven days later. Finally in March 1943, the cardinal was named the official state bird."]

Amundson, Rod. "The Carolina Otter." *Wildlife in North Carolina*, 14:8 (August 1950), 4-7. [Online description from "North Carolina Periodicals Index," East Carolina University: "Because of the superior quality of their fur, otters were almost trapped into extinction across the country. It wasn't many years ago that otters were extremely rare in North Carolina. Now, protected by strict game laws, the Carolina otter is sufficiently numerous again in the eastern part of the state to warrant an open season for trapping. Amundson discusses the otter's range, characteristics, food and breeding habits, management, general behavior, and having them as pets."]

Beane, Jeffrey C.; Alvin L. Braswell; Joseph C. Mitchell; William M. Palmer; and Julian R. Harrison, III. *Amphibians and Reptiles of the Carolinas and Virginia.* 2nd ed. Chapel Hill: University of North Carolina Press, 2010. [Publisher's description: "Revised and updated to reflect the most current science, and including 30 new species, this authoritative and comprehensive volume is the definitive guide to the amphibians and reptiles of the Carolinas and Virginia. The new edition features 189 species of salamanders, frogs, crocodilians, turtles, lizards, and snakes, with updated color photographs, descriptions, and distribution maps for each species. It is an indispensable guide for zoologists, amateur naturalists, environmentalists, backpackers, campers, hikers, and everyone interested in the outdoors."]

Beeland, T. Delene. *The Secret World of Red Wolves: The Fight to Save America's Other Wolf.* Chapel Hill: University of North Carolina Press, 2013.

Beeland, T. Delene. "The Secret World of Red Wolves: The Fight to Save America's Other Wolf." *Coastwatch*, 1 (Winter 2014), 33-35. [Online description from "North Carolina Periodicals Index," East Carolina University: "Northeastern North Carolina, specifically 1.7 acres of the Albemarle Peninsula, has the only wild red wolf mainland population in the world. Twenty-seven years ago the animal was on the brink of extinction, but now the U. S. Fish and Wildlife Service estimates there are between 90 and 110 ten wolves on the peninsula. In this excerpt from her book, titled above, Beeland recounts a night on the peninsula howling with the wolves."]

Blevins, David, and Michael P. Schafale. *Wild North Carolina: Discovering the Wonders of Our State's Natural Communities*. Chapel Hill: University of North Carolina Press, 2011. [Publisher's description: "Celebrating the beauty, diversity, and significance of the state's natural landscapes, Wild North Carolina provides an engaging, beautifully illustrated introduction to North Carolina's interconnected webs of plant and animal life. From dunes and marshes to high mountain crags, through forests, swamps, savannas, ponds, pocosins, and flatrocks, David Blevins and Michael Schafale reveal in words and photographs natural patterns of the landscape that will help readers see familiar places in a new way and new places with a sense of familiarity."]

Brotak, Ed; photographs by Todd Pusser. "Weather and Wildlife." *Wildlife in North Carolina*, 78:2 (March/April 2014), 10-15. [Online description from "North Carolina Periodicals Index," East Carolina University: "Stretching from the mountains to the coast, the state contains a diversity of wildlife and habitat. This includes the American alligator, the Southern flying squirrel, and elk herds. Brotak states that analyzing the climate of a particular region requires a close look at temperature and precipitation. 'These two elements to a large extent control the type of vegetation found in an area and therefore also determine the wildlife found there.' The article includes maps showing normal precipitation and normal mean temperatures from 1971-2000."]

Dean, Jim. "Uncommon Mammals." *Wildlife in North Carolina*, 50:2 (February 1986), 4-9. [Online description from "North Carolina Periodicals Index," East Carolina University: "North Carolina provides habitats to many mammals that are seldom seen. Some of them are rare, and some are merely secretive. Dean describes some of them, including the fox squirrel, swamp rabbit, river otter, nutria, nine-banded armadillo, coyote, mountain lion, and black-tailed jack rabbit."]

Draper, Grace S. "Our Blue Birds." *Wildlife in North Carolina*, 34:4 (April 1970), 17-19. [Online description from "North Carolina Periodicals Index," East Carolina University: "There are five birds that frequent North Carolina that show varying shades of blue plumage. They are the Eastern bluebird; the blue grosbeak, sometimes called the Big Indigo; the indigo bunting or indigo finch; the blue jay; and barn swallow. Draper provides a description of each bird."]

Frankenberg, Dirk. *The Nature of the North Carolina's Southern Coast.* Chapel Hill: University of North Carolina Press, 2012. [Publisher's description: "For some years, The Nature of North Carolina's Southern Coast has stood as an essential resource for all who treasure our coastal environment. In this book, Dirk Frankenberg describes the southern coast's beaches, inlets, and estuaries and instructs readers in the responsible exploration and enjoyment of some of North Carolina's most precious natural areas. From Ocracoke Inlet to the South Carolina border, this field guide provides a close-up look at a complex ecosystem, highlighting the processes that have shaped, and continue to shape, North Carolina's southern coast."]

Frankenberg, Dirk. *The Nature of the Outer Banks.* Chapel Hill: University of North Carolina Press, 2012. ["Publisher's description: "North Carolina's Outer Banks are in constant motion, responding to weather, waves, and the rising sea level. Beaches erode, sometimes taking homes or sections of highway with them into the surf; sand dunes migrate with the wind; and storms open new inlets and dump sand in channels and sounds. A classic guide, *The Nature of the Outer Banks* describes these dynamic forces and guides visitors to sites where they can see these phenomena in action."]

Frick-Ruppoert, Jennifer. *Mountain Nature: A Seasonal Natural History of the Southern Appalachians*. Chapel Hill: University of North Carolina Press, 2010. [Publisher's description: "The Southern Appalachians are home to a breathtakingly diverse array of living things – from delicate orchids to carnivorous pitcher plants, from migrating butterflies to flying squirrels, and from brawny black bears to more species of salamander than anywhere else in the world. *Mountain Nature* is a lively and engaging account of the ecology of this remarkable region. It explores the animals and plants of the Southern Appalachians and the webs of interdependence that connect them."]

Godfrey, Michael. "Three Carolinians." *Wildlife in North Carolina*, 36:6 (June 1972), 18-20. [Online description from "North Carolina Periodicals Index," East Carolina University: "Several well-known animals have the word "Carolina" attached to their common or scientific names. They are the eastern gray squirrel (*Sciurus carolinensis*), the red-bellied woodpecker (*Centurus carolinus*), and the Carolina wren. Godfrey describes them."]

Hudson, Arthur Palmer. "Animal Lore in Lawson's and Brickell's Histories of North Carolina." *North Carolina Folklore Journal*, 8:2 (December 1960), 1-15. [Online description from "North Carolina Periodicals Index," East Carolina University: "Two classics of North Carolina colonial writing are John Lawson's *History of North Carolina* and Dr. John Brickell's *The Natural History of North Carolina*. Each contains a systematic account of the 'beasts' found in North Carolina."]

Krautwurst, Terry. "Only in the Mountains." *Wildlife in North Carolina*, 65:7 (July 2001), 1-149. [Online description from "North Carolina Periodicals Index," East Carolina University: "The North Carolina mountains provide habitats to wildlife found nowhere else in the state. This wildlife includes the Appalachian cottontail, Carolina northern flying squirrel, brook trout, Virginia big-eared bat, and hellbender. While none of these species are endangered at the moment, air pollution and encroaching development are among threats they face."]

Lee, David. "Sing a Song of Redbirds." *Wildlife in North Carolina*, 62:3 (March 1998), 24-27. [Online description from "North Carolina Periodicals Index," East Carolina University: "The cardinal is one of the most popular of all songbirds. It is a favorite of bird watchers. Seven states use it as their state bird. It appears on many items at Christmas, and twenty-two college and two professional teams use it as their symbol."]

Lippson, Robert L., and Alice Jane Lippson. *Life along the Inner Coast*. Chapel Hill: University of North Carolina Press, 2012. [Publisher's description: "For decades, marine scientists Robert and Alice Jane Lippson have traveled the rivers, backwaters, sounds, bays, lagoons, and inlets stretching from the Chesapeake Bay to the Florida Keys aboard their trawler, Odyssey. The culmination of their leisurely journeys, *Life along the Inner Coast* is a guide to the plants, animals, and habitats found in one of the most biologically diverse regions on the planet. It is a valuable resource for naturalists, students, and anyone who lives or vacations along the Atlantic inner coast."]

Martin, Margaret. *A Long Look at Nature: The North Carolina State Museum of Natural Sciences*. Chapel Hill: University of North Carolina Press, 2001. [Publisher's description: "What does a jar of preserved leopard frogs or the articulated skeleton of a beached sperm whale say about the way we understand nature in North Carolina? Margaret Martin explores this question in the story of the North Carolina State Museum of Natural Sciences, founded over 120 years ago to serve as a keeper of natural history collections, a vital resource for the scientific community, and a public interpreter of our natural world. The book is organized around the museum's collections: Rocks and Minerals, Fossils, Invertebrates, Fishes, Reptiles and Amphibians, Birds, and Mammals. Martin looks at how these collections have been interpreted over time, tracing the shift away from a nineteenth-century presentation of nature as something ripe for exploitation to a more contemporary view of natural communities as complex, interconnected, and deserving of conservation. With 175 color and black-and-white photographs, *A Long Look at Nature* is both an engaging introduction to the museum and a striking visual tribute to its collections. The book celebrates North Carolina nature in all its diversity and highlights the museum's crucial role in interpreting North Carolina's natural heritage."]

Masterson, James R. "Travelers' Tales of Colonial Natural History." *Journal of American Folklore*, 59:231 (January-March 1946), 51-67.

McKinley, Daniel. "Historical Review of the Carolina Parakeet in the Carolinas." *Brimleyana*, 1 (March 1979), 81-98. [Online description from "North Carolina Periodicals Index," East Carolina University: "Many of the early voyagers and explorers, dating back to Thomas Hariot in 1588, reported sightings of parrots or parakeets in the Carolinas. McKinley discusses these early reports of the Carolina parakeet in North and South Carolina and what happened to it in later centuries."]

Norris, Jeannie Faris. "The State Bird." *The State: A Weekly Survey of North Carolina*, 20:31 (January 1953), 73; online: http://digital.ncdcr.gov/cdm/ref/collection/p16062coll18/id/29768. [Online description from "North

Carolina Periodicals Index," East Carolina University: "Selected on 4 March, 1943, for their abundance, color, singing abilities and tendency to remain in the state year round, the Cardinal became the state bird of North Carolina."]

Nickens, T. Edward. "A Brief Glance Backward." *Wildlife in North Carolina*, 64:1 (January 2000), 14-17. [Online description from "North Carolina Periodicals Index," East Carolina University: "As the state of North Carolina moves into the twenty-first century, Nickens takes a look back through the centuries at how humans interacted with the state's wildlife, from 1524, when Verrazano sailed along the coast, to the restoration of the wild turkey in 1999."]

North Carolina Birding Trail. *The North Carolina Birding Trail.* Chapel Hill: University of North Carolina Press, 2008. [Publisher's description: "North Carolina harbors an incredible diversity of habitats that provide food and shelter for more than 440 bird species throughout the year, making the state a destination for birders and nature lovers. The North Carolina Birding Trail is a driving trail linking birders and tourists with great birding sites across the state and the local communities in which they are found."]

Potter, Eloise F.; James F. Parnell; Robert P. Teulings; and Ricky Davis. *Birds of the Carolinas*. 2nd ed. Chapel Hill: University of North Carolina Press, 2006.

Powell, William S. "Creatures of Carolina from Roanoke Island to Purgatory Mountain." *North Carolina Historical Review*, 50:2 (April 1973), 155-168. [Online description from "North Carolina Periodicals Index," East Carolina University: "An examination of historical and modern records on animals, birds, and other forms of moving life that are native to North Carolina and whose presence predates European exploration."]

Powell, William S. "The Paroquet." *The State: Down Home in North Carolina*, 22:7 (August 1954), 15-16. [Online description from "North Carolina Periodicals Index," East Carolina University: "Slightly larger than a blue jay and containing a bigger wingspan, the paroquet of North Carolina vanished in 1909. First reported along the coast in 1586, by Thomas Hariot, the paroquet is a member of the parrot family. Living in large groups partial to orchards, paroquets fell to extinction as a result of destructive habits associated with human beings."]

Reynolds, Ryan. "Agile Acrobats." *Coastwatch*, (Early Summer 2005), 20-23. [Online description from "North Carolina Periodicals Index," East Carolina University: "River otters are known for their antics, whether performing in the wild or in an aquarium. This animal can grow to around three or four feet and weigh more than forty pounds. It can live up to fifteen years in the wild and sometimes longer in captivity. However, back in the 1800s and early 1900s, the river otter had all but vanished from the North Carolina landscape. Uncontrolled trapping, water pollution, and habitat destruction contributed to its demise. In the 1970s the state began an otter reintroduction program. Today the otter has been successfully restored throughout the state."]

Roberts, B. W. C. "Cockfighting: An Early Entertainment in North Carolina." *North Carolina Historical Review*, 42:3 (July 1965), 300-314; online: http://digital.ncdcr.gov/cdm/ref/collection/p16062coll9/id/4207. [Online description from "North Carolina Periodicals Index," East Carolina University: "This article looks at the history of cockfighting in North Carolina including various styles and rules of fighting as well as the raising and training of the fighting stock. Details on competitions, clubs, seasons, famous fights, laws and regulations are included."]

Schwarz, Frank J. *Sharks, Skates, and Rays of the Carolinas.* Chapel Hill: University of North Carolina Press, 2003.

Smith, Garrett. "Mount Mitchell." *Wildlife in North Carolina*, 76:4 (July/August 2012), 10-15. [Online description from "North Carolina Periodicals Index," East Carolina University: "Smith's article features one of North Carolina's great landmarks – Mount Mitchell – and the creatures that live there – mammals, birds, amphibians, reptiles."]

Webster, William David; James F. Parnell; and Walter Biggs, Jr. *Mammals of the Carolinas, Virginia, and Maryland.* Chapel Hill: University of North Carolina Press, 2004. [Publisher's description: "The only volume to deal specifically with the mid-Atlantic region, this practical guide describes in detail the 88 terrestrial mammals found there as well as the 33 marine species that inhabit the offshore waters. The authors offer expert descriptions of each species, including feeding habits, activity cycles, reproductive biology, and relation to other animals and humans. By emphasizing the relationships between mammals and their environments, the authors reveal how these animals live throughout the year. They guide readers to an appreciation of mammalian life and a keen awareness of the importance of conservation and habitat preservation."]

Wilson, Eddie W. "Some Tales about Snakes." *The State: A Weekly Survey of North Carolina*, 16:2 (June 1948), 9, 22; online: http://digital.ncdcr.gov/cdm/ref/collection/p16062coll18/id/22449. [Online description from "North Carolina Periodicals Index," East Carolina University: "The author outlines both Native American and contemporary lore about snakes, including religious and medicinal qualities. Cherokee religion believed rattlesnakes to be men in a different form. Dr. John Brickell's writing included snake folklore in *Natural*

History of North Carolina. There is also a discussion about North Carolina snake lore, with folktales and medicinal/therapeutic qualities of native snake species."]

Wilson, Kenneth A. "Nature's Playboy." *Wildlife in North Carolina*, 25:1 (January 1961), 16-18. [Online description from "North Carolina Periodicals Index," East Carolina University: "The otter is a sleek, elongated package of muscular energy with brains and playful disposition. Once facing the threat of extinction in the state, the otter has made a comeback and today produces valuable pelts. About 95 percent of the existing otter population is found in the coastal area of North Carolina, with the remainder scattered through the Piedmont counties in the Yadkin River watershed."]

Animals in North Carolina and Tennessee – Alligators

Amundson, Rod. "The American Alligator." *Wildlife in North Carolina*, 15:8 (August 1951), 4-6. [Online description from "North Carolina Periodicals Index," East Carolina University: "The American alligator is North Carolina's largest reptile and can weigh up to 600 pounds and measure 12 feet. Most range along the coastal swamps of the southeastern part of the state. Amundson describes the alligator's characteristics, breeding habits, food habits, and habitats."]

Beane, Jeffrey C.; Alvin L. Braswell; Joseph C. Mitchell; William M. Palmer; and Julian R. Harrison, III. *Amphibians and Reptiles of the Carolinas and Virginia*. 2nd ed. Chapel Hill: University of North Carolina Press, 2010. [Publisher's description: "Revised and updated to reflect the most current science, and including 30 new species, this authoritative and comprehensive volume is the definitive guide to the amphibians and reptiles of the Carolinas and Virginia. The new edition features 189 species of salamanders, frogs, crocodilians, turtles, lizards, and snakes, with updated color photographs, descriptions, and distribution maps for each species. It is an indispensable guide for zoologists, amateur naturalists, environmentalists, backpackers, campers, hikers, and everyone interested in the outdoors."]

Ellis, Marshall. "Swamp Thing." *Our State: Down Home in North Carolina*, 70:1 (June 2002), 76-78, 80, 82. [Online description from "North Carolina Periodicals Index," East Carolina University: "The American alligator is North Carolina's largest reptile. Alligators live mostly in swampy areas of the Coastal Plain, in places like Green Swamp in Columbus County and the Croatan National Forest in Carteret County. Areas like these are preferred living places because they are secluded, have a tolerable climate, and have plenty of food. Ellis describes these creatures and how they live."]

Fuller, Manley. "Carolina Gators." *Wildlife in North Carolina*, 48:6 (June 1984), 16-21. [Online description from "North Carolina Periodicals Index," East Carolina University: "The natural range of the alligator extends as far north as the coastal swamps of the southeastern part of North Carolina. These creatures are experiencing a modest population growth in the state, and Manley discusses what the future may hold for them."]

Funk, William H. "A Most Patient Predator." *Wildlife in North Carolina*, 78:4 (July/August 2014), 20-27. [Online description from "North Carolina Periodicals Index," East Carolina University: "In North Carolina alligators live in swamps and waterways from Brunswick County north to the Alligator River National Wildlife Refuge. It is the state's largest reptile and can weigh up to 600 pounds and measure 12 feet. North Carolina is one of nine states where the American alligator roams, and the state is the limit of its northern range."]

Horan, Jack. "NC Alligator Population Growing, Still Vulnerable." *Coastwatch*, 3 (Summer 2015), 32-33. [Online description from "North Carolina Periodicals Index," East Carolina University: "The alligator population in North Carolina is steadily growing, particularly in the southeastern part of the state. Despite recent growth and state laws that prohibit alligator hunting, North Carolina's gator population is still in danger."]

Lee, David. "Alligators." *Wildlife in North Carolina*, 57:5 (May 1993), 8-12.

Lee, David S. "Carolina Dragons." *Wildlife in North Carolina*, 66:5 (May 2002), 2-7. [Online description from "North Carolina Periodicals Index," East Carolina University: "The American alligator is North Carolina's largest reptile and can weigh up to 600 pounds and measure 12 feet. The state is the northern limit of their range, but they are not numerous here and live mostly on the outer Coastal Plain. Lee describes these creatures and how they live."]

Louder, Darrell E. "The Alligator: North Carolina's Link with the Past." *Wildlife in North Carolina*, 29:8 (August 1965), 4-5. [Online description from "North Carolina Periodicals Index," East Carolina University: "North Carolina is one of nine states where the American alligator roams, and its habitat in the swampy areas near the coast is the limit of its northern range. Its average size is eight to ten feet. North Carolina's largest living alligator measures thirteen feet and lives in the swamps of Carteret County. These creatures are extremely shy and prefer the wild areas far away from humans."]

Louder, Darrell E. "King of the Swamps." *The State: Down Home in North Carolina*, 26:8 (September 1958), 12-13. [Online description from "North Carolina Periodicals Index," East Carolina University: "The American alligator is found in the wildest part of southeastern North Carolina near the coast. Belonging to an order of reptiles known as the *Crocodilia* containing 25 species, only two species of alligator are known, and North Carolinians should consider ourselves fortunate to have such an animal in our midst. Unfortunately, many American alligators are killed by hunters for the 'thrill,' and unless a law is passed to protect the species, the alligator will fast disappear from the scene."]

Montgomery, Frank A., Jr. "Carolina Alligators." *The State: A Weekly Survey of North Carolina*, 2:52 (May 1935), 3. [Online description from "North Carolina Periodicals Index," East Carolina University: "The natural range of the alligator extends as far north as the coastal swamps of the southeastern part of North Carolina. Montgomery relates some interesting facts about their habits."]

Animals in North Carolina and Tennessee – Bears

Amundson, Rod. "The Black Bear." *Wildlife in North Carolina,* 30:9 (September 1966), 4-6. [Online description from "North Carolina Periodicals Index," East Carolina University: "The black bear, the smallest of the American bears, seldom attains over five feet in length or over 500 pounds in weight. Encroaching civilization has greatly reduced the bear population in this country since the first English settlers arrived. In North Carolina the black bear population is around 5,000. North Carolina has placed the bears on the list of protected game animals to keep them from becoming extinct in the state. Amundson discusses the bear's coloration, behavior, breeding habits, food habits, enemies, management, and hunting."]

Smith, Donna Campbell. "The Bears." *Carolina Country*, 45:10 (October 2013), 14-15. [Online description from "North Carolina Periodicals Index," East Carolina University: "The black bear is the only bear living in North Carolina, and the population in the Coastal Plain and in the state's mountains is at all-time high. This article provides information on the bears in the Coastal Plain that are often seen roaming the farms, communities, and wildlands."]

Venters, Vic. "Bears in the East." *Wildlife in North Carolina*, 60:1 (January 1996), 4-11. [Online description from "North Carolina Periodicals Index," East Carolina University: "In 1972, North Carolina was the first state in the nation to establish bear sanctuaries. Now, through habitat management, the black bear population in the Coastal Plain numbers almost 5,000, the largest in similar areas of the southeastern United States."]

Venters, Vic. "Bears in the West." *Wildlife in North Carolina*, 60:2 (February 1996), 10-15. [Online description from "North Carolina Periodicals Index," East Carolina University: "Almost extinct in the western counties by the 1920s, black bears were saved by the depression and the creation of the Great Smoky Mountains National Park. Black bears now number 2,200 and are found in 24 mountain counties."]

Animals in North Carolina and Tennessee – Beavers

Hester, F. Eugene. "Beneficial Beavers." *Wildlife in North Carolina,* 65:8 (August 2001), 22-27. [Online description from "North Carolina Periodicals Index," East Carolina University: "Beavers remake the environment to meet their needs. What's good for the beaver, though, sometimes causes problems for people, such as destruction of trees and crops and flooding caused by beaver dams. On the positive side, beaver ponds provide homes for waterfowl and habitats for other species including frogs and bitterns. The dams also help prevent harmful nutrients and pollutants from washing downstream by causing them to settle to the pond bottoms where bacteria destroy them.

Wilson, Kenneth A. "The Beaver in North Carolina." *Wildlife in North Carolina*, 19:5 (May 1955), 6-8, 10. [Online description from "North Carolina Periodicals Index," East Carolina University: "Once estimated at several hundred thousand in colonial North Carolina, the beaver was extinct across the state by the late 19th-century. In 1938, 29 beavers were released on what is now the Sandhills Wildlife Management Area in Richmond County. In 1955, the estimated beaver population was around 5,000. Wilson discusses the history of the beaver in North Carolina and its effect on the landscape."]

Animals in North Carolina and Tennessee – Buffalo/Bison

Earley, Lawrence S. "Buffalo in North Carolina." *Wildlife in North Carolina*, 60:6 (June 1996), 2-3; online: http://digital.ncdcr.gov/cdm/ref/collection/p16062coll9/id/4207. [Online description from "North Carolina Periodicals Index," East Carolina University: "Buffalo existed in the state into the early 18th century, but when settlers moved into the Piedmont, the small herds were soon hunted to extinction." "Images of the American West often contained herds of bison, but some historic accounts identified buffalo within the region that would become North Carolina. Several sources from John Lawson and Dr. John Brickell were studied for evidence of buffalo in the state, especially in the western mountain portion of the territory."]

Rights, Douglas L. "The Buffalo in North Carolina." *North Carolina Historical Review*, 9:3 (July 1932), 242-249.

Wadsworth, E. W. "From Buffalo Trails to Highways." *The State: Down Home in North Carolina*, 49:12 (May 1982), 8-10; online: http://digital.ncdcr.gov/cdm/ref/collection/p16062coll18/id/59657. [Online description from "North Carolina Periodicals Index," East Carolina University: "At one time, huge herds of buffalo crossed the Blue Ridge Mountains in order to winter along the east coast shoreline. Because these herds had a keen sense of direction, their trails were the same year after year. As a result, they were used as footpaths by the Cherokee Indians, and can still be followed today. Once in Boone, the buffalo trail is called the Wilderness Trail, and continues on into Kentucky. The last reported herd of buffalo to pass through North Carolina was in 1790."]

Animals in North Carolina and Tennessee – Dogs

"Our State Dog: North Carolina's Plott Hound." *Carolina Comments*, 59:4 (October 2011), 49.

Pittard, Janet C. "The State Dog." *Our State: Down Home in North Carolina*, 74:5 (October 2006), 26-29; online: http://digital.ncdcr.gov/cdm/ref/collection/p16062coll18/id/87516. [Online description from "North Carolina Periodicals Index," East Carolina University: "The story of the Plott hound begins in 1750 when Johannes Plott emigrated to colonial America from Heidelberg, Germany. He brought with him two Hanoverian-type Schweisshunds (bloodhounds). Plott eventually settled in New Bern, married, had three sons, and then moved on to Cabarrus County. His descendants continued to live in the Smoky Mountains and breed the dogs. The Plott hound is an intelligent animal, has a formidable reputation as a hunter, and tends to be a one-person dog. In 1946, the dog was recognized by the United Kennel Club, and years later by the American Kennel Club. On August 12, 1989, the North Carolina General Assembly officially recognized the Plott hound as the State Dog. At the time, few North Carolinians had ever heard of the hound, much less seen one."]

Plott, Bob. *Strike and Stay: The Story of the Plott Hound*. Charleston, S. C.: History Press, 2007.

Animals in North Carolina and Tennessee – Horses

Angione, Kathleen. "Healthy as a Horse." *Coastwatch*, (Early Summer 2006), 16-19. [Online description from "North Carolina Periodicals Index," East Carolina University: "Shackleford Banks, part of the Cape Lookout National Seashore, is a 3,000-acre uninhabited island near Atlantic Beach. A herd of 112 wild horses lives there, one of only a few wild herds remaining in the country. The herd's reproductive rate is carefully controlled to keep the horses from putting a strain on the island's food and water resources. To understand how the horses thrive and survive in the island's harsh environment, the National Park Service has undertaken a study of the horses' eating habits. The study will look at seasonal eating habits and whether different habitats provide different nutritional contents. No findings have been reported as yet, and the study will take another year to complete."]

Blackburn, Charles, Jr. "Off to the Races." *Our State: Down Home in North Carolina*, 71:9 (February 2004), 23-24; online: http://digital.ncdcr.gov/cdm/ref/collection/p16062coll18/id/78925. [Online description from "North Carolina Periodicals Index," East Carolina University: "While NASCAR and ACC basketball keep sports fans in the state occupied today, horse racing in eastern North Carolina during the 1700s and early 1800s was the most exciting sporting event around. Blackburn discusses the history of racing in the state, famous horses, like Sir Archie, and their owners."]

Bragdon, Douglas J. "The Wild Ponies of Ocracoke." *Tar Heel*, 8:6 (August 1980), 43-45. [Online description from "North Carolina Periodicals Index," East Carolina University: "The ponies on Ocracoke have been around for centuries. Some myths which have evolved around them say no one knows where they came from; the animals are wild; the animals are ponies; and the horses are unique to Ocracoke. Bragdon explores some of the more popular myths, such as these, and some 20th-century facts."]

Davis, Nancy. "Who'll Decide Horses' Future – Nature or Man?" *Coastwatch*, 10:5 (May 1983), 8-9. [Online description from "North Carolina Periodicals Index," East Carolina University: "With growing populations and harsh environmental conditions, many butt heads about what should be the fate of the wild horses on North Carolina's Shackleford Banks."]

Graff, Michael. "Where the Road Ends." *Our State: Down Home in North Carolina*, 78:12 (May 2011), 106-112, 114-121; online: http://digital.ncdcr.gov/cdm/ref/collection/p16062coll18/id/96673. [Online description from "North Carolina Periodicals Index," East Carolina University: "Spanish mustangs have roamed the dunes around Corolla for five hundred years. As late as 1920, there were 5,000 of them on the northern Outer Banks, but the population had dwindled to 113 by 2010 on the twelve mile strip of sand north of Corolla. As the beach population and summer tourism increases, the horses are pushed into a tighter, smaller habitat. Graff describes the work of Wesley Stallings, who is in his third year as manager of Corolla's famous wild horses."]

Hall, Lewis Philip. "Wild Horses of the Carolina Plain." *The State: Down Home in North Carolina*, 40:1 (June 1972), 12, 24; online: http://digital.ncdcr.gov/cdm/ref/collection/p16062coll18/id/55232. [Online description from "North Carolina Periodicals Index," East Carolina University: "Wild horses, thought to be descendants of domesticated horses that were abandoned by Spanish colonists in 1526, once roamed the grassy plains between the Great Caw Caw Swamp and the Waccamaw River in Brunswick County. Despite attacks by wolves and panthers, domestication by Indians and European settlers, and a yearly round-up that still occurred as late as 1897, the wild horses endured for approximately 400 years."]

Hart, Kathy. "Meet the Kin: Mr. Bob, Paint, and Owen K. Ballance." *Coastwatch*, 10:5 (May 1983), 3-5. [Online description from "North Carolina Periodicals Index," East Carolina University: "

Hause, Eric M. "Born to Roam." *The State: Down Home in North Carolina*, 64:2 (July 1996), 16-19; online: http://digital.ncdcr.gov/cdm/ref/collection/p16062coll18/id/34029. [Online description from "North Carolina Periodicals Index," East Carolina University: "Although they have roamed the Currituck Banks for centuries, wild horses there are being threatened by development. Concerned individuals, like Rowena Dorman - Corolla Wild Horse Fund director - are working to save the animals."]

Henning, Jeanneatta O. "Bringing Back the 'Wild' Horse Patrol." *The State: Down Home in North Carolina*, 47:5 (October 1979), 1-20; online: http://digital.ncdcr.gov/cdm/ref/collection/p16062coll18/id/58722. [Online description from "North Carolina Periodicals Index," East Carolina University: "Spanish conquistadors who ranged as far north as Chesapeake on the East Coast, left behind some of their horses. A line of these horses still survives today on Ocracoke Island. With the depletion of natural resources, the Park Service has reinstated the horse patrol of earlier days."]

Jenkins, Greg. "Unbridled Alliance." *Wildlife in North Carolina*, 69:2 (February 2005), 4-9; online: http://www.ncwildlife.org/Portals/0/Learning/documents/WINC/Sample_05/sample_feb05.swf. [Online description from "North Carolina Periodicals Index," East Carolina University: "The first family of Ocracoke is not human, but equine. Hart discusses the existence of wild horses on this area of North Carolina's Outer Banks from their Spanish ancestors to the modern herd."]

Kammerer, Roger. "Horse Racing and Breeding." *Greenville Times: Pitt's Past*, (July 24-August 6, 1985), 10. [Online description from "North Carolina Periodicals Index," East Carolina University: "Horseracing and horse breeding have been an important form of revenue and recreation for the county. In the 1700s, most horse breeding took place in the areas of Greenville, Yankee Hall, and Penny Hill. Horseracing became so entrenched in Greenville's culture that the winning horse made the front page of the paper…"]

Lewis, Henry W. "Horse and Horseman in Northampton before 1900." *North Carolina Historical Review*, 51:2 (April 1974), 125-148. [Online description from "North Carolina Periodicals Index," East Carolina University: "Between 1762 and 1900, Northampton County, North Carolina was well known the horses it produced for breeding and for sport. The established breeding families of the area were able to recite with pride the pedigrees of their prized horses."]

McAlpin, Karen. "Colonial Spanish Mustangs." *Tar Heel Junior Historian*, (Fall 2008); online: http://ncpedia.org/symbols/horse.

Peters, Sarah Friday. "A Haven for Horses: Horse Lore Steers Debate over Outer Banks Herds." *Coastwatch*, (May/June 1994), 2-9. [Online description from "North Carolina Periodicals Index," East Carolina University: "The wild horses on North Carolina's Outer Banks have spawned debate as to their true origin. The horses roam a 175-mile stretch from the Virginia line to Carrot Island, and face an uncertain future as development encroaches on their habitat."]

Smith, Donna. "Why Do They Round Up Wild Horses on Shackleford Banks?" *Carolina Country*, 32:7 (July 2000), 20-21. [Online description from "North Carolina Periodicals Index," East Carolina University: "The wild horses on Shackleford Banks, just off the coast of Carteret County, have survived there for 400 years. They are the descendants of horses brought by Spanish explorers. These tough animals have endured hurricanes, summer heat, insects, and a meager diet. Each year they are rounded up to take a count of the herd and to take blood samples to monitor diseases."]

Smith, Jason. "Horsepower Heaven." *Endeavors*, 18:3 (Spring 2002), 26-27; online: http://endeavors.unc.edu/spr2002/fulghum.html. [Online description from "North Carolina Periodicals Index," East Carolina University: "Horses races were once the most popular sporting event in North Carolina. Racing was so popular the legislature passed a law in 1764 curtailing gambling with two exceptions: backgammon and horse racing…"]

Westbrook, Kathy Grant. "Born Free." *Our State: Down Home in North Carolina*, 72:12 (May 2005), 78-80; online: http://digital.ncdcr.gov/cdm/ref/collection/p16062coll18/id/83383. [Online description from "North Carolina

Periodicals Index," East Carolina University: "In Currituck County, between Corolla and the Virginia border, around sixty wild horses roam free. They are the descendants of Spanish mustangs and have survived the fierce weather of the Outer Banks for over 400 years. In 1984, construction of a road has brought tourists and permanent homes to the area. By 1989, eleven horses had been killed along the highway. Westbrook discusses how contact between traffic and horses might be decreased."]

Archaeology of the Revolutionary Period in North Carolina and Tennessee

Babits, L. E. "Report of Investigations of Suspected Revolutionary War Entrenchment, Holly Springs [Wake County], North Carolina." Manuscript, Archaeology Branch, North Carolina Office of Archives and History, Raleigh.

Balko, Sheri L. "Richard Caswell, Lost Governor: Memory in Historical Archaeology." M. A. thesis, East Carolina University, 2009.

Beaman, Thomas E., Jr. "New Bern Archaeology: Digging Up the Past." *Journal of the New Bern Historical Society*, 10:2 (November 1997), 12-19. [Online description from "North Carolina Periodicals Index," East Carolina University: "Excavations at a small construction site near the Harvey Mansion in New Bern reveal items used in the 1700s and early 1800s, including pearl ware porcelain, moca ware, and black glass. The artifacts also reveal dietary practices."]

Brooks, Barbara Lynn; Ann M. Merriman; Madeline P. Spencer; and Mark Wilde-Ramsing. *Bibliography of North Carolina Underwater Archaeology*. Raleigh: Underwater Archaeology Branch, North Carolina Division of Archives and History, 2009; online: http://www.archaeology.ncdcr.gov/ncarch/UAB/pdf%20Files/Bibliography %20Updated %204-09.pdf.

Carnes-McNaughton, Linda F. "The Parity of Privies: Summary Research on Privies in North Carolina." *Historical Archaeology*, 34:1 (2000), 97-110; online: http://sha.org/wp-content/uploads/files/sha/files_2014/22264.pdf.

Collins, Carrie. "Archaeo-Genealogy: Adding Flesh to the Bones." *NCGS News: The Newsletter of the North Carolina Genealogical Society*, 32:1 (Winter 2008), 1-3.

Crass, David Colin, Steven D. Smith, Martha A. Zierden, and Richard D. Brooks. "Introduction: Southern Frontier Communities Viewed through the Archaeological Eye." In David Colin Crass, Steven D. Smith, Martha A. Zierden, and Richard D. Brooks, eds., *The Southern Colonial Backcountry: Interdisciplinary Perspectives on Frontier Communities* (Knoxville: University of Tennessee Press, 1998.)

Elliott, Rita Folse, and Daniel T. Elliott. "Guten Tag Bubba: Germans in the Colonial South." In J. W. Joseph and Martha Zierden, eds., Another's Country: Archaeological and Historical Perspectives on Cultural Interaction in the Southern Colonies (Tuscaloosa: University of Alabama Press, 2002), 79-92.

Foss, Robert W.; Patrick H. Garrow, and Silas D. Hurry. *Archaeological Investigations of the Edenton Snuff and Tobacco Manufacture.* (North Carolina Archaeological Council Publication no. 12) Raleigh: North Carolina Archaeological Council and the Office of State Archaeology, 1979; reprinted 1982; online: http://www.rla.unc.edu/NCAC/Publications/NCAC_12.pdf.

Funk, Thomas. "Archaeological Excavations at the Edenton Tea Party House Lot." Manuscript (1981), Historic Sites Section, Division of Archives and History, North Carolina Department of Cultural Resources, Raleigh.

Funk, Thomas; C. Terry Erlandson, and Jennifer Garlid. "Archaeological Excavations on the Edenton Tea Party House Lot." Manuscript (1979), Historic Sites Section, Division of Archives and History, North Carolina Department of Cultural Resources, Raleigh.

Gray, Anna L. "Return to the Port of Brunswick: An Analysis of Two Eighteenth Century North Carolina Sites." *North Carolina Archaeology*, 46 (October 1997), 69-83; online: http://www.rla.unc.edu/Publications/NCArch/NCA_46%28e-book%29.pdf.

Green, Ann. "ECU Students Uncover Edenton Shipwreck." *Coastwatch*, (Autumn 2001), 16-19. [Online description from "North Carolina Periodicals Index," East Carolina University: "An 18th-century shipwreck, discovered at the mouth of Pembroke Creek in Edenton, provides a teaching site for East Carolina University maritime archaeology students. The ocean-going vessel is approximately 85 feet long and 25 feet wide. Green describes the students' activities and artifacts discovered."]

Hargrove, Thomas H. *A Guide to Research Papers in the Archaeology of North Carolina on File with the Archaeology Branch of the North Carolina Division of Archives and History*. (North Carolina Archaeological Council, Pubilcation, no. 13) Raleigh: North Carolina Archaeological Council and the Office of State Archaeology, 1980; online: http://www.rla.unc.edu/NCAC/Publications/NCAC_13.pdf. *Addendum I* (1981); online: http://www.rla. unc.edu/NCAC/Publications/NCAC_14.pdf. Catherine E. Bollinger. *Addendum II* (1982): online: http://rla. unc.edu/ncac/Publications/ index.html. Susan G. Myers. *Addendum III* (1984); online:

http://www.rla.unc.edu/ NCAC/Publications/NCAC_21.pdf. Susan G. Myers. *Addendum IV* (1985); online: http://www.rla.unc.edu/ NCAC/Publications/NCAC_23.pdf.

Idol, Coy Jacob. "Investigations into the Oldest Standing Structure in North Carolina." M. A. thesis, East Carolina University, 2015; online: http://thescholarship.ecu.edu/handle/10342/5108. [Lane House, Edenton, along with discussion of other eighteenth-century structures in the town and the history of the community]

Nance, Benjamin C. *A Survey of Sites Related to the American Revolution and the War of 1812 in Tennessee.* Nashville: Tennessee Division of Archaeology, 2004.

Neidinger, Adriane Askins. "Archaeological and Historical Site investigation/Thesis of the John's Island Wreck." M. A. thesis, East Carolina University, 2000. [study of the site of the wrecked ship *Holy Heart of Jesus*, which sunk during the American Revolution near John's Island, in Pembroke Creek, close to Edenton, Chowan County]

Norris, Jeannie Faris. "Dendrochronology: A New Look at Old Wood." *North Carolina Preservation*, 83 (Fall 1991), 1. [Online description from "North Carolina Periodicals Index," East Carolina University: "Researchers are using the method of dendrochronology to determine the construction date of the historic Cupola House in Edenton."]

Norris, Jeannie Faris. "Underwater Archaeology Unit Investigates Shipwreck." *Carolina Comments,* 36:4 (July 1988), 88-90. [Online description from "North Carolina Periodicals Index," East Carolina University: "Near the Rose Hill Plantation outside of Wilmington, local divers discovered a shipwreck believed to be from the Revolutionary period. The plantation's age, built in 1730, and colonial-era wine bottles led archaeologists to speculate about the shipwrecks age. Preliminary fieldwork indicates the wreck was from a 65' long, 20' wide, 120 ton sloop."]

Reedy, James R. "Historical and Archaeological Investigations Concerning a Revolutionary War Vessel Burned at Beaufort, North Carolina, in 1778." M. A. thesis, East Carolina University, 1987.

Robinson, Kenneth W. "Port Brunswick and the Colonial Naval Stores Industry: Historical and Archaeological Observations." North Carolina Archaeology, 46 (1997), 51-68; online: http://www.rla.unc.edu/Publications/NCArch/NCA_46.pdf.

Sayers, Daniel O. *A Desolate Place for a Defiant People: The Archaeology of Maroons, Indigenous Americans, and Enslaved Laborers in the Great Dismal Swamp.* Gainesville: University Press of Florida, 2014.

Scott, Bob. "Secrets Dug from a Cornfield." *The State: Down Home in North Carolina*, 37:4 (July 1969), 14-15; online: http://digital.ncdcr.gov/cdm/ref/collection/p16062coll18/id/52742. [Online description from "North Carolina Periodicals Index," East Carolina University: "Archaeological excavations are currently being carried out in a mountain cornfield located near the east fork of the Tuckasegee River in Jackson County. The cornfield is thought to be the site of a Cherokee Village that once may have contained over 300 houses and that was destroyed in a raid in 1780 by John Sevier. Pottery, stone tools and weapons are among the artifacts that have been recovered. Additionally, several home sites have been excavated, revealing circular fireplaces in excellent condition, with ashes still intact."]

Ward, H. Trawick, and R. P. Stephen Davis, Jr. *Time before History: The Archaeology of North Carolina.* Chapel Hill: University of North Carolina Press, 1999. [Publisher's description: "North Carolina's written history begins in the sixteenth century with the voyages of Sir Walter Raleigh and the founding of the ill-fated Lost Colony on Roanoke Island. But there is a deeper, unwritten past that predates the state's recorded history. The region we now know as North Carolina was settled more than 10,000 years ago, but because early inhabitants left no written record, their story must be painstakingly reconstructed from the fragmentary and fragile archaeological record they left behind. *Time before History* is the first comprehensive account of the archaeology of North Carolina. Weaving together a wealth of information gleaned from archaeological excavations and surveys carried out across the state – from the mountains to the coast – it presents a fascinating, readable narrative of the state's native past across a vast sweep of time, from the Paleo-Indian period, when the first immigrants to North America crossed a land bridge that spanned the Bering Strait, through the arrival of European traders and settlers in the sixteenth and seventeenth centuries."]

Wheaton, Thomas R. "Colonial African American Plantation Villages." In J. W. Joseph and Martha Zierden, eds., Another's Country: Archaeological and Historical Perspectives on Cultural Interaction in the Southern Colonies (Tuscaloosa: University of Alabama Press, 2002), 30-44.

Wilde-Ramsing; Wilson Angley; Richard W. Lawrence; and Geoffrey J. Scofield. *The Rose Hill Wreck: Historical and Archaeological Investigations of an Eighteenth Century Vessel at the Colonial River Landing near Wilmington, North Carolina.* Kure Beach: Underwater Archaeology Branch, Division of Archives and History, North Carolina Department of Cultural Resources, 1992; online: http://www.archaeology.ncdcr.gov/ncarch/UAB/pdf%20Files/ Rose%20Hill%20Report.pdf.

Architecture, Historic Landscapes, and Gardens

Beaman, Thomas E., Jr. "The Archaeology of Morley Jeffers Williams and the Restoration of Historic Landscapes at Stratford Hall, Mount Vernon, and Tryon Palace." *North Carolina Historical Review*, 79:3 (July 2002), 47-372.

Bishir, Catherine W. *North Carolina Architecture*. Chapel Hill: University of North Carolina Press, 2005. [Publisher's description: "This award-winning, lavishly illustrated history displays the wide range of North Carolina's architectural heritage, from colonial times to the beginning of World War II. *North Carolina Architecture* addresses the state's grand public and private buildings that have become familiar landmarks, but it also focuses on the quieter beauty of more common structures: farmhouses, barns, urban dwellings, log houses, mills, factories, and churches. These buildings, like the people who created them and who have used them, are central to the character of North Carolina. Now in a convenient new format, this portable edition of *North Carolina Architecture* retains all of the text of the original edition as well as hundreds of halftones by master photographer Tim Buchman. Catherine Bishir's narrative analyzes construction and design techniques and locates the structures in their cultural, political, and historical contexts. This extraordinary history of North Carolina's built world presents a unique and valuable portrait of the state."]

Bishir, Catherine W., and Michael T. Southern. *A Guide to the Historic Architecture of Eastern North Carolina*. Chapel Hill: University of North Carolina Press, 1996. [Publisher's description: "Eastern North Carolina boasts some of the oldest and most distinctive architecture in the state, from colonial churches and antebellum plantation houses to the imperiled lighthouses of the late nineteenth century. The more recent history of this predominantly agricultural region includes landscapes of small farmsteads, country churches, factories, tobacco barns, quiet maritime villages, and market towns. In their guide to this rich and diverse architectural heritage, Catherine Bishir and Michael Southern introduce readers to more than 1,700 buildings in forty-one counties from the coast to Interstate 95. Written for travelers and residents alike, the book emphasizes buildings visible from the road and indicates which sites are open to the public. Featuring more than 400 photographs and 30 maps, the guide is organized by counties, which are grouped geographically. Sections typically begin with the county seat and work outward with concise entries that treat notable buildings, neighborhoods, and communities. The text highlights key architectural features and trends and relates buildings to the local and regional histories they represent. A project of the North Carolina State Historic Preservation Office of the Division of Archives and History, the book reflects more than twenty-five years of fieldwork and research in the agency's statewide architectural survey and National Register of Historic Places programs. Two future volumes will cover Western and Piedmont North Carolina."]

Bishir, Catherine W., and Michael T. Southern. *A Guide to the Historic Architecture of Piedmont North Carolina*. Chapel Hill: University of North Carolina Press for the North Carolina State Historic Preservation Office, 2003. [Publisher's description: "Central North Carolina boasts a rich and varied architectural landscape – from the early plantation houses and farms of its northeastern reaches, to the red brick textile mills and tobacco factories that line railroads across the region, to the glamorous New South skyscrapers of downtown Charlotte. This richly illustrated guide offers a fascinating look at the Piedmont's historic architecture, covering more than 2,000 sites in 34 counties. Highlights include cabins and stone houses dating to the region's early settlement; mill villages and main streets that depict its subsequent industrial and agricultural growth; and twentieth-century landmarks such as Durham's Duke University and Winston-Salem's Reynolds Building. As North Carolina faces massive changes in its economy and landscape, residents and travelers alike will value this unparalleled portrait of an American region, which traces its history and culture through its buildings and communities. A project of the North Carolina State Historic Preservation Office of the Division of Archives and History, this book completes a three-volume series. The project reflects more than twenty-five years of fieldwork and research in the agency's statewide architectural survey and National Register of Historic Places programs. Previous volumes cover the eastern and western portions of the state."]

Bishir, Catherine W.; Charlotte V. Brown; Carl R. Lousnbury; and Ernest H. Wood, III. *Architects and Builders in North Carolina: A History of the Practice of Building*. Chapel Hill: University of North Carolina Press, 1990. [Description: "A chronological history of the architecture of North Carolina, from 1650 to the present. The authors analyze building as a craft, an industry, and a profession, and discuss the people who produced the state's built landscape, from local artisans, contractors, and carpenters to celebrated architects. The illustrations include building plans and photographs of building sites and of the builders themselves."]

Bishir, Catherine W.; Michael T. Southern; and Jennifer F. Martin. *A Guide to the Historic Architecture of Western North Carolina.* Chapel Hill: University of North Carolina Press for the North Carolina State Historic Preservation Office, 1999.

Buck, Tara. "Knowing Your North Carolina Architecture: Georgian Style." *North Carolina Preservation*, 52 (August/September 1984), 14. [Online description from "North Carolina Periodicals Index," East Carolina University: "Based on the stylistic tradition of Wren's English Palladianism popularized in the 17th century, Georgian style architecture became popular in the 18th century in America. In North Carolina, many elements of the Georgian style are combined in imaginative and unconventional ways, producing unique visual effects."]

Butchko, Thoams R. *On the Shores of the Pasquotank: The Architectural Heritage of Elizabeth City and Pasquotank County, North Carolina.* Elizabeth City: Museum of the Albemarle, 1989.

Bynam, Flora Ann L. *Old Salem Garden Guide.* Winston-Salem: Old Salem, Inc., 1979.

Cockshutt, Catherine W. "Architectural Styles in North Carolina." *Tar Heel Junior Historian*, 15:2 (Winter 1976), 21-27. [Online description from "North Carolina Periodicals Index," East Carolina University: "The first installment in a series, Cockshutt, head of the Survey and Planning Branch, looks chronologically at changing architectural style and building techniques within the state. The earliest period between the 18th- and early 19th-century, builders relied heavily on wood and later brick. Structures were solid and well-crafted by skilled workmen from the state's abundant resources."]

Crutchfield, James A. "Pioneer Architecture in Tennessee." *Tennessee Historical Quarterly*, 35:2 (Summer 1976), 162-174.

Ewen, Charles; Patricia M. Samford; and Perry Mathewes. "The Sauthier Maps and the Formal Gardens at Tryon Palace: Myth or Reality?" *North Carolina Historical Review*, 79:3 (July 2002), 326-346.

Fox, Janet. "Gardens of Necessity." *The State: Down Home in North Carolina*, 56:12 (May 1989), 18-21; online: http://digital.ncdcr.gov/cdm/ref/collection/p16062coll18/id/63614. [Online description from "North Carolina Periodicals Index," East Carolina University: "The re-created gardens at the Moravian village of Old Salem in Winston-Salem remind visitors how much settlers depended on their fruits and vegetables, plants for medicines, and food for livestock."]

Herko, Carl. "How Do Our Gardens Grow?" *The Palace,* 1:2 (Winter 2001), 4-5. [Online description from "North Carolina Periodicals Index," East Carolina University: "Herko discusses the gardens and landscape of Tryon Palace in New Bern. Five staff gardeners work with an eye toward history in maintaining the grounds and presenting them as accurately as possible."]

Herzog, Lynda Vestal. "The Early Architecture of New Bern, North Carolina, 1750-1850." Ph. D. dissertation, University of California, Los Angeles, 1977.

Hood, Davyd Foard. *The Architecture of Rowan County, North Carolina: A Catalogue and History of Surviving 18th, 19th, and Early 20th Century Structures.* Salisbury: Historic Salisbury Foundation, 2000.

Hood, Davyd Foard. "Log Construction in Rowan County." *North Carolina Preservationist*, 9 (October 1977), 4-6. [Online description from "North Carolina Periodicals Index," East Carolina University: "This article details the log buildings found in Rowan County in terms of both architectural and cultural history, and preservation."]

Howard, J. Myrick. *Buying Time for Heritage: How to Save and Endandered Historic Property.* Chapel Hill: University of North Carolina Press, 2007. [Publisher's description: "As part of efforts to save endangered properties and encourage downtown and neighborhood revitalization, many of the nation's most successful historic preservation and downtown development organizations have become actively involved in real estate. *Buying Time for Heritage* explains how one nonprofit organization, Preservation North Carolina (PNC), has creatively employed common real estate strategies to save more than 500 endangered historic properties from destruction. As Myrick Howard explains, large sums of money are not always needed, but knowledge and passion are required. Howard provides practical tips on how a neighborhood, downtown, or preservation group can get involved in beneficial real estate work with only modest resources. Inspiring photographs illustrate his premise that a property is rarely 'too far gone' to be renovated, and the rewards of renovation are abundant. Buyers of PNC properties have put them to a multitude of new uses, adding millions of dollars to local tax rolls and creating numerous jobs. Several properties have been adapted into affordable housing, and thousands of acres of open space have been placed under protective covenants, perpetually restricting their development. Rather than face off against developers, PNC itself has become a developer – for community benefit. This volume offers a model for other organizations working to make historic communities thrive."]

Hunter, Priscilla Speed. "It's Beginning to Look at Lot Like Christmas." *The Palace*, 2:1 (Fall 2001), 4-5. [Online description from "North Carolina Periodicals Index," East Carolina University: "Tryon Palace's Christmas celebration encompasses two hundred years of North Carolina Christmas traditions including the African American Jonkonnu parade, historic greenery designs, and candle light tours of a Civil War Encampment."]

Johnston, Frances Benjamin, and Thomas Tileston Waterman. *The Early Architecture of North Carolina: A Pictorial Survey*. Chapel Hill: University of North Carolina Press, 1941; 1947.

Lounsbury, Carl. "The Development of Domestic Architecture in the Albemarle Region." *North Carolina Historical Review*, 54:1 (January 1977), 17-48. [Online description from "North Carolina Periodicals Index," East Carolina University: "This article is a systematic study of the development of vernacular domestic architecture in Gates, Perquimans, and Pasquotank counties in northeastern North Carolina, with a particular focus on the planning and structural character of farmhouses in the period between settlement and the American Civil War."]

Martin, Laura. "History in Flower." *North Carolina Home*, 2:2 (April 1993), 63-67. [Online description from "North Carolina Periodicals Index," East Carolina University: "History surrounds the origin, development and maintenance of Tryon Palace and its gardens in New Bern."]

McCrea, William J. "'History through Timber:' Dendrochronology Dating of Early North Carolina Architecture." *Carolina Comments*, 43:3 (May 1995), 69-74.

North Carolina (Colony and State). Office of State Treasurer. "Capital [*sic*] Buildings, 1767-1913." Manuscript Box 1-21 (MARS ID: 13.10; series), State Archives of North Carolina, Raleigh. [Online catalog description: "Fiscal material relating to the building and maintenance of Tryon Palace in New Bern (1767-1787), the 'Blue House' in Hillsborough (1790-1795), the State House (1792-1831), …"]

Pleasant, Paul. "Gum King, Dan Boone, Buffalo Bill." *The State: Down Home in North Carolina*, 29:19 (February 1962), 11-12, 31. [Online description from "North Carolina Periodicals Index," East Carolina University: "…Dan Boone came to North Carolina in 1750, building a prototype of what became a perpetual cabin building program."]

Rehder, John B. *Tennessee Log Buildings: A Folk Tradition*. Knoxville: University of Tennessee Press, 2012. [Contents: Discovering Folk Architecture; Two Tennessee Hearths: A Settlement History; Log Houses; Log Barns and Outbuildings; Exceptional Log Places; Appendix: Distribution Maps. Includes bibliographical references and index.]

Reimer, Rebecca. "Constructing Nature: The Eighteenth Century Garden and Tryon Palace." *The Palace*, 9:4 (Summer 2009), 4-5. [Online description from "North Carolina Periodicals Index," East Carolina University: "Reimer discusses the preservation of Tryon Palace's famous gardens, including labor intensive archaeological investigations, historical investigations into garden designs and horticulture."]

Sandbeck, Peter B. *The Historic Architecture of New Bern and Craven County, North Carolina*. New Bern: Tryon Palace Commission, 1988.

Spencer, Darrell. *The Gardens of Salem: The Landscape History of a Moravian Town in North Carolina*. Winston-Salem: Old Salem, 1997.

Spruill, Julia Cherry. "Virginia and Carolina Homes before the Revolution." *North Carolina Historical Review*, 12:4 (October 1935), 320-340; online: http://digital.ncdcr.gov/cdm/ref/collection/p16062coll9/id/4207. [Online description from "North Carolina Periodicals Index," East Carolina University: "This article provides details on the arrangement, form, style and diagnostic features of domestic architecture in Virginia and North Carolina in the pre-revolutionary period."]

Turnage, Sheila. "Mystery of the Palace Garden." *Our State: Down Home in North Carolina*, 67:11 (April 2000), 50-53; online: http://digital.ncdcr.gov/cdm/ref/collection/p16062coll18/id/70991. [Online description from "North Carolina Periodicals Index," East Carolina University: "There is a mystery on the Tryon Palace grounds. Where was the palace's original garden? There are three maps of it prepared by Claude Joseph Southier in the 18th-century, but they are contradictory. One, the Miranda Map of 1783, was lost and did not surface until 1991 in Venezuela. Using maps, historical documents, and dirt, an archaeological team from East Carolina University is working to solve the mystery. A 1999 north lawn dig eliminated that area as the possible site. The team will return in the summer of 2000 for a dig on the south lawn."]

Watson, Alan D. "County Buildings and Other Public Structures in Colonial North Carolina." *North Carolina Historical Review*, 82:4 (October 2005), 427-463. [Online description from "North Carolina Periodicals Index," East Carolina University: "This article examines the county buildings of colonial North Carolina and the importance they played with the local community. Courthouses, jails, and warehouses were specially built by counties and were indicative of the county's responsiveness to public needs."]

Wharton, Rachael, and Jeannie Faris Norris. "Tryon Palace Reconstructions of Christmases Past." *Coastwatch*, (November/December 1996), 2-7. [Online description from "North Carolina Periodicals Index," East Carolina University: "Christmas tours of New Bern's Tryon Palace and other historic sites, including the John Wright Stanley House, give visitors a feel for Christmas celebrations from the 1770s onward."]

Wilson, Everett B. *Fifty Early American Towns*. South Brunswick, N. J.: A. S. Barnes, 1966. [Includes Bath, Brunswick, Hillsborough, and Winston-Salem.]

Art, Decorative Art, Fine Art, and Portraiture

Bishir, Catherine W. *Crafting Lives: African American Artisans in New Bern, North Carolina, 1770-1900.* Chapel Hill: University of North Carolina Press, 2013. [Publisher's description: "From the colonial period onward, black artisans in southern cities – thousands of free and enslaved carpenters, coopers, dressmakers, blacksmiths, saddlers, shoemakers, bricklayers, shipwrights, cabinetmakers, tailors, and others – played vital roles in their communities. Yet only a very few black craftspeople have gained popular and scholarly attention. Catherine W. Bishir remedies this oversight by offering an in-depth portrayal of urban African American artisans in the small but important port city of New Bern. In so doing, she highlights the community's often unrecognized importance in the history of nineteenth-century black life. Drawing upon myriad sources, Bishir brings to life men and women who employed their trade skills, sense of purpose, and community relationships to work for liberty and self-sufficiency, to establish and protect their families, and to assume leadership in churches and associations and in New Bern's dynamic political life during and after the Civil War. Focusing on their words and actions, *Crafting Lives* provides a new understanding of urban southern black artisans' unique place in the larger picture of American artisan identity."]

Craig, James H. *The Arts and Crafts in North Carolina, 1699-1840.* Winston-Salem: Museum of Early Southern Decorative Arts, Old Salem, Inc., 1965.

Cutten, George Barton, and Mary Reynolds. *Silversmiths of North Carolina.* Raleigh: State Department of Archives and History, 1948; reprinted: 1984.

Foushee, Ola Marie. *Art in North Carolina: Episodes and Developments, 1585-1970.* Chapel Hill: [s. n.], 1972.

Hewlett, Crockette W.; foreword by Claude Howell. *Two Centuries of Art in New Hanover County.* Durham: Moore Publishing Company, 1976.

MacMillan, Laura. *The North Carolina Portrait Index.* Chapel Hill: University of North Carolina Press, 1963.

Art, Folk Art, Craftsmen, Artisans, Potters, etc.

Hewitt, Mark, and Nancy Sweezy. *The Potter's Eye: Art and Tradition in North Carolina Pottery.* Chapel Hill: University of North Carolina Press, 2005. [Publisher's description: "Classic North Carolina stoneware pots--with their rich textures, monochromatic glazes, and minimal decoration--belong to one of America's most revered stoneware pottery traditions. In a lavishly illustrated celebration of that tradition, Mark Hewitt and Nancy Sweezy trace the history of North Carolina pottery from the nineteenth century to the present day. They demonstrate the intriguing historic and aesthetic relationships that link pots produced in North Carolina to pottery traditions in Europe and Asia, in New England, and in the neighboring state of South Carolina. With hundreds of color photographs highlighting the shapes and surfaces of carefully selected pots, *The Potter's Eye* honors the keen focus vernacular potters bring to their materials, tools, techniques, and history. It is an evocative guide for anyone interested in the art of North Carolina pottery and the aesthetic majesty of this resilient and long-standing tradition."]

Owen, Ray, with Keitt Akin, *et al. Plain Style: The Work of 18th and 19th Century Craftsmen in Moore County, North Carolina: A Catalog.* Southern Pines: Moore County Historical Association, 1993.

Perry, Barbara Stone. *North Carolina Pottery: The Collections of the Mint Museum.* Chapel Hill: University of North Carolina Press, 2004. [Publisher's description: "North Carolina is home to the only continuing pottery tradition in the United States outside the Native American tradition of the Southwest. Noted for this rich tradition from Seagrove to Pisgah, work produced here has earned the attention of collectors, artists, and visitors from around the globe. The collection of The Mint Museums in Charlotte, numbering more than 1,600 pieces, is considered the most comprehensive in any public institution. This volume catalogs more than four hundred individual pieces in the Museums' collection and includes five essays by authorities in the field of ceramics, providing a visual and textual guide to a vibrant living tradition. Illustrated with hundreds of color photographs, the catalog includes descriptive entries on potters and potteries and details about individual pieces. These include traditional utilitarian wares from the eighteenth and nineteenth centuries, transitional or 'fancy wares' made during the first half of the twentieth century, and contemporary objects. Displaying works from the four major pottery-producing areas of the state – Moravian settlements, Seagrove, the Catawba Valley, and the mountains – the collection tells the entire story of the North Carolina pottery tradition. Essays by collector and patron Daisy Wade Bridges, scholar Charles G. Zug III, gallery director Charlotte V. Brown, potter Mark Hewitt, and curator Barbara Stone Perry survey the history and significance of one of the state's best-known art forms."]

Powell, Diana Barbara. "Artisans in the Colonial South: Chowan County, North Carolina, 1714-1776, as a Case Study." M. A. thesis, University of North Carolina at Chapel Hill, 1983.

Zug, Charles G., III. *Turners and Burners: The Folk Potters of North Carolina.* Chapel Hill: University of North Carolina Press, 1990. [Publisher's description: "This richly illustrated portrait of North Carolina's pottery traditions tells the story of the generations of 'turners and burners' whose creations are much admired for their strength and beauty. Perhaps no other state possesses such an active and extensive ceramic heritage, and one that is entirely continuous. This book is an attempt to understand both the past and the present, the now largely vanished world of the folk potter and the continuing achievements of his descendants. It is a tribute that is long overdue. From the middle of the eighteenth century through the second quarter of the twentieth century, folk potters in North Carolina produced thousands of pieces of earthenware and stoneware -- sturdy, simple, indispensable forms like jars and jugs, milk crocks and butter churns, pitchers and dishes, ring jugs and flowerpots. Their wares were familiar and everyday, not innovative or unusual, because they were shaped through generations of use for specific functions. The utilitarian forms were so commonplace and embedded in daily life that few individuals documented the craft. *Turners and Burners* is the first book to chronicle these pottery traditions, with close attention to distinct regional and temporal patterns and the major families involved. It explores in detail the traditional technologies used, from the foot-powered treadle wheel to the wood-fired groundhog kiln."]

Commemorations of the American Revolution in North Carolina and Tennessee

Barbee, Kathleen Elizabeth. "The Bicentennial: A Sociological View." Honors Essay, Department of Sociology, University of North Carolina at Chapel Hill, 1978.

Fries, Adelaide L. "An Early Fourth of July Celebration." *North Carolina Booklet*, 15:2 (October 1915), 122-127. [1783, in North Carolina]

Green, Fletcher M. "Listen to the Eagle Scream: One Hundred Years of the Fourth of July in North Carolina, 1776-1876." *North Carolina Historical Review*, 31:3 (July 1954), 295-320.

Griffin, Frances. *A Day of Thanksgiving, Salem, North Carolina, July 4, 1783: An Account of the First Fourth of July Observance by Legislative Enactment in America.* Winston-Salem: Old Salem, Inc., 1966.

Holmes, Pat. "Rebirth of the N. C. Brigade." *The State: Down Home in North Carolina*, 40:18 (April 1973), 9-13; online: http://digital.ncdcr.gov/cdm/ref/collection/p16062coll18/id/55888. [Online description from "North Carolina Periodicals Index," East Carolina University: "Originally organized in September of 1775 under the command of Col. James Moore, North Carolina's First Regiment of Continentals was reactivated on September 18, 1968 by Governor Bob Scott as part of North Carolina's observance of the National Bicentennial Celebration. Members of the modern First Regiment, which is commanded by Col. B. F. Jarrell of Burlington, take part in reenactments and drills staged as preliminaries to the actual start of the Bicentennial Celebration in 1976."]

How to Bicentennial: A Planning Guide. North Carolina Bicentennial Committee, Department of Cultural Resources, 1976.

North Carolina American Revolution Bicentennial Committee. "[Records]." Manuscript [MARS ID: 60], State Archives of North Carolina, Raleigh. [For a full description of the Archives' holdings for this commission, see either the MARS online catalog or the following publication: *Guide to Research Materials in the North Carolina State Archives: State Agency Records* (Raleigh: Department of Cultural Resources, Division of Archives and History, Archives and Records Section, 1995), 216-220.

Rauschenberg, Bradford L. "Discovery: A Documented Bow Bowl Made for Halifax-Lodge, North Carolina." *Journal of Early Southern Decorative Arts*, 1:1 (May 1975), 3-13; online: https://archive.org/details/journalofearlyso11muse. [Online description from "North Carolina Periodicals Index," East Carolina University: "This article presents information on a Masonic punch bowl made by the Bow factory in London for 'Halifax-Lodge/North-Carolina' that was part of a 1767 order for four Bow China bowls. This example is the first time a documented reference has been found specifying an order of Bow porcelain decorated especially for the American market. Archival and archaeological information on the bowl and its owners along with a diagnostic analysis of the bowl as an example of Bow porcelain are included."]

Rights, Douglas L. "First Observance of the Fourth." *The State: A Weekly Survey of North Carolina*, 19:4 (June 1951), 3, 18; online: http://digital.ncdcr.gov/cdm/ref/collection/p16062coll18/id/27191. [Online description from "North Carolina Periodicals Index," East Carolina University: "Among its many other 'firsts,' North Carolina can also claim the distinction of being the first state in the Union to observe the significance of Independence Day."]

Crowds and Mobs in North Carolina and the American Revolution

Lee, Wayne E.; foreword by Stanley Harrold and Randall M. Miller. *Crowds and Soldiers in Revolutionary North Carolina: The Culture of Violence in Riot and War.* Gainesville: University Press of Florida, 2001. [Contents: "Riotous disorderly persons;" "To fight the air:" The Careful Riots of the Regulators; The Road to Alamance; Colonial Ways of War: Tradition and Development; "A Fair Fight:" The Revolutionary Militias and the Struggle for Virtue, 1775-1776; Civil Consolidation: The "Peaceful" Years, 1777-1779; "The Law of Retaliation:" The War of the Militias, 1780-1782.]

Economic and Business History

Brown, David E. *North Carolina: New Directions for an Old Land: An Illustrated History of Tar Heel Enterprise.* Northridge, Calif.: Windsor Publications, 1985.

Combs, Edwin L., III. "Trading in Lubberland: Maritime Commerce in Colonial North Carolina." *North Carolina Historical Review*, 80:1 (January 2003), 1-27. [Online description from "North Carolina Periodicals Index," East Carolina University: "This article looks at the unique problems encountered by commercial interests in coastal North Carolina during the 18th century utilizing data contained in 1768-1772 British customs returns. This data was overlooked by historian Charles Christopher Crittenden in his 1936 article, 'Commerce of North Carolina, 1763-1789,' leading Combs to challenge Crittendens conclusions and place his focus on the delicate balance between maritime trade, mercantilism, and economic development."]

Crittenden, Charles C. *The Commerce of North Carolina, 1763-1789.* New Haven: Yale University Press, 1936.

Egnal, Marc. "The Economic Development of the Thirteen Continental Colonies, 1720-1775." *William and Mary Quarterly*, 3rd series, 37:1 (January 1980), 165-175.

Egnal, Marc, and Joseph A. Ernst. "An Economic Interpretation of the American Revolution." *William and Mary Quarterly*, 3rd series, 29:1 (January 1972), 3-32.

Haywood, C. Robert. "The Mind of the North Carolina Advocates of Mercantilism." *North Carolina Historical Review*, 33:2 (April 1956), 139-165.

John Hogg Company. "John Hogg Company, 1767-1812." Manscurpt AB.58 (MARS ID: 2958; record group), State Archives of North Carolina, Raleigh. [Online catalog description: "(Adie and Hogg, Chapel Hill, and Hillsborough; Hogg and Adam, Hillsborough; Hogg and Meng, Fayetteville; Huske and Hogg, Wilmington; Hogg and Campbell, Wilmington and Charleston, S. C.; and John Hogg, Hillsborough, Raleigh, and Wilmington.). General merchandise and commission merchants. Letterbook, daybooks, cash books, ledgers, and invoice books. See also A.B. 277 and A.B. 404."]

Keith, Alice Barnwell. "John Gray and Thomas Blount, Merchants, 1783-1800." *North Carolina Historical Review*, 25:2 (April 1948), 194-205.

Moody, Robert Earle; Crittenden, Charles C. "The Letter-book of Mills and Hicks." *North Carolina Historical Review*, 14:1 (1937), 39-83. [Trading with the firm of Champion and Dickenson, London, 1781-84]

Morgan, David T., and William J. Schmidt. "From Economic Sanctions to Political Separation: The North Carolina Delegation to the Continental Congress, 1774-1776." *North Carolina Historical Review*, 52:3 (July 1975), 215-234.

Morris, Francis Grave, and Phyllis Mary Morris. "Economic Conditions in North Carolina about 1780." *North Carolina Historical Review*,

(Part 1: Landholding) 16:2 (April 1939), 107-133 [Online description from "North Carolina Periodicals Index," East Carolina University: "This is the first article in a series on Revolutionary period economic conditions in North Carolina. This installment focuses on landholding, taxes, assessments, and related legislation. The article includes reprints of period tax and property forms, as well as tables logging various kinds of tax and landowner data."]

(Part 2: Ownership of Town Lots, Slaves, and Cattle) 16:2 (July 1939), 296-327; online: http://digital.ncdcr.gov/cdm/ref/collection/ p16062coll9/id/4207. [Online description from "North Carolina Periodicals Index," East Carolina University: "A look at the contributions of North Carolina delegates William Hooper, Joseph Hewes, and Richard Caswell to the Continental Congress. In 1775, John Penn replaced Caswell and eventually rose to political fame in North Carolina. The delegation made no lasting contributions to the Congress but did vote for independence despite an earlier reluctance;" and, "This is the second article in a series on Revolutionary period economic conditions in North Carolina. This installment focuses on those who owned town lots as opposed to those who owned and worked tracts of land for natural resources, as were discussed in the previous article … The article contains a number of tables and maps that address slave-holding, town lot ownership, free and slave population statistics, and cattle owner statistics.]

Parramore, Thomas C. "The Merchants Foote." *North Carolina Historical Review*, 46:4 (October 1969), 365-376. [Online description from "North Carolina Periodicals Index," East Carolina University: "This article finds a new source for material relating to the history of North Carolina in New England and New York mariner records who were involved in trade with North Carolina. Looking primarily at two sets of documents relating to the Foote family of Guilford, Connecticut, details of trade, nautical routes, and coastal towns are included as well as information on the Foote family and their business."]

Platt, Virginia Bever. "Tar, Slaves, and New England Rum: The Trade of Aaron Lopez of Newport, Rhode Island, with Colonial North Carolina." *North Carolina Historical Review,* 48:1 (January 1971), 1-22. [Online description from "North Carolina Periodicals Index," East Carolina University: "This article seeks to build upon previous historians' work on the history of commercial shipping activities in North Carolina including the naval stores trade, provisions trade, lumber products shipping, and tobacco exportation. The author examines the Aaron Lopez papers who was a Rhode Island merchant actively involved in dispatching at least 37 voyages to North Carolina between 1761 and 1775."]

Salstrom, Paul. *Appalachia's Path to Dependency: Rethinking a Region's Economic History, 1730-1940.* Lexington: University Press of Kentucky, 1994.

Sellers, Charles G., Jr. "Private Profits and British Colonial Policy: The Speculations of Henry McCulloh." *William and Mary Quarterly,* 3rd series, 8:4 (October 1951), 535-551.

Stover, John F. "French-American Trade during the Confederation, 1781-1789." *North Carolina Historical Review*, 35:4 (October 1958), 399-414; online: http://digital.ncdcr.gov/cdm/ref/collection/p16062coll9/id/4207. [Online description from "North Carolina Periodicals Index," East Carolina University: "French commerce and military aid to the colonies helped to fill the trade vacuum left by British commerce loss. French exports to America reached a high level in the 1780s. Trade directed toward North Carolina was extensive because larger American ports were blockaded or occupied by the British during the Revolution. Additionally, naval stores, North Carolina's major export, figured into the French-American trade, although only slightly."]

Surratt, Jerry L. "The Moravian as Businessman: Gottlieb Schober of Salem." *North Carolina Historical Review*, 60:1 (January 1983), 1-23. [Online description from "North Carolina Periodicals Index," East Carolina University: "An examination of the founding of the Moravian towns of Salem and Bethabara and the development of their businesses and economic systems. A particular focus is placed on the life and career of Gottlieb Schober, a Moravian who personified the successful community small businessman."]

Townsend, William Blair, 1723-1778. "William Blair Townsend Letter and Receipt Books, 1743-1805, bulk 1744-1777." Manuscript, Historical Collections – Business Manuscripts Mss:766 1743-1805 T752, Baker Library, Harvard University, Cambridge, Mass. [Online catalog description: The collection consists of two volumes, which date from 1743 to 1805, spanning his whole career as a merchant. Volume one is a letter book containing Townsend's business correspondence from November 23, 1743 to December 12, 1774. Most of the letters were written to American (many in North Carolina) and British (predominately in London) merchants. His earliest letters document his efforts to establish himself as a trader. Over time his letters turn to illustrate the common problems faced by many merchants: damaged goods, overpriced goods, embargos, and high freight costs. Particularly enlightening are his comments on the challenges of doing business throughout the French and Indian War and the years leading up to the American Revolution. He most frequently corresponded with London merchants Champion & Hayley, Lane & Booth, Lane Son & Fraser, Harrison & Ansley, and Leeds merchant Samuel Elam. In addition he frequently corresponded with Eliakim Palmer, colonial agent and merchant in London, as well as Dr. Walley Chauncy of North Carolina. He dealt in a wide variety of goods including molasses, rum, tar, medicines, pitch, saddles, tallow, hides, skins, pickled beef and pork, and wine. The letters also document Townsend's involvement in the slave trade through his occasional purchases of slaves."]

Virginia. General Assembly. House of Delegates. Speaker. "Report of the Commissioners of Virginia and North Carolina, 1778 March 3." Manuscript accession no. 36912, and on misc. microfilm reel 5372, Library of Virginia, Richmond. [Online catalog description: "Contains the report of the Commissioners of Virginia & North Carolina from a meeting held at Fredericksburg on 3 March 1778 for the purpose of regulating and ascertaining the price of labor, manufactures, internal produce, and commodities imported from foreign ports with the exception of military stores. Its purpose was also to regulate the charges of innholders. The commissioners propose that the price of salt be limited by law so as to never exceed ten dollars a bushel. They also recommend that the states import on account all such foreign articles as may be thought necessary for their respective quota of troops. Lastly, they recommend that the regulation of the innholders be continued with the justices of the county courts. They suggest an increase in the penalties for violation of the present laws. The

Commissioners consisted of Fielding Lewis, Charles Dick, & James Mercer from Virginia and Jacob Blount & James Coor from North Carolina. Fielding Lewis was named chairman. This report was referred to the Committee as a Whole on the State of the Commonwealth on 27 May 1778."]

Watson, Harry L. "'The Common Rights of Mankind:' Subsistence, Shad, and Commerce in the Early Republican South." *Journal of American History*, 83:1 (June 1996), 13-43.

Zornow, William F. "North Carolina Tariff Policies, 1775-1789." *North Carolina Historical Review*, 32:2 (April 1955), 151-164.

Education, Reading, Literature, Books, Libraries, Printing, etc.

Breytspraak, Charlotte and Jack. "Historical Profile: James Davis." *Journal of the New Bern Historical Society*, 1:1 (May 1988), 27-30. [first printer in New Bern and his support of the Revolution.]

Brown, Hugh Victor. *A History of Education of Negroes in North Carolina*. Raleigh: Irving Swain Press, 1961.

Bullock, Henry Allen. *A History of Negro Education in the South, from 1619 to the Present.* Cambridge: Harvard University Press, 1967.

Cometti, Elizabeth. "Notes and Documents: Some Early Best Sellers in Piedmont North Carolina." *Journal of Southern History*, 16:3 (August 1950), 324-337. [Guilford, Orange, Rockingham, Randolph, Durham, Person, Caswell, Chatham and Alamance counties portion of the Piedmont]

Connor, R. D. W. "The Genesis of Higher Education in North Carolina." *North Carolina Historical Review*, 28:1 (January 1951), 1-14.

Cumfer, Cynthia Dee. "'The Idea of Mankind Is So Various:' An Intellectual History of Tennessee, 1768-1810." Ph. D. dissertation, University of California, Los Angeles, 2001.

Davis, Richard Beale. *A Colonial Southern Bookshelf: Reading in the Eighteenth Century*. Athens: University of Georgia Press, 1979.

Eubanks, Georgann. *Literary Trails of Eastern North Carolina: A Guidebook*. Chapel Hill: University of North Carolina Press, 2013. [Publisher's description: "This concluding volume of the Literary Trails of North Carolina trilogy takes readers into an ancient land of pale sand, dense forests, and expansive bays, through towns older than our country and rich in cultural traditions. Here, writers reveal lives long tied to the land and regularly troubled by storms and tell tales of hardship, hard work, and freedom. Eighteen tours lead readers from Raleigh to the Dismal Swamp, the Outer Banks, and across the Sandhills as they explore the region's connections to over 250 writers of fiction, poetry, plays, and creative nonfiction. Along the way, Georgann Eubanks brings to life the state's rich literary heritage as she explores these writers' connection to place and reveals the region's vibrant local culture. Excerpts invite readers into the authors' worlds, and web links offer resources for further exploration. Featured authors include A. R. Ammons, Gerald Barrax, Charles Chesnutt, Clyde Edgerton, Philip Gerard, Kaye Gibbons, Harriet Jacobs, Jill McCorkle, Michael Parker, and Bland Simpson. The third volume focuses on the eastern portion of the state. Georgann Eubanks has organized the manuscript into three "trails": 'The Southeastern Corridor' from Raleigh to Wilmington, 'The Middle Corridor' from eastern Wake County to Carteret County, and 'The Northeastern Corridor' from Wake Forest to the northern Outer Banks. Each trail is further broken down into several tours of half-day segments. Each tour features a map detailing how to get from site to site, brief biographies of the writers included in the trail, passages from the writers that refer to the places along the trail, reading lists, and web addresses linking to further information about sites and authors."]

Eubanks, Georgann. *Literary Trails of the North Carolina Mountains: A Guidebook.* Chapel Hill: University of North Carolina Press, 2007. [Publisher's description: "The Mountains volume brings together more than 170 writers from the past and present, including Sequoyah, Elizabeth Spencer, Fred Chappell, Charles Frazier, Kathryn Stripling Byer, Robert Morgan, William Bartram, Gail Godwin, O. Henry, Thomas Wolfe, F. Scott Fitzgerald, Anne Tyler, Lillian Jackson Braun, Nina Simone, and Romulus Linney. Each tour provides information about the libraries, museums, colleges, bookstores, and other venues open to the public where writers regularly present their work or are represented in exhibits, events, performances, and festivals."]

Eubanks, Georgann. *Literary Trails of the North Carolina Piedmont*. Chapel Hill: University of North Carolina Press, 2010. [Publisher's description: "In the Piedmont volume featured authors include O. Henry, Doris Betts, Alex Haley, Langston Hughes, Zora Neale Hurston, John Hart, Betty Smith, Edward R. Murrow, Patricia Cornwell, Carson McCullers, Maya Angelou, Lee Smith, Reynolds Price, and David Sedaris."]

Fries, Adelaide L. *Historical Sketch of the Salem Female Academy.* Salem, N. C.: Crist & Keehn, Printers, 1902. [The Salem Female Academy in Winston-Salem founded in 1772 by Moravians.]

Haywood, Marshall Delancey. "In Spite of a King…" *The State: Down Home in North Carolina*, 23:25 (May 1956), 17-18, 25-26; online: http://digital.ncdcr.gov/cdm/ref/collection/p16062coll18/id/7031. [Online description from "North Carolina Periodicals Index," East Carolina University: "On January 10, 1771, the Assembly passed an act to incorporate an institution of higher learning to be called Queens College which will be located in Charlotte."]

Howard, Hannah Elizabeth. "Crafting Public Opinion: Printers and Publications in Revolutionary North Carolina, 1764-1776." M. A. thesis, University of North Carolina at Charlotte, 2010; Ph. D. dissertation, University of North Carolina at Charlotte, 2011. [Online catalog description: "This study examines colonial North Carolina's printers and surviving publications during the decade prior to the American Revolution. There has been very little analysis of North Carolina's printing business, and even less attention paid to the influence of its newspapers, pamphlets, and broadsides on public opinion and the events leading to the Revolution. These tracts confirm that North Carolinians saw their rebellion not as a break from British tradition, but as a desperate attempt to preserve their perception of British ideology and the rights. The decision of many colonists to revolt was not made suddenly, but as the culmination of increasing frustration at Parliament's failure to recognize their rights as British subjects. There still remained significant divisions throughout the province, on both the future of their relationship with Britain and their own arguments on unequal representation in the colonial assembly. But even as they struggled internally, their publications demonstrate an evolution of belief that included public contributions from all corners of North Carolina."]

Hubbell, Jay B[roadus]. *The South in American Literature, 1607-1900.* Durham: Duke University Press, 1954.

Kelly, James. "The Bicentennial and Tennessee History." *Tennessee Historical Quarterly*, 36:2 (Summer 1977), 224-236.

Kerr, Mary Hinton Duke. "Sarah DeRippe Falkener (1755-24 Feb. 1819)." In William S. Powell, ed., *Dictionary of North Carolina Biography, vol. 2: D-G* (Chapel Hill: University of North Carolina Press, 1979-1996), 178-179. [Falkener came from England to America in 1787 and later became "Lady Principal" of the Falkener Seminary for Young Ladies.]

King, Martha Joanne. "Making an Impression: Women Printers in the Southern Colonies in the Revolutionary Era." Ph. D. dissertation, College of William and Mary, 1992.

Knight, Edgar Wallace. "An Educational Practice in Colonial North Carolina." *North Carolina Booklet*, 16:1 (July 1916), 39-51.

Lawrence, R. C. "Schools of a Former Day." *The State: A Weekly Survey of North Carolina*, 6:52 (May 1939), 7, 18; online: http://digital.ncdcr.gov/cdm/ref/collection/p16062coll18/id/34979. [Online description from "North Carolina Periodicals Index," East Carolina University: "Before the development of public education in the state, private schools were the main source of education and these were generally for male students. Prior to 1825, 177 academies had been charted by the Legislature. All counties had at least one, except Ashe, Columbus, and Person. Lawrence comments on a few of the more well-known ones, Caldwell Academy, the Bingham School, military schools, and schools for girls."]

Lewis, Johanna Miller. "A Social and Architectural History of the Girls' Boarding School Building at Salem, North Carolina." *North Carolina Historical Review*, 66:2 (April 1989), 126-148. [This school for little girls opened by 1772 by Sister Elisabeth Osterlein]

Marshall, Roger Powell. "A Mythical Mayflower Competition: North Carolina Literature in the Half-Century Following the Revolution." *North Carolina Historical Review*, 27:2 (April 1940), 178-192.

McMurtrie, Douglas C. *Eighteenth Century North Carolina Imprints, 1749-1800.* Chapel Hill: University of North Carolina Press, 1938.

McMurtrie, Douglas Crawford. "A Bibliography of North Carolina Imprints, 1761-1800, I." *North Carolina Historical Review,* 13:1 (January 1936), 47-88; [part] II, 13:2 (April 1936), 143-166; [part] III, 13:3 (July 1936), 219-254.

Noble, M. C. S. *A History of the Public Schools in North Carolina.* Chapel Hill: University of North Carolina Press, 1930.

North Carolina (State). General Assembly. "[Document dated:] April 21, 1783: House Bill to Form Boards of Trustees for Martin Academy and Morgan Academy in the District of Morgan." Manuscript; General Assembly Record Group; Session Records, April-May 1783; Unidentified Amendments, Senate Bills, House Bills, Box 1 (MARS ID: 66.8.30.34; folder), State Archives of North Carolina, Raleigh. [Online catalog description: "Bill names trustees to the boards of Martin Academy in Washington County and Morgan Academy in Burke County."]

North Carolina (State). Office of State Treasurer. "Institutions, 1780-1937." Manuscript (MARS ID: 13.22), State Archives of North Carolina, Raleigh. [Includes: "The earliest records dating back to 1780 are sparse and concern the University of North Carolina." Source: *Guide to Research Materials in the North Carolina State Archives: State Agency Records* (Raleigh: Department of Cultural Resources, Division of Archives and History, Archives and Records Section, 1995), 666.]

O'Steen, Neal. "Pioneer Education in the Tennessee Country." *Tennessee Historical Quarterly*, 35:2 (Summer 1976), 199-219.

Powell, William S. "Eighteenth-Century North Carolina Imprints: A Revision and Supplement to McMurtrie." *North Carolina Historical Review*, 35:1 (January 1958), 50-73; online: http://digital.ncdcr.gov/cdm/ref/collection/p16062coll9/id/4207. [Online description from "North Carolina Periodicals Index," East Carolina University: "Powell provides an amended list of Douglas C. McMurtrie's 1938 bibliography of 18th century North Carolina imprints. The bibliography lists books printed in North Carolina in the 18th century, along with books which no longer survive, but are thought to be a product of North Carolina."]

Powell, William S. *North Carolina Fiction, 1734-1957: An Annotated Bibliography*. Chapel Hill: University of North Carolina Press, 1958.

Powell, William S. "Patrons of the Press: Subscription Book Purchases in North Carolina, 1733-1850." *North Carolina Historical Review*, 34:4 (October 1962), 423-499.

Purcell, James S. "Literary Culture in North Carolina before 1820." Ph. D. dissertation, Duke University, 1950.

Rehder, Barbara Beeland. "Development of Libraries in the Lower Cape Fear." *Lower Cape Fear Historical Society Bulletin*, 7:2 (February 1964), 3-7. [Online description from "North Carolina Periodicals Index," East Carolina University: "Rehder divides her discussion of early North Carolina libraries into three types. First to be established were parochial-public libraries. These were books that were sent to ministers by England's Society for the Propagation of the Gospel. Eventually these books met the needs of the whole community and became public property. Second were private libraries of individual citizens. Wills, inventories, existing collections, and a few books in the hands of descendants help to identify the books' original owners. Third was the Cape Fear Library. A group of area gentlemen donated a fee each year for the purchase of books, newspapers, and periodicals, and the acquisition of a reading room to hold them. This library lasted until 1781, when British soldiers and North Carolina Militia soldiers stole much of the material."]

Renfer, Betty Dishong. "Learning in Colonial Carolina." *Tar Heel Junior Historian*, 37:1 (Fall 1997), 1-3. [Online description from "North Carolina Periodicals Index," East Carolina University: "During colonial times education for the majority of the state's people was largely informal and accomplished through observing family members and the community. Those who would not become farmers could be apprenticed. Only the wealthy could afford to send their children to schools."]

Ring, Betty. "Salem Female Academy." *Antiques*, 106:3 (September 1974), 434-442. [Provides a brief, illustrated history of this school for girls established in 1772 by the Moravians of Salem, North Carolina.]

Rubin, Louis D., Jr., and J. A. Leo Lemay, eds. *A Bibliographical Guide to the Study of Southern Literature, with an Appendix Containing Sixty-Eight Additional Writers: The Colonial South*. Baton Rouge: Louisiana State University Press, 1969.

Sadler, Lynn Veach. *New Light on Eighteenth-Century North Carolina Literary Sources: Proceedings of the Tryon Palace Symposium, New Bern, North Carolina, September 22, 1989*. Fayetteville: Methodist College Press, 1989.

Salem Tells Its Story of the Education of American Girls. Winston-Salem: Salem College, 1946?

Samford, C. Clement, and John M. Hemphill II. *Bookbinding in Colonial Virginia*. Williamsburg: Colonial Williamsburg; Charlottesville: Distributed by University Press of Virginia, 1966.

Smith, Charles Lee. *The History of Education in North Carolina*. (Bureau of Education, Contributions to American History, no. 3) Washington, D. C.: Government Printing Office, 1888.

Smith, Charles Lee. "Schools and Education in Colonial Times." *North Carolina Booklet*, 8:4 (April 1909), 316-324. [Online description from "North Carolina Periodicals Index," East Carolina University: "This article chronicles the establishment of schools and implementation of education in North Carolina between the late 17th century and the mid-18th century."]

Sparrow, W. Keats. "Early North Carolina Literature: A Syllabus for Serious Readers." *North Carolina Literary Review*, 1:1 (Summer 1992), 138-145. [Online description from "North Carolina Periodicals Index," East Carolina University: "North Carolina boasts the longest literary heritage in English of any state, a distinguished heritage that begins before the first colonial narratives. Sparrow presents a syllabus of NC works that constitute this heritage."]

Spearman, R. Alan. "The Johnston Library at Hayes Plantation: The Character of the Eighteenth-Century Library and Its Evolution in the First Half of the Nineteenth Century." M. A. thesis, University of North Carolina, 1988.

Stem, Thad, Jr. "Absent with Leave, or How Musty Files Came Alive." *North Carolina Historical Review*, 51:2 (April 1974), 170-182. [Online description from "North Carolina Periodicals Index," East Carolina University: "This article discusses the history of printing in North Carolina beginning with the first public printer in 1749 through the many newspapers and editors of the 20th century. Despite being one of the last of the original colonies to get a printing press, the history of newspapers in North Carolina is an exciting one as told through the stories of many local papers and their editors."]

Stevenson, George, Jr. "Paper Mills in Eighteenth- and Nineteenth-Century North Carolina." *Carolina Comments*, 56:2 (April 2008), 70-75; online: http://www.ncpublications.com/comments/ccapr08.pdf.

Stokes, Durward T. "Adam Boyd, Publisher, Preacher, and Patriot." *North Carolina Historical Review*, 49:1 (January 1972), 1-21. [Online description from "North Carolina Periodicals Index," East Carolina University: "This article examines the multi-faceted career of Adam Boyd. During his life, Boyd was a minister, official of the court, member of the Committee of Safety, chaplain in the Continental Army, member of the North Carolina Society for the Cincinnati, and founder of the 'Cape Fear Mercury' one of North Carolina's earliest newspaper."]

Thornton, Mary Lindsay. "Public Printing in North Carolina, 1749-1815." *North Carolina Historical Review,* 21:3 (July 1944), 181-202; online: http://digital.ncdcr.gov/cdm/ref/collection/p16062coll9/id/4207. [Online description from "North Carolina Periodicals Index," East Carolina University: "The need for public printing within the state emerged from the necessity of distributing laws and other state documents for the consistent execution of the law. Stressing the need for printing official documents began with Governor Burrington in 1730 and would remain in legislative debates until 1749 when the first public printing occurred on October 17. The article compiles information concerning what documents were being printed, how many, and from which branches of government publications focused."]

Valentine, Patrick M. "Libraries and Print Culture in Early North Carolina." *North Carolina Historical Review*, 82:3 (July 2005), 293-325. [Online description from "North Carolina Periodicals Index," East Carolina University: "This article discusses the economic, geographic, social, and political factors that influenced literacy, the availability of printed materials, and the creation of libraries in North Carolina during the 17th and 18th centuries."]

Walser, Richard. *Literary North Carolina: A Brief Survey*. Raleigh: State Department of Archives and History, 1970.

Watson, Alan D. "The Role of Printing in Eighteenth-Century North Carolina." *Carolina Comments*, 48:3 (May 2000), 75-83.

Watson, Helen R. "The Books They Left: Some 'Liberies' in Edgecombe County, 1733-1783." *North Carolina Historical Review*, 48:3 (July 1971), 245-257. [Online description from "North Carolina Periodicals Index," East Carolina University: "An examination of the estates records of Edgecombe County during its first fifty years, through October court, 1783, reveals the type and size of private libraries."]

Weeks, Stephen B. "Libraries and Literature in North Carolina in the Eighteenth Century." *Annual Report of the American Historical Association for the Year 1895* (Washington, D. C.: The Association, 1896), 171-267.

Weeks, Stephen B. "The Pre-Revolutionary Printers of North Carolina: Davis, Steuart, and Boyd. *North Carolina Booklet*, 15:2 (October 1915), 104-121. [James Davis, Andres Steuart, and Adam Boyd.]

Foodways, Cooking, Beverages, Wine, Liquors, Homelife, Customs

Aldrich, April. *A History of Honey in Georgia and the Carolinas.* Charleston, S. C.: American Palate, 2015.

Cecelski, David. "What the Governor Grew." *Coastwatch*, (Winter 1998), 18-21. [Online description from "North Carolina Periodicals Index," East Carolina University: "The kitchen garden at Tryon Palace measured 16,200 square feet and was enclosed by an eight-foot-high wall. It provided the governor foods of American, European, and African origin, including squash and okra. Some, like salsify, are not common today."]

Crump, Nancy Carter. "Foodways of the Albemarle Region: Indulgent Nature Makes Up for Every Want." *Journal of Early Southern Decorative Arts,* 19:1 (May 1993), 1-36; online: https://archive.org/details/journalofearlyso1911993muse. [Online description from "North Carolina Periodicals Index," East Carolina University: "This article examines the early foodways of the Albemarle Region of North Carolina and the contributions made to Southern cuisine by the Native Americans and settlers of the region."]

Davis, Nancy. "Before the Fish Stick and Captain's Platter…" *Coastwatch*, 10:6 (June/July 1983), 4-5. [Online description from "North Carolina Periodicals Index," East Carolina University: "Boiled skate, baked turtle, and roasted eel may make some squeamish now, but these recipes were popular in 18th-century North Carolina. Joyce Taylor, NC Sea Grant's marine advisory agent at the NCSU Seafood lab is studying colonial recipes of underutilized species like eel, while archaeologists examine Native American fishing camps to understand early seafood consumption."]

Griffin, Frances. *Cooking in Old Salem*. Williamsburg: Williamsburg Publishing Company, 1981.

Hall, Robert L. "Africa and the American South: Culinary Connections." *Southern Quarterly*, 44:2 (Winter 2007), 19-52.

Hodge, Alan. "A Taste for History." *Our State: Down Home in North Carolina*, 75:1 (June 2007), 92-94, 96, 98-100; online: http://digital.ncdcr.gov/cdm/ref/collection/p16062coll18/id/89512. [Online description from "North Carolina Periodicals Index," East Carolina University: "The Historical Cooking Guild of the Catawba Valley base of operations is the James K. Polk Memorial near Pineville, and they demonstrate cooking techniques and foods of the 18th- and 19th-centuries. One of the group's main goals is having the food taste like it would have over 200 years ago. To add authenticity to their demonstrations, Cooking Guild members dress in period costumes. They also train interpreters at other historic sites. When doing a demonstration, guild members use only those fruits and vegetables that would have been in season and available to colonial cooks."]

Moss, Kay K. "Your Food Has Ancestors Too." *Tar Heel Junior Historian*, (Spring 2007); online: http://ncpedia.org/culture/food/history-of-food.

Patterson, Nancy. "How to Cook, Colonial Style." *New East*, 4:3 (June 1976), 19-22, 49. [Online description from "North Carolina Periodicals Index," East Carolina University: "Patterson takes the reader back to a colonial kitchen among the tryvets, spyettes, chauldrons, and gibcrokes, where cooks prepared 'possum laced with potatoes, Hopping John, and a frothy drink called Syllabub.' Readers will find the kitchen and utensils quite different from those of today."]

Reed, John Shelton, and Dale Volberg Reed, with William McKinney. *Holy Smoke: The Big Book of North Carolina Barbecue*. Chapel Hill: University of North Carolina Press, 2008.

Rogers, Amy. "North Carolina: A Culinary Crossroads." *Tar Heel Junior Historian*, (Spring 2007); online: http://ncpedia.org/culture/food/foodways.

Samford, Patricia M. "Discovering What Native North Carolinians Ate." *Tar Heel Junior Historian*, (Spring 2007); online with the title "American Indian Food" http://ncpedia.org/culture/food/american-indian-food.

Thompson, Michael D. "Everything But the Squeal: Pork as Culture in Eastern North Carolina." *North Carolina Historical Review*, 82:4 (October 2005), 464-498. [Online description from "North Carolina Periodicals Index," East Carolina University: "This article examines the importance of pork to the diet of residents of eastern North Carolina. Beginning in colonial North Carolina and continuing to current times, pork continues to be a tradition of the eastern North Carolina."]

Wilson, Eddie W. "The Gourd in Southern History." *North Carolina Historical Review*, 26:3 (July 1949), 300-305.

Wise, Steven M. *An American Trilogy: Death, Slavery, and Dominion on the Banks of the Cape Fear River*. New York: Da Capo Press, 2009. [Publisher's summary: "The Cape Fear River runs through Bladen County, North Carolina, population 33,000. On its western bank, in the town of Tar Heel, sits the largest slaughterhouse in the world. Deep below the slaughterhouse, one may find the arrowheads of Siouan-speaking peoples who roamed there for a millennium. Nearer the surface is evidence of slaves who labored there for a century. And now, the slaughterhouse kills the population of Bladen County, in hogs, every day. In this remarkable account, Wise traces the history of today's deadly harvest. From the colonies to the slave trade, from the artificial conception and unrecorded death of one single pig to the surreal science of the pork industry—whose workers continue the centuries of oppression—he unveils a portrait of this nation through the lives of its most vulnerable. His explorations ultimately lead to hope from a most unlikely source: the Baptist clergy, a voice in this wilderness proclaiming a new view of creation."]

Foodways, Cooking, Beverages, Wine, Liquors, Homelife, Customs – Taverns/Ordinaries/Inns

Clayton, LaReine Warden, Jane Gray Buchanan, ed. Stories of Early Inns and Taverns of the East Tennessee Country [endpapers map: "Routes of Migration in the Old East Tennessee Country, 1760-1860"]. Nashville: National Society of the Colonial Dames of America in the State of Tennessee, 1995.

Denny, Zeb. "Inns, Taverns, and Ordinaries." *The State: Down Home in North Carolina*, 50:5 (October 1982), 16-18; online: http://digital.ncdcr.gov/cdm/ref/collection/p16062coll18/id/59874. [Online description from "North Carolina Periodicals Index," East Carolina University: "In 1770, Captain John Collet's map of North Carolina showed a string of ordinaries from the Chowan River to the Yadkin River. An ordinary was a commercial building serving to satiate travelers during colonial times. By 1800, the term 'ordinary' was replaced by 'tavern,' to mean a place catering to social drinking, and later by 'inn' as taverns began to provide overnight accommodations. Many businesses that were run by farmers, however, remained taverns due to a lack of space for lodging. Taverns sprang up every few miles in the towns of the colonial period and thrived until the train became the popular means of transportation. The Halifax ordinary, 'Sign of the Thistle,' is where both the Halifax Resolves and the North Carolina Constitution were written over tankards of ale. Minstrels visiting the area came to entertain clientele. The building was remodeled and later called Eagle Hotel. The Marquis de Lafayette spent the night there on February 27, 1825. Both Andrew Jackson and James K. Polk visited another tavern, the York Tavern, in Rockford, North Carolina. By the end of the 1800s, the railroad had laid tracks in North Carolina and most of the taverns fell into disuse."]

Dunaway, Stewart E. *Caswell County, North Carolina, Ordinary (Tavern) Bonds, 1771-1815.* Hillsborough: North Carolina Historical Books, 2009. [Note: While not specifically concerning the Revolution, these sources can be used in tandem with land records and other documents to help locate places of residence, occupations, geographical features, and place names.]

Dunaway, Stewart E. *Chowan County, North Carolina, Tavern (Ordinary) Bonds, 1738-1799.* Hillsborough: North Carolina Historical Books, 2013. [Note: While not specifically concerning the Revolution, these sources can be used in tandem with land records and other documents to help locate places of residence, occupations, geographical features, and place names.]

Dunaway, Stewart E. *Granville County, North Carolina, Tavern (Ordinary) Bonds (1748-1838).* Hillsborough: North Carolina Historical Books, 2012. [Note: While not specifically concerning the Revolution, these sources can be used in tandem with land records and other documents to help locate places of residence, occupations, geographical features, and place names.]

Dunaway, Stewart E. *North Carolina Tavern (Ordinary) Bonds.* Hillsborough: North Carolina Historical Books, 2009- . [Contents: Vol. 1. 1755-1874: Orange, Rowan, Chatham, Surry, Bute, Randloph [*sic*], Carteret, Onslow, Hyde, Mecklenburg, and Guilford Co. v. 2. 1742-1867: Duplin, Franklin, Johnson [*sic*], Nash, Northampton, Pasquotank, Perquimans, Tyrrell, Wayne and Wilkes Co. v. 3. 1795-1859: Stokes and Warren County.] [Note: While not specifically concerning the Revolution, these sources can be used in tandem with land records and other documents to help locate places of residence, occupations, geographical features, and place names.]

Frye, Jason. "Town Center." *Our State: Down Home in North Carolina*, 78:11 (April 2011), 40-46, 48; online: http://digital.ncdcr.gov/cdm/ref/collection/p16062coll18/id/96430. [Online description from "North Carolina Periodicals Index," East Carolina University: "In many colonial towns, taverns were the only public building other than the courthouse. Using the Eagle Tavern, located in historic Halifax, Frye describes the many activities and services that a tavern could provide to citizens and travelers."]

Schwartz, Stuart. "Dudley's, an Important Gathering Place in Halifax." *Tar Heel Junior Historian*, 11:1 (September 1971), 10-11. [Online description from "North Carolina Periodicals Index," East Carolina University: "Archaeological excavations revealed the foundation of Dudley's tavern and artifacts from the era just prior to and during the American Revolution. Taverns served as an important meeting place for revolutionary colonists. Archaeologists from the Division of Historic Sites and Museums excavated tableware, architectural elements, and, of course, material culture related to alcohol."]

Thorp, Daniel B. "Taverns and Communities: The Case of Rowan County, North Carolina." In David Colin Crass, Steven D. Smith, Martha A. Zierden, and Richard D. Brooks, *The Southern Colonial Backcountry: Interdisciplinary Perspectives on Frontier Communities* (Knoxville: University of Tennessee Press, 1998), 76-86.

Thorp, Daniel B. "Taverns and Tavern Culture on the Southern Colonial Frontier: Rowan County, North Carolina, 1753-1776." *Journal of Southern History*, 62:4 (November 1996), 661-688.

Tucker, Harry Z. "Blackburne's Old Inn." The State: A Weekly Survey of North Carolina, 6:5 (July 1938), 3, 22; online: http://digital.ncdcr.gov/cdm/ref/collection/p16062coll18/id/38054. [Online description from "North Carolina Periodicals Index," East Carolina University: "This historic old building in Stokes County, built by Ambrose Blackburne and located on the highway between Walnut Cove and Danbury, has had an interesting history since it was built in the days before the Revolutionary War."]

Watson, Alan D. "Ordinaries in Colonial Eastern North Carolina." *North Carolina Historical Review* 45:1 (January 1968), 67-83.

Watson, Alan D. "The Extraordinary Ordinary." *Tar Heel Junior Historian*, 51:2 (Spring 2012), 20-23. [Online description from "North Carolina Periodicals Index," East Carolina University: "Among the most important businesses in early America was the ordinary, also called a tavern, a public house of entertainment, or an inn."]

Whitener, Daniel Jay. *Prohibition in North Carolina, 1715-1945.* Chapel Hill: University of North Carolina Press, 1946

Wilson, Eddie W. "Early Taverns in Carolina." *The State: A Weekly Survey of North Carolina*, 15:47 (April 1948), 11; online: http://digital.ncdcr.gov/cdm/ref/collection/p16062coll18/id/22190. [Online description from "North Carolina Periodicals Index," East Carolina University: "In addition to providing accommodations for the traveler, early taverns also were usually a local social center, where people gathered for various pastimes and to discuss the topics of the day."]

Furniture, Furnishings, and Furnituremakers

Beckerdite, Luke. "City Meets the Country: The Work of Peter Eddleman, Cabinetmaker." *Journal of Early Southern Decorative Arts*, 6:1 (May 1980), 58-73. [Online description from "North Carolina Periodicals Index," East Carolina University: "This article examines the furniture typology of the Catawba Valley of North Carolina through the works of cabinetmaker Peter Eddleman. The Catawba Valley groups of furniture were quite similar, influenced by the Delaware Valley where the families of Catawba Valley craftsmen originally came from."]

Beckerdite, Luke. "The Development of Regional Style in the Catawba River Valley: A Further Look." *Journal of Early Southern Decorative Arts*, 7:2 (November 1981), 31-48; online: https://archive.org/details/journalofearlyso721981muse. [Online description from "North Carolina Periodicals Index," East Carolina University: "This article examines the development of regional furniture styles in the Catawaba Valley of the North Carolina Piedmont through an anonymous group of furniture called the 'fluted pilaster group.' The Catawaba Valley style of furniture is heavily influenced by Delaware Valley settlers who moved to Catawaba Valley during the last half of the 18th century."]

Bivins, John, Jr. "Baroque Elements in North Carolina Moravian Furniture." *Journal of Early Southern Decorative Arts*, 2:1 (May 1976), 38-63; online: https://archive.org/details/journalofearlyso21muse. [Online description from "North Carolina Periodicals Index," East Carolina University: "A study of furniture produced in Wachovia, the Moravian settlement in North Carolina, focusing on the closely-knit stylistic trends – particularly baroque design elements – exhibited by decorative arts produced in within a cohesive societal sub-unit."]

Bivins, John, Jr. "Furniture of the North Carolina Roanoke River Basin in the Collection of Historic Hope Foundation." *Journal of Early Southern Decorative Arts*, 22:1 (Summer 1996), 1-90.

Comstock, Helen. "Furniture of Virginia, North Carolina, Georgia, and Kentucky." *Antiques*, 61:1 (January 1952), 40-100. [Covers 1640-1820.]

Couch, Dale L. "Four Mecklenburg County, North Carolina Chairs: An Examination of Style and Technology." *Journal of Early Southern Decorative Arts*, 14:1 (May 1988), 1-18; online: https://ia800502.us.archive.org/28/items/journalofearlyso1411988muse/journalofearlyso1411988muse.pdf. [Online description from "North Carolina Periodicals Index," East Carolina University: "This article examines the chair-making tradition of Mecklenburg County through the analysis of four chairs from the late 18th century. By analyzing the chairs, the tradition can be traced back to prior forms before the artisans migrated to North Carolina, which affected the style and technology of construction."]

Dahill, Betty. "The Sharrock Family: A Newly Discovered School of Cabinetmakers." *Journal of Early Southern Decorative Arts*, 2:2 (November 1976), 37-51; online: https://archive.org/details/journalofearlyso22muse. [Online description from "North Carolina Periodicals Index," East Carolina University: "An examination of the diagnostic features of furniture produced by members of the Sharrock family, a family of skilled cabinetmakers from Virginia and northeastern North Carolina. Particular attention is given to pieces by Thomas Sharrock and his son, George." George Sharrock (1765-1802); Thomas Sharrock (1741-1802).]

Horton, Frank L. "Carved Furniture of the Albemarle: A Tie with Architecture." *Journal of Early Southern Decorative Arts*, 1:1 (May 1975), 14-20; online: https://archive.org/details/journalofearlyso11muse. [Online description from "North Carolina Periodicals Index," East Carolina University: "This article examines pieces of unsigned carved furniture made in the Albemarle region of North Carolina that are associated with the architectural carving of the Blair-Pollock house of Edenton, circa 1766. Diagnostic analysis of the pieces, referred to as the 'Edenton Stair-Hall Group,' and of similar motifs and features found in the Blair-Pollock architectural carvings are compared and linked where appropriate."]

Lewis, Michael H. "American Vernacular Furniture and the North Carolina Backcountry." *Journal of Early Southern Decorative Arts*, 20:2 (November 1994), 1-37; online: https://archive.org/details/journalofearlyso2021994muse. [Online description from "North Carolina Periodicals Index," East Carolina University: "This article examines the origins of a particular walnut chest-on-frame, belonging to the Museum of Early Southern Decorative Arts, from the Piedmont of North Carolina as well as the study of Carolina backcountry furniture."]

Gambling and Lotteries in North Carolina

Blackburn, Charles, Jr. "Courting Dame Fortune." *Our State: Down Home in North Carolina*, 74:1 (June 2006), 28-31; online: http://digital.ncdcr.gov/cdm/ref/collection/p16062coll18/id/86492. [Online description from "North Carolina Periodicals Index," East Carolina University: "Two-and-a-half centuries ago, colonial settlers in North Carolina held legislatively authorized lotteries. The first held in 1759, raised 450 English pounds for construction of two Anglican churches. After the Revolutionary War, lotteries became a popular method for funding projects of all types. High-priority projects were internal improvements including waterways, bridges, canals, roads, and railroads. The University of North Carolina built South Building with money raised through 1801 legislation. Various county projects included a marine hospital, a poorhouse in Brunswick County, and a water system for Fayetteville in Cumberland County."]

Smith, Jason. "Horsepower Heaven." *Endeavors*, 18:3 (Spring 2002), 26-27; online: http://endeavors.unc.edu/spr2002/fulghum.html. [Online description from "North Carolina Periodicals Index," East Carolina University: "Horses races were once the most popular sporting event in North Carolina. Racing was so popular the legislature passed a law in 1764 curtailing gambling with two exceptions: backgammon and horse racing…"]

Watson, Alan D. "A Closer Look at Lotteries in Early North Carolina." *The State: Down Home in North Carolina*, 55:1 (June 1987), 7, 25; online: http://digital.ncdcr.gov/cdm/ref/collection/p16062coll18/id/62493. [Online description from "North Carolina Periodicals Index," East Carolina University: "Although the 1995 General Assembly defeated a lottery bill, colonial settlers held legislatively authorized ones. The first was held in 1759 to raise money for church construction. Others supported community needs and supplemented tax revenues."]

Watson, Alan D. "The Lottery in Early North Carolina." *North Carolina Historical Review*, 69:4 (October 1992), 365-387.

Ghosts, Superstitions, Folklore

Barefoot, Daniel W. *Piedmont Phantoms.* Winston-Salem: J. F. Blair, 2002.

Barefoot, Daniel W. *Seaside Spectres: North Carolina's Haunted Hundred.* Winston-Salem: John F. Blair, 2002. [Publisher's summary: North Carolina's Haunted Hundred, Barefoot's three-volume series, is a sampler of the diverse supernatural history of the Tar Heel State. One story is drawn from each of the state's hundred counties. You'll find tales of ghosts, witches, demons, spook lights, unidentified flying objects, unexplained phenomena, and more. Many of the stories have never before been widely circulated in print. *Seaside Spectres* contains 33 tales from the state's coastal region. In 'The Cursed Town,' the Beaufort County story, you'll read about the curse laid on Bath by an eighteenth-century preacher – a curse from which the town has never recovered. In 'Terrors of the Swamp,' the Camden County story, you'll learn of unexplained happenings in the Great Dismal Swamp – mysterious lights, a ghostly haunting from the American Revolution, and an awful creature called the Dismal Swamp Freak. In 'The Fraternity of Death,' the New Hanover County tale, you'll meet the nineteenth-century cult whose members mocked the Last Supper and died under mysterious circumstances soon afterward, inspiring a story by Robert Louis Stephenson." In volume 3, *Haints of the Hills*, "You'll want to travel the lonely stretch of road in Avery County where locals have witnessed the spirit of Captain Robert Sevier, the seven-foot-tall hero of the American Revolution, as laid out in 'The Long Trek Home'."]

Brewster, Paul G.; Archer Taylor; B. J. Whiting; George P. Wilson; and Stith Thompson. *The Frank C. Brown Collection of North Carolina Folklore, Vol. 1: Games and Rhymes, Beliefs and Customs, Riddles, Proverbs, Speech, Tales and Legends*. Durham: Duke University Press, 1952.

Cobb, Collier. "Greek, Roman, and Arabian Survivals on the North Carolina Coast: A Preliminary Sketch." *North Carolina Booklet*, 15:4 (April 1916), 218-226.

Haas, Mary R. "Southeastern Indian Folklore." *Journal of American Folkore*, 60:238 (October-December 1947), 403-406.

Hand, Wayland D. *North Carolina Folkore: Popular Beliefs and Superstitions 1-4783. The Frank C. Brown Collection, Vol. 6.* Durham: Duke University Press, 1961.

Harden, John. *The Devil's Tramping Ground and Other North Carolina Mystery Stories*. Chapel Hill: University of North Carolina Press, 1980. [Publisher's description: "From the first colonization at Roanoke Island, the bizarre and inexplicable have shrouded the Tar Heel State. From history and legend, John Harden records ominous events that have shaped or colored state history."]

Harden, John. *Tar Heel Ghosts*. Chapel Hill: University of North Carolina Press, 1980. [Publisher's description: "North Carolina's ghost stories have infinite variety. There are mountainous ghosts and seafaring ghosts; colonial ghosts and modern ghosts; gentle ghosts and roistering ghosts; delicate lady ghosts and fishwife ghosts; home ghosts and ghosts that just want to be noticed. Mysterious signs and symbols appear – small black crosses, galloping white horses, strangely moving lights, floating veils, lifelike apparitions, skulls, dripping blood, and 'things that go bump in the night.' At least one North Carolina ghost got himself into a court record, and other ghostly phenomena have attracted scientific investigation. These stories have a marked realistic North Carolina flavor. The reader finds mountain cabins and antebellum mansions, Indian trails, water wheels, river steamboats, railroad trains, slave labor on plantations, revenuers and stills in the mountains, a burial in St. James Churchyard in Wilmington, Winston-Salem before the days of Winston, Raleigh in the 1860s, Fayetteville during World War II, and even a new suburb haunted by old spooks."]

Holk, N. C. "Folk-Custom and Folk-Belief in North Carolina." *Journal of American Folklore*, 5:17 (April-June 1892), 112-120.
Johnson, F. Roy. *Legends and Myths of North Carolina's Roanoke-Chowan Area*. Murfreesboro: Johnson Publishing Company, 1966.
Johnson, F. Roy. *Tales from Old Carolina: Traditional and Historical Sketches of the Area between and about the Chowan River and Great Dismal Swamp*. Murfreesboro: Johnson Publishing Company, 1965.
Johnson, F. Roy. *Witches and Demons in History and Folklore*. Murfreesboro: Johnson Publishing Company, 1969.
Milnes, Gerald C. *Signs, Cures & Witchery: German Appalachian Folklore*. Knoxville: University of Tennessee Press, 2007.
Montgomery, G. T. *Ghosts of Old Salem, North Carolina*. Charleston, S. C.: Haunted American, 2014.Roberts, Nancy; Bruce Roberts, and LeGette Blythe. *Ghosts of the Carolinas*. Columbia: University of South Carolina Press, 1988.
Sprunt, James. *A Colonial Apparition: A Story of the Cape Fear*. Wilmington: Harper's Steamboat Line, 1909.
Starbuck, Richard W.; artwork by Lu Newman. *Ghosts of Salem and Other Tales*. Winston-Salem: Moravian Archives, 2002.
Walser, Richard, and Bill Ballard. *North Carolina Legends*. Raleigh: North Carolina Dept. of Cultural Resources, Division of Archives and History, 1980.
Whedbee, Charles Harry. *Legends of the Outer Banks and Tar Heel Tidewater*. Winston-Salem: J. F. Blair, 1966.
White, Newman Ivey; Henry M. Belden, *et al.*, assoc. eds. *The Frank C. Brown Collection of North Carolina Folklore: The Folklore of North Carolina, Collected by Dr. Frank C. Brown during the Years 1912-1943, in Colloboration with the North Carolina Folklore Society*. Durham: Duke University Press, 1952-1964. [Contents: v. 1. Games and Rhymes. Beliefs and Customs. Riddles. Proverbs. Speech. Tales and Legends; v. 2. Folk Ballads from North Carolina; v. 3. Folk Songs from North Carolina; v. 4. The Music of the Ballads; v. 5. The Music of the Folk Songs; v. 6-7. Popular Beliefs and Superstitions from North Carolina.]

Heraldry and Coats of Arms

Hinton, Mary Hilliard. "Heraldry and Its Usage in the Colony of North Carolina." *North Carolina Booklet*, 14:1 (July 1914), 3-27; online: http://digital.ncdcr.gov/cdm/ref/collection/p249901coll37/id/14180. [Online description from "North Carolina Periodicals Index," East Carolina University: "The art of heraldry served many public uses in colonial North Carolina. Several early North Carolina families also inherited the right to bear a coat of arms."]

Holidays in North Carolina

Brodie, Belinda Black. "Remnants of a German Past: Two Family Holiday Customs in Davidson County." *North Carolina Folklore Journal*, 37:2 (Summer-Fall 1990), 81-87. [Online description from "North Carolina Periodicals Index," East Carolina University: "Davidson County is witness to the survival of holiday rituals from a dark Germanic past into the 20th-century involving Easter and Christmas holidays with visits from Belsnickel and the building of the Easter nest."]
Bynum, Flora Ann L. *The Christmas Heritage of Old Salem*. Williamsburg, Va.: Williamsburg Publishing Company, 1983.
Carter, Spencer. "Colonial Christmas." *Carolina Country*, 7:12 (December 1975), 6-7. [Online description from "North Carolina Periodicals Index," East Carolina University: "Carter describes Christmas celebrations in North Carolina in the decades before the American Revolution. Christmas Day was considered a holy day, but the Christmas season, which ran from December 16 to January 6, was a time for social activities. The emphasis was on hunting, horse racing, games, courting, Christmas balls, family gatherings, and caroling. It was a season for leisure. Wassailing and burning the Yule log were traditions that early settlers brought from England, and mistletoe would have been one of the more popular decorations."]
Griffin, Frances. *A Day of Thanksgiving, Salem, North Carolina, July 4, 1783: An Account of the First Fourth of July Observance by Legislative Enactment in America*. Winston-Salem: Old Salem, Inc., 1966.
Hicklin, J. B. "Christmas in the South." *The State: A Weekly Survey of North Carolina*, 4:30 (December 1936), 1, 22; online: http://digital.ncdcr.gov/cdm/ref/collection/p16062coll18/id/10741. [Online description from "North Carolina Periodicals Index," East Carolina University: "Traditions and customs of the Old South, half-forgotten in the building of the new South, bob to the surface during the Christmas season. Firecrackers are common, Yule logs burn, and cowpeas and hog jowl are popular dishes. While the origin of these customs remains obscure, some trace them directly to the restricted life of early great plantations and poor communication

facilities, which made them communities within themselves. Customs brought by the pioneer settlers of Europe were also preserved and altered to meet conditions of the area."]

Jenkins, Emyl, ed. *The Book of American Traditions: Stories, Customs, and Rites of Passage to Celebrate Our Cultural Heritage*. New York: Crown Publishers, 1996.

Kammerer, Roger. "Old Christmas in North Carolina." *Greenville Times/Pitt's Past*, (December 18-January 7, 1991), 16-17. [Online description from "North Carolina Periodicals Index," East Carolina University: "Old Christmas, known as Welsh Night, occurs 12 days after Christmas. As of 1991, Rodanthe residents still practiced Old Christmas on the Outer Banks with Old Buck, not Santa, bringing gifts to people. Other North Carolina Christmas traditions include lighting the Yule log, decorating houses and lawns, and hanging stockings. In Edenton, Washington, New Bern, and Greenville, African Americans dressed in costumes and went to houses in wagons blowing horns and singing. If residents gave them something, they would have good luck throughout the rest of the year."]

Moose, Debbie. *Southern Holidays: A Savor of the South Cookbook*. Chapel Hill: University of North Carolina Press, 2014.

Nelson, Kay Shaw. "A Moravian Christmas: At Old Salem and Bethlehem, the Holidays Are Marked by the Warmth of the Hospitality and the Delectability of the Food." *Americana*, 7:5 (November/December 1979), 54-61, 92.

Norris, Jeannie Faris. "Christmas and Jonkonnu at Tryon Palace." *The Palace*, 7:1 (Fall 2006), 4. [Online description from "North Carolina Periodicals Index," East Carolina University: "A unique Christmas tradition at Tryon Palace is Jonkonnu. A blend of English, African, and Caribbean holiday and spiritual traditions brought to North Carolina by slaves, Jonkonnu celebrations at Tryon include parades and songs."]

Observance of Special Days. (Department of Public Instruction Publication no. 319) Raleigh: North Carolina State Superintendent of Public Instruction, 1959.

Parsons, Elsie Clews. "Tales from Guilford County, North Carolina." *Journal of American Folk-Lore*, 30:116 (April-June 1917), 168-200. [from page 169: "Between the Bahama Islands and the Carolinas there is an historical connection which may account in part for the number of tales they have, I find, in common. During the period of the Revolutionary War a number of Tories known as United Empire Loyalists migrated from the Carolinas to the Bahamas; and they took with them, of course, their household slaves. In connection with this migration, it was of interest to find that what is still current belief in the Bahamas serves as a tale in North Carolina. I refer to the magical beliefs embodied in Nos. 28, 34, 35."]

Perkins, George. "A Medieval Carol Survival: 'The Fox and the Goose'." *Journal of American Folkore*, 74:293 (July-September 1961), 235-244.

Robbins, Walter L. "Christmas Shooting Rounds in America and Their Backcountry." *Journal of American Folkore*, 86:339 (January-March 1973), 48-52.

Sharpe, Bill. "African American Holiday Celebration Returns to New Bern." *Carolina Comments*, 49:2 (March 2001), 25-26. [Online description from "North Carolina Periodicals Index," East Carolina University: "From the slave period until 1898, African Americans in Eastern North Carolina observed a Christmastime custom called Jonkonnu. The practice originated in Jamaica and spread to North Carolina, which was the only state where it was observed. Jonkonnu is a unique blend of West African and English customs. In 2000, the Christmas tradition was revived during New Bern's annual Holiday Candlelight Tours."]

Smith, Pam. "Christmas in Edenton: A Revolutionary Holiday." *Coastwatch*, (Holiday 2001); online: https://ncseagrant.ncsu.edu/coastwatch/previous-issues/2001-2/holiday-2001-table-of-contents/christmas-in-edenton/. [Publisher's summary: "Edenton residents are proud of the town's historic past. They keep the holiday spirit alive with a traditional candlelight tour of historic homes, complete with candles glowing in the window and a church decorated with greenery."]

Sowers, Betty. "Christmas Customs from the Germans." *North Carolina Folklore Journal*, 20:4 (November 1972), 171-173. [Online description from "North Carolina Periodicals Index," East Carolina University: "When German immigrants came to the Piedmont in the 18th-century, they brought with them their beliefs and customs, their ways and traditions, their lore and legends, and many of the customs associated with one of the most prominent religious holidays – Christmas. Many of the most beloved Christmas symbols are a part of the heritage received from the Germans."]

Spalding, Sara K., and Vina H. Farmer. "Two Centuries of American Christmas History." *The Palace*, 6:1 (February 2005), 4-5. [Online description from "North Carolina Periodicals Index," East Carolina University: "This article details the changes in Christmas traditions in North Carolina from the colonial period to the Civil War."]

Wharton, Rachael, and Jennie Faris Norris. "Tryon Palace Reconstructions of Christmases Past." *Coastwatch*, (November/December 1996), 2-7. [Online description from "North Carolina Periodicals Index," East Carolina

University: "Christmas tours of New Bern's Tryon Palace and other historic sites, including the John Wright Stanley House, give visitors a feel for Christmas celebrations from the 1770s onward."]

Iron Works in North Carolina

Butler, Lindley S. "Speedwell Furnace: The Ironworks on Troublesome Creek." Manuscript Cp553.3 B98s, North Carolina Collection, Louis Round Wilson Special Collections Library, University of North Carolina at Chapel Hill.

Butler, Lindley S. "Troublesome Creek Ironworks." In William S. Powell, ed.; Jay Mazzocchi, assoc. ed., *Encyclopedia of North Carolina* (Chapel Hill: University of North Carolina Press in association with the University of North Carolina Library, 2006), 1135-1136. [modern Rockingham County; active during the Revolution]

Cappon, Lester J. "Iron-Making: A Forgotten Industry of North Carolina." *North Carolina Historical Review*, 9:4 (October 1932), 331-348; online: http://digital.ncdcr.gov/cdm/ref/collection/p16062coll9/id/4207. [Online description from "North Carolina Periodicals Index," East Carolina University: "The Piedmont boasted a manufacturing strength in cotton and textile mills but during the late 18th- and early 19th- centuries iron smelting was a nascent industry. The earliest furnace was built by 1770 in Orange County and showed greatest promise in Lincoln County. A brief history of both discovering raw ore and iron manufacturing is presented."]

"Chatham Furnace Records, 1777." Manuscript 3398-z, Southern Historical Collection, Louis Round Wilson Special Collections Library, University of North Carolina, Chapel Hill; online finding aid available at http://www2.lib.unc.edu/mss/inv/c/Chatham_Furnace.html. [Online finding aid description: "The collection contains detailed letters, 25 March and 31 March 1777, and reports from James Milles, manager of the iron furnace on Tick Creek, Chatham County, N.C., for the Revolutionary government of North Carolina. The reports are directed to Archibald Maclaine (1728-1790), a state commissioner."]

Cowan, Thomas. "William Hill and the Aera Ironworks." *Journal of Early Southern Decorative Arts*, 13:2 (November 1987), 1-32; online: https://ia800308.us.archive.org/26/items/journalofearlyso1321987muse/journalofearlyso1321987muse.pdf. [Online description from "North Carolina Periodicals Index," East Carolina University: "This article discusses the iron furnaces in the Piedmont of North Carolina and South Carolina during the late 18th and early 19th centuries, with particular emphasis on the facilities owned by William Hill. While describing Hill's South Carolina Aera Ironworks, the article also examines the iron mining, smelting, and distribution practices of the region."]

"Dedication Ceremonies Set Sunday at Troublesome Creek." *Eden News* (August 9, 1972); Cb553.3 E22d, two copies in the in the North Carolina Collection, Louis Round Wilson Special Collections Library, University of North Carolina at Chapel Hill.

Fowler, Malcolm. "Iron Mining in Upper Cape Fear." *The State: A Weekly Survey of North Carolina*, 8:45 (April 1941), 8-9, 20; online: http://digital.ncdcr.gov/cdm/ref/collection/p16062coll18/id/39417; 8:47 (April 1941), 8-9, 20; online: http://digital.ncdcr.gov/cdm/ref/collection/p16062coll18/id/39355; [Online description from "North Carolina Periodicals Index," East Carolina University: "Iron mining was a one time a quite sizable industry in the Upper Cape Fear River region. There is a large body of rich ore particularly in Chatham County where numerous mills and blast furnaces took advantage of the many tributaries of the Cape Fear River."]

Gudger, E. W. "Early Iron Smelting." *The State: A Weekly Survey of North Carolina*, 8:39 (February 1941), 35; online: http://digital.ncdcr.gov/cdm/ref/collection/p16062coll18/id/39157. [Online description from "North Carolina Periodicals Index," East Carolina University: "Iron works have long been ubiquitous to the state of North Carolina. They were probably built before 1730 near coastal villages and have been in operation since before the American Revolution. The manufacture of iron in North Carolina includes the ancient works in the now forgotten town of Averasboro, and operations on the upper tributaries of the Dan, Cape Fear, and Yadkin Rivers."]

McNulty, Joe. "Troublesome Creek Revisited: Site of Historic Ironworks Is Marked with a Plaque." *Greensboro Daily News*, (August 14, 1792); Cb553.3 M15, two copies in the North Carolina Collection, Louis Round Wilson Special Collections Library, University of North Carolina at Chapel Hill.

Philadelphia, March 31, 1781: Intelligence from the Southward: Head-Quarters, Iron Works, North Carolina, March 10, 1781. Philadelphia: Printed by David C. Claypoole, 1781.

Labor and Servitude in North Carolina

Moore, Louis T. "Servants and Slaves in Colonial Carolina." *The State: A Weekly Survey of North Carolina*, 13:32 (January 1946), 6, 18; online:. [Online description from "North Carolina Periodicals Index," East Carolina

University: "In addition to Africans, there were also Indian and white slaves, and there were many rules and regulations in force with respect to their treatment."]

Winslow, Raymond A., Jr. "North Carolina Apprentice Indentures through 1850." *North Carolina Genealogical Society Journal*, 13:3 (August 1987), 164-171.

Music, Dancing, Theater, Sports, and Other Social Activities

Bryan, Sarah; Beverly Patterson; and Michelle Lanier. *African American Music Tales of Eastern North Carolina*. Chapel Hill: University of North Carolina Press, 2013. [Publisher's description: "Thelonius Monk, Billy Taylor, and Maceo Parker – famous jazz artists who have shared the unique sounds of North Carolina with the world – are but a few of the dynamic African American artists from eastern North Carolina featured in The African American Music Trails of Eastern North Carolina. This first-of-its-kind travel guide will take you on a fascinating journey to music venues, events, and museums that illuminate the lives of the musicians and reveal the deep ties between music and community. Interviews with more than 90 artists open doors to a world of music, especially jazz, rhythm and blues, funk, gospel and church music, blues, rap, marching band music, and beach music. New and historical photographs enliven the narrative, and maps and travel information help you plan your trip. Included is a CD with 17 recordings performed by some of the region's outstanding artists."]

Camus, Raoul F. *Military Music of the American Revolution*. Chapel Hill: University of North Carolina Press, 1976.

Clitherall, James. "James Clitherall Diary, 1776." Manuscript 159-z, Southern Historical Collection, Louis Round Wilson Special Collections Library, University of North Carolina, Chapel Hill; online finding aid available at http://www2.lib.unc.edu/mss/inv/c/Clitherall,James.html. [Online finding aid description: " James Clitherall travelled as an escort to Mary Izard Middleton (Mrs. Arthur) and Henrietta Middleton Rutledge (Mrs. Edward), wives of two members of the Continental Congress, from Charleston, S. C., to Philadelphia, Pa., in April-July 1776. The collection contains transcripts of the diary kept by Clitherall on this trip. Clitherall described land fertility, road conditions, tavern accommodations and entertainment, and leisure-time gatherings of local society on a trip through Camden, S. C.; Charlotte, N. C., Salisbury, N. C., and Guilford Court House, N. C.; Charlotte Court House and Orange Court House, Va.; and Lancaster, Pa. The volume includes the words of two songs, *New Song for Liberty* and *Liberty Song*, which the travelers heard at Charlotte, N. C."]

Fussell, Fred C., with Steve Kruger. *Blue Ridge Music Trails of North Carolina: A Guide to Music Sites, Artists, and Traditions of the Mountains and Foothills*. Chapel Hill: University of North Carolina Press, 2013. [Publisher's description: "The music and dance traditions of North Carolina's Blue Ridge Mountains are legendary. Residents continue a musical heritage that stretches back many generations. In this lively guidebook, noted folklorist Fred C. Fussell puts readers on the trail to discover the many sites in western North Carolina where this unique musical legacy thrives. Organized by region and county, *Blue Ridge Music Trails of North Carolina* welcomes readers into the rich worlds of bluegrass, old-time, gospel, and string band music, as well as clogging, flatfooting, and other forms of traditional dance."]

Grant, Emily. "Colonial Games." *Tar Heel Junior Historian*, 34:1 (Fall 1994), 2-5. [Online description from "North Carolina Periodicals Index," East Carolina University: "Colonial North Carolina's scattered rural population played games that were individualized or for small groups; among these were marbles, dolls, whittling, leapfrog, cards, hide-and-seek, and hopscotch."]

Henry, Mellinger E. "Notes and Queries: American Survival of an Old English Ballad [Barbara Allen]." *Journal of American Folklore*, 39:152 (April-June 1926), 211-212.

Maurer, Maurer. "Music in Wachovia, 1753-1800." *William and Mary Quarterly*, 3rd series, 8:2 (April 1951), 214-227.

Pfohl, Bernard J. "The Early Music of Salem Congregation." In *Salem's Remembrancers: Seven Moravian Historians Who Presented Their Papers before the Wachovia Historical Society of Salem, North Carolina, 1898-1910* (Winston-Salem: Wachovia Historical Society, 1976).

Rankin, Hugh F. *The Theater in Colonial America*. Chapel Hill: University of North Carolina Press, 1965.

Ritchie, Fiona, and Doug Orr. *Wayfaring Strangers: The Musical Voyage from Scotland and Ulster to Appalachia*. Chapel Hill: University of North Carolina Press, 2014. [Publisher's description: "Many of these Scots-Irish immigrants made their way into the mountains of the southern Appalachian region. They brought with them a wealth of traditional ballads and tunes from the British Isles and Ireland, a carrying stream that merged with sounds and songs of English, German, Welsh, African American, French, and Cherokee origin. Their enduring legacy of music flows today from Appalachia back to Ireland and Scotland and around the globe. In *Wayfaring Strangers*, Fiona Ritchie and Doug Orr guide readers on a musical voyage across oceans, linking people and songs through centuries of adaptation and change."]

Roberts, B. W. C. "Cockfighting: An Early Entertainment in North Carolina." *North Carolina Historical Review*, 42:3 (July 1965), 306-314.

Sickles, Dolly R. "Baroque'n Record." *Our State: Down Home in North Carolina*, 74:12 (May 2007), 164-166, 168, 170-171; online: http://digital.ncdcr.gov/cdm/ref/collection/p16062coll18/id/89271. [Online description from "North Carolina Periodicals Index," East Carolina University: "The Craven Historical Dancers and the New Bern Dancing Assembly re-create life in Tryon Palace in the days of the Royal Governor. Unlike modern day entertainment and entertainers, people in Colonial America provided entertainment for each other. The Baroque dance was a noble dance style and technique of the period. Sickles discusses the dance and the work of the two dance groups."]

White, Newman Ivey; Henry M. Belden, *et al.*, assoc. eds. *The Frank C. Brown Collection of North Carolina Folklore: The Folklore of North Carolina, Collected by Dr. Frank C. Brown during the Years 1912-1943, in Colloboration with the North Carolina Folklore Society.* Durham: Duke University Press, 1952-1964. [Contents: v. 1. Games and Rhymes. Beliefs and Customs. Riddles. Proverbs. Speech. Tales and Legends; v. 2. Folk Ballads from North Carolina; v. 3. Folk Songs from North Carolina; v. 4. The Music of the Ballads; v. 5. The Music of the Folk Songs; v. 6-7. Popular Beliefs and Superstitions from North Carolina.]

Whitley-Bauguess, Paige. "Dance in Eighteenth-Century New Bern." *New Bern Historical Journal*, 5:1 (May 1992), 3-15.

Wiggins, David K. "Sports and Recreation in the Slave Community." *Tar Heel Junior Historian*, 34:1 (Fall 1994), 6-8. [Online description from "North Carolina Periodicals Index," East Carolina University: "Such recreational activities as marbles, cards, dancing, swimming, and fishing enabled slaves in North Carolina to mitigate the difficulties and harshness of their lives in ways that were neither violent nor competitive."]

North Carolina Broadsides

Hummel, Ray O., Jr. *Southeastern Broadsides before 1877: A Bibliography*. Richard: Virginia State Library, 1971.

Postal Services in North Carolina

Johnston, Hugh Buckner. "The Journal of Ebenezer Hazard in North Carolina, 1777 and 1778." *North Carolina Historical Review*, 36:3 (July 1959), 358-381; online: http://digital.ncdcr.gov/cdm/ref/collection/p16062coll9/id/4207. [Online description from "North Carolina Periodicals Index," East Carolina University: "This article is a reprint of journal entries written by postmaster surveyor Ebenezer Hazard while on orders to regulate the Continental postal route between Philadelphia and Savannah. Published as a two volume manuscript entitled 'The Journal of Ebenezer Hazard,' the excerpts included here were written during a preliminary trip to Edenton and back between May 15 and July 8, 1777 and a complete round trip to Savannah between October 8, 1777 and March 5, 1778."]

North Carolina (State). General Assembly. "[Document dated:] May 15, 1782: Resolution to establish a post from the town of Hillsborough to the town of Richmond in Virginia (with messages and vote tally)." Manuscript; General Assembly Session Records; Session of May-June 1782; Committee Papers, Resolutions, Senate Bills, House Bills; Senate Joint Resolutions: May 7-May 15, 1782, Box 2 (MARS ID: 66.8.28.6.13), State Archives of North Carolina, Raleigh. [Online catalog description: "Resolution would establish a post to convey intelligence dispatches; includes vote tally; and message sending resolution to House for concurrence."]

Watson, Alan D. "The Ferry in Colonial North Carolina: A Vital Link in Transportation." *North Carolina Historical Review*, 51:3 (July 1974), 247-260. [Online description from "North Carolina Periodicals Index," East Carolina University: "Starting with one ferry in 1700, the ferry service has expanded since North Carolina's settlement to facilitate travel for various purposes. During the colonial period, ferries made it easier for colonists to go to court, church, taking livestock to market, traveling for muster and for quicker delivery of mail through the postal service."]

Poverty, Social Ills, and Charity in Revolutionary North Carolina

Brief History of Care of the Under-Privileged Child in North Carolina. Raleigh: North Carolina State Board of Charieits and Public Welfare, 1934.

Klebaner, Benjamin Joseph. "Some Aspects of North Carolina Poor Relief, 1700-1860." *North Carolina Historical Review*, 31:4 (October 1954), 479-492; online: http://digital.ncdcr.gov/cdm/ref/collection/p16062coll9/id/4207. [Online description from "North Carolina Periodicals Index," East Carolina University: "A system of tax-financed relief for the needy, which was administered by local governments was brought to the colonies from

England. In accordance with an act of 1701, likely the first poor law in the colony, Chowan precinct levied a tax for the support of the pauper. Thus began the various provisions for poor relief in North Carolina."]

Tillinghast, Anne. "The Social Work Activities of the Quakers in North Carolina from the Colonial Period to the Twentieth Century." Paper Submitted Social Work 265 at the University of North Carolina at Chapel Hill, Winter Quarter 1941; copy, Cp289.6 T57s, in the North Carolina Collection, Louis Round Wilson Special Collections Library, University of North Carolina at Chapel Hill.

Salt and Saltmaking

Littleton, Tucker R. "Wind Plus Water Equaled Salt." *The State: Down Home in North Carolina*, 49:9 (February 1982), 16-18, 28; online: http://digital.ncdcr.gov/cdm/ref/collection/p16062coll18/id/59506. [Online description from "North Carolina Periodicals Index," East Carolina University: "During the blockades of the Revolution, the War of 1812, and the Civil War, it became necessary for North Carolina to convert its gristmills to saltworks. Windmills were used to pump sea water into the plant, where it was then either boiled or evaporated, leaving only salt residue. Toward the end of the Civil War, several saltworks were destroyed by Yankee forces. So far, only thirteen saltworks that used windmills in production have been identified. They are in New Hanover, Carteret, and Brunswick counties."]

Hilldrup, R. L. "The Salt Supply of North Carolina during the Revolutionary War." *North Carolina Historical Review*, 22:4 (October 1945), 393-417.

North Carolina (State). General Assembly. "May 10, 1779: Petition of a Number of Inhabitants of New Hanover Co. for a Guard over the Salt Works (rejected)." Manuscript; General Assembly Record Group; Session Records, May 1779, Box 1 (MARS ID: 66.8.17.6.4; item), State Archives of North Carolina, Raleigh.

North Carolina (State). General Assembly. "[Document dated:] May 9, 1777: Re[specting] Salt Imported by John Cowper in the Brig. *Defiance* and sold in the Town of New Bern (with Message)." Manuscript; General Assembly Record Group; Session Records, April-May 1777: Joint Papers, Committee Papers, Resolutions, Miscellaneous Bills; House Joint Resolutions, folder 2, Box 1 (MARS ID: 66.8.9.13.26; item), State Archives of North Carolina, Raleigh. [Online catalog description: "Resolution allowing John Cowper to retain the money received from the sale of salt which he imported in the brigantine *Defiance*."]

North Carolina (State). General Assembly. "[Document Dated]: May 20, 1784: Report on Memorials of James Kerr, Commissioner of Rowan County." Manuscript; General Assembly Record Group; Session Records, April-June 1784; Committee Papers, Resolutions: Joint Select Committees: Reports and Papers: May 20-June 3, 1784, Box 2 (MARS ID:66.8.32.2.1; item), State Archives of North Carolina, Raleigh. [Online catalog description: "Report is on two memorials of James Kerr, Commissioner of Rowan County: The first memorial concerns the borrowing of salt by Kerr to fill a military requisition and asks for compensation to pay the donors. The second memorial concerns the collections of the specific tax in the county, where Kerr collected receipts instead of the money he was directed to collect in an act of the Assembly. Committee awards compensation for salt, but finds Kerr's conduct irregular in the collection of taxes."]

Street, Julia M. "When We Made Our Own Salt." *The State: Down Home in North Carolina*, 45:4 (September 1977), 16-18, 39; online: http://digital.ncdcr.gov/cdm/compoundobject/collection/p16062coll18/id/57449. [Online description from "North Carolina Periodicals Index," East Carolina University: "The author recounts the importance of salt in North Carolina's economy since the 1700s. During the American Revolution, salt was scarce, prompting towns on the coast of North Carolina to build their own salt works for local production."]

Williams, Isabel M., and Leora H. McEachern. *Salt – That Necessary Article.* Wilmington: [s. n.], 1973.

Textiles, Quilting, Samplers, Clothing, Needlework, etc.

Fries, Adelaide L. "One Hundred Years of Textiles in Salem." *North Carolina Historical Review*, 27:1 (January 1950), 1-19; online: http://digital.ncdcr.gov/cdm/ref/collection/p16062coll9/id/4207. [Online description from "North Carolina Periodicals Index," East Carolina University: "Gottfried Praezel owned the first loom in Salem and the town's textile history begins with him in 1766. The author traces the history of textile manufacture in Salem from humble beginnings to the end of the 19th century. The article describes the shift in textile workers from men and their apprentices to the Moravian women known as Single Sisters; linen produced and sales; and the introduction of more sophisticated machinery that changed Salem's textile manufacturing market."]

Poteat, RaeLana Vee. "'Both Plain and Ornamental': Professional Female Needleworkers in Eighteenth- and Early-Nineteenth Century North Carolina and Virginia." M. A. thesis, Western Florida University, 1997.

Sullivan, Kathy. "The Legacy of German Quiltmaking in North Carolina." In Jeannette Lasansky, ed., *Bits and Pieces: Textile Traditions* (Philadelphia: University of Pennsylvania Press, 1991), 65-71.

Weather in North Carolina and Tennessee during the Revolution

Barnes, Jay. *North Carolina's Hurricane History: Updated with a Decade of New Storms from Isabel to Irene.* Chapel Hill: University of North Carolina Press, 1995; Chapel Hill: University of North Carolina Press, 2013. [Publisher's description: "North Carolina's Hurricane History charts the more than fifty great storms that have battered the Tar Heel State from the colonial era through Irene in 2011 and Superstorm Sandy in 2012, two of the costliest hurricanes on record. Drawing on news reports, National Weather Service records, and eyewitness descriptions, hurricane historian Jay Barnes emphasizes the importance of learning from this extraordinary history as North Carolina prepares for the inevitable disastrous storms to come. Featuring more than 200 photographs, maps, and illustrations, this book offers amazing stories of destruction and survival. While some are humorous and some tragic, all offer a unique perspective on the state's unending vulnerability to these storms."]

Burgess, Christine G., *et al. Impacts of Hurricanes on North Carolina Fisheries*. Morehead City: North Carolina Department of Environmental and Natural Resources, Division of Marine Fisheries, 2007. [While examining the modern implications of hurricane strikes on the state, this study can also provide an idea of what North Carolinians dependent on the sea in earlier centuries experienced.]

Dunn, Gordon E., and Banner I. Miller. *Atlantic Hurricanes.* Baton Rouge: Louisiana State University Press, 1960.

Engel, Jonathan T. "The Force of Nature: The Impact of Weather on Armies during the American War of Independence, 1775-1781." M. A. thesis, Florida State University. [Author's summary: Examines the impact that weather had on armies during the American War of Independence. It argues that weather affected the operations of both American and British armies in three areas : strategy, influencing the planning of campaigns ; tactics, affecting the course of battles ; and administration, adding to the daily work of maintaining armies in the field and keeping them functional. Year after year, in all four seasons, generals and soldiers had to cope with phenomena such as rain, snow, heat and fog. Weather was capricious sometimes helping one army and harming the other and sometimes hindering both armies. Generals often tried to use the weather to gain an advantage and to mitigate the damage weather might do to their armies. The first chapter addresses weather's activity in early years of the war up to the end of 1777. The 2nd chapter focuses on the war in the north from 1778 to the end of major fighting in 1781, and the final chapter covers the impact of weather in that same period in the southern theater, concluding with the Franco-American victory at Yorktown ..."]

Fraser, Walter J., Jr. *Lowcountry Hurricanes: Three Centuries of Storms at Sea and Ashore*. Athens: University of Georgia Press, 2006.

Hairr, John. *The Great Hurricanes of North Carolina*. Charleston: History Press, 2008. [Includes the "Independence Hurrican of 1775."]

Kammerer, Roger. "Large Snows and Freezes in Greenville." *Greenville Times/Pitt's Past*, 32:3 (March5-April 2, 2014), 6. [Online description from "North Carolina Periodicals Index," East Carolina University: "Although snow is still considered a rare site in Greenville, there are tales of large snow storms and freezes in eastern North Carolina as far back as 1780."]

Ludlum, David M. *Early American Hurricanes, 1492-1870*. Boston: American Meteorological Society, 1963.

Ludlum, David M. *Early American Winters, 1604-1820* (History of American Weather series, no. 2) Boston: American Meteorological Society, 1966.

Mulcahy, Matthew. *Hurricanes and Society in the British Great Caribbean, 1624-1783*. Baltimore: Johns Hopkins University Press, 2006.

Robinson, Peter J.; foreword by Greg Fishel. *North Carolina Weather and Climate*. Chapel Hill: University of North Carolina Press, 2005. [Publisher's description: "From blue skies to raging hurricanes, from ice storms to droughts, North Carolina's weather varies widely from season to season and from day to day. In this delightful and informative book, Peter Robinson provides a layperson's guide to the state's weather and climate and an introduction to the science that describes it. What is North Carolina's 'typical' weather? How does it vary from the coast to the mountains? How do we forecast it? With dozens of color maps and tables to make understanding easier, Robinson covers big issues such as the role of weather and climate in daily life, severe weather threats and their causes, and the meteorological effects of seasons. He also explains more specific phenomena including the causes of heating and cooling, the effects of acid rain, and the role of groundwater in weather. Robinson addresses the state's weather history as well as long-term concerns associated with how air pollution affects weather and our health, and he explores why issues of local and global climate change matter. Throughout, he discusses weather in ways that can inform daily life, whether you're planting a garden, building a climate-friendly and energy-efficient home, or choosing a time and place for vacation."]

Williams, Tony. *Hurricane of Independence: The Untold Story of the Deadly Storm at the Deciding Moment of the American Revolution*. Naperville, Ill.: Sourcebooks, 2008.

Chapter Six: General Revolutionary War Sources

This publication focuses on the sources and studies that are available at the state and local level for research in North Carolina. It does not cover in depth the many records that are available relating to the Revolutionary War at the Federal level in the National Archives and Records Administration, Washington, D. C. Various guides to these sources have been published over the years, and the major ones are listed below. Many of the major record groups of documents were microfilmed many years ago and have now been digitized and available on various subscription websites. These are, of course, essential sources for research on Revolutionary War ancestors in any state.

There are innumerable publications on the history of the American Revolution. A search of the online catalog of any library, including the DAR Library in Washington, D. C. (www.dar.org/library), will reveal most of these. Use the subject search term: "United States – History – Revolution, 1775-1783" or the name of any state or locality in place of "United States" to discover what is available. The online and freely accessible WorldCat (www.worldcat.org) is a union catalog of the holdings of thousands of libraries in North America and elsewhere in the world. It is very useful for locating a library in a specific geographical area that owns a book of interest. The DAR Library catalog is not, however, presently included in WorldCat, so its many unique holdings must be searched on its own site.

Published Guides, Abstracts, and Transcriptions

Note: The website of the National Archives and Records Administration contains current information about the Archives' holdings: www.archives.gov. Many records in the National Archives have been or are being digitized and made available online at http://www.fold3.com.

Bockstruck, Lloyd de Witt. *Revolutionary War Pensions Awarded by State Governments, 1775-1874, the General and Federal Governments Prior to 1814, and by Private Acts of Congress to 1905.* Baltimore: Genealogical Publishing Company, 2011.

"Compiled Service Records of Soldiers Who Served in the American Army during the Revolutionary War." Record Group 93, National Archives and Records Administration, Washington, D. C. See also the descriptive pamphlet for this record group. These records are also available on microfilm as M881, 1,906 rolls Washington, D. C.: National Archives Trust Fund, 1976; and, on the subscription website *Fold3*.

Coren, Robert W. *Guide to the Records of the United States House of Senate at the National Archives, 1789-1989.* Washington, D. C: The Senate of the United States, 1989.

Davies, Kenneth Gordon, ed. *Documents of the American Revolution, 1770-1783; Colonial Office Series*. Shannon, Ire.: Irish University Press, 1972-1981. [Contents: 1: Calendar, 1770-71; 2: Transcripts, 1770; 3: Transcripts, 1771; 4: Calendar, 1772-73; 5: Transcripts, 1772; 6: Transcripts, 1773; 7: Calendar, 1774 to 30 June 1775; 8: Transcripts, 1774; 9: Transcripts, January to June 1775; 10: Calendar, 1 July 1775 to 1776; 11: Transcripts, July to December 1775; 12: Transcripts, 1776; 13: Calendar, 1777-78; 14: Transcripts, 1777; 15: Transcripts, 1778; 16: Calendar, 1779-80; 17: Transcripts, 1779; 18: Transcripts, 1780; 19: Calendar 1781-1783, and Addenda, 1770-1780; 20: Transcripts, 1781; 21: Transcripts, 1782. [Many references to North Carolina, its residents, and events in the state appear throughout this set.]

Emmet, Thomas Addis. "Thomas Addis Emmet Collection, 1483-1876, bulk 1700-1800)." Manuscript, MssCol 927, Manuscripts and Archives Division, Stephen A. Schwarzman Building, New York Public Library, New York City; also available online: http://archives.nypl.org/mss/927#detailed. [Online catalog description: "85 boxes; 13 microfilm reels; Twenty-eight series: I. The Albany Congress of 1754; II. The Stamp-Act Congress of 1765; III. The Continental Congress of 1774; IV. The Members of the Continental Congress, 1774-1789; V. The Presidents of Congress, and of the United States; VI. The Declaration of Independence; VII. The Signers to the Declaration of Independence; VIII. The Articles of Confederation; IX. Lossing's Field Book of the Revolution; X. The Siege of Savannah, 1779; XI. The Siege of Savannah; Lincoln Papers; XII. The Siege of Charleston; Lincoln Papers; XIII. The Generals of the American Revolution; XIV. Washington and His Military Family;

XV. The Annapolis Convention; XVI. The Federal Convention; XVII. The First Federal Administration; XVIII. The Republican Court; XIX. Booth's *History of New York*; XX. Francis's *Old New York*; XXI. Duer's *Old Yorker*; XXII. *Irving's Life of Washington*; XXIII. Boundary Line Controversy; XXIV. Howe's *Virginia*; XXV. Life of Edward Livingston; XXVI. Life of Marion; XXVII. Gen. Leslie's Letter Book; XXVIII. Miscellaneous Manuscripts." See also: New York Public Library. Emmet Collection. *Calendar of the Emmet Collection of Manuscripts, etc., Relating to American History*. New York: New York Public Library, 1900.]

Feinstone, Sol. "The Sol Feinstone Collection of the American Revolution, ca. 1760s-1850s." Manuscript Mss.B.F327, American Philosophical Society, Philadelphia; online description and inventory: http://www.amphilsoc.org/mole/view?docId=ead/Mss.B.F327-ead.xml. [The collection contains various letters of prominent residents of North Carolina of the period.]

Guide to Genealogical Research in the National Archives. Washington, D. C.: National Archives and Records Administration, 2000.

Heitman, Francis B[ernard]. *Historical Register of the Officers of the Continental Army during the War of the Revoluton, April 1775 to December 1783.* Washington, D. C. (Baltimore: Press of Nichols, Killam & Mafitt), 1893; reprinted as a new, revised, and enlarged edition: Washington, D. C.: Washington Rare Book Shop Publishing Company, 1914; reprinted with addenda by Robert H[endre] Kelby, New York: T. A. Wright, Inc., 1932; Baltimore: Genealogical Publishing Company, 1967; 1982; Baltimore: Genealogical Publishing Company for Clearfield Company, 1997. It is also available online at Google Books.

Index of Revolutionary War Pensions Applications in the National Archives. Arlington, Va.: National Genealogical Society, 1976. [Replaces Hoyt's *Index.*]

Matchette, Robert B., *et al. Guide to Federal Records in the National Archives of the United States.* 3 vols. Washington, D. C.: National Archives and Records Administration, 1995.

McConnell, Roland C. "Records in the National Archives Pertaining to North Carolina." *North Carolina Historical Review*, 25:3 (July 1948), 318-340.

Military Service Records: A Select Catalog of National Archives Microfilm Publications. Washington, D. C.: National Archives Trust Fund, 1985.

Neagles, James C. *Summer Soldiers: A Survey and Index of Revolutionary War Courts-Martial.* Salt Lake City: Ancestry, 1986.

Neagles, James C. *U. S. Military Records: A Guide to Federal and State Sources, Colonial America to the Present.* Salt Lake City: Ancestry, 1994. [Chapter 2: "Types of Records: Post-Service Records and Records Relating to Civilian Affairs" includes a timeline of significant dates in the history of American Revolutionary War pension legislation on page 58; Chapter 3: "Resources of the National Archives Microfilm Room" provides a good general overview on pages 90-92 of Revolutionary War and Post-Revolutionary Wars on microfilm collections that are available at the National Archives and many other libraries as well as (in most cases) online by 2014.]

Neagles, James C. and Lila L. *Locating Your Revolutionary War Ancestor: A Guide to the Military Records*. Logan, Ut.: The Everton Publishers, Inc., 1983. Mostly covers federal government records.

Peckham, Howard H., ed. Sources of American Independence: Selected Manuscripts from the Collections of the William L. Clements Library. 2 vols. Chicago: University of Chicago Press, 1978. [Robert G Mitchell, "After Yorktown: The Wayne-Greene Correspondence, 1782," 2:361-427.]

Peterson, Clarence Stewart. *Known Military Dead during the American Revolutionary War, 1775-1783.* Baltimore: Genealogical Publishing Company, 1959, 1967; reprinted: Baltimore: Clearfield Company, Inc., 1990.

Pierce, John. *Pierce's Register: Register of the Certificates Issued by John Pierce, Esquire, Paymaster General and Commissioner of Army Accounts for the United States, to Officers and Soldiers of the Continental Army under Act of July 4, 1783*. Originally published in: *Seventeenth Report of the National Society of the Daughters of the American Revolution, October 13, 1913 to October 11, 1914* (Senate Documents, vol. 9, no. 988, 63rd Congress, 3rd Session) Washington, D. C.: Government Printing Office, 1915; reprinted: Baltimore: Genealogical Publishing Company, 1973, 1976.

Prechtel-Kluskens, Claire. "Dig Deeper into Less Well Known Revolutionary War Records." *NGS Newsmagazine*, 35:2 (April-June 2009), 52-55.

Rose, Christine. *Military Pension Laws, 1776-1858.* San Jose, Calif.: Rose Family Association, 2001.

Schamel, Charles E., *et al. Guide to the Records of the United States House of Representatives at the National Archives, 1789-1989*. Washington, D. C: The House of Representatives, 1989.

Schweitzer, George K. *Revolutionary War Genealogy*. Knoxville: G. K. Schweitzer, 1982; reprinted: Knoxville, Tenn.: G. K. Schweitzer, 1984, 1987, 1997. [This book provides a short history of the Revolutionary War. It then broadly discusses the overall resources available at national and state archival repositories, state historical societies, the American Military History Institute, and other local level holdings. The book discusses locating military rosters, rolls, pension records, bounty land and other claim records, prison records, listings of clergy, French and Irish soldiers, and Loyalist and German lists. State publications and resources are listed. Approaches to locating local records are mentioned. The author also suggests researching other histories, such as: personal, regimental, battle, state, and group histories. Various resources are listed for each. Museums and historical sites are also mentioned as resources for research.]

Scott, Craig R. *The Lost Pensions: Settled Accounts of the Act of 6 April 1838.* Lovettsville, Va.: Willow Bend, 1996.

Scott, Craig R. *Revolutionary War Genealogy Research* (Genealogy at a Glance series) Baltimore: Genealogical Publishing Company, 2011. [4-page overview of the major sources and research centers]

Sherman, William F.; with additions and index by Craig R. Scott. *Records of the Accounting Officers of the Department of the Treasury, Inventory 14, Revised.* Lovettsville, Va.: Willow Bend Books, 1997.

United States. Adjutant General. "Lists of the Adjutant General's Office for Carded Records of Military Organizations: Revolutionary War through Philippine Insurrection," [aka "The Ainsworth List."] Record Group, National Archives and Records Administration, Washington, D. C. Also available on microfilm as National Archives microfilm publication T817, 112 rolls. Washington, D. C.: National Archives Trust Fund, 1963.

United States. Continental Army. "Revolutionary War Rolls, 1775-1783." Record Group 93, National Archives Trust Fund Board, Washington, D. C.; also available on microfilm as National Archives microfilm publication M246, 138 reels; also available online through the subscription website *Fold3*.

United States. Treasury Department. "Records of the Accounting Officers of the Department of the Treasury, Records of the Office of the Third Auditor 1775-1923." Record group 217, entry 722: "Selected Final Pension Payment Vouchers." National Archives and Records Administration, Washington, D. C. [Description: "The vouchers consist of pension agent files selected by National Archives staff for their genealogical value. The files contain details relating to the final payment to heirs of a pensioner after his death. Details in these accounts may include the name of the spouse, children, and other heirs; the date and place of death; and the date, place and amount of the final pension payment. The vouchers are filed by the state where the pensioner received payment and thereafter alphabetically by surname of the pensioner."]

United States. War Department. "Collection of Revolutionary War Records," Record Group 93, National Archives Trust Fund Board, Washington, D. C. [1775-1784]

Wehmann, Howard H.; revised by Benjamin L. Dewhitt. *A Guide to Pre-Federal Records in the National Archives.* Washington, D. C: National Archives and Records Administration, 1989.

Winslow, Raymond S., Jr. "Federal Records: Military Service and Veteran's Records." In Helen F. M. Leary, ed. *North Carolina Research: Genealogy and Local History.* 2nd ed. (Raleigh: North Carolina Genealogical Society, 1996), Chapter 36, 458-472.

Winslow, Raymond A., Jr. "Federal Records: The National Archives." In Helen F. M. Leary, ed. *North Carolina Research: Genealogy and Local History.* 2nd ed. (Raleigh: North Carolina Genealogical Society, 1996), Chapter 34, 427-432.

Wright, Robert K., Jr. *The Continental Army.* Washington, D. C.: Center for Military History, 1983

Peter Force Collection

Dirst, Tara, and Alan Kulikoff. "Was Dr. Benjamin Church a Traitor?: A New Way to Find Out." *Common-Place*, 6:1 (October 2005) online: http://www.common-place.org/vol-06/no-01/tales/. [Using the online *American Archives* site for research is the focus of the article.]

Force, Peter. "Peter Force and William Q. Force Collection, 1775-1875." Manuscript 2967, Southern Historical Collection, Louis Round Wilson Special Collections Library, University of North Carolina, Chapel Hill; online finding aid available at http://www2.lib.unc.edu/mss/inv/f/Force,Peter.html. [Online finding aid description: "The collection includes papers acquired by Peter Force, collector and historical editor of Washington, D. C., and his son, William Q. Force, concerning the dispute over the authenticity of the Mecklenburg County, N. C., declaration of independence of 1775, including correspondence of the Forces and other persons, copies of pertinent materials, and a scrapbook of clippings."]

Force, Peter, ed. *American Archives: Consisting of a Collection of Authentick Records, State Papers, Debates, and Letters and Other Notices of Publick Affairs, 4th series: From the King's Message of March 7th, 1774, to the Declaration of Independence, by the United States, in 1776.* 6 vols. Washington, D. C.: M. St. Clair Clarke and Peter Force, 1837-1846. [Includes many North Carolina documents (Note: The page numbers that appear are to the first page of a section in each volume dealing with the following groups or governmental bodies. There are, however, other significant segments of documents, usually in sections titled "Correspondence, Proceedings, etc." throughout *American Archives* that include other documents relating to the actions and interests of the different states and their subdivisions beyond those listed here. Consult the contents and index to each volume for additional entries and details). May be viewed online through HathiTrust.]

Force, Peter, ed. *American Archives: Consisting of a Collection of Authentick Records, State Papers, Debates, and Letters and Other Notices of Publick Affairs, 5th series: From the Declaration of Independence, in 1776, to the Definitive Treaty of Peace with Great Britain, in 1783.* 3 vols. Washington, D. C.: M. St. Clair Clarke and Peter Force, 1848-1853. [Includes many North Carolina documents (Note: The column numbers that appear are to the first column of a section in each volume dealing with the following groups or governmental bodies. There are, however, other significant segments of documents, usually in sections titled "Correspondence, Proceedings, etc.," throughout *American Archives* that include other documents relating to the actions and interests of the different states and their subdivisions beyond those listed here. Consult the contents and index to each volume for additional entries and details). May be viewed online through HathiTrust.]

Force, Peter, ed. *American Archives: Documents of the American Revolutionary Period, 1774-*1776; available online through Northern Illinois University Libraries, Digital Collections and Collaborative Projects: http://amarch.lib.niu.edu/redirect.

Goff, Frederick R. "Peter Force." *Papers of the Bibliographical Society of America*, 44:1 (1st quarter 1950), 1-16.

Library of Congress. Manuscript Division. *Peter Force: A Register of His Papers in the Library of Congress.* Washington, D. C.: The Library, [s. d.]. This appears online through the LOC catalog.

"Peter Force Library: Manuscripts and Maps Relating to American History, Early American Imprints, and Incunabula." Online: http://www.loc.gov/rr/mss/coll/084.html.

Stephenson, Richard W. "Maps from the Peter Force Collection." [U. S. Library of Congress]. *Quarterly Journal of the Library of Congress,* 30:3 (July 1973), 183-204.

Sung, Carolyn Hoover. "Peter Force: Washington Printer and Creator of the American Archives." Ph. D. dissertation, George Washington University, 1985.

Lyman Copeland Draper Papers

Draper's papers at the Wisconsin Historical Society in Madison are among the most important collections on the history of the western frontier from the Great Lakes to the Gulf of Mexico and from the western portions of the original Mid-Atlantic States, the Carolinas, and Georgia. A very well-written guide is available online:

Bennett, Edward Earl, Ruth Hardaker, Anne King Gregorie, and Isabel Thompson. *Calendar of the Tennessee and King's Mountain Papers of the Draper Collections of Manuscripts.* (Wisconsin Historical Publications. Calendar series, vol. 3) Madison: State Historical Society of Wisconsin, 1929.

Draper, Lyman Copeland. *Calendar of the Frontier Wars Papers of the Draper Collection of Manuscripts.* Utica, Ky.: McDowell Publications, 1991; indexed by Sam McDowell.

Draper, Lyman Copeland. "Draper Manuscripts, 1740-1891." Manuscript (Draper Mss; Micro 1034), Wisconsin Historical Society, Madison. [Originals and microfilm copies are housed at the Wisconsin Historical Society, and many other research institutions have the microfilm including the DAR Library, Washington, D. C.]

The following series contain Revolutionary North Carolina information:

Series B: Life of Boone Manuscript, ca. 1856-1898, by Draper (5 vols.)

Series C: Daniel Boone Papers (33 vols)

Series D: Border Forays (5 vols.)

Series P: Draper's Biographical Sketches (3 vols.)

Series R: Draper's Historical Miscellanies (8 vols.)

Series S: Draper's Notes, vols. 1-33.

Series U: Frontier War Papers, vols. 1-24.

Series DD (Vols. 1, 8-12, and 16), King's Mountain Papers, 1756-1887 [Description: "King's Mountain Papers: Papers about the Battle of King's Mountain, South Carolina, on October 7, 1780, in which some 1,400 frontier troops from Virginia and North Carolina trapped and routed 1,000 Loyalist soldiers and killed their commander, Patrick Ferguson. Besides his own notes and interviews, Draper gathered materials for over 40 years, acquired the papers of several of the prominent officers such as William Campbell, John Sevier, and Isaac Shelby."]. See: *Calendar of the Kings Mountain Papers.*

Series JJ (Vol. 1, Bk. B; Vol. 3, Bks. A and E), Newspaper Extracts, 1748-1840

Series XX (Vols. 1-2 and 4), Tennessee Papers, 1771-1883. See: *Calendar of the Tennessee and King's Mountain Papers of the Draper Collection of Manuscripts.* Madison: State Historical Society of Wisconsin, 1929; reprint, Hartford, Ky.: Cook & McDowell, 1979.

Harper, Josephine L. *Guide to the Draper Manuscripts.* Madison: State Historical Society of Wisconsin, 1983.

Hesseltine, William B. "Lyman Draper and the South." *Journal of Southern History*, 19:1 (February 1953), 20-31.
Hesseltine, William B. *Pioneer's Mission: The Story of Lyman Copeland Draper.* Madison: State Historical Society of Wisconsin, 1954.
Highsaw, James Leonard. *Transcriptions from the Lyman C. Draper Manuscripts Relating to the History of Tennessee from 1769-1850.* Madison: Wisconsin State Historical Society, 1914.
Kegley, George. "How Lyman Draper Saved History." *Journal of the Historical Society of Western Virginia*, 21:1 (2013), 20-22.
Lilienkamp, Daniel R. "Finding Your Ancestors in the Draper Manuscript Collection." Online, Special Collections Department, St. Louis County Library; online: http://www.slcl.org/sites/default/files/shared-files/Draper%20 Manuscript%20Collection%20guide.pdf
Moore, John Trotwood. *The Draper Manuscripts as Relating to Tennessee.* Nashville: Brandon Publishing, 1919.
Thwaites, Reuben Gold, ed. *Descriptive List of Manuscript Collections in the State Historical Society of Wisconsin,* Madison: The Society, 1906.

Numerous other publications utilize the content of the Draper Collection, including the following:

Allaire, Anthony. *Diary of Lieut. Anthony Allaire.* (Eyewitness Accounts of the American Revolution series) New York: New York Times, 1968; online: http://www.tngenweb.org/revwar/kingsmountain/allaire.html. [This originally appeared in Lyman Copeland Draper's *King's Mountain and Its Heroes* (Cincinnati: P.G. Thomson, 1881), 484-515. Allaire was a Loyalist.]
Allaire, Anthony; Lyman C. Draper, ed. "A Letter from a Royalist Officer." In *The Battle of Kings Mountain, October 7th, 1780 and the Events Which Led to It.* [S. l.: s. n.]: 1881; reprinted: Johnson City, Tenn.: Overmountain Press, 1996.
Draper, Lyman C[opeland]. "Draper Manuscripts: King's Mountain Papers, 1756-1843." Wisconsin Historical Society, Madison; also available on microfilm in many research libraries.
Draper, Lyman C[opeland]. *King's Mountain and Its Heroes: History of the Battle of King's Mountain, October 7th 1780 and the Events Which Led to It.* Cincinnati: P. G. Thomson, 1881; reprinted: Marietta, Ga.: Continental Book, 1954; (North Carolina Heritage series, no. 5) Spartanburg: The Reprint Company, 1967; Baltimore: Genealogical Publishing Company, 1967, 1971, 1978; Spartanburg: The Reprint Company, 1982; Johnson City, Tenn.: Overmountain Press, 1996.
Hardin, Vera. "Letters from Abraham Hardin to Lyman C. Draper." *Eswau Huppeday: Bulletin of the Broad River Genealogical Society,* 5:1 (February 1985), 6-15.
Hope, James Madison. "The Fight at Butterfly Spring." Broad River Journal, 14:4 (December 2006), 3-4. [from a letter by Hope to Lyman C. Draper dated August 10, 1874, relating a story about Loyalist and Patriot children in modern Gaston County, N. C. and events in 1780]
"Letters to Lyman C. Draper." *Bulletin of the Genealogical Society of Old Tryon County*, 6:2 (May 1978), 66-68.
Warmack, Joann A. "The Book of Leaves of Memory, No. 2." *Bulletin of the Genealogical Society of Old Tryon County*, 18:1 (February 1990), 59-60. [Dickey and Gray information from the Lyman Draper Papers]

Original Documents from the National Archives and Records Administration

[Note: Many important federal records relating to the American Revolution and containing information on the role of North Carolina and its citizens in the war effort are not included in this section. They are covered in detail in the many guides to the holdings of the National Archives.]

United States. War Department. "Compiled Military Service Records of Soldiers Who Served during the Revolutionary War, M881." National Archives Trust Fund Board, Washington, D. C.; RG 93; microfilm, 1,095 rolls; online at http://www.fold3.com. [Online description from "North Carolina Periodicals Index," East Carolina University: "These are compiled service records for the regular soldiers of the Continental Army, and for the militia, volunteers, and others who served with them. The records are arranged under the designation 'Continental Troops' or a state name, then by organization, and then alphabetically by a soldier's surname. Records consist of card abstracts of entries relating to each soldier from original records. Also included are regimental lists including muster rolls, pay lists, and caption cards."]
Lu, Helen M.; Gwen B. Neumann, Margaret Ann S. Hudson, J[oel] Chan Edmondson, John V. Sobieski, and Deidre Burridge Dagner. *Revolutionary War Period: Bible, Family & Marriage Records Gleaned from Pension Applications.* Dallas, Tex.: H. M. Lu [vols. 1-9], 1980-1990; Dallas, Tex.; Plano, Tex.: [J. Chan Edmondson, vols. 10-20], 1990-2002; Charlottesville, Va., and Louisa, Va.: D. B. Dagner, 2004-2006. [cumulative index vols. 1-10 by Chan Edmondson. Dallas, Tex., 1990] [This set contains North Carolina references.]

Papers of the Continental Congress, 1774-1789. Washington, D. C.: RG 360, M247, microfilm, 204 rolls. National Archives and Records Administration, Washington, D. C. [Online description from "North Carolina Periodicals Index," East Carolina University: Records "are arranged as bound by the State Department in the 19th century, primarily by type of record, such as journals, committee reports, correspondence, memorials, and petitions, and thereunder chronologically, alphabetically, or by subject. Records are arranged into 196 numbered units called 'Items.'"]

Pretchel-Kluskens, Claire. "Follow the Money: Tracking the Revolutionary War Army Pension Payments." *Prologue: Journal of the National Archives and Records Administration*, 40:4 (Winter 2008), 46-57; online: http://www.archives.gov/publications/prologue/2008/winter/follow-money.html. [This article provides a detailed explanation of the entire pension process at the federal level including final pension payments and other lesser-used sources.]

United States. Continental Congress. *Papers of the Continental Congress, 1775-1789.* National Archives and Records Administration, Washington, D. C.; RG 360, M247, microfilm, 204 rolls; online at http://www.fold3.com.

United States. Department of Veterans Affairs. "Records of Bounty Land Warrant Application Files Based on Revolutionary War Service, 1775-1855." Manuscript RG 15, M804, National Archives and Records Administration, Washington, D. C.; also available on 2,670 microfilm rolls. [Description: The warrant is a certificate which states that, based on the Soldier's service, he is entitled to a certain number of acres in one of the bounty land districts. Similar records may also be found in RG 127 (Records of the Treasury)."]

United States. Department of Veterans Affairs. "Final Payment Vouchers Index for Military Pensions, 1818-1864." National Archives and Records Administration; online at http://www.fold3.com. [Online description from "North Carolina Periodicals Index," East Carolina University: "These slips serve as an index to final and last payments to over 65,000 veterans of the Revolutionary War and some later wars." "While the title refers to 'final' payment vouchers, there are also 'last' payment vouchers included in this index. 'Last' refers to the last payment of record while the 'final' payment indicates that the pensioner has died and that a final payment was made on his account. A 'last' payment could have been made for several reasons, including death or that the pensioner no longer visited the pension office to receive further payments due."]

United States. Department of the Treasury, Accounting Officers. "Manuscript Final Pension Payment Vouchers are located at the National Archives." Manuscript, (Record Group 217: Records of the Accounting Officers of the Department of the Treasury, Records of the Office of the Third Auditor 1775-1923, Entry 722 Selected Final Pension Payment Vouchers, National Archives, Washington, D.C.). [The vouchers consist of pension agent files selected by National Archives staff for their genealogical value. The files contain details relating to the final payment to heirs of a pensioner after his death. Details in these accounts may include the name of the spouse, children, and other heirs; the date and place of death; and the date, place and amount of the final pension payment. The vouchers are filed by the state where the pensioner received payment and thereafter alphabetically by surname of the pensioner.]

United States. War Department. "Miscellaneous Numbered Records (The Manuscript File) in the War Department Collection of Revolutionary War Records, 1775-1790's." Washington, D. C.: National Archives and Records Administration, 1970. National Archives Microfilm Publication M859.

United States. Bureau of Pensions (Now Department of Veterans Affairs). "Revolutionary War Pension Files, Including Bounty-Land Warrant Application Files, M804." National Archives and Records Administration; online at http://www.fold3.com. [Online description from "North Carolina Periodicals Index," East Carolina University: "The records in this collection include entire pension files for soldiers and sailors who served in the Revolutionary War. Unlike selected records, which were typically chosen subjectively for genealogical content, these records reveal more details about each veteran's history and service, as well as more information about his family, state of health, and life after the war."]

United States. War Department. "Revolutionary War Rolls." National Archives Trust Fund Board; online at http://www.fold3.com. [Online description from "North Carolina Periodicals Index," East Carolina University: "NARA M246. Muster rolls, payrolls, strength returns, and other miscellaneous personnel, pay, and supply records of American Army units, 1775-83. Thousands of records from rolls of microfilm provide names and details about the men who fought for independence."]

United States. Department of the Navy. "Revolutionary War Service and Imprisonment Cards." National Archives and Records Administration; online at http://www.fold3.com. [Online description from "North Carolina Periodicals Index," East Carolina University: "These war service and imprisonment cards are also called 'War of the Revolution Navy and Privateer Records.' They cover 1) officers and men of captured American vessels taken to Forton Prison; 2) prize money due to men who served under John Paul Jones; and 3) captured seamen imprisoned at Old Mill Prison, with name, rank, vessel, nationality, and sometimes the circumstances of imprisonment and release. The cards are arranged alphabetically by surname."]

United States. War Department. "Revolutionary War Special Numbered Index." Washington, D. C.: National Archives and Records Administration, 1959, M847.

United States. Court of Appeals. "Revolutionary War Prize Cases: Records of the Court of Appeal in Cases of Capture, 1776-1787, M162." National Archives and Records Administration; online at http://www.fold3.com. [Online description from "North Carolina Periodicals Index," East Carolina University: "During the American Revolution, armed vessels serving under individual colonies began to prey upon British commerce. The lack of courts for the condemnation of prizes taken by the Continental vessels was a source of annoyance to General Washington. He saw a need for speedy and regular condemnation of the prizes taken by all these ships to avoid conflict among colonies. The cases in this publication cover the appeals process that resulted for dealing with prize cases."]

United States. Quartermaster General and the Commissary General of Military Stores. "Revolutionary War Service Records – Navy." M880. National Archives and Records Administration; online at http://www.fold3.com. [Online description from "North Carolina Periodicals Index," East Carolina University: "These compiled service records are for naval personnel and members of the Departments of the Quartermaster General and Commissary General of Military Store who served during the Revolutionary War. They consist of a jacket-envelope for each soldier, sailor, or civilian. Information on each card is abstracted from the original military records."]

United States. War Department, comp. "Numbered Record Books Concerning Military Operations and Service, Pay and Settlement of Accounts, and Supplies in the War Department Collection of Revolutionary War Records, M853." Washington, D. C.: National Archives & Records Administration, 1971; online at http://www.fold3.com. [Brief Online description from "North Carolina Periodicals Index," East Carolina University: "These document images are digitized from NARA microfilm publication M853, which reproduced 199 numbered record books, with related separate indexes and one unnumbered record book, concerning Revolutionary War military operations and service, pay and settlement of accounts, and supplies. These records are part of War Department Collection of Revolutionary War Records, Record series 93. Most of the numbered record books were created during the period 1775-1783 but some were continued in use or were begun in the early postwar years, and a few are copies made after 1800 of earlier records. The separate indexes were compiled in the 19th and 20th centuries by custodians of the records." These records are searchable by name and may also be browsed.]

White, Virgil D. *Genealogical Abstracts of Revolutionary War Pension Files.* 5 vols. Waynesboro, Tenn.: The National Historical Publishing Company, 1990.

White, Virgil D. *Index to Revolutionary War Service Records.* 4 volumes. Waynesboro, Tenn.: The National Historical Publishing Company, 1995.

General Records of the United States

Jenkins, William Sumner, ed. *Records of the States of the United States of America: A Microfilm Compilation.* 1,871 microfilm reels. Washington, D. C.: Library of Congress Photoduplication Service, 1949. [General contents: A. Legislative records; B. Statutory records; C. Constitutional records; D. Administrative records; E. Executive records; F. Court records; F. X. Special records; L. Local records, county and city; M. Records of American Indian nations; N. Newspapers; R. Rudimentary states and courts; X. Miscellany.] And: Lillian A. Hamrick. *A Guide to the Microfilm Collection of Early State Records, Prepared by the Library of Congress in Association with the University of North Carolina: Collected and Compiled under the Direction of William Sumner Jenkins.* Washington, D. C.: Library of Congress, Photoduplication Service, 1950. Also see: William Sumner Jenkins, ed. *Records of the States: Supplementary Microfilms.* Washington, D. C.: Library of Congress, Photoduplication Service, 1955.

Jenkins, William Sumner. State Document Microfilms as Research Sources for Law Libraries." *Law Library Journal,* 41:2 (1948), 77-87; offprint: New York: [s. l.], 1948.

Jenkins, William Sumner. *Collected Public Documents of the States: A Check List.* Boston: [s. n.], 1947.

Jenkins, William Sumner. *Collecting and Using the Records of the States of the United States: Twenty-five Years in Retrospection.* Chapel Hill: The University of North Carolina, Bureau of Public Records Collection and Research, 1960[?].

Records of the National Society Daughters of the American Revolution

The NSDAR, or more commonly just DAR, maintains a major collection of genealogical and historical material within the DAR Library in Washington, D. C. Many of the sources unique to the DAR have been digitized. A full explanation of these materials (including membership applications and supplemental applications) can be read online at: www.dar.org.

For ***the*** published guide to DAR's collections, see:

Grundset, Eric G., and Steven B. Rhodes. *American Genealogical Research at the DAR, Washington, D. C.* Washington, D. C.: NSDAR, 2004. [Note: This guide was published before the DAR's digitizing projects were completed, and it does not, therefore, provide information on the impact of reformatting of materials on research procedures and policies. Current updates are available online at the DAR's website: www.dar.org]

All DAR membership applications and supplemental applications have been digitized and may be ordered online by visiting the National Society's website: http://services.dar.org/public/dar_research/search. Documentation that supported these applications may or may not still be available at the DAR Library, but that which the Library does own as been digitized and is only available for viewing on-site. Researchers must contact the DAR Library Search Service for a search to be done to determine if pertinent documentation is available and to obtain copies. Research and copies may not be ordered by telephone. See: http://www.dar.org/library/search-services.

Since 1913, the DAR has had a Genealogical Records Committee (GRC) at the national, state, and chapter levels to seek out previously unpublished genealogical sources and to compile them into typescript volumes for placement in select libraries including the DAR Library. All of these volumes – nearly 20,000 in number – have been digitized and most have been indexed for every personal name that appears in them. The index is available to public research both at the DAR Library and online at: http://services.dar.org/public/dar_research/search/?Tab_ID=6 through the DAR's "Genealogical Research System" (GRS). Microfilm of the *Reports* that existed prior to 1972 is also available through the LDS Family History Library and its Family History Centers, but the series and volume numbers used for indexing the actual volumes in the DAR Library were added in the 1990s and will not match most of the numbering on the microfilmed volumes or on the volumes retained in most specific state research centers.

All of the *G. R. C. Reports* housed in the DAR Library have been digitized, but they can only be viewed on the Library's on-site computers in Washington, D. C., at the present time. As of 2015, the set for North Carolina contains 537 digitized typescripts, and the one for Tennessee has 314. Both include many Bible and cemetery transcriptions submitted by members in each state. Because records travelled with families and individuals, the sets of other states throughout the country may also contain North Carolina or Tennessee materials because descendants who were or are DAR members may have submitted transcriptions of family records in a *GRC Report* from the state in which they did or do reside. As a result, the online GRC National Index is an essential tool for North Carolina research.

Much information has appeared in the *DAR Magazine* over many decades. The magazine has had several titles: *American Monthly Magazine* (1892-1913), *Daughters of the American Revolution Magazine* (1913-1938), *National Historical Magazine* (1939-1945), *Daughters of the American Revolution Magazine* (1946-2001), and *American Spirit: Daughters of the American Revolution Magazine*, 2001 to the present. A three volume index to the magazine was published in 1998 and covers all volumes from 1982 through 1997. In late 2013, the entire run of the magazine was digitized.

Records of the National Society of the Daughters of the Revolution of 1776

The National Society of the Daughters of the Revolution of 1776 existed from 1891 to 1983. On its demise in the 1980s, the D of R's records were deposited at the Suffolk County Historical Society, 300 West Main Street, Riverhead, N. Y. 11901; 631.727.2881.

Because of the similarity of names, many researchers confuse this organization with the National Society Daughters of the American Revolution, but they were separate organizations. Volunteers indexed these records by the patriots' names and the names of members of the National Society. The searchable index is available online on the website of the German Genealogy Group along with a form to be used to request copies of application to the NSDR. Consult the index at: http://www.germangenealogygroup.com/records-search/daughters-of-the-revolution.php. Copies must be ordered from the Suffolk County Historical Society. None of these records are available from the DAR in Washington, D. C.

Records of the National Society of the Sons of the American Revolution

The Sons of the American Revolution (SAR) headquarters in Louisville, Kentucky, maintains the records of this lineage society for male descendants of Revolutionary War patriots. SAR's website provides full information on their collections and on how to access them. See: www.sar.org.

Records of the General Society, Sons of the Revolution

The Sons of the Revolution (SR) headquarters in Independence, Missouri, maintains the records of this lineage society for male descendants of Revolutionary War patriots. SR's website provides full information on their collections and on how to access them. See: www.sr1776.org.

North Carolina Records from the National Archives of the United Kingdom and Other British Sources

Andrews, Charles McLean. *Guide to the Materials for American History, to 1783, in the Public Record Office of Great Britain*. (Carnegie Institution of Washington publication no. 90A; Papers of the Department of Historical Research) Washington, D. C.: Carnegie Institution of Washington, 1912; reprinted: 2 vols. New York: Kraus Reprint Corporation, 1965.

Andrews, Charles McLean, and Frances G. Davenport. *Guide to the Manuscript Materials for the History of the United States to 1783, in the British Museum, in Minor London Archives, and in the Libraries of Oxford and Cambridge*. (Carnegie Institution of Washington publication no. 90) Washington, D. C.: Carnegie Institution of Washington, 1908; reprinted: 2 vols. New York: Kraus Reprint Corporation, 1965.

Cain, Robert J. "North Carolina's British Records Program." *Carolina Comments*, 38:5 (September 1990), 134-139. [Online description from "North Carolina Periodicals Index," East Carolina University: "The British Records Program of the North Carolina Colonial Records Project seeks to collect copies of state-related documents in English repositories and to make them available for public use at the State Archives in Raleigh."]

Cain, Robert J. *Preliminary Guide to the British Records Collection*. (Archives Information Circular, no. 16) Raleigh: North Carolina Department of Cultural Resources, Division of Archives and History, 1979.

Clinton, Henry, Sir, 1730-1795. *The American Rebellion: Sir Henry Clinton's Narrative of His Campaigns, 1775-1782, with an Appendix of Original Documents*. New Haven: Yale University Press, 1954.

Clinton, Henry, Sir, 1730-1795. "Sir Henry Clinton Papers, 1736-1850." Manuscript, William L. Clements Library, University of Michigan, Ann Arbor. [The online subject and geographic indices for this collection on the library's website provide the location of documents relating to North Carolina.]

"Dartmouth Manuscripts, 1720-1783." Transcriptions of original documents in the National Archives of the United Kingdom, Kew, London; "British Records Collection," State Archives of North Carolina, Raleigh. [These documents are cataloged individually in the MARS online catalog. They are listed individually within what was once called the "Dartmouth Manuscripts" in the 1920s.[14]

Goodloe, Daniel R[eaves]. *The Birth of the Republic: Compiled from the National and Colonial Histories and Historical Collections, from American Archives and from Memoirs, and from the Journals and Proceedings of the British Parliament*. Chicago and New York: Belford, Clarke, 1889; online: https://catalog.hathitrust.org/Record/009562705.

Great Britain. Board of Trade and Secretaries of State, America and West Indies. "Manuscripts in Collection CO 5." National Archives of the United Kingdom, Kew, Richmond, Surrey, England.

Great Britain. "British Public Records, c. 1600-1782." Manuscript 1609, Southern Historical Collection, Louis Round Wilson Special Collections Library, University of North Carolina, Chapel Hill; online finding aid

[14] "The Dartmouth Manuscripts, 1729-1783." In D. L. Corbitt, *Calendar of Manuscript Collections, Vol. 1* (Raleigh: Edwards & Broughton, 1926), 1-10.

available at http://www2.lib.unc.edu/mss/inv/b/British_Public_Records.html. [Online finding aid description: "The collection contains photostats, typed transcriptions, and microfilm copies of miscellaneous records from the British Public Record Office, arranged loosely into series as follows: records of cases in Chancery and the Star Chamber, 1600-circa 1630; port records of sailings, exports, imports, duties, etc., for forty British North American ports, 1768-1773; selected pages containing records, 1733-1770, relating to church silver supplied to North Carolina colonial governors Johnston, Dobbs, Tryon, and Martin; correspondence, 1758-1763, between North Carolina governor Arthur Dobbs (1689-1765) and the successive commanders of British forces in North America, including James Abercrombie, John Campbell, fourth Earl of Loudoun, and Jeffery Amherst (bound typescripts); fragment of a government account book, undated (18th century, 10 pages); account of the Gross Produce of the Stamp Duties for the year ending August 1, 1713; correspondence and reports, 1663-1782, of the royal governors of Carolina and North Carolina with various departments of the British government, including land records and legislative journals (30 microfilm reels); disbursement records of the militia and loyalist refugees at Charleston, 1780-1782 (5 microfilm reels); and a list of the names of members of the Company of the Levant, circa 1606."]

Great Britain. Colonial Office; Davies, K. G. (Kenneth Gordon), ed. *Documents of the American Revolution, 1770-1783; (Colonial Office series).* Shannon, Ireland: Irish University Press, 1972-1981. [Documents selected from Colonial Office records in the Public Record Office (now the National Archives of the United Kingdom, Kew, Richmond, Surrey, England). Includes bibliographical references and indexes.] [This set of books includes a calendar and transcriptions of selected documents from the British Colonial Office. There are many references to individual people and to the American colonies specifically in the index of each volume. ***Note that volumes 1-8 and most of volume 9 cover the period prior to the April 19, 1775 start of the actual hostilities of the Revolutionary War, so references to material in these early volumes of the set are not acceptable for proving Revolutionary War service of individuals for the DAR.***] [Many references to North Carolina, its residents, and events in the state appear throughout this set.]

Contents:

v. 1. Calendar, 1770-1771
v. 2. Transcripts, 1770
v. 3. Transcripts, 1771
v. 4. Calendar, 1772-1773
v. 5. Transcripts, 1772
v. 6. Transcripts, 1773
v. 7. Calendar, 1774-30 June 1775
v. 8. Transcripts, 1774
v. 9. Transcripts, 1775 January to June
v. 10. Calendar, 1 July 1775-1776
v. 11. Transcripts, 1775 July-December
v. 12. Transcripts, 1776
v. 13. Calendar, 1777-1778
v. 14. Transcripts, 1777
v. 15. Transcripts, 1778
v. 16. Calendar, 1779-1780; Vol. 16 has title: *Documents of the American Revolution, 1779-1780* Vol. 16 has spine title: *Documents of the American Revolution, 1770-1783*
v. 17. Transcripts, 1779
v. 18. Transcripts, 1780
v. 19. Calendar, 1781-1783 and addenda, 1770-1780
v. 20. Transcripts, 1781
v. 21. Transcripts, 1782-1783

Stevens, Benjamin Franklin, ed. *B. F. Stevens's Facsimiles of Manuscripts in European Archives Relating to America, 1773-1783, with Descriptions, Editorial Notes, Collations, References and Translations.* London: Photographed and printed by Malby & sons, 1889-1895.

Chapter Seven:
The Government of North Carolina as a Colony and a State in the Revolutionary Era

The government of every state has created records of historical and genealogical importance, and researchers need a full understanding of these sources. This chapter focuses on the materials relating to state government operations, services, and interactions with citizens in North Carolina, and, by extension, its daughter state of Tennessee. Many of these records are "name-heavy," containing the names of many residents and their involvement with the state government in a myriad number of ways. North Carolina's role in the Continental Congress and its citizen-participants therein is yet another facet of government.

North Carolina's Colonial Government and Its Records

Cheney, John L., Jr., ed. *North Carolina Government 1585-1979.* Raleigh: North Carolina Department of the Secretary of State, 1981.

Great Britain. Colonial Office. "Oxted, Near Godstone, Surry. Thomas Falkner to Lord George Germain, [Sec. of State]. 6 Jan., 1779." Copy of a manuscript in the National Archives of the United Kingdom (formerly the Public Records Office), Kew, Richmond, Surrey, England; 71.330.1-2, State Archives of North Carolina, Raleigh. [Online catalog description: "Requests Germain's approbation of his resignation from the position of secretary and clerk of the Crown for N. C."]

Great Britain. Colonial Office. "Paisley, [Scot.]. Neil Snodgrass, former Merchant in Va. and the Carolinas, to Lord George Germain, [Sec. of State]. 12 Mar., 1779." Copy of a manuscript in the National Archives of the United Kingdom (formerly the Public Records Office), Kew, Richmond, Surrey, England; 71.292.1-4, State Archives of North Carolina, Raleigh. [Online catalog description: "Expresses his interest in serving the Crown in the Carolinas and offers his knowledge and expertise on those colonies. He had been a very successful merchant in Va. and the Carolinas until the revolution forced him to flee for safety. See also Snodgrass to Germain, 13 May 1779 (21.20.131.1.3)."]

Governor of the Province of North Carolina

Cooke, Charles S. "The Governor, Council, and Assembly in Royal North Carolina." *James Sprunt Historial Publications,* 12:1 (Chapel Hill, N.C.: The University, 1912).

Cunningham, Carol Ruth. "The Southern Royal Governors and the Coming of the American Revolution, 1763-1776." Ph. D. dissertation, State University of New York at Buffalo, 1984.

Robinson, Blackwell P[ierce]. *The Five Royal Governors of North Carolina, 1729-1775.* Raleigh: Carolina Charter Tercentenar Commission, 1963.

Provincial/Royal/Colonial Council

Cooke, Charles S. "The Governor, Council, and Assembly in Royal North Carolina." *James Sprunt Historial Publications,* 12:1 (Chapel Hill, N.C.: The University, 1912).

Price, William S., J. "Men of Good Estates: Wealth among North Carolina's Royal Councillors." *North Carolina Historical Review,* 49:1 (January 1972), 72-82. [Online description from "North Carolina Periodicals Index," East Carolina University: "During North Carolina's colonial period members of the Royal Council were deemed 'men of good estates' and therefore the elite of North Carolina politics and society. The Royal Council served as the upper house of the Colonial Assembly as well as a higher court and board of advice and consent to the chief executive."]

Whitaker, Bessie Lewis. "The Provincial Council and the Committees of Safety in North Carolina." M. A. thesis, University of North Carolina at Chapel Hill, 1907; published: *The Provincial Council and Committees of Safety in North Carolina* (James Sprunt Studies in History and Political Science, no. 8) Chapel Hill: University of North Carolina Press, 1908.

The Provincial/Colonial Assembly

Cook, Florence. "Procedure in the North Carolina Colonial Assembly." *North Carolina Historical Review*, 8:3 (July

1931), 258-283; online: http://digital.ncdcr.gov/cdm/ref/collection/p16062coll9/id/4207. [Online description from "North Carolina Periodicals Index," East Carolina University: "This article examines procedure in the North Carolina assembly during the colonial period, 1731-1770. It includes descriptions of establishing operational policy, appointments and positions within the assembly, the role of religion within assembly operations, expulsion of members, member privileges, rules of decorum, acts of legislation, the passing and rejection of bills, the division of the houses and joint conferences, relations with the governor and committee systems."]

Cooke, Charles S. "The Governor, Council, and Assembly in Royal North Carolina." *James Sprunt Historial Publications,* 12:1 (Chapel Hill, N.C.: The University, 1912).

Franklin, W. Neil. "Some Aspects of Representation in the American Colonies." *North Carolina Historical Review*, 6;1 (January 1929), 38-66; online: http://digital.ncdcr.gov/cdm/ref/collection/p16062coll9/id/4207. [Online description from "North Carolina Periodicals Index," East Carolina University: "This article attempts to identify significant factors in the struggle for representation in the 13 original colonies with a special attention to sectionalism and the struggle between East and West within the states. Each colony is addressed individually."]

Greene, Jack P. "The North Carolina Lower House and the Power to Appoint Public Treasurers, 1711-1775." *North arolina Historical Review*, 40:1 (January 1963), 37-53; online: http://digital.ncdcr.gov/cdm/ref/collection/p16062coll9/id/4207. [Online description from "North Carolina Periodicals Index," East Carolina University: "Within the American colonial political structure, the elected lower houses of the assembly saw a rise in political power in the years before independence. Their ability to nominate and appoint public treasurers to collect, hold, and apply moneys from provincial revenues, and then control these officials, gave the lower houses a level of financial authority that encroached on executive power."]

Greene, Jack P. "The Role of the Lower Houses of Assembly in Eighteenth-Century Politics." *Journal of Southern History*, 27:4 (November 1961), 451-474.

Kammen, Michael. *Deputyes and Libertyes: The Origins of Representative Government in Colonial America.* New York: Knopf, 1969.

London, Lawrence F. "The Representation Controversy in Colonial North Carolina." *North Carolina Historical Review*, 11:4 (October 1934), 255-270. [sectionalism]

Main, Jackson Turner. *The Upper House in Revolutionary America, 1763-1788.* Madison: University of Wisconsin Press, 1967.

Colonial Agents

Lonn, Ella. *The Colonial Agents of the Southern Colonies.* Chapel Hill: University of North Carolina Press, 1945; reprinted: Gloucester, Mass.: Peter Smith, 1965.

Committees of Safety, 1774-1776
Patriotic Service[15]

Patriots of the Revolution are considered to be those men and women who by an act or series of actions demonstrated unfailing loyalty to the cause of American Independence from England. Patriotic service might begin as early as April 1774. We depend upon recorded actions to give us an indication of patriotism. What was the purpose of the action? What were the risks? The consequences? Answers to these questions can determine whether the action actually applied to an attempt to further the cause of independence or demonstrated loyalty to that cause.

Evidence of patriotic activity may be found in town, county, state, and federal records. Many records kept by the states have been indexed and often a letter to the state archives will be sufficient to determine if evidence exists to show that a person contributed supplies or made some other contribution to the war effort. Town and county records have usually not been indexed and a personal search of town minutes and court minutes is required. Minutes of the Continental Congresses have been published. *Old letters, diaries, and other family and personal papers can often be used as evidence of patriotic intent, provided the record was made at the time of the event described.*

---

[15] Office of the Registrar General's compilation, *Genealogy Guidelines* (Washington, D. C.: National Society Daughters of the American Revolution, 2014), 94-95.

Not all actions illustrating patriotism are mentioned here. Many others exist. When it is considered desirable to establish another type of patriotic service, proof of the action taken must be submitted with the application paper, together with historical justification to show that the action did indeed imply patriotic intent.

Committees of Safety: The Committees of Safety at the state level were successors to the Committees of Correspondence. Appointed by the Provincial Congresses or Conventions, they served as interim state governments until new state constitutions were implemented. Their primary focus was on security and defense, often including command of the militia.

Martin, Josiah. "Proclamation of Governor Josiah Martin Ordering County Committees of Safety and Unlawful Assemblies to Stop Meeting, August 13, 1774." Photograph of manuscript, N.2004.11.2 (MARS ID: 4.1.31.227; item), State Archives of North Carolina, Raleigh.

North Carolina (State). Secretary of State. "Committees of Safety, 1774-1776." Manuscript, Call Numbers: SS 305, SS 912-SS 913, SS 913A (MARS ID: 12.112; Series), General Assembly Record Group, Session Records, State Archives of North Carolina, Raleigh. [Online catalog description: "Journals, correspondence, and some miscellaneous material from county and municipal committees of safety, including New Hanover, Pitt, Rowan, Surry, and Tryon counties, New Bern District, and the Town of Wilmington. Correspondence concerns the requisition of supplies, commissioning of troops, and the Continental Congress in Philadelphia. Series includes printed, photocopied, or manuscript copies of some of the journals."]

Tryon County. Committee of Safety. "Minutes of Committees of Safety, Tryon County, 1775-1776." Manuscript 33MSS-17-7 (MARS ID: 5000.6.822.7; item), State Archives of North Carolina, Raleigh.

Watson, Alan D. "The Committees of Safety and the Coming of the American Revolution in North Carolina, 1774-1776." *North Carolina Historical Review*, 73:2 (April 1996), 131-155. [Online description from "North Carolina Periodicals Index," East Carolina University: "Created in 1774 at the urging of the Continental Congress, Committees of Safety were local organizations that were instrumental in the independence movement. While not completely legal when created, the committees eventually replaced local governments put in place by the Crown and assumed their duties. This included regulating the economy, politics, morality, and the militia within their communities. In December 1776, this authority was given to the Council of Safety, a more powerful central authority."]

Whitaker, Bessie Lewis. "The Provincial Council and Committees of Safety in North Carolina." *James Sprunt Studies in History and Political Science*, no. 8 (1909), 1-49.

Whitaker, Bessie Lewis. "The Provincial Council and the Committees of Safety in North Carolina." M. A. thesis, University of North Carolina at Chapel Hill, 1907.

Committees of Correspondence

Patriotic Service[16]

Patriots of the Revolution are considered to be those men and women who by an act or series of actions demonstrated unfailing loyalty to the cause of American Independence from England. Patriotic service might begin as early as April 1774. We depend upon recorded actions to give us an indication of patriotism. What was the purpose of the action? What were the risks? The consequences? Answers to these questions can determine whether the action actually applied to an attempt to further the cause of independence or demonstrated loyalty to that cause.

Evidence of patriotic activity may be found in town, county, state, and federal records. Many records kept by the states have been indexed and often a letter to the state archives will be sufficient to determine if evidence exists to show that a person contributed supplies or made some other contribution to the war effort. Town and county records have usually not been indexed and a personal search of town minutes and court minutes is required. Minutes of the Continental Congresses have been published. *Old letters, diaries, and other family and personal papers can often be used as evidence of patriotic intent, provided the record was made at the time of the event described.*

---

[16] Office of the Registrar General's compilation, *Genealogy Guidelines* (Washington, D. C.: National Society Daughters of the American Revolution, 2014), 94-95.

Not all actions illustrating patriotism are mentioned here. Many others exist. When it is considered desirable to establish another type of patriotic service, proof of the action taken must be submitted with the application paper, together with historical justification to show that the action did indeed imply patriotic intent.

Committees of Correspondence: These committees facilitated communication among the colonial assemblies; they represent a first step toward united action by the colonies, which eventually led to the call for a general Congress.

North Carolina (State). Committee of Correspondence. "Letter from the North Carolina Committee of Correspondence to the South Carolina Committee of Correspondence, June 10, 1774." *The Colonial and State Records, Volume 11 (1776-1777, with Supplement 1730-1776)*, 245-246; digital typescript available through *Documenting the American South* at University of North Carolina at Chapel Hill at http://docsouth.unc.edu/csr/index.html/document/csr11-0117.

North Carolina (State). Committee of Correspondence. "Letter from the North Carolina Committee of Correspondence to the Virginia Committee of Correspondence, June 21, 1774." *The Colonial and State Records, Volume 11 (1776-1777, with Supplement 1730-1776)*, 247-248; digital typescript available through *Documenting the American South* at University of North Carolina at Chapel Hill at http://docsouth.unc.edu/csr/index.html/document/csr11-0118.

The Five Provincial Congresses

Patriotic Service[17]

Patriots of the Revolution are considered to be those men and women who by an act or series of actions demonstrated unfailing loyalty to the cause of American Independence from England. Patriotic service might begin as early as April 1774. We depend upon recorded actions to give us an indication of patriotism. What was the purpose of the action? What were the risks? The consequences? Answers to these questions can determine whether the action actually applied to an attempt to further the cause of independence or demonstrated loyalty to that cause.

Evidence of patriotic activity may be found in town, county, state, and federal records. Many records kept by the states have been indexed and often a letter to the state archives will be sufficient to determine if evidence exists to show that a person contributed supplies or made some other contribution to the war effort. Town and county records have usually not been indexed and a personal search of town minutes and court minutes is required. Minutes of the Continental Congresses have been published. *Old letters, diaries, and other family and personal papers can often be used as evidence of patriotic intent, provided the record was made at the time of the event described.*

Not all actions illustrating patriotism are mentioned here. Many others exist. When it is considered desirable to establish another type of patriotic service, proof of the action taken must be submitted with the application paper, together with historical justification to show that the action did indeed imply patriotic intent.

The Provincial Congresses, State Governors, Legislators: The Provincial Congresses met in each of the colonies in 1774 and continued to meet until the new state governments were established. Minutes for many of these meetings have been published. DAR does not accept royal governors.

Butler, Lindley S. "Provincial Congresses." In William S. Powell, ed.; Jay Mazzocchi, assoc. ed., *Encyclopedia of North Carolina* (Chapel Hill: University of North Carolina Press in association with the University of North Carolina Library, 2006), 917-918. [1774-1775]

Engstrom, Mary Claire. "The War Congress." *The State: Down Home in North Carolina*, 42:2 (July 1975), 10-12; online: http://digital.ncdcr.gov/cdm/ref/collection/p16062coll18/id/9503. [Online description from "North Carolina Periodicals Index," East Carolina University: "On August 24, 1975, Historic Hillsborough and Orange County will celebrate the 200th anniversary of North Carolina's Third Provincial Congress, also called the War Congress. One hundred and eighty-four members from every county and borough in the state attended the congress, which lasted for twenty-one days. The congress decided on an interim government and officially declared war against England."]

---

[17] Office of the Registrar General's compilation, *Genealogy Guidelines* (Washington, D. C.: National Society Daughters of the American Revolution, 2014), 94-95.

Hobbie, Lawrence. "The Third Provincial Congress." *Tar Heel Junior Historian*, 14:3 (February 1975), 12-13. [Online description from "North Carolina Periodicals Index," East Carolina University: "One hundred eighty-four elected delegates met at Hillsborough for the Third Provincial Congress. From August 20 to September 11, 1775, members of the congress faced the problem of finding funds, general supplies, and men to prepare for war."]

The Journal of the Proceedings of the Provincial Congress of North Carolina, Held at Halifax on the 4th Day of April, 1776." New Bern, N. C.: Printed by James Davis, 1776.

North Carolina (Colony). Provincial Congress. *The Journal of the Proceedings of the Provincial Congress of North Carolina*. Raleigh: Lawrence & Lemay, Printers to the State, 1831.

North Carolina (Colony). Provincial Congress. *The Journal of the Proceedings of the Provincial Congress of North-Carolina, Held at Halifax the 12th Day of November, 1776, Together with the Declaration of Rights, Constitution & Ordinances of the Congress*. Newbern: Printed by James Davis, Printer to the Honourable the General Assembly, 1777. (*Hazard Pamphlets*, 39:1)

North Carolina (Colony). Provincial Congress. *North-Carolina. At a Convention of the Delegates for the Respective Counties and Towns, within This Province, Held at Newbern the 6th day of April, 1775. Mr Thomas Macknight ... having been called upon to sign (with other members of this convention) the Association approved of by the Continental Congress, thereupon refused, and withdrew himself. Resolved, that it is the opinion of this convention, that from the disingenious and equivocal behaviour of the said Thomas Macknight, it is manifest his intentions are inimical to the cause of American liberty*. Newbern: Printed by James Davis, 1775; micropublished: (Early American Imprints. First Series. No. 42912) New York: Readex Microprint, 1985.

North Carolina (Colony). Provincial Congress. *The Journal of the Proceedings of the Provincial Congress of North-Carolina, Held at Halifax on the Fourth Day of April, 1776*. New Bern: James Davis, printer, 1776; (facsimile reprint): Raleigh: Edwards & Broughton, 1976.

North Carolina (Colony). Provincial Conventions and Congresses. "Provincial Conventions and Congresses, 1774-1776." Manuscript SS 301-SS 304, SS 911, SS 911.1A-SS.911.1B (MARS ID: 12.114; series), "Secretary of State Record Group," State Archives of North Carolina, Raleigh. [Online catalog description: "Journals, proclamations, resolutions (including photographs of the Halifax Resolves), depositions, vouchers, receipts, certificates of election, and correspondence with delegates in Congress or concerning requisitioning of supplies. Records are for the First Provincial Convention (25-27 August 1774), the Second Provincial Convention (3-7 April 1775), the First Provincial Congress (20 August-10 September 1775), the Second Provincial Congress (4 April-14 May 1776), and the Third Provincial Congress (12 November-23 December 1776)."]

Pittman, Thomas Merritt. "The Revolutionary Congresses of North Carolina." *North Carolina Booklet*, 2:6 (October 10, 1902), 1-18. [Online description from "North Carolina Periodicals Index," East Carolina University: "This article examines the different Congresses that governed North Carolina during the Revolutionary War as well as some circumstances within the colony that led to the war."]

"Tyrrell Delegates to the Provincial Congresses at the Time of the Revolutionary War." *The Quarterly Review of the Eastern North Carolina Genealogical Society*, 7:4 (Fall 1980), 159.

Vidmar, Elizabeth. "A General Meeting of Delegates in Hillsborough, 1775." *Quarterly Review of the Eastern North Carolina Genealogical Society*, 14:4 (December 1987), 171-172.

Watson, Alan D. "The Fourth Provincial Congress at Halifax." *Tar Heel Junior Historian*, 14:3 (February 1975), 13-15. [Online description from "North Carolina Periodicals Index," East Carolina University: "Delegates met in Halifax on April 4, 1776 and took the first official action against the British crown. Despite victory at Moore's Creek, British soldiers harassed citizens in the Cape Fear region and forced the congress to acknowledge that reconciliation was not an option."]

Wilson, John Kenyon. "The Growth of the Revolutionary Spirit in North Carolina, as Shown in the Work of the Five Provincial Congresses." Senior thesis, University of North Carolina at Chapel Hill, 1905.

North Carolina's Revolutionary Government and Its Records

Cheney, John L., Jr., ed. *North Carolina Government 1585-1979*. Raleigh: North Carolina Department of the Secretary of State, 1981.

Ganyard, Robert L. *The Emergence of North Carolina's Revolutionary Government*. Raleigh: North Carolina Department of Cultural Resources, 1978.

Keith, Alice Barnwell. "The Revolutionary Government of North Carolina, 1774-1776." Typescript Cp970.32 K28r, North Carolina Collection, Louis Round Wilson Special Collections Library, University of North Carolina at Chapel Hill. [Online catalog note: "With MS. Corrections."]

Lewis, J. D. "NC Government during the American Revolution." Online: http://www.carolana.com/NC/Revolution/nc_revolution_government.html.

"Revolutionary War Papers, 1774-1782." Manuscript 2194-z, Southern Historical Collection, Louis Round Wilson Special Collections Library, University of North Carolina, Chapel Hill; online finding aid available at http://www2.lib.unc.edu/mss/inv/r/Revolutionary_War_Papers.html. [Online finding aid description: "The collection contains miscellaneous Revolutionary War papers, chiefly relating to North Carolina, South Carolina, and Georgia, 1781-1782. The collection includes letters, reports, invoices, and other papers of the North Carolina General Assembly and of Governor Richard Caswell concerning military activities and supplies, records of local proceedings, and other items."]

Rodabaugh, Karl. "Note de recherche: Ten Men in High Office in Revolutionary North Carolina, 1777-1783: A Test of the Martin Thesis in Men in Rebellion." *Histoire sociale/Social History*, 21 (May 1978), 224-232. [Samuel Ashe (New Hanover County), Thomas Benbury (Chowan County), Thomas Burke (Orange County), Richard Caswell (Dobbs County), Whitmel Hill (Martin County), Allen Jones (Northampton County), Alexander Martin (Guilford County), Abner Nash (Craven County), Edward Starkey (Onslow County), and John Williams (Granville County), all served in at least one office as either Governor, Speaker of the Senate, or Speaker of the House of Commons during the Revolutionary War.]

"State Records." In Helen F. M. Leary, ed. *North Carolina Research: Genealogy and Local History*. 2nd ed. (Raleigh: North Carolina Genealogical Society, 1996), Part III, 297-424. [Part III covers Chapters 28-33.]

North Carolina Censuses, Census Substitutes, Demographic Studies, and Similar Sources

Albright, Lee, and Helen F. M. Leary. "Strategy for the Census." In Helen F. M. Leary, ed. *North Carolina Research: Genealogy and Local History*. 2nd ed. (Raleigh: North Carolina Genealogical Society, 1996), Chapter Two: "Designing Research Strategies," 24-27.

Connor, Robert Diggs Wimberly. *Race Elements in the White Population in North Carolina*. (North Carolina State Normal & Industrial College Historical Publicatons series, no. 1) Raleigh: The College, 1920; reprinted: Spartanburg, S. C.: The Reprint Company, 1971; online: http://babel.hathitrust.org/cgi/pt?id=loc.ark:/13960/t5w66r92p;view=1up;seq=2. [Description: "A look at the English, Highland Scotch, Scotch-Irish, and German influences on the white population of North Carolina."]

Greene, Evarts, and Virginia Harrington. *American Population before the Federal Census of 1790*. New York: Columbia University Press, 1932: Gloucester, Mass., P. Smith, 1966; reprinted: Baltimore, Md.: Genealogical Publishing Company, 1993.

Kay, Marvin L., and Lorin Lee Cary. "A Demographic Analysis of Colonial North Carolina with Special Emphasis upon the Slave and Black Populations." In Jeffrey J. Crow and Flora J. Hatley, eds., *Black Americans in North Carolina and the South* (Chapel Hill: University of North Carolina Press, 1984), 71-121.

McGhee, Lucy Kate. *Partial Census of 1787 to 1791 of Tennessee as Taken from North Carolina Land Grants*. 3 vols. Washington, D. C.: L. K. McGhee, 1955.

Register, Alvaretta Kenan. *State Census of North Carolina, 1784 – 1787*. 2nd ed. rev. Norfolk, Va.: [s. n.], 1971; Baltimore, Md: Genealogical Publishing Co., 1973.

Stevenson, George. "State Records: State Census, 1785-1787." In Helen F. M. Leary, ed. *North Carolina Research: Genealogy and Local History*. 2nd ed. (Raleigh: North Carolina Genealogical Society, 1996), Chapter 28, 299-302.

United States. Department of Commerce and Labor, Bureau of the Census. *First Census of the United States, 1790, North Carolina*." Washington, D. C.: National Archives and Records Administration.

United States. Department of Commerce and Labor, Bureau of the Census. *Second Census of the United States, 1800, North Carolina*. Washington, D. C.: National Archives and Records Administration.

United States. Department of Commerce and Labor, Bureau of the Census. *Fifth Census of the United States, 1830, North Carolina, Orange County*. Washington, D. C.: National Archives and Records Administration.

"United States Census." In Helen F. M. Leary, ed. *North Carolina Research: Genealogy and Local History*. 2nd ed. (Raleigh: North Carolina Genealogical Society, 1996), Chapter 35, 433-457.

Wells, Robert V. *The Population of the British Colonies in America before 1776: A Survey of Census Data*. Princeton: Princeton University Press, 1975.

William L. Sauders and William Clark, Compiled and edited. The Colonial and State Records of North Carolina, 1662-1790. 28 volumes. Wilmington, N.C.: Broadfoot Pub. Co., 1993-94. Includes state laws, census of 1790, index, and historical review.

Wood, Peter H. "The Changing Population of the Colonial South: An Overview by Race and Region, 1685-1790." In Peter H. Wood, Gregory A. Waselkov, and M. Thomas Hatley, eds., *Powhatan's Mantle: Indians in the Colonial Southeast* (Lincoln: University of Nebraska Press, 1989), 35-103.

North Carolina Government and Politics (generally)

Blackwelder, Ruth. *The Age of Orange: Political and Intellectual Leadership in North Carolina, 1752-1861.* Charlotte: William Loftin, 1961.

Douglas, Elisha P. *Rebels and Democrats: The Struggle for Equal Political Rights and Majority Rule during the American Revolution.* Chapel Hill: University of North Carolina Press, 1955; reprinted: Chicago: I. R. Dee, 1989; Chapel Hill: University of North Carolina Press, 1995.

Golumbic, Lars C. 1996. "Who Shall Dictate the Law?: Political Wrangling Between 'Whig' Lawyers and Backcountry Farms in Revolutionary Era North Carolina." North Carolina Historical Review 73:1 (January 1996), 56-82.

Hayman, Wilson. "The American Revolution and the Transformation of North Carolina Politics, 1775 to 1778." Senior thesis, Princeton University, 1976.

Higginbotham, Don. "The Politics of Revolutionary North Carolina: A Preliminary Assessment." In Don Higginbotham, *War and Society in Revolutionary America: The Wider Dimensions of Conflict* (Columbia: University of South Carolina Press, 1988), 65-83.

Kirchner, Kevin Randall. "Twelve Days of Unity, Twenty Years of Division: The King's Mountain Volunteers in the Context of Land Speculation and Frontier Politics during the Revolutionary Era." Honors Paper, Duke University, Durham, 1998.

Leffler, Richard. "Political Parties in North Carolina before the Constitution, 1782-1787." Ph. D. dissertation, University of Wisconsin-Madison, 1994.

Maass, John R. "'The Cure for All Our Political Calamities': Archibald Maclaine and the Politics of Moderation in Revolutionary North Carolina." *North Carolina Historical Review*, 85:3 (July 2008), 251-281. [Online description from "North Carolina Periodicals Index," East Carolina University: "This article examines the arguements of Whig lawyer Archibald Maclaine who wished for moderation toward and reconciliation with Loyalists after the cessation of hostilities in North Carolina during the American Revolution."]

MacDonald, James M. "Politics of the Personal in the Old North State: Griffith Rutherford in Revolutionary North Carolina." Ph. D. dissertation, Louisiana State University, 2006. ["Traces the political climate of North Carolina throughout the Revolutionary period. Volume two contains an extensive bibliography."]

Smith, Martha M. "Loyalism as a Political Issue in Revolutionary North Carolina, 1775-1789." M. A. thesis, University of North Carolina, 1978. [Study of the impact of the loyalism issue on North Carolina's early political groups, especially in terms of the effects upon the establishment of a 'peaceful post-war security,' 'the government's respect for the provisions of the Treaty of Paris of 1783 and for private rights,' and the 'debates on the ratification of the Federal Constitution'."]

Smith, Penelope Sue. "Creation of an American State: Politics in North Carolina, 1765 - 1789." Ph. D. Dissertation, Rice University, 1980.

Wagstaff, Henry McGilbert. *State Rights and Political Parties in North Carolina – 1776-1861.* Baltimore: Johns Hopkins University Press, 1906.

Waldrup, J. Charles. "'Uneasy Lies the Head that Wears a Crown': Ruling Elites in North Carolina, 1776-1789." M. A. thesis, University of North Carolina at Chapel Hill, 1977.

Wood, Bradford J. "Politics and Authority in Colonial North Carolina: A Regional Perspective." *North Carolina Historical Review*, 81:1 (January 2004), 1-37. [Online description from "North Carolina Periodicals Index," East Carolina University: "This article examines the political landscape of the Lower Cape Fear region of colonial North Carolina, comparing it to the rest of the colony. The Lower Cape Fear region developed quite distinctly from nearby regions as it contained a stable and wealthy ruling class and a large, unruly slave population. The differences between the Lower Cape Fear region and the rest of the colony emphasize the problem with generalizing North Carolina's political environment."]

Wood, Walter Kirk. "The Union of the States: A Study of Radical Whig-Republican Ideology and Its Influence upon the Nation and the South, 1776-1861." Ph. D. dissertation, University of South Carolina, 1978.

Governor of the State of North Carolina

Hathaway, J. R. B. "Items relating to the Revolutionary War (From the Executive Letter Book at Raleigh, N. C.)" *North Carolina Historical and Genealogical Register*, 2:2 (April 1901), 234-255 [1777]; 2:3 (July 1901), 430-442 [1775-1777].

Hill, Michael, ed. *The Governors of North Carolina.* Raleigh: North Carolina Office of Archives and History, 2007.

Lewis, J. D. "North Carolina – From Statehood to 1800: North Carolina Governors from 1777 to 1800." Online: http://www.carolana.com/NC/Early_Statehood/nc_statehood_1800_governors.html.

Macmillan, Margaret Burnham. *The War Governors in the American Revolution.* (Studies in History, Economics, and Public Law, no. 503) New York: Columbia University Press; London: P. S. King & Staples, Ltd., 1943.

North Carolina (State). Governor's Office. "Governor's Office Records, 1663-1972." Manuscript G.O. 1 – G. O. 429.10 (MARS ID: 67.1; series), State Archives of North Carolina, Raleigh. [Online catalog description shows that this large collection contains: "Reports, minutes, commissions, oaths of office, accounts, receipts, warrants, surveys, appointments, requisitions, proclamations, reprieves extraditions, commutations, census and election returns, charters, and journals relating to the work of the Governor's Office." It includes: "…warrant books on the treasurer to pay individuals (1782-1883),…, election returns (1768-1783), census returns (1784),…, proclamation books (1766-1775),…"]

Prinz, Rudolph A. "Institutional Study of the Office of Governor in North Carolina during the War of Independence." M. A. thesis, University of North Carolina, 1976.

Council of State/Executive Council/Council of Safety

Jones, Joe. "From Royalist to Revolutionary." *The State: Down Home in North Carolina*, 41:9 (February 1974), 7-8; online: http://digital.ncdcr.gov/cdm/ref/collection/p16062coll18/id/56442. [Online description: "Willie Jones, a wealthy pre-Revolution aristocrat began his political career as a Royalist but deferred summons from His Majesty's Council of the Province to join radicals in support of the Revolution. Jones was known for his leadership abilities and acted as a virtual governor as president of the Council of Safety during the war. Jones was also instrumental in founding Raleigh, North Carolina."]

Great Britain. Colonial Office. Colonial Office. American and West Indies: North Carolina, Original Correspondence, Board of Trade. Secretary of State. (CO 5/318). "Order of N. C. Council of Safety. July 4, 1776." Copy of a manuscript in the National Archives of the United Kingdom (formerly the Public Records Office), Kew, Richmond, Surrey, England; (MARS ID: 21.1.27.92; folder), "British Records Collection," State Archives of North Carolina, Raleigh. [Online catalog description: "Persons claiming neutrality in the conflict must render an inventory of their property."]

Moore, Marie D. "Council of State in North Carolina, 1776-1868." M. A. thesis, Duke University, 1971.

North Carolina (Colony). Office of the Governor. "Council Journal, 1764-1775." Manuscript G. O. 117 (MARS ID: 67.1.12; box), State Archives of North Carolina, Raleigh.

North Carolina (State). Office of the Governor. "Council Journal, 1781-1782." Manuscript G. O. 120 (MARS ID: 67.1.125; box), State Archives of North Carolina, Raleigh.

North Carolina (Colony). Provincial Council of Safety. "Provincial Council of Safety Records, 1775-1776." Manuscript SS 306-SS 308 (MARS ID: 12.113; series), "Secretary of State Record Group," State Archives of North Carolina, Raleigh. [Online catalog description: "Journal, resolutions, petitions, a proclamation, and other records of the Provincial Council of Safety. Correspondence is largely that of Cornelius Harnett, president of the council, and includes correspondence with other states and Congress, messages to or about the Creek and Cherokee nations, and letters about the commissioning of officers and troops, requisitioning of supplies, and such subjects as Highlanders in North Carolina, ironworks, armed vessels, and salt."]

Towles, Louis P. "Council of Safety." In William S. Powell, ed.; Jay Mazzocchi, assoc. ed., *Encyclopedia of North Carolina* (Chapel Hill: University of North Carolina Press in association with the University of North Carolina Library, 2006), 296.

Council Extraordinary, 1781-1784

Norris, David A. "Council Extraordinary." In William S. Powell, ed.; Jay Mazzocchi, assoc. ed., *Encyclopedia of North Carolina* (Chapel Hill: University of North Carolina Press in association with the University of North Carolina Library, 2006), 296.

North Carolina (State). Council Extraordinary. "Council Extraordinary Papers, 1781-1784." Manuscript, PC.426, State Archives of North Carolina, Raleigh. [Online catalog description: "Order of Council Extraordinary to move military stores from New Bern to place of safety (1781); letter about Caswell Co. militia (1781); and statement (1784) about account (1776-1782) between the state and Adam Boyd, council secretary."]

North Carolina (State). General Assembly. Senate. "[Document dated:] February 2, [1781]): Joint Papers, Committee Papers, Resolutions, Senate Bills, House Bills, Bill to Establish a Council Extraordinary." Manuscript; General Assembly Record Group; Session Records, January-February 1781, Box 2 (MARS ID: 66.8.24.5; folder), State Archives of North Carolina, Raleigh. [Online catalog description: "The council extraordinary is to replace the board of war. Includes messages debating an amendment [*sic*]."]

Elections and Suffrage

Bassett, John Spencer. "Suffrage in the State of North Carolina (1776-1861). *Report of the American Historical Association for the Year 1895* (Washington, D. C.: American Historical Association, 1896), 269-285.

Ganyard, Robert L. "Radical and Conservatives in Revolutionary North Carolina: A Point at Issue: The October Election, 1776." *William and Mary Quarterly*, 3rd series, 24:4 (October 1967), 568-587.

McKinley, E[dward] Albert. "The Suffrage in North Carolina." In Albert E[dward] McKinley, *The Suffrage Movement in the Thirteen English Colonies in America.* (Publications of the University of Pennsylvania, Series in History, no. 2) (Philadelphia and Boston: Ginn & Co., Agents, for the University of Pennsylvania, 1905), 79-122.

North Carolina (Colony). General Assembly. "[Document dated:] 1775: Lower House Papers; Certificates of Election (Beaufort County-Tyrrell County); Borough of Bath-Borough of Wilmington." Manuscript; General Assembly Session Records: Colonial (Upper and Lower Houses), box 8 (MARS ID: 66.8.8.32; folder), State Archives of North Carolina, Raleigh.

North Carolina (State). General Assembly. "[Document dated:] 1777: Election Certificates and Oaths." Manuscript; General Assembly Session Records; Session of April-May 1777; Joint Papers, Committee Papers, Resolutions, Miscellaneous Bills, Box 1 (MARS ID: 66.8.9.7; folder), State Archives of North Carolina, Raleigh. [Online catalog description: "Oath of office taken by representatives to the North Carolina General Assembly; election certificates of Representatives Henry Rhodes and John King of Onslow County and Abner Nash of Craven County."]

North Carolina (State). General Assembly. "[Document dated:] May 8, 1779: "Report on the Election in Dobbs County (with Petition and List of Voters)." General Assembly Session Records; Session of May 1779; Joint Papers, Committee Papers, Resolutions, Senate Bills, House Bills; House Committee Reports (May 1779): Committee of Privileges and Elections, Box 1 (MARS ID: 66.8.17.11.2; item), State Archives of North Carolina, Raleigh. [Online catalog description: Etheldred Ruffin charges that the election to the Assembly in Dobbs County was in violation of the constitution, and the committee agrees with him."] [Voter lists are usually considered acceptable patriotic service because one would have to have taken an oath of allegiance before being eligible to vote (despite the absence of an oath list).]

North Carolina (State). General Assembly. "[Document dated:] April 17-24, 1780: Joint Papers, Committee Papers, Resolutions, Senate Bills, House Bills, Re[specting] the Election of William Hill of New Hanover County (with Petition, Letter of William Hill, and Poll List.)." Manuscript; General Assembly Record Group; Session Records, April-May 1780, Box 1 (MARS ID; 66.8.20.11.1; item), State Archives of North Carolina, Raleigh. [Online catalog description: "Fifteen inhabitants of Wilmington charge in a petition to the House that Hill's election was illegal because several voters were ineligible and because Hill already holds the positions of county trustee and customs official. By order of the committee, Thomas Person, chairman, issues a summons to Hill and to the sheriff of New Hanover County for the election returns. Upon receipt of the summons, Hill writes to Person, explaining the election, enclosing his certification of appointment as trustee, and resigning the seat. Also includes the poll list of the county."]

North Carolina (State). General Assembly. "[Document dated:] April-May 1780: Joint Papers, Committee Papers, Resolutions, Senate Bills, House Bills, Joint Papers: Election Certificates." Manuscript; General Assembly Record Group; Session Records, April-May 1780, Box 1 (MARS ID: 66.8.20.5; folder), State Archives of North Carolina, Raleigh. [Online catalog description: "Includes election certificate from Onslow County and the election returns for New Hanover County and Wilmington."]

North Carolina (State). General Assembly. "[Document dated:] May 5, 1780: Joint Papers, Committee Papers, Resolutions, Senate Bills, House Bills, Report on the Election of John Ashe of New Hanover County." Manuscript; General Assembly Record Group; Session Records, April-May 1780, Box 1 (MARS ID: 66.8.20.10.3), State Archives of North Carolina, Raleigh. [Online catalog description: "The committee reports that Ashe's election appears to be illegal because he is a resident of New Bern, not New Hanover County, and that his seat should be vacated."]

North Carolina (State). General Assembly. "[Document dated:] April 19, 1782: Joint Papers, Committee Papers, Resolutions, Senate Bills, House Bills, Regarding the Elections in New Hanover Co. and the Town of Willmington." Manuscript; General Assembly Record Group; Session Records, April-May 1782, Box 2 (MARS ID: 66.8.28.3.1), State Archives of North Carolina, Raleigh. [Online catalog description: "Committee report states that the elections for New Hanover Co. and Wilmington were illegally conducted and suggests that the seats be vacated; message from House to Senate refers petition of inhabitants of New Hanover County to committee."]

North Carolina (State). General Assembly. "[Document dated:] May 16, 1783: Papers Relating to Election for House of Commons in Craven County." Manuscript; General Assembly Record Group; Session Records, April-May 1783; Joint Papers, Committee Papers, Resolutions; House Committee of Privileges and Elections: Reports and Papers, Box 3 (MARS ID: 66.8.29.10; folder), State Archives of North Carolina, Raleigh.

North Carolina (State). General Assembly. "Election Certificates and Oaths, 1777." Manuscript; General Assembly Record Group; Session Records, April-May 1777: Joint Papers, Committee Papers, Resolutions, Miscellaneous Bills, Box 1 (MARS ID: 66.8.9.7; folder), State Archives of North Carolina, Raleigh. [Online catalog description: "Oath of office taken by representatives to the North Carolina General Assembly; election certificates of Representatives Henry Rhodes and John King of Onslow County and Abner Nash of Craven County."]

North Carolina (State). General Assembly. "Election Certificates, 1778." Manuscript; General Assembly Record Group; Session Records, April-May 1778; Miscellaneous, Joint Papers, Committee Papers, Senate Resolutions, Box 1 (MARS ID: 66.8.12.7; folder), State Archives of North Carolina, Raleigh.

North Carolina (State). General Assembly. "Election Writs and Certificates, 1778." Manuscript; General Assembly Record Group; Session Records, August 1778; Joint Papers, Committee Papers, Senate Bills, House Bills, Box 1 (MARS ID: 66.8.14.4; folder), State Archives of North Carolina, Raleigh.

North Carolina (State). General Assembly. "Election Writs and Certificates, 1779." Manuscript; General Assembly Record Group; Session Records, January-February 1779; Joint Papers, Committee Papers, Resolutions, Box 1 (MARS ID: 66.8.15.5; folder), State Archives of North Carolina, Raleigh. [Online catalog description: "Writs and certificates of election from New Hanover, Orange, and Pitt Counties; certificates of election from Beaufort and Washington Counties and Edenton."]

North Carolina (State). General Assembly. "Joint Papers (January-February 1779): Election Writs and Certificates." Manuscript; General Assembly Record Group; Session Records, January-February 1779; Box 1 (MARS ID: 66.8.15.5; folder), State Archives of North Carolina, Raleigh. [Online catalog description: "Writs and certificates of election from New Hanover, Orange, and Pitt Counties; certificates of election from Beaufort and Washington Counties and Edenton." The names that appear are: Timothy Bloodworth, Thomas Burke, Alderson Ellison, James Gorham, Joseph Hewes, Mark Patterson, Thomas Repass, Jr., James Simpson, and Jesse Walton.]

North Carolina (State). General Assembly. "Election Certificates (and Test Book), 1779." Manuscript; General Assembly Record Group; Session Records, May 1779; Joint Papers, Committee Papers, Senate Bills, House Bills, Box 1 (MARS ID: 66.8.17.7; folder), State Archives of North Carolina, Raleigh. [Online catalog description: "Includes five town certificates and forty-two county certificates as well as a test book containing the signed oath of allegiance to the state and oath of honesty in election." The counties {and towns} are: Anson, Beaufort, Bladen, Burke, Camden, Caswell, Chatham, Chowan, Craven, Cumberland, Currituck, Dobbs, Duplin, Edenton (town), Edgecombe, Franklin, Gates, Granville, Guilford, Halifax (town), Halifax, Hertford, Hyde, Johnston, Jones, Lincoln, Martin, Mecklenburg, Montgomery, Nash, New Bern (town), New Hanover, Northampton, Onslow, Orange, Pasquotank, Randolph, Rowan, Salisbury (town), Surry, Tyrrell, Wake, Warren, Washington, Wilkes, and Wilmington (town).]

North Carolina (State). General Assembly. "Election Writs and Certificates, 1779." Manuscript; General Assembly Record Group; Session Records, October-November 1779; Joint Papers, Committee Papers, Resolutions, Box 1 (MARS ID: 66.8.18.5; folder), State Archives of North Carolina, Raleigh. [Online catalog description: "Writs of election issued to Dobbs and Franklin Counties and New Bern at the close of the previous session in May; certificates of election from Dobbs County and New Bern."]

North Carolina (State). General Assembly. "Election Certificates, 1780." Manuscript; General Assembly Record Group; Session Records, April-May 1780; Joint Papers, Committee Papers, Resolutions, Box 1 (MARS ID: 66.8.20.5; folder), State Archives of North Carolina, Raleigh. [Online catalog description: "Includes election certificate from Onslow County and the election returns for New Hanover County and Wilmington."]

North Carolina (State). General Assembly. "Election Certificates, 1781." Manuscript; General Assembly Record Group; Session Records, January-February 1781; Joint Papers, Committee Papers, Resolutions, Box 1 (MARS ID: 66.8.23.5; folder), State Archives of North Carolina, Raleigh. [Online catalog description: "Includes a writ of election for New Bern and the certificate of William Blount's election to the seat vacated by James Green as well as the certificate of election for William Porter, of Rutherford County, to the seat vacated by Davis Whiteside's death."]

North Carolina (State). General Assembly. "Election Certificates for Members of the General Assembly and County Commissioners, 1783." Manuscript; General Assembly Record Group; Session Records, April-May 1783; Joint Papers, Committee Papers, Resolutions, Box 1 (MARS ID: 66.8.29.3; folder), State Archives of North Carolina, Raleigh.

The General Assembly

Greene, Jack P. "The Role of the Lower Houses of Assembly in Eighteenth-Century Politics." *Journal of Southern History*, 27:4 (November 1961), 451-474.

Main, Jackson Turner. *The Upper House in Revolutionary America, 1763-1788*. Madison: University of Wisconsin Press, 1967.

McBride, Ransom. "Revolutionary War Gems from the N. C. General Assembly Papers up to 1800." *North Carolina Genealogical Society Journal*, 28:1 (February 2002), 76-81. [petitions, widows, list of deceased officers and soldiers]

McBride, Janet and Ransom. "Revolutionary War Claims in NC Legislature after 1833." [Part 1] *North Carolina Genealogical Society Journal*, 18:1 (February 1992), 32-40; (Part 2) *North Carolina Genealogical Society Journal*, 18:3 (August 1992), 162-165.

North Carolina (State). General Assembly. "[Document dated:] April 27, 1778: Joint Papers, Committee Papers, Resolutions, Senate Bills, House Bills, Report on the Eligibility of Members from Washington, Tyrrell, Orange, Edgecombe, and New Hanover Counties (with Petition from Tyrrell Co.)." Manuscript General Assembly Record Group, Session Records, April-May 1778, Box 1 (MARS ID: 66.8.12.15.1), State Archives of North Carolina, Raleigh.

North Carolina (State). General Assembly. "[Documents dated:] 1780: Miscellaneous Statements, Certificates, and Protest." Manuscript, General Assembly Record Group, Session Records; Joint Papers, Committee Papers, Resolutions, April-May 1780, Box 1 (MARS ID: 66.8.20.6; folder), State Archives of North Carolina, Raleigh. [Online catalog description: "General John Butler certifies to the sheriff of Orange County that William Walker, a volunteer in a company of the North Carolina Brigade of Militia, has not yet received his bounty for service in South Carolina. In a document from February, Governor Caswell requires all civil and military officers to assist Peter Marlett in purchasing provisions for the militia. John Kennedy, jailer for the New Bern District, certifies the names of prisoners of war in his jail received from William Brown, a Justice for Beaufort County. John Everett, a Justice of the Peace of Martin County, attests to the deposition of Samuel Mitchell, master of the schooner *Rainbow*. Alexander Gilliland resigns as Justice of the Peace of Tryon (now Lincoln) County."]

North Carolina (State). General Assembly. "[Document dated:] April-May 1780: Joint Papers, Committee Papers, Resolutions, Senate Bills, House Bills, Joint Papers: Message from Governor and Material Sent for Perusal." Manuscript; General Assembly Record Group; Session Records, April-May 1780, Box 1 (MARS ID: 66.8.20.3; folder), State Archives of North Carolina, Raleigh. [Online catalog description: "Includes three resolutions from the Continental Congress pertaining to western lands, artificers, and troop quotas for the several states; A letter from outgoing Governor Caswell concerning the boundary with Virginia and a petition from Roanoke, North Banks, and Cape Hatteras; Caswell's final address to the House of Commons as governor; Abner Nash's first message to the Assembly as governor; and other messages from Nash to the Assembly concerning the war and the state's finances, one of which is accompanied by a letter from Henry Laurens, another by a letter from General William Caswell, and a third by a letter from Joseph Green, deputy contractor general."]

North Carolina (State). General Assembly. "[Document dated:] May 1, 1780: Resolution Impowering Governor to Pay Bounties (Assumed Rejected)." Manuscript; General Assembly Record Group; Session Records, April-May 1780 Joint Papers, Committee Papers, Resolutions, Senate Bills, House Bills:, Box 1 (MARS ID: 66.8.20.16.7), State Archives of North Carolina, Raleigh. [Online catalog description: "The resolution sought to empower the governor to draw on the treasurers for enough money to pay the bounties of the troops from Chowan, Tyrrell, and Hertford Counties at Kingston preparing to march to South Carolina."]

North Carolina (State). General Assembly. "[Document dated:] August 31, 1780: Joint Papers, Committee Papers, Resolutions, Senate Bills, House Bills, Resolutions of the Virginia Assembly, Letter to Richard and James Ellis,

Letter from James Iredell, and Petition of John Reddy." Manuscript; General Assembly Record Group; Session Records, August-September 1780, Box 1 (MARS ID: 66.8.22.3.2), State Archives of North Carolina, Raleigh. [Online catalog description: "Virginia encourages the Assembly to protect the land claims of Virginians who have found themselves to be in North Carolina following the extension of the boundary. The Ellises present the deposition and protest of Thomas Turner and other crew members of the brigantine *Bellona* explaining why they did not return from the West Indies with a supply of arms. Iredell discusses his inadequate salary. Reddy, of Tyrrell County, discusses his difficulties as a ferry and tavern keeper."]

North Carolina (State). General Assembly. "[Document dated:] August-September 1780: Joint Papers, Committee Papers, Resolutions, Senate Bills, House Bills, Joint Papers: Miscellaneous Correspondence." Manuscript General Assembly Record Group, Session Records, Box 1 (MARS ID: 66.8.22.5; folder), State Archives of North Carolina, Raleigh. [Online catalog description: "J. Sanders resigns as a justice of the peace for Johnston County; William Preston, in Montgomery County, writes Martin Armstrong, in Surry County, about a recent successful effort to break up a loyalist conspiracy; two letters on the progress of the war from Congressional delegates: one to Samuel Johnston and one to Gov. Nash."]

North Carolina (State). General Assembly. "[Document dated:] Miscellaneous Accounts, Certificates, Bonds, and Letters, 1781." Manuscript; General Assembly Record Group; Session Records, January-February 1781; Joint Papers, Committee Papers, Resolutions Senate Bills, House Bills, Joint Papers: Miscellaneous Accounts, Certificates, Bonds, and Letters." Box 1 (MARS ID: 66.8.23.6; folder), State Archives of North Carolina, Raleigh. [Online catalog description: "Includes certificates of assessment of the property in Bertie and Surry Counties; a bond of Jesse Miller, Patrick Boggan, and Stephen Miller to the chairman of the Anson County Court; a letter to the speakers from Martin Armstrong, of Surry County, describing the conduct of the insurgents following their defeat at Shallow Ford; and a letter to the speakers from Samuel Ashe describing the situation in the Wilmington area."]

North Carolina (State). General Assembly. "[Document dated:] June 27, [1781]: Governor Burke's Response to Major Craig." Manuscript; General Assembly Record Group; Session Records, June-July 1781 Joint Papers, Committee Papers, Resolutions, Senate Bills, House Bills; Messages from the Governor, Box 1 (MARS ID: 66.8.25.4.2; item), State Archives of North Carolina, Raleigh. [Online catalog description: "Burke sends for the Assembly's opinion his response to Major J. H. Craig, commander of the British army in Wilmington, in which Burke discusses the war and the treatment of prisoners."]

North Carolina (State). General Assembly. "[Documents dated:] April-May 1782: Materials Sent for Perusal (Governor's Messages, Resolves of Congress, Letters, Petitions, Resignments [*sic*]; Joint Papers, Committee Papers, etc.)." Manuscript, General Assembly Record Group, Session Records; Joint Papers, Committee Papers, April-May 1782, Box 1 (MARS ID: 66.8.27.4; folder), State Archives of North Carolina, Raleigh. [Online catalog description: "Messages from both houses and governor regarding papers; resignations of militia officers, auditors, justices, and the Commissioner of Trade; petitions of the inhabitants of New Hanover County concerning road to Wilmington, and of the justices, militia officers, and inhabitants of Onslow County in support of Stephen Shackleford; reports about exchange of prisoners while the British were in Beaufort; message from Secretary of State regarding listing of county justices; and resolutions and messages from Congress about military forces, the President of Congress, and suits against foreign powers."]

North Carolina (State). General Assembly. "[Document dated:] 1784: Miscellaneous, 1784." Manuscript, General Assembly Record Group, Session Records April-June 1784; Joint Papers, Committee Papers, Resolutions, Senate Bills, House Bills; Joint Papers, Box 1 (MARS ID: 66.8.31.7; folder), State Archives of North Carolina, Raleigh. [Online catalog description: "Includes: ... A letter from William Richards of the District of Edenton regarding accounts and land grants. A list of money owed soldiers in company of Col. John Sevier (damaged and faded)."]

North Carolina (State). General Assembly. "[Document dated:] May 18, 1782: Joint Papers, Committee Papers, Resolutions, Senate Bills, House Bills, Resolution in Favor of Joseph Pittman of Edgecombe County (Messages Only)." Manuscript; General Assembly Record Group; Session Records, April-May 1782, Box 2 (MARS ID: 66.8.28.7.2), State Archives of North Carolina, Raleigh. [Online catalog description: "Messages from both houses concurring with resolve."]

North Carolina (State). General Assembly. "[Document dated:] June 2, 1784: Joint Papers, Committee Papers, Resolutions, Senate Bills, House Bills, Resolution in Favor of Joseph Pittman of Edgecombe County." Manuscript; General Assembly Record Group; Session Records, April-June 1784, Box 2 (MARS ID: 66.8.32.5.43; item), State Archives of North Carolina, Raleigh. [Online catalog description: "Resolution awards an allowance to Joseph Pittman for carrying the journals of the Assembly and for carrying express messages."]

North Carolina. General Assembly. "North Carolina General Assembly Legislative Papers, 1784-1842." Manuscript 424-z, Southern Historical Collection, Louis Round Wilson Special Collections Library, University of North Carolina, Chapel Hill; online finding aid available at www2.lib.unc.edu/mss/inv/n/North_Carolina.General_Assembly.html. [Online finding aid description: "The collection includes records of early North Carolina state legislatures, consisting chiefly of papers, 1784-1809, pertaining to land fraud cases involving state officials, including correspondence and committee reports, messages between various governors and the two houses of the legislature, material from the legislative investigation, and petitions. The fraud involved land granted to Revolutionary War soldiers. Also included are miscellaneous papers, consisting of resolutions, governors' messages, and items for various legislative committees, 1793-1842."]

North Carolina (State). General Assembly. "Oaths of Office, General Assembly, 1780." Manuscript; General Assembly Record Group; Session Records, August-September 1780; Joint Papers, Committee Papers, Resolutions, Senate Bills, House Bills, Box 1 (MARS ID: 66.8.22.4), State Archives of North Carolina, Raleigh. [Online catalog description: "Includes an oath of honesty in election and an oath of allegiance to the state."]

North Carolina (State). General Assembly. Senate. "[Document dated:] April 25, 1780: Joint Papers, Committee Papers, Resolutions, Senate Bills, House Bills, Senate Bill Allowing Salaries to Governor, Council of State, and Others." Manuscript, General Assembly Record Group, April-May 1780, Box 2 (MARS ID: 66.8.21.11; folder), Session Records State Archives of North Carolina, Raleigh. [Online catalog description: "Includes two letters from Judge Samuel Spencer to the Speaker of the House concerning the salaries of judges; messages referring letters from Spencer and Samuel Ashe and a petition from the sheriff of Rowan County to a committee; the bill, some of which is deleted and which also authorized the governor, with the advice of the Council of State, to call the Assembly to meet earlier than scheduled if necessary; and messages relative to amendments."]

Shannon, George Ward, Jr. "225 Years and Counting." *The Palace,* 2:3 (Spring 2002), 4-5. [Online description from "North Carolina Periodicals Index," East Carolina University: "April 2002 marks the 225th anniversary of the first North Carolina General Assembly, which met at the Palace in New Bern where the state of North Carolina was born."]

The General Assembly – Legislation and Laws

Byrd, William L. *North Carolina Assembly Sessions Records: Slaves and Free Persons of Color, 1709-1789.* Bowie, Md.: Heritage Books, 2001.

Byrd, William L. *Villainy Often Goes Unpunished: Indian Records from the North Carolina General Assembly Sessions, 1675-1789.* Bowie, Md.: Heritage Books, 2002.

Cleaveland, Frederic N. "Service Legislation of the North Carolina General Assembly from 1777 to 1835." M. A. thesis, Duke University, 1942.

Cushing, John D. *The First Laws of the State of North Carolina.* Wilmington, Del.: Michael Glazier, Inc., 1984.

Graham, William A[lexander]. *General Joseph Graham and His Papers on North Carolina Revolutionary History, with Appendix: An Epitome of North Carolina's Military Services in the Revolutionary War and of the Laws Enacted for Raising Troops.* Raleigh: Edwards & Broughton, 1904. [Online description from Google.books: "This is a fascinating first hand account of the American Revolution in Southern Theatre in general and North Carolina in particular. Mecklenburg County native Joseph Graham provides one of the few complete primary sources for the Revolutionary War battles fought in the Carolina Backcountry. Graham opposed the British in the Race to the Dan and numerous battles and skirmishes including the Battle of Charlotte, the Battle of Cowan's Ford, and Pyle's Defeat. This is an important yet almost completely overlooked period of the American Revolution."]

Lawrence, R. C. "The Old Common Law." *The State: A Weekly Survey of North Carolina*, 11:37 (February 1944), 9, 29; online: http://digital.ncdcr.gov/cdm/ref/collection/p16062coll18/id/18543. [Online description from "North Carolina Periodicals Index," East Carolina University: "Lawrence reviews some of the common laws which the new nation and its states adopted from England. When the State and Federal Constitutions were adopted, there were more than fifty offenses punishable by death in North Carolina. The pillory, stocks, and whipping post were also in common use. Tongue slitting, branding, and ear croppings were frequent."]

Warren, Mary Bondurant. "Miscellaneous North Carolina Private Acts." *The Carolina Genealogist*, no. 29 (Winter 1997), State Records/N. C. Private Acts, 1-4; no. 30 (Spring 1977), State Records/N. C. Private Acts, 5-6; 31 (Winter 1977), 7-8; no. 32 (Fall 1977),), State Records/N. C. Private Acts, 9-10; no. 33 (Winter 1978-1979), State Records/N. C. Private Acts, 11-12. [Most of these acts dating from 1784 and 1785 relate to Revolutionary War matters such as bounty land, forfeited estates, veterans matters, etc.]

Williams, Samuel Cole. "Western Representation in North Carolina Assemblies, 1776-1790." *East Tennessee Historical Society's Publications*, 14 (1942), 106-112.

The General Assembly – Legislative Petitions

Many of these petitions relate to Revolutionary War service or expenditures. For the DAR's purposes, a petition must show some purpose related to support of the Revolutionary cause. A petition for the formation of a new county, for example, does not fall into this category unless it shows some purpose for the new county that has a baring on military activity.[18] Petitions for the construction of a new road or bridge, for a new ferry, or for other civil activities are not acceptable sources of proof of support of the Revolution. So, not every below petition is acceptable for proving service, nor is every petition in the State Archives.

One must study the wording of each petition available to determine if any are acceptable sources of service for the DAR or perhaps other lineage societies as well. In addition, a researcher would do well to continue the search in the State Archives catalog for the name of an individual or county of interest because the listings in this source guide to not include every petition sent to the General Assembly nor do they include the final results of all petitions. In short, there are many other petitions that do not appear in this publication that reside in the State Archives of North Carolina, and those that are cited in this publication are for illustrative purposes of what might appear in others.

During the Revolution, the area now known as Tennessee was claimed and loosely administered by North Carolina. The settlers in northeastern Tennessee, in the area around the Watauga River, drew up a compact of government called the Watauga Association. This association petitioned the North Carolina Legislature in August 1776 requesting annexation to North Carolina. In May 1780, persons from a settlement on the Cumberland River in Middle Tennessee drafted the Cumberland Compact. Signers of both documents are considered to have patriotic service as a signer of a petition. Men from the area that isnow Tennessee served in North Carolina units.][19]

Patriotic Service[20]

Patriots of the Revolution are considered to be those men and women who by an act or series of actions demonstrated unfailing loyalty to the cause of American Independence from England. Patriotic service might begin as early as April 1774. We depend upon recorded actions to give us an indication of patriotism. What was the purpose of the action? What were the risks? The consequences? Answers to these questions can determine whether the action actually applied to an attempt to further the cause of independence or demonstrated loyalty to that cause.

Evidence of patriotic activity may be found in town, county, state, and federal records. Many records kept by the states have been indexed and often a letter to the state archives will be sufficient to determine if evidence exists to show that a person contributed supplies or made some other contribution to the war effort. Town and county records have usually not been indexed and a personal search of town minutes and court minutes is required. Minutes of the Continental Congresses have been published. *Old letters, diaries, and other family and personal papers can often be used as evidence of patriotic intent, provided the record was made at the time of the event described.*

Not all actions illustrating patriotism are mentioned here. Many others exist. When it is considered desirable to establish another type of patriotic service, proof of the action taken must be submitted with the application paper, together with historical justification to show that the action did indeed imply patriotic intent.

---

[18] See: North Carolina (State). General Assembly [Document dated:] October 23, 1779: "Petition of a Number of Inhabitants of New Hanover, Duplin, and Bladen Counties for Erecting a Separate County from the Above Counties." New County, 1779." Manuscript. General Assembly Session Records; Session of October-November 1779, Joint Papers, Committee Resolutions, Resolutions, Box 1 (MARS ID: 66.8.18.7.11; item), State Library of North Carolina, Raleigh. [Online catalog description: "The petitioners refer to the difficulties they face in attending general musters and jury service at the courthouses of their respective counties and request that a new county be erected within the boundaries suggested." The purpose of the this request was to help facilitate attendance at general musters of the militia. http://www.rootsweb.ancestry.com/~aagriots/VA/main/1779Petition.htm.

[19] *Is That Service Right?* (Washington, D. C.: NSDAR, 2005), 44.

[20] Office of the Registrar General's compilation, *Genealogy Guidelines* (Washington, D. C.: National Society Daughters of the American Revolution, 2014), 94-95.

Signers of Petitions to the new provincial and state governments acknowledged the new government's right to represent the people. The content and wording of the petition must demonstrate loyalty to the cause of American independence. Petitions having to do with religious issues do not qualify.

Beck, John V. "1782 Legislative Petition." *Rowan County Register*, 3:1 (February 1988), 516-521.

Cates, Larry W. "Legislative Petitions, 1782." *North Carolina Genealogical Society Journal*, 39:1 (February 2013), 35-44; 40:1 (February 2014), 42-50; 40:2 (May 2014), 150-159; 40:3 (August 2014), 193-201.

Delamar, Marybelle. *Transcriptions of Petitions to the General Assembly of North Carolina relating to Revolutionary War Military Records.* 5 typescript volumes in the North Carolina Collection, University of North Carolina Library; photocopy at the State Archives of North Carolina,, Raleigh, 2007. [petitions from the legislative files of the North Carolina General Assembly] [Contents: vol. 1: Pages 1-240; vol. 2: Pages 241-480; vol. 3: Pages 481-720; vol. 4: Pages 721-944; vol. 5: Index to vols. 1-4.]

"The Delamar Transcriptions: A Little Known Source for Proving Revolutionary War Service." *NCGS News: The Newsletter of the North Carolina Genealogical Society*, 35:2 (Spring 2011), 6; online along with an index at the North Carolina Genealogical Society's member website: http://www.ncgenealogy.org/menu-resources/delamar-transcripts. [Description: "Marybelle Delamar identified petitions from 1778 to about 1833 concerning the Revolutionary War, which were found in the legislative files of the North Carolina General Assembly. These petitions may contain information about a soldier's service, widow, orphans, or other heirs. She transcribed each document and created an index to her transcripts. The index and transcripts have not been microfilmed and are not available through the Family History Library. They are only available at the North Carolina State Archives. However, Jo White Linn, and Ransom McBride abstracted the transcripts and published the abstracts in the North Carolina Genealogical Society Journal, volumes 1–6. The abstracts and Marybelle's index are now available in the "Member's Only" section of our website. The original petitions can also be found at the North Carolina State Archives. To find an original petition at the NC State Archives, go to the General Assembly card catalog index, then the year and session that corresponds to the date on the petition. Request the file box that has Revolutionary War Petitions for the appropriate session. For more information about the transcripts refer to *North Carolina Research, Genealogy, and Local History*, Second Edition, pages 393 and 395."]

Green, Virginia S. "1782 Legislative Petition." *Rowan County Register*, 2:3 (August 1987), 397-399.

Huddelston, John. "Petition of John Huddleston, N. C. General Assembly Session Records, Nov.-Dec. 1807." *Bulletin of the Genealogical Society of Old Tryon County*, 28:4 (November 2000), 155-156. [1779, Rutherford County]

Kierner, Cynthia A. *Southern Women in Revolution, 1776-1800: Personal and Political Narratives.* Columbia: University of South Carolina Press, 1998. [The author examines ninety-eight petitions submitted by North and South Carolina women to their state assemblies as an approach to study southern women's wartime experiences and their growing numbers in the public sphere.]

Lamkin, George. "Petition of George Lamkin, Former Sheriff of Tryon County, [to the] North Carolina General Assembly, 1780." *Bulletin of the Genealogical Society of Old Tryon County*, 20:4 (November 1992), 182. [The petition relates to the difficulties of performing his job because of the Indians and Loyalists in the area and the disruption of settlements.]

Lewis, J. D. "North Carolina – From Statehood to 1800." Online: http://www.carolana.com/NC/Early_Statehood/nc_statehood_1800_general_assembly.html. [Lists of legislators in the both the House of Commons and the Senate from 1777 to 1800]

Linn, Jo White. "Abstracts from the Delamar Transcripts – Revolutionary War Claims." [The title of this series of articles flips back and forth between the two parts.] *North Carolina Genealogical Society Journal*, 3:2 (1977), 91-98; 3:3 (August 1977), 160-165; 3:4 (November 1977), 222-228; 4:1 (February 1978), 40-45; 4:2 (May 1978), 102-107; 4:3 (August 1978), 171-176; 5:1 (February 1979), 24-30; 5:2 (May 1979), 100-104; 5:3 (August 1979), 158-164; 6:1 (February 1980), 9-16; 6:2 (May 1980), 100-106; 6:3 (August 1980), 175-177; 6:4 (November 1980), 236-240.

Linn, Jo White. "Private Petitions in the North Carolina Legislative Papers Abstracts of the Delamar Transcripts." *North Carolina Genealogical Society Journal*, 1:3 (July 1975), 141-168; 2:1 (January 1976), 39-47; 2:2 (April 1976), 108-116; 2:3 (July 1976), 148-153; 2:4 (October 1976), 198-203; 3:2 (May 1977), 84-89; 3:3 (August 1977), 160-165; 3:4 (November 1977), 222-228; 4:1 (February 1978), 40-45; 4:2 (May 1978), 102-107; 4:3 (August 1978), 171-176; 5:1 (February 1979), 24-30; 5:2 (May 1979), 100-104; 5:3 (August 1979), 158-164;

6:1 (February 1980), 9-16; 6:2 (May 1980), 100-106; 6:3 (August 1980), 175-177; 6:4 (November 1980), 236-240.

Linn, Jo White, and Benjamin Ransom McBride. "Private Petitions in the North Carolina Legislative Papers: Revolutionary War Service-Related Benefits, Abstracts of the Delamar Transcripts." *North Carolina Genealogical Society Journal*, 1:3 (July 1975), 141-168; 2:1 (January 1976), 38-47; 2:2 (April 1976), 108-116; 2:3 (July 1976), 148-153; 2:4 (October 1976), 198-203.

Moore, Mary. "Legislative Petition of Mary Moore, Fayetteville, N. C." Manuscript; Division of Archives and History Photograph Collection: Photographs Received in 1997, N.97.3.160 (MARS ID: 4.1.24.318; folder), State Archives of North Carolina, Raleigh. [Online catalog description: "View of the Legislative Petition of Mary Moore, of Fayetteville, Cumberland County, to the North Carolina General Assembly for Reimbursement of Provisions Provided during the Late Revolution, 29 December 1786."]

North Carolina (State). General Assembly. "[Document dated:] 1777: Memorial of Samuel Cooley and Robert Welson, Surgeons." Manuscript; General Assembly Record Group; Session Records, April-May 1777; Joint Papers, Committee Papers, Resolutions, Senate Bills, House Bills, Box 1 (MARS ID: 66.8.9.5.1; item), State Archives of North Carolina, Raleigh. [Online catalog description: "Appeal for a reasonable allowance for the purchase of horses and additional expenses incurred by Samuel Cooley and Robert Wilson, surgeons in the Fifth and Sixth Regiments of North Carolina."]

North Carolina (State). General Assembly. "[Document dated:] January 13, 1779: Joint Papers, Committee Papers, Resolutions, Senate Bills, House Bills, Petitions of Hardy Jones and Thomas Saint (Sent by Governor, Jan. 13. 1779)." Manuscript; General Assembly Record Group; Session Records, January-February 1779, Box 1 (MARS ID: 66.8.15.9.1; item), State Archives of North Carolina, Raleigh. [Online catalog description: "Hardy Jones petitions Gov. Caswell concerning alleged land fraud perpetrated by John Jacks in Rowan County; Thomas Saint, a Quaker, petitions the General Assembly to permit him to register his land without having to make a sworn declaration of fidelity to the state."]

North Carolina (State). General Assembly. "[Document dated:] January 23, 1779: Joint Papers, Committee Papers, Resolutions, Senate Bills, House Bills, Report of Committee on Citizenship on Petitions of Thomas Barker, Samuel Marshall, Robert Hogg, and Others (with Petitions and Messages)." Manuscript, General Assembly Record Group, Session Records, January-February 1779, Box 1 (MARS ID: 66.8.15.8.3), State Archives of North Carolina, Raleigh. [Online catalog description: "Includes testimony of Jonas Dunbibin and Thomas Walker, Justices of the Peace of New Hanover County." Names that appear are: Thomas Barker, John Burgwin, Jonas Dunbibin, Robert Hogg, Thomas Hooper, John London, Samuel Marshall, Samuel Peele, and Thomas Walker.]

North Carolina (State). General Assembly. "[Document dated:] May 10, 1779: Joint Papers, Committee Papers, Resolutions, Senate Bills, House Bills, Petition of a Number of Inhabitants of New Hanover Co. for a Guard over the Salt Works (rejected)." Manuscript; General Assembly Record Group; Session Records, May 1779, Box 1 (MARS ID: 66.8.17.6.4; item), State Archives of North Carolina, Raleigh.

North Carolina (State). General Assembly. "[Document dated:] October 25, 1779: Joint Papers, Committee Papers, Resolutions, Senate Bills, House Bills, Petition of Elizabeth Heron, Minor and Orphan Daughter of Benjamin Heron." Manuscript; General Assembly Record Group; Session Records, October-November 1779, Box 1 (MARS ID: 66.8.18.7.13; item), State Archives of North Carolina, Raleigh. [Online catalog description: "Heron, of New Hanover County, asks that the toll be raised for a bridge over the Cape Fear River which her father built at the request of the colonial assembly and bequeathed to her as her chief source of income. Given the depreciation of the currency and the bridge's need for repairs, the previous toll allowed by law is insufficient."]

North Carolina (State). General Assembly. "[Document dated:] October 25, 1779: Joint Papers, Committee Papers, Resolutions, Senate Bills, House Bills, House Bills (October 25): Bill to Amend an Act Entitled an Act to Encourage Benjamin Heron to Build a Bridge over the Northeast Branch of the Cape Fear River at or near the Place Where the Ferry Is Now Kept by Edward Davis (Rejected)." Manuscript; General Assembly Record Group; Session Records, October-November 1779, Box 2 (MARS ID: 66.8.19.39), State Archives of North Carolina, Raleigh. [Online catalog description: "The bill, as amended, would have permitted the New Hanover County Court to regulate the toll of the bridge."]

North Carolina (State). General Assembly. "[Document dated:] April-May 1780: Joint Papers, Committee Papers, Resolutions, Senate Bills, House Bills; Joint Papers, Committee Papers, Resolutions, Senate Bills, House Bills, Petition from the Inhabitants of Hanover (New Hanover) County." Manuscript; General Assembly Record Group; Session Records, April-May 1780, Box 1 (MARS ID: 66.8.20.7.3; item), State Archives of North Carolina, Raleigh. [Online catalog description: "The petitioners of Black River ask that Thomas Rogers be allowed to sell the horses and wagons he can take from a Tory neighborhood in order to recover the damages caused to him by Tories."]

North Carolina (State). General Assembly. "[Document dated:] January 29, [1781]: Joint Papers, Committee Papers, Resolutions, Senate Bills, House Bills, In Favor of John Wooton (With Petition)." Manuscript, Call Number General Assembly Record Group, Session Records, January-February 1781, Box 1 (MARS ID: 66.8.23.9.2; item), State Archives of North Carolina, Raleigh. [Online catalog description: "John Wotton, of Richmond County, informs the Assembly that he volunteered to help defend the state and was wounded so badly at the Battle of Camden that he can no longer work; he asks for assistance, as he is poor. Benjamin Seawell, commanding officer of Wotton's regiment, attests to the truth of the petition. The Assembly allows him twenty barrels of corn annually. Includes two copies of the resolution."]

North Carolina (State). General Assembly. "[Document dated:] February 9, [1781]: Joint Papers, Committee Papers, Resolutions, Senate Bills, House Bills, In Favor of George Harper (Message Only, with Petition). Manuscript, General Assembly Record Group, Session Records, January-February 1781, Box 1 (MARS ID: 66.8.23.13.5; item), State Archives of North Carolina, Raleigh. [Online catalog description: "Harper, of Franklin County, informs the Assembly that he volunteered for the militia and received a disabling wound at the Battle of Camden, thus preventing him from working."]

North Carolina (State). General Assembly. "[Document dated:] February 13, 1781: Joint Papers, Committee Papers, Resolutions, Senate Bills, House Bills, In Favor of John Wooten (with Petition)." Manuscript; General Assembly Record Group; Session Records, January-February 1781, Box 1 (MARS ID: 66.8.23.8.17; item), State Archives of North Carolina, Raleigh. [Online catalog description: "Medlock, of Richmond County, informs the Assembly that when the British forced him from his home on the Pee Dee River, a number of certificates of claims issued by the Assembly to several individuals were lost, and he asks that they be replaced. The committee recommends that his request be granted and also reports that a sum is due General Harrington. The Assembly concurs."]

North Carolina (State). General Assembly. "[Document dated:] June 13, [1781]: Joint Papers, Committee Papers, Resolutions, Senate Bills, House Bills, Petition of Henry O'Daniel." Manuscript; General Assembly Record Group; Session Records, June-July 1781, Box 1 (MARS ID: 66.8.25.7.3; item), State Archives of North Carolina, Raleigh. [Online catalog description: "O'Daniel asks that the Assembly pardon him for joining the British Army, for he did not actually fight and he has surrendered to an Orange County magistrate."]

North Carolina (State). General Assembly. "[Document dated:] May 5, 1782: Joint Papers, Committee Papers, Resolutions, Senate Bills, House Bills, Report Concerning Several Petitions." Manuscript; General Assembly Record Group; Session Records, Apr-May 1782, Box 1 (MARS ID: 66.8.27.7.1), State Archives of North Carolina, Raleigh. [Online catalog description: Draft and final report of the committee concerning the following petitions:

William Blount, on settlement of public accounts (report and messages)

William Tisdale, regarding his suspension as a judge of the Court of Admiralty for the Port of Beaufort (report, depositions, messages, and petition)

Justices of New Hanover County, regarding the delinquency of militia (report, petitions, and messages)

Prisoners of war at Charlestown, SC, regarding their distresses (report only)

Mary Mullen, of Richmond County, whose husband was killed and son wounded in battle, regarding monetary support for the family (report and petition)

John Cole of Richmond County, regarding the burning and plundering of his property by British soldiers (report and petition)

Inhabitants of Salisbury, regarding improper impression and confiscation of possessions by the Commissary General and the Quartermaster's Dept. (report, petitions, and messages)"]

North Carolina (State). General Assembly. "[Document dated:] May 4, 1784: Joint Papers, Committee Papers, Resolutions, Senate Bills, House Bills, Report on the Petitions of Thomas Sewell, Hugh Stanly, General Lillington, William Courtney, Roland Harris, Alexander Morrison, Elizabeth Hinkle, and Doctor Blyeth (Petitions, Messages, and Enclosures Only)." Manuscript, General Assembly Record Group, Session Records April-May 1782, Box 1 (MARS ID: 66.8.31.6; folder), State Archives of North Carolina, Raleigh. [Online catalog description: "Report on the petitions of:

Thomas Sewell, whose salt was requisitioned by Nathanael Greene's army, and requests compensation (petition only)

Hugh Stanly, of Jones County, who was wounded in battle and seeks an allowance (recommendation and messages only)

General Alexander Lillington, on his accounts (report from the District of Wilmington Board of Auditors only)

William Courtney, who had his lands destroyed by both the British and American armies and seeks compensation (petition only)
Roland Harris, who was involved in the construction of public buildings in Montgomery County, but due to the depreciation of currency, his worth has become nothing, and he wishes to be compensated (petition only)
Alexander Morrison, who was wounded in battle and seeks restitution for his services (petition only)
Elizabeth Hinkle, of Rowan County, whose husband was a tax collector for the Commissioner of Specific Supplies for the Southern Army and who because of the delinquents of the county was not able to settle accounts before he died. His wife asks for a halt in the judgement process until his accounts can be settled (petition and deposition only)
Doctor Blythe, on his accounts (deposition only)"]

North Carolina (State). General Assembly. "[Document dated:] Dec. 13, [1785]: Report on the Petition of James Britain (With Petition) (Rejected), 1785." Manuscript, General Assembly Record Group, Session Reports, November-December 1785; Joint Papers, Committee Papers, Resolutions, Senate Bills, House Bills; Senate Joint Resolutions: Decemer 14-Decembe 31, 1786; Box 3 (MARS ID: 66.8.37.9.12), State Archives of North Carolina, Raleigh. [Online catalog description: "Report concerns the petition of James Britain, who contends that land owned by his father by right of occupancy was left to him before the war, and when he went to fight in the war, the land was claimed by George Killian, who afterwards sold it. He requests a return of his land which should belong to him by right."]

North Carolina (State). General Assembly. "[Document dated:] Dec. 14, [1786]: Resolution for Secretary of State to Issue to Heirs of William Watts, Deceased, a Warrant for Bounty Land (Petition and Supporting Papers Only)." Manuscript; General Assembly Record Group; Session Records, November 1786-January 1787; Joint Papers, Committee Papers, Resolutions, Senate Bills, House Bills, Box 3 (MARS ID: 66.8.43.5.2; item), State Archives of North Carolina, Raleigh. [Online catalog description: "Memorial of Allie Watts of Anson County, requests payment for her husband's army service; includes depositions of officers attesting to William Watts' service."]

North Carolina (State). General Assembly. "[Document dated:] Dec. 26, [1786]: Resolution Re[specting] a Number of Officers of the Late Continental Line who Testified Concerning Frauds (Message Only)." Manuscript; General Assembly Record Group; Session Records, November1786-January 1787; Joint Papers, Committee Papers, Resolutions, Senate Bills, House Bills; House Joint Resolutions: December 16-December 31, 1786, Box 3 (MARS ID: 66.8.43.8.7; item), State Archives of North Carolina, Raleigh. [Online catalog description: "Legislative message concerns amending resolution by adding names to the list."]

North Carolina (State). General Assembly. "[Document dated:] n. d., 1787: Joint Papers, Committee Papers, Resolutions, Senate Bills, House Bills, Petitions to Council, 1787." Manuscript, General Assembly Record Croup, Session Records, November-December 1787, Box 1 (MARS ID: 66.8.46.3.5; item), State Archives of North Carolina, Raleigh. [Online catalog description: "Petitions to Council of State request leniency for prisoners John Price, James Holmes, John Sheppard, and others involved in fraudulent army accounts, and request a pardon from charge of horse stealing for James Connor (enclosing the indictment of Connor and jury's recommendation for mercy). Also in folder are signatures from an unidentified petition."]

North Carolina (State). General Assembly. "[Document dated:] Nov. 10, [1788]: Report on Petition of John Williams, Commissioner of Specific Tax, Caswell Co. (With Petition)." Manuscript; General Assembly Record Group; Session Records, November-December 1788; Joint Papers, Committee Papers, Resolutions, Senate Bills, House Bills; Joint Standing Committees: Committee of Propositions and Grievances: November 10-Novemer 24, 1788, Box 2 (MARS ID: 668.50.1.6; item), State Archives of North Carolina, Raleigh. [Online catalog description: "Report recommends that commissioner's accounts be considered balanced and settled by the comptroller; petition of John Williams asserts that the British Army took possession of a large number of supplies while passing through the county and asks for consideration of this in his arrearages on accounts; includes depositions of witnesses; and letter and copy of account from the comptroller."]

North Carolina (State). General Assembly. "[Document dated:] November 18, [1788]: Petition and Claim of Duncan Buie (Rejected)." Manuscript; General Assembly Record Group; Session Records, November-December 1788; Joint Papers, Committee Papers, Resolutions, Senate Bills, House Bills; Joint Papers: Petitions Rejectred or Not Acted Upon, Box 1 (MARS ID: 66.8.49.7.5), State Archives of North Carolina, Raleigh. [Online catalog description: "Petition requests compensation for cattle Duncan Buie lost during the war."]

North Carolina (State). General Assembly. "[Document dated:] December 7, 1789: Report on Petition of Daniel McCarthy (With Petition)." Manuscript; General Assembly Record Group; Session Records, November-December 1789; Joint Papers, Committee Papers, Resolutions, Senate Bills, House Bills, Box 2 (MARS ID: 66.8.52.19.12; item), State Archives of North Carolina, Raleigh. [Online catalog description: "Report recommended rejection of petition; petition of Daniel McCarthy requesting an allowance for injury received as a seaman during the war."]

North Carolina (State). General Assembly. "[Document dated:] December 11, 1789: Report on the Letters of Hugh Williamson and Abishai Thomas, Agents of This State." Manuscript; General Assembly Record Group; Session Records, November-December 1789; Joint Papers, Committee Papers, Resolutions, Senate Bills, House Bills, Box 2 (MARS ID: 66.8.53.4.8; item), State Archives of North Carolina, Raleigh. [Online catalog description: "Report of the committee resolves that the comptroller be instructed to obtain correspondence from the estate of Richard Caswell and Abner Nash relating to requisitions made by the Southern Department during the Revolutionary War. Also all papers that may relate to the accounts of this state against the United States should be forwarded to agents of this state."]

North Carolina (State). General Assembly. "[Document dated:] December 14, 1789: Report on Memorial of William Terrel Lewis and Alexander Long (With Petition and Enclosures)." Manuscript; General Assembly Record Group; Session Records, November-December 1789; Joint Papers, Committee Papers, Resolutions, Senate Bills, House Bills, Box 2 (MARS ID: 66.8.53.1.15; item), State Archives of North Carolina, Raleigh. [Online catalog description: "Memorial of William Terrel Lewis and Alexander Long asks for compensation due them for the apprehension of deserters from the state militia and Army of the United States during the American Revolution. Included are testimonies from individuals attesting that the deserters were apprehended. Committee report gives accounts of individual deserters and states that any person who apprehended deserters is entitled to four pounds each."]

North Carolina (State). General Assembly. "[Document dated:] December 7, 1789: Report on Petition of Daniel McCarthy (With Petition)." Manuscript; General Assembly Record Group; Session Records, November-December 1789; Joint Papers, Committee Papers, Resolutions, Senate Bills, House Bills, Box 2 (MARS ID: 66.8.52.19.12; item), State Archives of North Carolina, Raleigh. [Online catalog description: "Report recommended rejection of petition; petition of Daniel McCarthy requesting an allowance for injury received as a seaman during the war."]

North Carolina (State). General Assembly. "[Document dated:] December 14, 1789: Report on Petition of John Murphy (With Petition) (Rejected)." Manuscript; General Assembly Record Group; Session Records, November-December 1789; Joint Papers, Committee Papers, Resolutions, Senate Bills, House Bills, Box 2 (MARS ID: 66.8.53.1.17; item), State Archives of North Carolina, Raleigh. [Online catalog description: "Petition of John Murphy requests compensation and pay due him for time spent as a prisoner of the British in Wilmington and for loss of his property. Account of property loss is included. Committee recommends he be authorized to draw one third of the pay he is entitled, and the comptroller be directed to issue a certificate for the other two thirds of equal value to specie certificates."]

North Carolina (State). General Assembly. "[Document dated:] December 8, [1791]: Petition of Ezra Bostick." Manuscript; General Assembly Record Group; Session Records, December 1791-January 1792; Reports (Miscellaneous, Including Executive Messages; Petitions: Revolutionary War, Box 3 (MARS ID: 66.8.62.6.1; item), State Archives of North Carolina, Raleigh. [Online catalog description: "The petitioner claims that during his service in the war his wife ran off and eloped with another man. He asks the General Assembly for a divorce."]

North Carolina (State). General Assembly. "[Document dated:] December 8, 1791: Report of A. Thomas and James Taylor." Manuscript; General Assembly Record Group; Session Records,December 1791-January 1792; Reports (Miscellaneous, Including Executive Messages, Box 3 (MARS ID: 66.8.62.1.1; item), State Archives of North Carolina, Raleigh. [Online catalog description: "The report concerns the investigation of the army settlements at Warrenton in 1780. The investigators state that many soldiers have not received their compensation. The report describes the method of investigation and method of settling the accounts. It also makes remarks about non-commissioned officers and privates."]

North Carolina (State). General Assembly. "[Document dated:] December 9, [1791]: Petition of Ann Blount." Manuscript; General Assembly Record Group; Session Records, December 1791-January 1792; Reports (Miscellaneous, Including Executive Messages; Petitions: Revolutionary War, Box 3 (MARS ID: 66.8.62.6.2), State Archives of North Carolina, Raleigh. [Online catalog description: "The petitioner's deceased husband, James Blount, purchased many things for the public during his service in the military. Ann Blount, the petitioner, asks the General Assembly to settle his accounts and to grant her relief."]

North Carolina (State). General Assembly. "[Document dated:] December 10, [1791]: Petition of James McDowal." Manuscript; General Assembly Record Group; Session Records, December 1791-January 1792, Reports (Miscellaneous, Including Executive Messages; Petitions: Revolutionary War, Box 3 (MARS ID: 66.8.62.6.3; item), State Archives of North Carolina, Raleigh. [Online catalog description: "McDowal, who served in the militia, washed and, hence, destroyed his war payment certificates. He has received no compensation from the state for his services and asks the General Assembly for relief."]

North Carolina (State). General Assembly. "[Document dated:] December 12, [1791]: Petition of James Redfern." Manuscript General Assembly Record Group, Session Records, December 1791-January 1792; Reports (Miscellaneous, Including Executive Messages; Petitions: Revolutionary War, Box 3 (MARS ID: 66.8.62.6.4; item), State Archives of North Carolina, Raleigh. [Online catalog description: "Redfern was injured during the American Revolution and is no longer capable of working. He seeks relief from the state."]

North Carolina (State). General Assembly. "[Document dated:] December 13, [1791]: Petition of Thomas Blair." Manuscript; General Assembly Record Group; Session Records, December 1791-January 1792; Reports (Miscellaneous, Including Executive Messages; Petitions: Revolutionary War, Box 3 (MARS ID: 66.8.62.6.5; item), State Archives of North Carolina, Raleigh. [Online catalog description: "Blair claims that he lost his certificate which entitled him to payment for his service in the Continental Line. He asks the General Assembly for relief."]

North Carolina (State). General Assembly. "[Document dated:] December 13, [1791]: Petition of Cosimo Medici, (With Supporting Documents)." Manuscript; General Assembly Record Group; Session Records, December 1791-January 1792; Reports (Miscellaneous, Including Executive Messages); Petitios: Revolutionary War, Box 3 (MARS ID: 66.8.62.6.7; item), State Archives of North Carolina, Raleigh. [Online catalog description: "Medici was one of the prisoners of war held in Charleston. They were later exchanged for other prisoners. However, they incurred several debts necessary to their survival during their captivity. They made arrangements to pay off the debt but did not follow through with their plans because of dangerous circumstances. In the course of making these arrangements, Medici incurred more debt for which he asks the legislature for relief." Two other documents appear in the search results on this petition.]

North Carolina (State). General Assembly. "[Document dated:] December 13, [1791]: Petition of Joseph Wason (With Supporting Documents)." Manuscript; General Assembly Record Group; Session Records, December 1791-January 1792; Reports (Miscellaneous, Including Executive Messages); Petitions: Revolutionary War, Box 3 (MARS ID: 66.8.62.6.6; item), State Archives of North Carolina, Raleigh. [Online catalog description: "Wason suffered wounds during the war, and the General Assembly authorized allowances be paid to him from a special county tax. The county never collected the tax. Wason now seeks relief."]

North Carolina (State). General Assembly. "[Document dated:] December 7, [1792]: Petition of Brittain Matthews." Manuscript; General Assembly Record Group; Session Records, November 1792-January 1793; Joint Papers, Committee Papers, Resolutions, Senate Bills, House Bills, Box 3 (MARS ID: 66.8.66.11.30; item), State Archives of North Carolina, Raleigh. [Online catalog description: "A petition requesting compensation for a horse and for the petitioner's services. Includes legislative message changing the committee to whom the petition was referred."]

North Carolina (State). General Assembly. "[Document dated:] December 14, [1791]: Memorial and Petition of Stephen Moore, Late Deputy Quartermaster General for North Carolina during the Revolution." Manuscript; General Assembly Record Group; Session Records, December 1791-January 1792; Reports (Miscellaneous, Including Executive Messages); Petitions: Revolutionary War, Box 3 (MARS ID: 66.8.62.6.8; item), State Archives of North Carolina, Raleigh. [Online catalog description: "Concerning a repayment for forage borrowed during the revolution from Robert Kates."]

North Carolina (State). General Assembly. "[Document dated:] December 16, [1791]: Petition of Joseph Green." Manuscript; General Assembly Record Group; Session Records, December 1791-January 1792 Reports (Miscellaneous, Including Executive Messages); Petitions: Revolutionary War, Box 3 (MARS ID: 66.8.62.6.10; item), State Archives of North Carolina, Raleigh. [Online catalog description: "Concerning the depreciation of the money that Joseph Green received during the American Revolution."]

North Carolina (State). General Assembly. "[Document dated:] December 16, [1791]: Petition of John Williams, a Mariner." Manuscript; General Assembly Record Group; Session Records, December 1791-January 1792; Reports (Miscellaneous, Including Executive Messages); Petitions: Revolutionary War, Box 3 (MARS ID: 66.8.62.6.10; item), State Archives of North Carolina, Raleigh. [Online catalog description: "Concerning payment for use of his vessel, crew, and services during the American Revolution."]

North Carolina (State). General Assembly. "[Document dated:] December 19, [1791]: Petition of Captain George Samuel for Himself and for Others." Manuscript; General Assembly Record Group; Session Records, December 1791-January 1792; Reports (Miscellaneous, Including Executive Messages); Petitions: Revolutionary War, Box 3 (MARS ID: 66.8.62.6.14; item), State Archives of North Carolina, Raleigh. [Online catalog description: "Concerning George Samuel and others' service in the militia for which they have received no compensation."]

North Carolina (State). General Assembly. "[Document dated:] December 19, [1791]: Memorial of Presly Nelms (With Supporting Documents)." Manuscript; General Assembly Record Group; Session Records, December 1791-January 1792; Reports (Miscellaneous, Including Executive Messages); Petitions: Revolutionary War, Box 3 (MARS ID: 66.8.62.6.11; items), State Archives of North Carolina, Raleigh. [Online catalog description: "Concerning a wagon and a slave Nelms gave to the American Revolution and what he feels to be insufficient compensation for his property."]

North Carolina (State). General Assembly. "[Document dated:] December 19, [1791]: Petition of Samuel Hogan." Manuscript; General Assembly Record Group; Session Records, December 1791-January 1792, Reports (Miscellaneous, Including Executive Messages); Petitions: Revolutionary War, Box 3 (MARS ID: 66.8.62.6.12; item), State Archives of North Carolina, Raleigh. [Online catalog description: "Concerning payment that Samuel Hogan would like to receive for his late father's services in the American Revolution."]

North Carolina (State). General Assembly. "[Document dated:] December 21, [1791]: Petition of Elizabeth West (With Oath)." Manuscript; General Assembly Record Group; Session Records, December 1791-January 1792, Reports (Miscellaneous, Including Executive Messages); Petitions: Revolutionary War, Box 3 (MARS ID: 66.8.62.6.15), State Archives of North Carolina, Raleigh. [Online catalog description: "Concerns money that Elizabeth would like to collect from her late husband's service as a soldier."]

North Carolina (State). General Assembly. "[Document dated:] December 21, [1791]: Petition of Robert Fenner." Manuscript; General Assembly Record Group; Session Records, December 1791-January 1792; Joint Papers, Committee Papers, Resolutions, Senate Bills, House Bills, Box 3 (MARS ID: 66.8.62.6.16; item), State Archives of North Carolina, Raleigh. [Online catalog description: "Concerning compensation that Fenner thinks he is entitled to because of his services as an agent for the line (Contentinal Line?)."]

North Carolina (State). General Assembly. "[Document dated:] December 23, [1791]: Petition of David Speir." Manuscript; General Assembly Record Group; Session Records, December 1791-January 1792; Joint Papers, Committee Papers, Resolutions, Senate Bills, House Bills, Box 3 (MARS ID: 66.8.62.6.17; item), State Archives of North Carolina, Raleigh. [Online catalog description: "Concerning money that was owed to David Speir for his services in the Continental Line that was fraudently paid to John McNess."]

North Carolina (State). General Assembly. "[Document dated:] December 24, [1791]: Petition of Frederick Crucy." Manuscript; General Assembly Record Group; Session Records, December 1791-January 1792; Joint Papers, Committee Papers, Resolutions, Senate Bills, House Bills, Box 3 (MARS ID: 66.8.62.6.18; item), State Archives of North Carolina, Raleigh. [Online catalog description: "Concerning Frederick Crucy's request for compensation for his service in the militia."]

North Carolina (State). General Assembly. "[Document dated:] December 26, [1791]: Petition of Charles Medlock (With Oath)." Manuscript; General Assembly Record Group; Session Records, December 1791-January 1792; Joint Papers, Committee Papers, Resolutions, Senate Bills, House Bills, Box 3 (MARS ID: 66.8.562.6.19; item), State Archives of North Carolina, Raleigh. [Online catalog description: "The petitioner delivered supplies to the army for which he received payment in the form of a certificate from the state auditor. The certificate was destroyed by accident, and the petitioner asks that the state replace it."]

North Carolina (State). General Assembly. "[Document dated:] December 26, [1791]: Petition of Frances Bain, John Hall, William Hall, and Roger Hall." Manuscript; General Assembly Record Group; Session Records, December 1791-January 1792; Joint Papers, Committee Papers, Resolutions, Senate Bills, House Bills, Box 2 (MARS ID: 66.8.61.10.2; item), State Archives of North Carolina, Raleigh. [Online catalog description: "The siblings of Thomas Hall petition the assembly for the benefits of their dead brother's military service."]

North Carolina (State). General Assembly. "[Document dated:] December 28, [1791]: Petition of Janet Spurgin." Manuscript; General Assembly Record Group; Session Records, December 1791-January 1792, Box 3 (MARS ID: 66.8.62.6.20; item), State Archives of North Carolina, Raleigh. [Online catalog description: "Concerning reimbursement that Janet Spurgin feels is owed to her for supplies that she furnished to the militia during the war."]

North Carolina (State). General Assembly. "[Document dated:] December 28, [1791]: Petition of Jesse Benton, Executor for the Late Captain John Benton (With Supporting Documents)." Manuscript; General Assembly Record Group; Session Records, December 1791-January 1792; Joint Papers, Committee Papers, Resolutions, Senate Bills, House Bills, Box 3 (MARS ID: 66.8.62.6.20), State Archives of North Carolina, Raleigh. [Online catalog description: "Seeking reimbursement for clothes that the late Captain Benton furnished the militia."]

North Carolina (State). General Assembly. "[Document dated:] December 28, [1791]: Representation of Robert Burton." Manuscript; General Assembly Record Group; Session Records, December 1791-January 1792; Joint Papers, Committee Papers, Resolutions, Senate Bills, House Bills, Box 3 (MARS ID: 66.8.62.6.21; item), State Archives of North Carolina, Raleigh. [Online catalog description: "Concerning warrants that was lost by a

Deputy Quarter Master General named Varner which the petitioner, Burton, assumed credit for. Believing that the lost warrants should now be assumed by the state, Burton asks the General Assembly for relief."]

North Carolina (State). General Assembly. "[Documents dated:] 1791-1792: Petitions: Revolutionary War." Manuscript, General Assembly Record Group; Session Records, December 1791-January 1792; Reports (Miscellanous), including Executive Memorials, Box 3 (MARS ID: 66.8.62.6; folder), State Archives of North Carolina, Raleigh.

North Carolina (State). General Assembly. "[Document dated:] January 4, [1792]: Memorial of Robert Agnew." Manuscript; General Assembly Record Group; Session Records, December 1791-January 1792; Joint Papers, Committee Papers, Resolutions, Senate Bills, House Bills; Joint Papers, Committee Papers, Resolutions, Senate Bills, House Bills, Box 3 (MARS ID: 66.8.62.6.25; item), State Archives of North Carolina, Raleigh. [Online catalog description: "Concerning payment that Robert Agnew feels is owed to him by the General Assembly for his enlistment of an indentured servant in the militia."]

North Carolina (State). General Assembly. "[Document dated:] January 4, [1792]: Petition of Elizabeth Doughlass [*sic*]." Manuscript; General Assembly Record Group; Session Records, December 1791-January 1792; Joint Papers, Committee Papers, Resolutions, Senate Bills, House Bills, Box 3 (MARS ID: 66.8.62.6.24; item), State Archives of North Carolina, Raleigh. [Online catalog description: "Although Elizabeth Douglass [*sic*] missed the date for application to the legislature, she hopes that they will allow her half pay for her late husband's service in the Revolution."]

North Carolina (State). General Assembly. "[Document dated:] January 5, 1792: Report on the Petition of Thomas Blair." Manuscript; General Assembly Record Group; Session Records, December 1791-January 1792; House Resolutions, Senate Resolutions, Geovernor's Messages; Joint Committee Reports (Propositions and Grievances), Box 2 (MARS ID: 66.8.61.12.17; item), State Archives of North Carolina, Raleigh. [Online catalog description: "Due to a lack of evidence, the committee rejects the petition."]

North Carolina (State). General Assembly. "[Document dated:] January 6, [1792]: Petition of Joel Lewis." Manuscript; General Assembly Record Group; Session Records, December 1791-January 1792; Joint Papers, Committee Papers, Resolutions, Senate Bills, House Bills, Box 3 (MARS ID: 66.8.62.6.24; item), State Archives of North Carolina, Raleigh. [Online catalog description: "Concerning reimbursement for the petitioner's service in the militia which was complicated by the unexpected death of a another officer who with the petitioner had jointly given bond to another."]

North Carolina (State). General Assembly. "[Document dated:] January 12, [1792]: Report of the Petition of James Readfern." Manuscript, General Assembly Record Group Session Records, December 1791-January 1792; Joint Papers, Committee Papers, Resolutions, Senate Bills, House Bills, Box 2 (MARS ID: 66.8.61.11.21; item), State Archives of North Carolina, Raleigh. [Online catalog description: "The petition concerns the relief granted by the United States Congress for wounds incurred during the Revolutionary War. The committee reports that the legislature should not interfere in this business."]

North Carolina (State). General Assembly. "January 13, [1792]: Memorial of John Couch." Manuscript; General Assembly Record Group; Session Records, December 1791-January 1792; Joint Papers, Committee Papers, Resolutions, Senate Bills, House Bills, Box 3 (MARS ID: 66.8.62.6.28; item), State Archives of North Carolina, Raleigh. [Online catalog description: "Concerning money that the petitioner feels is owed to him by the state for debts that he incurred as a Quartermaster."]

North Carolina (State). General Assembly. "[Document dated:] November 21, 1792: Petition of Charles Jewkes. November 21, [1792]." Manuscript; General Assembly Record Group, Session Records, November 1792-January 1793; Joint Papers, Committee Papers, Resolutions, Senate Bills, House Bills, Box 3 (MARS ID: 66.8.66.11.21; item), State Archives of North Carolina, Raleigh. [Online catalog description: "A petition requesting compensation for the supplies furnished to the Continental Line."]

North Carolina (State). General Assembly. "[Document dated:] November 22, [1792]: Petition of John Hill, Thomas Bell, William Ireland, Joseph Houston, John Leech, William Neil, George Simmeral, and Dorcas Clark." Manuscript; General Assembly Record Group; Session Records, November 1792-January 1793; Joint Papers, Committee Papers, Resolutions, Senate Bills, House Bills, Box 3 (MARS ID: 66.8.66.11.9; item), State Archives of North Carolina, Raleigh. [Online catalog description: "A petition requesting the names of the people who settled the claims of James Douglas, George Bell, William Lusk, Moses Davis, Thomas Fleming, James Simmeral, and John Clark." To determine fraudulent land claims]

North Carolina (State). General Assembly. "[Document dated:] November 22, [1792]: Petition of William Gore." Manuscript; General Assembly Record Group; Session Records, November 1792-January 1793; Joint Papers, Committee Papers, Resolutions, Senate Bills, House Bills, Box 3 (MARS ID: 66.8.66.11.18; item), State

Archives of North Carolina, Raleigh. [Online catalog description: "A petition requesting formal recognition of the petitioner's patriotism in order to avoid slander."]

North Carolina (State). General Assembly. "[Document dated:] November 23, [1792]: Memorial of Joseph Shute, Executor of Thomas Pearson." Manuscript; General Assembly Record Group; Session Records, November 1792-January 1793; Joint Papers, Committee Papers, Resolutions, Senate Bills, House Bills, Box 3 (MARS ID: 66.8.66.11.39; item), State Archives of North Carolina, Raleigh. [Online catalog description: "A petition requesting compensation for rum provided to the soldiers by Thomas Pearson."]

North Carolina (State). General Assembly. "[Document dated:] November 23, [1792]: Petition of John Dickey and William Sharpe, Executors of William Lee Davidson." Manuscript; General Assembly Record Group; Session Records, November 1792-January 1793; Joint Papers, Committee Papers, Resolutions, Senate Bills, House Bills, Box 3 (MARS ID: 66.8.66.11.9; item), State Archives of North Carolina, Raleigh. [Online catalog description: "A petition requesting compensation for the services of William Lee Davidson."]

North Carolina (State). General Assembly. "[Document dated:] November 26, [1792]: Petition of James Kerr and John Alexander, Executors of Hugh Brevard." Manuscript; General Assembly Record Group; Session Records, November 1792-January 1793; Joint Papers, Committee Papers, Resolutions, Senate Bills, House Bills, Box 3 (MARS ID: 66.8.66.11.26; item), State Archives of North Carolina, Raleigh. [Online catalog description: "A petition stating that Brevard paid his debts to his soldiers and therefore his estate should not be held accountable."]

North Carolina (State). General Assembly. "[Document dated:] November 28, [1792]: Petition of Richard Copeland, Benjamin Dorton, John Boger, David Pae, Drury Parham, and John Dilliard." Manuscript; General Assembly Record Group; Session Records, November 1792-January 1793; Joint Papers, Committee Papers, Resolutions, Senate Bills, House Bills, Box 3 (MARS ID: 66.8.66.11.8; item), State Archives of North Carolina, Raleigh. [Online catalog description: "A petition requesting compensation for service in the militia."]

North Carolina (State). General Assembly. "[Document dated:] November 29, [1792]: Petition of Robert Hightower." Manuscript; General Assembly Record Group; Session Records, November 1792-January 1793; Joint Papers, Committee Papers, Resolutions, Senate Bills, House Bills, Box 3 (MARS ID: 66.8.66.11.17; item), State Archives of North Carolina, Raleigh. [Online catalog description: "A petition requesting reimbursement for supplies furnished to the militia."]

North Carolina (State). General Assembly. "[Document dated:] November 30, [1792]: Petition of Elias Hoell." Manuscript; General Assembly Record Group; Session Records, November 1792-January 1793; Joint Papers, Committee Papers, Resolutions, Senate Bills, House Bills, Box (MARS ID: 66.8.66.11.15; item), State Archives of North Carolina, Raleigh. [Online catalog description: "A petition stating that Elias Hoell never received full compensation for his services."]

North Carolina (State). General Assembly. "[Document dated:] November 30, [1792]: Petition of William Reed." Manuscript; General Assembly Record Group; Session Records, November 1792-January 1793; Joint Papers, Committee Papers, Resolutions, Senate Bills, House Bills, Box 3 (MARS ID: 66.8.66.11.35; item), State Archives of North Carolina, Raleigh. [Online catalog description: "A petition stating that William Reed bought a certificate for claiming militia wages from Isaac Etheridge but was then denied payment by the board of auditors because the name on their list was Isaac Everidge."]

North Carolina (State). General Assembly. "[Document dated:] December 3, [1792]: Petition of Gilbert Clarke, John Maclane, Hector Maclane, Daniel Munroe, and John Smith." Manuscript; General Assembly Record Group; Session Records, November 1792-January 1793; Joint Papers, Committee Papers, Resolutions, Senate Bills, House Bills, Box 3 (MARS ID: 66.8.66.1.23; item), State Archives of North Carolina, Raleigh. [Online catalog description: "A petition requesting that the state pay the money owed to the petitioners for the cattle they provided to the militia through the commissary Peter Malett."]

North Carolina (State). General Assembly. "[Document dated:] December 4, [1792]." Message from Governor. Manuscript; General Assembly Record Group; Session Records, November 1792-January 1793; Joint Papers, Committee Papers, Resolutions, Senate Bills, House Bills, Box 2, (MARS ID: 66.8.65.12.6; item), State Archives of North Carolina, Raleigh. [Online catalog description: "A message regarding a letter from Representative Williamson recommending that the widow of Brigadier General Davidson receive a pension. Includes the letter from Williamson detailing Mrs. Davidson's situation."]

North Carolina (State). General Assembly. "[Document dated:] December 4, [1792]." Petition of Benjamin Seawell. Manuscript; General Assembly Record Group; Session Records, November 1792-January 1793; Joint Papers, Committee Papers, Resolutions, Senate Bills, House Bills, Box 3 (MARS ID: 66.8.66.11.37; item), State Archives of North Carolina, Raleigh. [Online catalog description: "A petition stating that the petitioner has paid his account to the public but never received from the commissary, Christopher Lackey, the entire amount for paying the bounties of the soldiers and requesting reimbursement of the amount he never received but which was paid back to the state. Includes various oaths, warrants, and certification related to the matter."]

North Carolina (State). General Assembly. "[Document dated:] December 4, [1792]: Petition of Daniel Jones." Manuscript; General Assembly Record Group; Session Records, November 1792-January 1793; Joint Papers, Committee Papers, Resolutions, Senate Bills, House Bills, Box 3 (MARS ID: 66.8.66.11.22), State Archives of North Carolina, Raleigh. [Online catalog description: "A petition requesting compensation for Daniel Jones's services."]

North Carolina (State). General Assembly. "[Document dated:] December 5, [1792]: Petition of Richard Neckins." Manuscript; General Assembly Record Group; Session Records, November 1792-January 1793; Joint Papers, Committee Papers, Resolutions, Senate Bills, House Bills, Box 3 (MARS ID: 66.8.66.11.33; item), State Archives of North Carolina, Raleigh. [Online catalog description: "A petition requesting compensation for the petitioner's father's service as a soldier in the Continental Line, Dempsey Casey having already tried to obtain compensation with the board of commissioners."]

North Carolina (State). General Assembly. "Petition of Thomas Dwane. December 7, [1792]." Manuscript; General Assembly Record Group; Session Records, November 1792-January 1793; Joint Papers, Committee Papers, Resolutions, Senate Bills, House Bills, Box 3 (MARS ID: 66.8.66.11.10; item), State Archives of North Carolina, Raleigh. [Online catalog description: "A petition requesting compensation for services as a military officer."]

North Carolina (State). General Assembly. "[Document dated:] December 11, [1792]: Petition of Abner Flewellin." Manuscript; General Assembly Record Group; Session Records, November 1792-January 1793; Joint Papers, Committee Papers, Resolutions, Senate Bills, House Bills, Box 3 (MARS ID: 66.8.66.11.11; item), State Archives of North Carolina, Raleigh. [Online catalog description: "A petition stating that Abner Flewellin purchased from William Orange's widow the right to his army pay and is now being accused of forgery. Includes two depositions that he did everything with the consent of the widow Orange."]

North Carolina (State). General Assembly. "[Document dated:] December 11, [1792]: Petition of James Richardson." Manuscript; General Assembly Record Group; Session Records, November 1792-January 1793; Joint Papers, Committee Papers, Resolutions, Senate Bills, House Bills, Box 3 (MARS ID: 66.8.66.11.36; item), State Archives of North Carolina, Raleigh. [Online catalog description: "A petition requesting compensation for money paid to new recruits and for military supplies."]

North Carolina (State). General Assembly. "[Document dated:] December 11, [1792]: Petition of Thomas Amis." Manuscript; General Assembly Record Group; Session Records, November 1792-January 1793; Joint Papers, Committee Papers, Resolutions, Senate Bills, House Bills, Box 3 (MARS ID: 66.8.66.11.2; item), State Archives of North Carolina, Raleigh. [Online catalog description: "A petition requesting compensation for cattle purchased for the army and for which the petitioner is being held accountable."]

North Carolina (State). General Assembly. "[Document dated:] December 12, [1792]: Petition of Arthur Gatling." Manuscript; General Assembly Record Group; Session Records, November 1792-January 1793; Joint Papers, Committee Papers, Resolutions, Senate Bills, House Bills, Box 3 (MARS ID: 66.8.66.11.13; item), State Archives of North Carolina, Raleigh. [Online catalog description: "A petition stating that Arthur Gatling paid for the business of new recruits himself and asking for reimbursement."]

North Carolina (State). General Assembly. "[Document dated:] December 13, [1792]: Petition of John Tutle." Manuscript; General Assembly Record Group; Session Records, November 1792-January 1793; Joint Papers, Committee Papers, Resolutions, Senate Bills, House Bills, Box 3 (MARS ID: 66.8.66.11.40; item), State Archives of North Carolina, Raleigh. [Online catalog description: "A petition requesting compensation for a wagon team furnished to the militia. Includes oath that the petitioner did not receive compensation."]

North Carolina (State). General Assembly. "[Document dated:] December 13, 1792: Petition of Patrick McEahan and John Farley. December 13, [1792]." Manuscript; General Assembly Record Group; Session Records, November 1792-January 1793; Joint Papers, Committee Papers, Resolutions, Senate Bills, House Bills, Box 3 (MARS ID: 66.8.66.11.29; item), State Archives of North Carolina, Raleigh. [Online catalog description: "A petition requesting compensation for cattle supplied to the army through Bryan Best."]

North Carolina (State). General Assembly. "[Document dated:] December 14, [1792] Petition of Lodwick Alford." Manuscript; General Assembly Record Group; Session Records, November 1792-January 1793; "Joint Papers, Committee Papers, Resolutions, Senate Bills, House Bills, Box 3 (MARS ID: 66.8.66.11.28; item), State Archives of North Carolina, Raleigh. [Online catalog description: "A petition requesting compensation for the services of James Talton, Emanuel Talton, Thomas Hill, Green Hill, and William Coly for whom the petitioner has power of attorney."]

North Carolina (State). General Assembly. "[Document dated:] December 18 [1792]: Petition of Richard Singleton of Rutherford County." Manuscript; General Assembly Record Group; Session Records, November 1792-January 1793; Joint Papers, Committee Papers, Resolutions, Senate Bills, House Bills, Box 3 (MARS ID: 66.8.66.10.9; item), State Archives of North Carolina, Raleigh. [Online catalog description: "A petition requesting compensation for having paid the county taxes out of his own pocket during the war."]

North Carolina (State). General Assembly. "[Document dated:] December 20, 1792: Petition of Nathaniel Christmas." Manuscript; General Assembly Record Group; November 1792-January 1793; Joint Papers, Committee Papers, Resolutions, Senate Bills, House Bills, Box 3 (MARS ID: 66.8.66.11.6; item), State Archives of North Carolina, Raleigh. [Online catalog description: "A petition asking for compensation for the petitioner's services as lieutenant because he has been out of state and could not settle his account. Includes the letter from Alexander Martin appointing Nathaniel Christmas and certifications stating that he was never paid."]

North Carolina (State). General Assembly. "[Document dated:] December 20, [1792]: Petition of William Meredith." Manuscript; General Assembly Record Group; Session Records, November 1792-January 1793; Joint Papers, Committee Papers, Resolutions, Senate Bills, House Bills, Box 3 (MARS ID: 66.8.66.11.31; item), State Archives of North Carolina, Raleigh. [Online catalog description: "A petition requesting more time to pay the money made in the sale of public arms."]

North Carolina (State). General Assembly. "[Document dated:] December 21, [1792]: Petition of George Grimes." Manuscript; General Assembly Record Group; Session Records, November 1792-January 1793; Joint Papers, Committee Papers, Resolutions, Senate Bills, House Bills, Box 3 (MARS ID: 66.8.66.11.14; item), State Archives of North Carolina, Raleigh. [Online catalog description: "A petition concerning the discharge of the petitioner."]

North Carolina (State). General Assembly. "[Document dated:] December 22, [1792]: Petition of Samuel Jones." Manuscript; General Assembly Record Group; Session Records, November 1792-January 1793; Joint Papers, Committee Papers, Resolutions, Senate Bills, House Bills, Box 3 (MARS ID: 66.8.66.11.24; item), State Archives of North Carolina, Raleigh. [Online catalog description: "A petition requesting full compensation for Samuel Jones' services as an officer."]

North Carolina (State). General Assembly. "[Document dated:] December 24, [1792]: Memorial of Richard Mosson." Manuscript; General Assembly Record Group; Session Records, November 1792-January 1793; Joint Papers, Committee Papers, Resolutions, Senate Bills, House Bills, Box 3 (MARS ID: 66.8.66.11.32; item), State Archives of North Carolina, Raleigh. [Online catalog description: "A petition requesting compensation for the petitioner's services as an officer in the Continental Line."]

North Carolina (State). General Assembly. "[Document dated:] December 24, [1792]: Petition of James Shackleford." Manuscript; General Assembly Record Group; Session Records, November 1792-January 1793; Joint Papers, Committee Papers, Resolutions, Senate Bills, House Bills, Box 3 (MARS ID: 66.8.66.11.38; item), State Archives of North Carolina, Raleigh. [Online catalog description: "A petition requesting compensation for having transported prisoners in his boat. Includes certification that the deed was done and an oath that no compensation was received."]

North Carolina (State). General Assembly. "[Document dated:] December 24, [1792]: Petition of John Jones." Manuscript; General Assembly Record Group; Session Records, November 1792-January 1793; Joint Papers, Committee Papers, Resolutions, Senate Bills, House Bills, Box 3 (MARS ID: 66.866.11.23; item), State Archives of North Carolina, Raleigh. [Online catalog description: "A petition requesting compensation for John Jones's services as an officer. Includes an account of the money due to him."]

North Carolina (State). General Assembly. "[Document dated:] [undated]: Petition of Joseph McCulloch." Manuscript; General Assembly Record Group; Session Records, November 1792-January 1793; Joint Papers, Committee Papers, Resolutions, Senate Bills, House Bills, Box 3 (MARS ID: 66.8.66.11.28; item), State Archives of North Carolina, Raleigh. [Online catalog description: "A petition explaining the circumstances under which the petitioner acted during the revolution and asking for the restoration of his citizenship."]

North Carolina (State). General Assembly. "[Documents dated:] 1792-1793: Petitions Concerning the Revolutionary War." Manuscript; General Assembly Record Group; Session Records, November 1792-January 1793; House Committees, Senate Committees, Joint Committees, Box 3 (MARS ID: 66.8.66.11; folder), State Archives of North Carolina, Raleigh.

North Carolina (State). General Assembly. "[Document dated:] Jan. 2, [1793]: Report on the Petition of Thomas Devane (Rejected)." Manuscript; General Assembly Record Group; Session Records, December 1793-January 1794; Box 2 (MARS ID: 66.8.69.8.3; item), State Archives of North Carolina, Raleigh. [Online catalog description: "Devane had served as a commander of men for nine months and had fought another fourteen months in the land war. He is seeking compensation for his service."]

North Carolina (State). General Assembly. "[Document dated:] Dec 21, [1793]: Committee Report on the Petition of Thomas Childs." Manuscript, General Assembly Record Group; Session Records, December 1792-January 1794; Joint Papers, Committee Papers, Resolutions, Senate Bills, House Bills, Box 2 (MARS ID: 66.8.69.10.7; item), State Archives of North Carolina, Raleigh. [Online catalog description: "T. Childs had served as an active officer in the last war, during which he had sustained wounds that left him disabled and unable to earn a living. The treasurer is directed to pay to him thirty pounds for all his medical and travelling expenses as well as twelve pounds for every year since 1780. Petition included."]

North Carolina (State). General Assembly. "[Document dated:] Dec 30, [1793]. Committee Report on the Petition of Ann Langston and Sarah Bennett (Rejected)." Manuscript, General Assembly Record Group; Session Records, December 1793-January 1794; Box 2 (MARS ID: 66.8.69.10.11; item), State Archives of North Carolina, Raleigh. [Online catalog description: "The committee said that there was no evidence that showed that the two war widows had not received compensation and/or pension for the service of their husbands. Petition is rejected and the two are requested to provide a certificate from the court in Wayne County showing that they have not received anything. Petitions included."]

North Carolina (State). General Assembly. "[Documents dated:] 1793-1794: Petitions (Revolutionary War)." Manuscript; General Assembly Record Group; Session Records, December 1793-January 1794; Petitions, Amendments, Miscellaneous Correspondence, Box 3 (MARS ID: 66.8.70.5; folder), State Archives of North Carolina, Raleigh.

North Carolina (State). General Assembly. "[Documents dated:] 1794-1795: Petitions (Revolutionary War)." Manuscript; General Assembly Record Group; Session Records, December 1794-February 1795; Senate Committee Reports, Joint Committee Reports, Box 3 (MARS ID: 66.8.75.9; folder), State Archives of North Carolina, Raleigh.

North Carolina (State). General Assembly. "[Document dated:] Nov. 16, [1795]: The Petition of Philemon Hodge." Manuscript, General Assembly Record Group; Session Records, November-December 1795; Joint Papers, Committee Papers, Resolutions, Senate Bills, House Bills, Box 3 (MARS ID: 66.8.79.5.1; item), State Archives of North Carolina, Raleigh. [Online catalog description: "As administrator of the estates of soldiers of the late North Carolina line, the said petitioner, after applying to several places, requests that the General Assembly grant him certain claims."]

North Carolina (State). General Assembly. "[Document dated:] Nov 18, [1795]: Petition of Isaac Baits of Buncombe County." Manuscript, General Assembly Record Group; Session Records, November-December 1795; Joint Papers, Committee Papers, Resolutions, Senate Bills, House Bills, Box 3 (MARS ID: 66.8.79.5.2; item), State Archives of North Carolina, Raleigh. [Online catalog description: "The said petitioner was wounded in battle against the Cherokee Indians as a private in a company of rangers which resulted in the amputation of his wounded arm, for which he received allowances for two years. Due to the war, he stopped receiving said allowances and wishes to renew them. Sworn statements included."]

North Carolina (State). General Assembly. "[Document dated:] November 19, [1795]: The Representation and Petition of John Waddell of the County of Bladen." Manuscript; General Assembly Record Group; Session Records, November-December 1795; Joint Papers, Committee Papers, Resolutions, Senate Bills, House Bills, Box 3 (MARS ID: 66.8.79.5.3; item), State Archives of North Carolina, Raleigh. [Online catalog description: "Petitioner seeks the provisions due to him as an heir of General Nash. Other correspondence included."]

North Carolina (State). General Assembly. "[Document dated:] November 28, [1795]: Petition of William Gardner." Manuscript; General Assembly Record Group; Session Records, November-December 1795; Joint Papers, Committee Papers, Resolutions, Senate Bills, House Bills, Box 3 (MARS ID: 66.8.79.5.5; item), State Archives of North Carolina, Raleigh. [Online catalog description: "Petitioner's certificate for his services performed under Captain Barber was destroyed and he now wishes the General Assembly to provide him relief for such."]

North Carolina (State). General Assembly. "[Documents dated:] 1796: Petitions (Revolutionary War)." Manuscript; General Assembly Record Group; Session Records, November 1796-December 1796; Petitions, Amendments, Misc. Correspondence…, Box 3 (MARS ID: 66.8.82.2; folder), State Archives of North Carolina, Raleigh.

North Carolina (State). General Assembly. "[Document dated:] November 25, [1796]: The Petition of Colonel James Miller of Rutherford County." Manuscript; General Assembly Record Group; Session Records, November-December 1796; Joint Papers, Committee Papers, Resolutions, Senate Bills, House Bills, Box 3 (MARS ID: 66.8.82.2.2; item), State Archives of North Carolina, Raleigh. [Online catalog description: "Miller, as commissioner of confiscated property, allowed a certain Mary Potts to pay off a bond, for which she was indebted to John Goodbread for land belonging to Goodbread which had been confiscated by the state when he sided with the enemy, in beef cattle since his troops were in desperate need of provisions as they were battling the Indians. Miller receipted Potts for such and indemnified her against Goodbread's claim. After the war,

Goodbread reclaimed his estate from the state and brought suit against Mary Potts for the said bond who entered suit against Miller. Miller now requests to be refunded for the payment of the suit as he feels his actions were for the well-being of his troops and the general public, and had no personal incentives for himself. Affidavits also included."]

North Carolina (State). General Assembly. "[Document dated:] Dec. 3, [1795]: Petition of the Heirs of Colonel Edward Buncombe." Manuscript; General Assembly Record Group; Session Records, November-December 1795; Joint Papers, Committee Papers, Resolutions, Senate Bills, House Bills, Box 3 (MARS ID: 66.8.79.5.6; item), State Archives of North Carolina, Raleigh. [Online catalog description: "The petitioners, entitled to the said colonel's pay in certificates, request compensation for the trouble caused to them by the false issuing of the said certificates to a person in Philadelphia."]

North Carolina (State). General Assembly. "[Documents dated:] 1795: Petitions (Revolutionary War)." Manuscript; General Assembly Record Group; Session Records, November 1795-December 1795; Petitions, Amendments, Misc. Correspondence…, Box 3 (MARS ID: 66.8.79.5; folder), State Archives of North Carolina, Raleigh.

North Carolina (State). General Assembly. "[Document dated:] November 29, [1796]: The Petition and Remonstrance of Charles Frederic Mabius." Manuscript; General Assembly Record Group; Session Records, November-December 1796; Joint Papers, Committee Papers, Resolutions, Senate Bills, House Bills, Box 3 (MARS ID: 66.8.82.2.4; item), State Archives of North Carolina, Raleigh. [Online catalog description: "Charles Mabius of Rowan County, husband to the widow of the late Sergeant William Henry Bailley in the first regiment of the Continental Line of this state, requests that the Secretary of State issue a warrant to him for the remaining land granted to the said Bailley as a sergeant."]

North Carolina (State). General Assembly. "[Document dated:] November 30, [1796]: Report of the Committee of Propositions and Grievances on the Petition of Sundry Inhabitants of Rutherford County." Manuscript; General Assembly Record Group; Session Records, November-December 1796; Joint Papers, Committee Papers, Resolutions, Senate Bills, House Bills, Box 3 (MARS ID: 66.8.81.16.4; item), State Archives of North Carolina, Raleigh. [Online catalog description: "Committee rejects said inhabitants' request to repeal an act passed by the General Assembly of this state in 1785 disqualifying certain persons who allied with the British during the war from holding certain offices."]

North Carolina (State). General Assembly. "[Document dated:] Dec. 1, [1796]: The Petition of John Clark on Behalf of the Heirs of the Late Colonel Edward Buncombe." Manuscript; General Assembly Record Group; Session Records, November-December 1796; Joint Papers, Committee Papers, Resolutions, Senate Bills, House Bills, Box 3 (MARS ID: 66.8.82.2.7; item), State Archives of North Carolina, Raleigh. [Online catalog description: "The petition asks the General Assembly to order the Treasurer to pay the seventh year's half pay for the services of the said Colonel Buncombe to his heirs as instructed by an act of Assembly passed in 1785 concerning payment of such to the heirs of Buncombe as well as to the heirs of all other commanding officers of the Continental Line."]

North Carolina (State). General Assembly. "[Document dated:] Dec. 1, [1796]: The Petition of Robert Harris." Manuscript; General Assembly Record Group; Session Records, November-December 1796; Joint Papers, Committee Papers, Resolutions, Senate Bills, House Bills, Box 3 (MARS ID: 66.8.82.2.6; item), State Archives of North Carolina, Raleigh. [Online catalog description: "Robert Harris of Cabarrus County, as agent of the heirs of Lieutenant Colonel William Lee Davidson, requests that the General Assembly direct the full amount due to said Colonel for his service in the Continental Line of this state to be paid to his heirs either in cash or certificates."]

North Carolina (State). General Assembly. "[Document dated:] Dec. 2, [1796]: The Petition of Moses Lee." Manuscript; General Assembly Record Group; Session Records, November-December 1796; Joint Papers, Committee Papers, Resolutions, Senate Bills, House Bills, Box 3 (MARS ID: 66.8.82.2.8; item), State Archives of North Carolina, Raleigh. [Online catalog description: "The petitioner requests compensation for cattle and sheep furnished to the army of this state commanded by Colonel Thomas Brown of Bladen County."]

North Carolina (State). General Assembly. "[Document dated:] November 25, [1796]: Petition of Henry Blurton." Manuscript; General Assembly Record Group; Session Records, November-December 1796; Joint Papers, Committee Papers, Resolutions, Senate Bills, House Bills, Box 3 (MARS ID: 66.8.82.2.1; item), State Archives of North Carolina, Raleigh. [Online catalog description: "Henry Blurton of Johnston County wishes to be paid a certain sum for his eighteen months of service in Capt. Coleman's Company in the fifth North Carolina Regiment as a sergeant. Comptroller's certificate also included."]

North Carolina (State). General Assembly. "[Document dated:] November 25, [1796]: The Petition of Colonel James Miller of Rutherford County." Manuscript; General Assembly Record Group; Session Records, November-December 1796; Joint Papers, Committee Papers, Resolutions, Senate Bills, House Bills, Box 3

(MARS ID: 66.89.82.2.2; item), State Archives of North Carolina, Raleigh. [Online catalog description: "Miller, as commissioner of confiscated property, allowed a certain Mary Potts to pay off a bond, for which she was indebted to John Goodbread for land belonging to Goodbread which had been confiscated by the state when he sided with the enemy, in beef cattle since his troops were in desperate need of provisions as they were battling the Indians. Miller receipted Potts for such and indemnified her against Goodbread's claim. After the war, Goodbread reclaimed his estate from the state and brought suit against Mary Potts for the said bond who entered suit against Miller. Miller now requests to be refunded for the payment of the suit as he feels his actions were for the well-being of his troops and the general public, and had no personal incentives for himself. Affidavits also included."]

North Carolina (State). General Assembly. "[Document dated:] November 29, [1796]: The Petition and Remonstrance of Charles Frederic Mabius." Manuscript; General Assembly Record Group; Session Records, November-December 1796; Joint Papers, Committee Papers, Resolutions, Senate Bills, House Bills, Box 3 (MARS ID: 66.8.82.2.4; item), State Archives of North Carolina, Raleigh. [Online catalog description: "Charles Mabius of Rowan County, husband to the widow of the late Sergeant William Henry Bailley in the first regiment of the Continental Line of this state, requests that the Secretary of State issue a warrant to him for the remaining land granted to the said Bailley as a sergeant."]

North Carolina (State). General Assembly. "[Document dated:] November 30, [1796]: Report of the Committee of Propositions and Grievances on the Petition of Sundry Inhabitants of Rutherford County." Manuscript; General Assembly Record Group; Session Records, November-December 1796; Joint Papers, Committee Papers, Resolutions, Senate Bills, House Bills, Box 3 (MARS ID: 66.8.81.16.4; item), State Archives of North Carolina, Raleigh. [Online catalog description: "Committee rejects said inhabitants' request to repeal an act passed by the General Assembly of this state in 1785 disqualifying certain persons who allied with the British during the war from holding certain offices."]

North Carolina (State). General Assembly. "[Document dated:] Dec. 1, [1796]: The Petition of John Clark on Behalf of the Heirs of the Late Colonel Edward Buncombe." Manuscript; General Assembly Record Group; Session Records, November-December 1796; Joint Papers, Committee Papers, Resolutions, Senate Bills, House Bills, Box 3 (MARS ID: 66.8.82.2.7; item), State Archives of North Carolina, Raleigh. [Online catalog description: "The petition asks the General Assembly to order the Treasurer to pay the seventh year's half pay for the services of the said Colonel Buncombe to his heirs as instructed by an act of Assembly passed in 1785 concerning payment of such to the heirs of Buncombe as well as to the heirs of all other commanding officers of the Continental Line."]

North Carolina (State). General Assembly. "[Document dated:] Dec. 1, [1796]: The Petition of Robert Harris." Manuscript; General Assembly Record Group; Session Records, November-December 1796; Joint Papers, Committee Papers, Resolutions, Senate Bills, House Bills, Box 3 (MARS ID: 66.882.2.6; item), State Archives of North Carolina, Raleigh. [Online catalog description: "Robert Harris of Cabarrus County, as agent of the heirs of Lieutenant Colonel William Lee Davidson, requests that the General Assembly direct the full amount due to said Colonel for his service in the Continental Line of this state to be paid to his heirs either in cash or certificates."]

North Carolina (State). General Assembly. "[Document dated:] Dec. 2, [1796]: The Petition of Moses Lee." Manuscript; General Assembly Record Group; Session Records, November-December 1796; Joint Papers, Committee Papers, Resolutions, Senate Bills, House Bills, Box 3 (MARS ID: 66.8.82.2.8; item), State Archives of North Carolina, Raleigh. [Online catalog description: "The petitioner requests compensation for cattle and sheep furnished to the army of this state commanded by Colonel Thomas Brown of Bladen County."]

North Carolina (State). General Assembly. "[Document dated:] Dec 5, [1796]. Report of the Committee of Propositions and Grievances No. 2 on the Petition of Frances Bain, John Hall, William Hall, and Roger Hall." Manuscript; General Assembly Record Group; Session Records, November-December 1796; Joint Papers, Committee Papers, Resolutions, Senate Bills, House Bills, Box 2 (MARS ID: 66.881.17.2; item), State Archives of North Carolina, Raleigh. [Online catalog description: "As the brothers and sister of the late Thomas Hall who served as a Lieutenant in the continental line of this state and died as such, the petitioners request that a warrant be issued to them for seven years half pay of said Thomas. Committee rejects the petition. Petition included."]

North Carolina (State). General Assembly. "[Document dated:] Dec 8, [1796]. John Wooton's Petition." Manuscript; General Assembly Record Group; Session Records, November-December 1796; Joint Papers, Committee Papers, Resolutions, Senate Bills, House Bills, Box 3 (MARS ID: 66.882.2.9; item), State Archives of North Carolina, Raleigh. [Online catalog description: "John Wooton requests relief for a wound he received as a volunteer soldier in Colonel Benjamin Leawill's regiment of militia in the year 1780. Affidavits of Wooton and Colonel Leawill and a surgeon's certificate included."]

North Carolina (State). General Assembly. "[Document dated:] Dec 8, [1796]: Report of the Committee of Claims on the Certificate of John Smith in Favor of Shugar Dooling." Manuscript; General Assembly Record Group; Session Records, November-December 1796; Joint Papers, Committee Papers, Resolutions, Senate Bills, House Bills, Box 2 (MARS ID: 66.881.14.1; item), State Archives of North Carolina, Raleigh. [Online catalog description: "Committee rejects certificate for a horse lost in the war because they feel it is not a matter to be dealt with by said committee."]

North Carolina (State). General Assembly. "[Document dated:] Dec. 14, [1796]: The Petition of the Representatives of David Molborn, Soloman Molborn, and William Denail." Manuscript; General Assembly Record Group; Session Records, November-December 1796, Box 3 (MARS ID: 66.8.82.2.11; item), State Archives of North Carolina, Raleigh. [Online catalog description: "The petitioners request that they be issued their grants for bounties of land allotted by law to the three late soldiers of the Continental Line of this state aformentioned."]

North Carolina (State). General Assembly. "Dec 15, [1796]: The Petition of David Sayers of Franklin County." Manuscript; General Assembly Record Group; Session Records, November-December 1796; Joint Papers, Committee Papers, Resolutions, Senate Bills, House Bills, Box 3 (MARS ID: 66.882.1.12; item), State Archives of North Carolina, Raleigh. [Online catalog description: "The petitioner requests that the General Assembly examine a certificate issued to him by the Commissioners of Army Accounts, since he was unaware that before applying for payment of such, a law passed by the Legislature of this state requires certificates issued in said year to be reexamined by a board."]

North Carolina (State). General Assembly. "[Document dated:] Dec. 16, [1796]: The Petition of David Miller." Manuscript; General Assembly Record Group; Session Records, November-December 1796; Joint Papers, Committee Papers, Resolutions, Senate Bills, House Bills, Box 3 (MARS ID: 66.8.82.2.13; item), State Archives of North Carolina, Raleigh. [Online catalog description: "David Miller of Rutherford County furnished the army of this state with certain provisions for which he paid out of his own pocket. However, he had lost the vouchers and accounts for such when the Board of Auditors were liquidating such accounts. He has now recovered the same and wishes to present such before a committee so he may receive the relief he feels he deserves."]

North Carolina (State). General Assembly. "[Document dated:] Dec. 17, [1796]: The Petition of Thomas Griffith, a Soldier." Manuscript; General Assembly Record Group; Session Records, November-December 1796; Joint Papers, Committee Papers, Resolutions, Senate Bills, House Bills, Box 3 (MARS ID: 66.8.82.2.14; item), State Archives of North Carolina, Raleigh. [Online catalog description: "Thomas Griffith requests payment for his three months of service to his country under the command of Capt. Alexander Clark of Chatham County."]

North Carolina (State). General Assembly. "[Document dated:] Dec. 20, [1796]: Report of the Committee of Finance on the Petition of Thomas Griffith." Manuscript; General Assembly Record Group; Session Records, November-December 1796; Joint Papers, Committee Papers, Resolutions, Senate Bills, House Bills, Box 2 (MARS ID: 66.8.81.15.11; item), State Archives of North Carolina, Raleigh. [Online catalog description: "Committee rejects petitioner's request for compensation for military services performed in the war."]

North Carolina (State). General Assembly. "[Document dated:] Dec. 21, [1796]: The Petition of William Morrison and Robert Patton of the County of Burke." Manuscript; General Assembly Record Group; Session Records, November-December 1796; Joint Papers, Committee Papers, Resolutions, Senate Bills, House Bills, Box 3 (MARS ID: 66.8.82.2.15; item), State Archives of North Carolina, Raleigh. [Online catalog description: "Petitioners request compensation for a wagon and team furnished to the army under the command of General Butler in order to provide South Carolina with ammunition and provisions."]

North Carolina (State). General Assembly. "[Documents dated:] 1797: Petitions (Revolutionary War)." Manuscript; General Assembly Record Group; Session Records, November-December 1797, (MARS ID: 66.8.84.4; folder), State Archives of North Carolina, Raleigh. [Consult the State Archives for availability of this material.]

North Carolina (State). General Assembly. "[Documents dated:] 1798: Petitions (Revolutionary War)." Manuscript; General Assembly Record Group; Session Records, November-December 1798, (MARS ID: 66.8.86.14; folder), State Archives of North Carolina, Raleigh. [Consult the State Archives for availability of this material.]

North Carolina (State). General Assembly. "[Documents dated:] 1799: Petitions (Revolutionary War)." Manuscript; General Assembly Record Group; Session Records, November-December 1799, (MARS ID: 66.8.90.8; folder), State Archives of North Carolina, Raleigh. [Consult the State Archives for availability of this material.]

North Carolina (State). General Assembly. "[Documents dated:] 1800: Petitions (Revolutionary War)." Manuscript; General Assembly Record Group; Session Records, November-December 1800, (MARS ID: 66.8.94.8; folder), State Archives of North Carolina, Raleigh. [Consult the State Archives for availability of this material.]

North Carolina (State). General Assembly. Committee of Propositions and Grievances. "[Documents dated:] 1784: Joint Papers, Committee Papers, Resolutions, Senate Bills, House Bills, Reports and Papers, 1784." Manuscript

General Assembly Record Group, Session Records, October-November 1784, Box 1 (MARS ID: 66.8.35.7; folder), State Archives of North Carolina, Raleigh. [Note: Some of the these petitions appear to relate to Revolutionary War service or expenditures. Viewing each would be necessary to determine if any are acceptable sources of service for the NSDAR.] [Online catalog description: "Includes messages regarding appointment to the committee and acceptance of its report, as well as the report of the committee, on:
the petition of the inhabitants of Warren County, and the committee has decided that ample compensation has been made for the tobacco borrowed by Governor Burke, except interest to which they are entitled
the petition of Isles Simmons, who did not have sufficient proof that he was a member of the Continental Army to receive compensation for his services
the petition of Hardy Willie, regarding compensation for clothes
the petition (including deposition) of John Geddy, who requested payment on a bill of exchange, and the committee awards him an allowance based on the scale of depreciation
the claim of John Swayne, a soldier in the militia of Caswell County, and awards him an allowance
the petition of Richard Cogdell, and the committee awards allowance for services regarding currency as treasurer (not concurred with)
the accounts of Thornton Yancey, and the committee finds everything in order and awards an allowance
the petition of Matthew McClure, and the committee awards him an allowance for the interest on a settlement of his account from two years ago
the account of Josias Slack, coroner of Currituck County, and the committee awards him an allowance for the inquest and burial of Reuben Wright
the account of William Searcey, a witness for the state against Robert Young for horse stealing, and the committee awards him an allowance
the petition of Nathan Keais, and the committee awards him an allowance based on the scale of depreciation for a bill of exchange
the claim of Edward Williams, which was rejected for want of vouchers in support
the claim of Thomas Morris of Jones County, and the committee awards an allowance for the conveyance of a horse thief to the New Bern jail
the inquisition of Joseph Sandford, which was rejected for want of vouchers in proof
the petition of Captain Elijah Moore, which was rejected for lack of proof
the petition of inhabitants of Montgomery County, which the committee considers a judicial matter that should not come before the Assembly
the petition of William Borritz, who the committee allows a sum for the execution of a slave
the petition of Jacob Sikes, which was rejected for lack of information
the petition of John McCoy, who is awarded an allowance, the petition of William Moore and Philip Thomas who are awarded an allowance for wounds received in battle serving the Continental Army
the petition of Edward Proscell, and the committee believes the matter should be referred to the House
the matter of missing certificates, which the committee believe to have been taken by the British
the account of Andrew Bass, and he is awarded compensation for furnishing cattle to the District of New Bern
the account of William Graham, who is awarded allowance based on the scale of depreciation
the claim of Sampson Mosley, which is rejected for the presence of the missing certificate
and the claim of William Shaw of Wayne County, who is awarded an allowance"]

"Petition on Behalf of John Orsborn, N. C. Governor's Papers." *Bulletin of the Genealogical Society of Old Tryon County*, 28:4 (November 2000), 154-155. [Rutherford County]

"Petitioners from 'South Carolina', formerly Tryon County, 1775." *Bulletin of the Genealogical Society of Old Tryon County*, 38:2 (May 2010), 82-99.

Spurgin, Janet. "Legislative Petition of Janet Spurgin, New Bern, N. C." Manuscript, N.97.3.159. [Online catalog description: "View of the Legislative Petition of Janet Spurgin, of New Bern, Craven County, to the North Carolina General Assembly for Reimbursement for Provisions during the Late Revolution, 28 December 1791."]

Constitution of 1776

Dean, Earl. "Making History in Halifax." *The State: A Weekly Survey of North Carolina*, 17:26 (November 1949), 10; online: http://digital.ncdcr.gov/cdm/ref/collection/p16062coll18/id/24701. [Online description from "North Carolina Periodicals Index," East Carolina University: "November marks the 173rd birthday of North Carolina's first state constitution. This and many other important events took place in Halifax County."]

"Delegates to the North Carolina Constitutional Conventions." *Eswau Huppeday: Bulletin of the Broad River*

Genealogical Society, 7:4 (November 1987), 238-252.
Green, Fletcher Melvin. "Constitutional Development in the South Atlantic States, 1776-1860: A Study in the Evolution of Democracy." Ph. D. dissertation, University of North Carolina at Chapel Hill, 1927; published with the same title: Chapel Hill: University of North Carolina Press, 1930; reprinted: New York: W. W. Norton & Company, 1966. New York: Da Capo Press, 1971.
Ketchum, Earl H. "The Sources of the North Carolina Constitution of 1776." *North Carolina Historical Review*, 6:3 (July 1929), 215-236; online: http://digital.ncdcr.gov/cdm/ref/collection/p16062coll9/id/4207. [Online description from "North Carolina Periodicals Index," East Carolina University: "This article examines the creation and content of the North Carolina Constitution of 1776 looking at how each article of the Constitution was created as well as providing a short analysis of each article."]
Kruman, Marc W. *Between Authority and Liberty: State Constitution Making in Revolutionary America*. Chapel Hill: University of North Carolina Press, 1992.
Maddry, Charles Katharine. "North Carolina Constitution of 1776." M. A. thesis, University of North Carolina, 1929.
Mitchell, Memory F., ed. *North Carolina Documents, 1584-1868*. Raleigh: State Department of Archives and History, 1967. [Revolutionary War-era contents: Constitution of 1776.]
Nash, Frank. "The North Carolina Constitution of 1776 and Its Makers." *James Sprunt Historical Publications*, 11 (1912), 5-23.
Orth, John V. 'North Carolina Constitutional History." *North Carolina Law Review*, 70:6 (September 1992), 1759-1802. [Online description from "North Carolina Periodicals Index," East Carolina University: "John V. Orth, Kenan Professor of Law at the University of North Carolina at Chapel Hill, traces the development of the North Carolina Constitution."]
Sikes, Enoch Walter. "Our First Constitution, 1776." *The North Carolina Booklet,* 7:2 (October 1907), 131-137; online: http://digital.ncdcr.gov/cdm/ref/collection/p249901coll37/id/14180. [Online description from "North Carolina Periodicals Index," East Carolina University: "A short look at the creation of the state Constitution after the exodus of the British officials in 1776."]
Smiley, David L. "Revolutionary Origins of the South's Constitutional Defenses." *North Carolina Historical Review*, 44:3 (July 1967), 256-269.
Westbrook, Kathy Grant. "Halifax County." *Our State: Down Home in North Carolina*, 17:26 (November 1949), 10; online: http://digital.ncdcr.gov/cdm/ref/collection/p16062coll18/id/99313. [Online description from "North Carolina Periodicals Index," East Carolina University: "Halifax County, located in the northeastern part of the state, was the first colony to move toward independence from Great Britain. Westbrook describes what visitors will find in the areas of art, entertainment, nature, and aviculture."]

North Carolina and the Continental Congress; Signers of the Declaration of Independence

Patriotic Service[21]

Patriots of the Revolution are considered to be those men and women who by an act or series of actions demonstrated unfailing loyalty to the cause of American Independence from England. Patriotic service might begin as early as April 1774. We depend upon recorded actions to give us an indication of patriotism. What was the purpose of the action? What were the risks? The consequences? Answers to these questions can determine whether the action actually applied to an attempt to further the cause of independence or demonstrated loyalty to that cause.

Evidence of patriotic activity may be found in town, county, state, and federal records. Many records kept by the states have been indexed and often a letter to the state archives will be sufficient to determine if evidence exists to show that a person contributed supplies or made some other contribution to the war effort. Town and county records have usually not been indexed and a personal search of town minutes and court minutes is required. Minutes of the Continental Congresses have been published. *Old letters, diaries, and other family and personal papers can often be used as evidence of patriotic intent, provided the record was made at the time of the event described.*

[21] Office of the Registrar General's compilation, *Genealogy Guidelines* (Washington, D. C.: National Society Daughters of the American Revolution, 2014), 94-95.

Not all actions illustrating patriotism are mentioned here. Many others exist. When it is considered desirable to establish another type of patriotic service, proof of the action taken must be submitted with the application paper, together with historical justification to show that the action did indeed imply patriotic intent.

Continental Congress: The First such gathering convened on 5 September 1774 in Carpenter's Hall, Philadelphia, with delegates from every colony except Georgia. The Second Congress met from May 1775 until March 1781. It became the governing body of the United States and continued to meet until the Articles of Confederation were ratified in 1781. The minutes of the Continental Congress have been published, along with the correspondence of its members. Its business papers are microfilmed, with a five-volume printed index.

Baldwin, Simeon E. "The Contributions of North Carolina to the Development of American Institutions." *North Carolina Booklet,* 14:3 (January 1915), 141-154; online: http://digital.ncdcr.gov/cdm/ref/collection/p249901coll37/id/14180.

Biographical Directory of the United States Congress, 1774-Present. Online: http://bioguide.congress.gov/biosearch/biosearch.asp.

Braxton, Fairfax. "Patriots of North Carolina: Of the Twenty-Four Men Who Served This Colony in the Continental Congress, Many Were Soldiers in the Revolution." *National Republic*, (April 1930), 32-33, 48.

Burnett, Edmund C., ed. *Letters of Members of the Continental Congress*. 8 vols. Washington, D. C.: The Carnegie Institution of Washington, 1921-1936; reprinted: Gloucester, Mass.: Peter Smith, 1963.

Burnett, Edmund Cody. "Southern Statesmen and the Confederation." *North Carolina Historical Review*, 14:4 (October 1937), 343-360.

Butler, John P. *Index, The Papers of the Continental Congress, 1774-1789*. 5 vols. Washington, D. C.: National Archives, 1978.

Connor, Robert Digges Wimberly. "Joseph Hewes and the Declaration of Independence." *North Carolina Booklet*, 10:3 (January 1911), 155-164; online: http://digital.ncdcr.gov/cdm/ref/collection/p249901coll37/id/14180. [Online description from "North Carolina Periodicals Index," East Carolina University: "Colonial North Carolina politician Joseph Hewes enjoyed an undeserved reputation for being slow to embrace the cause independence."]

Davis, B. J. "Representatives to the Continental Congress." *Tar Heel Junior Historian*, (Fall 2008); online: http://ncpedia.org/history/usrevolution/continental-congress.

Gantt, Jonathan W. "The Relevance of the Declaration of Independence to Colonial North Carolina." M. A. thesis, University of North Carolina, Wilmington, 1990.

Kiernan, Denise. *Signing Their Lives Away: The Fame and Misfortune of the Men Who Signed the Declaration of Independence*. Philadelphia: Quirk Books, 2009. [Contents: Introduction; A Clarification: The Real Independence Day; {Chapters on the signers from each state}; Appendix: Text of the Declaration of Independence; Time Line; The Miscellany of Independence.] [XI: North Carolina; Joseph Hewes: The Signer Who Worked Himself to Death; William Hooper: The Signer Who Feared Democracy; John Penn: The Signer Who Taught Himself How to Read and Write.]

Lewis, J. D. "The American Revolution in North Carolina: The Signers of the Declaration of Independence from North Carolina." Online: http://www.carolana.com/NC/Revolution/nc_signers_of_declaration_of_independence.html.

Mitchell, Memory F. *North Carolina's Signers: Brief Sketches of the Men Who Signed the Declaration of Independence and the Constitution*. Raleigh: Division of Archives and History, North Carolina Department of Cultural Resources, 1964. [Online description from "North Carolina Periodicals Index," East Carolina University: "Simeon E. Baldwin, Governor of Connecticut, presented the commencement address at Wake Forest College on May 21, 1914. His speech surveyed the influence of North Carolina on the development of the Declaration of Independence, the United States Constitution, and the election process."]

Morgan, David T. and William J. Schmidt. *North Carolinians in the Continental Congress*. Winston-Salem, N. C.: J. F. Blair, 1976. [Chronological discussion 'of the North Carolinians who served in the Continental Congress between 1774 and 1789, including the years of the Revolutionary War'."]

Morgan, David T. and William J. Schmidt. "From Economic Sanctions to Political Separation: The North Carolina Delegation to the Continental Congress, 1774-1776." *North Carolina Historical Review,* 52:3 (July 1975), 215-234.

North Carolina (State). General Assembly. "June 30, [1781]: Re Letters from Delegates in Congress, Resolves of Congress, and Other Public Papers." Manuscript; General Assembly Record Group; Session Records, June-July 1781, Box 1 (MARS ID: 66.8.25.9.7; item), State Archives of North Carolina, Raleigh. [Online catalog description: "The committee is appointed and recommends several actions be taken regarding taxation, exports, prisoners of war, tariffs, and courts."]

North Carolina (State). Secretary of State. "Continental Congress Records, 1774-1779." Manuscript SS 317 (MARS ID: 12.115; series), State Archives of North Carolina, Raleigh. [Online catalog description: "Correspondence, reports and notes of the delegates from North Carolina to the Continental Congress. Included are talks with chiefs of the Creek and Cherokee Indians, notes about Arthur Lee, comments by Thomas Burke on the legality of the special courts of oyer and terminer, and observations on the draft constitution of North Carolina."]

Pierce, Eidth Louise. "The Relations between North Carolina and the Continental Congress." M. A. thesis, University of Tennessee, 1939.

Pyne, Frederick Wallace. *Descendants of the Signers of the Declaration of Independence: Volume 7: North Carolina, South Carolina, and Georgia.* Rockport, Me.: Picton Press, 2000; 2nd ed.: Rockport, Me., Picton Press, 2009.

Sanders, Jennings B. "Thomas Burke in the Continental Congress." *North Carolina Historical Review*, 9:1 (January 1932), 22-37.

Schmidt, William John. "The North Carolina Delegates in the Continental Congress, 1774-1781." Ph. D. dissertation, University of North Carolina at Chapel Hill, 1968. [Description: "Intends 'to determine whether these North Carolinians, collectively and individually, played a major or minor role in the proceedings of Congress, and to distinguish between the outstanding and the secondary figures from the North Carolina delegation'."]

Smith, Paul H., ed.; Rosemary Fry Plakas and Eugene R. Sheridan, assoc. eds. (vols. 1-12); Gerard W. Gawalt and Ronald M. Gephart, assoc. eds. (vols. 13-20); v. 21-25: Ronald M. Gephart, associate ed. (vol. 26): Ronald M. Gephart and Paul H. Smith, eds. (vol. 26) *Letters to Delegates to Congress, 1774-1789.* 26 vols. Washington, D.C.: Library of Congress, 1976-2000. [Contents: vol. 1. August 1774-August 1775; vol. 2. September-December 1775; vol. 3. January-May 1776; vol. 4. May-August 1776; vol. 5. August-December 1776; vol. 6. January-April 1777; vol. 7. May 1, 1777-September 18, 1777; vol. 8. September 18, 1777-January 31, 1778; vol. 9. February 1-May 31, 1778; vol. 10. June 1, 1778-September 30, 1778; vol. 11. October 1, 1778-January 31, 1779; vol. 12. February 1, 1779-May 31, 1779; vol. 13. June 1, 1779-September 30, 1779; vol. 14. October 1, 1779-March 31, 1780; vol. 15. April 1, 1780-August 31, 1780; vol. 16. September 1, 1780-February 28, 1781; vol. 17. March 1, 1781-August 31, 1781; vol. 18. September 1, 1781-July 31, 1782; vol. 19. August 1, 1782-March 11, 1783; vol. 20. March 12, 1783-September 30, 1783; vol. 21. October 1, 1783-October 31, 1784; vol. 22. November 1, 1784-November 6, 1785; vol. 23. November 7, 1785-November 5, 1786; vol. 24. November 6, 1786-February 29, 1788; vol. 25. March 1, 1788-July 25, 1789, with Supplement, 1774-87; vol. 26. Cumulative index with list of delegates to Congress 1774-1789.]

Sharpe, E. M. "Henry Downs: Signer of the Mecklenburg Declaration of Independence." *Olde Mecklenburg Genealogical Society Quarterly*, 11:3 (July-September 1993), 10-13.

Sheldon, George F., and William C. Friday. *Hugh Williamson: Physician, Patriot, and Founding Father.* Amherst, N.Y.: Humanity Books, 2010. [1735-1819; signer of the Declaration of Independence; North Carolina]

United States. Continental Congress. *Papers of the Continental Congress, 1774-1789.* Washington, D. C.: RG 360, M247, microfilm, 204 rolls. National Archives and Records Administration, Washington, D. C.; online at *http://www.fold3.com* [Online description from "North Carolina Periodicals Index," East Carolina University: Records "are arranged as bound by the State Department in the 19th century, primarily by type of record, such as journals, committee reports, correspondence, memorials, and petitions, and thereunder chronologically, alphabetically, or by subject. Records are arranged into 196 numbered units called 'Items.'"]

United States. National Archives and Records Service. *North and South Carolina State Papers, 1776-1788.* 1 microfilm reel. Washington, D. C.: NARS, 1959. [Description: "The official communications received by the Continental Congress from these two states."]

North Carolina Civil Service and Patriotic Service

Civil service is credited to those individuals who conducted public business under the authority of the new federal, state, county and town governments and displayed evidence of loyalty to the cause of political separation from England.

In New England, the business of ordinary government was conducted by the towns. The principal officers were selectmen and moderator. Additional officers were added to suit the needs of the particular town. Outside New

England, business was conducted at the county level and the types of offices held varied with the needs of the counties. Some states, notably New York, used both town and county forms of government.

Applicants seeking to establish civil service for an ancestor must first prove his place of residence. If the government unit was a town, the ancestor must have lived in that town at the time the service was performed. If the unit was a county or state, he must have resided in the place where the service was rendered. It was the law in all states during the Revolution that office holders be vested in the government they served.

Civil service began in the new American states when (1) the royal governor was removed from power and (2) a form of statewide American government was established.

Credit is not given for civil service in cities or states which were occupied by the British. Civil service is credited only when the Americans regained control of the locality.

Some offices classified as civil service include: State officials (other than governor and members of the legislature), county and town officers, Town Clerk, Selectman, Town Treasurer, Judge, Juror, Sheriff, Constable, Jailer, Overseer of the Roads, Justice of the Peace, Moderator, Overseer of the Poor, etc.

References to individuals with civil service or to records containing such information appear throughout this source guide.

Johnson, William Perry. "State and County Salaries and Fees, 1779." *Journal of North Carolina Genealogy*, 10:4 (Winter 1964), 1385-1387.

Courts, Court Records, Crime, Punishment, and Courthouses

Albright, Lee, and Helen F. M. Leary. "Strategy for Court Records." In Helen F. M. Leary, ed. *North Carolina Research: Genealogy and Local History*. 2nd ed. (Raleigh: North Carolina Genealogical Society, 1996), Chapter Two: "Designing Research Strategies," 52-53.

Arthur, Billy. "Plundering Sam Brown." *The State: Down Home in North Carolina*, 61:12 (May 1994), 17, 19-20; online: http://digital.ncdcr.gov/cdm/ref/collection/p16062coll18/id/66742. [Online description from "North Carolina Periodicals Index," East Carolina University: "Lincoln County's Sam Brown was a notorious robber and opponent of the American Revolution who, with his sister Charity, terrorized counties along the Yadkin River and in South Carolina. He was killed in 1780 by an outraged citizen."]

Boyd, Julian P. "County Court in Colonial North Carolina." M. A. thesis, Duke University, 1926.

Clark, Walter. "History of the Superior and Supreme Courts of North Carolina." *North Carolina Booklet*, 18:2 (October 1918), 78-104; published with the same title: Raleigh: North Carolina Society, Daughters of the Revolution, 1919. [Online description from "North Carolina Periodicals Index," East Carolina University: "The structure of the higher courts of North Carolina has changed considerably since their creation under Provincial government prior to the establishment of the State."]

Coates, Albert. "'A Declaration of Rights:' Wake County Courthouse Dedicated to Tradition of the Law." *Popular Government*, 37:2 (October 1970), 16-20. [Online description from "North Carolina Periodicals Index," East Carolina University: "With the event of the dedication of the new Wake County courthouse Coates discusses the history of the court system in North Carolina."]

Coates, Albert. "The Courts of Yesterday." *Popular Government*, 24:7 (April 1958), 2-6. [Online description from "North Carolina Periodicals Index," East Carolina University: "Three times in the history of North Carolina, its lawmakers have looked at the state's judicial system in an effort to develop and evolve."]

Corbitt, D. L. "Judicial Districts of North Carolina, 1746-1934." *North Carolina Historical Review*, 12:1 (January 1935; 45-61; online: http://digital.ncdcr.gov/cdm/ref/collection/p16062coll9/id/4207. [Online description from "North Carolina Periodicals Index," East Carolina University: "This article lists the judicial districts within North Carolina by year in the period of 1746-1934 including location and some service information. The introduction provides a brief history of the establishment of the state's district court system."]

Craig, Clifton M. "Jails in North Carolina." *Popular Government,* 37:6 (March 1971), 11-15, 25. [Online description from "North Carolina Periodicals Index," East Carolina University: "Craig discusses the evolution of jails in North Carolina as well as the statistics for jail renovation in the state."]

Edenton District Superior Court. "Miscellaneous Records, 1756-1806." Manuscript DSCR 2.024, 2.025.1-2.025.3 (MARS ID: 398.7; series), State Archives of North Carolina, Raleigh. [Online catalog description: "Ledger of court costs (1756-1763); jury lists and summonses for jury duty (1756-1806, n. d.); slave records (1762-1806); and other miscellaneous records (1763-1806). Slave records are writs from actions and cases involving slaves. Miscellaneous records include execution dockets (1763, 1783-1787); minute dockets (1790, 1802, 1803, 1805); prosecution dockets (1804); state dockets (1794-1795), and lists of judgments. Also included are records relating to assignees, ejectments, trustees, and governor's pardons."]

Fayetteville District Superior Court. "Miscellaneous Records, 1761-1801." Manuscript DSCR 4.008 (MARS ID: 398.9; series), State Archives of North Carolina, Raleigh. [Online catalog description: "Accounts of fees, fines and forfeitures (1788-1800), fraud and embezzlement trials (Revolutionary army accounts, 1786); officials' bonds and oaths (1790-1805); certificate of land recovered (1794); and other claims. Also included are criminal actions."]

Halifax District Superior Court. "Miscellaneous Records, 1760-1808." Manuscript DSCR 5.004 (MARS ID: 398.11; series), State Archives of North Carolina, Raleigh. [Online catalog description: "Miscellaneous records of the court, including one civil action, a few criminal actions, and clerk's records. Included are partial dockets (1772-1791), jury tickets (1760-1787), recommendations for sheriff, officials' bonds and oaths, accounts of fees, fines, and charges, records from criminal cases involving slaves, and records relating to prisoners. Land records include some relating to confiscated property and to the Granville Proprietary Land Office."]

Hardesty, Fred. "The Church Courts." *The State: Down Home in North Carolina*, 37:5 (August 1969), 11-12; online: http://digital.ncdcr.gov/cdm/ref/collection/p16062coll18/id/52787. [Online description from "North Carolina Periodicals Index," East Carolina University: "Bath's St. Thomas Episcopal Church, North Carolina's oldest church in its oldest town, was not merely the center of religious study in the community. Like most early American denominations, it was also the local community's primary center of discipline and legal recourse. Most churches forbade its members from taking a fellow member to court before 'gospel steps' had been taken. As the antebellum period progressed and the church began to gradually lose control of its members, church courts became less and less effective."]

Haun, Weynette Parks. *Morgan District North Carolina, Superior Court of Law & Equity*. 4 vols. Durham, North Carolina: W. P. Haun, 1987-[1995]. [Online description from FamilySearch.org: "Volume 2 has land records for 1773–1807. This district was created in 1782 and included Lincoln, Burke, and Wilkes counties and all counties west of these three. In 1784 this district only covered the western counties of what is now the state of North Carolina. This book contains a detailed name index."]

Hillsborough District Superior Court. "Miscellaneous Records, 1768-1808." Manuscript DSCR 204.928.1 – 204.298.3 (MARS ID: 398.17; series), State Archives of North Carolina, Raleigh. [Online catalog description: "Miscellaneous records of the Hillsborough District Superior Court. Major files include: accounts, fines collected, bills of sale, certificates, lists of confiscated property, claims, coroners' inquests, deeds, grand jury presentments, guardians' records, jury tickets, jury excuses, justices, jury lists, land records, letters, officials' bonds, promissory notes, receipts, and wills."]

Linn, Stahle. "The History of the North Carolina Judiciary from the Time of the Revolution to the Present Date." Ph. D. thesis, University of North Carolina at Chapel Hill, 1907.

McCain, Paul M. "Magistrates Courts in Early North Carolina." *North Carolina Historical Review*, 48:1 (January 1971), 23-30. [Online description from "North Carolina Periodicals Index," East Carolina University: "This article looks at the establishment, structure, and function of the magistrates courts in colonial North Carolina. Information on single and multiple justice courts, on laws passed pertaining to magistrates courts, on areas of the courts purview, and of the justices' administrative duties is included."]

Moore, Peter N. "The Mysterious Death of William Richardson: Kinship, Female Vulnerability, and the Myth of Supernaturalism in the Southern Backcountry." *North Carolina Historical Review*, 80:3 (July 2003), 279-296. [Online description from "North Carolina Periodicals Index," East Carolina University: "Discusses the 1771 case of the Agnes Richardson and the death of her husband, of Presbyterian minister William Richardson, in the Waxhaw settlement, a Scots-Irish American community along the North Carolina-South Carolina border. The story that emerged regarding Agnes' possible role in the death, and a harrowing trial and accusation, reveal a focus on supernaturalism and folk justice that are commonly associated with the backcountry. Investigation of historical evidence reveals that her accusation has much to say about the social and legal constructs of early American society."]

Morgan District Superior Court. "Miscellaneous Records, 1778-1806, n. d." Manuscript DSCR 205.928.1-DSCR 205.928.2, (MARS ID: 398.23; series), State Archives of North Carolina, Raleigh. [Online catalog description: "Accounts of fees, fines and monies received (1782-1792); affidavits (1784, 1794); portions of appearance and trial dockets (1782-1806); court orders (1781, 1783, 1801); grand jury presentments, jury lists and excuses (1784-1806); records of actions and cases involving slaves (1778-1806); and tax records (1784). Also includes some correspondence (1791-1804); governors' pardons (1797, 1806); road records (1791-1799); suits concerning the confiscation act (1781-1783); and insolvent debtors (1797-1803)."]

New Bern District Superior Court. "Miscellaneous Records, 1758-1806 and no date." Manuscript DSCR 206.928.1 – DSCR 206.928.3 (MARS ID: 398.30; series), State Archives of North Carolina, Raleigh. [Online catalog description: "Miscellaneous records of New Bern District Superior Court including civil and criminal actions relating to ships and merchants (1764, 1783-1803); accounts of fees, fines and charges (1758-1806); confiscations of slaves (1779-1786); other records involving slaves (1766-1806); partial dockets (1779-1805); prosecution docket (1769-1771); Superior Court minutes (1761); jury lists (1774-1807); state actions concerning treason (1777, 1780, 1781, 1783); lists of suits (1785, 1790-1800); naturalization oaths (1799-1806) and a list of three decisions appealed from New Bern District Superior Court to the Court of Conference (1800). Also included are road and bridge records (1792-1796, 1800-1805); petitions to build grist mills (1795, 1799, 1804); correspondence (1787, 1790); and insolvent debtors (1788, 1798, 1799). "]

North Carolina (State). Office of State Treasurer. "Miscellaneous records of the Hillsborough District Superior Court. Major files include: accounts, fines collected, bills of sale, certificates, lists of confiscated property, claims, coroners' inquests, deeds, grand jury presentments, guardians' records, jury tickets, jury excuses, justices, jury lists, land records, letters, officials' bonds, promissory notes, receipts, and wills., Vols. 1-91 (with gaps), 1775-1939." Manuscript S.115.1-S.115.15 (MARS ID: 13.24; series), State Archives of North Carolina, Raleigh. [Online catalog description: "Journals and ledgers recording the income and expenses of the state. Earlier volumes indicate income from confiscated property, expenditures for militia, and receipts from sheriffs. Also payments by counties into special or general purpose funds, and expenditures for state agencies and programs."]

Rose, William. "[Letter of] William Rose [to] Governor." Manuscript letter, digital surrogates available online at: http://image.lva.virginia.gov/GLR/04735, Library of Virginia, Richmond. [Online catalog description: "Part of a collection of letters and other documents received in the Governor's Office during the period June 29, 1776-Nov. 30, 1784. Re expediency of erecting a wall around the prison rather than recruiting guards; re pay for the present guard. (Enclosures - (1) House resolution; (2) return of guards - lacking.) July 4, 1783, Warrant: John Pleasants to Keeper of Henrico Public Jail, for arrest and confinement of David Miller and John Wilkinson, accused of mutiny and murder while on board a privateer, who had escaped from a jail in North Carolina."]

Salisbury District Superior Court. "Miscellaneous Records, 1754-1807." Manuscript DSCR 207.928.1 (MARS ID: 398.36; series), State Archives of North Carolina, Raleigh. [Online catalog description: "Miscellaneous records of Salisbury District Superior Court, including docket cases (1806); jury list (1756); grand jury presentments (1772); accounts of fees, fines and charges (1758, 1769-1806); depositions; list of prisoners held for treason (1782); records involving slaves (1757-1808); and coroners' inquests (1778-1788). Also included are guardians' records (1793); bastardy records (1757, 1761, 1777, 1782); road records (1765-1807); tax records (1758, 1788-1789); actions involving mills (1787, 1791); power of attorney and certified testimony (1769); a license to practice law (1804); correspondence (1778, 1805); and a promissory note given by Daniel Boone (1770)."]

Salisbury District Superior Court. "Miscellaneous Records, 1753-1809." Manuscript DSCR 206.403.1 (MARS ID: 398.34; series), State Archives of North Carolina, Raleigh. [Online catalog description: "Ejectments, writs, affidavits, judgments, declarations, and plats relating to property cases heard in the Salisbury District Superior Court. Miscellaneous land papers include agreements, surveys, plats, complaints and answers concerning confiscated land (1782-1800), and two land grants."]

Smith, Michael R. "History of Jails in North Carolina." *Popular Government*, 51:3 (Winter 1986), 30-34, 48.

Spindel, Donna J. "Law and Disorder: The North Carolina Stamp Act Crisis." *North Carolina Historical Review*, 57:1 (January 1980), 1-16. [Online description from "North Carolina Periodicals Index," East Carolina University: "In 1766, opposition to the Stamp Act in North Carolina was met with weak police action in stamping out anti-British activity. Governor William Tryon was unable to effectively enforce the Stamp Act in the Wilmington area due to several acts of civil disobedience. Police often supported these conflicts or did not have the means to suppress them"]

Spindel, Donna J. *Crime and Society in North Carolina, 1663-1776*. Baton Rouge: Louisiana State University Press, 1989. [Online description from "North Carolina Periodicals Index," East Carolina University: "Often people complain about the state of jails today, but Smith argues they are quite different from the jails of yesteryear and will differ greatly from the jails of tomorrow as well. This article takes a look at the history of jails in North Carolina, as well as the evolving standards of the ideal."]

Stevenson, George. "State Records: Higher Court Records." In Helen F. M. Leary, ed. *North Carolina Research: Genealogy and Local History*. 2nd ed. (Raleigh: North Carolina Genealogical Society, 1996), Chapter 32, 329-354.

Stewart, Stephen Alexander. "Court System of North Carolina before the Revolution." *Trinity College Historical Society Annual Publication of Historical Papers*, series 4 (1900), 12-20.

Turner, Grace. "The Robbery of Rebecca Watkins, 1780, Caswell Co., NC, Criminal Actions." *Bulletin of the Genealogical Society of Old Tryon County*, 21:3 (August 1993), 131.

Waldrup, John Charles. "Role of the Judiciary in Revolutionary North Carolina." Office of Continuing Education, Duke University, 1985. Typescript. North Carolina Collection. University of North Carolina Library, Chapel Hill. ["A paper presented at the conference 'All the Powers Vested, North Carolina and the Federal Constitution, 1780-1800,' held 4-5 Oct. 1985, Duke University."]

Watson, Alan D. "'A Great Number of Pore People Is a Relaying on His Conduct & Politeness:' The County Clerk in Colonial North Carolina." *North Carolina Historical Review*, 85:2 (April 2008), 133-162.

Watson, Alan D. "The Constable in Colonial North Carolina." *North Carolina Historical Review*, 68:1 (January 1991), 1-16. [Online description from "North Carolina Periodicals Index," East Carolina University: "An examination of the role of the constable, the lowest position on the peace keeping hierarchy in the colony, along with the establishment, organization, and duties of the constabulary office in Colonial North Carolina."]

Wilmington. "Miscellaneous Records, 1782-1806." Manuscript DSCR 12.032 and 12.034, (MARS ID: 398.38; series), State Archives of North Carolina, Raleigh. [Online catalog description: "Miscellaneous civil and criminal action records and records of the clerk of Wilmington District Superior Court. Included are cases concerning high treason (1784-1786); copies of wills (1791-1806); summonses and bonds (1782-1784); records and accounts for the district court (1786-1791); lists of suits and executions (1793)."]

Winslow, Raymond S., Jr. "County Records: Civil and Criminal Action Papers." In Helen F. M. Leary, ed. *North Carolina Research: Genealogy and Local History*. 2nd ed. (Raleigh: North Carolina Genealogical Society, 1996), Chapter 18, 256-257.

Winslow, Raymond S., Jr. "County Records: County Court Minutes." In Helen F. M. Leary, ed. *North Carolina Research: Genealogy and Local History*. 2nd ed. (Raleigh: North Carolina Genealogical Society, 1996), Chapter 15, 240-248.

Winslow, Raymond S., Jr. "County Records: Dockets." In Helen F. M. Leary, ed. *North Carolina Research: Genealogy and Local History*. 2nd ed. (Raleigh: North Carolina Genealogical Society, 1996), Chapter 19, 261-264.

Winslow, Raymond S., Jr. "County Records: Equity Court Minutes." In Helen F. M. Leary, ed. *North Carolina Research: Genealogy and Local History*. 2nd ed. (Raleigh: North Carolina Genealogical Society, 1996), Chapter 17, 254-255.

Winslow, Raymond S., Jr. "County Records: Superior Court Minutes." In Helen F. M. Leary, ed. *North Carolina Research: Genealogy and Local History*. 2nd ed. (Raleigh: North Carolina Genealogical Society, 1996), Chapter 16, 249-253.

Oaths of Allegiance and Other Oaths

Patriotic Service[22]

Patriots of the Revolution are considered to be those men and women who by an act or series of actions demonstrated unfailing loyalty to the cause of American Independence from England. Patriotic service might begin as early as April 1774. We depend upon recorded actions to give us an indication of patriotism. What was the purpose of the action? What were the risks? The consequences? Answers to these questions can determine whether the action actually applied to an attempt to further the cause of independence or demonstrated loyalty to that cause.

Evidence of patriotic activity may be found in town, county, state, and federal records. Many records kept by the states have been indexed and often a letter to the state archives will be sufficient to determine if evidence exists to show that a person contributed supplies or made some other contribution to the war effort. Town and county records have usually not been indexed and a personal search of town minutes and court minutes is required. Minutes of the Continental Congresses have been published. *Old letters, diaries, and other family and personal papers can often be used as evidence of patriotic intent, provided the record was made at the time of the event described.*

[22] Office of the Registrar General's compilation, *Genealogy Guidelines* (Washington, D. C.: National Society Daughters of the American Revolution, 2014), 94-95.

Signers of the Oaths of Allegiance: Most states required their adult male inhabitants to swear (or, for certain groups, affirm) an Oath of Allegiance to the new state government. For example, Virginia enacted such a law in May 1777, which applied to all free males above the age of sixteen. The men who took these oaths qualify for patriotic service. Some lists of names have been published, usually at the town or county level.

Blassingame, John W. "American Nationalism and Other Loyalties in the Southern Colonies, 1763-1775." *Journal of Southern History*, 34:1 (February 1968), 50-75.

Granville County. "Miscellaneous Records, 1722, 1747-1920, no date." Manuscript CR.044.928.22-CR.044.928.26, State Archives of North Carolina, Raleigh. [Online catalog description shows that this collection includes: "…; military records, 1766 - 1870 (broken series);…; oath of allegiance, Joseph Hart ordered to take, 1778;…; treason trial, State vs. John Williams, 1777;…"]

Hathaway, J. R. B. "Thomas Barker of Edenton and the Oath of Allegiance in 1778." *The North Carolina Historical and Genealogical Register*, 1:4 (October 1900), 515.

Johnson, William Perry. "1779 Tax List of Randolph County." *North Carolinian: A Quarterly Journal of Genealogy and History,* 2:2 (June 1956), 179-186. [DAR Genealogy Office Note: "While a tax list, there are notes stating that certain individuals had not taken the oath of allegiance and returned the inventories of their taxable property, thereby implying that those that did return their inventories had taken the oath of allegiance."]

Kimbrough, John N. "John Kimbrough's Parole, 1781." Manuscript, Special Collections SFC4:414, J. Murrey Atkins Library, University of North Carolina at Charlotte. [Online catalog description: "A parole, signed by John Kimbrough and witnessed by O. H. Williams, swearing Kimbrough's pledge to no longer take up arms on behalf of the King of England, against the United States, dated April 11, 1781." This is not necessarily an oath of allegiance to North Carolina, but rather an oath not to support the British war effort.]

North Carolina (State). General Assembly. "[Document dated:] January 23, 1779: Joint Papers, Committee Papers, Resolutions, Senate Bills, House Bills, Granting Citizenship to Thomas Britain (with Messages and Petition)." Manuscript; General Assembly Record Group; Session Records, January-February 1779, Box 1 (MARS ID: 66.8.15.11.8; item), State Archives of North Carolina, Raleigh. [Online catalog description: "The resolution grants citizenship to Thomas Britain, of Edenton, without making him take the oath of allegiance, for in his petition he stated that he had taken a similar oath as a member of the Chowan County militia."]

North Carolina (State). General Assembly. "[Document dated]: April 17, 1782: Petition from the Inhabitants of Rowan Co. in Favor of Edward Turner." Manuscript; General Assembly Record Group; Session Records, April-May 1782; Joint Papers, Committee Papers; Miscellaneous Petitions: April-May 1782, Box 1 (MARS ID: 66.8.27.5.3), State Archives of North Carolina, Raleigh. [Online catalog description: "Petition in favor of Edward Turner to regain citizenship."]

North Carolina (State). General Assembly. "[Document Dated]: May 6, 1782: House Bill to Bring Certain Persons to Trial for Treason, Pardon Others, Repeal Acts v. Nonjurors (with Petition, etc.) (Laid Over)." Manuscript; General Assembly Record Group; Session Records, April-May 1782; Committee Papers, Resolutions, Senate Bills, House Bills, Box 2 (MARS ID: 66.8.28.26; folder), State Archives of North Carolina, Raleigh. [Online catalog description: "Petition of sundry non-jurors of Granville County protests the deprivation of the rights of citizenship and the increased taxation that is punishment for not taking oath of allegiance; bill would distinguish between non-jurors and those guilty of treasonous acts; and messages from both houses amend bill. List of names included." Note: A "non-juror" is someone who does not swear a specific oath.]

North Carolina (Colony and State). Office of State Treasurer. "Oaths, Bonds, and Sureties, 1738-1929." Manuscript Box 1-67 (MARS ID: 13.42; series), State Archives of North Carolina, Raleigh. [Online catalog description: "Oaths, bonds, and sureties required by law of sheriffs, clerks of county and superior courts, registers of deeds, tax collectors, constables, county and state treasurers, treasurers of institutions, the secretary of state, comptroller, state auditor, and other county and state officials responsible for funds. Miscellaneous bonds include ordinary (tavern) bonds, 1778-1805."]

North Carolina Oath of Allegiance, 1778, Granville District. Signal Mountain, Tenn.: Mountain Press, 2007.

"Oaths of Allegiance." *Bute County Committee of Safety Minutes, 1775-1776* (Warrenton: Warren County Bicentennial Committee, 1977), Appendix II 56-64.

"Oath of Allegiance in 1777. *North Carolina Historical and Genealogical Register*, 2:2 (April 1901), 205-206. [signers of the Chowan County oath to North Carolina]

"Oaths of Allegiance-Rowan County, North Carolina, 1778." *Daughters of the American Revolution Magazine,* 82:2 (February 1948), 208-209.

"Oath of Allegiance and Jurors." In Walter Clark, ed., *State Records of North Carolina: Laws, 1715-1776*, 22 (Goldsboro: Nash Bros., Book and Job Printers, 1904; reprinted: Wilmington: Broadfoot Publishing Company, 1994), 168-179.

"Patriots Oath of Allegiance." *Journal of the Genealogical Society of Rowan County, North Carolina*, 3:2 (March 1989), 55.

Smith, Martha M. "Loyalism as a Political Issue in Revolutionary North Carolina, 1775-1789." M. A. thesis, University of North Carolina, 1978. [Study of the impact of the loyalism issue on North Carolina's early political groups, especially in terms of the effects upon the establishment of a 'peaceful post-war security,' 'the government's respect for the provisions of the Treaty of Paris of 1783 and for private rights,' and the 'debates on the ratification of the Federal Constitution'."]

Spencer, Samuel, 1734-1793. "Samuel Spencer Petition, 1777." Manuscript 684-z, Southern Historical Collection, Louis Round Wilson Special Collections Library, University of North Carolina, Chapel Hill; online finding aid available at http://www2.lib.unc.edu/mss/inv/s/Spencer,Samuel.html. [Online finding aid description: "Samuel Spencer was a North Carolina Superior Court judge. The collection is a petition to Spencer asking that certain suspected Loyalists in the Salisbury, N. C., area be allowed to take the oath of allegiance to the state."]

Warren, Mary Bondurant. "Loyalty Oaths to Independent Government, 1778." *The Carolina Genealogist*, no. 5 (Fall-Winter 1971), State Records/Loyalty Oaths, 1-8. [Tar River, Oxford (Granville County), Dutch (Granville County), Beaver Dam (Granville County), Island Creek, Nutbush, County Line, and Goshen Districts; Petition of Persons Whose Lands Have Lately Been Cut off from North Carolina into South Carolina, 1775; Granville County Petitioners]; no. 11 (Summer 1972), State Records/Loyalty Oaths, 7-8 [includes one from Craven County, June 15, 1778].

Relocation of the State Capital

Kirwan, Virginia. "New Bern as Colonial and State Capital." *New Bern Historical Journal*, 1:2 (November 1988), 3-13.

North Carolina (Colony and State). Office of State Treasurer. "Capital [*sic*] Buildings, 1767-1913." Manuscript Box 1-21 (MARS ID: 13.10; series), State Archives of North Carolina, Raleigh. [Online catalog description: "Fiscal material relating to the building and maintenance of Tryon Palace in New Bern (1767-1787), the 'Blue House' in Hillsborough (1790-1795), the State House (1792-1831), …"]

Zagarri, Rosemarie. "Representation and the Removal of State Capitals, 1776-1812." *Journal of American History*, 67:4 (October 1988), 1239-1256; reprinted in: Peter S. Onuf, ed., *The New American Nation, 1775-1820, Volume 3: The Revolution in the States* (New York: Garland Publishing, Inc., 1991), 18-36.

Sheriffs, Constables, and Justices of the Peace of the Counties of North Carolina

Boyd, Julian P. "The Sheriff in Colonial North Carolina." *North Carolina Historical Review*, 5:2 (April 1928), 151-180; online: http://digital.ncdcr.gov/cdm/ref/collection/p16062coll9/id/4207. [Online description from "North Carolina Periodicals Index," East Carolina University: "Tension existed between the ruling class living in the colonies and the authoritative Crown throughout the early history of North Carolina. The sheriff became a key figure in the political struggle of the colony because of the administrative and punitive powers granted his office. The article reviews the various roles of sheriffs in colonial government and how this could exploit both the ruling class families and the Crown."]

Campbell, Ruby G. "North Carolina's Justices of the Peace – 1776." *Argyll Colony Plus*, 6:2 (August 1992), 98-105.

Davis, James. *The Office and Authority of a Justice of the Peace. And Also, the Duty of Sheriffs, Coroners, Constables, Churchwardens, Overseers of roads and Other Officers. Together with precedents of Warrants, Judgments, Executions and Other Legal Process, Issuable by magistrates within Their Several Juristictions, in Cases Civil and Criminal, with the Method of Judicial Proceedings before Justices of the Peace out of Sessions. Also Some Directions for Their Conduct within Their County Courts. To Which Is Added, an Appendix Containing Many Useful Precedents, and Directions for the Execution of Them. Collected from the Common and Statute Laws of England, and the Acts of Assembly of This Province, and Adapted to Our Constitution and Practice.* New Bern: J. Davis, 1774; online: http://digital.lib.ecu.edu/16960.

"Names of Men & Their Respective Counties (Counties throughout the State) Who Were Appointed as Justices of the peace, Sheriffs, and Constables, 23 December 1778." In Walter Clark, ed., *State Records of North Carolina: Laws, 1715-1776*, 23 (Goldsboro: Nash Bros., Book and Job Printers, 1904; reprinted: Wilmington: Broadfoot Publishing Company, 1994), 992-996.

North Carolina (State). General Assembly. "[Document dated:] April-May 1777: Joint Papers, Committee Papers, Resolutions, Senate Bills, House Bills, Papers Concerning Justices of the Peace and Militia Officer Appointments, 1777." Manuscript; General Assembly Record Group; Session Records, Apr-May 1777, Box 1 (MARS ID: 66.8.9.8), State Archives of North Carolina, Raleigh. [Online catalog description: "Documents concerning Governor Caswell's appointment of officers to the militia regiments of Cumberland and Chatham counties, and his appointments of Justices of the Peace for Onslow and Pasquotank counties."]

North Carolina (State). General Assembly. "[Document Dated]: June-July 1781: Justices of the Peace and Militia Officers – Recommendations and Resignations." Manuscript; General Assembly Record Group; Session Records, June-July 1781; Joint Papers, Committee Papers, Resolutions, Box 1 (MARS ID: 66.8.25.5; folder), State Archives of North Carolina, Raleigh. [Online catalog description: "Contains several recommendations, resignations, and appointments for justices of the peace and the militia, as well as one commission from the governor for the justices of the peace for Onslow County."]

Watson, Watson, Alan D. "The Appointment of Sheriffs in Colonial North Carolina: A Reexamination." *North Carolina Historical Review*, 53:4 (October 1976), 385-398. [Online description from "North Carolina Periodicals Index," East Carolina University: "This article challenges and reevaluates several of historian Julian Boyd's interpretations regarding the appointments of sheriffs in colonial North Carolina. The author uses quantitative evidence from 14 counties, the number of sheriffs who were justices of the peace, the frequency of self-recommendation, the frequency of county court recommendations and the governor's use of independent judgment in the appointment of sheriffs."]

Watson, Alan D. "The Constable in Colonial North Carolina." *North Carolina Historical Review*, 68:1 (January 1991), 1-16. [Online description from "North Carolina Periodicals Index," East Carolina University: "An examination of the role of the constable, the lowest position on the peace keeping hierarchy in the colony, along with the establishment, organization, and duties of the constabulary office in Colonial North Carolina."]

Chapter Eight: North Carolina Finances and Taxation during the Revolutionary Era

Financial and taxation records can be very important sources for the study of the Revolutionary War in any state. They can often reveal contacts between residents and the state government. Tax records may be useful for help in establishing a place of residence for an individual and possibly as sources for documenting patriotic service in support of the American war effort depending of the wording of the enabling legislation that created any given tax. North Carolina had many taxes during the period of the Revolution, but there are few concentrated collections of these sources except for the holdings of the State Archives in Raleigh. Many appear to remain in the individual towns if they have survived. This chapter presents the survivors and their usefulness to modern researchers.

In every state archive, the financial records that have evolved and been retained over the last few centuries constitute the most voluminous portion of the holdings. Those for North Carolina are certainly no exception.

"From 1740 to 1779, the colony was divided into a Northern District and a Southern District with a Treasurer for each. The 1779 General Assembly provided for six treasurers to serve 'the newly created districts of Edenton, Wilmington, New Bern, Hillsboro, Halifax, and Salisbury. In 1782 the district of Morgan was added." [State Archives of North Carolina unpublished finding aid "Treasurer's and Comptroller's Papers," first page of the section titled "Brief History of the Treasurer."]

Albright, Lee, and Helen F. M. Leary. "Strategy for Tax Records." In Helen F. M. Leary, ed. *North Carolina Research: Genealogy and Local History*. 2nd ed. (Raleigh: North Carolina Genealogical Society, 1996), Chapter Two: "Designing Research Strategies," 48-52.

Baker, Mary. "Taxation in the Colonial Period of North Carolina." *Journal of the New Bern Historical* 11:2 (November 1998), 7-12; online: https://www.evernote.com/shard/s5/res/2f622494-ca64-47a1-8c31-ae16b72314de/Taxation %20in%20the%20Colonial%20Period%20of%20NC%20Vol%20XI%20No%20II.pdf. [Online description from "North Carolina Periodicals Index," East Carolina University: "Taxation was a fact of life for the colonists as early as the 1600s. The main tax was the poll, or capitation, tax. However, as specific needs arose, taxes were levied for them. For example, in 1714-15, a tax paid for the Tuscarora War, and forts were built at Cape fear and Ocracoke with a eight-year tax levied in 1748."]

Becker, Robert A. *Revolution, Reform, and the Politics of American Taxation, 1763-1783.* Baton Rouge: La., State University Press, 1980.

Becker, Robert A. "Revolution and Reform: An Interpretation of Southern Taxation, 1763 to 1783." *William and Mary Quarterly*, 3rd series, 32:3 (July 1975), 417-442.

[Chatham, Thurmond, collector]. "Thurmond Chatham (1796-1957) Papers, 1776-1956." Manuscript PC.1139 (MARS ID: 1649; record group), State Archives of North Carolina, Raleigh. [Online catalog description shows that this collection includes: "…pages from *Pennsylvania Magazine* (June, 1776) containing 'An Account of the Colonies of North and South Carolina, with Georgia' and map. Also Rutherford Co. parole of a tory (Oct. 9, 1780); instructions from Gov. Thomas Burke on collecting taxes (1782);…"]

"Collecting Taxes, 'In his Majesties Name.'" ID # 36383, *Jonathan Putnam Papers*, Tennessee State Library & Archives, Nashville; digital surrogate available through the Revolutionary War Collection, Tennessee Virtual Archive at http://cdm15138.contentdm.oclc.org/cdm/singleitem/collection/p15138coll16/id/39/rec/11. [Description from TeVA: "Jonathan Putnam, constable, is directed to collect taxes, 'In his Majesties Name.' The document also details the consequences for individuals who are unable or unwilling to pay."]

Einhorn, Robin L[eigh]. *American Taxation, American Slavery.* Chicago: University of Chicago Press, 2006. [Examines the colonial tax systems of Virginia and Massachusetts and the changes brought by the Revolutionary War.]

Ferguson, E[lmer] James. *The Power of the Purse: A History of American Public Finance, 1776-1790.* Chapel Hill: University of North Carolina Press for the Institute of Early American History and Culture, 1961.

Hamilton, Alexander, 1757-1804. "Letters, 1780; 1791." Manuscript Sec. A Box 57 items 1-2, David M. Rubenstein Rare Book & Manuscript Library, Duke University, Durham. [Online catalog description: "Letters, 1780, from Hamilton to Elizabeth Schuyler concerning the Benedict Arnold affair and the death of Major John André, and a letter, 1791, to Alisha and James Thomas, treasury agents for North Carolina, enquiring whether North Carolina had ever issued its own certificates of indebtedness in lieu of those of the United States."]

Kay, Marvin L. Michael. "The Payment of Provincial and Local Taxes in North Carolina, 1748-1771." *William and Mary Quarterly,* 3rd series, 26:2 (April 1969), 218-240.

Kay, Marvin L. Michael. "Provincial Taxes in North Carolina during the Administrations of Dobbs and Tryon." *North Carolina Historical Review,* 42:4 (October 1965), 440-453. [Online description from "North Carolina Periodicals Index," East Carolina University: "This article looks at the provincial tax structure of colonial North Carolina while under the governance of colonial Governors Dobbs and Tryon. Characterized as inequitable, maladministered, inefficient, and plagued by corruption, the tax structure depended highly on the poll tax and imported liquor duties for provincial tax revenue. Details on how taxes were collected, accounted for, and disbursed as well as the common abuses are included."]

Morrill, James R. *The Practice and Politics of Fiat Finance: North Carolina in the Confederaton, 1783-1789.* Chapel Hill: University of North Carolina Press, 1969.

North Carolina (State). General Assembly. "[Document dated:] February 14, [1781]: Relieving Persons Who Have Furnished Arms with Provisions Greater in Amount Than Their Specific Tax, Etc." Manuscript; General Assembly Record Group; Session Records, January-February 1781; Joint Papers, Committee Papers, Resolutions, Senate Bills, House Bills, Box 1 (MARS ID: 66.8.23.19.19; item), State Archives of North Carolina, Raleigh. [Online catalog description: "The resolution exempts from penalty persons who cannot pay their specific tax for the reasons mentioned."]

North Carolina (State). General Assembly. "[Document dated:] October 20, 1779: Joint Papers, Committee Papers, Resolutions, Senate Bills, House Bills, Exempting Certain Persons from Taxes (Granville County and Pasquotank County) (with Messages)." Manuscript; General Assembly Record Group; Session Records, October-November 1779, Box 1 (MARS ID: 66.8.18.12.4), State Archives of North Carolina, Raleigh. [Online catalog description: "John Duncan, James Stanly, and James Head, of Granville County, and Christopher Nicholson, of Pasquotank County, are exempted from poll taxes."]

North Carolina (State). General Assembly. "[Document dated]: September 6, 1780: Bill for Levying a Specific Provision Tax." Manuscript; General Assembly Record Group; Session Records, August-September 1780; Joint Papers, Committee Papers, Resolutions, Senate Bills, House Bills, Box 1 (MARS ID: 66.8.22.16; folder), State Archives of North Carolina, Raleigh. [Online catalog description: "Includes appointments to a committee to write the bill and two copies of the bill. The bill levies a tax for the military which is to be paid in food, and the bill establishes how a commissioner to carry out the act in each county is to be appointed and what powers he will have."]

North Carolina (State). General Assembly. "[Document Dated]: July 14, 1781: Resolution Releasing Ephraim Washington from Fourfold Tax (with Deposition)." Manuscript; General Assembly Record Group; Session Records, June-July 1781; Joint Papers, Committee Papers, Resolutions, Senate Bills, House Bills, House Joint Resolutions: July 14, 1781, Box 1 (MARS ID: 66.8.25.16.4, State Archives of North Carolina, Raleigh. [Online catalog description: "Washington, of Granville County, was a prisoner of the British at Charleston."]

North Carolina (State). General Assembly. "[Document dated:] May 1, 1782: Joint Papers, Committee Papers, Resolutions, Senate Bills, House Bills, In Favor of John Devane of New Hanover Co. (Message and Petition Only)." Manuscript; General Assembly Record Group; Session Records, April-May 1782, Box 2 (MARS ID: 66.8.28.5.7; item), State Archives of North Carolina, Raleigh. [Online catalog description: "Petition of John Devane requests that he be released from taxation in Duplin County because he is only a transient resident there while avoiding the British; messages from both houses concurring with resolution."]

North Carolina (State). General Assembly. "[Document dated]: May 18, 1784: House Bill to Authorize That the Specific Tax of 1782 Be Collected by Richmond Pearson in Rowan County and the Commissioners in Franklin County (with Petition)." Manuscript; General Assembly Record Group; Session Records, April-June 1784; House Bills, Box 4 (MARS ID: 66.8.34.23; folder),), State Archives of North Carolina, Raleigh.

North Carolina (State). General Assembly. "[Document dated:] Oct. 26, [1784]: House Bill for Payment on Interest of Certificates Granted to the Continental Line (Laid over), 1784." Manuscript, General Assembly Record Group, Session Records October-November, 1784; Joint Papers, Committee Papers, Resolutions, Senate Bills, House Bills, Box 2 (MARS ID: 66.8.36.3; folder), State Archives of North Carolina, Raleigh. [Online catalog description: "Bill levies a tax to be specifically used for the payment of interest on the certificates granted to officers and soldiers of the Continental Line. The bill also directs the state treasurer in the handling of certificates and the payment of interest."]

North Carolina (State). General Assembly. "[Document dated:] January 2, [1792]: Report of the Memorial of Joseph Wason." Manuscript; General Assembly Record Group; Session Records, December 1791-January 1792; Joint

Papers, Committee Papers, Resolutions, Senate Bills, House Bills, Box 2 (MARS ID: 66.8.61.11.54; item), State Archives of North Carolina, Raleigh. [Online catalog description: "The report concerns the taxes paid by Joseph Wason who was injured in the Revolutionary War. The committee recommends that Wason be reimbursed for the taxes he paid."]

North Carolina (State). "Office of State Treasurer." "Correspondence of the State Treasurer, 1783-1949." Manuscript Box 1-78; Box 1-31; 1.27.D.18-33 (Old Records Center); Records Series (RS) Number: 3193; Records Series (RS) Number: 16271 (MARS ID: 13.1; series), State Archives of North Carolina, Raleigh. [Online catalog description: "Chiefly letters written to the state treasurer concerning state income, expenditures, investments, and financial conditions."]

North Carolina (State). "Office of State Treasurer." "County Settlements with the State, 1733-1938." Manuscript Box 1-170 (MARS ID: 13.13; series), State Archives of North Carolina, Raleigh. [Online catalog description: "Records relating to the settlement of accounts between local officials and the state or between individuals and the state. Most concern the collection of state taxes at the local level or the rendering of other services to the state. County Tax Lists (1755-1868) are an incomplete collection and are available only on microfilm. Settlements with Individuals (alphabetical by last name) concern payment of taxes or exemptions. County Settlements (1733-1910, arranged by county) are chiefly settlements with sheriffs, clerks of court, collectors of arrears, tax collectors, entry takers, tax assessors, and registers of deeds, for fees, salaries, and expenses of collecting taxes and fees on land entries, licenses, deeds and grants, suits, forfeitures, marriages, etc. Expenses were also incurred for apprehending, trying, and punishing criminals prosecuted by the state, and for having seals made for the county or court… Claims for Election Expenses (1754-1877, chronological); Attendance Certificates and Salaries for Judges, Solicitors, and the Attorney General (1764-1887, by county); and claims of county coroners (1742-1828, chronological)."]

North Carolina (State). Office of State Treasurer. "Journals and Ledgers, 1775-1939." Manuscript Vol. 1-Vol. 65, etc. (MARS ID: 13.24; series), State Archives of North Carolina, Raleigh. [Online catalog description: "Journals and ledgers recording the income and expenses of the state. Earlier volumes indicate income from confiscated property, expenditures for militia, and receipts from sheriffs. Also payments by counties into special or general purpose funds, and expenditures for state agencies and programs."]

North Carolina (State). Office of State Treasurer. State Comptroller. "Correspondence of the State Comptroller, 1782-1868." Manuscript, Office of the State Comptroller, Box 1 – Box 4 (MARS Id: 13.2; Series), State Archives of North Carolina, Raleigh. [Online catalog description: "Correspondence of the comptroller. Early letters are primarily from entry takers concerning their appointments and bonds, revenue, confiscated property, and counterfeit or stolen vouchers. Other letters from veterans of the Revolutionary War and the War of 1812 request verification of militia service for pension benefits. Topics include sale of public tobacco and public lands, licenses for retail goods stores, and the tax on the slave trade"]

North Carolina (State). State Treasurer; State Comptroller. "Military Papers – General Records, 1747-1909." Manuscript, Office of State Treasurer, Office of Comptroller, Boxes 1-12, 74, 89, 93-98, 120-121-A (MARS ID: 13.26; series), State Archives of North Carolina, Raleigh. [Online catalog description: "Records relating to the financing of military activities in North Carolina, including accounts, certificates, claims against the state, receipts, returns, inventories, promissory notes, payrolls, contracts, officials' bonds and oaths, correspondence, petitions, affidavits, testimony, powers of attorney, resolutions and committee reports of the General Assembly, governors' messages to the assembly and memorials to Congress, insurance policies, and railroad passes. Records from the colonial and Revolutionary periods concern scouting on the frontier; the purchase, impressment, seizure, and issuance of provisions, supplies, arms, ammunition, accoutrements, horses, cattle, and tobacco; pay, clothing, and ration allowances for Continental Line and militia units, guards of public property, and the governors' escort; the development of public salt works, lead mines, fisheries, and gun factories; work on fortifications by slaves; capture and imprisonment of Loyalists, deserters, felons, and fugitive slaves; county commissioners of the specific tax; lost certificates; expenses of the commissioners of army accounts, the Board of Trade, and the Board of War; instructions to surveyors of the bounty land tract; accounts with the federal government; and postwar sales of public property. In the antebellum period the records concern settlement of outstanding claims for Revolutionary War service; surveying bounty lands; payments to militia officers; government premiums to encourage the manufacture of arms and powder…"] There are online finding aids for this collection. Those pertinent to the Revolutionary period are:

"Military Collection. II. Frontier Scouting and Indian Wars, 1754-1777." Online: http://www.archives.ncdcr.gov/Portals/3/PDF/findingaids/pdf/MilColl_IndianWars.pdf. [a few payrolls and other records]

"Military Collection. III. War of the Regulation, 1768-1779." Online: http://www.archives.ncdcr.gov/Portals/3/PDF/findingaids/pdf/MilColl_WarofRegulation.pdf. [a considerable collection of materials on the Regulators]

"Military Collection. IV. Troop Returns, 1747-1893." Online: http://archives.ncdcr.gov/Portals/3/PDF/findingaids/pdf/MilColl_TroopReturns.pdf. [Covering a long period in the state's history, this collection contains many muster rolls and pay rolls for the militia during the Colonial period, the Revolution (Militia and Continental Line), and subsequent years. Some of these have been published, but most have not. This is a very important source for documentation of Revolutionary War service and tracing unit histories.]

Boxes 2-3: Militia, 1775-1779. [Contains many county militia lists.]

Box 4: Continental Line, 1775-1778 (Includes drafts and enlistments from militia)

Box 5: Continental Line, 1779-1780

Box 6: Continental Line, 1780-1783

Box 7: Militia, 1780-1799

"Military Collection. V. War of the Revolution." Online: http://www.archives.ncdcr.gov/Portals/3/PDF/findingaids/pdf/MilColl_WaroftheRevolution.pdf. [A lengthy finding aid of records of North Carolina for the period of the Revolution, this online listing contains correspondence, depositions relating to pension applications, a list of those receiving "State Pensions to Invalids and Widows," and Loyalist materials.]

North Carolina Office of Archives and History. Department of Cultural Resources. "Treasurer's and Comptroller's Papers." Unpublished finding aid in the reading room of the State Archives of North Carolina, Raleigh.

Parker, Coralie. *The History of Taxation in North Carolina during the Colonial Period, 1663-1776.* New York: Columbia University Press: 1928.

Price, William Solomon, Jr. *Not a Conquered People: Two Carolinians View Parliamentary Taxation.* (Bicentennial Pamphlet series, no. 2). Raleigh: Department of Cultural Resources, Division of Archives and History, North Carolina Bicentennial Committee, 1975.

"State Revolutionary War Debt Certificates, 1775-1789." Manuscript Special Colls. Currency, Massachusetts Historical Society, Boston; online finding aid available at http://www.masshist.org/collection-guides/view/fao0004. [Online finding aid description: "This collection consists of fiscal paper issued by the individual state loan offices during the course of the Revolutionary War. Predominantly loan certificates for funds borrowed by the states to arm and provision their quota of the troops raised for the Continental Army, the collection also includes army certificates used to pay the troops, certificates of interest payments due on the loans, certificates issued to pay the states' adjusted account of pay owed to the army, lottery certificates, and certificates of interest on the liquidated debt owed by individual states." Includes five North Carolina certificates issued to William Spinnney, William Clifton, John Jones, Alexander Simmons, and Levi Rice.]

Watson, Alan D. "County Fiscal Policy in Colonial North Carolina." *North Carolina Historical Review*, 55:3 (July 1978), 284-305. [Online description from "North Carolina Periodicals Index," East Carolina University: "The county as a unit of government became very important during the Colonial Period of the 18th century in North Carolina. The county was instrumental in the disbursement of public funds for a variety of purposes. This included construction and maintenance of public buildings, salaries for sheriffs, clerks of court and tobacco inspectors, provision of public services, construction of bridges and operation of ferries, standardizing weights and measures, surveying of county boundaries and provision of charitable services."]

Winslow, Raymond A., Jr. "County Records: Tax and Fiscal Records." In Helen F. M. Leary, ed. *North Carolina Research: Genealogy and Local History.* 2nd ed. (Raleigh: North Carolina Genealogical Society, 1996), Chapter 14, 231-239.

Fiscal Districts in North Carolina

Fiscal Districts [established by the General Assembly in 1780]: Each district was presided over by a board of auditors who were authorized to hear claims for public service. The authority of the auditors did not extend beyond their fiscal districts.[23]

Knowledge of these districts is useful for the interpretation of various financial documents that reside in the State Archives of North Carolina, Raleigh. For example, since the names of the individual auditors can be associated with

[23] Note: Portions of this section were written by various staff genealogists, past and current, of the Genealogy Office, Office of the Registrar General, National Society Daughters of the American Revolution, Washington, D. C. Forrest C. Crosley, Assistant Director of Genealogy, contributed additional text.

a particular fiscal district, which encompassed several different counties, knowing which district an individual lived in can be helpful when studying records. If one encounters a North Carolina voucher for some service performed for the state during the Revolution, it may shows that a "John Smith" was reimbursed for goods or services by an auditor for the Edenton District. But if, however, all available information for the individual of interest indicates that the man in question actually resided in one of the counties within the Morgan District, this is a problem. The authority of the auditors did not extend beyond their own fiscal district. Therefore, the man being reimbursed in Edenton District most likely would have been a different man than the one in the Morgan District with the same name.

The districts were:
Edenton District: Bertie, Camden, Chowan, Currituck, Gates, Hertford, Pasquotank, Perquimans, and Tyrrell counties.
Halifax District: Edgecombe, Franklin, Halifax, Martin, Nash, Northampton, and Warren counties.
Hillsborough District: Caswell, Chatham, Granville, Orange, Randolph, and Wake counties.
Morgan District after 1782: Burke, Lincoln, Rutherford, Sullivan, Washington, and Wilkes counties.
New Bern District: Beaufort, Carteret, Craven, Dobbs, Hyde, Johnston Jones, Pitt, and Wayne counties.
Salisbury District before 1782: Anson, Burke, Guilford, Lincoln, Mecklenburg, Montgomery, Richmond, Rowan, Rutherford, Sullivan, Surry, Washington, and Wilkes counties.
Salisbury District after 1782: Anson, Guilford, Mecklenburg, Montgomery, Richmond, Rowan, and Surry counties.
Wilmington District: Bladen, Brunswick, Cumberland, Duplin, New Hanover, and Onslow counties.[24]

North Carolina Revolutionary War Pay Vouchers and Certificates and Public Claims

[Note: Some problems exist in the use and interpretation of the voucher records. Please read the first entry for some basic information on this subject. Another helpful reading is found at the beginning of *Treasurer & Comptroller's Records: Revolutionary War Pay Vouchers*, microfilmed by the North Carolina Department of Cultural Resources, Division of Archives and History, Archives and Records Section, Raleigh. In addition, researchers should be aware of the fact that some vouchers were counterfeit. A clue to this fact would be the presence in the records of a voucher that was either/or rejected or did not have a whole punched through the middle of it in much the same fashion as movie or train tickets were once punched to show that they had been used. Always read the reverse of any certificate of interest, because it may contain additional important detail about the claimant and circumstances of the claim for the voucher. Some rejected vouchers may also have been turned down because the claimant had reached the payment limit that he was allowed to collect. In short, careful study of these records is warranted.]

Coker, Charles Frederick William, and Donald R. Lemon. *North Carolina's Revolutionary War Pay Records.* (North Carolina State Archives Information Circular 1) Raleigh: North Carolina Department of Cultural Resources, 1966; updated: 1973, 1976.
"Index to North Carolina Revolutionary Pay Vouchers." *The North Carolinian: A Quarterly Journal of Genealogy and History,* 6:1 (March 1960), 660-662.
Johnson, William Perry. "Halifax District Revolutionary Pay Vouchers." *Journal of North Carolina Genealogy*, 12:2 (Summer 1996), 1671.
Johnson, William Perry. "Index to N. C. Revolutionary War Pay Vouchers." *The North Carolinian: A Quarterly Journal of Genealogy and History*, 3:4 (December 1957), 358-361; 4:4 (December 1958), 502-506; 6:1 (March 1960), 660-662; 7:2 (June 1961), 816-820; 7:3 (September 1961), 854-862; [The journal ceased publication without publishing any additional articles in this series.] [This series of abstracts was published in reverse alphabetical order, because so many similar projects end before completing the alphabet. It only covers, however, the surnames Vaden to Zollicoffer.]
North Carolina (State). State Treasurer. "Military Papers – Revolutionary War Pay Vouchers." Manuscript, Office of the State Treasurer, Boxes 31.1-31.154, 31.155-31.216, State Archives of North Carolina, Raleigh; also

[24] For a map of these Fiscal Districts, see: "NC Auditors Map," a handout at the State Archives of North Carolina. This map uses the base map by L. Polk Denmark titled "North Carolina at the Beginning of 1780 Showing Approximate County Divisions within the Present State Boundaries" that appears on page [287] of David Leroy Corbitt's *The Formation of the North Carolina Counties, 1663-1943* as the base map for the hand-drawn boundaries of the Fiscal Districts. The listing of the districts themselves appears on this handout as well and comes from information at the State Archives that is published in Helen F. M. Leary's *North Carolina Research* (2nd ed.), 368, 370.

available on 73 microfilm reels. [Online catalog description: "Vouchers and certificates issued in lieu of cash for military service or for supplies furnished to the army. Typically, a voucher will show the name of the payee, number of the certificate, and the amount due. It may also give the date of issuance and the fiscal district or county in which issued. Certificates issued in payment for supplies or provisions may specify the material furnished. When a voucher was redeemed, it was cancelled by punching a hole through it. The issuance and redemption of certificates are recorded in the Revolutionary Army Account Books."]

North Carolina (State). State Treasurer. "Public Claims of Individuals against the State, 1733-1906." Manuscript, MARS Id: 13.44 (Series), State Archives of North Carolina, Raleigh. [Online catalog description: "Vouchers and claims by individuals against the colony and state, 1733-1906. Included are claims for such things as transporting goods; room, board, and refreshment for travelers on state business; services of various kinds rendered to the state; office supplies and furniture purchased. There are also some Revolutionary vouchers and claims included here because it is impossible to determine the last name of the claimant. The names were either mutilated when the voucher was paid and canceled, or the writing has faded and the name cannot be determined."]

"Reports of the Committees of Public Claims, North Carolina General Assembly, 1778-1787." *North Carolina Genealogical Society Journal*, 31:4 (November 2006), 323-358.

Stanford, Richard, 1767-1816. "Richard Stanford (1767-1816) Papers, 1798-1827, 1888-1914." Manuscript, Call Number PC.177 (MARS ID: 686; folder), State Archives of North Carolina, Raleigh. [Online catalog description: "Chiefly letters from Stanford of Hawfields, Democratic-Republican congressman (1791-1816) in Philadelphia and Washington, to his wife and to Capt. William Lytle about Revolutionary vouchers (1798-1799), events in Congress, slaves, his children, and peace (1815)."]

Turner, Grace W., and Raymond A. Winslow, Jr. "Reports of Committees of Public Claims, North Carolina General Assembly, 1778-1787." *North Carolina Genealogical Society Journal*, 31:4 (November 2005), 323-358; (1787-1788) 32:1 (February 2006), 3-59; (1789) 32:2 (May 2006), 153-170; (1789) 32:3 (August 2006), 248-265.

North Carolina Revolutionary Army Accounts

Allen, Penelope Johnson. *Tennessee Soldiers in the Revolution: A Roster of Soldiers Living during the Revolutionary War in the Counties of Washington and Sullivan, Taken From the Revolutionary Army Accounts of North Carolina.* Bristol, Tenn.: The King Printing Company, 1935; reprinted: Baltimore: Genealogical Publishing Company, 1996. [Contents: Introduction; Index to Revolutionary Soldiers; Revolutionary Pensioners of Tennessee, Act of 1828; Index to Wills of Washington County, Tennessee; Abstracts of Wills of Washington County; Marriage Records of Blount County; Marriage Records of Davidson County; Revolutionary Grants of Davidson County.]

"An Explanation of the 'Revolutionary Army Accounts' in the North Carolina Department of Archives & History." In William Doub Bennett, ed., *North Carolina State Archives State Agency Finding Aids of Interest to Genealogists: Volume I: Colonial Higher Courts, District Superior Courts, North Carolina Supreme Court, Treasurers & Comptrollers Papers, State Auditors Papers* (Raleigh: W. D. Bennett, 1997), 101-144. [This is an essential guide to this very confusing material that has been published as detailed in the next entry.]

Haun, Weynette Parks. *North Carolina Revolutionary Army Accounts*, in 18 volumes. [Note: Researchers should read the introductions to each of these volumes to gain an understanding of the contents of the *Army Accounts*. One observer stated that this is one of the most important and also one of the most "perplexing" set of records in the State Archives of North Carolina.][25] [Note: Throughout the entire 18-volume set, the pagination of the text pages is consequetive from 1 to 2,774 (exclusive of the indexes in each published volume).]

---

[25] Jo White Linn. "Introduction." *North Carolina Revolutionary Army Accounts: North Carolina Revolutionary Army Accounts, Secretary of State, Treasurer's & Comptroller's Papers, Journal "A" (Public Accounts), 1775-1776.* (Durham: W. P. Haun, 1988), i. This writer cites the following as the source for a quotation, but the quote does not appear in the cited 2002 revision of this *Archives Information Circular.* It may have been in the original 1973 version. See: C. Fred W Coker and Donald R. Lemon. *North Carolina's Revolutionary War Pay Records.* (North Carolina State Archives Information Circular 1) (Raleigh: North Carolina Department of Cultural Resources, 1976).

Part I. [= Haun vol. 1 or A, pages 1-170] Introduction by Jo White Linn. *North Carolina Revolutionary Army Accounts: North Carolina Revolutionary Army Accounts, Secretary of State, Treasurer's & Comptroller's Papers, Journal "A" (Public Accounts), 1775-1776.* Durham: W. P. Haun, 1988. [Taken from microfilm S.115.51, State Archives of North Carolina, Raleigh.]

Part II. [= Haun vol. 2, pages 171-288] *North Carolina Revolutionary Army Accounts, Secretary of State, Treasurer's & Comptroller's Papers, Vol. I and Vol. II.* Durham: W. P. Haun, 1990. [Taken from microfilm S.115.38N, State Archives of North Carolina, Raleigh.]
Contains:

{Vol. I, Books 1-5 Specie Certificates Paid into the Comptroller's Office by John Armstrong, Entry Taker for Lands in North Carolina. [Volume I = Old Series Vol. I, Nos. 1-5]

{Vol. II, Books 1-2, (1) Continental Line 1783, (2) Allowances Made to Continental Officers & Soldiers, … at Hillsborough, May 1, 1792 [Volume II = Old Series Vol. 2, Nos. 7-10]

Part III. [= Haun, vol. 3, pages 289-428] *North Carolina Revolutionary Army Accounts, Secretary of State, Treasurer's & Comptroller's Papers, Vol. III and Vol. IV.* Durham: W. P. Haun, 1991. [Taken from microfilm S.115.39N, State Archives of North Carolina, Raleigh.] Contains:

Vol. III, Books 1-7 [Encompasses = {]

{Book 1: Statement of Accounts of Non-Commissioned Officers & Privates of NC Line… as Passed by the Commissioner of Army Accounts.

{Book 2: "B-Journal of Remarks on Accounts … (in Book 1)

{Book 3: Statement… Non-Commissioned Officers & Privates…Settled at Warrenton, 1786.

{Book 4: Remarks … (on Book 3)

{Book 5: (Identical in form to Book 1)

{Book 6: Journal C – Remarks &c… Appended to Book 5

{Book 7: Account of Due Bills & Certificates Drawn by (Various Persons) Out of Commissioners Office Appointed to Liquidate Accounts of Officers & Soldiers of the Continental Line of North Carolina.

Vol. IV, Books 1-7.

{Book 1: Journal of Remarks…as Settled at Warrenton in 1786…

{Book 2: Accounts…Forwarded by Comptroller of NC…to Philadelphia…1791

{Book 3: "Heading Missing" … of Same Nature as Book 2

{Book 4: State of NC in Accot with Sundry Persons for Errors…

{Book 5: US Is Indebted to NC…Vouchers Are Missing

{Book 6: US to NC for Disbursements…for Army Contingencies

{Book 7: State of NC for Certificates Issued

Part IV. [= Haun vol. 4, pages 429-566]. *North Carolina Revolutionary Army Accounts, Secretary of State, Treasurer's & Comptroller's Papers, Vols. V & VI.* Durham: W. P. Haun, 1992.

Vol. V, Books 1-9 [Encompasses = {] [Taken from S.115.39N, State Archives of North Carolina, Raleigh]

{Book 1: Alphabetical Book Containing (Allowances) by Committee of Claims, 18th April 1776 to __ May 1779.

{Book 2: An Account of Claims Allowed by the Board of Auditors for the District of Wilmington for Militia Pay No. 5701-6014.

{Book 3: An Acount & Return of All the Claims Passed by the Auditors of the District of Wilmington from 16th May 1786 to 26th June 1786, Inclusive.

{Book 4: Report of the Auditors of Wilmington District from March 1784 to April 1785. Allowances made by the Board of Audi[tors] of Wilmington District from No. 3349 to No. 3918, Inclusive.

{Book 5: Warrants from Treasurer Haywood.

{Book 6: An Accot. of Cloathing, Currency, & Specie Certificates Sent to the Commissioners at New York by the Comptroller of Public Accots. of the State of North Carolina, May 1790. [Note: Although most of the material in this book relates to payments to soldiers during the Third Chickamauga Expedition in 1787 and to other activities after the American Revolution, a portion of the records deals with payments for earlier Revolutionary War service by individuals.[26]

---

[26] Forrest C. Crosley (Assistant Director for Genealogy, Office of the Registrar General, National Society Daughters of the American Revolution, Washington, D. C.) made the comments relative to the use of certain portions of this document as proof of Revolutionary War service in an internal memorandum dated May 1, 2006. Portions of his

{Book 7: Report of the Several Claims Allowed and Signed by the Board of Auditors for the District of Wilmington from the 17th of October 1781, to the 19th of April 1782, being in Currency.

{Book 8: Report of the Several Claims Allowed and Signed by the Board of Auditors for the District of Wilmington, from the 17th of October 1781 to the 15th July 1783.

{Book 9: Claims Allowed and passed by the Board of Auditors for the District of Wilmington from the 16th July 1783 (included) to the 19th of March 1784 for which Certificates are issued from No. (1459) to No. (3348) Inclusive & returned into the Comptroller's office…

Vol. VI, Books 1-4 [Encompasses = {] [Taken from microfilm S.115.40N, State Archives of North Carolina, Raleigh.]

{Book 1: Accounts of Claims Exhibited into the Comptrollers Office Agreeable to Resolve of the General Assembly of North Carolina passed December 1787.

{Book 2: Hillsborough Treasury Office.

{Book 3: A List of Certificates paid into the Treasury on (A)ccot. of Taxes, 1785 & 1786.

{Book 4: Certificates Received for the Year 1786.

Part V. [= Haun vol. 5, pages 567-672] *North Carolina Revolutionary Army Accounts, Secretary of State, Treasurer's & Comptroller's Papers, Vol. VII & Warrenton Settlements in 1786.* Durham: W. P. Haun, 1994. [Encompasses = {] [Taken from microfilms S.115.40N, S.115.41N and S.115.63]

{Book 26: A List of Certificates to Be Paid to the Comptroller for the Taxes for 1787, Including Those Due for the Years 1784, 1785 & 1786. [pages 567-582]

{Book 90: Certificates Paid the Comptroller by John Haywood Public Treasurer in the Fall of 1791. [pages 583-586]

{Book C-13: Due Bills Paid to Comptroller by Treasurer Haywood, 1787; Cash Claims Paid to Comptroller by Treasurer Haywood for 1786; Army Certificates; Certificates Paid by Bazile Grant Entry Taker of Onslow [County]; Certificates Paid by Sundries; Continental Loan Office Certificates; Cash Claims; Certificates for Currency Received from Richard Cogdal for New Bern District. [pages 587-604]

{Book C-17: List of Specie Certificates Paid by Green Hill Treasurer for the District of Halifax, 1783[?]; G. Hill Specie. [pages 605-614]

{Book G-16: Certificates Paid by the treasurer to the Comptroller July 1790 (by County) [pages 615-629.]

{Book G-17: Statement of the Accounts Paid the Officers and Soldiers of the Continental Line since 1784; A List of Officers Accots; Soldiers['] Cloathing from Kedar Powell Sheriff of Johnston

---

analysis follow with his consent: "In Weynette Parks Haun's *North Carolina Revolutionary Army Accounts, Secretary of State, Treasurer's & Comptrollers' Papers, Vol. V, Vol. VI, in Vol. VI*, pp. 485-489 are accounts that clearly refer to various types of payments made to North Carolina Continental Line & militia troops, and the furnishing of supplies and other kinds of patriotic service. Therefore, these pages are acceptable Revolutionary War service. Beginning at the bottom of p. 489 and continuing through p. 504 are the certificates issued to those who participated in the 1787 Third Chickamauga Expedition. Their certificates are numbered sequentially 1-1422 and include the heading 'for militia service performed in Davidson County' or 'for services against the Chicamaga Indians.' These entries are not acceptable as Revolutionary service. Starting on p. 505 and continuing through p. 531 the accounts are vaguer. In her explanation found between pp. 484-485, Haun states that these entries from the 'Hillsborough Treasury Office are certificates paid into the State Treasury office at Hillsborough by the sheriffs and entry takers of the different counties. The certificates originally were issued by the district boards of auditors for militia pay and for supplies furnished the militia and Continental troops, by the county commissioners of specific taxes for supplies furnished Continental troops, and by the various boards of commissioners to liquidate the claims of the Continental officers and soldiers. They were redeemed by the sheriffs, who accepted them for taxes, and by the entry takers, who them for land entry fees. The sheriffs and entry takers, in settling their accounts with the State, paid the certificates into the office of the Treasurer.' Therefore, while pp. 505-531 appear to be valid Revolutionary service, the service description is likely to be more general ('Paid for services rendered.') Do not use pp. 532-566 as a source for service. While these are found in Vol. VI, they appear in a separate book and were used to pay taxes in 1785 & 1786. While this may seem a bit confusing at first, if one reads the introductory material in Haun's published version of Vol. VI of the *North Carolina Revolutionary Army Accounts*, it will become clearer."

[County] for 1781. Also: Register of the Settlement of Army Acounts at Warrenton in the Year 1786. [pages 630-637]

{Register of the Settlements of Army Accounts at Warrenton in the Year 1786. [pages 639-672]

Part VI. [= Haun vol. 7, pages 673-839] *North Carolina Revolutionary Army Accounts (Secretary of State's Papers), Vol. VIII.* Durham: W. P. Haun, 1995. [Includes: Book G-18, Army Account Book E, Army Account Book F-1; Army Acount Book F-2; Book K Militia.]

Part VII. [= Haun vol. 7, pages 840-992] *North Carolina Revolutionary Army Accounts (Secretary of State's Papers) Vol. IX.* Durham: W. P. Haun, 1995. [Includes: Book 21; Book L-1; Book L-2; Book L-3; Book P-39; Book S-26; Book No. 12; Book 14.]

Part VIII. [= Haun vol. 8, pages 993-1124]. *North Carolina Revolutionary Army Accounts (Treasurer's & Comptroller's Papers) Vol. X.* Durham: W. P. Haun, 1996. [Includes Book No. 18, Book No. 19, Book A. No 40; Remarks on Book A. No. 40; US to NC for payments made to Continental Line in 1792, C & D, etc.]

Part IX. [= Haun vol. 9, pages 1125-1248] *North Carolina Revolutionary Army Accounts (Treasurer's & Comptroller's Papers) North Carolina Continental Line, 1776-1783.* Durham: W. P. Haun, 1997.

Part X. [1 = Haun vol. 10, pages 1249-1408] *North Carolina Revolutionary Army Accounts (Treasurer's and Comptroller's Papers), Vol. XI.* Durham: W. P. Haun, 1999.

Part XI. [= Haun vol. 11, pages 1409-1520] *North Carolina Revolutionary Army Accounts (Treasurer, State), vol. XII.* Durham: W. P. Haun, 1999.

Part XII. [= Haun vol. 12, pages 1521-1724] *North Carolina Revolutionary Army Accounts, Book A [Treasurer, State]* Durham: W. P. Haun, 1999.

Part XIII. [= Haun vol. 13, pages 1725-1862] *North Carolina Revolutionary Army Accounts (Treasurer, State) Book B.* Durham: W. P. Haun, 1999.

Part XIV. [= Haun vol. 14, pages 1863-2012] *North Carolina Revolutionary Army Accounts, (Treasurer, State), Accounts of the United States with North Carolina, Book C.* Durham: W. P. Haun, 1999.

Part XV. [= Haun vol. 15, pages 2013-2158] *North Carolina Revolutionary Army Accounts, Military Land Warrant Book, 1783-1841; Continental Line, 1783-1841 (Secretary of State: SS.981.1 : S.108.264),* Durham: W. P. Haun, 1999.

Part XVI. [= Haun vol. 16, pages 2159-2356] *North Carolina Revolutionary Army Accounts, (Treasurer, State), Accounts of the United States with North Carolina, Book D, Book 1.* Durham: W. P. Haun, 2000.

Part XVII. [= Haun vol. 17, pages 2357-258 *North Carolina Revolutionary Army Accounts, Treasurer: State, Books: E-G, H, J.* Durham: W. P. Haun, 2004.

Part XVIII. [= Haun vol. 18, pages 2581-2774] *North Carolina Revolutionary Army Accounts,Treasurer: State, Book K.* Durham: W. P. Haun, 2004.

Coker, Charles Frederick William and Donald R. Lemon. *North Carolina's Revolutionary War Pay Records.* (North Carolina State Archives Information Circular, no. 1) Raleigh: North Carolina Department of Cultural Resources, 1966; revised: 1973, 1976, 2002.

Kammerer, Roger. "NC Revolutionary War Public Accounts, 1776." *Pitt County Genealogical Quarterly*, 22:1 (February 2016), 1-2.

Kellam, Ida Brooks. *North Carolina Revolutionary Army Accounts: north Carolina Amount of Claims by the Auditors of Wilmington District from the 16th of October, 1781 to the __ of August 1783 (Book W, No. 1 1781-1783).* Wilmington: Old New Hanover County Genealogical Society, 1993. [The Wilmington District included the counties of Bladen, Brunswick, Cumberland, Duplin, New Hanover, and Onlsow.]

North Carolina (State). State Comptroller. "Abstract of the Army Accounts of the North-Carolina Line, Settled by the Commissioners at Halifax from the 1st September 1784, to the 1st February, 1785; and at Warrenton in the Year 1786; Designating by Who the Claims Were Receipted for Respectively." Halifax: [s. n.], 1794. Manuscript VC970.341 N87c1, North Carolina Collection, Louis Round Wilson Special Collections Library, University of North Carolina at Chapel Hill. [Online catalog description: "Includes: Statement of the settlements of army accounts by Willie Jones, Benjamin McCulloch and Henry Montfort, commissioners, at Halifax in the years 1783 & 1784; Abstract of claims of officers and soldiers of the North Carolina line, settled by James Coor, John Hawks & William Blount, April 1782; Statement of the final settlement certificates by Abishai Thomas; List of final settlement certificates delivered by John Haywood, public treasurer; List of final settlement certificates issued by the late comptroller, those marked J. C. by John Craven, Feb. 1, 1785; Abstract of the settlement of army accounts at Hillsborough in 1792. Signed J. Craven, Comptroller."]

North Carolina (State). State Comptroller, State Treasurer. "Military Papers – Revolutionary War Army Accounts, 1780-1795." Manuscript, Office of State Comptroller, State Treasurer Record Group, Volumes 40-66 (MARS

ID: 13.30), State Archives of North Carolina, Raleigh. [Online catalog description: "Account books, accounts, abstracts, lists, warrants, registers, certificates, receipts, reports, resolutions, ordinances, correspondence, and memoranda concerning the issuance and redemption of certificates or vouchers for Revolutionary War and postwar frontier militia service, and for supplies and provisions rendered to Continental and militia forces. The records also relate to the settlement of the state claim against the federal government for expenses incurred in the prosecution of the war. The account books are of various kinds, some created in the office of the treasurer and some by the comptroller, and they record both the issuance and redemption of certificates. Others relate to several postwar efforts to settle accounts of individual soldiers and the North Carolina claim against the United States. The other records include lists of certificates paid into the treasury for taxes or land entry fees, 1780-1795; counterfeit certificates; miscellaneous accounts, lists, and affidavits; and General Assembly resolutions concerning the issuance and redemption of certificates. There are as well abstracts of certificates presented as claims against the United States, usually including the number of the certificate, date of issue, by whom and to whom issued, and the amount of principal and interest. Records relating to the settlement of the North Carolina claim include accounts and abstracts of state credits and debits, expense accounts and warrants in favor of the state claim commissioners, presentments of the commissioners to the General Assembly and Congress, and congressional and legislative resolutions and committee reports. The series also includes the Register of the Continental Line, 1776-1783, compiled in 1791 from pay and muster rolls; and a copy of the printed abstract of the several settlements of Revolutionary army accounts, ca. 1794."] [Most, if not all, of this collection was published by Weynette Parks Haun. See the next entry.]

Sullivan, Kathy Gunter. "Understanding Revolutionary Army Accounts Book V: A Source for Evidence of Patriotic Service in North Carolina." *North Carolina Genealogical Society Journal*, 35:1 (February 2009), 15-18.

Continental Loan Office for North Carolina

[Note: There are no records of the North Carolina Continental Loan Office in the National Archives, Washington, D.C., althought records do exist for some of the other original states. Some records of the Continental Loan Office for North Carolina are, however, located in the "Military Papers Collection." These include general records, "Continental Loan Office Certificates," and others. "The Revolutionary Audited Accounts" contain some of these sources in Vol. VII.] These are detailed in the State Archives of North Carolina's unpublished finding aid "Treasurer's and Comptroller's Papers."]

North Carolina (State). General Assembly. "[Document dated:] December 6, 1777: Bill for Establishing a Loan Office in This State." Manuscript; General Assembly Record Group; Session Records, November-December 1777; Miscellaneous, Joint Papers, Committee Papers, Resolutions, Senate Bills, House Bills; Senate Joint Resolution, Box 1 (MARS ID: 66.8.10.21; item), State Archives of North Carolina, Raleigh.

North Carolina (State). General Assembly. "[Document dated:] May 14, 1779: Resolution Impowering Treasurers to Receive Continental Loan Office Certificates (with Message)." Manuscript; General Assembly Record Group; Session Records, May 1779; Joint Papers, Committee Papers, Resolutions, Senate Bills, House Bills; House Joint Resolution, May 3-15, 1779, Box 1 (MARS ID: 66.8.17.13.22; item), State Archives of North Carolina, Raleigh. [Online catalog description: "The resolution directs the treasurers to receive the certificates from the county treasurers and entry takers and draw the money for the use of the state."]

North Carolina (State). General Assembly. "[Document dated:] November 4, 1779: Resolution Impowering Sheriffs to Receive Claims Allowed and Loan Office Certificates in Payment for Taxes (with Messages)." Manuscript; General Assembly Record Group; Session Records, October-November 1779; Joint Papers, Committee Papers, Resolutions, Senate Bills, House Bills; Senate Joint Resolution, Box 1 (MARS ID: 66.8.18.12.20; item), State Archives of North Carolina, Raleigh.

North Carolina (State). General Assembly. "[Document dated:] December 18, 1787: Resolution Concerning Loan Office Certificates." Manuscript; General Assembly Record Group; Session Records, November-December 1787; Joint Select Committees, Senate Standing Committees, House Standing Committees; House Joint Resolutions (Nov. 19-Dec. 22, 1787), Box 2 (MARS ID: 66.8.47.6.9; item), State Archives of North Carolina, Raleigh. [Online catalog description: "Resolution directing treasurer to receive loan office certificates; includes portion of petition." "See also Joint Selecte Committee report on petition from inhabitants of Rowan Co., Dec. 12, 1787."]

North Carolina (State). General Assembly. "[Document dated:] December 15, 1790: Report on Letter from William Skinner, Commissioner of the United States Loan Office about Checks to Certificates (Letter Only)." Manuscript; General Assembly Record Group; Session Records, November-December 1790; Joint Standing Committees (November 12-25), Box 2 (MARS ID: 66.8.57; box), State Archives of North Carolina, Raleigh.

Currency, Money, Specie, Counterfeiting, etc., in North Carolina

Abernethy, Edgar. "North Carolina Currency." *The State: A Weekly Survey of North Carolina*, 11:32 (January 1944), 1-2; online: http://digital.ncdcr.gov/cdm/ref/collection/p16062coll18/id/18376.

Baker, Mary. "Money of the Colonial Period and Its Value." *New Bern Historical Journal*, 9:2 (November 1996), 31-36; online: https://www.evernote.com/shard/s5/res/1ece722d-661e-4ddf-891f-54f94116574a/Money%20of%20the%20Colonial%20Period%20and%20its%20Value%20Vol%20IX%20No%20II.pdf.

Corbitt, D. L. "Brunswick Committee Takes Action against Counterfeiters: Brunswick Committee, July 29, 1776." *North Carolina Historical Review,* 4:2 (April 1927), 202-203.

Corbitt, D. L. "William Edwards Acquitted of Counterfeiting by the Council of Safety, North Carolina in the Council of Safety, August 3, 1776." *North Carolina Historical Review,* 4:2 (April 1927), 203-204.

Davis, Sallie Joyner. "Sallie Joyner Davis Collection." Manuscript Collection #133, Joyner Library, East Carolina University, Greenville; online finding aid and digital surrogates available at https://digital.lib.ecu.edu/special/ead/findingaids/0133. [Online catalog description: "The collection contains a letter (1916) from Colonel Fred A. Olds of the North Carolina Historical Commission to Miss Davis in which he proposes that East Carolina develop a historical collection. In order to encourage the collection, Colonel Olds enclosed a quantity of currency, including colonial proclamation money (1754, 1768, 1771), Revolutionary War currency (1780), and a variety of Civil War money. The letter describes the type of shelving needed for storing documents and provides commentary on the history of the currency."]

"Duke University Currency Collection, 1746-1982." Manuscript, David M. Rubenstein Rare Book & Manuscript Library, Duke University, Durham; online finding aid available at http://library.duke.edu/rubenstein/findingaids/currency/. [Online finding aid description: "There are 67 pieces of Revolutionary paper currency and one copper plate for printing a bill. They include the Continental Currency issued by the Continental Congress and also the Revolutionary War state issues. There is currency from: The Continental Congress (10), 1776-1779; Georgia (18), 1776-1778; North Carolina (23), 1776-1780; South Carolina (14), 1775-1779; Virginia (2), 1777-1780. From North Carolina there is a copper plate used for the printing of one of the $2 1/2 bills of the issue of April 2, 1776 (the bill with a vignette of a Liberty Cap over an altar). The other side of the same copper plate was used to print $5 bills of the same issue (version with vignette of a raven). Signatories include five members of the Continental Congress: William Sharpe and John Williams from N. C. and William Few, William Gibbons, and Edward Telfair from Georgia. Telfair signed the Articles of Confederation, and Few signed the Constitution."]

Fries, Adelaide L. "North Carolina Certificates of the Revolutionary War Period." *North Carolina Historical Review*, 9:3 (July 1932), 229-241. [Online description from "North Carolina Periodicals Index," East Carolina University: "Certificates printed during the American Revolution functioned to replace hard currency which, for North Carolina, was largely depleted by 1780. The article carefully reviews *Colonial* and *State Records of North Carolina* as wells as diaries and minute books from the Moravian Church of Salem to better understand the legislation and distribution of certificates within the state."]

Kammerer, Roger. "John and Benjamin Garris, Counterfeiters, 1780." *Pitt County Genealogical Quarterly*, 12:2 (May 2005), 26.

Lawrence, R. C. "Colonial Money." *The State: A Weekly Survey of North Carolina*, 12:50 (May 1945), 7, 18; online: http://digital.ncdcr.gov/cdm/ref/collection/p16062coll18/id/13151. [Online description from "North Carolina Periodicals Index," East Carolina University: "There were many interesting features in connection with the issuance of paper money during the early history of North Carolina. The first bills were issued in 1712, and taxes collected were used to build forts and applied to public debt. The bills were printed on ordinary paper and were signed by Generals, Governors, Attorneys General."]

McCusker, John J. *Money and Exchange in Europe and America, 1600-1775: A Handbook.* Chapel Hill: University of North Carolina Press for the Institute of Early American History and Culture, Williamsburg, Va., 1978.

Norris, David A. "Cash Crop." *Our State: Down Home in North Carolina*, 73:4 (September 2005), 100-102, 104-106; online: http://digital.ncdcr.gov/cdm/ref/collection/p16062coll18/id/84263. [Online description from "North Carolina Periodicals Index," East Carolina University: "Norris traces the history paper currency and coins issued in North Carolina from the time of the Lords Proprietors in 1694 through the Civil War."]

"North Carolina Paper Currency." Online at the Craven County Digital History Exhibits: http://newbern.cpclib.org/digital/money.html.

"Paper Currency of the Revolution, 1775-1781." Manuscript Special Colls. Currency, Massachusetts Historical Society, Boston; online finding aid available at http://www.masshist.org/collection-guides/view/fao0006. [Includes North Carolina Issues from April 2, 1776, August 8, 1778, May 15, 1779, and May 10, 1780.]

Raper, Charles Lee. "The Finances of the North Carolina Colonists." *North Carolina Booklet*, 7:2 (October 1907), 86-104; online: http://digital.ncdcr.gov/cdm/ref/collection/p249901coll37/id/14180. [Online description from "North Carolina Periodicals Index," East Carolina University: "An account of the history of the use of currency and economic and financial systems in colonial North Carolina with sections addressing coins, barter systems, and paper money."]

Roberts, Frank M. "When Tar Heels Issued $3 Bills." *The State: Down Home in North Carolina*, 42:2 (July 1974), 16-17, 45; online: http://digital.ncdcr.gov/cdm/ref/collection/p16062coll18/id/56711. [Online description from "North Carolina Periodicals Index," East Carolina University: "David Cox Jr. of Hertford, collector of Tar Heel currency, maintains that, 'North Carolina issued far more paper money than any other state in the union.' His collection of N. C. printed currency contains money, scrip, and bank notes from the Revolutionary and Civil wars and has been displayed at the Smithsonian. N. C. currency began circulating in 1712 but was prohibited in 1786 upon joining the union. Many counties and municipalities issued Confederate money between 1861 and 1864."]

Scott, Kenneth. *Counterfeiting in Colonial America*. New York and Oxford: Oxford University Press, 1957.

Scott, Kenneth. "Counterfeiting in Colonial North Carolina." *North Carolina Historical Review*, 34:4 (October 1957), 467-482. [Online description from "North Carolina Periodicals Index," East Carolina University: "This article looks at the history of counterfeiting in colonial North Carolina including detailing occurrences of counterfeiting as well as laws, trials, and punishments levied on offenders."]

Watson, Alan D. "Counterfeiting in Colonial North Carolina: A Reassessment." *North Carolina Historical Review*, 79:2 (April 2002), 182-197. [Online description from "North Carolina Periodicals Index," East Carolina University: "This article examines counterfeit currency in colonial North Carolina, especially between the 1760s and 1770s. Like most of the colonies, North Carolina often suffered from a shortage of legal tender during this period, leading to counterfeiting of paper money. While the western part of the colony was particularly vulnerable to counterfeiting, it did not pose a significant threat to legitimate currency."]

Watson, Alan D. *Money and Monetary Problems in Early North Carolina*. Raleigh: North Carolina Department of Cultural Resources, Division of Archives and History, 1980.

Weir, Robert M. "North Carolina's Reaction to the Currency Act of 1764." *North Carolina Historical Review*, 40:2 (April 1963), 183-199. [Online description from "North Carolina Periodicals Index," East Carolina University: "This article details the currency act of 1764 extending previous bans on paper legal tender to all of the continental colonies, the impact of the act and its role in moving the colonies towards revolution."]

Select Tax Sources for North Carolina or Tennessee Revolutionary War Residence

The lists below include a number of sources that may be used to help establish residence in various towns, townships and counties that existed during the Revolutionary War. It is not, however, all inclusive, and numerous other sources such as alternative tax lists, petitions, store account ledgers, and land, probate, court, church, voter and vital records may also be used. In geographic areas where county and state boundaries were disputed during the Revolution, researchers should investigate the available records for each respective county and state, as Revolutionary War patriots may have multiple residences as well as military, civil or patriotic service in more than one state. In some instances, certain sources of residence cited here may also qualify as a source of Revolutionary War service.

At the present time, the NSDAR has not established specific guidelines for the acceptance of an individual's name appearing on a tax list during the years of the American Revolution as falling into the category of having paid a supply tax. The wording of an act of the North Carolina General Assembly must specifically state that a new tax in any given year was to be used for the support of the war effort. Careful examination of these acts and correlation with a specific tax list would be necessary for an applicant to use such a list as a supply tax payment. Discussion is advised (before submission of an application with this documentation) with the staff of the Genealogy Office, Office of the Registrar General, National Society Daughters of the American Revolution, 1776 D. Street, NW, Washington, D. C. 20006-5303.

Statewide:

North Carolina (State). General Assembly. "Tax Lists, 1771-1785." Manuscript GA 11.1 (MARS ID: 66.30.1, box), State Archives of North Carolina, Raleigh. [Contains: Bertie County, 1774; Brunwick County, 1772; Granville County, 1771; Perquimans County, 1772; Onslow County, 1772; Surry County, 1771, 1772.]

North Carolina (State). General Assembly. "Tax Lists, 1779." Manuscript GA 30.1 (MARS ID: 66.30.2; box), State Archives of North Carolina, Raleigh. [Contains: Beaufort County, Carteret County, Craven County, Currituck County, Hertford County, Jones County, Martin County, Orange County, Pasquotank County, Warren County, New Bern District]

North Carolina (State). General Assembly. "Tax Lists, 1780-1782." Manuscript GA 46.1 (MARS ID: 66.30.3, box), State Archives of North Carolina, Raleigh. [These records are for the following counties and years: Bertie County, 1781; Brunswick County, 1782; Camden County, 1782; Caswell County, 1780; Dobbs County, 1780; Gates County, 1782, Granvillke County, 1782; Halifax County, 1782; Montgomery County, 1782; Nash County, 1782; Northampton County, 1780; Pasquotank County, 1782; Rutherford County, 1782; Surry County, 1782; Wilkes County, 1782. See the above paragraph for further information on the possible use of these lists as supply tax lists.]

North Carolina (State). General Assembly. "Tax Lists, 1783-1785." Manuscript GA 64.1 (MARS ID: 66.30.4; box), State Archives of North Carolina, Raleigh. [These records are for the following counties and years: Beaufort County, 1784; Bladen County, 1784; Brunswick County, 1784; Caswell County, 1784; Chowan County, 1785; Granville County, 1785; Halifax County, 1783; Hertford County, 1784; Johnston County, 1784; Sampson County, 1784; Tyrrell County, 1784; Warren County, 1784; Wilkes County, 1784. Note that all but one of these lists if from 1784 and 1785, after the conclusion of the Revolution. Examination of the 1783 Halifax County tax list and correlation with a specific Act of Assembly that authorized its collection is necessary to determine if this particular list was a supply tax list. See the above paragraph for further information.]

North Carolina (Colony and State). Office of Secretary of State. "Tax Lists, 1720-1839." Manuscript SS 837.1-SS.837.2 (MARS ID: 12.97; series), State Archives of North Carolina, Raleigh. [Online catalog description: "Thirty-four tax lists of households subject to taxation in fifteen counties. Information generally includes name of the head of household, acreage, valuation, and number of polls in household, black and white."] [Note: Consult the State Archives of North Carolina for years and counties included in this collection.]

North Carolina (Colony and State). General Assembly. "Tax Lists, 1771-1774, 1779-1790." Manuscript GA 11.1, GA 30.1, GA 46.1.1-GA 46.1.2, GA 64.1, GA 101.1 (MARS ID: 66.30), State Archives of North Carolina, Raleigh. [Online catalog description: "Alphabetical by county. Lists sent to the General Assembly from various counties, giving the names of the heads of household that were subject to taxation."] [Note: Consult the State Archives of North Carolina for years and counties included in this collection.]

Ratcliff, Clarence E. *North Carolina Taxpayers, 1679-1790.* 2 vols. Baltimore: Genealogical Publishing Company, 1984.

Beaufort County:

Beaufort County. "Tax Lists and Scrolls, 1779-1927." 24 microfilm reels, State Archives of North Carolina, Raleigh. [Consult the State Archives to determine the exact years that are available.]

"List of Taxables for Beaufort County, North Carolina for 1779." *North Carolina Genealogical Society Journal,* 15:3 (August 1989), 137-146.

Willis, Laura. *Beaufort County, North Carolina, 1779, 1784, 1786, 1789 Tax Lists*. Mayfield, Ky.: Simmons Historical Publications, 2009.

Bertie County:

Bertie County. Clerk of Superior Court; Clerk of Court of Pleas and Quarter Sessions; Register of Deeds. "Tax Lists, 1755-1860, 1877, 1906, 1908-1909." Manuscript CR.010.701.1-CR.010.70.13 and 7 microfilm reels (MARS ID: 201.7.1; box), State Archives of North Carolina, Raleigh. [Consult the State Archives to determine the exact exact years that are available.]

Pruitt, Albert Bruce. *List of Taxables, 1765-1771, Bertie County, NC.* Whitakers: A. B. Pruitt, 2009.

Bladen County:

1763 Tax List of Bladen County. [Elizabethtown?]: Bladen County Historical Society, 1976.

Byrd, William L. *Bladen County, North Carolina Tax Lists*. 2 vols. [S. l.: North Carolina?]: W. L. Byrd, 1998-2000.

Campbell, Wanda S. *1784 Tax List, Bladen County, N. C.* [S. l.: s. n., 197?]

A List of Persons in Bladen Exempt from Paying Specie Tax for the Year 1781. [Elizabethtown?]: Bladen County Historical Society, 1975.

A List of the Taxable Property in Bladen County for the Year 1784. Elizabethtown, N. C.: Bladen County Historical Society, [1976?].

A List of the Taxable Property in Bladen County for the Year of Our Lord 1788. Elizabethtown, N. C.: Bladen County Historical Society, 1975.

Brunswick County:

1769 Brunswick County, North Carolina, Tax List. Signal Mountain, Tenn.: Mountain Press, 1999.

1772 Brunswick County, North Carolina, Tax List. Signal Mountain, Tenn.: Mountain Press, 1999.

Burke County:

[Burke County. Clerk]. "Tax List, 1771." In the "Thomas Merritt Pittman (1857-1932) Collection, 1747-1934." Manuscript PC.123 (MARS ID: 632; record group), State Archives of North Carolina, Raleigh.

Burke County. "Tax Records, 1782-1894." Manuscript, State Archives of North Carolina, Raleigh.

Bute County:

1771 Bute County, North Carolina, Tax List. Signal Mountain, Tenn.: Mountain Press, 1999.

[Bute County.] "[Bute County Tax List, 1771]." Manuscript in the "Thomas Merritt Pittman (1857-1932) Collection, 1747-1934," PC.123, State Archives of North Carolina, Raleigh.

Bute County. "List of Taxables, 1771." 1 microfilm reel, State Archives of North Carolina, Raleigh.

Bute County. "Tax and Fiscal Records, 1765-1778." Manuscript, State Archives of North Carolina, Raleigh.

Bute County. "Taxables, 1766." Manuscript, 1 folder, CRX Records, State Archives of North Carolina, Raleigh.

Bute County. "Taxables, List of, 1777-1780." Manuscript, 1 vol., CRX Records, State Archives of North Carolina, Raleigh.

Camden County:

1782 Camden County, North Carolina, Tax List. Signal Mountain, Tenn.: Mountain Press, 1999.

Johnson, William Perry. "Camden Co.: 1782 Tax List." *Journal of North Carolina Genealogy*, 9:2 (Summer 1963), 1138-1145.

Carteret County:

Carteret County. "Tax Records, 1745-1899." Manuscript, State Archives of North Carolina, Raleigh. [Consult the State Archives to determine the exact years that are available.]

"Currituck and Carteret County Tax Lists, 1779-1825." Microfilm 33MSS-0-138 [MARS ID: 5000.6.805.138; item], Outer Banks History Center, Manteo. [Consult the Center for the exact years that appear on the role.]

Johnson, William Perry. "Carteret County: 1779 Tax List." *The North Carolinian: A Quarterly Journal of Genealogy and History*, 7:1 (March 1961), 771-773.

Caswell County:

Caswell County. Clerk of Superior Court; Clerk of Court of Pleas and Quarter Sessions; Register of Deeds. "Lists of Taxables, 1777-1867." Manuscript CR.202.701.10-CR.020.701-12 (MARS ID: 220.71.2; box), State Archives of North Carolina, Raleigh. [Online catalog description: "1777-1803 (broken series) 1804-1829 (broken series) 1830-1867 (broken series)." Consult the State Archives to determine the exact years that are available.]

Caswell County. Clerk of Superior Court; Clerk of Court of Pleas and Quarter Sessions; Register of Deeds. "Lists of Taxables, 1780-1867." Manuscript CR.020.701.1-CR.701.9 (MARS ID: 220.7.1; box), State Archives of North Carolina, Raleigh. [Online catalog description: "1780 – 1787, 1788 – 1796, 1805 – 1806, 1823 - 1824 (This book appears to be a record of taxes for several districts of Caswell County, kept by Col. George W. Williamson, sheriff and presumably tax collector. It was presented to the State Department of Archives and History by Mrs. John W. Williams, Durham, N. C.), 1838 – 1839, 1844 – 1847, 1863 – 1864, 1866 1867."]

Johnson, William Perry. "Caswell County: 1779 Tax List." *Journal of North Carolina Genealogy*, 20:1 (Spring/Summer 1974), 2908-2920.

Winslow, Raymond A., Jr. "Caswell Co., N. C., 1777 Tax List." *North Carolina Genealogical Society Journal*, 27:1 (February 2001), 3-32.

Chowan County:

Chowan County. Clerk of Superior Court; Clerk of Court of Pleas and Quarter Sessions; Register of Deeds. "Taxables, List of, 1717-1909." Manuscript CR.024.701.2-CR.024.71.10 (MARS ID: 224.71.2; box), State Archives of North Carolina, Raleigh. [Online catalog description: "Box 2 contains undated records. Box 10 contains Insolvent Taxables, 1754 - 1840, no date; Corporation Taxes, 1901 - 1906; Tax Alterations, 1830 - 1836; Tax Notices, 1853; Tax Receipts, 1810 - 1879; Property Valuation, 1777, 1847, no date." Consult the State Archives to determine the exact years that are available.]

Smith, Robert Bland, and Grayson Hamilton Harding. *Chowan County Taxables, 1784*. Edenton: [s. n.], 1965.

Craven County:

"1779 Craven County Tax List (Two Districts)." *Pitt County Genealogical Quarterly,* 14:2 (May 2007), 1-3.

Craven County. "Tax Records, 1764-1904." Manuscript, State Archives of North Carolina, Raleigh.

Cumberland County:

[Cumberland County]. "List of Insolvents, 1783." In Cumberland County Clerk of Superior Court; Clerk of Court of Pleas and Quarter Sessions; Register of Deeds. "Cumberland County Miscellaneous Records, 1758-1965, no date," Manuscript CR.029.928.3-CR.029.928.9 (MARS ID: 229.103.2; box), State Archives of North Carolina, Raleigh.

Cumberland County. "Lists of Taxables, 1771-1783,…" Microfilm, State Archives of North Carolina, Raleigh.

Cumberland County. "List of Taxables, 1775." In Cumberland County Clerk of Superior Court; Clerk of Court of Pleas and Quarter Sessions; Register of Deeds. "Cumberland County Miscellaneous Records, 1758-1965, no date," Manuscript CR.029.928.3-CR.029.928.9 (MARS ID: 229.103.2; box), State Archives of North Carolina, Raleigh.

Cumberland County. "Lists of Taxables, 1777-1884." Manuscript, State Archives of North Carolina, Raleigh.

Pruitt, Albert Bruce. *Cumberland County, NC, Taxables, 1777-1783, 1815 and 1767.* Whitakers: A. B. Pruitt, 2015. [Publisher's description: "This book contains lists of taxables in Cumberland County in a book (1777-1783 in book CR 029.701.1) and two lists (1815 and 1767 in Treasurer & Comptroller records box 3) in the North Carolina archives."]

Currituck County:

Bennett, William Doub. *Currituck County, North Carolina, Eighteenth Century Tax & Militia Records*. Baltimore: Clearfield Company, 1993.

"Currituck and Carteret County Tax Lists, 1779-1825." Microfilm 33MSS-0-138 [MARS ID: 5000.6.805.138; item], Outer Banks History Center, Manteo. [Consult the Center for the exact years that appear on the role.]

Jones, Gordon C., comp. Abstracts of Land-Grants, Tax Lists, Orphans Dockets, Inventories and Other Records: Currituck and Dare Counties, North Carolina (1666-1831). 2nd ed. Elizabeth City: Family Research Society of Northeastern North Carolina, 2003. Includes:

"List of Taxables, Married Men Poll Tax, Single Men Poll Tax, Currituck County, 1779." In Gordon C. Jones. *Abstracts of Wills and Other Records, Currituck and Dare Counties, North Carolina, 1663-1850* (Philadelphia: [s. n.], 1958; reprinted: Baltimore: Genealogical Publishing Company, 1977), 10-15.

Dobbs County:

"Dobbs County 1780 Tax List." Manuscript, File Box G. A. 46.1, State Archives of North Carolina, Raleigh.

Murphy, William L. *Two 1780 Dobbs County, North Carolina Tax Lists*. Raleigh, N. C.: W. L. Murphy, 1987. [One of the tax lists was a "provisions tax." Includes: "Commissioner's List for 1780 Provision Taxes," 1-25, 28. [These pages contain the names of those who helped supply the American Army by paying the 1780 provisions tax.]

Duplin County:

"Duplin County Tax List, 1783 (Including the area that became Sampson County in 1784)." *North Carolina Genealogy,* 18:2 (Fall-Winter 1972), 2778-2782; 19:1 (Spring-Summer 1973), 2813-2821.

Duplin County. Clerk of Superior Court; Clerk of Court of Pleas and Quarter Sessions; Register of Deeds. "Tax Lists, 1783-1817." Manuscript, CR.035.701.1 (MARS ID: 235.71.1; box), State Archives of North Carolina, Raleigh. [Consult the State Archives to determine the exact years that are available.]

[Duplin County]. Clerk of Superior Court; Clerk of Court of Pleas and Quarter Sessions; Register of Deeds. "[A Partial Tax List, 1783]." Manuscript in the Albert Timothy Outlaw (1894-1962) Papers." Microfilm MfP.149 (MARS ID: 2649; record group), State Archives of North Carolina, Raleigh.

[Duplin County]. "[A Partial Tax List, 1783]." Manuscript in the Albert Timothy Outlaw (1894-1962) Papers." Microfilm MfP.149 (MARS ID: 2649; record group), State Archives of North Carolina, Raleigh.

Granville County:

1771 Granville, North Carolina, Tax List. Signal Mountain, Tenn.: Mountain Press, 1999.

Granville County. Clerk of Superior Court; Clerk of Court of Pleas and Quarter Sessions; Register of Deeds. "Taxables, 1747-1887." Manuscript CR.044.701.20-CR.044.701.28 (MARS ID: 244.71.2; box), State Archives of North Carolina, Raleigh. [Consult the State Archives to determine the exact years that are available.]

Granville County. "Tax Lists, 1755-1902, ..." Microfilm, State Archives of North Carolina, Raleigh. [Consult the State Archives to determine the exact years that are available.]

Greene County [now in Tennessee]:

Reynolds, Louise Wilson. "Tax List of Greene County, State of Tennessee, for the Year 1783." *Daughters of the American Revolution Magazine*, 53:4 (April 1919), 196-203. ["The following tax list is perhaps the oldest county tax assessment of the state in existence. The original, like many court records of value to genealogists, has been carelessly misplaced or destroyed and is no longer accessible. With few exceptions the men whose names appear on the list were Revolutionary soldiers and patriots."]

Halifax County:

Halifax County. Clerk of Superior Court; Clerk of Court of Pleas and Quarter Sessions; Register of Deeds. "Lists of Taxables, 1784-1834." Manuscript CR.047.701.1-CR.047.701.2 (MARS ID: 247.7.1; box), State Archives of North Carolina, Raleigh. [Consult the State Archives to determine the exact years that are available.]

Hertford County:

"1779 Hertford County Tax List." Manuscript, State Archives of North Carolina, Raleigh; published: Winslow, Raymond A., Jr. *North Carolina Genealogical Society Journal*, 20:1 (February 1994), 2-22; 20:2 (May 1994), 96-117; and, 20:4 (November 1994), 242-276.

Hertford County. "Tax List, 1782." Manuscript, State Archives of North Carolina, Raleigh.

Johnson, William Perry. "Hertford Co.: 1779 Tax List." *Journal of North Carolina Genealogy*, 13:2 (Summer 1997), 1871-1875.

Murfree, William. "William Murfree Tax Receipt Book, 1768-1770." Manuscript PC.1801 (MARS ID: 2311; record group), State Archives of North Carolina, Raleigh. Published: Raymond Parker Fouts. *William Murfree Tax Receipt Book, Hertford County, North Carolina, 1768-1770*. Cocoa Beach, Fla.: GenRec Books, 1993. [Online catalog description: "This volume appears to be a private record kept by William Murfree, sheriff of Hertford County, as a result of an investigation into the public accounts by the General Assembly of 1768 which reported that many of the county sheriffs were in arrears in their settlements with the colonial treasury. Murfree seems to have kept this record to show precisely what had been collected in his name and from whom. He not only names the taxpayers of the county, but indicates which of the three years they were subject to pay tax in the county, the sum collected, and, frequently, to whom they had paid the tax and the medium of exchange."]

Hyde County:

Hyde County. "Tax Records, 1740-1936." Manuscript, State Archives of North Carolina, Raleigh. [Consult the State Archives to determine the exact years that are available.]

Johnston County:

Brown, Claudia Stephenson. *1784 through 1840 Census of Johnston County, North Carolina*. Smithfield: Johnston County Genealogical and Historical Society, 2001. [Includes the 1784-1787 tax lists.]

Haun, Weynette Parks. *Johnston County, North Carolina, Taxables, 1784-1820*. Durham: W. P. Haun, 1983.

Jones County:

"Jones County, North Carolina List of Taxables for 1779." *North Carolina Genealogical Society Journal,* 26:4 (November 2000), 407-418.

Jones County. "Tax List, 1779." One microfilm reel, State Archives of North Carolina, Raleigh.

Lincoln County:

Lincoln County. "Tax Lists, 1784-1886,..." Manuscript, State Archives of North Carolina, Raleigh. [Consult the State Archives to determine the exact years that are available.]

Martin County:

"Martin County Insolvents, 1779." *Pitt County Genealogical Quarterly,* 13:2 (May 2006), 9. [Although a tax list, there are notations after the names of some men that state "in the Service."]

Martin County. "Miscellaneous Records, 1774-1906." Manuscript, State Archives of North Carolina, Raleigh. [Consult the State Archives to determine the exact years that are available.]

Montgomery County:

"Montgomery County, North Carolina Tax List of 1782." *North Carolina Genealogical Society Journal,* 9:2 (May 1983), 109-114.

Nash County:

Brantley, Jason Edward. *1782 Tax List Nash County, North Carolina, Tax List.* Bailey, N. C.: T. E. Brantley, [198?].

New Hanover County:

New Hanover County. New Hanover County. "Tax Records, 1779-1816,..." Manuscript, State Archives of North Carolina, Raleigh. [Consult the State Archives to determine the exact years that are available.] "Tax Records, 1779-1816,..." Manuscript (MARS ID: 270.71; series), State Archives of North Carolina, Raleigh. [Consult the State Archives to determine the exact years that are available.]

Reaves, Bill. "A List of Taxables for the County of New Hanover as Returned by the Magistrates to the September Court, 1767." *Clarendon Courier: Journal of the Old New Hanover Genealogical Society*, 6:3 (June 1994), 14-18.

Northampton County:

"Northampton County Tax Records, 1784-1879." Manuscript and microfilm, State Archives of North Carolina, Raleigh.

Onslow County:

1769 Onslow County, North Carolina, Tax List. Signal Mountain, Tenn.: Mountain Press, 1999.

"Onslow County Tax Records, 1774-1879." Manuscript and microfilm, State Archives of North Carolina, Raleigh.

Onslow County. "Tax Records, 1774-1912." Manuscript and one microfilm reel (1774-1790), State Archives of North Carolina, Raleigh. [Consult the State Archives to determine the exact years that are available.]

Orange County:

Bennett, William Doub. "Freeholders of Orange County, N .C. – 1776." *North Carolina Genealogical Society Journal*, 10:2 (May 1984), 98-106.

Johnson, William Perry. "Orange County, 1779 Tax List (Early Settlers in Alamance, Orange, and Durham Counties)." *Journal of North Carolina Genealogy*, 15:2 (Summer 1969), 2349-2365.

"List of Taxable Property in Orange County, North Carolina, 1780-1781." *North Carolina Genealogical Society Journal,* 11:3 (August 1985), 150-160; 11:4 (November 1985), 227-238

Orange County. "List of Taxables, 1780-1827." 3 microfilm reels, State Archives of North Carolina, Raleigh. [Consult the State Archives to determine the exact years that are available.]

Orange County. "Tax Lists, 1779-1783." 2 microfilm reels, State Archives of North Carolina, Raleigh. [Consult the State Archives to determine the exact years that are available.]

Orange County. Clerk of Superior Court; Clerk of Court of Pleas and Quarter Sessions; Register of Deeds. "Tax Lists, 1780-1801..." Manuscript (MARS ID: 273.71; series), State Archives of North Carolina, Raleigh. [Consult the State Archives to determine the exact years that are available.]

Warren, Mary Bondurant. "A List of the Taxable Persons in the County of Orange with the Amt. of Their Taxable Property, vizt., for the Year 1779 [tax amount omitted in transcription]." *The Carolina Genealogist*, no. 17 (Winter 1974), County Records/Orange County Tax List 1779, 1-12.

Pasquotank County:

1769 Pasquotank County, North Carolina, Tax Listing. Signal Mountain, Tenn.: Mountain Press, 1999.

Forehand, Steven. *1770 Taxables for Pasquotank County, North Carolina.* Camden: S. Forehand, 2006.
Forehand, Steven. *1777-78 Taxables for Pasquotank County, North Carolina.* Camden: S. Forehand, 2006.
Pasquotank County. Clerk of Superior Court; Clerk of Court of Pleas and Quarter Sessions; Register of Deeds. "Tax Lists, 1735-1882." 7 manuscript vols. CR.075.701.1-CR.075.701.3 (MARS ID: 275.71.1; box), State Archives of North Carolina, Raleigh. [Online catalog description: "1735-1799 (broken series), 1800-1829 (broken series), 1830-1882 (broken series)." Consult the State Archives to determine the exact years that are available.]

Perquimans County:
Perquimans County. Clerk of Superior Court; Clerk of Court of Pleas and Quarter Sessions; Register of Deeds. "Lists of Taxables, 1742-1859." Manuscript CR.077.701.1-CR.077.701.5 (MARS ID: 277.71.1; box), State Archives of North Carolina, Raleigh. [Consult the State Archives to determine the exact years that are available.]

Pitt County:
"A List of the Inhabitants of Pitt County Taken by order of the Continental and Provincial Congress August 25, 1775." *North Carolina Genealogical Society Journal,* 7:4 (November 1981), 188-196.

Randolph County:
Johnson, William Perry. "1779 Tax List of Randolph County." *North Carolinian: A Quarterly Journal of Genealogy and History,* 2:2 (June 1956), 179-186. [DAR Genealogy Office Note: "While a tax list, there are notes stating that certain individuals had not taken the oath of allegiance and returned the inventories of their taxable property, thereby implying that those that did return their inventories had taken the oath of allegiance."]
Randolph County. "Lists of Taxables, 1784-1867." Manuscript, State Archives of North Carolina, Raleigh. [Consult the State Archives to determine the y exact ears that are available.]
Randolph County. "Lists of Taxables, 1785-1848." Manuscript, CRX Records, State Archives of North Carolina, Raleigh. [Consult the State Archives to determine the exact years that are available.]
Randolph County. Clerk of Superior Court; Clerk of Court of Pleas and Quarter Sessions; Register of Deeds. "Miscellaneous Tax Records, 1784-1886." Manuscript CR.081.701.1-CR.081.701.4 (MARS ID: 281.71.1; box), State Archives of North Carolina, Raleigh. [Consult the State Archives to determine the exact years that are available.]

Richmond County:
Richmond County. "Tax Records, 1783-1898." Manuscript, State Archives of North Carolina, Raleigh. [Consult the State Archives to determine the exact years that are available.]

Rowan County:
Linn, Jo White. *Abstracts of the Wills & Estate Records of Rowan County, North Carolina, 1753-1805 and Rowan County Tax Lists of 1759 and 1778.* Salisbury: J. W. Linn, 19779.
Linn, Jo White. *Rowan County, North Carolina Tax Lists, 1757-1800: Annotated Transcriptions.* Salisbury: J. W. Linn, 1995.
"Rowan County Tax Records, 1758-1910." Manuscript and microfilm, State Archives of North Carolina, Raleigh.
Rowan County: "Tax Records, 1758-1910." Manuscript, State Archives of North Carolina, Raleigh. [Consult the State Archives to determine the exact years that are available.]
Rowan County. "Tax Records, 1758-1894." Manuscript, CRX Records, State Archives of North Carolina, Raleigh. [Consult the State Archives to determine the exact years that are available.]

Rutherford County:
Holcomb, Brent H. *1785 Tax List (Partial), Rutherford County, North Carolina.* Chapel Hill: B. H. Holcomb, 1974.

Surry County:
1772 Surry County, North Carolina, Tax List. Signal Mountain, Tenn.: Mountain Press, 1999.
Scates, Beulah, and Mrs. Myron R. McKinley. *1782 Tax List of Surry County, North Carolina.* Cimarron, Kans.: Mrs. R. J. Taylor, 1974.
Surry County. "Tax Records, 1775-1888." Manuscript, State Archives of North Carolina, Raleigh. [Consult the State Archives to determine the exact years that are available.]

Tyrrell County:

"A List of Taxables, Tyrrell County, North Carolina, 1782." *North Carolina Genealogical Society Journal,* 10:4 (November 1984), 242-247.

Tyrrell County. "Lists of Taxables, 1782, 1850." One microfilm reel, State Archives of North Carolina, Raleigh.

Tyrrell County. "Tax Records, 1782-1929." Manuscript, State Archives of North Carolina, Raleigh. [Consult the State Archives to determine the exact years that are available.]

Wake County:

Wake County. Clerk of Superior Court; Clerk of Court of Pleas and Quarter Sessions; Register of Deeds. "Wake County Tax Lists, 1781-1860." Manuscript CR.099.701.1- CR.099.701.2, State Archives of North Carolina, Raleigh; also available on microfilm. [Consult the State Archives to determine the exact years that are available.]

Wake County. "Tax Lists, 1781-1867." Manuscript, State Archives of North Carolina, Raleigh. [Consult the State Archives to determine the exact years that are available.]

Wake County. "Tax Lists, 1781-1817." One microfilm reel, State Archives of North Carolina, Raleigh. [Consult the State Archives to determine the exact years that are available.]

Warren County:

Warren County. "Lists of Tithables, 1781-1801,..." Manuscript, State Archives of North Carolina, Raleigh. [Consult the State Archives to determine the exact years that are available.]

Warren County. "Miscellaneous Tax Records, 1780-1935." Manuscript, State Archives of North Carolina, Raleigh. [Consult the State Archives to determine the exact years that are available.]

Warren County. "Tax Lists, 1779-1808." One microfilm reel, State Archives of North Carolina, Raleigh. [Consult the State Archives to determine the exact years that are available.]

Washington County, now the State of Tennessee:

Creekmore, Pollyanna. "Washington County, Tennessee, 1778 Taxpayers List." *East Tennessee Historical Society Special Publication,* no. 34 (1962), 118-131.

Wayne County:

Hill, Martha Ellis. *Wayne County, North Carolina, Court House Records, Four Books, 1780-1896*. La Grange: M. E. Hill, 1995.

Wayne County. "Tax Records, 1780-1920." Manuscript, State Archives of North Carolina, Raleigh. [Consult the State Archives to determine the exact years that are available.]

Wilkes County:

Hayes, Mae R., *1782 Tax List Wilkes County, North Carolina*. North Wilksboro: Genealogical Society of the "Original" Wilkes County, [197?]; 2nd rev. ed. [Ruby Tuttle] Mrs. W[illiam] O[liver] Absher and Mrs. W. C. [Nancy F.] Sidden. North Wilksboro: Wilkes Genealogical Society, 1975.

Wilkes County. "Tax Lists, 1778-1823, 1904." One microfilm reel, State Archives of North Carolina, Raleigh. [Consult the State Archives to determine the exact years that are available.]

Wilkes County. Clerk of Superior Court; Clerk of Court of Pleas and Quarter Sessions; Register of Deeds. "Tax Records, 1781-1908." Manuscript CR.104.701.1-CR.104.701.5 (MARS ID: 304.71.1; box), State Archives of North Carolina, Raleigh. [Consult the State Archives to determine the years that are available.]

Yadkin County:

Byrd, William L., and John H Smith. *North Carolina Slaves and Free Persons of Color: Stokes and Yadkin Counties*. Bowie, Md.: Heritage Books, 2001.

Pruitt, Albert Bruce. *Index to North Carolina County Maps: Davie, Guilford, Montgomery, Randolph, Rockingham, Stokes, Surry, & Yadkin*. Whitakers: A. B. Pruitt, 1988.

Chapter Nine:
North Carolina and Tennessee Land and Land Records

North Carolina land records are extensive in quantity and not always easy to use. Beyond county records, such as deeds and that are not covered in this source guide intentionally, land records at the state level are voluminous. Most reside in the State Archives of North Carolina in Raleigh, and the agency's online MARS catalog is the first place to go to investigate these materials. Perhaps concurrently, the related chapters in Leary's *North Carolina Research* are essential reading. The following materials will help a researcher wade through the mass of materials relating to North Carolina's land records, their locations, and their uses. Because the Old North State included Tennessee until 1796, North Carolina laws and procedures prevailed and set the basis for the land system and records of the future Volunteer State after its admission to the Union.

North Carolina gave military bounty warrants to its Continental Line soldiers. The Military Land District, where these grants were to be located, was in Middle Tennessee mainly in the area then Davidson and Sumner Counties. No military bounty land was given within the present boundaries of North Carolina. These military warrants could be sold or assigned, so the person receiving the grant was not necessarily the person who performed the military service. Not all land grants in Tennessee at this time period were given for military serive. The State Archives of North Carolina may be able to help in determining the person to whom the Revolutionary military bounty land warrant was awarded.[27]

Albright, Lee, and Helen F. M. Leary. "Strategy for Land Records." In Helen F. M. Leary, ed. *North Carolina Research: Genealogy and Local History*. 2nd ed. (Raleigh: North Carolina Genealogical Society, 1996), Chapter Two: "Designing Research Strategies," 42-48.

Anderson, John Huske. "John Huske Anderson Collection, 1820-1856." Manuscript, Call Number PC.279, State Archives of North Carolina, Raleigh. [Online catalog description: "Deeds, letters, bills of complaint, and other legal papers of Alfred M. Slade, Bertie and Martin counties, concerning lawsuits, the estate of Thomas Monk of Martin Co., and Revolutionary land grants to John Ludum and William Flury of Bertie and Chowan counties."]

Battle, Kemp P. "The Lords Proprietor of North Carolina." *North Carolina Booklet*, 4:4 (August 1904), 5-37; online: http://digital.ncdcr.gov/cdm/ref/collection/p249901coll37/id/14180. [Online description from "North Carolina Periodicals Index," East Carolina University: "This article discusses the Lords Proprietors who helped settle North Carolina. It covers the forfeiture of the land rights of Sir Walter Raleigh because of treason and regranted in 1606 all the way through the post-American Revolution Supreme Court decision that retracted the land claims of the heirs of the last Lords Proprietor, Earl Granville."]

Brown, W. Vance. "W. Vance Brown Papers." Manuscript, PC.121, State Archives of North Carolina, Raleigh. [Online catalog description: "Papers of four generations of the Brown family in Pennsylvania, western North Carolina, and New Zealand. Papers of John Brown (1772-1845), Pennsylvania congressman, land speculator, and agent in western North Carolina for William Cathcart, George and James Latimer, and other Pennsylvanians, and the North Carolina Land Company include diary of trip to Burke and Buncombe counties (1794-1795) and correspondence (1795-1841), notebooks, court records, and tax receipts concerning land. One earlier letter (1779) is from Joseph Reed, president of the Pennsylvania Executive Council, about the war in that state."]

Chaffin, Nora C. "The Colonial Land System in North Carolina, 1578-1754." M. A. thesis, Duke University, 1930.

Cooper, Jim. "Some of North Carolina's Granting of Land during the Revolutionary War." *North Carolina Genealogical Society Journal*, 22:4 (November 1996), 378-381.

Corbitt, D. L. "Ceding Our Western Claims to the United States." *North Carolina Historical Review,* 3:2 (April 1926), 372.

Corbitt. D. L. "The Landjobbers in the Western Territory." *North Carolina Historical Review,* 3:2 (April 1926), 373.

Corbitt, D. L. "What is a Liberal Cession of Western Territory?" *North Carolina Historical Review,* 3:2 (April 1926), 372.

Cowdrey, Albert E. *This Land, This South: An Environmental History*. Lexington: University Press of Kentucky, 1983.

---

[27] *Is That Service Right?* (Washington, D. C.: NSDAR, 2005), 44.

Hofmann, Julian G., and B. Ransom McBride. "Mapping." In Helen F. M. Leary, ed. *North Carolina Research: Genealogy and Local History*. 2nd ed. (Raleigh: North Carolina Genealogical Society, 1996), Chapter 7: "Mapping," 117-133.

Hofmann, Margaret M. "State Records: Land Grants." In Helen F. M. Leary, ed. *North Carolina Research: Genealogy and Local History*. 2nd ed. (Raleigh: North Carolina Genealogical Society, 1996), Chapter 31, 313-328.

Kirchner, Kevin Randall. "Twelve Days of Unity, Twenty Years of Division: The King's Mountain Volunteers in the Context of Land Speculation and Frontier Politics during the Revolutionary Era." Honors Paper, Duke University, Durham, 1998.

Lacy, Dan. "Records in the Offices of Registrars of Deeds in North Carolina." *North Carolina Historical Review*, 14:3 (July 1937), 213-229; online: http://digital.ncdcr.gov/cdm/ref/collection/p16062coll9/id/4207. [Online description from "North Carolina Periodicals Index," East Carolina University: "This article describes the contents of the archives of the office of register of deeds in North Carolina based on the detailed catalogues created by The Historical Records Survey, a Works Progress Administration project begun in North Carolina in 1936 and still underway at the time of press. The article provides a history of the office of register of deeds and highlights records or groups of records of interest."]

Laub, C. Herbert. "British Regulation of Crown Lands in the West: The Last Phase, 1775-1775." *William and Mary Quarterly*, 3rd series, 10:1 (January 1930), 52-55.

McNamara, Billie R. *Tennessee Land: Its Early History and Laws*. Knoxville, Tenn.: B. R. McNamara, 1996.

Moore, Terry. "Finding Your North Carolina Revolutionary War Soldier or Patriot, Part 4: NC Revolutionary War Bounty Land Grants." *NCGS News: The Newsletter of the North Carolina Genealogical Society*, 38:5 (September 2014), 10-11; online: http://www.ncgenealogy.org/articles_tools/Finding_Your_Rev_War_Soldier.pdf.

Moore, Terry. "Starting at a Post Oak: Genealogical Gems among the Rocks and Streams." *NCGS News: The Newsletter of the North Carolina Genealogical Society*, 37:4 (July 2013), 10-11; online: http://www.ncgenealogy.org/articles_tools/Starting_at_a_Post_Oak.pdf.

Moore, Terry. "This Land Was Their Land." *NCGS News: The Newsletter of the North Carolina Genealogical Society*, 38:1 (January 2014), 10-11.

Moore, Terry. "Who Owns the Land? A Brief History of North Carolina Land Grants." *NCGS News: The Newsletter of the North Carolina Genealogical Society*, 10-11; online: http://www.ncgenealogy.org/articles_tools/Who_Owns_the_Land.pdf. [The article notes two important dates in North Carolina that affected land records during the Revolution: "1776: Empty lands in the Granville District and other parts of North Carolina were taken over by the revolutionary North Carolina government," and, "1777-1959: North Carolina land offices were established in each county and the state of North Carolina issued land patents during this time period."]

Morgan, Lawrence N. "Land Tenure in Proprietary North Carolina." *James Sprunt Historial Publications,* 12:1 (Chapel Hill: The University, 1912), 43-63.

"North Carolina Land and Property." FamilySearch Wiki: https://familysearch.org/wiki/en/North_Carolina_Land_and_Property.

North Carolina (State). General Assembly. "[Document dated:] Aprill [*sic*] 18, 1778: Petition of the Inhabitants of Mecklenburg Co., 1778." Manuscript; General Assembly Record Group; Session Records, April-May 1778; Joint Papers, Committee Papers, Resolutions, Senate Bills, House Bills, Box 1 (MARS ID: 66.8.12.11.3; item), State Archives of North Carolina, Raleigh. [Online catalog description: "Petition in which the inhabitants of Mecklenburg Co. express concern over an act which provides officers and soldiers with grants of land in return for military service. The petitioners fear that the act provides insufficient protection against greed and speculation."]

North Carolina (State). General Assembly. "[Document dated:] May 2, 1780: Resolution Requesting Governor to Require Persons Settled in Indian Lands to Move Off (Message Only)." Manuscript; General Assembly Session Records; Session of April-May 1780; Joint Papers, Committee Papers, Resolutions; House Joint Resolutions: May 2-10, 1780, Box 1 (MARS ID: 66.8.20.17.1; item), State Archives of North Carolina, Raleigh.

North Carolina (State). General Assembly. "[Document dated:] April 29, 1784: Report on Petition of Robert Rowan and Others (Rejected)." Manuscript; General Assembly Record Group; Session Records, April-June 1784; Joint Papers, Committee Papers, Resolutions, Senate Bills, House Bills, Box 2 (MARS ID: 66.8.32.1.6; item), State Archives of North Carolina, Raleigh. [Online catalog description: "Memorials are all from officers or heirs of officers who served with the late Col. Hugh Waddell in the provincial army and were promised land for their service from George the Third by proclamation. Memorialists hope to claim this land which is now vested in the state of North Carolina. Committee awards land to officers who served, but asks the consideration of the House in regards to the memorials of the heirs."]

North Carolina (State). General Assembly. "[Document dated:] November 16, 1784: Resolution Permitting Dr. John Fergus to Enter Vacant Land in the District of Wilmington (Petition Only)." Manuscript; General Assembly Record Group; Session Records, October-November 1784; Joint Papers, Committee Papers, Resolutions, Senate Bills, House Bills, Box 1 (MARS ID: 66.8.35.14.10; item), State Archives of North Carolina, Raleigh. [Online catalog description: "Petition asks for grant of land in the District of Wilmington as compensation for services as surgeon in the war."]

North Carolina (State). General Assembly. "[Document dated:] Dec. 26, [1785]: Resolution in Favor of Colonel Hardy Murfree Respecting Certain Lands (Petition Only)." Manuscript; General Assembly Record Group; Session Records, November-December 1785; Joint Papers, Committee Papers, Resolutions, Senate Bills, House Bills, Box 2 (MARS ID: 66.8.38.6.18; item), State Archives of North Carolina, Raleigh. [Online catalog description: "Resolution regards the memorial of Colonel Hardy Murfree concerning the land set aside for those who fought with the Continental Line. After surveying the land alloted him, he discovered there were two claims already within the boundaries of his land. He seeks the ability to claim another parcel of land."]

North Carolina (State). General Assembly. "[Document dated:] 1795: A Bill to Authorize the Secretary to Issue Grants for Military Lands, in the Manner Therein Described; and to Direct the Secretary and Comptroller to Issue Warrants in Certain Cases Therein Mentioned." Manuscript; General Assembly Record Group; Session Records, November-December 1795; Joint Papers, Committee Papers, Resolutions, Senate Bills, House Bills, Box 2 (MARS ID: 66.8.78.14.1; item), State Archives of North Carolina, Raleigh.

North Carolina (State). General Assembly. "[Document dated:] 1794-1795: A Bill to Confirm the Titles of Certain Persons Who Entered and Obtained Grants for Land after the Land Office Was Shut in 1781 and before it was Opened in 1783. (Rejected)." Manuscript; General Assembly Record Group; Session Records, December 1974-February 1795; Joint Papers, Committee Papers, Resolutions, Senate Bills, House Bills, Box 1 (MARS ID: 66.8.73.34.1; item), State Archives of North Carolina, Raleigh.

North Carolina (Colony and State). Office of State Treasurer. "Indian Affairs and Lands, 1712, 1739-1957)." Manuscript Box 1-Box 17 (MARS ID: 13.21; series), State Archives of North Carolina, Raleigh. [Online catalog description: "An artificial and diverse collection of accounts, certificates, warrants, survey plats, reports, receipt books, depositions, court papers, deeds, and correspondence relating to the Cherokee and Tuscarora Indians, 1739-1900, 1911, 1923, 1956-1957. For the former, most of the records are of the antebellum period and concern lands sold and leased by the state and by the Cherokee, and also the 'life reservations' created for them by the state. Public claims and payrolls (1759-1760, 1771, 1791) concern expeditions against the Cherokee. Other records concern treaties, and the furnishing of provisions and supplies. Miscellaneous items include copies of Col. George Washington's orders for escorting Cherokees from Virginia to the Nation; a typed copy of a journal of a visit to the Cherokee by Thomas Griffin, 1767; an 1846 history of the *Cherokee in North Carolina since 1809*; a census of the Eastern Cherokee in 1923; and photographs of the Qualla Reservation. Records relating to the Tuscarora mainly concern leases and sales of land in Bertie County. Most of them date from the antebellum period, but there is also a Tuscarora petition (1956-1957) before the Indian Claims Commission for rights to lands in North Carolina. There is also a copy of a treaty of 1712. Other material concerns the service of Tuscaroras in the French and Indian War, and supplies furnished them by the state."]

North Carolina (State). Office of State Treasurer. "Lands, Estates, Boundaries, and Surveys." Manuscript Box 1-Box 25; State Treasurer Record Group (MARS ID: 13.25; series), State Archives of North Carolina, Raleigh. [Online catalog description: "Records of the treasurer and the comptroller relating to various land matters. Material on confiscated lands includes surveys of property formerly owned by Loyalists, including Henry Eustace McCulloh and Arthur Dobbs; bonds for commissioners of confiscated property; and requests for payment by surveyors. Miscellaneous land papers include records relating to the Glasgow Land Frauds, including caveats from Washington and Sullivan counties (1782-1784) and papers relating to prosecution of the land fraud case. Also entries and warrants for the Western Lands (1784-1793); records of state land sold, including plots in Raleigh (1795-1891); land entry receipts (1795-1859) and settlements of estates with no counties given; and fiscal records relating to the running of various state boundary lines (1767-1815)."]

North Carolina (State). Office of State Treasurer. "Military Papers – Board of Adjudicators of Revolutionary War Bounty Land Warrants, 1821-1824." Manuscript, Office of State Treasurer Record Group, Box 66.3 (MARS ID: 13.31; series), State Archives of North Carolina, Raleigh. [Online catalog description: "Copies of a list of Continental Line soldiers whose bounty land rights had not been claimed as of 1821. List was apparently created either by the Board of Adjudicators, which was appointed in 1819 and was composed of the governor, treasurer, and comptroller, or by the agent of the Board of Trustees of the University of North Carolina, who was instructed to identify unclaimed bounty lands that would escheat to the university. One of the two copies contains additions noting acreage and warrant numbers, issued in 1824."]

"North Carolina Land Grants: http://www.nclandgrants.com." *NCGS News: The Newsletter of the North Carolina Genealogical Society*, 11.

"North Carolina and Tennessee Revolutionary War Land Warrants, 1783-1843." Searchable online database: http://search.ancestry.com/search/db.aspx?dbid=2885. [The site is also browsable and includes the introductory material from the original microfilm publication from the Tennessee State Archives, Nashville.]

Parker, Brett F. "A Landed Elysium? "Proprietors, Planters, and the Law of Real Property in Carolina." M. A. thesis, Middle Tennessee State University, Murfreesboro, 1999.

Pomeroy, Kenneth B. and James G. Yoho. *North Carolina Lands: Ownership, Use, and Management of Forest and Related Lands*. Washington: American Forestry Association [distributed by the Livingston Publishing Company, Narberth, PA.], 1964.

Pruitt, Albert Bruce. *Abstracts of Henry E. McCulloh's Survey Book and Petition to the Crown and Warrants (Money) Issued in 1787 by Gov. Richard Caswell.* Whitakers: A. B. Pruitt, 1992. [Henry Eutace McCulloh (?-ca. 1810)]

Rodman, Lida T. "Lida T. Rodman Collection, 1776-83." Manuscript, (presumably) at State Archive of North Carolina, Raleigh. ["Photostats of letters and documents relating to the American Revolution. There are two copies of an agreement with British merchants of Savannah, Ga. Signed by General Wayne, a list of the North Carolina officers entitled to bounty of lands by act of Congress, 1776, and several letters from outstanding persons. Among the correspondents are William Blount, Richard Caswell, Samuel Johnston, and William Savage."[28]]

"The Secretary of Loyalist Descendants Seeks Information on NC's 'Truce Lands' during the Revolutionary War." *North Carolina Genealogical and Historical News*, 4:1 (January-February 1988), 6-8. [Discusses this area mostly in South Carolina to the northeast of the Pee Dee River and supposedly crossing over into portions of North Carolina's modern Robeson and Columbus Counties. It includes a map of the region where Loyalists led by "Colonel David Fanning attempted to have the Cumberland County area of North Carolina 'neutralized' into a truce area during 1781 and 1782. Strong opposition, however, prevented the realization of this attempt'." While there is more information on the "Truce Lands," the term coming from a truce agreement between General Francis Marion and Loyalist Colonel Micajah Ganey/Gainey, there is not a lot on this general subject in print.]

Sellers, Charles G., Jr. "Private Profits and British Colonial Policy: The Speculations of Henry McCulloh." *William and Mary Quarterly*, 8:4 (October 1951), 535-551. [Henry McCulloh was a land speculator in North Carolina who had ties to both the Tory and Patriot causes during the Revolutionary War.]

Sioussat, St. George L. "Breakdown of the Royal Management of Land in the Southern Provinces, 1773-1775." *Agricultural History*, 3:2 (April 1929), 67-98.

Smathers, George H. *The History of Land Titles in Western North Carolina. A History of the Cherokee Land Laws Affecting the Title to Land Lying West of the Meigs and Freemand Line, and Laws Affecting the Title of Land Lying East of the Meigs and Freeman Line Back to the Top of the Blue Ridge, Including all the Land on the Waters of the French Broad River in What Was Formerly Buncombe County as Created by the Act of 1792.* Asheville: Miller Printing Company, 1938.

Swann, Lee Ann Caldwell. "Land of Their Own: Land Grants to Women in the Lower Colonial South." Ph. D. dissertation, University of Georgia, 1986. [North Carolina, South Carolina, Georgia]

"Tennessee Land and Property." FamilySearch Wiki: https://familysearch.org/wiki/en/Tennessee_Land_and_Property.

Winn, John, d. 1844; and Philip James Winn. "John Winn and Philip James Winn Papers, 1780-1889, 1925." Manuscript 5839, David M. Rubenstein Rare Book & Manuscript Library, Duke, Durham. [Online catalog description shows that this collection contains materials of John Winn relating to legal cases relating to Revolutionary bounty land; …"]

Winslow, Raymond S., Jr. "County Records: Land Records." In Helen F. M. Leary, ed. *North Carolina Research: Genealogy and Local History.* 2nd ed. (Raleigh: North Carolina Genealogical Society, 1996), Chapter 13, 209-230.

[28] North Carolina Historical Records Survey Project. *Guide to the Manuscript Collections in the Archives of the North Carolina Historical Commission* (Raleigh: North Carolina Historical Commission, 1942), 118.

The Granville District and the Revolution

Connor, Henry G. "The Granville Estate and North Carolina." *University of Pennsylvania Law Review*, 62:9 (October 1, 1914), 671-697.

Dunaway, Stewart E. *Lord John Carteret, Earl Granville and the Granville Grants in N. C.: A History.* Hillsborough: North Carolina Historical Books, 2013.

Hofmann, Margaret M. *The Granville District of North Carolina: Abstracts of Land Grants.* 5 vols. Ahoskie: M. M. Hofmann, 1986-1995. [Contents: v. 1. Anson, Beaufort, Bertie, Bladen, Chowan, Cumberland, Currituck, Dobbs, Edgecombe Cos.; v. 2. Granville, Halifax, Hyde, Johnston, Northampton, Orange, Tyrrell Cos.; v. 3. Pasquotank, Perquimans, Pitt and Rowan Cos.; v. 4. Abstracts of miscellaneous land office records: Anson, Beaufort, Bertie, Bladen, Bute, Chowan, Cumberland, Currituck, Dobbs, Edgecombe, Granville Cos.; v. 5. Abstracts of miscellaneous land office records: Halifax, Hertford, Hyde, Johnston, Northampton, Orange, Pasquotank, Perquimans, Pitt, Tyrrell, and Rowan Cos.]

Lefler, Hugh Talmadge. "The Biggest Piece of Rental Property in Carolina's History." The State: A Weekly Survey of North Carolina, 21:31 (January 1954), 1-2, 12; online: http://digital.ncdcr.gov/cdm/ref/collection/p16062coll18/id/31422; 21:32 (January 1954), 4, 19; online: http://digital.ncdcr.gov/cdm/ref/collection/p16062coll18/id/31447. [Online description from "North Carolina Periodicals Index," East Carolina University: "Some two million North Carolinians now live on land which was once the property of an English nobleman, John Lord Carteret, the first Earl of Granville - the largest individual landholder in North Carolina history."]

Mitchell, Thornton W. "Granville Grant and District." Online: http://ncpedia.org/granville-grant-and-district.

Mitchell, Thornton W. "The Granville District and Its Land Records." *North Carolina Historical Review*, 70:2 (April 1993), 103-129. [Online description from "North Carolina Periodicals Index," East Carolina University: "A look at the establishment in 1742 of the Granville District, an area of North Carolina that was created from the consolidation of Lord John Carteret's (later Earl Granville) land claims totaling to 1/8th of the royal Carolina grant. Information on the establishment of the Granville District just south of the Virginia-North Carolina border, on its administration by various land agents, its settlement, its eventual confiscation by the state of North Carolina during the American Revolution, and the heirs' attempts to recover it are included."]

Moore, Terry. "Who Owns the Land? A Brief History of North Carolina Land Grants." *NCGS News: The Newsletter of the North Carolina Genealogical Society*, 10-11; online: http://www.ncgenealogy.org/articles_tools/Who_Owns_the_Land.pdf. [The article notes two important dates in North Carolina that affected land records during the Revolution: "1776: Empty lands in the Granville District and other parts of North Carolina were taken over by the revolutionary North Carolina government," and, "1777-1959: North Carolina land offices were established in each county and the state of North Carolina issued land patents during this time period."]

North Carolina (State). Secretary of State. Land Office. "Lord Granville's Land Office: Office Administrative Papers, 1746-1778." Manuscript SS 1091, SS 1091.1-SS 1091.3 (MARS ID: 12.65; series), State Archives of North Carolina, Raleigh (Online catalog description: "Memoranda and instructions to agents, officers, surveyors, and others; lists of surveys returned; books and lists of entries (1750-1763) sent in by subagents and recorded in the office; quit rent lists (1750-1758, 1761) giving landowners and acreage; and an inventory of the office papers, ordered in 1778 by the General Assembly (listing entries and warrants only, not the 'grants')."]

North Carolina Oath of Allegiance, 1778, Granville District. Signal Mountain, Tenn.: Mountain Press, 2007.

Watt, W. N. *The Granville District.* [S. l.]: W. N. Watt, 1992.

North Carolina Land Entries, 1778-1783, and Oaths of Allegiance

The North Carolina Colonial Land Office closed in 1775, and the state did not reopen its own office until early 1778. The State Archives of North Carolina maintains the records of both offices. Of particular interest for Revolutionary War research and for an ancestor's patriotic service for a descendant's application for membership in the National Society Daughters of the American Revolution (and perhaps other Revolutionary-War based lineage societies) are the Land Entry records from the State Land Office. A search of the MARS online catalog of the State Archives will reveal the many records for land entries that exist. Consultation with the staff of the Archives can help a researcher obtain the information they desire. [Note: Search the catalog using the terms "entry" and "entries" to obtain all possible references.]

The National Society Daughters of the American Revolution accepts an individual's application for a North Carolina land entry between certain dates as proof of patriotic service because in order to qualify for an entry one had to swear and oath of Allegiance to the state. This is based on the following:

As a designation of patriotic service is given to any person who entered a land claim for a land grant between 1 January 1778 and 26 November 1783 (the date of the law and the lastest date accepted by NSDAR for any service). The law states (*State Records of North Carolina*, vol. 24, p. 44) "That every person … before he shall enter a claim for any of the lands aforesaid, shall take and subscribe the Oath or Affirmation of Allegiance and Abjuration prescribed by the law of this state."[29]

Published abstracts exist for most of the counties [Note: Counties not listed below either did not have records from the period 1778-1783 or they had not yet been formed.]:

Griffey, Irene M. *Earliest Tennessee Land Records & Earliest Tennessee Land History*. Baltimore: Clearfield, 2000. [Includes records of men who took the oath of allegiance in order to make a land entry in a specific county.]

North Carolina (State). Secretary of State. Land Office. "Land Entries (Original) Papers, 1778-1905, n. d." Manuscript SS 435-SS 435.1, State Archives of North Carolina, Raleigh. [Online catalog description: "Miscellaneous land entry papers."]

North Carolina (State). Secretary of State. Land Office. "Transcriptions of County Land Entry Books, 1778-1795." Manuscript (70 vols) SS 948.1-SS 968.4 (MARS ID: 12.67; series), State Archives of North Carolina, Raleigh. [Online catalog description: "Transcriptions of county land entry books, forwarded to the secretary of state pursuant to an act of 1795 (c. 17)."]

Pruitt, Albert Bruce. *Abstracts of Land Entrys: Anson Co., NC, 1778-1795*. Whitakers: A. B. Pruitt, 1987.

Pruitt, Albert Bruce. *Abstracts of Land Entries: Bertie Co., NC, 1778-1794; Martin Co., NC, 1778-1795*. Whitakers: A. B. Pruitt, 1992.

Pruitt, Albert Bruce. *Abstracts of Land Entries: Bladen Co., 1778-1781*. Whitakers: A. B. Pruitt, 1989.

Pruitt, Albert Bruce. *Abstracts of Land Entries: Bute Co., NC, 1778-1779; Franklin Co., NC, 1779-1781; Warren Co., NC, 1779-1791*. Whitakers: A. B. Pruitt, 1992.

Pruitt, Albert Bruce. *Abstracts of Land Entries: Carteret Co., NC, 1778-1803*. Whitakers: A. B. Pruitt, 1990.

Pruitt, Albert Bruce. *Abstracts of Land Entries: Caswell Co., NC, 1778-1795, 1841-1863; and Person Co., NC, 1792-1795*. Whitakers: A. B. Pruitt, 1990.

Pruitt, Albert Bruce. *Abstracts of Land Entries: Chatham Co., NC, 1778-1790*. Whitakers: A. B. Pruitt, 1990.

Pruitt, Albert Bruce. *Abstracts of Land Entries: Craven Co., NC, 1778-1796*. Whitakers: A. B. Pruitt, 1991.

Pruitt, Albert Bruce. *Abstracts of Land Entrys: Cumberland Co., NC, 1778-1795*. Whitakers: A. B. Pruitt, 1988.

Pruitt, Albert Bruce. *Abstracts of Land Entries: Duplin Co., NC, 1778-1795; Sampson Co., NC, 1784-1795 and 1853-1860*. Whitakers: A. B. Pruitt, 1990.

Pruitt, Albert Bruce. *Abstracts of Land Entries: Edgecombe Co., NC, 1783-1795; Nash Co., NC, 1778-1794; Halifax Co., NC, 1778-1795; Northampton Co., NC, 1778-1794*. Whitakers: A. B. Pruitt, 1992.

Pruitt, Albert Bruce. *Abstracts of Land Entries: Gates Co., NC, 1779-1794, Chowan Co., NC, 1787-1795; Perquimans Co., NC, 1778-1795; Pasquotank Co., NC, 1778-1795; Camden Co., NC, 1778-1795; Currituck Co., NC, 1778-1795*. Whitakers: A. B. Pruitt, 1992.

Pruitt, Albert Bruce. *Abstracts of Land Entries: Granville Co., NC, 1778-1790*. Whitakers: A. B. Pruitt, 1988.

Pruitt, Albert Bruce. *Abstracts of Land Entrys: Guilford Co., NC, 1778-1796, and Rockingham Co., NC, 1790-1795*. Whitakers: A. B. Pruitt, 1987.

Pruitt, Albert Bruce. *Abstracts of Land Entries: Hyde Co., 1778-1795*. Whitakers: A. B. Pruitt, 1991.

Pruitt, Albert Bruce. *Abstracts of Land Entries: Lincoln Co., NC, 1778-1780*. Whitakers: A. B. Pruitt, 1987.

Pruitt, Albert Bruce. *Abstracts of Land Entries: Lincoln Co., NC, 1780 & 1795-1796*. Whitakers: A. B. Pruitt, 1987.

Pruitt, Albert Bruce. *Abstracts of Land Entries: Lincoln Co., NC, 1778-1780*. Whitakers: A. B. Pruitt, 1987.

Pruitt, Albert Bruce. *Abstracts of Land Entries: Mecklenburg Co., NC, 1778-1795*. Whitakers: A. B. Pruitt, 1988.

Pruitt, Albert Bruce. *Abstracts of Land Entries: Montgomery Co., NC, 1778-1795*. Whitakers: A. B. Pruitt, 1988.

Pruitt, Albert Bruce. *Abstracts of Land Entries: New Hanover Co., NC, 1778-1796*. Whitakers: A. B. Pruitt, 1990.

Pruitt, Albert Bruce. *Abstracts of Land Entries: Onslow Co., NC, 1778-1796; Jones Co., NC, 1795-1797*. Whitakers: A. B. Pruitt, 1990.

Pruitt, Albert Bruce. *Abstracts of Land Entries: Orange Co., NC, 1778-1795*. Whitakers: A. B. Pruitt, 1990.

Pruitt, Albert Bruce. *Abstracts of Land Entries: Pitt Co., NC, 1778-1797*. Whitakers: A. B. Pruitt, 1991.

Grigg, Barbara N., Carolyn N. Hager, & A. B. Pruitt. *Randolph County, NC, Land Entries, 1779, 1780 & 1783-1801*. [S. l.]: The Compilers, 1994.

Pruitt, Albert Bruce. *Abstracts of Land Entries: Richmond Co., NC, 1780-1795*. Whitakers: A. B. Pruitt, 1987.

---

[29] *Is That Service Right?* (Washington, D. C.: NSDAR, 2005), 43-44.

Pruitt, Albert Bruce. *Abstracts of Land Entrys: Rowan Co., NC, 1778-1795.* Whitakers: A. B. Pruitt, 1987.
Pruitt, Albert Bruce. *Abstracts of Land Entries: Rutherford Co., NC, 1779-1795.* Whitakers: A. B. Pruitt, 1987.
Pruitt, Albert Bruce. *Abstracts of Land Entries: Tryon & Lincoln Co., NC, 1778-1780.* Whitakers: A. B. Pruitt, 1987.
Pruitt, Albert Bruce. *Abstracts of Land Entries: Tyrrell Co., NC, 1778-1794.* Whitakers: A. B. Pruitt, 1991.
Pruitt, Albert Bruce. *Abstracts of Land Entries: Wilkes Co., NC, 1783-1795.* Whitakers: A. B. Pruitt, 1989.
Pruitt, Albert Bruce. *North Carolina Land Warrants in Tennessee, Valid and Invalid.* Whitakers: A. B. Pruitt, 2004. [Includes listings for men who would have had to take the oath of allegiance in order to quality for making a land entry in a specific county.]
Pruitt, Albert Bruce. *Tennessee Land Entries: Washington County, 1778-1796.* Whitakers: A. B. Pruitt, 1997.
Wells, Agnes M.; Virginia G. Phillips, and Carol J. Leonard. *Joseph Winston: His Entry Book Surry County, North Carolina Land Entries 1778-1781.* Mount Airy: A. M. Wells, 1987.

The following multi-county indexes have been published to accompany the above titles:

Pruitt, Albert Bruce. *Index to Land Entries: Beaufort County, NC, 1778-1795; Johnston Co., NC, 1778-1805; Wake Co., NC, 1778-1846; and Land Warrants: Johnston Co., NC, 1737-1763.* Durham: W. P. Haun, 1980, 1983, 1993.

North Carolina Land Grants in Tennessee

North Carolina Land Grants in Tennessee[30]

Important Dates

North Carolina initially opened land offices to sell vacant land because of the need to raise funds for Revolutionary War Expenses.

1777. North Carolina General Assembly passed land office legislation. Land could be sold to any citizen or person willing to become a citizen of the state of North Carolina, which was indicated when the person took an oath of Allegiance to the State of North Carolina. The land office entry taker administered the Oath of Allegiance. Men serving in the military of North Carolina or the United States were exempt from taking the oath when entering land grants.
1777. Washington County, North Carolina, comprising the entire modern state of Tennessee, was created, to facilitate disposal of North Carolina frontier land. Sullivan County was created in 1779 from Washington.
1780. North Carolina General Assembly passes legislation to encourage enlistment in the Continental Line.
1782. The Assembly passes other legislation to correct problems resulting from the 1780 legislation.
1783. Soldiers were required to apply for warrants from the Secretary of State. Military bound land was located in north central Tennessee near modern Nashville.
1784. North Carolina determines that if there is not sufficient tillable land within the boundaries of the land set aside for the officers and soldiers of the Continental Line, the deficiency will be made up by an unappropriated lands within the state. This requirement is included in the agreement of transfer of the land from North Carolina to the United States, and again from the United States when the State of Tennessee was created.
1784. Person who served and lived in, or served and died in Davidson Co, North Carolina (Tennessee), were awarded land.
1784. North Carolina entry takers were instructed to keep a book of entries.

Types of Grants.

Once the warrant had been received, the process of obtaining possession of the land was similar for all persons.

- Purchase Grants.

[30] This section (down to the bibliographic entries) is the work of Penelope L. Secord, Staff Genealogist, Office of the Registrar General, National Society Daughters of the American Revolution, Washington, D. C. It has been used with her consent.

- Pre-emption Grants. (made to persons who were living on the land before it was legally available for settlement).
- Commissioners Grants. These grants were given to persons sent to middle Tennessee by theNorth Carolina legislature to determine the boundaries for the military reservations. Commissioners and their assistants were given land grants within the military reservation.
- Legislative Grants. Given by the General Assembly to specific persons because of their service
- Service Grants, or Service Rights, for surveyors, markers, guards and hunters. Service Grants are not for military service during the Revolutionary War, and are not accepted as Revolutionary War service.
- Military. North Carolina provided military land grants to soldiers of the Continental Line only, and required a minimum of 2 years service. The amount of land granted depended upon soldier's rank, and was located in theNorth Carolina Military Reservation, located in north, central Tennessee.

Procedure for Obtaining Land

- Warrant. A warrant, which specified why a person was entitled to obtain land, and how much land could be obtained, was obtained from whatever office had been designated to certify the person was eligible to obtain land.

In North Carolina, a soldier applied to the Secretary of State, who verified the soldier's service, and then provided the soldier with a warrant stating the amount of land the soldier could receive. The warrant was delivered to the surveyor of the Military Reservation, Martin Armstrong. Initially, it was not necessary to record the warrants in a book, because the courts ruled that the title was vested in the applicant from the date the endorsement of the location was made on the warrant of the survey.

- Location (the term referring to the step prior to entering the grant). A person desiring land either had to go himself or send an agent to make a preliminary description of the desired land. These land locations were not entered in the book in chronological order. After the description of the land had been recorded, the land was surveyed. (In Public Land States, surveying the land was the first task completed).
- Entry. The earliest date the grant was intended to be obtained. The soldier or his agent had already visited the property, and provided a written description of the land. The entry taker entered the information in the book, and endorsed the back of the paper of the written description with the name of the claimant, the estimated number of acres in the desired tract of land, and the date and time the entry taker received the written description. Entries also included the number of the warrant.

  Frequently a person made an entry for land previously entered by another person. He was not required to obtain a new warrant because the warrant certified that he was eligible to make a land entry. He could choose another location, which is indicated by the term "removed to another location.

  Entries could be purchased and sold, meaning that the claimant may or may not have performed the service. The grant will list the person entitled to the grant and the assignee. The county record will be under the name of the last recipient of the grant, who may not have performed the military service.

- Survey. This is the legal description of the natural boundaries of the land. Surveyors were government employees whose services were paid for by the person requesting the survey...the person who had entered the land. The Surveyors paid the markers, hunters and guards, which was usually part of the land being surveyed. Surveys were to be performed in the order the entries had been made.

Grants were valid whether or not a survey had been completed. However, title to the property could not be conveyed to the person entering the grant unless the survey had been returned to the office of the Secretary.

- Platt. A scale drawing of the land. Each surveyor was required to make two copies. One copy was returned to the Secretary's office; the second was attached to the grant when it was issued.

- Grant. The certificate that passed title from the government to the person. The secretary of state prepared all grants which were given to the governor for his signature. Once signed by the governor, title for the property passed from the state to the person applying for the land.

Cautions

1. See: Irene M Griffey, *Earliest Tennessee Land Records & Earliest Tennessee Land History,* pg. 72, regarding the column Assignee in her book. "The assignee in some instances was the person from whom the grant was obtained. In other instances it was the person to whom the grant was assigned. Spreadsheet space did not permit distinguishing between the two."
2. Early land grants were provided to persons living on the land before the government had opened the land to settlement.
3. Early land grants were also provided to surveyors, markers (chain carriers, who took an oath "the truth to tell"), hunters and guards who assisted the surveyors. Law determined the amount of land awarded for each category.
4. Early grants were given to the commissioners and their assistants, who were sent to Middle Tennessee to determine the boundaries of the Military Reserve.
5. Military grants were given to members of Evans Battalion, a military unit formed to protect Davidson County settlers from American Indians, but this is not Revolutionary War Service. Their term of service was two years. They received one portion of land for one year of service, and a second portion for the second year of service.
6. North Carolina militia members did not receive Military Bounty Land. They may have applied for warrants for land under a category other than military service.
7. Records for these Tennessee land grants were recorded in North Carolina after Tennessee became a state.

Conclusion

Because many persons received Tennessee land grants for reasons other than military service, caution needs to be used when using the various indexes of early Tennessee land grants. Tennessee county deeds may include the reason the first person holding title to the property received the property. Obtaining title to property included many legal considerations not discussed here. Frequently, there was confusion over who had claim to the land, and many cases were settled in the courts over a period of years. The court cases may provide a good history of who obtained the land and how title to the land was passed from one individual to another.

Discussion of North Carolina military land grants is found in Griffey's *Earliest Tennessee Land Records & Earliest Tennessee Land History*, and in A. B. Prutt's *Tennessee Land Entries, Military Bounty Land, Martin Armstrong's Office, Part 1, Location Book (#3138-4839).* Pruitt's book provides details about each North Carolina legislature act concerning military land and is an excellent resource for determining the location of various North Carolina military land records.

Armstrong, Martin. "Martin Armstrong Paper, 1782." Manuscript, PC.288, State Archives of North Carolina, Raleigh. [Online catalog description: "Letter from Armstrong of Surry Co. to the commissioners of western lands, declining appointment as commissary for the expedition to lay off Cumberland lands for Continental Line officers and soldiers. Recommends a substitute."]

Battey, George M[agruder]. "The 'Tennessee Bee-Hive;' or Early (1778-1791) North Carolina Land Grants in the Volunteer State, Being an Index with Some 3100 Names of Revolutionary Soldiers and Settlers Who Participated in the Distribution of More than 5,000,000 Acres of Land." Typescript (Washington, D. C.: G. M. Battey, 1949). ["Accompanied by an excellent 1837 map drawn by cartographer S. Augustus Mitchell, of Philadelphia." A copy is owned by the Library of Congress, Washington, D. C. The classification number is E225.B27.]

Bramlet, Albert Lincoln. "North Carolina's Western Lands." Ph. D. dissertation, University of North Carolina, 1928.

Burgner, Goldene Filler. *North Carolina Land Grants in Tennessee, 1778-1791*. Easley, S. C.: Southern Historical Press, 1981. [revision of the book with the same title by Cartwright and Gardiner below.]

Cartwright, Betty Goff, and Lillian Johnson Gardiner. *North Carolina Land Grants in Tennessee, 1778-1791.* Easley, S.C.: Southern Historical Press, 1981; revised by Goldene Filler Burgner and published as noted above.

"Early North Carolina/Tennessee Land Grants at the Tennessee State Library and Archives." Online: http://sos.tn.gov/products/tsla/early-north-carolina-tennessee-land-grants-tennessee-state-library-and-archives.

Griffey, Irene M. *Earliest Tennessee Land Records & Earliest Tennessee Land History*. Baltimore: Clearfield, 2000. [Includes records of men who took the oath of allegiance in order to make a land entry in a specific county.]

Griffey, Irene M. The Preemptors: Middle Tennessee's First Settlers. Clarksville, TN: The Compiler, 1989.

Haywood, John, ed. A Revisal of All the Public Acts Of The State Of North-Carolina and of the State of Tennessee, Now in Force in the State of Tennessee [Issued With]: The Laws of North Carolina and Tennessee, Respecting Vacant Lands and Deeds, Which Are No Longer in Force, But Necessary to the Investigation of Land Titles in Tennessee. *Nashville: Thomas G. Bradford, 1810.*

Hollis, Shirley Ann. *The Hidden Revolutionary War Land Grants in the Tennessee Military Reservation*. Lawrenceburg, Tenn: Family Tree Press, 1992.

Jansen, Daniel. "A Case of Fraud and Deception: The Revolutionary War Military Land Bounty Policy in Tennessee." *Journal of the East Tennessee Historical Society*, 64 (1992), 41-67.

Jones, Thomas B. "The Public Lands of Tennessee." *Tennessee Historical Quarterly*, 27:1 (Spring 1968), 13-36.

Kammerer, Roger. "Revolutionary War Land Warrants in Tennessee." *Pitt County Genealogical Quarterly*, 22:2 (May 2015), 1-5. ["abstracts of Tennessee Revolutionary War Land Warrants, compiled by Edythe Rucker Whitley in pamphlets in the 1930's found in the Tennessee State Archives, Nashville, TN."]

The Land Laws of Tennessee, Being a Compilation of the Various Statutes of North Carolina, the United States, and Tennessee, Relative to Titles to Lands within the State of Tennessee. Chattanooga: J. M. Deardorff & Sons, Printers, 1891.

"List of Soldiers." ID # 37946, Early Tennessee Land Records – Revolutionary War Land Grants to University of N. C., Tennessee State Library & Archives, Nashville; digital surrogate available through the Revolutionary War Collection, Tennessee Virtual Archive at http://cdm15138.contentdm.oclc.org/cdm/compoundobject/collection/p15138coll16/id/145/rec/47. [Description on TeVA: "List of {North Carolina} soldiers who died in service United States without issue or heir, their land escheated to the University of North Carolina… If a North Carolina war veteran died without heirs, his state land grant property reverted (escheated) to the University of North Carolina. (Tennessee was then a part of North Carolina.) These escheats made the University of North Carolina one of the most heavily-endowed colleges in the country."]

Matlock, J. W. L. "John Cotten: Reluctant Pioneer." *Tennessee Historical Magazine*, 27:3 (Fall 1968), 277-286.

McGill, John T. "Andrew Greer." *Tennessee Historical Magazine*, 2:3 (September 1916), 204-207. [Andrew Greer was one of the first settlers in what is now Tennessee. This article gives a brief description of his life, and mentions his time as a magistrate in Tennessee.]

McNamara, Billie R. "An Introduction to the History of Tennessee's Confusing Land Laws." *Tennessee Ancestors: A Tri-Annual Publication of the East Tennessee Historical Society*, 12:1 (April 1996), 11-24. [Covers legislation put in place by North Carolina during the Revolution and after].

Murphey, Archibald D; William Henry Hoyt, ed. *The Papers of Archibald D. Murphey*. Raleigh: E. M. Uzzell & Co., State Printers, 1914. [Contents: v. 1. William A. Graham. Chronological List of the Murphey Papers Here Printed. Memoir of Murphey; Correspondence 1801-1832; v. 2. *Public Papers. Historical, Biographical, and Literary Papers. Papers on the North Carolina-Tennessee Land Controversy. Petition of Rev. John Debow to the General Assembly, 1777*. Appendix. Also: *General Joseph Graham's Narrative of the Revolutionary War in North Carolina, in 1780 and 1781*, 443-444.]

"North Carolina Judicial Papers, 1798-1800." Manuscript 391-z, Louis Round Wilson Special Collections Library, University of North Carolina, Chapel Hill. [Online catalog description: "The collection contains papers, mostly June 1800, related to a court called by the legislature to investigate frauds in connection with land grants to Revolutionary War veterans."]

"North Carolina Land Grants in East Tennessee: John Carter and the Carter Family." *East Tennessee Roots*, 9:1 (May 2001), 1-3; "North Carolina Land Grants in East Tennessee Part 2: North Carolina's Frontier Settlements. The Land Act of 1777 and the Land Act of 1783." *East Tennessee Roots*, 9:2 (Spring 2003), 87-129; "North Carolina Land Grants in East Tennessee Part 3: Washington County Entries Continue..." *East Tennessee Roots*, 9:3 (Fall 2003), 189-215.

"North Carolina Military Bounty Land Acreage in Tennessee." *Olde Mecklenburg Genealogical Society Quarterly*, 26:1 (January-March 2008), 6.

"North Carolina Revolutionary Warrants." Undated flyer from the Tennessee State Library and Archives, Nashville.

North Carolina (State). General Assembly. "[Document dated:] May 6, [1782]: Joint Papers, Committee Papers, Resolutions, Senate Bills, House Bills, Report on Memorial of the Officers of the N. C. Line (With Messages)." Manuscript; General Assembly Record Group; Session Records, April-May 1782, Box 1 (MARS ID:

66.8.27.12), State Archives of North Carolina, Raleigh. [Online catalog description: "Report of committee recommends granting of land and allowances to soldiers; messages from both houses appoint members to committee to draft a bill in concurrence with report."]

North Carolina (State). General Assembly. "[Document dated:] May ?, [1783]: Joint Papers, Committee Papers, Resolutions, Senate Bills, House Bills, Report of Committee Examining Memorial of Anthony Bledsoe and Absalom Tatum." Manuscript; General Assembly Record Group; Session Records, April-May 1783, Box 1 (MARS ID: 66.8.29.9.12), State Archives of North Carolina, Raleigh. [Online catalog description: "Anthony Bladsoe [*sic*] and Absalom Tatum were commissioners assigned to lay off land for officers and soldiers. Report was apparently never given. It details the parcel of land to be laid off for soldiers and officers of the Continental Army."]

North Carolina (State). General Assembly. "[Document dated:] May 7, [1783]: Joint Papers, Committee Papers, Resolutions, Senate Bills, House Bills, House Bill to Amend the Act for Relief of Soldiers and Officers of the Continental Line." Manuscript; General Assembly Record Group; Session Records, April-May 1783, Box 2 (MARS ID: 66.8.30.75), State Archives of North Carolina, Raleigh. [Online catalog description: "Bill lays out process by which members of the North Carolina Continental Line can claim the land awarded to them for their service. Includes provisions regarding the commission to lay off the land in question and for settlement of accounts. Includes legislative messages concerning amendments."]

North Carolina (State). General Assembly. "[Document dated:] April 1784: Joint Papers, Committee Papers, Resolutions, Senate Bills, House Bills, A Bill to Repeal an Act for the Relief of Such as Have Been Disabled by Wounds or Rendered Incapable of Providing for Themselves and Their Families Subsistence in the Militia Service of the State, and Providing for the Widows and Orphans Such as Have Died. Passed at Hillsborough in April 1784 (Rejected), 1793." Manuscript; General Assembly Record Group; Session Records, December 1793-January 1794, Box 1 (MARS ID: 66.8.68.30.2), State Archives of North Carolina, Raleigh. [Online catalog description: "Bill attempted to repeal an earlier act that had been passed."]

North Carolina (State). General Assembly. "[Document dated:] May 1, [1784]: Joint Papers, Committee Papers, Resolutions, Senate Bills, House Bills, Resolution in Favor of Robert Brownfield and Nathaniel Alexander." Manuscript; General Assembly Record Group; Session Records, April-June 1784, Box 2 (MARS ID: 66.8.32.5.12), State Archives of North Carolina, Raleigh. [Online catalog description: "Resolution awards Robert Brownfield and Nathaniel Alexander with one thousand acres each for their services as surgeons in the Continental hospitals."]

North Carolina (State). General Assembly. "[Document dated:] May 11, [1784]: Joint Papers, Committee Papers, Resolutions, Senate Bills, House Bills, Report on Memorial of Elijah Robertson." Manuscript; General Assembly Record Group; Session Records, April-June 1784, Box 1 (MARS ID: 66.8.31.8.10), State Archives of North Carolina, Raleigh. [Online catalog description: "Petition states that Elijah Robertson was commissary for the commission assigned to lay off land for the officers and soldiers of the N. C. Continental Line and was promised land for his services. He did not receive his land and requests redress. The committee suggests a grant of nine hundred and sixty acres of land."]

North Carolina (State). General Assembly. "[Document dated:] May 15, [1783]: Joint Papers, Committee Papers, Resolutions, Senate Bills, House Bills, Memorial of Abishai Thomas." Manuscript; General Assembly Record Group; Session Records, April-May 1783, Box 1 (MARS ID: 66.8.29.5.4), State Archives of North Carolina, Raleigh. [Online catalog description: "Memorial requests grant of land as an officer."]

North Carolina (State). General Assembly. "[Document dated:] May 15, [1784]: Joint Papers, Committee Papers, Resolutions, Senate Bills, House Bills, Senate Bill to Amend Act for Relief of Officers and Soldiers of the Continental Line (Messages Only)." Manuscript; General Assembly Record Group; Session Records, April-June 1784, Box 3 (MARS ID: 66.8.33.24), State Archives of North Carolina, Raleigh.

North Carolina (State). General Assembly. "[Document dated:] June 1, [1784]: Joint Papers, Committee Papers, Resolutions, Senate Bills, House Bills, Report on the Committee to which was Recommitted the Proceedings of the Commissioners to Lay off Lands Reserved for the NC Continental Line (Messages only), 1784." Manuscript; General Assembly Record Group; Session Records, April-June, 1784, Box 2 (MARS ID: 66.8.32.2.12), State Archives of North Carolina, Raleigh. [Online catalog description: "Messages concern the House's unwillingness to concur with the report of the committee in regards to acres laid off for specific officers."]

North Carolina (State). General Assembly. House of Delegates. "[Document dated:] Nov. 8, [1784]: Joint Papers, Committee Papers, Resolutions, Senate Bills, House Bills, House Bill to Prevent the Issuing of Grants for Lands on the Western Waters." Manuscript; General Assembly Record Group, Session Records October-November 1784, Box 2 (MARS ID: 66.8.36.44), State Archives of North Carolina. [Online catalog description: "Bill disallows the issuing of land grants in the west to those persons who used counterfeit certificates to obtain land from John Armstrong's entry-taker office. Bill also indemnifies Armstrong from any misconduct in the course of his duties as entrytaker. Includes memorial from Armstrong bringing the matter to the Assembly's attention."]

North Carolina (State). General Assembly. "[Document dated:] Dec. 29, [1785]: Joint Papers, Committee Papers, Resolutions, Senate Bills, House Bills, Resolution that the Secretary Not Issue Grants for Lands Lying on the West Side of the Cumberland Mountains until the Next Assembly." Manuscript; General Assembly Record Group; Session Records, November-December, 1785, Box 2 (MARS ID: 66.8.38.6.30), State Archives of North Carolina, Raleigh. [Online catalog description: "Resolution temporarily suspends the granting of lands to the east of the Cumberland Mountains because of the instances of fraud being committed. Excepted are the lands set aside for officers and soldiers of the N. C. Continental Line."]

North Carolina (State). General Assembly. "[Document dated:] December 26, [1791]: Joint Papers, Committee Papers, Resolutions, Senate Bills, House Bills, Resolution that the Secretary of State Continue to Issue Warrants to Officers and Soldiers of the Continental Line." Manuscript; General Assembly Record Group, Session Records, December, 1791-January, 1792, Box 2 (MARS ID: 66.8.61.2.4), State Archives of North Carolina, Raleigh. [Online catalog description: "Resolution states that officers and soldiers of the Continental Line are still entitled to the lands that other bills specify."]

North Carolina (State). General Assembly. "[Document dated:] January 2, [1792]: Joint Papers, Committee Papers, Resolutions, Senate Bills, House Bills, Memorial of Martin Armstrong." Manuscript; General Assembly Record Group, Session Records, December 1791-January 1792, Box 3 (MARS ID: 66.8.62.6.23), State Archives of North Carolina, Raleigh. [Online catalog description: "Armstrong, the petitioner, has been assigned to survey the lands alloted for officers and soldiers of the Continental Line. Because of hostile Indians, he feels he will be unable to complete his assignment in the allotted time and asks the General Assembly to offer him more time to complete his task."]

North Carolina (State). General Assembly. *A Bill to Authorize the Secretary to Issue Grants for Military Lands, in the Manner Therein Described, and to Direct the Secretary and Comptroller to Issue Warrants in Certain Cases Therein Mentioned.* Halifax: Printed by Hodge & Wills, [1795?]; micropublished: (Early American Imprints. First Series, no. 47522) New York: Readex Microprint, 1985. [Broadside; "Concerning land grants to officers and soldiers from North Carolina who fought in the Continental Army during the Revolution."]

North Carolina (State). General Assembly. "[Document dated:] Dec. 2, [1785]: Joint Papers, Committee Papers, Resolutions, Senate Bills, House Bills; Joint Papers, Committee Papers, Resolutions, Senate Bills, House Bills, Report on the Petition of Timothy De Momroe (Petition and Enclosures Only)." Manuscript; General Assembly Record Group, Session Records November-December, 1785, Box 2 (MARS ID: 66.8.38.2.11), State Archives of North Carolina, Raleigh. [Online catalog description: "Petition is from Timothy De Momroe, who served as an officer with the French in western Virginia during the war and, through oversight, did not receive land that was promised the officers of the line. Now, he resides in Nashville and wishes to be granted a portion of land for the support of his family. Included are depositions as to his worthiness as an officer and defender of the American cause."]

North Carolina (State). General Assembly. "[Document dated:] Dec. 17, [1787]: Joint Papers, Committee Papers, Resolutions, Senate Bills, House Bills; Joint Papers, Committee Papers, Resolutions, Senate Bills, House Bills, Memorial of Martin Armstrong on the Shortage of Good Land for Military Warrants in the Cumberland District." Manuscript; General Assembly Record Group; Session Records, November-December 1787, Box 1 (MARS ID: 66.8.46.2.12), State Archives of North Carolina, Raleigh. [Online catalog description: "Report concerning the surveyors' inability to find enough contiguous, arable land for large warrants, because of the terrain and the placement of earlier grants. Requests instructions from General Assembly."]

North Carolina (State). General Assembly. House of Delegates. "[Document dated:] Dec. 19, [1785]: Joint Papers, Committee Papers, Resolutions, Senate Bills, House Bills, House Bill to Explain and Amend the Act for Opening the Land Office and for Adding Lands to the County of Davidson (Laid Over)." Manuscript; General Assembly Record Group; Session Records, November-December, 1785, Box 4 (MARS ID: 66.8.40.25), State Archives of North Carolina, Raleigh. [Online catalog description: "Bill provides direction in the instance of two entries being made on the same plot of land, gives instruction to the entrytaker of Davidson County, and adds all land that was given to officers and soldiers of the line to Davidson County. Includes legislative messages regarding amendments."]

North Carolina (State). General Assembly. "[Document dated:] Dec 23, [1796]. Joint Papers, Committee Papers, Resolutions, Senate Bills, House Bills, Secretary to Forbear to Issue Grants in Certain Instances." Manuscript; General Assembly Record Group; Session Records, November 1796-December 1796, Box 2 (MARS ID:

66.8.81.5.13), State Archives of North Carolina, Raleigh. [Online catalog description: "Resolved that the Secretary, in order to issue warrants for land, must in all cases compare the certificate with the muster rolls to make sure that such applicant served agreeably to law."]

North Carolina (State). Office of Secretary of State. Office of the Secretary. Land Office. "James Saunders Service Right, 1785." ID # 37944, Early Tennessee Land Records – Revolutionary War Land Warrants, 1784-1840 Guard Rights, Tennessee State Library & Archives, Nashville; digital surrogate available through the Revolutionary War Collection, Tennessee Virtual Archive at http://cdm15138.contentdm.oclc.org/cdm/singleitem/collection/p15138coll16/id/43/rec/32. [Description from TeVA: "Two hundred-acre service right to land around Bledsoe's Lick. The community was named for Isaac Bledsoe, a pioneer and long hunter who built a fort on the site. Settlers in the region were open to attack by Native Americans who believed their hunting grounds were being destroyed. The town is now known as Castalian Springs and is located in Sumner County, Tennessee."]

North Carolina (State). Office of Secretary of State. Office of the Secretary. Land Office. "Land Warrents, Plats of Survey, and Related Records. Tennessee, Davidson County, 1783-1824." Manuscript S.108.350-S.108.361, 12 microfilm reels (MARS ID: 12.14.2; folder), State Archives of North Carolina, Raleigh. [Online catalog description: "Davidson County (formed in 1783 from Washington County, Tennessee) was named after General William Lee Davidson. The county seat was named Nashville after General Francis Nash. A portion of Davidson became Sumner County in 1787, and another portion of Davidson became Tennessee County in 1799. Part of Davidson became Williamson County in 1799."]

North Carolina (State). Office of Secretary of State. Office of the Secretary. Land Office. "Land Warrents, Plats of Survey, and Related Records. Tennessee, Eastern District, 1779-1802." Manuscript S.108.361-S.108.363, 3 microfilm reels (MARS ID: 12.14.3; folder), State Archives of North Carolina, Raleigh.

North Carolina (State). Office of Secretary of State. Office of the Secretary. Land Office. "Land Warrents, Plats of Survey, and Related Records. Tennessee, Middle District, 1783-1797." Manuscript S.108.363-S.108.365, 3 microfilm reels (MARS ID: 12.14.4; folder), State Archives of North Carolina, Raleigh.

North Carolina (State). Office of Secretary of State. Office of the Secretary. Land Office. "Land Warrents, Plats of Survey, and Related Records. Tennessee, Western, 1783-1802." Manuscript S.108.366-S.108.367, 3 microfilm reels (MARS ID: 12.14.3; folder), State Archives of North Carolina, Raleigh.

North Carolina (State). Office of Secretary of State. Office of the Secretary. Land Office. "Land Warrents, Plats of Survey, and Related Records. Tennessee, Greene County, 1778-1803." Manuscript S.108.367-S.108.373, 7 microfilm reels (MARS ID: 12.14.3; folder), State Archives of North Carolina, Raleigh. [Online catalog description: "Greene County (formed in 1783 from Washington County, Tennessee) was named for General Nathaniel Greene, as was Greeneville, the county seat. Portions of Greene County became Jefferson and Knox counties in 1792."]

North Carolina (State). Office of Secretary of State. Office of the Secretary. Land Office. "Land Warrents, Plats of Survey, and Related Records. Tennessee, Grainger County, 1783-1807." Manuscript S.108.367-S.108.373, 7 microfilm reels (MARS ID: 12.14.7; folder), State Archives of North Carolina, Raleigh. [Online catalog description: "Grainger County (formed in 1796 from Hawkins and Knox counties, Tennessee) was named in honor of William Blount's wife, Mary Grainger Blount. The county seat of Rutledge was named after George Rutledge. The courthouse was erected in 1801."]

North Carolina (State). Office of Secretary of State. Office of the Secretary. Land Office. "Land Warrents, Plats of Survey, and Related Records. Tennessee, Giles County, 1778-1820." Manuscript S.108.373.1 microfilm reel (MARS ID: 12.14.8; folder), State Archives of North Carolina, Raleigh. [Online catalog description: "Giles County (formed in 1809 from Maury County, Tennessee) was named after Virginia Governor William B. Giles, upon the suggestion of Andrew Jackson. The county seat of Pulaski was named after Casimir Pulaski, a Polish patriot who served as a Revolutionary War cavalry leader. The site of the county seat was below the Congressional Indian Reservation line and land titles in that area were not clear until 1812 when restrictions on settlement in the Indian lands were removed."]

North Carolina (State). Office of Secretary of State. Office of the Secretary. Land Office. "Land Warrents, Plats of Survey, and Related Records. Tennessee, Hawkins County, 1778-1804." Manuscript S.108.373-S.108.378, 5 microfilm reels (MARS ID: 12.14.9; folder), State Archives of North Carolina, Raleigh. [Online catalog description: "Hawkins County (formed in 1787 from Sullivan County, Tennessee) was named for Benjamin Hawkins. The county seat of Rogersville was founded in 1789 on the land of Joseph Rogers and James Hogan. Portions of Hawkins County became Jefferson and Knox counties in 1792, and another portion became Grainger County in 1796."]

North Carolina (State). Office of Secretary of State. Office of the Secretary. Land Office. "Land Warrents, Plats of Survey, and Related Records. Tennessee, Jefferson County, 1779-1803." Manuscript S.108.378, 1 microfilm reel (MARS ID: 12.14.10; folder), State Archives of North Carolina, Raleigh. [Online catalog description: "Jefferson County (formed in 1792 from Greene and Hawkins counties, Tennessee) was named in honor of Thomas Jefferson. The county seat of Dandridge was established in 1793. A portion of Jefferson County became Sevier County in 1794."]

North Carolina (State). Office of Secretary of State. Office of the Secretary. Land Office. "Land Warrents, Plats of Survey, and Related Records. Tennessee, Knox County, 1778-1796." Manuscript S.108.378, 1 microfilm reel (MARS ID: 12.14.11; folder), State Archives of North Carolina, Raleigh. [Online catalog description: "Knox County (formed in 1792 from Greene and Hawkins counties, Tennessee) was named in honor of General Henry Knox. Knoxville, the county seat, was established in 1791-1792. Prior to that, the location was known as White's Fort. In 1792 Governor William Blount made Knoxville the territorial capital, and the town continued as the Tennessee state capital from 1796 to 1813, when Nashville became the capital. A portion of Knox County became Grainger County in 1796."]

North Carolina (State). Office of Secretary of State. Office of the Secretary. Land Office. "Land Warrents, Plats of Survey, and Related Records. Tennessee, Maury County, 1778-1815." Manuscript S.108.378, 1 microfilm reel (MARS ID: 12.14.12; folder), State Archives of North Carolina, Raleigh. [Online catalog description: "Maury County (formed in 1807 from Williamson County, Tennessee) was named after Major Abram P. Maury. Columbia was selected as the county seat in 1808 and was incorporated in 1817. A portion of Maury County became Giles County in 1809."]

North Carolina (State). Office of Secretary of State. Office of the Secretary. Land Office. "Land Warrents, Plats of Survey, and Related Records. Tennessee, Montgomery County, 1785-1802." Manuscript S.108.378, 1 microfilm reel (MARS ID: 12.14.13; folder), State Archives of North Carolina, Raleigh. [Online catalog description: "Montgomery County (along with Robertson County) was formed in 1796 when Tennessee County was split to form two new counties. The county was named after John Montgomery. In 1784 John Montgomery and Martin Armstrong laid off the town of Clarksville on a parcel of land for which they had entered a claim. They named the town after George Rogers Clark. It became Montgomery County's seat after serving as county seat for Tennessee County."]

North Carolina (State). Office of Secretary of State. Office of the Secretary. Land Office. "Land Warrents, Plats of Survey, and Related Records. Tennessee, Robertson County, 1785-1804." Manuscript S.108.378, 1 microfilm reels (MARS ID: 12.14.14; folder), State Archives of North Carolina, Raleigh. [Online catalog description: "Robertson County (along with Montgomery County) was formed in 1796 when Tennessee County was split to form two new counties. It was named after James Robertson. The county seat of Springfield was established in 1798."]

North Carolina (State). Office of Secretary of State. Office of the Secretary. Land Office. "Land Warrents, Plats of Survey, and Related Records. Tennessee, Sevier County, 1799." Manuscript S.108.378, 1 microfilm reel (MARS ID: 12.14.15; folder), State Archives of North Carolina, Raleigh. [Online catalog description: "Sevier County (formed in 1794 from Jefferson County) was named after John Sevier. The county seat of Sevierville was laid off in 1795. [The area was once known as the 'State of Franklin,' formed extra legally 1785-1788."]

North Carolina (State). Office of Secretary of State. Office of the Secretary. "Land Office: Land Warrents, Plats of Survey, and Related Records. Tennessee, Smith County, 1783-1804." Manuscript S.108.378, 1 microfilm reel (MARS ID: 12.14.16; folder), State Archives of North Carolina, Raleigh. [Online catalog description: "Smith County (formed in 1799 from Sumner County, Tennessee) was named for General Daniel Smith. In 1804 the county seat was established at the location of the present-day town of Carthage. The courthouse was erected in 1805."]

North Carolina (State). Office of Secretary of State. Office of the Secretary. Land Office. "Land Warrents, Plats of Survey, and Related Records. Tennessee, Sullivan County, 1770-1798." Manuscript S.108.378-S.108.382, 5 microfilm reel (MARS ID: 12.14.17; folder), State Archives of North Carolina, Raleigh. [Online catalog description: "Sullivan County (formed in 1779 from Washington County, Tennessee) was named for John Sullivan. Blountsville was made the county seat. A portion of Sullivan County became Hawkins County in 1787, and a portion of Washington County was annexed to Sullivan County in 1788."]

North Carolina (State). Office of Secretary of State. Office of the Secretary. Land Office. "Land Warrents, Plats of Survey, and Related Records. Tennessee, Sumner County, 1780-1803." Manuscript S.108.382-S.108.387, 6 microfilm reels (MARS ID: 12.14.9; folder), State Archives of North Carolina, Raleigh. [Online catalog description: "Sumner County (formed in 1787 from Davidson County, Tennessee) was named for General Jethro Sumner. The county seat of Gallatin, named for Albert Gallatin, was established in 1804. A portion of

Sumner County became Davidson County in 1787, and other portions became Smith County and Wilson County in 1799."]

North Carolina (State). Office of Secretary of State. Office of the Secretary. Land Office. "Land Warrents, Plats of Survey, and Related Records. Tennessee, Tennessee County, 1780-1819." Manuscript S.108.387-S.108.390, 4 microfilm reel (MARS ID: 12.14.19; folder), State Archives of North Carolina, Raleigh. [Online catalog description: "Tennessee County (formed in 1788 from Davidson County, Tennessee) was named after the ancient capital of the Cherokee Indians. The county seat was Clarksville. The town was laid off in 1784 by John Montgomery and Martin Armstrong on a parcel of land for which they had entered a claim. The town was named after George Rogers Clark. Clarksville later served as the county seat of Montgomery County. Upon the admission of the state of Tennessee into the Union in 1796, the county of Tennessee was split to form Montgomery and Robertson counties."]

North Carolina (State). Office of Secretary of State. Office of the Secretary. Land Office. "Land Warrents, Plats of Survey, and Related Records. Tennessee, Washington County, 1770-1803." Manuscript S.108.390-S.108.395, 6 microfilm reels (MARS ID: 12.14.20; folder), State Archives of North Carolina, Raleigh. [Online catalog description: "Washington County, Tennessee began as the District of Washington (a part of North Carolina) in 1776. The county designation was granted in 1777. A portion of the district along with a portion of Surry County, NC were formed into Wilkes County, NC in 1777. Washington County encompassed the territory west of Wilkes County (between Wilkes, the Virginia line, the hunting grounds of the Cherokee Indians, and the Mississippi River). It was named in honor of George Washington. The county seat of Jonesboro was named after Willie Jones and was established in 1779. A portion of Washington County became Sullivan County in 1779, and portions of Washington County became Davidson and Greene counties in 1783. Other areas of Washington were annexed to Sullivan County in 1788 and Wilkes County, NC in 1792. Carter County was formed from Washington County in 1796."]

North Carolina (State). Office of Secretary of State. Office of the Secretary. Land Office. "Land Warrents, Plats of Survey, and Related Records. Tennessee, Wilson County, 1783-1802." Manuscript S.108.395, 1 microfilm reel (MARS ID: 12.14.9; folder), State Archives of North Carolina, Raleigh. [Online catalog description: "Wilson County (formed in 1799 from Sumner County, Tennessee) was named for Major David Wilson. Lebanon was chosen as the county seat in 1802."]

North Carolina (State). Office of Secretary of State. Office of the Secretary. Land Office. "Land Warrents, Plats of Survey, and Related Records. Tennessee, Williamson County, 1800-1801." Manuscript S.108.373-S.108.378, 5 microfilm reels (MARS ID: 12.14.22; folder), State Archives of North Carolina, Raleigh. [Online catalog description: "Williamson County (formed in 1799 from Davidson County, Tennessee) was named for General Williamson of North Carolina or Dr. Hugh Williamson (also from North Carolina) and the county seat was supposed to have been named for Dr. Williamson's good friend, Benjamin Franklin. Part of Williamson County became Maury County in 1807."]

North Carolina (State). Office of Secretary of State. Office of the Secretary. Land Office. "Land Warrents, Plats of Survey, and Related Records. Tennessee, No County Given." Manuscript S.108.395, 1 microfilm reel (MARS ID: 12.14.23; folder), State Archives of North Carolina, Raleigh.

North Carolina (State). Office of Secretary of State. Office of the Secretary. Land Office. "Land Office, State Land Office, Western Lands (John Armstrong's Office): Land Patents (Undelivered Originals), 1786-1797." Manuscript; Call Number SS 1089 (MARS ID: 12.78; series), Secretary of State Record Group (MARS ID: 12.80), State Archives of North Carolina, Raleigh. [Online catalog description: "Land patents apparently not delivered to the grantee. Included are some patents for land in the Military District (now in Tennessee)."]

North Carolina (State). Office of Secretary of State. Office of the Secretary. Land Office. "Land Office, State Land Office, Western Lands (Military District): Miscellaneous Land Records, Continental Line, 1782-1826." Manuscript; Call Number SS 758-SS 759, Office of the Secretary of State (MARS ID: 12.36), State Archives of North Carolina, Raleigh. [Online catalog description: "Miscellaneous records including material relating to land grants for surveyors' chainbearers and bodyguards, a list (1783) of military bounty land entries by officers and soldiers, and a volume of surveys made by virtue of military land warrants (1800-1801)."]

North Carolina (State). Office of Secretary of State. Office of the Secretary. Land Office. "Land Office, State Land Office, Western Lands (Military District): Military Land Warrant Returns, 1786-1799." Manuscript; SS 804.1, Office of the Secretary of State (MARS ID: 12.82) State Archives of North Carolina, Raleigh. [Online catalog description: "Lists of warrants and plats of survey that had been returned to the land office from the surveyor of military bounty lands in the Military District (now in Tennessee)."]

North Carolina (State). Office of Secretary of State. Office of the Secretary. Land Office. "Land Office, State Land Office, Western Lands (Military District): Register of Military Land Warrants for the Continental Line, 1783-

1841." Manuscript; SS 979-SS 981.1, Office of the Secretary of State (MARS ID: 12.83), State Archives of North Carolina, Raleigh. [Online catalog description: "Register of land warrants given to former members of the Continental Line and their heirs. The information includes warrant number, name and rank of grantee, acreage, to whom the warrant was delivered, and the number of months served in the army. The transcribed copy of the first volume (the first one is now bound in three sections) of the register includes the second series of warrants issued."]

North Carolina (State). Office of Secretary of State. Office of the Secretary. Land Office. "Land Office, State Land Office, Western Lands (Military District): Revolutionary Military Papers, 1767-1855." Manuscript, SS760-SS791 (MARS ID: 12.81), State Archives of North Carolina, Raleigh. [Online catalog description: "Papers and claims concerning military bounty land in the Military District (now in Tennessee)."]

North Carolina (State). Office of Secretary of State. Office of the Secretary. Land Office. "Military Land Warrant for Elijah Roberts, 1995 (1786)." Manuscript, Call Number N.95.2.67, Photographic Collections (MARS ID: 4.1.22.136), State Archives of North Carolina, Raleigh. [Online catalog description: "Secretary of State Military Land Warrant for Elijah Roberts' Services as a Private in the Continental Line #3319. Secretary of State Land Office, Warrants, Plats, Surveys, Davidson County, Tennessee, File # 2135, James Mulherrin, Assignee of Elijah Roberts (Military Warrant #3319)."]

North Carolina (State). Office of Secretary of State. Office of the Secretary. Land Office. "North Carolina Grant." ID # 37945, Early Tennessee Land Records – Revolutionary War Land Warrants, 1784-1840 Guard Rights, Tennessee State Library & Archives, Nashville; digital surrogate available through the Revolutionary War Collection, Tennessee Virtual Archive at http://cdm15138.contentdm.oclc.org/cdm/compoundobject/collection/p15138coll16/id/136/rec/52. [Description from TeVA: "North Carolina grant to James Sanders, 1790."]

North Carolina (State). Office of Secretary of State. Office of the Secretary. Land Office. "Land Grant Given to John Winton." ID # 37949, Early Tennessee Land Records – Revolutionary War Land Warrants, 1784-1840 Guard Rights, Tennessee State Library & Archives, Nashville; digital surrogate available through the Revolutionary War Collection, Tennessee Virtual Archive at http://cdm15138.contentdm.oclc.org/cdm/compoundobject/collection/p15138coll16/id/155/rec/38. [Description from TeVA: "North Carolina land grant given to John Winton, assignee for Robert White, guard right for Davidson County in the Territory South of the River Ohio, 1794."]

North Carolina (State). Office of Secretary of State. Office of the Secretary. Land Office. "North Carolina Land Warrant." ID # 37943, Early Tennessee Land Records, Tennessee State Library & Archives, Nashville; digital surrogate available through the Revolutionary War Collection, Tennessee Virtual Archive at http://cdm15138.contentdm.oclc.org/cdm/compoundobject/collection/p15138coll16/id/133/rec/53. [Description from TeVA: North Carolina land warrant for 5,760 acres of land in Davidson County to Colonel Samuel Lockart, 1787 (Hand copy of original. Original probably in North Carolina.)"]

North Carolina (State). Office of Secretary of State. Office of the Secretary. Land Office. "North Carolina Land Warrant, No. 94." #39494, Early Tennessee Land Records, Revolutionary War Land Warrants, 1784, Tennessee State Library and Archives, Nashville; digital surrogate available through the Revolutionary War Collection, Tennessee Virtual Archive at http://cdm15138.contentdm.oclc.orgcdmcompoundobjectcollection/p15138coll16/id/362/rec/54. [Description from TeVA: "North Carolina land warrant, No. 94, for 2,500 acres of land to George Doherty, dated September 4, 1785 and July 10, 1788. The land adjoins James Robertson's. Includes seal."]

North Carolina (State). Office of Secretary of State. Office of the Secretary. "File No. 1449. John Baker, Capt., Continental Line (Military Warrant No. 717), 1800." Manuscript; Call Number S.108.387, Secretary of State Record Group, Land Office: Land Warrants, Plats of Survey, and Related Records (MARS ID: 12.14.18.1316), State Archives of North Carolina, Raleigh. [Online catalog description: "Warrant issued to John Baker for service as a captain in the Continental Line." 1,462 acres of land were granted in Round Lick Creek, Tennessee.]

North Carolina (State). Secretary of State. Land Office "File No. 1451, Samuel Freeman, Private, Continental Line (Military Warrant No., 8, Office of Secretary of State. Office of the Secretary. Second Series, 1800." Manuscript; S.108.387, Secretary of State Record Group, Land Office: Land Warrants, Plays of Survey, and Related Records (MARS ID: 12.14.18.1318), State Archives of North Carolina, Raleigh. [Online catalog description: "Warrant issued to Samuel Freeman a soldier in the Continental Line by resolve of the General Assembly dated December 20, 1799." 640 acres of land were granted "on the barren fork of Drakes Creek."]

North Carolina (State). Office of Secretary of State. Office of the Secretary. Land Office. "Western Lands (John Armstrong's Office): Land Entries, 1783-1784." Manuscript SS 436-SS 439.1 (MARS ID: 12.78; series), State

Archives of North Carolina, Raleigh. [Online catalog description: "Land entries from John Armstrong's office for western lands (now in Tennessee)."]

North Carolina (State). Office of Secretary of State. Office of the Secretary. Land Office. "Western Lands (John Armstrong's Office): Land Entry Book, 1783-1784." Manuscript SS 1080 (MARS ID: 12.79; series), State Archives of North Carolina, Raleigh. [Online catalog description: "Land entry book from John Armstrong's office for western lands (now in Tennessee)."]

North Carolina (State). Office of Secretary of State. Office of the Secretary. Land Office. "Western Lands (Military District): Revolutionary Military Papers, 1767-1855." Manuscript SS 760-SS 791 (MARS ID: 12.81; series), State Archives of North Carolina, Raleigh. [Online catalog description: "Papers and claims concerning military bounty land in the Military District (now in Tennessee)."]

North Carolina (State). Office of Secretary of State. Office of the Secretary. Land Office. "Western Lands (Military District): Register of Military Land Warrants for the Continental Line, 1783-1841." Manuscript SS 979-SS 981.1 (MARS ID: 12.83; series), State Archives of North Carolina, Raleigh. [Online catalog description: "Register of land warrants given to former members of the Continental Line and their heirs. The information includes warrant number, name and rank of grantee, acreage, to whom the warrant was delivered, and the number of months served in the army. The transcribed copy of the first volume (the first one is now bound in three sections) of the register includes the second series of warrants issued."]

North Carolina (State). Office of Secretary of State. Office of the Secretary. Land Office. "Western Lands (John Armstrong's Office): Land Patents (Undelivered Originals), 1786-1797." Manuscript SS 1089 (MARS ID: 12.34; series), Secretary of State Record Group (MARS ID: 12.80), State Archives of North Carolina, Raleigh. [Online catalog description: "Land patents not delivered to the grantee, for reasons unknown. Those dated 1877 to 1908 were not delivered due to some failure in payment."]

North Carolina (State). Office of Secretary of State. Office of the Secretary. Land Office. "Western Lands (Military District): Miscellaneous Land Records, Continental Line." Manuscript SS 7658-SS759 (MARS ID: 12.36; series), State Archives of North Carolina, Raleigh. [Online catalog description: "Miscellaneous records including material relating to land grants for surveyors' chainbearers and bodyguards, a list (1783) of military bounty land entries by officers and soldiers, and a volume of surveys made by virtue of military land warrants (1800-1801)."]

Potter, Henry, 1766-1857. "Henry Potter (1766-1857) Papers, 1795-1821, 1859-1861, 1953, 1966." Manuscript; PC.213 (MARS ID: 723), State Archives of North Carolina, Raleigh. [Online catalog description: "Papers of Judge Potter of Raleigh and Fayetteville, U. S. circuit and district court judge (1801-1857), concerning Tennessee land claims of his father-in-law Maj. James Easton of Pitt Co. Letters to Easton (1803-1811) are from agents Thomas Dillon in Tennessee and Philemon Beecher in Ohio about land and land warrants sold him by speculators Stockley Donelson and William Tyrrell; from Congressmen William Dickson, William Blackledge, and John Rhea about bill allowing Tennessee to grant land (1804-1805); and from Dillon about the Tennessee legislature and its land act (1806-1807). Potter's correspondence (1811-1821) concerns his children's claims to land willed them by Easton, with letters from Dillon, Beecher, John Haywood, John C. McLemore, Col. John McIver, and Judge James Trimble about military warrants granted Thomas Massey and Robert Young; confusion and fraud in land warrants; and the Tennessee land acts. Other papers include depositions about Massey's Revolutionary service and information on Donelson's movements in 1796. Donelson's papers (1795-1797) include letters to him about western land, Revolutionary War certificates, and slaves, and his surveying instructions to Tyrrell and James W. Lackey. Also auction advertisement listing cargo from France (Beaufort, 1813), and pamphlets about Judge Potter."]

Presley, (Mrs.) Leister E. *North Carolina Land Grants in Tennessee, 1778-1791*. Searcy, Ark.: Presley, 1970.

Pruitt, Albert Bruce. *Corrections or Alterations to Land Grants in North Carolina (1714-1783) & Tennessee (1778-1796*. Whitakers: A. B. Pruitt, 2002.

Pruitt, Albert Bruce. *North Carolina Land Warrants in Tennessee, Valid and Invalid*. Whitakers: A. B. Pruitt, 2004. [Includes listings for men who would have had to take the oath of allegiance in order to quality for making a land entry in a specific county.]

Pruitt, Albert Bruce. *Petitions for Land Grant Suspensions in North Carolina, 1776-1836*. 2 vols. Whitakers: A. B. Pruitt, 1993.

Pruitt, Albert Bruce. *Tennessee Land Entries: Military Bounty Land, Martin Armstrong's Office*. Whitakers: A. B. Pruitt, 1996. [Contents: Pt. 1. Location book (#3138-4839); Pt. 2. Location book (#5572-7490 & 2754-3111); Pt. 3. Warrants first series (#1-2500) Oct. 1783-Sept. 1785; Pt. 4. Warrants first series (#2501-5312) Sept. 1785-Dec. 1797; Pt. 5. Warrants second series (#1-1242) Dec. 1799-Feb. 1841; Pt. 6. Locations #2-2742 and #4840-5569; Pt. 7. Index.]

Rice, Shirley Hollis. *The Hidden Revolutionary War Land Grants in the Tennessee Military Reservation*. Lawrenceburg, Tenn.: Family Tree Press, 1991.

Rosenthal, Patricia, and Jean K. Ramsey. "Bounty Land [for Joseph Eller, Davidson County, Tennessee]." *Journal of the Genealogical Society of Rowan County, North Carolina*, 8:2 (June 1994), 57.

Sistler, Barbara; Byron Sistler; and Samuel Sistler. *Tennessee Land Grants*. Nashville: Byron Sistler & Associates, 1998.

United States. National Archives and Records Service. *List of North Carolina Land Grants in Tennessee, 1778-1791*. 1 microfilm reel. Washington, D. C.: NARS, 1944. [Description: "File microcopies of records in the National Archives, no. 68.]

Warren, Mary Bondurant. "List of North Carolina Land Grants in Tennessee, 1778-1791." *The Carolina Genealogist*, no. 10 (Spring 1972), State Records/N. C. Grants in Tenn., 1-4; no. 11 (Summer 1972), State Records/N. C. Grants in Tenn., 5-10; no. 12 (Fall 1972), State Records/N. C. Grants in Tenn., 11-20; no. 13 (Winter 1973), State Records/N. C. Grants in Tenn., 13-30; no. 14 (Spring 1973), State Records/N. C. Grants in Tenn., 31-40; no. 15 (Summer 1973), State Records/N. C. Grants in Tenn., 41-42; no. 16 (Fall 1973), State Records/N. C. Grants in Tenn., 43-44; no. 18 (Spring 1974), State Records/N. C. Grants in Tenn., 45-48; no. 19 (Summer 1974), State Records/N. C. Grants in Tenn., 49-50; no. 20 (Fall 1974), 51-60; no. 22 (Spring 1975),), State Records/N. C. Grants in Tenn., 61-68; no. 23 (Summer 1975), State Records/N. C. Grants in Tenn., 69-78; no. 24 (Winter 1975), State Records/N. C. Grants in Tenn., 79-88; no. 25 (Winter 1976), State Records/N. C. Grants in Tenn., 89-98; no. 26 (Spring 1976), State Records/N. C. Grants in Tenn., 99-108; no. 27 (Summer 1976), State Records/N. C. Grants in Tenn., 109-118; no. 28 (Fall 1976), State Records/N. C. Grants in Tenn., 119-126; no. 29 (Winter 1977), State Records/N. C. Grants in Tenn., 127-132; no. 30 (Spring 1977), State Records/N. C. Grants in Tenn., 133-134; no. 31 (Summer 1977), State Records/N. C. Grants in Tenn., 135-136; no. 32 (Fall 1997), State Records/N. C. Grants in Tenn., 137-138; no. 33 (Winter 1978-1979), State Records/N. C. Grants in Tenn., 139-140; no. 34 (Spring 1978-1979), State Records/N. C. Grants in Tenn., 141-142; no. 35 (Summer 1978-1979), State Records/N. C. Grants in Tenn., 143-144; no. 36 (Fall 1978-1979), State Records/N. C. Grants in Tenn., 145-146; no. 37 (Winter 1980), State Records/N. C. Grants in Tenn., 147-150; no. 38 (Spring 1980), State Records/N. C. Grants in Tenn., 151-158; no. 39 (Summer 1980), State Records/N. C. Grants in Tenn., 159-162; no. 40 (Fall 1980), State Records/N. C. Grants in Tenn., 163-172; no. 41 (Winter 1981), State Records/N. C. Grants in Tenn., 173-182; no. 42 (Spring 1981), State Records/N. C. Grants in Tenn., 183-190; no. 43 (Summer 1981), 191-202.

White, Katharine Keogh. "Land Warrants for Military Service." *Daughters of the American Revolution Magazine*, 60:1 (January 1926), 37-39 [Describes land grants given in Tennessee]

Whitley, Edith Johns Rucker. "Revolutionary Soldiers Who Were Granted Land in Tennessee for Their Services in That War." Typescript VCp970.34 W61r, North Carolina Collection, Louis Round Wilson Special Collections Library, University of North Carolina at Chapel Hill.

Fraudulent Bounty Land Claims in Tennessee

Arthur, John Preston. *Western North Carolina: A History (From 1730 to 1913)*. Raleigh: Edwards & Broughton Printing Co., 1914; reprinted: Johnson City, Tenn.: Overmountain Press, 1996.

Jackson, Andrew. "Letter from Andrew Jackson to Governor Samuel Ashe." Manuscript, Call Number N.95.3.2, Photographic Collections, State Archives of North Carolina, Raleigh. [Online catalog description: "Letter from Andrew Jackson to Governor Samuel Ashe Referring to the Military Land Fraud in Tennessee, 6 December 1797."]

North Carolina (State). General Assembly. "[Document dated:] Dec. 26, [1786]: Joint Papers, Committee Papers, Resolutions, Senate Bills, House Bills, Resolution Re[specting] a Number of Officers of the Late Continental Line who Testified Concerning Frauds (Message Only), 1786." Manuscript; General Assembly Record Group; Session Records, November, 1786-January, 1787, Box 3 (MARS ID: 66.8.43.8.7), State Archives of North Carolina, Raleigh. [Online catalog description: "Legislative message concerns amending resolution by adding names to the list."]

North Carolina (State). General Assembly. "[Document dated:] Dec. 28, [1787]: Joint Papers, Committee Papers, Resolutions, Senate Bills, House Bills, Resolution Directing Secretary of State to Issue Military Land Warrants to Representatives of Samuel Griffith, Deceased (With Certifications) (Rejected)." Manuscript, General Assembly Record Group, Session Record, November 1786-January 1787, Box 3 (MARS ID: 66.8.43.5.13), State Archives of North Carolina, Raleigh. [Online catalog description: "Resolution directs the Secretary of State to issue land warrants to Isaac Hicks, John Murray, Martin Miller, John Brooks, and the representatives of Samuel Griffith; includes certificates of service for Isaac Hicks, John Murray, and others."]

North Carolina (State). General Assembly. "North Carolina General Assembly Legislative Papers, 1784-1842." Manuscript 424-z, Southern Historical Collection, Louis Round Wilson Special Collections Library, University of North Carolina, Chapel Hill; online finding aid available at www2.lib.unc.edu/mss/inv/n/North_Carolina.General_Assembly.html. [Online finding aid description: "The collection includes records of early North Carolina state legislatures, consisting chiefly of papers, 1784-1809, pertaining to land fraud cases involving state officials, including correspondence and committee reports, messages between various governors and the two houses of the legislature, material from the legislative investigation, and petitions. The fraud involved land granted to Revolutionary War soldiers. Also included are miscellaneous papers, consisting of resolutions, governors' messages, and items for various legislative committees, 1793-1842."]

North Carolina (State). General Assembly. "[Document dated:] Dec. 26, [1793]. Joint Papers, Committee Papers, Resolutions, Senate Bills, House Bills, Committee Report on the Resolution of the Last General Assembly Temporarily Suspending the Execution of Grants in the Counties of Rutherford and Buncombe." Manuscript; General Assembly Record Group; Session Records, December 1793-January 1794, Box 2 (MARS ID: 66.8.69.6.18), State Archives of North Carolina, Raleigh. [Online catalog description: "The committee reported that the suspension had had its effect and the fraud had been stopped. The committee had destroyed the books of the entrytaker and instructed the comptroller to participate in looking into the fraud."]

Stone, David 1770-1818. "David Stone (1770-1818) Papers, 1793-1942." Manuscript, PC.82, State Archives of North Carolina, Raleigh. [Online catalog description: "Papers of Stone, U. S. senator (1801-1807, 1813-1814) and governor (1808-1810), including letters (1800-1813) from Peter Browne, Robert Burton, Solomon Pinto of Connecticut, and others about land frauds in North Carolina, the N. C. Court of Conference, funding of the Revolutionary debt, Halifax Co. politics, and foreign policy (1806)..."]

Fraudulent Bounty Land Claims in Tennessee – The Glasgow Land Frauds

Koonts, Russell Scott. "'An Angel has Fallen!:' The Glasgow Land Frauds and the Establishment of the North Carolina Supreme Court." M. A. thesis, North Carolina State University, 1995; available online at http://www.danielhaston.com/history/rev-war/glasgow-frauds.htm.

Landis, Ira D. "The 1797 North Carolina Land Swindle." *Mennonite Historical Bulletin*, 7:1 (March 1946), 1-3.

North Carolina (State). Secretary of State. "Glasgow Land Fraud Records, 1798-1800." Manuscript SS 753-SS 756.2 (MARS ID: 12.32; series), Secretary of State Record Group, State Archives of North Carolina, Raleigh. [Online catalog description: "Reports to the General Assembly and to the governor by the legislative committee appointed under the resolution of 1798, and the board created by the act of 1798 (c. 14) to investigate suspected fraud in the granting by the secretary's office of western lands in John Armstrong's office and Martin Armstrong's office (military bounty lands). Also included are the related files pertaining to that investigation, as well as the proceedings and related papers of the Court of Oyer and Terminer convened under the act of 1799 (c. 4) to try Secretary of State James Glasgow and others for culpability. Also includes the 'keys' (prepared by Archives staff) used for locating material in the related files of investigation."]

Pruitt, Albert Bruce. *Glasgow Land Fraud Papers*. 2 vols. Whitakers: A. B. Pruitt, 1988, 1993.

Pruitt, Albert Bruce. "Military Bounty Land Warrants and the Glasgow Land Fraud." Online: http://www.tngenweb.org/tnland/pruitt3.htm.

United States. Congress (4th, 2nd session: 1796-1797), *In Senate of the United States, March 1st, 1797: Mr. Hillhouse, from the committee to whom was referred the letter and enclosures from the governor of North Carolina, relative to the extinguishment of the Indian title to lands granted to T. Glasgow & Co. by the state of North Carolina – the address of the legislature of the state of Tennessee, on the same subject – and also the petition of J. Glasgow and others, relative to lands entered in the Office of John Armstrong, Esq., and since ceded to the United States – reported.* Philadelphia: [Printed by John Fenno?], 1797.

Whyte, Robert, 1767-1844. "Whyte, Robert Papers, 1755-[1800-1840]-1896." Manuscript Accession Number: 141, Microfilm Accession Number: 1780, Tennessee State Library and Archives, Nashville; online finding aid available at http://share.tn.gov/tsla/history/manuscripts/findingaids/141.pdf. [Online finding aid description: "The Robert Whyte papers containing approximately 2.5 cubic feet of material and 686 documents spanning the period 1755-1896, although concentrated between approximately 1800-1840... The majority of the documents in the collection are legal in nature: indentures, land grants, legal correspondence, legal briefs, notes on cases, court dockets, summons, warrants, etc... Researchers should note that there are several documents in the collection that list Whyte as 'Robert White.' The variations in his name are the result of a spelling change which Whyte himself made. Whyte's father spelled his name "White," and Whyte's name was listed as "Robert White" at the time of his election to the North Carolina House of Commons in 1797 (Mitchell 1951, 5). Whyte appears to have changed the spelling around the time he relocated to Nashville in 1802-1804. The reason for the change remains unclear, but some sources have speculated that it was to distance himself from the scandal over fraudulent land grants which surrounded his father-in-law, Col. James Glasgow (Mitchell 1951, 5-6).”][31]

Speculation Lands

Justice, George W.; Justice, C. B.; Justice, W. B.; Justice, S. J.; Justice, T. B.; Justice Family Members; Speculation Land Company. “Speculation Lands Collection (1752-1930).” Manuscript, Special Collections, D. H. Ramsey Library, University of North Carolina at Ashville; online: http://toto.lib.unca.edu/findingaids/mss/speculation_lands/context/finding_aid.htm. [Online description: “In Philadelphia in September of 1795, two agents, Andrew Baird and Lewis Beard, approached Tench Coxe, assistant to Alexander Hamilton, the Secretary of the Treasury of the United States under Washington’s administration, regarding land holdings of some half million acres in western North Carolina. The Baird agents represented the interests of the Rutherford Land Company that consisted of some 18 members or Trustees, including William W. Erwin , James Greenlee, and others. The Rutherford Land Company was apparently created by Greenlee who owned extensive tracts in Burke County, North Carolina. Andrew Baird, a former New Jersey iron master, knew members of the Coxe family and this possibly accounts for the primary interest in Coxe as an investor. The Bairds offered Coxe an opportunity to purchase some or all of the land holdings of the Company, described as “east of the Blue Ridge Mountains” for 9 cents an acre. The tracts Tench Coxe eventually purchased included land in present day Rutherford County, Polk County, Henderson County, Cleveland County, McDowell County and Buncombe County. [William W. Ervin and Andrew Baird to Coxe, Sept. 17, 1795, Coxe Papers. Tench Coxe through a series of purchases obtained some 400,000 acres in western North Carolina. He managed to retain many of the land holdings for some twenty years by placing his real estate into a land trust. The first trust was held by William Tilghman, a trusted cousin and family lawyer, another friend and relative Abraham Kintzing, and a close relative, Richard Coxe, his wife’s brother. It is believed that Pierre-Estienne DuPonceau, a family friend and lawyer was also appointed a trustee at this time. This collection details the Tench Coxe purchase, the subsequent trusteeships and ownerships, the ensuing financial intrigue, and the substantial survey activity generated by various real estate activities.”]

Patton, Sadie Smathers. *Buncombe to Mecklenburg Speculation Lands.* Forest City: The Western North Carolina Historical Association, 1955.

Sakolski, Aaron Morton. *The Great American Land Bubble: The Amazing Story of Land-Grabbing, Speculations, and Booms from Colonial Days to the Present Time.* New York: Harper & brothers, 1932.

Speculation Land Company. “Speculation Land Company Records, 1775-1992.” Manuscript Collection 124, “W.L. Eury Appalachian Collection,” Special Collections, Belk Library, Appalachian State University, Boone; online finding aId: http://collections.library.appstate.edu/findingaids/ac124. [Online catalog description: “The Specula-tion Land Company sold and leased real estate in many southwestern North Carolina counties, particularly Rutherford, Polk, and Henderson. The owners, Isaac Bronson and Goold Hoyt, were based in New York, local agents were based in Rutherfordton, N. C. The Justice family, whose male members worked as agents of the company for several generations, generated or received most documents. Members of the Justice family also served as Baptist ministers for two generations.”]

Transylvania Company/Colony/Purchase

Allin, Benjamin Casey. *Some Notes Regarding Thomas Allin, Surveyor of the Transylvania Company: Report of Colonel Thomas Allin to the Transylvania Company or the Richard Henderson & Co. on the Layong off of Henderson, Kentucky, April 6, 1797.* [United States?: Society of Transylvanians; Evansville, Ind.: Keller-Crescent Co., 1945].

Clark, Walter. “The Colony of Transylvania.” *North Carolina Booklet*, 3:9 (January 1904), 5-39; online: http://digital.ncdcr.gov/cdm/ref/collection/p249901coll37/id/14180. [Online description from “North Carolina Periodicals Index,” East Carolina University: “This article describes a 1775 scheme to acquire, settle, and hold a large piece of land, called “Transylvania County,” lying between the Kentucky and Cumberland rivers, in what is now Tennessee and Kentucky. Details include Boonesborough’s establishment by a group of men led by North Carolina Judge Richard Henderson and frontiersman Daniel Boone. A reprint of Henderson’s journal documenting his journey into this territory is included.”]

---

[31] Mitchell References are from: Mitchell, Enoch L. “Robert Whyte, Agrarian, Lawyer, Jurist.” *Tennessee Historical Quarterly*, 10:1 (March 1951): 3-24.

Fowles, Susan S., and Susan S. Toules. "Col. Richard Henderson of the Famous Transylvania Company." Register of the Kentucky State Historical Society, 7:20 (May 1909), 37-45.

Henderson, Archibald. The Significance of the Transylvania Company in American History. [S. l.: s. n., 1935?].

Lester, William Stewart. "The Transylvania Colony." Ph. D. Dissertation, University of Kentucky, 1934; published: Spencer, Ind.: S. R. Guard & Co., 1935.

North Carolina. Secretary of State. "Miscellaneous Papers, 1689-1912." Manuscript PC.21 (MARS ID: 530; record group), State Archives of North Carolina, Raleigh. [Online catalog description shows that this collection includes: "...Photocopies are chiefly material relating to western lands, especially those of the Transylvania Company, with descriptions of Tennessee and Kentucky."]

North Carolina. Secretary of State. "Miscellaneous Papers, 1741-1921." Manuscript Records Series (RS) Number 15680 (MARS ID: 12.23). State Archives of North Carolina, Raleigh. [Online catalog description shows that this collection includes: "...photostatic copies of important documents in the records of the General Assembly including the 1775 Cherokee Indian deed to the Transylvania Company; ..."]

Swift, Vance E. "The 14th Colony." *The State: Down Home in North Carolina*, 46:6 (November 1978), 16-17, 39; online: http://digital.ncdcr.gov/cdm/ref/collection/p16062coll18/id/58157. [Online description from "North Carolina Periodicals Index," East Carolina University: "On March 17, 1775, a group of nine North Carolina proprietors called the Transylvania Company participated in the largest private purchase of Indian land ever in North America. The Cherokee Indians sold some 22,000,000 acres of land to the men who immediately began colonizing it. After independence, Virginia governor Patrick Henry declared the deal null and void, and both Virginia and North Carolina each granted the men 200,000 acres."]

Toomey, Michael. "Transylvania Purchase." Online (2009): http://tennesseeencyclopedia.net/entry.php?rec=1398.

Towles, Susan S. "A Sketch of Colonel Richard Henderson of the Transylvania County." *Register of the Kentucky State Historical Society*, 7:20 (May 1909), 39-48.

Williams, John. "John Williams (1731-1799) Papers, 1772-1784." Manuscript, PC.176 (MARS ID: 1943), State Archives of North Carolina, Raleigh. [Online catalog description: "Correspondence of Col. John Williams, Granville Co. lawyer, legislator, delegate to Continental Congress (1778-1779), judge, Revolutionary officer, and proprietor of the Transylvania Company. Letters concern family and business matters such as lawsuits and horse racing; suspension of the courts (1773); need for paymaster of troops (1777); the 1778 General Assembly; Tryon Co. loyalists; Transylvania Company's claim before the Virginia Assembly (1778); Williams's resignation from Congress; need to provide the Virginia- North Carolina Boundary Commission with militia protecion [*sic*] against the Cherokee (1779); and the illegitimate daughter of Gen. Francis Nash. Among the correspondents are Robert Burton, Isaac Edwards, Richard Henderson, Robert Morris, Francis Nash, and William B. Smith."]

Chapter Ten:
North Carolina Military Records

Major Battles and Events in North Carolina and Tennessee during the Revolution

Lewis, J. D. "The American Revolution in North Carolina: The Known Battles & Skirmishes in North Carolina." Online: http://www.carolana.com/NC/Revolution/NC_Revolutionary_War_Known_Battles_Skirmishes.htm.

Lewis, J. D. "The American Revolution in North Carolina: North Carolinians Outside of North Carolina during the Revolution." Online: http://www.carolana.com/NC/Revolution/nc_troops_outside_nc.html. [Contains links to maps and websites of battles outside of North Carolina where North Carolina troops fought.]

Colonial Military Records of North Carolina

Stevenson, George. "North Carolina's Colonial Era Military Records." *Recall*, 5:1 (April 1999), 4-8. [Online description from "North Carolina Periodicals Index," East Carolina University: "Documents relating to North Carolina's military activities from the reign of Queen Anne down to the 20th century have survived in varying quantities. Stevenson discusses the military activities in the state during the Colonial Period and the records that resulted from it. All conflict is arranged in chronological order--the Tuscarora War, 1711-1715; The Spanish Alarm, 1739-1748; The French and Indian War, 1755-1763; The War of the Regulation, 1768-1771; and the Colonial and State Militias during the Revolutionary War."]

General Military Studies and Documents

Battle, Jane Hyde Hall Liddell. "Jane Hyde Hall Liddell Battle Papers, 1693-1930." Manuscript 2769-z, Southern Historical Collection, Louis Round Wilson Special Collections Library, University of North Carolina, Chapel Hill; online finding aid available at http://www2.lib.unc.edu/mss/inv/b/Battle,Jane_Hyde_Hall_Liddell.html. [Online finding aid description: "Unrelated letters collected for their autograph value by Jane Battle and a few personal letters to S. Westray Battle. Included are the following: … a letter, 1780, from Abner Nash (1740-1786) about North Carolina troops…"]

Bower, Jacob, 1757-1818. "[Orderly Book: General, Brigade, and Division Orders, Middlebrook, Smith's Clove, New Windsor, and Elsewhere, 27 April – July 1779]. Manuscript MSS L1998F206.2 [Bound], Society of the Cincinnati Library, Anderson House, Washington, D. C. [Online catalog description: "Brigade orders signed Fr. Johnston. Col. Commandant. Daily orders concern courts martial, equipment and supply shortages and reporting methods, officers' promotions and claims. Also, allusions to Steuben's recently published *Regulations for the Order and Discipline of the Troops* (p. 5-11; 19-20; 32-37; 63; 73-75; 88-89; 144) and to the duties of the newly appointed Inspector General (p. 5-11; 33; 145). Many references to civil military relations (p. 29-30; 70-71; 89-90; 160- 161), to the reorganization of the Continental Army and various officers' duties (p. 31-32; 67; 80-81). Other units in camp: the Delaware regiment, various Maryland, North Carolina and Virginia Continental and state regiments, and several other Pennsylvania state and continental regiments."]

"Captain Arthur Council." In Weynette Parks Haun, *North Carolina Revolutionary Army Accounts Secretary of State Treasurer's and Comptroller's Papers Journal "A" (Public Accounts), 1775-1776* (Durham: W. P. Haun, 1988), 6-7. [Arthur Council was appointed as a captain in the militia of Wilmington District on April 10, 1776.) Tuesday, April 16th, 1776, The Congress met according to adjournment. The several districts, by direction of the Congress, having nominated sundry persons as officers to the battalions directed to be raised in this Province; the House taking the same in consideration, Resolved, That the persons be, and they are hereby appointed accordingly, …" In William L. Saunders, col. and ed., *The Colonial Records of North Carolina, Vol. 10: 1775-1776* (Raleigh: Josephus Daniels, 1890), 517-518.]

Carrington, Henry B. *Battles of the American Revolution, 1775-1781. Historical and Military Criticism, with Topographical Illustration*. New York: A. S. Barnes & Co., 1871, 1876.

Cate, Redfford. "Redfford Cate Collection." Manuscript MfP.159 (MARS ID: 2669; record group), State Archives of North Carolina, Raleigh. [The online catalog record for this collection shows that it contains: "…a note from Gen. Horatio Gates at Hillsborough about lack of cavalry at Battle of Camden (Aug., 1780); and letters from James Moore at Wilmington to the provincial congress on the situation of American troops (Mar., 1776), from Thomas Burke to the General Assembly on powers of Congress (1777), from Willie Jones to Gov. Abner Nash with news of Congress and the war (1780); …; accounts of John Penn with the state (1775-1780);…"]

Chartrand, Rene. *Colonial American Troops, 1610-1774*. Oxford: Osprey Publishing, 2003.

Clark, Henry Toole. "List of Revolutionary War Officers Compiled by Clark." Manuscript in the "Shiloh Mill Books Collection, 1800-1867," 1950-z, Southern Historical Collection, Louis Round Wilson Special Collections Library, University of North Carolina at Chapel Hill.

Clark, Walter. "North Carolina's Record in War: Troops and Generals." *North Carolina Booklet*, 4:6 (October 1904), 18-24. [Includes a section: "In the Revolution – 1775-'83," 19-21.

Davis, Robert S., Jr. "Continental Officers from the South in the *American State Papers*." *Georgia Genealogical Magazine: A Magazine of Genealogical Source Material Concerning Georgians,* no. 100 (Spring 1986), 167-172. [Virginia, North Carolina, South Carolina, and Georgia listings]

"Descriptive List of Troops Raised from Morgan District to Serve 18 Months in Continental Army, 1782." *North Carolinian: Journal of Genealogy and History,* 6:4 (December 1960), 752. [Gives names and ages of soldiers]

"Descriptive List of Men Raised from the Morgan District for B. General Sumner." *Eswau Huppeday: Bulletin of the Broad River Genealogical Society*, 14:4 (November 1994), 262-264.

Dickins, Francis Asbury. "Papers, 1840-1856." Manuscript Mss 2 D5605 b, Virginia Historical Society, Richmond. [Online catalog description shows that this collection includes: "list of North Carolina soldiers in the Revolutionary War and the War of 1812; list, 1856, of letters written to Revolutionary War claimants; list of Maryland soldiers killed at Camden, S. C., 16 August 1780;…"]

Dunn, Lewie. "'Lost' Now 'Found' North Carolina Revolutionary War Records." *Georgia Genealogical Society Quarterly*, 42:1 (Spring 2006), 2-4.

Durham, J. Lloyd. "Outfitting an American Revolutionary Soldier." *Tar Heel Junior Historian*, (Fall 1992); online: http://ncpedia.org/history/usrevolution/soldiers.

Gaines, George Towns. *Fighting Tennesseans*. [S. l.: s. n.], 1931.

Great Britain. Colonial Office. "Edenton, [N.C.]. Extract of William Knight to Richard Bone, a Wine Merchant in Kensington [London]. 1 Nov., 1775." Copy of a manuscript in the National Archives of the United Kingdom (formerly the Public Records Office), Kew, Richmond, Surrey, England, (MARS ID: 21.20.115.3), State Archives of North Carolina, Raleigh. [Online catalog description: "Three thousand minutemen raised in N. C., 200 of which are stationed at Edenton."]

Grundset, Eric G., Briana L. Diaz, Hollis L. Gentry, and Jean D. Strahan. *Forgotten Patriots: African American and American Indian Patriots in the Revolutionary War* (2008). Free online at: http://www.dar.org/library/fp.cfm.

Haywood, Marshall DeLancey. *The Citations Contained within This Leaflet Are Designed to Aid Those Who Have Occasion to Search for Records of the Services of Revolutionary Ancestors in North Carolina: Prepared for General Distribution*. [Raleigh: North Carolina Society, Sons of the Revolution, 1909]. [A copy is located at the Wisconsin Historical Society, Madison.]

Haywood, Marshall DeLancey. "Number of North Carolinians in the Revolutionary War." *North Carolina Booklet*, 15:1 (July 1915), 28-32.

Holmes, Pat. "Rebirth of the N. C. Brigade." *The State: Down Home in North Carolina*, 40:18 (April 1973), 9-13; online: http://digital.ncdcr.gov/cdm/ref/collection/p16062coll18/id/55888. [Online description from "North Carolina Periodicals Index," East Carolina University: "Originally organized in September of 1775 under the command of Col. James Moore, North Carolina's First Regiment of Continentals was reactivated on September 18, 1968 by Governor Bob Scott as part of North Carolina's observance of the National Bicentennial Celebration. Members of the modern First Regiment, which is commanded by Col. B. F. Jarrell of Burlington, take part in reenactments and drills staged as preliminaries to the actual start of the Bicentennial Celebration in 1976."]

Johnson, William Perry. "N. C. Revolutionary Military Papers." *The North Carolinian: A Quarterly Journal of Genealogy and History*, 7:4 (December 1961), 886-898; *Journal of North Carolina Genealogy,* 8:1 (March 1962), 930-939; 8:4 (December 1962), 1049-1062; *Journal of North Carolina Genealogy*, 9:2 (Summer 1963), 1125-1130; 10:2 (Summer 1964), 1329-1345; 12:3 (Fall 1966), 1728-1734; 14:2 (Summer 1968), 2093-2098; 16:2 (Fall/Winter 1970), 2578-2583; 20:1 (Spring/Summer 1974), 2928-2932. [The journal ceased publication without publishing any additional articles in this series.]

King, Clyde L. "Military Organizations of North Carolina during the American Revolution." *North Carolina Booklet*, 8:1 (July 1908), 42-55; online: http://digital.ncdcr.gov/cdm/ref/collection/p249901coll37/id/14180. [Online description from "North Carolina Periodicals Index," East Carolina University: "This article chronicles various military organizations of the North Carolina during the American Revolution. Through this, the author hopes to determine whether North Carolina or the Continental Congress exercised control or authority over them."]

Lawrence, R. C. "Revolutionary Generals." *The State: A Weekly Survey of North Carolina*, 11:41 (March 1944), 6, 14; online: http://digital.ncdcr.gov/cdm/ref/collection/p16062coll18/id/18687. [Online description from "North

Carolina Periodicals Index," East Carolina University: "Lawrence lists North Carolina's twelve Revolutionary War generals and gives a brief summary of their careers."]

Lewis, J. D. "The American Revolution in North Carolina: The Patriots and Their Forces." Online: http://www.carolana.com/ NC/Revolution/revolution_patriot_troops_nc.html. [Includes sections titled: "How the NC Military Organization Changed over the Course of the War;" "The Different Military Units in North Carolina during the Revolutionary War;" "All Known North Carolina Ground Troops." The sections have links to chronological information, unit information, officer listings, soldier listings, etc.]

Lewis, J. D. "North Carolina Military Organization Charts, 1775-1783." Online: http://www.carolana.com/NC/Revolution/revolution_nc_troops_1775_03_10.html. [Charts of the organization for specific dates throughout the war.]

"List, 1779, of North Carolina Militiamen." Manuscript Mss12: 1779 Jul[?]:1, Virginia Historical Society, Richmond. [Online catalog description: "List, 1779 July-November, of North Carolina militiamen drafted for service in the U. S. Continental Army."]

"List of North Carolina Soldiers in the Revolutionary War and the War of 1812." Manuscript in Mss2 D5605 b, "Francis Aubrey Dickins Papers, 1840-1856," Virginia Historical Society, Richmond.

"List of Virginia and North Carolina Officers, Undated." Manuscript accession no. 45186, "State Government Records Collection," Library of Virginia, Richmond; also available on miscellaneous microfilm reel. [Online catalog description: "Contains a printed list of Virginia Revolutionary Officers and North Carolina Revolutionary Officers. The list provides the name of the officer, their rank, and state."]

Lutz, Paul V. "A State's Concern for the Soldiers' Welfare: How North Carolina Provided for Her Troops during the Revolution." *North Carolina Historical Review*, 42:3 (July 1965), 315-318; online: http://digital.ncdcr.gov/cdm/ref/collection/p16062coll9/id/4207. [Online description from "North Carolina Periodicals Index," East Carolina University: "This article looks at the provisions, payments, and rewards offered to North Carolina soldiers in the Revolutionary War."]

Lynn, John W. *North Carolina Lineages of Revolutionary War Regiments*. Grand Junction, Colo.: Lynn Research, 1986.

Lytle, William, 1755-1829. "William Lytle Papers, 1773-1841 (bulk 1773-1805)." Manuscript 445-z, Southern Historical Collection, Louis Round Wilson Special Collections Library, University of North Carolina, Chapel Hill; online finding aid and some digital surrogates available at http://www2.lib.unc.edu/mss/inv/l/Lytle,William.html. [Online finding aid description: "William Lytle, of Hillsboro, N. C., was the son of Robert Lytle (1729-1774) and Sarah Mebane Lytle, and served in the Sixth, First, and Fourth regiments of the North Carolina Line during the Revolutionary War. He entered as a lieutenant in 1776, and became a captain in 1779. He moved to Tennessee about 1790. The collection includes personal correspondence, military and business papers of William Lytle, chiefly before 1805. Includes Revolutionary muster rolls, information about the Cherokee Treaty of 1791 and Indian affairs in Tennessee in the 1790s, accounts, inventories, deeds, court papers concerning Tennessee lands, bills, and receipts. Correspondents include Nicholas Long, Alexander Mebane, William Norwood, Montfort Stokes, Absalom Tatom, and James Taylor."]

Maddox, Joseph T., and Mary Carter. *North Carolina Revolutionary Soldiers, Sailors, Patriots and Descendants*. 2 vols. Albany, Ga.: Georgia Pioneers Publications, [1976?]

McBride, Ransom. "Killed and Wounded by Indians, 1782, 1788." *North Carolina Genealogical Society Journal*, 9:4 (November 1983), 236.

McDonald, Hugh, ed. "Extract from a Revolutionary Journal." *North Carolina University Magazine*, 2:10 (December 1853). [The author of the journal is not identified.]

McIntyre, Jim. "The Role of the Rifleman in the Southern Campaigns of the American War of Independence." Online: http://lib.jrshelby.com/mcintyre-riflemen%20in%20the%20south.pdf.

McMaster, Fitzhugh. "Some Notes on North Carolina." *Military Collector and Historian*, 33:2 (Summer 1981), 80.

"Military Engagements and Military Casualties in North Carolina during the American Revolution. [Abstracted from Howard H. Peckham, editor, The Toll of Independence: Engagements & Battle Casualties of the American Revolution." (Chicago: 1974).] [19--?]. [Lists all battles and casualties in North Carolina during the war.]

Moore, Terry. "Finding Your North Carolina Revolutionary War Soldier or Patriot, Part 1: [Continental Line]." *NCGS News: The Newsletter of the North Carolina Genealogical Society*, 38:2 (March 2014), 10-11; online: http://www.ncgenealogy.org/articles_tools/Finding_Your_Rev_War_Soldier.pdf.

Moore, Terry. "Finding Your North Carolina Revolutionary War Soldier or Patriot, Part 2: [Continental Line and Militia]." *NCGS News: The Newsletter of the North Carolina Genealogical Society*, 38:3 (May 2014), 10-11; online: http://www.ncgenealogy.org/articles_tools/Finding_Your_Rev_War_Soldier.pdf.

Moss, Bobby Gilmer, and Michael Scoggins. *African-American Patriots in the Southern Campaign of the American*

Revolution. Blacksburg, S. C.: Scotia-Hibernia Press, 2004. [Description: "Provides biographical and military service information on African-Americans who participated with American forces patriots in the southern campaign of the American Revolution. The coverage area includes Maryland, Virginia, North Carolina, South Carolina, Georgia, and Florida."]

"Muster and Pay Rolls of the War of the Revolution, 1775-1783: North Carolina Troops." *Collections of the New-York Historical Society for the Year 1915* (New York: The Society, 1916), 512-515; reprinted: 2 volumes in 1. Baltimore: Genealogical Publishing Company, 1996. [The original page numbers remain in the facsimile reprint. The original documents are in the Muster Roll Collection of the Patricia D. Klingenstein Library of the New-York Historical Society.]

North Carolina (State). General Assembly. "[Document dated:] July 7, 1781: Joint Papers, Committee Papers, Resolutions, Senate Bills, House Bills, Concerning a Defect in the Militia Law." Manuscript; General Assembly Record Group; Session Records, June-July 1781, Box 1 (MARS ID: 66.8.25.4.6), State Archives of North Carolina, Raleigh. [Online catalog description: "Burke informs the Assembly that the mutiny of an entire squadron of light horse has demonstrated a flaw in the militia law, in that the officers who are supposed to be the court martial are in this case also offenders."]

North Carolina (State). General Assembly. House of Delegates. "[Document dated:] December 6, [1777]: Joint Papers, Committee Papers, Resolutions, Senate Bills, House Bills, Bill to Enable the Governor to Send an Aid from the Militia to Oppose the Enemies of the U. S., etc." Manuscript; General Assembly Record Group; Session Records, November-December 1777, House Bills, Box 2 (MARS ID: 66.8.11.28), State Archives of North Carolina, Raleigh.

North Carolina (State). General Assembly. House of Delegates. "House Bills (July 3), [1781]: Joint Papers, Committee Papers, Resolutions, Senate Bills, House Bills, Bill for the More Effectually Punishing the Enemies of This of the United States (Failed)." Manuscript; General Assembly Record Group; Session Records, June-July 1781, Box 2 (MARS ID: 66.8.26.27), State Archives of North Carolina, Raleigh. [Online catalog description: "The bill would have forced those individuals who broke their oaths of allegiance during the British invasion to serve as Continental soldiers and established a company of light horse in each county to enforce the act."]

North Carolina (State). General Assembly. House of Delegates. "House Bills (June 30), [1781]: Joint Papers, Committee Papers, Resolutions, Senate Bills, House Bills, Bill for Raising Troops for the Defense of the State (Failed)." Manuscript; General Assembly Record Group; Session Records, June-July 1781, Box 2 (MARS ID: 66.8.26.23), State Archives of North Carolina, Raleigh.

North Carolina Daughters of the American Revolution. "North Carolina – Revolutionary Soldiers." *North Carolina DAR Genealogical Records Committee Report, Series 1, Volume 2: Records* (typescript, 1926), 37-42; digital surrogate, DAR Library, Washington, D. C.

North Carolina Daughters of the American Revolution. "North Carolina Revolutionary Soldiers." *North Carolina DAR Genealogical Records Committee Report, Series 1, Volume 75: Genealogical Records* (typescript, 1941), 71; digital surrogate, DAR Library, Washington, D. C.

North Carolina Daughters of the American Revolution; foreword by Gertrude Sloan Hay (Mrs. R. Duke). *Roster of Soldiers from North Carolina in the American Revolution with an Appendix Containing a Collection of Miscellaneous Records* Durham: North Carolina Daughters of the American Revolution, 1932: reprinted: Baltimore: Genealogical Publishing Company, 1967, 1972, 1977, 1984, 1988, 2000. [Provides name, rank, company, dates of enlistment and commission, period of service, and any notable occurrences.] [**Note: The National Society Daughters of the American Revolution does not accept this publication as a source for proof of service during the American Revolution. It should only be used as a guide and for clues**.][32]

---

[32] Note: One example of the problems with this publication is the following information provided by Forrest C. Crosley, Assistant Director of Genealogy, Office of the Registrar General, National Society Daughters of the American Revolution (2013). "Do not use North Carolina military bounty warrants found in Roster of Soldiers from North Carolina in the American Revolution, pp 233-312, per Lloyd De Witt Bockstruck's *Revolutionary War Bounty Land Grants Awarded by State Governments* (Introduction, p. xix). It states that the list of bounty land warrants on pages 233-312 is a 'transcription made from an incomplete and faulty register of the military bounty land warrants. Many of the names do not agree with the original…all warrant numbers from 237 to 1170 are incorrectly given. They should be one number higher. The most serious flaw in this publication, however, is the omission of 1,579 warrants included in the Military Land Warrant Book. In other words, forty percent of the North Carolina entries are missing from the only published source heretofore available'."

North Carolina (State). General Assembly. "[Document dated:] February 8, [1781]: Joint Papers, Committee Papers, Resolutions, Senate Bills, House Bills, Recommending Colonel Malmedy to the Commanding Officer (with Three Letters from Malmedy)." Manuscript; General Assembly Record Group; Session Records, January-February 1781, Box 1 (MARS ID: 66.8.23.17.4), State Archives of North Carolina, Raleigh. [Online catalog description: "The resolution recommends Malmedy to Major General Caswell for appointment to a military position. Malmedy's letters discuss the Assembly's actions and his plans for light horse."]

North Carolina. "Troop Returns, 1747-1893." Manuscript (MARS ID: 5864; record group), State Archives of North Carolina, Raleigh. [Online catalog description: "Troop Returns include lists, returns, records of prisoners, and records of draftees. Lists are usually pay or muster rolls. Most of the returns are field or general returns, and report the names of the officers and the number of enlisted men under their command (but not the names of each soldier). Prisoners records may be lists of British prisoners or of North Carolina Line officers captured by the British. Drafts and enlistments records give the names of enlisted men and sometimes take the form of descriptive lists that also include height, age, coloring, etc., of each soldier. Except for the drafts and enlistments, most of the Continental Line records are field and general returns; the militia records, on the other hand, generally record the names of both officers and soldiers."]

North Carolina Daughters of the American Revolution; foreword by Gertrude Sloan Hay (Mrs. R. Duke). Roster of Soldiers from North Carolina in the American Revolution with an Appendix Containing a Collection of Miscellaneous Records Durham: North Carolina Daughters of the American Revolution, 1932: reprinted: Baltimore: Genealogical Publishing Company, 1967, 1972, 1977, 1984, 1988, 2000.

Pendleton, Nathaniel. "A Signed Letter of Nathaniel Pendleton to Holland Summer's 10 Miles from Mores, March 10, 1781: to an Unidentified Person [Possibly Nathanael Greene]." Manuscript MSS 189-A M, Society of the Cincinnati Library, Anderson House, Washington, D. C. [Online catalog description: "'One mile beyond this place, on the way to Mores [i. e. Col. Moore's?], I met the bearer of this [not included] with two or three other men, belonging to Genl. Butler's detachment.' 'The packet from Baron Steuben I took from a man who took it from an express, who was taken sick on the road. I thought best to send the bearer with it, & the above information. Agreeable to your direction I shall go in search of General Butler ... & hasten his march as much as I possibly can; he has neglected to leave his baggage behind. Of consequence it must retard his march.' Context: General Nathanael Greene was camped at High Rock Ford on this date, awaiting reinforcements before engaging Cornwallis or Tarleton before the battle of Guilford Courthouse. General John Butler had taken over command of North Carolina militiamen and joined Greene 'on or about 10 March' – *Papers of General Nathanael Greene*, vol. VII, p. 421 note 3. See also, on the same page, Greene's March 10 letter to Col. Henry Lee: 'I am anxiously waiting for the arrival of the North Caro[li]nia Militia'."]

Prall, Mrs. C. E. and Mrs. G. S. Miles for the Guilford Battle Chapter, North Carolina Daughters of the American Revolution. "Revolution Soldiers." *North Carolina DAR Genealogical Records Committee Report, Series 1, Volume 277: Family Records, Histories of Families, Bounty Lands* (typescript, 1960), 1-2; digital surrogate, DAR Library, Washington, D. C.

"Revolutionary Military Papers Index." Online at the North Carolina Genealogical Society's member website: http://www.ncgenealogy.org/menu-resources/revolutionary-military-papers-index. [Description: Secretary of State's Office. "Revolutionary Military Papers, 1767-1855." Manuscript Box 760-804.1, State Archives of North Carolina, Raleigh. "The Secretary of State Revolutionary Military Papers, 1767-1855, are indexed in a card catalog at the State Archives of North Carolina. These index cards were microfilmed at one time, and those images have been converted to JPG images. The State Archives has provided the North Carolina Genealogical Society with a copy of these images. NCGS is currently undertaking a project to convert these images to searchable PDF files, to provide as a member benefit. More comprehensive information about these index cards, and the papers they represent, will be forthcoming. The original index cards, and associated images, are in the Public Domain, free for anyone to see. The pdf files found on this website are a derivitive work, and as such are the property of the North Carolina Genealogical Society."]

Rider, Thomas A. "Massacre or Myth: No Quarter at the Waxhaws, 29 May 1780." M. A. thesis, University of North Carolina at Chapel Hill, 2002.

Robertson, John K. "Southern Campaigns." Website: http://www.southerncampaign.org/. [Includes: "Online Library of the Revolutionary War;" "Global Gazetteer of the American Revolution;" "Southern Campaign Revolutionary War Pension Statements & Rosters;" "Southern Campaigns of the American Revolution"]newsletter with many historical articles.]

Robertson, John K., and Bob McDonald. "Index of Continental Army Orderly Books." Online: http://revwar75.com/ob/index.htm [Provides references to the location of original North Carolina orderly books with very brief histories of the units.]

Sherman, William T. *Calendar and Record of the Revolutionary War in the South: 1780-1781*. Seattle: W. T. Sherman, 2003; online: http://www.virginia1774.org/Southern%20Record.pdf. [Contents: The American Revolution and the Southern War in Perspective; Leaders and Units; I. American Leaders; The Continental Army; Virginia Militia and State Troops; North Carolina Militia and State Troops; Frontier Militia; South Carolina Militia and State Troops; Georgia Militia and State Troops. II. American Units; The Continental Army; State Troops; III. British Leaders; The British Army and Provincials; German; North Carolina Loyalists; South Carolina Loyalists; Georgia Loyalists. IV. British Units; The British Army; Provincials and Loyalist Militia; German; V. Calendar and Record; Appendix. A. Totals for Greene's Continentals in the South; B. Totals for the British Army in the Carolinas and Georgia; C. Loyalties and Population in the South in 1780.]

Snow, Carol Leonard. *Volunteer Revolutionary War Soldiers from North Carolina*. Toast, N. C.: C. L. Snow, 1993.

"Some Defense Problems – The American Revolution." *North Carolina Genealogical Society Journal*, 9:2 (May 1983), 102.

State Archives of North Carolina. "Military Collection Finding AId: V. War of the Revolution." Online at the State Archives of North Carolina website: http://archives.ncdcr.gov/Portals/3/PDF/findingaids/pdf/MilColl_WaroftheRevolution.pdf. [This collection includes papers of the Board of War, 1780-1781; Commissary Correspondence, 1779-1783; British and Loyalist Papers; Miscellaneous Papers, 1776-1789; Jeffrey Coltraine Jr. Collection; Declarations of Service to Accompany U. S. Pension Applications (with a list of names prepared by Betty Camin); State Pensions to Invalids and Widows (with a list of names); and Loyalist Records (including documents relating to confiscated Loyalist property arranged by county). The finding aid provides greater detail on this collection than the listing in this entry.]

Stevenson, George. *North Carolina Revolutionary War Records of Primary Interest to Genealogists* (Archives Information Circular, no. 13) Raleigh: State of North Carolina, Department of Cultural Resources, Division of Archives and History, 1975; revised March 2002.

United States. Department of War. Adjutant-General's Office. *Index to Compiled Service Records of Volunteer Soldiers Who Served during the Revolutionary War in Organizations from the State of North Carolina*. 2 microfilm reels (M-257). Washington, D. C.: National Archives and Records Service, 1958.

White, Emmett R. *Revolutionary War Soldiers of Western North Carolina*. 3 vols. Easley, S. C.: Southern Historical Press, 1984; 2011. [List of entires in alphabetical order that provide details about the individual soldiers of the Revolutionary War from the western part of North Carolina. Covers Burke, Catawba, Caldwell, and McDowell Counties.]

Yates Mill Chapter, North Carolina Daughters of the American Revolution. "Revolutionary War Troop Returns, North Carolina." *North Carolina DAR Genealogical Records Committee Report, Series 2, Volume 57: Miscellaneous State Records* (typescript, 2009), 86-112; digital surrogate, DAR Library, Washington, D. C. [Includes "Beaufort County Drafted Men – 1779"; "Beaufort Regiment of Militia – 1781"; "Descriptive List of Bladen County Militia – 1782"; "Descriptive List of the Delinquents from Bladen County"; "Descriptive List of Bute County Continental Soldiers – 1778"; "Carteret County Militia – 1777"; "Descriptive List of Carteret County Continental Soldiers – 1778"; "Chowan County Enlistments – 1779"; "Duplin County Militia – 1779"; "Hyde County Field Returns – 1774"; Descriptive List of Hyde County Continental Soldiers – 1778"; "Hyde County Militia – 1780"; "Onslow County Recruiting Officer Report"; "Onslow Field Return – 1777"; "Onslow County Conscripts – 1778"; "Onslow County Militia Volunteers and Draftees – 1779"; "Pitt County Militia – 1775"]

North Carolina Board of War

North Carolina (State). General Assembly. House of Delegates. "[Document dated:] September 5, [1780]: Bill for Establishing a Board of War." Manuscript; General Assembly Record Group; Session Records, August-September 1780; Joint Papers, Committee Papers, Resolutions, Senate Bills, House Bills, House Bill: Box 1 (MARS ID: 66.8.22.23), State Archives of North Carolina, Raleigh.

North Carolina (State). Office of Secretary of State. "Board of War Records, 1780-1781." Manuscript SS 911.1C (MARS ID: 12.116; series), State Archives of North Carolina, Raleigh. ["Journal. Correspondence of the Board is presently in the Military Collection (3 manuscript boxes)." *Guide to Research Materials in the North Carolina State Archives: State Agency Records* (Raleigh: Department of Cultural Resources, Division of Archives and History, Archives and Records Section, 1995), 623.]

North Carolina (State). General Assembly. "[Document Dated: September 5, 1780]: House Bill: Bill for Establishing a Board of War." Manuscript; General Assembly Record Group; Session Records, August-September 1780;

Joint Papers, Committee Papers, Resolutions, Senate Bills, House Bills, Box 1 (MARS ID: 66.8.22.23; folder), State Archives of North Carolina, Raleigh.

North Carolina (State). General Assembly. "[Document Dated: January 29, 1781]: Resolution Requesting Journals of the Board of War." Manuscript; General Assembly Record Group; Session Records, January-February 1781; Joint Papers, Committee Papers, Resolutions, Senate Bills, House Bills, Box 1 (MARS ID: 66.8.23.15.2; item), State Archives of North Carolina, Raleigh.

North Carolina (State). General Assembly. "[Document Dated: May 17, 1782]: Report on the Settlement of the Accounts of John Haywood, Secretry to the Late Board of War (with Messages and Letter)." Manuscript; General Assembly Record Group; Session Records, April-May 1782; Joint Papers, Committee Papers, Box 1 (MARS ID: 66.8.27.11.19; item), State Archives of North Carolina, Raleigh. [Online catalog description: "Letter from John Haywood requesting that his accounts be sent to committee for settlement; committee report detailing account settlement; and messages from both houses referring letter to committee and concurring with report."]

Troxler, George W. "Board of War." In William S. Powell, ed.; Jay Mazzocchi, assoc. ed., *Encyclopedia of North Carolina* (Chapel Hill: University of North Carolina Press in association with the University of North Carolina Library, 2006), 136-137.

Conscription, Recruitment, Enlistment, and Service Exemptions

Cometti, Elizabeth. "Impressment during the American Revolution." In Vera Largent, ed., *The Walter Clinton Jackson Essays in the Social Sciences, by the Members of the Faculty of the Woman's College of the University of North Carolina* (Chapel Hill: University of North Carolina Press, 1942).

Graham, William A[lexander]. *General Joseph Graham and His Papers on North Carolina Revolutionary History, with Appendix: An Epitome of North Carolina's Military Services in the Revolutionary War and of the Laws Enacted for Raising Troops.* Raleigh: Edwards & Broughton, 1904.

Lewis, Giles F. "Giles F. Lewis Collection, 1782-1850." Manuscript, PC.1283, State Archives of North Carolina, Raleigh. [Online catalog description: {Includes} "army receipt for horse as partial payment for a substitute for Lewis in the Continental draft (1782)."]

Maass, John. "'Too Grievous for a People to Bear': Impressment and Conscription in Revolutionary North Carolina." *Journal of Military History*, 73:4 (October, 2009), 1091-1115.

North Carolina. General Assembly. "June 1781: Petition of John Evans of Nash County (Laid Over)." Manuscript; General Assembly Record Group; Session Records, June-July 1781, Box 1 (MARS ID: 66.8.25.7.2), State Archives of North Carolina, Raleigh. [Online catalog description: "Evans asks the Assembly to discharge him from the militia, as he feels he was threatened into enlisting."]

North Carolina and Tennessee Militia

Babits, L. E. "The Militia." *Tar Heel Junior Historian*, 15:2 (Winter 1976), 33-36. [Online description from "North Carolina Periodicals Index," East Carolina University: "The most effective unit of the state's militiamen was organized under Lieutenant Colonel Henry Dixon. His men must have been drilled continuously based on their discipline in battle. A second noteworthy group of North Carolina militia were the 'over mountain men.' This unit lacked formal military training but, as a group, functioned as a disciplined and organized regiment."]

Baldwin, Samuel, 1754-1850. "Papers, 1780-1849 (Bulk dates: March 20-April 29, 1780)." Manuscript MG 540, New Jersey Historical Society, Newark. [Online finding aid description: "The papers consist of two folders of materials dating from 1780-1849. The main document in the papers is the diary of Samuel Baldwin, written from March 20 - April 20, 1780 in Charleston, South Carolina during the British attack on that city. Baldwin describes such things as British troop movements; the departure of the North Carolina militia as their term of service expired; the sinking of ships; desertion; offensive and defensive preparations; fighting; and the capture and killing of men on both sides."]

Branton, Yvonne M. "Lost to Posterity." *Daughters of the American Revolution Magazine*, 119:2 (February 1985), 93-94. [John Singletary, who fought in North and South Carolina and was part of the North Carolina Militia]

Brevard Family, McDowell Family. "Brevard and McDowell Family Papers, 1754-1953." Manuscript 86 and microfilm M-86, 2 rolls, Southern Historical Collection, Louis Round Wilson Special Collections Library, University of North Carolina, Chapel Hill; online finding aid and some digital surrogates available at http://www2.lib.unc.edu/mss/inv/b/Brevard_and_McDowell_Family.html. [Online finding aid description: "...The collection consists of papers of members of the Brevard, McDowell, and related families. Papers of Alexander Brevard include land grants, deeds, wills, and business papers relating to Mount Tirzah Forge in

Lincoln County, including some relating to slaves working at the Forge; North Carolina Revolutionary War militia papers, including a muster roll, 1780-1781; and an account, 1827, of his war service."]

Churchill, Robert H. "Gun Ownership in Early America: A Survey of Manuscript Militia Returns." *William and Mary Quarterly*, 3rd series, 60:3 (July 2003), 615-642.

"Estimate of Militia, April 1782." *North Carolinian: A Quarterly Journal of Genealogy and History*, 6:3 (September 1960), 725-726.

Ferguson, Clyde R. "Carolina and Georgia Patriot and Loyalist Militia in Action, 1778-1783." In Jeffrey J. Crow and Larry E. Tise, eds., *The Southern Experience in the American Revolution* (Chapel Hill: University of North Carolina Press, 1978), 174-199.

Ferguson, Clyde R. "Functions of the Partisan-Militia in the South during the American Revolution: An Interpretation." In W. Robert Higgins, ed., *The Revolutionary War in the South: Power, Conflict, and Leadership: Essays in Honor of John Richard Alden* (Durham: Duke University Press, 1979), 239-258.

Gobbel, Luther Lafayette. "Militia in North Carolina in Colonial and Revolutionary Times." *Trinity College Historical Society Historical Papers*, 13 (1919), 35-61.

Holden, John Marion. "Revolutionary War Patriot Militiamen of Southeastern North Carolina." Graduate thesis, University of North Carolina, Chapel Hill: 1988. [Description: "This study examines the nature of Patriot militia service during the American Revolution and the socioeconomic status of citizen-soldiers. Profiles of eighteen militiamen of southeastern North Carolina are based on pension applications, tax lists, wills, and estate inventories."]

Johnson, William Perry. "Descriptions of Soldiers from Militia Returns, 1778-1782." *North Carolinian: A Quarterly Journal of Genealogy and History*, 6:3 (September 1960), 725-730, 751-758.

Kay, Marvin, and William S. Price, Jr. "'To Ride the Wood Mare': Road Building and Militia Service in Colonial North Carolina, 1740-1775." *North Carolina Historical Review*, 57:4 (October 1980), 361-409. [Online description from "North Carolina Periodicals Index," East Carolina University: "In colonial North Carolina, road building and militia service laws were a product of a highly divided class system. Wealthy landowners and slave-owners comprised the governmental bodies that decided when roads were built, where they went as well as whom would be exempt from militia and road service duties. Slaves and members of the lower economic classes were required to at least 12 days per year on road service and whites were also required to spend additional time with the militia. These duties often placed a larger economic burden on members of the lower classes."]

Kearney, Timothy. *Abstracts of Letters of Resignations of Militia Officers in North Carolina, 1779-1840*. Raleigh: North Carolina Genealogical Society, 1992; reprinted: 2004.

Lee, Wayne E.; foreword by Stanley Harrold and Randall M. Miller. *Crowds and Soldiers in Revolutionary North Carolina: The Culture of Violence in Riot and War*. Gainesville: University Press of Florida, 2001. [Contents: "Riotous disorderly persons;" "To fight the air:" The Careful Riots of the Regulators; The Road to Alamance; Colonial Ways of War: Tradition and Development; "A Fair Fight:" The Revolutionary Militias and the Struggle for Virtue, 1775-1776; Civil Consolidation: The "Peaceful" Years, 1777-1779; "The Law of Retaliation:" The War of the Militias, 1780-1782.]

Lee, Wayne E. "Restraint and Retaliation: The North Carolina Militias and the Backcountry War of 1780-1782." In John Resch and Walter Sargent, eds.; introduction by John Shy. *War & Society in the American Revolution: Mobilization and Home Fronts* (DeKalb: Northern Illinois University Press, 2007), 163-190.

Lee, Wayne Emmett. "Careful Riot, Virtuous War: The Legitimation of Public Violence in Eighteenth-Century North Carolina." Ph. D. dissertation, Duke University, 1999.

Lewis, J. D. "The American Revolution in North Carolina: Adjutants." Online: http://www.carolana.com/NC/Revolution/nc_patriot_military_adjutants.html.

Lewis, J. D. "The American Revolution in North Carolina: Captains." Online: http://www.carolana.com/NC/Revolution/nc_patriot_military_captains.html.

Lewis, J. D. "The American Revolution in North Carolina: Cornets." Online: http://www.carolana.com/NC/Revolution/nc_patriot_military_cornets.html.

Lewis, J. D. "The American Revolution in North Carolina: Corporals." Online: http://www.carolana.com/NC/Revolution/nc_patriot_military_corporals.html.

Lewis, J. D. "The American Revolution in North Carolina: Ensigns." Online: http://www.carolana.com/NC/Revolution/nc_patriot_military_ensigns.html.

Lewis, J. D. "The American Revolution in North Carolina: Generals." Online: http://www.carolana.com/NC/Revolution/nc_patriot_military_generals.html. [Provides brief descriptions of the careers of the North Carolina generals of the militia and Continental Line: James Armstrong, John Ashe, Thomas Benbury, William Bryan,

John Butler, Richard Caswell, William Caswell, William Lee Davidson, Thomas Eaton, Isaac Gregory, Henry William Harrington, James Hogun, Robert Howe, Allen Jones, James Kenan, John Alexander Lillington, Charles McDowell, Alexander Mebane, James Moore, Francis Nash, Thomas Person, Andrew Pickens, Ambrose Ramsey, Griffith Rutherford, John Simpson, William Skinner, William Smallwood, Jethro Sumner, Edward Vail, and John Pugh Williams.]

Lewis, J. D. "The American Revolution in North Carolina: Lieutenants." Online: http://www.carolana.com/NC/Revolution/nc_patriot_military_lieutenants.html.

Lewis, J. D. "The American Revolution in North Carolina: Lt. Colonels." Online: http://www.carolana.com/NC/Revolution/nc_patriot_military_lt_colonels.html.

Lewis, J. D. "The American Revolution in North Carolina: Majors." Online: http://www.carolana.com/NC/Revolution/nc_patriot_military_majors.html.

Lewis, J. D. "The American Revolution in North Carolina: Quarter Masters (QMs)." Online: http://www.carolana.com/NC/Revolution/nc_patriot_military_miscellaneous.html.

Lewis, J. D. "The American Revolution in North Carolina: Matrosses & Gunners." Online: http://www.carolana.com/NC/Revolution/nc_patriot_military_matrosses_and_gunners.html.

Lewis, J. D. "The American Revolution in North Carolina: The North Carolina Militia." Online: http://www.carolana.com/NC/Revolution/revolution_patriots_militia_nc.html.

Lewis, J. D. "The American Revolution in North Carolina: The Patriots and Their Forces: How the NC Military Organization Changed over the Course of the War." Online: http://www.carolana.com/NC/Revolution/revolution_patriot_troops_nc.html

Lewis, J. D. "The American Revolution in North Carolina: Privates, Horsemen, Fifers, Drummers, etc." Online: http://www.carolana.com/NC/Revolution/nc_patriot_military_privates_etc.html.

Lewis, J. D. "The American Revolution in North Carolina: Quarter Masters (QMs)." Online: http://www.carolana.com/NC/Revolution/nc_patriot_military_quarter_masters.html.

Lewis, J. D. "The American Revolution in North Carolina: Sergeants." Online: http://www.carolana.com/NC/Revolution/nc_patriot_military_sergeants.html.

Lunderberg, Philip Karl. "A History of the North Carolina Militia, 1784-1848." M. A. Thesis, Duke University, 1947. [post-Revolution]

Moore, Terry. "Finding Your North Carolina Revolutionary War Soldier or Patriot, Part 2: [Continental Line and Militia]." *NCGS News: The Newsletter of the North Carolina Genealogical Society*, 38:3 (May 2014), 10-11; online: http://www.ncgenealogy.org/articles_tools/Finding_Your_Rev_War_Soldier.pdf.

North Carolina (State). General Assembly. "[Document dated:] September 2, [1780]: Re[specting] Militia Lately Defeated in South Carolina and Dispersed." Manuscript; General Assembly Record Group; Session Records, August-September 1780; Joint Papers, Committee Papers, Resolutions, Senate Bills, House Bills, Box 1 (MARS ID: 66.8.22.10.6; item), State Archives of North Carolina, Raleigh. [Online catalog description: "The resolution recommends that the governor require the commanding officers of the districts or counties to return the deserted members of the militia to service under General Caswell."]

North Carolina (State). General Assembly. "[Document dated:] September 5, [1780]: Re[specting] Forwarding Part of Militia for Relief of Frontiers (Rejected)." Manuscript; General Assembly Record Group; Session Records, August-September 1780; Joint Papers, Committee Papers, Resolutions, Senate Bills, House Bills, Box 1 (MARS ID: 66.8.22.9.10; item), State Archives of North Carolina, Raleigh. [Online catalog description: "In light of the belief that the British plan to march into Mecklenburg and Rowan Counties, the resolution would have directed the governor to send some of the militia in the Hillsborough District to the southwest and insured that each soldier would have a horse and receive an additional bounty."]

North Carolina (State). General Assembly. House of Delegates. "[Document dated:] Nov. 20, [1788]: House Bill to Amend Militia Law to Establish Office of Inspector General (With Petitions) (Laid Over)." Manuscript; General Assembly Record Group; Session Records, November-December 1788; Joint Papers, Committee Papers, Resolutions, Senate Bills, House Bills, Box 3 (MARS ID: 66.8.51.55; folder), State Archives of North Carolina, Raleigh. [Online catalog description: "Petition of Henry Emanuel Lutterloh proposing that he be made Inspector General of the North Carolina Militia, with the commission of Brigadier General; second petition of H. E. Lutterloh requesting grant of land as was given to other Continental Army officers; and bill establishing the office of inspector general to regulate and train the state militia."]

North Carolina (State). General Assembly. House of Delegates. "[Document dated:] July 3, [1781]: House Bill for Drafting Militia to Reinforce the Southern Army (With Messages about Bill from Governor Burke)." Manuscript; Assembly Record Group; Session Records, June-July 1781; Joint Papers, Committee Papers, Resolutions, Senate Bills, House Bills, Box 2 (MARS ID: 66.8.26.25; folder), State Archives of North Carolina,

Raleigh. [Online catalog description: "Includes appointments to a committee to write the bill. Burke's first message notes two possible flaws in the bill, which a committee is appointed to consider. Burke's second message informs the Assembly that the second of the two flaws remains."]

North Carolina (State). General Assembly. Senate. "[Document dated:] July 9, [1791]: Senate Bill for Raising Troops out of the Militia of this State for the Defense Thereof." Manuscript, , General Assembly Record Group, Session Records, June-July 1781; Joint Papers, Committee Papers, Resolutions, Senate Bills, House Bills, Box 2 (MARS ID: 66.8.26.9; folder), State Archives of North Carolina, Raleigh.

North Carolina (State). State Treasurer; State Comptroller. "Military Papers – General Records, 1747-1909." Manuscript, Office of State Treasurer, Office of Comptroller, Boxes 1-12, 74, 89, 93-98, 120-121-A (MARS ID: 13.26; series), State Archives of North Carolina, Raleigh. [This portion of the Military Papers contains numerous muster rolls, pay rolls, and other documents for the militias and the Continental Line regiments/brigades.]

Philips, Abraham, 1755-1836. "Abraham Philips Journal with Affidavit, 1781-1783, 1853." Manuscript MSS5945, Manuscript Division, Madison Building, Library of Congress, Washington, D. C. [Online catalog description: "Journal kept by Philips during his Revolutionary War service with the North Carolina militia. Pertains chiefly to troop movements and skirmishes with Loyalists in North Carolina and Virginia. Individuals mentioned include John Butler, Nathanael Greene, Alexander Martin, and William Washington. Also includes Philips's accounts reflecting, in part, his work as a surveyor. Affidavit (1853 May 31) confirms that the journal was written by Philips."]

Pugh, Robert C. "The Revolutionary Militia in the Southern Campaign, 1780-1781." *William and Mary Quarterly*, 3rd series, 14:2 (April 1957), 154-175.

Shriner, Kevin Nelson. "African-Americans in the Militias of Virginia, Georgia, and the Carolinas, 1639-1792." M. A. thesis, University of Arkansas, Fayetteville, 1994.

Smith, Trevor Augustine. "Pioneers, Patriots, and Politicians: The Tennessee Militia System, 1772-1857." Ph. D. dissertation, University of Tennessee, Knoxville, 2003.

Stevenson, George. "The Colonial and State Militia." In Helen F. M. Leary, ed. *North Carolina Research: Genealogy and Local History*. 2nd ed. (Raleigh: North Carolina Genealogical Society, 1996), Chapter 33: "Military Records," 362-366. [Contains subheadings: "Eligibility," and "Structure."]

Stevenson, George. "North Carolina's Colonial Era Military Records." *Recall*, 5:1 (April 1999), 4-8. [Online description from "North Carolina Periodicals Index," East Carolina University: "Documents relating to North Carolina's military activities from the reign of Queen Anne down to the 20th century have survived in varying quantities. Stevenson discusses the military activities in the state during the Colonial Period and the records that resulted from it. All conflict is arranged in chronological order--the Tuscarora War, 1711-1715; The Spanish Alarm, 1739-1748; The French and Indian War, 1755-1763; The War of the Regulation, 1768-1771; and the Colonial and State Militias during the Revolutionary War."]

United States. Continental Army. Lee's Legion. "Proclamation, 1781 March 20, of Henry Lee as Commander of Lee's Legion." Manuscript Mss13 1781 March 20:1, Virginia Historical Society, Richmond. [Online catalog description: "Proclamation issued to the commanders of North Carolina militia in Mecklenburg, Roane and Surry counties recounting recent military events and urging the aid of their troops in harassing British forces under General Lord Cornwallis currently on route to Wilmington." VHS historical note: "Following the Battle of Guilford Court House, N. C., in March 1781, American General Nathanael Greene dispatched Colonel Henry Lee of Virginia and his Legion to watch and harass British forces under General Lord Cornwallis with a view to engaging in battle again. Lee called on North Carolina militia to aid in this effort and their combined operations led Cornwallis to turn north into Virginia and toward Yorktown."]

Vollmer, Arthur. *Military Obligation: The American Tradition: A Compilation of the Enactments of Compulsion from the Earliest Settlements of the Original Thirteen Colonies in 1607 through the Articles of Confederation 1789: Special Monograph No. 1, Volume II, Part 10: North Carolina Enactments*. Washington, D. C.: Government Printing Office for the Selective Service System, 1947.

Wheeler, E. Melton. "Development and Organization of the North Carolina Militia," *North Carolina Historical Review,* 41:3 (July 1964), 307-323; online: http://digital.ncdcr.gov/cdm/ref/collection/p16062coll9/id/4207. [Online description from "North Carolina Periodicals Index," East Carolina University: "The state militia began with a charter in 1663 allowing the eight Lords Proprietors of Carolina to enlist and train a force for the defensive purposes. Militia was to defend early North Carolinians from Native Americans, pirates along the coast, and England's European foes, especially the Spanish. From this initial act the author describes the history of the state's militia, statistics concerning recruitment, and the legislative measures to both form and maintain the state's defensive force through the 18th century."]

Wheeler, Earl Melton. "The Role of the North Carolina Militia in the Beginning of the American Revolution." Ph. D. dissertation, Tulane University, 1969. ["Examines the role of the North Carolina militia from 1774-1776."]

Whisker, James Biser. *The American Colonial Militia, Volume V: The Colonial Militia of the Southern States, 1606-1785.* Lewiston, N. Y.: The Edwin Mellen Press, 1997. ["The North Carolina Militia," 95-113.]

Wyche, Kathleen B, trans. "North Carolina Militia Paroled by Lord Cornwallis in 1781." *The North Carolina Genealogical Society Journal*, 4:3 (August 1978), 147-151; correction: 13:3 (August 1987), 140-141. [Note from the Genealogy Office, Office of the Registrar General, National Society Daughters of the American Revolution, Washington, D. C.: Believed to be a list of North Carolina militiamen captured by British forces during the fall of Charleston, South Carolina in 1780. Men are listed by their home county. Originally this was believed to be a listed of men taken at Guilford Court House in 1781, but further research showed it to be a list of men taken at Charleston."]

North Carolina Continental Line and Its Regiments

Babits, L. E. "The Continental Soldier." *Tar Heel Junior Historian*, 15:1 (Fall 1975), 6-9. [Online description from "North Carolina Periodicals Index," East Carolina University: "The Revolutionary Army can be broken down into two separate entities, the militia and the continentals. Militia were required to fight but generally remained within their own state, whereas, the continentals were enlisted and fought wherever they were needed. North Carolina sent nine continental regiments into battle; comprised of farmers and merchants sent for training at Halifax."]

Babits, Lawrence E. and Joshua B. Howard. *Fortitude and Forbearance: The North Carolina Continental Line in the Revolutionary War, 1775-1783.* Raleigh: Office of Archives and History, North Carolina Department of Cultural Resources, 2004. [List of regiments, officers, engagements of the North Carolina Continentals, with useful appendix.]

Berg, Fred Anderson. *Encyclopedia of Continental Army Units, Battalions, Regiments and Independent Corps.* Harrisburg, Pa.: Stackpole, 1972.

Bush, John. "John Bush Order Book, 1777, 1807." Manuscript 1452-z, Southern Historical Collection, Louis Round Wilson Special Collections Library, University of North Carolina, Chapel Hill; online finding aid available at http://www2.lib.unc.edu/mss/inv/b/Bush,John.html. [Online finding aid description: "John Bush was an adjutant officer to North Carolina troops in the Revolutionary War. The collection contains the officer's order book of Bush, 1777, containing copies of brigade and regimental orders issued to units of the North Carolina Continental Line camped in the vicinity of Trenton, N. J., and Wilmington, Del, 1777; and some personal accounts of John Bush and estate accounts of William Bush, 1807."]

Collins, James Potter. *Autobiography of a Revolutionary Soldier.* Clinton, La.: Feliciana Democrat Press, 1859. [James Potter Collins (1763-1844)]

Daves, Graham. *A Sketch of the Military Career of Captain John Daves of the North Carolina Continental Line of the Army of the Revolution, Together with Some Facts of Local and Family History, by His Grandson, Major Graham Daves.* Baltimore: Press of the Friedenwald Company, 1892. [John Daves (1748-1804)]

Daves, Graham. "Officers of the North Carolina Continental Line on the Continental Establishment." *North Carolina University Magazine*, old series, 26:2 (May 1894); new series vol. 13, 369-379. [

Davis, Charles Lukens, and Henry Hobart Bellas. *A Brief History of the North Carolina Troops on the Continental Establishment in the War of the Revolution, With a Register of Officers of the Same; Also a Sketch of the North Carolina Society of the Cincinnati from Its Organization in 1783, to Its So-Called Dissolution after 1790.* Philadelphia: [s. n.], 1896. [Includes: Henry Hobart Bellas' "A Sketch of the North Carolina Society of the Cincinnati from Its Organization in 1783, to Its So-Called Dissolution after 1790," 75-106.]

Dixon, Henry. "Henry Dixon Paper." Manuscript, PC.456, State Archives of North Carolina, Raleigh. [Online catalog description: "Typed copy of drill regulations of North Carolina Continental troops."]

Hathaway, J. R. B. "North Carolina Troops in the Continental Line: A Register of Officers, with Dates of Commissions, Made up under Direction of the Secretary of State from Records in His Office, October 1884." *The North Carolina Historical and Genealogical Register*, 1:3 (July 1900), 415-426.

Hathaway, J. R. B. "Soldiers of the N. C. Continental Line, Revolutionary War." *North Carolina Historical and Genealogical Register*, 2:1 (January 1901), 125-129; 2:2 (April 1901), 179-186; 2:3 (July 1901), 383-390; 2:4 (October 1901), 578-585; 3:1 (January 1903), 95-104; 3:2 (April 1903), 291-298: 3:3 (July 1901), 454-462.

Hintze, Fred M., Jr. *North Carolina Continental Line of the American Revolutionary, an Alphabetic List of Enlisted Soldiers.* Richlands: Privately Printed, 2003.

Howard, Joshua B. "Fortitude and Forbearance: The North Carolina Continental Line at Eutaw Springs – September 8, 1781." *Southern Campaigns of the American Revolution*, 3:9 (September 2006), 20-24; online: www.southerncampaign.org.

Howard, Joshua B. "NC Continental Line at Eutaw Springs." *Southern Campaigns of the American Revolution*, 3:9 (September 2006), 22-24.

Lewis, J. D. "The American Revolution in North Carolina: Adjutants." Online: http://www.carolana.com/NC/Revolution/nc_patriot_military_adjutants.html.

Lewis, J. D. "The American Revolution in North Carolina: Captains." Online: http://www.carolana.com/NC/Revolution/nc_patriot_military_captains.html.

Lewis, J. D. "The American Revolution in North Carolina: Cornets." Online: http://www.carolana.com/NC/Revolution/nc_patriot_military_cornets.html.

Lewis, J. D. "The American Revolution in North Carolina: Corporals." Online: http://www.carolana.com/NC/Revolution/nc_patriot_military_corporals.html.

Lewis, J. D. "The American Revolution in North Carolina: Ensigns." Online: http://www.carolana.com/NC/Revolution/nc_patriot_military_ensigns.html.

Lewis, J. D. "The American Revolution in North Carolina: Generals." Online: http://www.carolana.com/NC/Revolution/nc_patriot_military_generals.html. [Provides brief descriptions of the careers of the North Carolina generals of the militia and Continental Line: James Armstrong, John Ashe, Thomas Benbury, William Bryan, John Butler, Richard Caswell, William Caswell, William Lee Davidson, Thomas Eaton, Isaac Gregory, Henry William Harrington, James Hogun, Robert Howe, Allen Jones, James Kenan, John Alexander Lillington, Charles McDowell, Alexander Mebane, James Moore, Francis Nash, Thomas Person, Andrew Pickens, Ambrose Ramsey, Griffith Rutherford, John Simpson, William Skinner, William Smallwood, Jethro Sumner, Edward Vail, and John Pugh Williams.]

Lewis, J. D. "The American Revolution in North Carolina: Lieutenants." Online: http://www.carolana.com/NC/Revolution/nc_patriot_military_lieutenants.html.

Lewis, J. D. "The American Revolution in North Carolina: Lt. Colonels." Online: http://www.carolana.com/NC/Revolution/nc_patriot_military_lt_colonels.html.

Lewis, J. D. "The American Revolution in North Carolina: Majors." Online: http://www.carolana.com/NC/Revolution/nc_patriot_military_majors.html.

Lewis, J. D. "The American Revolution in North Carolina: Quarter Masters (QMs)." Online: http://www.carolana.com/NC/Revolution/nc_patriot_military_miscellaneous.html.

Lewis, J. D. "The American Revolution in North Carolina: Matrosses & Gunners." Online: http://www.carolana.com/NC/Revolution/nc_patriot_military_matrosses_and_gunners.html.

Lewis, J. D. "The American Revolution in North Carolina: The Patriots and Their Forces: How the NC Military Organization Changed over the Course of the War." Online: http://www.carolana.com/NC/Revolution/revolution_patriot_troops_nc.html

Lewis, J. D. "The American Revolution in North Carolina: Privates, Horsemen, Fifers, Drummers, etc." Online: http://www.carolana.com/NC/Revolution/nc_patriot_military_privates_etc.html.

Lewis, J. D. "The American Revolution in North Carolina: Quarter Masters (QMs)." Online: http://www.carolana.com/NC/Revolution/nc_patriot_military_quarter_masters.html.

Lewis, J. D. "The American Revolution in North Carolina: Sergeants." Online: http://www.carolana.com/NC/Revolution/nc_patriot_military_sergeants.html.

Lewis, J. D. *NC Patriots, 1775-1783: Their Own Words*. 3 vols. Little River, S. C.: J. D. Lewis, 2012. [Contents: Volume 1: The NC Continental Line; Volume 2, Part 1: The Provincial and State Troops; Volume 2, Part 2: The Provincial and State Troops.] [Note: This recently published study of nearly 3,000 pages of text, may be a researcher's first reference when checking for North Carolina soldiers during the Revolution. The lengthy introductory chapters provide extensive information on the organization and changes to North Carolina units and on the entire war effort. The references to individual soldiers throughout the three volumes, however, are not sourced directly, i. e. each man's entry does not state where the information appeared. A list of sources used throughout the study appears in Volume 1 on pages 692-693.]

"List of Colonels and Lieutenant Colonels Who Served in the Continental Army during the Revolutionary War, ca. 1783." Manuscript accession no. 44627, Library of Virginia, Richmond. [Online catalog description: "Contains a list of colonels and lieutenant colonels who served in the Continental Army during the Revolutionary War. The list is arranged by colony and provides the last name of the officers, their rank, and dates of service." Contains North Carolinians.]

"List of Virginia and North Carolina Officers, Undated." Manuscript accession no. 45186, Library of Virginia, Richmond. [Online catalog description: "Contains a printed list of Virginia Revolutionary Officers and North Carolina Revolutionary Officers. The list provides the name of the officer, their rank, and state. These records are part of the Revolutionary Government record group (RG# 2)."]

McBride, Ransom. "A 'Lost' List of Continental Soldiers from the Western Counties." *North Carolina Genealogical Society Journal*, 9:3 (August 1983), 146. [Contains names of men residing in Lincoln County, Burke County, Wilkes County, and Rutherford County]

McBride, Ransom. "Another Account of Missing Records Pertaining to North Carolina Soldiers during the American Revolution." *North Carolina Genealogical Society Journal*, 22:4 (November 1996), 385-387.

McBride, Ransom. "Revolutionary War Papers." *North Carolina Genealogical Society Journal*, 3:1 (February 1977), 22-31; 4:1 (February 1978), 24-29; 4:2 (May 1978), 121-131; 4:3 (August 1978), 188-194; 5:1 (February 1979), 44-51; 5:2 (May 1979), 89-95: (Warren and Wilkes Counties), 5:4 (November 1979), 248-255; (Supplement #1), *North Carolina Genealogical Society Journal*, 7:3 (August 1981), 163-166.

McBride, Ransom. "Revolutionary War Service Records and Settlements."

(1st in series). *North Carolina Genealogical Society Journal*, 8:2 (May 1982), 95-101.

(2nd in series: A-B). *North Carolina Genealogical Society Journal*, 8:3 (August 1982), 154-161.

(3rd in series, Cail-Chav(e)rs). *North Carolina Genealogical Society Journal*, 8:4 (November 1982), 209-214.

(4th in series, Ltr. "C"). *North Carolina Genealogical Society Journal*, 9:3 (August 1983), 147-154.

(5th in series, Letter "D"). *North Carolina Genealogical Society Journal*, 9:2 (May 1983), 85-91.

(6th in series, Letters E & F) *North Carolina Genealogical Society Journal*, 9:3 (August 1983), 147-154.

(6th [oops] in series, Letter G), *North Carolina Genealogical Society Journal*, 9:4 (November 1983), 221-228.

(7th in series, letter "Ha" only). *North Carolina Genealogical Society Journal*, 10:2 (May 1984), 107-113.

(8th in series, surname letter "He-I"). *North Carolina Genealogical Society Journal*, 10:4 (November 1984), 235-241.

(9th in series, surname letters "Ja-Jo" only), *North Carolina Genealogical Society Journal*, 11:2 (May 1985), 113-118.

(10th in series, surname letter "K" only), *North Carolina Genealogical Society Journal*, 11:4 (November 1985), 239-242.

(11th in series). *North Carolina Genealogical Society Journal*, 12:2 (May 1986), 95-104.

(12th in series, "Mc" surnames). *North Carolina Genealogical Society Journal*, 12:4 (November 1986), 228-233.

(13th in series, "M" surnames). *North Carolina Genealogical Society Journal*, 13:2 (May 1987), 92-99.

(14th in series, Moldin-Myers). *North Carolina Genealogical Society Journal*, 13:4 (November 1987), 235-240.

(15th in series, N and O surnames). *North Carolina Genealogical Society Journal*, 14:2 (May 1988), 109-116.

(16th in series, P surnames). *North Carolina Genealogical Society Journal*, 14:4 (November 1988), 227-235.

(17th in series, Ra-Ro surnames). *North Carolina Genealogical Society Journal*, 15:2 (May 1989), 101-107.

(18th in series, Ro-Sh surnames). *North Carolina Genealogical Society Journal*, 15:4 (November 1989), 228-235.

(19th in series, Sh-Sp surnames). *North Carolina Genealogical Society Journal*, 16:2 (May 1990), 107-114.

(20th in series, Sp-Sy surnames). *North Carolina Genealogical Society Journal*, 16:4 (November 1990), 233-239.

(21st in series, T surnames). *North Carolina Genealogical Society Journal*, 17:2 (May 1991), 108-116.

(22nd in series, Va-Wa surnames). *North Carolina Genealogical Society Journal*, 17:4 (November 1991), 216-223.

(23rd in series, We-Wi surnames). *North Carolina Genealogical Society Journal*, 18:2 (May 1992), 92-100.

(24th and last in series). *North Carolina Genealogical Society Journal*, 18:4 (November 1992), 236-245.

McRee, Griffith John. *Memoir of Major Griffith J. McRee of the Continental Line of North Carolina,* [North Carolina: s. n., 1853].

"Military Procedures." ID # 36421, Tennessee Historical Society, Nashville; digital surrogate available through the Revolutionary War Collection, Tennessee Virtual Archive at http://cdm15138.contentdm.oclc.org/cdm/compoundobject/collection/p15138coll16/id/89/rec/49. [Description from TeVA: "Manual Exercises – Military procedures for loading and firing the flintlock musket, charging with bayonets, forming troops for battle, written by Lt. Col. Henry Dickson of North Carolina Continental Troops, during the American Revolution… Henry Dixon, (ca. 1750-17 July 1782), was a Revolutionary War officer, born in the part of Granville County that later became Orange and then Caswell. In 1763, he married Martha Wynne in Halifax County, Va. Dixon was commissioned captain of the First Regiment and charged to form North Carolina's first units of the Continental line in September 1775. In 1778 the North Carolina legislature appointed Dixon 'Inspector General over Militia' a post he held for the remainder of the war. He worked with Generals Jethro Sumner and Nathaniel Greene in the defense of the southern states."]

Mosher, Merrill Hill. "Babits and Howard. 'Fortitude and Forbearance': The North Carolina Continental Line in the American Revolution 1775-1783." *National Genealogical Society Quarterly*, 93:3 (June 2005), 151.

Nash, Frank. "The Continental Line of North Carolina." *North Carolina Booklet*, 17:3 (January 1981), 105-135. [Online description from "North Carolina Periodicals Index," East Carolina University: "The nine regiments of North Carolina soldiers of the Continental Line during the American Revolution fought from the Battle of Brandywine through the Southern Campaign."]

North Carolina (State). General Assembly. "[Document dated:] April 14, [1777]: Respecting the Marching of the Continental Troops (With Messages)." Manuscript; General Assembly Record Group; Session Records, April-May 1777; Joint Papers, Committee Papers, Resolutions, Senate Bills, House Bills, Box 1 (MARS ID: 66.8.9.12.3; item), State Archives of North Carolina, Raleigh. [Online catalog description: "Resolution to send all available troops in the North Carolina contingent of the Continental Army to reinforce the regiments commanded by General Washington."]

North Carolina (State). General Assembly. "[Document dated:] April 16, [1777]: Treasurers Advance Money to Nicholas Long (With Messages)." Manuscript; General Assembly Record Group; Session Records, April-May 1777; Joint Papers, Committee Papers, Resolutions, Senate Bills, House Bills, Box 1 (MARS ID: 66.8.9.12.4; item), State Archives of North Carolina, Raleigh. [Online catalog description: "Resolution supporting the payment of Nicholas Long for the expenses he incurred during the march of North Carolina troops to the assistance of General Washington."]

North Carolina (State). General Assembly. "[Document dated:] April 17, [1777]: Appointing Col. Abraham Sheppard to the Command of a Regiment, etc. (With Message)." Manuscript; General Assembly Record Group; Session Records, April-May 1777; Joint Papers, Committee Papers, Resolutions, Senate Bills, House Bills, Box 1 (MARS ID: 66.8.9.12.8; item), State Archives of North Carolina, Raleigh. [Online catalog description: "Resolution giving Colonel Abraham Sheppard the command of a regiment, and the authority to appoint his own officers and recruit his own men."]

North Carolina (State). General Assembly. "[Document dated:] April 17, [1777]: Governor to Fill up Commissions for the Officers of the Army (With Message)." Manuscript; General Assembly Record Group; Session Records, April-May 1777; Joint Papers, Committee Papers, Resolutions, Senate Bills, House Bills, Box 1 (MARS ID: 66.8.9.12.7; item), State Archives of North Carolina, Raleigh. [Online catalog description: "Resolution empowering Governor Caswell to fill commissions in the Army."]

North Carolina (State). General Assembly. "[Document dated:] April 18, [1778]: Allowing James Williams Rent on Houses in Halifax (With Messages and Petition)." Manuscript; General Assembly Record Group; Session Records, April-May 1778; Joint Papers, Committee Papers, Resolutions, Senate Bills, House Bills, Box 1 (MARS ID: 66.8.12.16.7; item), State Archives of North Carolina, Raleigh. [Online catalog description: "James Williams to be paid rent for lodging Continental troops in houses owned by him."]

North Carolina (State). General Assembly. "[Document dated:] April 21, [1777]: Preventing Officers from South Carolina and Georgia from Recruiting Soldiers in N. C. (With Messages)." Manuscript; General Assembly Record Group; Session Records, April-May 1777; Joint Papers, Committee Papers, Resolutions, Senate Bills, House Bills, Box 1 (MARS ID: 66.8.9.12.11; item), State Archives of North Carolina, Raleigh. [Online catalog description: "Resolution preventing the recruiting officers from South Carolina and Georgia from recruiting soldiers in North Carolina, because the Assembly was concerned about the deficient numbers of men in the Continental regiments of this state."]

North Carolina (State). General Assembly. House of Delegates. "[Document dated:] April 24, [1780]: Re[specting] Sundry Dispatches, Resolutions, Etc. from Continental Congress." Manuscript; General Assembly Record Group; Session Records, April-May 1780, Joint Papers; Committee Papers, Resolutions, Senate Bills, House Bills, Box 1 (MARS ID: 66.8.20.8.5; item), State Archives of North Carolina, Raleigh. [Online catalog description: "The committee reports that the Congressional plan for reducing inflation is impractical for the state. On the subject of the state's quota of troops for Continental service, the committee recommends an immediate call for volunteers along with suitable bounties for service. The committee also makes a tax recommendation. The Assembly concurs with the report."]

North Carolina (State). General Assembly. "[Document dated:] August-September, [1780]: Petition from Captains William Chronicle, David Cowan, and James Jack." Manuscript; General Assembly Record Group; Session Records, August-September 1780; Joint Papers, Committee Papers, Resolutions, Senate Bills, House Bills, Box 1 (MARS ID: 66.8.22.6.5; item), State Archives of North Carolina, Raleigh. [Online catalog description: "The petitioners inform the Assembly that the troops raised from the Salisbury District to fill up the Continental battalions have been prevented from marching by the commanding officer; they ask for assistance, given their limited terms of service and the low number of wagons they have been given."]

North Carolina (State). General Assembly. House of Delegates. "[Document dated:] January 30, [1781]: House Bill to Reduce the Six Continental Battalions to Four, and Complete Them." Manuscript; General Assembly Record Group; Session Records, January-February 1781; Joint Papers, Committee Papers, Resolutions, Senate Bills, House Bills, Box 2 (MARS ID: 66.8.24.12; folder), State Archives of North Carolina, Raleigh.

North Carolina (State). General Assembly. "[Document dated:] Apr. 23, [1782]: Report on Memorial of the Officers of the N. C. Line (Messages and Memorial Only)." Manuscript; General Assembly Record Group; Session Records, April-May 1782; Joint Papers, Committee Papers, Resolutions, Senate Bills, House Bills, Box 1 (MARS ID: 66.8.27.8.12; item), State Archives of North Carolina, Raleigh. [Online catalog description: "Petition of the officers and soldiers of the N. C. Continental Line requesting that a proposed county not be formed on land which was designated for the soldiers and officers. Also mentions under payment of soldiers and those who should be released from duty. Messages from both houses concern appointments to committee to consider petition."]

North Carolina (State). General Assembly. "[Document dated:] Apr. 26, [1782]: Resolution Permitting Certain Officers of N. C. Line to Retire at Half Pay (Messages and Letter Only)." Manuscript; General Assembly Record Group; Session Records, April-May 1782; Joint Papers, Committee Papers, Resolutions, Senate Bills, House Bills, Box 2 (MARS ID: 66.8.28.8.7; item), State Archives of North Carolina, Raleigh. [Online catalog description: "Letter from Brig. Gen. Jethro Sumner concerning arrangement of officers of Continental Line and recommending officers to retire on half pay; with messages from both houses about concurrence with resolution."]

North Carolina (State). General Assembly. "[Document dated:] Apr. 29, [1784]: Resolution Appointing Committee of Claims and Depreciation." Manuscript, General Assembly Record Group, Session Records, April-June 1784; Joint Papers, Committee Papers, Resolutions, Senate Bills, House Bills, Box 2 (MARS ID: 66.8.32.5.8; item), State Archives of North Carolina, Raleigh. [Online catalog description: "Resolution appoints committee to take up claims of wounded soldiers and officers from the war and to deal with the problem of depreciated certificates that have been presented."]

North Carolina (State). General Assembly. "[Document dated:] Nov 13, [1784]: Report on the Memorial of Major Thomas Harris, 1784." Manuscript; General Assembly Record Group; Session Records, October-November 1784; Joint Papers, Committee Papers, Resolutions, Senate Bills, House Bills, Box 1 (MARS ID: 66.8.35.9.6; item), State Archives of North Carolina, Raleigh. [Online catalog description: "Petition regards the service and wounding of Thomas Harris, who served as an officer in the North Carolina Continental Line. The committee awards him compensation, both monetary and land."]

North Carolina (State). General Assembly. "[Document dated:] Dec. 14, [1785]: Senate Bill to Empower Commissioner to Liquidate the Accounts of Officers and Soldiers of the Continental Line." Manuscript; General Assembly Record Group; Session Records, November-December, 1785; Joint Papers, Committee Papers, Resolutions, Senate Bills, House Bills, Box 3 (MARS ID: 66.8.39.13; folder), State Archives of North Carolina, Raleigh. [Online catalog description: "Bill appoints Benjamin McCulloch, John Macon, and Henry Montfort to be commissioners to liquidate any remaining accounts of the officers and soldiers of the North Carolina Continental Line and directs them in their duties. The bill also authorizes the temporary reinstatement of the various district Boards of Auditors."]

North Carolina (State). General Assembly. "[Document dated:] Dec. 9, 1786: Resolution Concerning Soldiers in Continental Line, 1786." Manuscript; General Assembly Record Group; Session Records, November 1786-January 1787; Joint Papers, Committee Papers, Resolutions, Senate Bills, House Bills, Box 3 (MARS ID: 66.8.43.7.10; item), State Archives of North Carolina, Raleigh. [Online catalog description: "Resolution directs Secretary of State and Robert Fenner to furnish to the committee to examine the state prisoners, a list of names of those that that have served in the Continental Line."]

North Carolina (State). General Assembly. House of Delegates. "[Document dated:] February 3: Re[specting] Sundry Letters, Resolves of Congress, Petitions, and Other Public Papers (Enclosing Petition of Captain Thomas Armstrong)." Manuscript; General Assembly Record Group; Session Records, January-February 1781; Joint Papers, Committee Papers, Resolutions, Senate Bills, House Bills, Box 1 (MARS ID: 66.8.23.8.8; item), State Archives of North Carolina, Raleigh. [Online catalog description: "Thomas Armstrong, a captain in the state's Continental line, informs the Assembly that he has received little relief as a result of being a prisoner of war compared to that given by other states. The committee recommends that the speakers write General Greene requesting that he arrange an exchange of prisoners; that the governor issue a proclamation permitting loyalists in the state to receive a pardon by serving a year in the Continental army; that Colonel Martin Armstrong be suspended pending investigation of charges of misconduct following the Battle of Kings Mountain; that the resolutions of Congress pertaining to provisions and forage be adopted; and that Captain Armstrong be allowed almost ten thousand pounds. The House rejected the report."]

North Carolina (State). General Assembly. "[Document dated:] November 25, 1789: Report on Petition of the Sundry Officers Late of the Continental Line (Petition Only), 1789." Manuscript; General Assembly Record Group; Session Records, November-December, 1789; Joint Papers, Committee Papers, Resolutions, Senate Bills, House Bills, Box 2 (MARS ID: 66.8.53.3.8; item), State Archives of North Carolina, Raleigh. [Online catalog description: "Petition of sundry officers of the Continental Line requests that they be compensated for their services, as the General Assembly is bound by the Constitution to pay its debts."]

North Carolina (State). General Assembly. Committee of Propositions and Grievances. "[Document dated:] 1784: Reports and Papers." Manuscript; General Assembly Record Group; Session Records, October-November 1784, Joint Papers, Committee Papers, Resolutions, Senate Bills, House Bills, Reports and Papers, 1784, Box 1 (MARS ID: 66.8.35.7; folder), State Archives of North Carolina, Raleigh. [Online catalog description: "Includes messages regarding appointment to the committee and acceptance of its report, as well as the report of the committee, on: the petition of Isles Simmons, who did not have sufficient proof that he was a member of the Continental Army to receive compensation for his services...the claim of John Swayne, a soldier in the militia of Caswell County, and awards him an allowance...the petition of John McCoy, who is awarded an allowance, the petition of William Moore and Philip Thomas, who are awarded an allowance for wounds received in battle serving the Continental Army...the matter of missing certificates, which the committee believe to have been taken by the British..."]

North Carolina (State). [Treasurer?]. "Blank Form of Indebtness of State for Service in the Continental Line, North Carolina, 1785." Manuscript, Houghton 42-6092, Houghton Library, Harvard University, Cambridge, Mass. [Online catalog description: "Filled out in manuscript: No. 498, December 1785, to Isaac Owell [?], in the amount of £138.19.3, 'interest to 1 August 1789.' Autograph signatures of commissioners John Macon and Benjamin McCulloch."]

"North Carolina Continental Army Troops Letter Collection." Manuscript #0455, Historical Society of Pennsylvania, Philadelphia. [Online catalog description: "The participation of North Carolina troops in the Revolution is described in letters of General Robert Howe, Stephen Moore, R. Rutherford, Allen Jones, John Armstrong, Thomas Burke, William Davidson, Richard Caswell, John Penn, and others, 1777-1783; and in orders of the Assembly, 1777. The letters discuss the resolutions of the Assembly on the ratification of the Constitution, 1787-1788; the question of imposts by North Carolina, 1788; paper currency, 1785; treaties and sales of Indian lands, 1827; slavery, laws, finances, freemasonry, religion, local affairs, political and military appointments. Also included in this volume are: manuscript map of the dividing line between Virginia and Carolina, 1728; printed copy of the amendment to the Constitution of North Carolina and of the Declaration of Rights, 1788; and muster roll of British troops in Charleston, S. C., 1782. This collection also includes an orderly book, 'North Carolina Line,' 1777 {formerly Am .6515} that is currently missing."]

North Carolina (State). General Assembly. "[Document dated:] April 29, [1777]: Report re[arding] Supernumerary Officers (Message Only)." Manuscript; General Assembly Record Group; Session Records, April-May 1777; Joint Papers, Committee Papers, Resolutions, Senate Bills, House Bills; Box 1 (MARS ID: 66.8.9.10.11; item), State Archives of North Carolina, Raleigh. [Online catalog description: "Messages concerning the expense of retaining supernumerary officers in the North Carolina Continental Regiment."]

North Carolina (State). General Assembly. "[Document dated:] November 25, 1789. Report on the Petition of the Sundry Officers Late of the Continental Line (Petition Only). November 25, 1789." Manuscript; General Assembly Record Group; Session Records, November-December 1789; Joint Papers, Committee Papers, Resolutions, Senate Bills, House Bills, Box 2 (MARS ID: 66.8.53.3.8; item), State Archives of North Carolina, Raleigh. [Online catalog description: "Petition of sundry officers of the Continental Line requests that they be compensated for their services, as the General Assembly is bound by the Constitution to pay its debts."]

North Carolina Troops in the Continental Line: A Register of Officers, with Dates of Commissions, Made Up under Direction of the Secretary of State from Records in His Office, October 1884. [Raleigh: s. n., 1884?]; online: http://digital.ncdcr.gov/u?/p249901coll22,285653.

"An Odd Correspondence." *Washington County Genealogical Society Journal*, 5:3 (December 1997), 82-84. [Col. Robert Howe of the North Carolina Continental Line with Lord Dunmore in 1775; three letters relating to prisoners and other matters]

Rankin, Hugh F. *The North Carolina Continentals*. Chapel Hill: University of North Carolina Press, 1971; reprinted: 2005. [Publisher's description: "In this classic account of the Revolutionary War experiences of the North

Carolina Continentals, Hugh F. Rankin traces the events leading to war in North Carolina and follows all the campaigns and battles in which the North Carolina Continentals took part – Brandywine, Germantown, Charleston, Savannah, Camden, Eutaw Springs, and others. He also provides descriptions of almost all of the significant personalities in the Continental Army. Originally published in 1971, this new edition contains a foreword by Lawrence Babits, introducing the book to a new generation of scholars and general readers interested in the Revolutionary War."]

Rankin, Hugh F. *The North Carolina Continental Line in the American Revolution.* (Bicentennial Pamphlet Series, no. 12) Raleigh: Department of Archives and History, 1977.

North Carolina Daughters of the American Revolution; foreword by Gertrude Sloan Hay (Mrs. R. Duke). Roster of Soldiers from North Carolina in the American Revolution with an Appendix Containing a Collection of Miscellaneous Records Durham: North Carolina Daughters of the American Revolution, 1932: reprinted: Baltimore: Genealogical Publishing Company, 1967, 1972, 1977, 1984, 1988, 2000. Roster of the Continental Line from North Carolina, 1783. Signal Mountain, Tenn.: Mountain Press, 2004.

"Roster of the Continental Line from North Carolina, 1783." In William L. Saunders, ed., *The State Records of North Carolina* (Goldsboro, N. C.: Nash Brothers, 1899; reprinted Wilmington, N. C.: Broadfoot, 1993), 16:1002-1197.

Royster, Charles. *A Revolutionary People at War: The Continental Army and American Character, 1775-1783.* New York: W. W. Norton, 1979.

"Shiloh Mill Books, 1800-1867." Manuscript 1950-z, Southern Historical Collection, Louis Round Wilson Special Collections Library, University of North Carolina, Chapel Hill, online finding aid available at http://www2.lib.unc.edu/mss/inv/s/Shiloh_Mill.html. [Online catalog description: "The Shiloh (Grist) Mill, Edgecombe County, N. C., was owned by North Carolina Governor Henry Toole Clark. The collection includes …, and list of North Carolina Revolutionary War officers, compiled by Clark."]

"Some Unredeemed Revolutionary War Vouchers of the Continental Line of North Carolina." *North Carolina Genealogical Society Journal*, 10:4 (November 1984), 249.

"Tarheels of the Line." *Washington County Genealogical Society Journal*, 5:3 (December 1997), 74. [statistics on North Carolina's troops in the Continental Line, 1775-1783]

Turner, Jacob. "Jacob Turner Order Book, 1777-1778." Manuscript, Call Number PC.1014, State Archives of North Carolina, Raleigh. [Online catalog description: "Book kept by Capt. Jacob Turner of the North Carolina Continental Line (killed Sept., 1777) and a successor, containing each day's orders from General Washington's headquarters in New Jersey, Pennsylvania, and New York, July 5-Aug. 29, 1777, and July 5-Aug. 27, 1778. These give officers of the day, guard duty, marching orders, findings of courts-martial, advertisements of items lost, and general orders concerning discipline, sanitation, care of sick, camp followers, damage to civilian property, organization, and promotion."]

United States. Continental Army. "Payroll of a Detachment of Virginia and North Carolina Troops, 1778 Jan.-Feb." Manuscript accession no. 20135a, Library of Virginia, Richmond. [Online catalog description: "Located in Organization records (military records) oversize box 1. Payroll, January-February 1778, of a detachment of Virginia and North Carolina troops commanded by Ensign John Steel at Yorktown, Virginia. Includes name, rank, and payment."]

Warren, Mary Bondurant. "Revolutionary War Rolls – A Guide." *The Carolina Genealogist*, no. 32 (Fall 1977), State Records/Revolutionary War Guide, 1-4. [North and South Carolina units found in the National Archives and Records Administration's Microfilm Publication M246 titled "Revolutionary War Rolls, 1775-83."]

Williams, Benjamin. *Newbern, October 6th, 1794: Dear sir, I find that the people, in the district I have the honor to represent, are much displeased at the disproportion, between the pay of the militia officers and that of the private. In some counties, I am told, the cause of uneasiness is charged to me. ...* [New Bern, N. C.: François Xavier Martin, 1794].

1st North Carolina Regiment

"American Revolutionary War Collection: Civil War [*sic*; i. e. Revolutionary War] Inspection Return – 1783." North Carolina Collection, Pack Memorial Library, Asheville. [Online catalog description: "One 'Inspection Return' of the 1st? North Carolina Regiment of Foot form by Lt. Col. Com. Lytle. Date 5/12/1783, 16" x 22". List of ranks of men, arms, accoutrements and ammunition; numbers present and fit for duty, sick, absent, prisoners, etc., as well as numbers for individual clothing articles. Additional comments at bottom half: '33 camp kettles, 69 lanterns, 7 axes, 1 spade, were lost by accident'; also list and number of items lost 'in consequence of desertion & unavoidable accidents...' Signed by Lytle and also examined by a Lt. Col, [illegible]. Document was torn at several of the fold lines; taped with archival tape and sleeved in mylar 6/2001. Stored in vault in Oversize Box B."]

Brown, John. "John Brown Journal and Orderly Book, 1775-1799." Manuscript MSS4979, Manuscript Division, Madison Building, Library of Congress, Washington, D. C. [Online catalog description: "Orderly and memorandum book kept by Brown while serving with the First North Carolina Regiment, U. S. Continental Army, consisting of general and regimental orders issued on the march from Halifax, N. C., through Maryland and Virginia to New Jersey and Pennsylvania (1777 May 21-1778 January 3). Subjects include the Battle of Brandywine, Pa., 1777; Battle of Germantown, Philadelphia, Pa., 1777; winter at Valley Forge, Pa., 1777-1778; and camp life. Also contains personal memoranda including financial accounts and copies of legal documents pertaining to Brown family farms and related enterprises in Bladen County, N. C. The journal (1775-1778) records company rations, expenses, enlistments, casualties, and desertions as well as personal memoranda regarding debts, loans, purchases, and slaves."]

Carr, James. "James Carr Papers, 1781." Manuscript, PC.392, State Archives of North Carolina, Raleigh. [Online catalog description: "Papers of Sgt. James Carr of Duplin Co., 1st Battalion N. C. Continental Line, relating to his being drafted from militia, his weapon, wound received at Eutaw Springs, and furlough."]

Greisser, Edith. "Declaration for a Pension, John Riser, Veteran of the Revolutionary War." *Old Newberry District Quarterly*, 11:4 (Winter 2002), 34-35. [1st North Carolina Regiment; pensioned in South Carolina]

Holmes, Pat. "Rebirth of the N. C. Brigade." *The State: Down Home in North Carolina*, 40:18 (April 1973), 9-13; online: http://digital.ncdcr.gov/cdm/ref/collection/p16062coll18/id/55888. [Online description from "North Carolina Periodicals Index," East Carolina University: "Originally organized in September of 1775 under the command of Col. James Moore, North Carolina's First Regiment of Continentals was reactivated on September 18, 1968 by Governor Bob Scott as part of North Carolina's observance of the National Bicentennial Celebration. Members of the modern First Regiment, which is commanded by Col. B. F. Jarrell of Burlington, take part in reenactments and drills staged as preliminaries to the actual start of the Bicentennial Celebration in 1976."]

Lewis, J. D. "The American Revolution in North Carolina: 1st North Carolina Regiment." Online: http://www.carolana.com/NC/Revolution/revolution_nc_first_regiment.html.

North Carolina (State). State Treasurer; State Comptroller. "Military Papers – General Records, 1747-1909." Manuscript, Office of State Treasurer, Office of Comptroller, Boxes 1-12, 74, 89, 93-98, 120-121-A (MARS ID: 13.26; series), State Archives of North Carolina, Raleigh. [This portion of the Military Papers contains numerous muster rolls, pay rolls, and other documents for the militias and the Continental Line regiments/brigades.]

Rauch, Steven J. "Major Pinketham [Pinkethman] Eaton, First North Carolina Regiment in 1781." *Southern Campaigns of the American Revolution*, 3:6-7 (June-July 2006), 50-53; online: www.southerncampaign.org.

"Steel Creek Grave-Yard, North Carolina." *Daughters of the American Revolution Magazine*, 44:4 (April 1914), 239. [Steel Creek Presbyterian Church, Mecklenburg County, N. C. Contains the grave of Captain Henry Neel of the 1st North Carolina Regiment.]

Warren, Mary Bondurant. "Unpaid Revolutionary Soldiers, Probably Members of the First North Carolina Continental Line, from Published List in *North Carolina Chronicle or Fayetteville Gazette*, October 25; November 1 and 8, 1790." *The Carolina Genealogist*, no. 8 (Fall 1971), Military Records/Unpaid N. C. Soldiers, 1-9.

2nd North Carolina Regiment

Lewis, J. D. "The American Revolution in North Carolina: 2nd North Carolina Regiment." Online: http://www.carolana.com/NC/Revolution/revolution_nc_second_regiment.html.

Lewis, J. D. "Patriot Leaders in North Carolina: Alexander Martin: Lt. Colonel in the 2nd NC Regiment (NC Continental Line) - 1775-1776; Colonel over the 2nd NC Regiment (NC Continental Line) - 1776-1777; Member of Board of War - 1780-1781; 4th Governor of North Carolina - 1782-1784 & 1789-1792." Online: http://www.carolana.com/NC/Revolution/patriot_leaders_nc_alexander_martin.html.

Moultrie, William, 1730-1805. "Orderly Books of William Moultrie, 1775, June 20-1780, Dec. 15." Manuscript mssHM 681, Huntington Library, San Marino, Calif. [Online catalog description: "The manuscript contains two orderly books. The first covers the time period from June 20, 1775 to October 16, 1776, and comprises orders issued by William Moultrie during his command of the defense of Sullivan's Island. Also included are orders issued by Cristopher Gadsen, and Robert Howe, then Colonel of the 2nd Regiment of North Carolina. The second part of the manuscript covers the period from April 15, 1779 to February 12, 1780 and consists of orders issued by William Moultrie and Benjamin Lincoln during Lincoln's operations on the Southern theater. Also included is a list of 'General officers of the American Army, Dec. 15, 1780' and Moultrie's note on his aides."]

North Carolina (State). State Treasurer; State Comptroller. "Military Papers – General Records, 1747-1909." Manuscript, Office of State Treasurer, Office of Comptroller, Boxes 1-12, 74, 89, 93-98, 120-121-A (MARS ID: 13.26; series), State Archives of North Carolina, Raleigh. [This portion of the Military Papers contains numerous muster rolls, pay rolls, and other documents for the militias and the Continental Line regiments/brigades.]

"Welcome to the 2nd NC Regt's Site on the Web." Online: http://www.2nc.org/. Includes:

"A Brief History of the 2nd North Carolina Regiment."

"A Roster of the Men That Served in the 2nd North Carolina Regiment."

"A List of the Effects of an Officer of the 4th North Carolina Regiment Who Died at Wilmington, NC, on 7 September 1776." ["Benaiah Turner of Captn Mores Company."]

"Recruiting Orders for Lt. Rolston of the 2nd Battalion of NC Troops Signed by Maj. Hardy Murfree on 10 May 1777.

"October 27, 1777, A Return of Clothing Wanting for the Soldiers of the Diferant Regts in Halifax."

3rd North Carolina Regiment

Anderson, William Lee, III. "Lieutenant Colonel Robert Mebane: Revolutionary War Continental Army Officer, Commander of North Carolina's Third Regiment: Military Timeline Notes." Online: http://elehistory.com/amrev/RobertMebane.pdf. [Robert Mebane (1745-1781); Orange County]

"A Descriptive Roll of the Drafts Deser(ters? and Delinquents) recd. (?) by Lt. John McNees of the 3rd North Carolina Regiment at Halifax." *North Carolinian Quarterly Journal of Genealogy & History*, 6:3 (September 1960), 729. [No date, but all enlistments are in the year 1781]

Lewis, J. D. "The American Revolution in North Carolina: 3rd North Carolina Regiment." Online: http://www.carolana.com/NC/Revolution/revolution_nc_third_regiment.html.

North Carolina (State). General Assembly. "[Document dated:] April 24, [1777]: William Ridley Appointed chirurgeon to the Third Regiment (with Messages)." Manuscript, General Assembly Record Group, Session Records April-May 1777; Joint Papers, Committee Papers, Resolutions, Senate Bills, House Bills, Box 1 (MARS ID: 66.8.9.11.4; item), State Archives of North Carolina, Raleigh. [Online catalog description: "Senate resolution to appoint William Ridley as surgeon to the Third Regiment of Continental Troops."]

North Carolina (State). State Treasurer; State Comptroller. "Military Papers – General Records, 1747-1909." Manuscript, Office of State Treasurer, Office of Comptroller, Boxes 1-12, 74, 89, 93-98, 120-121-A (MARS ID: 13.26; series), State Archives of North Carolina, Raleigh. [This portion of the Military Papers contains numerous muster rolls, pay rolls, and other documents for the militias and the Continental Line regiments/brigades.]

Sumner, Jethro, 1733?-1785. "Jethro Sumner Papers, 1775-1791 (bulk 1781-1782)." Manuscript 705, Southern Historical Collection, Louis Round Wilson Special Collections Library, University of North Carolina, Chapel Hill; online finding aid and digital surrogates available at http://www2.lib.unc.edu/mss/inv/s/Sumner,Jethro.html. [Online finding aid description: "Jethro Sumner (1733?-1785) was a brigadier general in the Continental Army. Sumner served in the Virginia militia, 1755-1761; was justice of the peace, 1768, and sheriff, 1772-1777, of Bute (now Warren) County, N.C.; and was colonel of the 3rd Battalion, North Carolina Continentals, 1776-1778, and brigadier-general 1779-1780. The collection contains Revolutionary War military correspondence of Continental Brigadier General Jethro Sumner. The bulk of the collection relates to the period 1781-1782, when Sumner was raising troops for General Nathanael Greene, whom he reinforced at the Battle of Eutaw Springs, and while he was in charge of forces in North Carolina. Letters are chiefly concerned with strategic matters including reports on engagements and the movement of British forces, procurement of arms and supplies, and issues of manpower including drafting of men and desertion. A few items pertain to his earlier service in the North. Among the correspondents are Martin Armstrong, Reading Blount, Thomas Burke, John B. Ashe, Baron Steuben, Alexander Martin, Benjamin Lincoln, Nathanael Greene, John Alexander Lillington, William Christmas, William R. Davie, Thomas Eaton, Joseph Hewes, Willie Jones, Nicholas Long, James Cole Mountflorence, Benjamin Seawell, H. Tatum, and Hugh Williamson."]

4th North Carolina Regiment

Lewis, J. D. "The American Revolution in North Carolina: 4th North Carolina Regiment." Online: http://www.carolana.com/NC/Revolution/revolution_nc_fourth_regiment.html.

North Carolina (State). State Treasurer; State Comptroller. "Military Papers – General Records, 1747-1909." Manuscript, Office of State Treasurer, Office of Comptroller, Boxes 1-12, 74, 89, 93-98, 120-121-A (MARS ID: 13.26; series), State Archives of North Carolina, Raleigh. This portion of the "Military Papers" contains numerous muster rolls, pay rolls, and other documents for the militias and the Continental Line regiments/brigades.]

5th North Carolina Regiment

Haywood, Marshall De Lancey. *Colonel Edward Buncombe, Fifth North Carolina Continental Regiment: His life, Military Career, and Death While a Wounded Prisoner in Philadelphia during the War of the Revolution. Address Delivered before the North Carolina Society of the Cincinnati at Its Meeting Held in Hillsborough, July 4, 1901.* North Carolina Society of the Cincinnati. Raleigh [N. C.]: Alford, Bynum & Christophers, printers, 1901.

Lewis, J. D. "The American Revolution in North Carolina: 5th North Carolina Regiment." Online: http://www.carolana.com/NC/Revolution/revolution_nc_fifth_regiment.html.

"North Carolina Gazette, New Bern, North Carolina, July 25, 1777, List of Deserters from the 5th Battalion, North Carolina Continental Line." *Quarterly Review of the Eastern North Carolina Genealogical Society*, 14:2 (June 1987), 63.

North Carolina (State). State Treasurer; State Comptroller. "Military Papers – General Records, 1747-1909." Manuscript, Office of State Treasurer, Office of Comptroller, Boxes 1-12, 74, 89, 93-98, 120-121-A (MARS ID: 13.26; series), State Archives of North Carolina, Raleigh. This portion of the Military Papers contains numerous muster rolls, pay rolls, and other documents for the militias and the Continental Line regiments/brigades.]

6th North Carolina Regiment

"Compiled Service Records of Revolutionary Soldiers Serving in the 6th North Carolina Regiment." *Southern Genealogist's Exchange Quarterly*, 22: whole no. 97 (Spring 1981), 6-10; 22: whole no. 98 (Summer 1981), 82-88.

Council, Arthur. "[A Signed Letter of Arthur Council, Cross Creek 9 June 1776 to an Unidentified Person]." Manuscript MSS L1995F237, Society of the Cincinnati Library, Anderson House, Washington, D. C. [Online catalog description: "In June 1777, Council was authorized to receive arms for the 6th North Carolina regiment -- see *Dict. of N. C. Biography*, v. 1 p. 440. Requests formal orders so that Col. Folsom can purchase arms for Council's regiment. Recommends Deny [i.e. Dennis] Porterfield be promoted from ensign to 2nd lieutenant."]

Lamb, Gideon, 1740-1781. "Gideon Lamb (1740-1781) Papers, 1776, 1779." Manuscript, Call Number PC.258, State Archives of North Carolina, Raleigh. [Online catalog description: "Papers of Lamb, Currituck Co. legislator and colonel of the 6th N. C. Regt. [Militia], consisting of bill of lading for salt shipped to New Bern (1776); and letter from Colonel Lamb at Campbellton to Gov. Richard Caswell about small number of North Carolina troops in the state and in Charleston (1779)."]

Lewis, J. D. "The American Revolution in North Carolina: 5th North Carolina Regiment." Online: http://www.carolana.com/NC/Revolution/revolution_nc_sixth_regiment.html.

North Carolina (State). State Treasurer; State Comptroller. "Military Papers – General Records, 1747-1909." Manuscript, Office of State Treasurer, Office of Comptroller, Boxes 1-12, 74, 89, 93-98, 120-121-A (MARS ID: 13.26; series), State Archives of North Carolina, Raleigh. This portion of the Military Papers contains numerous muster rolls, pay rolls, and other documents for the militias and the Continental Line regiments/brigades.]

"North Carolina Historical Re-Enactment Society: Home of the 6th North Carolina Regiment." Online: http://www.6nc.org/.

United States. Continental Army. North Carolina Battalion, 6th. "United States Continental Army Orderly Book, 1777-1778." Manuscript BG S625, Filson Historical Society, Louisville, Ky. [Online catalog description: "Orderly book recording military events of this unit from ca. 26 May 1777 to 12 June 1778. Included are orders, appointments, promotions, courts of inquiry, courts-martial and the punishments they meted out, troop movements, and encouraging and congratulatory messages from George Washington to the troops. It also reflects Washington's concern about camp hygiene, and the avoidance of smallpox and venereal disease, the practice of 'marooning' (plundering horses, fence rails, and supplies from friendly citizens), gaming, desertions, and other discipline problems. This book appears to have been kept by Benjamin Coffield, adjutant of the battalion, 17 May 1777 to 1 July 1778. It was later kept in the possession of Benjamin Carter, a lieutenant in 1776 and a captain in 1779 in the Fourth North Carolina who transferred to the Second in 1782."]

7th North Carolina Regiment

Lewis, J. D. "The American Revolution in North Carolina: 7th North Carolina Regiment." Online: http://www.carolana.com/NC/Revolution/revolution_nc_seventh_regiment.html.

North Carolina (State). State Treasurer; State Comptroller. "Military Papers – General Records, 1747-1909." Manuscript, Office of State Treasurer, Office of Comptroller, Boxes 1-12, 74, 89, 93-98, 120-121-A (MARS ID: 13.26; series), State Archives of North Carolina, Raleigh This portion of the Military Papers contains numerous muster rolls, pay rolls, and other documents for the militias and the Continental Line regiments/brigades.]

8th North Carolina Regiment

Lewis, J. D. "The American Revolution in North Carolina: 8th North Carolina Regiment." Online: http://www.carolana.com/NC/Revolution/revolution_nc_eighth_regiment.html.

North Carolina (State). General Assembly. "[Document dated:] 1777: Messages from Governor." Manuscript; General Assembly Record Group; Session Records, April-May 1777, Box 1 (MARS ID: 66.8.9.6; folder), State Archives of North Carolina, Raleigh. [Online catalog description: "Appointments made by Governor Richard Caswell to the Eighth North Carolina Battalion of the Army of the United States; discussion of probable peace treaty with the Cherokee Indians; report of complaints about inadequate ration allowance for the battalion."]

North Carolina (State). State Treasurer; State Comptroller. "Military Papers – General Records, 1747-1909." Manuscript, Office of State Treasurer, Office of Comptroller, Boxes 1-12, 74, 89, 93-98, 120-121-A (MARS ID: 13.26; series), State Archives of North Carolina, Raleigh. This portion of the Military Papers contains numerous muster rolls, pay rolls, and other documents for the militias and the Continental Line regiments/brigades.]

9th North Carolina Regiment

Lewis, J. D. "The American Revolution in North Carolina: 9th North Carolina Regiment." Online: http://www.carolana.com/NC/Revolution/revolution_nc_ninth_regiment.html.

Lewis, J. D. "Patriot Leaders in North Carolina: John Luttrell: Lt. Colonel in the 9th NC Regiment - 1776-1778; Lt. Colonel in the Chatham County Regiment of Militia - 1779-1781; Colonel in the Chatham County Regiment of Militia – 1781." Online: http://www.carolana.com/NC/Revolution/patriot_leaders_nc_john_luttrell.html.

North Carolina (State). General Assembly. "[Document dated:] April 25, [1778]: In Favor of James Christian, Soldier (With Messages)." Manuscript; General Assembly Record Group; Session Records, April-May 1778, Box 1 (MARS ID: 66.8.12.13.16; item), State Archives of North Carolina, Raleigh. [Online catalog description: "Resolved that James Christian is to be paid the sum of twenty pounds as compensation for a broken arm he suffered while serving in the 9th Battalion."]

North Carolina (State). State Treasurer; State Comptroller. "Military Papers – General Records, 1747-1909." Manuscript, Office of State Treasurer, Office of Comptroller, Boxes 1-12, 74, 89, 93-98, 120-121-A (MARS ID: 13.26; series), State Archives of North Carolina, Raleigh. This portion of the Military Papers contains numerous muster rolls, pay rolls, and other documents for the militias and the Continental Line regiments/brigades.]

10th North Carolina Regiment

Grady, Benjamin. "Benjamin Grady Collection, 1756-1853, 1909." Manuscript PC.521 (MARS ID: 1031; record group), State Archives of North Carolina, Raleigh. [Online catalog description: "Photocopies collected by B. F. Grady of Clinton, including wills of John Sampson (1783), Penelope Clinton (1814), Vice-President William R. King of North Carolina and Alabama (1853), and their relatives; a quitrent receipt (1756); list of Lieutenant Wilkinson's Company, 10th Regt. (1782)…"]

Lewis, J. D. "The American Revolution in North Carolina: 10th North Carolina Regiment." Online: http://www.carolana.com/NC/Revolution/revolution_nc_tenth_regiment.html.

Ralls, Stephen A. "A Case Study of the Tenth Regiment, North Carolina Continental Line." *North Carolina Genealogical Society Journal*, 18:2 (May 1992), 66-72.

North Carolina (State). State Treasurer; State Comptroller. "Military Papers – General Records, 1747-1909." Manuscript, Office of State Treasurer, Office of Comptroller, Boxes 1-12, 74, 89, 93-98, 120-121-A (MARS ID: 13.26; series), State Archives of North Carolina, Raleigh. This portion of the Military Papers contains numerous muster rolls, pay rolls, and other documents for the militias and the Continental Line regiments/brigades.]

North Carolina Light Dragoons

"An Account of Goods Delivered Sundry Persons Belonging to the Continental Army: To be Charged to Them Respectively and to Be Accounted for By the Regimental Pay Masters, [Fort Pitt?], 20 Sept. 1778-3 May 1779." Manuscript MSS L1995F171, Society of the Cincinnati Library, Anderson House, Washington, D. C. [Online catalog description: "Acco{un}t of goods d{e}l{ivere}d at Fort Pitt by order of Brigr. Genl. McIntosh. Goods mentioned include linen, serge, thread, buttons, ruffled shirts, bandanas, shoes, sheeting, and blankets, with prices for each. Among the military units mentioned are the 8th Pennsylvania under Daniel Brodhead, the 13th Virginia under William Russell, and Capt. Ash's {i.e. Ashe's?} North Carolina Light Dragoons."]

North Carolina (State). General Assembly. "[Document dated:] February 2, 1779: Resolution Re[lating] to Discharging the Light Dragoons (Messages Only)." Manuscript; General Assembly Record Group; Session Records, January-February 1779; Joint Papers, Committee Papers, Resolutions, Box 1 (MARS ID: 66.8.15. 10.18; item), State Archives of North Carolina, Raleigh.

North Carolina Invalid Corps

North Carolina (State). General Assembly. "[Document dated:] August 31, [1780]: Recommending Commission for Captain William Williams as Captain of Invalid Corps (With Petition)." Manuscript; General Assembly Record Group; Session Records, August-September 1780, Box 1 (MARS ID: 66.8.22.9.2; item), State Archives of North Carolina, Raleigh. [Online catalog description: "Williams informs the Assembly that although he became an invalid at Valley Forge while with the North Carolina Brigade, he still wishes to serve the state as commander of an invalid corps, if the Assembly would create one. The resolution does, and it recommends that the governor issue Williams a commission as its captain."]

Maryland and Delaware Forces in North Carolina

"1st Maryland/Southern Campaign (NC)." Online: http://www.revwar.com/1msc/.

"Alamance Battleground Research Project Concludes Extensive Work." *Carolina Comments,* 59:1 (January 2011), 5-8. [Includes a couple of paragraphs on a Continental Army button with the initials "USA" on it found at the battlefield. It is likely from a skirmish on the old battleground in 1781 "between Capt. Robert Kirkwood's Delaware Continental company and a detachment of General Cornwallis' army."]

Seymour, William. "A Journal of the Southern Expedition, 1780-1783." *Papers of the Historical Society of Delaware*, 15 (1896).

Smallwood, William, 1732-1792. "Letters, 1780." Manuscript Sec. A Box 121 items 1-2, David M. Rubenstein Rare Book & Manuscript Library, Duke University, Durham. [Online catalog description: "U. S. major general in the Revolutionary War. Collection consists of letters from Smallwood relating to the need for food and supplies for his troops, then on duty in N. C.; and describing the strength of the Tories in western N. C." William Smallwood was from Charles County, Maryland.]

Smallwood, William, 1732-1792. "William Smallwood Papers, 1780." Manuscript MSS96107, Peter Force Collection, Library of Congress Manuscript Division, Madison Building, Washington, D. C.; [Online catalog description: "Orderly book (1780 July 3-October 2) with general, division, and brigade orders received by Gen. Smallwood's Maryland regiment from Generals Baron de Kalb and Horatio Gates, Chatham County, N.C. Includes returns (July 1780) of Maryland and Delaware troops."]

Smallwood, William, 1732-1792. "William Smallwood Papers, 1780." 1 manuscript vol. (also microfilm edition, 17,137, reel 67), Manuscript Reading Room, Madison Building, Library of Congress, Washington, D. C. [Online catalog description: "Orderly book (1780 July 3-October 2) with general, division, and brigade orders received by Gen. Smallwood's Maryland Regiment from Generals Baron de Kalb and Horatio Gates, Chatham County, N. C. Includes returns (July 1780) of Maryland and Delaware troops."]

Virginia Forces in North Carolina and North Carolina-Virginia Connections

[See also the section on the Battle of King's Mountain.]

Abercrombie, Janice L. "Louisa County Troops Called to Assist North Carolina, 1776." *Louisa County Historical Magazine*, 41:1 (Spring 2010), 40.

Abercrombie, Janice L., and Richard Slatten. *Virginia Revolutionary "Publick" Claims.* 3 vols. Athens, Ga.: Iberian Publishing Company, 1992; *Index to the Virginia Revolutionary "Publick" Claims: County Booklets.* Athens, Ga.: Iberian Publishing Company, 1992. [Description: "Index to the county court booklets in the public service claims. The county governments acted as local procurement agencies, to provide livestock, foodstuffs, arms and other supplies for the use of the militia and for the Virginia and Continental armies." Some North Carolinians appear in these records.]

Brandon, Lawrence. "They, Too, Were Patriots: Supplies Furnished a Hampshire County Regiment." *North Carolina Genealogical Society Journal,* 40:3 (August 2014), 182. ["The following list of claims relates to Captain Daniel Richardson's march of Hampshire County, Virginia, militia to Hillsboro in 1780." The people listed are those who gave supplies to the unit in Caswell and Orange Counties, North Carolina.]

"Colonel Nicholas Long, for the services of the Battalion of Minute Men & Volunteers of the District of Halifax on an Expedition to Norfolk in Virginia, also to Wilmington and Moore's Creek." In Weynette Parks Haun, *North Carolina Revolutionary Army Accounts, Part I, Secretary of State Treasurer's & Comptroller's Papers Journal "A", (Public Accounts) 1775-1776* (Durham: W. P. Haun, 1988), 144-160.

Davis, John. "John Davis Diaries." Manuscript #Am.6565, Historical Society of Pennsylvania, Philadelphia. [Online catalog description: "John Davis was captain of the 1st Pennsylvania Battalion, Continental Army, under General Anthony Wayne. His diary covers the Virginia campaign, Yorktown, and the march to North and South Carolina to join Nathanael Greene."]

Gaines, Daniel, active 1780s. "Letter, 1781 June 23, Mount Tirzah [Person County, N. C.], to William Cabell." Manuscript Mss 2 G1273 a 1, Virginia Historical Society, Richmond. [Online catalog description: "Concerns the Virginia Militia in North Carolina. Printed in Alexander Brown. *The Cabells and Their Kin* (Richmond: Garrett and Massie, 1939), 212.

"Henry County Militia Officers under the Command of Colonel Martin Armstrong of North Carolina, Oct. 1780 (includes Col. Abraham Penn and six captains from the Henry County militia), *The State Records of North Carolina, 1780-1781*, Vol. XV, p. 123-124.

Lawson, Robert, ?-ca.1802. "Papers, 1776-1825 bulk 1781." Library Service Center items 1-40, David M. Rubenstein Rare Book & Manuscript Library, Duke University, Durham. [Online catalog description: "Chiefly letters to Lawson, Brigadier-General in the Virginia Militia, concerning the raising, reenforcement, and movement of troops in Virginia and North Carolina, during the Revolutionary War in 1781. Some papers concern military promotions and family affairs. Later letters indicate that Lawson moved to Kentucky, having considered South Carolina. Several concern Lawson's possible reenforcement of Nathanael Greene's troops. Included also are a letter of America Lawson Lewis to Lafayette in 1825 sending him some of her father's papers for brief examination, and routine letters of Thomas Jefferson while governor of Virginia. Correspondents include Thomas Jefferson, Jonathan Beckley, A. L. Lewis, S. Hardy, Baron Von Steuben, John P. Muhlenberg, and Richard Henry Lee. Also an account book (1776, Sept.-Dec.) relating to Lawson's service with the 4th Virginia Battalion, military commissions, letters of introduction (1787) for Lawson from George Mason and Henry Lee to Pierce Butler, Charles Pinckney, and William Few and other miscellany items."]

Lee, Henry. *The Campaign of 1781 in the Carolinas, with Remarks Historical and Critical on Johnson's Life of Greene; to Which is Added an Appendix of Original Documents, Relating to the History of the Revolution.* Philadelphia: E. Littell, 1824; Chicago: Quadrangle, 1824; reprinted: Spartanburg: Reprint Company, 1975.

Lee, Henry. *Memoirs of the War in the Southern Department of the United States*. Philadelphia and New York: Bradford and Inskeep, 1812; Philadelphia: Fry and Kammerer, 1812; 2nd edition edited by "Colonel Howard;" Washington, D. C.: Peter Force, 1827; 3rd edition edited by Robert E. Lee: New York: University Publishing, 1869; (Eyewitness Accounts of the American Revolution series) New York: New York Times, 1969.

Lee, Henry. "Henry Lee Papers, 1768-1816." Manuscript Accession 26824, Library of Virginia, Richmond; online finding aid available at http://ead.lib.virginia.edu/vivaxtf/view?docId=lva/vi01136.xml. [Online finding aid description: "Papers, 1768-1816, of Henry Lee (1756-1818) of Westmoreland County, Virginia, and Barbados, containing bonds, correspondence, deeds, depositions, notes and reminiscences. Correspondence includes transcripts of letters and depositions discussing the quartering of British troops in Boston, Massachusetts, possible efforts by British officers to encourage African Americans to rebel, and general unrest in Massachusetts, all before the Revolution. Also contains letters from George Washington (1732-1799), the Marquis de Lafayette (1757-1834), and Nathanael Greene (1742-1786) regarding the military situation in New York, North Carolina, and South Carolina during the American Revolution; letters concerning politics in the United States during the 1780s and 1790s; and correspondence containing recollections by other officers of the Continental Army about campaigns in North Carolina and South Carolina, including the battles of Guilford Court House and Hobkirk's Hill."]

Liles, Frankie. "Washington County Militia at Kings Mountain." *Magazine of Virginia Genealogy*, 52:1 (February 2014), 78-82. [Contents: A Pay Roll of Lieutenant Reece Bowen's Company of Militia from Washington County, under Command of Colonel William Campbell; A Pay Roll of a Part of the Washington Militia in

Actual Service under the Command of Ensign Rob[t] Mcfarlon; "A Pay Roll fore Capt. James Dysarts Company of Light Horse in Actuall Service on a Touer to North Carolina under the Command of Col. Wm. Campbell."]

O' Neill, Terri Bradshaw. "Artificers and Laborers at Mount Tirzah in Caswell County, N. C., 1781-1782." *North Carolina Genealogical Society Journal,* 25:4 (November 1999), 411-417.

Page, John. "John Page Letters, 1776." Manuscript Accession 24721, Library of Virginia, Richmond; online finding aid available at http://ead.lib.virginia.edu/vivaxtf/view?docId=lva/vi00722.xml. [Online finding aid description: "Letters, 1776, from John Page (1743-1808) to Charles Lee (1731-1782) consisting of: letter, 12 July 1776, describing the defense of Gwynn{'s} Island against the fleet of Lord Dunmore; and letter, 13 August 1776, discussing Lee's military maneuvers, campaigns against the Cherokee by the militias of Virginia and North Carolina, the arrival of the Chevalier de St. Aubin, and mail difficulties. These letters are printed in *Lee Papers* volume II, volume 5 of the New York Historical Society, pp. 131-136 and 214-216."]

"A Pay Roll of Capt. Dysart's Company of Light Horse in Actual Service on a Tour of North Carolina under Col. William Campbell – Orders of Gen'l Green." *Georgia Genealogical Society Quarterly*, 2:3 (March 1966), 114.

Penn, Abraham, 1743-1801. "Roster, n. d." Manuscript accession no. 41633, Library of Virginia, Richmond. [Online catalog description: "Roster, undated, of soldiers who marched with Colonel Abraham Penn to the Battle of Guilford Courthouse in 1781. Col. Abraham (Abram) Penn was born in Goochland or Amherst County Virginia in 1743. He married Ruth Stovall in 1767 in Amherst County, Virginia. Shortly thereafter, he moved to Henry County, Virginia and lived on Beaver Creek on land which was later the home of Col. George Hairston. When Henry County was formed in 1776, Abram Penn was the presiding justice of the County Court. He organized and commanded the Henry County troops in the Battle of Guilford Courthouse in the American Revolution and was at the Surrender in Yorktown…"]

"Roll of Captain (Turner) Bynum's Company of Militia, taken April 7, 1781" (no county designation given), *State Records of North Carolina, Clark, Vol. 17, p. 1042* [DAR Genealogy Office analysis of this document: "Though no county designation appears on this list, this actually appears to be a list of Virginia militia from neighboring Greensville County, Virginia. The captain in this company was Turner Bynum and the lieutenant was Isaac Rowell. On 26 April 1781, Isaac Rowell was appointed a 2nd lieutenant in the Greensville County militia, and on 22 August 1782 Turner Bynum was commissioned a captain in the Greensville County militia (*William & Mary Quarterly, 1st Series, Volume 27, p. 96*). In the DAR Genealogical Research System, the residence of Captain Turner Bynum is given as Greensville County, Virginia. Also, in the Revolutionary War pension record of Isaac Rowell, *W9634, his widow states that he served not only in the North Carolina line, but also "Captain Binum's Company of Virginia militia". In the DAR GRS, the residence of Isaac Rowell is listed as Greensville County, Virginia. While this list does appear to be a Greensville County, Virginia, militia list, it does not preclude the possibility of some North Carolinians who resided in areas nearby from having served in the unit."]

Virginia (State). General Assembly. House of Delegates. "Resolution, House of Delegates, Agreed to by Senate 20 May 1780, 1780 May 15." Manuscript accession no. 44393, Library of Virginia, Richmond: online: http://image.lva.virginia.gov/GLR/00281. [Online catalog description: "These records are part of the Governor's Office record group (RG# 3) - Executive Papers of Governor Thomas Jefferson, 1779-1781. Resolution to supply North Carolina with such arms as can be spared by state magazine. Certified by John Beckley, C. H. D. Agreed to by the Senate, Will[iam] Drew, C. S."]

Virginia. General Assembly. House of Delegates, Speaker. "Letters, 1782, May 6." Manuscript 36912 and on misc. microfilm reel 5373, Library of Virginia, Richmond. [Online catalog description: "Contains a letter from Governor Benjamin Harrison, in Council, to {John Tyler, Speaker of the House of Delegates}, regarding various issues and enclosing two letters from George Washington & Nathanael Green… In his original letter, Harrison discusses the proceedings of Congress regarding back lands, Gen. Greene's demand for assistance from Virginia militia, laws for the seizure of British goods, the recruitment of men to fill battalions, the incident between a Virginia privateer seizing a North Carolina vessel in port at Edenton, stolen slaves in North Carolina,…"]

Virginia. General Assembly. House of Delegates, Speaker. "Letters, 1782 June 10." Manuscript 36912, and on misc. microfilm reel 5373, Library of Virginia, Richmond. [Online catalog description: "Contains a letter from Governor Benjamin Harrison to [John Tyler], Speaker of the House of Delegates, enclosing letters from Governor Alexander Martin of North Carolina and the General Assembly of North Carolina. The Governor indicates that he also encloses letters from Gen. Greene and Admiral Rodney's letter to the Governor of Jamaica, but these are not present. Harrison briefly mentions the content of these letters including Gen. Greene's 'wants' for his army and Admiral Rodney's account of the capture of Count de Grass[e] and the loss of six line of battle ships in his fleet to the British. The letter from Governor Alexander Martin, dated 1782 May

20, encloses the General Assembly of North Carolina's answer to the General Assembly of Virginia, dated 1782 May 17, respecting certain lands in North Carolina which fell into dispute by the extension of the boundary line. This document is signed by Thomas Benbury & R[ichard] Caswell, Speaker of the Senate."]

Virginia (State). Governor. "Bounty Land Warrants, 1779-1860." Manuscript accession no. 41429, 29 microfilm reels, Library of Virginia, Richmond. [These documents contain the names various North Carolinians supporting the claims of Virginia veterans for bounty land or of men who may have served in Virginia units but were either from North Carolina originally or had resettled there. Their names appear in the Library of Virginia's online catalog in the title field with links to images of the actual documents. These men include:

John Wallis (with an affidavit by Samuel Blankinship, Iredell County, N. C., and a letter from Lewis Williams; 1827)

John Dixon, Surry County, N. C. (with a certificate from J. L. Edwards, Supt. Pensions, and a letter from Lewis Williams; 1826)

Edline Willoughby (with an affidavit from Willoughby, Anson County, N. C.; 1822)

William Thompson (with an affidavit from James Carter and William Pike, Halifax County, N. C.; 1821)

Harrison Wade (with affidavits of Micajah Bullock, Granville County, N. C.; 1823)

Benjamin Wade (with affidavits of Micajah Bullock, Granville County, N. C.; and William Fowler, Senr., and certificates for Stephen K. Snead and Thomas Miller; 1823)

Drewry Pattiford, Granville County, N. C. (with a certificate of L. Holmes. Note: "Assigns all his land &c. due for services in the Continental army to Saml. Parker, dated 1784."]

James Monroe, Lieutenant Colonel (with certificates from James E. Heath, Auditor; W. W. Parker, 1st Clerk, Land Office; Ro[bert] Johnston, 1st Auditor; 2 letters from Th[omas] Jefferson (copies); letter from James Monroe (copy); letter from A[bner] Nash, Governor of North Carolina (copy); and other documents; 1850)

John Adam (with affidavits for Ben Jones, Wake County, N. C.; Dudley Ballard, Caswell, N C.; James Young, Amos Bridges, and Susania Jones, all of Franklin County, N. C.; 1804)

Herod Gibbs (with affidavits of Stephen Young, late Captain, Mecklenburg County, N. C.; James Alverson, Chester District, S. C.; Thomas Wills, Fairfield District, S. C.; and certificates of Hod Turpin, late ensign, and Hezekiah Morton. "See also papers of Thomas Wills, Rejected Claims, 1811; 1813; see also papers of James Gassaway, 1813.")

Christopher Daniell (with affidavits of Christopher Daniell, Orange County, N. C.; Thomas Miller; a certificate of James S. Smith, to Governor Randolph; and an advise from Thomas M. Randolph; 1822)

Ransome Colquett (with affadavits of Ransome Colquett, Rockingham County, N. C.; William Roane; Berryman Green, late Pay Master); certificates for Thomas Green, late soldier and J. Roberston, Jr.; letter of William Roane; 1823)

William Chapman, Rowan County, N. C. (with affidavits of William Chapman, J. H. Chapman, and Randolph Mitchell; letter from William Chapman; 1824)

Virginia (State). Governor. "Rejected Claims for Bounty Land Warrants, 1779-1860." Manuscript accession no. 41986, 15 microfilm reels, Library of Virginia, Richmond. These documents contain the names various North Carolinians supporting the claims of Virginia veterans for bounty land or of men who may have served in Virginia units but were either from North Carolina originally or had resettled there. Their names appear in the Library of Virginia's online catalog in the title field with links to images of the actual documents. These men include:

Charles Pearson (with a certificate from Wilkes County, North Carolina, Court, and a letter signed M. Stokes; 1823)

Martin Maney, Buncombe County, N. C. (with a letter signed by William Roane; 1823)

John Houghland, Mecklenburg County, N. C. (with a certificate signed by V. D. Ingham, Secretary of the Treasury, and a letter from Henry W. Connor; 1831)

Peter Barrett, Person County, N. C. (with an affidavit from the said Peter Barrett; 1831)

Virginia (State). Militia. Henry County. "List, 1781 Mar. 11." Manuscript accession nos. 20442, 22585 and 22586, Organization Records Collection," Library of Virginia, Richmond. [Online catalog description: "List, 11 March 1781, of Henry County, Virginia, militia sent to the assistance of General Nathanael Greene (1742-1786) in North Carolina. Includes photostat copy. Accessions 20442 and 22586 for more complete lists of the militia."]

Virginia (State). Militia. Parker's Brigade (1780-1781). "Order Book, 1781 March 8-27." Manuscript Mss 1 P2266 a 9, Virginia Historical Society, Richmond. [Online catalog description: "Concerns the military activities of the combined Virginia and North Carolina militia forces under Josiah Parker's command at Edmonds Hill, Norfolk County {now Chesapeake} and Northwest Bridge {Portsmouth}, Va."]

[Waddell, Joseph A.] "Mrs. Breckenridge's Brewery." *Journal of the History Museum and Historical Society of Western Virginia*, 14:2 (2001), 20. [Description: "Describes March 1, 1781, encampment of a Rockbridge County militia company near the residence of Colonel Robert Breckinridge in Botetourt County on its way to the battle at Guilford Court House in North Carolina. Source: *Annals of Augusta County, Virginia, 1726 – 1781*, Joseph A. Waddell. Staunton, Va., 1902."]

Deserters and Desertion from the Army

Boyle, Joseph Lee. *"He Loves a Good Dea of Rum...:" Military Desertions during the American Revolution, 1775-1783*. 2 vols. Baltimore: Clearfield Company, 2009. [Publisher's description: "This compilation is from thirty-eight newspapers published from Massachusetts to North Carolina from 1775 to 1783." Contents: v.1. 1775-June 30, 1777; v. 2. June 30, 1777-1783.]

"D. A. R. Entry on These Lines? Doubtful!" *Pamteco Tracings*, 11:1 (June 1995), 17-20. [Criminal Action Papers against a group of people who set up an asylum for deserters from the Continental army and also set deserters free from jail. The article lists names of specific individuals.]

North Carolina (State). General Assembly. "[Document dated:] Dec. 5, [1788]: Report on Claims No. 38-47 – William Terrell Lewis and Others (Petition Only)." Manuscript; General Assembly Record Group; Session Records, November-December 1788, Box 1 (MARS ID: 66.8.49.11.14; item), State Archives of North Carolina, Raleigh. [Online catalog description: "Petition requests payment for capture and delivery of deserters during the war."]

Roebuck, Haywood. "Some Continental Line Deserters from Rowan, Surry, and Mecklenburg Counties, N. C. 1780-1782." *North Carolina Genealogical Society Journal*, 1:2 (April 1975), 102-104.

Smith, Clifford Neal. *British and German Deserters, Discharges, and Prisoners of War Who May Have Remained in Canada and the United States, 1774-1783, Part 1 and Part 2* [*and*] *Deserters and Disbanded Soldiers from British, German, and Loyalist Military Units in the South, 1782*. Baltimore: Genealogical Publishing Company, 2004.

Tate, Thad W. "Desertion from the American Revolutionary Army." M. A. thesis, University of North Carolina at Chapel Hill, 1948.

Courts Martial

Ball, Farlin Q. "Farlin Q. Ball Collection, 1779-1784." Manuscript, Call Number PC.298, State Archives of North Carolina, Raleigh. [Online catalog description: "Proceedings of court-martial presided over by Col. Charles Cotesworth Pinckney in South Carolina, 1779, hearing disobedience charge against Lt. William Lytle of the N.C. Continental Line. Testimony in the case concerns extra captains appointed by North Carolina and includes quotes from pertinent state and federal records."]

North Carolina (State). General Assembly. "[Document dated:] May 5, 1783: Resolution Concerning the Court Martial of Col. James Blount of Chowan County." Manuscript; General Assembly Record Group; Session Records, April-May 1783; Joint Papers, Committee Papers, Resolution; House Joint Resolutions: May 1-17, 1783, Box 1 (MARS ID: 66.8.29.14.3), State Archives of North Carolina, Raleigh. [Online catalog description: "Resolution asks the governor to order a court martial to determine the facts regarding Col. James Blount's conduct in the taking of a flag vessel into Virginia. Includes a message from the governor requesting action from the assembly."]

North Carolina (State). General Assembly. "[Document dated]: April 26, 1784: Resolution Confirming the Court Martial Sentence of Colonel James Blount (Governor's Message and Court Martial Proceedings Only)." Manuscript; General Assembly Record Group; Session Records, April-June 1784; Committee Papers, Resolutions; House Joint Resolutions, Box 2 (MARS ID: 66.8.32.5.5; item), State Archives of North Carolina, Raleigh. [Online catalog description: "Resolution affirms the court martial of Col. James Blount, who was ordered to apprehend Capt. Scimmerhorn of the flag vessel the *Grand Turk* in Edenton Harbor, and declined to do so for several days, thereby allowing him to escape to Virginia. The court martial found him guilty and unfit to serve the state in the military. Court proceedings and depositions included."][33]

McDowell, Charles. "Charles McDowell Papers, 1782." Manuscript, PC.29, State Archives of North Carolina, Raleigh. [Online catalog description: "Proceedings of court-martial in Burke Co. of McDowell, accused of

---

[33] A fuller description of this material appears in D. L. Corbitt, ed., *Calendar of Manuscript Collections, Vol. 1* (Raleigh: Edwards & Broughton, 1926), 223.

'countenancing Tories,' and a letter from Gen. Griffith Rutherford transmitting proceedings to the General Assembly with recommendation that McDowell's commission be restored."]

Micajah Petway Chapter, North Carolina Daughters of the American Revolution. "Court Martial Held for Nash County, 1780: Exemption of Soldiers from Service, 1782." 7 leaves. [copy at the Middle Georgia Regional Library, Washington Memorial Library, Macon Genealogical and Historical Department.]

"N. C. Brigade Courts Martial, Camp Valley Forge [1778]." In Mary Bondurant Warren, ed., *Revolutionary Memoirs and Muster Rolls* (Athens, Ga.: Heritage Papers, 1994), 91-92 and 93-94.

United States. Continental Army. "Valley Forge Court Martial Records." Manuscript #AM.6315, Historical Society of Pennsylvania, Philadelphia. [Online catalog description: "Records of the court-martial of Lieutenant Matthew McCalley of the 10th North Carolina Battalion and other prisoners, before Colonel Thomas Clark at Valley Forge."]

Uniforms

Babits, Lawrence E. "A North Carolina Revolutionary War Button." *Military Collector and Historian*, 26 (Spring 1974), 52.

Gillgam, Jim. "Uniforms of the Continental Line, 1776." Online: http://ncrevwar.lostsoulsgenealogy.com/uniforms1776.htm.

Lefferts, Charles Mackubin. *Uniforms of the American, British, French and German Armies in the War of the Revolution*. New York: New-York Historical Society, 1924.

Arms, Armaments, Armories, Gunsmiths, and Gunmaking in North Carolina

Bivens, John. *Longrifles of North Carolina.* Lancaster, Pa.: George Shumway, 1968.

Harrington, Hugh T. "Roundball Ballistics in the Revolutionary War: What Cause Rifle Shots to Go over the Heads of the Enemy." *Southern Campaigns of the American Revolution*, 3:5 (May 2006), 12-14; online: southerncampaign.org.

Mahler, Grace H. "Old Weapons of North Carolina." *The State: Down Home in North Carolina*, 28:12 (November 1960), 17; online: http://digital.ncdcr.gov/cdm/ref/collection/p16062coll18/id/43054. Online description from "North Carolina Periodicals Index," East Carolina University: "A new permanent exhibit of weapons is on display in North Carolina's Hall of History, located in Raleigh. One of the finest gun collections in the South, this exhibit demonstrates the craft and art of handmade guns."]

Supplying the Army and Soldiers' Families in North Carolina: The Commissary General and Related Procurement Functions

Patriotic Service[34]

Patriots of the Revolution are considered to be those men and women who by an act or series of actions demonstrated unfailing loyalty to the cause of American Independence from England. Patriotic service might begin as early as April 1774. We depend upon recorded actions to give us an indication of patriotism. What was the purpose of the action? What were the risks? The consequences? Answers to these questions can determine whether the action actually applied to an attempt to further the cause of independence or demonstrated loyalty to that cause.

Evidence of patriotic activity may be found in town, county, state, and federal records. Many records kept by the states have been indexed and often a letter to the state archives will be sufficient to determine if evidence exists to show that a person contributed supplies or made some other contribution to the war effort. Town and county records have usually not been indexed and a personal search of town minutes and court minutes is required. Minutes of the Continental Congresses have been published. *Old letters, diaries, and other family and personal papers can often be used as evidence of patriotic intent, provided the record was made at the time of the event described.*

Not all actions illustrating patriotism are mentioned here. Many others exist. When it is considered desirable to establish another type of patriotic service, proof of the action taken must be submitted with the application paper, together with historical justification to show that the action did indeed imply patriotic intent.

---

[34] Office of the Registrar General's compilation, *Genealogy Guidelines* (Washington, D. C.: National Society Daughters of the American Revolution, 2014), 94-95.

Those who rendered material aid, such as furnished supplies, with or without remuneration, loaned money or provided munitions or guns. Some states enacted special tax laws to raise money for supplies. Payment of such "supply" taxes is considered patriotic service [although each case may be judged on its merits before approval of this service is given.]

Babits, Lawrence E. "Supplying the Southern Army, March 1780-September 1781." *Military Collector and Historian* , 48:4 (Winter 1995), 163-171.

Barringer, Rufus. "Rufus Barringer Collection, 1770-1778." Manuscript, PC.855, State Archives of North Carolina, Raleigh. [Online catalog description: "Typed copy of memorandum book apparently kept by William Alexander, fur trader, on trips through North Carolina, Virginia, Maryland, and Pennsylvania, containing diary of travels and expenses, furs bought, purchases made for others; receipts to him as 'comisar,' for rations of various military companies (1777-1778); and copies of drafts for payment, one by Gov. Richard Caswell on the Georgia delegates in Congress (1777). Also references to Alexander's father Hezekiah, and to John McKnitt Alexander."]

Brooks, Aubrey Lee. "Collection, 1758-1875." Manuscript, CP.359 (MARS ID: 869; record group), State Archives of North Carolina, Raleigh. [The online catalog description of this collection shows that it includes a letter of: "Gov. Richard Caswell to justices of Craven Co. on profiteering, suggesting seizure of clothing needed for troops (1778);…"]

Carp, E. Wayne. *To Starve the Army at Pleasure: Continental Army Administration and American Political Culture, 1775-1783.* Chapel Hill: University of North Carolina Press, 1984.

Cobb, Collier. "Collier Cobb Collection, 1779, 1780." Manuscript PC.413 (MARS ID: 923; record group), State Archives of North Carolina, Raleigh. [Online catalog description: "Draft of letter from assistant commissary Joseph Green, Dobbs Co., to Capt. John Estes about provisions for troops and record keeping (1779); and warrant from New Bern Superior Court for arrest of man charged with trespass."]

Gibson, John. "Quartermaster Waste Book. Hillsborough, South [i. e. North] Carolina; September-November 1780." Manuscript, Special Collections and Moore Wing Orderly Book Collections, Cadet Library, United States Military Academy at West Point, N. Y.

Greene, Nathanael, 1742-1786. "Nathanael Greene Papers, 1778-1786 [manuscript]." Library Service Center Box 1, David M. Rubenstein Rare Book & Manuscript Library, Duke University, Durham. [Online catalog description: "Reports, requisitions, and correspondence pertaining to the quartermaster department of the Continental Army while Greene was quartermaster general, 1778-1780; papers concerning the war in South Carolina and Georgia during Greene's term as commander of the troops in the southern states, 1780-1783; and papers, 1783-1786, pertaining to Greene's business affairs. Correspondents include John Habersham, Wade Hampton, John Houston, Henry Lee, Andrew Pickens, Charles Cotesworth Pinckney, Thomas Posey, and Anthony Wayne."]

Horgan, Lucille E. *Forged in War: The Continental Congress and the Origin of the Military Supply and Acquisition System.* Westport, Conn.: Greenwood Press, 2002.

Lewis, J. D. "The American Revolution in North Carolina: Deputy Quarter Master General's (DQMG) Department." Online: http://www.carolana.com/NC/Revolution/revolution_nc_dqmg.html.

Lutz, Paul V. "A State's Concern for the Soldiers' Welfare: How North Carolina Provided for Her Troops during the Revolution." *North Carolina Historical Review*, 42:3 (July 1965), 315-318.

North Carolina (State). General Assembly. "[Document dated:] May 7, [1777]: Re[specting] Removal of Military Stores if Exposed to Danger of Enemy (With Messages)." Manuscript; General Assembly Record Group; Session Records, April-May 1777; Joint Papers, Committee Papers, Resolutions, Senate Bills, House Bills, Box 1 (MARS ID: 66.8.9.13.2; item), State Archives of North Carolina, Raleigh.

North Carolina (State). General Assembly. "[Document dated:] May 9, [1777]: Re[specting] Rations to Commissaries." Manuscript; General Assembly Record Group; Session Records, Apr-May 1777; Joint Papers, Committee Papers, Resolutions, Senate Bills, House Bills, Box 1 (MARS ID: 66.8.9.11.18; item), Archives of North Carolina, Raleigh. [Online catalog description: "Resolution allowing an increase in the amount of money spent on rations and supplies for Continental troops."]

North Carolina (State). General Assembly. "[Document dated:] May 9, [1777]: Respecting Militia Frontiers and Magazines (With Message)." Manuscript; General Assembly Record Group; Session Records, April-May 1777; Joint Papers, Committee Papers, Resolutions, Senate Bills, House Bills, Box 1 (MARS ID: 66.8.9.11.15; item), State Archives of North Carolina, Raleigh. [Online catalog description: "Resolution supporting the creation of additional companies of militia to use in the war against the Cherokee."]

North Carolina (State). General Assembly. "[Document dated:] December 6, 1777: Bill for the Ease and Convenience of the Militia on the West Side of New Port in Carteret Co." Manuscript; General Assembly Record Group; Session Records, November-December 1777, House Bills, Box 2 (MARS ID: 66.8.11.25; folder), State Archives of North Carolina, Raleigh.

North Carolina (State). General Assembly. "[Document dated:] April 21, [1778]: Appointing John Council Bryan as Commissary (With Messages)." Manuscript; General Assembly Record Group; Session Records, April-May 1778; Joint Papers, Committee Papers, Resolutions, Senate Bills, House Bills, Box 1 (MARS ID: 66.8.12.16.13; item), State Archives of North Carolina, Raleigh.

North Carolina (State). General Assembly. House of Delegates. "[Document dated:] April 24, [1778]: Re[specting] John Council Bryan (With Message)." Manuscript; General Assembly Record Group; Session Records, April-May 1778; Joint Papers, Committee Papers, Resolutions, Senate Bills, House Bills, Box 1 (MARS ID: 66.8.12.16.21), State Archives of North Carolina, Raleigh. [Online catalog description: "Governor empowered to advance money to John Council Bryan for the purchase of provisions for the army."]

North Carolina (State). General Assembly. "[Document dated:] August 14, [1778]: In Favor of Jonathan Dunbibbin (With Message and Petition)." Manuscript; General Assembly Record Group; Session Records, August 1778, Joint Papers, Committee Papers, Resolutions, Senate Bills, House Bills, Box 1 (MARS ID: 66.8.14.9.4), State Archives of North Carolina, Raleigh. [Online catalog description: "Resolution to pay Dunbibbin for supplying lumber to the Continental Army."]

North Carolina (State). General Assembly. "[Document dated:] April 28, 1778: "Bill to Prevent the Exportation of Beef, Pork, Bacon and Indian Corn." Manuscript; General Assembly Session Records; Session of April-May 1778; House Resolutions (April 27-May 1), Senate Bills, House Bills, Box 2 (MARS ID: 66.8.13.34; folder), State Archives of North Carolina, Raleigh.

North Carolina (State). General Assembly. "[Document Dated]: February 4, 1779: Report on Petiton of Isaiah Paschal (with Messages and Petitions)." Manuscript; General Assembly Record Group; Session Records, January-February 1779; Joint Papers, Committee Papers, Resolutions; Joint Select Committees, box 1 (MARS ID: 66.8.15.8.12; item), State Archives of North Carolina, Raleigh. [Online catalog description: "After reviewing the petitions, the committee recommends that Isaiah Paschal of Granville County be discharged from the militia due to his age and infirmity; the Assembly concurs."]

North Carolina (State). General Assembly. "[Document dated:] Feb. 5, [1779]: Report Re the Memorial of Rev. Adam Boyd for Clothing Troops (With Messages and Petition)." Manuscript, General Assembly Record Group, Session Records January-February 1779; Joint Papers, Committee Papers, Resolutions, Senate Bills, House Bills,Box 1 (MARS ID: 66.8.15.8.13; item), State Archives of North Carolina, Raleigh. [Online catalog description: "After investigating Boyd's petition, which concerns his efforts to provide clothing for the militia, the committee recommends appropriating fifteen thousand pounds for the clothing of every North Carolina officer in Continental service."]

North Carolina (State). General Assembly. "[Document dated:] September 6, 1780: Bill for Leying a Specific Provision Tax." Manuscript; General Assembly Record Group; Session Records, August-September, 1780; Joint Papers, Committee Papers, Resolutions, Senate Bills, House Bills, Box 1 (MARS ID: 66.8.22.16; folder), State Archives of North Carolina, Raleigh. [Online catalog description: "Includes appointments to a committee to write the bill and two copies of the bill. The bill levies a tax for the military which is to be paid in food, and the bill establishes how a commissioner to carry out the act in each county is to be appointed and what powers he will have."]

North Carolina (State). General Assembly. "[Document dated:] September 6, [1780]: Directing Delivery of Tobacco to Captain William Borritz as Payment for Cannon Imported." Manuscript; General Assembly Record Group; Session Records, August-September 1780; Joint Papers, Committee Papers, Resolutions, Senate Bills, House Bills, Box 1 (MARS ID: 66.8.22.9.13; item), State Archives of North Carolina, Raleigh. [Online catalog description: "Borritz, master of the ship *Fair America* (formerly the *Holy Heart of Jesus*), informs the Assembly that he has yet to receive the full amount of tobacco promised for delivery of cannons to the state. The Assembly appoints a committee to investigate, which recommends that the commissioners of the board of trade be ordered to deliver to Borritz the the [*sic*] remainder of the tobacco due him. The resolution so directs."]

North Carolina (State). General Assembly. "[Document dated]: February 1, 1781: "Resolution to Ascertain Adequate and Proper Allowances to Be Made for Articles Furnished the Public." Manuscript; General Assembly Record Group; Session Records, January-February 1781; Joint Papers, Committee Papers, Resolutions; January-February 1781: Joint Select Committees, Box 1 (MARS ID: 66.8.23.8.5; item), State Archives of North Carolina, Raleigh. [Online catalog description: "A joint committee is appointed, and it recommends a list of prices to be paid by the state for food and other articles, with special prices listed for certain counties in the Halifax and Hillsborough Districts."]

North Carolina (State). General Assembly. "[Document Dated]: February 6, 1781: Resolution Re[specting] Hogs Impressed by Philip Vass, Granville County Commissioner (Rejected)." Manuscript; General Assembly Record Group; Session Records, January-February 1781; Joint Papers, Committee Papers, Resolutions, Senate Bills, House Bills, Senate Joint Resolutions: February 6-7, 1781, Box 1 (MARS ID: 66.8.23.12.1; item), State Archives of North Carolina, Raleigh. [Online catalog description: "The resolution would have permitted Vass to keep the hogs in his possession by order of the board of war for the use of the state after giving the former owners, such as Mr. Taylor, certificates for them. Includes two copies of the resolution."]

North Carolina (State). General Assembly. "[Document Dated]: February 7, 1781: Resolution Re[specting] Hogs Impressed by Philip Vass, Granville County Commissioner." Manuscript; General Assembly Record Group; Session Records, January-February 1781; Joint Papers, Committee Papers, Resolutions, Senate Bills, House Bills, House Joint Resolution: February 6-9, 1781, Box 1 (MARS ID: 66.8.23.17.2; item), State Archives of North Carolina, Raleigh. [Online catalog description: "In addition to the provisions of the Senate resolution for which it is a substitute, the resolution directs Vass and all other commissioners in the counties in the Hillsborough and Halifax Districts to send all public livestock to the army."]

North Carolina (State). General Assembly. "[Document dated:] February 7, [1781]: Directing Quartermaster to Furnish Continental Line Officers with Horses (Messages only), 1781." Manuscript; General Assembly Record Group; Session Records, January-February, 1781; Joint Papers, Committee Papers, Resolutions, Senate Bills, House Bills, Box 1 (MARS ID: 66.8.23.12.4; item), State Archives of North Carolina, Raleigh. [Online catalog description: "The resolution alluded to only pertains to the officers in the Halifax District who take commands in the militia immediately.

North Carolina (State). General Assembly. Senate. "[Document dated:] July 2, [1781]): Senate Bill for Vesting Power in the Continental Congress to Levy Duty on Foreign Merchandise." Manuscript; General Assembly Record Group; Session Records, June-July 1781, Joint Papers, Committee Papers, Resolutions, Senate Bills, House Bills, Box 2 (MARS ID: 66.8.25.3; folder), State Archives of North Carolina, Raleigh. [Online catalog description: "The bill provides exemptions for certain articles necessary for the war effort."]

North Carolina (State). General Assembly. "[Documents dated:] April 22, 1783: Resolution Directs Halifax District Auditors to Credit Supplies to Matthew Rabun (Petition Only)." Manuscript; General Assembly Record Group; Session Records, Apri-May 1783; Joint Papers, Committee Papers, Resolutions; House Joint Resolutions: April 21-30, 1783, Box 1 (MARS ID: 66.8.29.13.4; item), State Archives of North Carolina, Raleigh. [Online catalog description: "Petition asks that Matthew Rabun, Commissioner of Specific Supplies for Halifax County, be credited supplies to carry out his duties."]

North Carolina (State). General Assembly. "[Document dated:] May 12, 1783: Resolution in Favor of Samuel Caswell of Dobbs County." Manuscript; General Assembly Record Group; Session Records, April-May 1783; Joint Papers, Committee Papers, Resolutions: Senate Joint Resolutions: April 20-May 17, 1783, Box 1 (MARS ID: 66.8.29.12.13; item), State Archives of North Carolina, Raleigh. [Online catalog description: "Resolution is to settle the accounts of Samuel Caswell of Dobbs County, who was commander of the guard at Kingston (Kinston) and furnished the guard with supplies. Includes petition."]

North Carolina (State). General Assembly. "[Document dated:] May 11, [1784]: Resolution Regarding the Memorial of Col. Nicholas Long (Message, Committee Report, and Memorial, Only) (Rejected)." Manuscript; General Assembly Record Group; Session Records, April-June 1784; Joint Papers, Committee Papers, Resolutions, Senate Bills, House Bills, Box 2 (MARS ID: 66.8.32.5.17; item), State Archives of North Carolina, Raleigh. [Online catalog description: "Memorial states that Col. Nicholas Long acted as Deputy Quartermaster for the North Carolina Continental Line and now requests a grant of land similar to the one given other officers from the line. A committee report rejects this request."]

North Carolina (State). General Assembly. "[Document Dated]: May 12, 1784: Resolution to Order the Comptroller to Settle Account of Philip Vass, Late Commissioner of Granville County." Manuscript; General Assembly Record Group; Session Records, April-June 1784; Committee Papers, Resolutions; House Joint Resolutions: April 21-June 3, 1784, Box 2 (MARS ID: 68.8.32.5.18; item), State Archives of North Carolina, Raleigh.

North Carolina. General Assembly. "[Document dated:] May 25, 1784: Joint Papers, Committee Papers, Resolutions, Senate Bills, House Bills, Report on the Petition of Michael Hearn of Edgecombe County." Manuscript; General Assembly Record Group; Session Records, April-June 1784, Box 1 (MARS ID: 66.8.31.9.11), State Archives of North Carolina, Raleigh. [Online catalog description: "Petition awards compensation for a portion of pork lost at sea that Michael Hearn had sold to the commissary of the army. The committee awards compensation."]

North Carolina (State). General Assembly. "[Document Dated]: December 17, 1785: Senate Bill Vesting Certain Property in Granville County in Mary Alston Bell." Manuscript; General Assembly Record Group; Session Records, November-December 1785; Senate Bills (December 10-22), House Bills (November 2-…), Box 3 (MARS ID: 66.8.39.14; folder), State Archives of North Carolina, Raleigh. [Online catalog description: "Bill vests the title to certain tracts of land and a slave in Mary Alston Bell. The property was given to her by George Alston previous to the point that his property was confiscated."]

North Carolina (State). General Assembly. "[Document dated:] Dec. 3, [1788]: Report on Petition of Neil Ray (with Petition)." Manuscript; General Assembly Record Group; Session Records, November-December, 1788; Joint Papers, Committee Papers, Resolutions, Senate Bills, House Bills, Box 2 (MARS ID: 66.8.50.2.18; item), State Archives of North Carolina, Raleigh. [Online catalog description: "Report rejects petition because the comptroller is authorized to settle such accounts; with petition of Neil Ray requests compensation for property taken when the militia camped on his property during the war."]

North Carolina (State). General Assembly. "[Document dated:] Dec. 5, [1788]: Report on Petition of Neal McLean (With Petition)." Manuscript; General Assembly Record Group; Session Records, November-December 1788; Joint Papers, Committee Papers, Resolutions, Senate Bills, House Bills, Box 1 (MARS ID: 66.8.49.11.18; item), State Archives of North Carolina, Raleigh. [Online catalog description: "Petition of Neal McLean requests compensation for articles supplied to the army during the war; committee report suggests that case is a matter for the comptroller."]

North Carolina (State). General Assembly. "[Document dated:] Dec 5., [1796]: Report of the Committee of Propositions and Grievances on the Petition of Charles Oxendine." Manuscript; General Assembly Record Group; Session Records, November-December 1796; Joint Papers, Committee Papers, Resolutions, Senate Bills, House Bills, Box 2 (MARS ID: 66.8.49.11.18; item), State Archives of North Carolina, Raleigh. [Online catalog description: "Committee denies said petitioner compensation for military supplies furnished by him to the army during the war."]

North Carolina (State). General Assembly. "[Document dated:] Dec. 12, [1796]: Report of the Committee of Propositions and Grievance No.1 on the Petition of James Outlaw" Manuscript, General Assembly Record Group, Session Reports, November-December 1796; Joint Papers, Committee Papers, Resolutions, Senate Bills, House Bills, Box 2 (MARS ID: 66.8.81.17.4; item), State Archives of North Carolina, Raleigh. [Online catalog description: "Said petitioner of Duplin County furnished a certain captain of militia by the name of James Gillispie with ten heads of sheep and one of beef during the war and was issued a certificate for such supplies by Capt. Gillispie which has somehow become lost. Outlaw therefore requests that he be issued another certificate for supplies. Committee rejects the petition. Petition included."]

North Carolina (State). General Assembly. Senate. "[Document dated:] 1792-1793: Senate Bill to Make Compensation to Those Citizens Who Have Never Received Any for Militia Services or Supplies during the Late Was [*sic*] (Laid Over)." Manuscript, General Assembly Record Group, Session Records November 1792-January 1793; Joint Papers, Committee Papers, Resolutions, Senate Bills, House Bills, Box 3 (MARS ID: 66.8.65.8.1; item), State Archives of North Carolina, Raleigh. [Online catalog description: "A bill to appoint commissioners to receive claims for payment of military service or supplies."]

United States. National Archives and Records Service. *Letters, Orders for Pay, Accounts, Receipts, and Other Supply Records Concerning Weapons and Military Stores, 1776-1801*. (Pamphlets Describing National Archives Microfilm Publications, M927) Washington, D. C.: National Archives and Records Service, General Services Administration, 1974.

United States. National Archives and Records Service. *Letters, Returns, Accounts, and Estimates of the Quartermaster General's Department, 1776-1783 in the War Department Collection of Revolutionary War Records*. (National Archives Microfilm Publications, Pamphlet Describing M 926) Washington, D. C.: National Archives and Records Service, General Services Administration, 1973.

United States. War Department, comp. "Numbered Record Books Concerning Military Operations and Service, Pay and Settlement of Accounts, and Supplies in the War Department Collection of Revolutionary War Records, M853." Washington, D. C.: National Archives & Records Administration, 1971; online at http://www.fold3.com. [Online description from "North Carolina Periodicals Index," East Carolina University: "These document images are digitized from NARA microfilm publication M853, which reproduced 199 numbered record books, with related separate indexes and one unnumbered record book, concerning Revolutionary War military operations and service, pay and settlement of accounts, and supplies. These records are part of War Department Collection of Revolutionary War Records, Record series 93. Most of the numbered record books were created during the period 1775-1783 but some were continued in use or were begun in the early postwar years, and a few are copies made after 1800 of earlier records. The separate indexes were compiled in the 19th and 20th centuries by custodians of the records." These records are searchable by name and may also be browsed.]

Webb, James. "James Webb (1774-1855) Papers, 1781-1846." Manuscript, PC.127, State Archives of North Carolina, Raleigh. [Online catalog description shows that this collection includes: "A letter from District Quartermaster Nicholas Long to Gov. Thomas Burke concerns ammunition supplies (Aug., 1781), and there is a copy of a military grant of land in Tennessee to Col. Martin Armstrong (1786)."]

Battles and Skirmishes of the Revolution in North Carolina and Tennessee

"[Campaigns in North Carolina during the Revolutionary War." Reference Vertical File, State Library of North Carolina, Raleigh.

Gillgam, Jim. "Links to Revolutionary War Battlefields in North Carolina." Online: http://ncrevwar.lostsouls genealogy.com/battlefieldsnc.htm.

Robinson, Blackwell Pierce. *Battles and Engagements of the American Revolution in North Carolina.* [S. l.]: LaFayette Chapter of the Daughters of the Revolution, 1961.

1775

Destruction of Fort Johnson, July 1775

"Fort Johnson." North Carolina Department of Cultural Resources, Historical Marker Program. Online: http://www.ncmarkers.com/Markers.aspx?MarkerId=D-11.

Lee, Wayne E. "Fortify, Fight, or Flee Great Britain. Colonial Office. "Ft. Johnson. Letter from Gov. Josiah Martin to Ld. Dartmouth, Sec. of State, #34, June 20, 1775." Copy of a manuscript in the National Archives of the United Kingdom (formerly the Public Records Office), Kew, Richmond, Surrey, England; (MARS ID: 21.1.27.48; folder), State Archives of North Carolina, Raleigh. [Online catalog description: "Has fled to this place and sent his family to New York; expects arms from Gen. Gage; still sure that highlanders and western counties could be relied on, and requests arms and restoration of his rank as lt. colonel; Mecklenburg Resolves; Wilmington; John Ashe; S. C. congress attempting to recruit in N. C.; assembly prorogued to Sept 12; thinks better of council than he previously did, with the exception of Mr. Dry."]

Great Britain. Colonial Office. "Ft. Johnson. Letter from Gov. Josiah Martin to Ld. Dartmouth, Sec. of State, #35, July 6, 1775." Copy of a manuscript in the National Archives of the United Kingdom (formerly the Public Records Office), Kew, Richmond, Surrey, England; (MARS ID: 21.1.27.49; folder), State Archives of North Carolina, Raleigh. [Online catalog description: "Acknowledges despatches; has at last been able to communicate with Gen. Gage; Dartmouth's despatches to Martin were opened by 'the Mob at Charles Town'; this despatch being delivered by Alexander Schaw, who can furnish news of potential support for government of N. C. and neighboring colonies; bridles at instruction that generals' orders to be supreme in military matters in colonies."]

Great Britain. Colonial Office. "Fort Johnston, N. C. [Copy] John Collet [Commander of Fort Johnston] to [Francis] Parry Aboard *Cruizer*. 20 May, 1775." Copy of a manuscript in the National Archives of the United Kingdom (formerly the Public Records Office), Kew, Richmond, Surrey, England; Z.5.108N, State Archives of North Carolina, Raleigh. [Online catalog description: "Letter states that Collet expects attack by provincial militia, begs for spare powder and urges *Cruizer* to anchor near fort and remain there. Enclosed in Vice Admiral Graves to Admiralty Lords, 16 July 1775 (21.20.104.1.8).

Great Britain. Colonial Office. "Ft. Johnson. Minutes of the Executive Council. June 25, 1775." Copy of a manuscript in the National Archives of the United Kingdom (formerly the Public Records Office), Kew, Richmond, Surrey, England; (MARS ID: 21.1.27.51), State Archives of North Carolina, Raleigh.

Hogan, Michael D. "North Carolina Forts (Part 2): Ft. Johnson in Transition." Online, Historic Southport: http://www.southportncmagazine.com/forts_2_johnston.html.

Battle of Great Bridge, Norfolk County, Virginia, December 9, 1775

[See also the section in Chapter Eighteen on Betsy Dowdy.]

"Battle of Great Bridge." Online on Wikipedia: http://en.wikipedia.org/wiki/Battle_of_Great_Bridge

"The Battle of the Great Bridge." *Virginia Historical Register and Literary Companion*, 6:1 (January 1853), 1-6.

Creecy, Richard Benbury. "Legend of Betsy Dowdy: An Historical Tradition of the Battle of Great Bridge." *North Carolina Booklet,* 1:5 (10 September 1901), 3-7. [In 1775, Betsy Dowdy from the coast of North Carolina warned General William Skinner that the Lord Dunmore's army was heading towards North Carolina. Online description from "North Carolina Periodicals Index," East Carolina University: "The recounting of the

Revolutionary War legend of a young girl who, facing fear that the British may steal Outer Banks' ponies, rode on a perilous journey to alert the militia and thus aided in the victory at Great Bridge."]

Fuss, Norman. "Billy Flora and the Battle of Great Bridge." *Journal of the American Revolution*, 14 October 2014; online: www.allthingsliberty.com

Grisson, E. Preston. "Virginia's Bridge to Victory." *Patriots of the American Revolution*, 4:6 (November/December 2011), 40-46. ["The article focuses on the victory of the Battle of Great Bridge in Virginia on December 9, 1775, which was the first pitched land combat in the country involving British troops. It says that the battle has led to the end of the sovereignty of Great Britain over the colony of Virginia and the loss of the most important port of the former. It adds that the Great Bridge was a center of activity in transporting the products from the forests and fields south of the Chesapeake Bay."]

Hanbury, Elizabeth, and Jim Hodges. *The Battle of Great Bridge.* Chesapeake, Va.: Great Bridge Battlefield & Waterways Foundation.

Henry, Patrick. "Letter: Williamsburg to Governor Johnstone, Maryland, 1779 May 12." Manuscript accession no. 19775, Personal Papers Collection, Library of Virginia, Richmond. [Online catalog description: "Henry informs Johnson about the loss of Portsmouth to the British. The commanding officers of the fort were retreating toward the Great Bridge pursued by the enemy. He was uncertain if the British meant to establish a permanent fort in Virginia."]

Jarvis, James, 1791-1862. "Remiscences, 1846 February 22, of the War of 1812 and of the American Revolution." Manuscript Mss. Sm Coll Jarvis, Special Collections, Earl Gregg Swem Library, College of William and Mary in Virginia, Williamsburg. [Online catalog description: "Concerns the Battle of Great Bridge, Norfolk County, Va., 9 December 1775; …"]

Muhlenberg, John Peter Gabriel. "Muhlenburg Papers. Orderly Book." Manuscript, Historical Society of Pennsylvania, Philadelphia; also on microfilm at the John D. Rockefeller, Jr., Library, Colonial Williamsburg Foundation, Williamsburg. [Online catalog description: "Copies of general orders issued at College Camp, Great Bridge Camp, and Norfolk, mainly by Col. Thomas Bullett and Col. Patrick Henry, Jr."]

Noël Hume, Ivor. "The Battle of Great Bridge: in the First Engagement of the Revolution in Virginia, as in the Last, Americans Besieged and Beat the British." *Colonial Williamsburg: The Journal of the Colonial Williamsburg Foundation*, (Spring 2008), 62-67. [Description: "In the first and little known engagement of the American Revolution, the Americans beseiged and beat the British at Great Bridge south of Norfolk. Then in the last battle at Yorktown, they defeated the British once again."]

Scott, C. "Letters Concerning the Battle of Great Bridge, and Action at Norfolk." In Peter Force, ed., *American Archives*, series 4, vol. 4 (Washington, D. C.: M. St. Claire Clarke and P. Force, 1843), cols. 171-172, 183-184, 245, 292. [Dated: December 1775]

Shultice, Alice Lee. "The Battle of Great Bridge." *Daughters of the American Revolution Magazine*, 85:10 (October 1951), 775-776.

Whetstone, J. Thomas. "The Amazing Complete Victory at Great Bridge." *SAR Magazine*, 106:2 (Fall 2011), 18-23.

Wilson, David K. "'This I Was Determined Not to Suffer': The Humiliation of Lord Dunmore in the Second Bunker Hill Affair (Great Bridge)." *Southern Campaigns of the American Revolution*, 4:1 (January-March 2007), 41-55; online: www.southerncampaign.org

Wilson, David K. "Great Bridge: The Battle for Norfolk." In *The Southern Strategy: Britain's Conquest of South Carolina and Georgia, 1775-1780.* (Columbia: University of South Carolina Press, 2005), 5-18; reprinted with modifications: *Southern Campaigns of the American Revolution*, 4:1 (January-March 2007), 41-55; online: www.southerncampaign.org

Wingo, Elizabeth B. *The Battle of Great Bridge*. Chesapeake, Va.: Norfolk County Historical Society of Chesapeake, 1964.

Woodford, William, 1734-1780. "[Letters to Edmund Pendleton, President of the Convention.]" In Peter Force, ed., *American Archives*, series 4, vol. 4 (Washington, D. C.: M. St. Claire Clarke and P. Force, 1843), cols. 224, 228, 233, 244-245, 278-279, 292-294, 794. [Battle of Great Bridge and events at Norfolk.]

1776

Massacre at the Piney Bottom, 1776

Evans, Robert B. "Massacre at the Piney Bottom and the Revenge Taken by the Whigs." In Eli W. Caruthers, Revolutionary Incidents and Sketches of Character Chiefly in the "Old North State." Philadelphia, Pa: Hayes & Zell, 1854, 1856; reprinted: Greensboro: Guilford County Genealogical Society, 1994, 94-98.

Battle of Moore's Creek/Moore's Creek Bridge, February 27, 1776

Baker, Thomas E. *Redeemed from Oblivion: An Administrative History of Guilford Courthouse National Military Park.* Washington, D. C.: National Park Service, United States Department of the Interior, 1995.

Barefoot, Daniel W. "Moore's Creek, Battle of." In William S. Powell, ed., Jay Mazzocchi, assoc. ed., *Encyclopedia of North Carolina* (Chapel Hill: University of North Carolina Press in association with the University of North Carolina Library, 2006), 762-763.

"The Battle of Moore's Creek." *Daughters of the American Revolution Magazine*, 70:9 (September 1936), 929.

"The Battle of Moore's Creek Bridge." *Daughters of the American Revolution Magazine*, 85:2 (February 1951), 119-120.

"Battle of Moore's Creek Bridge, February 27, 1776, at Wilmington, North Carolina." Online: http://www.myrevolutionarywar.com/battles/760227-moores-creek-bridge/. [The battle actually took place in Pender County.]

Blankenship, Jamie. *Background Study on Fences and Monuments at Moores Creek National Battlefield.* Washington, D. C.: National Park Service, United States Department of the Interior, 1989.

Brewer, David M. *Report on an Archeological Survey and Testing of Moores Creek National Battlefield.* Washington, D. C.: National Park Service, United States Department of the Interior, 1983.

Capps, Michael A., and Steven A. Davis. *Moores Creek National Battlefield: An Administrative History.* Washington, D. C.: National Park Service, United States Department of the Interior, 1999; online: http://www.nps.gov/parkhistory/online_books/mocr/.

Carraway, Gertrude S. "Revolutionary Battlefield Now National Park." *Daughters of the American Revolution Magazine*, 61:1 (January 1927), 41-42.

Carraway, Gertrude Sprague. "[Scrapbook of Clippings and Other Material Dealing with the Moore's Creek Battleground Celebration and North Carolina's part in the Sesqui-Centennial Exposition at Philadelphia]." Scrapbook FCp970.33 M82, North Carolina Collection Folio, Louis Round Wilson Special Collections Library, University of North Carolina at Chapel Hill; online: https://archive.org/details/scrapbookofclipp00carr.

Chase, Harry; Mark Lee Gardner; Chris Wheeler; and Sonny Hutchison. *In the Most Furious Manner: Liberty Forged at Moores Creek*. Columbia, Md.: National Park Service, [200?]

Cheatham, James T. "English Southern Strategy Failed in 1776: The Moores Creek Bridge Campaign." *Recall: the North Carolina Military Historical Society*, 18:2 (Fall 2012), 16-17.

Cheatham, James. "The Year the Revolution Should Have Ended." *Recall: The North Carolina Military History Society's Newsletter*, 15:2 (Fall 2009), 1-3; online: http://ns50.webmasters.com/*ncmhs.net/httpdocs/RecallF09.pdf. [Online description from "North Carolina Periodicals Index," East Carolina University: "When England went to war with its American colonies, it was at a distinct disadvantage – 3,000 miles of ocean separated them. Communication to and from England could take as much as five months, and there were 1,200 miles of shoreline along the coastal colonies. Cheatham presents six events that should have, for all intents and purposes, proven to King and Parliament that the war was over at the end of 1776. These include the Battle of Moore's Creek Bridge, the British evacuation of Boston, the Declaration of Independence, and Washington's surprise attack on Trenton, New Jersey, in December of that year."]

Corbitt, D. L. "Battle of Moore's Creek Bridge." *North Carolina Historical Review,* 4:2 (April 1927), 208-209.

Daniel, Robert Williams. "Collection: of Robert Williams Daniel, 1776-1882." Manuscript Mss1/D2266/a, Virginia Historical Society, Richmond. [Description on ArchiveGrId: "The collection contains a letter from Edmund Pendleton to James Mercer, 19 March 1776, concerning Sir Andrew Snape Hamond and Charles Lee, the Virginia Committee of Safety, the arming of slaves by Lord Dunmore, raids in Virginia by British navy ships, and the Battle of Moore's Creek Bridge (N.C.)."]

"Decision at Moore's Creek Bridge." *Cincinnati Fourteen: Journal of the Society of the Cincinnati.* 48:2 (Spring 2012), 30-39.

Elking, Thomas. "Unsung Hero of Moore's Creek." *The State: Down Home in North Carolina*, 24:24 (April 1957), 11; online: http://digital.ncdcr.gov/cdm/ref/collection/p16062coll18/id/41051. [Online description from "North Carolina Periodicals Index," East Carolina University: "A private in the North Carolina Militia during the Revolutionary War, John Colwell fired the first shot in the Battle of Moore's Creek Bridge. On February 27th, 1776, the North Carolina Militia halted advancing Tories, preventing a rendezvous with British troops waiting in Wilmington."]

Fryar, Jack E., Jr. "The Battle at Widow Moore's Creek." In Jack E. Fryar, Jr., ed., *The Coastal Chronicles: Volume II: Popular History Stories of the Coastal Carolinas as Seen in* Coastal Chronicles Magazine (Wilmington, N. C.: Dram Tree Books, 2004), 10-22.

Fryar, Jack E., Jr. "An Ounce of Prevention." In Jack E. Fryar, Jr., ed., *The Coastal Chronicles: Volume II: Popular History Stories of the Coastal Carolinas as Seen in Coastal Chronicles* Magazine (Wilmington, N. C.: Dram Tree Books, 2004), 2-8. [Richard Caswell, Moore's Creek, Josiah Martin, Loyalists]

Gibbs, Russell A. *A History of Moores Creek National Military Park.* Washington, D. C.: National Park Service, United States Department of the Interior, 1965.

Great Britain. Colonial Office. "Chatham, Nantasket Road, Ma. Copy of Evan Nepean to Admiral [Samuel] Graves. 25 Mar., 1776." Copy of a manuscript in the National Archives of the United Kingdom (formerly the Public Records Office), Kew, Richmond, Surrey, England; 70.90.1-4, British Records, Colonial Office, Secretary of State, "Intercepted Letters to and from American Colonists," State Archives of North Carolina, Raleigh. [Online catalog description: "General topics: the state of affairs in the Boston area and an erroneous account of the Battle of Moore's Creek Bridge claiming a highlander victory over the rebels."]

Green, Paul. *Fighting over the Battle of Moore's Creek Bridge: Notes on the Memorial Service Held at the National Park, February 27, 1949.* [North Carolina?: N. C. Society of County Historians?, 1949?]. [Contains: George Moore's "The Battle of Moores Creek Bridge," 14-19.]

Hall, Mary Melda. "The Battle of Moore's Creek – A Test of Loyalty." (American History Essay Topic) *Daughters of the American Revolution Magazine*, 111:8 (October 1977), 820, 822.

Hatch, Charles E., Jr. *The Battle of Moores Creek Bridge.* Washington, D. C.: National Park Service, United States Department of the Interior, 1969.

Higginbotham, Don. "The Battle of Moore's Creek Bridge." *Tar Heel Junior Historian*, 14:3 (February 1975), 10-11. [Online description from "North Carolina Periodicals Index," East Carolina University: "The first battle of the American Revolution within the state's boundaries occurred at Widow Moore's Creek Bridge on February 27, 1776. No British troops were involved; rather it was a battle between patriots, also called Whigs, supporting American independence and loyalists, also called Tories, in favor of remaining under the crown's control. Patriots won the battle which discouraged British troops on the coast from landing on North Carolina soil."]

Hubbell, S. Michael. *Mary Slocumb's Ride to the Battle of Moore's Creek Bridge.* Washington, D. C.: National Park Service, United States Department of the Interior, 1962.

Hubbell, W. K. "Military Movements in the Battle of Moore's Creek Bridge." Manuscript, MC.175.1952h, State Archives of North Carolina, Raleigh. [Online catalog description: "This map was prepared by W. K. Hubbell and portrays the movements of the British, Loyalist, and American forces during the campaign culminating in the Battle of Moore's Creek Bridge on February 27, 1776. The counties in the Cape Fear region are shown as they existed in 1778, and major rivers are depicted and identified; but little other detail is provided. A key to the symbols used to indicate the marches of the various armies appears along with the title in an inset in the lower left corner of the map."]

Johnston, Peter R. "The Last Highland Charge." *Military History*, 22:10 (January/February 2006), 30-36. [Moore's Creek Bridge]

King, Clyde B. *Moores Creek Battlefield.* Hubbell, S. Michael. Washington, D. C.: National Park Service, United States Department of the Interior, 1939.

Lawrence, R. C. "Battle of Moore's Creek." *The State: A Weekly Survey of North Carolina*, 12:25 (November 1944), 6-7; online: http://digital.ncdcr.gov/cdm/ref/collection/p16062coll18/id/19837.

MacDonald, Donald. "An Address to the Whigs the Day before the Battle of Moore's Creek." Manuscript, PC.721, Donald MacDonald Paper, State Archives of North Carolina, Raleigh; and: "Donald MacDonald's Letter to Patriot Commanders at Moore's Creek Demanding Their Surrender, February 26, 1776." Photograph of a manuscript, N.2004.11.1 (MARS ID: 4.1.31.226).

MacNeill, Cameron. "Moore's Creek – Highland Nemesis." *The State: A Weekly Survey of North Carolina*, 21:16 (September 1953), 19, 21-22; online: http://digital.ncdcr.gov/cdm/ref/collection/p16062coll18/id/30953. [Online description from "North Carolina Periodicals Index," East Carolina University: "One of the most historic spots in southeastern North Carolina is Moore's Creek National Military Park, located in the southern part of Pender County, a place visited by thousands every year. It was here in 1776 that the Tory Scotch Highlanders were defeated by the Whigs, the first victory gained on North Carolina soil by American armies in the Revolution."]

"Major James Moore for his Services as Major of the Minute Men on an Expedition to Moore's Creek against the Insurgents." In Weynette Parks Haun, *North Carolina Revolutionary Army Accounts, Part I, Secretary of State Treasurer's & Comptroller's Papers Journal "A", (Public Accounts) 1775-1776* (Durham: W. P. Haun, 1988), 5. [County designation determined by *North Carolina State Records*, Volume 10, p. 944, John Rochell appointed captain in Hillsborough District, November 1776; *North Carolina State Records*, Volume 10, p. 969, reference to a petition from soldiers in Wake County under the command of Captain James Jones of the Light

Horse, December 1776; Revolutionary War pension of Lewis Bledsoe W17315. {This analysis was performed by genealogists in the Genealogy Office, Office of the Registrar General, National Society Daughters of the American Revolution, Washington, D. C.}]

McCrain, Gerald R., and Barbara H. Church. *An Analysis of Past and Present Plant Community Patterns in Moores Creek National Battlefield.* [S. l.]: Resource Management Company, 1985.

Misenheimer, John. "Mecklenburg Militia at Battle of Moores Creek Bridge." *Olde Mecklenburg Genealogical Society Quarterly*, 20:3 (2002), 31-34.

"Miscellaneous Papers, 1689-1912." Manuscript, PC.21, State Archives of North Carolina, Raleigh. [Online catalog description: "Revolutionary War letters discuss the Battle of Moores Creek Bridge and southern campaigns, loyalists, privateers, condition of soldiers, parole of Governor Burke, and surrender of Cornwallis at Yorktown."]

Moore, Louis T. "Mary Slocumb's Famous Ride." *The State: A Weekly Survey of North Carolina*, 16:1 (June 1948), 41-42; online: http://digital.ncdcr.gov/cdm/ref/collection/p16062coll18/id/22420. [Online description from "North Carolina Periodicals Index," East Carolina University: "Mary Slocumb ran to her husband in battle after believing she dreamed he cried out for her. At the Battle of Moore's Creek Bridge during the Revolutionary War, Colonel Slocumb was engaged with British troops. His wife Mary believed she heard him call to her while she slept and decided to make a daring run to Moore's Creek from Goldsboro a sixty mile journey. Most of the article is a reprint of Mary Slocumb's own description of events, ending with the author mentioning the internment of Colonel Slocumb and his wife at Moore's Creek National Park."]

"Moore's Creek Bridge & Lasting Ramifications of a Victory." *Washington County Genealogical Society Journal*, 5:3 (December 1997), 72-73.

Moores Creek National Battlefield. "Park Files." Moores Creek National Battlefield, Currie, North Carolina.

Moores Creek National Battlefield. *Report on the Reconstruction of the Historic Moores Creek Bridge.* Washington, D. C.: National Park Service, United States Department of the Interior, 1993.

Moores Creek National Battlefield. *Statement for Management.* Washington, D. C.: National Park Service, United States Department of the Interior, 1994.

Moss, Bobby Gilmer. *Roster of the Loyalists at the Battle of Moores Creek Bridge*. Blacksburg, S. C.; Scotia-Hibernia Press, 1992.

Moss, Bobby Gilmer. *Roster of the Patriots in the Battle of Moores Creek Bridge*. Blackburg, S. C.: Scotia-Hibernia Press, 1992.

Murphy, John Gerald. "The Battle at Moore's Creek Bridge." B. S. dissertation, University of North Carolina at Chapel Hill, 1901.

National Military Park At Battle Field of Moores Creek, N. C. *Hearings before the United States House Committee on Military Affairs, Sixty-Ninth Congress, First Session, on Apr. 20, 21, 1926.*Washington: U. S. G. P. O., 1926.

Noble, M. C. S. "The Battle of Moore's Creek Bridge, February 27, 1776." *North Carolina Booklet*, v. 3, no. 11 (March 1904), 1-36.

Norris, Jeannie Faris. "Lowlander vs. Highlander." *The State: Down Home in North Carolina*, 26:8 (September 1958), 17; online: http://digital.ncdcr.gov/cdm/ref/collection/p16062coll18/id/51771. [Online description from "North Carolina Periodicals Index," East Carolina University: "The Battle of Moores Creek Bridge, February 27, 1776, was a complete victory for the Patriots, contributing to the Revolutionary cause in the South, with the Colony remaining in the Patriot's possession until British invasion in 1780. Some elements among settlers had not been amalgamated by the general population in 1775, chief of these was a large number of Scottish Highlanders, largely from clans MacDonald (Isles) and McLeod. These clans settled in the central part of the Colony between 1765 and 1775."]

Page, G. G. *The Battle of Moore's Creek Bridge*. Kings Mountain, N. C.: Herald Publishing House, 1926.

Perkins, Betty. "A Patriot's Return to Moore's Creek." *The State: Down Home in North Carolina*, 42:8 (January 1975), 17-18, 55; online: http://digital.ncdcr.gov/cdm/ref/collection/p16062coll18/id/9203. [Online description from "North Carolina Periodicals Index," East Carolina University: "John Grady of Duplin County, the first North Carolinian casualty in the Revolutionary War, died at the Battle of Moore's Creek. Grady's remains have been exhumed from his monument in Wilmington and shall be re-interred with full military honors at the 199th anniversary celebration at Moore's Creek."]

Rankin, Hugh F. "The Moore's Creek Bridge Campaign, 1776." *North Carolina Historical Review*, 30:1 (January 1953), 23-60.

Rankin, Hugh F. *The Moore's Creek Bridge Campaign, 1776*. Conshohocken, Pa.: Eastern National Park and Monument Association, 1986. [Includes fold-out map of the battlefield.]

Rogers, Edmund B. *History of Legislation Relating to the National Park System Through the 82[d] Congress: Moores Creek.* Washington, D. C.: National Park Service, United States Department of the Interior, 1958.

Scott, Ralph. "Carolina's First Strike for Freedom: The Battle of Moore's Creek Bridge." *New East*, 3:2 (May/June 1975), 32-34.

Sparrow, W. Keats. "The Battle of Moore's Creek Bridge." *Recall: The North Carolina Military History Society's Newsletter*, 3:2 (October 1997), 5-6. [Online description from "North Carolina Periodicals Index," East Carolina University: "The Battle of Moore's Creek Bridge, February 27, 1776, was a complete victory for the Patriots over the Scottish Highlanders and their Tory allies. It gave a tremendous morale boost to the other colonies. Desperately needed equipment was captured, including 35 guns, 1,500 excellent rifles, and medicine and surgical supplies. The Patriots also captured 800 prisoners. Significantly, the Patriot victory brought an end to royal rule in North Carolina."]

Swilley, Monroe F. "David Blackshear." In Kenneth Coleman and Charles Stephen Gurr, eds., *Dictionary of Georgia Biography*. 2 vols. (Athens: University of Georgia Press, 1983), 1:85-86. 1764-1837; child participant in the Battle of Moore's Creek Bridge in 1776; moved to Georgia in 1790]

Thompson, Timothy A. *Report on Excavations at Moores Creek National Military Park, Pender County, North Carolina*. Raleigh: North Carolina Department of Cultural Resources, Division of Archives and History, 1975.

United States. Congress. House Military Affairs Committee. *Hearings before the Committee on Military Affairs, House of Representatives, Sixty-Ninth Congress, First Session, on H. R 3796: National Military Park at Battle Field of Moores Creek, N. C.* Washington, D. C.: Government Printing Office, 1926.

United States. Department of the Interior. National Park Service. *Master Plan, Moores Creek National Military Park.* Washington, D. C.: National Park Service, United States Department of the Interior, 1969.

United States. Department of the Interior. National Park Service. *Development Concept Plan, Moores Creek National Military Park.* Washington, D. C.: National Park Service, United States Department of the Interior, 1972.

United States. Department of the Interior. National Park Service. Southeast Regional Office. *Completion Report, Moores Creek National Battlefield, Cleaning and Preservation of Six Monuments.* Atlanta: National Park Service, United States Department of the Interior, 1993.

Watson, Alan D. "Prelude to Moore's Creek: The Coming of the Revolution in North Carolina: The Cape Fear." *Rowan County Register*, 4:1 (March 1992), 4-9. [Includes a list of the members of the Safety Committees of the counties in the Cape Fear area.]

Wright, Joshua Granger. *Address Delivered at the Celebration of the Battle of Moore's Creek Bridge, February 27th, 1857*. Wilmington: Fulton & Price, 1857.

Skirmish at Fort Johnson, March 10-12, 1776

Fryar, Jack E., Jr. *Under Three Flags: The Fort Johnson Story*. Wilmington: Dram Tree Books, 2008.

"Revolutionary War Raids & Skirmishes in 1776: March 10-12 at Fort Johnson, North Carolina." Online: http://www.myrevolutionarywar.com/battles/1776-skirmish/.

Skirmish at Fort Johnston, May 1-3, 1776

Bentley, Joseph H. "Fort Johnston in the History of the Lower Cape Fear." Typescript (1970), [A copy is located in the North Carolina Room, Main Library, New Hanover County Public Library, Wilmington.]

de Roulhac Hamilton, J. G. "The Site of Fort Johnston." In Addresses Delivered under the Auspices of the North Carolina Society of the Colonial Dames of America, 1900-1926. [S. l.]: Jackson & Bell, [1927?].

Fryar, Jack E., Jr. *Under Three Flags: The Fort Johnson Story*. Wilmington: Dram Tree Books, 2008.

"Revolutionary War Raids & Skirmishes in 1776: May 1-3 at Fort Johnson, North Carolina." Online: http://www.myrevolutionarywar.com/battles/1776-skirmish/.

Skirmish at Orton Plantation, May 11, 1776

"Revolutionary War Raids & Skirmishes in 1776: May 11, 1776, at Orton, North Carolina." Online: http://www.myrevolutionarywar.com/battles/1776-skirmish/.

Burning of Brunswick Town, May 17, 1776

"Revolutionary War Raids & Skirmishes in 1776: May 17, 1776, at Brunswick Town, North Carolina." Online: http://www.myrevolutionarywar.com/battles/1780-skirmish/.

Skirmish at Quaker Meadows, July 1776

"Revolutionary War Raids & Skirmishes in 1776: July ??, 1776 at Quaker Meadows, North Carolina." Online: http://www.myrevolutionarywar.com/battles/1776-skirmish/.

Siege at McDowell's Station, July 3-13, 1776

"Revolutionary War Raids & Skirmishes in 1776: July 3-12, 1776, at McDowell's Station, North Carolina." Online: http://www.myrevolutionarywar.com/battles/1776-skirmish/.

Battle of Island Flats, Tennessee, July 20, 1776

"Revolutionary War Raids & Skirmishes in 1776: July 20, 1776, at Island Flats, Tennessee." Online: http://www.myrevolutionarywar.com/battles/1776-skirmish/.

Siege of Fort Caswell/Watauga, Tennessee, July 20-August 2, 1776

"Revolutionary War Raids & Skirmishes in 1776: July 20-August 2, 1776, at Watauga, Tennessee (Siege of Fort Caswell/Watauga." Online: http://www.myrevolutionarywar.com/battles/1776-skirmish/.

British Raid at Roanoke Inlet, August 15, 1776

"Revolutionary War Raids & Skirmishes in 1776: August 15, 1776, at Roanoke Inlet, North Carolina." Online: http://www.myrevolutionarywar.com/battles/1776-skirmish/.

Battle of Bald Head Island, September 6-7, 1776

"North Carolina Historical Marker: Revolutionary War Fort." Online: http://www.waymarking.com/gallery/image.aspx?f=1&guid=07228896-028e-4b15-8d65-33c42eb7eff6.

"Revolutionary War Raids & Skirmishes in 1776: September 6-7, 1776, at Bald Head Island, North Carolina." Online: http://www.myrevolutionarywar.com/battles/1776-skirmish/.

Rutherford's Expedition against the Cherokees, August 17-October 7, 1776

Ashe, Samuel A'Court. "Rutherford's Expedition against the Indians, 1776." *North Carolina Booklet*, 4:8 (December 1904), 3-28; online: http://penelope.uchicago.edu/Thayer/E/Gazetteer/Places/America/United_States/North_Carolina/_Texts/journals/The_North_Carolina_Booklet/4/8*.html.

Ashe, Samuel A'Court. *Rutherford's Expedition against the Indians, 1776*. Raleigh: E. M. Uzzel, 1904.

Beadle, Michael. "Rutherford Trace." *Smoky Mountain News*, (week of August 23, 2006); online: http://history.fohcg.org/time-frame/1700s/rutherford-trace/.

Brown, John P. *Old Frontiers: The Story of the Cherokee Indians from the Earliest Times to the Date of Their Removal to the West, 1838*. Kingsport: Southern Publishers, 1938.

"Cherokee Expedition 1776 – Col. William Christian's Campaign." Online: http://www.carolana.com/NC/Revolution/Cherokee_Expedition_1776_TN.pdf. [The information is taken from various pension applications of participants.]

"Cherokee Expedition 1776 – "Rutherford's Campaign." Online: http://www.carolana.com/NC/Revolution/revolution_cherokee_expedition_1776.html.

"Cherokees Seek Peace after Rutherford Expedition." Online: https://nchistorytoday.wordpress.com/2013/07/20/cherokees-seek-peace-after-rutherford-expedition/.

Dean, Nadia. *A Demand of Blood: The Cherokee War of 1776*. Cherokee: Valley River Press, 2012. [Publisher's description: "A Demand of Blood chronicles the frontier war fought in the shadows of the American Revolution. As southern colonists engaged in rebellion against the Crown, Dragging Canoe, Cherokee warrior and British ally, waged guerilla warfare throughout the southern colonies. In retaliation, patriot powers sent 6,000 militiamen to destroy Cherokee towns. In 1777, Cherokees sued for peace, ceding land their young warriors had fervently fought to regain."]

Dickins, Roy S., Jr. "The Route of Rutherford's Expedition against the North Carolina Cherokee." *Southern Indian Studies*, 19 (October 1967), 3-24.

Ganyard, Robert L. "Threat from the West: North Carolina and the Cherokee, 1776-1778." *North Carolina Historical Review*, 45:1 (January 1968), 47-66.

Hamer, Philip M. "The Wataugans and the Cherokee Indians in 1776." *East Tennessee Historical Society Publications*, 3 (1931), 108-127.

Harding, Gary Rutherford. "General Griffith Rutherford." Online: https://familysearch.org/patron/v2/TH-303-45048-222-0/dist.pdf?ctx=ArtCtxPublic&session=USYSF50010E8A7680769D137036A27C97548_idses-prod02.a.fsglobal.net.

Hatley, Tom. *The Dividing Paths: Cherokees and South Carolinians through the Era of Revolution*. New York: Oxford University Press, 1995.

Lenoir, William. "An Account of the Expedition against the Cherokee Indians in 1776, under Gen'l Griffith Rutherford, from 17th August to 7th October, 1776." Typescript Cp970.2 L574a, North Carolina Collection, Wilson Library, University of North Carolina at Chapel Hill. [Lenoir wrote the account in June 1835.]

Lenoir, William; J. G. DeRoulhac Hamilton. "The Revolutionary Diary of William Lenoir." *Journal of Southern History*, 4:2 (May 1940), 247-259.

Mooney, James. "Myths of the Cherokees." *Nineteenth Annual Report of the Bureau of American Ethnology to the Secretary of the Smithsonian Institution, 1897-98.* (Washington, D. C.: Government Printing Office, 1900), 19:Part 1:3-548.

Moore, William. "Letter from Captain William Moore to General Griffith Rutherford, 17 November 1776." Online on the LearnNC website: http://www.learnnc.org/lp/editions/nchist-revolution/4291.

Norris, David A. "Rutherford's Expedition." Online: http://ncpedia.org/rutherfords-campaign.

North Carolina. "Miscellaneous Papers, 1689-1912." Manuscript PC.21 (MARS ID: 530; record group), State Archives of North Carolina, Raleigh. [Online catalog description shows that this collection includes: "… reminiscences by Lewis Williams and others on the Cherokee expedition of 1776; …"]

O'Donnell, James H. "The Virginia Expedition against the Overhill Cherokee, 1776." *East Tennessee Historical Society Publications*, 9 (April 1925), 13-25.

Ramsey, J. G. M. [James Gettys McGready]. "Letter (Copy), J. G. M. Ramsey in Knoxville, Tenn., to [Gov.] Albert S. Marks in Nashville, Tenn., 1879, Nov. 18." Ramsey Family. "Ramsey Family Papers, 1790-1912." Manuscript MS.0253, Box 2, folder 6 (Correspondence, 1876-1879), Special Collections Library, University of Tennessee, Knoxville; online: http://dlc.lib.utk.edu/spc/view?docId=tei/0012_000060_000457_0000/0012_000060_000457_0000.xml. [Online catalog description: "Expresses appreciation for the honor of being appointed a delegate to the Yorktown Centennial. Gives account of Tennessee's part in the founding of American independence. Declines the appointment because of his lameness."]

Rockwell, E[lijah] F[rink], ed. "Parallel and Combined Expeditions against the Cherokee Indians in South and in North Carolina, in 1776." *Historical Magazine with Notes and Queries*, new series, 2 (October 1867), 212-220.

"The Rutherford Expedition." Online on the LearnNC website: http://www.learnnc.org/lp/editions/nchist-revolution/4300. [Includes a map of the route of the North Carolina forces and a timeline keyed to the map.]

"The Rutherford's Expedition against the Cherokees." *University Magazine* [University of North Carolina at Chapel Hill], new series, 7 (February 1888), 89-95.

Williams, Samuel C. "Col. Joseph Williams' Battalion in Christian's Campaign." *Tennessee Historical Magazine*, 9:2 (July 1925), 102-114.

1777

North Carolina Forces at the Valley Forge Encampment, 1777-1778; North Carolina Brigade

Ashe, Samuel A'Court. "History Given of Valley Forge." *North Carolina Booklet,* 23:1-4 (1926), 25-27.

Fore, Mrs. J. A. "North Carolinians at Valley Forge." *Daughters of the American Revolution Magazine*, 70:9 (September 1936), 924.

Haywood, Marshall DeLancey. "North Carolina's Memorial at Valley Forge." *North Carolina Booklet,* 23:1-4 (1926), 17-24.

McLean, Angus Wilton. *North Carolina in the War of Independence: Address by Angus Wilton McLean, Governor of North Carolina, Valley Forge, June 17, 1926*. [S. l.: s. n., 1926?]

Nash, Robert T. "From Germantown and Valley Forge to Middle Tennessee: A Research Note on Land Grants and Paying for the North Carolina Continental Line." *Tennessee Historical Quarterly*, 78:4 (Winter 2014), 312-331.

"N. C. Brigade Courts Martial, Camp Valley Forge [1778]." In Mary Bondurant Warren, ed., *Revolutionary Memoirs and Muster Rolls* (Athens, Ga.: Heritage Papers, 1994), 91-92 and 93-94.

"North Carolina Brigade, Lafayette's Division." Online listing of officers in each of the ten North Carolina regiments under Brigadier General Lachlan McIntosh at Valley Forge: http://valleyforgemusterroll.org/brigades/nc.asp.

North Carolina Society of Pennsylvania. *North Carolina at Valley Forge*. Philadelphia: The Society, 1923.

North Carolina Society of Pennsylvania. *North Carolina State Sunday at Valley Forge*. Philadelphia: The Society, 1926.

North Carolina Society of Pennsylvania. *Thirteenth Annual North Carolina State Sunday at Valley Forge, March 22, 1936*. Philadelphia: The Society, 1936.

Rubincam, Milton, and Frank J. Metcalf. "Muster Rolls Compiled for the Valley Forge Park Commission, 1947-1949." Typescript in the DAR Library, Washington, D. C. [The reference gives the general abbreviation, the state, and the page number within that state's listings.] [Includes: North Carolina: An analysis was made of the 1st, 2nd, 3rd, 4th, 5th, 6th, 7th, 8th, and 9th Regiments to determine whether they were at Valley Forge.]

Tyson, Lawrence. *Tennessee's Part in the Revolution: Address at Valley Forge, at the Presentation of the Tennessee Flag & Inauguration of Tennessee, Sunday, April 24, 1927*. Valley Forge, Pa.: Tennessee Society Colonial Dames, 1927.

United States. Continental Army. "Valley Forge Court Martial Records." Manuscript #AM.6315, Historical Society of Pennsylvania, Philadelphia. [Online catalog description: "Records of the court-martial of Lieutenant Matthew McCalley of the 10th North Carolina Battalion and other prisoners, before Colonel Thomas Clark at Valley Forge."]

1780

Battle of Ramsour's/Ramsaur's Mill, June 20, 1780

"An Account of the Battle of Ramsour's Mill." *Iredell County Tracks*, 33:2 (Spring 2010), 17-20. [Originally published in *The Carolina Watchman*, Salisbury, April 26, 1846.]

Barefoot, Daniel W. "Ramsour's Mill, Battle of." In William S. Powell, ed., Jay Mazzocchi, assoc. ed., *Encyclopedia of North Carolina* (Chapel Hill: University of North Carolina Press in association with the University of North Carolina Library, 2006), 945-946.

Barringer, Rufus. "Battle of Ramsour's Mill." *Davidson College Studies in History,* 1 (1898), 43-57.

"The Battle of Ramsour's Mill, June 20, 1780 at Ramsour's Mill, North Carolina." Online: http://www.my revolutionary war.com/battles/800620-ramsours-mill/.

Butler, Amelia Phelps. "A Little Journey to the Battlefield of Ramsour's Mill." *American Monthly Magazine* [DAR], 21:5 (November 1902), 361-364.

Carpenter, William L. *The Battle of Ramsour's Mill*. [Lincolnton, NC]: Lincoln County Historical Association and Lincoln County Museum of History, 1995. Includes map showing chronological progression of the battle.

Carpenter, William L. "Surprise Attack at Ramsour's Mill." *The State: Down Home in North Carolina*, 43:12 (May 1976), 10-11; online: http://digital.ncdcr.gov/cdm/compoundobject/collection/p16062coll18/id/11657. [Online description from "North Carolina Periodicals Index," East Carolina University: "This article details a skirmish between Patriots and Tories during the American Revolutionary War in 1780. Taking place at Ramsour's Mill in Lincoln County, about 400 Patriots defeated 1,200 Tories."]

Davis, Thomas R. "Battle of Ramsour's Mill." *The State: A Weekly Survey of North Carolina,* 9:33 (January 1942), 9, 22; online: http://digital.ncdcr.gov/cdm/ref/collection/p16062coll18/id/43298. [Online description from "North Carolina Periodicals Index," East Carolina University: "On June 20, 1780 Whigs and Torries faced off at Ramsour's Mill near Lincolnton. The battle was indecisive and ended with estimated 75 dead and 100 wounded for each side. The Whigs may have prevailed had a messenger from General Griffith Rutherford's not been murdered on his way to Colonel Locke."]

"Descriptive List of Men Raised from Morgan District to Serve Eighteen Months in the Continental Army. Received by Capt. Brevard at Ramsour's Mill between the 20th day of August & 12th October 1782." *Eswau Huppeday: Bulletin of the Broad River Genealogical Society*, 14:2 (May 1994), 132-133. [Lincoln County, North Carolina]

"Descriptive List of Men Returned to Me at Ramsours Mill & Receipted for by Captain Brevard, 1782." *North Carolinian: A Quarterly Journal of Genealogy and History,* 6:4 (December 1960), 751. [Gives the names and ages of the soldiers, the county they were from, and the "company they lived." List includes the names of twelve men: 7 from Burke County, 3 from Lincoln County, 1 from Rutherford County, and 1 from Wilkes County]

Echerd, John E. "The Battle of Ramsour's Mill." *SAR Magazine*, 47:4 (Spring 2003), 16-19.

"Expeditions to Ramseurs Mills, Captain William Lenoir, June 17-August 20, 1780." In Paul W. Gregory, *Early Settlers of Reddies River* (Wilkes Co.: Wilkes Genealogical Society, 1976), 44.

Fair, Warren A. *Ramsour's Mill: A Detailed Account of This Noted Conflict as Told to the Late Wallace M. Reinhardt by Reliable Men Who Took Part in the Bloody Fight*. Lincolnton: Warren A. Fair, 1937.

Gillgam, Jim, and Darrell Harkey. "Battle of Ramsour's Mill GPR Research." *Southern Campaigns of the American Revolution*, 4:2 (April-June 2007), 21; online: www.southerncampaign.org.

Graham, Joseph. *Battle of Ramsour's Mill*. Lincolnton: J. R. Nixon, 1955. [Alternate title: *General Benjamin Lincoln*.]

Graham, William A. "The Battle of Ramsaur's Mill, June 20, 1780." *The North Carolina Booklet*, 4:2 (June 1904), 1-23; online: http://digital.ncdcr.gov/cdm/ref/collection/p249901coll37/id/14180. [Online description from "North Carolina Periodicals Index," East Carolina University: "This article examines the Battle of Ramsaur's Mill, a military engagement between Patriot and Loyalist forces during the Revolutionary War. On June 20, 1780 near present-day Lincolnton, 400 Patriot militiamen defeated 1,200 Loyalist militia in a battle that demoralized Loyalist forces throughout the Southern theater of war."]

Hodges, J. E. "Ramsours Mill Battle Ground Fought June 20, 1780 Between 400 Whigs and 1300 Tories and was a Complete Victory for the Whigs." Manuscript, MC.175.1780h, State Archives of North Carolina, Raleigh. [Online catalog description: "This undated manuscript map was made by Dr. J. E. Hodges of Maiden from an earlier map by Wallace Reinhardt. The Reinhardt map was prepared based on information provided by Adam Reep, a participant in the battle of Ramsour's Mill. The map portrays the location of and troop positions at the battle."]

Jonas, Charles Andrew. *Revolutionary War Epics: Battle of Ramsours Mills, Battle of King Mountain: Speeches in the House of Representatives, June 11 and 20, 1930.* Washington, D. C.: Government Printing Office, 1930. [Ramsour's Mill is near Lincolnton, N. C.]

"Ramsour's Mill Battle Letter, 1849." Manuscript 617-z, Southern Historical Collection, Louis Round Wilson Special Collections Library, University of North Carolina, Chapel Hill; online finding aid available at http://www2.lib.unc.edu/mss/inv/r/Ramsour's_Mill_Battle.html. [Online catalog description: "The collection is a letter, 1849, containing an account of the Revolutionary battle at Ramseur's (or Ramsour's) Mill, 20 June 1780, told to the writer by a participant when he was 90. Also included is a typed transcription."]

Reinhardt, Wallace M. *The Battle of Ramsaur's Mill: A Detailed Account of This Noted Conflict as Told to the Late Wallace M. Reinhardt by Reliable Men Who Took Part in the Bloody Fight*. Lincolnton: Warren A. Fair, 1937.

Rockwell, E[lijah] F[rink]. "The Battle of Ramsours Mill." *Historical Magazine*, 2d series, 2 (July 1867), 24-27.

"Roster of William Lenoir's Company, March 30, 1776." In Paul W. Gregory, *Early Settlers of Reddies River* (Wilkes Co.: Wilkes Genealogical Society, 1976), 44.

"Society Celebrates Ramsour's Mill Victory." *Palmetto Patriot: South Carolina Society Sons of the American Revolution*, 2012:3 (Fall 2012), 4.

Battle of the Big Glades, Ashe County July 1780,

"[The Battle of the Big Glades]." Online: http://www.werelate.org/wiki/Place:Ashe,_North_Carolina,_United_States. [Text: "During the Revolutionary War one skirmish was fought in Ashe County. It is called the 'Battle of the Big Glades.' The battle was fought in July 1780 between a force of Americans, led by Captain Robert Love, and a force of 150 British Loyalists on their way to Charlotte to join Lord Cornwallis, the British commander in the Southern colonies. The Americans won the skirmish."]

Battle of South Pacolet River, July 14-15, 1780; Grindal Shoals

Bailey, J[ames] D[avis]. *History of Grindal Shoals and Some Early Adjacent Families*. Gaffney, S. C.: The Ledger Print, 1927; reprinted: Greenville, S. C.: A Press, 1981.

Bell, John L. "South Pacolet River, Battle of." In William S. Powell, ed.; Jay Mazzocchi, assoc. ed., *Encyclopedia of North Carolina* (Chapel Hill: University of North Carolina Press in association with the University of North Carolina Library, 2006), 1062-1063; online at NCpedia: http://ncpedia.org/south-pacolet-river-battle.

Most, Rachel. *An Archaeological Reconnaissance of the Proposed Pacolet River Reservoir, Spartanburg County, South Carolina*. (Research Manuscript Series, no. 116) Columbia: Institute of Archeology and Anthropology, University of South Carolina, 1977.

Robertson, John A. "The Historic Significance of Grindal Shoals, Pacolet River, Cherokee/Union Counties, South Carolina." Online: http://lib.jrshelby.com/grindal-shoals3.pdf.

Battle of Earle's Ford, South Carolina, July 15, 1780

Hairr, John. "Earle's Ford, Battle of." In William S. Powell, ed.; Jay Mazzocchi, assoc. ed., *Encyclopedia of North Carolina* (Chapel Hill: University of North Carolina Press in association with the University of North Carolina

Library, 2006), 366-367; online: http://ncpedia.org/earles-ford-battle. [The battle took place adjacent to the modern boundary of Polk County, North Carolina.]

Pancake, John S. *This Destructive War: The British Campaign in the Carolinas, 1780-1782*. Tuscaloosa, Ala.: The University of Alabama Press, 1985.

Battle of Colson's Mill, July 21, 1780 [in modern Stanly County]

"Battle of Colson's Mill." Online: https://en.wikipedia.org/wiki/Battle_of_Colson's_Mill.

Dunaway, Stewart E. *Colson's Ferry, Mill, Ordinary, Fort: A Revolutionary War Overview.* Hillsborough: North Carolina Historical Books, 2010. [Publisher's description from p. 4: "Colson's Plantation was at the junction of the Rocky River and the Pee Dee River and became a strategic location during the Revolutionary War."]

"Revolutionary War Raids & Skirmishes in 1780: July 21, 1780, at Colson, North Carolina." Online: http://www.myrevolutionarywar.com/battles/1780-skirmish/.

Stonestreet, O. C., IV. *The Battle of Colson's Mill: Death Knell of the Carolina Tories*. Mooresville, North Carolina: Createspace Publishing, 2014. [A forgotten skirmish of the American Revolutionary War was fought just outside of present-day Norwood, North Carolina in the sweltering heat of July 21st, 1780. A small but determined force of Patriot militia under the command of Colonel William Lee Davidson launched a surprise attack in the early morning hours against the gathering Tories at Colson's Mill. Though tired by a fast-paced march, and outnumbered at least two to one, the Patriots carry the day at this critical moment of the Southern Campaign. The victory will deny the British much needed supplies, men, and intelligence as they advance northward into the heart of the Carolina]

Skirmish at Mask's Ferry, September 10, 1780

"Revolutionary War Raids & Skirmishes in 1780: September 20, 1780, at Mask's Ferry, North Carolina." Online: http://www.myrevolutionarywar.com/battles/1780-skirmish/.

First Skirmish at Cane Creek, September 12, 1780

"The Skirmish at Cane Creek (First), September 12, 1780, at Cane Creek, McDowell County, North Carolina." Onilne: http://www.myrevolutionarywar.com/battles/800912-cane-creek/.

Battle of Wahab's Plantation, September 21, 1780

Pope, David L. "Wahab's Plantation, Battle of." In William S. Powell, ed.; Jay Mazzocchi, assoc. ed., *Encyclopedia of North Carolina* (Chapel Hill: University of North Carolina Press in association with the University of North Carolina Library, 2006), 1171-1172. [1780]

"Revolutionary War Raids & Skirmishes in 1780: September 21, 1780, at Wahab's Plantation, Lancaster County, South Carolina." Online: http://www.myrevolutionarywar.com/battles/1780-skirmish/.

Battle of Charlotte, September 26, 1780

Anderson, William Lee, III. "Where Did Cornwallis's Army Invade North Carolina? (Also the Battle of Charlotte, 26 September 1780)." Online: http://www.elehistory.com/amrev/CornwallisNCInvasion.pdf.

"Battle of Charlotte, September 26, 1780 at Charlotte, North Carolina." Online: http://www.myrevolutionary war.com/battles/800926-charlotte/.

Blythe, Dolores S. "Hornets at Work." *The State: Down Home in North Carolina*, 64:6 (November 1978), 12; online: http://digital.ncdcr.gov/cdm/_ref/collection/p16062coll18/id/58157. [Online description from "North Carolina Periodicals Index," East Carolina University: "Lord Cornwallis and his British army had been in Charlotte for almost a week when Cornwallis dispatched a foraging party led by Major John Doyle on October 3, 1780. Captain James Thompson and thirteen other local residents surrounded the party and ambushed them, causing the British to believe they were under attack of a large force. Soon after, British forces retreated from Charlotte."]

"Cornwallis' Attack on Charlotte Town." *Southern Campaigns of the American Revolution*, 2:10.1 (October 2005), 1-2; online: www.southerncampaign.org [September 1780]

Norris, David A., and Daniel W. Barefoot. "Charlotte, Battle of." In William S. Powell, ed.; Jay Mazzocchi, assoc. ed., *Encyclopedia of North Carolina* (Chapel Hill: University of North Carolina Press in association with the University of North Carolina Library, 2006), 201-202. [1780]

Phifer, Cordelia White. *Revolutionary Historical Spots in Charlotte and Mecklenburg County; Also Some Confederate History of Charlotte & Mecklenburg County*. Charlotte: Chamber of Commerce, [193?].

Poteet, Ellen. "Banastre Tarlton's Description of Charlotte in 1780." *Olde Mecklenburg Genealogical Society Quarterly*, 24:2 (2006), 18-22.

North Carolina, Tennessee, and the Battle of King's Mountain, October 7, 1780 (fought in South Carolina)

"229th Anniversary of Victory at Kings Mountain." *Palmetto Patriot: South Carolina Society Sons of the American Revolution, Palmetto Patriot: South Carolina Society Sons of the American Revolution*, 2009:4 (Winter 2009), 16; online: http://www.scssar.org/.

"Abstract of William Lenoir's Payroll for the Expedition to Kings Mountain, September 7, 1780 to __." In Paul W. Gregory, *Early Settlers of Reddies River* (Wilkes Co.: Wilkes Genealogical Society, 1976), 43.

Adams, Randolph G. "Two Documents on the Battle of King's Mountain." *North Carolina Historical Review,* 8 (1931), 348-352.

Addison, Stephen O.; Polly Fowler and Cheryl Hunt, eds. *Profile of a Patriot: Colonel Benjamin Cleveland, Hero of Kings Mountain*. Cleveland, Tenn.: S. O. Addison, 1993. [Benjamin Cleveland, 1738-1806]

Alderman, Pat. *One Heroic Hour at King's Mountain: Battle of Kings Mountain, October 7, 1780*. Erwin, Tenn.: P. Alderman, 1968; reprinted: Johnson City, Tenn.: Overmountain Press, 1990.

Alderman, Pat. *The Overmountain Men; Early Tennessee History, 1760-1795*. Johnson City, Tenn.: Overmountain Press, 1970.

Alderman, Pat, Lee B. Andrews, and Verna Alderman. *Overmountain Men; Early Tennessee History, 1760-1780. The Exploration, Settlement and Founding of the First Free Government in America; Its Struggles for Survival, Culminating in the Battle of King's Mountain*. [Erwin?, Tenn.]: Privately printed, 1958; Reprinted Erwin, Tenn.: Wintergreen Print Co., 1968.

Allaire, Anthony. *Diary of Lieut. Anthony Allaire*. (Eyewitness Accounts of the American Revolution series) New York: New York Times, 1968; online: http://www.tngenweb.org/revwar/kingsmountain/allaire.html. [This originnally appeared in Lyman Copeland Draper's *King's Mountain and Its Heroes* (Cincinnati: P.G. Thomson, 1881), 484-515. Allaire was a Loyalist.]

Allaire, Anthony; Lyman C. Draper, ed. "A Letter from a Royalist Officer." In *The Battle of Kings Mountain, October 7th, 1780 and the Events Which Led to It*. [S. l.: s. n.]: 1881; reprinted: Johnson City, Tenn.: Overmountain Press, 1996.

Anderson, William Lee. "Lincoln County Men at Kings Mountain." *Footprints in Time, Gaston-Lincoln County Genealogical Society*, (June 2011), 55-74; Online: http://www.elehistory.com/amrev/LincolnCountyMenAtKingsMountain.pdf.

"Another Revolutionary Hero Gone." *American Monthly Magazine* [DAR], 42:3 (March 1913), 141. [Colonel Benjamin Hardin, from Rutherford County, North Carolina; fought at the Battle of King's Mountain.]

Anthony, Mark C. "230th Anniversary of Kings Mountain Celebrated." *Palmetto Patriot: South Carolina Society Sons of the American Revolution, Palmetto Patriot: South Carolina Society Sons of the American Revolution*, 201:4 (Winter 2010), 16; online: http://www.scssar.org/.

Armstrong, Zella. "Participants in the Battle of Kings Mountain." *The Lookout*, (1921). [copy at the DAR Library, Washington, D. C. (GEOFC/S.C./MILITARY/1775-1776/KINGS-MT).]

Bailey, James D[avis]. *Commanders at King's Mountain*. Gaffney, S. C.: E. H. DeCamp, 1926; reprinted: Greenville, S. C.: A Press, 1980.

Bales, Clarence A. "Kings Mountain: Turning Point of the Revolution." Typescript (Jefferson City, Tenn., 1958) (GEOFC/S.C./MILITARY/1775-1783/KINGS-MT), DAR Library, Washington, D. C.

Bartholomees, James Boone. "Fight or Flee: The Combat Performance of the North Carolina Militia in the Cowpens-Guilford Courthouse Campaign, January to March 1781." Ph. D. dissertation, Duke University, 1977.

Bass, Robert D. "The Last Campaign of Major Patrick Ferguson." *South Carolina Historical Association Proceedings*, 5 (1968), 16-28.

"Battle of Kings Mountain." *Daughters of the American Revolution Magazine*, 70:9 (September 1936), 920-921.

"Battle of Kings Mountain." *MHQ: The Quarterly Journal of Military History*, 11:1 (Autumn 1998).

"Battle of Kings Mountain." *Old Pendleton District Newsletter*, 13:8 (October 1999).

"Battle of Kings Mountain: A Civil War." *New Greenville Mountaineer*, 22:3 (May 2002).

"Battle of Kings Mountain: Lincoln and Gaston County, NC Participation, 1775." *Gaston County Historical Bulletin*, 53:1 (2007).

"Battle of Kings Mountain Roster." *Tennessee Rifleman*, 3:3 (July 1962), 61-62; 5:3 (July 1964), 113; 5:4 (October 1964), 118-119; 6:1 (January 1965), 124-125; 6:3 (July 1965), 137; 6:4 (October 1965), 143; 7:1 (January 1966), 149; 7:2 (April 1966), 154; 7:3 (July 1966), 161; 7:4 (October 1966), 167; 8:1 (January 1967), 172; 8:2 (April 1967), 180.

Bayless, Bell. "The Battle of King's Mountain, Taken From an Account Written By Capt. David Vance in 1799." *American Monthly Magazine* [DAR], 17:6 (December 1900), 507-517.

Beach, Peggy. "Battle of Kings Mountain." *A Lot of Bunkum*, 20:2 (May 1999), 65-71.

Bearce, Robert. "Backwater Barbarians." *Baroid News Bulletin*, 31:1 (Spring 1980), 4-12. [Battle of King's Mountain]

Bennett, Edward Earl, Ruth Hardaker, Anne King Gregorie, and Isabel Thompson. *Calendar of the Tennessee and King's Mountain Papers of the Draper Collections of Manuscripts*. (Wisconsin Historical Publications. Calendar series, vol. 3) Madison: State Historical Society of Wisconsin, 1929.

Bennett, William Doub. "Captain William Lenoir's Company and the Battle of King's Mountain." *North Carolina Genealogical Society Journal*, 9:4 (November 1983), 234-235.

Berg, Gordon, and Bruce Adams. *Laboring for Independence: Workers in the Revolution*. Washington, D. C.: U. S. Department of Labor, [1976?]. [Includes "Gunpowder Made by a Woman Helped Colonists Win Crucial Battle" (Kings Mountain, S. C.), 20].

Blythe, Robert W., Maureen A. Carroll, and Steven H. Moffson. *Kings Mountain National Military Park: Historic Resource Study*. Atlanta: National Park Service,1995.

Boyd, William K. "The Battle of King's Mountain." *The North Carolina Booklet*, 8:4 (April 1909), 299-315; online: http://digital.ncdcr.gov/cdm/ref/collection/p249901coll37/id/14180. [Online description from "North Carolina Periodicals Index," East Carolina University: "The Battle of Kings Mountain took place near the town of Kings Mountain, North Carolina on the prominence across the border in South Carolina. The decisive defeat of Loyalist militia under Patrick Ferguson ended Cornwallis advance into North Carolina in October 1780." Includes maps.]

Brown, Robert Wilburn. *Kings Mountain and Cowpens: Our Victory Was Complete*. Charleston: History Press, 2009. [Contents: The beginning; Balance of Forces; Turning the Tide in the North; Civil War, Terrain, Weapons and Revolutionary Tactics; The South Carolina Campaign; Prelude to Kings Mountain; The Battle of Kings Mountain; Aftermath of Kings Mountain; The Winter of 1780-1781; Prelude to Cowpens; Double Envelopment at Cowpens; Aftermath of Cowpens; Race to the Dan; Conclusion.]

Buchanan, John. "The Importance of the Battle of Kings Mountain." *Flintlock and Powderhorn*, 17:2 (Fall 1999), 8-13.

Campbell, David, 1779-1859; Emily Jane Hubble, ed. "List of King's Mountain Volunteers in 1780." *Daughters of the American Revolution Magazine*, 45:2&3 (August-September 1914), 154-155.

Campbell, Robert. "King's Mountain: Battle of King's Mountain by Ensign Robert Campbell." *Genealogist's Post*, 3:10 (October 1966), 25-36. [Includes: "List of King's Mountain Volunteers in 1780, Copied from Gov. D. Campbell's Manuscript at Madison, Wis., State Library [Wisconsin Historical Society]."]

Capps, W. R. *Condensed History of the Battle of King's Mountain: Together with Cards of the Leading Business Houses of Charlotte*. Charlotte: Harper J. Elam, 1880.

Carpenter, Hugh. *King's Mountain, an Epic of the Revolution, with Historical and Biographical Sketches and Illustrations*. Knoxville, Tenn.: Privately Printed, 1936.

Carrillo, Richard F. *Colonial Road Survey at King's Mountain National Military Park, South Carolina.* (Research Manuscript series, no. 66) Columbia: Division of Advanced Studies and Research, Institute of Archeology and Anthropology, University of South Carolina, 1974.

Casper, David R. "Joseph Beeler at King's Mountain." *Tennessee Ancestors: A Tri-Annual Publication of the East Tennessee Historical Society*, 10:3 (December 1994), 177-181.

Celebration of the Battle of King's Mountain, October, 1855, and the Address of the Hon. John S. Preston. Together with the Proceedings of the Meetings and Accompanying Documents. Yorkville, S. C.: For the Committees by Miller & Melton; Charleston: James & Williams, Printers, 1855.

Chandler, Helen Deane. *A Brief Description of the Battle of Kings Mountain: The Turning Point of the American Revolution, Fought in York County, S. C., October 7, 1780; Together with Brief Accounts of Previous Celebrations, Illustrations Showing the Battlefield and Monuments and Interesting Data Concerning the 150th Anniversary Celebration to be Held on the Battleground October 7, 1930*. Gastonia, N. C.: Publicity Committee of the Sesqui-Centennial Committee, 1930.

Chesney, Alexander; Bobby Gilmer Moss, ed. *Journal of Capt. Alexander Chesney: Adjutant to Maj. Patrick Ferguson.* Blacksburg, S. C.: Scotia-Hibernia Press, 2002.

"Col. William Campbell Certificate." ID # 36597, Tennessee Historical Society, Nashville; digital surrogate available through the Revolutionary War Collection, Tennessee Virtual Archive at http://cdm15138.contentdm.oclc.org/cdm/compoundobject/collection/p15138coll16/id/96/rec/10. [Description from TeVA: "Certificate regarding the conduct of Col. William Campbell at the Battle of King's Mountain."]

Collins, Robert L. "The Overmountain Men March Again." *The State: Down Home in North Carolina*, 47:3 (August 1979), 16-17, 33; online: http://digital.ncdcr.gov/cdm/ref/collection/p16062coll18/id/58624. [Online description from "North Carolina Periodicals Index," East Carolina University: "Beginning in 1975 and held each September since, a reenactment of the Overmountain Victory March takes place. The march honors a the mountain men who were victorious at Kings Mountain during the Revolutionary War. Armed with a horn, a scroll, and Bible, and dressed in clothing of the time period, the group begins at Sycamore Shoals and marches 160 miles to Kings Mountain."]

Collins, Robert L. "Retracing Bright's Trace." *The State: Down Home in North Carolina*, 43:1 (June 1975), 8-12; online: http://digital.ncdcr.gov/cdm/compoundobject/collection/p16062coll18/id/9458. [Online description from "North Carolina Periodicals Index," East Carolina University: "Today, hikers can walk the historic trail that 'Backwater men' or 'Overmountain men' took when combating British forces during the American Revolutionary War in 1780. These men traveled the Big Yellow Mountain Gap to Kings Mountain and defeated Major Patrick Ferguson's troops."]

"Compensation for Revolutionary Service." Online: http://www.rootsweb.ancestry.com/~scyork/RevWar/KingsMtn.html.

Corbitt, D. L. "Two Documents on the Battle of King's Mountain." *North Carolina Historical Review*, 8 (1931), 348-352.

"Corps of Discovery at Kings Mountain." *Southern Campaigns of the American Revolution*, 3:12 (December 2006), 9; online: www.southerncampaign.org.

Cox, William E. *Battle of Kings Mountain Participants, October 7, 1780.* [S. l.]: Eastern National Park & Monument Association, 1972.

Cranke, H. P. "The Indian Play at Kings Mountain." *Daughters of the American Revolution Magazine*, 55:11 (November 1921), 622-626.

Crowson, E. T. "Colonal William Campbell and the Battle of King's Mountain." *Virginia Cavalcade*, 30:1 (Summer 1980), 22-29.

Dameron, J. David. *King's Mountain: The Defeat of the Loyalists, October 7, 1780.* (Battleground America series). Cambridge, Mass.: Da Capo Press, 2003. [Examination of the battle with information about touring the site; includes pictures of the site as it appears today.]

De Peyster, J. Watts. "The Affair at King's Mountain, 7th October 1780." *Magazine of American History*, 5:6 (December 1880), 401-424.

de Peyster, J. Watts. *The Battle or Affair of King's Mountain, Saturday, 7th October 1780: Being an Address Delivered at the Annual Meeting of the New York Historical Society on the Evening of Tuesday, 4th January 1881.* New York: [New York Historical Society?], 1881.

de Peyster, J. Watts. "Kings Mountain: The Oriskany of the South." *Historical Magazine with Notes and Queries*, 2d series, 5 (March 1869), 189-197.

Dean, Earl. "Battle of Kings Mountain." *The State: A Weekly Survey of North Carolina*, 18:42 (March 1951), 28-29; online: http://digital.ncdcr.gov/cdm/ref/collection/p16062coll18/id/26745. [Online description from "North Carolina Periodicals Index," East Carolina University: "Kings Mountain was one of the most important battles of the Revolutionary War; it helped turn the tide in favor of the rebels."]

"Death of Col.Williams at the Kings Mountain Battle: Correct Story of Notable Local Battle." *Eswau Huppeday*, 32:3 (August 2012), 133-136.

Draper, Lyman Copeland. "Draper Manuscripts: King's Mountain Papers, 1756-1843." Wisconsin Historical Society, Madison; also available on microfilm in many research libraries.

Draper, Lyman Copeland. *King's Mountain and Its Heroes: History of the Battle of King's Mountain, October 7th 1780 and the Events Which Led to It.* Cincinnati: P. G. Thomson, 1881; reprinted: Marietta, Ga.: Continental Book, 1954; (North Carolina Heritage series, no. 5) Spartanburg: The Reprint Company, 1967; Baltimore: Genealogical Publishing Company, 1967, 1971, 1978; Spartanburg: The Reprint Company, 1982; Johnson City, Tenn.: Overmountain Press, 1996.

Draper, Lyman C. "Letter, Lyman C. Draper, in Madison, Wis., to J[ames] G[ettys] M[cGready] Ramsey in Knoxville, Tenn., 1880 Aug. 2." Ramsey Family. "Ramsey Family Papers, 1790-1912." Manuscript MS.0253, Box 2, folder 7 (Correspondence, 1881-1883), Special Collections Library, University of Tennessee, Knoxville; online: http://dlc.lib.utk.edu/spc/view?docId=tei/0012_000060_000472_0000/0012_000060_000472_0000.xml.

[Online catalog description: "Informs J.G.M. of the writer's need for information concerning the Western part of the route of the King's Mountain men. Discussion of Tennesseans who could have been at the Cowpens."]

Drayton, John (prepared from material collected by the author's father William H. Drayton). *Memoirs of the American Revolution, From its Commencement to the Year 1776, Inclusive; as Relating to the State of South-Carolina; and Occasionally Relating to the States of North-Carolina and Georgia.* 2 vols. Charleston: A. E. Miller, 1821; reprinted with the title *Memoirs of the American Revolution as Relating to the State of South Carolina* (Eyewitness Accounts of the American Revolution) New York: New York Times, 1969; Bedford, Mass.: Applewood Books, 2009. [A biographical sketch of William Henry Drayton appears in vol. 1, xiii-xxvii.]

Dugger, Shepherd Monroe; foreword by Cratis Williams. *The War Trails of the Blue Ridge: Containing an Authentic Description of the Battle of Kings Mountain, the Incidents Leading up to and the Echoes of the Aftermath of This Epochal Engagement and Other Stories Whose Scenes Are Laid in the Blue Ridge.* Banner Elk, N. C.: Puddingstone Press, 1974.

Dunaway, Stewart E. *The Fulkersons in the Battle of King's Mountain: A Revolutionary War Story.* Hillsborough: North Carolina Historical Books, [201?].

Dunkerly, Bert. "Kings Mountain 225th Commemoration." *Southern Campaigns of the American Revolution*, 2:11.1 (November 2005); online: www.southerncampaign.org.

Dunkerly, Robert, ed. *The Battle of King's Mountain: Eyewitness Accounts.* Charleston: History Press, 2007. [Contents: American Accounts; The Shelby-Campbell Controversy; Loyalist Accounts.]

Dunkerly, Robert M. "The 225th Anniversary of the Battle of Kings Mountain." *Southern Campaigns of the American Revolution*, 2:9 (September 2005), 22-23; online: www.southerncampaign.org.

Dunkerly, Robert M. *Kings Mountain Walking Tour Guide.* Pittsburgh: Dorrance Publishing Company, 2003.

Dunkerly, Robert M. "Worshipping at the Shrine of Liberty: The Preservation of the Kings Mountain Battlefield." 2:2 (February 2005), 5-8; online: www.southerncampaign.org.

Dykeman, Wilma; Louis S. Glanzman, illus. *With Fire and Sword: The Battle of Kings Mountain.* Washington, D. C.: Office of Publications, National Park Service, U. S. Department of the Interior; for sale by the Superintendent of Documentss., U. S. Govt. Printing Office, 1978.

Eakin, Stephen Robert. "'Gunpowder Mary' McKeehan, A Tennessee Heroine of the Revolution." *Flintlock & Powderhorn: Magazine of the Sons of the Revolution*, 9:1 (April 1991), 21-23. [Discusses McKeehan's involvement in the Battle of King's Mountain.]

Essington, Meghan. "Memory, Manhood, and Military Service: Gentlemen and Common Planters in the Battle of King's Mountain." *Journal of East Tennessee History*, no. 86 (2014), 2-17.

Ervin, Sam James, Jr. *The Battle of King's Mountain: An Appraisal of Its Historical Significance.* [S. l., N. C.?: s. n.], 1980?

Ferguson, James. *Two Scottish Soldiers: A Soldier of 1688 and Blenheim; A Soldier of The American Revolution, and A Jacobite Laird and His Forbears.* Aberdeen: D. Wyllie & Son, 1888. [Patrick Ferguson, 1744-1780; Battle of King's Mountain]

Ferguson, Patrick. "Patrick Ferguson Papers, 1780, 1931." Manuscript PC.495 (MARS ID: 1005; record group), State Archives of North Carolina, Raleigh. [Online catalog description: "Photocopy of letter written by Colonel Ferguson, British officer in command of loyalist troops camped on Kings Mountain, about the strength of his troops relative to the Americans (Oct. 6, 1780). Original is in the William L. Clements Library, University of Michigan. Also newspaper article (1931) by Randolph G. Adams about the letter."]

Fink, Madge C. "Colonel James William: A Sketch of a Patriot and the Events Leading to the Battle of King's Mountain." *Daughters of the American Revolution Magazine*, 119:7 (August/September 1985), 572-575, 623.

Fink, Paul M. "Jacob Brown of Nolichucky." *Tennessee Historical Quarterly*, 21:3 (September 1962), 235-250. [Fink was one of the men who started purchasing land in Tennessee from American Indians; this article also discusses his involvement in the Washington Co. militia and the Battle of King's Mountain.]

Finley, David Edward. "Kings Mountain." *American Monthly Magazine* [*Daughters of the American Revolution Magazine*], 36:1 (January 1910), 3-8. [Includes the text of a speech given by D. E. Finley at the dedication ceremony of the fifth monument at the King's Mountain Battlefield on October 7, 1909.]

Fiske, John. "From King's Mountain to Yorktown." *Atlantic Monthly*, 66:398 (December 1890), 789-807.

Fiske, John. "The Disasters of 1780." *Atlantic Monthly*, 66:395 (September 1890), 337-354.

Flowers, Charles. "The Long Road to Victory." *WNC Magazine*, 4:1 (January/February 2010), 42-47. [Online description from "North Carolina Periodicals Index," East Carolina University: "The Overmountain Men steered the Revolutionary War in the Patriots' favor at King's Mountain, when they won against one of King George's most successful fighting force in the South."]

Foster, Stephen. "Battle of Kings Mountain." *American Historical Magazine*, 1 (1896), 22-45; reprinted: *Holston Pastfinder*, 19:2 (December 2000), 4-11.

Foster, Stephen. "Battle of Kings Mountain." Undated typescript ("Reuben T. Durrett Collection on Kentucky and the Ohio River Valley," Durrett Codex 71), Special Collections Research Center, University of Chicago, Chicago. [Online catalog description: "Copied from the original manuscript in the hand of T. W. Preston, Vicksburg, Mississippi, May, 1895."]

Frink, Madge G. "A Day to Remember: October 7, 1780." *Daughters of the American Revolution Magazine*, 114:8 (October 1980), 996-999. [Includes a map: "Troop Positions, Battle of Kings Mountain."]

Gaston, Arthur Lee. *Gaston is Heard. Chester Lawyer Makes Principal Address at Kings Mountain, Friday; 148th Anniversary is Observed.* [S. l.]: Yorktown Chapter, South Carolina DAR, 1928?

Gilchrist, Marianne McLeod. *Patrick Ferguson: "A Man of Some Genius.* Edinburgh: NMS Enterprises, 2003. [Patrick Ferguson, 1744-1780. Online catalog description: "Patrick Ferguson: born May 24, 1744 (Julian calendar) to James and Anne Ferguson of Edinburgh; designed the British Army's first breech-loading rifle; commanded the American Volunteers (drawn from the King's American Regiment, the Loyal American Regiment, the 1st, 2nd, and 4th New Jersey Battalions, and De Lancey's 3rd Battalion); died in the Battle of King's Mountain, S. C., in Oct. 1780."]

Gilliam, Hubert. "An Unexpected Enemy and the Turn of the Tide: Andrew Creswell's King's Mountain Letter." *Smithfield Review: Studies in the History of the Region West of the Blue Ridge*, 10 (2006), 5-19; 12 (2008), 99-101.

Gist, Margaret Adlum. "King's Mountain." *American Monthly Magazine* [*Daughters of the American Revolution Magazine*], 36:2 (February 1901), 168-171.

Gordon, John. "Kings Mountain, South Carolina." In Larry E. Selesky, chief ed., *Encyclopedia of the American Revolution.* 2nd ed. (Library of Military History) (Detroit: Thomson Gale, 2006), 1:582-588.

Greenawalt, Greg. "State Societies Mark Patriot Victory at Kings Mountain." *Palmetto Patriot: South Carolina Society of the Sons of the American Revolution*, 2012: issue 4 (Winter 2012), 1, 4-5; online: http://www.scssar.org.

Greisser, Edith. "James Williams." *The Carolina Herald and Newsletter: Official Publication of the South Carolina Genealogical Society*, 32:3 (July-September 2004), 28-36.

Griffin, Clarence. "History-Making Court-Martial of 1780 Led to Nine Hangings." *Bulletin of the Genealogical Society of Old Tryon County*, 17:3 (August 1989), 116-117. [the trial of thirty-two Tories and the hanging of nine of them after the Battle of Kings Mountain]

Hall, Reid, and Jack F. Westmoreland. *Battle of King's Mountain, October 7, 1780.* [S. l.: s. n.], 1980.

Hamilton, J. G. de Roulhac. "King's Mountain: Letters of Colonel Isaac Shelby." *Journal of Southern History*, 4:3 (August 1938), 367-377.

Harris, Joe. "Memorial Service & Grave Marking Ceremony for a Revolutionary War Hero." *Recall*, 7:2 (Fall 2001), 9-10. [Online description from "North Carolina Periodicals Index," East Carolina University: "Harris, a descendant of a Revolutionary War soldier, Samuel Johnson of Wilkes County, recounts his war experiences and the battle at King's Mountain. He entered the war as a private 1776 and eventually promoted and received an officer's commission as Captain. Harris conducted a memorial service for his ancestor in August 2001 at the Little Stone Mountain Baptist Church in Traphill, N. C. Later at the graveyard, a new marble headstone which was supplied by the US Veterans Administration was unveiled."]

Hart Family, Shelby Family. "Shelby and Hart Family Papers, 1775-1814; 1899-1900." Manuscript 659-z, Southern Historical Collection, Louis Round Wilson Special Collections Library, University of North Carolina, Chapel Hill; online finding aid available at http://www2.lib.unc.edu/mss/inv/s/Shelby_and_Hart_Family.html. [Online finding aid description: "Members of the Shelby family and the Hart family resided in Kentucky. Prominent family members include Isaac Shelby (1750-1826), a Revolutionary officer and the first governor of Kentucky, 1792-1796 and 1812-1816, and Nathaniel Hart (1734-1782), Revolutionary officer and pioneer… Many items concern lands claims and titles of members of the Hart family in Kentucky. Also included is a ten-page manuscript description by Isaac Shelby of the Battle of King's Mountain and other events of the Revolution in the South after 1780, and two related letters to him."]

Headspeth, W. Carroll, and Spurgeon Compton. *A Masterful Maneuver: The Retreat to the Dan: An Important Link in a Chain of Events That Led in Rapid Succession from Kings Mountain to Yorktown — and Victory.* South Boston, Va.: South Boston News, 1974.

Henderson, W. A. *Kings Mountain and Its Campaign: An Address on Occasion of the Unveiling of a Monument to Its Heroes at Guilford Battlefield, July 4, 1903.* Greensboro, N. C.: Guilford Battleground Company, 1903?

Hill, Reid, and Jack F. Westmoreland. *Battle of King's Mountain, October 7, 1780.* Richburg, S. C.: Chester County Genealogical Society, 1980?

Historical Statements Concerning the Battle of Kings Mountain and the Battle of Cowpens, South Carolina. (70th Congress, 1st Session, House Document 328) Washington, D. C.: U. S. Government Printing Office, 1928.

Hoover, Herbert. *Address of President Hoover on the Occasion of the Celebration of the One Hundred and Fiftieth Anniversary of the Battle of King's Mountain, October 7, 1930.* Washington, D. C.: Government Printing Office, 1930.

Hopkins, Alfred F. "Testing the Ferguson Rifle, Modern Marksmen Attains High Precision with Arm of 1776." In *Rifles and Riflemen at the Battle of Kings Mountain* (National Park Service Popular Studies series. History, no. 12) (Washington, D. C.: National Park Service, 1941).

Hoss, E[lijah] E[mbree]. *The Battle of King's Mountain.* Nashville: Published for the Methodist Episcopal Church, Souht, by Smith & Lama, 1918.

Hudgins, Bill. "The Battle of Kings Mountain: A Brief Battle on the South Carolina Frontier Changed the Course of the Revolutionary War." *American Spirit: Daughters of the American Revolution Magazine*, 145:1 (January/February 2011), 30-34.

Hunter, Elizabeth. "Over the Hill." *The State: Down Home in North Carolina*, 61:4 (September 1993), 37-39; online: http://digital.ncdcr.gov/cdm/ref/collection/p16062coll18/id/66314. [Online description from "North Carolina Periodicals Index," East Carolina University: "The Overmountain Victory Trail Celebration in Spruce Pine honors a band of Southern patriots who won a key battle at King's Mountain during the Revolution."]

Jackson, W. Garrett. "King's Mountain: A Virginia Perspective." *Drumbeat, with Flintlock & Powderhorn: News of the Sons of Revolution*, 29:4 (Winter 2011), 14-15.

Jenkins, Paul B. "The Fight at King's Mountain." *Field and Stream*, 33:10 (October 1930), 38-40, 77-79.

Johnson, Uzal, 1757?-1827. Manuscript [part of the Thorne-Boudinot Collection," Box 3, folder 10], Manuscript Division, Department of Rare Books and Special Collections, Harvey S. Firestone Library, Princeton University, Princeton, N. J. [a copy is also available as P 900002, Personal Papers Collection, South Carolina Department of Archives and History, Columbia. ["Memorandum of Occurances during the Campaigne" or "Diary of Military Service in South Carolina, 1780-1781."]

Johnson, Uzal, 1757?-1827. "Memorandum of Occurances during the Campaigne, 1780-1781." Typescritten transcript (43/103), South Carolina Historical Society, Charleston. [Online catalog description: "Continental Army surgeon. He served with the New Jersey Volunteers (Loyal American Volunteers)."]

Johnson, Uzal; Bobby Gilmer Moss, ed. *Uzal Johnson, Loyalists: Revolutionary Diary of Surgeon to Ferguson's Command.* Blacksburg, S. C.: Scotia-Hibernia Press, 2000.

Johnson, Uzal; Wade S. Kolb III and Robert M. Weir, eds., with the assistant of Anne H. Weir. *Captured at Kings Mountain: The Journal of Uzal Johnson, a Loyalist Surgeon.* Columbia: University of South Carolina Press, 2011. [Johnson (1757?-1827) was from New Jersey and came to South Carolina in a Loyalist unit under Colonel Patrick Ferguson (1744-1780). He was captured and imprisoned at Hillsborough, N. C.]

Jonas, Charles Andrew. *Revolutionary War Epics: Battle of Ramsours Mills, Battle of Kings Mountain: Speeches in the House of Representatives, June 11 and 20, 1930.* Washington, D. C.: Government Printing Office, 1930.

Jones, K. Randall. *Before They Were Heroes at King's Mountain.* Winston-Salem, N. C.: Daniel Boone Footsteps, 2011.

Jones, Randall. *Guide to the Overmountain Victory National Historic Trail.* Winston-Salem: Daniel Boone Footsteps, 2011.

Keller, S. Roger. *Isaac Shelby: A Driving Force in America's Struggle for Independence.* Shippensburg, Pa.: Burd Street Press, 2000. [Shelby,1750-1826, was later a governor of Kentucky.]

Kelly, James C., and William C. Bakker III. *The Sword of the Lord and Gideon: A Catalogue of the Historical Objects Relating to the Battle of King's Mountain.* Boone, N. C.: Appalachian Consortium Press, 1980.

"King's Mountain, the Decisive Battle of the Revolution." *American Monthly Magazine*, 22:6 (June 1903), 967-969.

King's Mountain Centennial Association. *Battle at King's Mountain, October 7, 1780: Proposed Centennial Celebration, October 7, 1880.* Yorkville, S. C.: Printed at the Office of the Enquirer, 1880.

King's Mountain Centennial Association. "King's Mountain Centennial Association Records, 1880-1910." Manuscript collection (I&O), Manuscripts Division, South Caroliniana Library, University of South Carolina, Columbia.

King's Mountain Monument Association. "King's Mountain Monument Association Records, 1909, Aug. 10-Oct. 8." Manuscript (Manuscripts I&O), Manuscripts Division, South Caroliniana Library, University of South Carolina, Columbia.

"King's Mountain Expedition, September 7-November 7, 1780." In Paul W. Gregory, *Early Settlers of Reddies River* (Wilkes Co.: Wilkes Genealogical Society, 1976), 48.

Kings Mountain. Washington, D. C.: Government Printing Office, 1970.

"Kings Mountain." *Historical Magazine with Notes and Queries*, 5:3 (March 1869), 189-197.

"Kings Mountain and Cowpens Newspaper Excerpts, 1871-1908." *York County Genealogical and Historical Society Quarterly*, 18:2 (September 2006),

Kings Mountain Celebration Committee (N. C.) and Kings Mountain Celebration Committee (S. C.). *Official Programme of the Sesqui-Centennial Celebration of the Battle of Kings Mountain: On the Battlefield in York County, South Carolina, Tuesday, Oct. 7, 1930, on the One Hundred and Fiftieth Anniversary of the Engagement Which Proved to Be the Turning Point of the American Revolution.* [S. l.: s. n., 1930?]

Kirchner, Kevin Randall. "Twelve Days of Unity, Twenty Years of Division: The King's Mountain Volunteers in the Context of Land Speculation and Frontier Politics during the Revolutionary Era." Honors Paper, Duke University, Durham, 1998.

Kughler, Francis V. "Mural Six: On to King's Mountain." *The State: Down Home in North Carolina*, 29:2 (June 1961), 2, 8; online: http://digital.ncdcr.gov/cdm/ref/collection/p16062coll18/id/8523. [Online description from "North Carolina Periodicals Index," East Carolina University: "Francis V. Kughler discusses the design and creation of his sixth mural 'On To King's Mountain.' The mural, created for the Institute of Government building in Chapel Hill, represents the celebrated mountaineers who made a surprise attack on the Tories encamped on King's Mountain. Kughler discusses his historical research, and the study of human subjects which aided in the creation of his latest work."]

Kurz, Barbara. "Dr. McLean's Kings Mountain Memorial Address." *The Quarterly: A Publication of the York County Genealogical and Historical Society*, 22:4 (March 2011), 10-14.

Lathan, R[obert]. *Historical Sketch of the Battle of King's Mountain, Fought between the American and British Troops, at King's Mountain, York Co., S. C., October 7, 1780.* Yorkville, S. C.: Printed at the Office of the Enquirer, 1880.

Lea, John M. "Letter, John M. Lea in Nashville, Tenn., to J[ames] G[ettys] M[cGready] Ramsey in Knoxville, Tenn., 1880 Aug. 12." Ramsey Family. "Ramsey Family Papers, 1790-1912." Manuscript MS.0253, Box 2, folder 7 (Correspondence, 1881-1883), Special Collections Library, University of Tennessee, Knoxville; online: http://dlc.lib.utk.edu/spc/view?docId=tei/0012_000060_000471_0000/0012_000060_000471_0000.xml. Online catalog description: "Long discussion of Tennessees part in the Battle of King's Mountain, research done on this subject by Mr. Lea, and further research planned."]

"Letter from Isaac Shelby to John Sevier." ID # 36384, Tennessee State Historical Society, Nashville; digital surrogate available through the Revolutionary War Collection, Tennessee Virtual Archive at http://cdm15138.contentdm.oclc.org/cdm/compoundobject/collection/p15138coll16/id/70/rec/41. [Description from TeVA: "Letter from Isaac Shelby to John Sevier regarding misrepresentations of the part Colonel William Campbell took in the Battle of King's Mountain, October 7, 1780."]

"Letter from Isaac Shelby to John Sevier." ID # 36388, Tennessee State Historical Society, Nashville; digital surrogate available through the Revolutionary War Collection, Tennessee Virtual Archive at http://cdm15138.contentdm.oclc.org/cdm/compoundobject/collection/p15138coll16/id/86/rec/40. [Description from TeVA: "Letter from Isaac Shelby to John Sevier asking for corroborative testimony as to Shelby's services in the Battle of King's Mountain, South Carolina. Letter written on August 12, 1812."]

"Lieutenant-Colonel Patrick Ferguson: A Career of the American Revolution." *Living Age*, 155 (October 7, 1882), 24-34. [Patrick Ferguson (1744-1780)]

Lynch, Michael. "Creating Regional Heroes: Traditional Interpretations of the Battle of King's Mountain." *Tennessee Historical Quarterly*, 68:3 (Fall 2009), 224-249.

Mackenzie, George C. "The Battle of King's Mountain." *Daughters of the American Revolution Magazine*, 99:2 (February 1965), 132-134, 206, 208.

Mackenzie, George C. *Kings Mountain National Military Park.* (United States Historical Handbook Series, no. 22) Washington, D. C.: National Park Service, 1955; reprinted 1961.

Malgee, David G. "A Frontier Biography: William Campbell of Kings Mountain." M. A. thesis, University of Richmond, 1983.

Massey, De Van. *An Administrative History of Kings Mountain National Military Park.* Washington, D. C.: National Park Service, 1985.

Massey, Tim. "Did the Road to Kings Mountain Begin at Valley Forge?" *The Encampment*, 33:3 (Fall 2009), 8, 10.

McAfee, Hoyte. "Judge Webb's Version of Kings Mountain Battle." *Charlotte Observer*, October 2, 1938; section 3, page 7; reprinted in: *Eswau Huppeday*, 32:4 (November 2012), 191-201. [Judge E. Yates Webb, North

Carolina congressman]
McCown, Mary Hardin. "A King's Mountain Diary." *East Tennessee Historical Society's Publications*, 14 (1942), 102-106.
McDowell, Franklin Brevard. *The Battle of King's Mountain, October 7, 1780: Address Delivered before the Society of the Cincinnati in the State of North Carolina, at Charlotte, April 19, 1907*. Raleigh: Commercial Printing Company for the Society of the Cincinnati in the State of North Carolina, 1907.
McIntyre, Debby. "The Revolutionary War Battle at Kings Mountain." *Essau Huppeday*, 33:1 (February 2013), 23-36.
McLean, William, 1757-1828. "Memorial Address Given by Dr. William McLean: Incomplete Typescript Copy, 1814 July 4." *Gastonia Gazette,* (1891?); copy at the Wisconsin Historical Society Library, Madison. [Online catalog description: "Dr. William McLean was from Lincoln (Gaston) County, North Carolina and served as a physician during the America Revolution and was present at the King's Mountain Battle. Incomplete memorial address delivered at King's Mountain battleground, South Carolina, in celebration of the erection of the first monument to the men who fell in the battle there October 7, 1780."]
Messick, Hank. *King's Mountain: The Epic of the Blue Ridge "Mountain Men" in the American Revolution*." Boston: Little, Brown, 1976.
Morris, Glenn. *Over the Mountain to Victory*. Birmingham, Ala.: Progressive Farmer Company, 1980.
Moss, Bobby Gilmer. *The Patriots at Kings Mountain.* Blacksburg, S. C.: Scotia-Hibernia Press, 1990.
Moss, Bobby Gilmer. *Roster of the Loyalists in the Battle of Kings Mountain*. Blacksburg, S. C.: Scotia-Hibernia Press, 1998.
Norris, Jeannie Faris. "A Battleground is Dedicated." *The State: Down Home in North Carolina*, 29:15 (December 1961), 11; online: http://digital.ncdcr.gov/cdm/ref/collection/p16062coll18/id/9142. [Online description from "North Carolina Periodicals Index," East Carolina University: "Orators, politicians, and citizens were present during the 100th anniversary of the Battle of Kings Mountain, celebrated on 5 October 1880. The ceremonies lasted for two days, as the first monument was unveiled, and the 'relic house' was opened to the public. Governors of North Carolina, South Carolina, and Virginia were on hand to witness the military display that included the Cleveland Guard of Shelby, King's Mountain High School Cadets, and others."]
North Carolina (State). General Assembly. "[Document dated:] February 1, [1781]: Re[specting] Purchase of Arms Captured at Kings Mountain (Rejected)." Manuscript; General Assembly Record Group; Session Records, January-February 1781; Joint Papers, Committee Papers, Resolutions, Senate Bills, House Bills, Box 1 (MARS ID: 66.8.23.10.2; item), State Archives of North Carolina, Raleigh. [Online catalog description: "The resolution would have appointed commissioners to receive and value the arms captured from Major Ferguson's party by Colonel Cleveland, of Wilkes County, and grant certificates of purchase to the captors."]
North Carolina (State). General Assembly. "[Document dated:] February 3, [1781]: Re[specting] Purchase of Arms Captured at Kings Mountain (Rejected)." Manuscript; General Assembly Record Group; Session Records, January-February 1781; Joint Papers, Committee Papers, Resolutions, Senate Bills, House Bills, Box 1 (MARS ID: 66.8.23.16.4; items), State Archives of North Carolina, Raleigh. [Online catalog description: "The resolution appoints commissioners from Wilkes and Surry Counties to receive and value any arms captured from the enemy, such as the ones from the Battle of Kings Mountain taken by Colonel Cleveland, and grant certificates of purchase to the captors."]
"Obituary of Thomas Snoddy, One of the Last of the King's Mountain Men." *Tennessee Ancestors: A Tri-Annual Publication of the East Tennessee Historical Society*, 6:1 (April 1990), 76.
"Over Mountain Men at the Battle of Kings Mountain, 1780." *Gaston County Historical Bulletin*, 49:2 (2003),
Overmountain Victory. Blacksburg, S. C.: Overmountain Victory National Historic Trail, 2011.
Page, G. G. *The Battle of Kings Mountain, October 7, 1780; The Battle of Yorktown, October 18-19, 1781*. Kings Mountain, N. C.: Herald Publishing House, 1929.
Page, G. G. *Battle of Kings Mountain Fought October 7, 1780, and Other Important Data*. Kings Mountain, N. C.: Herald Publishing House, 1926.
Page, G. G. *A Patriotic Address to the Shelby Kiwanis Club at Cleveland Springs Hotel, October 7, 1926, 7 p. m.: The 146th Anniversary of the Battle of Kings Mountain*. Kings Mountain, N. C.? G. G. Page, 1926.
"Participants in Battle of Kings Mountain from Washington County, TN; from Green County, TN, from Holston Area." *Bristol Tennessean*, 23 September 1977; reprinted in: *Holston Pastfinder,* 18:1 (no. 68) (September 1999), 38-39; *Holston Pastfinder,* 18:3 (no. 70) (March 2000), 1.
"Patriot's [sic] Attack Loyalists at King's Mountain, 1780." *Old News*, (December 2007).
Patterson, Donald Preston, Jr. "The Battle of King's Mountain" (American History Essay Topic), *Daughters of the American Revolution Magazine*, 111:10 (October 1977), 821-822.

Pettus, Louise. "Enoch Gilmer, King's Mountain Spy." Online: http://www.rootsweb.ancestry.com/~scyork/Pettus.htm#49.

Pettus, Louise. "John Craig's Story Sheds Light on Revolutionary War." Online: http://www.rootsweb.ancestry.com/~scyork/Pettus1.html#John Craig's.

Pettus, Louise. "Kings Mountain's National Status Was Hard-Fought Battle." Online: http://www.rootsweb.ancestry.com/~scyork/Page1.html.

Preston, Francis, 1765-1836. "Oration Delivered by Gen'l. Francis Preston on Oct. 7, 1810, at Abington, Va." *Publications of the Historical Society of Washington County, Virginia,* 3 (1939; published 1964), 15-19.

Preston, John S. *Celebration of the Battle of King's Mountain, October, 1855, and the Address of the Hon. John S. Preston; Together with the Proceedings of the Meetings and the Accompanying Documents*. Yorkville, S. C.: Miller 7 Melton, 1855.

Putnam, Albigence W. "Another Account of the Battle of Kings Mountain, by Robert Campbell & 'A Letter Relative to the Battle of Kings Mountain." *American Historical Magazine*, 1:1 (January 1896), 40-47.

Reeves, Enos. "Enos Reeves Papers, 1780-1781." Library Service Center Box 1, David M. Rubenstein Rare Book & Manuscript Library, Duke University, Durham. [Online catalog description: "Incomplete journal kept in letter form. Subjects of comment include …; the battles of King's Mountain, N. C., and Yorktown, Va.; problems of discipline in the Continental Army; troop movements; social affairs; counterfeiting and the depreciation of the currency; and service in North Carolina."]

"Revolutionary Records: Some Heroes of the Battle of King's Mountain." *American Monthly Magazine* [DAR], 17:6 (December 1900), 541.

Rifles and Riflemen at the Battle of Kings Mountain. (National Park Service Popular Studies series. History, no. 12) Washington, D. C.: National Park Service, 1941. [Contains: "Kings Mountain, a Hunting Rifle Victory," by Rogers W. Young; "The American Rifle at the Battle of Kings Mountain," by C. P. Russell; "Testing the Ferguson Rifle, Modern Marksman Attains High Precision with Arm of 1776," by Dr. Alfred F. Hopkins.]

Robertson, Mason G., and June N. Stubbs. "The Strange Campbell/Shelby Controversy and the Role of John Broady at the Battle of Kings Mountain, 1780." *Smithfield Review*, 7 (2003), 27-47.

"'Rock House' Beyond Kings Mountain: The Old Battleground." *Eswau Huppeday*, 32:3 (August 2012), 132-133.

"Roster of Men Who Accompanied Colonel William Campbell to the Battle of King's Mountain, October 7th, 1780 (County Lieutenant of Washington County, Virginia; Col. Arthur Campbell, Colonel of Washington County, Va.; Col. William Campbell, Major of Militia; Major William Edmondson." *Publications of the Historical Society of Washington County, Virginia,* 3 (1939; published 1964), 23-27.

Russell, C. P. "The American Rifle at the Battle of Kings Mountain." In *Rifles and Riflemen at the Battle of Kings Mountain* (National Park Service Popular Studies series. History, no. 12) (Washington, D. C.: National Park Service, 1941), 8-18.

"Sesquicentennial Celebration Prayer, Battle of Kings Mountain, 7 October 1930." *Eswau Huppeday*, 32:3 (August 2012), 130-131.

Shackleton, Robert. "A Battle-Field That Is Seldom Visited, King's Mountain." *Magazine of History*, (July-August 1893), 38-46.

Shelby, Isaac. "Battle of Kings Mountain." Manuscript (portion of collection 00659-z, "Shelby and Hart Family Papers, 1775-1814; 1899-1900," Southern Historical Collection, The Louis Round Wilson Special Collections Library, University of North Carolina at Chapel Hill.]

Shelby, Isaac. "Battle of King's Mountain, October 7, 1780: reprinted from a Rare Tract in the Possession of the Shelby Family of Kentucky." *Magazine of American History with Notes and Queries*, 5 (1880), 351-369; reprinted in: *Recall*, 3:2 (October 1997), 7-9. [Online description from "North Carolina Periodicals Index," East Carolina University: "General Martin D. Hardin of Kentucky spoke with Isaac Shelby in 1815 and again in 1819 about the Battle of King's Mountain. The notes he took were later communicated to the *American Review* in 1848 by his son John J. Hardin and are included in this article."]

Shelby, Isaac. "Isaac Shelby Papers, 1792-1823." Manuscript (MSS2769), Manuscript Division, Madison Building, Library of Congress, Washington, D. C. [Online catalog description: "Transcript of Shelby's account (1823) of the battle of King's Mountain during the Revolution, together with letters and certificates relating to Col. William Campbell; …"]

Shelby, Isaac; William T. Graves, transc. "Col. Isaac Shelby's Account of His Exploits during the Revolutionary War." *Southern Campaigns of the American Revolution*, 2:3 (March 2005), 19-21; online: www.southerncampaign.org [annotated with footnotes]

Simpson, Elizabeth. "The Hero of Graham's Fort." *The State: Down Home in North Carolina*, 40:7 (September 1972), 8-9; online: http://digital.ncdcr.gov/cdm/ref/collection/p16062coll18/id/55470. [Online description from

"North Carolina Periodicals Index," East Carolina University: "Colonel William Graham, Cleveland County delegate to the Third and Fifth Provincial Congresses in 1775 and 1776, ran afoul of public opinion during his tenure as Commander of the South Fork militia during the Battle of King's Mountain in 1780. After leaving the area with permission to attend to his ailing wife, his successor in command, Major Chronicle, as well as eight of Graham's men, was killed in the battle. Additionally, Chronicle's replacement, Lt. Col. Frederick Hambright and eight enlisted men were seriously wounded. Graham emerged unscathed physically but was branded by some as a cowardly deserter, despite conflicting reports that he participated vigorously in the battle."]

Singleton, Lucy Ann Blanchard. "The Sword of the Lord and of Gideon!: Rallying Call for the Overmountain Victory Trail." *Daughters of the American Revolution Magazine*, 114:7 (August-September 1980), 893-896.

Smith, Ed. "…'all the rebells in hell'…" *The State: A Weekly Survey of North Carolina*, 20:15 (September 1952), 5-6; online: http://digital.ncdcr.gov/cdm/ref/collection/p16062coll18/id/29158. [Online description from "North Carolina Periodicals Index," East Carolina University: "This article discusses the Battle of King's Mountain and includes an old sketch of King's Mountain and the original marker. During a Revolutionary War battle fought on October 7, 1780, the outnumbered American forces defeated British troops on the border of North and South Carolina."]

Smith, Ed. "The Kings of King's Mountain." *The State: A Weekly Survey of North Carolina*, 22:11 (October 1954), 10-11, 26-27; online: http://digital.ncdcr.gov/cdm/ref/collection/p16062coll18/id/32588. [Online description from "North Carolina Periodicals Index," East Carolina University: "Part of the Third Red Coat Army from England, Colonel Patrick Ferguson fought and died while fighting against local militia at the Battle of King's Mountain, 7 October 1780. Scotsman, tactician, and military leader, Ferguson led some 1,000 men in battle alongside Lord Cornwallis. He is buried on King's Mountain, North Carolina."]

Souvenir Program. Sesqui-centennial Celebration. Battle of Kings Mountain. Oct. 7th, 1930, on the Battlefield in York County, South Carolina. [York, S. C.?: s. n.], 1930.

Stewart, H. Leroy. Turn of the Tide: The Battle of Kings Mountain. *Old Pendleton District Newsletter*, 13:8 (October 1999), 27-30.

Stone, Maggie H. "Joseph Greer, 'Kings Mountain Messenger:' A Tradition of the Greer Family." *Tennessee Historical Magazine*, 2:1 (March 1916), 40-42.

Summers, Lewis Preston. "An Address by L. P. Summers before the Washington County Historical Society at the court House in Abington, on October 7th, 1938, Being the 158th Anniversary of the Battle of King's Mountain, South Carolina." *Publications of the Historical Society of Washington County, Virginia,* 3 (1939; published 1964), 19-22.

Sumner, Jethro, 1733-1785. "Jethro Sumner Papers, 1780-1781." Manuscript (1937. M-343.), Manuscript Division, William L. Clements Library, University of Michigan, Ann Arbor. [Online catalog description: "The Jethro Sumner Papers contain incoming and outgoing letters relating to the progress of the Southern Campaign of the Revolutionary War, including the battles of Charlotte and King's Mountain, logistical and personnel concerns, and Sumner's resignation." The finding aid for this collection is accessible through the online catalog record.]

Swoope, Scott. "King's Mountain: A South Carolina Perspective." *Drumbeat, with Flintlock & Powderhorn: News of the Sons of Revolution*, 29:4 (Winter 2011), 13-14.

Thornton, Mary Lindsay. "The Battle of King's Mountain: A Bibliography." *North Carolina Library Bulletin*, 7 (1930), 275-276.

"Tide Begins Turning at Kings Mountain." In *South Carolina in Revolution: Conflict: Bicentennial Edition The State, Book Two – March 21, 1976* (Columbia: The State Newspaper, 1976), 36-37.

Van Blarcom, Leigh. "Document Preservation along the Overmountain Trail." *The Quarterly: A Publication of the York County Genealogical and Historical Society*, 18:1 (June 2006), 16-18.

Vance, David, and Robert Henry. "King's Mountain Expedition." *Historical Papers, Historical Society of Trinity College*, Series 3 (1899), 24-35, 78-89.

Vance, David, and Robert Henry. "Narrative of the Battle of Cowan's Ford, February 1st, 1781, by Robert Henry, and Narrative of the Battle of Kings Mountain, by Captain David Vance." Greensboro, N.C.: Reece & Elam, Printers, 1891.

Vincent, Susan Hart. *Kings Mountain National Military Park: Cultural Landscape Report.* Atlanta: Cultural Resources Division, Southeast Regional Office, National Park Service, 2003.

Walker, Melissa. *The Battles of Kings Mountain and Cowpens: The American Revolution in the Southern Backcountry.* (Critical Moments in American History series) New York: Routledge, 2013.

Warner, Mary Reid Goss, and Mary Nelson Moss White. "On Kings Mountain." *Surry County Genealogical Association Journal*, 22:1 (Spring 2002), 16-19.

"Washington Co., Va. Men at Kings Mountain." *Holston Pastfinder* [Bristol, Va.], 17:3 (March 1999), 11-13.

Whaley, Dave. "King's Mountain: Kinfolk at War." *Drumbeat, with Flintlock & Powderhorn: News of the Sons of Revolution*, 29:4 (Winter 2011), 9-12.
Webb, Edwin Yates. *The Battle of Kings Mountain: Speech of Hon. E. Y. Webb, of North Carolina, in the House of Representatives, Saturday, May 5, 1906*. Washington, D. C.: U. S. Government Printing Office, 1930.
White, Kate. "'King's Mountain Men'." *Tennessee Historical Magazine*, 8:4 (January 1925), 309-310.
White, Katherine K. *The King's Mountain Men: The Story of the Battle, with Sketches of the American Soldiers Who Took Part.* Dayton, Va.: Joseph K. Reubush Company, 1924; reprinted: Baltimore: Genealogical Publishing Company, 1966; 1970.
Wicker, Tom. "Turning Point in the Wilderness." *MHQ: The Quarterly Journal of Military History*, 11:1 (Autumn 1998), 62-71.
Williams, Mark. "Preston Goforth and the Battle of Kings Mountain: A Historical Poem." *Carologue: A Bulletin of South Carolina History*, 17:1 (Spring 2001), 13-19.
Williams, Samuel G. "Battle of King's Mountain." *Tennessee Historical Magazine*, 7:1 (April 1921), 51-66.
Williams, Samuel G. "Battle of King's Mountain as Seen by British Officers." *Tennessee Historical* Magazine, 7:1 (April 1921), 51-66; 7:2 (July 1921), 104-110; 7
"Winning the Battle of Kings Mountain, 1780." *Flintlock and Powderhorn*, 24:1 (Spring 2006).
Wood, W. J. *Battles of the Revolutionary War, 1775-1781*. Chapel Hill: Algonquin Books of Chapel Hill, 1990. [Chapter Seven: "Battle of King's Mountain."]
Yancey, Noel. "King's Mountain, Battle of." In William S. Powell, ed.; Jay Mazzocchi, assoc. ed., *Encyclopedia of North Carolina* (Chapel Hill: University of North Carolina Press in association with the University of North Carolina Library, 2006), 649-650.
Young, Rogers W. "Kings Mountain, a Hunting Rifle Victory." In *Rifles and Riflemen at the Battle of Kings Mountain* (National Park Service Popular Studies series. History, no. 12) (Washington, D. C.: National Park Service, 1941), 1-7.
Young, Rogers W. *Rifles & Riflemen at the Battle of Kings Mountain*. Washington, D. C.: National Park Service, 1941.

Skirmish at Richmond Town, October 8, 1780

"Revolutionary War Raids & Skirmishes in 1780: October 8, 1780, at Richmond Town, North Carolina." Online: http://www.myrevolutionarywar.com/battles/1780-skirmish/. [Surry County]

Skirmish at Polk's Mill, October 9, 1780

"Revolutionary War Raids & Skirmishes in 1780: October 9, 1780, at Polk's Mill, North Carolina." Online: http://www.myrevolutionarywar.com/battles/1780-skirmish/.
Williams, James H. "Battle of Polk's Mill." *Olde Mecklenburg Genealogical Society Quarterly*, 26:1 (2008), 10-13.

Skirmish at Great Swamp, November 3, 1780

"Revolutionary War Raids & Skirmishes in 1780: November 3, 1780, at Great Swamp, North Carolina." Online: http://www.myrevolutionarywar.com/battles/1780-skirmish/.

1781

North Carolina and Tennessee and the Battle of Cowpens, January 17, 1781 (fought in South Carolina)

Babits, Lawrence E. "Battle of Cowpens (17 January 1781)." In Gregory Fremont-Barnes and Richard Alan Ryerson, eds., *The Encyclopedia of the American Revolutionary War: A Political, Social and Military History* (Santa Barbara, Calif.: ABC Clio, 2006), 1:305-310.
Babits, Lawrence Edward. *Cowpens Battlefield: A Walking Guide*. Johnson City, Tenn.: Overmountain Press, 1993.
Babits, Lawrence Edward. *A Devil of a Whipping: The Battle of Cowpens*. Chapel Hill: University of North Carolina Press, 1998. [Online catalog description: "The author uses veterans' sworn pension statements, long-forgotten published accounts, and a thorough knowledge of weaponry, tactics, and the art of moving men across the landscape where they on the battlefield, when they were there, and what they saw in this minute-by-minute account of the fighting as their victory at Cowpens puts the British army on the road to the Yorktown surrender and, ultimately, clearing the way for American independence."]

Babits, Lawrence E. "Table of Organization: The American Main Line at Cowpens, 17 January 1781." *Military Collector & Historian*, 46:4 (Winter 1994), 158-162.

Bearss, Edwin C. "The Battle of Cowpens: A Documented Narrative and Troop Movement Maps." Unpublished report: Washington, D. C.: Office of Archeology and Historic Preservation, National Park Service, 1967; published: Johnson City, Tenn.: The Overmountain Press, 1996.

Binkley, Cameron. *Cowpens National Battlefield: An Administrative History*. Atlanta: Cultural Resources Stewardship, Southeast Regional Office, National Park Service, 2002.

"British Flee; Patriot Victory at Cowpens Called Tactical Masterpiece; Tarleton Humiliated by Militiamen." In *South Carolina in Revolution: Conflict: Bicentennial Edition The State, Book Two – March 21, 1976* (Columbia: The State Newspaper, 1976), [46], 47-49.

Brown, Robert Wilburn. *Kings Mountain and Cowpens: Our Victory Was Complete*. Charleston: History Press, 2009. [Contents: The beginning; Balance of forces; Turning the tide in the North; Civil war, terrain, weapons and revolutionary tactics; The South Carolina campaign; Prelude to Kings Mountain; The Battle of Kings Mountain; Aftermath of Kings Mountain; The winter of 1780-1781; Prelude to Cowpens; Double envelopment at Cowpens; Aftermath of Cowpens; Race to the Dan; Conclusion.]

Byars, Billy. "A Vignette of the Battle at Cowpens." *Upper South Carolina Genealogy & History*, 21:4 (November 2007), 140-141.

"Cow Pens." *Historical Magazine with Notes and Queries*, 2:6 (December 1867).

"Cowpens." *American Monthly Magazine* [DAR], 35:2 (August 1909), 380-383.

"Cowpens 225th Anniversary – Living History." *Southern Campaigns of the American Revolution*, 3:2.3 (February 2006), 18-23; online: www.southerncampaign.org.

Cowpens Centennial Committee. *Cowpens Centennial*. Charleston: [s. n.], 1881.

Cowpens Centennial Committee. *Daniel Morgan of New Jersey: The Hero of Saratoga* [and] *Cowpens*. Charleston, S. C.: The Committee, 1880.

Cowpens Centennial Committee. *Proceedings at the Unveiling of the Battle Monument in Spartanburg, S. C., in Commemoration of the Centennial of the Battle of Cowpens*. Charleston: The Committee, 1896.

Cowpens National Battlefield, South Carolina: on This Field on January 17, 1781, Daniel Morgan Led His Army of Tough Continentals and Backwoods Militia to a Brilliant Victory over Banastre Tarleton's Larger Force of British Regulars. [S. l.]: National Park Service, 1984.

Crawley, Ron. "Cavalry Tactical Demonstration at Cowpens." *Southern Campaigns of the American Revolution*, 3:12 (December 2006), 12; online: www.southerncampaign.org [3rd Continental Light Dragoons (reenactor group)]

Davis, Burke. *The Cowpens-Guilford Courthouse Campaign*. (Great Battles in History series) Philadelphia: Lippincott, 1962; reprinted: Philadelphia: University of Pennsylvania Press, 2003.

DePriest, Virginia Greene. "Aftermath of Cowpens." *Eswau Huppeday: Bulletin of the Broad River Genealogical Society*, 4:3 (August 1984), 197-207.

"Description of a Monument at Cowpens in 1856." *Upper South Carolina Genealogy & History*, 21:4 (November 2007), 141.

Dillion, Dorothy Vernon. "The Cowpens National Battlefield Is Established." *Daughters of the American Revolution Magazine,* 107:9 (November 1973), 850-851.

Draper, Lyman C. "Letter, Lyman C. Draper, in Madison, Wis., to J[ames] G[ettys] M[cGready] Ramsey in Knoxville, Tenn., 1880 Aug. 2." Ramsey Family. "Ramsey Family Papers, 1790-1912." Manuscript MS.0253, Box 2, folder 7 (Correspondence, 1881-1883), Special Collections Library, University of Tennessee, Knoxville; online: http://dlc.lib.utk.edu/spc/view?docId=tei/0012_000060_000472_0000/0012_000060_000472_0000.xml. [Online catalog description: "Informs J.G.M. of the writer's need for information concerning the Western part of the route of the King's Mountain men. Discussion of Tennesseans who could have been at the Cowpens."]

Draper, Lyman C. "Letter, Lyman C. Draper, in Madison, Wis., to J[ames] G[ettys] M[cGready] Ramsey in Knoxville, Tenn., 1880 Aug. 12." Ramsey Family. "Ramsey Family Papers, 1790-1912." Manuscript MS.0253, Box 2, folder 7 (Correspondence, 1881-1883), Special Collections Library, University of Tennessee, Knoxville. [Online catalog description: "Presents evidence showing that very few Tennesseans were at the Cowpens. Believes that only four Tennesseans took part and these were volunteers. Mentions that a sketch of the writer's life has just been written."]

Edgar, Walter. *Partisans and Redcoats: The Southern Conflict That Turned the Tide of the American Revolution*. New York: Perennial/Harper Collins Publishers, 2003. [Battle of Cowpens]

Extract from the Minutes of the Meeting of the Society of the Cincinnati of the State of South Carolina, Held in the City of Charleston on the 19th of April, 1897, the Anniversary of the Battle of Lexington. Charleston: Walker,

Evans & Cogswell Co., Printers, 1897. [Online catalog description: "Reproduces a letter by William A. Courtenay, chairman for the Cowpens Centennial Committee, and Capt. H.A. DeSaussure's remarks regarding the monument built by the Washington Light Infantry to commemorate the centennial of the Battle of Cowpens, S. C., of Jan. 17, 1781."]

Farley, M. Foster. "The 'Old Wagoner' and the 'Green Dragon'." [from an unknown London periodical], 1975. [A copy is located at the South Caroliniana Library, University of South Carolina, Columbia. The subjects are Daniel Morgan, Banastre Tarleton, and the Battle of Cowpens.]

Fleming, Thomas. *Cowpens: "Downright Fighting": The Story of Cowpens*. (National Parks Handbook series, no. 135) Washington, D. C.: Division of Publications, National Park Service, U. S. Department of the Interior, 1988.

Fleming, Thomas. "The Cowpens: What Attila was to his Roman enemies, Banastre Tarleton was to the American continentals - a leader feared, and rightly so. But he met his match in a Carolina backwoods pasture." *MHQ: The Quarterly Journal of Military History*, 1:4 (Summer 1989), 56-69.

Fowler, V. G. "Lieutenant Colonel John Eager Howard." Online: http://web.archive.org/web/20050404132923/http://www.nps.gov/cowp/howard.htm

Graham, James. *The Life of General Daniel Morgan, of the Virginia Line of the Army of the United States, with Portions of His Correspondence; Compiled from Original Sources*. New York: Derby & Jackson; Cincinnati: H. W. Derby & Co., 1856; reprinted: New York: Derby & Jackson, 1859; Bloomingburg, N. Y.: Zebroski Historical Services Publishing Company, 1993; online at Googlebooks.

Haines, Melissa Jean. "A British Perspective of the Aftermath of the Battle of Cowpens." Typescript (Dec. 14, 1988) in the Michael Scardaville Collection (Manuscripts P Scardaville – 1988 – Haines), Manuscripts Division, South Caroliniana Library, University of South Carolina, Columbia.

Haller, Stephen E. *William Washington: Cavalryman of the Revolution*. Bowie, Md.: Heritage Books, 2001.

Harris, Joe. "SAR's Mark Battle of Cowpens, South Carolina." *SAR Magazine*, 100:4 (Spring 2006), 22-23.

The Hero of Cowpens: A Centennial Sketch. New York: A. S. Barnes, 1881. [Daniel Mogan]

Historical Statements Concerning the Battle of Kings Mountain and the Battle of Cowpens, South Carolina. (70th Congress, 1st Session, House Document 328) Washington, D. C.: U. S. Government Printing Office, 1928.

History of Cowpens: Cowpens, South Carolina. [S. l.]: Inter-Collegiate Press, 1982.

Hughes, Nathaniel C., Jr. "Cowpens, Battle of." In William S. Powell, ed.; Jay Mazzocchi, assoc. ed., *Encyclopedia of North Carolina* (Chapel Hill: University of North Carolina Press in association with the University of North Carolina Library, 2006), 308-309.

Intelligence from the South: Major Giles, Aide-de-Camp to General Morgan, Passed through This Place Yesterday Morning with the Following Intelligence." Richmond, Va.: [s. n.], 1781; electronically published: (Early American Imprints, First Series, no. 43984) Chester, Vt.: Readex, a Division of Newsbank, 2002-2004. ["Reporting the defeat of Tarleton's forces at Cowpens."]

"John Savage Fired First Shot at Battle of Cowpens; Descendant Dr. J. H. Saye Proud in 1899." *Broad River Journal*, 12:4 (September 2004),

Kennedy, Fronde. "Fronde Kennedy Papers, 1841-1930." Manuscript collection (Manuscripts Annex), South Caroliniana Library, University of South Carolina, Columbia. [Includes: "biographical sketch of Mrs. Fannie Monroe, whose father fought at Cowpens during the American Revolution."]

"Kings Mountain and Cowpens Newspaper Excerpts, 1871-1908." *York County Genealogical and Historical Society Quarterly*, 18:2 (September 2006),

Lampman, Charles R. "The Battle of Cowpens, South Carolina." *SAR Magazine*, 100:3 (Winter 2006), 4-7.

M'Conkey, Rebecca. *The Hero of Cowpens: A Centennial Sketch*. New York: A. S. Barnes, 1881. [Daniel Morgan (1736-1802)]

Manning, Sam Philips. "Samuel P. Manning Papers, 1937-1996." Manuscript collection (South Carolina Political Collections), Manuscripts Division, South Caroliniana Library, University of South Carolina, Columbia. [This collection illustrates Manning's work while a member of the South Carolina House to commemorate events in South Carolina history and particularly the Battle of Cowpens.]

McConkey, Rebecca. *The Hero of Cowpens: A Revolutionary Sketch*. Rev. ed. New York: Funk & Wagnalls, 1885.

McIntyre, Debby. "The Revolutionary War Battle of Cowpens." *Essau Huppeday*, 33:2 (May 2013).

Miller, Mary Montgomery. "Kate Barry." *Daughters of the American Revolution Magazine*, 118:11 (November 1984), 644-646. [her contribution to the Battle of Cowpens]

Moncure, John. *The Cowpens Staff Ride and Battlefield Tour*. Fort Leavenworth, Kans.: U. S. Army Command and General Staff College, 1996.

Montross, Lynn. "America's Most Imitated Battle: At Cowpens, Dan Morgan Showed How Militia Can Be Used: The Formula Worked in Three Later Fights." *American Heritage*, 7:3 (April 1956), 34-37, 100-101.

Moss, Bobby Gilmer. *The Patriots at the Cowpens*. Greenville, S. C.: A Press, 1985; rev. ed.: Blacksburg, S. C.: Scotia-Hibernia Press, 1991.

Murphey, Daniel. "The Cavalry at Cowpens." *Southern Campaigns of the American Revolution*, 3:2.3 (February 2006), 23-28; online: www.southerncampaign.org.

Myers, Theodorus Bailey. *Cowpens Papers, Being Correspondence of General Morgan and the Prominent Actors; from the Collection of Theodorus Myers. Contributed to the Centennial Celebration, May 11th, 1881. First Published in the News and Courier, Charleston, S. C., 1881*. Charleston: News and Courier Book Press, 1881.

Myers, Theodorus Bailey. *One Hundred Years Ago. The Story of the Battle of Cowpens. The Carolinas in 1780; A Glance at the Military Situation - Morgan's Command – The Chain of Events as Shown in Letters of Greene, Morgan, Pickens, Rutledge and Others, Hitherto Unpublished.* Charleston: News and Courier, May 10, 1881.

Nelson, Anson. "Letter, Anson Nelson in Nashville, Tenn., to J[ames] G[ettys] M[cGready] Ramsey in Knoxville, Tenn., 1880 March 18 Ramsey Family. "Ramsey Family Papers, 1790-1912." Manuscript MS.0253, Box 2, folder 7 (Correspondence, 1881-1883), Special Collections Library, University of Tennessee, Knoxville; online: http://dlc.lib.utk.edu/spc/view?docId=tei/0012_000060_000473_0000/0012_000060_000473_0000.xml.

O'Hara, Geoffrey, and Harry Russell Wilkins. *Cowpens Battleground: A Song*. Spartanburg: Cowpens Chapter, South Carolina Daughters of the American Revolution, 1947.

"Patriot Minorities at the Battle of Cowpens." Online: http://web.archive.org/web/20060106210720/http://www.nps.gov/cowp/minority.htm.

Peay, [Lila Augusta] (Mrs. George Keats Peay). "Battle of Cowpens." *American Monthly Magazine* [DAR], 21:3 (September 1902), 197-205.

Perry, Benjamin Franklin. *An Address, Delivered at the Celebration of the 54th Anniversay of the Battle of the Cowpens, on the Battle Ground, in Spartanburgh District, S. C., January 17, 1835*. Greenville, S. C.: Printed at the Mountaineer Office, 1835.

Rankin, Hugh F. "Cowpens: Prelude to Yorktown." *North Carolina Historical Review*, 31:3 (July 1954), 336-369.

Pugh, Robert Coplin. "The Cowpens Campaign and the American Revolution." Ph. D. thesis, University of Illinois, 1951.

Rankin, Hugh F. *Greene and Cornwallis: The Campaign in the Carolinas* (North Carolina Bicentennial Pamphlet series, no. 10) Raleigh: North Carolina Department of Cultural Resources, Division of Archives and History, 1976. [Covers the Battle of Cowpens, 1781.]

"The Revolutionary War Battle of (the) Cowpens." *Tennessee Rifleman*, 40:4 (Fall 1999), 1064.

Roberts, Kenneth Lewis. "900 Men Who Shook and Empire." *Collier's*, 138:4 (August 17, 1956), 58-67.

Roberts, Kenneth Lewis. *The Battle of Cowpens: The Great Morale-Builder*. Garden City, N. Y.: Doubleday, 1957; reprinted: Philadelphia: Eastern Acorn Press, 1989. [novel]

Rockwell, E[lijah] F[rink]. "The Battle of Cow-Pens." *Historical Magazine with Notes and Queries*, 2d series, 2 (December 1867), 356-358.

"SCSSAR Marks 231st Anniversary of Victory at Cowpens." Palmetto Patriot: South Carolina Society Sons of the American Revolution, 2012:1 (Spring 2012), 16; online: http://www.scssar.org.

Shackelton, Robert. "Hannah's Cowpens: A Battle Field of the Revolution." *Magazine of American History*, 30:3-14 (1893), 207-213.

Singleton, William N. "Cowpens: 'The Patriots Best-Fought Battle'." *Daughters of the American Revolution Magazine*, 111:5 (May 1977), 472-481.

Smith, Mrs. William H. "Cowpens." *American Monthly Magazine* [DAR], 35:2 (August 1909), 380-383.

Swager, Christine R; John Robertson, illus. *Come to the Cow Pens! The Story of the Battle of Cowpens*. Spartenburg, S. C.: Hub City Writers Project, 2002. [Contents: Scots-Irish settlement; Come to the cow pens; Major General Nathaniel Greene; Brigadier General Daniel Morgan; Adversaries; The militia; The battle; The chase; The aftermath.]

Swisher, James K. "Duel in the Backwoods." *Military Heritage*, 4:3 (2002), 50-57, 96-97.

United States. Congress. House. Committee on Military Affairs. Subcommittee No. 6. *National Military Park at Cowpens Battle Ground. Hearings before the Committee on Military Affairs, House of Representatives, Sixty-Ninth Congress, First Session, on H.R. 4532. February 24, 1926. Statements of Hon. Wm. F. Stevenson, of South Carolina, Hon. John J. McSwain of South Carolina, and a Committee of Citizens of South Carolina.* Washington, D. C.: Government Printing Office, 1926.

United States. Congress. House. Committee on Military Affairs. *To Create a National Military Park at Cowpens Battle Ground, March 29, 1926. Mr. McSwain, from the Committee of Military Affairs, Submitted the Following Report (to Accompany H. R. 4532.* Washington, D. C.: U. S. Government Printing Office, 1926

Walker, Melissa. *The Battles of Kings Mountain and Cowpens: The American Revolution in the Southern Backcountry.* (Critical Moments in American History series) New York: Routledge, 2013.

Withrow, Scott. "The Battle of Cowpens." Online: http://web.archive.org/web/20060108161104/http://www.nps.gov/cowp/batlcowp.htm.

Withrow, Scott. "The Southern Campaign: Cowpens in the Context of Other Battles in the South." Online: http://web.archive.org/web/20050922045939/http://www.nps.gov/cowp/socampn.htm.

Wood, James W. *Cowpens Hero.* Spartanburg, S. C.: Wofford Library Press, 1970. [Daniel Morgan, 1736-1802]

Zollars, Malvine L. B. "Buried Treasure." *Cornerstone Clues* [Waynesburg, Pa.], 24:4 (November 1999), 94-95. [Cowpens and Guilford Courthouse]

British Capture and Occupation of Wilmington, January 28-29 or February 1-November 18, 1781

"Revolutionary War Raids & Skirmishes in 1781: February 1 (also given as 28-29 January)-November 18-1781, at Wilmington, New Hanover County, N. C." Online: http://www.myrevolutionarywar.com/battles/1781-skirmish/.

Skirmish at Heron Bridge, January 30, 1781

Hall, Wes. "An Underwater Archaeological Survey of Heron's Colonial Bridge Crossing Site over the Northeast Cape Fear River near Castle Hayne, North Carolina." M. A. thesis, East Carolina University, 1992.

"Revolutionary War Raids & Skirmishes in 1781: January 30, at Heron Bridge, North Carolina." Online: http://www.myrevolutionarywar.com/battles/1781-skirmish/.

Battle of Cowan's Ford, February 1, 1781

Anthony, Mark. "SCSSAR Represented at Cowan's Ford Ceremony." *Palmetto Patriot: South Carolina Society Sons of the American Revolution,* 2009:1 (Spring 2009), 12; online: http://www.scssar.org.

"Battle of Cowan's Ford." *Southern Campaigns of the American Revolution*, 3:2.3 (February 2006), 2; online: http://southerncampaign.org/newsletter/v3n2.pdf. [Image of the David Teague painting of the battle.]

"Battle of Cowan's Ford, February 1, 1781, at Huntersville, Lincoln and Mecklenburg County Border, North Carolina (aka McCowan's Ford)." Online: http://www.myrevolutionarywar.com/battles/810201-cowans-ford/.

"Battle of Cowan's Ford, February 1, 1781, Mecklenburg County, NC." Online: http://www.benjamincleveland chapter.org/cowensford.html.

Cross, Jerry L. "Cowan's Ford, Battle of." In William S. Powell, ed.; Jay Mazzocchi, assoc. ed., *Encyclopedia of North Carolina* (Chapel Hill: University of North Carolina Press in association with the University of North Carolina Library, 2006), 308.

Crow, Judson. "The Battle of Cowan's Ford." *Olde Mecklenburg Genealogical Society Quarterly*, 12:4 (1994), 6-13; 13:1 (1995), 26-35.

Graham, Joseph. "Sketch of the Vicinity of Beaties and Cowans Fords on the Cataba River and Position of the American and British Forces..., [1781], 1820-1821." Manuscript, MC.175.1821g, State Archives of North Carolina, Raleigh. [Online catalog description: "This map was prepared by Joseph Graham (1759-1836) to accompany his account of Revolutionary War military action in western North Carolina. The map portrays the location of the Battle of Cowans Ford fought on February 1, 1781 between the British under Lord Cornwallis and the American forces consisting of North Carolina militia led by General William Lee Davidson. In addition to the camps and positions of both armies, roads and residences are also shown."]

Graham, W. A. "The Battle of Cowan's Ford - The Passage of the Catawba River by Lord Cornwallis, February 1, 1781." *North Carolina Booklet*, 5 (1906), 232-246.

Henry, Robert, and David Vance, *Narrative of the Battle of Cowan's Ford, February 1st, 1781, by Robert Henry, and Narrative of the Battle of King's Mountain, by Captain David Vance. Manuscript Preserved by Robert Henry, Esq. Published by D. Schenck, Sr.* Greensboro, N. C.: Reece & Elam, Printers, for D. Schenck, Sr., 1891. [Robert Henry, 1765-1863; David Vance, 1745?-1813]

Lawrence, R. C. "Gen. William Lee Davidson." *The State: A Weekly Survey of North Carolina*, 14:7 (July 1946), 9, 18; online: http://digital.ncdcr.gov/cdm/ref/collection/p16062coll18/id/15813. [Online description from "North

Carolina Periodicals Index," East Carolina University: "Davidson was an outstanding soldier/patriot during the Revolutionary War. He was killed at the Battle of Cowan's Ford, February 1, 1781, at age 35."]

Misenheimer, John E. "Battle of Cowan's Ford: Important to American Victory." *Olde Mecklenburg Genealogical Society Quarterly*, 21:2 (2003), 19-22.

Misenheimer, John E., Jr. "The Battles of Cowpens and Cowan's Ford." *The Golden Nugget (Cabarrus Genealogical Society)*, 13:2 (Summer 2005), 46-53.

Reuwer, David P. "The Battle of Cowan's Ford – Trouble in Their Rear." *Southern Campaigns of the American Revolution*, 3:2.3 (February 2006), 3-4; online: www.southerncampaign.org.

"Revolutionary Records: Patriots in the Battle of Cowan's Ford." *American Monthly Magazine* [DAR], 17:4 (December 1900), 541.

Stedman, Charles. "Sketch of the Catawba River at McCowans Ford, [1781], 1794." Manuscript, MC.175.1794s, State Archives of North Carolina, Raleigh. [Online catalog description: "This map was engraved for publication in Charles Stedman, History of the American War (London, 1794). It portrays the location of the battle of Cowans Ford on the Catawba River (now under the waters of Lake Norman) fought on February 1, 1781 between British forces under Lord Cornwallis and North Carolina militia commanded by General William Lee Davidson. The positions and routes of the British and American troops are shown."]

Stonestreet, O. C., IV. *The Battle of Cowan's Ford: General Davidson's Stand on the Catawba River and Its Place in North Carolina History*. [United States]: Createspace Publishing, 2012. [Local Patriot militia under the command of Brigadier General William Lee Davidson clash with the British forces under Lord Charles Cornwallis along the banks of the Catawba River in the early morning hours of Feb.1st, 1781.]

Skirmish at Tarrant's Tavern, February 1, 1781

"Revolutionary War Raids & Skirmishes in 1781: February 1, 1781 at Tarrant's Tavern (Torrence's Tavern), Mecklenburg County, North Carolina." Online: http://www.myrevolutionarywar.com/battles/1781-skirmish/.

Stonestreet, O. C., IV. *A Quick and Bloody Affair: The Shirmish at Torrence's Tavern.* [United States: O. C. Stonestreet, 2014.

Battle of Trading Ford, February 2-3, 1781, Yadkin River Crossing between Rowan and Davidson Counties

Brownlee, Ann. "Fateful Day at Trading Ford." *Salisbury Post,* (February 6, 2005); online: http://www.trading-ford.org/fateful.html.

"Trading Ford Area Recognized in Report to Congress as At-Risk Site." *The Dispatch: Davidson County's New Source*, (June 17, 2008); online: http://www.the-dispatch.com/article/20080617/NEWS/806170303?p=1&tc=pg.

Skirmish at Grant's Creek, Rowan County, February 6, 1781

"Revolutionary War Raids & Skirmishes in 1781: February 6, 1781 at Grant's Creek, Rowan County, North Carolina." Online: http://www.myrevolutionarywar.com/battles/1781-skirmish/.

Battle of Shallow Ford, February 7, 1781

Ashe, S. A. "The Battle of Shallow Ford." *Tylers Quarterly Historical and Genealogical Magazine*, 9 (July 1927), 48-51.

North Carolina. General Assembly. "[Document dated:] January-February 1781: Joint Papers, Committee Papers, Resolutions, Senate Bills, House Bills, Joint Papers: Miscellaneous Accounts, Certificates, Bonds, and Letters." Manuscript; General Assembly Record Group; Session Records, January-February 1781, Box 1 (MARS ID: 66.8.23.6), State Archives of North Carolina, Raleigh. [Online catalog description shows that this collection includes: "…a letter to the speakers from Martin Armstrong, of Surry County, describing the conduct of the insurgents following their defeat at Shallow Ford;…"]

"Revolutionary War Raids & Skirmishes in 1781: February 7, 1781 at Shallow Ford, Forsyth County, North Carolina." Online: http://www.myrevolutionarywar.com/battles/1781-skirmish/.

Battle of Brice's Crossroads, February 12, 1781

Barefoot, Daniel W. "Bruce's Cross Roads, Battle of." In William S. Powell, ed.; Jay Mazzocchi, assoc. ed., *Encyclopedia of North Carolina* (Chapel Hill: University of North Carolina Press in association with the University of North Carolina Library, 2006), 151-152.

Buchanan, John. *The Road to Guilford Courthouse: The American Revolution in the Carolinas*. New York: John Wiley, 1996.

Butler, Lindley S. "New Garden, Battle of." In William S. Powell, ed.; Jay Mazzocchi, assoc. ed., *Encyclopedia of North Carolina* (Chapel Hill: University of North Carolina Press in association with the University of North Carolina Library, 2006), 791-792. [1781]

Caruthers, Eli Washington. *Revolutionary Incidents and Sketches of Character Chiefly in the Old North State*. Philadelphia: Hayes & Zell, 1854.

Historic Summerfield, North Carolina. Online: http://www.summerfieldgov.com/vertical/sites/%7BC25D1811-CF89-415D-A5B8-0412F39A34CB%7D/uploads/%7BA3831436-02A5-479F-9620-514CA44DBDF%7D.PDF.

Hoskins, Joseph A. "Bruce's Cross Roads." *North Carolina Booklet*, 19:1-2 (July-October 1919), 51-54.

"Revolutionary War Raids & Skirmishes in 1781: February 11 (also given as 13), 1781 at Bruce's Crossroads (aka Gillies' Death, Reedy Fork, and Summerfield, Guilford County, North Carolina." Online: http://www.myrevolutionarywar.com/battles/1781-skirmish/.

Skirmish on the Road to Dix's Ferry, February 13, 1781

"Revolutionary War Raids & Skirmishes in 1781: February 13, 1781, on the Road to Dix's Ferry in Rockingham County, North Carolina." Online: http://www.myrevolutionarywar.com/battles/1781-skirmish/.

Skirmish at Hart's Mill, February 17, 1781

Bright, Jeffrey G., and Stewart E. Dunaway. *Like a Bear with His Stern in a Corner: The NC Campaign during the American Revolution: The Battles of Hart's Mill, Pyle's Defeat, Clapp's Mill, Weitzel's Mill*. Hillsborough: North Carolina Historical Books, 2009.

"Revolutionary War Raids & Skirmishes in 1781: February 7, 1781 at Shallow Ford, Forsyth County, North Carolina." Online: http://www.myrevolutionarywar.com/battles/1781-skirmish/.

Pyle's Massacre/Battle of Pyle's Defeat/Pyle's Hacking Match/Battle of Haw River, February 24, 1781

"The Battle of Haw River, February 25, 1781 at the Haw River, Alamance County, North Carolina (aka Pyle's Defeat, also Pyles' Massacre." Online: http://www.myrevolutionarywar.com/battles/810225-haw-river/.

Bright, Jeffrey G., and Stewart E. Dunaway. *Like a Bear with His Stern in a Corner: The NC Campaign during the American Revolution: The Battles of Hart's Mill, Pyle's Defeat, Clapp's Mill, Weitzel's Mill*. Hillsborough: North Carolina Historical Books, 2009.

Dunaway, Stewart, and Jeff Bright. *Pyle's Defeat: The Most Comprehensive Guide: Case Closed*. [North Carolina: J. Bright and S. Dunaway; Morrisville, N.C.: Distributed by Lulu], 2011.

McGowan, Molly. "History, Revised: State Corrects Alamance County Revolutionary War Marker." *The Times-News*, April 26, 2013; online: http://www.thetimesnews.com/news/top-news/history-revised-state-corrects-alamance-county-revolutionary-war-marker-1.134549. [Pyle's Defeat marker]

McLeod, Marshall W. "Henry Lee and the Pyle Massacre." *Northern Neck of Virginia Historical Magazine*, 33:1 (December 1983), 3796-3823. [John Pyle, d. 1781; Pyle's Massacre, February 1781, North Carolina]

Piecuch, Jim. "'Light Horse Harry' Lee and Pyle's Massacre." *Journal of the American Revolution*, 1 (2013), 188-197.

Troxler, Carole W. *Pyle's Defeat: Deception at the Racepath*. Graham, N. C.: Alamance County Historical Association, 2003. [near Burlington, N. C.]

Troxler, George. *Pyle's Massacre: February 23, 1781*. Burlington: Alamance County Historical Association, 1973.

Battle of Clapp's Mills/Alamance Creek, March 2, 1781

"The Battle of Clapp's Mills, March 2, 1781, at Clapp's Mills, Alamance County, North Carolina (aka Alamance Creek)." Online: http://www.myrevolutionarywar.com/battles/810302-clapps-mills/.

Bright, Jeffrey G. *Clapp's Mill: The Battle on Foust Plantation*. [Morrisville, N. C.: Lulu.com], 2013.

Bright, Jeffrey G., and Stewart E. Dunaway. *Like a Bear with His Stern in a Corner: The NC Campaign during the American Revolution: The Battles of Hart's Mill, Pyle's Defeat, Clapp's Mill, Weitzel's Mill.* Hillsborough: North Carolina Historical Books, 2009.

Clapp, Steve. "Battle of Clapp's Mill." Online: http://www.steveclapp.com/places/ClappMill.htm.

Graham, Joseph. "Scetch [*sic*] of the Ground and Position of the British and Americans at the Battle Near Claps Mill Fought on the 1st. Day of March 1781, [1781], 1820-1821." Manuscript, MC.175.1820g, State Archives of North Carolina, Raleigh. [Online catalog description: "This map was prepared by Joseph Graham (1759-1836) to accompany his account of Revolutionary War military action in western North Carolina. The map portrays the location of the battle of Clapp's Mill fought in Chatham County on March 2, 1781 and shows the positions of Colonel Banastre Tarleton's British forces and the American troops under the command of Colonel Henry Lee."]

"Revolutionary War Raids & Skirmishes in 1781: March 3, 1781, at Alamance River, Alamance County, North Carolina." Online: http://www.myrevolutionarywar.com/battles/1781-skirmish/.

"A Short Note on Clapp's Mill: Prelude to the Battle of Weitzel's Mill." Online: http://blog.tradingpath.org/ Steele, Rollin M., Jr. *The Lost Battle of the Alamance Also Known as the Battle of Clapp's Mill: A Turning Point in North Carolina's Struggle with Their British Invaders in the Very Unuual Year of 1781.* 3rd printing: Burlington: Powell Enterprises, 1999.

Steele, R. M., and Pat Bailey. "Clapps' Mill, Battle of." In William S. Powell, ed.; Jay Mazzocchi, assoc. ed., *Encyclopedia of North Carolina* (Chapel Hill: University of North Carolina Press in association with the University of North Carolina Library, 2006), 241. [1781]

"Tarleton's Mistake," March 3-4 or 4-5, 1781

"Revolutionary War Raids & Skirmishes in 1781: March 3-4 (possibly 4-5), 1781 ("Tarleton's Mistake, and Tory Cattle Drovers); location uncertain but possibly Alamance and Orange County, North." Online: http://www.myrevolutionarywar.com/battles /1781-skirmish/.

Battle of Wetzell's/Weitzell's Mill, March 6, 1781

"The Battle of Wetzell's Mill, March 6, 1781." Online: http://www.carolana.com/NC/Revolution/revolution_battle_of_weitzells_mill.html.

Bright, Jeffrey G., and Stewart E. Dunaway. *Like a Bear with His Stern in a Corner: The NC Campaign during the American Revolution: The Battles of Hart's Mill, Pyle's Defeat, Clapp's Mill, Weitzel's Mill.* Hillsborough: North Carolina Historical Books, 2009.

Buchanan, John. *The Road to Guilford Courthouse: The American Revolution in the Carolinas*. New York: John Wiley & Sons, 1997.

Hairr, John. "Wetzell's Mill, Battle of." In William S. Powell, ed.; Jay Mazzocchi, assoc. ed., *Encyclopedia of North Carolina* (Chapel Hill: University of North Carolina Press in association with the University of North Carolina Library, 2006), 1192-1193; online: http://ncpedia.org/wetzells-mill-battle.

Haynes, Kenneth R., Jr. "The Race to Weitzel's Mill, 6 March 1781." *Gorget & Sash: Journal of the Early Modern Warfare Society*, 3:1 (n. d.), 1-14.

Pancake, John S. *This Destructive War: The British Campaign in the Carolinas, 1780-1782*. Tuscaloosa, Ala.: The University of Alabama Press, 1985.

Scotti, Anthony J. *Brutal Virtue: The Myth and Reality of Banastre Tarleton*. Westminster, Md.: Heritage Books, 2002.

"Some Notes on the Battle of Weitzel's Mill, March 6th, 1781." Online: http://blog.tradingpath.org/2013/03/some-notes-on-battle-at-weitzels-mill-v.html.

Skirmish at Heron's Bridge, March 9, 1781

"Revolutionary War Raids & Skirmishes in 1781: March 9, 1781, Heron's Bridge, Pender County, North Carolina." Online: http://www.myrevolutionarywar.com/battles/1781-skirmish/.

Skirmish at South Buffalo Creek, March 12, 1781

"Revolutionary War Raids & Skirmishes in 1781: March 12, 1781, South Buffalo Creek, Guilford County, North Carolina." Online: http://www.myrevolutionarywar.com/battles/1781-skirmish/.

Battle of New Garden Meetinghouse, March 15, 1781

"The Battle of New Garden Meetinghouse, March 15, 1781, at the New Garden Meeting House, Guilford County, North Carolina." Online: http://www.myrevolutionarywar.com/battles/810315-newgarden-meetinghouse/.

Newlin, Algie Innman. *The Battle of New Garden*. Greensboro: North Carolina Friends Historical Society, 1977; reprinted: Greensboro: Thomson-Shore, 1995.

Battle of Guilford Courthouse, March 15, 1781

Alderman, Edwin Anderson, and C. F Thomas. *An Address, Delivered Oct. 15th, 1892, Greensboro, N. C. at the Guilford Battle Ground, on the Occasion of the Dedication of the Monument to the Maryland Soldiers*. Greensboro, N. C.: C. F. Thomas, Book and Job Printer, for the Guilford Battle Ground Co., 1893.

Babits, Lawrence E., and Joshua B. Howard. *Long, Obstinate, and Bloody: The Battle of Guilford Courthouse*. Chapel Hill: University of North Carolina Press, 2009. [Publisher's description: "On March 15, 1781, the armies of Nathanael Greene and Lord Charles Cornwallis fought one of the bloodiest and most intense engagements of the American Revolution at Guilford Courthouse in piedmont North Carolina. In *Long, Obstinate, and Bloody*, the first book-length examination of the Guilford Courthouse engagement, Lawrence E. Babits and Joshua B. Howard piece together what really happened on the wooded plateau in what is today Greensboro, North Carolina, and identify where individuals stood on the battlefield, when they were there, and what they could have seen, thus producing a new bottom-up story of the engagement."]

Baker, Thomas. *Another Such Victory:The Story of the American Defeat at Guilford Courthouse That Helped Win the War for Independence*. National Park Service Publication, Eastern Acorn Press, 1999.

Baker, Thomas E. "The Battle of Guilford Courthouse." *Tar Heel Junior Historian*, 20:2 (Winter 1981), 21-24.

Baker, Thomas E. *The Monuments at Guilford Courthouse National Military Park, North Carolina*. Pamphlet. Greensboro, N. C.: Guilford Courthouse National Military Park, 1979. [Martha Bell (1735-1820?), spy]

Bartholomees, James Boone, Jr. "Fight or Flee: The Combat Performance of the North Carolina Militia in the Cowpens-Guilford Courthouse Campaign, January to March 1781." Ph. D. Dissertation, Duke University, 1978.

"The Battle of Guilford Courthouse." *Daughters of the American Revolution Magazine*, 70:9 (September 1936), 928.

The Battle of Guilford Courthouse, 1781-1981. [Washington, D. C.: National Park Service? 1981.]

The Battle-Ground Oak, Revolutionary Battlefield, March 15, 1781. Greensboro: Greensboro, N. C. Chamber of Commerce, [s. d.]

Boynton, Henry Van. *Oration by Gen. H. V. Boynton, Delivered at Guilford Battle Ground, July 4, 1900*. Greensboro: Guilford Battle Ground Company, 1900.

Bradshaw, G[eorge] S[amuel]. *Mrs. Kerenhappuch Turner, A Heroine of 1776: An Address by* G.S. *Bradshaw, Esq., on Occasion of the Unveiling of a Monument to Her Memory, at the Guilford Battle Ground, July 4th, 1902*. Greensboro, N. C.: Guilford Battle Ground Company, 1902. [The Maryland mother of Revolutionary War soldiers, her travel to North Carolina to nurse the wounded after the Battle of Guilford Courthouse, and the statue erected to her at this even in 1902.]

"British Memorial Monument, Guilford Courthouse National Military Park, Greensboro, North Carolina." *Southern Campaigns of the American Revolution*, 4:1 (January-March 2007), 22; online: www.southerncampaigns.org.

Browning, R. Getty. "The Battle of Guilford C. H." *The State: A Weekly Survey of North Carolina*, 8:17 (September 1940), 10-11; online: http://digital.ncdcr.gov/cdm/ref/collection/p16062coll18/id/6122. [Online description from "North Carolina Periodicals Index," East Carolina University: "Browning says there are many erroneous statements made about the famous conflict at the Guilford Courthouse, but to the contrary, the North Carolina troops gave an excellent attempt to obey instructions to try and annihilate the British troops."]

Buchanan, John. *The Road to Guilford Courthouse: The American Revolution in the Carolinas*. New York: Wiley, 1997. [Contents: 1. The Battle of Sullivan's Island; 2. The Rice Kings; 3. Southern Strategy; 4. The Approach March; 5. Charleston Besieged; 6. The Rise of Banastre Tarleton; 7. Into the Back Country; 8. Hearts and Minds; 9. Trouble in the Back Country; 10. More Trouble in the Back Country; 11. A Hero Takes Charge; 12. The Battle of Camden; 13. The Partisans Fight On; 14. The Rise of Patrick Ferguson; 15. To Catch Ferguson; 16. King's Mountain; 17. Retreat and Turmoil; 18. A General from Rhode Island; 19. The Stage is Set; 20. Tarleton Pursues Morgan; 21. Cowpens; 22. Bayonets and Zeal; 23. Patience and Finesse; 24. Guilford Courthouse: "Long, Obstinate, and Bloody".]

Byrd, Clara Booth. "The Battle of Guilford Courthouse." *Daughters of the American Revolution Magazine*, 84:8 (August 1950), 655-656.

Chastellux, François Jean, Marquis de, 1734-1788. "Extract from 'Travels in North America, in the years 1780, 1781, and 1782' [manuscript] 1924." Manuscript MSS 10616-d, Special Collections, University of Virginia Library, Charlottesville. [Online catalog description: "The typed extract relates the visit of the Marquis de Chastellux to David Steele, Revolutionary War soldier. Chastellux tells of seeing the bone fragment sabered from Steele's head by a British soldier at the battle of Guilford Courthouse, March 15, 1781."]

Chastellux, Francois Jean, Marquis de, 1734-1788. *Travels in North America in the Years 1780-1781-1782.* London: G. G. J. and J. Robinson, 1787; reprinted: Dublin: Printed for Messrs. Colles, Moncrieffe, White, H. Whitestone, Byrne [and 4 others in Dublin], 1787; Jamaica, N. Y.: White, Gallaher & White, 1827.

Cissna, Bill. "History on the March." *Our State: Down Home in North Carolina*, 73:10 (March 2006), 34-36, 38-39; online: http://digital.ncdcr.gov/cdm/ref/collection/p16062coll18/id/85697. [Online description from "North Carolina Periodicals Index," East Carolina University: "Reenactments of battles gained popularity when the United States celebrated its 1976 bicentennial. Reenactments started for the Battle of Guilford Courthouse in Greensboro in 1981. In March 2006, the 225th anniversary of the battle will take place with a variety of activities, including the reenactment. Cissna discusses the battle and talks with a number of reenactors."]

Corbitt, D. L. "Battle near Guilford Court House." *North Carolina Historical Review,* 4:2 (April 1927), 213.

Corbitt, D. L. "The Rebel Army Routed at Guilford." *North Carolina Historical Review*, 3:1 (January 1926), 131.

Cox, Edwin, III. "The Battle of Guilford Courthouse and Some of Its Lessons." *Flintlock and Powderhorn: Magazine of the Sons of the Revolution*, 6:2 (September 1988), 13-19.

Daniel, Jim. "History of the Battle of Guilford Courthouse." Online: http://www.6nc.org/history-of-the-battle-of-guilford-courthouse/.

Daniels, Dennis. "Guilford Courthouse National Military Park: The Early Years with a Concentration on 1930s and 40s." M. A. thesis, University of North Carolina-Greensboro, 1994.

Daves, Edward Graham. *Maryland and North Carolina in the Campaign of 1780-1781, with a Preliminary Notice of the Earlier Battles of the Revolution, in Which the Troops of the Two States Won Distinction.* Baltimore: John Murphy, 1893.

Davis, Burke. "Cornwallis Slept Here." *The State: A Weekly Survey of North Carolina*, 19:48 (April 1952), 3, 12; online: http://digital.ncdcr.gov/cdm/ref/collection/p16062coll18/id/28530. [Online description from "North Carolina Periodicals Index," East Carolina University: "A Tar Heel author enjoys the ghosts, wasps, and tourists which infest the old Guilford battleground home."]

Davis, Burke. *Cowpens-Guilford Courthouse Campaign*. Philadelphia: Lippincott, 1962; reprinted: Philadelphia: University of Pennsylvania Press, 2003.

Davis, Burke. "From 1 to 3 p. m." *The State: Down Home in North Carolina*, 23:5 (July 1955), 13, 60; online: http://digital.ncdcr.gov/cdm/ref/collection/p16062coll18/id/81776. [Online description from "North Carolina Periodicals Index," East Carolina University: "The Southern campaign of the American Revolution came to a climax in Guilford County on March 15, 1781. Some 4,000 Americans, under the command of Nathanael Greene, waited as Lord Cornwallis approached from the west. Although some men ran from their lines, others fought hard to drive down the British ranks, who continued to push forward despite flanks of riflemen. The men often fought hand-to-hand, but Cornwallis gained the ground, losing many of his own men in the battle. Despite controversy over those who ran, a monument stands to one of the brave, Peter Francisco, at Guilford Battleground."]

Davis, Curtis Carroll. "The Tribulations of Mrs. Turner: An Episode after Guilford Court House." *Maryland Historical Magazine*, 76:4 (Winter 1981), 376-379. [Kerenhappuch Norman Turner mother of Revolutionary soldiers from Maryland, her trip to nurse the wounded following the Battle of Guilford Courthouse in North Carolina, and the statue erected to her in 1902.]

Dunkerly, Robert M. "Prelude to Guilford Courthouse." *Southern Campaigns of the American Revolution*, 3:3 (March 2006), 34-43; online: http://southerncampaign.org/newsletter/v3n3.pdf.

Elam, Harper J. *A Sketch of the Battle of Guilford Court House*. Greensboro: H. J. Elam; Thomas, Reece & Company, 1887.

Elzemeyer, Mary Vanstory. "Historic Carolina Trees." *The State: A Weekly Survey of North Carolina*, 10:33 (January 1943), 4-5; online: http://digital.ncdcr.gov/cdm/ref/collection/p16062coll18/id/16633. [Online description from "North Carolina Periodicals Index," East Carolina University: "There are quite a number of historic trees which are associated with important historical events during the early history of North Carolina and they are found in all sections of the State. Outstanding among them are three which are located at the Guilford Battleground, formerly known as Guilford Courthouse, near Greensboro."]

Erection of Monument to Commemorate the Battle of Guilford Courthouse, N. C., and in Memory of Maj. Gen. Nathanael Greene and the Officers and Soldiers of the Continental Army Who Participated with Him in the Battle of Guilford Courthouse. Washington: G. P. O., 1912.

"Extracts from the Memorial Volume of the Guilford Battle Ground Company, Greensborough Guilford Battleground Co." Greensboro, N.C.: [The Company?], 1894.

Faden, William, 1749-1836. "Battle of Guilford Fought on the 15th of March 1781." *Atlas of the Battles of the American Revolution, Together with Maps Shewing the Routes of the British and American Armies, Plans of Cities, Surveys of Harbors, &c.* London: [for T. Cadell], 1787; digitized map available online at http://digital.tcl.sc.edu/cdm/ref/collection/schmscl/id/266.

Gels, Douglas J. "Finding the Trail to Troublesome Creek: An Application of GIS to Identify Nathanael Greene's Withdrawal Route and Position after the Battle of Guilford Courthouse, 15-16 March 1781." M. A. thesis, University of North Carolina-Greensboro, 2005.

Guilford Battleground Company. *Extracts from the Memorial Volune of the Guilford Battle County Company.* Greensborough [*sic*]: The Company, 1894.

Guilford Battle Ground Co., Greensboro, N. C. *Addresses of Hon/ Chas. B Aycock and R. G. Beasley, Esq., on the Occasion of the Unveiling of the Colonial Column and the Monument to Captain Hames Morehead, at Guilford Battle Ground, July 4, 1901*. Greensboro, 1901.

"Guilford Courthouse National Military Park." Website: http://www.nps.gov/guco/index.htm. [Contains the following documents: "A History of Guilford Courthouse National Military Park;" "Touring the Battlefield;" "A Walking Guide to Guilford Courthouse N. M. P.;" "Order of Battle;" "Black Soldiers at Guilford Courthouse;" "Women Honored at Guilford Courthouse [Kerenhappuck Norman Turner and Martha Bell];" "The North Carolina Militia Flag;" "George Washington's Visit to Guilford Courthouse Battlefield, June 2, 1791;" "After the Battle: A Short History of Post-Battle Lives;" "Map of the Southern Campaign of the American Revolution;" "The Militia;" "The 18th Century Tailor;" "Fishes of Guilford Courthouse NMP;" "NC Signers of the Declaration of Independence;" "Exploring Trees in the Park: Another Kind of Living History;" "Life in the 1700s: Coping with Disease;" "Maps of Monuments and Memorials."]

"Guilford Courthouse National Military Park: National Park Service Museum Collections, American Revolutionary War." Online: http://www.nps.gov/museum/exhibits/revwar/guco/gucoweapons.html. [The site includes images of artifacts and materials relating to an overview of the battlefield, "Weapons of War;" "Leisure Hours;" "Medicine;" "Food and Spirits;" "Women;" and a park image gallery.]

Hairr, John. *Guilford Courthouse: Nathanael Greene's Victory in Defeat, March 15, 1781*. (Battleground America series) Cambridge, Mass.: Da Capo Press, 2002. [Examination of the battle with information about touring the site; includes pictures of the site as it appears today.]

Hall, Karen Lynn Jones. *Guilford Courthouse Battleground Monuments*. [North Carolina: K. L. J. Hall, 2013?]

Harrison, Richard. "On the Day of the Battle of Guilford Courthouse, 1781." *North Carolina Genealogical Society Journal*, 5:2 (May 1979), 95. [letter from Richard Harrison to his wife Ann in Granville County, N. C.]

Harrison, R[ichard]. "R. Harrison Letter, 15 March 1781." Manuscript 2031-z, Southern Historical Collection, Louis Round Wilson Special Collections Library, University of North Carolina, Chapel Hill; online finding aid available at http://www2.lib.unc.edu/mss/inv/h/Harrison,R.html. [Online finding aid description: "Major R. Harrison fought in the Battle of Guilford Courthouse during the Revolutionary War. The collection is a letter from Harrison at Camp Guilford Court House, N. C., to his wife in Granville County, N. C., and an undated noted from Henry Pattillo added to the letter. Harrison discussed the current military situation; Pattillo gave a report of recent military action."]

Hatch, Jabez, 1738?-1802. "Return of Opposing Force, 15 March 1781." Manuscript, Misc. Bd. 1781 March 15, Massachusetts Historical Society, Boston. [Online catalog description: "Return of an estimate of strength of Lord Cornwallis' forces in the Carolinas before the Battle of Guilford Courthouse."]

Hinton, Mary H. "Martha McFarlane Bell." *North Carolina Bulletin,* 16:4 (October 1916), 88-96.

Jackson, Solomon. "Newspaper Articles, 1873." Manuscript SC 2131, Indiana Historical Society Library Manuscript Collection, Indiana Historical Society Library, Indianapolis. [Online catalog description: "The collection consists of photocopies of typewritten transcripts of two newspaper articles, 1873, describing Solomon Jackson's part in the Battles of Camden and Guilford Courthouse in the Revolutionary War, and his life in Lexington, Ind., after his family moved there in 1814 from North Carolina."]

Jones, Joe. "Second-Guessing at Guilford Courthouse." *The State: Down Home in North Carolina*, 48:9 (February 1981), 7-8; online: http://digital.ncdcr.gov/cdm/ref/collection/p16062coll18/id/60050. [Online description from "North Carolina Periodicals Index," East Carolina University: "This year marks the 190th anniversary of George

Washington's visit to the Guilford Courthouse Battlefield. This year is the bicentennial celebration of that battle, and events will take place at the courthouse on April 14th and 15th."]

Jones, Nellie Rowe and Louise A. Sharp. *Roster of Troops Who Fought at Guilford Court House March 15, 1781.* [S. l., s. n. 19-??]. ["Contains bibliographic citations for where discussion of each soldier can be found."]

Jordan, Paula Stahls, and Kathy Warden Manning. *Women of Guilford County, North Carolina: A Study of Women's Contributions, 1740-1979.* Greensboro, N. C.: Women of Guilford, 1979. [Chapter I: "Women in the Early Colonies," 1-8; Chapter II: "The Revolution," 9-20, includes "The War in Guilford County," "Martha McFarlain McGee Bell," "Rachel Craighead," and "Women under the Constitution." Chapter III: "The New Nation and the Era of Reform," 21-44.

Kieron, Francis. "The Battle of Guilford Courthouse." *Journal of American History*, 7:1 (First Quarter 1913), 809-819; reprinted: *Recall: The North Carolina Military History Society*, 19:1 (Spring 2013), 18-22; online: http://ns50.webmasters.com/*ncmhs.net/httpdocs/RecallSp13.pdf.

Killebrew, Joseph Buckner. *The Battle of Guilford Court House: An Address before the Tennessee Division of the Sons of the American Revolution.* Knoxville: Press of S. B. Newman & Co., 1902.

King, Mrs. J. A. "The Revolutionary Oak at Guilford Court House, North Carolina." *Daughters of the American Revolution Magazine*, 92:8 (October 1959), 723, 756.

Konstam, Angus. *Guilford Courthouse, 1781: Lord Cornwallis's Ruinous Victory.* Oxford, Eng.: Osprey Publishing, 2002. [Publisher's description: "By the Spring of 1781, the American Revolutionary War had dragged on for almost six years and the outcome still hung in the balance. When the British commander Lord Cornwallis launched his invasion. In the Spring of 1781, the American Revolutionary War had dragged on for almost six years, and neither side had gained a decisive advantage. When the British commander Lord Cornwallis launched his invasion of North Carolina in early 1781, his objective was to destroy General Nathaniel Greene's army, not to capture territory. Greene fell back before him into Virginia, and his force grew daily as militia flocked to the colours, and a revitalised American army took the offensive. At Guilford Courthouse on 15 March 1781 the two armies met. In a see-saw battle, victory seemed to be within the American grasp, but the British held off a fierce counterattack by American infantry and cavalry, forcing Greene to concede the field. It was a British victory but at a terrible cost - Cornwallis lost over a quarter of his command. When news of the 'victory' reached Britain, a politician remarked; 'Another such victory would ruin the British army.' The battle led to the recapture of the Carolinas by Greene, and set in motion a chain of events that would culminate in the surrender of Cornwallis and his army at Yorktown seven months later."]

"Map of the Battle of Guilford Courthouse." *Journal of North Carolina Genealogy*, 12:1 (Spring 1966), 1630.

A Memorial Volume of the Guilford Battle Ground Company: organized May 6, 1887, at Greensboro, N.C.: with numerous beautiful illustrations: It contains a brief history of the battle of Guilford Court House: an account of the organization and progress of the Guilford Battle Ground Company, biographical sketches, and a full account of the Holt monument and its dedication, July the 4th, 1893 Guilford Battleground Co. Greensboro: Reece & Elam, 1893.

Morehead, Joseph M. *James Hunter: "The Country Is as Much Master Now as Ever." An Address by Joseph M. Morehead, Esq., at Guilford Battle Ground, July 3, 1897* [cover title]; *Address of Joseph M. Morehead, Esq., of Guilford, on the Life and Times of James Hunter, "General" of the Regulators, at the Guilford Battle Ground, Saturday, July 3, 1897* [from the title page; Second and Enlarged Edition] Greensboro: C. F. Thomas, Book and Job Printer, 1898.

Morehead, Joseph M. "Short Sketch of the Battle of Guilford Court-House from the View-Point of Results." *North Carolina Booklet*, 4:12 (March 1905), 3-8; online: http://digital.ncdcr.gov/cdm/ref/collection/p249901coll37/id/14180. [Online description from "North Carolina Periodicals Index," East Carolina University: "This article provides a brief overview of the activities and decisions made by Revolutionary War commanders on both sides of the conflict before and after the Battle of Guilford Court-House, when Patriot forces under the command of Nathaniel Greene defeated Loyalist forces commanded by General Cornwallis."]

Morehead, Joseph M. "Joseph M. Morehead Papers, 1753-1919 (bulk 1880-1913)." Manuscript 523, Southern Historical Collection, Louis Round Wilson Special Collections Library, University of North Carolina, Chapel Hill; online finding aid available at http://www2.lib.unc.edu/mss/inv/m/Morehead,Joseph_M.html. [Online finding aid description: "The collection includes legal and business papers, chiefly 1880-1913, of lawyers Joseph Motley Morehead and James Turner Morehead Jr. (1838-1919) of Guilford County, N. C. ... Also included are papers concerning United States and North Carolina military history and monuments, particularly related to the Guilford Battleground Company of which Joseph Morehead was president."]

Morehead, Joseph Motley. *Battle of Guilford Court House, and the Preservation of That Historic Field.* Greensboro: Jos. J. Stone & Co., 1906; reprinted: 1907, 1908; Greensboro: The Record Job Office, 1909.

Norris, Jeannie Faris. "Peter the Great." *The State: A Weekly Survey of North Carolina*, 7:39 (February 1940), 6-7; online: http://digital.ncdcr.gov/cdm/ref/collection/p16062coll18/id/5158. [Online description from "North Carolina Periodicals Index," East Carolina University: "On the Guilford Battleground near Greensboro is a monument to the exploits of Peter Francisco, giant of the American Revolution. He was said to have performed a deed of unparalleled bravery, cutting down eleven men with his sword, although badly wounded. At the battle of Camden, horses drawing a cannon were killed and Francisco shouldered the gun weighting eleven hundred pounds and carried it where it was needed." For more on Peter Francisco, see the companion publication *Virginia in the American Revolution: A Source Guide for Genealogists and Historians*. Washington, D. C.: NSDAR, 2015.]

North Carolina (State). General Assembly. "[Document dated:] July 4, [1781]: Recommending that Major General Greene Discharge Persons Who Fled from Action at Guilford Court House (Message Only)." Manuscript; General Assembly Record Group; Session Records, June-July 1781; Joint Papers, Committee Papers, Resolutions, Senate Bills, House Bills, Box 1 (MARS ID: 66.8.25.14.5; item), State Archives of North Carolina, Raleigh.

Poquette, Nancy. "History of the Guilford Militia: Whitesell's Mill and Battle of Guilford Courthouse." *The Guilford Genealogist*, 35:2 (Summer 2008), 26-60.

Powell, William S. "The Battle of Guilford Courthouse: A Pyrrhic Victory for the Crown." *Tar Heel: The Magazine of North Carolina*, 9:3 (March 1981), 34-36.

Rachel Caldwell Chapter, North Carolina Daughters of the American Revolution. *North Carolina DAR Genealogical Records Committee Report, Series 1, Volume 269: Biographical Sketches of Soldiers and Patriots in the Battle of Guilford Courthouse, March 15, 1781* (typescript, 1959); digital surrogate, DAR Library, Washington, D. C.

Rachel Caldwell Chapter, North Carolina Daughters of the American Revolution. *North Carolina DAR Genealogical Records Committee Report, Series 1, Volume 286: Biographical Sketches of Soldiers and Patriots in the Battle of Guilford Courthouse, March 15, 1781, Volume II* (typescript, 1960); digital surrogate, DAR Library, Washington, D. C.

Rachel Caldwell Chapter, North Carolina Daughters of the American Revolution. *North Carolina DAR Genealogical Records Committee Report, Series 1, Volume 299: Biographical Sketches of Soldiers and Patriots in the Battle of Guilford Courthouse, March 15, 1781, Volume III* (typescript, 1961); digital surrogate, DAR Library, Washington, D. C.

Rachel Caldwell Chapter, North Carolina Daughters of the American Revolution. *North Carolina DAR Genealogical Records Committee Report, Series 1, Volume 304: Biographical Sketches of Soldiers and Patriots in the Battle of Guilford Courthouse, March 15, 1781, Volume IV* (typescript, 1962); digital surrogate, DAR Library, Washington, D. C.

Rachel Caldwell Chapter, North Carolina Daughters of the American Revolution. *North Carolina DAR Genealogical Records Committee Report, Series 1, Volume 309: Biographical Sketches of Soldiers and Patriots in the Battle of Guilford Courthouse, March 15, 1781, Volume V*. Digitized typescript (1962), DAR Library, Washington, D. C.

Rachel Caldwell Chapter, North Carolina Daughters of the American Revolution. *North Carolina DAR Genealogical Records Committee Report, Series 1, Volume 315: Biographical Sketches of Soldiers and Patriots in the Battle of Guilford Courthouse, March 15, 1781, Volume VI* (typescript, 1964); digital surrogate, DAR Library, Washington, D. C.

Rachel Caldwell Chapter, North Carolina Daughters of the American Revolution. *North Carolina DAR Genealogical Records Committee Report, Series 1, Volume 337: Biographical Sketches of Soldiers and Patriots in the Battle of Guilford Courthouse, March 15, 1781, Volume VII* (typescript, 1968); digital surrogate, DAR Library, Washington, D. C.

Rachel Caldwell Chapter, North Carolina Daughters of the American Revolution. *North Carolina DAR Genealogical Records Committee Report, Series 1, Volume 342: Biographical Sketches of Soldiers and Patriots in the Battle of Guilford Courthouse, March 15, 1781, Volume VIII* (typescript, 1969); digital surrogate, DAR Library, Washington, D. C.

Rachel Caldwell Chapter, North Carolina Daughters of the American Revolution. *North Carolina DAR Genealogical Records Committee Report, Series 1, Volume 363: Biographical Sketches of Soldiers and Patriots in the Battle of Guilford Courthouse, March 15, 1781, Volume IX*. Digitized typescript (1971), DAR Library, Washington, D. C.

Rachel Caldwell Chapter, North Carolina Daughters of the American Revolution. *North Carolina DAR Genealogical Records Committee Report, Series 1, Volume 364: Biographical Sketches of Soldiers and Patriots in the Battle of Guilford Courthouse, March 15, 1781, Volume X* (typescript, 1971); digital surrogate, DAR Library, Washington, D. C.

Reid, Courtland T. *Guilford Courthouse National Military Park, North Carolina (Based on Historical Narrative by William P. Brandon).* Washington, D. C.: National Park Services, 1959; 1961; online: http://purl.access.gpo.gov/GPO/LPS74181.

"Return of Opposing Forces, 15 March 1781." Manuscript Misc. Bd. 1781 March 15, Massachusetts Historical Society, Boston. [Online catalog description: "Return of an estimate of strength of Lord Cornwallis' forces in the Carolinas before the Battle of Guilford Courthouse."]

Schenck, David. "David Schenck (1835-1902) Papers, 1772-1894." Manuscript, PC.35, State Archives of North Carolina, Raleigh. [Online catalog description: "Papers of Schenck, attorney, superior court judge, and president of Guilford Battleground Company, including copies of Gen. Jethro Sumner's appointment as sheriff of Bute Co. (1772) and his estate papers (1785), wills of Thomas and Mary Sumner Blount, and Revolutionary pension records. Several correspondents (1887- 1893) report family stories of the Battle of Guilford Courthouse; and an essay claims that Alexander Lillington, not Richard Caswell, commanded at the Battle of Moores Creek Bridge."]

Schenck, David. *A Historical Address, Delivered by the Hon. David Schenck, Saturday, May 5th, 1888, at the Guilford Battle Ground: Subject, the Battle of Guilford Court House, Fought Thursday, March 15, 1781.* Greensboro: Thomas Brothers, Printers, for Guilford Battle Ground Co., 1888.

Seymour, Mary E. "Revolutionary Heroines." *Daughters of the American Revolution Magazine*, 70:9 (September 1936), 933-934. [Includes Mrs. Keren-happuch Turner, who rode all the way on horseback from her home in Maryland to Guilford Court House, North Carolina, and was able to nurse her son back to health after the battle there.]

Smith, Edward. "The King of King's Mountain." *The State: Down Home in North Carolina*, 22:1 (October 1954), 10-11, 26-27; online: http://digital.ncdcr.gov/cdm/ref/collection/p16062coll18/id/32588. [Online description from "North Carolina Periodicals Index," East Carolina University: "Part of the Third Red Coat Army from England, Colonel Patrick Ferguson fought and died while fighting against local militia at the Battle of King's Mountain, 7 October 1780. Scotsman, tactician, and military leader, Ferguson led some 1,000 men in battle alongside Lord Cornwallis. He is buried on King's Mountain, North Carolina."]

Stine, Linda France; Roy S. Stine; and Kristen S. Selikoff. "Multidisciplinary Landscape Research at Tannenbaum Historic Park, Guilford County, North Carolina." *North Carolina Archaeology*, 52 (October 2003), 20-52. . [Online description from "North Carolina Periodicals Index," East Carolina University: "Archaeology and geography staff and students from the University of North Carolina at Greensboro used multidisciplinary research to explore the occupation of Tannenbaum Historic Park in Greensboro from the American Revolution to the present. The Park is part of the Guilford Courthouse Battlefield National Historic Landmark and is believed to be the location where General Cornwallis formed the first British line of attack which proceeded into the current Guilford Courthouse National Military Park."]

Stoesen, Alexander R. "Guilford Courthouse, Battle of." In William S. Powell, ed.; Jay Mazzocchi, assoc. ed., *Encyclopedia of North Carolina* (Chapel Hill: University of North Carolina Press in association with the University of North Carolina Library, 2006), 544-545.

Suggs, Joseph R. "Martha McFarlane McGee Bell (1735-9 Sept. 1820)." In William S. Powell, ed., *Dictionary of North Carolina Biography, vol. 1: A-C* (Chapel Hill: University of North Carolina Press, 1979-1996), 132.

Swanson, Julia Rankin. "Caroline Close Stuart." *The State: A Weekly Survey of North Carolina*, 13:20 (October 1945), 9, 29-30; online: http://digital.ncdcr.gov/cdm/ref/collection/p16062coll18/id/13819. [Online description from "North Carolina Periodicals Index," East Carolina University: "Carolina Close Stuart was one of the early nurses who cared for the wounded at the Battle of Guilford Courthouse; she was a remarkable woman in many other ways as well."]

Thurmond, George. "The Battle of Guilford Courthouse, North Carolina." *SAR Magazine*, 100:4 (Spring 2006), 20-22.

[Tucker, St. George]; Charles Washington Coleman, ed. "The Southern Campaign 1781 from Guilford Court House to the Siege of Yorktown Narrated by St. George Tucker in Letters to His Wife, Part II: The Peninsula Campaign." *Magazine of American History*, 7:3 (September 1881), 201-216.

Van Noppen, Addie Donnell. *The Battle Field of Guilford Court House.* Greensboro: Guilford Battle Chapter of the Daughters of the American Revolution, 1915; reprinted: 1927

Vance, Zebulon Baird. *Address At the Guilford Battle Ground, May 4, 1889*. [Greensboro, N. C.]: Reece & Elam, Printers, 1889.

Vogler, Bob. "Searching for Mass Graves at Guilford Courthouse." *Southern Campaigns of the American Revolution*, 4:2 (April-June 2007), 8; online: www.southerncampaign.org.

Voigt, Robert C. "Guilford Courthouse Flag." In William S. Powell, ed.; Jay Mazzocchi, assoc. ed., *Encyclopedia of North Carolina* (Chapel Hill: University of North Carolina Press in association with the University of North Carolina Library, 2006), 545.

Walser, Richard. "Yorktown." *The State: A Weekly Survey of North Carolina*, 20:20 (October 1952), 5-6, 24; online: http://digital.ncdcr.gov/cdm/ref/collection/p16062coll18/id/29311. [Online description from "North Carolina Periodicals Index," East Carolina University: "Burke Davis of Greensboro, North Carolina is writing a historic novel about the Battle of Guilford Courthouse. Author of several novels illuminating neglected or hidden early American History, Burke's latest work was inspired by his most recent home, the location of Lord Cornwallis's stay during the battle."]

Wellborn, Jennifer M. *Martha MacFarlane McGee Bell: Heroine, Patriot, and Spy, and the Case for Caruthers.* Rock Hill, S. C.: J. M. Wellborn, 2002. [Examines the story of and evidence relating to the life of this North Carolinian.]

Whitfield, Theodore M. "Kerenhappuch Turner." *Baltimore Sunday Sun Magazine*, (July 18, 1976), 32.

Winston, George T. *The Oration of George T. Winston, LL. D., President of the University of North Carolina, at Guilford Battle Ground, July 4th, 1895: Subject: The Life and Times of Major Joseph Winston; To This Are Added Other Speeches Delivered on This Occasion*. Greensboro: Reece & Elam, Printers, 1895.

"Women Honored at Guilford Courthouse." Online: http://www.nps.gov/guco/planyourvisit/upload/Women%20 Honored.doc [Features the stories of Kerenhappuch Turner and Martha McFarland McGee Bell and the wording on monuments to them at the battlefield park.]

Wood, Ernie. "Martha Bell Tolled the War for Tories." *News and Observer,* [Raleigh], February 1, 1976.

Wood, W. J. *Battles of the Revolutionary War, 1775-1781*. Chapel Hill: Algonquin Books of Chapel Hill, 1990. [Chapter nine examines the Battle of Guilford County Courthouse.]

Skirmish on the Road to Ramsey's Mill, March 24-25, 1781

"Revolutionary War Raids & Skirmishes in 1781: March 24-25, 1781, on the Road to Ramsey's Mill, Chatham County, North Carolina." Online: http://www.myrevolutionarywar.com/battles/1781-skirmish/.

Skirmish at Cole's Bridge, March 31 or April 1, 1781

"Revolutionary War Raids & Skirmishes in 1781: April 1 (possibly 31 March) 1781, Skirmish at Cole's Bridge, Scotland County, North Carolina." Online: http://www.myrevolutionarywar.com/battles/1781-skirmish/.

Skirmish at Fort Nashborough, Tennessee, April 2-3, 1781

"Revolutionary War Raids & Skirmishes in 1781: April 2-3, 1781, at Fort Nashborough, Tennessee." Online: http://www.myrevolutionarywar.com/battles/1781-skirmish/.

Raid on Wolf's Den, April 15 or 16, 1781

"Revolutionary War Raids & Skirmishes in 1781: 15 or 16 April, 1781, Raid on Wolf's Den (aka Big Glades or Riddle's Knob), Ashe County, North Carolina." Online: http://www.myrevolutionarywar.com/battles/1781-skirmish/.

Skirmish at Tarboro, May 5 or 6, 1781

"Revolutionary War Raids & Skirmishes in 1781:6 (also possibly 5th) May, 1781, Skirmish at Tarboro, Edgecombe County, North Carolina." Online: http://www.myrevolutionarywar.com/battles/1781-skirmish/.

Skirmish at Peacock's Bridge, May 6, 1781

"Revolutionary War Raids & Skirmishes in 1781: 6 May, 1781, Skirmish at Peacock's Bridge, Wilson County, North Carolina." Online: http://www.myrevolutionarywar.com/battles/1781-skirmish/.

Skirmish at Cox's Mill, May 11-12, 1781

"Revolutionary War Raids & Skirmishes in 1781: May 11-12, 1781, Cox's Mill, Randolph Co., North Carolina." Online: http://www.myrevolutionarywar.com/battles/1781-skirmish/.

Burning of Wyanoke Ferry, June 1781

"Revolutionary War Raids & Skirmishes in 1781: June 1781, Burning of Wyanoke Ferry in North Carolina." Online: http://www.myrevolutionarywar.com/battles/1781-skirmish/.

Battle of the House in the Horseshoe, July 29, 1781

"225th Anniversary Battle of House in the Horseshoe." *Southern Campaigns of the American Revolution*, 3:9 (September 2006), 5-6; online: southerncampaign.org [Alston Plantation, near Carthage, N. C.]

"House in the Horseshoe, July 29, 1781." Online: http://www.carolana.com/NC/Revolution/revolution_house_in_the_horseshoe.html.

"House in the Horseshoe Overview." Online: http://www.nchistoricsites.org/horsesho/main.htm.

"House in the Horseshoe, Revolutionary War." Online: http://www.nchistoricsites.org/horsesho/.

Thompson, Jessica Lee. "House in the Horseshoe." Online at the North Carolina History Project website: http://www.northcarolinahistory.org/encyclopedia/411/entry.

Thompson, William H., Jr. "House in the Horseshoe." *Encyclopedia of North Carolina* (Chapel Hill: University of North Carolina Press, 2006), 592.

White, Thadd. "House in the Horseshoe." *Greenville Times/Pitt's Past*, 28:2 (January 20, 2010), 118-121. [Online description from "North Carolina Periodicals Index," East Carolina University: "House in the Horseshoe was built in 1772 as a plantation house and was later the site of American Revolutionary War battles. The historical home is now the location of reenactments."]

Wicker, Jim. "The Bullet Holes Are Still There: The Tory Victory at the House in the Horseshoe Was One of the Last for N. C. Loyalists." *The State: Down Home in North Carolina*, 54:5 (October 1986), 16-17; online: http://digital.ncdcr.gov/cdm/ref/collection/p16062coll18/id/62125. [Online description from "North Carolina Periodicals Index," East Carolina University: "On August 5, 1781, a battle between Revolutionary War Patriots and Tories took place at the home of Mrs. Phillip Alston in Moore County. Mrs. Alston surrendered to the Patriots to save the lives of her children. Known as the 'House in the Horseshoe' because it is located in a C-like bend in Deep River, the Alston home changed ownership several times before the Moore County Historical Society acquired it in 1954. The state then took ownership, restored it, and furnished it with colonial period decorations. Each year, during the first weekend in August, a reenactment battle is held."]

The Race/Retreat to the Dan, 1781

Aaron, Larry G. *The Race to the Dan: The Retreat That Rescued the American Revolution*. Halifax: Halifax County Historical Society, 2007.

"Crossing of the Dan." Archives website at: http://web.archive.org/web/20080212182408/http://www.prizery.com/CrossingPage2.htm.

"Crossing the Dan Exhibit." Online: http://www.prizery.com/index.php?option=com_content&view=article&id=101&Itemid=200.

Headspeth, W[illiam] Carroll. *The Retreat to the Dan: A Masterful Maneuver*. South Boston: South Boston News, 1974.

Battle of Rockfish Creek, August 2, 1781, Duplin County

Carr, J. O. "The Battle of Rockfish Creek in Duplin County." *North Carolina Booklet*, 6:3 (January 1907), 177-184; online: http://digital.ncdcr.gov/cdm/ref/collection/p249901coll37/id/14180. [Online description from "North Carolina Periodicals Index," East Carolina University: "This article describes the Battle of Rockfish Creek, which took place on August 2, 1781 between a Whig militia of 330 troops and 500 British. The British defeated the militia and took over 30 prisoners. The British troops were marching through the counties surrounding Wilmington arresting Whigs and enlisting more Loyalist supporters."]

"Chronology of Events in the History of Duplin County, NC." Online: http://www.duplincountync.com/aboutDuplin County/chronologyOfEvents.html. ["General Cornwallis' troops marched through Duplin on their way to Virginia and defeat. They encamped briefly at old Duplin Court House on Turkey Swamp. Battle of Rockfish Creek: The Duplin Militia, under the command of Col. Thomas Kenan, was routed by the British on August 2, 1781 near Wallace."]

Tetterton Beverly. "Rockfish, Battle of." In William S. Powell, ed.; Jay Mazzocchi, assoc. ed., *Encyclopedia of North Carolina* (Chapel Hill: University of North Carolina Press in association with the University of North Carolina Library, 2006), 984.

Battle of Bettis' Bridge, August 5, 1781

Ney, Wilbur Sturtevant. 'The Battle of Bettis' Bridge, August 5, 1781." Typescript Cp970.33 N99b, North Carolina Collection, Louis Round Wilson Special Collections Library, University of North Carolina at Chapel Hill.

Battle of Elizabethtown/Tory Hole, August 28, 1781

Beasley, Rowland Fowler. *The Battle of Elizabethtown: Speech Delivered on the Occasion of the Annual Celebration at the Guilford Battle Ground, July 4th, 1901, at Which Time Was Unveiled the Colonial Column, and a Monument to Captain James Morehead of the 10th Regiment North Carolina Continental Line.* Greensboro: Guilford Battle Ground Company, 1901. [James Morehead (1750-1815); Battle of Elizabethtown, 1781.]

Bladen County Historical Society. *Battle of Elilzabethtown: Whigs Broke Tory Power in Bladen County, August 1781, Driving Them into Tory Hole.* [Bladen County, N. C.]: The Society, 1957.

McMillan, Hamilton. "The Battle of Elizabethton." *Fayetteville Observer*, (June 25, 1901), letter to the editor.

Norris, Jeannie Faris. "Bladen County." *The State: A Weekly Survey of North Carolina*, 10:23 (November 1942), 1-3, 19-21; online: http://digital.ncdcr.gov/cdm/ref/collection/p16062coll18/id/33426. [Online description from "North Carolina Periodicals Index," East Carolina University: "The mother of 55 other counties, Bladen County was the scene of the Battle of Elizabethtown and is the location of many historic homes."]

Tetterton, Beverly. "Elizabethtown, Battle of." In William S. Powell, ed.; Jay Mazzocchi, assoc. ed., *Encyclopedia of North Carolina* (Chapel Hill: University of North Carolina Press in association with the University of North Carolina Library, 2006), 390-391.

Troy, Robert E. "Robert E. Troy Letter, 1845." Manuscript 729, Southern Historical Collection, Louis Round Wilson Special Collections Library, University of North Carolina, Chapel Hill; online finding aid available at http://www2.lib.unc.edu/mss/inv/t/Troy,Robert_E.html. [Online finding aid description: "Robert E. Troy was a prominent lawyer in Lumberton, N. C., and served as mayor of the town in 1852. He also was Master of St. Alban's Lodge A. F. & A. M. James Cain (circa 1748-1826) was a resident of Bladen County, N.C. He was wounded in the Battle of Elizabethtown. Colonel Thomas Robeson (1740-1785) led Whig troops in defeating Tories at the Battle of Elizabethtown on 28 August 1781. The collection consists of a typed transcription of a letter, 12 March 1845, originally sent by Robert E. Troy in Lumberton, N.C., to the *Robesonian* following an interview with James Cain, a veteran of the Revolutionary War. The letter describes the leadership of Whig officer Colonel Thomas Robeson in defeating Tory troops in the Battle of Elizabethtown, N. C., on 28 August 1781. Also includes a photocopy of the typed transcription."]

Battle of Lindley's Mill/Cane Creek, September 13, 1781

Arthur, Billy. "The Midnight Ride of Alexander Mebane." *Our State: Down Home in North Carolina*, 67:3 (August 1999), 18-20; online: http://digital.ncdcr.gov/cdm/ref/collection/p16062coll18/id/68131. [Online description from "North Carolina Periodicals Index," East Carolina University: "North Carolina's Paul Revere was Col. Alexander Mebane. Captured by Tory Colonel David Fanning, Mebane escaped the night of September 12, 1781, and rode through Orange and Alamance Counties to warn the patriots of the Tories' approach. On September 13, Tories and Patriots fought at Lindley's Mill, with neither side achieving victory. After the war Mebane's activities included serving in the U. S. Congress, as a member of the Constitutional Convention, and as an original trustee of the University of North Carolina."]

"The Battle of Lindley's Mill/Cane Creek, September 12, 1781, at Hillsboro, North Carolina (aka Hillsboro Raid)." Online: http://www.myrevolutionarywar.com/battles/810912-lindleys-mill/.

Butler, Lindley S. "200 Years Ago and Lindley's Mill." *The State: Down Home in North Carolina*, 49:5 (October 1981), 12-13; online: http://digital.ncdcr.gov/cdm/ref/collection/p16062coll18/id/60425. [Online description from "North Carolina Periodicals Index," East Carolina University: "On September 12, 1781, Loyalist partisan Colonel David Fanning and his militia surrounded the temporary state capital, Hillsborough. The one-thousand-man force successfully captured state officers, army officials, and Governor Thomas Burke. While Fanning marched his men to loyalist stronghold Wilmington, Whig general John Butler quickly assembled 400 militia at the mill of Quaker Thomas Lindley to block Fanning. The Whigs were overpowered, however, and the Loyalists were able to deliver their prisoners to Major James H. Craig in Wilmington."]

Dunaway, Stewart E. *The Battle at Lindley's Mill.* 2nd ed. Hillsborough: North Carolina Historical Books, 2009.

Newlin, Algie. *The Battle of Lindley's Mill.* Burlington: Alamance Historical Association, 1975.

Vocci, Robert Blair. "Lindley's Mill, Battle of." In William S. Powell, ed.; Jay Mazzocchi, assoc. ed., *Encyclopedia of North Carolina* (Chapel Hill: University of North Carolina Press in association with the University of North Carolina Library, 2006), 678-679. [1781]

Battle of Brown's Marsh, between September 28 and October 2, 1781

"Battle of Brown's Marsh." Online: http://www.carolana.com/NC/Revolution/revolution_brown_marsh.html.

Hairr, John. "Brown's Marsh, Battle of." In William S. Powell, ed.; Jay Mazzocchi, assoc. ed., *Encyclopedia of North Carolina* (Chapel Hill: University of North Carolina Press in association with the University of North Carolina Library, 2006), 150-151; online: http://ncpedia.org/browns-marsh-battle. [between September 28 and October 2, 1781 near Clarkton in Bladen County]

Pancake, John S. *This Destructive War: The British Campaign in the Carolinas, 1780-1782*. Tuscaloosa, Ala.: The University of Alabama Press, 1985.

Battle of McPhaul's Mill, October 1781

"Battle of McPhaul's Mill." In E. W. Caruthers. *Interesting Revolutionary Incidents and Skethces of Character Chiefly in the Old North State* (Philadelphia: Hayes & Zell, 1854); online: http://www.capefearclans.com/McPhaulsMillSketch.html.

McPhaul, John Henry. "The Battles of McPhaul's Mill and Raft Swamp, 1781." Online: http://www.capefearclans.com/ColonialMuster.html.

Tyler, Blake. "Revolution in Robeson." Online: http://ncvisitorcenter.com/Battle_of_Raft_Swamp.html.

Skirmish at Bee's/Mcintyre's Farm, October 3 or 4, 1781

Charlotte-Mecklenburg Historic Landmarks Commission. "McIntyre Site Report." Online: http://www.cmhpf.org/Properties%20Foundation%20Reports/McIntyreFarm.html.

Lowrance, Anne. "A Battle Won with Hornets." *Olde Mecklenburg Genealogical Society Quarterly*, 14:1 (1996), 16-17. [Battle of McIntyre Farm.]

Norris, David A. "McIntyre's Farm, Battle of." Online: http://ncpedia.org/mcintyres-farm-battle.

Vocci, Robert Blair. "McIntyre's Farm, Battle of." In William S. Powell, ed.; Jay Mazzocchi, assoc. ed., *Encyclopedia of North Carolina* (Chapel Hill: University of North Carolina Press in association with the University of North Carolina Library, 2006), 723.

Battles of Raft Swamp and Drowning Creek/Beattie's Bridge, October 15, 1781

"The American Revolution in North Carolina: Raft Swamp, October 15, 1781

"The Battle of Little Raft Swamp, September 1, 1781, at Little Raft Swamp, North Carolina." Online: http://www.myrevolutionarywar.com/battles/810901-little-raft-swamp/.

Butler, Lindley S. "Raft Swamp, Engagement at." In William S. Powell, ed.; Jay Mazzocchi, assoc. ed., *Encyclopedia of North Carolina* (Chapel Hill: University of North Carolina Press in association with the University of North Carolina Library, 2006), 936; online: http://ncpedia.org/raft-swamp-engagement. [Loyalist refuge]

McPhaul, John Henry. "The Battles of McPhaul's Mill and Raft Swamp, 1781." Online: http://www.capefearclans.com/ColonialMuster.html.

Tyler, Blake. "Revolution in Robeson." Online: http://ncvisitorcenter.com/Battle_of_Raft_Swamp.html.

1782

Battle of Lookout Mountain, Tennessee, June 1782; Cherokee Expedition

Echerd, John C. "September 20, 2007, Marks the 225th Anniversary of the Last Overmountain Battle of the American Revolution." *Chattanooga Regional Historical Journal*, 12:1 (Summer 2009), 68-73. [This article poses the argument that the last battle of the American Revolution was fought in June of 1782 at Lookout Mountain in Tennessee, led by John Sevier and his "Nolichucky Riflemen" against the Cherokee. John Sevier later went on to serve as a public official in both Tennessee and North Carolina.]

Evans, E. Raymond. "Was the Last Battle of the American Revolution Fought on Lookout Mountain?" *Journal of Cherokee Studies*, 5:1 (Spring 1980), 30-49; reprinted in *Chattanooga Regional Historical Journal*, 12:1 (Summer 2009), 74-98. [This article examines various alleged primary and secondary source documents regarding John Sevier's fight against the Cherokee on Lookout Mountain in 1782. It proposes there is no solid evidence the battle even took place.]

Jolley, LaVonne C. "Additional References: 'Last Battle'." *Chattanooga Regional Historical Journal*, 12:1 (Summer 2009), 99-101. [LaVonne C. Jolley, editor of the *Chattanooga Regional Historical Journal*, provides additional, historical details and references to two separate articles within the same journal issue. Those other two articles, one by John C. Echerd and the other by E. Raymond Evans, make alternate arguments regarding whether or not the last battle of the American Revolution was Lookout Mountain of Tennessee.]

Lewis, J. D. *NC Patriots, 1775-1783: Their Own Words*. Little River, S. C.: J. D. Lewis, 2012. [Lewis states in volume 2, page 133, that Isaac Butler died at this battle; on page 225, that Joseph Bullard, of Washington County (now Tennessee) was killed at the "Battle of Lookout Mountain" in 1782; and on page 409 that John Harden died there as well. From 1779-1782, Bullard was a captain under Lt. Col./Col. John Sevier and a Major under Col. John Sevier.]

Revolutionary War Size Rolls and Descriptive Lists from North Carolina

While uncommon, descriptive lists such as these, that include information such as the soldier's age, residence, birthplace, & place of enlistment can be extremely valuable in helping to determine whether someone who is being assigned a particular service matches the individual as shown in the lineage on page two of an application or supplemental application.

"Descriptive List of the Men of Bladen County Delivered Augt. 20th, 1782." *Quarterly Review of the Eastern North Carolina Genealogical Society*, 14:2 (June 1987), 64. [Includes ages, physical description, and occupation.]

"A Descriptive List of the Men Raised in the Dobbs Regiment of Militia for Twelve Months Service in the Continental Service under an act of the General Assembly passed in February 1781." *North Carolinian: Quarterly Journal of Genealogy & History*, 6:3 (September 1960), 729-730. [This list includes ages, height, complexion, occupation, and the name of the militia captain under whom they served.]

"Granville County, North Carolina: A Descriptive List of Men Raised under the Present Act of Assembly – 1778 (Abstracted from the Original, NC Archives, Granville County Records, {Mil TR4-40})." *Granville Connections, Journal of the Granville County Genealogical Society*, 1:1 (Winter 1995), 10-15. [This list gives age, height, and occupation.]; also printed in *North Carolinian, Quarterly Journal of Genealogy & History*, 6:3 (September 1960), 726-727; Also printed in *The Roster of Soldiers from North Carolina in the American Revolution* (Baltimore: Geneal. Pub., 1972), 600. [This copy does not include ages.]

"Men from Onslow County Volunteering for Duty in the North Carolina Continental Line, September 3, 1778." *Quarterly Review of the Eastern North Carolina Genealogical Society*, 14:1 (March 1987), 30. [Includes residence, place of birth, age, physical description.]

"Onslow County Conscripts, 1778." *Quarterly Review of the Eastern North Carolina Genealogical Society*, 14:1 (March 1987), 30. [This includes residence, place of birth, age, and physical description.]

North Carolina Cavalry and Light Horse Company

"Captain John Coleclough of Bute County for the Services of Self & Company of Militia of Light Horse on an Expedition to Currituck." In Weynette Parks Haun, *North Carolina Revolutionary Army Accounts, Part I, Secretary of State Treasurer's & Comptroller's Papers Journal "A", (Public Accounts) 1775-1776* (Durham: W. P. Haun, 1988), 97.

Howe, Robert. "Robert Howe (1732-1786) Papers, 1777, 1780." Manuscript, PC.612, State Archives of North Carolina, Raleigh. [Online catalog description: "Letters from Major General Howe of Brunswick Co., including note to Gov. Richard Caswell about Cosmo de Medici, appointed captain of light horse; one to New York Gov. George Clinton about relocation of two families near Stony Point, N.Y., with draft of Clinton's reply (Apr., 1780); and one to Gen. Nathanael Greene about a staff appointment (June, 1780)."]

Lewis, J. D. "Patriot Leaders in North Carolina: Joel Lewis: Ensign in the NC Continental Line - 1776-1779; Lieutenant in the 2nd NC Regiment – 1779; Captain in the Surry County Regiment of Militia - 1780-1781; Captain in the NC Light Horse Regiment – 1781; 1st Major in the NC State Regiment (State Troops) – 1781; Lt. Colonel/Colonel over the NC State Regiment (State Troops) - 1781-1783." Online: http://www.carolana.com/NC/Revolution/patriot_leaders_nc_joel_lewis.html.

North Carolina (State). General Assembly. "[Document Dated]: February 12, 1779; Resolution to Appointment Officers of Light Horse (with Messages)." Manuscript; General Assembly Record Group; Session Records,

January-February 1779; Joint Papers, Committee Papers, Resolutions; January-February, 1779: House Joint Resolutions: February 6-13, 1779, Box 1 (MARS ID: 66.8.15.12.17), State Archives of North Carolina, Raleigh. [Online catalog description: "The resolution makes numerous military appointments." The appointments were in the following counties: Anson, Burke, Caswell, Granville, Guilford, Halifax, Mecklenburg, Orange, Surry, Tryon, and Wilkes, and in the Districts of Hillsborough, Salisbury, and Wilmington.]

North Carolina (State). General Assembly. "[Document dated]: September 4, 1780: Resolution Requesting Governor to Lend Volunteer Light Horse to Western Counties." Manuscript; General Assembly Record Group; Session Records, August-September 1780; Joint Papers, Committee Papers, Resolutions; House Joint Resolutions: August 31-September 6, 1780, Box 1 (MARS ID: 66.8.22.10.13), State Archives of North Carolina, Raleigh. [Online catalog description: "The resolution also makes provisions for acquiring volunteers and for supplying them. Includes an amendment from the Senate."]

North Carolina (State). General Assembly. "[Document dated:] February 11, [1781]: Impowering [*sic*] Major General Caswell to Raise a Regiment of Light Horse from Districts of New Bern and Wilmington; Directing General Butler to Raise a Regiment of Volunteer Light Horse in District of Hillsborough (Messages Only)." Manuscript; General Assembly; Session Records, January-February 1781; Joint Papers, Committee Papers, Resolutions; House Joint Resolutions: February 10-11, 1781, Box 1 (MARS ID: 66.8.23,18.8; item), State Archives of North Carolina, Raleigh.

North Carolina (State). General Assembly. "[Document Dated]: June 29, 1781: For Raising Company of Light Horse in Onslow County (Messages Only)." Manuscript; General Assembly Record Group; Session Records; Joint Papers, Committee Papers, Resolutions, June-July 1781, Box 1 (MARS ID: 66.8.25.13.4), State Archives of North Carolina, Raleigh.

Battle Flags of North Carolina in the Revolution

Edmonds, W. R. *The North Carolina State Flag*. Raleigh, N. C.: Edwards & Broughton Print Co., 1913; reprinted: Raleigh: North Carolina Historical Commission, 1942; Raleigh: State Department of Archives and History, 1946.

Gillgam, Jim. "First Flag of North Carolina, June 1775." Online: http://ncrevwar.lostsoulsgenealogy.com/flag 1775.htm.

Kerr, Tom. "Bonnie Banner." *Our State: Down Home in North Carolina*, 72:9 (February 2005), 112-114; online: http://digital.ncdcr.gov/cdm/ref/collection/p16062coll18/id/82684. [Online description from "North Carolina Periodicals Index," East Carolina University: "W. R. Edmonds's small pamphlet *The North Carolina State Flag*, published in 1911, is the most authoritative resource available on the state's flag. Edmonds was a member of the North Carolina Historical Commission when he wrote the pamphlet, which is about three and a half pages in length, followed by four pages of footnotes. Kerr discusses some of the interesting facts from the text."]

Lawrence, R. C. "Some Insignia of State." *The State: A Weekly Survey of North Carolina*, 13:46 (April 1946), 8, 18-19; online: http://digital.ncdcr.gov/cdm/ref/collection/p16062coll18/id/15374. [Online description from "North Carolina Periodicals Index," East Carolina University: "Lawrence tells about the origin of North Carolina's state flag, great seal and also the legislation which brought about the adoption of a state flower and state bird."]

Rankin, Hugh F. "The Naval Flag of the American Revolution." *William and Mary Quarterly*, 3rd series, 11:3 (July 1954), 339-353.

Richardson, Edward W. Standards and Colors of the American Revolution. [Philadelphia]: University of Pennsylvania Press and the Pennsylvania Society of Sons of the Revolution and its Color Guard, 1982.

Schermerhorn, Frank Earle. *American and French Flags of the Revolution, 1775-1783.* Philadelphia: Pennsylvania Society of the Sons of the Revolution, 1948.

Tyrrell, Anne M. "The Flag Collection of the North Carolina Museum of History." *Tar Heel Junior Historian*, 20:2 (Winter 1981), 18-20. [Online description from "North Carolina Periodicals Index," East Carolina University: "One of the nation's largest flag collections, which contains over 320 items dating from the American Revolution to the present, is housed in Raleigh in the North Carolina Museum of History. The oldest flag dates from 1781 and is thought to have been carried at the Battle of Guilford Courthouse."]

Voigt, Robert C. "Guilford Courthouse Flag." In William S. Powell, ed.; Jay Mazzocchi, assoc. ed., *Encyclopedia of North Carolina* (Chapel Hill: University of North Carolina Press in association with the University of North Carolina Library, 2006), 545.

Health, Medicine, Medical Treatment, Sexuality in North Carolina during the Revolutionary War

Medical Patriotic Service[35]

Patriots of the Revolution are considered to be those men and women who by an act or series of actions demonstrated unfailing loyalty to the cause of American Independence from England. Patriotic service might begin as early as April 1774. We depend upon recorded actions to give us an indication of patriotism. What was the purpose of the action? What were the risks? The consequences? Answers to these questions can determine whether the action actually applied to an attempt to further the cause of independence or demonstrated loyalty to that cause.

Evidence of patriotic activity may be found in town, county, state, and federal records. Many records kept by the states have been indexed and often a letter to the state archives will be sufficient to determine if evidence exists to show that a person contributed supplies or made some other contribution to the war effort. Town and county records have usually not been indexed and a personal search of town minutes and court minutes is required. Minutes of the Continental Congresses have been published. *Old letters, diaries, and other family and personal papers can often be used as evidence of patriotic intent, provided the record was made at the time of the event described.*

Not all actions illustrating patriotism are mentioned here. Many others exist. When it is considered desirable to establish another type of patriotic service, proof of the action taken must be submitted with the application paper, together with historical justification to show that the action did indeed imply patriotic intent.

Doctors, nurses and others who rendered aid to the American wounded, other than their immediate families, qualify for patriotic service.

Austin, Anne L. *History of Nursing Source Book.* New York: G. P. Putnam's Sons, 1957. [Part II: "Some Sources for the Study of Nursing in the Western Hemisphere before 1873," includes Chapter 8: "Some References to Early American Nursing in Homes and Hospitals," 303-363, section 252: "Records of the Moravians in North Carolina 1758-1783," 326-328, mentions some men and women as nurses.]

Bordley, James, III, and A. McGehee Harvey. *Two Centuries of American Medicine.* Philadelphia: W. B. Saunders Company, 1976.

Cavender, Anthony. *Folk Medicine in Southern Appalachia.* Chapel Hill: University of North Carolina Press, 2003. [Publisher's description: "In the first comprehensive exploration of the history and practice of folk medicine in the Appalachian region, Anthony Cavender melds folklore, medical anthropology, and Appalachian history and draws extensively on oral histories and archival sources from the nineteenth century to the present. He provides a complete tour of ailments and folk treatments organized by body systems, as well as information on medicinal plants, patent medicines, and magico-religious beliefs and practices. He investigates folk healers and their methods, profiling three living practitioners: an herbalist, a faith healer, and a Native American healer. The book also includes an appendix of botanicals and a glossary of folk medical terms. Demonstrating the ongoing interplay between mainstream scientific medicine and folk medicine, Cavender challenges the conventional view of southern Appalachia as an exceptional region isolated from outside contact. His thorough and accessible study reveals how Appalachian folk medicine encompasses such diverse and important influences as European and Native American culture and America's changing medical and health-care environment. In doing so, he offers a compelling representation of the cultural history of the region as seen through its health practices."]

Cox, Lisa D. "Rachel Allen, Medicine Woman." *Alamance Genealogist*, 30:3 (September 2013), 124-125. [1760?-1840; Pennsylvania to Alamance County ca. 1762 with her parents and siblings]

Duffy, John. *Epidemics in Colonial America.* Baton Rouge, Louisiana State University Press, 1953; reprinted: Port Washington, N. Y.: Books for Libraries, 1972.

Fischer, Kirsten. "Common Disturbers of the Peace: The Politics of White Women's Sexual Misconduct in Colonial North Carolina." In Janet L. Coryell, Martha H. Swain, Sandra Gioia Treadway, and Elizabeth Hayes Turner,

---

[35] Office of the Registrar General's compilation, *Genealogy Guidelines* (Washington, D. C.: National Society Daughters of the American Revolution, 2014), 94-95.

eds., *Beyond Image and Convention: Explorations in Southern Women's History* (Columbia and London: University of Missouri Press, 1998), 10-27.

Fischer, Kirsten. *Suspect Relations: Sex, Race, and Resistance in Colonial North Carolina.* Ithaca, N. Y.: Cornell University Press, 2002. [This book covers the topics through the entire Colonial period, but includes references specific to the Revolutionary era throughout as well.]

Forbus, Wiley Davis. *Medicine in North Carolina: A Survey of the Development of Medican Science in Carolina "North and East of the Cape Fear."* 2 vols. Durham: W. D. Forbus, 1973.

Fulghum, R. Neil. "Hugh Walker and North Carolina's 'Smallpox Currency' of 1779." *Colonial Newsletter*, 45:3 (December 2005), 2895-2920.

Graham, Charles P. *A Glimpse of Carolina Medicine and the Lower Cape Fear Area: From Colonial Times to 1860.* Wilmington: Wilmington-New Hanover County American Revolution Bicentennial Association, 1975.

Guion, Isaac. "Isaac Guion Papers, ca. 1780." Manuscript, PC.543, State Archives of North Carolina, Raleigh. [Online catalog description: "Letter from Dr. Guion, member of Council of State, to Brig. Gen. John Ashe in camp at Wilmington about surgeons, assistants, and medicines for militia brigades."]

Jones, Thomas B. "Calvin Jones, M. D.: A Case Study in the Practices of Early American Medicine." *North Carolina Historical Review*, 49:1 (January 1972), 56-71. [Online description from "North Carolina Periodicals Index," East Carolina University: "This article examines the career of physician and surgeon Calvin Jones of North Carolina. During his career, Jones bridged the gap between a method of medicine characterized by speculative systems of pathology and heroic practice (1729-1820) and a period (1820-1870) that saw to the implementation of a method of modern pathology and clinical studies."]

Kopperman, Paul E. "The Medical Dimension of Cornwallis's Army, 1780-1781." *North Carolina Historical Review*, 89:4 (October 2012), 367-398. [Online description from "North Carolina Periodicals Index," East Carolina University: "This article examines the medical and health concerns of the military force in the Southern theater under the command of Lord Cornwallis during the Revolutionary War. It also discusses the impact the shortage of medical supplies and services has on military strategy and execution."]

Lawrence, R. C. "Some Colonial Physicians." *The State: A Weekly Survey of North Carolina*, 10:11 (August 1942), 3; online: http://digital.ncdcr.gov/cdm/ref/collection/p16062coll18/id/33095. [Online description from "North Carolina Periodicals Index," East Carolina University: "Physicians were in the North Carolina colony almost as early as there were preachers. John King practiced in Chowan as early as 1694, and Godfrey Spruill was practicing at Edenton as early as 1702. Lawrence lists other outstanding doctors, including one he considers the most famous, Dr. Hugh Williamson of Chowan, who was appointed Surgeon-General of the North Carolina troops by Governor Richard Caswell."]

Lawrence, R. C. "Some Pioneer Physicians." *The State: A Weekly Survey of North Carolina*, 10:31 (January 1943), 4, 17; online: http://digital.ncdcr.gov/cdm/ref/collection/p16062coll18/id/14879. [Online description from "North Carolina Periodicals Index," East Carolina University: "North Carolina has a number of well-known physicians dating from its earliest days. One signed the Constitution. Another became Governor of the state. Others were outstanding in the service they rendered to the state. Among them were Ephraim Brevard, Thomas Burke, Hugh Williamson, and Edward Warren."]

Long, Dorothy. *Early North Carolina Medicine: Army Surgeons of the American Revolution*. [Winston-Salem?: Medical Society of the State of North Carolina], 1953.

Long, Dorothy. *Medicine in North Carolina: Essays in the History of Medical Science and Medical Service, 1524-1960*. Raleigh: North Carolina Medical Society, 1972. [Contents: Volume 1: *Development of Medical Science, Medical Administrative Agencies, and Medical Service Facilities in North Carolina*. Volume II: *Medical Education and Medical Service in North Carolina*.]

Moss, Kay. *Southern Folk Medicine, 1750-1820.* Columbia: University of South Carolina Press, 1999.

North Carolina (State). General Assembly. "[Document dated:] May 1, 1777: Re[spectin] *Pennsylvania Farmer* and Small Pox (with Messages)." Manuscript; General Assembly Record Group; Session Records, April-May, 1777; Joint Papers, Committee Papers, Resolutions, Miscellaneous Bills and Amendments; Senate Joint Resolutions, Box 1 (MARS ID: 66.8.9.11.5; item), State Archives of North Carolina, Raleigh. [Online catalog description: Resolution to prevent the passengers on board the *Pennsylvania Farmer* from coming ashore until the threat of small pox has been removed."]

North Carolina (State). General Assembly. "[Document dated:] September 8, [1780]: Joint Papers, Committee Papers, Resolutions, Senate Bills, House Bills, On Petition of Doctor Isaac Alexander, Re[specting] Hospital at Charlotte (with Petition)." Manuscript; General Assembly Record Group; Session Records, August-September 1780, Box 1 (MARS ID: 66.8.22.7.6; item), State Archives of North Carolina, Raleigh. [Online catalog description: "Alexander informs the Assembly that he and his associates have been providing medical care to the sick and wounded arriving in Charlotte as a result of the fighting in the western part of the state. Their resources are limited, though, so they ask the Assembly to make some arrangement for the care of the injured. The chambers appoint a committee, which recommends that a hospital be established in Charlotte and that Alexander be named director. The Assembly concurs."]

North Carolina (State). General Assembly. "[Document dated:] Apr. 26, [1784]: Joint Papers, Committee Papers, Resolutions, Senate Bills, House Bills, Report Regarding the Petitions of Dr. Miles King and Robert Hunter (Petition Only)." Manuscript; General Assembly Record Group; Session Records, April-June 1784, Box (MARS ID: 66.8.32.1.4; item), State Archives of North Carolina, Raleigh. [Online catalog description: "Petition of Dr. Miles King regards his request for compensation for medical services he provided the North Carolina Continental Line. Petition of Robert Hunter requests compensation promised for three saddles he provided to the Army."]

North Carolina (State). General Assembly. "[Document dated:] May 1, [1784]: Joint Papers, Committee Papers, Resolutions, Senate Bills, House Bills, Resolution in Favor of Robert Brownfield and Nathaniel Alexander, 1784." Manuscript; General Assembly Record Group; Session Records, April-June 1784, Box 2 (MARS ID: 66.8.32.5.12), State Archives of North Carolina, Raleigh. [Online catalog description: "Resolution awards Robert Brownfield and Nathaniel Alexander with one thousand acres each for their services as surgeons in the Continental hospitals."]

Parramore, Thomas C. "The County Distemper in Colonial North Carolina." *North Carolina Historical Review*, 48:1 (January 1971), 44-52. [Online description from "North Carolina Periodicals Index," East Carolina University: This article examines documented accounts and cases of a disease referred to as 'yaws' in an attempt to determine whether it was contracted as extensively as some accounts make it seem, or if it was just one among many health problems faced by the early settlers. An important distinction between two diseases known as 'yaws' is made, with one being a topical disease restricted to rural areas and populations whose living conditions, knowledge of sanitation, and personal hygiene are rudimentary. The other was known at the time of press as endemic (or non-venereal) syphilis. Details of period symptoms, diagnoses, and identification of the types of 'yaws' as well as modern distinctions made by the author based on his research are included."]

Parramore, Thomas C. "Doctors Whig and Tory." *North Carolina Medical Journal*, (February 1968), 65-68. [William Houston, Ephraim Brevard, Alexander Gaston, Soloman Halling, Thomas Burke, Hugh Williamson, Thomas Cobham, Robert Lenox, Alexander Morrison.]

Tannenbaum, Rebecca J. *Health and Wellness in Colonial America*. Santa Barbara: Greenwood, 2012.

Watson, Alan D. "Combating Contagion: Smallpox and the Protection of Public Health in North Carolina, 1750 to 1825." *North Carolina Historical Review,* 90:1 (January 2013), 26-48.

Well, Warner. "Indian Medicine in North Carolina." *The State: Down Home in North Carolina*, 25:21 (March 1958), 11-12, 20; online: http://digital.ncdcr.gov/cdm/ref/collection/p16062coll18/id/50973. [Online description from "North Carolina Periodicals Index," East Carolina University: "Utilizing empiricism as well as methods passed down from previous generations of Native American 'doctors,' used a variety of techniques to cure illnesses. Sweathouses (bagnios), flagellation with rattlesnake teeth, moxabustion, inunctions with bear grease, deer tendons as sutures, use of ground up shells, and ingesting local plant life, are a few methods."]

Wiley, Mary C. "Medicine in Old Wachovia." *The State: Down Home in North Carolina*, 22:4 (July 1954), 10-12; online: http://digital.ncdcr.gov/cdm/ref/collection/p16062coll18/id/32241. [Online description from "North Carolina Periodicals Index," East Carolina University: "When pioneer Moravian physicians came to the Salem community, they brought the skills they learned in the Old World with them. To this they added the healing qualities of native herbs in their cures. Many of these items, such as dental surgery equipment, brass mortar and pestle, small wooden pill bottles, and apothecary scales, may be viewed at the Moravian Museum, which is located in the old Boys' School in the heart of Old Salem."]

British Forces and Their German Allies

Blagden, Charles, Sir, 1748-1820. "[Diaries], 1776-1788." Manuscript Osborn fc16, Beinecke Library, Yale University, New Haven. [Online catalog description: "Manuscript, in a single hand, consisting primarily of scientific and travel notes. The manuscript begins with Blagden's notes during his service as a surgeon in the army during the American Revolutionary War between 1776 and 1780. Stationed in the Carolinas and in Virginia, Blagden reports extensively on the temperature and weather as well as on the movements of troops; information about ships captured and officers killed both in the British and Continental armies; and the outcomes of battles both in his vicinity and elsewhere in North America. He also records disputes with other hospital administrators about how to tend or house the sick, and dines with various generals. In 1777, he gives an account of Native Americans in the town in which he is staying. Throughout, he also records many observations about local birds and fish, including plover, mackerel, and trout."]

Cameron, Rebecca. "A Sprig of English Oak: Lieutenant Colonel Wilson Webster, of His Majesty's 33[d] Regiment of Foot, 1781." *North Carolina Booklet*, 12:3 (January 1913), 195-202.

Cary, A. D. L., and Stouppe McCane; Forster Groom, illus. *Regimental Records of the Royal Welch Fusiliers (Late the 23rd Foot)*. 4 vols. London: Published for the Royal United Service Institution by Forster Groom, 1921-1929.

Causey, Ellen Fitzgibbons. "Dunmore's Ethiopian Regiment." In William S. Powell, ed.; Jay Mazzocchi, assoc. ed., *Encyclopedia of North Carolina* (Chapel Hill: University of North Carolina Press in association with the University of North Carolina Library, 2006), 360.

Clinton, Henry, Sir; William B. Willcox, ed. *The American Rebellion: Sir Henry Clinton's Narrative of His Campaigns, 1775-1782, with an Appendix of Original Documents*. New Haven: Yale University Press, 1954.

Ferrar, Michael Lloyd. *A History of the Services of the 19th Regiment, Now Alexandra, Princess of Wale's Own (Yorkshire Regiment), from Its Formation in 1688 to 1911*. London: Eden Fisher & Company, 1911.

Forbes, John; James Alfred Proctor, ed. *Writings of General John Forbes Relating to Service in North America*. Menasha, Wisc.: Collegiate Press, 1938.

Fortesque, J[ohn] W[illiams]. *A History of the 17th Lancers (Duke of Cambridge's Own)*. London and New York: Macmillan and Company, 1895; online: http://babel.hathitrust.org/cgi/pt?id=mdp.39015027428823;view=1up;seq=13.

Foss, Michael. *The Royal Fusiliers: The 7th Regiment of Foot* (Famous Regiments series). London: Hamish Hamilton, 1967.

Great Britain. Colonial Office. "Charleston, S. C. Duplicate of J[ames] Simpson, [Intendant General of the S. C. Civil Police]. To Lord George Germain, [Sec. of State]. 13 Aug., 1780." Copy of a manuscript in the National Archives of the United Kingdom (formerly the Public Records Office), Kew, Richmond, Surrey, England; 71.347.1-7, British Records, Colonial Office, Secretary of State, Peace Commissioners' Reports, State Archives of North Carolina, Raleigh. [Online catalog description: "General topics: S. C. merchants desire to export commodities to Great Britain to pay debts owed to British merchants; General Horatio Gates's arrival at Deep Creek, N. C. to head a large rebel army; general military affairs in S. C., including troop movements and skirmishes."]

Great Britain. Colonial Office. "List of Field Officers of the Established Provincial Corps of North America." Copy of a manuscript in the National Archives of the United Kingdom (formerly the Public Records Office), Kew, Richmond, Surrey, England; 70.429.1-3, State Archives of North Carolina, Raleigh. [Online catalog description: "Includes the commanding officers of the N. C. Rangers and the N. C. Volunteers."]

Great Britain. Colonial Office. "No. 28 South Molton Street, London. Josiah Martin, [Former Gov. Of N.C.], to Welbore Ellis, [Sec. of State]. 7 Mar., 1782." Copy of a manuscript in the National Archives of the United Kingdom (formerly the Public Records Office), Kew, Richmond, Surrey, England; 71.338.1-4, State Archives of North Carolina, Raleigh. [Online catalog description: "The odyssey of N. C. Highlander soldiers and officers during the Am. Revolution."]

Great Britain. Colonial Office. "St. James's Palace, [London]. Copy of 'Orders and Instructions' for Sir Henry Clinton, Commander-in-Chief in America, 22 Jly., 1779." Copy of a manuscript in the National Archives of the United Kingdom (formerly the Public Records Office), Kew, Richmond, Surrey, England; 72.176.1-7, British Records, Colonial Office, Secret Despatches, State Archives of North Carolina, Raleigh. [Online catalog description: "General instructions concerning a commission (not included) authorizing Clinton to issue Crown pardons to rebels: conditions for pardon eligibility (1) all illegal assemblies, conventions, and congresses to be dissolved and British colonial government to be recognized as the only legal governing authority and (2) armed rebel bodies are to be disbanded and rebel forts to be turned over to British authorities; Clinton to issue a peace proclamation recognizing pardoned rebels; Parliament repeals both the remaining Townshend Act (1767) on tea and the Massachusetts Bay Regulating Act (1774); a council of advisers (including North Carolina Governor Josiah Martin) appointed to assist Clinton in his duties as peace commissioner; Clinton to make regular reports to the secretary of state."]

Great Britain. Colonial Office. "Whitehall. Letter from Ld. Dartmouth, Sec. of State, to Gov Josiah Martin, #21. Oct 27, 1775." Copy of a manuscript in the National Archives of the United Kingdom (formerly the Public Records Office), Kew, Richmond, Surrey, England; (MARS Id: 21.1.27.58; folder), "British Records Collection," State Archives of North Carolina, Raleigh. [Online catalog description: "Seven regiments, with two companies of artillery, being sent to Cape Fear and to be commanded by one of Gen. Howe's officers; Martin to command any provincial troops raised; Martin secretly to procure pilots; encloses King's speech to Parliament."]

Great Britain. Colonial Office. Secret Despatches. "Whitehall, [London]. Copy of Ld. George Germain, [Secretary of State], to Sir Henry Clinton, [Commander-in- Chief in America], no. 76. 3 Jan, 1781 Copy of a manuscript in the National Archives of the United Kingdom (formerly the Public Records Office), Kew, Richmond, Surrey, England; 72.181.1-5 (MARS ID: 21.21.43.9; folder), "British Records Collection," State Archives of North Carolina, Raleigh. [Online catalog description: "General topics: acknowledges receipt of recent Clinton correspondence; British defeat in the Battle of King's Mountain results in Ld. Cornwallis's withdrawing from North Carolina and Maj. Gen. Leslie withdrawing from Virginia; British loss of Portsmouth, Virginia; plans for the 1781 campaign to emphasize bringing the American War to an end; British recruits and reinforcements being sent to Charleston, South Carolina, which is to serve as primary depot for the southern campaign."]

Great Britain. Public Record Office [now the National Archives]. "Public Record Office. Carleton Papers. Headquarters Papers of the British Army in America (PRO 30/55, Selections)." Copy of a manuscript in the National Archives of the United Kingdom (formerly the Public Records Office), Kew, Richmond, Surrey, England; (MARS ID: 21.214; series), "British Records Collection," State Archives of North Carolina, Raleigh. [Online catalog description: "Headquarters papers of Sir Guy Carleton, last commander in chief in America during the Revolutionary War. Items copied concern North Carolina's participation in that war."]

Great Britain. Royal Artillery Institution. "Papers of James Pattison. (RAI Pattison, Selections)." Copy of a manuscript in the National Archives of the United Kingdom (formerly the Public Records Office), Kew, Richmond, Surrey, England; (MARS Id: 21.298; series), "British Records Collection," State Archives of North Carolina, Raleigh. [Online catalog description: "Maj. Gen. James Pattison was for part of the Revolutionary War commander of Royal Artillery in North America and superintendent general of police for the City of New York. North Carolina items in this collection concern various aspects of the American Revolution."]

Great Britain. Treasury. "Adjutant General's Office, [Charleston, South Carolina]. Jno. [John] Stapleton to Colonel [Robert] Gray, Paymaster of Militia. 2 Jly. 1782" Copy of a manuscript in the National Archives of the United Kingdom (formerly the Public Records Office), Kew, Richmond, Surrey, England; Number: Z.5.143N (MARS ID: 21.102.5.7 and 21.102.5.8; folders), State Archives of North Carolina, Raleigh. [Online catalog description: "To pay Ensign Martin of North Carolina Militia for six months' service under Colonel {David} Fanning. {See 21.102.5.1.9.}"]

Great Britain. Treasury. "Adjutant General's Office, Charleston, South Carolina. Jno. [John] Stapleton to Colonel [Robert] Gray, Paymaster of Militia. 2 Jly. 1782" Copy of a manuscript in the National Archives of the United Kingdom (formerly the Public Records Office), Kew, Richmond, Surrey, England; Z.5.143N, State Archives of North Carolina, Raleigh. [Online catalog description: "To pay Captain McLeod of North Carolina Militia for six months' service under Colonel {David} Fanning. {See 21.102.5.1.9.}"]

Johnson, Uzal, 1757?-1827. "War Diary, 1780-1781." Mauscript, "Thorne Collection of Elias Boudinot," Manuscript C0001, Box 3, Folder 10, Firestone Library, Princeton University, Princeton, N. J. [Online finding aid description: "Among papers of others in the collection are Loyalist surgeon Uzal Johnson's journal (5 March 1780 to 6 March 1781), including accounts of the battle of King's Mountain and other military movements in and around Charleston, South Carolina, while serving under General Patterson in the 71st Regiment of Light Infantry…"]

Jones, Eldon. "The British Withdrawal from the South, 1781-85." In W. Robert Higgins, ed., *Revolutionary War in the South: Power, Conflict and Leadership* (Durham: Duke University Press, 1979), 259-286.

Lewis, J. D. "The American Revolution in North Carolina: The British Army and the Loyalists." Online: http://www.carolana.com/NC/Revolution/revolution_british_allies_loyalists.html.

Perry, James, 1756-1821. "Papers, 1812." Manuscript RUB Bay 0039:07, David M. Rubenstein Rare Book & Manuscript Library, Duke University, Durham. [Online catalog description: "A letter from James Perry (1756-1821), British journalist, asking George Hanger for a statement concerning a parliamentary investigation of funds awarded Hanger for his services during the War of the American Revolution."]

Tallent, Fran. "Hessians in Cabarrus." *The Golden Nugget (Cabarrus Genealogical Society)*, 13:3 (Autumn 2005), 77.

Urban, Mark. *Fusiliers: The Saga of a British Redcoat Regiment in the American Revolution*. New York: Walker & Company, 2007.

Webb, Edward Arthur Howard. *A History of the Services of the 17th (the Leicestershire) Regiment: Containing an Account of the Formation of the Regiment in 1688, and of Its Subsequent Services, Revised and Continued to 1910*. London: Vacher, 1911.

Winslow, Raymond A., Jr. "Two Lists of North Carolinians and Others Serving in British Armies during the American Revolution." *North Carolina Genealogical Society Journal*, 16:3 (August 199), 142-146; (part 2), 20:2 (May 1994), 96-117; (part 3), 20:4 (November 1994), 242-276.

Wray, George, d. 1793. "Letter, 1781 Jan 15, Charleston, S. C., Peter Traille to George Wray." Manuscript (5849), Manuscript Division, South Caroliniana Library, University of South Carolina, Columbia. [Online catalog description: "Commissary for the Royal Artillery of the British Army during American Revolution. Letter from Peter Traille, Charleston, S. C., directing Wray to issue to 'Mr. Samuel French, Conductor of Stores to the Royal Artillery' certain supplies and equipment, receipted by French for the 'Ordnance Ammunition and Stores ... for the Expedition under the Command of Major [James] Craig.' Less than a week after Traille wrote this letter, Craig captured the town of Wilmington, North Carolina."]

British Forces and Their German Allies – Cornwallis' Campaign through North Carolina

Anderson, William Lee, III. "Where Did Cornwallis's Army Invade North Carolina? (Also the Battle of Charlotte, 26 September 1780)." Online: http://www.elehistory.com/amrev/CornwallisNCInvasion.pdf.

Arthur, Billy. "Cornwallis' Chatham County Surrender?" *The State: Down Home in North Carolina*, 60:5 (October 1992), 10; online: http://digital.ncdcr.gov/cdm/ref/collection/p16062coll18/id/65703. [Online description from "North Carolina Periodicals Index," East Carolina University: "Speculation centers on the possibility that British general Cornwallis might have surrendered in Chatham County (March 1781) except for the detection of colonial troops that caused the British to flee south to Fayetteville."]

Balfour, Nisbet. [Letterbook of Lieut. Col. Nisbet Balfour, British Commandant of Charleston, S. C. 1 Jan. - 1 Dec. 1781]. Manuscript MSS L2001F617, Society of the Cincinnati Library, Anderson House, Washington, D. C.; digital surrogate available at http://cdm16923.contentdm.oclc.org/cdm/ref/collection/p16923coll6/id/547. [Online catalog description: "Most in a single, unidentified secretarial hand and signed N. B.; 3 are in a different hand, possibly that of Balfour himself, and signed N. Balfour. Correspondents: Benedict Arnold (2 letters), Sir Henry Clinton (18 letters), Lord Sackville, Secretary of State (12 letters), Sir James Wright, British governor of Georgia (4 letters), and others. Context: Sir Henry Clinton captured Charleston in January, 1780; and Balfour, appointed commandant six months later, played a strategic role in evaluating and transmitting information, money, and supplies north to Clinton and south to Tarleton during the southern campaign, many details of which are recorded here." Includes reports of actions by Americans Light Horse Harry Lee, General Nathanael Greene, Francis Marion, and Daniel Morgan; and British officers Col. Cruger, Col. Brown, Cornwallis, Tarleton, Rawdon and others.]

Blythe, Dolores S. "Hornets at Work." *The State: Down Home in North Carolina*, 64:6 (November 1978), 12; online: http://digital.ncdcr.gov/cdm/ref/collection/p16062coll18/id/58157. [Online description from "North Carolina Periodicals Index," East Carolina University: "Lord Cornwallis and his British army had been in Charlotte for almost a week when Cornwallis dispatched a foraging party led by Major John Doyle on October 3, 1780. Captain James Thompson and thirteen other local residents surrounded the party and ambushed them, causing the British to believe they were under attack of a large force. Soon after, British forces retreated from Charlotte."]

Boynton, Robert P. "British Activities near Cabarrus during the Revolutionary War." *The Golden Nugget (Cabarrus Genealogical Society)*, 13:3 (Autumn 2005), 76-77.

Bright, Jeffery G., and Stewart E. Dunaway. *Like a Bear with His Stern in a Corner: The NC Campaign during the American Revolution: The Battles of Hart's Mill, Pyle's Defeat, Clapp's Mill, Weitzel's Mill.* [North Carolina: J. Bright and S. Dunaway; Morrisville: Lulu.com, [2009?] [Publisher's description: "This book documents a part of the Southern Campaign of the American Revolution immediately after the Race to the Dan and leading up to the Battle at Guilford Courthouse. The period between February and March 1781 was an important time for North Carolina as well as America as a whole. Patriot forces continued to skirmish with British Gen Cornwallis. Although none of these events were paramount or decisive, they illustrated the fortitude of the American Spirit. This strong resolve sent a clear message to the British that the patriots would rather fight than remain loyal to the King. Read about Hart's Mill, Pyle's Defeat, Clapp's Mill and Weitzel's Mill. Learn what occurred, the issues and impacts surrounding each of these unique events. The title of this book comes from a letter written by Col. Otho Williams to Gen Greene describing Cornwallis' tactics during this time period, detailing one of the many aspects that are fully documented in this book."]

Broughton-Mainwaring, Rowland. *Historical Record of the Royal Welch Fusiliers, Late the Twenty-Third Regiment, or, Royal Welsh Fusiliers (the Prince of Wales's Own Regiment of Welsh Fusiliers), Containing an Account of the Formation of the Regiment in 1689, and of Its Subsequent Services to 1889.* London: Hatchards, 1889; online: http://catalog.hathitrust.org/Record/006066251.

Carter, William H[arding]. "A British Dragoon in the American Revolution." *Cavalry Journal*, 32:133 (October 1923), 400-411. [Banastre Tarleton]

Corbitt, D. L. "General Green Avoids Encounter with Lord Cornwallis; Great Numbers Join Royal Army." *North Carolina Historical Review*, 3:1 (January 1926), 130-131.

Cornwallis, Charles Cornwallis, Marquis, 1738-1805. *Answer to That Part of the Narrative of Lieutenant-General Sir Henry Clinton, K. B., Which Relates to the Conduct of Lieutenant-General Earl Cornwallis, during the Campaign in North America, in the Year 1781.* London: J. Debrett, 1783; reprinted: New York: Research Imprints, 1970.

Cornwallis, Charles, Marquis, 1738-1805. "Proclamation, 1781 March 18, North Carolina." Manuscript, Rosenbach A. S. W. Collected cats. 16:446, 30:105, Rosenbach Museum and Library, Philadelphia, Pa. [Description on ArchiveGrId: "After his costly victory at Guilford Court House, Cornwallis offers protection to any rebels who will surrender."]

Cornwallis, Charles, Marquis, 1738-1805; Ian Saberton, ed. *The Cornwallis Papers: The Campaigns of 1780 and 1781 in the Southern Theatre of the American Revolutionary War.* 5 vols. Uckfield, East Sussex, Eng.: Naval & Military Press, 2010. [Publisher's description: "This work deals with Britain's last throw of the dice in the American Revolutionary War. Comprising six volumes, it contains a fully edited transcript of almost all the papers that were written by, or came before, Lord Cornwallis during his command in the south. The papers cover the siege of Charlestown, his tenuous occupation of South Carolina and Georgia, the autumn, winter and Virginia campaigns, and ultimately his capitulation at Yorktown. Volume I (1st April to 15th August 1780) begins with Cornwallis's involvement in the siege of Charlestown and his consolidation of British authority in South Carolina. It ends as British ascendancy there begins so soon to unravel in the face of internal uprisings and an external threat."]

"Cornwallis' Attack on Charlotte Town." *Southern Campaigns of the American Revolution*, 2:10.1 (October 2005), 1-2; online: www.southerncampaign.org [September 1780]

Dauphinee, Andrew D. "Lord Cornwallis and the Loyalists: A Study in British Pacification during the American Revolution." Ph. D. dissertation, Temple University, 2011.

Davenport, John Scott; cartography by Garland P. Stout. *Cornwallis' Invasion of North Carolina in 1781, Involving the Piedmont and the Dunker Congregations therein, with Notation of Tory Uprisings in 1780 Counter to His Lordship's Strategy (Not Including Skirmishes, Pyle's Massacre, or Fanning's Activities).* Charlotte: Carolina Maps by Mail, 2004.

Dukes, Richard Sears, Jr. "Anatomy of Failure: British Military Policy in the Southern Campaign of the American Revolution, 1775-1781." Ph. D. dissertation, University of South Carolina, 1993.

Faden, William. *The Marches of Lord Cornwallis in the Southern Provinces, Now States of North America, Comprehending the Two Carolinas, with Virginia and Maryland, and the Delaware Counties.* London: William Faden, 1787; reprinted and annotated with additional information by David Schenck and with the title: *The Marches of Lord Cornwallis and Major General Greene in the Southern Provinces, Now States of North America, Comprehending the Two Carolinas.* Raleigh: Edwards & Broughton, 1889.

Ferguson, Patrick, 1744-1780. "Address, 1780." Manuscript File 1780 October 1 MAD 4/14/File, Memorial Library, University of Wisconsin, Madison. [Online catalog description: "Brief address by Major Patrick Ferguson of the British Army to the inhabitants of North Carolina, dated Denard's Ford, Broad River, Tryon County, imploring them to gather arms against a 'barbaric force,' copied from the Virginia paper {*Virginia Gazette*} printed by Dixon and Nicolson, Nov. 11, 1780."]

Fiske, John. "The Disasters of 1780." *Atlantic Monthly*, 66:395 (September 1890), 337-354.

Frasche, Louis D. F. "Problems of Command: Cornwallis, Partisans and Militia, 1780." *Military Review*, 57:2 (April 1977), 60-74.

Graham, W. A. "The Battle of Cowan's Ford - The Passage of the Catawba River by Lord Cornwallis, February 1, 1781." *The North Carolina Booklet*, 5 (1906), 232-246.

Graham, George Washington. "Cornwallis's Campaign in North Carolina." Senior thesis, University of North Carolina at Chapel Hill, 1903.

"General Cornwallis' Opinion of North Carolina, 1781." *North Carolina Genealogical Society Journal*, 6:2 (May 1980), 106.

Gibson, George H. "Twenty-Seven Tickets." *North Carolina Historical Review*, 37:4 (October 1960), 477-487. [Online description from "North Carolina Periodicals Index," East Carolina University: "During the American Revolution, the British came to North Carolina when the Colonial armies crossed the Catawba River and began the retreat to the Dan River. During this time, the arrival of British troops to the Moravian settlements at Bethania, Bethabara, and Salem caused anxiety and heavy losses in livestock, forage, and provisions. To provide for the losses, the acting Commissary A. Knect wrote reimbursement tickets to those residents who supplied the British with supplies."]

Graham, Joseph. "Revolutionary History of North Carolina: British Invasion of 1780-81." *North Carolina University Magazine*, 4:8 (October 1855), 337-352.

Great Britain. Army. "Charles Cornwallis Orderly Book, 1780-1781." Manuscript M-1815, William L. Clements Library, University of Michigan, Ann Arbor; online finding aid available at http://quod.lib.umich.edu/cgi/f/findaid/findaid-idx?c=clementsmss;idno=umich-wcl-M-1815cor. [Online catalog description: "The Charles Cornwallis orderly book (148 pages), contains orders from Cornwallis' moving headquarters in the southern theater of the American Revolutionary War. These document the British march across North Carolina, the aftermath of the Guilford Courthouse campaign, and Cornwallis' campaign in Virginia. The book contains lists of promotions and reports of courts martial, as well as general marching orders and information on supplies, transportation, and the sick and wounded." The finding aid for this collection is accessible through the online catalog record.]

Great Britain. Colonial Office. "Charleton [*sic*], S. C. Printed Analysis of the Costs of Transporting Cornwallis's Army through N. C. and Va. in 1780 and 1781. 2 Aug., 1780-1782." Copy of a manuscript in the National Archives of the United Kingdom (formerly the Public Records Office), Kew, Richmond, Surrey, England; 70.415.1-12 (MARS ID: 21.20.6.1; folder), "British Records Collection," State Archives of North Carolina, Raleigh.

Great Britain. Colonial Office. "Copy of 'The Army to Be Employed by the British United Colonies – Campaign 1776.'" Copy of a manuscript in the National Archives of the United Kingdom (formerly the Public Records Office), Kew, Richmond, Surrey, England; 71.238.1-3 (MARS ID: 21.20.120.2; folder), "British Records Collection," State Archives of North Carolina, Raleigh. [Online catalog description: "Includes commanding officers, numbers of companies and troops, and general area of employment. Three battalions are to be raised in N. C. Copy referred to in Hart to Weymouth, 21 July 1776 (21.20.120.1.1)."]

Great Britain. Colonial Office. "Headquarters, Waxhaw, S. C. Josiah Martin, [Former Gov. of N.V.], to Lord George Germain, [Sec. of State]. 21 Sep., 1780." Copy of a manuscript in the National Archives of the United Kingdom (formerly the Public Records Office), Kew, Richmond, Surrey, England; 71.337.1-3 (MARS ID: 21.20.140.14; folder), "British Records Collection," State Archives of North Carolina, Raleigh. [Online catalog description: General topics: praise for Cornwallis's actions at Camden; pro-British sentiments in N. C."]

Great Britain. Colonial Office. "Portsmouth, Va. Extract of a Letter from [Benedict] Arnold to ____. 13 Feb., 1781." Copy of a manuscript in the National Archives of the United Kingdom (formerly the Public Records Office), Kew, Richmond, Surrey, England; 70.422.1-4 (MARS ID: 21.20.6.8; folder), "British Records Collection," State Archives of North Carolina, Raleigh. [Online catalog description: "General letter of his activities in Va. including his proposal for a raid on Albemarle Sound, Edenton, and New Bern to disrupt N. C. shipping and divert attention from the movements of Generals Cornwallis and Leslie."]

Great Britain. Colonial Office. "Return of Provisions, etc. Issued by the Commissary of Capture in the Army under the Command of… Cornwallis. 16 May-31 Aug. 1781)." Copy of a manuscript in the National Archives of the United Kingdom (formerly the Public Records Office), Kew, Richmond, Surrey, England; 71.299.1-3 (MARS ID: 21.20.133.2; folder), State Archives of North Carolina, Raleigh. [Online catalog description: "Provisions include beef, flour, coffee, sugar, tobacco, bacon, salt, butter, corn, cattle, horses, sheep, hats, shoes, and wagons. Among the regiments receiving these provisions is the North Carolina Loyalists Regiment. Enclosed in Hay to Germain, 11 October 1781 (21.20.133.1.1)."]

Great Britain. Colonial Office. "St. James's, [London]. Opinion of [David Murray], Viscount Stormont, [Sec. of State]. 30 Sep., 1780." Copy of a manuscript in the National Archives of the United Kingdom (formerly the Public Records Office), Kew, Richmond, Surrey, England; 71.239.1-2 (MARS ID: 221.20.121.1; folder), "British Records Collection," State Archives of North Carolina, Raleigh. [Online catalog description: "Questions the propriety of publishing extracts from Lord Cornwallis's dispatches in *The Gazette*. Restates offer by N. C. Highlanders to form a pro-British regiment."]

Great Britain. Colonial Office. "St. Augustine, [Fl.]. Thomas Brown, Superintendent of Indian Affairs, to ____. 1 Jun, 1783." Copy of a manuscript in the National Archives of the United Kingdom (formerly the Public Records Office), Kew, Richmond, Surrey, England; 71.114.1-4 (MARS ID: 21.20.69.15; folder), "British Archives Collection," State Archives of North Carolina, Raleigh. [Online catalog description: "Brief narrative of Brown's military endeavors during the American Revolution in service to the Crown. Mention of a map (not located) of the southern district to be enclosed."]

Great Britain. Colonial Office. "Yarmouth, [Eng.]. William Tryon, [Former Gov. of N. C.], to Lord George Germain, [Sec. of State]. 10 Jun., 1781." Manuscript, 71.305.1-2, State Archives of North Carolina, Raleigh. [Online catalog description: "Comments on the strategic importance of the arrival of Lord Cornwallis in Wilmington."]

Great Britain. Public Record Office [now the National Archives]. "Public Record Office. Gifts and Deposits. Cornwallis Papers. (PRO 30/11, Selections." Copy of a manuscript in the National Archives of the United Kingdom (formerly the Public Records Office), Kew, Richmond, Surrey, England; (MARS Id: 21.208; series), "British Records Collection," State Archives of North Carolina, Raleigh. [Online catalog description: "The papers of Charles, Lord Cornwallis. The North Carolina items all relate to the Revolutionary War in the south."]

Gruber, Ira D. "Britain's Southern Strategy." In W. Robert Higgins, ed. *The Revolutionary War in the South: Power, Conflict, and Leadership: Essays in Honor of John Richard Allen* (Durham: Duke University Press, 1979), 205-238.

Guedalla, Philip. "Portrait of a Red-Faced General: Lieutenant-General Earl Cornwallis." *Harper's Magazine*, (December 1925), 102-106; online through the magazine's subscription website: https://www.unz.org/Pub/Harpers-1925dec-00102. Also: Gerald W[hite] Johnson. "A Footnote to Mr. Guedalla's *Portrait of a Red-Faced General.*" *Harper's Magazine*, (March 1926), 530.

Hanger, George. *An Address to the Army; in Reply to Strictures, by Roderick M'Kenzie, (Late Lieutenant in the 71st Regiment) on Tarlton's History of the Campaigns of 1780 and 1781*. London: Printed for J. Ridgway, 1789.

Hayes, John T. *Massacre: Tarleton vs. Buford, May 29, 1780; Lee vs. Pyle, 1781*. Fort Lauderdale, Fla.: Saddlebag Press, 1997.

Heaton, Charles. "The Failure of Enlightenment Military Doctrine in Revolutionary America: The Piedmont Campaign and the Fate of the British Army in the Lower South." *North Carolina Historical Review*, 87:2 (April 2010), 127-157. [Online description from "North Carolina Periodicals Index," East Carolina University: "This article examines British military forces and strategy in the American South during the Revolutionary War. The commander of British forces in the Lower South, Lord Cornwallis, wished to revise British strategy in North America. The article also looks at his attempts to seize North Carolina and the strategic management styles of both the British and American armies during the 'Piedmont Campaign'."]

Hill Brown, Richard K. "Lord Cornwallis, a Military Man in the South, 1780-1781." M. A. thesis, University of North Carolina at Chapel Hill, 1967.

Hill, Daniel Harvey. "Greene's Retreat." *North Carolina Booklet*, 1:7 (November 1901), 3-26. [Online description from "North Carolina Periodicals Index," East Carolina University: "A look at General Cornwallis' campaign against North Carolina during the Revolutionary War beginning in Charlotte, where he was opposed by Continental General Nathaniel Greene. Cornwallis' and Greene's maneuvers, as well as positions of the other British and Continental Army forces over the course of a year are discussed."]

Hill Brown, Richard K. "Lord Cornwallis, a Military Man in the South, 1780-1781." M. A. thesis, University of North Carolina at Chapel Hill, 1967.

Hinshaw, Ida C. "Cornwallis in North Carolina: Episodes of the Revolutionary Period." *Journal of American History*, 6 (1912), 385-389.

Holder, Edward M. "Cornwallis in Wachovia." *The State: A Weekly Survey of North Carolina*, 10:38 (February 1943), 6-7, 20; online: http://digital.ncdcr.gov/cdm/ref/collection/p16062coll18/id/16810. [Online description from "North Carolina Periodicals Index," East Carolina University: "Holder describes the invasion of the Moravian territory on the northwest corner of the Wachovian tract, by the British forces who were in pursuit of General Nathanael Greene. British soldiers spent two days in the vicinity of Bethania."]

Jackson, James William. "Guerrilla Warfare in the Carolinas: The Defeat of Lord Cornwallis, 1780-1781." M. A. thesis, University of Tennessee, 1969.

Jenkins, Charles Francis. "Charles Francis Jenkins Collection, 1786-1808." Manuscript PC.1090 (MARS ID: 1600; record group), State Archives of North Carolina, Raleigh. [Online catalog description: "Edenton District Court attendance certificate (1786) and receipt for John Williams, superior court judge in Granville District; letter from Speaker Joseph B. Varnum, U. S. House of Representatives, to the governor of North Carolina informing him of a vacancy in North Carolina's delegation (1808); and recollections (n.d.) dictated by Dr. A. J. DeRosset, Sr. (b. 1767), of the British occupation of Wilmington in 1781, the home of Col. John Swann on the Northeast Cape Fear River, the fight at 'Big Bridge' there, the British gunboat and barge, and Generals Cornwallis and Tarleton."]

Johnson, Gerald W. "A Footnote to Mr. Guedalla's 'Portrait of a Red-Faced General'." *Harper's Magazine*, (March 1926), 530.

Kopperman, Paul E. "The Medical Dimension of Cornwallis's Army, 1780-1781." *North Carolina Historical Review*, 89:4 (October 2012), 367-398. [Online description from "North Carolina Periodicals Index," East Carolina University: "This article examines the medical and health concerns of the military force in the Southern theater under the command of Lord Cornwallis during the Revolutionary War. It also discusses the impact the shortage of medical supplies and services has on military strategy and execution."]

Kyte, George W. "Strategic Blunder: Lord Cornwallis Abandons the Carolinas, 1781." *The Historian*, 22 (1960), 129-144.

Lee, Henry, Jr. *The Campaign of 1781 in the Carolinas: with Remarks Historical and Critical on Johnson's Life of Greene; to Which is Added an Appendix of Original Documents, Relating to the History of the Revolution.* Philadelphia: E. Little, 1824; reprinted: Chicago: Quadrangle Books, 1962; Spartanburg, S. C.: The Reprint Co., 1975; Cranbury, N. J.: Scholar's Bookshelf, 2006.

Lee, Henry, Jr. "Letters of H. Lee, Jr., to R. H. Lee." *Historical Magazine with Notes and Queries*, 9 (September 1865), 281-283.

Lumpkin, Henry. *From Savannah to Yorktown: The American Revolution in the South.* Columbia: University of South Carolina Press, 1981.

"Memorials Related to Service in America, 1760-1804." Manuscript Mss Collection (BV War of Revolution, Memorials Non-circulating), Patricia D. Klingenstein Library, New-York Historical Society, New York. [Online catalog description: "Memorials, 1760-1804, of British officers and soldiers, detailing their service in America during the French and Indian War and the American Revolution, with some supporting documents. The memorials appeal for disability pensions, promotions, and in some cases commissions for their sons. One memorialist, Daniel Manson, also mentions the loss of his property in North Carolina."]

Newsome, Albert Ray. "A British Orderly Book, 1780-1781." *North Carolina Historical Review*, [part I] 9:1 (January 1932), 57-78; [part II] 9:2 (April 1932), 163-186; [part III] 9:3 (July 1932), 2; [part IV] 9:4 (October 1932), 366-392. [Online description from "North Carolina Periodicals Index," East Carolina University: "...British orderly Book which covers military operations and orders from August 28, 1780 through March 20, 1781. Sections specific to North Carolina include: Cornwallis' march across the state, the Guilford Court House Campaign, and some coverage of the British retreat from Wilmington. Alexander Leslie (?-1781)]

Nifong, Michael R. "In the Provincial Service: The British Legion in the American Revolution, 1778-1783." M. A. thesis, University of North Carolina at Chapel Hill, 1976.

Observations on Some Parts of the Answer of Earl Cornwallis to Sir Henry Clinton's Narrative; to Which Is Added an Appendix; Containing Extracts of Letters and Other Papers, to Which Reference is Necessary. London: J. Debrett, 1783; reprinted: New York: Research Imprints, 1970.

Pearson, Jesse T. "The Failure of British Strategy during the Southern Campaign of the American Revolutionary War, 1780-81." M. A. thesis, Master of Military Art and Science, United States Army, Command and General Staff College, 2005; online: http://cgsc.cdmhost.com/utils/getfile/collection/p4013coll2/id/366/filename/367.pdf.

Rankin, Hugh F. "Greene and Cornwallis: The Campaign in the Carolinas, 1780-1781." M. A. thesis, University of North Carolina at Chapel Hill, 1950; published with the same title: Raleigh: N. C. Divison of Archives & History, 1976.

Reese, George H. *The Cornwallis Papers: Abstracts of Americana.* Charlottesville: Published for Virginia Independence Bicentennial Commission [by] University Press of Virginia [1970].

Ross, C. R. "A Clock That Kept Time for Cornwallis." *North Carolina Historical and Genealogical Record: A Quarterly Magazine of North Carolina Genealogy, Biography and Local History*, 1:1 (January 1932), 14-15; and: Frank Nash. "More about the Hillsboro Clock." *North Carolina Historical and Genealogical Record: A Quarterly Magazine of North Carolina Genealogy, Biography and Local History*, 1:2 (April 1932), 88-89.

Schenck, David. *North Carolina, 1780-'81, Being a History of the Invasion of the Carolinas by the British Army, with the Particular Design of Showing the Part Borne by North Carolina in That Struggle for Liberty and Independence, and to Correct Some of the Errors of History in Regard to That State and Its People.* Raleigh: Edwards & Broughton Printing Company, 1889; reprinted: Spartanburg, S. C.: The Reprint Company, 1967; Bowie, Md.: Heritage Books, 2000.

Scotti, Anthony J. *Brutal Virtue: The Myth and Reality of Banastre Tarleton.* Westminster, Md.: Heritage Books, 2002.

Tarleton, Banastre, Lieutenant General, 1754-1833. *A History of the Campaigns of 1780 and 1781, in the Southern Provinces of North America.* Dublin, Printed for Colles, Exshaw, White, H. Whitestone, Burton, Byrne, Moore, Jones, and Dornin, 1787; reprinted: London: printed for T. Cadell, 1787; (South Carolina Heritage Series, no. 11) Spartanburg, S. C.: Reprint Company, 1967; (Eyewitness Accounts of the American Revolution series) New York: New York Times, 1968; North Stratford, N. H.: Ayer, 2001; Cranbury, N. J.: Scholars Bookshelf, 2005.

Torrence, Jedediah. *The Jed Letters: Reprinted from the Charlotte Observer from May 1, 1980 through April 12, 1981.* Charlotte: The Observer, [1988?].

Trudeau, Noah Andre. "Steeplechase in the Carolinas, 1781." *MHQ: Quarterly Journal of Military History*, 27:4 (Summer 2015), 40-47.

Weigley, Russell F. *The Partisan War: The South Carolina Campaign of 1780-1782.* (Tricentennial Booklet no. 2) Columbia: University of South Carolina Press for the South Carolina Tricentennial Commission, 1970. [Contents: Charleston and the Waxhaws: 1779-May 29, 1780; Thomas Sumter: May 29-July 25, 1780; Camden, King's Mountain, and Francis Marion: July 25-December 2, 1780; Cowpens: December 2, 1780-January 17, 1781; The Race to the Dan: January 17-February 14, 1781; Guilford Court House and Greene's Return to South Carolina: February 14-April 5, 1781; The Conquest of the British Garrisons: April 5-June 5, 1781; Ninety-Six: May 22-July 1, 1781; Eutaw Springs: July 1-September 8, 1781; The Fire Gutters out: September 8, 1781-December 14, 1782.]

Weil, Emily. *Cornwallis' Campaign: Wilmington to Yorktown.* Goldsboro: Wayne County Historical Association, 2010. [Online catalog description from the State Library of North Carolina: "A fictionalized description of the movement of the British Army from Wilmington, N. C. to Yorktown, Va., prior to the defining Battle of Yorktown in 1781."]

Wickwire, Franklin, and Mary Wickwire. *Cornwallis: The American Adventure.* Boston: Houghton Mifflin, 1970.

Willcox, William B. "The British Road to Yorktown: A Study in Divided Command." *American Historical Review*, 52:1 (Oct. 1946), 1-35.

Wilson, David K. *The Southern Strategy: Britain's Conquest of South Carolina and Georgia, 1775-1780.* Columbia: University of South Carolina Press, 2005. [Publisher's description: "America's popular memory of the Revolutionary War casts New England minutemen facing off against redcoats at Concord Bridge and George Washington's frostbitten soldiers huddled together at Valley Forge, but David K. Wilson's new study challenges the generally accepted notion that the war was fought primarily in the North. Recalling that the ramparts of Savannah were no less bloodstained than Bunker Hill and the siege of Charleston no less important than the battle for New York, Wilson considers the waging of war in the southern colonies during the critical and often overlooked period from 1775 to the spring of 1780. He suggests that the paradox of the British defeat in 1781 - after Crown armies had crushed all organized resistance in South Carolina and Georgia - makes sense only if one understands the fundamental flaws in what modern historians label Britain's Southern Strategy. Wilson closely examines battles and skirmishes in North Carolina, South Carolina, and Georgia to coristruct a comprehensive military history of the American Revolution in the South through May 1780. battle maps and orders of battle for each engagement. Appraising the strategy and tactics of the most significant conflicts, he tests the thesis that the British could raise the manpower they needed to win the war in the South by tapping a vast reservoir of southern Loyalists. According to Wilson, the policy was flawed in both its conception and execution. The sheer amount of empirical data Wilson has amassed here distinguishes this work and makes Wilson's recounting an invaluable guide to the war in the South."]

Winn, Richard. "[Unsigned account of Revolutionary War battles in Georgia, South Carolina, and North Carolina] 1780." Online through the University of Georgia Libraries: http://purl.galileo.usg.edu/gdir?code=zlna&id=krc119. [Online catalog description from the University of South Carolina Libraries: "The author (General Richard Winn?) writes in detail about important American and British military figures including: William Few, Lacey Bratton, Thomas Sumter, Paddy Carr, George Turnbull, Christian Huck, Banastre Tarleton, and Lord Cornwallis. Also discussed is the assistance rendered to the American forces by Catawba Indians under the leadership of their General New River. New River rose to power after the death of Chief Hagler (also Haigler)."]

Woodward, Joel A. "Comparative Evaluation of British and American Strategy in the Southern Campaign of 1780-1781." Master of Military Art and Science, United States Army, Command and General Staff College, 2002; online: http://cgsc.cdmhost.com/cdm/singleitem/collection/p4013coll2/id/ 306/rec/6.

Wyche, Kathleen B, trans. "North Carolina Militia Paroled by Lord Cornwallis in 1781." *The North Carolina Genealogical Society Journal*, 4:3 (August 1978), 147-151; correction: 13:3 (August 1987), 140-141. [Note from the Genealogy Office, Office of the Registrar General, National Society Daughters of the American Revolution, Washington, D. C.: Believed to be a list of North Carolina militiamen captured by British forces during the fall of Charleston, South Carolina in 1780. Men are listed by their home county. Originally this was believed to be a listed of men taken at Guilford Court House in 1781, but further research showed it to be a list of men taken at Charleston."]

British Claims against North Carolina and North Carolinians after the Revolution

"Claims against Bladen (Robeson) Residents by British Merchants after the Revolutionary War." *The Robeson County Register*, 6:3 (August 1991), 123.

Great Britain. Exchequer and Audit Department, Claims, American Loyalists, Series I (AO 12, Selections). Documents Communicated by State Governments – North Carolina (with Report) (AO 12/91). "Copy of Judgment in John Fleetwood v. John Hamilton, Wayne County Court, October 1782." Copy of a manuscript in the National Archives of the United Kingdom (formerly the Public Records Office), Kew, Richmond, Surrey, England; (MARS ID: 21.2.14.36), "British Records Collection," State Library of North Carolina, Raleigh.

Great Britain. Exchequer and Audit Department. Claims, American Loyalists, Series II (AO 13, Selections), Various Papers. (AO 13/91). "[Claim of] Alexander Munn, 21 Oct. 1783." Copy of a manuscript in the National Archives of the United Kingdom, formerly the Public Records Office, Kew, Richmond, Surrey, England), 77.1745.1-5 (MARS ID: 21.3.45.58), "British Records Collection," State Archives of North Carolina, Raleigh. [Online catalog description: "Debts due to Munn in Wake and Granville counties, North Carolina, as of 1 Oct. 1777."]

Great Britain. Exchequer and Audit Department. Claims, American Loyalists, Series II (AO 13, Selections), Claims, Miscellaneous. (AO 13/138). "[Claim of] Alexander Munn. 13 Mar. 1784." Copy of a manuscript in the National Archives of the United Kingdom, formerly the Public Records Office, Kew, Richmond, Surrey, England), 77.2282.1-16 (MARS ID: 21.3.71.66; folder), "British Records Collection," State Archives of North Carolina, Raleigh. [Online catalog description: "Memorial to the Loyalist Commissioners presented on Munn's behalf by Thomas Macknight. Includes power of attorney, certificates, and list of debts owing to Munn. The list of debts is made up of debtors in Wake and Granville counties, 1777."]

Great Britain. Exchequer and Audit Department. Claims, American Loyalist, Series II (AO 13, Selections), Claims, North Carolina, M.P-W. (AO 13/124). "[Papers in the Loyalist Claim of] Nicholas Walsh (Resident of Tryon Co. for 30 Years prior to the Revolution). n. d." Copy of a manuscript in the National Archives of the United Kingdom (formerly the Public Record Office), Kew, Richmond, Surrey, England; (MARS ID: 21.3.7.20; folder), "British Records Collection," State Archives of North Carolina, Raleigh. [Online catalog description: "Memorials and affidavit concerning his losses; schedule of same; certificates by Archibald McArthur and others; affidavit of Jonas Bedford; letter from Josiah Martin concerning his case."]

Great Britain. Exchequer and Audit Department. Audit Office. "[Claim of] Francis Williamson, 17 March 1784." Copy of a manuscript in the National Archives of the United Kingdom (formerly the Public Records Office), Kew, Richmond, Surrey, England; X77.1078.1-3 (MARS ID: 21.3.35.4; folder), "British Records Collection," State Archives of North Carolina, Raleigh. [Online catalog description: "Memorial of Thomas Macknight on behalf of the family of this deceased Currituck County loyalist."]

Great Britain. Exchequer and Audit Department. Audit Office. "[Claim of] James McNiel. 17 March 1784." Copy of a manuscript in the National Archives of the United Kingdom (formerly the Public Records Office), Kew, Richmond, Surrey, England; X77.1120.1-5 (MARS ID: 21.3.45.11; folder), State Archives of North Carolina, Raleigh. [Online catalog description: "Memorial of loyalist losses in Halifax and Edgecombe counties, North Carolina."]

Great Britain. Exchequer and Audit Department. Audit Office. "[Claim of James Parker.] 19 June 1784." Copy of a manuscript in the National Archives of the United Kingdom (formerly the Public Records Office), Kew, Richmond, Surrey, England;77.21244.1 (MARS ID: 21.3.67.11; folder), "British Records Collection," State Archives of North Carolina, Raleigh. [Online catalog description: "Lincoln's Inn Fields. Deposition of Caleb Church, cooper, born in Currituck County, North Carolina and now of Stanhope Street, St. Clement Dane, concerning losses of Parker."]

Great Britain. Exchequer and Audit Department. Audit Office. "[Claim of Juan DuBois]. 9 Feb. 1784." Copy of a manuscript in the National Archives of the United Kingdom (formerly the Public Records Office), Kew, Richmond, Surrey, England; 77.1872.1 (MARS ID: 21.3.50.8), "British Records Collection," State Archives of North Carolina, Raleigh. [Online catalog description: "Brunswick County. Deposition of John Kirkwood, watchmaker, and Archibald Ronaldson, joiner and house carpenter, both of Wilmington, concerning their valuation of losses of Mrs. Jean DuBois."]

Great Britain. Exchequer and Audit Department. Audit Office. "[Claim of] Logan, Gilmour and Co., 8 Jun. 1784." Copy of a manuscript in the National Archives of the United Kingdom (formerly the Public Records Office), Kew, Richmond, Surrey, England; 77.1463.1-2 (MARS ID: 21.3.26.6; folder), "British Records Collection," State Archives of North Carolina, Raleigh. [Online catalog description: "Affidavit of Thomas Macknight late of Belville, Currituck County, North Carolina, in behalf of Isabella Logan, widow of a partner in the firm trading in Pasquotank County."]

Great Britain. Exchequer and Audit Department. Audit Office. "[Claim of] William Aitcheson, 13 Aug. 1774." Copy of a manuscript in the National Archives of the United Kingdom (formerly the Public Records Office), Kew, Richmond, Surrey, England; 77.1443.1-4 (MARS ID: 21.3.22.4; folder), "British Records Collection,"

State Archives of North Carolina, Raleigh. [Online catalog description: "Will, leaving lands in Pasquotank County, North Carolina, to his son William; directing that the copartnery of the North Carolina firms Tho[mas] Macknight & Co., and William McCormick & Co. should continue after his death; etc."]

Great Britain. Exchequer and Audit Department. Audit Office. Claims, American Loyalists, Series II (AO 13, Selections), Claims. South Carolina, C, F, M. (AO 13/131). "[Claim of] William Mackenzie. 20 March 1779." Copy of a manuscript in the National Archives of the United Kingdom, formerly the Public Records Office, Kew, Richmond, Surrey, England), 77.2082.1-3 (MARS ID: 21.3.67.17, folder), "British Records Collection," State Archives of North Carolina, Raleigh. [Online catalog description: "Memorial (Copy) to the Treasury Commissioners setting forth his sufferings as a loyal Anglican clergyman in Granville County, North Carolina, during the Revolution."]

Great Britain. Exchequer and Audit Department. Audit Office. "[Claim of] William Scarborough. 17 Mar. 1784." Copy of a manuscript in the National Archives of the United Kingdom (formerly the Public Records Office), Kew, Richmond, Surrey, England; X77.1081.1-3 (MARS ID: 21.3.38.1), "British Records Collection," State Archives of North Carolina, Raleigh. [Online catalog description: "Memorial of Thomas Macknight, with a schedule of losses, on behalf of this Pasquotank County loyalist."]

Great Britain. Exchequer and Audit Department. Audit Office. "[Claim of] William Simpson. 31 January 1784." Copy of a manuscript in the National Archives of the United Kingdom (formerly the Public Records Office), Kew, Richmond, Surrey, England; 77.1604.1-2 (MARS ID: 21.3.38.17), "British Records Collection," State Archives of North Carolina, Raleigh. [Online catalog description: "Brunswick County, North Carolina, loyalist losses sustained 1 Apr. 1776."]

Great Britain. Exchequer and Audit Department. Audit Office. "[Claim of] William Simpson, 22 March 1784." Copy of a manuscript in the National Archives of the United Kingdom (formerly the Public Records Office), Kew, Richmond, Surrey, England; 77.1605.1 (MARS ID: 21.3.38.18), "British Records Collection," State Archives of North Carolina, Raleigh. [Online catalog description: "Memorial of Colonel John Hamilton on behalf of Simpson, forced to abandon his Brunswick County, North Carolina, property in April 1776."]

Great Britain. Exchequer and Audit Department. Audit Office. "Examination and Decision on [Application for Immediate Relief as a Suffering Loyalist] of Joseph Johnston of Brunswick Co, N. C. Mar. 11, 1784." Copy of a manuscript in the National Archives of the United Kingdom (formerly the Public Records Office), Kew, Richmond, Surrey, England; X77.228.1 (MARS ID: 21.2.17.18), "British Records Collection," State Archives of North Carolina, Raleigh.

Great Britain. Exchequer and Audit Department. Audit Office. "Schedule of North Carolina Loyalist Losses of John Slingsby. 9 Feb. 1784." Copy of a manuscript in the National Archives of the United Kingdom (formerly the Public Records Office), Kew, Richmond, Surrey, England; 77.1607.1-3 (MARS ID: 21.3.38.20; folder), "British Records Collection," State Archives of North Carolina, Raleigh. [Online catalog description: "With affidavits by Thomas Eason and Archibald Ranaldson of Brunswick County."]

Great Britain. Exchequer and Audit Department. Audit Office. "[Claim of James Parker.] 26 Jan. 1785." Copy of a manuscript in the National Archives of the United Kingdom (formerly the Public Records Office), Kew, Richmond, Surrey, England; X77.1181.1-4 (MARS ID: 21.3.67.4; folder), British Records Collection," State Archives of North Carolina, Raleigh. [Online catalog description: "Irvine, Ayrshire [Scotland]. Deposition of Thomas Macknight concerning loyalist services and losses of James Parker, including his exerting his influence among the population of Currituck and Pasquotank counties, 'to keep them steady and firm in their opposition to the measures of Congress . . .'."]

Great Britain. Exchequer and Audit Department. Audit Office. Exchequer and Audit Department, Claims, American Loyalists, Series I (AO 12, Selections). Documents Communicated by State Governments – North Carolina (with Report). (AO 12/91). "Deposition of Ephraim Knight, Halifax Co., Apr. 23, 1777; 1781, 1788." Copy of a manuscript in the National Archives of the United Kingdom (formerly the Public Records Office), Kew, Richmond, Surrey, England; (MARS ID: 21.2.14.49; folder), "British Records Collection," State Archives of North Carolina, Raleigh. [Online catalog description: "States that in Oct., 1777, Archibald and John Hamilton delivered to him for safekeeping the books and papers of their store at Hamilton Hill, and that Knight's wife destroyed them in 1781."]

Great Britain. Exchequer and Audit Department. Audit Office. Claims, American Loyalists, Series II (AO 12, Selections), Documents Communicated by State Governments – North Carolina (with Report). (AO 12/91). "Copy of Judgment in John Pope v. John Hamilton, Granville County Court, February 1785." Copy of a manuscript in the National Archives of the United Kingdom, formerly the Public Records Office, Kew, Richmond, Surrey, England), (MARS ID: 21.2.14.44; folder), "British Records Collection," State Archives of North Carolina, Raleigh. [

Great Britain. Exchequer and Audit Department. Audit Office. Claims, American Loyalists, Series II (AO 12, Selections), Documents Communicated by State Governments – North Carolina (with Report). (AO 12/91). "Copy of Judgment in John Winnington v. Hamilton and Co., Granville County Court, February 1785." Copy of a manuscript in the National Archives of the United Kingdom, formerly the Public Records Office, Kew, Richmond, Surrey, England), (MARS ID: 21.2.14.46; folder), "British Records Collection," State Archives of North Carolina, Raleigh. [

Great Britain. Exchequer and Audit Department. Audit Office. Claims, American Loyalists, Series II (AO 12, Selections), Various. (AO 12/107). "Letter from Thomas Mutter, Granville Co., N. C., to Archibald Hamilton. Extract. Feb. 28, 1785." Copy of a manuscript in the National Archives of the United Kingdom, formerly the Public Records Office, Kew, Richmond, Surrey, England), 77.40.2-3 (MARS ID: 21.2.21.11; folder), "British Records Collection," State Archives of North Carolina, Raleigh. [Online catalog description: "On difficulties of collecting pre-Revolutionary War debts, confiscation of Hamilton's property in N. C., and the likelihood of having to surrender the books and bonds belonging to the company [Archibald Hamilton and Co.]. 'No. 46.'"]

Great Britain. Exchequer and Audit Department. Audit Office. Claims, American Loyalists, Series II (AO 13, Selections), Claims. South Carolina, C, F, M. (AO 13/131). "Hill Street, [London]. [Stuart] Mackenzie to John Robinson, [junior secretary of the Treasury]. 21 Feb. 1780." Copy of a manuscript in the National Archives of the United Kingdom, formerly the Public Records Office, Kew, Richmond, Surrey, England), 77.2083.1 (MARS ID: 21.3.64.18), "British Records Collection," State Archives of North Carolina, Raleigh. [Online catalog descrip-tion: "Copy of letter inquiring about the status of the loyalist memorial of Reverend W[illia]m Mackenzie formerly of Granville County, North Carolina."]

Great Britain. Exchequer and Audit Department. Audit Office. Claims, American Loyalists, Series II (AO 13, Selections), Various Papers. (AO 13/106). "Glasgow, [Scotland]. Archibald Hamilton to Thomas Miller, [Granville County, North Carolina]. 13 August 1784." Copy of a manuscript in the National Archives of the United Kingdom, formerly the Public Records Office, Kew, Richmond, Surrey, England), 77.1955.1-2 (MARS ID: 21.3.58.3), "British Records Collection," State Archives of North Carolina, Raleigh. [Online catalog description: "Extract. Introduces John Sym agent of the Hamilton's affairs in North Carolina. Please deliver to him the firm's papers, and send a certified account of the land the firm made over to Edward Moore, Benjamin McCulloch, and James Martin in 1777."]

Great Britain. Exchequer and Audit Department. Audit Office. Claims, American Loyalists, Series II (AO 13, Selections), Various Papers. (AO 13/106). "Glasgow, [Scotland]. Archibald Hamilton to Thomas Miller, [Granville County, North Carolina]. 16 Aug. 1784." Copy of a manuscript in the National Archives of the United Kingdom, formerly the Public Records Office, Kew, Richmond, Surrey, England), 77.1956.1 (MARS ID: 21.3.58.4; folder), "British Records Collection," State Archives of North Carolina, Raleigh. [Online catalog description: "Sym has been detained by unfavorable winds. In addition to other evidences wanted (for loyalist claim) please make a list of every debtor who has paid money into the state treasury on account of the Hamiltons or of Miller."]

Great Britain. Exchequer and Audit Department. Audit Office. Claims, American Loyalists, Series II (AO 13, Selections), Various Papers. (AO 13/106). "Glasgow, [Scotland]. Archibald Hamilton to Thomas Miller, [Granville County, North Carolina]. 28 Sept. 1784." Copy of a manuscript in the National Archives of the United Kingdom, formerly the Public Records Office, Kew, Richmond, Surrey, England), 77.1957.1-2 (MARS ID: 21.3.58.5; folder), "British Records Collection," State Archives of North Carolina, Raleigh. [Online catalog description: "Extract. Colonel [Nisbet] Balfour let David Oliphant free when Hamilton was suing the latter in Charleston. Now that Balfour is back in Britain, Hamilton means to see whether or not British law will hold the colonel liable. Please send an account of what part of the 30,000 wt. of tobacco was delivered to Oliphant. Hopes the General Assembly has become more moderate in respect to British debts."]

Great Britain. Exchequer and Audit Department. Audit Office. Claims, American Loyalists, Series II (AO 13, Selections), Various Papers. (AO 13/106). "Glasgow, [Scotland]. Archibald Hamilton to Thomas Miller, [Granville County, North Carolina]. 2 Apr. 1785." Copy of a manuscript in the National Archives of the United Kingdom, formerly the Public Records Office, Kew, Richmond, Surrey, England), 77.1958.1-2 (MARS ID: 21.3.58.6; folder), "British Records Collection," State Archives of North Carolina, Raleigh. [Online catalog description: "Extract. Hopes soon to hear from Miller. Needs badly to have an account of lands made over to McCulloch and Moore, lands and Negroes made over to Martin, and Virginia property made over to John Cowper, etc. Hopes Miller will pay something on account."]

Great Britain. Exchequer and Audit Department. Audit Office. Claims, American Loyalists, Series II (AO 13, Selections), Various Papers. (AO 13/106). "Glasgow, [Scotland]. Archibald Hamilton to Thomas Miller, [Granville County, North Carolina]. 16 May 1785." Copy of a manuscript in the National Archives of the

United Kingdom, formerly the Public Records Office, Kew, Richmond, Surrey, England), 77.1959.1-6 (MARS ID: 21.3.58.7; folder), "British Records Collection," State Archives of North Carolina, Raleigh. [Online catalog description: "Ack[nowledge receipt] of Miller's letter from Petersburg dated in Feb. 1784; much pained by contents. Expresses dissatisfaction with Miller, with John Abernethie, with North Carolina confiscation laws, and with the state of the firm's business affairs in America."]

Great Britain. Exchequer and Audit Department. Audit Office. Claims, American Loyalists, Series II (AO 13, Selections), Various Papers. (AO 13/106). "Glasgow, [Scotland]. Archibald Hamilton to Thomas Miller, [Granville County, North Carolina]. 6 Aug. 1785." Copy of a manuscript in the National Archives of the United Kingdom, formerly the Public Records Office, Kew, Richmond, Surrey, England), 77.1960.1-2 (MARS ID: 21.3.58.8; folder), "British Records Collection," State Archives of North Carolina, Raleigh. [Online catalog description: "Extract. Has had no reply to letter of 16 May. Have you delivered the firm's papers to Mr. Sym? Please keep me informed on the North Carolina assembly."]

Great Britain. Treasury. "[Claim of] Cuming, Mackenzie and Co., 1 Jly, 1775." Copy of a manuscript in the National Archives of the United Kingdom (formerly the Public Records Office), Kew, Richmond, Surrey, England; X77.1239.1-30 (MARS ID: 21.11.20.1, "British Records Collection," State Archives of North Carolina, Raleigh. [Online catalog description: "'List of Debts due . . . at Hillsborough . . .' etc. Includes debtors living in Anson, Bertie, Brunswick, Bute, Chatham, Chowan, Cumberland, Dobbs, Granville, Halifax, New Hanover, Northampton, Orange, Pasquotank, Rowan, and Wake counties, the towns of Edenton, Hillsborough and Wilmington, and on Tar and Holston rivers."]

Great Britain. Treasury. "[Claim of] Cuming, Warwick and Co., North Carolina and Virginia, 1 Aug. 1775." Copy of manuscript in the National Archives of the United Kingdom (formerly the Public Record Office), 77.2393.1-2 (MARS ID: 21.111.29.20; folder), "British Records Collection," State Archives of North Carolina, Raleigh. [Online catalog description: "An abstract of a 'List of debts due . . . Northampton Store, No. Carolina, August, 1st 1775.' {Prepared, 1798?}."]

Great Britain. Treasury. "[Claim of] William Cunningham and Co. 1 Sep. 1775." Copy of a manuscript in the National Archives of the United Kingdom (formerly the Public Records Office), Kew, Richmond, Surrey, England; X77.1198.1-3 (MARS ID: 21.111.1.4). "British Records Collection," State Archives of North Carolina, Raleigh. [Online catalog description: "List of Debts Brunswick [County] Store, [Virginia. Includes Carolina and North Carolina debtors, one of whom is John Marshall of Bute County.] Extract."] Copy of manuscript in the National Archives of the United Kingdom (formerly the Public Record Office), Z.5.140N (MARS ID: 21.111.21.19; folder), State Archives of North Carolina, Raleigh.

Great Britain. Treasury. "[Claim of] Spiers, Bowman and Co. 1 May 1777." Copy of manuscript in the National Archives of the United Kingdom (formerly the Public Record Office), X77.1262.1-13 (MARS ID: 21.111.31.2; folder), "British Records Collection," State Archives of North Carolina, Raleigh. [Online catalog description: "Debts due at the Petersburg, Virginia, store. Extract. Debtors from Bute, Granville, and Halifax counties, North Carolina."]

Great Britain. Treasury. "[Loyalist Claim of Buchanans, Hastie and Co.] 'Depositions of Sarah and Thomas Yuille Relating to the Books and the Concern Having Been Defaced by Being Buried Underground during the [Revolutionary] War.' 30 June, 1783; 10 August 1798." Microfilmed copy of manuscript in the National Archives of the United Kingdom (formerly the Public Record Office), Z.5.140N (MARS ID: 21.111.221.19; folder), "British Records Collection," State Archives of North Carolina, Raleigh. [Online catalog description: "1783 Jun. 30. Halifax, [Va.]. Thomas Yuille to Neill Buchanan, Merchant in Chesterfield. Recounts the obliteration of the account books by having been buried. 1798 Aug. 10. [Halifax County, Virginia]. Affidavit (with certifications) of Sarah, widow of Thomas Yuille, concerning the damage to account books by burying them in 1777."]

Great Britain. Treasury. "[Loyalist Claim of Gibson, Donaldson and Hamilton and Co., and George Miller and Co.] 28 October 1773." Microfilmed copy of manuscript in the National Archives of the United Kingdom (formerly the Public Record Office), Z.5.139N (MARS ID: 21.11.10.3), "British Records Collection," State Archives of North Carolina, Raleigh. [Online catalog description: "Articles of a Copartnership … between James Gibson … George Miller of Dobbs County, North Carolina (regarding the stores at Neuse River and Duplin Court House). {A true copy made in 1799; attested in 1806.} {4 post folio pages}."]

Great Britain. Treasury. Board Papers. American Loyalist Claims. (T-79, Selections), Special Agents' Report on Claims, Vol. IV. (T 79/77). "Reports of special agent William H. Williams on [loyalist] claims for debts contracted mostly before the Revolution by persons living mainly in counties of Duplin, Sampson, New Hanover, Wayne, Bladen, Robeson, and Cumberland." [n. d. – 1801] Copy of a manuscript in the National Archives of the United Kingdom (formerly the Public Record Office), Kew, Richmond, Surrey, England;

(MARS ID: 21.111.43.1; folder), "British Records Collection," State Archives of North Carolina, Raleigh. [Online catalog description: "In addition to names of debtors, the reports often include details concerning their property, place of current residence, emigration to other states, death, marriage and remarriage, heirs, relatives, etc., as well as a few copies of pre-revolutionary correspondence and accounts. Claimants as follows: [fols.] 1-4 Cornell, Samuel, administrators of [fols.] 3-6 Hanna, assignee of Cruden [Fols.] 5-6 Buchanan, Hastie, & Co. [fols.] 6-7 Alston, Young & Co. [fols.] 7-9 Gibson, Donaldson, & Hamilton [Fols.] 10-24 Harford, John [fols.] 25-113 John Hay & Co. [fols.] 114 Mclellan & WALLACE [fols.] 115-158 James Gammel & Co. [fols.] 159-180 Mcdonnell, John."]

Great Britain. Treasury. Board Papers. American Loyalist Claims. (T-79, Selections), Special Agents' Report on Claims, Vol. XI. (T 79/84). "Reports of special agent William Duffy on claims for debts contracted mostly before the Revolution by persons living mainly in the counties of Granville, Franklin, and Orange, and southern counties of Virginia." [n. d. - 1801] Copy of a manuscript in the National Archives of the United Kingdom (formerly the Public Record Office), Kew, Richmond, Surrey, England; (MARS ID: 21.111.48.1; fodler), "British Records Collection," State Archives of North Carolina, Raleigh. [Online catalog description: "In addition to names of debtors, the reports often include details concerning their property, place of current residence, emigration to other states, death, marriage and remarriage, heirs, relatives, etc., and occasionally copies of accounts, bonds, receipts, and court proceedings. Claimants as follows: [fols.] 1-49, 132-133 Alston, Young, & Co. [fols.] 49-81, 162-197 Young, Miller, & Co. [fols.] 82-93, 205-207 Spiers, Bowman, & Co. [fols.] 94-117 Alexander Donald & Co. [fols.] 118-122 Dinwiddie Crawford & Co. [fols.] 122-125 Cilbeck, Chambers, ROSS, & Co. [fols.] 126-131, 146-161, 213-225 Buchanan, Hastie, & Co. [fols.] 134 Dunlop and assignees of Wilson [fols.] 135-137, 202-203 Michael and John Wallace & Co. [fols.] 138-140 Dreghorn Murdock & Co. [fols.] 198-200 James Gammell & Co. [fols.] 201-202 Gibson, Donaldson, & Hamilton [fols.] 204-205 Ramsay Monteath & Co. [fols.] 208-213 John Hay & Co. [fols.] 225-227 William Cunningham & Co. [fols.] 227-228 Munn, Alexander, administrators of."]

Great Britain. Treasury. Board Papers. American Loyalist Claims. (T-79, Selections), Special Agents' Report on Claims, Vol. XII. (T 79/85). [1800] "Report of Special Agent Henry Potter on Claims for Debts Contracted Mostly before the Revolution by Persons Living Mainly in the Counties of Granville, Franklin, Martin, Warren, Bute, Halifax, Northampton, Edgecombe, Nash, Pitt, Wayne, and Orange." [n. d. - 1800]Copy of a manuscript in the National Archives of the United Kingdom (formerly the Public Record Office), Kew, Richmond, Surrey, England; (MARS ID: 21.111.49.1; folder), "British Records Collection," State Archives of North Carolina, Raleigh. [Online catalog description: "In addition to names of debtors, the reports often include details concerning their property, place of current residence, emigration to other states, death, marriage and remarriage, heirs, relatives, etc., as well as copies of court proceedings, and correspondence. Major claimants as follows: [fols.] 1-14, 107-121 Gibson, Donaldson, & Hamilton [fols.] 15-49 Mclellan & Wallace [fols.] 50-70 McNiel, James [fols.] 71-79, 95-104, 131-147 Alston, Young, & Co. [fols.] 80-95 Munn, Alexander [fols.] 104-106 Gammell & Co. [fols.] 130-147 Dreghorn, Murdock, & Co. [fols.] 122-129 Alexander Donald & Co."]

Great Britain. Treasury. Board Papers. Claims, American Loyalists, T 79, Selections. Claimants' Papers. (T 79/1). "[Claim of] William Cunningham and Co. 1 Sep. 1775." Copy of a manuscript in the National Archives of the United Kingdom, formerly the Public Records Office, Kew, Richmond, Surrey, England), 77.2314.1-26 (MARS ID: 21.111.1.14), "British Records Collection," State Archives of North Carolina, Raleigh. [Online catalog description: "'List of Debts Cabinpoint Store, [Virginia].' Contains accounts of numerous North Carolina debtors from Bute, Granville, Orange and Rowan counties, Broad and Yadkin rivers, Salisbury, and other North Carolina accounts not located specifically. Noteworthy names included among debtors are Thomas Person, Captain Chesley Daniel and David Royster of Granville County, and Colonel William Kennon."]

Great Britain. Treasury. Board Papers. Claims, American Loyalists, T 79, Selections. Claimants' Papers. (T 79/9). "[Claim of] Henry Eustace McCulloh. 14 Jan. 1775." Copy of a manuscript in the National Archives of the United Kingdom, formerly the Public Records Office, Kew, Richmond, Surrey, England), Z.5.146N (MARS ID: 21.111.8.91; folder), "British Records Collection," State Archives of North Carolina, Raleigh. [Online catalog description: "Account current of William Johnston, [Granville County, North Carolina], debtor to Henry Eustace McCulloh, from 4 Jun. 1774 to 3 Jly. 1775."]

Great Britain. Treasury. Board Papers. Claims, American Loyalists, T 79, Selections. Claimants' Papers. (T 79/9). "[Claim of] Henry Eustace McCulloh." Copy of a manuscript in the National Archives of the United Kingdom, formerly the Public Records Office, Kew, Richmond, Surrey, England), Z.5.146N (MARS ID: 21.111.8.97; folder), "British Records Collection," State Archives of North Carolina, Raleigh. [Online catalog description: "A list of sundry bonds due from persons in Granville, Orange, and Wake counties left in the hands of William Johnston of Orange County, with Johnston's receipt."]

Great Britain. Treasury. Board Papers. American Loyalist Claims. (T-79, Selections), Claimants' Papers. (T 79/13). "[Loyalist Claim]. Memorial of Charles Duncan to the Commissioners for Loyalist Claims as Agent for the Surviving Partners of the Mercantile Firm of Dinwiddie, Crawfurd and Co. Trading in Virginia and North Carolina before the Revolution. 19 Nov. 1794." Copy of a manuscript in the National Archives of the United Kingdom (formerly the Public Record Office), Kew, Richmond, Surrey, England; (MARS ID: 21.111.12.37; folder), State Archives of North Carolina, Raleigh. [Online catalog description: "[5 post folio pages and endorsement]."]

Great Britain. Treasury. Board Papers. Claims, American Loyalists, T 79, Selections. Claimants' Papers. (T 79/24). '[Claim of] Cuming, Mackenzie and Co. 1 July 1775." Copy of a manuscript in the National Archives of the United Kingdom, formerly the Public Records Office, Kew, Richmond, Surrey, England), X77.1239.1-30 (MARS ID: 21.111.20.1; folder), "British Records Collection," State Archives of North Carolina, Raleigh. [Online catalog description: "'List of Debts due . . . at Hillsborough . . .' etc. Includes debtors living in Anson, Bertie, Brunswick, Bute, Chatham, Chowan, Cumberland, Dobbs, Granville, Halifax, New Hanover, Northampton, Orange, Pasquotank, Rowan, and Wake counties, the towns of Edenton, Hillsborough and Wilmington, and on Tar and Holston rivers."]

Great Britain. Treasury. Board Papers. American Loyalist Claims. (T-79, Selections), Claimants' Papers. (T 79/25). "[Loyalist Claim of Buchanans, Hastie and Co.] Depositions of Sara and Thomas Yuille Relating to the Books and of the Cocnern Having Been Defaced by Being Buried Underground during the [Revolutionary] War. 30 June, 1783, and 10 August 1789." Copy of a manuscript in the National Archives of the United Kingdom (formerly the Public Record Office), Kew, Richmond, Surrey, England; (MARS ID: 21.111.21.19), State Archives of North Carolina, Raleigh. [Online catalog description: "1783 Jun. 30. Halifax, [Va.]. Thomas Yuille to Neill Buchanan, Merchant in Chesterfield. Recounts the obliteration of the account books by having been buried. 1798 Aug. 10. [Halifax County, Virginia]. Affidavit (with certifications) of Sarah, widow of Thomas Yuille, concerning the damage to account books by burying them in 1777."]

Great Britain. Treasury. Board Papers. Claims, American Loyalists, T 79, Selections. Claimants' Papers. (T 79/40). "[Claim of] Spiers, Bowman and Co. 1 May 1777." Copy of a manuscript in the National Archives of the United Kingdom, formerly the Public Records Office, Kew, Richmond, Surrey, England), X77.1262.1-13 (MARS ID: 21.111.31.2; folder), "British Records Collection," State Archives of North Carolina, Raleigh. [Online catalog description: "Debts due at the Petersburg, Virginia, store. Extract. Debtors from Bute, Granville, and Halifax counties, North Carolina."]

Great Britain. Treasury. Board Papers. Claims, American Loyalists, T 79, Selections. Claimants' Papers. (T 79/40). "[Claim of] Spiers, Bowman and Co. 1 May 1777." Copy of a manuscript in the National Archives of the United Kingdom, formerly the Public Records Office, Kew, Richmond, Surrey, England), X77.1267.1-5 (MARS ID: 21.11.31.7; folder), "British Records Collection," State Archives of North Carolina, Raleigh. [Online catalog description: "List of debts owing to the firm's store in Mecklenburg County, Va. A large percentage of the debtors lived in Bute, Granville, Guilford and Orange counties, North Carolina."]

McBride, Ransom. "British Mercantile Claims." *The North Carolina Genealogical Society Journal*, 5 (1979), 7.

McBride, Ransom. "Claims of British Merchants after the Revolutionary War."
(1st in series). *North Carolina Genealogical Society Journal*, 4:3 (August 1978), 152-161.
(2nd in series). *North Carolina Genealogical Society Journal*, 5:1 (February 1979), 4-13.
(3rd in series). *North Carolina Genealogical Society Journal*, 5:3 (August 1979), 177-183.
(4th in series). *North Carolina Genealogical Society Journal*, 6:1 (February 1980), 17-26.
(5th in series). *North Carolina Genealogical Society Journal*, 6:2 (May 1980), 110-118.
(6th in series). *North Carolina Genealogical Society Journal*, 6:3 (August 1980), 195-200.
(7th in series). *North Carolina Genealogical Society Journal*, 7:3 (August 1981), 155-159
(8th in series). *North Carolina Genealogical Society Journal*, 8:1 (February 1982), 18-23.
(9th in series). *North Carolina Genealogical Society Journal*, 9:3 (August 1983), 155-164.
(10th in series), *North Carolina Genealogical Society Journal*, 11:1 (February 1985). 25-32.
(11th in series). *North Carolina Genealogical Society Journal*, 11:4 (November 1985), 243-251.
(12th in series). *North Carolina Genealogical Society Journal*, 17:1 (February 1991), 20-29.
(13th in series). *North Carolina Genealogical Society Journal*, 17:2 (May 1991), 97-107.
(14th in series) *North Carolina Genealogical Society Journal*, 17:3 (August 1991), 144-150.
(15th in series). *North Carolina Genealogical Society Journal*, 18:1 (February 1992), 41-47.
(16th in series), *North Carolina Genealogical Society Journal*, 19:3 (August 1993), 150-159.

Rolleston, Christopher. "Christopher Rolleston Indenture, 1789." In *Miscellaneous Papers*, Manuscript 517, Southern Historical Collection, Louis Round Wilson Special Collections Library, University of North Carolina,

Chapel Hill. [Description on ArchiveGrId: "'Indenture tripartite,' 1789, an instrument of assignment by Christopher Rolleston of London, England, surviving partner of the late Edward Neufville of Bristol, England, of the firm of Neufville and Rolleston, merchants and exporters and importers, to various attorneys acting for the creditors of Neufville and Rolleston. The indenture explains that difficulties in collecting debts had arisen as a result of the American Revolution and that Edward Neufville had journeyed to Carolina in 1780 to try to collect on these debts, returning to England in 1788 without having had much success."]

[Tryon, William]. "Memorial of Governor William Tryon for the Recovery of Losses of Personal and Real Property Incurred during the American Revolution, States of North Carolina and New York." Manuscript; Office of the Governor; "Colonial Governors' Papers Record Group: William Tryon (8 July 1729-27 January 1788) Papers," CGP 6 and CGP 9 (MARS ID: 308.8.98; box), State Archives of North Carolina, Raleigh. [Online catalog description: "Evidence supporting memorial, including list of real estate owned in North Carolina with estimate of value; sworn testimony to memorial."]

Williams, Wiley J. "British Debts." In William S. Powell, ed.; Jay Mazzocchi, assoc. ed., *Encyclopedia of North Carolina* (Chapel Hill: University of North Carolina Press in association with the University of North Carolina Library, 2006), 148-149.

North Carolina Accounts with and Claims against the United States from the Revolution

Duffy, William. "William Duffy (d. 1810) Papers.' Manuscript PC.9 (MARS ID: 518; record group). State Archives of North Carolina, Raleigh. [Online catalog description: "Papers relating chiefly to business and legal matters of Duffy (d. 1810), prominent North Carolina lawyer and speaker. There are a few documents and letters relating to the settlement of Revolutionary accounts of the state of North Carolina with the United States. Among the correspondents are Blake Baker, John Read, Jr., John Haywood, Edmund Hones, Henry Seawell, and James Taylor."[36]

North Carolina (State). General Assembly. "[Document dated:] May 28, 1784: Resolution Ordering the Comptroller to Adjust and Finalize the Accounts between This State and the United States." Manuscript; General Assembly Record Group; Session Records, April-June 1784; Committee Papers, Resolutions; House Joint Resolutions: April 21-June 3, 1784, Box 2 (MARS ID: 66.8.32.5.30; item], State Archives of North Carolina, Raleigh. [Online catalog description: "Resolution directs the comptroller to settle with the commissioner appointed by the United States based on the scale of depreciation and the delegates to congress are only authorized to approve a commissioner from Delaware, Maryland, Virginia, South Carolina, or Georgia."]

North Carolina (State). General Assembly. "[Document dated:] November 25, 1784: Resolution Directing the Comptroller General to Pay All Continental Currency into the Hands of the Commissioner Assigned to Liquidate the Accounts of North Carolina with the United States." Manuscript; General Assembly Record Group; Session Records, October-November 1784; Joint Papers, Committee Papers, Resolutions, Unidentified Amendments, Senate Bills, Box 1 (MARS ID: 66.8.35.13.6; item), State Archives of North Carolina, Raleigh.

North Carolina (State). General Assembly. "[Document dated:] Dec. 20, [1787]: Report on Representation of Robert Fenner, Agent of Continental Line (With Representation and Messages, 1787." Manuscript; General Assembly Record Group; Session Records, November-December, 1787; Joint Papers, Committee Papers, Resolutions, Senate Bills, House Bills, Box 1 (MARS ID: 66.8.46.13.16; ITEM), State Archives of North Carolina, Raleigh. [Online catalog description: "Letter from Robert Fenner concerning exchange of warrants for credit with the U.S.; report from committee recommends directing governor to issue warrant on treasury for credit with the U.S.; and messages from both houses concerning amending agreement."]

North Carolina (State). General Assembly. "[Document dated:] 1789: Resolution Concerning Muster Rolls, etc., in the Hands of General Clarke (Rejected). Concerning Muster Rolls, etc., in the Hands of Various People. Comptroller to Forward to Edenton All Such Accounts and Claims against the United States." Manuscript; General Assembly Record Group; Session of November-December 1789; House Joint Resolutions, Bills, Senate Bills House Bills; House Joint Resolutions: November 5-December 9, 1789, Box 3 (MARS ID: 66.8.54.1.12; item), State Archives of North Carolina, Raleigh. [Online catalog description: "Resolution states that General Clarke be requested to deliver to Doctor Williamson musters, or papers that relate to the accounts of this state with the United States. Resolution also states that the same papers be obtained from Generals Sumner and Hogan as well as Colonels Dixon and Litle as they may relate to the service performed by this state during the

---

36 North Carolina Historical Records Survey Project. *Guide to the Manuscript Collections in the Archives of the North Carolina Historical Commission* (Raleigh: North Carolina Historical Commission, 1942), 44.

American Revolution. Resolution directs the comptroller to forward to Edenton, old Continental money in the Treasury, as well as vouchers and accounts against the United States."]

North Carolina (State). General Assembly. "[Document dated:] November 25, 1789: Bill for Procuring Testimony Concerning Accounts of This State against the United States." Manuscript; General Assembly Record Group; Session of November-December 1789; House Bills, Box 4 (MARS Id: 66.8.55.31; folder), State Archives of North Carolina, Raleigh. [Online catalog description: "Bill directs the comptroller to obtain any musters, or payrolls that may be among the papers of the late Governor or military officers. It also directs the commanding officer of every county militia to inquire about wagons that may have been furnished to the militia in 1782."]

North Carolina (State). General Assembly. "[Document dated:] December 12, 1789: [Resolution for the] Comptroller to Collect Evidence to Support the Accounts of This State against the United States (American Revolution)." Manuscript; General Assembly Record Group; Session of November-December 1789; House Joint Resolutions, Bills, Sentae Bills, House Bills, Box 3 (MARS ID: 66.8.54.2.3; item), State Archives of North Carolina, Raleigh. [Online catalog description: "Resolution directs the executors of the estates of the late Abner Nash, and Richard Caswell to forward to officers of the state, correspondence relating to the Southern Department during the American Revolution."]

North Carolina (State). "Accounts of the United States with North Carolina, War of the Revolution, Books A-C, 1776-1792." Manuscript and 1 microfilm reel, State Archives of North Carolina, Raleigh.

Thomas, Abishai. "Abishai Thomas Papers, 1789-1795." Manuscript, PC.86, State Archives of North Carolina, Raleigh. [Online catalog description: "Papers of Thomas, clerk of the General Assembly and agent for North Carolina in the settlement of public accounts after the American Revolution. Letters concern settlement of accounts between the state and the United States; settlement of accounts with Col. Thomas Polk and deputy quartermaster general Nicholas Long; settlement of individual claims for damages done by American troops or for payment on certificates; problem of fraudulent certificates; allegation of collusion between agents and certificate speculators; and method of paying pensions. Correspondents include William Dickson, William Skinner, Hugh Williamson, Thomas Polk, and Alexander Martin, with drafts of letters from Thomas and fellow agent James Taylor to Alexander Hamilton, Comptroller Oliver Wolcott, and others. Also copy of request from Francis Child for any papers in the estates of Richard Caswell and William Blount relating to war- time requisitions; and depreciation accounts and service summaries for 34 officers in the North Carolina Line."]

Chapter Eleven:
Spies and Espionage in North Carolina during the Revolution

As with most other states, it is surprising to see how little has been published for North Carolina and Tennessee about espionage and spies during the American Revolution. By its very nature, the subject is shrouded in mystery and secrecy, so it is not difficult to understand why there is a lack of original material for use in building historical studies. There are other references to spies and the like throughout the text, and the index reveals these.

Collins, James Potter; revised and prepared by John M. Roberts. *A Revolutionary Soldier*. (American Military Experience series) New York: Arno Press, 1979. [spies; James Potter Collier, 1763-1844]

Daigler, Kenneth A. *Spies, Patriots, and Traitors: American Intelligence in the Revolutionary War*. Washington, D. C.: Georgetown University Press, 2014.

Jordan, Paula S. "Hannah Millikan Blair (1756-14 Jan. 1852)." In William S. Powell, ed., *Dictionary of North Carolina Biography, vol. 1: A-C* (Chapel Hill: University of North Carolina Press, 1979), 171.

Markle, Donald E. *The Fox and the Hound: The Birth of American Spying*. New York: Hippocrene Books, 2014. [See: Chapter IX: The Southern Department – Where the War Was Won: North Carolina (Including Present-Day Tennessee): The Buffer State between North and South," 119-123.

O'Toole, G. J. A. [George J. A.]. *The Encyclopedia of American Intelligence and Espionage from the Revolutionary War to the Present*. New York: Facts on file, 1988.

O'Toole, G. J. A. [George J. A.]. *Honorable Treacher: A History of U. S. Intelligence, Espionage, and Covert Action from the American Revolution to the CIA*. New York: Atlantic Monthly Press, 1991.

Seielstad, Kristen M. "'Upon Secrecy, Success Depends': Intelligence Operations during the Southern Campaign of the American Revolution." M. A. thesis, College of Charleston and the Citadel, 2010. [Online catalog description: "Intelligence gathering played a major role in both British and American military operations during the American Revolution. This study presents an analysis of these intelligence activities during the southern campaign of the war as it was fought in the Georgia and the Carolinas between 1779 and 1781. It will analyze the methods by which soldiers and civilians collected information about the enemy during this campaign, and seek to determine how military commanders utilized such information as intelligence prior to battle. This study differentiates between passive and active intelligence gathering in effort to illustrate the degree to which both methods were relied upon to gain accurate information about enemy forces."]

Trawick, Gary E. "The Egg Peddler." *The State: Down Home in North Carolina*, 37:10 (October 1969), 10, 20; online: http://digital.ncdcr.gov/cdm/ref/collection/p16062coll18/id/52935. [Online description from "North Carolina Periodicals Index," East Carolina University: "On August 29, 1781, a small group of Patriots launched a surprise attack against Tories encamped at Elizabethton. The Patriots believed that they were outnumbered but were unsure of the Tories exact numbers and who, specifically, was in command of their forces. A young woman named Sally (Sallie) Salter volunteered to infiltrate the Tory camp under the guise of a loyalist egg seller, seeking only to help feed the troops while garnering a small amount of business for herself. She identified the joint commanders as Colonels Slingby and Godden and placed the number of troops at approximately three to four hundred. Patriot commander, Col. Thomas Robeson, led the ensuing attack based on Salter's information, leading to a Patriot rout of the Tory forces in which both Colonels Slingby and Godden, as well as most of their troops were killed."]

Chapter Twelve
Naval and Maritime Records of North Carolina

Allegood, Jerry. "No Haunting, Just History." *Coastwatch*, (Winter 2009), 22-24. [Online description from "North Carolina Periodicals Index," East Carolina University: "Worn-out workboats left in the backwaters of North Carolina's coastal waterways provide researchers with a wealth of information about the state's maritime history. Allegood describes research conducted by students in the East Carolina University's Program in Maritime Studies along the Pungo River in Beaufort County."]

Babits, Lawrence E., and Joshua Howard. "Our Captain Quinn, North Carolina's Benedict Arnold." *Tributaries*, 15:1 (October 2008), 13-26. [Online description from "North Carolina Periodicals Index," East Carolina University: "New details about Captain Michael Quinn are revealed by combining archaeological and historical. He was a captain in the North Carolina Continental Line, a Revolutionary War group of troops. Later during his army career he turned from the Continental army to become a loyalist. After turning his loyalty, Quinn and his ship were captured outside of Edenton and killed during an attempted escape."]

Bussell, E[verett] Wayne. *Matthew Bussell and the American Revolution: Sailor and Soldier*. Lexington, Ky.: E. W. Bussell, 2012. [Virginia State Navy; ship *Dragon*; 1st Continental Artillery, Captain Anthony Singleton's Artillery Company; military campaigns in South Carolina, North Carolina, and Virginia]

Butler, Lindley S. *Pirates, Privateers, and Rebel Raiders of the Carolina Coast*. Chapel Hill: University of North Carolina Press, 2000. [Publisher's description: "North Carolina possesses one of the longest, most treacherous coastlines in the United States, and the waters off its shores have been the scene of some of the most dramatic episodes of piracy and sea warfare in the nation's history. Now, Lindley Butler brings this fascinating aspect of the state's maritime heritage vividly to life. He offers engaging biographical portraits of some of the most famous pirates, privateers, and naval raiders to ply the Carolina waters. Covering 150 years, from the golden age of piracy in the 1700s to the extraordinary transformation of naval warfare ushered in by the Civil War, Butler sketches the lives of eight intriguing characters: the pirate Blackbeard and his contemporary Stede Bonnet; privateer Otway Burns and naval raider Johnston Blakeley; and Confederate raiders James Cooke, John Maffitt, John Taylor Wood, and James Waddell. Penetrating the myths that have surrounded these legendary figures, he uncovers the compelling true stories of their lives and adventures."]

Cecelski, David S. *The Waterman's Song: Slavery and Freedom in Maritime North Carolina.* Chapel Hill: University of North Carolina Press, 2001. [Publisher's description: "The first major study of slavery in the maritime South, *The Waterman's Song* chronicles the world of slave and free black fishermen, pilots, rivermen, sailors, ferrymen, and other laborers who, from the colonial era through Reconstruction, plied the vast inland waters of North Carolina from the Outer Banks to the upper reaches of tidewater rivers. Demonstrating the vitality and significance of this local African American maritime culture, David Cecelski also reveals its connections to the Afro-Caribbean, the relatively egalitarian work culture of seafaring men who visited nearby ports, and the revolutionary political tides that coursed throughout the black Atlantic. Black maritime laborers played an essential role in local abolitionist activity, slave insurrections, and other antislavery activism. They also boatlifted thousands of slaves to freedom during the Civil War. But most important, Cecelski says, they carried an insurgent, democratic vision born in the maritime districts of the slave South into the political maelstrom of the Civil War and Reconstruction."]

Coggins, Jack. *Ships and Seamen of the American Revolution: Vessels, Crews, Weapons, Gear, Naval Tactics, and Actions of the War for Independence.* Harrisburg, Pa.: Stackpole Books, 1969.

Combs, Edwin L., III. "Trading in Lubberland: Maritime Commerce in Colonial North Carolina." *North Carolina Historical Review*, 80:1 (January 2003), 1-27. [Online description from "North Carolina Periodicals Index," East Carolina University: "This article looks at the unique problems encountered by commercial interests in coastal North Carolina during the 18th century utilizing data contained in 1768-1772 British customs returns. This data was overlooked by historian Charles Christopher Crittenden in his 1936 article, 'Commerce of North Carolina, 1763-1789,' leading Combs to challenge Crittendens conclusions and place his focus on the delicate balance between maritime trade, mercantilism, and economic development."]

Crittenden, Charles Christopher. *The Commerce of North Carolina, 1763-1789*. New Haven: Yale University Press, 1936.

Crittenden, Charles Christopher. "Inland Navigation in North Carolina, 1763-1789." *North Carolina Historical Review*, 8:2 (April 1931), 145-154.

Crittenden, Charles Christopher. "The Seacoast in North Carolina History, 1763-1789." *North Carolina Historical Review*, 7:4 (October 1930), 433-442; online: http://digital.ncdcr.gov/cdm/ref/collection/p16062coll9/id/4207.

[Online description from "North Carolina Periodicals Index," East Carolina University: "The author examines the 18th century coastline and the geographical impediments which hindered the state's overseas commerce. Discussed are the major bodies of water throughout eastern North Carolina including the Cape Fear River, the sounds, and Ocracoke Inlet and the men who sailed these waters and attempted to improve navigation throughout the period."]

Crittenden, Charles Christopher. "Ships and Shipbuilding in North Carolina, 1763-1789." *North Carolina Historical Review*, 8:1 (January 1931), 1-13.

Day, Jean [Stella Jean]. *The Revolutionary War in Coastal North Carolina: Ma Britain's Apron Strings*. Morehead City: Carteret County Historical Society, 2005. [Contents: Seeds of Mutiny; The Battle of Moore's; A difficult Choice; Cut Them Apron Strings! War: Ready or Not; That Old Arch-Traitor Goodrich; Beaufort, the Little Port That Wasn't; Eighty-Four Hogsheads of Rum; Edenton, Gateway to the North; Season It with Salt – Blacks in the Revolution; The Frenchman's Fort; The North Carolina Navy; War Winding Down; The British Invade Beaufort; Coastal North Carolina after the War.]

Day, Jean [Stella Jean]; Hervie Day, ed. *Revolutionary Patriots along the North Carolina Coast*. Newport, N. C.: Golden Age Press, 2006. [Contents: Payback time; Damned If He Did; Faith of Our Fathers; Slippery Bridge; Brash Courage; Where's the Navy? 'Hongry Towne;' That Virginian Traitor; Ocracoke Militia; Edenton, the Port City; Blacks in the Revolution; When Rum Was Gold; Fort Hancock; Wilmington, the End of War in Sight; British Attack Beaufort; After the War.]

Dean, Earl. "Carolina-Built Ships." *The State: A Weekly Survey of North Carolina*, 16:42 (March 1949), 11, 17; online: http://digital.ncdcr.gov/cdm/ref/collection/p16062coll18/id/23635. [Online description from "North Carolina Periodicals Index," East Carolina University: "During the Revolutionary War, ports at Wilmington, Elizabeth City, and New Bern were producing wooden vessels to add to the nation's naval fleet. The Carolina ships were used to run the blockade during this period and crewed by remarkable seamen."]

Drane, Robert Brent. "The Expedition against the Row Galley *General Arnold* – A Side Light on Colonial Edenton." *North Carolina Booklet*, 7:4 (April 1908), 267-277.

Drayton, John (prepared from material collected by the author's father William H. Drayton). *Memoirs of the American Revolution, From its Commencement to the Year 1776, Inclusive; as Relating to the State of South Carolina; and Occasionally Relating to the States of North Carolina and Georgia*. 2 vols. Charleston: A. E. Miller, 1821; reprinted: (Eyewitness Accounts of the American Revolution) New York: New York Times, 1969; Bedford, Mass.: Applewood Books, 2009. [A biographical sketch of William Henry Drayton appears in vol. 1, xiii-xxvii.]

Drew, Jonathan. "Shipwreck Found off North Carolina, Possibly from Late 1700s." *US News Online*, July 17, 2015. [Publisher's abstracts: "Duke University says scientists using underwater vehicles and sonar have found a shipwreck off the North Carolina coast that may date back to the American Revolution. The expedition led by Duke marine scientist Cindy Van Dover found the previously unknown wreck in mile-deep waters July 12 using an underwater robot and a manned submarine."]

Duffus, Kevin P. *Shipwrecks of the Outer Banks: An Illustrated Guide.* Raleigh, N.C.: Looking Glass Productions, Inc., 2007.

Fitzpatrick, John C. "A Sea Captain of the Revolution." *Daughters of the American Revolution Magazine*, 54:8 (August 1920), 44-448. [Andrew Paton, active 1778].

Frye, Barry E. "Privateers and Letters of Marque in North Carolina during the American Revolution." M. A. thesis, East Carolina University, 1980.

Goerch, Doris. "Early Days of Shipping." *The State: A Weekly Survey of North Carolina*, 11:10 (August 1943), 1, 24; online: http://digital.ncdcr.gov/cdm/ref/collection/p16062coll18/id/17630. [Online description from "North Carolina Periodicals Index," East Carolina University: "The history of shipping throughout the eastern portion of the state began during the colonial period. During that time, trading points were established along the Pamlico Sound in Bath Town, on Lionel Reading and Emanuel Cleaves' plantations, and in Washington for local planters to exchange goods with foreign shippers. Out of those ports listed, Washington became the more integral town. In the 1780s a flourishing trade developed between Washington and points in eastern North Carolina. Washington trade also expanded during this period to Europe and the West Indies."]

Goldenberg, Joseph A. *Shipbuilding in Colonial America.* Charlottesville: Published for the Mariners Museum, Newport News, Virginia, by the University Press of Virginia, 1976.

Great Britain. Admiralty. "[Extract from Journal of Samuel Lord Hood]. 5-20 Sep., 1781." Copy of a manuscript in the National Archives of the United Kingdom (formerly the Public Records Office), Kew, Richmond, Surrey, England; X76.378-.1-26 (MARS ID: 21.124.9.3; folder), "British Records Collection," State Archives of North Carolina, Raleigh. [Online catalog description: "Off coast of North Carolina, including battle of 6 Sep."]

Great Britain. Admiralty. "List of Rebel Vessels Taken by [Admiral Clark] Gayton's Squadron at Jamaica. 21 Dec.-26 Feb." Copy of a manuscript in the National Archives of the United Kingdom (formerly the Public Records Office), Kew, Richmond, Surrey, England; 73.41.1-22 (MARS ID: 21.114.47.6; folder), "British Records Collection," State Archives of North Carolina, Raleigh. [Online catalog description: "{Lists date of capture, name of captured vessel and its master, place of origin, lading, name of seizing vessel and its commander, and agents' name.} Including numbers from North Carolina."]

Great Britain. Admiralty. "[Sandy Hook, New Jersey]. List of Prizes Taken by [Vice Admiral Marriot] Arbuthnot's. [Commander of North American Station], Squadron, 4 Aug. to 20 Nov. 1779, and Condemned at New York. 16 Dec., 1779." Copy of a manuscript in the National Archives of the United Kingdom (formerly the Public Records Office), Kew, Richmond, Surrey, England; Z.5.48N (MARS ID: 21.114.25.51; folder), "British Records Collection," State Archives of North Carolina, Raleigh. [Online catalog description: "Includes the *Boston*, schooner from North Carolina, master William Cooper, taken off Cape Cod [Massachusetts] with cargo of tar and turpentine."]

Great Britain. Admiralty. "Whitehall [London]. Copy of Lord George Germain, [Secretary of State,] to Lord [Charles] Cornwallis. 6 Dec. 1775." Copy of a manuscript in the National Archives of the United Kingdom (formerly the Public Records Office), Kew, Richmond, Surrey, England; (MARS Id: 21.114.208.46; folder), "British Records Collection," State Archives of North Carolina, Raleigh. [Online catalog description: "Plan of operations for expedition to Cape Fear. Encl{osed} in Germain to Admiralty, 6 Dec. 1775. {See 21.114.209.1.45}."]

Great Britain. Colonial Office. "Boston, [Massachusetts]. Vice Admiral [Samuel] Graves to Admiralty Lords. 16 Jly., 1775." Copy of a manuscript in the National Archives of the United Kingdom (formerly the Public Records Office), Kew, Richmond, Surrey, England; Z.5.108N (MARS ID: 21.20.104.8; folder), "British Records Collection," State Archives of North Carolina, Raleigh. [Online catalog description: "Letter notes that Graves has had letter from Parry aboard *Cruizer* in North Carolina. Rebels there proposing to arm vessels and attack *Cruizer*. Expects no further provisions can be delivered there. Report of letter from Governor Martin in New Bern, North Carolina, 27 May, 1775, asking for a cutter to be moored near his residence in case escape necessary. Enclosing John Collet, commander of Fort Johnston, to Parry aboard *Cruizer*, 20 May 1775 (21.20.104.1.9)."]

Great Britain. Colonial Office. "Customhouse, Plymouth. Henry Folcher, Jr., Customs Collector, and R. Widger, Customs Comptroller, to [The Treasury Bd.]. 16 Jan., 1776." Copy of a manuscript in the National Archives of the United Kingdom (formerly the Public Records Office), Kew, Richmond, Surrey, England; 71.252.1-2 (MARS ID: 21.20.124.3; folder), "British Records Collection," State Archives of North Carolina, Raleigh. [Online catalog description: "The arrival of the *Elizabeth* from New Bern. Significant because the Provincial Congress permitted it to be loaded after the beginning of the trading prohibition between N. C. and Great Britain."]

Great Britain. Colonial Office. "Extract from the Journal of the *Lord Hyde* Packet Boat. 20 Aug., 1775." Copy of a manuscript in the National Archives of the United Kingdom (formerly the Public Records Office), Kew, Richmond, Surrey, England; 71.191.1-2 (MARS ID: 21.20.115.8; folder), "British Records Collection," State Archives of North Carolina, Raleigh. [Online catalog description: "Entry relates the burning of Fort Johnson and Gov. Josiah Martin's withdrawal to the *Cruizer*."]

Great Britain. Colonial Office. "Fort Johnston, N. C. [Copy] John Collet [Commander of Fort Johnston] to [Francis] Parry Aboard *Cruizer*. 20 May, 1775." Copy of a manuscript in the National Archives of the United Kingdom (formerly the Public Records Office), Kew, Richmond, Surrey, England; Z.5.108N (MARS ID: 21.20.104.1.8; folder), "British Records Collection," State Archives of North Carolina, Raleigh. [Online catalog description: "Letter states that Collet expects attack by provincial militia, begs for spare powder and urges *Cruizer* to anchor near fort and remain there. Enclosed in Vice Admiral Graves to Admiralty Lords, 16 July 1775."]

Great Britain. Colonial Office. "[No. 28] South Molton Street, [London]. Josiah Martin, [Former Gov. of N. C.], to the Earl of Shelburne, [Sec. of State]. 23 May, 1782." Copy of a manuscript in the National Archives of the United Kingdom (formerly the Public Records Office), Kew, Richmond, Surrey, England; 71.339.1-4 (MARS ID: 21.20.140.16; folder, "British Records Collection," State Archives of North Carolina, Raleigh. [Online catalog description: "Report on the actions of Capt. Linzee of the Crown sloop *Fakon* that eventually resulted in the death of James E. Bowen, a N. C. vice admiralty court judge."]

Great Britain. Colonial Office. "No. 36 Snow Hill, London. Robert Nelson, Former N. C. Merchant, to Lord George Germain. 9 Jun., 1781." Copy of a manuscript in the National Archives of the United Kingdom (formerly the Public Records Office), Kew, Richmond, Surrey, England; 71.302.1-4 (MARS ID: 21.20.133.5; folder), "British Records Collection," State Archives of North Carolina, Raleigh. [Online catalog description: "Detailed narrative of his Loyalist service; the seizure of his ship, the *Polly*, and her cargo near R. I. by Sir Peter Parker in accordance with an act of Parliament; and his request for the return of the ship and cargo or payment of compensation for the seizure. Encloses a letter of introduction by Josiah Martin, 14 March 1777 (21.20.133.1.6).”]

Great Britain. Colonial Office. “Orange Co., Certification by John Taylor, [1783].” Copy of a manuscript in the National Archives of the United Kingdom (formerly the Public Records Office), Kew, Richmond, Surrey, England; (MARS ID: 21.1.14.54; folder), “British Records Collection,” State Archives of North Carolina, Raleigh. [Online catalog description: “Concerns commission from Gov. Abner Nash to James Spicer to command flag vessel *Endeavour* sailing to Charles Town with British prisoners and commodities for relief of N. C. prisoners there.”]

Habersham, John, 1754-1799. “A Signed Letter of John Habersham, Savannah, 31 Aug. 1782: to Mjr. Gen. Nathanael Greene.” Manuscript MSS L1991.1.348 M, Society of the Cincinnati Library, Anderson House, Washington, D. C. [Online catalog description: “‘A prize has been brought into this place by Captain Goodloe, belonging to North Carolina. One captain, two lieutenants and ten privates of the British militia were on board, bound for St. Augustine.’ Habersham expresses his hope to exchange the prisoners, for, among others, ‘Capt. Brigg of the late lieutenant-colonel {Ephraim} Jackson’s State Legion, Lieutenants Cowan and Hillary of the Regiment of the State ....’ He also mentions a report that ‘Lieut. Colonel Laurens was lately killed....’ Habersham was an original member of the Georgia Society of the Cincinnati.”]

Haywood, Marshall DeLancey. “The State Navy of North Carolina in the War of the Revolution.” *North Carolina Booklet*, 17:1 (July 1917), 48-56. [Online description from “North Carolina Periodicals Index,” East Carolina University: “The State Navy of North Carolina and her privateers during the American Revolution contributed significant resources to the cause, but records of their activities are scarce.”]

Howard, Joshua B. “‘The Most Abandoned Sett of Wretches’: North Carolina’s Privateering Efforts during the American Revolution, 1775-1783.” M. A. thesis, East Carolina University, 2004.

Jackson, Claude V., III. *The Cape Fear-Northeast Cape Fear Rivers Comprehensive Study: A Maritime History and Survey of the Cape Fear and Northeast Cape Fear Rivers, Wilmington Harbor, North Carolina: Vol. 1: Maritime History*. Raleigh: North Carolina Department of Archives and History and United States Army Corps of Engineers, 1996; republished: Jack E. Fryar, Jr., ed. *The Big Book of the Cape Fear*. Wilmington: Dram Tree Books, 2008. [Publisher’s description: “In 1993-1994, the North Carolina Department of Cultural Resources’ Underwater Archaeology Unit teamed with the U. S. Army Corps of Engineers to conduct a comprehensive survey of Cape Fear River. The volume has been enhanced with more than 250 photos, illustrations, and maps.”]

“Jolidon Revolutionary Collection, 1778-1783.” Manuscript Library Service Center Box 1, David M. Rubenstein Rare Book & Manuscript Library, Duke University, Durham. [Online catalog description: “Military and official correspondence passing between French agents and French naval officers during the closing years of the Revolution. They relate to such matters as the obtaining of supplies for the French forces off the Carolina coast. Chiefly in French, some English.”]

Kammerer, Roger. “Early Shipbuilding in Pitt County.” *Greenville Times/Pitt’s Past*, (March 1-14, 1989), 18. [Online description from “North Carolina Periodicals Index,” East Carolina University: “Compared to agriculture, shipbuilding has been a minor industry in eastern North Carolina. The first vessel, built in 1776, was a 25-ton sloop named *Peggy*. Thirty years later, in 1807, Yankee Hall became Pitt County’s center for shipbuilding building the 99-ton brig *Minerva* that year, followed by the building in 1810 of the 153-ton brig the *Charleston Packet*. Pillsboro, located near Falkland, was the site of shipbuilding in 1860 and the *Lillian* was the final ship in Pitt County, built by J. L. Fountain and Company in 1904.”]

Lawrence, R. C. “Fleets of the State.” *The State: A Weekly Survey of North Carolina*, 6:42 (March 1939), 11, 18; online:. [Online description from “North Carolina Periodicals Index,” East Carolina University: “North Carolina has had its own navy in several wars, including the Revolutionary and Civil.”]

Merriman, Ann. “S. R. Fowle Company: Coastal Trade and Schooners.” *Tributaries*, 5 (October 1995), 22-27. [Online description from “North Carolina Periodicals Index,” East Carolina University: “Schooners figured prominently in the state’s water commerce during the 18th and 19th Centuries. Records of the S. R. Fowle Company of Washington provide important information on the use of these vessels for commerce.”]

Minford, Rob. “Industries of a Feather, Part One: Naval Stores, Cotton, and Agriculture.” *Lower Cape Fear Historical Society Bulletin*, 56:3 (November 2012), 1-7. [Online description from “North Carolina Periodicals Index,” East Carolina University: “Although now faded into the landscape, industries such as naval stores, cotton, and agriculture once dominated on the shores opposite the hub of Wilmington providing a once significant economic enterprise to Eagles Island.”]

Mires, Calvin H. "The Value of Maritime Archaeological Heritage; An Exploratory Study of the Cultural Capital of Shipwrecks in the Graveyard of the Atlantic." Ph. D. dissertation, East Carolina University, 2014.

Montgomery, Frank A., Jr. "The Tar Burners." *The State: Down Home in North Carolina*, 35:15 (January 1968), 12-13, 15; online: http://digital.ncdcr.gov/cdm/ref/collection/p16062coll18/id/103404. [Online description from "North Carolina Periodicals Index," East Carolina University: "When prices for tar and pitch were increased by their suppliers, England turned to their American colonies as a new source around 1700. Southeastern North Carolina became a major supplier of naval stores, which included tar, rosin, turpentine, and pitch. For decades Wilmington was recognized as the largest export point in the world for naval stores."]

Norris, Jeannie Faris. "The Odyssey of the Periauger." *Carolina Comments,* 52:4 (October 2004), 107-111; online: http://www.ncpublications.com/comments/ccOct04.pdf. [Online description from "North Carolina Periodicals Index," East Carolina University: "A replica of a periauger was built at the North Carolina Maritime Museum Watercraft Center in Beaufort in 2004. The construction took seven months and involved 30 volunteers working 8,400 hours. The log boat was the state's workboat during the 18th- and early 19th-centuries. The replica will be moored at the Newbold-White House near Hertford, where it will serve as an interpretive teaching tool. The article describes the boat's three-week journey to its home port in Hertford."]

Norris, Jeannie Faris. "Underwater Archaeology Unit Investigates Shipwreck." *Carolina Comments,* 36:4 (July 1988), 88-90. [Online description from "North Carolina Periodicals Index," East Carolina University: "Near the Rose Hill Plantation outside of Wilmington, local divers discovered a shipwreck believed to be from the Revolutionary period. The plantation's age, built in 1730, and colonial-era wine bottles led archaeologists to speculate about the shipwrecks age. Preliminary fieldwork indicates the wreck was from a 65' long, 20' wide, 120 ton sloop."]

North Carolina. "Miscellaneous Papers, 1689-1912." Manuscript PC.21 (MARS ID: 530; record group), State Archives of North Carolina, Raleigh. [Online catalog description shows that this collection includes: "photocopies relating to …privateering (1778, 1812)."]

North Carolina (State). General Assembly. "[Document dated:] April 25, [1777]: Report re[specting] Row Galleys (Message Only), 1777." Manuscript; General Assembly Record Group; Session Records, April-May, 1777; Joint Papers, Committee Papers, Resolutions, Senate Bills, House Bills, Box 1 (MARS ID: 66.8.9.10.8; item), State Archives of North Carolina, Raleigh. [Online catalog description: "Messages concerning the situation of the row galleys built by Virginia, and whether North Carolina should bear part of the expenses for their upkeep."]

North Carolina (State). General Assembly. "[Document dated:] April 26, 1777: Report on Defense Necessary for Ocracock Inlet and the Ports of Beaufort and Roanoke (Messages Only)." Manuscript; General Assembly Session Records; Session of April-May 1777; Joint Papers, Committee Papers, Resolutions, Miscellaneous Bills, Box 1 (MARS ID: 66.8.9.10.10; item), State Archives of North Carolina, Raleigh. [Online catalog description: "Message concerning the report on defense measures to be taken for the security of Ocracock Inlet, Beaufort, and Roanoke; reference made to defense capability of the row galleys constructed by Virginia."]

North Carolina (State). General Assembly. "[Document dated:] May 1, 1777: Re[spectin] *Pennsylvania Farmer* and Small Pox (with Messages)." Manuscript; General Assembly Record Group; Session Records, April-May, 1777; Joint Papers, Committee Papers, Resolutions, Miscellaneous Bills and Amendments; Senate Joint Resolutions, Box 1 (MARS ID: 66.8.9.11.5; item), State Archives of North Carolina, Raleigh. [Online catalog description: Resolution to prevent the passengers on board the *Pennsylvania Farmer* from coming ashore until the threat of small pox has been removed."]

North Carolina (State). General Assembly. "[Document dated:] 1777: Joint Papers: Misc. Account and Sworn Statement to Committees." Manuscript; General Assembly Record Group; Session Records, April-May, 1777; Joint Papers, Committee Papers, Resolutions, Miscellaneous Bills and Amendments, Senate Bills, House Bills, Box 1 (MARS ID: 66.8.9.10.15; item), State Archives of North Carolina, Raleigh. [Online catalog description: "Record of payment made for a ship chartered by the State of North Carolina;…"]

North Carolina (State). General Assembly. "[Document dated:] 1779: Miscellaneous." Manuscript; General Assembly Record Group; Session Records, May 1779; Joint Papers, Committee Papers, Resolutions, Senate Bills, House Bills, Box 1 (MARS ID: 66.8.17.8; folder), State Archives of North Carolina, Raleigh. Online catalog description: "Contains a letter from James Green, Jr., to the Speaker of the House of Commons concerning the lack of an officer to receive Continental taxes; a list of militia draftees who failed to appear when required; an inventory of accounts settled by committees from May, 1776 to January, 1779; and two letters to Thomas Younghusband, of Currituck County, describing attacks on that county by privateers."]

North Carolina (State). General Assembly. "[Document dated:] June 2, 1779: Petition of James Beaton, John Johnston, and Alex MacLean." Manuscript; General Assembly Record Group; Session Records, October-

November 1779; Joint Papers, Committee Papers, Resolutions, Senate Bills, House Bills:Box 1 (MARS ID: 66.8.18.6.1), State Archives of North Carolina, Raleigh. [Online catalog description: "The petitioners were on a British privateer that wrecked off the coast of the state; as a result, they lost all their clothes and were taken prisoner by John Humphrey of Currituck County. They request parole to Philadelphia to be exchanged."]

North Carolina (State). General Assembly. "[Document dated:] September 4, [1780]: Re[specting] the French Fleet and Thomas Buckle." Manuscript, Assembly Record Group, Session Records, August-September 1780; Joint Papers, Committee Papers, Resolutions, Senate Bills, House Bills, Box 1 (MARS ID: 66.8.22.35.5; item), State Archives of North Carolina, Raleigh. [Online catalog description: "Governor Nash informs the Assembly of the probable arrival of the French fleet despite a lack of official confirmation by the Continental Congress. He also refers to a letter concerning the confiscated property of Thomas Buckle, whom Nash considers a loyalist for signing a letter to General Henry Clinton at Charleston."]

North Carolina (State). General Assembly. "[Document Dated]: February 13, 1781: That Militia Company Be Raised for Defense of Sea Coast of Onslow County." Manuscript; General Assembly Record Group; Session Records, January-February 1781; Joint Papers, Committee Papers, Resolutions, House Joint Resolutions: February 12-14, Box 1 (MARS ID: 66.8.23.19.11; item), State Archives of North Carolina, Raleigh. [Online catalog description: "The resolution directs that the company be stationed at the mouth of the White Oak River."]

North Carolina (State). General Assembly. "[Document dated:] Dec. 22, [1787]: Resolution Directing Comptroller to Settle Accounts of John McCrohone (Petition Only)." Manuscript; General Assembly Record Group; Session Records, November-December 1787; Joint Papers, Committee Papers, Resolutions, Senate Bills, House Bills, Box 2 (MARS ID: 66.8.47.6.16; item), State Archives of North Carolina, Raleigh. [Online catalog description: "Petition of owners of ship impressed into service of the state, requests compensation because ship was destroyed during the war."]

North Carolina. Office of State Treasurer; Office of State Comptroller. "Ports, 1682-1887." Manuscript [MARS ID: 13.43; series), Vols. 1-38; Boxes 1-15, State Archives of North Carolina, Raleigh. [Online catalog description: Shipping lists, entries and clearances, and other records kept at the various ports of North Carolina, practically all of them from the colonial period and early statehood, but also including a few from the later nineteenth century. The records consist of volumes and loose papers of diverse types, all of them in some way concerning the collection of customs duties; the enforcement of laws relating to privateering, health, and the welfare of seamen; or the gathering of data regarding the movement of vessels and commodities in and out of the ports. Accounts, registers, and certificates record such information as duties received or secured; exports and imports; oaths taken; bonds entered into; vessels entered and cleared; drawbacks and reshipments; arrearages; relief of sick and disabled seamen; the imposition of quarantine; and sales of cargoes. There is also some correspondence, and several files relating to individual vessels. The following ports are represented in this series: Bath (1761-1794), Beaufort (1760-1790), Brunswick (1787-1790), Currituck (1783-1790), Edenton (1792-1807), Elizabeth City (1826-1827), Roanoke (1682-1794), Swansboro (1788-1790), Wilmington (1793, 1868-1887), and unidentified (1756-1830, 1876)."]

Nowitzky, George I. *Norfolk: The Marine Metropolis of Virginia, and the Sound and River Cities of North Carolina.* Norfolk: G.I. Nowitzky, 1888; reprinted: Whitefish, Mont.: Kessinger Publishing, 2007.

Page, John. "John Page Letter, 1777, September 26." Manuscript MS 1932.8, John D. Rockefeller, Jr. Library, Colonial Williamsburg Foundation, Williamsburg, Va.; online finding aid available at http://ead.lib.virginia.edu/vivaxtf/view?docId=cw/viwc00236.xml. [Online finding aid description: "Concerns an agreement between Virginia and North Carolina to combine resources to build new vessels to help defend the coast. Has heard Ocracoke Inlet is blocked and believes additional vessels would help rout the enemy. Champion Travis is to examine the state of the existing galleys. Mentions the North Carolina militia and states that {George} Washington has received reinforcements. Also, Gen. {William} Howe has retired from Brandywine at Wilmington."]

Parramore, Thomas C. *Southampton County, Virginia.* Charlottesville: University Press of Virginia for the Southampton County Historical Society, 1978. [See particularly, Chapter 3, "The Tale of the Spanish Cannons," for a discussion of the row galleys of Virginia and North Carolina during the Revolution.]

Petrey, Whitney R. "Weapemeoc Shores: The Loss of Traditional Maritime Culture among the Weapemeoc Indians." M. A. thesis, East Carolina University, 2014.

Platt, Virginia Bever. "Tar, Slaves, and New England Rum: The Trade of Aaron Lopez of Newport, Rhode Island, with Colonial North Carolina." *North Carolina Historical Review,* 48:1 (January 1971), 1-22. [Online description from "North Carolina Periodicals Index," East Carolina University: "This article seeks to build upon previous historians' work on the history of commercial shipping activities in North Carolina including the naval stores trade, provisions trade, lumber products shipping, and tobacco exportation. The author examines the Aaron Lopez papers who was a Rhode Island merchant actively involved in dispatching at least 37 voyages to North Carolina between 1761 and 1775."]

Rankin, Hugh F. "The Naval Flag of the American Revolution." *William and Mary Quarterly*, 3rd series, 11:3 (July 1954), 339-353.

Reedy, James R. "Historical and Archaeological Investigations Concerning a Revolutionary War Vessel Burned at Beaufort, North Carolina, in 1778." M. A. thesis, East Carolina University, 1987.

Rimler, Rose. "Revolutionary War-Era Shipwreck Discovered off North Carolina Coast." *New & Observer* (Raleigh), July 17, 2015.

Robinson, Kenneth W. "Port Brunswick and the Colonial Naval Stores Industry: Historical and Archaeological Observations." *North Carolina Archaeology*, 46 (1997), 51-68; online: http://www.rla.unc.edu/Publications/NCArch/NCA_46.pdf. [Online description from "North Carolina Periodicals Index," East Carolina University: "Port Brunswick along the Cape Fear River became a major exporter of pitch, tar, and raw turpentine. Robinson reviews the production of naval stores and the arrangement of port facilities through archaeological research."]

Shepherd, James F., and Samuel H. Williamson. "The Coastal Trade of the British North American Colonies, 1768-1772." *Journal of Economic History*, 32:4 (December 1972), 783-810.

Shutz, Geza. "Ships and Shipping in North Carolina, 1763-1789." *North Carolina Historical Review*, 8;1 (January 1931), 1-13; online: http://digital.ncdcr.gov/cdm/ref/collection/p16062coll9/id/4207. [Online description from "North Carolina Periodicals Index," East Carolina University: "A general history of ships and shipping in North Carolina between 1763-1789. Includes descriptions of vessel types popular to that period such as sloops, schooners and brigs, descriptions of shipping cargoes, ports, shipbuilding, shipwrecks, passenger vessels, and maritime industry in the state in general."]

"Some Americans Aboard *HMS Blonde* during the Revolution, 1780-1781." *North Carolina Genealogical Society Journal*, 7:3 (August 1991), 184.

Sprunt, James, "A Colonial Admiral of the Cape Fear." *North Carolina Booklet*, 6:1 (July 1906), 49-75. [Thomas Frankland (1718-1784)]

Stick, David. *Graveyard of the Atlantic: Shipwrecks of the North Carolina Coast*. Chapel Hill: University of North Carolina Press, 1989. [Publisher's description: "This is a factual account, written in the pace of fiction, of hundreds of dramatic losses, heroic rescues, and violent adventures at the stormy meeting place of northern and southern winds and waters – the Graveyard of the Atlantic off the Outer Banks of North Carolina."]

Still, William N[orwood]. *North Carolina's Revolutionary War Navy*. (Bicentennial Pamphlet Series, no. 7) Raleigh: North Carolina Department of Cultural Resources, Division of Archives and History, 1976. [Examination of the role of North Carolina in the maritime fight for independence. Bibliographic essay in the back is an excellent reference for researchers seeking primary source material on the subject.]

Street, Julia M. "We Led the World in Naval Stores." *The State: Down Home in North Carolina*, 44:5 (October 1976), 14-16; online: http://digital.ncdcr.gov/cdm/ref/collection/p16062coll18/id/72796. [Online description from "North Carolina Periodicals Index," East Carolina University: "During the Colonial Period, North Carolina accounted for three fifths of all naval stores shipped from the American colonies to England. Naval stores include tar, rosin, turpentine, and pitch. In 1705, England, no longer dependent on Sweden and the Baltic countries for stores, passed the Naval Stores Bounty Act, authorizing large payments for the goods from the colonies. Although the turpentine industry boomed in the 1840s and 50s, the Civil War was devastating to the industry which never fully recovered after the war."]

Taylor, Mark T. "Seiners and Tongers: North Carolina Fisheries in the Old and New South." *North Carolina Historical Review*, 69:1 (January 1992), 1-36.

Ubbelohde, Carl. *The Vice-Admiralty Courts and the American Revolution*. Chapel Hill: University of North Carolina Press for the Institute of Early American History and Culture, Williamsburg, Va., 1960.

United States. Navy. Naval History Division. "Selected Papers Relating to North Carolina and North Carolinians, 1778-1957." Manuscript 3417-z, Southern Historical Collection, Louis Round Wilson Special Collections Library, University of North Carolina, Chapel Hill; online finding aid available at http://www2.lib.unc.edu/329mss/inv/u/United_States.Naval_History_Division.html. [Online catalog description: "The collection includes copies of papers relating to North Carolinians in the United States Navy, naval vessels whose names have North Carolina associations, and Revolutionary and Civil War naval actions off the North Carolina coast. Included are biographical sketches of Edwin Alexander Anderson, David Worth Bagley, Osborne Bennett Hardison, Felix Leslie Johnson, William Durwood Leggett Junior, Andrew Theodore Long, John Wesley Roper, and John Wilkes; photocopies of letters and official communications relating to the *USS Croatan*, *USS*

Currituck, *USS North Carolina*, and *USS Raleigh*; communications relating to John Paul Jones, 1778, 1779, and 1782, and to David Dixon Porter, 1864 and 1865; and histories of the *USS Albemarle* (three different ships), *USS Bogue*, *USS Croatan*, and *USS Currituck*."]

Watson, Alan D. "Pilotage and Pilots in Colonial North Carolina: The Case of Ocracoke Inlet." *Tributaries*, 3:1 (October 1993), 20-25. [Online description from "North Carolina Periodicals Index," East Carolina University: "Pilots directed ships through the often tricky inlet system separating state rivers from ocean-going commerce. Specifically, the history of Ocracoke pilots and legislation governing them is presented."]

Williams, Justin. "English Mercantilism and Carolina Naval Stores, 1705-1776." *Journal of Southern History*, 1:2 (May 1935), 169-185.

Wilson, Jim. "Sailing Out of History." *Wildlife in North Carolina*, 69:11 (November 2005), 20-25. [Online description from "North Carolina Periodicals Index," East Carolina University: "The periauger was flat-bottomed, dugout workboat in the state's waterways during the 18th- and early 19th-centuries that disappeared in the first half of the 19th-century. Improved roadways, the opening of more railroad lines, and the steamboat contributed to its demise. Archaeologists have yet to find the remains of a vessel of this type in the state. In 2004, a group of marine historians successfully planned, built, and sailed a reproduction of periauger. Wilson discusses the project."]

Yocum, Thomas. "The War on Water." *Our State: Down Home in North Carolina*, 68:10 (March 2001), 55-57, 59-61; online: http://digital.ncdcr.gov/cdm/ref/collection/p16062coll18/id/72796. [Online description from "North Carolina Periodicals Index," East Carolina University: "For those on the Outer Banks and Carteret County, conflict with the British Navy was continual between 1776 and 1782. Yocum describes the six-year struggle and the patriots who defended coastal Carolina."]

Fishing Industry

Burgess, Carla B. "A Million Herring in One Night." *Coastwatch*, 17:4 (April 1990), 4-5. [Online description from "North Carolina Periodicals Index," East Carolina University: "A little digging in coastal North Carolina shows that some communities rest on herring bones. Burgess discusses the history the herring fishery in North Carolina."]

Leary, William J., Jr. "The Fisheries of Eastern Carolina." *North Carolina Booklet*, 14:4 (April 1915), 173-194; online: http://digital.ncdcr.gov/cdm/ref/collection/p249901coll37/id/14180. [Online description from "North Carolina Periodicals Index," East Carolina University: "From the colonial periods to the early twentieth century, fishing constituted a major economic activity in North Carolina. There is early evidence of commercial fisheries and distinct traditions of fishing shad, herring, rock, bass and sturgeon."]

Norris, Jeannie Faris. "The Great Fisheries of the Nineteenth Century." *The State: Down Home in North Carolina*, 31:24 (April 1964), 15-16; online: http://digital.ncdcr.gov/cdm/ref/collection/p16062coll18/id/46710. [Online description from "North Carolina Periodicals Index," East Carolina University: "A fishing county since the early 18th century, Bertie County benefitted from the introduction of seine nets as early as 1713, utilizing this method through 1915. The last seine to operate in the county was the Sutton Beach station, also known as Avoca, the largest and most successful of all the Albemarle Sound fisheries."]

Shannon, Renee Walcott. "The Fate of a Fishery – Shad and River Herring at the Turn of the 21st Century." *Coastwatch*, (Spring 2000), 6-13. [Online description from "North Carolina Periodicals Index," East Carolina University: "Shad and herring fisheries on coastal rivers have fed generations of eastern Carolinians. However, technological innovations, pollution, and overfishing have decreased the size of the annual harvest. Shannon describes the fisheries at Lock and Dam No. 1, Cape Fear River; Contentnea Creek, in Grifton; and the Roanoke River at Jamesville; and their prospects in the twenty-first century."]

Whaling and North Carolina

Barfield, Rodney. "A Whale of a Job." *The State: Down Home in North Carolina*, 60:2 (July 1992), 12-14; online: http://digital.ncdcr.gov/cdm/ref/collection/p16062coll18/id/65546. [Online description from "North Carolina Periodicals Index," East Carolina University: "The whaling industry on the Outer Banks is of historical interest for North Carolina."]

Bradley, Ryan, and Nathan Richards. "Where Were the Whalers? An Investigation of the Archaeological, Historical, and Cultural Infuences of North Carolina Whaling. M. A. thesis, East Carolina University, 2016. [Online catalog description: "

The purpose of this study is to examine ex situ material culture associated with North Carolina shore whaling in an attempt to clarify, contest, or confirm the nature of the industry as it existed on the coast of North Carolina.

Previous research on the subject reveals a fragmented history with more questions than answers. The paucity of in situ archaeological signatures found in the shifting sands of the Outer Banks makes an ex situ material culture study particularly important. By locating, examining, and geospatially analyzing artifacts associated with North Carolina shore whaling it may be possible to answer a few of the questions and perhaps provide better places to look for the answers."]

Curci, Jessica. "The North Carolina Whaling Industry." *Tributaries*, 14:1 (October 2006), 23-32. [Online description from "North Carolina Periodicals Index," East Carolina University: "The state continued its shore whaling activities into the early 20th-century. Being situated near the Gulf Stream, whalers caught whales first near Albemarle and later Cape Lookout, Shackleford Banks and Bogue Banks. The author discusses local whaling traditions and the history of the industry throughout eastern North Carolina."]

Dean, Jim. "Diamond City Whales." *Wildlife in North Carolina*, 46:3 (March 1982). [Online description from "North Carolina Periodicals Index," East Carolina University: "Diamond City, which had a population of several hundred people, once filled the land between Cape Lookout Lighthouse and the point of Core Banks Island. All that remains are a few family graveyards. Dean discusses the city and the whaling industry that flourished there for 150 years, ending in 1909."]

Great Britain. Parliament. House of Commons. *Reasons Most Humbly Offered to the Honourable House of Commons for Caring on an American Fishery upon the Coast of New England and North Carolina, for Whale, Cod, Macrell and Herring*. [London: His Majesty's Stationary Office? 1720?]

Jateff, Emily. *Hain't Been Found Yet: The Search for Archaeological Evidence of Shore Whaling at Diamond City*. (Flinders University of South Australia Maritime Archaeology Monograph series, no. 14). Bedford Park, South Australia: Department of Archaeology, Flinders University, 2007.

Reeves, Randall R., and Edward Mitchell. *History of Whaling in and near North Carolina*. (National Oceanic and Atmospheric Administration Technical Report NMFS 65) Seattle: United States Department of Commerce, National Oceanic and Atmospheric Administration, National Marine Fisheries Service, 1988.

Simpson, Marcus B., Jr. *Whaling on the North Carolina Coast*. Raleigh: Division of Archives and History, North Carolina Department of Cultural Resources, 1990.

Simpson, Sallie W., and Maucus B. Simpson, Jr. "The Pursuit of Leviathan: A History of Whaling on the North Carolina Coast." *North Carolina Historical Review*, 65:1 (January 1988), 1-51. [Online description from "North Carolina Periodicals Index," East Carolina University: "Between the 17th and 20th centuries, the waters off of North Carolina were some of the most fruitful for whaling in North America. While never a large industry for local fishermen who usually participated in shore-whaling, pelagic whalers from New England were common visitors, stalking the whale pods."]

Street, Julia M. "Whaling on the Outer Banks." *The State: Down Home in North Carolina*, 44:1 (June 1976), 14-16; online: http://digital.ncdcr.gov/cdm/ref/collection/p16062coll18/id/60612. [Online description from "North Carolina Periodicals Index," East Carolina University: "By 1700, ships from the New England Whaling Fleet took advantage of beached whales along North Carolina's coast, using the carcasses to make oil. By 1885, a town of over 500 people lived in Lookout Woods, later called Diamond City, chiefly to whale live specimens. Most of the whales killed were Right Whales, yielding an average of 200 barrels of oil each. Due to a decreased number of whales swimming off the coast, whaling in North Carolina ended around 1899."]

Chapter Thirteen:
Prisoners of War, Prisons, Prison Ships, and Refugees

Patriotic Service[37]

Patriots of the Revolution are considered to be those men and women who by an act or series of actions demonstrated unfailing loyalty to the cause of American Independence from England. Patriotic service might begin as early as April 1774. We depend upon recorded actions to give us an indication of patriotism. What was the purpose of the action? What were the risks? The consequences? Answers to these questions can determine whether the action actually applied to an attempt to further the cause of independence or demonstrated loyalty to that cause.

Evidence of patriotic activity may be found in town, county, state, and federal records. Many records kept by the states have been indexed and often a letter to the state archives will be sufficient to determine if evidence exists to show that a person contributed supplies or made some other contribution to the war effort. Town and county records have usually not been indexed and a personal search of town minutes and court minutes is required. Minutes of the Continental Congresses have been published. *Old letters, diaries, and other family and personal papers can often be used as evidence of patriotic intent, provided the record was made at the time of the event described.*

Not all actions illustrating patriotism are mentioned here. Many others exist. When it is considered desirable to establish another type of patriotic service, proof of the action taken must be submitted with the application paper, together with historical justification to show that the action did indeed imply patriotic intent.

Prisoners of War or *refugees from occupying forces. Prisoners on the British Ship New Jersey and other prison ship:* Since there is no positive residence or unit identification of these lists of names, the applicant must supply documentation which proves without a doubt that the prisoner is indeed the person from whom the applicant descends.

"American Continental Prisoners of War Captured at Charleston and Camden Who Enlisted in the British Army" - *North Carolina Genealogical Society Journal*, 9:3 (August 1983), 168-172.

"American Prisoners aboard *Gorbay* at Charleston, S. C., 1781." *North Carolina Genealogical Society Journal*, 8:2 (May 1982), 82.

"American Prisoners at Ft. Chambly, 1779-1780." *North Carolina Genealogical Society Journal*, 17:4 (November 1991), 209-212. [This list contains names of American soldiers from all colonies held as prisoners at Ft. Chambly, near Montreal, Canada.]

"American Prisoners in Mill Prison, England, 1781." *North Carolina Genealogical Society Journal*, 9:1 (February 1983), 48.

"Benjamin Tarver for Conveying Prisoners to Virginia by Order of Congress." In Weynette Parks Haun, *North Carolina Revolutionary Army Accounts, Part I, Secretary of State Treasurer's & Comptroller's Papers Journal "A", (Public Accounts) 1775-1776* (Durham: W. P. Haun, 1988), 81-82. [County determined by Revolutionary War pensions of John Maholland R6832A; R7348 John Moore. Also, a number of the names in this account appear in the 1790 census of Northampton County, North Carolina. {This analysis was performed by genealogists in the Genealogy Office, Office of the Registrar General, National Society Daughters of the American Revolution, Washington, D. C.}]

Butler, Lindley S. "200 Years Ago and Lindley's Mill." *The State: Down Home in North Carolina*, 49:5 (October 1981), 12-13; online: http://digital.ncdcr.gov/cdm/ref/collection/p16062coll18/id/60425. [Online description from "North Carolina Periodicals Index," East Carolina University: "On September 12, 1781, Loyalist partisan Colonel David Fanning and his militia surrounded the temporary state capital, Hillsborough. The one-thousand-man force successfully captured state officers, army officials, and Governor Thomas Burke. While Fanning marched his men to loyalist stronghold Wilmington, Whig general John Butler quickly assembled 400 militia at

[37] Office of the Registrar General's compilation, *Genealogy Guidelines* (Washington, D. C.: National Society Daughters of the American Revolution, 2014), 94-95.

the mill of Quaker Thomas Lindley to block Fanning. The Whigs were overpowered, however, and the Loyalists were able to deliver their prisoners to Major James H. Craig in Wilmington."]

Courtney, William and William O'Neel. "William Courtney and William O'Neel Letter, ca. 1780." Manuscript 5403-z, Southern Historical Collection, Louis Round Wilson Special Collections Library, University of North Carolina, Chapel Hill; online finding aid available at http://www2.lib.unc.edu/mss/inv/c/Courtney,William_and_William_O'Neel.html. [Online finding aid description: "William Courtney and Major William O'Neel were in the Continental Army during the American Revolutionary War. They were taken as prisoners of war by forces led by Lord Cornwallis, possibly in North Carolina during the summer of 1780. The collection consists of a copy of a letter written by William Courtney and William O'Neel while they were prisoners of war. The letter, written to General Nathanael Greene on behalf of more than 100 fellow prisoners, asks that Greene take up their cause and relieve them from inhumane treatment."]

Great Britain. Army. "[American Officers Taken in the Southern Department by the British Army Previous to 26 Nov. 1782.]" Manuscript, University of North Carolina at Chapel Hill. [Online catalog description: "Ms., signed: Ashley Ferry, Robert Cooke, and L. Warren. …A register of those captured from North Carolina, Georgia, Virginia, Maryland, Delaware, South Carolina and Pennsylvania with the dates of their captures."]

Great Britain. Colonial Office. "List of 23 American Prisoners of War who Served on French Vessels. 13 May, 1782." Copy of a manuscript in the National Archives of the United Kingdom (formerly the Public Records Office), Kew, Richmond, Surrey, England; 70.425.1-2 (MARS ID: 21.20.6.11; folder), "British Records Collection," State Archives of North Carolina, Raleigh. [Online catalog description: "One prisoner, John Davis from N. C., desired to remain in Great Britain."]

Great Britain. Colonial Office. "New Bern. Commission from Gov. Abner Nash to James Spicer, Apr 25, 1781." Copy of a manuscript in the National Archives of the United Kingdom (formerly the Public Records Office), Kew, Richmond, Surrey, England; (MARS ID: 21.1.14.53; folder), "British Archives Collection," State Archives of North Carolina, Raleigh. [Online catalog description: "To command flag vessel *Endeavour* sailing to Charles Town with British prisoners and commodities for relief of N. C. prisoners there."]

Great Britain. Colonial Office. "Deposition of James Spicer. [ca. Sept, 1781]." Copy of a manuscript in the National Archives of the United Kingdom (formerly the Public Records Office), Kew, Richmond, Surrey, England; (MARS ID: 21.1.14.63; folder), "British Records Collection," State Archives of North Carolina, Raleigh. [Online catalog description: "Loss of flag of truce *Endeavour* and return of Spicer and crew to Beaufort, N. C."]

Great Britain. Colonial Office. "Orange Co., Certification by John Taylor, [1783]." Copy of a manuscript in the National Archives of the United Kingdom (formerly the Public Records Office), Kew, Richmond, Surrey, England; (MARS Id: 21.1.14.54; folder), "British Records Collection," State Archives of North Carolina, Raleigh. [Online catalog description: "Concerns commission from Gov. Abner Nash to James Spicer to command flag vessel *Endeavour* sailing to Charles Town with British prisoners and commodities for relief of N. C. prisoners there."]

Great Britain. Treasury. "Charles Town [South Carolina]. Memorial of John Sherwood and Enoch Andrews to Colonel Alexander Leslie. 23 May, 1782." Copy of a manuscript in the National Archives of the United Kingdom (formerly the Public Records Office), Kew, Richmond, Surrey, England; 77.342.1-2 (MARS ID: 21.102.2.10; folder), State Archives of North Carolina, Raleigh. [Online catalog description: "Carried arms in George Town district Dec. 1780; were captured 'and carried with Hand Cuffs on, to a place near Nubern {*sic*} in North Carolina where they were confined in a log Pen - but by the assistance of friends they escaped . . .'; etc. Including certification by James Cassels, colonel, George Town militia."]

Great Britain. Treasury. "Charles Town [South Carolina]. Memorial to [Lieutenant General] Alexander Leslie from Private W[illi]am Beams. Formerly of David Fanning's Regiment in North Carolina. 10 Jly. 1782." Copy of a manuscript in the National Archives of the United Kingdom (formerly the Public Records Office), Kew, Richmond, Surrey, England; (MARS Id: 21.102.5.15), "British Records Collection," State Archives of North Carolina, Raleigh. [Online catalog description: "Including order for payment."]

Great Britain. Treasury. "Charles Town, [South Carolina]. [Request from John MacLeod and Six Others.] 17 Dec. 1782." Copy of a manuscript in the National Archives of the United Kingdom (formerly the Public Records Office), Kew, Richmond, Surrey, England; 77.350.1 (MARS ID: 21.102.2.21; folder), State Archives of North Carolina, Raleigh. [Online catalog description: "'It is our orders soon to march from here,' therefore request their pay for services in North Carolina Militia be given Donald MacInnes. Marks of John MacLeod and six others."]

Great Britain. Treasury. "[Charleston, South Carolina. 'A List of Men from No. Carolina Bound for Augustine Who Acted in the Militia Service Never Recd. No Pay for their Service.' 6 Oct. 1782." Copy of a manuscript in the

National Archives of the United Kingdom (formerly the Public Records Office), Kew, Richmond, Surrey, England; (MARS Id: 21.102.5.21), "British Records Collection," State Archives of North Carolina, Raleigh.
Great Britain. Treasury. "[Charleston, South Carolina. 'Abstract of Pay Due to Captain Stephen Scarborough and Matthew Parker Ensn. Of the No. Carolina Militia...' [May 1782]." Copy of a manuscript in the National Archives of the United Kingdom (formerly the Public Records Office), Kew, Richmond, Surrey, England; (MARS Id: 21.102.5.13), "British Records Collection," State Archives of North Carolina, Raleigh.
Great Britain. Treasury. "[Charleston], South Carolina. Abstract of Pay Due Quarter Masters of Refugees from Various Districts. 30 Jun. 1782." Copy of a manuscript in the National Archives of the United Kingdom (formerly the Public Records Office), Kew, Richmond, Surrey, England; 77.410.1-2 (MARS ID: 21.102.4.13; folder), State Archives of North Carolina, Raleigh. [Online catalog description: "Including W{illia}m McQueen for North Carolina, and Joseph Brinkley for sick refugees from North Carolina."]
Great Britain. Treasury. "[Charleston, South Carolina]. 'Abstract of Pay Due to Officers and Privates' off David Fanning's Regiment, 'Who Came Lately from North Carolina'. [Aug. 1782]." Copy of a manuscript in the National Archives of the United Kingdom (formerly the Public Records Office), Kew, Richmond, Surrey, England; (MARS ID: 210102.5.19), "British Records Collection," State Archives of North Carolina, Raleigh. [Online catalog description: "Including order for payment, and certificate by Fanning."]
Great Britain. Treasury. "[Charleston, South Carolina]. 'Abstract of Pay Due to Subbeltons {Subalterns} and Privates Belonging to Anson County Regement [*sic*] Commanded by Duncan Ray Collonel [*sic*]... Those Men Came Lately to Charlestown from North Carolina.' [May 1782]." Copy of a manuscript in the National Archives of the United Kingdom (formerly the Public Records Office), Kew, Richmond, Surrey, England; (MARS Id: 21.102.5.11), "British Records Committee," State Archives of North Carolina, Raleigh. [Online catalog description: "Names given."]
Great Britain. Treasury. "[Charleston, South Carolina]. A[rchibald] Taylor, Major, North Carolina M[ilitia] to Colonel [Robert] Gray, [Paymaster to Royal Militia]. 10 Sep. 1782." Copy of a manuscript in the National Archives of the United Kingdom (formerly the Public Records Office), Kew, Richmond, Surrey, England; 77.363.1 (MARS ID: 21.90.255.31; folder), State Archives of North Carolina, Raleigh. [Online catalog description: "Concerning his pay."]
Great Britain. Treasury. "Charleston, [South Carolina]. Certificate by David Fanning [in Claim of Meredith Edwards, Captain of Militia, Formerly of His Regiment in North Carolina.] 10 Jly. 1782." Copy of a manuscript in the National Archives of the United Kingdom (formerly the Public Records Office), Kew, Richmond, Surrey, England; (MARS Id: 21.102.5.18), "British Records Collection," State Archives of North Carolina, Raleigh.
Great Britain. Treasury. "[Charleston, South Carolina]. Certificates [Relating to American Loyalists]. 26 July 1782." Copy of a manuscript in the National Archives of the United Kingdom (formerly the Public Records Office), Kew, Richmond, Surrey, England; 77.407.1-2 (MARS ID: 21.102.4.7; folder), "British Records Collection," State Archives of North Carolina, Raleigh. [Online catalog description: "Concerning Aaron Dickson 'of the North Carolina refugees [who] did attend the said refugees during the time they underwent the small pox in the Scots meetinghouse.' Including on back an order dated 2 Aug. 1782."]
Great Britain. Treasury. "[Charleston, South Carolina]. Certificates etc. [Relating to American Loyalists.] Mar.-May (Various Dates), 1782." Copy of a manuscript in the National Archives of the United Kingdom (formerly the Public Records Office), Kew, Richmond, Surrey, England; 77.405.1-2 (MARS ID: 21.102.4.7; folder), "British Records Collection," State Archives of North Carolina, Raleigh. [Online catalog description: "Concerning payments to James Crosby of North Carolina Militia."]
Great Britain. Treasury. "[Charleston, South Carolina]. Certification that Two Sergeants and 13 Men of the Royal Refugees are Now Serving in Captain [Kenneth] Stewart's Company of North Carolina Militia. 31 Dec. 1781." Copy of a manuscript in the National Archives of the United Kingdom (formerly the Public Records Office), Kew, Richmond, Surrey, England; 77.341.1 (MARS ID: 21.102.2.9; folder), "British Records Collection," State Archives of North Carolina, Raleigh.
Great Britain. Treasury. "Charleston, [South Carolina]. Daniel McFattar and Two Others to Colonel Robert Gray, Paymaster of Royal Militia. 30 Jun. 1782." Copy of a manuscript in the National Archives of the United Kingdom (formerly the Public Records Office), Kew, Richmond, Surrey, England; 77.360.1 (MARS ID: 21.102.2.39; folder), "British Records Collection," "British Records Collection," State Archives of North Carolina, Raleigh. [Online catalog description: "Concerning pay for service in North Carolina Regiment of Royal Militia."]
Great Britain. Treasury. "[Charleston, South Carolina]. Dugal Duncan to Colonel [Robert] Gray, [Paymaster to Royal Militia]. 18 May 1782." Copy of a manuscript in the National Archives of the United Kingdom (formerly the Public Records Office), Kew, Richmond, Surrey, England; 77.370.1 (MARS ID: 21.102.2.53; folder),

"British Records Collection," State Archives of North Carolina, Raleigh. [Online catalog description: "Concerning his pay (North Carolina Militia)."]

Great Britain. Treasury. "[Charleston, South Carolina]. Dugald Blue to Colonel [Robert]Gray, [Paymaster to Royal Militia]. 26 May 1782." Copy of a manuscript in the National Archives of the United Kingdom (formerly the Public Records Office), Kew, Richmond, Surrey, England; 77.370.1 (MARS ID: 21.102.2.55; folder), "British Records Collection," State Archives of North Carolina, Raleigh. [Online catalog description: "Concerning his pay, North Carolina Militia."]

Great Britain. Treasury. "[Charleston, South Carolina]. End. 'Distressed Refugees from Savannah, North Carolina andc [*sic*].' 6 Aug. 1782." Copy of a manuscript in the National Archives of the United Kingdom (formerly the Public Records Office), Kew, Richmond, Surrey, England; 77.419.1-3 (MARS ID: 21.102.4.22; folder), "British Archives Collection," State Archives of North Carolina, Raleigh. [Online catalog descriptions: "(And orders for payment, 11 Aug.)"]

Great Britain. Treasury. "[Charleston, South Carolina]. George Lifener to Colonel Robert Gray, Paymaster of Royal Militia. 12 Sep. 1782." Copy of a manuscript in the National Archives of the United Kingdom (formerly the Public Records Office), Kew, Richmond, Surrey, England; 77.358.1 (MARS ID: 21/102.2.35), "British Archives Collection," State Archives of North Carolina, Raleigh. [Online catalog description: "Concerning his pay for service in North Carolina militia."]

Great Britain. Treasury. "[Charleston, South Carolina]. John Blue to Colonel Robert Gray, Paymaster of Royal Militia. 28 Jun. 1782." Copy of a manuscript in the National Archives of the United Kingdom (formerly the Public Records Office), Kew, Richmond, Surrey, England; 77.357.1 (MARS ID: 21.102.2.33; folder), "British Records Collection," State Archives of North Carolina, Raleigh. [Online catalog description: "Concerning his pay for service in North Carolina militia."]

Great Britain. Treasury. "[Charleston, South Carolina]. John Morison to colonel [Robert] Gray, [Paymaster to Royal Militia]. 11 May 1782." Copy of a manuscript in the National Archives of the United Kingdom (formerly the Public Records Office), Kew, Richmond, Surrey, England; (MARS ID: 21.102.2.51; folder), "British Records Collection," State Archives of North Carolina, Raleigh. [Online catalog description: "Concerning his pay (North Carolina Militia)."]

Great Britain. Treasury. "[Charleston, South Carolina]. John Murphy to Colonel [Robert] Gray, [Paymaster to Royal Militia]. 28 May 1782." Copy of a manuscript in the National Archives of the United Kingdom (formerly the Public Records Office), Kew, Richmond, Surrey, England; 77.369.1 (MARS ID: 21.102.2.52; folder), "British Records Collection," State Archives of North Carolina, Raleigh. [Online catalog description: "Concerning his pay. (North Carolina Militia."]

Great Britain. Treasury. "[Charleston, South Carolina]. John Murphy to Colonel Robert Gray, Paymaster of Royal Militia. 22 Jly. 1782." Copy of a manuscript in the National Archives of the United Kingdom (formerly the Public Records Office), Kew, Richmond, Surrey, England; 77.359.1 (MARS ID: 21.102.2.52; folder), "British Records Collection," State Archives of North Carolina, Raleigh. [Online catalog description: "Concerning his pay for service in North Carolina militia."]

Great Britain. Treasury. "[Charleston, South Carolina]. List No. 7, Payments at Charles Town to Major [Thomas] Torrants of North Carolina. 15 Feb. 1782." Copy of a manuscript in the National Archives of the United Kingdom (formerly the Public Records Office), Kew, Richmond, Surrey, England; X77.302.1 (MARS ID: 21.102.1.2; folder), "British Records Collection," State Archives of North Carolina, Raleigh.

Great Britain. Treasury. "[Charleston, South Carolina]. List No. 9, Payments at Charles Town to Militia Officers of North and South Carolina. 20 Feb.-24 Apr. [1782]." Copy of a manuscript in the National Archives of the United Kingdom (formerly the Public Records Office), Kew, Richmond, Surrey, England; X77.303.1-2 (MARS ID: 21.102.1.3; folder), "British Records Project," State Archives of North Carolina, Raleigh.

Great Britain. Treasury. "[Charleston, South Carolina]. List No. 10, 'Distressed Refugees Paid on Order…' [n. d.], [1782]." Copy of a manuscript in the National Archives of the United Kingdom (formerly the Public Records Office), Kew, Richmond, Surrey, England; X77.303.2 (MARS ID: 21.102.1.4; folder), "British Records Collection," State Archives of North Carolina, Raleigh. [Online catalog description: "Including several from North Carolina."

Great Britain. Treasury. "[Charleston, South Carolina]. List No. 19, 'Distressed Refugees from Different Places.' 4-27 April 1782." Copy of a manuscript in the National Archives of the United Kingdom (formerly the Public Records Office), Kew, Richmond, Surrey, England; X77.304.1 (MARS ID: 21.102.1.5; folder), "British Records Collection," State Archives of North Carolina, Raleigh.

Great Britain. Treasury. "[Charleston, South Carolina]. List No. 21, 'Distressed Refugees from Different Places.' 4 May-13 Jly. 1782." Copy of a manuscript in the National Archives of the United Kingdom (formerly the Public

Records Office), Kew, Richmond, Surrey, England; X77.305.1 (MARS ID: 21.102.1.6; folder), "British Records Collection," State Archives of North Carolina, Raleigh. [Online catalog description: "Including several from North Carolina."]

Great Britain. Treasury. "[Charleston, South Carolina]. List No. 23, 'Refugees of the Second Class Now in Charlestown.' 28 May [1782]." Copy of a manuscript in the National Archives of the United Kingdom (formerly the Public Records Office), Kew, Richmond, Surrey, England; X77.306.1 (MARS ID: 21.102.1.7; folder), "British Records Collection," State Archives of North Carolina, Raleigh. [Online catalog description: "One only, from North Carolina."]

Great Britain. Treasury. "[Charleston, South Carolina]. List No. 24, 'Militia Officers at Present Refugees in Charlestown.' (Various Dates), 1782." Copy of a manuscript in the National Archives of the United Kingdom (formerly the Public Records Office), Kew, Richmond, Surrey, England; X77.307.1-2 (MARS ID: 21.102.1.8; folder), "British Records Collection." State Archives of North Carolina, Raleigh. [Online catalog description: "Including two from North Carolina."]

Great Britain. Treasury. "[Charleston, South Carolina]. List No. 36, 'Distressed Refugees from Different Places' 23 July-29 November 1782." Copy of a manuscript in the National Archives of the United Kingdom (formerly the Public Records Office), Kew, Richmond, Surrey, England; X77.316.1 (MARS ID: 21.102.1.17; folder), "British Records Collection." State Archives of North Carolina, Raleigh. [Online catalog description: "Including two from North Carolina."]

Great Britain. Treasury. "[Charleston, South Carolina]. List No. 28, 'Refugee Women and Children Going Back to the Country.' 27 May-3 Jun 1782." Copy of a manuscript in the National Archives of the United Kingdom (formerly the Public Records Office), Kew, Richmond, Surrey, England; X77.309.1 (MARS ID: 21.102.1.10; folder), "British Records Collection," State Archives of North Carolina, Raleigh. [Online catalog description: "Including one from North Carolina."]

Great Britain. Treasury. "[Charleston, South Carolina]. List No. 29, 'North Carolina Refugees Colo. Duncan Ray.' 8 Jun. 1782." Copy of a manuscript in the National Archives of the United Kingdom (formerly the Public Records Office), Kew, Richmond, Surrey, England; X77.310.1 (MARS ID: 21.102.1.11; folder), "British Records Collection,:" State Archives of North Carolina, Raleigh.

Great Britain. Treasury. "[Charleston, South Carolina]. List No. 31, 'Quarter Masters of the Refugees from Different Districts.' (Various Dates), 1781-1782." Copy of a manuscript in the National Archives of the United Kingdom (formerly the Public Records Office), Kew, Richmond, Surrey, England; X77.311.1 (MARS ID: 21.102.1.12; folder), "British Records Collection," State Archives of North Carolina, Raleigh. [Online catalog description: "Including one from North Carolina."]

Great Britain. Treasury. "[Charleston, South Carolina]. List No. 32, 'Refugees of the First Class in Charles Town.' (Various Dates), 1782." Copy of a manuscript in the National Archives of the United Kingdom (formerly the Public Records Office), Kew, Richmond, Surrey, England; X77.312.1-2 (MARS ID: 21.102.1.13; folder), "British Records Collection," State Archives of North Carolina, Raleigh. [Online catalog description: "Including two from North Carolina, Raleigh."]

Great Britain. Treasury. "[Charleston, South Carolina]. List No. 33, 'Refugees of the Second Class in Charles Town.' (Various Dates), 1782." Copy of a manuscript in the National Archives of the United Kingdom (formerly the Public Records Office), Kew, Richmond, Surrey, England; X77.313.1 (MARS ID: 21.102.1.20; folder), "British Records Collection," State Archives of North Carolina, Raleigh. [Online catalog description: "Including several from North Carolina."]

Great Britain. Treasury. "[Charleston, South Carolina]. List No. 34, 'Refugees of the Third Class in Charles Town.' (Various Dates), 1782." Copy of a manuscript in the National Archives of the United Kingdom (formerly the Public Records Office), Kew, Richmond, Surrey, England; X77.314.1 (MARS ID: 21.102.1.15; folder), "British Records Collec-tion," State Archives of North Carolina, Raleigh. [Online catalog description: "Including one from North Carolina."]

Great Britain. Treasury. "[Charleston, South Carolina]. Lists Nos. 38 and 39. 'Distressed Refugees under Different Inspectors.' (Various Dates), [1782]." Copy of a manuscript in the National Archives of the United Kingdom (formerly the Public Records Office), Kew, Richmond, Surrey, England; X77.318.1-9 (MARS ID: 21.102.1.19; folder), "British Records Collection," State Archives of North Carolina, Raleigh. [Online catalog description: "Including (f. 17b) from George Town, Orangeburg, North Carolina, and Pensacola; and (ff. 18b, 19) 'from North Carolina &c recommended by Colo. Samuel Campbell.'"]

Great Britain. Treasury. "[Charleston, South Carolina]. List No. 40. 'Refugees of the First Class in Charles Town.' (Various Dates), 1782." Copy of a manuscript in the National Archives of the United Kingdom (formerly the Public Records Office), Kew, Richmond, Surrey, England; X77.319.1-2 (MARS ID 21.102.1.20; folder),

"British Records Collection,"State Archives of North Carolina, Raleigh. [Online catalog description: "Including several from North Carolina."]

Great Britain. Treasury. "[Charleston, South Carolina]. List No. 42, 'Refugees of the Second Class in Charlestown.' Sep. (Various Dates), 1782." Copy of a manuscript in the National Archives of the United Kingdom (formerly the Public Records Office), Kew, Richmond, Surrey, England; X77.320.1 (MARS ID: 21/102.1.21; folder), "British Records Collection," State Archives of North Carolina, Raleigh. [Online catalog description: Including one from North Carolina."]

Great Britain. Treasury. "[Charleston, South Carolina]. List No. 43, 'Refugees of the Third Class in Charlestown.' Sep. (Various Dates), 1782." Copy of a manuscript in the National Archives of the United Kingdom (formerly the Public Records Office), Kew, Richmond, Surrey, England; X77.321.1 (MARS ID: 21.102.1.22; folder), "British Records Collection," State Archives of North Carolina, Raleigh. [Online catalog description: "Including one from North Carolina."]

Great Britain. Treasury. "[Charleston, South Carolina]. List No. 44. 'Inspectors of the Country Refugees in Charlestown.' Sep. (Various Dates), 1782." Copy of a manuscript in the National Archives of the United Kingdom (formerly the Public Records Office), Kew, Richmond, Surrey, England; X77.322.1 (MARS ID: 21.102.1.23; folder), "British Records Collection," State Archives of North Carolina, Raleigh. [Online Catalog description: "Including James Cassils for those from North Carolina and elsewhere."]

Great Britain. Treasury. "[Charleston, South Carolina]. List No. 45. 'Quarter Masters of the Refugees from Different Districts.' Sep. (Various Dates), 1782." Copy of a manuscript in the National Archives of the United Kingdom (formerly the Public Records Office), Kew, Richmond, Surrey, England; X77.323.1 (MARS ID: 21.102.1.24; folder), "British Records Collection," State Archives of North Carolina, Raleigh. [Online catalog descriptions: "Including Will[iam] McQueen for North Carolina district."]

Great Britain. Treasury. "[Charleston, South Carolina]. List No. 46. 'Second Officers of the Militia on James Island.' Sep. and Oct. (Various Dates), 1782." Copy of a manuscript in the National Archives of the United Kingdom (formerly the Public Records Office), Kew, Richmond, Surrey, England; X77.324.1 (MARS ID: 21.102.1.25; folder), "British Records Collection," State Archives of North Carolina, Raleigh. [Online catalog description: "Including a Number from North Carolina, Raleigh."]

Great Britain. Treasury. "[Charleston, South Carolina]. List No. 51. 'Inspectors of the Country Refugees in Charlestown.' Oct. (Various Dates), 1782." Manuscript, X77.329.1 (MARS ID: 21.102.1.30; folder), State Archives of North Carolina, Raleigh. [Online catalog description: "Including James Cassels for North Carolina and other districts."]

Great Britain. Treasury. "[Charleston, South Carolina]. List No. 52. 'Quarter Masters of the Refugees from Different Districts.' Oct. and Nov. (Various Dates), 1782." Manuscript, X77.330.1 (MARS ID: 21.102.1.31; folder), State Archives of North Carolina, Raleigh. [Online catalog description: "Including W[ilia]m McQueen for North Carolina district."]

Great Britain. Treasury. "[Charleston, South Carolina]. List No. 53. 'Second Officers on James Island.' Oct. and Nov. (Various Dates), 1782." Manuscript, X77.331.1 (MARS ID: 21.102.1.32; folder), State Archives of North Carolina, Raleigh. [Online catalog description: "Including a number from North Carolina."]

Great Britain. Treasury. "[Charleston, South Carolina]. Lt. Col. J. Allen to Colonel [Robert] Gray, [Inspector of Refugees. Post 1 Jun. 1782]." Manuscript, 77.423.1 (MARS ID: 21.102.4.26; folder), State Archives of North Carolina, Raleigh. [Online catalog description: "Ordering that Colonel [Hector] McNeil, Lt. Col. McRay, and Captain Molloy [?] of North Carolina Militia be 'put on the same footing with other Militia Officers.'"]

Great Britain. Treasury. "[Charleston, South Carolina]. Malcolm McFatter to Colonel [Robert] Gray, [Paymaster to Royal Militia]. 9 May 1782." Manuscript, 77.370.1 (MARS ID: 21.102.2.54; folder), State Archives of North Carolina, Raleigh. [Online catalog description: "Concerning his pay (North Carolina Militia)."]

Great Britain. Treasury. "Charleston, [South Carolina]. Memorial to [Lieutenant General] Alexander Leslie from Meredith Edwards, Captain of Militia, Formerly of David Fanning's Regiment in North Carolina. 10 Jly. 1782." Manuscript, [MARS Id: 21.102.5.17], State Archives of North Carolina, Raleigh. [Online catalog description: "Including certificate by Fanning. {See 21.102.5.1.16.}"]

Great Britain. Treasury. "[Charleston, South Carolina]. Memorial to Lt. Col. [Nisbet] Balfour, [Commandant], from Daniel Doty of North Carolina. [n.d.], [1782]." Manuscript, MARS Id: 21.102.5.10, State Archives of North Carolina, Raleigh. [Online catalog description: "His services, including 'being employ'd by . . . Josiah Martin . . . to Raise Men in Support Government'. Including certificate by Z. Gibbs and others."]

Great Britain. Treasury. "Charleston, [South Carolina]. Neil Curry to Colonel Robert Gray, Paymaster of Royal Militia. 21 Jly. 1782." Manuscript, 77.359.1 (MARS ID: 21.102.2.37; folder), State Archives of North Carolina,

Raleigh. [Online catalog description: "Concerning his pay for service in North Carolina Regiment of Royal Militia."]

Great Britain. Treasury. "Charleston, [South Carolina]. No.1. Receipts for Payments to 'North Carolina Militia, Colo. Faithful Grahams Regiment Who Came to Charlestown with Major Craig.' Dec.-Feb. (Various Dates), 1781-1782." Manuscript, X77.376.1-4 (MARS ID: 21.102.3.6; folder), State Archives of North Carolina, Raleigh. [Online catalog description: "Including names of officers and men of the regiment, with their signatures."]

Great Britain. Treasury. "Charleston, [South Carolina]. No. 2. [Receipts for Payment] to 'North Carolina Militia, from Different Counties, Omitted in Abstract No. 1.' Feb. (Various Dates), 1782." Manuscript, X77.377.1-2 (MARS ID: 21.102.3.7; folder), State Archives of North Carolina, Raleigh.

Great Britain. Treasury. "Charleston, [South Carolina]. No. 3. [Receipts for Payment] to 'North Carolina, Anson County Militia.' Jan., Feb. 1782." Manuscript, X77.378.1 (MARS ID: 21.102.3.8], State Archives of North Carolina, Raleigh.

Great Britain. Treasury. "Charleston, [South Carolina]. No. 3: Receipts for Payments to Anson County Militia. Feb. (Various Dates), 1782." Manuscript, 77.338.1-2 (MARS ID: 21.102.2.6; folder), State Archives of North Carolina, Raleigh.

Great Britain. Treasury. "[Charleston, South Carolina]. No. 4: Receipts for Payments to 'Colo. Faithful Graham's Regiment who Came to Charlestown.' 4, 15 Feb, 1782." Manuscript, 77.339.1-2 (MARS ID: 21.102.2.7; folder), State Archives of North Carolina, Raleigh.

Great Britain. Treasury. "[Charleston, South Carolina]. No. 5: Receipts for Payments to Cumberland County Militia. 7 Feb. 1782." Manuscript, 77.340.1-2 (MARS ID: 21.102.2.8; folder), State Archives of North Carolina, Raleigh.

Great Britain. Treasury. "Charleston, [South Carolina]. No. 6: Receipts for Payments to Bladen County Militia. 7, 9 Feb. 1782." Manuscript, 77.337.1-2 (MARS ID: 21.102.2.5; folder), State Archives of North Carolina, Raleigh.

Great Britain. Treasury. "Charleston, [South Carolina]. No. 7. [Receipts for Payment] to 'No. Carolina Militia, Colonel Hector McNiel.' 2 Apr. 1782." Manuscript, X77.380.1 (MARS ID: 21.102.3.12; folder), State Archives of North Carolina, Raleigh.

Great Britain. Treasury. "Charleston, [South Carolina]. No. 8. [Receipt for Payment] to 'North Carolina Militia, Lt. Colo. John Moore.' Apr. (Various Dates), 1782." Manuscript, X77.381.1 (MARS ID: 21.102.3.13; folder), State Archives of North Carolina, Raleigh.

Great Britain. Treasury. "Charleston, [South Carolina]. No. 9. [Receipts for Payment] to 'North Carolina Militia. Colonel Samuel Campbell.' Apr.-Jun. (Various Dates), 1782." Manuscript, X77.382.1-3 (MARS ID: 21.102.3.14; folder), State Archives of North Carolina, Raleigh.

Great Britain. Treasury. "Charleston, [South Carolina]. No. 10. [Receipts for Payment] to 'North Carolina Militia from Different Counties.' 19 Apr. [1782]." Manuscript, X77.383.1 (MARS ID: 21.102.3.15; folder), State Archives of North Carolina, Raleigh.

Great Britain. Treasury. "Charleston, [South Carolina]. No. 11. [Receipts for Payment] to 'North Carolina Militia now Inlisted in Governor Martins Corps in Charlestown.' 25 Apr. 1782." Manuscript, X77.384.1 (MARS ID: 21.102.3.16; folder), State Archives of North Carolina, Raleigh.

Great Britain. Treasury. "Charleston, [South Carolina]. No. 12. [Receipts for Payment] to 'Sergeants McLeod and McLellan of the Anson County Militia.' 28 May 1782." Manuscript, X77.385.1 (MARS ID: 21.102.3.17; folder), State Archives of North Carolina, Raleigh.

Great Britain. Treasury. " Charleston, [South Carolina]. No. 13. [Receipts for Payment] to Col. Gideon Wright of North Carolina Militia. 3 Jun. 1782." Manuscript, X77.385.1 (MARS ID: 21.102.3.18; folder), State Archives of North Carolina, Raleigh.

Great Britain. Treasury. "Charleston, [South Carolina]. No. 14. [Receipts for Payment] to 'North Carolina Regiment of Colo. Samuel Campbell.' May-Jun. 1782." Manuscript, X77.386.1-3 (MARS ID: 21.102.3.19; folder), State Archives of North Carolina, Raleigh.

Great Britain. Treasury. "Charleston, [South Carolina]. No. 15. [Receipts for Payment] to 'North Carolina Militia who Served in South Carolina under Major Ferguson Andca [?] [Andrews?].' 14 Aug. 1782." Manuscript, X77.387.1-2 (MARS ID: 21.102.3.20; folder), State Archives of North Carolina, Raleigh.

Great Britain. Treasury. "Charleston, [South Carolina]. No. 16. [Receipts for Payment to 'North Carolina Militia, Anson County Regiment, Colo. Duncan Ray.' Jly-Aug. (Various Dates), 1782." Manuscript, X77.388.1 (MARS ID: 21.102.3.21; folder), State Archives of North Carolina, Raleigh.

Great Britain. Treasury. "Charleston, [South Carolina]. No. 17. [Receipts for Payment] to 'North Carolina Bladen County Militia Colo. Hector McNeil.' 17 Jly." Manuscript, 77.371.374, X77.375.398 (MARS ID: 21.102.3.22; folder), State Archives of North Carolina, Raleigh.
Great Britain. Treasury. "Charleston, [South Carolina]. No. 18. [Receipts for Payment] to 'North Carolina Cumberland County Militia.' 13 Jly. 1782." Manuscript, X77.390.1 (MARS ID: 21.102.3.23; folder), State Archives of North Carolina, Raleigh.
Great Britain. Treasury. "[Charleston, South Carolina]. No. 19. [Receipts for Payment] to 'Partial Payments and Omissions to the North Carolina Militia.' Jly.-Oct. (Various Dates), 1782." Manuscript, X77.391.1 (MARS ID: 21.102.3.24; folder), State Archives of North Carolina, Raleigh.
Great Britain. Treasury. "Charleston, [South Carolina]. No. 20. [Receipts for Payment] to 'North Carolina Militia, Colo. David Fanning.' Jly.-Oct. (Various Dates), 1782." Manuscript, X77.392.1 (MARS ID: 21.102.3.25; folder), State Archives of North Carolina, Raleigh.
Great Britain. Treasury. "Charleston, [South Carolina]. No. 21. [Receipts for Payment] to 'North Carolina Militia Colo. Samuel Bryan.' Jly.-Nov. (Various Dates), 1782." Manuscript, X77.393.1 (MARS ID: 21.102.3.26; folder), State Archives of North Carolina, Raleigh.
Great Britain. Treasury. "Charleston, [South Carolina]. No. 22. [Receipts of Payment] to 'North Carolina Militia.' 24-25 Jly. 1782." Manuscript, X77.394.1 (MARS ID: 21.102.3.27; folder), State Archives of North Carolina, Raleigh.
Great Britain. Treasury. "Charleston, [South Carolina]. No. 23. [Receipts for Payment] of 'Donations to the North Carolina Militia.' 23 Jly. 1782." Manuscript, 77.385.1 (MARS ID: 21.102.3.28; folder), State Archives of North Carolina, Raleigh.
Great Britain. Treasury. "Charleston, [South Carolina]. No. 24. [Receipts for Payment to 'North Carolina Regiment of Colo. Samuel Campbell.' Sep. (Various Dates), 1782." Manuscript, X77.396.1-3 (MARS ID: 21.102.3.19; folder), State Archives of North Carolina, Raleigh.
Great Britain. Treasury. "Charleston, [South Carolina]. No. 25. [Receipts for Payment] to 'North Carolina Regiment of Colo. Samuel Campbell.' Oct.-Nov. (Various Dates), 1782." Manuscript, X77.397.1-2 (MARS ID: 21.102.3.30), State Archives of North Carolina, Raleigh.
Great Britain. Treasury. "Charleston, [South Carolina]. No. 26. [Receipts for Payment] to 'Cumberland County Militia.' 6 Oct. 1782." Manuscript, X77.398.1 (MARS ID: 21.102.3.31; folder), State Archives of North Carolina, Raleigh.
Great Britain. Treasury. "[Charleston], South Carolina. No. 32 (Endorsement). 'Abstract of Pay Due Refugees of the First Class Now in Charlestown' to 30 Jun. 1782. 30 Jly. 1782." Manuscript, 77.411.1-3 (MARS ID: 21.102.4.14; folder), State Archives of North Carolina, Raleigh.
Great Britain. Treasury. "[Charleston, South Carolina]. No. 46. Abstract [of Pay Due] the Following Officers of the Militia Who Were Seconded at the Last Arrangement at James Island....' 5 Sep. 1782." Manuscript, 77.429.1 (MARS ID: 21.102.4.32; folder), State Archives of North Carolina, Raleigh. [Online catalog description: "(Order for payment). Including several from North Carolina."]
Great Britain. Treasury. "[Charleston, South Carolina]. Petition to General [Alexander] Leslie, from Charles Molloy, Captain in Loyal North Carolina Militia. [Oct. 1782]." Manuscript, Z.5.143N (MARS ID: 21.102.5.4; folder), State Archives of North Carolina, Raleigh. [Online catalog description: "His services and present distress. Including endorsement by Colonel David Fanning, 6 Oct. 1782, and order for payment of same date."]
Great Britain. Treasury. "[Charleston, South Carolina]. Petition to General [Alexander] Leslie from Lt. Allan Carmichael, Royal Militia of North Carolina. [n.d.], [1782]." Manuscript, 77.421.1 (MARS ID: 21.102.4.24; folder), State Archives of North Carolina, Raleigh. [Online catalog description: "His services and present distress."]
Great Britain. Treasury. "Charleston, [South Carolina]. Request from Angus McAlister. 11 Dec. 1781." Manuscript, 77.343.1, State Archives of North Carolina, Raleigh. [Online catalog description: "That Captain Archibald Seller [?] be paid McAlister's wages as militia soldier of North Carolina Refugees."]
Great Britain. Treasury. [Charleston, South Carolina]. Request from Dick Hall of North Carolina Militia. 10 Dec. 1781." Manuscript, 77.343.1, State Archives of North Carolina, Raleigh. [Online catalog description: "That Captain Prevatt be paid Hall's wages."]
Great Britain. Treasury. "Charleston, [South Carolina]. [Request] from Donald McAlister. 11 Dec. 1781." Manuscript, 77.343.1, State Archives of North Carolina, Raleigh. [Online catalog description: "That Captain Duncan Morison be paid McAlister's wages as militia soldier of North Carolina Refugees."]

Great Britain. Treasury. "[Charleston, South Carolina]. Request from John Baley and His Son Thomas. 22 Feb. 1782." Manuscript, 77.345.1, State Archives of North Carolina, Raleigh. [Online catalog description: "That their pay as militiamen in North Carolina be given to Arch[ibal]d Murray."]

Great Britain. Treasury. "[Charleston, South Carolina]. Request from John Stewart and Donald McInnes. 24 Dec. 1781." Manuscript, 77.349.1, State Archives of North Carolina, Raleigh. [Online catalog description: "That their pay be given Captain Alex[ande]r McLeod of the North Carolina."]

Great Britain. Treasury. "Charleston, [South Carolina]. Samuel McAlester to Colonel [Robert] Gray, [Paymaster to Royal Militia]. 11 Dec. 1781." State Archives of North Carolina, Raleigh. [Online catalog description: Concerning his pay as militia soldier of North Carolina Refugees."]

Great Britain. Treasury. "Charleston, [South Carolina]. Statement by John Campbell, North Carolina Royal Militia, 'Now Bound for North Carolina by Furlow and Flagg.' 28 Jun. 1782." Manuscript, 77.355.1-2. State Archives of North Carolina, Raleigh. [Online catalog description: "Nominating Lt. John Campbell to receive his wages. On back: statement signed by Lt. John Campbell."]

Great Britain. Treasury. "[Charleston, South Carolina]. Unsigned Request to Pay Joseph Brinckle 'my Dowery or Wages as Alowable to the North [Ca]rrilinan Melitia….' 10 Dec. 1781." Manuscript, 77.352.1, State Archives of North Carolina, Raleigh.

Great Britain. Treasury. "Charlestown, [South Carolina]. 'A List of the Women and Children on James Island…' and 'Distressed Refugees on James Island.' 11 Aug. 1782." Manuscript, 77.418.1-2, State Archives of North Carolina, Raleigh. [Online catalog description: "(Order for payment). Including Colonel {Samuel} Campbell's North Carolina list."]

Great Britain. Treasury. "Charlestown, [South Carolina]. Abstract of Pay Due Carious Persons at the Refugee Hospital. 3 Apr. 1782." Manuscript, 77.408.1, State Archives of North Carolina, Raleigh. [Online catalog description: "Including Aaron Dickson, nurse to North Carolinians 'in the Scotch Meeting.'"]

Great Britain. Treasury. "Charlestown, [South Carolina]. [Abstract] No. 3: [Pay Due] North Carolina Royal Militia of Anson County. 17 Jan. 1782." Manuscript, 77.336.1, State Archives of North Carolina, Raleigh.

Great Britain. Treasury. "Charlestown, [South Carolina]. [Abstract] No. 5: [Pay Due] Royal Militia of Cumberland County, North Carolina. 17 Jan. 1782." Manuscript, 77.335.1, State Archives of North Carolina, Raleigh.

Great Britain. Treasury. "Charlestown, [South Carolina]. Abstract No. 6: Pay Due Sundry Officers and Privates of Royal North Carolina Militia of Bladen County. 17 Jan. 1782." Manuscript, 77.334.1, State Archives of North Carolina, Raleigh.

Great Britain. Treasury. "Charlestown, [South Carolina]. Alexander McColl to Colonel Robert Gray, Paymaster of Royal Militia. 27 Jun. 1782." Manuscript, 77.361.1, State Archives of North Carolina, Raleigh. [Online catalog description: "Concerning pay for service in North Carolina Regiment of Royal Militia."]

Great Britain. Treasury. "Charlestown, [South Carolina]. Certificate by Lt. Col. Faithful Graham and Two Others. 3 May, 1782." Manuscript, MARS Id: 21.102.5.12, State Archives of North Carolina, Raleigh. [Online catalog description: "Concerning services of Captain Stephen Scarborough, who recently escaped from a rebel prison at Wilmington."]

Great Britain. Treasury. "Charlestown, [South Carolina]. Donald McDonald's Statement. 12 Jun. 1782." Manuscript, 77.366.1, State Archives of North Carolina, Raleigh. [Online catalog description: "Concerning his pay for service in North Carolina Militia, Anson County."]

Great Britain. Treasury. "Charlestown, [South Carolina]. List 38. Report on Refugees 'Under the Inspection of 'Colo. Casels.' 11 Aug. 1782." Manuscript, 77.417.1-2, State Archives of North Carolina, Raleigh. [Online catalog description: "(Order for Payment). Including Several from North Carolina."]

Great Britain. Treasury. "Charlestown, [South Carolina]. Memorandum and Petition to Lt. General [Alexander' Leslie from Captain Moses Moore, for 'Many Years… a Magistrate and Captain of Militia in the County of Tyron in North Carolina.' 24 May, 1782." Manuscript, 77.412.1-2, State Archives of North Carolina, Raleigh.

Great Britain. Treasury. "Charlestown, [South Carolina]. Memorial of Stephen Brown to Lt. General [Alexander' Leslie. 24 May, 1782." Manuscript, 77.413.1-2, State Archives of North Carolina, Raleigh. [Online catalog description: "Was lieutenant in George Town militia; captured by Americans and taken to Hillsborough, North Carolina; etc."]

Great Britain. Treasury. "Charlestown, [South Carolina]. No. 33 [Endorsement]. 'Abstract of Pay Due the Refugees of the Second Class now in Charlestown' to 30 Jun. 1782." Manuscript, 77.414.1, State Archives of North Carolina, Raleigh. [Online catalog description: "Including two from North Carolina."]

Great Britain. Treasury. "Charlestown, [South Carolina]. No. 34. 'Abstract of Pay Due to the Refugees of the Third Class now in Charlestown; to 30 Jun. 1782." Manuscript, 77.415.1, State Archives of North Carolina, Raleigh. [Online catalog description: "Including one from North Carolina."]

Great Britain. Treasury. "Charlestown, [South Carolina]. No. 38. 'Return of Distressed Refugees under the Inspection of Robert Gray, [Inspector of Refugees].' 8 Aug. 1782." Manuscript, 77.416.1-2, State Archives of North Carolina, Raleigh. [Online catalog description: "Including several from North Carolina and order for payment dated 11 Aug. 1782."]

Great Britain. Treasury. "Charlestown, [South Carolina]. Order to Pay Colonel [Duncan] Ray 25 Guineas 'As a Refugee in this Garrison, from North Carolina.' 8 Jun. 1782." Manuscript, 77.409.1, State Archives of North Carolina, Raleigh.

Great Britain. Treasury. "Charlestown, [South Carolina]. Report from Robert Gray, Inspector of Refugees, on 'Sundry Distressed Refugees under My Inspection Who Were Not Included in My Former Reports to the Commander.' 23 May, 1782." Manuscript, 77.406.1-3, State Archives of North Carolina, Raleigh. [Online catalog description: "Including Elizabeth Brooks and Margaret Evans of North Carolina."]

Great Britain. Treasury. "Charlestown, [South Carolina]. Report No. 2 on 'Distressed Refugees Who Have Applied for Relief to [Lt. Colonel] Nisbet Balfour, [Commandant], ...' 22 Sep. 1781." Manuscript, Call Number 77.399.1-4. State Archives of North Carolina, Raleigh. [Online catalog description: "Including Captain Lewis Lowry of North Carolina. (Case 12)"]

Great Britain. Treasury. "Charlestown, [South Carolina]. Report No. 5 on 'Distressed Refugees Who Have Applied for Relief to [Lt. Colonel] Nisbet Balfour, [Commandant], ..." 1 Oct. 1781." Manuscript, 77.400.1-2, State Archives of North Carolina, Raleigh. [Online catalog description: "Including (case 36) Captain Scrimgeour of North Carolina Militia; and (case 39) William Owens from North Carolina."]

Great Britain. Treasury. "Charlestown, [South Carolina]. Report No. 7 on 'Distressed Refugees Who Have Applied for Relief to [Lt. Colonel] Nisbet Balfour, [Commandant], ..." 8 Oct. 1781." Manuscript, 77.404.1-2, State Archives of North Carolina, Raleigh. [Online catalog description: "Including reference to case 36, Captain Scrimgeour of North Carolina."]

Great Britain. Treasury. "Charlestown, [South Carolina]. Report No. 11 on 'Distressed Refugees Who Have Applied for Relief to [Lt. Colonel] Nisbet Balfour, [Commandant], ..." 23 Oct. 1781." Manuscript, 77.403.1-2, State Archives of North Carolina, Raleigh. [OnlineMc catalog description: "Including (Case 63) Martha Morgan of North Carolina."]

Great Britain. Treasury. "(Charlestown, [South Carolina]). Report No. 12 on 'Distressed Refugees Who Have Applied for Relief to [Lt. Colonel] Nisbet Balfour, [Commandant], ..." [Dec. 1781]." Manuscript, 77.402.1-2, State Archives of North Carolina, Raleigh. [Online catalog description: "Including (case 68) John Doak of Cross Creek."]

Great Britain. Treasury. "Charlestown, [South Carolina]. Report No. 13 on 'Distressed Refugees Who Have Applied for Relief to [Lt. Colonel] Nisbet Balfour, [Commandant, ..." 25 Dec. 1781." Manuscript, 77.401.1-2, State Archives of North Carolina, Raleigh. [Online catalog description: "Including (case 87) John Owens from North Carolina."]

Great Britain. Treasury. "Charlestown, [South Carolina]. Request from Alex[ande]r McLeod. 20 Jan. 1782." Manuscript, 77.347.1, State Archives of North Carolina, Raleigh. [Online catalog description: "That his pay be given to Ensign Jno. [John] McLeod of North Carolina Highland Regiment."]

Great Britain. Treasury. "Charlestown, [South Carolina]. [Request] from Arch[ibal]d McKeithan, North Carolina Militia. 29 Jun. 1782." Manuscript, 77.355.1-2, State Archives of North Carolina, Raleigh. [Online catalog description: "[That his wages for service be paid] to Arch[ibal]d Taylor."]

Great Britain. Treasury. "Charlestown, [South Carolina]. Request from Captain Donald McKeithan. 27 Jun. 1782." Manuscript, Call Number 77.353.1, State Archives of North Carolina, Raleigh. [Online catalog description: "That his wages for service in North Carolina militia be paid Major Arch[ibal]d Taylor."]

Great Britain. Treasury. "Charlestown, [South Carolina]. Request from John McDonald and Donald McKenzie. 16 Jan. 1782." Manuscript, 77.346.1, State Archives of North Carolina, Raleigh. [Online catalog description: "That their pay be given Lt. Duncan McNab of North Carolina Highland Regiment."]

Great Britain. Treasury. "Charlestown, [South Carolina]. [Request] from Lt. Andrew Riddell, North Carolina Royal Militia, to Captain Duncan Morison. 15 Aug. 1782." Manuscript, 77.353.1, State Archives of North Carolina, Raleigh.

Great Britain. Treasury. "Cover: 'No. Carolina Militia Abstracts and Rects.' [1782]." Manuscript, 77.333.1, State Archives of North Carolina, Raleigh.

Great Britain. Treasury. "'Headquarters', [Charleston, South Carolina]. 'Abstract of Pay Due to Colonel David Fanning of the Loyal Militia of Randolph and Chatham Counteys in the Provance of North Carolina...' 11 Jly. [1782]." Manuscript, MARS Id: 21.102.5.14, State Archives of North Carolina, Raleigh.

Great Britain. Treasury. "Headquarters, [Charleston, South Carolina]. Edward Scott to Colonel Robert Gray, [Paymaster of Militia]. 8 May 1782." Manuscript, MARS Id: 21.102.5.22, State Archives of North Carolina, Raleigh. [Online catalog description: "Order to pay Colonel [Gideon] Wright of North Carolina. Including receipt signed by Wright."]

Great Britain. Treasury. "Headquarters, [Charleston, South Carolina]. Edward Scott, Secretary, to Colonel Rob[ert] Gray, Paymaster of Militia. 25 Jly. 1782." Manuscript, Z.5.143N, State Archives of North Carolina, Raleigh. [Online catalog description: "Sums advanced 'as a gratuitous consideration for their Services' to Colonel [David] Fanning, Colonel [Samuel] Bryan, Lt. Col. [John] Hampton, and Captain [Nicholas] White. Endorsed 'Voucher for North Carolina'."]

Great Britain. Treasury. "James Island, [South Carolina]. ' A Return of the Distressed Women and Children of the North Carolina Regt. Of Militia Commanded by Coll. Saml. Campbell.' 6 Aug. 1782." Manuscript, 77.420.1-2, State Archives of North Carolina, Raleigh. [Online catalog description: "(And order for payment, 11 Aug.) Columns: 'Company they Belong'; names, women; children; widows; orphans; and payments made to each."]

Great Britain. Treasury. "James Island [South Carolina]. Certificate [Relating to American Loyalists.] 28 Jly. 1782." Manuscript, 77.407.1-2, State Archives of North Carolina, Raleigh. [Online catalog description: "Concerning Aaron Dixson's attendance on the sick of the North Carolina refugees."]

Great Britain. Treasury. "James Island, [South Carolina]. Certification by D[uncan] Morison, Captain. Feb. 1782." Manuscript, 77.348.1, State Archives of North Carolina, Raleigh. [Online catalog description: "That Lt. John Campbell is ill and cannot attend to receive pay for services in loyal militia of Bladen County."]

Great Britain. Treasury. "James Island, [South Carolina]. George Ronnalds to Colonel Robert Gray, Paymaster of Royal Militia. 29 Aug. 1782." Manuscript, 77.357.1, State Archives of North Carolina, Raleigh. [Online catalog description: "Concerning his pay for service in North Carolina militia."]

Great Britain. Treasury. "James Island, [South Carolina]. [Request] from Arthur Johnston. 17 Apr. 1782." Manuscript, 77.344.1, State Archives of North Carolina, Raleigh. [Online catalog description: "That Captain W[illia]m Lane be paid Johnston's wages as soldier in North Carolina Regiment of militia."]

Great Britain. Treasury. "James Island, [South Carolina]. Statement by Richard Teer. 16 Jly. 1782." Manuscript, 77.362.1, State Archives of North Carolina, Raleigh. [Online catalog description: "Concerning his pay: witnessed by F[aithful] Graham, Lt. Col. North Carolina Mil[itia]."]

Great Britain. Treasury. "James Island, [South Carolina]. Will[ia]m Conner to Colonel Robert Gray, Paymaster of Royal Militia. 9 Aug. 1782." Manuscript, 77.360.1, State Archives of North Carolina, Raleigh. [Online catalog description: "Concerning pay for service in North Carolina Regiment of Royal Militia."]

Great Britain. Treasury. "Militia Pay Office, Charlestown, [South Carolina]. 'Abstract [of Pay Due the] Second Officers of the Militia on James Island.' 1 Sep. 1782." Manuscript, 77.436.1, State Archives of North Carolina, Raleigh. [Online catalog description: "Including several from North Carolina."]

Great Britain. Treasury. "Militia Pay Office, Charlestown, [South Carolina]. No. 40. 'Abstract of Pay due the Refugees of the First Class….' 29 Aug. 1782." Manuscript, 77.424.1-4, State Archives of North Carolina, Raleigh. [Online catalog description: "Including several from North Carolina."]

Great Britain. Treasury. "Militia Pay Office, Charlestown, [South Carolina]. No. 42. 'Abstract of Pay due the Refugees of the Second Class….' 29 Aug. 1782." Manuscript, 77.425.1, State Archives of North Carolina, Raleigh. [Online catalog description: "Including several from North Carolina."]

Great Britain. Treasury. "Militia Pay Office, Charlestown, [South Carolina]. No. 43. 'Abstract [of Pay due the Refugees of the] Third Class….' 29 Aug. 1782." Manuscript, 77.426.1, State Archives of North Carolina, Raleigh. [Online catalog description: "Including two from North Carolina."]

Great Britain. Treasury. "Militia Pay Office, Charlestown, [South Carolina]. No. 44. 'Abstract [of Pay Due] Inspectors of the Refugees in Charlestown.' 29 Aug. 1782." Manuscript, 77.427.1, State Archives of North Carolina, Raleigh. [Online catalog description: "Including James Cassels for North Carolina, etc."]

Great Britain. Treasury. "Militia Pay Office, Charlestown, [Charlestown, [South Carolina]. No. 45. 'Abstract [of Pay Due] Quarter Masters of the Refugees….' 1 Sep. 1782." Manuscript, 77.431.1-3, State Archives of North Carolina, Raleigh. [Online catalog descriptions: "Including several from North Carolina."]

Great Britain. Treasury. "Militia Pay Office, Charlestown, [South Carolina]. No. 48. 'Abstract of Pay due the Refugees of the First Class….' 1 Sep. 1782." Manuscript, 77.431.1-3, State Archives of North Carolina, Raleigh. [Online catalog description: "Including several from North Carolina."]

Great Britain. Treasury. "Militia Pay Office, Charlestown, [South Carolina]. No. 49. 'Abstract [of Pay due the Refugees of the] Second Class….' 1 Sep. 1782." Manuscript, 77.432.1, State Archives of North Carolina, Raleigh. [Online catalog description: "Including two from North Carolina."]

Great Britain. Treasury. "Militia Pay Office, Charlestown, [South Carolina]. No. 50. 'Abstract [of Pay due the Refugees of the] Third Class….' 1 Sep. 1782." Manuscript, 77.433.1, State Archives of North Carolina, Raleigh. [Online catalog description: "Including two from North Carolina."]

Great Britain. Treasury. "Militia Pay Office, Charlestown, [South Carolina]. No. 51. 'Abstract [of Pay Due the] Inspectors of the Country Refugees….' 1 Sep. 1782." Manuscript, 77.434.1, State Archives of North Carolina, Raleigh. [Online catalog description: "Including James Cassels for North Carolina, etc."]

Great Britain. Treasury. "Militia Pay Office, Charlestown, [South Carolina]. No. 52.' Abstract [of Pay Due the Quarter Masters of the Different Districts of Refugees…' 1 Sep. 1782." Manuscript, 77.435.1, State Archives of North Carolina, Raleigh. [Online catalog description: "Including W[illia]m McQueen for North Carolina."]

Great Britain. Treasury. "[Treasury, London. Extract from List of Provincial Officers Serving during American Revolution, 1782]." Manuscript, X76.3397.1, State Archives of North Carolina, Raleigh. [Online catalog description: "North Carolina Independent Company."]

Great Britain. Treasury. "[Treasury, London. Extract from List of Provincial Officers Serving during American Revolution, 1782]." Manuscript, X76.3398.1, State Archives of North Carolina, Raleigh. [Online catalog description: "North Carolina Highland Regiment."]

Great Britain. Treasury. "[Treasury, London. Extract from List of Provincial Officers Serving during American Revolution, 1782]." Manuscript, X76.3399.1, State Archives of North Carolina, Raleigh. [Online catalog description: "North Carolina Provincials."]

Great Britain. Treasury. "[Treasury, London. Extract from List of Provincial Officers Serving during American Revolution, 1782]." Manuscript, X76.3400.1, State Archives of North Carolina, Raleigh. [Online catalog description: "Indian Department, Southern District."]

Great Britain. Treasury. "[Treasury, London. Extract from List of Provincial Officers Serving during American Revolution, 1782]." Manuscript, X76.3396.1, State Archives of North Carolina, Raleigh. [Online catalog description: "North Carolina Volunteers."]

Great Britain. Treasury. "Board Papers. Miscellanea – Documents Relating to Refugees. (T 50/1-56, Selections)." Manuscript, MARS Id: 21.102 (Series), State Archives of North Carolina, Raleigh. [Online catalog description: "Letters, memorials, petitions, reports, vouchers, receipts, returns, muster rolls, accounts, pension lists, etc., concerning Loyalists. Includes numbers of documents relating to Loyalist military units and civilian refugees from North Carolina, and various payments made to them, including pensions."]

Great Britain. Treasury. "Board Papers, Miscellanea – Documents Relating to Refugees. (T-50/1-56, Selections): American: Carolina Militia. Receipt Books, Pay Lists, etc. (T.50/5): [Charleston, South Carolina]. (Certificate by Archibald McDugald and Others), 6 Mar. 1782." Microfilm of a manuscript in the Public Records Office (now the National Archives of the United Kingdom), Z.5.143N (Archive Stacks 47-47b; MARS ID: 21.102.5.34; folder), State Archives of North Carolina, Raleigh. [Online catalog description: "Roll of Soldiers belonging to the No. Carolina Highland Regt. who served in the No. Carolina Militia before their Inlistment."]

Great Britain. War Office. "War Office. Commissariat Department: Accounts, New York. (WO 60, Selections), 1776-1784." Manuscript, MARS Id: 21.236 (Series), State Archives of North Carolina, Raleigh. [Online catalog description: "The archives of the War Office include many records relating to the British Army in the colonies. The North Carolina items in WO 60 concern mainly provisions and other supplies, and transportation, issued Loyalist refugees, and military units and their families in the closing months of the Revolutionary War and beyond."]

Great Britain. War Office. "War Office. Miscellanea: Headquarters Records, America. (WO 28, Selections), 1775-1805." Manuscript, MARS Id: 21.230 (Series), State Archives of North Carolina, Raleigh. [Online catalog description: "The archives of the War Office include many records relating to the British Army in the colonies. The items concerning North Carolina in the series WO 28 have to do with Loyalist troops."]

Great Britain. War Office. "War Office. Private Collections: American Revolution Entry Books. (WO 36, Selections), 1776-1782." Manuscript, MARS Id: 21.232 (Series), State Archives of North Carolina, Raleigh. [Online catalog description: "The archives of the War Office include many records relating to the British Army in the colonies. The North Carolina items in WO 36 concern the Revolutionary War."]

Great Britain. War Office. "War Office. Returns: Annual Printed Army Lists. List of Reduced Officers on Half Pay. British American Half Pay Lists. (WO 65, Selections), 1782-1783." Manuscript, MARS Id: 21.237 (Series), State Archives of North Carolina, Raleigh. [Online catalog description: "The archives of the War Office include many records relating to the British Army in the colonies. The North Carolina items in WO 65 concern Loyalist officers on half pay following the Revolutionary War."]

Great Britain. War Office. "War Office. Returns: Monthly Returns, Canada. (WO 17, Selections), 1775-1786." Manuscript, MARS Id: 21.227 (Series), State Archives of North Carolina, Raleigh. [Online catalog description:

"The archives of the War Office include many records relating to the British Army in the colonies. Items concerning North Carolina in WO 17 consist of returns and lists from the Revolutionary War, especially Loyalist troops."]

Haywood, Marshall De Lancey. *Colonel Edward Buncombe, Fifth North Carolina Continental Regiment: His life, Military Career, and Death While a Wounded Prisoner in Philadelphia during the War of the Revolution. Address Delivered before the North Carolina Society of the Cincinnati at Its Meeting Held in Hillsborough, July 4, 1901*. North Carolina Society of the Cincinnati. Raleigh [N. C.]: Alford, Bynum & Christophers, printers, 1901.

"Joseph Simpson, Prisoner in Quebec, 1780." *North Carolina Genealogical Society Journal*, 5:2 (May 1979), 144. [Most of the prisoners in the list were from Massachusetts, and Simpson is the only one included in the abstract because he was from North Carolina.]

Kimbrough, John N., ca. 1735-ca. 1799. "John Kimbrough Parole." Manuscript SFC4, J. Murrey Atkins Library Special Collections, University of North Carolina, Charlotte. [Online catalog description: "A parole, signed by John Kimbrough and witnessed by O. H. Williams, swearing Kimbrough's pledge to no longer take up arms on behalf of the King of England, against the United States, dated April 11, 1781. Transcription: 'I John Kimbrough having borne arms in the service of the King of England against the United States of America and having surrendered myself as a Prisoner of War do hereby pledge my word of Honor that I will remain at and within the limits of ten miles of my own House upon little river until Exchang'd or call'd for by the Legislature of the state of North Carolina or the Commanding Officer of the Southern Army; And that I will not at any time during my Captivity say or do anything injurious to the Interest of the United States. Witness my hand this 11th of April 1781.Test. O. H. Williams, [signed] John Kimbrough'"]

Knight, Betsy. "Prisoner Exchange and Parole in the American Revolution." *William and Mary Quarterly,* 3rd series, 48:2 (April 1991), 201-222.

"List of American Prisoners of War, North Carolina & South Carolina Militiamen Held Aboard Prison Ship *Torbay* in Charleston, SC Harbor, May 1781." In Walter Clark, ed., *State Records of North Carolina, 1781-1785*, 17 (Goldsboro: Nash Brothers, Book and Job Printers, 1899; reprinted: Wilmington: Broadfoot Publishing Company, 1994), 1044-1046.

"A List of American Who Died on Board the Prison Ship, at St. Lucia, 1781." *New England Historical and Genealogical Register*, 18:3 (July 1864), 290. [Most of the twenty-one men were from Massachusetts, but others are from Pennsylvania, North Carolina, and Virginia.]

"A List of the Continental Officers, Prisoners of War in South Carolina, the Order They Are to Be Exchanged." In Mary Bondurant Warren, ed., *Revolutionary Memoirs and Muster Rolls* (Athens, Ga.: Heritage Papers, 1994), 116-122. [The men were from Georgia, North Carolina, South Carolina, Virginia (mostly) and had been captured at the Battle of Charleston on May 12, 1780.]

Maxwell, William. "William Maxwell, A.L.S. 'Gard House, Fryday, 12 O'Clock' [1776]: to the North Carolina Council of Safety." Manuscript MSS L2013F226, Society of the Cincinnati Library, Anderson House, Washington, D. C. [Online catalog description: "A letter of petition for his release from jail where Maxwell was being held under suspicion of being a Loyalist to the British Crown. 'As I stand justsify'd in my consiance in not having acted anything contrary to the Resolves of the Continental or Provincial Congress's ... I shall, gentlemen, in as few words as possible give you my real sentiments. The interest of America, I never look't upon separable from my own ... I am a citizen of the world and would defend the liberty of the country I live & expect to die in, America is my country, with her I must rise & fall, live & die.' On July 26, 1776, Maxwell wrote to Governor Hartnett to say his petitions and letters had not been answered – From records of the Secretary of State of North Carolina."]

McBride, Ransom. "American Continental POW's Captured at Charleston & Camden Who Enlisted in the British Army." *North Carolina Genealogical Society Journal*, 9:3 (August 1983), 168-172.

McBride, Ransom. "American Prisoners at Fort Chambly, 1779-1780." *North Carolina Genealogical Society Journal*, 17:4 (November 1991), 209-212. [Prisoners were from all over the country, not just North Carolina]

McBride, Ransom. "Some American Prisoners of the British Army in North Carolina, 1781." *North Carolina Genealogical Society Journal*, 5:2 (May 1979), 74-83. [This also includes some Maryland and Virginia prisoners.]

McBride, Ransom. "Some Recommended Pensioners of Warren County, NC, 1799." *North Carolina Genealogical Society Journal*, 12:3 (August 1986), 160-167.

North Carolina (State). General Assembly. "[Documents dated:] October 18, 1779: Petiton of Solomon Smith, Captain of the Sloop *Sally*." Manuscript; General Assembly Record Group; Session Records, October-November 1779; Joint Papers, Committee Papers, Resolutions; Joint Papers (October-November 1779):

Petitions Addressed to Governor and Council; Box 1 (MARS ID: 66.8.18.6.7; item), State Archives of North Carolina, Raleigh. [Online catalog description: "The petitioner, a prisoner of war in Halifax County, asks to be paroled to New York to be exchanged."]

North Carolina (State). General Assembly. "[Document dated:] October-November 1779: Resolutions: October 22: To Extend Parole of John Lane (with Message)." Manuscript; General Assembly Record Group; Session Records, October-November 1779; Joint Papers, Committee Papers, box 1 (MARS ID: 66,8.18.13.9; item), State Archives of North Carolina, Raleigh. [Online catalog description: "Lane, a prisoner of war in Halifax, is permitted to go to Wake County."]

North Carolina (State). General Assembly. "[Documents dated:] August 31, 1780: Granting Citizenship to William Dowl, Prisoner of War at Halifax (with Petition) (Rejected)." Manuscript; General Assembly Record Group; Session Records, August-September 1780; Joint Papers, Committee Papers, Resolutions, Senate Bills, House Bills; Senate Joint Resolutions: August 30-September 13, 1780; Box 1 (MARS ID: 66.8.22.9.4; item), State Archives of North Carolina, Raleigh. [Online catalog description: "Dowl informs the Assembly that he thinks he might be of service to the state as a weaver."]

North Carolina (State). General Assembly. "[Document dated:] February 1, [1781]: Re[specting] Sending Flag of Truce to Charles Town with Supplies for Prisoners." Manuscript; General Assembly Record Group; Session Records, January-February 1781; Joint Papers, Committee Papers, Resolutions, Senate Bills, House Bills, Box (MARS ID: 66.8.23.10.1; item), State Archives of North Carolina, Raleigh. [Online catalog description: "The resolution requests that the governor send the flag with clothing and other supplies now in the possession of Colonel Long to the prisoners and recommends that Captain Thomas Armstrong bear the flag."]

North Carolina (State). General Assembly. "[Document dated:] July 3, [1781]: Impowering Governor to Exercise Law of Retaliation on British Prisoners." Manuscript; General Assembly Record Group; Session Records, June-July 1781; Joint Papers, Committee Papers, Resolutions, Senate Bills, House Bills, Box 1 (MARS ID: 66.8.25.14.2; item), State Archives of North Carolina, Raleigh.

North Carolina (State). General Assembly. "[Document dated:] Dec. 9: Resolution Concerning Soldiers in Continental Line, 1786." Manuscript, Call Number General Assembly Record Group, Session Records, November, 1786-January, 1787; Joint Papers, Committee Papers, Resolutions, Senate Bills, House Bills, Box 3 (MARS ID: 66.8.43.7.10; item), State Archives of North Carolina, Raleigh. [Online catalog description: "Resolution directs Secretary of State and Robert Fenner to furnish to the committee to examine the state prisoners, a list of names of those that that have served in the Continental Line."]

Parramore, Thomas C. "The Great Escape from Forten Gaol: An Incident of the Revolution." *North Carolina Historical Review*, 45:4 (October 1968), 349-356. [Online description from "North Carolina Periodicals Index," East Carolina University: "From its home port of Edenton, North Carolina the brig *Fair American* was to make war on British shipping during the American Revolution as a privateer. During its maiden voyage, it was taken by a British frigate and its crew imprisoned at Forten Gaol near Gosport, England. While in Forten Gaol, the crew of *Fair American* participated in one of the largest prisoner escapes of the American Revolution. About 60 sailors escaped the prison in a tunnel dug into a nearby house, while most were recaptured within days, the captain and lieutenant of *Fair American* made it back to Boston and back into military service for the war."]

"Prisoners from Battle of Moore's Creek Bridge." *A Lot of Bunkum*, 18:2 (May 1997), 30.

"Prisoners from the American Brig, *Triumph*, 1783." *North Carolina Genealogical Society Journal*, 7:4 (November 1981), 222.

"Return of the North Carolina Militia Prisoners of War Who Were Wounded on the 16 and 18 of Aug. 1780." *Eswau Huppeday: Bulletin of the Broad River Genealogical Society*, 19:3 (August 1999), 177. [A note at the end says "To be continued," but it was not.]

Sammons, Helen. "Loyalists or Helpless Prisoners?" *Clarendon Courier*, 6:3 (September 1994), 9. [residents of Wilmington and vicinity; 1781]

Snyder, Vivian J. "Vivian J. Snyder Collection, 1781, 1808, 1815, 1933." Manuscript PC.1565 (MARS ID: 2075; record group), State Archives of North Carolina, Raleigh. [Online catalog description shows that this collection includes: "Photocopies of order from Gen. George Washington to a Colonel Wood concerning prisoners of war to be exchanged (1781);..."]

"Some American Prisoners of the British at St. Augustine, Florida, Feb-Mar. 1781." *North Carolina Genealogical Society Journal*, 5:3 (August 1979), 157.

Teller, Susan Moore. *Obadiah Moore, Revolutionary Patriot, Private, North Carolina Continental Line, Battle of Charleston, Prisoner of War*. Sun City, Ariz.: Moore Teller Associates, 2014. [Obadiah Moore, 1754-1839; Pitt County resident]

"Tories Held in Halifax Jail, 1776." *North Carolina Genealogy*, 20:1 (Spring-Summer, 1974), 2921.

Thorndale, William. "North Carolina Militiamen Paroled at Charleston, South Carolina, May 1780." *North Carolina Genealogical Society Journal*, 13:3 (August 1987), 140-141.

Warren, Mary Bondurant. "Return of the North Carolina Militia Prisoners of War Who Were Wounded on the 16th and 18th of Aug., 1780 at Camden." *The Carolina Genealogist*, no. 5 (Fall-Winter 1971), Military Records/Militia, 1-2.

Chapter Fourteen:
Records and Sources Relating to Veterans of the American Revolution in North Carolina

This chapter illustrates the great variety of materials that a researcher may encounter relating to a veteran of the American Revolution from North Carolina or Tennessee. A substantial literature along with manuscript original sources exists for the study of veterans of the war, and a considerable amount of material has been transcribed and published. A large percentage of such publications appear below, but not every reference to a Revolutionary pension transcription in a periodical is in this guide since the pensions are readily available through online subscription websites.

Admiral David Farragut Chapter, Tennessee Daughters of the American Revolution. *Tennessee DAR Genealogical Records Committee Report, Series 1, Volume 68: Some Tennessee Heroes of the Revolution* (typescript, 1954); digital surrogate, DAR Library, Washington, D. C.

Alexander, Elijah. "Elijah Alexander Papers." Typescript, PC.269, State Archives of North Carolina, Raleigh. [Online catalog description: "Typed copy of statement by Alexander about his Revolutionary service in western North and South Carolina, 1780-1781."]

Ames, Fisher, 1758-1808. "Letters, 1790-1808." Manuscript RUB Bay 0042:05 Box 1, David M. Rubenstein Rare Book & Manuscript Library, Duke University, Durham. [Online catalog description: "A letter, 1790, from Ames to U. S. Judge John Lowell of Massachusetts concerning legislation to prevent frauds in the payment of North Carolina veterans of the Revolutionary War, and reviews the character of John Jay. A letter, 1801, to Benjamin Bourne evaluates an unidentified applicant for an editorial position with a Federalist paper."]

Aptheker, Herbert. "Edward Griffin, Revolutionary Soldier." *Negro History Bulletin*, XIII: 2 (November 1949), 38, 45.

"At Least Two David Ivey/Ivys in the Rev. War, NC." *North Carolina Genealogical Society Journal*, 9:4 (November 1983), 235.

Atwood, Zula. "Aaron Wood, Revolutionary Soldier." *The Quarterly – York County, South Carolina: A Publication of the York County Genealogical and Historical Society*, 7:4 (March 1996), 11-12.

Bailey, James Davis. *A Sketch of the Life and Career of Col. James D. Williams: A Martyr-Hero of the Revolution*. [Gaffney, S. C.: Gaffney Ledger Company, 1988]. [James D. Williams (1740-1780)]

Battle, Kemp Davis. "Life and Services of Colonel Jonas Johnston." *North Carolina Booklet*, 18:4 (April 1919), 178-187.

Berrien, John MacPherson. "John MacPherson Berrien Papers, 1778-1938." Manuscript 63, Southern Historical Collection, Louis Round Wilson Special Collections Library, University of North Carolina, Chapel Hill; online finding aid available at http://www2.lib.unc.edu/mss/inv/b/Berrien,John_McPherson.html. [Online finding aid description: "... Also includes papers (1778-1786) relating to the military service during the Revolution of Berrien's father, John Berrien; ..."]

Blanton, Evelyn. "Colonel John Walker." *Eswau Huppeday: Bulletin of the Broad River Genealogical Society,* 5:2 (May 1985), 88-99.

Bowman, John Eliot. "Some Southern States Veterans of the American Revolution: About 340 Newspaper Items, Alphabetically Arranged, 1790-1857." Typescript [carbon] C970.341 B78s, North Carolina Collection, Louis Round Wilson Special Collections Library, University of North Carolina at Chapel Hill.

Browder, Blanche Penland. "Research Files, 1967-1984." Manuscript 33124, Personal Papers Collections, Library of Virginia, Richmond. [Includes Isham Browder's Revolutionary War record.]

Brunson, Mattie M. "Col. Elias Alexander." *American Monthly Magazine* [DAR], 40:4 (October 1912), 176-177. [From Floyds Creek, Rutherford County, N. C.; fought at Cowpens, King's Mountain, Ramseur's Mill, and Guilford Court House]

Burnett, Fred M. "A Sketch of the Ancestors, Life and War Experience of Marcus Lafayette Burnett, 1928." Manuscript 107-z, Southern Historical Collection, Louis Round Wilson Special Collections Library, University of North Carolina, Chapel Hill; online finding aid available at http://www2.lib.unc.edu/mss/inv/b/Burnett,Fred_M.html. [Online finding aid description: "The collection consists of a typescript copy of an account of the life and Confederate service of Marcus LaFayette Burnett (b. 1845), describing his family history, his grandfather's emigration to Old Fort, N. C., in 1770; pioneer life; hunting; Revolutionary War battles in North Carolina and South Carolina; ..."]

Cameron, Rebecca. "A Partisan Leader in 1776." *North Carolina Booklet*, 12:1 (July 1912), 53-58. [Colonel William Shepperd of Long Meadows, North Carolina]

Clark, Wanda L. *The Trosper Tree: Descendants of Nicholas Trosper, Soldier of the Revolution, from Morganton District, Burke County, North Carolina, with Col. Charles McDowell, 1784, Captain of Militia, DAR No. 269369*. McAlester, Okla.: W. L. Clark, 1985.

Cook, Gerald Wilson. *The Descendants of Claiborne Howard, Soldier of the American Revolution, Including the Following Major Family Groups: Barnard, Brindle, Campbell, Clemons, Cook, Denny, Everidge, Felts, Hadley, Hobson, Howard, Hutchens, Mayberry, Messick, Tulburt, and information on families in Iredell, Surry, Wilkes, and Yadkin Counties, North Carolina; Hardin County, Iowa; Missouri, California, Oregon and Washington.* Cholon, Vietnam: Hoang-Van Print Shop, 1960. [Claiborne Howard (1763-1846)]

Cook, Thomas; William Montgomery Sweeny. *Captain Thomas Cook (1752-1841): A Soldier of the Revolution*. New York: [s. n.], 1909; online: https://archive.org/stream/captainthomascoo00cookiala#page/n4/mode/1up. [Commander of the Independent Company of Light Horse, North Carolina Continental Line]

Cooke, Martha Jean Clark, for the Tennessee Daughters of the American Revolution. "Joseph Hannah Revolutionary Soldier." *Tennessee DAR Genealogical Records Committee Report, Series 1, Volume 132: Tennessee Genealogical Records Committee NSDAR [bk. 8]* (typescript, 1974), 29-39; digital surrogate, DAR Library, Washington, D. C.

[Craig, Gerrald]. "A Power of Attorney from Revolutionary Soldier Gerrald Craig, in Case of His Death (1776)." Manuscript in the "John M. and Ruth Hodges Papers, 1735-1966," PC.1242, State Archives of North Carolina, Raleigh.

Davis, Robert S. "Revolutionary Relic." *North Carolina Genealogical Society Journal*, 11:4 (November 1985), 226. [rifle ball removed from the body of John Duckworth "an aged Revolutionary soldier." (apparently living in Georgia in 1842)]

Davis, Robert Scott, Jr. "North Carolina, South Carolina, and Georgia Revolutionary War Soldiers Claims." *Georgia Genealogical Magazine*, no. 81 (Summer 1981), 203-210; no. 82 (Fall 1981), 285-292.

"Died in Hampton, on Jan. 1, 1827, Thomas A. B. Jones, Age 90, Soldier of the Revolution, Born in North Carolina." *American Beacon and Norfolk and Portsmouth Daily Advertiser* [Norfolk], (Saturday, January 6, 1839), 2:col. 6. [Thomas A. B. Jones (1749-1839)]

Dulin, Sugar, 1763-1845. "Sugar Dulin Autobiographical Sketch, ca. 1833." Manuscript 5339-z, Southern Historical Collection, Louis Round Wilson Special Collections Library, University of North Carolina, Chapel Hill; online finding aid available at http://www2.lib.unc.edu/mss/inv/d/Dulin,Sugar.html. [Online finding aid description: "Sugar Dulin was born in Onslow County, N. C. He moved to Mecklenburg County, N. C., in 1791, where he bought a large tract of land east of Charlotte and lived until his death in 1845. Dulin fought as a soldier in the Revolutionary War. The collection consists of an autobiographical sketch, written by Dulin circa 1833. Most of the information relates to his time as a soldier during the Revolutionary War. Dulin detailed troop movements, locations, and orders. He described his surroundings and mentioned the names of fellow soldiers and officers. At one point, Dulin repeated a friend's story of being shot by the Whigs while at home. Also included is a short overview of his life, giving his place and date of birth and describing his joining the army and later moving to Mecklenberg County. The only date mentioned in the sketches is 1781."]

Dumont, William Henry. "Heirs of Some North Carolina Revolutionary Soldiers." *The North Carolinian: A Quarterly Journal of Genealogy and History*, 4:4 (December 1958), 484-486.

Ferguson, Moses, and Robert McCormick. "Oaths of Moses Ferguson and Robert McCormick Stating That Adam Miller Served in the Revolutionary War, 1831." Manuscript 36378, Tennessee State Library and Archives, Nashville; online: http://teva.contentdm.oclc.org/cdm/singleitem/collection/p15138coll16/id/37/rec/30.

"Frederick Rivenbark, Revolutionary War Soldier." *Rivenbark Family Review*, 18 (September 1985), 3.

Futrell, Nathan, 1773-1829. "Futrell Family Collection, 1829-1966." Manuscript Mss. C F, Filson Historical Society, Louisville, Ky. [Online catalog description: "Collection includes an 1829 affidavit stating that Nathan Futrell served as a drummer boy, at the age of seven, with the North Carolina militia during the American Revolution. It is witnessed by Bryan Futrell. The affidavit is mounted. Remaining items include a metal presentation plaque and a typed note describing the affidavit signed by Roger H. L. Futrell and dated 3 November 1966."]

Gay, Allen, 1765-1847. "Allen Gay Manuscript, 1800s." Manuscript MS 275, Georgia Historical Society, Savannah. [Online catalog description: "The collection consists of a manuscript, 'Sketch of the life & Revolutionary incidents of Allen Gay,' … Allen Gay (1765-1847), a native of North Carolina, moved to Georgia around the year 1785. At the age of 16, he volunteered to take his father's place as a soldier in the Revolutionary War when his father was called for a one-year tour of duty. Gay fought in the 1st Battalion under Colonel Dickerson, in Captain Robert Raford's Company."]

Gipson, William, 1753-1835. "[Revolutionary War Memoir]." In John C. Dann, ed. *The Revolution Remembered: Eyewitness Accounts of the War for Independence* (Chicago: University of Chicago Press, 1980), Chapter 6: "War in the Carolinas," 185-192. [William Gipson, Moncks Corner, South Carolina, and North Carolina]

Griffin, Clarence. *Revolutionary Service of Col. John Walker and Family, and Memoirs of Hon. Felix Walker*. Forest City: The Forest City Courier, 1930.

Griffin, Clarence. "Thomas Hutchins, Sr., Revolutionary Patriot." *North Carolina Historical and Genealogical Record: A Quarterly Magazine of North Carolina Genealogy, Biography and Local History*, 1:1 (January 1932), 10-14.

Gunn, Drewey Wayne. *The Descendants of Barnett Moore of Rockingham County, North Carolina, Identifying 3192 Family Members Born between 1780 and 1980 of Barnett Moore (ca. 1758-1822), Veteran of the American Revolution*. Kingsfille, Tex.: D. W. Gunn, 1997.

Harkness, David J. *Forgotten Heroes of the American Revolution*. Knoxville: University of Tennessee Press, 1974. [Includes Nathan Futrell and Jimmy Blair of North Carolina.]

Haynes, Donald E. "A Family Divided: The Shuford Family during the Revolutionary War." *A Lot of Bunkum*, 30:4 (November 2009), 9-11.

Haynsworth, James L. "Major Adam McDonald." *The Carolinas Genealogical Society Bulletin*, 12:1 (Summer 1975), 16.

Haywood, Marshall DeLancey. *Joel Lane, Pioneer and Patriot*. Raleigh: Alford, Bynum and Christophers, Printers, 1900; 2d rev. ed.: Raleigh: Alfred Williams & Co., 1925; 3rd ed.: Raleigh: Wake County Committee of the Colonial Dames of America, 1952.

Haywood, Marshall De Lancey. "Major George Farragut." *Gulf States Historical Magazine*, 5:1 (September 1903), 90-98.

Heath, (Mrs.) R. E. "Revolutionary Soldiers: Two Robert Wilsons Who Fought in North Carolina." *The Carolinas Genealogical Society Bulletin*.13:2 (Fall 1976), 23-25.

Henry, Louis Carr. "Revolutionary Service of George Bannerman." *National Genealogical Society Quarterly*, 21 (June 1933), 69.

Hubard Family. "Hubard Family Papers, 1741-1907." Manuscript 360, Southern Historical Collection, Louis Round Wilson Special Collections Library, University of North Carolina, Chapel Hill; online finding aid available at http://www2.lib.unc.edu/mss/inv/h/Hubard_Family.html. [Online finding aid description: "In this period there appear, in larger numbers, the papers of William Hubard (d. 1805), first at Gloucester County, where some members of his family remained, then at Charlotte County, Va. These papers include a number concerning business transactions with John Thruston, also at Gloucester County, whose daughter, Frances Thruston Hubard (1752-1781) married William Hubard in 1768. William Hubard served in the state militia, attaining the position of major (circa 1778)… 1776: The will, dated 22 March 1776, of Joseph Montford of Halifax, N. C. There is a letter, dated 6 April 1776, from William Cabell to Edmund Wilcox to the effect that he, Wilcox, had attended Colonel Corbin on board Lord Dunmore's ship, with permission of the Committee of Safety; also referring to ministerial troops at Boston and to General Washington… 1780: There is a receipt, dated 24 August 1780, for furnishing a substitute soldier."]

"Information of North Carolina Soldier Josiah Martin Who Died in Tennessee." Manuscript FC/Families/Martin, Josiah, DAR Library, Washington, D. C.

"Information on Descendants of North Carolina Revolutionary Soldier David Lew Who Died in South Carolina." Manuscript FC/Families/Lewis/S. C., DAR Library, Washington, D. C. [Includes transcript of Lew's will]

"Information on Descendants of North Carolina Revolutionary Soldier Harrison Macon." Manuscript, FC/Families Macon/N. C., DAR Library, NSDAR, Washington, D. C. [Includes land grant information.]

"Information on North Carolina Revolutionary Soldier Exum Lewis and Some of His Descendants." Manuscript, FC/Families/Lewis/N. C., DAR Library, Washington, D. C.

"John Gillon: A Hero of the Revolution." *Carolinas Genealogical Society Bulletin*, 8:1 (Summer 1971), 5-6.

"John Hubbard, Veteran." *Carolinas Genealogical Society Bulletin*, 31:1 (Summer 1994), 7.

John Penn Chapter, North Carolina Daughters of the American Revolution. *North Carolina DAR Genealogical Records Committee Report, Series 1, Volume 133: Certified Records of Revolutionary Soldiers from North Carolina Historical Commission* (typescript, 1949); digital surrogate, DAR Library, Washington, D. C.

Jones, Richard Bowdenm, Sr. *Some Descendants of Nicholas Bourden, and His Wife Prudence, the Great-Granddaughter of Captain John Moore*. Wimauma, Fla.: R. B. Jones, 1994.

Julich, Louise Milam. "Walter Ross, Revolutionary War Soldier." *The Carolinas Genealogical Society Bulletin*, 35:1 (Summer 1998-1999), 10.

Leonard, Jacob Calvin. "Valentin Leonhardt, the Revolutionary War Patriot of North Carolina." *The Pennsylvania-German*. 11:1 (January 1910), 10-20. [Valentin Leonhardt (1718-1781)]

McDonald, Hugh. "Hugh McDonald Paper." Manuscript, PC.1178, State Archives of North Carolina, Raleigh. [Online catalog description: "Eight-page fragment of Revolutionary War memoirs, apparently by Hugh McDonald of Cumberland Co., telling of his release after capture as a loyalist at Moores Creek Bridge; enlistment in the American army under Capt. Arthur Council; organization at Wilmington of Gen. Francis Nash's brigade; movements (1776-1777) to South Carolina, North Carolina, and Philadelphia; celebration in Philadelphia (July 4, 1777); contest with British ships at Mud Fort near Wilmington on the Delaware; battles of Brandywine and Germantown; death of General Nash; retreat from Germantown; and Col. Archibald Lytle. Also contains part of sketch of Revolutionary leader Robert Rowan of Cumberland Co."]

McMurty, David Cornelius. *Inaccuracies in the Family Records and Revolutionary War Period Military Service Records of Three Contemporary John McMurties: Report to the National Societies of the Daughters of the American Revolution and the Sons of the American Revolution on the Inaccuracies in the Family and Revolutionary War Service Records of John McMurtrie of Philadelphia, John McMurtry of New Jersey and Tennessee, Captain John McMurtry of Kentucky as Recorded by Frederick James McMurtrie*. Lexington, Ky.: D. C. McMurty, 1983.

Misenheimer, John E. "Johann Jacob Meisenheimer/Misenheimer." *Golden Nugget (Cabarrus Genealogical Society)*, 13:1 (Spring 2005), 10-13.

Misenheimer, John E. "Misenheimer Men of the American Revolution." *The Golden Nugget (Cabarrus Genealogical Society)*, 13:3 (Autumn 2005), 78-81.

Murrell, William, 1746-1829. "William Murrell Account Books, 1784-1806." Manuscripts P (4 holograph vols.; 1 microfilm roll), Manuscripts Department, South Caroliniana Library, University of South Carolina, Columbia. ["Portions of ledger, 1784-1806, Vol. I, transcribed as 'Lists of Revolutionary Soldiers or Executors of Estates Involving Indents Issued to Various Parties by the State of S. C.;' volume lists names of veterans from South Carolina, North Carolina, Georgia, Virginia, Maryland, Pennsylvania, New York, and Connecticut [filed in Manuscripts-P as 'Revolutionary Soldiers']; index, 15-18."]

Nash, Gary B. "Thomas Peters: Millright and Deliverer." In David Sweet and Gary B. Nash, eds., *Struggle and Survival in Colonial America* (Berkeley and Los Angles: University of California Press, 1981), 69-85; reprinted with minor changes as "Thomas Peters: Millwright, Soldier and Deliverer." In Gary B. Nash, ed., *Race, Class and Politics: Essays on American Colonial and Revolutionary Society* (Urbana and Chicago: University of Illinois Press, 1986), 269-281.

"Nathan Musselwhite, Revolutionary War Soldier." *North Carolina Genealogical Society Journal*, 9:4 (November 1983), 9:4 (November 1983), 235.

North Carolina DAR. "Col. James Campbell Jr., Rev. Sol." *North Carolina DAR Genealogical Records Committee Report, Series 1, Volume 128: [Records] [bk.4]* (typescript, 1948), 1); digital surrogate, DAR Library, Washington, D. C.

North Carolina (State). General Assembly. "[Document dated:] January 10, 1780: Petition of Ann Glover, Widow of Samuel Glover, Late Soldier in the Continental Service." Manuscript; General Assembly Session Records; Session of April-May 1780; Joint Papers, Committee Papers, Resolutions; Miscellaneous Petitions, Box 1 (MARS ID: 66.8.20.7.1), State Archives of North Carolina, Raleigh. [Online catalog description: "Glover, citing her husband's generally good conduct while in the service, asks for a yearly allowance for her support and the support of her two children." Samuel Glover served in the 2nd North Carolina Regiment.]

North Carolina (State). General Assembly. "[Document dated]: 1784: Resolution in Favor of Andrew Allison of Rowan County." Manuscript; General Assembly Record Group; Session Records, April-June 1784: Committee Papers, Resolutions: Senate Joint Resolutions: April-June 1784, Box 2 (MARS ID: 66.8.32.4.10; item), State Archives of North Carolina, Raleigh. [Online catalog description: "Resolution awards compensation for service and wounds received in the war."]

North Carolina (State). General Assembly. Senate. "Resolved that the Treasurer be Directed to Pay to Daniel Houston Sums of Money per Year for the Settlement of his Account." Manuscript; General Assembly Record

Group; Session Records, December 1793-January 1794, Box 1 (MARS ID: 66.8.68.48.9; item), State Archives of North Carolina, Raleigh. [Online catalog description: "Thomas Daniel Houston had served in the American Revolution under the command of Col. Francis Lock and Capt. David Calwell and had sustained wounds that made him eligible for compensation. Houston had been a soldier and was wounded while fighting against British troops. His wounds left him incapable of fighting again or laboring for a living. He is therefore, eligible for public allowances."]

North Carolina (State). Secretary of State. "Correspondence Concerning Revolutionary War Veterans and Pensioners, 1818-1859." Manuscript SS 25.1-SS 25.3 (MARS ID: 12.35; series), State Archives of North Carolina, Raleigh. [Online catalog description: "Correspondence concerning proof of service during the American Revolution, which was needed for federal pension applications or for claims for military bounty land."]

Oden, John, III. "Samuel Freeman's Revolutionary Service." *Washington County Genealogical Society Journal*, 4:3 (December 1996), 72.

Organ Lutheran Church (Salisbury, N. C.) and Mary Pegram West. *Dedication of Memorial, John Bost, Soldier of the American Revolution: October 17, 1976, 3 P. M., Organ Lutheran Church, Rowan County, North Carolina.* Salisbury: [s. n.], 1976. [John Bost (1743-1793)]

Pannill, Ruth Hairston. "Capt. Peter Hairston – Virginia and North Carolina." *Daughters of the American Revolution Magazine*, 96:4 (April 1962), 430

Pruette, Ola Falls. "Joseph Brown, Revolutionary War Soldier." *Eswau Huppeday: Bulletin of the Broad River Genealogical Society,* 4:2 (May 1984), 115-122.

Pyle, C. Homer; Bessie E. Pyle, ed. *Colonel John Pyle and His People.* Bethany, Mo.: BB Engraving and Printing Company, 1970.

Royall, Henry Estil. "The Administration of Veterans Affairs in North Carolina from 1715 to 1790." M. A. thesis, University of North Carolina at Chapel Hill, 1952.

Sammons, Helen Moore. "William Pridgeon, Patriot." *Clarendon Courier*, 6:3 (September 1994), 10-11. [See also: "Extraordinary Longevity," *Clarendon Courier*, 6:4 (December 1994), 18. [Pridgeon's obituary from 1845 stating that he lived to be 123 years old.]

Sams, Parker Chastaine. *Fighting Charles Reese: His Life and His Family.* [Findlay, Ohio: P. C. Sams], 1996. [Charles Reese (ca. 1756-1830)]

[Sanders, Amy Warren]. "Revolutionary Soldier Being Honored." *Family Puzzlers: The Next Generation*, no. 15 (September 1999), 1-2. [William Morris of North Carolina; died in DeKalb County, Ga.]

[Sanders, Amy Warren]. "Revolutionary Soldiers to Be Honored." *Family Puzzlers: The Next Generation*, no. 16 (October 1999), 1-2. [John Biffle (1744-1850; Germany to North Carolina; died in DeKalb County, Ga. Joseph Emanuel Lyon (1754-1830; England to North Carolina; died in DeKalb County, Ga.]

Saxon, John L. "The Spirit of 1776." *The State" Down Home in North Carolina,* 44:2 (July 1976), 15; online: http://digital.ncdcr.gov/cdm/ref/collection/p16062coll18/id/11791. [Online description from "North Carolina Periodicals Index," East Carolina University: "A flask originally carried by a Revolutionary War soldier from North Carolina is in perfect condition and in the home of a descendant of the soldier in Paducah, Ky. The soldier's name was Smothers and he was from North Carolina. In a painting of Washington looking at his troops at Valley Forge, a similar looking object can be seen dangling from a soldier. Although often a gill of rum was given to soldiers, perhaps they were also allowed to bring extra rum into battle."]

Schenck, David. "Biographical Sketch of Lieut. Col. 'Hal' Dixon." *North Carolina University Magazine,* old series, 28; new series 15:1 (October 1895), 16 pages.

Sellers, Charles, Jr. "Making a Revolution: the North Carolina Whigs, 1765-1775." In Joseph Carlyle Sitterson, ed., *Studies in Southern History* (James Sprunt Historical Publications, v. 39) (Chapel Hill: University of North Carolina Press, 1957), 23-46.

Shelby Family. "Shelby Family Papers, 1738-1916." Manuscript MSS39669, Library of Congress Manuscript Division, Madison Building, Washington, D. C.; online finding aid available at http://hdl.loc.gov/loc.mss/eadmss.ms013008. [Online finding aid description: "Correspondence, memoranda, legal and financial papers, military records, genealogical data, and memorabilia relating mainly to Evan Shelby, soldier and frontiersman, and to his son, Isaac Shelby, soldier and political leader, providing a record of frontier life and political and economic developments in Pennsylvania, Maryland, Virginia, North Carolina, Tennessee, and Kentucky."]

"Some Anderson County Tennessee, Revolutionary Soldiers' Testimonies: James Blackbourn, Page Portwood, Aaron Smith, and John McEntire." *East Tennessee Roots*, 8:1 (Summer 1996), 42-44.

"Some Descendants of Nicholas Nall, a Revolutionary Soldier." *North Carolina Genealogical Society Journal*, 5:2 (May 1979), 141.

"Some Information on North Carolina Revolutionary Soldier Richard Minter." Manuscript FC Families Minter Richard, DAR Library, Washington, D. C.

"Some Revolutionary War Papers of John Jenkins." *Eswau Huppeday: Bulletin of the Broad River Genealogical Society,* 2:2 (May 1982), 31-36.

Spears, Kenneth Sherrill. "1845 Query from Shelby [N. C.] about Revolutionary War Soldiers." *Eswau Huppeday: Bulletin of the Broad River Genealogical Society,* 9:2 (May 1989), 91. [A. R. Homesley letter to the governor looking for whereabouts of Capt. John Morphis]

Splawn, Jane Long. "Colonel Nicholas Long." *Eswau Huppeday: Bulletin of the Broad River Genealogical Society,* 6:1 (February 1986), 51-53.

Steed, Paul P. *Jesse Steed: Soldier of the American Revolution, North Carolina Continental Line.* Dallas: P. P. Steed, 2010. [Jesse Steed (1749-1787)]

Strother, William H. "William H. Strother Paper, 1847." Manuscript, PC.974, State Archives of North Carolina, Raleigh. [Online catalog description: "Sworn statement by Ailsey Medlin of Franklin Co. that she is the daughter and only heir of Benjamin Schoolfield, who died in service with the North Carolina militia in 1778. Accompanied by sworn statements about her character, one by Strother, and certifications. See also P.C. 955."]

"Sullivan. Revolutionary War Record of Daniel Sullivan, 1763-1841." Mimeograph (MARS ID: 400.1890; folder), State Archives of North Carolina, Raleigh. [Mentions Richard Byrd and Joseph Pyatt.]

"Survivors of the Revolution." *Olde Mecklenburg Genealogical Society Quarterly*, 24:3 (2006), 6. [elderly veterans of the Revolution living in North Carolina, ages 96-102. [Originally published in *North Carolina Whig*, 17 January 1859.]

"Thomas Lewis, Veteran." *Carolinas Genealogical Society Bulletin*, 31:1 (Summer 1994), 6.

"Two Soldiers, Both Named John Gibbs, Who Served in the American Revolution in North Carolina." *The Carolinas Genealogical Society Bulletin*, 11:1 (Summer 1974), 3-5.

Waggoner, Martha. "1st Black Joins NC's Sons of American Revolution." *Associated Press; AP Regional State Report: Massachusetts,* February 20, 2012. [Publisher's summary: "Raleigh, N. C. (AP) A chapter of the Sons of the American Revolution in North Carolina is inducting its first black member, a firefighter who only recently learned his ancestor was freed from slavery after fighting for American independence. Thirty-year-old Chaz Moore is a descendant of Toby Gilmore, the son of a chieftain in coastal West Africa who was kidnapped at the age of 16 and sold into slavery in Massachusetts. He gained his freedom by joining the fight for what would become the United States."]

Walker, James Alves. *Life of Col. John (Jack) Walker*. Wilmington: J. A. Walker, 1902. [John Walker (1741-1813); John Walker (1789-1862); Thomas Davis (1764-1822).

Wall, Bonneta B. "Daughters of the American Revolution Papers: Richard Wall." *Eswau Huppeday: Bulletin of the Broad River Genealogical Society,* 2:4 (November 1982), 100-104.

Weeks, Milton D. "The Ancestry of Theophilus Weeks, A Soldier of the American Revolution." *Quarterly Review of the Eastern North Carolina Genealogical Society*, 8:2 (Spring 1981), 53-55.

Welborn, [Leo Cadia Lucile Barbee] (Mrs. John Scott) for the Alexander Martin Chapter, North Carolina Daughters of the American Revolution. *North Carolina DAR Genealogical Records Committee Report, Series 1, Volume 139: List of Soldiers of North Carolina in the American Revolution* (typescript, 1949); digital surrogate, DAR Library, Washington, D. C.

Wilds, Scott. "North Carolina Revolutionary War Service of Four Darlington Residents." *Darlington Flag*, 25:3 (Summer 2013), 100-102. [John Grant, William Gee, and John Huse appear in documents.]

Willcox, George W. *John Willcox, 1728-1793, of Chester County, Pennsylvania, Cumberland County, North Carolina, and Chatham County, North Carolina.* [United States]: Historical Research Co., 1988.

"William Graham (1745-1835), Revolutionary War Soldier & Wife, Susan Twitty Graham (1751-1825)." Manuscript, FC/Families/Graham.William/N. C., DAR Library, Washington, D. C.

Payments to Veterans and Veterans Claims to North Carolina

"Captain Thomas Stockton's Claim against the State, N. C. General Assembly Session Records, November-December 1787." *Bulletin of the Genealogical Society of Old Tryon County*, 29:4 (November 2001), 174.

Fenner, Julian B. "Julian B. Fenner Papers, 1727-1894." Manuscript PC.1530 (MARS ID: 2040; record group), State Archives of North Carolina, Raleigh. [Online catalog description: "Papers of Maj. Robert Fenner of Halifax Co., son John H. Fenner, and grandson William E. Fenner, primarily Halifax Co. deeds, plats and wills relating to their estate settlements and to former owners of the land, including free Negro Joseph Bartley (1855). Letter to Gov. Richard Caswell (Aug. 1, 1786) from Maj. Robert Fenner, agent for the late North Carolina [Continental] Line, explains his refusal to relinquish the final settlement certificates."]

[Johnson, William Perry]. "Revolutionary War – Final Settlements." *The North Carolinian: A Quarterly Journal of Genealogy and History*, 6:4 (December 1960), 753-758; 7:2 (June 1961), 821-822; 8:3 (September 1962), 1012.

North Carolina (State). State Treasurer. "Military Papers – Service Records and Final Settlements." Manuscript Box 13-Box 24 (MARS ID: 13.27; series), State Archives of North Carolina, Raleigh. [Online catalog description: Records relating to the settlement of approximately six hundred outstanding claims against the state by individual soldiers for their Revolutionary War service pay. Folders frequently concern more than one soldier, and may include affidavits, depositions, and certifications concerning military service; furlough and discharge papers; powers of attorney; assignments of interest; certifications concerning letters of administration on the estates of deceased soldiers; and accounts of final settlements."]

Pensions

Absher, Mrs. W. O. "Some Stokes County Revolutionary War Pensioners Deaths." *North Carolina Genealogical Society Journal*, 3:1 (February 1977), 40-42.

Absher, Mrs. W. O. "Stokes County, N. C. Revolutionary War Pension Abstracts." *North Carolina Genealogical Society Journal*, 1:4 (October 1975), 174-178.

"Aged, Impoverished, and Infirm: Two Pension Petitions in Randolph County Court Minutes." *The Genealogical Journal by the Randolph County Genealogical Society*, 26:1 (Spring 2002), 23-25. [John Slack and Jesse Gatlin]

Allen, Penelope Johnson. *Tennessee Soldiers in the Revolution: A Roster of Soldiers Living during the Revolutionary War in the Counties of Washington and Sullivan, Taken From the Revolutionary Army Accounts of North Carolina.* [Bristol, Tenn.: The King Printing Company for the Tennessee Society, Daughters of the American Revolution], 1935; reprinted: Baltimore: Genealogical Publishing Company, 1975. [Contents: Introduction; Index to Revolutionary Soldiers; Revolutionary Pensioners of Tennessee, Act of 1828; Index to Wills of Washington County, Tennessee; Abstracts of Wills of Washington County; Marriage Records of Blount County; Marriage Records of Davidson County; Revolutionary Grants of Davidson County.]

"American Revolution: Stephen Billew (Billue), Pension File No. 5,280. Allowed Feb. 25, 1833." *The Carolinas Genealogical Society Bulletin*, 14:3 (Winter 1977-1978), 57-58.

"American Revolution Soldier Pension Lists." Manuscript Am.6552, Historical Society of Pennsylvania, Philadelphia. [Online catalog description: "This collection contains photostatic copies of lists, 1780-1784, of soldiers who served in Connecticut, Delaware, Georgia, Massachusetts, Maryland, North Carolina, New Hampshire, New Jersey, Pennsylvania, Rhode Island, and Virginia and were awarded pensions for their military service during the American Revolution."]

"Anson County Revolutionary War Pensions, 1841." *Carolinas Genealogical Society Bulletin*, 11:3 (Winter 1974-1975), 58.

Anthony, Elizabeth C. "Revolutionary Pension Application of William Bradley." *Eswau Huppeday: Bulletin of the Broad River Genealogical Society*, 13:1 (February 1993), 50-52.

Anthony, Libby. "Revolutionary Pension Application of Mayfield Crane." *Eswau Huppeday: Bulletin of the Broad River Genealogical Society,* 9:1 (February 1989), 30-31.

"Application for Revolutionary War Pension, James Gardner." *Genealogical Journal by the Randolph County Genealogical Society*, 13:4 (Fall 1989), 12-14.

Armstrong, Zella. *Twenty-Four Hundred Tennessee Pensioners; Revolution – War of 1812*. Chatanooga, Tenn.: Lookout Publishing Company, [1937].

Baer, Mabel van Dyke, for the Monticello Chapter, District of Columbia DAR. *District of Columbia DAR Genealogical Records Committee Report, Series 3, Volume 272: Revolutionary War Pension Abstracts, Volume IV: Soldiers Serving from North Carolina, South Carolina, and Georgia* (typescript, 1970); digital surrogate, DAR Library, Washington, D. C.

Banes, Verna Baker. "Hugh McCrory's Pension and Revolutionary War Records." *Olde Mecklenburg Genealogical Society Quarterly*, 5:4 (Winter-Spring 1987), 159-160.

Bayer, Mabel Van Dyke for the Monticello Chapter, D. C. Daughters of the American Revolution. *D. C. DAR Genealogical Records Committee Report, Series 3, Volume 269: Revolutionary War Pension Abstracts [Bk. 1 Soldiers Residing in Indiana, Kentucky and Ohio and Tennessee* (typescript, 1971); digital surrogate, DAR Library, Washington, D. C. [Tennessee Records start on page 187]

Bazwell, David, 1759-1836. "Declaration of Revolutionary Service, 1833 April 11." Manuscript 20419, Library of Virginia, Richmond. [Online catalog description: "Declaration of Revolutionary service, 11 April 1833, of David Bazwell (1759-1836) of Williamson County, Tennessee. Bazwell was applying for a pension under an act of Congress passed in 1832. Bazwell lists his service as a member of the Virginia militia from Mecklenburg

County, Virginia, and of the North Carolina militia from Person County, North Carolina. Bazwell's declaration was attested to by Samuel Dunnaway, his brother-in-law, his brother John Bazwell, and William Warren. On 16 November 1840 Dunnaway appeared before a justice of the Davidson County, Tennessee, Court, and made a separate statement concerning Bazwell's marriage to Susan Price in North Carolina in 1793 and his death in 1836."]

Benton, Carol, Linda Smith, Eleanor Waters, James Goodbread, and Samuel Weaver. "Some North Carolina Revolutionary War Soldiers Pensioned in Other States." *North Carolina Genealogical Society Journal*, 21:4 (November 1995), 353-374.

Blaylock, George. "Revolutionary War Pension Claim Documents, 1829." Manuscript VFM 4885, Ohio History Center, Ohio History Connection, Columbus. [Online catalog description: "Partially printed letters from the U.S. Treasury Department to George H. Blaylock regarding his Revolutionary War pension claim with instructions for proving his enlistment in Matthew Ramsay's Company in Chatham County, North Carolina and transfer to William Lytle's Company."]

Bockstruck, Lloyd de Witt. *Revolutionary War Pensions Awarded by State Governments, 1775-1874; the General and Federal Governments Prior to 1814; and by Private Acts of Congerss to 1905*. Baltimore: Genealogical Publishing Company, 2011.

Bolling, Aletha. "Pension Application of Jonathan Davis." Journal of the Greenville Chapter of the South Carolina Genealogical Society, 2:2 (Summer 1991), 56-57. [Caswell County, N. C.]

Brooks, Roy. "Revolutionary War Pension Fille of Captain William Davis." *Bulletin of the Genealogical Society of Old Tryon County*, 7:1 (February 1979), 28-29.

Bryan, John Heritage. "John Heritage Bryan (1798-1870) Collection, 1716-1907." Manuscript, PC.6 (MARS ID: 515; record group), State Archives of North Carolina, Raleigh. [Online catalog description: "...Miscellaneous papers include some relating to Revolutionary War claims..."]

Buie, Rufus T. "Revolutionary War Pension Document of John Buie of Hardin County, Tennessee (1835)." *Argyll Colony Plus*, 4:4 (Fall 1989), 139-140.

Bundy, Harry. "Application of Revolutionary War Pension of John Harris, Pasquotank County, NC." *Carolina Trees & Branches: Family Research Society of Northeastern North Carolina,* 19:3 (July 2010), 77.

"Burke County Revolutionary War Pension Files: An Index." *Journal of the Burke County Genealogical Society*, 22:4 (November 2004), 111-117; 23:1 (February 2005), 11-15.

Burns, Annie Walker. *Abstract of Pensions of North Carolina Soldiers of the Revolution, War of 1812 & Indian Wars*. 15 vols. Washington, D.C.: Burns, 1959-1966.

Cain, Robert J. "Loyalist Widow Pension Document of Rebecca McDugald of Moore County, North Carolina." *Argyll Colony Plus*, 4:4 (Fall 1989), 140-141.

Caldwell, Juanita "Nita" Evans. "Martin and Elizabeth Roberts, Petition for Pension, W. 4785 and 19732." *Eswau Huppeday: Bulletin of the Broad River Genealogical Society*, 23:3 (August 2003), 127-135.

Camin, Betty J. *North Carolina Revolutionary War Pension Applications*. Raleigh, N. C: B. J. Camin, 1983.

Camin, Betty J. "Revolutionary War Pension Applications at the North Carolina Archives."

(1st in series). *North Carolina Genealogical Society Journal*, 10:1 (February 1984), 39-43.

(2nd in series). *North Carolina Genealogical Society Journal*, 10:3 (August 1984), 160-169.

(3rd in series). *North Carolina Genealogical Society Journal*, 11:1 (February 1985), 16-24.

(4th in series: Carter-Cuthbertson). *North Carolina Genealogical Society Journal*, 11:3 (August 1985), 170-176.

(5th in series: D surnames). *North Carolina Genealogical Society Journal*, 12:1 (February 1986), 36-49.

(6th in series, E-G surnames). *North Carolina Genealogical Society Journal*, 12:3 (August 1986), 173-187.

(7th in series, H surnames). *North Carolina Genealogical Society Journal*, 13:1 (February 1987), 32-44.

(8th in series, I-K surnames). *North Carolina Genealogical Society Journal*, 13:3 (August 1987), 153-163.

(9th in series). *North Carolina Genealogical Society Journal*, 14:1 (February 1988), 38-47.

(10th in series). *North Carolina Genealogical Society Journal*, 14:3 (August 1988), 167-178.

(11th in series). *North Carolina Genealogical Society Journal*, 15:1 (February 1989), 23-32.

(12th in series). *North Carolina Genealogical Society Journal*, 15: 15:3 (August 1989), 155-165.

(13th in series). *North Carolina Genealogical Society Journal*, 16:1 (February 1990), 25-35.

(14th in series). *North Carolina Genealogical Society Journal*, 16:3 (August 1990), 156-161. [page 161 blank – need copy.]

(15th in series). *North Carolina Genealogical Society Journal*, 17:1 (February 1991), 30-36.

(16th in series). *North Carolina Genealogical Society Journal*, 17:3 (August 1991), 154-161.

(17th in series). *North Carolina Genealogical Society Journal*, 19:1 (February 1993), 36-47.

(18th in series). *North Carolina Genealogical Society Journal*, 19:3 (August 1993), 169-177.

(19th and last in series). *North Carolina Genealogical Society Journal*, 20:1 (February 1994).

Campbell Chapter, Tennessee Daughters of the American Revolution. *Tennessee DAR Genealogical Records Committee Report, Series 1, Volume 41: Applications for Pensions, Made under Acts of 1832 and Later by Revolutionary War Soldiers of Bledsoe County, Tenn.* (typescript, 1947); digital surrogate, DAR Library, Washington, D. C.

Carpenter, Frances. "Revolutionary Pension Application of John Harmon." *Eswau Huppeday: Bulletin of the Broad River Genealogical Society,* 10:3 (August 1990), 198-201.

Carpenter, Frances. "Revolutionary Pension Application of William Ledford." *Eswau Huppeday: Bulletin of the Broad River Genealogical Society,* 10:3 (August 1990), 202-205.

Carpenter, Frances. "Revolutionary Pension Application of William Logan." *Eswau Huppeday: Bulletin of the Broad River Genealogical Society,* 10:4 (November 1990), 242-247.

Carrére, Charlotte R. "Revolutionary War Pension Applications." *Wake Treasures*, 1:3 (Fall 1991), 2-4. [From: Wake County, N. C. Miscellaneous Records, State Archives of North Carolina]

Carrére, Charlotte R. "State Pensions to Invalids and Widows." *Wake Treasures*, 1:4 (Winter 1991), 18-19. [pensions based on the 1784 North Carolina law "An Act for the relief of such persons was have been disabled by wounds, or rendered incapable of procuring for themselves and families subsistence in the militia service of this state, and providing for the widows and orphans of such as have died." North Carolina. Treasurer's and Comptroller's papers, Papers, Military Papers, State Archives of North Carolina]

Cartee, Bob G. "Revolutionary Pension Application for James M. Cartee." *Eswau Huppeday: Bulletin of the Broad River Genealogical Society,* 9:4 (November 1989), 219-225.

Cashin, Edward J. "The Pension Claim of Joshua Burnett." *Richmond County History* [Augusta, Ga.], 10:1 (Winter 1978), 14-19. [from North Carolina]

Casper, Jean A. "The Revolutionary War Pension Application of Aaron Lewis." *The Robeson County Register*, 9:3 (August 1994), 98-103.

Cate, Ruth. "Tennessee Pensioners of the Revolution: Jesse Perry (S3655)." *Tennessee Ancestors: A Tri-Annual Publication of the East Tennessee Historical Society*, 6:1 (April 1990), 64-68.

Cates, Larry W. "Revolutionary War Pension Application of John Daffron." *The Genealogical Journal by the Randolph County Genealogical Society*, 31:3 (Fall 2007), 46-53.

Cates, Larry W. "Revolutionary War Pension Application of John Knight (Wife Sarah)." *The Genealogical Journal by the Randolph County Genealogical Society*, 30:4 (Winter 2006), 6-13.

Chaney, J. G. "John Chaney's Revolutionary Pension." *The Genealogical Journal by the Randolph County Genealogical Society*, 2:3 (Spring 1978), 32-38.

Conner, Tennga S. "The Revolutionary War Pension Application of Andrew Beaty of Fentress County, Tennessee. " *Tennessee Ancestors: A Tri-Annual Publication of the East Tennessee Historical Society*, 16:3 (December 2000), 202-206.

"Correspondence Concerning Revolutionary War Veterans and Pensioners, 1818-1859." Manuscript, SS 25.1 – SS 25.3, State Archives of North Carolina, Raleigh. [Online catalog description: "Correspondence concerning proof of service during the American Revolution, which was needed for federal pension applications or for claims for military bounty land."]

Craig, Marion Stark. "Revolutionary War Pension Application and Obituary of Benjamin Hardin." *Bulletin of the Genealogical Society of Old Tryon County*, 4:1 (February 1976), 12-17.

Crawford, Sybil F. "John Crawford, a Migration Story." *Rowan County Register*, 4:3 (August 1989), 884-886. [Followed by "Revolutionary War Pension Record of John Crawford," 887-888.]

Crowder, Louise. "Revolutionary War Pension." *Georgia Genealogical Magazine: A Magazine of Genealogical Source Material Concerning Georgians,* no.74 (Fall 1979), 303-304. [Stephen Crain, of Halifax County, N. C., and Chester District, S. C., 1832]

Culbreth, (Mrs.) Hubert. "Revolutionary War Pension Application and Biography of Richard Ledbetter." *Bulletin of the Genealogical Society of Old Tryon County*, 4:1 (February 1976), 17-20.

Curry, Mrs. Elmer E. "Veterans' Administration. North Carolina Pension Agency Book. Act of March 18, 1818. List of Pensioners Whose Dates of Death are Recorded in Said Book." *District of Columbia. DAR Genealogical Records Committee Report, Series 1, Volume 29.2: Miscellaneous Records* (typescript, 1938), 62-64); digital surrogate, DAR Library, Washington, D. C.

Dann, John C., ed. *The Revolution Remembered: Eyewitness Accounts of the War for Independence*. Chicago: University of Chicago Press, 1980. [Chapter 6: "War in the Carolinas," 174-233.] Based on the personal views expressed in seventy-nine Revolutionary War pension applications stored in the National Archives.

Davis, Robert S., Jr. "Revolutionary War Pensioners in the South, 1813." *Georgia Genealogical Magazine: A Magazine of Genealogical Source Material Concerning Georgians,* no. 105 (Summer 1987), 249-255. [Virginia, North Carolina, South Carolina, Georgia, and Kentucky]

Deberry, Edmund. "Edmund Deberry (1787-1859) Papers, 1745-1850." Call Number MfP.9, State Archives of North Carolina, Raleigh. [Online catalog description: "Papers of Deberry of Montgomery Co., state senator (1806-1828) and Whig member of Congress (1829-1851), including… [o]ther letters (1829-1854) relate to claims of Deberry's constituents to military pensions and land grants."]

Dellinger, Paul. "John Dellinger Revolutionary War Soldier Pension Information." *Eswau Huppeday: Bulletin of the Broad River Genealogical Society,* 10:2 (May 1990), 128-130.

Denmark, Stephen. "Abstracts of Revolutionary Pensions: Furna Cannon." *Pitt County Genealogical Quarterly*, 1:1 (Winter 1994), 13-16.

DePriest, Virginia Greene. "The Revolutionary War Pension Application of William Holland from the Collection of Virginia Greene DePriest." *Eswau Huppeday: Bulletin of the Broad River Genealogical Society*, 28:2 (May 2008), 92-96.

Dippel, Myra Davis. "Revolutionary Pension Application for John Wheeler." *Eswau Huppeday: Bulletin of the Broad River Genealogical Society,* 7:4 (November 1987), 269-278.

Draughon, Mrs. Wallace. "Mrs. Wallace Draughon Collection, 1801-1856." Manuscript, PC.1352, State Archives of North Carolina, Raleigh. [Online catalog description: "Photocopies of pension applications and related papers in the National Archives based on service of eight Revolutionary soldiers of North Carolina: James Brown of Granville Co., James Brown of North Carolina and Pennsylvania, David Quinn, Jacob Seagraves, Benjamin Smith, David Smith, John Smith, and John Thompson. Papers include depositions about Revolutionary service and experiences such as John Smith's imprisonment on British vessel in Georgia (1778-1779); record of birth dates of David Quin's slaves and children (1801-1836); and letter from heirs of Jacob Seagraves in Illinois (1851)."]

Elmore, Larry. "Brothers-in-Law: The Revolutionary War Pension Applications of Edward Rippy and William Elmore." *Eswau Huppeday: Bulletin of the Broad River Genealogical Society*, 16:2 (May 1996), 95-109.

Ferguson, Nancy Ellen. "Revolutionary War Pension Application of Daniel Allen." *Bulletin of the Genealogical Society of Old Tryon County*, 24:2 (May 1996), 83-84.

Fergusson Family. "Fergusson Family Papers, 1784-1927." Manuscript 1260, Tennessee State Library and Archives, Nashville; online finding aid available at http://share.tn.gov/tsla/history/manuscripts/findingaids/478.pdf. [Online finding aid description: "Adam Fergusson (1796-1862) born in North Carolina of Scottish parentage moved to Tennessee when he was eight years of age. He became an attorney and was appointed pension agent for Tennessee. A great deal of his correspondence concerns applications for pensions. Several business trips were made to Washington in the 1850s on behalf of claims and in some of his letter he wrote of pension frauds." Box 20 contains some Revolutionary War military records; Boxes 22-23 contain Pension Data from the Revolutionary, 1812, Mexican, and Civil Wars.]

Fuller, Elijah. "Elijah Fuller Papers, 1786-1911." Manuscript 1573, Southern Historical Collection, Louis Round Wilson Special Collections Library, University of North Carolina, Chapel Hill; online finding aid available at http://www2.lib.unc.edu/mss/inv/f/Fuller,Elijah.html. [Online finding aid description: "Elijah Fuller was born in 1810 to Bartholomew Fuller of Franklin County, N. C., Revolutionary patriot and Baptist preacher, and Sarah Cooke Fuller… In addition to his activities as a merchant, he was a Revolutionary War pension agent and an assignee in bankruptcy court for Cumberland County… [Includes r]eceipts, bills of sale, account statements, shipping statements, notes, bankruptcy cases, invoices, Revolutionary War pension claims, insurance policies, promissory notes, and other material relating to William MacLennan's and Elijah Fuller's business activities in Fayetteville, N. C."]

Galbreath, Carol J. "Revolutionary War Pensioners of Randolph County: Dan Merrell." *The Genealogical Journal by the Randolph County Genealogical Society*, 16:4 (Fall 1992), 36-38.

Goode Family. "Goode Family Papers, 1781-1887." Manuscript Collection #184, J. & Y. Joyner Library, East Carolina University, Greenville; online finding aid available at https://digital.lib.ecu.edu/special/ead/findingaids/0184/. [Online finding aid description: "The collection contains information on a variety of subjects and covers a period of more than one hundred years. Two items deal with the Revolutionary War in that one Luke Wiles was wounded in battle in Guilford County, N.C., and was discharged from the militia due to his wound. In 1825, Wiles sought relief from the national government in the form of a pension."]

Gossett, Jeff. "William Gossett Revolutionary War Pension Application." *Bulletin of the Genealogical Society of Old Tryon County*, 19:3 (August 1991), 116-119.

Greisser, Edith. "Declaration for a Pension, John Riser, Veteran of the Revolutionary War." *Old Newberry District Quarterly*, 11:4 (Winter 2002), 34-35. [1st North Carolina Regiment; pensioned in South Carolina]

Hackett, James Gordon. "James Gordon Hackett Collection, 1806-1887." Manuscript PC.112 (MARS ID: 621; record group), State Archives of North Carolina, Raleigh. [Online catalog description: "Papers (1833-1856) of Wilkesboro lawyer A. A. Scroggs relate to Revolutionary and War of 1812 pensions, with letters from Congressman David S. Reid (1844) and others and affidavits of service and marriage."]

Hathaway, J. R. B. "Affidavit of Willis Boon for Pension as a Revolutionary Soldier." *North Carolina Historical and Genealogical Register*, 1:3 (July 1900), 426.

Haywood, Ernest. "Ernest Haywood Collection of Haywood Family Papers, 1752-1967." Manuscript 1290, Southern Historical Collection, Louis Round Wilson Special Collections Library, University of North Carolina, Chapel Hill; online finding aid available at http://www2.lib.unc.edu/mss/inv/h/Haywood,Ernest.html. [The online finding aid shows that this collection contains correspondence and other information relating to Revolutionary War pensions in North Carolina.]

Hensley, Laura W. "Tennessee Pensioners of the Revolution: Nathaniel Watson (S3454)." *Tennessee Ancestors: A Tri-Annual Publication of the East Tennessee Historical Society*, 7:1 (April 1991), 67-70.

Hill, Jane Smith. "Revolutionary War Pensions: Edmond Hays/Edmund Hayes." *The Genealogical Journal by the Randolph County Genealogical Society*, 16:1 (Winter 1992), 37.

Holdaway, Boyd J. "Tennessee Pensioners of the Revolution: Timothy Holdaway." *Tennessee Ancestors: A Tri-Annual Publication of the East Tennessee Historical Society*, 5:2 (August 1989), 101-107.

Homesley, Ray. "Revolutionary War Pension Application of Joshua Roberts." *Eswau Huppeday: Bulletin of the Broad River Genealogical Society,* 11:4 (November 1991), 240-242.

Hughes, Stevie. "Revolutionary War Pension Application of Zepher Johnson (Johnston)." *Tennessee Ancestors: A Tri-Annual Publication of the East Tennessee Historical Society*, 17:1 (April 2001), 18-20.

Hutchins, Ann. "Ann Hutchins Pension Claim, 1841." Manuscript 361-z, Southern Historical Collection, Louis Round Wilson Special Collections Library, University of North Carolina, Chapel Hill; online finding aid available at http://www2.lib.unc.edu/mss/inv/h/Hutchins,Ann.html. [Online finding aid description: "Ann Hutchins was the widow of James Hutchins, a private in the Continental Army. The collection is an approved claim for Ann Hutchins's United States pension."]

Inghrim, Ellen Williams, and Mary S. Williams. "Robert Williams, Rev. War Pension." *Pitt County Genealogical Quarterly*, 14:1 (February 2007), 10-12.

Isaac, Stan. "Matthew Sparks's Pension Application." *Rowan County Register*, 16:1 (February 2001), 3591-3593.

"Jesse Mills, Patriot of Cooper's Gap, Polk County, North Carolina, War Department, Widow's Pension." *Bulletin of the Genealogical Society of Old Tryon County*, 19:3 (August 1991), 132-141.

Johnson, Sydney E. "Whitehurst Pensions." *Pitt County Genealogical Quarterly*, 10:2 (May 2003), 8-10. [One of the pensions is that of Arthur Whitehurst, Sr., for Revolutionary War service.]

Johnson, William Perry. "Abstracts of Pension Applications of North Carolina Soldiers of the Revolutionary War." *The North Carolinian: A Quarterly Journal of Genealogy and History*, 1:1 (March 1955), 27-30; 1:2 (June 1955), 59-60; 1:3 (September 1955), 68-74; 1:4 (December 1955), 120-125; 2:1 (March 1956), 145-150; 2:4 (December 1956), 245-248; 3:4 (December 1957), 373-375; 5:2 (June 1959), 549-554; 7:1 (March 1961), 773-780; [The journal ceased publication without publishing any additional articles in this series.]

Johnson, William Perry. "An Unusual Revolutionary War Experience." *Journal of North Carolina Genealogy*, 10:2 (Summer 1964), inside front cover. [Presents information from the pension of John Hancock of Montgomery County, who was captured by the British and put on a prison ship, escaped, and then enlisted in the American army.]

Johnson, William Perry. "Lee Family: N. C. Revolutionary War Pensioners" *Journal of North Carolina Genealogy*, 13:3 (Fall 1967), 1936-1940. [Pensions of 12 men surnamed "Lee," "Lea," or "Leigh."]

Johnson, William Perry. "N. C. Revolutionary War Pensioners: Crabtree." *Journal of North Carolina Genealogy*, 20:2 (Fall/Winter 1974), 2994-2996.

Johnson, William Perry. "N. C. Revolutionary War Pensioners: Grider, Gryder." *Journal of North Carolina Genealogy*, 20:2 (Fall/Winter 1974), 2979-2981.

Johnson, William Perry. "N. C. Revolutionary War Pensioners: Hicks." *Journal of North Carolina Genealogy*, 17:1 (Spring/Summer 1972), 2711-2716.

Johnson, William Perry. "N. C. Revolutionary War Pensioners: Strahan, Strain, Strayhorn." *Journal of North Carolina Genealogy*, 19:1 (Spring/Summer 1973), 2831-2833.

Jones, Jean E. "Tennessee Pensioners of the Revolution: Samuel Rayl." *Tennessee Ancestors: A Tri-Annual Publication of the East Tennessee Historical Society*, 6:2 (August 1990), 161-165.

Jordan, Harriet. "The Revolution in Tennessee, from Pension Applications." *Tennessee Ancestors: A Publication of the East Tennessee Historical Society*, 29:1 (June 2013), 66-75; 29:2 (December 2013), 165-180; 30:1 (June 2014), 82-91.

Lee, Mrs. I. F., and the Anders Family. "Mrs. I. F. Lee Collection." Manuscript PC.130 (MARS ID: 639; Record Group), State Archives of North Carolina, Raleigh. [Online catalog description: "Papers of the Anders family of Bladen and New Hanover counties, including grants, deeds, plats and other land papers;... ; draft power of attorney from Penelope Lewis to William Anders for collecting pay of soldier in the N. C. Continental Line (1791), bearing names and addresses of several widows and former soldiers in the New Hanover (Pender) Co. area."]

Kammerer, Roger. "Britain Meeks, Rev. War Pension." *Pitt County Genealogical Quarterly*, 16:4 (November 2009), 1-2.

Kammerer, Roger. "Hezekiah Nobles, Rev. War Pension." *Pitt County Genealogical Quarterly*, 16:1 (February 2009), 1.

Kammerer, Roger. "Jacob Grimmer, Rev. War Pension." *Pitt County Genealogical Quarterly*, 15:2 (May 2008), 1-2.

Kammerer, Roger. "Jeremiah Dixon Rev. War Pension." *Pitt County Genealogical Quarterly*, 14:4 November 2007), 1-2.

Kammerer, Roger. "Jesse Shivers Rev. War Pension." *Pitt County Genealogical Quarterly*, 15:2 (February 2008), 2-3.

Kammerer, Roger. "John Corey, Revolutionary War Soldier." *Pitt County Genealogical Quarterly*, 16:2 (May 2009), 1.

Kammerer, Roger. "John Kinsaul, Rev. War Pension." *Pitt County Genealogical Quarterly*, 15:3 (August 2008), 1-2.

Kammerer, Roger. "John Mills, Rev. War Pension." *Pitt County Genealogical Quarterly*, 27:1 (February 2010), 1.

Kammerer, Roger. "John Moore, Revolutionary War Pension." *Pitt County Genealogical Quarterly*, 9:2 (May 2002), 11-12.

Kammerer, Roger. "Joshua Dinkins, Rev. War Pension." *Pitt County Genealogical Quarterly*, 16:3 (August 2009), 1-4

Kammerer, Roger. "Martin County Insolvents, 1779." *Pitt County Genealogical Quarterly*, 13:2 (May 2006), 9.

Kammerer, Roger. "Rev. War Pension, Henry Tyson." *Pitt County Genealogical Quarterly*, 7:1 (February 2000), 3-7.

Kammerer, Roger. "Rev. War Pension: Thomas Jenkins." *Pitt County Genealogical Quarterly*, 7:2 (May 2000), 6-7.

Kammerer, Roger. "Rev. War Soldiers, Letters." *Pitt County Genealogical Quarterly*, 7:3 (August 2000), 1-3. [More records from the North Carolina Secretary of State's Office, "Correspondence of Revolutionary War Veterans and Pensioners."]

Kammerer, Roger. "Revolutionary War Papers [relating to Pitt County men]." *Pitt County Genealogical Quarterly*, 6:2 (May 1999), 1-3. [Includes some pensions Declaims recorded in the county court, "List of Deserters from Beaufort and Pitt Counties," and "Field Return of the Pitt Regiment Militia [1779];" 6:3 (August 1999), 1-4 [Includes petitions and enlistment records [1779]; 6:4 (November 1999), 1-4 [Includes similar records from state records]; 8:4 (November 2001), 1-7; 9:1 (February 2002), 1-3; 9:2 (May 2002), 1-5; 9:3 (August 2002), 1-5; 9:4 (November 2002), 1-3; 10:1 (February 2003), 1-5; 11:2 (May 2004), 1-4;

Kammerer, Roger. "Revolutionary War Pension: William Hardee." *Pitt County Genealogical Quarterly*, 2:1 (February 1995), 8-9.

Kammerer, Roger. "Thomas Jenkins, Rev. War Pension." *Pitt County Genealogical Quarterly*, 15:4 (November 2008), 1.

Kesler, Juanita Jackson. "Revolutionary War Pension for Mannering Brookshire, Lt. of Cavalry." *The Genealogical Journal by the Randolph County Genealogical Society*, 24:3 (Fall 2000), 51-54.

Kesler, Juanita. "Revolutionary Pension Declaration of Thomas Yeargan." *The Genealogical Journal by the Randolph County Genealogical Society*, 30:1 (Spring 2006), 53-54.

Ketchum, (Mrs.) Cecil R. "Revolutionary War Pensions: Dennis Hopkins." *The Genealogical Journal by the Randolph County Genealogical Society*, 16:1 (Winter 1992), 37-42.

Lands, Rosemary. "The Pension Application of James Jack." *Olde Mecklenburg Genealogical Society Quarterly*, 16:1 (1998), 4-12.

Lassiter, Becky N. "James Nickleston of Stokes County – Revolutionary War Pension Claim." *The Journal of the Genealogical Society of Rockingham and Stokes Counties, North Carolina*, 13:2 (September 2006), 1752-1756.

Lazenby, Mary Elinor. *Catawba Frontier, 1775-1781: Memories of Pensioners*. Washington, D. C.: M. E. Lazenby, 1950. [Nearly all of the pensioners were from North Carolina.]

Lind, Helen Y. "Revolutionary War Pension Application of Aaron Thomas." *Bulletin of the Genealogical Society of Old Tryon County*, 34:2 (May 2006), 78-83.

Lindsey, June Murtishaw. "James & Liddy Ross Revolutionary War Pension File." *The Carolinas Genealogical Society Bulletin*, 15:4 (Spring 2003-2004), 119-122.

Lindsey, June Murtishaw. "Revolutionary War Pension Application of Jacob Little." *The Carolinas Genealogical Society Bulletin*, 16:2 (Fall 2004-2005), 52-55.

Linn, Jo White, and B. R. McBride. "Delamar Revolutionary War Pension Abstracts." *The North Carolina Genealogical Society Journal,* 2:2 (April 1976), 108-116.

Linn, Jo White. "Genealogical Gleanings from Revolutionary War Pension Applications." *Rowan County Register*, 8:1 (February 1993), 1725-1730.

Linn, Jo White. "Some Genealogical Information on Some Burke Families from Revolutionary War Pension Records." *Journal of the Burke County Genealogical Society*, 8:3 (September 1990), 65-66.

"List of Revolutionary Pensioners Residing in Rowan County, N. C. in 1840." *Journal of the Genealogical Society of Rowan County, North Carolina*, 9:3 (September 1995), 93.

Lollis, Talforn C. "Revolutionary War Pension Application: James Dobbins." *Eswau Huppeday: Bulletin of the Broad River Genealogical Society,* 3:3 (August 1983), 66-69.

[Lossing, Benson J.] "Last Survivors of the Pensioned Soldiers of the Revolution." *American Historical Record and Repertory of Notes and Queries Concerning the History and Antiquities of America and Biography of Americans*, 2:23 (November 1873), 531-534. [There are entries for each man that the author identified that vary in length from a short paragraph to longer ones with considerable information about the individual. The North Carolinians included are:

Peter Bashaw, White's Creek, Davidson County, Tennessee. He enlisted at Hillsborough, North Carolina in 1780.

John Brooks, Robeson County, North Carolina, died in 1861, aged 103 years.

Elijah Denny, Rockcastle County, Kentucky; died April 24, 1863, aged 101; served from Wilkes County, N. C.

Moses Jones, Orange County, North Carolina, died in 1861, aged 99. He was from Granville County.

George Roberts, Buncombe County, North Carolina, died January 1, 1864, aged 106. He enlisted in Wilkes County.

Lu, Helen M.; Gwen B. Neumann, Margaret Ann S. Hudson, J[oel] Chan Edmondson, John V. Sobieski, and Deidre Burridge Dagner. Revolutionary War Period: Bible, Family & Marriage Records Gleaned from Pension Applications. Dallas, Tex.: H. M. Lu [vols. 1-9], 1980-1990; Dallas, Tex.; Plano, Tex.: [J. Chan Edmondson, vols. 10-20], 1990-2002; Charlottesville, Va., and Louisa, Va.: D. B. Dagner, 2004-2006. [cumulative index vols. 1-10 by Chan Edmondson. Dallas, Tex., 1990] [This set contains many North Carolina references.]

Lucas, John V. "Revolutionary War Pension, Giles Nelson." *Pitt County Genealogical Quarterly*, 8:1 (February 2001), 11-13.

Lucas Family. "Papers, 1813-1867 and n. d." Manuscript Sec. A Box 86, items 1-31, David M. Rubenstein Rare Book & Manuscript Library, Duke University, Durham. [Online catalog description: "Family residing in Raleigh, N. C. Correspondence, legal papers, and financial papers of the Lucas family of Raleigh, N. C. Early letters (1813-1816) were written by Alexander Lucas to his wife Mary while he visited Pennsylvania and Washington, D. C. Legal papers pertain to a lawsuit involving William Lucas, Henderson Lucas, and Margaret Lucas and concerning the estate and Revolutionary War military bounty of their grandfather, Thomas Lucas."]

Macon, Nathaniel, 1758-1837. "Papers, 1798-1854." Manuscript Sec. A Box 90 items 1-37, David M. Rubenstein Rare Book & Manuscript Library, Duke University, Durham. [Online catalog description: "Revolutionary War figure and member of the U. S. Congress; from Monroe (Warren Co.), N. C. Papers concerning the settlement of claims from the Revolution…"]

Manning, Nancy. "Isaac Bates' State Revolutionary War Pension." *A Lot of Bunkum*, 26:2 (May 2005), 38.

McBride, Ransom. "An Ex-Pensioner's Re-Application." *North Carolina Genealogical Society Journal*, 19:2 (May 1993), 121. [John Curry of Richmond Co., N. C.]

McBride, Ransom. "Invalid Pensioners, Widows and Orphans of the N. C. Continental Line about 1795." *North Carolina Genealogical Society Journal*, 13:4 (November 1987), 240.

McBride, Ransom. "Some Recommended Pensioners of Warren County, NC, 1799." *North Carolina Genealogical Society Journal*, 12:3 (August 1986), 160-167.

McCurdy Family. "McCurdy Family Papers, 1852-1889 and Undated." Manuscript Library Service Center Box 1, David M. Rubenstein Rare Book & Manuscript Library, Duke University, Durham. [Online catalog description:

"The McCurdy family was based in Concord (Cabarrus Co.), N. C. Archibald McCurdy (1752-1843) emigrated from Ireland, served in the Revolutionary War and in the War of 1812 and rose to the rank of Captain. In 1826, he married his third wife, Elizabeth 'Maggie' Goodman Greely (1791-1880) … [P]resent is a set of letters written by S. L. Jeffers and her husband, Frank, to her parents, but their relationship to the McCurdys is not clear. In addition, includes business letters directed to Jacob M. McCurdy regarding land pensions {!!} and purchases, accounts, taxes, although the majority deal with the transfer of Archibald McCurdy's Revolutionary War pension to Elizabeth. Other items include an 8-pg manuscript song book, probably for guitar; an undated handwritten program for an instrumental music performance; several sets of travel instruction for areas around Salem, N. C.; and an undated copy of *Milns's Geographical Running Hand* copybook."]

McDowell, William Wallis. "William Wallis McDowell Papers, 1772-1893." Manuscript 3160, Southern Historical Collection, Louis Round Wilson Special Collections Library, University of North Carolina, Chapel Hill; online finding aid available at http://www2.lib.unc.edu/mss/inv/m/McDowell,William_Wallis.html. [Online finding aid description: "William Wallis McDowell was a landowner, merchant, and banker of Asheville, N. C. The collection contains business and some personal and military papers of McDowell. Among the papers are … a ledger pertaining to Revolutionary War pensions in ten western North Carolina counties, 1851-1852…"]

McGee, Norman T. "Tennessee Pensioners of the Revolution: John McGee." *Tennessee Ancestors: A Tri-Annual Publication of the East Tennessee Historical Society*, 6:3 (December 1990), 251-259.

McGhee, Lucy Kate (Mrs. Carl). *Tennessee Revolutionary War Pensioners and Other Patriotic Records*. Washington, D. C.: L. K. McGhee, 1954.

McIntyre, Debby. "Pension Application Papers of William Falls." *Eswau Huppeday: Bulletin of the Broad River Genealogical Society*, 27:4 (November 2007), 192-195.

McIntyre, Debby. "The Revolutionary War Pension Application of Colonel Fredrick Hambright and Wife, Mary." *Eswau Huppeday: Bulletin of the Broad River Genealogical Society*, 30:1 (February 2010), 12-15.

McIntyre, Debby. "The Revolutionary War Widows Pension Application for Nancy Hughes, Wife of William Hughes." *Eswau Huppeday*, 29:3 (August 2009), 137-140.

"Mecklenburg Co., N. C. Revolutionary War Pensioners, 1841. *The Carolinas Genealogical Society Bulletin*, 11:1, 10.

"Military Records; N. C. State Revolutionary Pensions: Isaac Kennedy." *The Robeson County Register*, 11:1 (February 1996), ibc.

Miles, Millard. "Tennessee Pensioners of the Revolution: Richard Grantham." *Tennessee Ancestors: A Tri-Annual Publication of the East Tennessee Historical Society*, 5:3 (December 1989), 208-211.

Misenheimer, John E. "American Revolution Pensioners with Ties to Mecklenburg County." *Olde Mecklenburg Genealogical Society Quarterly*, 22:2 (2004), 27-36.

Moore, Terry. "Finding Your North Carolina Revolutionary War Soldier or Patriot, Part 3: Pensions." *NCGS News: The Newsletter of the North Carolina Genealogical Society*, 38:4 (July 2014), 10-11; online: http://www.ncgenealogy.org/articles_tools/Finding_Your_Rev_War_Soldier.pdf.

Morgan, Tom. "Revolutionary War Pensioners of Randolph County: Henry Morgan and James Morgan." *The Genealogical Journal by the Randolph County Genealogical Society*, 16:4 (Fall 1992), 35.

Morton, Mrs. Roy J. "Mrs. Roy J. Morton Collection, 1853." Manuscript, PC.1426, State Archives of North Carolina, Raleigh. [Online catalog description: "Photocopies of Stokes Co. depositions by William Moore and Revolutionary War pensioner James Nichelston concerning Revolutionary service of Capt. Joshua Cox, Surry Co. militia."]

Normandy, Dixie Mathey. "Revolutionary War Pension Application of William Matheny." *Eswau Huppeday: Bulletin of the Broad River Genealogical Society*, 5:1 (February 1985), 1-5.

"North Carolina: Names of the Revolutionary Pensioners Which Have Been Placed on the Roll of North Carolina, Under the Law of the 18th of March, 1818, from the Passage Thereof to This Day, Inclusive, with the Rank They Held, and the Lines in Which They Served, Viz." *The Carolina Genealogist*, no. 1 (Fall 1969): 1-5. [Virginia is among the states of service represented.]

"North Carolina Pension Roll, U. S. Dept. [of] War Report on Pensions, 1835." *A Lot of Bunkum*, 26:4 (November 2005), 20-22.

"North Carolina Revolutionary War Pensioners, 1841." *The Carolinas Genealogical Society Bulletin*, 11:1, 10. [Cabarrus and Mecklenburg Counties]

North Carolina Revolutionary War Pensioners under the Acts of 1818 and 1832 as Reported by Secretary of State to Congress in 1835. Signal Mountain, Tenn.: Mountain Press, 2008.

"North Carolina: Names of the Revolutionary Pensions Which Have Been Placed on the Roll of North Carolina under the Law of the 18th of March, 1818, from the Passage Thereof to This Day, Inclusive, with the Rank They

Held, and the Lines in Which They Served, viz: ..." *The Carolina Genealogist*, no. 1 (Fall 1969), 1-8. [The states of service represented are Georgia, Maryland, Massachusetts, North Carolina, Pennsylvania, South Carolina, and Virginia.]

North Carolina Daughters of the American Revolution. "Summary of Pension Record for Inlow, John." *North Carolina DAR Genealogical Records Committee Report, Series 1, Volume 376: Miscellaneous North Carolina Records* (typescript, 1972), 290; digital surrogate, DAR Library, Washington, D. C.

North Carolina Daughters of the American Revolution. "Summary of Pension Record for Larimore or Larrimore, James." *North Carolina DAR Genealogical Records Committee Report, Series 1, Volume 376: Miscellaneous North Carolina Records* (typescript, 1972), 289; digital surrogate, DAR Library, Washington, D. C.

North Carolina (State). General Assembly. "[Document dated:] Apr. 30, [1784]: Report on Memorial of Sarah Galloway (Memorial Only) (Rejected)." Manuscript; General Assembly Record Group; Session Records, April-June 1784; Joint Papers, Committee Papers, Resolutions, Senate Bills, House Bills, Box 1 (MARS ID: 66.8.31.8.5; item), State Archives of North Carolina, Raleigh. [Online catalog description: "Memorial of Sarah Galloway of Wayne County claims that her husband died in the service of the Continental Army and as she is not able to support her family, she requests an allowance. Includes a referral from the county court."]

North Carolina (State). General Assembly. Senate. "[Document dated:] January 3, 1792: Bill to Repeal an Act Entitled an Act to Amend an Act for the Relief of Persons that Have Been Disabled by Wounds or Rendered Incapable of Procuring a Subsistance [*sic*] for Themselves and for their Families in the Militia and to Provide for the Widows and Orphans of Such." Manuscript; General Assembly Record Group; Session Records, December 1791-January 1792; Joint Papers, Committee Papers, Resolutions, Senate Bills, House Bills, Senate Bills, Box 1 (MARS ID: 66.8.60.40; item), State Archives of North Carolina, Raleigh. [Online catalog description: "Bill repeals an act that amended a previous act. It states that persons disabled by wounds in the militia or their widows are entitled to relief."]

North Carolina (State). General Assembly. [Documents Dated]: 1796-1925: House and Senate Miscellaneous File." Manuscript GA AO Vol. 1 – GA AO Vol. 3; GA AO Vol. 12 – GA AO Vol. 56 (MARS ID: 66.29; series; General Assembly Record Group, State Archives of North Carolina, Raleigh. [The online catalog description shows that this collection contains: "...some other accounts to be paid, including payments to invalid Revolutionary War pensioners (1796-1798)..."]

North Carolina (State). Secretary of State. "Correspondence Concerning Revolutionary War Veterans and Pensioners, 1818-1859." Manuscript SS 25.1-SS 25.3 (MARS ID: 12.35; series), State Archives of North Carolina, Raleigh. [Online catalog description: "Correspondence concerning proof of service during the American Revolution, which was needed for federal pension applications or for claims for military bounty land."]

North Carolina (State). State Treasurer. "Military Papers – State Pensions and Widows, 1784-1826." Manuscript, State Treasurer Record Group, Boxes 25-30, Volume 69, (MARS ID: 13.28; series), State Archive of North Carolina, Raleigh. [Online catalog description: "Petitions of Revolutionary War veterans and their heirs; affidavits concerning service, infirmity, or kinship; powers of attorney; receipts, and certificates of payment, all concerning qualification for and payment of state pensions to disabled militia veterans and to widows and orphans of militia soldiers killed in service. The volume of state pension accounts (1802-1826) records payments made to invalid soldiers and indicates the pensioners assumed by the federal government in 1808."]

"North Carolina Miscellaneous Papers, 1772-1948." Manuscript, Manuscript 1135-z, Southern Historical Collection, Louis Round Wilson Special Collections Library, University of North Carolina, Chapel Hill; online finding aid available at http://www2.lib.unc.edu/mss/inv/n/North_Carolina_Miscellaneous_Papers.html. [Online finding aid description: "The collection contains miscellaneous financial and legal papers, including documents relating to the settlement of accounts, tax returns, estate inventories, bills of sale for the purchase and rental of slaves, court papers, and other items from many dates and locations in North Carolina. Individual units have been cataloged separately." Unit 1 contains "One bond, three notes, a Revolutionary pension claim, and three estate papers, 1772-1837..."]

"Oath that Adam Miller Served in the Revolutionary War." ID # 36378, Tennessee State Library & Archives, Nashville; digital surrogate available through the Revolutionary War Collection, Tennessee Virtual Archive at http://cdm15138.contentdm.oclc.org/cdm/singleitem/collection/p15138coll16/id/37/rec/56. [Description from TeVA: "Oaths of Moses Ferguson and Robert McCormick stating that Adam Miller served in the Revolutionary War, 1831."] [Miller served in North Carolina]

Padgett, Charles B. "Revolutionary War and Pension Records of William McCarter (McArthur) and Wife Isabella Carson McArthur." *Eswau Huppeday: Bulletin of the Broad River Genealogical Society,* 4:1 (February 1984), 11-21.

Patterson, Barbara Glenn Ellis. "The Revolutionary War Pension Records of Micajah Morris & Sarah Moore Morris." *Bulletin of the Genealogical Society of Old Tryon County*, 19:1 (February 1991), 18-20. [soldier from Virginia; pensioner from Rutherford County, North Carolina]

Pease, Janet. "Michael Leonard's Pension Application." *Rowan County Register*, 16:1 (February 2001), 3587-3590.

"Pension Application – John Richards." *Olde Mecklenburg Genealogical Society Quarterly*, 7:2 (Spring-Summer 1989), 52-54.

"Pension Application – William Chapman [Rowan County]." *Journal of the Genealogical Society of Rowan County, North Carolina*, 7:3 (March 1994), 27.

"Pension Application of Richard Cavett for Revolutionary War Service in Sullivan County, Tennessee." *East Tennessee Roots*, 8:2 (Winter1997), 114-115.

"Pension Application of Samuel Riggs, Revolutionary Soldier." *East Tennessee Roots*, 7:3 (Summer 1995), 124-127. [Resident of Hawkins County]

"Pension Application of Sarah Cole, Widow of Revolutionary Soldier Joseph Cole." *East Tennessee Roots*, 8:1 (Summer 1996), 40-41.

"Pension Lists, 1780-1784." Photostatic copies, Historical Society of Pennsylvania Library, Philadelphia. [ArchiveGrid Online description from "North Carolina Periodicals Index," East Carolina University: "Photostatic copies of lists, 1780-1784, of soldiers who served in Connecticut, Delaware, Georgia, Massachusetts, Maryland, North Carolina, New Hampshire, New Jersey, Pennsylvania, Rhode Island and Virginia and were awarded pensions for their military service during the American Revolution."]

"Petition of Col. James Miller." *Bulletin of the Genealogical Society of Old Tryon County*, 25:1 (February 1997), 32-34. [relating to his Revolutionary War service]

Philbeck, Miles S. "The Service of Wilhelm Ernst Felback in the Revolutionary War." *Bulletin of the Genealogical Society of Old Tryon County*, 26:4 (November 1998), 173-174.

Piecuch, James. *"Cool Deliberate Courage:" John Eager Howard in the American Revolution*. Charleston, S. C.: Nautical and Aviation Publishing Company of America, 2009. [Contents: Baltimore's Farewell to a Revolutionary War Hero; Campaigning in the North; Battling for South Carolina; Triumph at the Cowpens; The Race to the Dan; Guilford Courthouse; The Second Fight for Camden: Hobkirk's Hill; The Final Campaign; Politician and Businessman. John Eager Howard (1752-1827)]

Pittman, Betsy Dodd. "Revolutionary War Pension Claim, Burke County Court of Pleas and Quarter Sessions." *Journal of the Burke County Genealogical Society*, 14:4 (November 1996), 30. [Thomas Wallace, 1823]

Polk, James K. (James Knox), 1795-1849. "Papers, 1831-1846." Manuscript RUB Bay 3340 1-4, David M. Rubenstein Rare Book & Manuscript Library, Duke University, Durham. [Online catalog description: "Papers include a letter, 1846, from Cave Johnson about an affair involving a committee of claims, and correspondence, 1831-1832, concerning Revolutionary war claims."]

Poteet, Ellen. "Mecklenburg Pensioners in 1840 Census." *Olde Mecklenburg Genealogical Society Quarterly*, 22:4 (2004), 23-27.

Poteet, Ellen. "N. C. State Pensioners of the Revolution." *Olde Mecklenburg Genealogical Society Quarterly*, 24:2 (2006), 23-29.

Potts, Guy. "Revolutionary War Pension for Frederick Rigsby [Rigsbee], Wake County, North Carolina." *Wake Treasures*, 18:1 (Winter/Spring 2007), 10-13.

Powell, John W. "George Reed." *Clarendon Courier*, 7:4 (Winter 1995), 79-81. [Revolutionary War pension application of Reed who was originally from Onslow County, North Carolina, but moved to Warrick County, Indiana]

Price, Betty K. "The 1840 Mecklenburg County, North Carolina Census Contains the Following Pensioners of Revolutionary War or Military Service." *Olde Mecklenburg Genealogical Society Quarterly*, 5:1 (Spring-Summer 1987), 9.

"Rev. War Pension of Reuben Gurganus." *Pitt County Genealogical Quarterly*, 3:3 (August 1996), 19-20.

"Rev. War Pension of Willis Wilson." *Pitt County Genealogical Quarterly*, 3:4 (November 1996), 1-5.

Revel, Barbara Modlin. "Samuel Freeman's Revolutionary Service." *Washington County Genealogical Society Journal*, 4:3 (December 1996), 72.

"Revolutionary and Military Pensioners – List for Tennessee, June 1, 1840." *American Historical Magazine*, 3:2 (April 1898), 120-132.

"Revolutionary Pension Application for William Dalton." *Eswau Huppeday: Bulletin of the Broad River Genealogical Society,* 3:1 (February 1983), 10-12.

Revolutionary Pension Application of Richard Ledbetter. *Eswau Huppeday: Bulletin of the Broad River Genealogical Society,* 9:2 (May 1989), 81-88.

"Revolutionary Pension Application, James Owenby." *Eswau Huppeday: Bulletin of the Broad River Genealogical Society*, 19:2 (May 1999), 107-118.

"Revolutionary Soldiers and Patriots of North Carolina [in Pension Papers of Other Soldiers]." *The Carolinas Genealogical Society Bulletin*, 9:1 (Summer 1972), 8-10; 9:2 (Fall 1972), 29-30; 9:3 (Winter 1972), 45-46; 9:3 (Spring 1973), 71-74; 10:1 (Summer 1973), 5-8; 10:2 (Fall 1973), 29-30; 10:3 (Winter 1973), 47-48.

"Revolutionary War Pension Application for William Graham, Colonel." *Eswau Huppeday: Bulletin of the Broad River Genealogical Society,* 29:4 (November 2009), 195-198.

"Revolutionary War Pension Application of Edward Rippy." *Eswau Huppeday: Bulletin of the Broad River Genealogical Society,* 11:2 (May 1991), 77-84.

"Revolutionary War Pension Application of John Padgett – W2331." *Bulletin of the Genealogical Society of Old Tryon County*, 20:2 (May 1992), 71, 78-82.

"Revolutionary War Pension Application of John Presnell." *The Genealogical Journal by the Randolph County Genealogical Society*, 19:1 (Spring 1995), 35-36.

"Revolutionary War Pension Application of Joseph Dickson." *Eswau Huppeday: Bulletin of the Broad River Genealogical Society,* 11:3 (August 1991), 188-192.

"Revolutionary War Pension Application of Thomas Jones." *The Genealogical Journal by the Randolph County Genealogical Society*, 14:4 (Fall 1990), 20-21.

"Revolutionary War Pension Application: James Owenby." *Eswau Huppeday: Bulletin of the Broad River Genealogical Society,* 3:2 (May 1983), 33-37.

"Revolutionary War Pension Application: John Dickson." *Eswau Huppeday: Bulletin of the Broad River Genealogical Society,* 11:1 (February 1991), 39-45.

"Revolutionary War Pension Applications: [Rowan County Court of Pleas & Quarter Sessions, 1819-1820]." *Journal of the Genealogical Society of Rowan County, North Carolina*, 16:4 (December 2002), 163-166. [Stephen Baily, William Lomax, William Folk, Philipp Eagle, Robert Faucett, John Yeoman, John Lard, William Chapman, and William West.]; 17:2 (June 2003), 69-75. [Philip Agle, Michael Shaw, William Lomax, Jacob Rusher, and Cohart Walling.]

"Revolutionary War Pension File of James Parks, N. C. Treasurer and Comptroller's Papers, Military Papers, State Pensions." *Bulletin of the Genealogical Society of Old Tryon County*, 29:4 (November 2001), 175-176.

"Revolutionary War Pension File of James Patterson." *Bulletin of the Genealogical Society of Old Tryon County*, 8:2 (May 1980), 77-82.

"Revolutionary War Pension of John Green (S6914)." *Bulletin of the Genealogical Society of Old Tryon County*, 38:2 (May 2010), 52-56.

"Revolutionary War Records: [John Merrell, Rowan County]." *Journal of the Genealogical Society of Rowan County, North Carolina*, 3:4 (December 1999), 149-150.

"Revolutionary War Service for George Kiker. *The Carolinas Genealogical Society Bulletin*, 24:3 (Winter 1987-88), 47, 49.

"Revolutionary War Soldier Pension Application: John Ellison (Allison)." *Eswau Huppeday: Bulletin of the Broad River Genealogical Society,* 1:1 (February 1981), 15-18.

"Revolutionary War Soldier Pension Application: Simon Davis." *Eswau Huppeday: Bulletin of the Broad River Genealogical Society,* 1:2 (May 1981), 44-50.

"Revolutionary War Soldiers: Thomas Potts of Maryland and Anson County, N. C., Pension No. S-7326." *The Carolinas Genealogical Society Bulletin*.13:3 (Winter 1976), 55.

Richardson, Louise Goins. "Tennessee Pensioners of the Revolution: William Goings (W930)." *Tennessee Ancestors: A Tri-Annual Publication of the East Tennessee Historical Society*, 7:3 (December 1991), 301-302.

Rose, Christine. *Military Pension Laws, 1776-1858 from the Journals of the Continental Congress and the United States Statues-at-Large*. San Jose, Calif.: Rose Family Association, 2001.

"Roster of North Carolina Soldiers in the American Revolution: Rowan County." *Journal of the Genealogical Society of Rowan County, North Carolina*, 8:2 (June-July 1985), 77 [This is actually a listing from the pension rolls.]

"Samuel Martin Revolutionary War Pension Application, R15990." *The Genealogical Journal by the Randolph County Genealogical Society*, 18:2 (Fall 1994), 13-14.

Saupe, Pat. "William and Jesse Henson's Pension Applications." *The Genealogical Journal by the Randolph County Genealogical Society*, 27:1 (Spring 2003), 56-59.

Schmidt, Anita. "David Allen, Revolutionary War Pension Claim S16601." *Rabbit Tracks: Conejo Valley Genealogical Society, Inc.*, 27:1 (Spring 2009), 17-18. [Served from Surry County, North Carolina; pensioned while living in Franklin County, Alabama in 1832.]

Armstrong, Zella. *Some Tennessee Heroes of the Revolution, Compiled from Pension Statements.* 6 vols. Chattanooga: Lookout Publishing Company, 1934-1944; reprinted: Baltimore: Genealogical Publishing Company, 2009.

Southern Campaigns of the American Revolution, 1-7 (September 2004-2011), online: www.southerncampaign.org. [Contains many articles and news accounts of Revolutionary War events, personages, etc., and modern Revolutionary War activities, commemorations, seminars, etc., including: "Southern Campaign Revolutionary War Pension Statements & Rosters."]

Southern Campaigns of the American Revolution, 1-7 (September 2004-2011), online: www.southern campaign.org. [Contains many articles and news accounts of Revolutionary War events, personages, etc., and modern Revolutionary War activities, commemorations, seminars, etc., including: "Southern Campaign Revolutionary War Pension Statements & Rosters."]

Stokes, Gladys. "Revolutionary War Pension Application of James Patterson." *Eswau Huppeday: Bulletin of the Broad River Genealogical Society,* 8:2 (May 1988), 128-133.

Styles, Marshall L. *Benjamin Merrell: Pension File S8891, Randolph & Buncombe Counties, North Carolina* (Western North Carolina's Revolutionary War Patriot Soldiers: A Collection of their Records Series, vol. 10). [Simpsonville, S. C.: M. L. Styles], 2010. [Copy available at University of North Carolina at Chapel Hill.]

Styles, Marshall L. *Blake Piercy: Pension File R8243, Burke, Buncombe & Yancy Counties* (Western North Carolina's Revolutionary War Patriot Soldiers: A Collection of their Records Series, Vol. 14). [Simpsonville, S. C.: Marshall L. Styles], 2010. [Copy available at University of North Carolina at Chapel Hill.]

Styles, Marshall L. *Bradley Powers: Pension File R8410, Randolph & Buncombe Counties* (Western North Carolina's Revolutionary War Patriot Soldiers: A Collection of their Records Series, Vol. 17). [Simpsonville, S. C.: Marshall L. Styles], 2010. [Copy available at University of North Carolina at Chapel Hill.]

Styles, Marshall L. *Captain Herndon Haralson, a Revolutionary War Soldier from Caswell County, North Carolina.* Asheville, NC: Old Buncombe County Genealogical Society, 2010. [Copy available at University of North Carolina at Chapel Hill.]

Styles, Marshall L. *James Jennings: Pension File W7897, Surry, Buncombe & Madison Counties* (Western North Carolina's Revolutionary War Patriot Soldiers: A Collection of their Records Series, Vol. 7). [Simpsonville, S. C.: Marshall L. Styles], 2010. [Copy available at University of North Carolina at Chapel Hill.]

Styles, Marshall L. *Jesse Mills: Pension File W7448, Rutherford County, North Carolina* (Western North Carolina's Revolutionary War Patriot Soldiers: A Collection of their Records Series, Vol. 12). [Simpsonville, S. C.: Marshall L. Styles], 2010. [Copy available at University of North Carolina at Chapel Hill.]

Styles, Marshall L. *John Allen: Pension File S6481, Rutherford, Buncombe & Yancey Counties* (Western North Carolina's Revolutionary War Patriot Soldiers: A Collection of their Records Series, Vol. 1). [Simpsonville, S. C.: Marshall L. Styles], 2010. [Copy available at University of North Carolina at Chapel Hill.]

Styles, Marshall L. *John Lanning: Pension File S7314, Edgecombe & Burke Counties* (Western North Carolina's Revolutionary War Patriot Soldiers: A Collection of their Records Series, Vol. 8). [Simpsonville, S. C.: Marshall L. Styles], 2010. [Copy available at University of North Carolina at Chapel Hill.]

Styles, Marshall L. *John M. Massey: Pension File W4724, Granville, Bute & Haywood Counties, NC, Union County, SC* (Western North Carolina's Revolutionary War Patriot Soldiers: A Collection of their Records Series, Vol. 9). [Simpsonville, S. C.: Marshall L. Styles], 2010. [Copy available at University of North Carolina at Chapel Hill.]

Styles, Marshall L. *John Merrell: Pension File S7220, Randolph & Buncombe Counties* (Western North Carolina's Revolutionary War Patriot Soldiers: A Collection of their Records Series, Vol. 11). [Simpsonville, S. C.: Marshall L. Styles], 2010. [Copy available at University of North Carolina at Chapel Hill.]

Styles, Marshall L. *John Shope: Pension File R9530, Buncombe County* (Western North Carolina's Revolutionary War Patriot Soldiers: A Collection of their Records Series, Vol. 19). [Simpsonville, S. C.: Marshall L. Styles], 2010. [Copy available at University of North Carolina at Chapel Hill.]

Styles, Marshall L. *John Stiles: Pension File W4820, Lincoln, Buncombe, Haywood & Jackson Counties* (Western North Carolina's Revolutionary War Patriot Soldiers: A Collection of their Records Series, Vol. 20). [Simpsonville, S. C.: Marshall L. Styles], 2010. [Copy available at University of North Carolina at Chapel Hill.]

Styles, Marshall L. *Joseph Pitman, Jr.: Pension File S7314, Edgecombe & Burke Counties* (Western North Carolina's Revolutionary War Patriot Soldiers: A Collection of their Records Series, Vol. 15). [Simpsonville, S. C.: Marshall L. Styles], 2010. [Copy available at University of North Carolina at Chapel Hill.]

Styles, Marshall L. *Nathan Horton: Pension File W7779, Ashe, Wilkes & Watauga Counties* (Western North Carolina's Revolutionary War Patriot Soldiers: A Collection of their Records Series, Vol. 5). [Simpsonville, S. C.: Marshall L. Styles], 2010. [Copy available at University of North Carolina at Chapel Hill.]

Styles, Marshall L. *Phillip Brittain: Pension File S39243, Burke & Buncombe Counties, NC, & Bedford County, TN* (Western North Carolina's Revolutionary War Patriot Soldiers: A Collection of their Records Series, Vol. 2). [Simpsonville, S. C.: Marshall L. Styles], 2010. [Copy available at University of North Carolina at Chapel Hill.]

Styles, Marshall L. *Samuel Murray, Sr., Buncombe County: For Service with Colonel Francis "The Swamp Fox" Marion* (Western North Carolina's Revolutionary War Patriot Soldiers: A Collection of their Records Series, Vol. 13). [Simpsonville, S. C.: Marshall L. Styles], 2010. [Copy available at University of North Carolina at Chapel Hill.]

Styles, Marshall L. *Thomas Pitman: Pension File R8275, Edgecombe & Buncombe Counties* (Western North Carolina's Revolutionary War Patriot Soldiers: A Collection of their Records Series, Vol. 16). [Simpsonville, S. C.: Marshall L. Styles], 2010. [Copy available at University of North Carolina at Chapel Hill.]

Styles, Marshall L. *William Brittain: Pension File S8100, Burke & Buncombe Counties* (Western North Carolina's Revolutionary War Patriot Soldiers: A Collection of their Records Series, Vol. 3). [Simpsonville, S. C.: Marshall L. Styles], 2010. [Copy available at University of North Carolina at Chapel Hill.]

Styles, Marshall L. *William Gragg, Jr.: Pension File W7897, Surry, Buncombe & Madison Counties* (Western North Carolina's Revolutionary War Patriot Soldiers: A Collection of their Records Series, Vol. 4). [Simpsonville, S. C.: Marshall L. Styles], 2010. [Copy available at University of North Carolina at Chapel Hill.]

Styles, Marshall L. *William Lewis Queen: Pension File S9462, Burke, Rutherford, Macon, Haywood Counties* (Western North Carolina's Revolutionary War Patriot Soldiers: A Collection of their Records Series, Vol. 18). [Simpsonville, S. C.: Marshall L. Styles], 2010. [Copy available at University of North Carolina at Chapel Hill.]

Styles, Marshall L. *Zephaniah Horton: Pension File W3997, Wilkes, Buncombe & Yancey Counties* (Western North Carolina's Revolutionary War Patriot Soldiers: A Collection of their Records Series, Vol. 6). [Simpsonville, S. C.: Marshall L. Styles], 2010. [Copy available at University of North Carolina at Chapel Hill.]

Sullivan, (Mrs.) John T. "Revolutionary War Pension File of Benjamin Gunter: W19558." *Bulletin of the Genealogical Society of Old Tryon County*, 14:2 (May 1986), 79-80.

Sullivan, Thomas C. "Cover of Pension Application, Dooly County, Georgia." *The Robeson County Register*, 4:2 (May 1989), 77. [mentions William Hawthorn and George Willis, both formerly of Bladen County, N. C. during the Revolution.]

Surratt, Jo Ann Freeman. "One Who Served: The Revolutionary Pension Application of Thomas Dalton." *Eswau Huppeday: Bulletin of the Broad River Genealogical Society*, 25:3 (August 2005), 131-143.

Surratt, Jo Ann F. "Revolutionary War Pension Application of William C. Cuthbertson." *Eswau Huppeday: Bulletin of the Broad River Genealogical Society,* 12:2 (May 1992), 102-118.

Swann, Family. "Swann Family Papers, 1784-1983." Manuscript 2827, Southern Historical Collection, Louis Round Wilson Special Collections Library, University of North Carolina, Chapel Hill; online finding aid available at http://www2.lib.unc.edu/mss/inv/s/Swann_Family.html. [Online finding aid description: "Correspondence, Financial and Legal Papers, Writings, and Genealogical Materials of the Swann family of Wilmington and Pittsboro, N. C., and Fernandina, Fla. … Papers from 1853 to 1865 relate primarily to Ann Sophia Green Swann, including letters documenting her activities in Revolutionary War claims, a volume in which she recorded family history and childhood experiences, and a diary/commonplace book in which she wrote many melancholy entries, mainly having to do with the deaths of several of her children."]

Sweeny, William M[ontgomery], ed. *Captain Thomas Cook (1752-1841), a Soldier of the Revolution*. [New York?: s. n.], 1909.

Twe, Jerome. "Private Arthur Matthis of the North Carolina Militia: Trials of Securing a Pension." *Footnotes: Duplin County Historical Society*, issue 108 (October 2009), 8-13.

United States. Congress (3rd, 1st Session: 1792-1793). House. *The Committee to Whom Were Referred Sundry Petitions of Persons, Stating, That They Have Been Rendered Invalids in the Service of the United States during the Late War, and Praying to Be Placed on the Pension List – and Also a Letter from the Judges of the Circuit Court for the District of North-Carolina, Relative to the Act Passed the Last Session of Congress, Regulating Claims to Invalid Pensions…Report*. Philadelphia: [s. n.], 1793; micropublished: (Early American Imprints. First Series. No. 46902) New York: Readex Microprint, 1985.

United States. Congress. "[Congressional Reports Relating to North Carolinians in the American Revolution]." Manuscript C970.314 U58c, North Carolina Collection, Louis Round Wilson Library Special Collections, University of North Carolina, Chapel Hill. [Online catalog description: "Reports deal with claims made to the Committee on Revolutionary Pensions."]

United States. Congress. House. Committee on Pensions. *Hannah Dowd Vanderford: Mr. Loudenslager, from the Committee on Pensions, Submitted the Following Report (to accompany H.R. 8689)*. [Washington: G. P. O., 1896]. [Online catalog description: "Hannah Dowd Vanderford, daughter of Connor Dowd of Captain Patrick's

Company, North Carolina Volunteers, American Revolution, requests a pension. Report on pension request of George Hughes printed on verso."]

United States. Congress. House. Committee on Revolutionary Claims. *Daniel Williams – Representatives of: To Accompany Bill H. R. no. 686: Mr. Underwood, from the Committee on Revolutionary Claims, Made the Following Report.* [Washington: s. n., 1838]. [Online catalog description: "Executor of Daniel Williams requests military pension owed to Williams, a captain in the continental army of the Revolution, North Carolina line.]

United States. Congress. House. Committee on Revolutionary Pensions. *A Bill for the Relief of Peter Hendrick, of the State of North Carolina.* [Washington: s. n., 1839].

United States. Congress. House. Committee on Revolutionary Pensions. *Heirs, &c. of William Lomax: To Accompany Bill H. R. no. 608: Mr. Taliaferro, from the Committee on Revolutionary Pensions, Submitted the Following Report.* [Washington: s. n., 1842]. [Online catalog description: "The heirs of William Lomax of North Carolina request a military pension."]

United States. Congress. House. Committee on Revolutionary Pensions. *Mary Rand: To Accompany Bill H. R. no. 269: Mr. Fornance, from the Committee on Revolutionary Pensions, Submitted the Following Report.* [Washington: s. n., 1842]. [Online catalog description: "Mary Rand of North Carolina, widow of Walter Rand, requests a widow's pension."]

United States. Congress. House. Committee on Revolutionary Pensions. *William Harper: To Accompany Bill H. R. no. 136: Mr. Taliaferro, from the Committee on Revolutionary Pensions, Made the Following Report.* [Washington: s. n., 1842]. [Online catalog description: "William Harper, formerly of North Carolina, requests a pension for his service in the Revolutionary War."]

United States. Congress. House. Committee on Revolutionary Pensions. *William Harper: To Accompany Bill H. R. no. 435: Mr. Taliaferro, from the Committee on Revolutionary Pensions, Made the Following Report.* [Washington: s. n., 1842]. [Online catalog description: "William Harper, formerly of North Carolina, requests a pension for his service in the Revolutionary War."]

United States. Congress. House. Committee on Revolutionary Pensions. *William Harper: To Accompany Bill H. R. no. 893: Mr. Taliaferro, from the Committee on Revolutionary Pensions, Made the Following Report.* [Washington: s. n., 1842]. [Online catalog description: "William Harper, formerly of North Carolina, requests a pension for his service in the Revolutionary War."]

Vopelak, Mark, and Elizabeth E. Ross. "Revolutionary War Pension Records at the North Carolina State Archives." *North Carolina Genealogical Society Journal*, 27:3 (August 2001), 295-300. [Includes "Alphabetical Index to North Carolina Revolutionary War Pensioners."]

Warmack, Joann. "Pension File of Anthony Dickey." *Bulletin of the Genealogical Society of Old Tryon County*, 18:1 (February 1990), 8-22; 18:2 (May 1990), 52-58.

Warren, Mary Bondurant. "State of North Carolina's Pensions Paid to Invalid Veterans of the Revolutionary War, Their Widows or Heirs." *The Carolina Genealogist*, no. 25 (Winter 1976), Military Records/N. C. State Revolutionary Pensions, 1-8; no. 26 (Spring 1976), Military Records/N. C. State Revolutionary Pensions, 11-18; no. 27 (Summer 1976), Military Records/N. C. State Revolutionary Pensions, 19-22; no. 28 (Fall 1976), Military Records/N. C. State Revolutionary Pensions, 23-26; no. 29 (Winter 1977), Military Records/N. C. State Revolutionary Pensions, 27-36; no. 30 (Spring 1977), Military Records/N. C. State Revolutionary Pensions, 37-42; no. 31 (Summer 1977), Military Records/N. C. State Revolutionary Pensions, 43-44; no. 32 (Fall 1977), Military Records/N. C. State Revolutionary Pensions, 45-46; no. 33 (Winter 1978-1979), Military Records/N. C. State Revolutionary Pensions, 47-48; no. 34 (Spring 1978-1979), Military Records/N. C. State Revolutionary Pensions, 49-50; no. 35 (Summer 1978-1979), Military Records/N. C. State Revolutionary Pensions, 51-52; no. 36 (Fall 1978-1979), Military Records/N. C. State Revolutionary Pensions, 53-62; no. 37 (Winter 1980), Military Records/N. C. State Revolutionary Pensions, 63-64; no. 40 (Fall 1980), Military Records/N. C. State Revolutionary Pensions, 65-70.

White, Cotton. "Papers, n. d." Manuscript accession no. 37625, Library of Virginia, Richmond. [Online catalog description: "Papers of Cotton White containing research material on two Revolutionary War Virginia infantry soldiers: Henry Lynch (1764-1849) of Cumberland County, Virginia, and Missouri; and Elijah Lynch (1765-1839) of Culpeper County, Virginia, and North Carolina. Material consists of wills, pension claims statements, Revolutionary War muster rolls, and correspondence in reference to Henry and Elijah Lynch."]

"William Gudger, War Pension Claim, W15772." *A Lot of Bunkum*, 26:4 (November 2005), 19.

Located and Marked Graves of Revolutionary War Veterans in North Carolina and Tennessee

Various publications list the burial locations of many Revolutionary War veterans from North Carolina. Use these with caution because many do not provide supporting documentation to show that the graves are indeed those of a specific veteran as opposed to someone with the same name. Such compilations cannot be used as sources of proof from Revolutionary War service in applications to the National Society Daughters of the American Revolution.

Many of these graves have been marked by DAR Chapters over the years, but frequently there is no supporting information to verify the marking. The NSDAR's Office of the Historian General (NSDAR Headquarters, 1776 D. Street, N. W., Washington, DC 20006-5303; 202-879-3257) maintains records of some grave markings and locations. The staff of this office will attempt to assist researchers, but because many early markings and locations were done by local chapters there is often no proof available at NSDAR national headquarters.

The following indexes are available in the Office of the Historian General:

Index of Reported Located Graves of Revolutionary War Soldiers and Patriots

This index is a finding aid to the located graves, which have been reported by DAR members and others since the late 1890s. It provides access to those listings published in the Reports to the Secretary of the Smithsonian from 1898 to 1974 (see below), as well as to others that have been listed since then. A few cards include photographs of the tombstones. Listings of located graves which appeared in the *Smithsonian Reports* were also collected, indexed, and published in a four volume, privately printed, non–DAR sponsored work by Patricia Law Hatcher, *Abstract of Graves of Revolutionary Patriots*. 4 vols. Dallas, Texas: Pioneer Heritage Press, 1987–1988. The DAR published lists in pamphlet form in the mid to late 1970s noting additional reported located graves. This pamphlet is entitled *Located Graves of Soldiers and Patriots of the American Revolution, March 1, 1974—March 1, 1976*. Some further lists appeared in *The DAR Magazine* in the years immediately after 1978. There have been no subsequent publications other than those in the magazine. This index has been digitized enabling the employees in the Office of the Historian General quicker access to the information it contains.

Index of Reported Marked Graves of Revolutionary War Soldiers and Patriots

The DAR Magazine provides researchers with frequent references to grave marking ceremonies by DAR chapters. No comprehensive index to these activities exists; however, any information concerning the date of placement and dedication of a marker may provide clues about when an article may have appeared in *The DAR Magazine* describing the event. Some of these entries include photographs of the ceremony. Since the late 1980s the Office of the Historian General has maintained files containing proof of these locations and markings. This index has been digitized enabling the employees in the Office of the Historian General quicker access to the information it contains.

Index of Reported Marked Graves of Wives and Daughters of Revolutionary War Patriots and Soldiers

Index of Reported Marked Graves of Signers of the Declaration of Independence

Index of Reported Marked Graves of DAR Members

These multi–drawer card indexes gives useful information relating to marked graves of deceased DAR members prior to the 1990s. They are not comprehensive since not all markings have been reported. Currently, all reports received of the placement of DAR insignia markers are entered into iMIS, an internal database at DAR headquarters. This index has been digitized enabling the employees in the Office of the Historian General quicker access to the information it contains.

Index of Reported Marked Graves of Real Daughters

This index notes the graves of DAR members who were actually daughters of Revolutionary War participants. See section 7.4 for more information. This index has been digitized enabling the employees in the Office of the Historian General quicker access to the information it contains.

Index of Reported Historical Markers Placed by DAR Chapters (arranged by state)

Many native North Carolinians as well as men who moved to North Carolina after the Revolution appear in these volumes.

Bates, Lucy Womack. *Roster of Soldiers and Patriots of the American Revolution Buried in Tennessee*. Johnson City: Tennessee Society Daughters of the American Revolution, 1974.

Blair, Anna. "Revolutionary War Soldiers Buried in North Carolina." In Daughters of the American Revolution. *Historical Collections of the Georgia Chapters of the Daughters of the American Revolution, Volume 1: Seventeen Georgia Counties.* (Atlanta: Charles P. Byrd, 1926; 2 vols. in 1; reprinted with an index by Lelia Thornton Gentry. Baltimore: Clearfield Company, 1995), 352-364.

Bonner, R. T. "Revolutionary Grave Marked." *Pamtico Tracings*, 13:1 (June 1997), 10. [grave of Joseph Guilford].

"DAR Seeking Location of Graves of Revolutionary War Soldiers." *Bulletin of the Genealogical Society of Old Tryon County, North Carolina*, 3:2 (May 1975), 93-96. [Cleveland County, Lincoln County and McDowell County, North Carolina; York County, South Carolina.]

"Department of Veterans Affairs Provides Marker for Revolutionary War Soldier." *Olde Mecklenburg Genealogical Society Quarterly*, 25:1 (2007), 30-31. [John Bearden]

Gentry, Susie. "Graves of Revolutionary Soldiers in Tennessee." *American Monthly Magazine* [DAR], 35:6 (December 1909), 1188-1191. [burials in Bedford, Davidson, Franklin, Jefferson, Lincoln, Madison, Maury, Robertson, Rutherford, Smith, Weakley, and Williamson Counties]

Kivett, William D. "My Patriot: Peter Kivett, a Common Patriot." *Palmetto Patriot: South Carolina Society Sons of the American Revolution,* 2009:1 (Spring 2009), 3. [McMaster's Cemetery, "about 30 miles south of Greensboro, North Carolina."]

Kobrin, Lisa. "Local Revolutionary War Soldiers' Graves." *Alamance Genealogist,* 30:3 (September 2013), 136-137.

North Carolina Daughters of the American Revolution. "Graves of Revolutionary Soldiers." *North Carolina DAR Genealogical Records Committee Report, Series 1, Volume 128: [Records] [bk.4]* (typescript, 1948), 6-7); digital surrogate, DAR Library, Washington, D. C.

North Carolina Daughters of the American Revolution. *Roster of Revolutionary War Gravesites of Soldiers, Patriots, and Ancestors Buried in North Carolina.* New Bern: The Society, 2007; and: *Index -- Roster of Revolutionary War Gravesites of Soldiers, Patriots, and Ancestors Buried in North Carolina.* [New Bern: The Society, 2008. [Copy available at the DAR Library, Washington, D. C.]

"Revolutionary Records: Revolutionary Soldiers in Tennessee." *American Monthly Magazine* [DAR], 19:1 (July 1901), 29.

"Revolutionary Records: Revolutionary Soldiers' Graves in Tennessee Soil." *American Monthly Magazine* [DAR], 24:2 (February 1904), 109; 24:3 (March 1904), 210; 24:4 (April 1904), 306; 24:5 (May 1904), 414; 24:6 (June 1904), 514-515.

"Revolutionary War Veterans Buried in Western North Carolina." *A Lot of Bunkum*, 25:1 (February 2004), 7-12; 25:2 (May 2004), 15-18; plus: "RW Veterans: Corrections & Additions," 25:4 (November 2004), 22.

"Revolutionary War Marker Dedicated 22 March 2009 in Davie County." *NCGS News: Newsletter of the North Carolina Genealogical Society*, 33:3 (Summer 2009), 10. [marker on the grave of Richmond Pearson (1751-1819) near Cooleemee]

Reynolds, Elizabeth Parker for the Yadkin River Patriot's Chapter, North Carolina Daughters of the American Revolution. "Revolutionary Soldiers' Graves Located." *North Carolina DAR Genealogical Records Committee Report, Series 1, Volume 7: Historian's Report for Yadkin River Patriot's Chapter, Vol. 2* (typescript, 1927), 90-92); digital surrogate, DAR Library, Washington, D. C.

"Scrapbook on Revolutionary War Soldiers' Graves in Tennessee, 1924-1936." Manuscript Files Collection, M-18, Scrapbook, ac. no. 67-096, Tennessee State Library and Archives, Nashville. [Online catalog description: "Scrapbook of clippings, letters, and notes, arranged alphabetically by soldier's name. Probably prepared by Mrs. John Trotwood Moore, former Tennessee State Librarian and D.A.R. member. Many of the clippings relate to D.A.R. efforts to place markers on soldiers' graves."]

"Steel Creek Grave-Yard, North Carolina." *Daughters of the American Revolution Magazine*, 44:4 (April 1914), 239. [Steel Creek Presbyterian Church, Mecklenburg County, N. C. Contains the grave of Captain Henry Neel of the 1st North Carolina Regiment.]

Tennessee Daughters of the American Revolution. "Tennessee – Revolutionary Soldiers' Graves." *Tennessee DAR Genealogical Records Committee Report, Series 1, Volume 2: Miscellaneous Records* (typescript, 1929), 19-22; digital surrogate, DAR Library, Washington, D. C.

Thompson, Doris Lancaster; sketches by Morgan Harris. *Revolutionary War Gravesites of Soldiers, Patriots, and Ancestors Buried in North Carolina.* [Oxford]: John Penn Chapter, North Carolina Society Daughters of the American Revolution, 2007; and *Index – Roster of Revolutionary Gravesites of Soldiers, Patriots, and Ancestors Buried in North Carolina.* [North Carolina: North Carolina Society Daughters of the American Revolution, 2008?]

Grave Markings and Related Compilations for the Migration States from North Carolina

[Note: *These publications should only be used as guides because many of the burials are not accurately documented. The DAR does not accept listings in these publications as proof of Revolutionary War service or lineage despite the publication of some of them by DAR state societies or members.*]

Alabama

Owen, Thomas McAdory, for the Alabama Department of Archives and History. *Revolutionary Soldiers in Alabama, Being a List of Names, Compiled from Authentic Sources, of Soldiers of the American Revolution, Who Resided in the State of Alabama.* Montgomery: The Brown Printing Company, Printers, 1911; reprinted: Baltimore: Genealogical Publishing Company, 1967.

Illinois

Davis, James E. *Frontier Illinois*. Bloomington: Indiana University Press, 1998.

Devanny, [Mildred E. Smith] (Mrs. John S.). *Soldiers of the American Revolution Buried in Illinois*. Springfield: Illinois State Genealogical Society, 1976.

Meyer, Harold I. (Mrs.). *Roster of the Revolutionary War Soldiers and Widows Who Lived in Illinois Counties*. Chicago: Illinois Daughters of the American Revolution, 1962.

Walker, E. S. "Revolutionary Heroes Honored in Madison County." *Journal of the Illinois State Historical Society (1908-1984),* 5:3 (October 1912), 372-381. [Includes: George Bridges (1762-after 1832); John Carnelison (ca. 1758-1840); John Long (1732-1839); Henry Revis (1752-after 1832; from Northampton County); Francis Roach (1739-1845; born Virginia; served from North Carolina); and, Laban Smart (1759-after 1832).]

Walker, E. S. "Revolutionary Heroes Honored in Madison County." *Journal of the Illinois State Historical Society*, 5:3 (October 1912), 372-381.

Walker, E. S., Mrs. "Revolutionary Heroes Honored." *Journal of the Illinois State Historical Society*, 5:1 (April 1912), 106-115. [Sangamon County, Illinois. Includes the following men from North Carolina: George Bryan (1758-1845); Michael Crawford (1759-1835; born in New Jersey; served from North Carolina); William Penny (1751-?).]

Walker, Edwin S. "Revolutionary Soldiers Buried in Clark County, Ill." *Journal of the Illinois State Historical Society*, 6:2 (July 1913), 232-234. [Including Peter Dozier (1762-1838) and Samuel McClure (1748-1845) from Virginia.]

Walker, Edwin S. "Soldiers of the American Revolution Buried in Illinois." *Journal of the Illinois State Historical Society (1908-1984)*, 7:1 (April 1914), 92-98; 8:3 (October 1915), 440-447; 9:2 (July 1916), 172-176.

Walker, Harriet J. (Mrs. E. S.) "Revolutionary Soldiers Buried in Illinois." *Journal of the Illinois State Historical Society*, 6:1 (April 1913), 112-118; 6:3 (October 1913), 445-451; 7:1 (April 1914), 92-98; 7:2 (July 1914), 70-73; 7:3 (October 1914), 195-199; 7:4 (January 1915), 402-407; 8:1 (April 1915), 46-54; 8:2 (July 1915), 288-299; 8:3 (October 1915), 440-447; 9:1 (April 1916), 43-45; 9:2 (July 1915), 172-176; 19:1-2 (April-July 1926), 49-62; consolidated and republished: Los Angles: The Standard Printing Company, 1917; reprinted: Baltimore: Genealogical Publishing Company, 1967.

Walker, Harriet J. "Some Revolutionary War Soldiers Buried in Illinois [from North Carolina]." *The Carolinas Genealogical Society Bulletin*, 26:1 (Summer 1999-2000), 9.

Indiana

Cayton, Andrew Robert Lee. *Frontier Indiana*. Bloomington: Indiana University Press, 1996.

"Graves of Revolutionary Soldiers." *Indiana Magazine of History*, 8:1 (January 1912), 15-21.

Morris, Louise Elizabeth B. *Indiana: Revolutionary Soldiers Buried in Indiana.* Typescript, 1925. [copy in the DAR Library, Washington, D. C.]

O'Bryne, Estalle Armstrong (Mrs. Roscoe C.) "Roster of Revolutionary Soldiers Buried in Indiana." Ragan, W. H. "Revolutionary Soldiers in Putnam County." *Indiana Magazine of History*, 33:4 (December 1937), 524-526.

O'Byrne, Estalla Armstrong, for the Indiana Daughters of the American Revolution. *Roster of Soldiers and Patriots of the American Revolution Buried in Indiana.* Brookville, Ind.: [Indiana DAR], 1938; reprinted: Baltimore: Genealogical Publishing Company, 1968.
Ticusan, Sarah G. H. *An Index to Roster of Soldiers and Patriots of the American Revolution Buried in Indiana, Published by the Indiana Daughters of the American Revolution, 1938.* Indianapolis: Indiana State Library, 1974.
Waters, Margaret R. *Revolutionary Soldiers Buried in Indiana: 300 Names Not Listed in the "Roster of Soldiers and Patriots of the American Revolution Buried in Indiana."* Indianapolis: M. R. Waters, 1949; reprinted: Baltimore: Genealogical Publishing Company, 1970.
Waters, Margaret R. *Revolutionary Soldiers Buried in Indiana: A Supplement; 485 Names Not Listed in the "Roster of Soldiers and Patriots of the American Revolution Buried in Indiana" (1939); nor in "Revolutionary Soldiers Buried in Indiana" (1949).* Indianapolis: M. R. Waters, 1954; reprinted: Baltimore: Genealogical Publishing Company, 1970.
Wolfe, Barbara Ellen Schull. *Index to Revolutionary Soldiers of Indiana and Other Patriots.* Indianapolis: Ye Olde Genealogie Shoppe, 1977.

Ohio

Curry, W. L. *Register of the Ohio Society of the Sons of the American Revolution, 1912-13. Roster of Revolutionary Soldiers Residing in Ohio in 1840; Names and Location of Burial of Eight Hundred Revolutionary Soldiers in Ohio.* Columbus, Ohio: [s. p.], 1913.
Ohio. Adjutant General's Department. *Official Roster of the Soldiers of the American Revolution Buried in the State of Ohio.* 3 vols. Columbus: F. J. Herr Printing Co., 1929; [S. l.]: State Society Daughters of the American Revolution of Ohio, 1938; [S. l.]: State Society Daughters of the American Revolution of Ohio, 1959.
Slager, A. L. "Revolutionary War Soldiers Buried in Clark County, Ohio." *Ohio Archaeological and Historical Quarterly*, 37:1 (January 1938), 86-100.

Contemporary Newspaper Sources for North Carolina Research during and after the Revolution

Andrlik, Todd. *Reporting the Revolutionary War: Before It Was History, It Was News.* Naperville, Ill.: Sourcebooks, 2012.
Broughton, Carrie L. *Marriage and Death Notices from Raleigh Register and North Carolina State Gazette, 1799-1825.* Baltimore, Md.: Genealogical Publishing Co., 1975.
Broughton, Carrie L. *Marriage and Death Notices from Raleigh Register and North Carolina State Gazette, 1826-1845.* Baltimore, Md.: Genealogical Publishing Co., 1968.
Broughton, Carrie L. *Marriage and Death Notices from Raleigh Register and North Carolina State Gazette, 1846-1867.* Baltimore, Md.: Genealogical Publishing Co., 1975.
Broughton, Carrie L. "Marriage Notices from the *Raleigh Register and North Carolina State Gazette.*" *Daughters of the American Revolution Magazine*, 84:10 (October 1950), 832-835, 840; 84:11 (November 1950), 889-893.
Broughton, Carrie L, and North Carolina State Library. *Marriage and Death Notices in Raleigh Register, North Carolina State Gazette, Daily Sentinel, Raleigh Observer and News and Observer, 1867-1887.* Raleigh : State Library, 1951.
Broughton, Carrie L. and North Carolina State Library. *Marriage and Death Notices from Raleigh, N. C. Newspapers, 1796-1826.* Easley, S.C.: Southern Historical Press, 1977.
Corbitt, D. L. "Historical Notes: *The North Carolina Gazette.*" *North Carolina Historical Review*, 2:1 (January 1925), 83-89; online: http://digital.ncdcr.gov/cdm/ref/collection/p16062coll9/id/4207. [Online description from "North Carolina Periodicals Index," East Carolina University: "The North Carolina Gazette was the first newspaper published in North Carolina. The oldest found edition was published on November 15, 1751 by James Davis and was number 15. The paper was printed in New Bern, and included information on a range of topics including period laws for tavern and ordinary keepers."]
Dickerson, O. M. "British Control of American Newspapers on the Eve of the Revolution." *New England Quarterly*, 24:4 (December 1951), 453-468.
Elliott, Robert N., Jr. "James Davis and the Beginning of the Newspaper in North Carolina." *North Carolina Historical Review*, 42:1 (January 1965), 1-20; online: http://digital.ncdcr.gov/cdm/ref/collection/p16062coll9/id/4207. [Online description from "North Carolina Periodicals Index," East Carolina University: "This article examines the beginnings of newspapers in the American colonies starting with papers in Boston in the late 17th

century and continuing to the Baltimore province in Maryland, to Charleston, and then to Williamsburg in Virginia. The latter became the first newspaper to be read in North Carolina due to the two colonies' commercial and cultural ties. Further information on the spread of printing to North Carolina and the development of papers there as well as information on period printing and printing offices are included."]

Fouts, Raymond Parker. *Abstracts from Newspapers of Edenton, Fayetteville, & Hillsboro, North Carolina, 1785-1800*. Cocoa, Fla.: GenRec Books, 1984.

Fouts, Raymond Parker. *Abstracts from Newspapers of Wilmington, North Carolina*. 5 vols. Cocoa, Fla.: GenRec Books, 1984-1987.

Fouts, Raymond Parker. *Abstracts from the North Carolina Gazette of New Bern, North Carolina*. 2 vols. Cocoa, Fla.: GenRec Books, 1983.

Harrell-Sesniak, Mary. *500+ Revolutionary War Obituaries and Death Notices*. Houston, Tex.: M. Harrell-Sesniak, 2010.

Johnston, Hugh Buckner. *Deaths and Marriages from Tarboro, North Carolina Newspapers, 1824-1865*. Easley, S. C.: Southern Historical Press, 1985.

Jones, H. G., and Julius H. Avant. *Union List of North Carolina Newspapers, 1751-1900*. Raleigh: State Dept. of Archives and History, 1963.

Kellam, Ida Brooks. *Marriage and Death Notices in Newspapers Published in Wilmington, North Carolina, 1797-1842; Marriage Contracts of New Hanover County Citizens, 1728-1855*. Wilmington: I. B. Kellam, 1959.

Navey, William R. "Death Notices from *The Charlotte Journal* [1835-1851]. *The Carolinas Genealogical Society Bulletin*, 6:1 (July-September 1969); 7:4 (Spring 1971), 65-68; 8:1 (Summer 1971), 15-16; 8:2 (Fall 1971), 35-38; 8:3 (Winter 1971), 50-51; 8:4 (Spring 1972), 68-69 [information printed in reverse order]; 9:1 (Summer 1972) 11-12; 9:2 (Fall 1972), 25-26; 9:3 (Winter 1972), 47, 50 [printing error]; 9:3 (Winter 1972), 75-76. [Contains obituaries for many Revolutionary War veterans scattered throughout the abstracts. Not all of these men were from the Carolinas.]

Neal, Lois Smathers. *Abstracts of Vital Records from Raleigh, North Carolina, Newspapers, 1799-1839*. 4 vols. in 3. Raleigh: North Carolina Genealogical Society, 1979-1995.

"Obituaries of Revolutionary War Patriots." *A Lot of Bunkum*, 30:4 (November 2009), 7-8.

Topkins, Robert M. *Marriage and Death Notices from the Western Carolinian (Salisbury, North Carolina), 1820-1842: An Indexed Abstract*. Spartanburg, S. C.: The Reprint Company, 1983.

Topkins, Robert M. "Private Records: Newspapers." In Helen F. M. Leary, ed. *North Carolina Research: Genealogy and Local History*. 2nd ed. (Raleigh: North Carolina Genealogical Society, 1996), Chapter 40, 520-533.

Wallace, Wesley H. "Cultural and Social Advertising in Early North Carolina Newspapers." *North Carolina Historical Review*, 33:3 (July 1956), 281-309. [1751-1778; mostly about *The North Carolina Gazette*, New Bern]

Wallace, Wesley H. "Property and Trade: Main Themes of Early North Carolina Newspaper Advertisements." *North Carolina Historical Review*, 32:4 (October 1955), 451-482. [1751-1778; mostly about *The North Carolina Gazette*, New Bern]

Warren, Mary Bondurant. "Marriage, Death and Individual Notices from North Carolina Newspapers before 1792 (Library of Congress [holdings])." *The Carolina Genealogist*, no. 8 (Fall 1971), State Records/Newspapers North Carolina, 1-10; no. 9 (Winter 1972), 11-20; no. 31 (Summer 1997), State Records/Newspapers North Carolina, 21-30; no. 32 (Fall 1977), State Records/Newspapers North Carolina, 31-34; no. 33 (Winter 1978-1979), State Records/Newspapers North Carolina, 35-36; no. 34 (Spring 1978-1979), State Records/ Newspapers North Carolina, 37-40; no. 35 (Summer 1978-1979), State Records/Newspapers North Carolina, 41-44; no. 36 (Fall 1978-1979), State Records/Newspapers North Carolina, 45-49; no. 37 (Winter 1980), State Records/ Newspapers North Carolina, 51-56; no. 42 (Spring 1981), State Records/ Newspapers North Carolina, 57-64; no. 41 (Fall 1981), State Records/ Newspapers North Carolina, 65-72; no. 45 (Winter 1982), State Records/ Newspapers North Carolina, 73-80; no. 46 (Spring 1982), State Records/Newspapers North Carolina, 81-90; no. 47 (Summer 1982), State Records/ Newspapers North Carolina, 91-94; no. 48 (Fall 1982), State Records/ Newspapers North Carolina, 95-96. [This series begins in the late colonial period and continues to 1778. *The Carolina Genealogist* ceased publication with no. 52 and the remainder of this serialized article was never published.]

Chapter Fifteen:
Regions, Counties, Towns, Districts, and Localities in North Carolina and Tennessee during the American Revolution

Every county, town, and village history for localities in North Carolina has some material on the history of those places during the American Revolution. Time and space do not allow for listings of all of these publications in this source guide. Searches in the online catalogs of such research centers the State Archives of North Carolina, the State Library of North Carolina, the libraries of the University of North Carolina at Chapel Hill, the Tennessee State Library and Archives, the East Tennessee Historical Society, and the DAR Library and the Library of Congress, both in Washington, D. C., will reveal these histories and studies. This section will be mostly comprised of very specific studies and publications relating to the subdivisions of North Carolina during the period of the American Revolution.

Note that the Revolutionary War lists of soldiers that often appear in local histories in North Carolina are rarely cited giving the location of the original document when the book was published. Because many of these studies were done in the late nineteenth and early twentieth centuries, modern researchers may have a difficult time locating such records in the early twenty-first century. Many Revolutionary War materials come from town and county records, but others were in private hands decades ago. Researchers should seek out the originals in the local government sources and at local historical societies for comparison against the printed versions and to gain context for the printed versions.

Lewis, J. D. "North Carolina – From Statehood to 1800: North Carolina counties Formed between 1775 and 1800." Online: http://www.carolana.com/NC/Early_Statehood/nc_statehood_1800_counties_established.html. Includes "Map of NC Counties as of 1775," "Map of NC Counties 1775-1777," "Map of NC Counties 1778-1780."]

Lewis, J. D. "North Carolina – The Counties from 1664 to Present." Online: http://www.carolana.com/NC/Counties/home.html. [Two sections: "In Order of Creation" and "In Alphabetical Order."]

Lewis, J. D. "The Known Towns/Villages of North Carolina." Online: http://www.carolana.com/NC/Towns/home.html. [This includes a list of towns established in the state from 1776-1800.]

"North Carolina Counties 1775 to 1777." Online: http://www.carolana.com/NC/Revolution/nc_counties_during_revolution.html. [map]

North Carolina Coast and the Outer Banks (generally)

Alexander, John, and James Lazell. *Ribbon of Sand: The Amazing Convergence of the Ocean and the Outer Banks.* Chapel Hill: University of North Carolina Press, 2000.

Barfield, Rodney. *Seasoned by Salt: A Historical Album of the Outer Banks.* Chapel Hill: University of North Carolina Press, 1995. [Publisher's description: "The Outer Banks of North Carolina have had a lively and sometimes lurid history going back four centuries. These barrier islands, frequently battered by storms and hurricanes, were the site of the first English colony in North America and figured prominently in the Civil War. The hundreds of shipwrecks off their shores have earned the Outer Banks a reputation as the 'Graveyard of the Atlantic'."]

Butler, Lindley S. *Pirates, Privateers, and Rebel Raiders of the Carolina Coast.* Chapel Hill: University of North Carolina Press, 2000.

Cecelski, David. "A World of Fisher Folks." *North Carolina Literary Review*, 1:2 (1994), 183-199. [Online description from "North Carolina Periodicals Index," East Carolina University: "The unique maritime culture of North Carolina has been an inspiration for naturalists, folklorists, historians, poets and novelists for centuries as they have been drawn to the coasts. A strong North Carolina fishing culture initially drew many people, however, pollution, over-development, and poor fishery management, the culture is in decline. Writers and historians continue to record and preserve this culture in their respective works."]

Cobb, Collier. "Some Changes in the North Carolina Coast since 1585." *North Carolina Booklet*, 4:9 (January 1905), 3-13; online: http://digital.ncdcr.gov/cdm/ref/collection/p249901coll37/id/14180. [Online description from "North Carolina Periodicals Index," East Carolina University: "This article details recorded changes in the North Carolina coast between 1585 and 1900 by comparing historical maps with modern observations. Details include changed feature names, shifting shoals, moving inlets, and altered water ways."]

Crittenden, Charles C. "The Seacoast in North Carolina History, 1763-1789." *North Carolina Historical Review*, 7:4

(October 1930), 433-442; online: http://digital.ncdcr.gov/cdm/ref/collection/p16062coll9/id/4207. [Online description from "North Carolina Periodicals Index," East Carolina University: "The author examines the 18th century coastline and the geographical impediments which hindered the state's overseas commerce. Discussed are the major bodies of water throughout eastern North Carolina including the Cape Fear River, the sounds, and Ocracoke Inlet and the men who sailed these waters and attempted to improve navigation throughout the period."]

Cumming, William P. "Wimble's Maps and the Colonial Cartography of the North Carolina Coast." *North Carolina Historical Review*, 42:2 (April 1969), 171-177.

Delaney, Norman C. "The Outer Banks for North Carolina during the Revolutionary War." *North Carolina Historical Review*, 36:1 (January 1959), 1-16; online: http://digital.ncdcr.gov/cdm/ref/collection/p16062coll9/id/4207. [Online description from "North Carolina Periodicals Index," East Carolina University: "This article provides a history of the Outer Banks during the period of the Revolutionary War with a particular focus on Ocracoke Island and Ocracoke Inlet. Progressing chronologically, the author details troop positions, defenses, and naval maneuvers made on the barrier islands during the war years."]

Downing, Sarah. *Hidden History of the Outer Banks* Charleston, S. C.: History Press, 2013. [Includes a section titled: "Windmills Once Dotted the Coast," 30-32.]

Dunbar, Gary S. and Fred Kniffen. *Historical Geography of the North Carolina Outer Banks*. (Louisiana State University Studies, Costal Studies series) Baton Rouge: Louisiana State University, [1958].

Fisher, John Joseph. "Geomorphic Expression of Former Inlets along the Outer Banks of North Carolina." M. S. thesis, University of North Carolina, 1962.

Frankenberg, Dirk. *The Nature of the North Carolina's Southern Coast.* Chapel Hill: University of North Carolina Press, 2012. [Publisher's description: "For some years, The Nature of North Carolina's Southern Coast has stood as an essential resource for all who treasure our coastal environment. In this book, Dirk Frankenberg describes the southern coast's beaches, inlets, and estuaries and instructs readers in the responsible exploration and enjoyment of some of North Carolina's most precious natural areas. From Ocracoke Inlet to the South Carolina border, this field guide provides a close-up look at a complex ecosystem, highlighting the processes that have shaped, and continue to shape, North Carolina's southern coast."]

Frankenberg, Dirk. *The Nature of the Outer Banks.* Chapel Hill: University of North Carolina Press, 2012. [Publisher's description: "North Carolina's Outer Banks are in constant motion, responding to weather, waves, and the rising sea level. Beaches erode, sometimes taking homes or sections of highway with them into the surf; sand dunes migrate with the wind; and storms open new inlets and dump sand in channels and sounds. A classic guide, *The Nature of the Outer Banks* describes these dynamic forces and guides visitors to sites where they can see these phenomena in action."]

Hart, Kathy. "Coastal Beginnings." *Coastwatch*, 13:1 (January 1986), 1-3. [Online description from "North Carolina Periodicals Index," East Carolina University: "Millions of years ago, North Carolina looked very different from what it is today. Hart discusses the geologic formation of North Carolina with particular attention to the coast."]

Hart, Kathy. "What Sets These Woods Apart." *Coastwatch*, 15:6 (June/July 1988), 2-3. [Online description from "North Carolina Periodicals Index," East Carolina University: "North Carolina has a unique resource: oceanfront forests. Despite the inhospitable environment, maritime forests such as these provide barrier islands along the state's coast with special benefits that include anchoring the shifting sands, storing fresh water, and adding soil."]

Hoag, Ronald Wesley. "Hatteras Blues: Greatness and Grace on the Edge." *North Carolina Literary Review*, 15 (2006), 84-92. [Online description from "North Carolina Periodicals Index," East Carolina University: "Hatteras native and author Tom Carlson paints a splendid picture of the people, issues, and ideas of the Outer Banks in his book *Hatteras Blues: A Story from the Edge of America*. During the course of the book, Carlson conveys the uniqueness of culture and character found on the Outer Banks."]

Horan, Jack. "Trail Mix: Scenic Byway, Maritime Trail Beckon to Vistors." *Coastwatch*, 3 (Summer 2013), 6-13; https://ncseagrant.ncsu.edu/. [Online description from "North Carolina Periodicals Index," East Carolina University: "Whether you are traveling by car or simply cruising the internet, the Outer Banks offers unique ways to visit important cultural, historical, geographical, and environmental features of North Carolina's Outer Banks. The Outer Banks National Scenic Byway connects sea and soundside villages, museums, lighthouses, wildlife refuges, ferries, and the coastal shared heritage. The Outer Banks Maritime Heritage Trail provides a virtual travel experience with videos and oral histories highlighting landmarks on land or under water, along N.C. 12 from Nags Head to Hatteras Inlet."]

Huling, Billie Jean. *The Lore and Lure of the Coastal Banks.* Mount Olive: Mount Olive College Press, 1994.

Lippson, Robert L., and Alice Jane Lippson. *Life along the Inner Coast*. Chapel Hill: University of North Carolina Press, 2012. [Publisher's description: "For decades, marine scientists Robert and Alice Jane Lippson have traveled the rivers, backwaters, sounds, bays, lagoons, and inlets stretching from the Chesapeake Bay to the Florida Keys aboard their trawler, *Odyssey*. The culmination of their leisurely journeys, *Life along the Inner Coast* is a guide to the plants, animals, and habitats found in one of the most biologically diverse regions on the planet. It is a valuable resource for naturalists, students, and anyone who lives or vacations along the Atlantic inner coast."]

Littleton, Tucker R. "Strange Pasture." *The State: Down Home in North Carolina*, 47:4 (September 1979), 10-13; online: http://digital.ncdcr.gov/cdm/ref/collection/p16062coll18/id/58669. [Online description from "North Carolina Periodicals Index," East Carolina University: "As early as 1694, livestock was being raised and sold on the Outer Banks. Although subject to the onslaught of storms, livestock was well fed and protected by the marshes. Because of overpopulation, free ranging stock has been almost completely eliminated in recent decades."]

Littleton, Tucker R. "When Windmills Whirled on the Tar Heel Coast." *The State: Down Home in North Carolina*, 48:5 (October 1980), 8-12; online: http://digital.ncdcr.gov/cdm/ref/collection/p16062coll18/id/59318.

Manuel, John. *The Natural Traveler along the North Carolina Coast*. Winston-Salem: John F. Blair, 2003.

McGowan, Thomas. "David Stick: Outer Banks Historian." *North Carolina Folklore Journal*, 36:2 (Summer-Fall 1989), 70-72. [Online description from "North Carolina Periodicals Index," East Carolina University: "David Stick has written four major histories of the North Carolina coast. Through Stick's books and articles, the reader gains not only a factual chronicle of the history of the North Carolina coast, but also a lively appreciation of the details of regional traditional life – of the forms and functions of the folk-life of communities and occupational groups along the Outer Banks."]

Merriman, Ann. "S. R. Fowle Company: Coastal Trade and Schooners." *Tributaries*, 5 (October 1995), 22-27. [Online description from "North Carolina Periodicals Index," East Carolina University: "Schooners figured prominently in the state's water commerce during the 18th and 19th Centuries. Records of the S. R. Fowle Company of Washington provide important information on the use of these vessels for commerce."]

"Outer Banks Windmills." Online: http://beaufortartist.blogspot.com/2008/03/outer-banks-windmills.html.

Riggs, Stanley R.; Dorothea V. Ames; Stephen J. Culver; and David J. Mallinson. *The Battle for North Carolina's Coast: Evolutionary History, Present Crisis, and Vision for the Future*. Chapel Hill: University of North Carolina Press, 2011. [Publisher's description: "The North Carolina barrier islands, a 325-mile-long string of narrow sand islands that forms the coast of North Carolina, are one of the most beloved areas to live and visit in the United States. However, extensive barrier island segments and their associated wetlands are in jeopardy. In *The Battle for North Carolina's Coast*, four experts on coastal dynamics examine issues that threaten this national treasure.

Senter, Jim. "Live Dunes and Ghost Forests: Stability and Change in the History of North Carolina's Maritime Forests." *North Carolina Historical Review*, 80:3 (July 2003), 334-371. [Online description from "North Carolina Periodicals Index," East Carolina University: "An examination of the Outer Banks ecological history focusing on forests and the idea suggesting human intervention brought about its destruction. Evidence suggests that geological and climactic changes were the causes of the live dunes that threatened the forests rather than anthropogenic processes."]

Sharpe, Bill. "The Cape of Three Oceans." *The State: Down Home in North Carolina*, 22:15 (December 1954), 10-11, 19; online: http://digital.ncdcr.gov/cdm/ref/collection/p16062coll18/id/32776. [Online description from "North Carolina Periodicals Index," East Carolina University: "Including Core Sound, Core Bank, Shackleford Bank, and Cape Lookout, this article discusses the water and history of this region of North Carolina's southern Outer Banks."]

Sharpe, Bill. "Fascinating Empire of War." *The State: A Weekly Survey of North Carolina*, 19:53 (May 1952), 3-5, 20-27; online: http://digital.ncdcr.gov/cdm/ref/collection/p16062coll18/id/28699. [Online description from "North Carolina Periodicals Index," East Carolina University: "North Carolina's coastland is more than just a beach; it is a breezy land of heroic memory and salty people."]

Sharpe, Bill. "How Did the Coast Get Like That?" *The State: A Weekly Survey of North Carolina*, 19:2 (June 1951), 8-9, 21-22; online: http://digital.ncdcr.gov/cdm/ref/collection/p16062coll18/id/27133. [Online description from "North Carolina Periodicals Index," East Carolina University: "Many people have been puzzled by the unusual formation of the North Carolina coast, and Sharpe explains how such a strange thing came about."]

Simpson, Bland. *Little Rivers and Waterway Tales: A Carolinian's Eastern Streams*. Chapel Hill: University of North Carolina Press, 2015. [Publisher's description: "Bland Simpson regales us with new tales of coastal North Carolina's 'water-loving land,' revealing how its creeks, streams, and rivers shape the region's geography as well as its culture. Drawing on deep family ties and coastal travels, Simpson and wife and collaborator Ann Cary Simpson tell the stories of those who have lived and worked in this country, chronicling both a distinct environment and a way of life. Whether rhapsodizing about learning to sail on the Pasquotank River or eating oysters on Ocracoke, he introduces readers to the people and communities along the watery web of myriad 'little rivers' that define North Carolina's sound country as it meets the Atlantic."]

Simpson, Bland. *The Coasts of Carolina: Seaside to Sound Country*. Chapel Hill: University of North Carolina Press, 2010. [Publisher's description: "The Coasts of Carolina captures the vibrancy of the North Carolina oceanfront, sound country, and interior shores behind the barrier islands. Scott Taylor, who has been photographing the coast for almost thirty years, and Bland Simpson, whose many coastal books have delighted readers for two decades, come together to offer an inviting visual and textual portrait organized around coastal themes such as nature, fishing, and community life, with an emphasis on particular places and seasons. Evocative text is woven together with 145 vivid color images to present a unique and welcoming vision of the coastal region. As natives of the area, the collaborators venture beyond the familiar to show us swamp, marsh, river, sound, and seashore, uncovering places of uncommon delight that most visitors rarely lay eyes on. Their work celebrates the beauty of this amazing region and embodies their distinctive sense of what makes the North Carolina coast so special."]

Stick, David. *Graveyard of the Atlantic: Shipwrecks of the North Carolina Coast*. Chapel Hill: University of North Carolina Press, 1989. [Publisher's description: "This is a factual account, written in the pace of fiction, of hundreds of dramatic losses, heroic rescues, and violent adventures at the stormy meeting place of northern and southern winds and waters – the Graveyard of the Atlantic off the Outer Banks of North Carolina."]

Stick, David. *The Outer Banks of North Carolina, 1584-1958*. Chapel Hill: University of North Carolina Press, 1990. [Publisher's description: "The Outer Banks have long been of interest to geologists, historians, linguists, sportsmen, and beachcombers. This long series of low, narrow, sandy islands stretches along the North Carolina coast for more than 175 miles. Here on Roanoke Island in the 1580s, the first English colony in the New World was established. It vanished soon after, becoming the famous 'lost colony.' At Ocracoke, in 1718, the pirate Blackbeard was killed; at Hatteras Inlet and Roanoke Island important Civil War battles were fought; at Kitty Hawk and Kill Devil Hills the Wright brothers experimented with gliders and in 1903 made their epic flight. The Graveyard of the Atlantic, scene of countless shipwrecks, lies all along the ever-shifting shores of the Banks. This is the fascinating story of the Banks and the Bankers; of whalers, stockmen, lifesavers, wreckers, boatmen, and fishermen; of the constantly changing inlets famous for channel bass fishing; and of the once thriving Diamond City that disappeared completely in a three-year period."]

Stick, David. "Windmills." Online: http://ncpedia.org/windmills.

Stick, David, ed. *An Outer Banks Reader*. Chapel Hill: University of North Carolina Press, 1998. [Publisher's description: "For half a century, David Stick has been writing books about the fragile chain of barrier islands off the North Carolina coast known as the Outer Banks. Two of his earliest, *Graveyard of the Atlantic* and *The Outer Banks of North Carolina*, were published by the UNC Press in the 1950s, and continue to be best-sellers. More recently, Stick embarked on another project, searching for the most captivating and best-written examples of what others have said about his beloved Outer Banks. In the process, more than 1,000 books, pamphlets, periodicals, historical documents, and other writings were reviewed. The result is a rich and fascinating anthology. The selections in *An Outer Banks Reader* span the course of more than four and a half centuries, from the first known record of a meeting between Europeans and Native Americans in the region in 1524 to modern-day accounts of life on the Outer Banks. Together, Stick hopes, the sixty-four entries may provide both 'outlanders' and natives with an understanding of why the Outer Banks are home to a rapidly growing number of people who would rather spend the rest of their lives there than any place else on earth."]

Watson, Alan D. "Pilotage and Pilots in Colonial North Carolina: The Case of Ocracoke Inlet." *Tributaries*, 3:1 (October 1993), 20-25. [Online description from "North Carolina Periodicals Index," East Carolina University: "Pilots directed ships through the often tricky inlet system separating state rivers from ocean-going commerce. Specifically, the history of Ocracoke pilots and legislation governing them is presented."]

Westbrook, Kathy Grant. "Very Estuary." *Our State: Down Home in North Carolina*, 69:11 (April 2002), 80-83; online: http://digital.ncdcr.gov/cdm/ref/collection/p16062coll18/id/74893. [Online description from "North Carolina Periodicals Index," East Carolina University: "The North Carolina Estuarium, located in Washington, focuses on the unique environment of the Albemarle-Pamlico estuarine system, which covers all or part of 36 counties. It is the state's largest system, and the country's second behind the Chesapeake Bay. The facility opened in 1998 with exhibits presenting ecosystem, history, fish and wildlife, and human interaction with the estuary."]

Wrenn, Warren. "The Outer Banks: Hindrance to Ships, Barrier to Progress." *Tar Heel Junior Historian*, 28:2 (Spring 1989), 10-13. [Online description from "North Carolina Periodicals Index," East Carolina University: "Known as the 'Graveyard of the Atlantic,' the state's Outer Banks hindered settlement and caused the loss of hundreds of ships throughout history. Inaccessible waterways deterred growth during the colonial period and slowed growth of shipping during the 19th- and early 20th-century. Recently, the Outer Banks have transformed from deterrent to economic boom, generating revenue from vacationers seeking beaches and fishing."]

Yocum, Thomas. "Windmill History on the Outer Banks." Online: http://www.coastalguide.com/windmill-history-outer-banks.html.

North Carolina Coastal Plain, Sounds, Estuaries, and Tidewater

Cecelski, David S. *A Historian's Coast: Adventures into the Tidewater Past.* Winston-Salem: John F. Blair, 2000.

Davis, Nancy, and Kathy Hart. "Estuaries." *Coastwatch*, 10:7 (August 1983), 3-69. [Online description from "North Carolina Periodicals Index," East Carolina University: "This article looks at the social, biological, historical, and economic dimensions of one of North Carolina's most valuable assets: estuaries."]

Edgerton, C. R. "Amazing Journey into the Sounds." *Coastwatch*, 17:2 (February 1990), 2-3. [Online description from "North Carolina Periodicals Index," East Carolina University: "The Pamlico and Albemarle Sounds of North Carolina are dynamic mergers of water, wind, and currents that prompt the growth of many fish species. Edgerton discusses how fish migration into these sounds from birth in the Gulf of Mexico. "]

Edgerton, C. R. "Currituck Sound: Lessons Learned the Hard Way." *Coastwatch*, 17:3 (March 1990), 4-6. [Online description from "North Carolina Periodicals Index," East Carolina University: "Once upon a time, the shallow waters of Currituck Sound were clear, drinkable, and harbored abundant fish. Thanks to the native submerged seagrasses, ecology in the Sound flourished. Through the years, the quality of Currituck Sound has hinged on the survival of the Sound's seagrass beds, and its ups and downs."]

Hart, Kathy. "Cookin Up an Estuary." *Coastwatch*, (May/June 1994), 21. [Online description from "North Carolina Periodicals Index," East Carolina University: "North Carolina boasts the third largest estuarine system in the United States. The state has 2.3 million acres of estuaries, from which come ninety percent of commercial and recreational species of fish and shellfish."]

Hart, Kathy. "Sound Value." *Friends of Wildlife*, 42:2 (Spring 1994), 16. [Online description from "North Carolina Periodicals Index," East Carolina University: "The North Carolina estuarine system, third largest in the U.S., produces 90% of the state's commercial and recreational species of fish and shellfish. Hart briefly describes the variety of life that inhabits the sounds, marshes, and open waters."]

Humber, John L. *The Coastal Plain of North Carolina in 1776.* Chapel Hill: J. L. Humber, 1965. [map]

Lee, David S. *Gulf Stream Chronicles: A Naturalist Explores Life in an Ocean River.* Chapel Hill: University of North Carolina Press, 2015. [Publisher's description: "Off the shore of Hatteras Island, where the inner edge of the Gulf Stream flows northward over the outer continental shelf, the marine life is unlike that of any other area in the Atlantic. Here the powerful ocean river helps foster an extraordinarily rich diversity of life, including Sargassum mats concealing strange creatures and exotic sea beans, whales and sea turtles, sunfish and flying fish, and shearwaters and Bermuda petrels. During his long career as a research scientist, David S. Lee made more than 300 visits to this area off the North Carolina coast, documenting its extraordinary biodiversity. In this collection of twenty linked essays, Lee draws on his personal observations and knowledge of the North Atlantic marine environment to introduce us to the natural wonders of an offshore treasure. Lee guides readers on adventures miles offshore and leagues under the sea, blending personal anecdotes with richly detailed natural history, local culture, and seafaring lore. These journeys provide entertaining and informative connections between the land and the diverse organisms that live in the Gulf Stream off the coast of North Carolina. Lee also reminds us that ocean environments are fragile and vulnerable to threats such as pollution, offshore energy development, and climate change, challenging those of us on land to consider carefully the costs of ignoring sea life that thrives just beyond our view."]

McMullan, Phil; Cy Rich, Jr.; Steve Barnes; and, Joe Landino. *North Carolina's Blacklands Treasure.* Nags Head: Pamlico & Albemarle Publishing, 2016. [Publisher's description: "Bounded by the Albemarle Sound on the north and the Pamlico Sound on the south, the Blacklands of Northeastern North Carolina boast some of the most productive agricultural soils in the nation. But throughout much of its history, this region - filled with murky swamps and impenetrable wilderness - has defeated many an adventurer trying to tame it. *North Carolina's Blacklands Treasure* tells the story of the determined, steadfast and downright stubborn pioneers who turned this seeming wasteland into a bountiful breadbasket."]

Norris, Jeannie Faris. "The Peninsula of Pamlico." *The State: Down Home in North Carolina*, 22:3 (July 1954), 21, 23, 66-67; online: http://digital.ncdcr.gov/cdm/ref/collection/p16062coll18/id/32196. [Online description from "North Carolina Periodicals Index," East Carolina University: "With the exception of Long Island Sound, Pamlico Sound, at 1,700 square miles and reaching over eighty miles in length, is the East Coast's largest sound. This article describes the sound and a number of towns located along it, including Stumpy Point, Engelhard, Swam Quarter, and Germantown."]

Norris, Jeannie Faris. "Where Five Great Sounds Meet." *The State: Down Home in North Carolina*, 22:3 (July 1954), 17-18, 69; online: http://digital.ncdcr.gov/cdm/compoundobject/collection/p16062coll18/id/32196. [Online description from "North Carolina Periodicals Index," East Carolina University: "Roanoke Island is the place where North Carolina's five great sounds meet. In the north the Albemarle flows into the Currituck Sound. The water then moves into either the Roanoke or the Croatan Sound as it passes on either side of the island, and finally merges at the south end with the Pamlico Sound. An individual taking a boat ride around the island can truthfully say that in one day he or she has sailed through the state's five sounds."]

Peters, Sarah Friday. "Coastal Dialects: Queen's English or a Language of Their Own?" *Coastwatch*, (September/October 1993), 12-17. [Online description from "North Carolina Periodicals Index," East Carolina University: "A survey of the various dialects heard along the Outer Banks, this article addresses both the unique language patterns and the settlement pattern of the North Carolina coast."]

Pusser, Todd. "North Carolina's Wildest Landscape." *Wildlife in North Carolina*, 79:5 (September/October 2015), 8-13. [Online description from "North Carolina Periodicals Index," East Carolina University: "The Albemarle Peninsula is a wetland located between the Albemarle and Pamlico Sounds. The peninsula covers 3,200 square miles of land in five different counties. The wetland environment is home to a variety of wildlife, including bobcats, black bears, red wolves, tundra swans, river otters, snake species, and the American Alligator, among others."]

Saxon, John L. "Down East." *Coastwatch*, (March/April 1996), 2-7. [Online description from "North Carolina Periodicals Index," East Carolina University: "When referring to the eastern part of the state, 'Down East' is a term widely used. However, the real 'Down East' is found in locales like Smyrna, Stacy, Harkers Island, and Cedar Island."]

Settlage, Sharon. "The Pamlico Sound: Fishing Gem of North Carolina." *Coastwatch*, 3 (Summer 2012), 12-17; online: https://ncseagrant.ncsu.edu/. [Online description from "North Carolina Periodicals Index," East Carolina University: "The Pamlico Sound, the largest body of water in the four distinct coastal regions of North Carolina, is known as the fishing gem of the state. As a prime habitat for numerous aquatic animals and vegetation, the Pamlico Sound is a strategic habitat area for the North Carolina Coastal Habitat Protection Plan."]

Simpson, Bland and Ann Cary Simpson. *Into the Sound Country: a Carolinian's coastal plain.* Chapel Hill: University of North Carolina Press, 1997. [Publisher's description: "Into the Sound Country is a story of rediscovery--of two North Carolinians returning to seek their roots in the state's eastern provinces. It is an affectionate, impressionistic, and personal portrait of the coastal plain by two natives of the region, writer Bland Simpson and photographer Ann Cary Simpson. Here Bland Simpson tours his old waterfront haunts in Elizabeth City, explores scuppernong vineyards from Hertford to Southport, tramps through Pasquotank swamps and Croatan pine savannas, and visits Roanoke River oyster bars and Core Banks fishing shanties. Ann Simpson's original photographs capture both the broad vistas of the sounds and rivers and the quieter corners of mossy creeks and country churchyards. Her selection of archival illustrations ranges from the informative to the humorous, from a turpentine scraper at work in the 1850s to a pair of little girls playing with a horseshoe crab on a Beaufort porch at the turn of the century."]

Watson, Alan D. "Arrivals in the East: Settlement of the Coastal Plain, 1650-1775." *Tar Heel Junior Historian*, 34:2 (Spring 1995), 8-15; online: http://ncpedia.org/history/colonial/coastal-plain. [Online description from "North Carolina Periodicals Index," East Carolina University: "The state's Coastal Plain is divided into three sub regions: the Albemarle, middle Coastal Plain, and the Cape Fear. Each area is different geographically, and each had a different settlement history."]

North Carolina Coastal Plain – Albemarle Sound Region (Northeastern North Carolina)

Catherine Albertson. *In Ancient Albemarle.* Raleigh: Commercial Printing Company for the North Carolina Society Daughters of the American Revolution, 1914.

Griffen, A. Ray, Jr. "North Carolina Genealogical Geography: Northeastern North Carolina – Old Albemarle County." *Piedmont Lineages: Quarterly Journal of the VA-NC Piedmont Genealogical Society*, 20:1 (February 1998), 15-18.

Lossing, Benson J. *Benson J. Lossing's Pictorial Field-Book of the Revolution in Virginia and Maryland (Including West Virginia, Washington, D. C., and the Albemarle of North Carolina.* [Lossing's original publication: 2 vols.: New York: Harper & Brothers, 1851-1852; reprinted [extracts from the original publication] Wilmington, N. C.: Dram Tree Books, 2008.

Lounsbury, Carl. "The Development of Domestic Architecture in the Albemarle Region." *North Carolina Historical Review*, 54:1 (January 1977), 17-48. [Online description from "North Carolina Periodicals Index," East Carolina University: "This article is a systematic study of the development of vernacular domestic architecture in Gates, Perquimans, and Pasquotank counties in northeastern North Carolina, with a particular focus on the planning and structural character of farmhouses in the period between settlement and the American Civil War."]

Mann and Midyett Families. "Mann and Midyett Family Papers, 1751-1941." Manuscript, Outer Banks History Center, State Archives of North Carolina, Manteo. [Online finding aid description: "The Mann and Midyett families have had a long presence in Northeastern North Carolina and can trace their roots back to the early 18th century. The papers in this collection are from the descendants of Joseph and Elizabeth Lockhart Mann, and William and Esther Midyett. The Mann and Midyett Family Papers include correspondence, receipts, deeds, financial information, and ephemera. There are also many documents on the sale, purchase, and hiring out of slaves belonging to the Mann and Midyett families." See also the online exhibit of selections from these family papers at: http://exhibits.archives.ncdcr.gov/mann_midyett/index.html.]

Monty, Brenda. "Historic Albemarle Tour." *North Carolina's Eastern Living Magazine*, 3:3 (Spring 2012), 95-98. [Online description from "North Carolina Periodicals Index," East Carolina University: "Created in 1975, the Historic Albemarle Tour is the oldest organized Heritage Trail in the southeast. The tour covers 17 eastern counties and 29 natural and historic sites, including lighthouses and life-saving stations, the state's oldest surviving colonial architecture, museums, formal gardens, and an aquarium. Historic Albemarle Tour signposts along the roads guide travelers."]

Norris, Jeannie Faris. "The Great Fisheries of the Nineteenth Century." *The State: Down Home in North Carolina*, 31:24 (April 1964), 15-16; online: http://digital.ncdcr.gov/cdm/ref/collection/p16062coll18/id/46710. [Online description from "North Carolina Periodicals Index," East Carolina University: "A fishing county since the early 18th century, Bertie County benefitted from the introduction of Seine nets as early as 1713, utilizing this method through 1915. The last seine to operate in the county was the Sutton Beach station, also known as Avoca, the largest and most successful of all the Albemarle Sound fisheries."]

Norris, Jeannie Faris. "Historic, Quaint and Varied." *The State: Down Home in North Carolina*, 22:26 (May 1955), 16-18; online: http://digital.ncdcr.gov/cdm/ref/collection/p16062coll18/id/81519. [Online description from "North Carolina Periodicals Index," East Carolina University: "Discussing the varied history of northeastern North Carolina, there is information about historic locations, beloved past times, and reasons to visit this portion of the state."]

North Carolina (State). General Assembly. "[Document dated:] February 5, [1781]: Letter from Colonel Gideon Lamb and Bonds Given by Tories." Manuscript; General Assembly Record Group; Session Records, January-February 1781; Joint Papers, Committee Papers, Resolutions, Senate Bills, House Bills, Box 1 (MARS ID: 66.8.23.3.3), State Archives of North Carolina, Raleigh. [Online catalog description: "Lamb informs the Assembly that in his opinion the only way to deal with the numerous loyalists in Currituck, Camden, Pasquotank, and Perquimans Counties is to forgive them on the condition that they sign bonds for their good behavior, which he has done. He includes several of the bonds."]

Stevens, J. Howard. *Albemarle People and Places*. Elizabeth City: Family Research Society of Northeastern North Carolina, 1999.

Yocum, Thomas. "Touring Historic Albemarle." *Our State: Down Home in North Carolina*, 68:4 (September 2000), 89-92; online: http://digital.ncdcr.gov/cdm/ref/collection/p16062coll18/id/71710. [Online description from "North Carolina Periodicals Index," East Carolina University: "Twenty-five years ago the Historic Albemarle Tour was created. The tour covers fifteen eastern counties and twenty-seven natural and historic sites, including lighthouses and life-saving stations, the state's oldest surviving colonial architecture, museums, formal gardens, and an aquarium. Many feared for these sites when floods from Hurricane Floyd swept over the Albemarle region, but most tour sites weathered the storm."]

Yocum, Thomas. "The War on Water." *Our State: Down Home in North Carolina*, 68:10 (March 2001), 55-57, 59-61; online: http://digital.ncdcr.gov/cdm/ref/collection/p16062coll18/id/72796. [Online description from "North Carolina Periodicals Index," East Carolina University: "For those on the Outer Banks and Carteret County, conflict with the British Navy was continual between 1776 and 1782. Yocum describes the six-year struggle and the patriots who defended coastal Carolina."]

North Carolina Coastal Plain – Albemarle Sound Region – Great Dismal Swamp

Blackburn, Charles, Jr. "The Great Dismal Swamp." *New East*, 4:2 (March/April 1976), 40-42. [Online description from "North Carolina Periodicals Index," East Carolina University: "Located on the marshy coast of North Carolina and Virginia, the Great Dismal Swamp, once covering 2,200 square miles, has been described as an area of history and mystery. Blackburn discusses historical events and persons connected with the swamp, such as George Washington, who designed a plan to drain the swamp."]

Bond, Tillie. "Tillie Bond Collection." Manuscript PC.16 (MARS ID: 525), State Archives of North Carolina, Raleigh. [Online catalog description: "Papers relating to the Albemarle region of North Carolina, especially Chowan Co., including deeds, grants, and plats from Chowan, Bertie, Tyrrell, Currituck, and Perquimans counties, and estate papers or wills of Thomas and Penelope Barker, James Craven, James Flood, Edmund Gale, Robert Halton, Edward Pagett, Elizabeth and Samuel Padgett, and John, Samuel, and Thomas Hodgson. Also court papers, bonds licenses, appointments, accounts, a New York Court of Vice-Admiralty libel of an American prize vessel (1778), …, an attempt to collect a debt owed to loyalist creditor, …. Papers of Thomas and Penelope Barker include letters from Peter Elmsley, Henry E. McCulloh, and Joseph Hewes; items relating to agent Barker's return via France (1778); and his application for restoration of property and citzenship (1779)."]

de Rageot, Roger H. "An Introduction to the Great Dismal Swamp." *Wildlife in North Carolina*, 29:5 (May 1965), 7-9, 23. [Online description from "North Carolina Periodicals Index," East Carolina University: "Although the history and folklore of the Great Dismal Swamp are well documented, very little comprehensive study has been made to this day of the swamp's flora and fauna. Rageot gives a general description of the swamp and discusses its geology and flora and fauna, including birds, mammals, and fishes."]

Dean, Earl. "The Great Dismal Swamp." *The State: A Weekly Survey of North Carolina*, 17:9 (July 1949), 3, 17-18. [Online description from "North Carolina Periodicals Index," East Carolina University: "The Great Dismal Swamp is still one of the wildest places in the eastern part of the United States, and there are some sections that never have been explored by man."]

Dean, Earl. "Lake Drummond and Its Name." *The State: A Weekly Survey of North Carolina*, 17:3 (August 1949), 3-4; online: http://digital.ncdcr.gov/cdm/ref/collection/p16062coll18/id/24326. [Online description from "North Carolina Periodicals Index," East Carolina University: "Some claim Lake Drummond was named for a deer hunter who lost his way, while others insist it was named for the first governor of North Carolina under the Lords Proprietors."]

Derks, Scott. "The Dismal." *Wildlife in North Carolina*, 46:5 (May 1982), 24-28. [Online description from "North Carolina Periodicals Index," East Carolina University: "Once covering 1.4 million acres, the Great Dismal Swamp has been reduced to 210,000 acres over the last 200 years. Eroding water tables, 200 years of logging, especially of the Atlantic white cedar, and an elaborate network of ditches cut through the swamp have all contributed to the reduction of this mysterious, dank, and nearly impenetrable area. Yet, the swamp stubbornly clings to survival."]

Kent, Harriette Thorne. *Swampers: Free Blacks and the Great Dismal Swamp*. [S. l.]: H. T. Kent, 1991.

"Man in the Dismal Swamp." *New East*, 1:3 (June/July 1973), 24-26, 28-29. [Online description from "North Carolina Periodicals Index," East Carolina University: "The Great Dismal Swamp, an area of history and mystery, sprawls across North Carolina's northeastern corner and southeastern Virginia. No one knows who discovered it or when. The author discusses historical events and persons connected with the swamp."]

McIlvenna, Noeleen. "Escape through the Great Dismal Swamp." *Tar Heel Junior Historian*, 47:1 (Fall 2007), 27-29. [Online description from "North Carolina Periodicals Index," East Carolina University: "The Great Dismal Swamp presented a refuge for 17th-century Europeans hoping to become independent. The first English explorer in the Albemarle area was Nathaniel Batts in 1660 and he settled in the region after purchasing land from the native population. Eventually this initial settlement developed into a community of male and female craftsmen function in cooperation with the native population and free of society's constraints."]

Norris, Jeannie Faris. "Man in the Dismal Swamp." *New East*, 1:3 (June/July 1973), 24-26, 28-29. [Online description from "North Carolina Periodicals Index," East Carolina University: "The Great Dismal Swamp, an area of history and mystery, sprawls across North Carolina's northeastern corner and southeastern Virginia. No one knows who discovered it or when. The author discusses historical events and persons connected with the swamp."]

North Carolina (State). General Assembly. "[Document dated:] February 1, 1779: Petition of Gideon Lamb and Others Re Road through Great Dismal Swamp." Manuscript, General Assembly Record Group; Session Records, January-February 1779; Joint Papers, Committee Papers, Resolutions, Senate Bills, House Bills, Box 1 (MARS ID: 66.8.15.9.11), State Archives of North Carolina, Raleigh. [Online catalog description: "The petitioners refer to and include a petition to Governor Josiah Martin and the colonial assembly requesting a law permitting Gideon Lamb to collect a toll to pay for the maintenance of a road he built through the Great Dismal Swamp." Personal names that appear in this document are Richard Caswell, Gideon Lamb, and Josiah Martin.]

North Carolina (State). General Assembly. "[Document dated:] October 26, 1779: Petition of Gideon Lamb for Road through Great Dismal Swamp." Manuscript; General Assembly Record Group; Session Records, October-November 1779; Joint Papers, Committee Papers, Resolutions, Senate Bills, House Bills, Box 1 (MARS ID: 66.8.18.7.15; item), State Archives of North Carolina, Raleigh. [Online catalog description: "Lamb requests a law to permit him to build a toll road through the great Dismal Swamp and includes a list of subscribers who support his action."]

Pettie, Sharon T. "Preserving the Great Dismal Swamp." *Journal of Forest History*, 20:1 (January 1976), 28-33.

Royster, Charles. *The Fabulous History of the Dismal Swamp Company: A Story of George Washington's Times*. New York: Knopf, 1999.

Simpson, Bland. *The Great Dismal: A Carolinians Swamp Memoir*. Chapel Hill: University of North Carolina Press, 1998. [Publisher's description: "Just below the Tidewater area of Virginia, straddling the North Carolina-Virginia line, lies the Great Dismal Swamp, one of America's most mysterious wilderness areas. The swamp has long drawn adventurers, runaways, and romantics, and while many have tried to conquer it, none has succeeded. In this engaging memoir, Bland Simpson, who grew up near the swamp in North Carolina, blends personal experience, travel narrative, oral history, and natural history to create an intriguing portrait of the Great Dismal Swamp and its people. For this edition, he has added an epilogue discussing developments in the region since 1990."]

Turnage, Sheila. "Anything But Dismal." *The State: Down Home in North Carolina*, 63:5 (October 1995), 24-28. [Online description from "North Carolina Periodicals Index," East Carolina University: "Sprawling across the state's northeastern corner and in southeastern Virginia, the Great Dismal Swamp attracts visitors interested in history, wildlife, and outdoor adventure."]

North Carolina Coastal Plain – Pamlico Sound Region

Cheatham, James T. *Sailing the Carolina Sounds: Historical Places and My Favorite People*. Charlotte: Delmar Printing & Publishing, 1993.

Yocum, Thomas. "The War on Water." *Our State: Down Home in North Carolina*, 68:10 (March 2001), 55-57, 59-61; online: http://digital.ncdcr.gov/cdm/ref/collection/p16062coll18/id/72796. [Online description from "North Carolina Periodicals Index," East Carolina University: "For those on the Outer Banks and Carteret County, conflict with the British Navy was continual between 1776 and 1782. Yocum describes the six-year struggle and the patriots who defended coastal Carolina."]

Cape Fear River Valley and Region

Adams, Natalie P. "A Pattern of Living: A View of the American Slave Experience in the Pine Forests of the Lower Cape Fear." In J. W. Joseph and Martha Zierden, eds., *Another's Country: Archaeological and Historical Perspectives on Cultural Interaction in the Southern Colonies* (Tuscaloosa: University of Alabama Press, 2002), 65-78.

Dunkerly, Robert M. *Redcoats on the River: Southeastern North Carolina in the Revolutionary War*. Wilmington: Dram Tree Books, 2008; revised edition with new title: *Redcoats on the Cape Fear: The Revolutionary War in Southeastern North Carolina.* Jefferson: McFarland & Company, 2012. [Publisher's summary: "Nestled on the banks of the Cape Fear River, Wilmington, North Carolina, remains famous as a blockade-running port during the Civil War, and was equally vital during the Revolution. Based on more than 100 eyewitness accounts and other primary sources, this volume chronicles the fascinating story of Wilmington and Lower Cape Fear during the Revolution."]

Fowler, Malcolm. "Iron Mining in Upper Cape Fear." *The State: A Weekly Survey of North Carolina*, 8:45 (April 1941), 8-9, 20. [Online description from "North Carolina Periodicals Index," East Carolina University: "Iron mining was a one time a quite sizable industry in the Upper Cape Fear River region. There is a large body of rich ore particularly in Chatham County where numerous mills and blast furnaces took advantage of the many tributaries of the Cape Fear River."]

Fryar, Jack E., Jr. "Cape Fear's Ablest Soldier." In Jack E. Fryar, Jr., ed., *The Coastal Chronicles: Volume II: Popular History Stories of the Coastal Carolinas as Seen in Coastal Chronicles Magazine* (Wilmington: Dram Tree Books, 2004), 44-48. [James Moore]

Garrison, Roy Charles. "Migration, Settlement and Revolution: The Highland Scots in the Cape Fear Region of Colonial North Carolina." M. A. thesis, University of North Carolina at Charlotte, 1998. [Online catalog description: "Cultural traditions and new environment have generally been opposing influences on the behavior of immigrants. Under some circumstances these forces can fragment a community of newcomers. Such was the case of the Highland Scots in colonial North Carolina. Choosing to migrate as a result of economic hardship in Scotland and opportunity in the Cape Fear region, they established a distinct community that initially preserved many of their cultural traditions. However, in their efforts to establish themselves successfully in their new home, many adopted new behaviors such as the production of naval stores and lumber, as well as the purchase and development of land throughout the Upper Cape Fear region. When the American Revolution broke out, many Scots fought to maintain their ties to Britain, but many others chose neutrality or embraced insurrection as a method of preserving their newly established economic security."]

Harrington, Sion H., III. "The Tory War of 1781-1782 in North Carolina's Upper Cape Fear Country." *Recall: North Carolina Military History Society Newsletter*, 3:2 (October 1997), 9-14. [Online description from "North Carolina Periodicals Index," East Carolina University: "The partisan warfare that took place in North Carolina during the Revolutionary War is both fascinating and disturbing. However, it is beyond the range and scope of this article which concentrates on the people and events of the Upper Cape River Valley between 1781-1782. Harrington attempts 'to explain this significant historical event in terms of what it was, when and where it occurred, who participated and why, the nature of the conflict and, most importantly, its impact both on society in the near term as well as the subsequent history of the area'."]

Mackenzie, James. "Over the Isle to America." *The State: Down Home in North Carolina*, 40:3 (July 1972), 12-14; online: http://digital.ncdcr.gov/cdm/ref/collection/p16062coll18/id/55330. [Online description from "North Carolina Periodicals Index," East Carolina University: "In 1773, thousands of Scottish citizens from the Isle of Skye immigrated to North Carolina's Cape Fear Valley region to escape unaffordable rent increases. To celebrate their new lives, the immigrants created a new dance called *America*, which was performed to a brisk reel. The accompanying song, *Over the Isles to America*, is still a popular folk song in Scotland, according to Scottish folk song authority James E. Scott."]

Sheppard, Joseph. "Revisiting SPG Missionaries in the Lower Cape Fear and Some Sources for Anglican Research in Colonial North Carolina." *Lower Cape Fear Historical Society Bulletin*, 46:1 (February 2002), 1-8. [Online description from "North Carolina Periodicals Index," East Carolina University: "The Society for the Propagation of the Gospel in Foreign Parts played an important role in the early religious life of colonial North Carolina. The SPG, chartered on June 16, 1701, sent Christian missionaries to the colony until the Revolutionary War. Between 1701 and 1783, about forty-six Anglican clergymen served in North Carolina. Sheppard discusses the role they played, the difficulties of procuring missionaries for the colony, and some notable missionaries from this period, including Richard Marsden. Sources for Anglican research are provided at the end of the article."]

Watson, Alan D. "Travel Conditions in Colonial North Carolina: The Case of the Lower Cape Fear." *Lower Cape Fear Historical Society Bulletin*, 41:2 (February 1997), 1-8. [Online description from "North Carolina Periodicals Index," East Carolina University: "Colonial travel in the lower Cape Fear region was by water and often slow and hazardous. As the population spread inland, a system of roads, bridges, ferries, and taverns developed. Since counties provided the upkeep, some routes were better than others."]

Wood, Bradford J. "'For Want of a Social Set': Networks and Social Interaction in the Lower Cape Fear Region of North Carolina, 1725-1775." In Robert Olwell and Alan Tully, eds., *Cultures and Identities in Colonial British America* (Baltimore: Johns Hopkins University Press, 2006), 45-69.

North Carolina Piedmont

Bright, Jeffery G., and Stewart E. Dunaway. *The American Revolution in North Carolina: An Exhaustive Reference of the Piedmont*. [United States]: Lulu.com, 2013. [Description: "This book documents a part of the Southern Campaign of the American Revolution immediately after the Race to the Dan and leading up to the Battle at Guilford Courthouse. The period between February and March 1781 was an important time for North Carolina as well as America as a whole. Patriot forces continued to skirmish with British Gen Cornwallis. Although none of these events were paramount or decisive, they illustrated the fortitude of the American Spirit. This strong resolve sent a clear message to the British that the patriots would rather fight than remain logy to the King. Read about Hart's Mill, Pyle's Defeat, Clapp's Mill and Weitzel's Mill. Learn what occurred, the issues and impacts surrounding each of these unique events. The title of this book comes from a letter written by Col. Otho Williams to Gen. Greene describing Cornwallis' tactics during this time period, detailing one of the many aspects that are fully documented in this book."]

Bright, Jeffery G., and Stewart E. Dunaway. *Like a Bear with His Stern in a Corner: The NC Campaign during the American Revolution: The Battles of Hart's Mill, Pyle's Defeat, Clapp's Mill, Weitzel's Mill.* [North Carolina: J. Bright and S. Dunaway; Morrisville: Lulu.com, [2009?] [Publisher's description: "This book documents a part of the Southern Campaign of the American Revolution immediately after the Race to the Dan and leading up to the Battle at Guilford Courthouse. The period between February and March 1781 was an important time for North Carolina as well as America as a whole. Patriot forces continued to skirmish with British Gen Cornwallis. Although none of these events were paramount or decisive, they illustrated the fortitude of the American Spirit. This strong resolve sent a clear message to the British that the patriots would rather fight than remain loyal to the King. Read about Hart's Mill, Pyle's Defeat, Clapp's Mill and Weitzel's Mill. Learn what occurred, the issues and impacts surrounding each of these unique events. The title of this book comes from a letter written by Col. Otho Williams to Gen Greene describing Cornwallis' tactics during this time period, detailing one of the many aspects that are fully documented in this book."]

Cometti, Elizabeth. "Notes and Documents: Some Early Best Sellers in Piedmont North Carolina." *Journal of Southern History*, 16:3 (August 1950), 324-337. [Guilford, Orange, Rockingham, Randolph, Durham, Person, Caswell, Chatham and Alamance counties portion of the Piedmont]

Duke Power Company. *What Makes the Piedmont Great?* [Durham?: Duke Power Company?, 1969?]. [The online catalog of the University of North Carolina at Chapel Hill shows that this is "Reprints of a series of advertisements recounting incidents in North Carolina during the American Revolution." A copy is located at North Carolina Collection, Folio FCp970 D87p, Louis Round Wilson Special Collections Library.]

Hendricks, Christopher E., and J. Edwin Hendricks. "Expanding to the West: Settlement of the Piedmont Region, 1730-1775." *Tar Heel Junior Historian*, 34:2 (Spring 1995), 16-21; online: http://ncpedia.org/history/colonial/piedmont. [Online description from "North Carolina Periodicals Index," East Carolina University: "Following the Great Wagon Road and the Great Indian Trading Path, settlers began moving into the Piedmont shortly before the Revolution. Despite Indian warfare and the Regulator conflict, the best land was occupied by farms and towns by the 1770s."]

Kars, Marjoleine. "'Breaking Loose Together': Religion and Rebellion in the North Carolina Piedmont, 1730-1790." Ph. D. dissertation, Duke University, 1994; published: *Breaking Loose Together: The Regulator Rebellion in Pre-Revolutionary North Carolina*. Chapel Hill: University of North Carolina Press, 2002. [Online abstract: "Because the North Carolina Piedmont was the center of the Great Awakening in the South, the site of the largest uprising among colonial farmers before 1776, and the theater of intense partisan warfare during the Revolution, it provides an ideal site to investigate how religion, economics, and politics interacted to shape rural life in the eighteenth century. In the first part of the work, I use land and court records, and loyalty claims to sketch the changing economy of the Piedmont from the beginning of settlement in the 1740s to the 1770s. I argue that local elites tried as much as possible to manipulate the chaotic land market to their own advantage. While growing integration into the Atlantic economy created opportunities for some Piedmont inhabitants, many others fell into debt. A scarcity of currency and the collusion of creditors and court officials created great hardships for farmers trying to pay off debts and taxes. The majority of Piedmont settlers came from northern colonies and brought with them much of the radical ferment of the Great Awakening. Using church records and the diaries of itinerant ministers, I argue in part two that denominational divisions among Piedmont inhabitants have been exaggerated and that the religious enthusiasm of the unchurched has been overlooked. In fact, many backcountry immigrants, whether they officially belonged to a church or not, were deeply influenced by the radical religious climate unleashed by the Great Awakening. As people grew increasingly exasperated with the corruption of their officials, they fused radical Protestant ideas about the importance of individual conscience with radical Whig ideas about the right to resist unjust government to fuel and justify their rebellion. In the third and last part of the dissertation, I examine the Regulation and its relationship to the American Revolution. I use petitions, participants' papers, and government sources to discuss the rebellion in terms of the enfolding revolutionary conflict at home and in the larger context of agrarian conflict and popular resistance elsewhere in the world. I argue that the Regulation foreshadowed many of the social struggles which accompanied the conflict with Britain."]

Morgan, Adam. *North Carolina's Wild Piedmont: A Natural History*. Charleston: History Press, 2015.

Raynor, George. *Piedmont Passages: Volume 2: Patriots and Tories in Piedmont Carolina*. Salisbury: Salisbury Post, 1991.

Scroggins, Michael C. *Relentless Fury: The Revolutionary War in the Southern Piedmont.* Rock Hill, S. C.: Culture & Heritage Museums, 2006.

North Carolina Backcountry and Western North Carolina

Arthur, Billy. "Plundering Sam Brown." *The State: Down Home in North Carolina*, 61:12 (May 1994), 17, 19-20; online: http://digital.ncdcr.gov/cdm/ref/collection/p16062coll18/id/66742. [Online description from "North Carolina Periodicals Index," East Carolina University: "Lincoln County's Sam Brown was a notorious robber and opponent of the American Revolution who, with his sister Charity, terrorized counties along the Yadkin River and in South Carolina. He was killed in 1780 by an outraged citizen."]

Arthur, John Preston. *Western North Carolina: A History (From 1730 to 1913)*. Raleigh: Edwards & Broughton Printing Co., 1914; reprinted: Johnson City, Tenn.: Overmountain Press, 1996. [Ashe and Bucombe Counties]

Beeman, Richard R. "The Political Response to Social Conflict in the Southern Backcountry: A Comparative View of Virginia and the Carolinas during the Revolution." In Ronald Hoffman, Thad W. Tate, and Peter J. Albert, eds., *An Uncivil War: The Southern Backcountry during the American Revolution* (Charlottesville: University Press of Virginia for the United States Capitol Historical Society, 1985), 213-239.

Beeman, Richard R. "The Unsettling Political Cultures of the Backcountry: The Southern Backcountry." In Beeman, Richard R., ed., *The Varieties of Political Experience in Eighteenth-Century America* (Philadelphia: University of Pennsylvania Press, 2004), 157-182. [Virginia and the Carolinas].

Blackmun, Ora. *Western North Carolina and Its People to 1880*. Boone: Applachian Consortium Press, 1977.

Bramlet, Albert Lincoln. "North Carolina's Western Lands." Ph. D. dissertation, University of North Carolina at Chapel Hill, 1928.

Boyd, William K. "Early Relations of North Carolina and the West." *North Carolina Booklet*, 7:3 (January 1908), 193-209.

Calhoon, Robert. "Ordered Liberty in the Southern Backcountry and the Middle-West." *Journal of Backcountry Studies,* 1:2 (Fall 2006); online: http://libjournal.uncg.edu/jbc/article/view/52/38.

Caruso, John Anthony. *Appalachian Frontier: America's First Surge Westward.* Indianapolis: Bobbs-Merrill, 1959.

Cashin, Edward. "From Creeks to Crackers." In David Colin Crass, Steven D. Smith, Martha A. Zierden, and Richard D. Brooks, *The Southern Colonial Backcountry: Interdisciplinary Perspectives on Frontier Communities* (Knoxville: University of Tennessee Press, 1998), 69-75.

Crass, David Colin; Steven D. Smith; Martha A. Zierden; and Richard D. Brooks. "Epilogue: Interdisciplinary Dialogues on the Southern Colonial Backcountry, 1893-1998." *The Southern Colonial Backcountry: Interdisciplinary Perspectives on Frontier Communities* (Knoxville: University of Tennessee Press, 1998), 237-248.

Crass, David Colin, Steven D. Smith, Martha A. Zierden, and Richard D. Brooks. "Introduction: Southern Frontier Communities Viewed through the Archaeological Eye." In David Colin Crass, Steven D. Smith, Martha A. Zierden, and Richard D. Brooks, eds., *The Southern Colonial Backcountry: Interdisciplinary Perspectives on Frontier Communities* (Knoxville: University of Tennessee Press, 1998.)

Crass, David C., et al. *The Southern Colonial Back Country: Interdisciplinary Perspectives on Frontier Communities*. Knoxville: University of Tennessee Press, 1998.

Crow, Jeffrey J. "Liberty Men and Loyalists: Disorder and Disaffection in the North Carolina Backcountry." In Ronald Hoffman, Thad W. Tate, and Peter J. Albert, eds., *An Uncivil War: The Southern Backcountry during the American Revolution* (Charlottesville: University Press of Virginia for the U. S. Capitol Historical Society, 1985), 125-178.

Davidson, Philip. "The Southern Backcountry on the Eve of the Revolution." In Avery Craven, ed., *Essays in Honor of William E. Dodd, by His Former Students at the University of Chicago* (Chicago: University of Chicago Press, 1935), 1-14.

Dick, Everett. *The Dixie Frontier: A Social History of the Southern Frontier from the First Tranmontane Beginnings to the Civil War*. New York: Knopf, 1948; reprinted: Norman: University of Oklahoma Press, 1993.

Durham, Walter T. "Westward with Anthony Bledsoe: The Life of an Overmountain Frontier Leader." *Tennessee Historical Quarterly*, 53:1 (Spring 1994), 2-19. [Anthony Bledsoe was in the House of Delegates in North Carolina throughout the Revolutionary War.]

Ekirch, A. Roger. "'A New Government of Liberty:' Hermon Husband's Vision of Backcountry North Carolina, 1755." *William and Mary Quarterly*, 3rd series, 34:4 (October 1977), 632-646

Ekirch, A. Roger. "Whig Authority and Public Order in Backcountry North Carolina, 1776-1783." In Ronald Hoffman, Thad W. Tate, and Peter J. Albert, eds., *An Uncivil War: The Southern Backcountry during the American Revolution* (Charlottesville: University Press of Virginia for the United States Capitol Historical Society, 1985), 99-124.

Fecher, Rebecca Taft. "The Trading Path and North Carolina." *Journal of Backcountry Studies* (online) 3:2 (Fall 2008); online: http://libjournal.uncg.edu/ojs/index.php/jbc/issue/view/10 [18th century].

Fiske, John. "Border Warfare of the Revolution." *Atlantic Monthly*, 64:386 (December 1889), 813-824.

Golumbic, Lars. "Dueling Legal Visions: Lawyers, the Backcountry, and the Law in Revolutionary Era North Carolina." M. A. thesis, University of North Carolina-Chapel Hill, 1994.

Golumbic, Lars C. "Who Shall Dictate the Law?: Political Wrangling Between 'Whig' Lawyers and Backcountry Farms in Revolutionary Era North Carolina." North Carolina Historical Review 73:1 (January 1996), 56-82.

Graves, William T. *Backcountry Revolutionary: James Williams (1740-1780) with Source Documents*. Lugoff, S. C.: Southern Campaigns of the American Revolution Press, 2012.

Graves, William T. *James Williams: An American Patriot in the Carolina Backcountry*. San Jose: Writers Club Press, 2002.

Greene, Jack P. "Independence, Improvement, and Authority: Toward a Framework for Understanding the Histories of the Southern Backcountry during the Era of the American Revolution." In Ronald Hoffman, Thad Tate, and Peter Albert, eds., *An Uncivil War: The Southern Backcountry during the American Revolution* (Charlottesville: University Press of Virginia, 1985), 3-36; also in: Jack P. Greene, *Imperatives, Behaviors, and Identities: Essays in Early American Cultural History* (Charlottesville: University Press of Virginia for the U. S. Capitol Historical Society, 1992), 181-207.

Griffin, Clarence W. *Western North Carolina Sketches.* Forest City: Forest City Courier, 1941.

Hartsoe, Kenneth David. "Governor Josiah Martin and His 1772 Journey to the North Carolina Backcountry." M. A. thesis, San Jose State University, 2001. [Online abstract: "During the summer of 1772, North Carolina Governor Josiah Martin visited the backcountry region of his colony. His objective was to acquaint himself with settlers of the frontier counties who were socially and politically isolated from the established provincial leadership on the colony's eastern seaboard. Many of these settlers were Regulators defeated by Governor William Tryon at the Battle of Alamance in May 1771. As a result, Martin inherited a colony smoldering from several years of backcountry violence and disregard for government authority. Martin's trip to the backcountry was the first attempt by North Carolina's royal government to reach out to a bitter and defeated populace. This thesis examines the many challenges Martin faced while in the backcountry and how his response to these challenges secured the trust and respect of a defeated populace."]

Hendricks, Christopher E. "The Backcountry Grows Up." *Tar Heel Junior Historian*, 45:2 (Spring 2006), 12-14. [Online description from "North Carolina Periodicals Index," East Carolina University: "Hendricks describes the settlement of the Piedmont region, or the backcountry of the state, during the 1700s. The first European settlers in the area were English. Many came down the Great Wagon Road or moved from the Coastal Plain. Population grew in the state from 35,000 in 1730 to 180,000 in 1770; much of the growth took place in the Piedmont. New towns were created to serve as government and trade centers or cultural centers for groups, such as German Moravians, and new counties formed."]

Hoffman, Ronald. "The Disaffected in the Revolutionary South." In Alfred F. Young, ed., *The American Revolution: Explorations in the History of American Radicalism* (DeKalb: Northern Illinois University Press, 1976), 273-316.

Hoffman, Ronald, Thad Tate, and Peter J. Albert, eds. *An Uncivil War: The Southern Backcountry during the American Revolution*. Charlottesville: University Press of Virginia, 1985.

Hofstra, Warren R. "Epilogue: Interdisciplinary Dialogues on the Southern Colonial Backcountry, 1893-1998." In David Colin Crass, Steven D. Smith, Martha A. Zierden, and Richard D. Brooks, eds., *The Southern Colonial Backcountry: Interdisciplinary Perspectives on Frontier Communities* (Knoxville: University of Tennessee Press, 1998), 221-236.

Holland, Ron. "North Carolina's Final Frontier: Settlement of the Mountain Region, 1775 to 1838." *Tar Heel Junior Historian*, 34:2 (Spring 1995), 23-26; online with the title: "Settlement of the Mountains, 1775-1838:" http://ncpedia.org/history/1776-1860/mountain-settlement. [Online description from "North Carolina Periodicals Index," East Carolina University: "Though land was cheap, rugged mountains, the lack of good roads, political conflict with the east, and isolation were challenges to those who came to the mountains to farm, start businesses, or search for gold."]

Hsiung, David C. "Seeing Early Appalachian Communities through the Lenses of History, Geography, and Sociology." In David Colin Crass, Steven D. Smith, Martha A. Zierden, and Richard D. Brooks, eds., *The Southern Colonial Backcountry: Interdisciplinary Perspectives on Frontier Communities* (Knoxville: University of Tennessee Press, 1998), 162-181.

Hunter, Cyrus Lee. *Sketches of Western North Carolina Historical and Biographical, Illustrating Principally the Revolutionary Period of Mecklenburg, Rowan, Lincoln and Adjoining Counties, Accompanied with Miscellaneous Information, Much of It Never Before Published.* Raleigh: Raleigh News Steam Job Print, 1877;

reprinted: Raleigh: Edwards & Broughton, 1930; Baltimore: Regional Publishing Company, 1970; Charleston, S. C.: BiblioBazaar, 2006.

Inscoe, John C. "Mountain Masters: Slaveholding in Western North Carolina." *North Carolina Historical Review*, 61:2 (April 1984), 143-173.

Irvin, Ned L. "Collecting Memory: Antiquarians and the Preservation of the Early History of the Trans-Appalachian Frontier." *Journal of East Tennessee History*, 72 (2000), 62-81.

Lee, Wayne E. "Restraint and Retaliation: The North Carolina Militias and the Backcountry War of 1780-1782." In John Resch and Walter Sargent, eds.; introduction by John Shy. *War & Society in the American Revolution: Mobilization and Home Fronts* (DeKalb: Northern Illinois University Press, 2007), 163-190.

Lewis, Johanna Miller. "Women and Economic Freedom in the North Carolina Backcountry." In Larry D. Eldridge, ed., *Women and Freedom in Early America* (New York: New York University Press, 1997), 191-208.

Lewis, Johanna Miller. "Women Artisans in Backcountry North Carolina, 1753-1790." *North Carolina Historical Review*, 68 (July 1991), 214-236. [Online description from "North Carolina Periodicals Index," East Carolina University: "An examination of women artisans in Rowan County, which in the late 18th century encompassed the entire northwestern quadrant of the modern state. While the actual number of women artisans will never be known because the business activities of some married women were run by their husbands, but the count of women artisans evidenced in county records grew in the last half of the 18th century with spinning and weaving being the most popular craft."]

Lewis, Johanna Miller. *Artisans in the North Carolina Backcountry*. Lexington: University Press of Kentucky, 1995.

Maass, John R. "'From Principles of Humanity and Virtue': Moderation and the Revolutionary Settlement in North Carolina." *Journal of Backcountry Studies*, 2:2 (Fall 2007); online: http://libjournal.uncg.edu/jbc/article/view/41/28.

McBride, Ransom. "A 'Lost' List of Continental Soldiers from the Western Counties." *North Carolina Genealogical Society Journal*, 9:3 (August 1983), 146. [Contains names of men residing in Lincoln County, Burke County, Wilkes County, and Rutherford County]

McDowell, William Wallis. "William Wallis McDowell Papers, 1772-1893." Collection Number 03160, Southern Historical Collection, Louis Round Wilson Special Collections Library, University of North Carolina, Chapel Hill; online finding aid available at http://www2.lib.unc.edu/mss/inv/m/McDowell,William_Wallis.html. [Online finding aid description: "William Wallis McDowell was a landowner, merchant, and banker of Asheville, N. C. The collection contains business and some personal and military papers of McDowell. Among the papers are ... a ledger pertaining to Revolutionary War pensions in ten western North Carolina counties, 1851-1852..."]

McKaughan, Joshua Lee. "People of Desparate Fortune: Power and Populations in the North Carolina Backcounty." *Journal of Backcountry Studies*, 2:1 (Spring 2007); online: http://libjournal.uncg.edu/jbc/issue/view/13.

Miller, Randall M. "A Backcountry Loyalist Plan to Retake Georgia and the Carolinas, 1778." *South Carolina Historical Magazine*, 75:4 (October 1974), 207-214.

Millett, Nathaniel. "Defining Freedom in the Atlantic Borderlands of the Revolutionary Southeast." *Early American Studies*, 5 (Fall 2007), 367-397.

Misenheimer, John E., Jr. "Mary Brevard Davidson and Others after the American Revolution." *The Golden Nugget (Cabarrus Genealogical Society)*, 13:3 (Autumn 2005), 82-84. [Mary Davidson, Ann Christenbury, Sarah Rounsevall, and Nancy Horah of Western North Carolina. The latter's husband was a Loyalist.]

Mitchell, Robert D. "Southern Backcountry: A Geographical House." In David Colin Crass, Steven D. Smith, Martha A. Zierden, and Richard D. Brooks, eds., *The Southern Colonial Backcountry: Interdisciplinary Perspectives on Frontier Communities* (Knoxville: University of Tennessee Press, 1998), 1-35.

Montgomery, Michael. "Searching for Security: Backcountry Carolina, 1760s-1780s." In Warren R. Hofstra, ed. *Ulster to America: The Scots-Irish Migration Experience, 1680-1830* (Knoxville: University of Tennessee Press, 2012), 147-163.

Moore, Peter N. "The Mysterious Death of William Richardson: Kinship, Female Vulnerability, and the Myth of Supernaturalism in the Southern Backcountry." *North Carolina Historical Review*, 80:3 (July 2003), 279-296. [Online description from "North Carolina Periodicals Index," East Carolina University: "Discusses the 1771 case of the Agnes Richardson and the death of her husband, of Presbyterian minister William Richardson, in the Waxhaw settlement, a Scots-Irish American community along the North Carolina-South Carolina border. The story that emerged regarding Agnes' possible role in the death, and a harrowing trial and accusation, reveal a focus on supernaturalism and folk justice that are commonly associated with the backcountry. Investigation of historical evidence reveals that her accusation has much to say about the social and legal constructs of early American society."]

Moore, Peter N. *World of Toil and Strife: Community Transformation in Backcountry South Carolina, 1750-1805.* Columbia: University of South Carolina Press, 2007. [Contains a discussion of slavery during this period and offers information on the role of the Catawba Indians during the Revolutionary War.]

Mosseller, Lillian Mills. "Landed Gentry of the Blue Ridge." *The State: Down Home in North Carolina*, 42:6 (November 1974), 18-20, 38; online: http://digital.ncdcr.gov/cdm/ref/collection/p16062coll18/id/56923. [Online description from "North Carolina Periodicals Index," East Carolina University: "The landed gentry colonized a part of the Appalachian Mountains. The first white settlers in the area were Ambrose and son, William Mills. The Mills family faced multiple attacks, some due in part to their Royalist persuasion, but mostly from Native Americans who pillaged and burned their homes on several occasions."]

Nixon, Joseph R. "German Settlers in Lincoln County and Western North Carolina." *James Sprunt Historical Publications*, 11:2 (1912), 25-62. [Contents: Chapter I: The German Migration; Chapter II: German Life in North Carolina; Chapter III: The Ramsour Family.]

Nobles, Gregory H. "Breaking into the Backcountry: New Approaches to the Early American Frontier, 1750-1800." *William and Mary Quarterly*, 3rd series, 46:4 (October 1989), 641-670.

North Carolina (State). General Assembly. "[Document dated]: September 4, 1780: Resolution Requesting Governor to Lend Volunteer Light Horse to Western Counties." Manuscript; General Assembly Record Group; Session Records, August-September 1780; Joint Papers, Committee Papers, Resolutions; House Joint Resolutions: August 31-September 6, 1780, Box 1 (MARS ID: 66.8.22.10.13), State Archives of North Carolina, Raleigh. [Online catalog description: "The resolution also makes provisions for acquiring volunteers and for supplying them. Includes an amendment from the Senate."]

North Carolina (State). General Assembly. "[Document dated]: September 5, 1780: Resolution Re[specting] Forwarding Part of Militia for Relief of Frontiers (Rejected). "Manuscript; General Assembly Record Group; Session Records, August 30-September 13, 1780; Joint Papers, Committee Papers, Resolutions; Joint Senate Resolutions: August 30-September 13, 1780, Box 1 (MARS ID: 66.8.22.9.10; item), State Archives of North Carolina, Raleigh. [Online catalog description: "In light of the belief that the British plan to march into Mecklenburg and Rowan Counties, the resolution would have directed the governor to send some of the militia in the Hillsborough District to the southwest and insured that each soldier would have a horse and receive an additional bounty."]

Osborne, Anne. "Charles Woodmason: Peripatetic Prelate of the Backwoods." *Newberry County Historical Society Bulletin*, 7:1 (December 1975), 19-29.

Posey, Walter Brownlow. *Frontier Mission: A History of Religion West of the Southern Appalachians to 1861.* Lexington: University of Kentucky Press, 1966.

Preyer, Norris W. *Hezekiah Alexander and the Revolution in the Backcountry*. Charlotte: Heritage Printers, 1987. [Hezekiah Alexander, 1728-1801]

Puglisi, Michael J. "Muddied Water: A Discussion of Current Interdisciplinary Backcountry Studies." In David Colin Crass, Steven D. Smith, Martha A. Zierden, and Richard D. Brooks, eds., *The Southern Colonial Backcountry: Interdisciplinary Perspectives on Frontier Communities* (Knoxville: University of Tennessee Press, 1998), 36-55.

Ramsey, Robert. *Carolina Cradle: Settlement of the Northwest Carolina Frontier, 1747-1762*. Chapel Hill: University of North Carolina Press, 1964. [Publisher's description: "This account of the settlement of one segment of the North Carolina frontier -- the land between the Yadkin and Catawba rivers -- examines the process by which the piedmont South was populated. Through its ingenious use of hundreds of sources and documents, Robert Ramsey traces the movement of the original settlers and their families from the time they stepped onto American shores to their final settlement in the northwest Carolina territory. He considers the economic, religious, social, and geographical influences that led the settlers to Rowan County and describes how this frontier community was organized and supervised."]

Revolutionary War: Carolina's Backcountry Revolutionary War Trail. Raleigh: North Carolina Division of Tourism, Film, and Sports Development, 2008. [map]

"Revolutionary War Veterans Buried in Western North Carolina." *A Lot of Bunkum*, 25:1 (February 2004), 7-12; 25:2 (May 2004), 15-18; plus: "RW Veterans: Corrections & Additions," 25:4 (November 2004), 22.

Rohrbough, Malcolm J. *Trans-Appalachian Frontier: People, Societies, and Institutions, 1775-1850*. New York: Oxford University Press, 1978.

Smathers, George H. *The History of Land Titles in Western North Carolina. A History of the Cherokee Land Laws Affecting the Title to Land Lying West of the Meigs and Freemand Line, and Laws Affecting the Title of Land Lying East of the Meigs and Freeman Line Back to the Top of the Blue Ridge, Including all the Land on the*

Waters of the French Broad River in What Was Formerly Buncombe County as Created by the Act of 1792. Asheville: Miller Printing Company, 1938.

Sosin, Jack. *The Revolutionary Frontier, 1763-1783.* New York: Holt, Rinehart, and Winston, 1967.

Stewart, Cory Joe. "The Affairs of Boston in the North Carolina Backcountry during the American Revolution." Ph. D. dissertation, University of North Carolina at Greensboro, 2010.

Stewart, Cory Joe. "Elizabeth Maxwell Steele: 'A Great Politician' and the Revolution in the Southern Backcountry." In Michele Gillespie and Sally G. McMillen, eds. *North Carolina Women: Their Lives and Times.* 2 vols. (Athens: University of Georgia Press, 2014), 1:54-72.

Swisher, James K. *The Revolutionary War in the Southern Back Country.* Gretna, La.: Pelican Publishing Company, 2008. [Contents: Revolution – Clash at Point Pleasant; The Cherokee War of 1776: Unconscionable Betrayal; Thunder on Spring Hill: The Struggle for Savannah; The Redcoats Return to Charlestown; The Battle of Camden: A Disparaging Defeat; The Rise of Partisan Warfare; Battle at Kings Mountain: The Fatal Miscalculations of Patrick Ferguson; The Fight at Hannah's Cowpens: A Complete Victory of Tactical Ingenuity; Duel in North Carolina: The Battle of Guilford Court House.]

Thorp, Daniel B. "Doing Business in the Backcountry: Retail Trade in Rowan County, North Carolina." *William and Mary Quarterly,* 3rd series, 48:3 (July 1991), 387-408.

Thorp, Daniel B. "Taverns and Communities: The Case of Rowan County, North Carolina." David Colin Crass, Steven D. Smith, Martha A. Zierden, and Richard D. Brooks, *The Southern Colonial Backcountry: Interdisciplinary Perspectives on Frontier Communities* (Knoxville: University of Tennessee Press, 1998), 76-86.

Thorp, Daniel B. "Taverns and Tavern Culture on the Southern Colonial Frontier: Rowan County, North Carolina, 1753-1776." *Journal of Southern History*, 62:4 (November 1996), 661-688.

Tillson, Albert H., Jr. "The Southern Backcountry: A Survey of Current Research." *Virginia Magazine of History and Biography*, 98:3 (July 1990), 387-422.

Turrentine, Joseph Dempsey. "Why Neighbor Fought Neighbor." B. A. thesis, University of Georgia, 2009. [Thesis description: "During the Revolutionary War, western North Carolina maintained one of the highest loyalist populations of any region in the thirteen colonies. Nearly one hundred years later, this same region contained widespread unionist sentiment during the Civil War. In a region just tame enough to settle yet too wild to firmly control, the ruling class chose repression to maintain their grip on the region. In both centuries, conditions were ripe for internal conflict, but for different reasons. Eventually, in both conflicts neighbor executed neighbor and western North Carolina populations descended into anarchy. In Wilkes Country during the Revolutionary War, Benjamin Cleveland personified the western ruling class, their overall impact on the outcome of the American Revolution, and Cleveland's story represents a good starting point for comparison. By comparing and contrasting these two internal conflicts, I hope to more fully expose the societal parallels that led to total breakdown, and to detect what impacts, if any, that the first struggle had on the second."]

Weeks, Stephen B[eauregard]. "General Joseph Martin and the War of the Revolution in the West." *Annual Report of the American Historical Association for the Year 1892* (Washington, D. C.: The Association, 1893), 403-477.

White, Ed. *The Backcountry and the City: Colonization and Conflict in Early America.* Minneapolis: University of Minnesota Press, 2005.

White, Emmett R. *Revolutionary War Soldiers of Western North Carolina.* 3 vols. Easley, S. C.: Southern Historical Press, 1984; 2011. [List of entires in alphabetical order that provide details about the individual soldiers of the Revolutionary War from the western part of North Carolina.]

Williams, Cratis. "The Mountain Folk of Western North Carolina." *Tar Heel Junior Historian*, 17:1 (Fall 1977), 2-6. [Online description from "North Carolina Periodicals Index," East Carolina University: "Settlers in the western portion of the state were far removed from both their state and national government. In an effort to organize, this group created the Watauga Association in 1772. The Watauga Settlements encompassed an area in western North Carolina and eastern Tennessee and was populated primarily by Scotch-Irish and German settlers."]

Williams, John Alexander. *Appalachia: A History.* Chapel Hill: University of North Carolina Press, 2002. [Publisher's description: "Interweaving social, political, environmental, economic, and popular history, John Alexander Williams chronicles four and a half centuries of the Appalachian past. Along the way, he explores Appalachia's long-contested boundaries and the numerous, often contradictory images that have shaped perceptions of the region as both the essence of America and a place apart."]

Wise, Larry E., Jr. "'A Sufficient Competence to Make Them Independent': Attitudes Towards Authority, Improvement and Independence in the Carolina-Virginia Backcountry, 1760-1800." Ph. D. dissertation, University of Tennessee, 1997.

Woodmason, Charles; Richard J. Hooker, ed. *The Carolina Backcountry on the Eve of the Revolution: The Journal and Other Writings of Charles Woodmason, Anglican Itinerant.* Chapel Hill: University of North Carolina Press, 1953. [Contains Woodmason's observations on the residents of frontier areas of the Carolinas briefly mentioning business women, lewd women, American Indian women, widows, wives, and daughters.]

Woodson, Carter G. "Freedom and Slavery in Appalachian America." *Journal of Negro History*, 1:2 (April 1916), 132-150.

Counties and Towns of North Carolina in the Revolutionary Era

[Note: The entries that appear in this chapter are by no means a complete listing of all of the local histories for North Carolina counties, towns, and cities. Consultation of online catalogs of local, regional, state, university and college online catalogs can provide details on many more such publications. Compiled bibliographies of North Carolina local histories are also another useful resource. One example is George Stevenson's *North Carolina Local History: A Select Guide,* which despite its age remains useful.[38]

Albright, Lee, and Helen F. M. Leary. "Strategy for 'Burned' Counties." In Helen F. M. Leary, ed. *North Carolina Research: Genealogy and Local History*. 2nd ed. (Raleigh: North Carolina Genealogical Society, 1996), Chapter Two: "Designing Research Strategies," 57-61.

Albright, Lee, and Helen F. M. Leary. "Strategy for Court Records." In Helen F. M. Leary, ed. *North Carolina Research: Genealogy and Local History*. 2nd ed. (Raleigh: North Carolina Genealogical Society, 1996), Chapter Two: "Designing Research Strategies," 52-53.

Albright, Lee, and Helen F. M. Leary. "Strategy for Finding the 'Right' County." In Helen F. M. Leary, ed. *North Carolina Research: Genealogy and Local History*. 2nd ed. (Raleigh: North Carolina Genealogical Society, 1996), Chapter Two: "Designing Research Strategies," 53-57.

Battle, Kemp P. "Glimpses of History in the Names of Our Counties." *North Carolina Booklet*, 6:1 (July 1906), 27-49; online: http://digital.ncdcr.gov/cdm/ref/collection/p249901coll37/id/14180. [Online description from "North Carolina Periodicals Index," East Carolina University: "This article examines the formation of the counties of North Carolina throughout the state's history as well as the historical figures, places, and peoples that the counties are named after."]

Black, Roy W. "The Genesis of County Organization in the Western District of North Carolina and in the State of Tennessee." *West Tennessee Historical Society Papers*, 2 (1948), 95-118; online: http://register.shelby.tn.us/wths/?acc=Y.

Corbitt, David Leroy. *The Formation of the North Carolina Counties, 1663-1943.* Raleigh: Division of Archives and History, North Carolina Department of Cultural Resources, 1969.

"County Records." In Helen F. M. Leary, ed. *North Carolina Research: Genealogy and Local History*. 2nd ed. (Raleigh: North Carolina Genealogical Society, 1996), Part II, 149-296. [Part II encompasses Chapters 10-27.]

Ellis, C. T. "Counties That Have Vanished." *The State: A Weekly Survey of North Carolina*, 10:51 (May 1943), 7, 14; online: http://digital.ncdcr.gov/cdm/ref/collection/p16062coll18/id/17263. [Online description from "North Carolina Periodicals Index," East Carolina University: "You will look in vain on the North Carolina map for Tryon, Bute, Glasgow, and Dobbs Counties, but many years ago they were a part of the State."]

Great Britain. Colonial Office. "Philadelphia. Circular Letter from William Hooper, Joseph Hewes, and Richard Caswell to 'the Committees of the Several Towns and Counties of North-Carolina, Appointed for the Purpose of Carrying into Execution the Resolves of the Continental Congress.' June 19, 1775." Manuscript, MARS Id: 21.1.27.65 (Folder), State Archives of North Carolina, Raleigh.

Guess, William Conrad. "County Government in Colonial North Carolina." *James Sprunt Historical Publications*, 11:1 (Chapel Hill: University of North Carolina Press, 1911), 3-23.

"How Counties Got Their Names." *The State: Down Home in North Carolina*, 26:5 (August 1958), 53-56; online: http://digital.ncdcr.gov/cdm/ref/collection/p16062coll18/id/51628. [Online description from "North Carolina Periodicals Index," East Carolina University: "A list of all the North Carolina counties and the origin of their names is listed alphabetically in this article. From Alamance County to Yancey, the dates and inspiration for these names hold a long history of the state."]

Nash, Francis. "The Borough Towns of North Carolina." *North Carolina Booklet*, 6:2 (October 1906), 82-102. [Online description from "North Carolina Periodicals Index," East Carolina University: "This article examines

---

[38] George Stevenson, *North Carolina Local History: A Select Bibliography.* Raleigh: North Carolina Department of Cultural Resources, Division of Archives and History, 1984.

the formation and establishment of boroughs or franchised towns in the early colonial settlement of North Carolina during the 18th century."]

Norris, Jeanie Faris. "How We Grew." *The State: Down Home in North Carolina*, 28:12 (November 1960), 11; online: http://digital.ncdcr.gov/cdm/ref/collection/p16062coll18/id/43054. [Online description from "North Carolina Periodicals Index," East Carolina University: "Containing progressive maps that depict the growth of North Carolina counties from 1700 through 1912, this is an illustrated chronology as opposed to an article."]

Norris, Jeanie Faris. "Ten 'Lost' North Carolina Counties Abandoned When Names Were Changed." *We the People of North Carolina*, 9:6 (November 1951), 8-9, 21. [Online description from "North Carolina Periodicals Index," East Carolina University: "Ten counties in North Carolina have been abolished, absorbed, or otherwise are gone off the maps of today's North Carolina. A map accompanying the article indicates where the counties were formerly located."]

North Carolina (State). General Assembly. "[Document dated:] April 16, 1778: Bill to Impower the County Court of Each County to Take into Their Possession the Records Belonging to Each Respective County (Rejected)." Manuscript; General Assembly Record Group; Session Records, April-May 1778, Senate Bills, House Bills, House Resolutions (April 27-May 1, 1778), Box 2 (MARS ID: 66.8.13.14; folder), State Archives of North Carolina, Raleigh.

North Carolina (State). General Assembly. "[Document dated:] April 25, 1783: House Bill to Preserve County Records (Rejected)." Manuscript: General Assembly Record Group; Session Records, April-May 1783; Unidentified Amendements; Senate Bills, House Bills, Box 2 (MARS ID: 66.8.30.48; folder), State Archives of North Carolina, Raleigh. [Online catalog description: "Bill requires all county records to be maintained in a suitable repository and kept until required by the Clerk of the County Courts."]

North Carolina. Office of the Secretary of State. "County Boundary Lines, 1747-1922." Manuscript SS.XX, Box 1 (MARS ID: 12.110.1; box), State Archives of North Carolina, Raleigh. [Online catalog description: "These are reports, maps, and related materials concerning county boundary lines."]

Sanders, John L. "Guide to Pronouncing County Names." *Popular Government*. 63:3 (Spring 1998), 38. [Online description from "North Carolina Periodicals Index," East Carolina University: "There are one hundred counties in North Carolina and probably several hundred pronunciations of their names. Recognizing that there are local variations in the way the name is said, Sanders offers a list to provide a ready guide to customary county name pronunciation."]

Wager, Paul Woodford. *County Government and Administration in North Carolina.* Chapel Hill: University of North Carolina Press, 1928.

Walser, Richard. "Sifting the Past." *The State: Down Home in North Carolina*, 23:15 (December 1955), 14, 23; online: http://digital.ncdcr.gov/cdm/ref/collection/p16062coll18/id/82234. [Online description from "North Carolina Periodicals Index," East Carolina University: "Walser says 'that all any county history can do is to put down as many facts as possible, make them readable, then supply an index.' Presently {1955}, one-third of the state's one hundred counties have a published history. Walser reviews some of the published ones and provides a partial list and date of publication."]

Watson, Alan D. "County Buildings and Other Public Structures in Colonial North Carolina." *North Carolina Historical Review*, 82:4 (October 2005), 427-463. [Online description from "North Carolina Periodicals Index," East Carolina University: "This article examines the county buildings of colonial North Carolina and the importance they played with the local community. Courthouses, jails, and warehouses were specially built by counties and were indicative of the county's responsiveness to public needs."]

Watson, Alan D. "The County Clerk in Colonial North Carolina." *North Carolina Historical Review*, 85:1 (January 2008), 133-162. [Online description from "North Carolina Periodicals Index," East Carolina University: "This article examines the role of the county clerk in colonial North Carolina. The clerk's duties included maintaining court records, processing documents, and offering legal advice, making it a very influential position. The abuse of power by clerks was a factor in the violent actions of the Regulator movement between 1766 and 1781."]

Watson, Alan D. "County Fiscal Policy in Colonial North Carolina." *North Carolina Historical Review*, 55:3 (July 1978), 284-305. [Online description from "North Carolina Periodicals Index," East Carolina University: "The county as a unit of government became very important during the Colonial Period of the 18th century in North Carolina. The county was instrumental in the disbursement of public funds for a variety of purposes. This included construction and maintenance of public buildings, salaries for sheriffs, clerks of court and tobacco inspectors, provision of public services, construction of bridges and operation of ferries, standardizing weights and measures, surveying of county boundaries and provision of charitable services."]

Winslow, Raymond S., Jr. "County Records: Bonds." In Helen F. M. Leary, ed. *North Carolina Research: Genealogy and Local History*. 2nd ed. (Raleigh: North Carolina Genealogical Society, 1996), Chapter 20, 265-271.

Winslow, Raymond S., Jr. "County Records: Civil and Criminal Action Papers." In Helen F. M. Leary, ed. *North Carolina Research: Genealogy and Local History*. 2nd ed. (Raleigh: North Carolina Genealogical Society, 1996), Chapter 18, 256-257.

Winslow, Raymond S., Jr. "County Records: County Court Minutes." In Helen F. M. Leary, ed. *North Carolina Research: Genealogy and Local History*. 2nd ed. (Raleigh: North Carolina Genealogical Society, 1996), Chapter 15, 240-248.

Winslow, Raymond S., Jr. "County Records: Dockets." In Helen F. M. Leary, ed. *North Carolina Research: Genealogy and Local History*. 2nd ed. (Raleigh: North Carolina Genealogical Society, 1996), Chapter 19, 261-264.

Winslow, Raymond S., Jr. "County Records: Election Records." In Helen F. M. Leary, ed. *North Carolina Research: Genealogy and Local History*. 2nd ed. (Raleigh: North Carolina Genealogical Society, 1996), Chapter 25, 286-287.

Winslow, Raymond S., Jr. "County Records: Equity Court Minutes." In Helen F. M. Leary, ed. *North Carolina Research: Genealogy and Local History*. 2nd ed. (Raleigh: North Carolina Genealogical Society, 1996), Chapter 17, 254-255.

Winslow, Raymond S., Jr. "County Records: Military and Pension Records." In Helen F. M. Leary, ed. *North Carolina Research: Genealogy and Local History*. 2nd ed. (Raleigh: North Carolina Genealogical Society, 1996), Chapter 21, 272-275.

Winslow, Raymond S., Jr. "County Records: Miscellaneous Records." In Helen F. M. Leary, ed. *North Carolina Research: Genealogy and Local History*. 2nd ed. (Raleigh: North Carolina Genealogical Society, 1996), Chapter 27, 290-296.

Winslow, Raymond S., Jr. "County Records: Records of County Officials." In Helen F. M. Leary, ed. *North Carolina Research: Genealogy and Local History*. 2nd ed. (Raleigh: North Carolina Genealogical Society, 1996), Chapter 24, 282-285.

Winslow, Raymond S., Jr. "County Records: Roads and Bridges." In Helen F. M. Leary, ed. *North Carolina Research: Genealogy and Local History*. 2nd ed. (Raleigh: North Carolina Genealogical Society, 1996), Chapter 22, 276-279.

Winslow, Raymond S., Jr. "County Records: School Records." In Helen F. M. Leary, ed. *North Carolina Research: Genealogy and Local History*. 2nd ed. (Raleigh: North Carolina Genealogical Society, 1996), Chapter 23, 280-281.

Winslow, Raymond S., Jr. "County Records: Superior Court Minutes." In Helen F. M. Leary, ed. *North Carolina Research: Genealogy and Local History*. 2nd ed. (Raleigh: North Carolina Genealogical Society, 1996), Chapter 16, 249-253.

Alamance County

[Note: For various state government documents relating to Alamance County during the Revolutionary period, search the MARS online catalog using the advanced search: http://mars.archives.ncdcr.gov/AdvancedSearch.aspx. Use the "Year" search box to restrict the searching to 1775-1783 and enter the county's name in the "Subjects" box, and hit the "Search" button near the top. This will retrieve any cataloged document for the county from that time period. These materials can vary considerably from personal or county petitions to the General Assembly, Loyalist matters, land disputes and claims, tax collection, exemptions from taxation, payments to county veterans, county divisions, personal collections, genealogical material, British claims against North Carolinians, etc. There is considerable information in these materials that could provide interesting documentation for persons living during the Revolution. The results will also include all of the wills and probates recorded in the county during the period set for the search. We had hoped to include many of these listings in this guide, but they are too voluminous. Citations to many of these search results for the eastern counties do, however, appear in the text.]

Bailey, Pat. "Final Roll Call at Frieden's for Revolutionary War Soldier John Boon." *Alamance Genealogist,* 30:3 (September 2013), 138-139.

Bolden, Don. "The Braxtons Still Live Here." *The State: Down Home in North Carolina*, 48:10 (March 1981), 21, 25; online: http://digital.ncdcr.gov/cdm/ref/collection/p16062coll18/id/60087. [Online description from "North Carolina Periodicals Index," East Carolina University: "William Braxton was granted a 265 acre plat from Lord

Granville in 1756. The land is in Alamance County, and the Braxton family lives there still. They own the entire plat and even have the deed granting Braxton the land."]

Cox, Lisa D. "Rachel Allen, Medicine Woman." *Alamance Genealogist,* 30:3 (September 2013), 124-125. [1760?-1840; Pennsylvania to Alamance County ca. 1762 with her parents and siblings]

Kobrin, Lisa. "Local Revolutionary War Soldiers' Graves." *Alamance Genealogist,* 30:3 (September 2013), 136-137.

McGowan, Molly. "History, Revised: State Corrects Alamance County Revolutionary War Marker." *The Times-News*, April 26, 2013; online: http://www.thetimesnews.com/news/top-news/history-revised-state-corrects-alamance-county-revolutionary-war-marker-1.134549. [Pyle's Defeat marker]

Stanford, Richard, 1767-1816. "Richard Stanford (1767-1816) Papers, 1798-1827, 1888-1914." Manuscript, Call Number PC.177 (MARS ID: 686; record group), State Archives of North Carolina, Raleigh. [Online catalog description: "Chiefly letters from Stanford of Hawfields, Democratic-Republican congressman (1791-1816) in Philadelphia and Washington, to his wife and to Capt. William Lytle about Revolutionary vouchers (1798-1799), events in Congress, slaves, his children, and peace (1815)."]

Stockard, Sallie W. *The History of Alamance*. Raleigh: Capital Printing Company, 1900.

Troxler, Carole Watterson, and William Murray Vincent. *Shuttle & Plow: A History of Alamance County, North Carolina*. Graham: Alamance County Historical Association, 1999.

Anson County [Salisbury District]

[Note: For various state government documents relating Anson County to during the Revolutionary period, search the MARS online catalog using the advanced search: http://mars.archives.ncdcr.gov/AdvancedSearch.aspx. Use the "Year" search box to restrict the searching to 1775-1783 and enter the county's name in the "Subjects" box, and hit the "Search" button near the top. This will retrieve any cataloged document for the county from that time period. These materials can vary considerably from personal or county petitions to the General Assembly, Loyalist matters, land disputes and claims, tax collection, exemptions from taxation, payments to county veterans, county divisions, personal collections, genealogical material, British claims against North Carolinians, etc. There is considerable information in these materials that could provide interesting documentation for persons living during the Revolution. The results will also include all of the wills and probates recorded in the county during the period set for the search. We had hoped to include many of these listings in this guide, but they are too voluminous. Citations to many of these search results for the eastern counties do, however, appear in the text.]

Allen, Sara C., ed. *The Heritage of Alexander County, North Carolina.* Winston-Salem: Hunter Publishing Company, 1986.

"The Anson County Courthouse Fire, 1868." *North Carolina Genealogical Society Journal*, 3:1 (February 1977), 62.

"Anson County Revolutionary War Pensions, 1841. *The Carolinas Genealogical Society Bulletin*, 11: 58.

Anson County. "Anson County Miscellaneous Records, 1759-1960: Depositions Concerning Probable Seditious Activity, 1775, 1785." Manuscript C.R.05.928.1, State Archives of North Carolina, Raleigh.

Anson County. "Anson County Miscellaneous Records, 1759-1960: Deposition of William Pickett Concerning the Regulators." Manuscript C.R.05.928.1, State Archives of North Carolina, Raleigh.

Ashe, Sarah William. "The Story of Sneedsboro." *The State: A Weekly Survey of North Carolina*, 17:25 (November 1949), 4-5, 20; online: http://digital.ncdcr.gov/cdm/ref/collection/p16062coll18/id/24672. [Online description from "North Carolina Periodicals Index," East Carolina University: "Once a bustling city, Sneedsboro soon declined. All that remains today are crumbling ruins and a graveyard."]

"Captain Thomas Wade of Anson County for the Service of His Light Horse & Independent Company of Foot to Cross Creek against the Insurgents, February 1776." In Weynette Parks Haun, *North Carolina Revolutionary Army Accounts, Part I, Secretary of State Treasurer's & Comptroller's Papers Journal "A", (Public Accounts) 1775-1776* (Durham: W. P. Haun, 1988), 101-104.

Daves, Graham. "Town and County Resolutions of 1774." *Magazine of American History with Notes and Queries*, 30:1-2 (July-August 1893), 88-90. [Wilmington; Rowan County; Anson County; New Bern and Craven County]

"Depositions in Connection with the Accusation of James Chiles as a Loyalist, Anson County, N. C., 1776." *The Carolinas Genealogical Society Bulletin*, 12:4 (Spring 1976), 64-65.

Harrison, James T. "James T. Harrison Papers, 1770-1896." Manuscript 2441, Southern Historical Collection, Louis Round Wilson Special Collections Library, University of North Carolina, Chapel Hill; online finding aid available at http://www2.lib.unc.edu/mss/inv/h/Harrison,James_T.html. [Online finding aid description: "1770-1802 - legal Papers, bills, receipts, and miscellaneous items relating chiefly to individuals in Anson and Richmond Counties, North Carolina. Among them were William Love, John Crawford, David Love, Thomas Blewett (probably father of Thomas G. Blewett), John Cole, and William Colson. There are a few items relating to the Revolutionary War, such as receipts for supplies furnished to troops, notes concerning payments to volunteer soldiers of Anson County (whose names are listed), agreements relating to locating and surveying land claims of veterans in North Carolina, and a deed of sale for military land claim by Benjamin Simmons to Thomas Evans."]

Henderson, Archibald. *Revolution in North Carolina in 1775: Transylvania, Craven, Anson, and Mecklenburg.* [S. l.: s. n.], 1916. [According to the online catalog of the University of North Carolina at Charlotte, this volume examines "[t]he Mecklenburg Declaration of Independence and the revolution in North Carolina in 1775."]

Hilke, Ann Christnacht, and Linda K. Reid. "1777 Petition of John Smith of Anson County." *The North Carolina Genealogical Society Journal*, 35:2 (May 2009), 129-130.

Medley, Mary L. *History of Anson County, North Carolina, 1750-1976*. Wadesboro: Anson County Historical Society; Charlotte: Heritage Printers, Inc., 1976.

Merrens, Roy H., and Herbert R. Paschal. "A Map-Maker's View of Anson County in 1769." *North Carolina Historical Review*, 59:4 (October 1982), 271-278.

McBride, Robert Martin. *Portrait of an American Loyalist, James Cotton of Anson County, North Carolina.* Nashville: R. M. McBride, 1954.

Merrens, Roy H., and Herbert R. Paschal. "A Map-Maker's View of Anson County in 1769." *North Carolina Historical Review*, 59:4 (October 1982), 271-278. [Online description from "North Carolina Periodicals Index," East Carolina University: "In 1769, map-maker John Abraham Collet provided a short description of Anson County, North Carolina to promote the interior of the state. Collet wrote quite positively about the area on everything from agriculture to roads, even if the information was at sometimes inaccurate."]

Moore, Terry. "Anson County, North Carolina, Created from Bladen County in 1750." *NCGS News: The Newsletter of the North Carolina Genealogical Society*, 39:6 (November 2015), 12-13; online: http://www.ncgenealogy.org/articles_tools/Anson_County_North_Carolina.pdf.

Norris, Jeannie Faris. "The Boggan-Hammond House, in Wadesboro." *The State: Down Home in North Carolina*, 38:11 (November 1970), 14-16, 19; online: http://digital.ncdcr.gov/cdm/ref/collection/p16062coll18/id/53874. [Online description from "North Carolina Periodicals Index," East Carolina University: "The Anson County Historical Society, under the leadership of Linn D. Garibaldi, took possession of the oldest and most historically significant house in Wadesboro from Major L. P. McLendon, prominent Greensboro lawyer, state civic leader, and descendant of Capt. Patrick Boggan, the original builder of the house. The historical society's efforts to preserve the home for a museum and for educational purposes was aided by a 1969 General Assembly grant of $20,000 and a Richardson Foundation grant of $3,000. Capt. Boggan was one of the Anson Regulators who stormed the county courthouse on April 28, 1768 demanding relief from the injustices of Royal Local Magistrates. The Regulators nominated their own Assembly representative, Charles Robinson, making them possibly the first citizens group in America to make a political nomination and certainly among the first to forcibly demand justice from local officers." (Patrick Henry Boggan (1725-1817)]

Norris, Jeannie Faris. "Ghost Town." *The State: Down Home in North Carolina*, 29:9 (September 1961), 11; online: http://digital.ncdcr.gov/cdm/ref/collection/p16062coll18/id/8848. [Online description from "North Carolina Periodicals Index," East Carolina University: "Originally planned as a great inland port, only a scrawny chimney and a cemetery mark the location of the once flourishing Sneedsborough, North Carolina. Attracting many leaders of the day, Sneedsborough thrived for approximately 30 years, until the lack of commerce and the spread of epidemics forced most of the residents to move elsewhere."]

North Carolina (State). General Assembly. "[Documents dated:] April 20, 1780: Resolution Exempting from Poll Taxes William Whitfield of Pitt County and James Smith of Anson County (with Anson County Court Recommendation and Whitfield's Petition." Manuscript; General Assembly Record Group; Session Records, April-May 1780; Joint Papers, Committee Papers, Resolutions; House Joint Resolutions: April 17-27, 1780; Box 1 (MARS ID: 66.8.20.15.4; folder), State Archives of North Carolina, Raleigh. [Online catalog description: "The Anson County Court recommends exemption for James Smith, as he is poor, aged, and infirm. Whitfield informs the Assembly in his petition that he is disabled and must care for small children."]

Picket, James. "James Pickett Paper, 1776." Manuscript, Call Number PC.844 (MARS ID: 1354; record group), State Archives of North Carolina, Raleigh. [Online catalog description: "James Pickett's deposition, dated in Anson Co., Nov. 12, 1776, and witnessed by Matthew Raiford, attesting James Terry's public stand against the tory views of John Collson in 1775."]

Pleasant, Paul. "No Man's Land." *The State: Down Home in North Carolina*, 29:9 (September 1961), 16-17, 29. [Online description from "North Carolina Periodicals Index," East Carolina University: "The boundary dispute in the 1740s between North and South Carolina found Anson County caught in the middle. Continued confusion over land rights resulted in forced land seizures, and land holders refusing to pay taxes to North or South Carolina. The dispute and confusion continued until after the Revolutionary War."]

Williams, Jacob. "Deposition of Jacob Williams Concerning the Treatment of Loyalists in Anson County, August 18, 1775." *The Carolinas Genealogical Society*, 46:1 (Summer 2009), 6.

Ashe County

Arthur, John Preston. *Western North Carolina: A History (From 1730 to 1913)*. Raleigh: Edwards & Broughton Printing Company for the Edward Buncomb Chapter, North Carolina Daughters of the American Revolution, 1914; reprinted: Johnson City, Tenn.: Overmountain Press, 1996. [Ashe and Bucombe Counties]

Fletcher, Arthur L. *Ashe County: A History.* Jefferson, N. C.: Ashe County Research Association, [1963].

Avery County

Avery County Bicentennial Commission. *Avery County Heritage*. 4 vols. [Banner Elk]: Puddingston Press, 1976-[1986]. [Contents: {v. 1} Biographies and Genealogies; v. 2. Biographies, Genealogies and Church Histories; v. 3. (compiled by the Avery County Historical Society) Biographies, Genealogies and Church Histories; v. 4. Historical Sites.]

Bailey, Lloyd Richard, Sr., ed. *The Heritage of the Toe River Valley*. 12 vols. Durham: L. R. Bailey, 1994-2007. [Avery, Mitchell, and Yancey Counties]

Davis, William Michael. *The Revolutionary War Military Record of William Davis of Three Mile Creek of Avery County, North Carolina.* Taylorsville: W. M. Davis, 2007. [William Avery (1725 or 1727-1841)]

Beaufort County, Bath, and Washington [New Bern District]

[Note: For various state government documents relating to Beaufort County and Beaufort during the Revolutionary period, search the MARS online catalog using the advanced search: http://mars.archives.ncdcr.gov/AdvancedSearch.aspx. Use the "Year" search box to restrict the searching to 1775-1783 and enter the county's or town's name in the "Subjects" box, and hit the "Search" button near the top. This will retrieve any cataloged document for the county from that time period. These materials can vary considerably from personal or county petitions to the General Assembly, Loyalist matters, land disputes and claims, tax collection, exemptions from taxation, payments to county veterans, county divisions, personal collections, genealogical material, British claims against North Carolinians, etc. There is considerable information in these materials that could provide interesting documentation for persons living during the Revolution. The results will also include all of the wills and probates recorded in the county during the period set for the search. We had hoped to include many of these listings in this guide, but they are too voluminous. Citations to many of these search results for the eastern counties do, however, appear in the text.]

"Beaufort County Militia, 1781." Online at North Carolina Beaufort County History and Genealogy: http://homepages.rootsweb.com/~rosslibr/beaufortco/bmilitia.html.

Bonner, R. T. "Revolutionary History: The Graves of Our Revolutionary Ancestors Who Took Part in the Revolutionary War in Civil Capacities from Beaufort County, North Carolina." *Pamtico Tracings*, 4:1 (June 1988), 15; reprinted: 13:1 (June 1997), 12. [Originally published in *The Washington Progress*, May 9, 1912.] Also printed in *Pitt County Genealogical Quarterly*, 13:4 (November 2006), 34.

"Bounty Paid Members of the Beaufort County, N. C. Militia, 1780." *North Carolina Genealogical Society Journal*, 9:1 (February 1983), 22.

"Burial Sites of Veterans, Beaufort County." *Pamtico Tracings*, 4:1 (June 1988), 15.

Byrd, William L., and John H Smith. *North Carolina Slaves and Free Persons of Color: Hyde and Beaufort Counties*. Bowie, Md.: Heritage Books, 2002.

Carraway, Gertrude. "The Restoration of Bath." *The State: A Weekly Survey of North Carolina*, 9:20 (October 1941), 18-19; online: http://digital.ncdcr.gov/cdm/ref/collection/p16062coll18/id/40317. [Online description from "North Carolina Periodicals Index," East Carolina University: "During the early 1940s, ambitious plans were made to transform Bath into a living history town much like Colonial Williamsburg. Bath presented the perfect locale for such a project because it is the oldest incorporated town in North Carolina. By 1941, some of the restoration had already been completed. The state's oldest church building, St. Thomas Episcopal, had just been restored and work begun on restoring the Marsh Home dated to 1744."]

Casto, Marilyn D. "Historic Houses of Beaufort County, North Carolina, 1744-1899." Ph. D. dissertation, University of North Carolina at Greensboro, 1982.

Hardesty, Fred. "The Church Courts." *The State: Down Home in North Carolina*, 37:5 (August 1969), 11-12; online: http://digital.ncdcr.gov/cdm/ref/collection/p16062coll18/id/52787. [Online description from "North Carolina Periodicals Index," East Carolina University: "Bath's St. Thomas Episcopal Church, North Carolina's oldest church in its oldest town, was not merely the center of religious study in the community. Like most early American denominations, it was also the local community's primary center of discipline and legal recourse. Most churches forbade its members from taking a fellow member to court before 'gospel steps' had been taken. As the antebellum period progressed and the church began to gradually lose control of its members, church courts became less and less effective."]

Jones, Plummer Alston, Jr. "List of Taxables for Beaufort County, NC, for 1779." *North Carolina Genealogical Society Journal*, 15:3 (August 1989), 137-146.

Latham, Bea. "Bath: North Carolina's First Town." *Tar Heel Junior Historian*, 45:2 (Spring 2006), 3-5: online: http://ncpedia.org/geography/bath. [Online description from "North Carolina Periodicals Index," East Carolina University: "North Carolina's early immigrants were a mixed group that included well-to-do planters, laborers, apprentices, indentured servants, and convicts. In 1701, John Lawson first sighted the land where Bath would be built. Word of this desirable area quickly spread, attracting new immigrants from other colonies to move to North Carolina. In 1704, Lawson drew plans for the town, and in 1705, Bath incorporated. The surrounding area was a source of tar, turpentine, and other naval stores. Latham discusses the town's history."]

Lea, Diane. "Historic Bath: North Carolina's Oldest Town Celebrates 300th Birthday." *Metro Magazine*, 6:8 (August 2005), 21-25, 27-28; online: http://www.metronc.com/article/?id=22. [Online description from "North Carolina Periodicals Index," East Carolina University: "Bath is North Carolina's oldest incorporated town and its first port, chartered by an act of the Colonial General Assembly in 1705 in the picturesque country between the eastern Piedmont and the barrier islands of the Outer Banks."]

"A List of the Several Divisions of Affective Men in the Beaufort Regiment of Militia Made the 20th of April 1781." *Quarterly Review of the Eastern North Carolina Genealogical Society*, 14:2 (June 1987), 65-67.

Major Reading Blount Chapter, North Carolina Daughters of the American Revolution. *Historical Highlights of Washington and Beaufort County: Bicentennial Edition, 1776-1976*. Washington: The Chapter, 1976.

McBride, Ransom. "Officers and Soldiers of Beaufort Co., NC, Whose Estates Were Administered by June 1792." *North Carolina Genealogical Society Journal*, 18:2 (May 1992), 72.

North Carolina (State). General Assembly. "[Document dated:] February 11, 1779: Re[specting] Petition of Carlin Wallard and William Congleton (with Message and Petition)." Manuscript, General Assembly Record Group, Session Records; Joint Papers, Committee Papers, Resolutions; Joint Select Committees, January-February 1779, Box 1 (MARS ID: 66.8.15.8.16; item), State Archives of North Carolina, Raleigh. [Online catalog description: "Wallard and Congleton, of Beaufort County, are discharged from the militia because they were improperly selected for service."]

North Carolina (State). General Assembly. "[Document dated:] May 16, 1783: Papers Relating to an Election for the House of Commons in Beaufort County." Manuscript, General Assembly Record Group, Session Records; Joint Papers, Committee Papers, Resolutions: House Committee of Privileges and Elections: Reports and Papers, April-May 1783, Box 1 (MARS ID: 66.8.29.10.4; item), State Archives of North Carolina, Raleigh. [Online catalog description: "Memorial claims that the seat taken by John Blount rightfully belongs to William Palmer and requests remedy of the situation. Includes election returns."]

"Regiment of Superanuated & Invalids [Beaufort County?]." *Pamtico Tracings*, 3:2 (September 1987), 6.

"Return of Men Raised in Beaufort County, 1st July 1779." *Pamtico Tracings*, 6:2 (December 1990), 14.

"A Return of the Drafted Men in the State Service in Beaufort County, 9th March 1779." *Quarterly Review of the Eastern North Carolina Genealogical Society*, 14:2 (June 1987), 67; also published in: *Pamtico Tracings*, 6:2 (December 1990), 14.

Rodman, Lida Tunstall. "Historic Homes and People of Old Bath Town." *North Carolina Booklet*, 2:8 (December 1902), 1-13; online: http://digital.ncdcr.gov/cdm/ref/collection/p249901coll37/id/14180. [Online description from "North Carolina Periodicals Index," East Carolina University: "This article discusses the significant homes and people of Bath. Included in the article are the old Marsh home, the first library in the state, and the old Fort, as well as residents such as Christopher Gayle, Mary Evans, and Tobias Knight."]

Sanders, Rebecca. *Early Carteret County, North Carolina, Court Minutes 1764-1777, Vol. 3*. Beaufort: J. Sanders, 1992.

Sanders. *Early Carteret County, North Carolina, Court Minutes 1778-1789, Vol. 4*. Beaufort: J. Sanders, 1992.

Tucker, Harry Z. "Maule's Point." *The State: A Weekly Survey of North Carolina*, 11:12 (August 1943), 2, 23; online: http://digital.ncdcr.gov/cdm/ref/collection/p16062coll18/id/17696. [Online description from "North Carolina Periodicals Index," East Carolina University: "Maule's Point was a historic plantation located on Pamlico River twelve miles from Bath. The plantation was named after a noted Scotch family which lived and worked the lands around Olde Bath Towne. The head of this family was Dr. Patrick Maule who studied medicine in his native Scotland before moving to Bath County to further his practice. After his death in 1736, son John Maule inherited the property an erected the family mansion in 1750 which stood until 1930. The house that stood in 1943 was believed to have been built by John's son Moses following the Revolutionary War."]

Turnage, Sheila. "Bath." *The State: Down Home in North Carolina*, 62:3 (August 1994), 10-12; online: http://digital.ncdcr.gov/cdm/ref/collection/p16062coll18/id/66889. [Online description from "North Carolina Periodicals Index," East Carolina University: "The town of Bath was Britain's first seat of power in colonial North Carolina. The Palmer-Marsh House, the political and economic heart of colonial Bath, was recently restored after suffering fire damage in 1989."]

Turnage, Sheila. "Three Towns on the Eve of Revolution." *Our State: Down Home in North Carolina*, 68:10 (March 2001), 56-59; online: http://digital.ncdcr.gov/cdm/ref/collection/p16062coll18/id/72796. [Online description from "North Carolina Periodicals Index," East Carolina University: "Turnage gives a brief look at what was happening in New Bern, Beaufort, and Bath on the eve of the American Revolution."]

Turner, Grace. "Some Revolutionary Soldiers of Beaufort County, N. C." *Pamtico Tracings*, 7:2 (December 1991), 43-44.

Watson, Alan D.; Eva C. (Bea) Latham; and Patricia M. Samford. *Bath: The First Town in North Carolina*. Raleigh: Office of Archives and History, North Carolina Department of Cultural Resources, 2005.

Bertie County [Edenton District]

[Note: For various state government documents relating to Bertie County during the Revolutionary period, search the MARS online catalog using the advanced search: http://mars.archives.ncdcr.gov/AdvancedSearch.aspx. Use the "Year" search box to restrict the searching to 1775-1783 and enter the county's name in the "Subjects" box, and hit the "Search" button near the top. This will retrieve any cataloged document for the county from that time period. These materials can vary considerably from personal or county petitions to the General Assembly, Loyalist matters, land disputes and claims, tax collection, exemptions from taxation, payments to county veterans, county divisions, personal collections, genealogical material, British claims against North Carolinians, etc. There is considerable information in these materials that could provide interesting documentation for persons living during the Revolution. The results will also include all of the wills and probates recorded in the county during the period set for the search. We had hoped to include many of these listings in this guide, but they are too voluminous. Citations to many of these search results for the eastern counties do, however, appear in the text.]

Bennett, William Doub. "Some Revolutionary War Service Veterans in Bertie County, NC." *North Carolina Genealogical Society Journal*, 12:1 (February 1986), 50.

Bertie County. "Bertie County Miscellaneous Records, 1723-1898: Jury Lists, 1746-1868, and no date." Manuscript C.R.010.928.10, State Archives of North Carolina, Raleigh.

Bertie County. "Bertie County Miscellaneous Records, 1723-1898: Revolutionary War Records, 1775-1854, and no date." Manuscript C.R.010.928.12, State Archives of North Carolina, Raleigh. [This collection probably includes a document with a poor citations to its location: "[A Revolutionary Oath of Allegiance, 1777]."

"Bertie Co., North Carolina Powers of Attorney, 1820 and 1821." Manuscript MssColl 511. DAR Library, NSDAR, Washington, D. C. [Online catalog description: "Photocopies of documents from the North Carolina State Archives. These are powers of attorney granted by heirs to file for land warrants, 1820 and 1821. Some are copies of documents filed in other counties."]

"Charles W. Jacocks on an Expedition against the Insurgents." In Weynette Parks Haun, *North Carolina Revolutionary Army Accounts, Part I, Secretary of State Treasurer's & Comptroller's Papers Journal "A", (Public Accounts) 1775-1776* (Durham: W. P. Haun, 1988), 58-61. [A comparison with period tax records points to this list being from Bertie County.]

Dunaway, Stewart E. *Bertie County, North Carolina, Mill Records (1736-1827) and Ferry Records (1747-1842)*. Hillsborough: North Carolina Historical Books, 2010. [Note: While not specifically concerning the Revolution, these sources can be used in tandem with land records and other documents to help locate places of residence, occupations, geographical features, and place names.]

*The Episcopal Church in Bertie County, 1701-1990, from Its Anglican roots to the Twentieth Century.*Windsor: St. Thomas' Episcopal Church, 1990.

Everett, Vernon L. "The Waddell Tombstone." *Washington County Genealogical Society Journal*, 4:3 (December 1996), 85. [stone of Elizabeth Waddell Davison, wife of Captain Robert Davison, along with information on the Davison and Hawkins families of Bertie County]

Great Britain. Exchequer and Audit Department. Audit Office. "Certificate Addressed to Governor Richard Caswell from John Johnson, Clerk of Bertie County Court, 14 Aug. 1777." Manuscript 77.2203.1 (MARS ID: 21.3.70.19), State Archives of North Carolina, Raleigh. [Online catalog description: "Stating that Reverend Francis Johnston has given bond that he will depart the state within 60 days, having been banished for refusing to take an oath of allegiance to the state."]

Haun, Weynette Parks. *Bertie County, North Carolina, County Court Minutes, 1772-1780, Book IV.* Durham: W. P. Haun, 1979.

Haun, Weynette Parks. *Bertie County, North Carolina, County Court Minutes, 1781 thru 1787, Book V.* Durham: W. P. Haun, 1982.

Haun, Weynette Parks. *Bertie County, North Carolina, County Court Minutes (Court of Pleas & Quarter Sessions), 1778 thru 1792, Book VI, Book V.* Durham: W. P. Haun, 1982.

Jones, Doward N. "Tide Me Over." *Our State: Down Home in North Carolina*, 73:6 (November 2005), 200-202, 204; online: http://digital.ncdcr.gov/cdm/ref/collection/p16062coll18/id/84831. [Jones recounts the history of the Sans Souci ferry, a small two-car cable ferry that carries traffic across Cashie River in Bertie County. In 1722, a man named Tomlinson applied for and received permission to build a ferry. Since then a ferry has operated at that crossing. Artist Francis Speight's famous painting of the idyllic ferry crossing brought the scene to wider audience beyond the state."]

[Meredith, Lewis, and David Meredith]. "Lewis and David Meredith Account Book, 1775-1786." Manuscript AB.331 (MARS ID: 3231; record group), State Archives of North Carolina, Raleigh. [Online catalog description: "General merchandise. Account book."]

Norris, Jeannie Faris. "The Great Fisheries of the Nineteenth Century." *The State: Down Home in North Carolina*, 31:24 (April 1964), 15-16; online: http://digital.ncdcr.gov/cdm/ref/collection/p16062coll18/id/46710. [Online description from "North Carolina Periodicals Index," East Carolina University: "A fishing county since the early 18th century, Bertie County benefitted from the introduction of Seine nets as early as 1713, utilizing this method through 1915. The last seine to operate in the county was the Sutton Beach station, also known as Avoca, the largest and most successful of all the Albemarle Sound fisheries."]

Norris, Jeannie Faris. "King House Wins Incentive Grant." *The North Carolina Preservationist*, 3 (January 1976), 6. [Online description from "North Carolina Periodicals Index," East Carolina University: "The King House, built in 1763 by William King, has been selected as a recipient of the 1975 Incentive Grant sponsored by the Historic Preservation Society of North Carolina. The house was given to the Historic Hope Foundation in 1974; they propose to move the King House to Hope Plantation located west of Windsor."]

North Carolina. General Assembly. "December 22, 1777: Joint Papers, Committee Papers, Resolutions, Senate Bills, House Bills, Appointing Commissioners to Superintend Affairs of the Tuscarora Indians in Bertie Co. (Message Only)." Manuscript; General Assembly Record Group; Session Records, November-December 1977, Box 1 (MARS ID: 66.8.10.8.15; item), State Archives of North Carolina, Raleigh.

North Carolina. General Assembly. "Feb. 2, 1779: Joint Papers, Committee Papers, Resolutions, Senate Bills, House Bills, Petition of the Sundry Inhabitants of Bertie Co. in Favor of William Berkitt." Manuscript; General Assembly Record Group; Session Records, January-February 1779, Box 1 (MARS ID: 66.8.15.9.12), State Archives of North Carolina, Raleigh. [Online catalog description: "The petitioners request that William Berkitt be excused from military service because he exposed a conspiracy, thus placing his life in danger."]

North Carolina. General Assembly. Senate. "[Document dated:] January 26, 1779: Joint Papers, Committee Papers, Resolutions, Senate Bills, House Bills, Senate Bill to Empower the Court of Bertie County to Levy a Further Tax for Completing the Public Buildings of Said County." Manuscript; General Assembly Record Group; Session Records, January-February 1779, Box 2 (MARS ID: 66.8.16.7), State Archives of North Carolina, Raleigh.

North Carolina (State). General Assembly. "[Document dated:] May 15, 1779: Joint Papers, Committee Papers, Resolutions, Senate Bills, House Bills, For Granting Commissions to Persons in Bertie County (Messages Only)." Manuscript General Assembly Record Group, Session Records, May 1779, Box 1 (MARS ID: 66.8.17.13.31), State Archives of North Carolina, Raleigh. [Online catalog description: "Copies of a list of Continental Line soldiers whose bounty land rights had not been claimed as of 1821. List was apparently created either by the Board of Adjudicators, which was appointed in 1819 and was composed of the governor, treasurer, and comptroller, or by the agent of the Board of Trustees of the University of North Carolina, who was instructed to identify unclaimed bounty lands that would escheat to the university. One of the two copies contains additions noting acreage and warrant numbers, issued in 1824."]

North Carolina. General Assembly. "[Document dated:] October 20, 1779: Joint Papers, Committee Papers, Resolutions, Senate Bills, House Bills, Exempting Richard Hays from Taxes (Bertie County) (with Petition and Messages)." Manuscript; General Assembly Record Group; Session Records, October-November 1779, Box 1 (MARS ID: 66.8.18.13.15), State Archives of North Carolina, Raleigh. [Online catalog description: "The petitioners ask that Hays, a poor and crippled man, be exempted from taxes, and the Assembly complies."]

North Carolina. General Assembly. "[Document dated:] April-May, 1780: Joint Papers, Committee Papers, Resolutions, Senate Bills, House Bills, Petition of the Tuscarora Indians of Bertie County." Manuscript; General Assembly Record Group; Session Records, April-May 1780, Box 1 (MARS ID: 66.8.20.7.4), State Archives of North Carolina, Raleigh. [Online catalog description: "The petitioners inform the Assembly that an act appointing commissioners to settle disputes between the Tuscaroras and the whites is not serving its purpose due to the fact that jurors often fail to attend when summoned; they ask for assistance."]

North Carolina. General Assembly. House. "House Bills (Session of April 28, 1780): Joint Papers, Committee Papers, Resolutions, Senate Bills, House Bills, House Bill to Amend Act for Quieting and Securing the Tuscarora Indians." Manuscript; General Assembly Record Group; Session Records, April-May 1780, Box 2 (MARS ID: 66.8.21.30), State Archives of North Carolina, Raleigh. [Online catalog description: "Correcting an oversight in the original act, the bill imposes a penalty on jurors and witnesses, duly summoned, who fail to attend. The fines are to be levied by the commissioners appointed to hold a court for the Tuscarora claims and are to be applied to the charges of Bertie County. Clauses relating to overseers of the poor were deleted."]

"Oath of Allegiance Signed by James Bazemore, His Brothers John Jr. & Jesse and His Father John Sr. Already Established." Manuscript in "Bertie County Revolutionary War Papers, 1774-1777, 1821," State Archives of North Carolina, Raleigh.

"Revolutionary Patriots, Bertie and Granville Counties, N. C." *Mississippi DAR Genealogical Records Committee Report, Series 1, Volume 141: Genealogical Records* (typescript, 1986), 38-44; digital surrogate, DAR Library, Washington, D. C.

Sharpe, Bill. "First Choice of the First Settlers, Bertie Has Been in Use for 300 Years." *The State: Down Home in North Carolina*, 31:24 (April 1964), 8-10, 24-28; online: http://digital.ncdcr.gov/cdm/ref/collection/p16062coll18/id/46710. [Online description from "North Carolina Periodicals Index," East Carolina University: "Encompassing 682 square miles, two major rivers, and several small creeks, Bertie County served as the unofficial seat during early colonial times. Predominately an agricultural region assisted by a mild climate and a 214 day growing season, Bertie has little industrial wealth outside of lumber and tobacco. Established in 1722 and home to historic conflicts such as Culpepper's Rebellion as well as the Battle of Batchelor's Bay, Bertie County grew in prosperity with the onset of the steamboat age and improved transportation within the state."]

Smallwood, Arwin D. *Bertie County: An Eastern Carolina History*. Charleston, S. C.: Arcadia, 2002. [Publisher's description: "The lives of the Native American, African, and European inhabitants of Bertie County over its 400 years of recorded history have not only shaped, but been shaped by its landscape. One of the oldest counties in North Carolina, Bertie County lies in the western coastal plains of northeastern North Carolina, bordered to the east by Albemarle Sound and the tidewater region and to the west by the Roanoke River in the piedmont. The county's waterways and forests sustained the old Native American villages that were replaced in the eighteenth century by English plantations, cleared for the whites by African slaves. Bertie County's inhabitants successfully developed and sustained a wide variety of crops including the 'three sisters' - corn, beans, and squash - as well as the giants: tobacco, cotton, and peanuts. The county was a leading exporter of naval stores and mineral wealth and later, a breadbasket of the Confederacy. *Bertie County: An Eastern Carolina History* documents the long history of the region and tells how its people, at first limited by the landscape, radically altered it to support their needs. This is the story of the Native Americans, gone from the county for 200 years but for arrowheads and other artifacts. It is the story of the African slaves and their descendants and the chronicle of their struggles through slavery, the Jim Crow era, and the Civil Rights Movement. It is also the story of the Europeans and their rush to tame the wilderness in a new land. Their entwined history is clarified in dozens of new maps created especially for this book, along with vivid illustrations of forgotten faces and moments from the past."]

Society for the Propagation of the Gospel in Foreign Parts. "Bertie Co. Letter from Rev. C. E. Taylor to [Sec., SPG], Oct. 13, 1783." Manuscript Z.5.294 (MARS ID: 21.6.3.21; folder), State Archives of of North Carolina, Raleigh. [Online catalog description: "Report on his activities during the war. Was before 1776 'happy in St. George's Parish,' Northampton Co., with 'two new and elegant Churches built for me, and two others enlarged and beautified,' but all was changed by war; resigned his parish on declaration of independence, when establishment ceased; "I could not labour, and to beg was ashamed," therefore was reduced to selling his land and houses to support his wife and five children; during war officiated on the coast and elsewhere, baptising many; serves Halifax Town since July, because a sum was raised for him there; no more than five clergy in province, and Methodists make great inroads; 'The Gentleman who presides at present in No. Carolina' has told him that he would encourage an orthodox clergy, but the assembly refuses any establishment; wishes to be recalled to England, but in any event wants assistance from the Society since he has received no salary for seven years and is in danger of confinement for debt'."]

Society for the Propagation of the Gospel in Foreign Parts. "London. Extract from Minutes of the General Meeting of the Society for the Propagation of the Gospel. March 19, 1784." Manuscript, (MARS ID: 21.9.23.5; microfilm volume), State Archives of of North Carolina, Raleigh. [Online catalog description: "Letter read from Mr. Charles Edward Taylor dated Bertie Co., N. C., 13 Oct 1783. Agreed that Taylor be informed that his connection with the Society ceased in 1772."]

Thomas, Gerald W. *Rebels and King's Men: Bertie County in the Revolutionary War.* Raleigh: North Carolina Department of Cultural Resources, Office of Archives and History, 2013.

Thompson, Harry Lewis. *Bertie Folklore: Tales from Bertie County, North Carolina.* Plymouth: Beacon Printing & Imaging, 1999.

"Tories in Bertie County." Online: http://www.rootsweb.ancestry.com/~ncbertie/conspiracy.htm.

Watson, Alan D. *Bertie County: A Brief History.* Raleigh: North Carolina Division of Archives and History, 1982.

White, Thadd. "A Little River with a Lot of History." *North Carolina's Eastern Living Magazine*, 5:2 (Winter 2013), 14-15. [Online description from "North Carolina Periodicals Index," East Carolina University: "The Cashie River in Bertie County is historically significant to the small town of Windsor, which is the reason it sits in its present location."]

Bladen County [Wilmington District]

[Note: For various state government documents relating to Bladen County during the Revolutionary period, search the MARS online catalog using the advanced search: http://mars.archives.ncdcr.gov/AdvancedSearch.aspx. Use the "Year" search box to restrict the searching to 1775-1783 and enter the county's name in the "Subjects" box, and hit the "Search" button near the top. This will retrieve any cataloged document for the county from that time period. These materials can vary considerably from personal or county petitions to the General Assembly, Loyalist matters, land disputes and claims, tax collection, exemptions from taxation, payments to county veterans, county divisions, personal collections, genealogical material, British claims against North Carolinians, etc. There is considerable information in these materials that could provide interesting documentation for persons living during the Revolution. The results will also include all of the wills and probates recorded in the county during the period set for the search. We had hoped to include many of these listings in this guide, but they are too voluminous. Citations to many of these search results for the eastern counties do, however, appear in the text.]

Bladen County. "Bladen County Miscellaneous Records, 1761-1958: A List of the Mob Riotously Assembled Together in Bladen County, Oct. 13, 1773." Manuscript C.R.011.928.7, State Archives of North Carolina, Raleigh.

"Bladen County Militia under Command of Captain Nathaniel Richardson." In Weynette Parks Haun, *North Carolina Revolutionary Army Accounts, Part I, Secretary of State Treasurer's & Comptroller's Papers Journal "A", (Public Accounts) 1775-1776* (Durham: W. P. Haun, 1988), 19-20.

Burke, James C. "A Cultural Geography of the Lower Cape Fear Basin Region of Bladen County." M. A. L. S. thesis, University of North Carolina Wilmington, 2001.

Byrd, William L., III. "Some Bladen County Petitions, 1769-1785." *North Carolina Genealogical Society Journal*, 30:2 (May 2004), 198-209.

[Byrne, Matthew, and Margaret Byrne]. "Matthew and Margaret Byrne, 1757-1784." Manuscript AB.76 (MARS ID: 2976; record group), State Archives of North Carolina, Raleigh. [Online catalog description: "General merchandise. Also contains record of slave births (1762-1862), and love poems. Ledger." Bladen County]

"Captain James Council's Company, Bladen County Militia, 1775." *Robeson County Register*, 9:4 (November 1994), 154-155, and in Weynette Parks Haun, *North Carolina Revolutionary Army Accounts, Part I, Secretary of State Treasurer's & Comptroller's Papers Journal "A", (Public Accounts) 1775-1776* (Durham: W. P. Haun, 1988), 154-155.

"Descriptive List of the Men of Bladen County Delivered Augt. 20th, 1782." *Quarterly Review of the Eastern North Carolina Genealogical Society*, 14:2 (June 1987), 64. [Includes ages, physical description, and occupation.]

Fryer, Hazel Herndon. "Oakland – The Legend Goes On." *The State: Down Home in North Carolina*, 46:5 (October 1978), 16-18, 22; http://digital.ncdcr.gov/cdm/ref/collection/p16062coll18/id/58116. [Online description from "North Carolina Periodicals Index," East Carolina University: "Oakland Plantation in Carvers, a 200-year-old mansion on the National Registry of Historic Places, is currently used as a hunting lodge. Oakland was built in 1781 and is rumored to be haunted. The Neisler family who currently owns the house and lives there invites local residents to fish fries and barbeques on a regular basis, and the family's hospitality is endless. Lena Neill has been the cook at Oakland since before 1941 and her cooking makes guests reluctant to leave."]

Great Britain. Treasury. "[Treasury: Claim of Samuel Andrews]. Copy of commission appointing Andrews Major in Loyal Militia of Bladen County. 27 Sep., 1781." Manuscript (copy) 76.2347.1 (MARS ID: 21.90.250.28), State Archives of North Carolina, Raleigh. [Online catalog description: "Including notarization dated St. John, N{ew} B{runswick}, 3 Nov. 1787. Seal. {Enclosed in 21.90.250.1.26.}"]

Haines, Jeffrey L. "Petition from the Adjoining Inhabitants of the Counties of New Hanover, Duplin, and Bladen, 23 October 1779." *North Carolina Genealogical Society Journal*, 33:3 (August 2007), 244-249. [for a new county]

Johnson, William Perry. "Descriptions of Soldiers from Militia Returns, 1778-1782." *North Carolinian: A Quarterly Journal of Genealogy and History*, 6:3 (September 1960), 725-730, 751-758. [Includes: "Bladen County Militia, 1782," 751.]

Lewis, J. D. "Patriot Leaders in North Carolina: Thomas Owen: 1st Major in the Bladen County Regiment of Militia - 1775-1776; Colonel in the Bladen County Regiment of Militia - 1776-1783." Online: http://www.carolana.com/NC/Revolution/patriot_leaders_nc_thomas_owen.html.

Norris, Jeannie Faris. "Bladen County." *The State: A Weekly Survey of North Carolina*, 10:23 (November 1942), 1-3, 19-21; online: http://digital.ncdcr.gov/cdm/ref/collection/p16062coll18/id/33426. [Online description from "North Carolina Periodicals Index," East Carolina University: "The mother of 55 other counties, Bladen County was the scene of the Battle of Elizabethtown and is the location of many historic homes."]

North Carolina (State). General Assembly. "[Document dated:] January 28, 1779: Petition of a number of Inhabitants of New Hanover, Duplin, and Bladen Counties for Erecting a Separate County from the Above Counties." Manuscript; General Assembly Record Group; Session Records, January-February 1779, Box 1 (MARS ID: 66.8.15.9.8; item), January-February 1779, State Archives of North Carolina, Raleigh. [Online catalog description: "The petitioners refer to the difficulties they face in attending general musters and jury service at the courthouses of their respective counties and request that a new county be erected within the boundaries suggested."]

North Carolina (State). General Assembly. [Document dated:] October 23, 1779: Petition from the Adjoining Inhabitants of the Counties of New Hanover, Duplin & Bladen." Manuscript; General Assembly Session Records; Session of October-November 1778; Joint Papers, Committee Papers, Resolutions, Box 1 (MARS ID: 66.8.18.7.11; item), State Archives of North Carolina, Raleigh. [The purpose of this petition was to form a New County in Order to Help Facilitate Attendance of General Muster."]

Royal, Lee. "Town and Country." *Our State: Down Home in North Carolina*, 76:5 (October 2008), 178-180, 182, 184; online: http://digital.ncdcr.gov/cdm/ref/collection/p16062coll18/id/100420. [Online description from "North Carolina Periodicals Index," East Carolina University: "Royal takes the reader on a tour of Elizabethtown, the county seat of Bladen County. Among the sights are the Corner Café, Tory Hole Park, where a Revolutionary War battle took place in 1781; Jones Lake State Park; and the Front Porch Restaurant."]

Wise, Steven M. *An American Trilogy: Death, Slavery, and Dominion on the Banks of the Cape Fear River*. New York: Da Capo Press, 2009. [Publisher's summary: "The Cape Fear River runs through Bladen County, North Carolina, population 33,000. On its western bank, in the town of Tar Heel, sits the largest slaughterhouse in the world. Deep below the slaughterhouse, one may find the arrowheads of Siouan-speaking peoples who roamed there for a millennium. Nearer the surface is evidence of slaves who labored there for a century. And now, the slaughterhouse kills the population of Bladen County, in hogs, every day. In this remarkable account, Wise traces the history of today's deadly harvest. From the colonies to the slave trade, from the artificial conception and unrecorded death of one single pig to the surreal science of the pork industry—whose workers continue the centuries of oppression—he unveils a portrait of this nation through the lives of its most vulnerable. His explorations ultimately lead to hope from a most unlikely source: the Baptist clergy, a voice in this wilderness proclaiming a new view of creation."]

Brunswick County [Wilmington District]

[Note: For various state government documents relating to Brunswick County during the Revolutionary period, search the MARS online catalog using the advanced search: http://mars.archives.ncdcr.gov/AdvancedSearch.aspx.

Use the "Year" search box to restrict the searching to 1775-1783 and enter the county's name in the "Subjects" box, and hit the "Search" button near the top. This will retrieve any cataloged document for the county from that time period. These materials can vary considerably from personal or county petitions to the General Assembly, Loyalist matters, land disputes and claims, tax collection, exemptions from taxation, payments to county veterans, county divisions, personal collections, genealogical material, British claims against North Carolinians, etc. There is considerable information in these materials that could provide interesting documentation for persons living during the Revolution. The results will also include all of the wills and probates recorded in the county during the period set for the search. We had hoped to include many of these listings in this guide, but they are too voluminous. Citations to many of these search results for the eastern counties do, however, appear in the text.]

Baldridge, Ede Dunn. "The South Brunswick Isles: It's Only Natural." *The State: Down Home in North Carolina*, 67:1 (June 1999), 50-57; online: http://digital.ncdcr.gov/cdm/ref/collection/p16062coll18/id/67897. [Online description from "North Carolina Periodicals Index," East Carolina University: "When the state's barrier islands are mentioned, many people think of the Outer Banks. However, off the coast of Brunswick County lies another chain of islands - Oak Island, Holden Beach, Ocean Isle Beach, and Sunset Beach - that are similar in climate, flora, and fauna, but different in character, history, and appearance."]

"Brunswick Town/Fort Anderson: Colonial Period-Civil War." Online: http://www.nchistoricsites.com/brunswic/brunswic.htm.

Corbitt, D. L. "Brunswick Deserted; Several Houses Burned Including William Hooper's." *North Carolina Historical Review*, 4:2 (April 1927), 207-208.

Early, Lawrence S. "Stew in Brunswick." *Wildlife in North Carolina*, 55:6 (June 1991), 14-21. [Online description from "North Carolina Periodicals Index," East Carolina University: "Brunswick County has more natural communities of rare plants and animals than any other county in the state. Among the communities are more than 100 rare plants and over 20 natural areas of national and statewide significance. Brunswick County also has development proceeding at an unchecked pace. Earley discusses why this is of concern to conservationists and what could be done about it."]

Ewen, Charles R. "The Once and Future Project: The Role of Brunswick Town in Historical Archaeology." *North Carolina Archaeology*, 46 (1997), 84-90.

Gray, Anna L. "Return to the Port of Brunwick: An Analysis of Two Eighteenth Century North Carolina Sites." *North Carolina Archaeology*, 46 (October 1997), 69-83; online: http://www.rla.unc.edu/Publications/NCArch/NCA_46%28e-book%29.pdf.

Great Britain. Exchequer and Audit Department. Audit Office. "Examination and Decision on [Application for Immediate Relief as a Suffering Loyalist] of Joseph Johnston of Brunswick Co, N. C. Mar. 11, 1784." Manuscript (copy) X77.228.1 (MARS ID: 21.2.17.18), State Archives of North Carolina, Raleigh.

Great Britain. Colonial Office. "Brunswick. Letter from 'The People' to Gov. Josiah Martin. July 16, 1775." Manuscript (MARS ID: 21.1.27.54; folder), State Archives of North Carolina, Raleigh. [Online catalog description: "Accuses Capt. Collet of a variety of arbitrary and illegal acts and informs governor that they intend to recover the dismounted cannon at Ft. Johnston for King's use."]

Hartsoe, Kenneth D. "Double Duty." *Our State: Down Home in North Carolina*, 71:10 (March 2004), 25-26; online: http://digital.ncdcr.gov/cdm/ref/collection/p16062coll18/id/79084. [Online description from "North Carolina Periodicals Index," East Carolina University: "Fort Johnson, an obscure fort located in Brunswick County, has the unique distinction of being the location where both the Revolutionary War and Civil War began in North Carolina. Hartsoe recounts the events."]

Lee, E. Lawrence, Jr. "Old Brunswick: The Story of a Colonial Town." *North Carolina Historical Review*, 29:2 (April 1952), 230-245.

Lee, Enoch Lawrence. *The History of Brunswick County, North Carolina*. [Southport?: Brunswick County, 1978?].

Murray, James, 1713-1781. "Papers, 1760-1786." Copies of manuscript, PC.71 (MARS ID: 580; record group), State Archives of North Carolina, Raleigh. [Online catalog description: "Copies of correspondence of James Murray and family, Scottish merchant and planter in Brunswick and Wilmington, member of the governor's Council (1740-1757), and secretary of the province. Letters from Murray in 1760-1761) refer to his suspension from office (1757) by Gov. Arthur Dobbs, efforts of John Rutherfurd (also suspended) for reinstatement, Murray's hopes to succeed Dobbs, the unprofitability of planting in North Carolina, and the difficulty of selling a plantation. After moving to Boston his letters concern family and business matters, Boston Massacre, Sons of Liberty, journey with daughter to England and Scotland (1770-1771), problems during the siege of Boston, and smallpox inoculations. His later letters (1776-1781) were written as a Loyalist refugee in New York, Philadelphia, Rhode Island, and Halifax, Nova Scotia. Letters from daughter Elizabeth refer to her education and social life in Boston and England, British prisoners in Boston (June, 1776), and postwar efforts to recover property in Carolina. Two letters (1770) are from Gen. Alexander Mackay in Britain. Originals are in the Massachusetts Historical Society." {"James Murray Papers," Manuscript, Ms. N-571}]

North Carolina. General Assembly. "[Document dated:] April 25, 1777: Joint Papers, Committee Papers, Resolutions, Senate Bills, House Bills, In Favor of Richard Quince for Lumber (with Messages)." Manuscript; General Assembly Record Group; Session Records, April-May 1777, Box 1 (MARS ID: 66.8.9.12.16; item), State Archives of North Carolina, Raleigh. [Online catalog description: "Resolution offering payment to Richard Quince for a quantity of lumber purchased by the state and to be used in Brunswick."]

North Carolina. General Assembly. Senate. "[Document dated:] September 7, 1780: Joint Papers, Committee Papers, Resolutions, Senate Bills, House Bills, Senate Bill to Re-establish the County Court of Brunswick, etc. (Failed)." Manuscript; General Assembly Record Group; Session Records, August-September 1780, Box 1 (MARS ID: 66.8.22.17; folder), State Archives of North Carolina, Raleigh. [Online catalog description: "The court had been disrupted by careless clerks and a relocation to Lockwood's Folly. The bill would have re-established the court in the town of Brunswick and made specific provisions for the appointment of tax assessors."]

Pleasant, Paul. "In Open Daylight." *The State: Down Home in North Carolina*, 23:26 (May 1956), 10, 36-37. [Online description from "North Carolina Periodicals Index," East Carolina University: "Eighty years before Boston's celebrated tea party, Brunswick's resistance to Britain took play in open daylight, was led by the most prominent men of the community, with arms in their hands, who defied His Majesty's governor, his navy, and his tax collectors. Today, Old Brunswick is a ghost town on the banks of the Cape Fear River."]

Reaves, Bill. *Shallotte in Time: A Chronology of Events from 1728 to 1992*. [North Carolina?: s. n.], 1999.

Robinson, Kenneth W. "Port Brunswick and the Colonial Naval Stores Industry: Historical and Archaeological Observations." *North Carolina Archaeology*, 46 (1997), 51-68.

Smith, Scott. "Brunwick Town." *The State: Down Home in North Carolina*, 61:10 (March 1994), 29-30; online: http://digital.ncdcr.gov/cdm/ref/collection/p16062coll18/id/66618. [Online description from "North Carolina Periodicals Index," East Carolina University: "Founded in 1726 as a business venture by Maurice Moore, Brunswick Town prospered as a sea port but declined after the American Revolution and was in ruins by 1830. Now a state historic site on the Cape Fear River, it attracts over 50,000 visitors a year."]

South, Stanley A. *Archaeology at Colonial Brunswick*. Raleigh: Office of Archives and History, North Carolina Department of Cultural Resources, 2010. [Publisher's description: "In *Archaeology at Colonial Brunswick*, Stan South recounts the decade-long excavation of this important North Carolina colonial port. He provides historical context and detailed interpretation of the many hundreds of objects uncovered. South's narrative guides the reader through a town and a way of life that ended more than two centuries ago. The experience is enhanced by 196 illustrations that include photographs of excavated buildings and artifacts, archaeological site plans, and interpretive drawings. *Archaeology at Colonial Brunswick* meets the inquisitive needs of the general public while answering the scientific queries of archaeologists."]

South, Stanley A. "Russellborough: Two Royal Governors' Mansion at Brunswick Town." *North Carolina Historical Review*, 44:4 (October 1967), 360-372; online: http://digital.ncdcr.gov/cdm/ref/collection/p16062coll9/id/4207. [Online description from "North Carolina Periodicals Index," East Carolina University: "This article looks at the history of the colonial era, Brunswick County property known as Russellborough, which served as home to Royal governors Dobbs and Tryon. Details of the property, structures, and use-life of the estate as well details discovered via archaeological excavations done in the late 1960's are included."]

Southport (Smithville): A Chronology. 4 vols. Southport: Southport Historical Society, 1978-1990.

Waddell, Alfred M. *A Colonial Officer and His Times, 1754-1773: A Biographical Sketch of General Hugh Waddell of North Carolina; with Notices of the French and Indian War in the Southern Colonies, the Resistance to the Stamp Act in North Carolina...The Regulators War, and an Historical Sketch of the Former Town of Brunswick, on the Cape Fear River*. Raleigh: Edwards & Broughton, 1890.

Waddell, James Iredell, 1824-1886. "Papers, 1775-1919." Manuscript PC.87 (MARS ID: 596; record group), State Archives of North Carolina, Raleigh. [Online catalog description shows that this collection includes: "...Papers of the Moore and Waddell families include will of Judge Alfred Moore (1755-1810), with land and slave papers for his plantation in Brunswick Co. (1762-1842) including map of Eagle Island; land and slave papers and will (1837) of Alfred Moore of 'Moorefields' in Orange Co. (1755-1837); a few New Hanover and Greene County wills and land papers (1771-1810);..."]

Webb, Mack. "Villages That Vanished." *The State: A Weekly Survey of North Carolina*, 13:17 (September 1945), 11; online: http://digital.ncdcr.gov/cdm/ref/collection/p16062coll18/id/13716. [Online description from "North Carolina Periodicals Index," East Carolina University: "At one time Gaston, Buffalo City, Williamsboro,

Waynesboro, Brunswick, Sneedsboro, Parkewood, and Tuckertown were thriving and prosperous communities. Then along came business and transportation changes, with the result that these towns and others had to fold up."]

Wyche, Blonnie Bunn. *An Abbreviate Sketch: Colonial Brunswick and Wilmington.* [Wilmington?]: Lower Cape Fear Historical Society, [2000?].

Buncombe County [Morgan District]

[Note: For various state government documents relating to Buncombe County during the Revolutionary period, search the MARS online catalog using the advanced search: http://mars.archives.ncdcr.gov/AdvancedSearch.aspx. Use the "Year" search box to restrict the searching to 1775-1783 and enter the county's name in the "Subjects" box, and hit the "Search" button near the top. This will retrieve any cataloged document for the county from that time period. These materials can vary considerably from personal or county petitions to the General Assembly, Loyalist matters, land disputes and claims, tax collection, exemptions from taxation, payments to county veterans, county divisions, personal collections, genealogical material, British claims against North Carolinians, etc. There is considerable information in these materials that could provide interesting documentation for persons living during the Revolution. The results will also include all of the wills and probates recorded in the county during the period set for the search. We had hoped to include many of these listings in this guide, but they are too voluminous. Citations to many of these search results for the eastern counties do, however, appear in the text.]

Arthur, John Preston. *Western North Carolina: A History (From 1730 to 1913).* Raleigh: Edwards & Broughton Printing Co., 1914; reprinted: Johnson City, Tenn.: Overmountain Press, 1996. [Ashe and Bucombe Counties]

Arthur, Billy. "Word of Mouth." *Our State: Down Home in North Carolina*, 67:5 (October 1999), 18-20; online: http://digital.ncdcr.gov/cdm/ref/collection/p16062coll18/id/68379. [Online description from "North Carolina Periodicals Index," East Carolina University: "Revolutionary War soldier, frontiersman, U. S. Congressman, and skilled orator, Felix Walker claims fame not for the foregoing positions but for the meaning he gave to a word in Webster's Dictionary. During the Missouri Compromise debate in the Sixteenth Congress, Walker felt compelled to give a speech and talk for Buncombe County. Soon afterwards 'buncombe' came to mean speech-making to please constituents, or just plain bunk."]

Edward Buncombe and Buncombe County: A British-Born American Patriot Lost His Family, His Wealth, and His Life in Helping Establish Independence for the Thirteen Colonies. Ashville: Buncombe County Bicentennial Commission, 1976.

"The Indian Incursion of 1776." *A Lot of Bunkum*, 19:1 (February 1998), 24-25.

Israel, Kenneth D. "A True List of Names of Captain Porter's Company, 1777." *A Lot of Bunkum,* 29:1 (February 2008), 30-31.

"Obituaries of Revolutionary War Patriots." *A Lot of Bunkum*, 30:4 (November 2009), 7-8.

Price, Betty Kuykendall. "Phillip Guise, Revolutionary War Patriot of Old Buncombe County, Now Henderson Co., North Carolina." *A Lot of Bunkum*, 18:2 (May 1997), 45-46.

Price, Betty Kuykendall. "The Revolutionary War Service of Captain Abraham Kuykendall." *A Lot of Bunkum*, 26:1 (February 2005), 9-13.

"Revolutionary War Veterans for Harrison." *A Lot of Bunkum*, 26:3 (August 2005), 33. [Originally published in *The Highland Messenger* (Ashville), October 9, 1840.]

Styles, Marshall L. *Colonel Ambrose Mills, a Soldier in the King's Army during the American Revolution: A Genealogy of the No. Carolina Cos. Buncombe, Henderson, Madison, Polk, Rutherford, Yancey, 1650-1995, Including the Primary Families of Edney & Styles*. (My North Carolina Heritage series, vol. 5). Salem, Mass.: Higginson Book Company, 1996.

"Wars/American Revolutionary War – Buncombe County." Buncombe County Pamphlet Collection, North Carolina Collection, Pack Memorial Library, Asheville. [Online catalog description: "Programs and brochures relating to American Revolutionary War, Buncombe County. 1. Application to bureau of Pensions for pension records regarding Peter Carter? (ink/water spot over part of last name) from Hyde Co. dated 12/3/1898 and written by Mrs. T. F. Davidson of Asheville." 2. List of Revolutionary Soldiers who have lived in Buncombe County and excerps from pensioners reports."]

Burke County [Salisbury District before 1782; Morgan District after 1782]

[Note: For various state government documents relating to Burke County during the Revolutionary period, search the MARS online catalog using the advanced search: http://mars.archives.ncdcr.gov/AdvancedSearch.aspx. Use the

"Year" search box to restrict the searching to 1775-1783 and enter the county's name in the "Subjects" box, and hit the "Search" button near the top. This will retrieve any cataloged document for the county from that time period. These materials can vary considerably from personal or county petitions to the General Assembly, Loyalist matters, land disputes and claims, tax collection, exemptions from taxation, payments to county veterans, county divisions, personal collections, genealogical material, British claims against North Carolinians, etc. There is considerable information in these materials that could provide interesting documentation for persons living during the Revolution. The results will also include all of the wills and probates recorded in the county during the period set for the search. We had hoped to include many of these listings in this guide, but they are too voluminous. Citations to many of these search results for the eastern counties do, however, appear in the text.]

Bennett, William Doub. "Josiah Brandon's Burke County, N. C., 1777-1800." *North Carolina Genealogical Society Journal*, 7:1 (February 1981), 2-11.

"Burke County Revolutionary War Pension Files: An Index." *Journal of the Burke County Genealogical Society*, 22:4 (November 2004), 111-117; 23:1 (February 2005), 11-15.

Burke County. "Burke County Miscellaneous Records, 1776-1949: Military Records, 1778-1864." Manuscript C.R.014.928.2, State Archives of North Carolina, Raleigh.

Burke, County. "Burke County Miscellaneous Records, 1776-1949: Slave Records, 1776-1869." Manuscript C.R.014.928.4, State Archives of North Carolina, Raleigh.

Childers, Jeannine Ballew. "Richard Ballew [of Burke County, North Carolina]." *Journal of the Burke County Genealogical Society*, 16:1 (February 1998), 18-20.

Clark, Larry R. "Red, White, and Black: Early Settlers in the Region of Burke County." *Journal of the Burke County Genealogical Society*, 21:1 (February 2003), 12-16.

"Davidson's Fort Historic Park, Inc.: Re-Learn History." Online: http://www.davidsonsfort.com/.

"Descriptive List of Men Raised for 18 Months from Burke County, N. C. [Alexander Brevard's Papers, Private Collection no. 2]." *Eswau Huppeday: Bulletin of the Broad River Genealogical Society*, 14:3 (August 1994), 174.

"Extant Tax Records (Delinquents), Burke County, N. C., 1782-1783." *North Carolina Genealogical Society Journal*, 6:3 (August 1980), 185.

Heavner, Phillip McCall. "14 Revolutionary Vets Lived in 1840 [in Burke County]." *Journal of the Burke County Genealogical Society*, 22:3 (August 2004), 68.

Huggins, Edith Warren, *Burke County, North Carolina Land Records.* Easley: Southern Historical Press, 1977-1987. [Volume 1: *Burke County North Carolina, Land Records, 1778*; Volume II: *Burke County North Carolina, Land Records 1779-1790 and Important Miscellaneous Records 1777-1800*, includes "Militia Returns" and "Revolutionary War Final Settlements, 1777-1792"; Volume III: *Burke County North Carolina Land Records and More Important Miscellaneous Records 1751-1809*; Volume IV: *Burke County, North Carolina Records, 1755-1821 (Including Wills Index 1784-1900).*]

Linn, Jo White. "Burke County, NC, Confiscation Proceeding, 1780: Bond of John Bowman." *Journal of the Burke County Genealogical Society*, 17:1 (February 1999), 4.

Linn, Jo White. "Burke County, NC, Road Orders, 1777, 1778, 1782." *Journal of the Burke County Genealogical Society*, 15:3 (August 1997), 4-7.

"A 'Lost' List of Continental Solders from the Western Counties." *North Carolina Genealogical Society Journal*, 9:3 (August 1983), 142. [Lincoln, Burke, Wilkes, and Rutherford Counties]

Moore, Terry. "Burke County, North Carolina, Research." *NCGS News: The Newsletter of the North Carolina Genealogical Society*, 40:1 (January 2016), 4-5; online: http://www.ncgenealogy.org/articles_tools/Burke_County_North_Carolina_Research.pdf.

North Carolina (State). General Assembly. "[Document dated:] December 6, 1777: Bill for appointing commissioners to lay off and mark a road from the courthouse in the county of Washington through the mountains into the country of Burke." Manuscript; General Assembly Session Records; Session of November-December 1777; House Bills, Box 2 (MARS ID: 66.8.11.27), State Archives of North Carolina, Raleigh.

Pearson, William S[impson]. "William S. Pearson Letter, 1880." Collection Number: 00583, Southern Historical Collection, Louis Round Wilson Special Collections Library, University of North Carolina, Chapel Hill; online finding aid available at http://www2.lib.unc.edu/mss/inv/p/Pearson,William_S.html. [Online finding aid description: "The collection contains two handwritten copies and a typed transcription of a letter dated 17 June 1880 from G. W. Michal to William S. Pearson. Based on information gathered from longtime residents of Burke County, N. C., the letter describes and differentiates between Joseph McDowell (1756-1801) and Joseph

McDowell (1758-1799), both of whom were Revolutionary War officers and United States congressman. Both men also died in Burke County, N. C."]

Phifer, Edward W., Jr. *Burke: The History of a North Carolina County, 1777-1920, with a Glimpse Beyond.* Morganton: Phifer, 1977.

Phifer, Edward W., Jr. "Slavery in Microcosm: Burke County, North Carolina." *Journal of Southern History*, 28:2 (May 1962), 137-165.

Pittman, Betsy Dodd. "Burke County Bypasses." *North Carolina Genealogical Society Journal*, 15:2 (May 1989), 68-72.

Pittman, Betsy Dodd. "Revolutionary War Pension Claim, Burke County Court of Pleas and Quarter Sessions." *Journal of the Burke County Genealogical Society*, 14:4 (November 1996), 30. [Thomas Wallace, 1823]

Sharpe, Bill. "Burke, Corridor of History." *The State: Down Home in North Carolina*, 22:24 (April 1955), 16-17, 19-23, 26; online: http://digital.ncdcr.gov/cdm/ref/collection/p16062coll18/id/81405. [Online description from "North Carolina Periodicals Index," East Carolina University: "Settled in 1750 and comprised of two mountain ranges averaging 1,200 feet, Burke County also has numerous lakes and a rich history as well as industry and agriculture."]

"A Short History of Davidson's Fort (As We Know It So Far)." Online: http://www.davidsonsfort.com/Site/photos_to_use/Short%20History%20of%20Davidson.pdf.

Surratt, Jo Ann F. "Burke County Records of the Revolutionary War." *Eswau Huppeday: Bulletin of the Broad River Genealogical Society,* 7:2 (May 1987), 117-121.

Surratt, Jo Ann F. "Pre-1800 List of names, Miscellaneous Records of Burke County, 1776-1949." *Eswau Huppeday: Bulletin of the Broad River Genealogical Society,* 7:2 (May 1987), 122.

West, Sandra J. "A Petition for the Inhabitants of Burke." *Journal of the Burke County Genealogical Society*, 20:2 (May 2002), 7.

White, Emmett R. "Revolutionary War Soldiers of Burke County, NC: A Roster of 500 Participants with Service Documentation." *Journal of the Burke County Genealogical Society*, 15:4 (November 1997), 6-13.

Bute County (1764-1779) [Hillsborough District]

[In 1779, the North Carolina legislature divided Bute County into Franklin and Warren Counties, and Bute became extinct. The former county's records became the property of the Warren County clerk.]

[Note: For various state government documents relating to Bute County during the Revolutionary period, search the MARS online catalog using the advanced search: http://mars.archives.ncdcr.gov/AdvancedSearch.aspx. Use the "Year" search box to restrict the searching to 1775-1783 and enter the county's name in the "Subjects" box, and hit the "Search" button near the top. This will retrieve any cataloged document for the county from that time period. These materials can vary considerably from personal or county petitions to the General Assembly, Loyalist matters, land disputes and claims, tax collection, exemptions from taxation, payments to county veterans, county divisions, personal collections, genealogical material, British claims against North Carolinians, etc. There is considerable information in these materials that could provide interesting documentation for persons living during the Revolution. The results will also include all of the wills and probates recorded in the county during the period set for the search. We had hoped to include many of these listings in this guide, but they are too voluminous. Citations to many of these search results for the eastern counties do, however, appear in the text.]

Abernethy, George. "Linville Gorge." *The State: A Weekly Survey of North Carolina*, 13:24 (November 1945), 3-5; online: http://digital.ncdcr.gov/cdm/ref/collection/p16062coll18/id/13955. [Online description from "North Carolina Periodicals Index," East Carolina University: "Linville Gorge lies in Burke County. Beginning at Linville Falls, it is some fifteen or twenty miles in length and the mountains along the sides rise from 1500 to 2000 feet above the Linville River."]

"1.) Balloted Men and Volunteers from Bute County to Serve Nine Months as Continental Soldiers, Beginning 1 March 1779." *North Carolinian: A Quarterly Journal of Genealogy & History*, 6:3 (September 1960), 727-728. [Gives names, ages, and places of birth.]

Bute County. "Bute County Miscellaneous Records, 1762-1779 and no date." Manuscript C.R.105.928.1, State Archives of North Carolina, Raleigh.

[Bute County. Citizens]. "Oath of Allegiance, Bute Co., North Carolina [no date given]." Online at the Bute Co., North Carolina Gen Web 1764-1779 site: http://www.ncgenweb.us/ncstate/historical/Bute/other/oath.htm.

[Bute County. Citizens]. "Copy of State Oath of Allegiance and List of Persons Taking Oath (1778; Presumably Bute Co.)." In the "Thomas Merritt Pittman (1857-1932) Collection, 1747-1934)." Manuscript PC.123, State

Archives of North Carolina, Raleigh. [A comparison with Holcomb's Bute County, NC Minutes of the Court of Pleas & Quarter Sessions, 1767-1779 indicates that this list is from Bute County.]

[Bute County. Committee of Safety]. "Minutes, Resolutions, and Lists of Members and Association Subscribers for the Bute Co. Committee of Safety and Letters to Them from Samuel Johnston and Thomas Person (1774-1776)." In the "Thomas Merritt Pittman (1857-1932) Collection, 1747-1934." Manuscript PC.123 (MARS ID: 632; record group), State Archives of North Carolina, Raleigh.

Bute County. Committee of Safety. *Bute County Committee of Safety Minutes, 1775-1776.* Warrenton: Warren County Bicentennial Committee, 1977. [Also includes information on local Freemasons and the names of those who took the oath of allegiance to North Carolina on pages 56-64.]

[Bute County.] "Copy of State Oath of Allegiance and List of Persons Taking Oath (1778, Presumably Bute Co.)" Manuscript in the "Thomas Merritt Pittman (1857-1932) Collection, 1747-1934," PC.123, State Archives of North Carolina, Raleigh. [A comparison with Holcomb's *Bute County, NC Minutes of the Court of Pleas & Quarter Sessions, 1767-1779* indicates that this list is from Bute County.]

"Bute County Militia List 1778." *The Quarterly Review of the Eastern North Carolina Genealogical Society*, 5:4 (Fall 1978), 170-172.

"Captain John Coleclough of Bute County for the Services of Self & Company of Militia of Light Horse on an Expedition to Currituck." In Weynette Parks Haun, *North Carolina Revolutionary Army Accounts, Part I, Secretary of State Treasurer's & Comptroller's Papers Journal "A", (Public Accounts) 1775-1776* (Durham: W. P. Haun, 1988), 97.

"Captain William Green of Bute County for the Services of his Company of Militia on an Expedition to Currituck, December 1775." In Weynette Parks Haun, *North Carolina Revolutionary Army Accounts, Part I, Secretary of State Treasurer's & Comptroller's Papers Journal "A", (Public Accounts) 1775-1776* (Durham: W. P. Haun, 1988), 80-81.

Christmas-Beattie, Ginger. "Bute County Safety Committee Meeting Minutes, 1775-1776." Online at the Bute Co., North Carolina Gen Web 1764-1779 site: http://www.ncgenweb.us/ncstate/historical/Bute/other/com-safety.htm.

Corbitt, D. L. "Slaves Ran Away; Horses Stolen; Reward Offered; Thirty Pounds Reward: Bute County, North Carolina, 1775." *North Carolina Historical Review*, 4:1 (January 1927), 112-113.

Dunaway, Stewart E. *Bute County, North Carolina, County Records: Road, Bridge, Ferry (1765-1779)* Hillsborough: North Carolina Historical Books, 2009. [Note: While not specifically concerning the Revolution, these sources can be used in tandem with land records and other documents to help locate places of residence, occupations, geographical features, and place names.]

Ervin, Sam J. "200 Years Refute Bob Brown's Theory." *The State: Down Home in North Carolina*, 39:1 (June 1971), 13-14; online: http://digital.ncdcr.gov/cdm/ref/collection/p16062coll18/id/54384. [Online description from "North Carolina Periodicals Index," East Carolina University: "Senator Sam Ervin, Jr. refutes Bob Brown's theory that the famed Brown Mountain Lights, visible from Ripshin Ridge in Burke County, are merely electric lights from towns across the mountains claiming that sightings of the lights pre-date electric lights and go back as far as the 1760s."]

Hawkins, John D. "Colonel Philemon Hawkins, Sr." *North Carolina Booklet*, 19:3 (April 1920), 92-106.

Kerr, Mary Hinton. "Bute County Record Book 2." Online at the Bute Co., North Carolina Gen Web 1764-1779 site: http://www.ncgenweb.us/ncstate/historical/Bute/data-idx.htm.

"List of Bute County Militia under Command of Colonel Philemon Hawkins [date?]." In Weynette Parks Haun, *North Carolina Revolutionary Army Accounts, Part I, Secretary of State Treasurer's & Comptroller's Papers Journal "A", (Public Accounts) 1775-1776* (Durham: W. P. Haun, 1988), 24-25.

McBride, Ransom. "Continental Soldiers for Nine Months from Bute County, NC, 1779." *North Carolina Genealogical Society Journal*, 15:2 (May 1989), 108-110.

North Carolina (State). General Assembly. "[Document dated: February 5, 1781: Resolution Re[specting] Remnants of Gun Factory, Bute County (Messages Only)." Manuscript, General Assembly Record Group; Session of January-February 1781: Joint Papers, Committee Papers, Resolutions: House Joint Resolutions: February 3-4, 1781, Box 1 (MARS Id: 66.8.23.16.5; item), State Archives of North Carolina, Raleigh.

"Oaths of Allegiance." *Bute County Committee of Safety Minutes, 1775-1776* (Warrenton: Warren County Bicentennial Committee, 1977), Appendix II 56-64.

Pittman, Thomas Merrit. "Thomas Merritt Pittman (1857-1932) Collection, 1747-1934." Manuscript, Call Number PC.123, State Archives of North Carolina, Raleigh. [Online catalog description: Includes "minutes, resolutions, and lists of members and Association subscribers for the Bute Co. Committee of Safety and letters to them from Samuel Johnston and Thomas Person (1774-1776); copy of state oath of allegiance and list of persons taking oath (1778, presumably Bute Co.) … James Cary papers (1776-1807) include letter book (1782-1789) recording letters to former North Carolina agent Alexander Elmsley and British officials regarding his claims for losses as a loyalist and for pay as loyalist militia officer; papers relating to his property in South Carolina, Jamaica, and Virginia; and papers of his wife Mary Cary"]

Cabarrus County

[Note: For various state government documents relating to Cabarrus County during the Revolutionary period, search the MARS online catalog using the advanced search: http://mars.archives.ncdcr.gov/AdvancedSearch.aspx. Use the "Year" search box to restrict the searching to 1775-1783 and enter the county's name in the "Subjects" box, and hit the "Search" button near the top. This will retrieve any cataloged document for the county from that time period. These materials can vary considerably from personal or county petitions to the General Assembly, Loyalist matters, land disputes and claims, tax collection, exemptions from taxation, payments to county veterans, county divisions, personal collections, genealogical material, British claims against North Carolinians, etc. There is considerable information in these materials that could provide interesting documentation for persons living during the Revolution. The results will also include all of the wills and probates recorded in the county during the period set for the search. We had hoped to include many of these listings in this guide, but they are too voluminous. Citations to many of these search results for the eastern counties do, however, appear in the text.]

Bridges, Kathryn L, et al. *Cabarrus Revolutionary Patriot Roll*. Concord: Cabarrus Genealogical Society, [2005?]

"Cabarrus County Watercourses." *Cabarrus Golden Nugget,* 23:4 (Winter 2015), 118. [map of the waterways of the county to assist with locating land and residences]

Caldwell, Rosa E. "The Old McCurdy Home." *The State: A Weekly Survey of North Carolina,* 10:33 (January 1943), 6; online: http://digital.ncdcr.gov/cdm/ref/collection/p16062coll18/id/16633. [Online description from "North Carolina Periodicals Index," East Carolina University: "The log home of Captain Archibald McCurdy, of Revolutionary War fame, still stands in a secluded spot of the most picturesque section of Cabarrus County. Although in dilapidated condition after 160 years, the home still contains many relics such as spinning wheels, clocks, chests, and candle snuffers."]

Fesperman, Linda Martin. "George Michael Heilig – Revolutionary War Hero." *The Golden Nugget (Cabarrus Genealogical Society)*, 8:2 (June 2000), 53-55.

Goerch, Carl. "The Black Boys." *The State: A Weekly Survey of North Carolina,* 8:29 (December 1940), 1-5, 21; online: http://digital.ncdcr.gov/cdm/ref/collection/p16062coll18/id/6532. [Online description from "North Carolina Periodicals Index," East Carolina University: "Cabarrus County boasts some interesting features and stories, such as 'The Black Boys,' a band of Cabarrus County men that prevented the shipment of ammunitions to the British government during the Revolutionary War. Cabarrus County is also the location of the first gold mine in the United States and the first organ in a private home in North Carolina."]

McCurdy Family. "McCurdy Family Papers, 1852-1889 and Undated." Manuscript (OCLC no. 906048305), David M. Rubenstein Rare Book & Manuscript Library, Duke University, Durham. [Online catalog description: "The McCurdy family was based in Concord (Cabarrus Co.), N.C. Archibald McCurdy (1752-1843) emigrated from Ireland, served in the Revoluntionary War and in the War of 1812 and rose to the rank of Captain… Collection comprises primarily family and personal letters sent to and by members of the McCurdy family, … In addition, includes business letters directed to Jacob M. McCurdy regarding land pensions and purchases, accounts, taxes, although the majority deal with the transfer of Archibald McCurdy's Revolutionary War pension to Elizabeth…"]

Rights, Douglas. "Indians of Cabarrus County." *The State: A Weekly Survey of North Carolina*, 19:27 (December 1951), 16-17; online: http://digital.ncdcr.gov/cdm/ref/collection/p16062coll18/id/27853. [Online description from "North Carolina Periodicals Index," East Carolina University: "Before the first settlers arrived in colonial days to find a home in what is now Cabarrus County, Siouan Indians claimed the land."]

[Smoot, James Edward]. "Dr. James Edward Smoot (1868-1949) Collection." Manuscript PC.1362 (MARS ID: 1872; record group), State Archives of North Carolina, Raleigh. [Online catalog description: "Papers of Dr. Smoot, physician and historian of Cabarrus Co., consisting primarily of his unpublished typescript, 'An Encyclopedic History of Cabarrus County and Territory from 1732-1944,' with indexes and photographs. In the typescript are extracts from records of the county and the town of Concord, from Civil War letters, and from newspapers; and information on early settlers, notable families, historic events, Indians, Negroes, schools and colleges, churches, public health, doctors, participation in various wars, utilities and transportation, crafts such as organ building, and business and industry, especially gold mining, cotton mills, and iron manufacture…"]

Tallent, Fran. "Hessians in Cabarrus." *The Golden Nugget (Cabarrus Genealogical Society)*, 13:3 (Autumn 2005), 77.

Walter, Gary Douglas. "Paul Walter, Sr. – Revolutionary War Minute Man." *The Golden Nugget (Cabarrus Genealogical Society)*, 13:1 (Spring 2005), 8-9.

Caldwell County

Alexander, Nancy. *Here Will I Dwell: The Story of Caldwell County*. Salisbury: Rowan Printing Company, 1956.

Camden County [Edenton District]

[Note: For various state government documents relating to Camden County during the Revolutionary period, search the MARS online catalog using the advanced search: http://mars.archives.ncdcr.gov/AdvancedSearch.aspx. Use the "Year" search box to restrict the searching to 1775-1783 and enter the county's name in the "Subjects" box, and hit the "Search" button near the top. This will retrieve any cataloged document for the county from that time period. These materials can vary considerably from personal or county petitions to the General Assembly, Loyalist matters, land disputes and claims, tax collection, exemptions from taxation, payments to county veterans, county divisions, personal collections, genealogical material, British claims against North Carolinians, etc. There is considerable information in these materials that could provide interesting documentation for persons living during the Revolution. The results will also include all of the wills and probates recorded in the county during the period set for the search. We had hoped to include many of these listings in this guide, but they are too voluminous. Citations to many of these search results for the eastern counties do, however, appear in the text.]

Camden County. "Camden County Miscellaneous Records, 1786-1928: Revolutionary War Account of Robert Staples, a Musician (1829)." Manuscript C.R.018.928.3, State Archives of North Carolina, Raleigh.

Camden County. "Camden County Miscellaneous Records, 1786-1928: Revolutionary War Records, 1792, 1819." Manuscript C.R.018.928.3, State Archives of North Carolina, Raleigh.

North Carolina (State). General Assembly. "[Document dated:] February 5, 1781: Joint Papers, Committee Papers, Resolutions, Senate Bills, House Bills, Letter from Colonel Gideon Lamb and Bonds Given by Tories." Manuscript, General Assembly Record Group, Session Records, January-February 1781, Box 1 (MARS ID: 66.8.23.3.3; item), State Archives of North Carolina, Raleigh. [Online catalog description: "Lamb informs the Assembly that in his opinion the only way to deal with the numerous loyalists in Currituck, Camden, Pasquotank, and Perquimans Counties is to forgive them on the condition that they sign bonds for their good behavior, which he has done. He includes several of the bonds."]

North Carolina (State). General Assembly. "[Document dated:] 1785: Joint Papers, Committee Papers, Resolutions, Senate Bills, House Bills, Report on the Memorial of Benjamin Jones (Petition Only)." Manuscript; General Assembly Record Group; Session Records, November-December 1785, Box 2 (MARS ID: 66.8.38.2.7), State Archives of North Carolina, Raleigh. [Online catalog description: "Petition is from Benjamin Jones, entrytaker for Camden County, who upon settlement of his account with the treasurer discovered that interest did not accrue [*sic*] on auditors certificates. Therefore, he asks the General Assembly to grant him relief in some way."]

Pugh, Jesse Forbes. *Three Hundred Years along the Pasquotank: A Biographical History of Camden County*. Old Trap: [s. n.], 1957.

Carteret County and Beaufort [New Bern District]

[Note: For various state government documents relating to Beaufort during the Revolutionary period, search the MARS online catalog using the advanced search: http://mars.archives.ncdcr.gov/AdvancedSearch.aspx. Use the "Year" search box to restrict the searching to 1775-1783 and enter the town's name in the "Subjects" box, and hit the "Search" button near the top. This will retrieve any cataloged document for the county from that time period. These materials can vary considerably from personal or county petitions to the General Assembly, Loyalist matters, land disputes and claims, tax collection, exemptions from taxation, payments to county veterans, county divisions, personal collections, genealogical material, British claims against North Carolinians, etc. There is considerable information in these materials that could provide interesting documentation for persons living during the Revolution. The results will also include all of the wills and probates recorded in the county during the period set for the search. We had hoped to include many of these listings in this guide, but they are too voluminous. Citations to many of these search results for the eastern counties do, however, appear in the text.]

"1777, A Return of the Commissioned Officers of Carteret Regiment of Militia as Follows." *Quarterly Review of the Eastern North Carolina Genealogical Society*, 14:1 (March 1987), 27.

Allcott, John V. "Colonial Beaufort." *North Carolina Historical Review*, 42:2 (April 1965), 139-152; online: http://digital.ncdcr.gov/cdm/ref/collection/p16062coll9/id/4207. [Online description from "North Carolina Periodicals Index," East Carolina University: "This article examines the first permanent colonies established in North Carolina and the settlement that became Beaufort. Article details land patents, area trade, town layout, town incorporation, Lord Proprietors relations, real estate speculation, land transfers, population growth, resident occupations, justice system, religion, land surveying, and period maps are included."]

Arrington, Joel. "Portsmouth Yesterday & Today." *Wildlife in North Carolina*, 48:3 (March 1984), 7-13. [Online description from "North Carolina Periodicals Index," East Carolina University: "The village of Portsmouth, located on North Core Banks, was founded in 1753 and was once a bustling fishing village. Today it is empty - a village of deserted buildings and no residents, except for a few visiting fishermen and beachcombers."]

Bailey, Josiah W. "Cape of Neglected History." *The State: Down Home in North Carolina*, 33:4 (July 1965), 9-10, 28. [Online description from "North Carolina Periodicals Index," East Carolina University: "Cape Lookout is an important maritime site that has remained neglected in the history books. Directly off the Graveyard of the Atlantic, the area off the North Carolina Outer Banks, Cape Lookout was home to pirates and Indians. Sir Walter Raleigh's expedition to the New World sent Captain Arthur Barlow in 1584 to explore the area. Cape Lookout remained an uninhabited region since 1854, with occupation minimized in the area. President Lyndon Johnson has recently recommended to Congress that the area become the newest addition to the nation's National Seashore Park."]

"Ballotted Men and Volunteers from Carteret County to Serve Nine Months as Continental Soldiers Beginning 1 March 1779." *North Carolinian: Quarterly Journal of Genealogy & History*, 4:3 (September 1960), 728. [Gives, names, ages, and places of birth.]

Branch, Paul. "Battle of Beaufort." In William S. Powell, ed.; Jay Mazzocchi, assoc. ed., *Encyclopedia of North Carolina* (Chapel Hill: University of North Carolina Press in association with the University of North Carolina Library, 2006), 105.

"Captain Enoch Ward of Carteret County for the Services of His Company of Militia on Various Alarms." In Weynette Parks Haun, *North Carolina Revolutionary Army Accounts, Part I, Secretary of State Treasurer's & Comptroller's Papers Journal "A", (Public Accounts) 1775-1776* (Durham: W. P. Haun, 1988), 136-137.

"Cartrite [Carteret] County Militia List 1778." *The Quarterly Review of the Eastern North Carolina Genealogical Society*, 5:4 (Fall 1978), 166.

Carteret County. "Carteret County Miscellaneous Records, 1741-1932: Bounty Claims, 1772-1778." Manuscript C.R.019.928.4, State Archives of North Carolina, Raleigh.

Carteret County. "Carteret County Miscellaneous Records, 1741-1932: List of Those Not Taking Oath of Allegiance (no date)." Manuscript C.R.019.928.4, State Archives of North Carolina, Raleigh.

Cheatham, James T. "Beaufort Scene of the Last Revolutionary Battle." *The Researcher: Carteret County Historical Society*, 24:2 (Fall 2008/Spring 2009), 9-10. [1782]

"Colonel Richard Caswell for the Services of the New Bern Battalion of Minute Men on an Expedition to Moore's Creek, Wilmington against the Insurgents, 1775." In Weynette Parks Haun, *North Carolina Revolutionary Army Accounts, Part I, Secretary of State Treasurer's & Comptroller's Papers Journal "A", (Public Accounts) 1775-1776* (Durham: W. P. Haun, 1988), 106-119.

Crow, Jeffrey J. "What Price Loyalism? The Case of John Cruden, Commissioner of Sequestered Estates." *North Carolina Historical Review*, 58:3 (July 1981), 215-233. [Online description from "North Carolina Periodicals Index," East Carolina University: "An examination of the two week occupation and plundering of Beaufort by British troops that began on April 5, 1782, a full six months after Lord Cornwallis' surrender at Yorktown, to identify why the battle took place, what the purpose of the invasion was, and why coastal North Carolina was targeted so late in the Revolutionary War. Particular attention is given to the career of the mastermind of the attack, North Carolina loyalist John Cruden, the commissioner of sequestered estates for Lord Cornwallis, and his motives for attachment to the British cause."]

Davis, Nancy. "Chronicle of a Seaport Village." *Coastwatch*, 11:2 (February 1984), 2-3. [Online description from "North Carolina Periodicals Index," East Carolina University: "Portsmouth Village is quiet now, but its history tells the story of a once-bustling community established on trans-shipment. Today, it stands as part of National Register of Historic Places."]

Doughton, Sammy Pou. "The Forgotten Fort Hancock at Cape Lookout." *The State: Our State Magazine*: (July 1977); reprinted: *The Researcher: Carteret County Historical Society*, 23:2 (Fall 2007-Winter 2008), 6-7. [1778]

Dunaway, Stewart E. *Carteret County Road Records (1774-1905), Bridge Record (1888), Ferry Record (1813).* Hillsborough: North Carolina Historical Books, 2013. [Note: While not specifically concerning the Revolution, these sources can be used in tandem with land records and other documents to help locate places of residence, occupations, geographical features, and place names.]

Faulkner, Janice Hardison. "Old Beaufort: The Town Where Time Stands Still." *New East*, 3:2 (May/June 1975), 5-10. [Online description from "North Carolina Periodicals Index," East Carolina University: "Beaufort in Carteret County is the state's fourth oldest town. Faulkner discusses the town's history and architecture. A walking tour map identifying historic sites and a map of the town plan from 1713 are included."]

Fryar, Jack E., Jr. "Redcoats on the Waterfront: The British Invasion of Beaufort." In Jack E. Fryar, Jr., ed., *The Coastal Chronicles: Volume II: Popular History Stories of the Coastal Carolinas* as seen in *Coastal Chronicles Magazine* (Wilmington, N. C.: Dram Tree Books, 2004), 176-188.

Haines, Jeffrey L. "1777 Petition of Inhabitants of Carteret County." *North Carolina Genealogical Society Journal*, 35:3 (August 2009), 259-262. [relating to Old Topsail Inlet and its importance as a supply route, with a contemporary map]

Kell, Jean. "The Day the British Took Beaufort." *New East*, 4:2 (March/April 1976), 10-14. [Online description from "North Carolina Periodicals Index," East Carolina University: "Jean Kell, who was doing research in the North Carolina State Archives, discovered a new and unknown chapter in the state's history. One year after Cornwallis surrendered at Yorktown and before the peace treaty was signed, the last battle of the Revolutionary War was fought at Beaufort in Carteret County in April 1782. Kell recounts the battle which ended just seven years, lacking a day, from the opening battle on April 18, 1775."]

Kell, Jean B., ed. *North Carolina's Coastal Carteret County during the American Revolution, 1765-1785*. Morehead City, N. C.: Carteret County Historical Society, 2000.

"A List of the Several Divisions of Affective Men in the Beaufort Regiment of Militia Made the 20th of April 1781." *Quarterly Review of the Eastern North Carolina Genealogical Society*, 14:2 (June 1987), 65-67.

"Major Thomas Chadwick for the Services of the Carteret Militia on Duty, April 1776." In Weynette Parks Haun, *North Carolina Revolutionary Army Accounts, Part I, Secretary of State Treasurer's & Comptroller's Papers Journal "A", (Public Accounts) 1775-1776* (Durham: W. P. Haun, 1988), 138.

Masters, Phillip. "The Historical Geography of Beaufort Inlet." *Tributaries*, 8 (October 1998), 24-33. [Online description from "North Carolina Periodicals Index," East Carolina University: "By studying the historical geography of Beaufort Inlet, Intersal, Inc. was able to determine inlet boundaries, features, and obstacles in the 18th-century. Using this data, the firm conducted a ten-year search that discovered what is thought to be the wreck of Blackbeard's flagship *Queen Anne's Revenge*."]

North Carolina (State). General Assembly. "[Document dated:] April 26, 1777: Report on Defense Necessary for Ocacock Inlet and the Ports of Beaufort and Roanoke (Messages Only)." Manuscript; General Assembly Session Records; Session of April-May 1777; Joint Papers, Committee Papers, Resolutions, Miscellaneous Bills, Box 1 (MARS ID: 66.8.9.10.10; item), State Archives of North Carolina, Raleigh. [Online catalog description: "Message concerning the report on defense measures to be taken for the security of Ocacock Inlet, Beaufort, and Roanoke; reference made to defense capability of the row galleys constructed by Virginia."]

North Carolina (State). General Assembly. "[Document dated:] May 8, 1777: Senate Bill for Cutting a Canal from Clubfoots Creek to Join the Neuse River with Old Topsail Inlet." Manuscript; General Assembly Session Records; Session of April-May 1777; Joint Papers, Committee Papers, Resolutions, Miscellaneous Bills, Box 1 (MARS ID: 66.8.9.13.16; item), State Archives of North Carolina, Raleigh. [Online catalog description: "Resolution allowing the Independent Company at Core Sound one half of the money received from the sale of anchors belonging to the *Aurora*, which the soldiers saved."]

North Carolina (State). General Assembly. "[Document dated:] December 4, 1777: Petition of the Sundry Inhabitants of Carteret Co. (with Plan of Old Topsail Inlet and the Harbor of Beaufort." Manuscript; General Assembly Session Records; Session of November-December 1777; Miscellaneous, Joint Papers, Committee Papers, Resolutions, Box 1 (MARS ID: 66.8.10.10.8; item), State Archives of North Carolina, Raleigh. [Online catalog description: "Petition requesting the construction of a fortification at Old Topsail Inlet to protect the flow of trade at that location."]

North Carolina (State). General Assembly. "[Document dated:] December 6, 1777: Bill for the Ease and Convenience of the Militia on the West Side of New Port in Carteret Co." Manuscript; General Assembly Record Group; Session Records, November-December 1777, House Bills, Box 2 (MARS ID: 66.8.11.25; folder), State Archives of North Carolina, Raleigh.

North Carolina (State). General Assembly. "[Document dated:] May 5, 1780: Disbanding Garrison at Fort Hancock." Manuscript; General Assembly Record Group; Session Records, April-May 1780; Joint Papers,

Committee Papers, Resolutions, Box 1 (MARS ID: 66.8.20.14.4; item), State Archives of North Carolina, Raleigh.

North Carolina (State). General Assembly. "[Document dated:] May 6, 1782: Resolution regarding petition of William Borden (messages only, with petition and a letter from William Tisdale regarding Gov. Josiah Martin's papers)." Manuscript; General Assembly Record Group; Session Records, April-May 1782, Committee Papers, Resolutions, Senate Bills, House Bills, Box 2 (MARS ID: 66.8.28; box), State Archives of North Carolina, Raleigh.

North Carolina (State). General Assembly. "[Document dated:] April 26, 1783: Senate Bill for Cutting a Canal from Clubfoots Creek to Join the Neuse River with Old Topsail Inlet." Manuscript; General Assembly Session Records; Session of April-May 1783; Unidentified Amendments, Senate Bills, House Bills, Box 2 (MARS ID: 66.8.30.7; folder), State Archives of North Carolina, Raleigh. [Online catalog description: "Bill creates a commission to supervise the creation of the canal and to collect private money for its building. An amendment was added to ensure that the canal would be property of the state and free from tolls."]

Paul, Charles L. "Beaufort, North Carolina: Its Development as a Colonial Town." *North Carolina Historical Review*, 47:4 (October 1970), 370-387. [Online description from "North Carolina Periodicals Index," East Carolina University: "This article archives the growth of Beaufort, North Carolina between its founding in 1713 and the end of the colonial period in 1782."]

Paul, Charles L. "Colonial Beaufort." *North Carolina Historical Review*, 42:2 (April 1965), 139-152.

Paul, Charles L. "Factors in the Economy of Colonial Beaufort." *North Carolina Historical Review*, 44:2 (April 1967), 111-134.

Paul, Mary C. *Carteret County, North Carolina: History & Folklore*. Charleston, S. C.: History Press, 2008.

Payne, Peggy. "Island Ghost Town." *Carolina Country*, 8:2 (February 1976), 7-9. [Online description from "North Carolina Periodicals Index," East Carolina University: "Founded in 1753, the town of Portsmouth on the Outer Banks was a lively place of 505 people. Shipping was an important activity because inbound ships were stopped by the shallow waters and had to unload cargo at Portsmouth into smaller, shallow-draft vessels that could carry it across to the mainland. Activity in the town reached a peak in the mid-19th-century, afterward declined because of hurricanes, channels that filled with sand, and shipping activities falling off. By the early 1970s, the last residents had departed. All that remains of the town are 20 structures, including a post office, church, a schoolhouse, and several cemeteries."]

Powers, Julie Ann. "Whispers from a Village: Portsmouth Legacy Lives On." *Coastwatch*, (Early Summer 1999), 6-12. Online description from "North Carolina Periodicals Index," East Carolina University: "The village of Portsmouth on North Core Banks, a once bustling fishing village, stands uninhabited since the last residents left in 1971. The village, founded in 1753, is listed on the National Register of Historic Places and contains twenty structures, including a post office, church, and several cemeteries. Around 700 people visit Portsmouth each month in warm weather."]

Reedy, James R. "Historical and Archaeological Investigations Concerning a Revolutionary War Vessel Burned at Beaufort, North Carolina, in 1778." M. A. thesis, East Carolina University, 1987.

"A Return of the Commissioned Officers of the Carteret Regiment of Militia, 1777." *Quarterly Review of the Eastern North Carolina Genealogical Society*, 14:4 (March 1987), 27.

Rippy, J. Fred. "A View of the Carolinas in 1783." *North Carolina Historical Review,* 6:4 (October 1929), 362-370; online: http://digital.ncdcr.gov/cdm/ref/collection/p16062coll9/id/4207. [Online description from "North Carolina Periodicals Index," East Carolina University: "A summary of descriptions and accounts of visits to several towns in North and South Carolina in 1783 culled from the diary of Francisco de Miranda, known best as a leader and proponent of the independence movement in the Spanish-American Colonies. Includes details of the Ocracroke Inlet area, New Bern, Beaufort, and Wilmington."]

Ross, Kirk. "High Tide on the Sound Side." *Independent Weekly*, 23:23 (June 2006), 14; online: http://www.indyweek.com/indyweek/high-tide-on-the-sound-side/Content?oid=1197725. [Online description from "North Carolina Periodicals Index," East Carolina University: "Since the mid-1970s, beach development has been largely confined to North Carolina's shoreline. Hotels, family homes, and campgrounds gradually changed to condos, high-end housing, and gated communities. As the shoreline filled up, development began moving inland from the coasts, and condominium complexes and housing communities are springing up along inland waterways. In Carteret County, the development is threatening a way of life for many families who can trace their ancestry back to the mid-1700s. Fishing families and boat builders find surviving difficult when dealing with rising taxes, poor markets, and loss of fish houses, boat yards, and boat docks."]

Sanders, Rebecca. *Early Carteret County, North Carolina Court Minutes, Vol. 3,1764-1777; Vol. 4, 1778-1789.* Beaufort: R. W. Sanders, 1991.

Simpson, Bland. "At Large on Cedar Island." *Wildlife in North Carolina*, 61:2 (February 1997), 8-15. [Online description from "North Carolina Periodicals Index," East Carolina University: "Cedar Island National Wildlife Refuge, lying at the eastern end of Carteret County, holds 10,000 acres of the largest unchanged salt marsh in the state."]

Turnage, Sheila. "Three Towns on the Eve of Revolution." *Our State: Down Home in North Carolina*, 68:10 (March 2001), 56-59; online: http://digital.ncdcr.gov/cdm/ref/collection/p16062coll18/id/72796. [Online description from "North Carolina Periodicals Index," East Carolina University: "Turnage gives a brief look at what was happening in New Bern, Beaufort, and Bath on the eve of the American Revolution."]

Watson, Alan D. "Pilotage and Pilots in Colonial North Carolina: The Case of Ocracoke Inlet." *Tributaries*, 3:1 (October 1993), 20-25. [Online description from "North Carolina Periodicals Index," East Carolina University: "Pilots directed ships through the often tricky inlet system separating state rivers from ocean-going commerce. Specifically, the history of Ocracoke pilots and legislation governing them is presented."]

White, Franc. "Portsmouth – Village in Limbo." *New East*, 1:2 (March/April 1973), 12-15, 29. [Online description from "North Carolina Periodicals Index," East Carolina University: "The village of Portsmouth, located on North Core Banks, was founded in 1753 and was once a bustling fishing village. Today it is empty - a village of deserted buildings and no residents. White describes life in the village as it used to be."]

White, James E., III. "The Clubfoot Creek Canal." *Journal of the New Bern Historical Society*, 19:1 (May 2006), 3-14. [Online description from "North Carolina Periodicals Index," East Carolina University: "From its founding, New Bern was an ideal place for a port. Ships brought goods in using Ocracoke and Old Topsail inlets, but ships coming in at Old Topsail had to travel around Carteret County and Cedar Island to get to and from New Bern. This added time to the voyages. A plan was put forth in 1766 to dig a canal to connect the Neuse River to Old Topsail Inlet. Travel time for the ships would be cut in half, and trade would increase. The ideal place to dig a canal was between Clubfoot Creek and Harlowe Creek. White discusses the canal's progress after the General Assembly enacted a law to build the canal in 1766 down to present-day."]

Yocum, Thomas. "The War on Water." *Our State: Down Home in North Carolina*, 68:10 (March 2001), 55-57, 59-61; online: http://digital.ncdcr.gov/cdm/ref/collection/p16062coll18/id/72796. [Online description from "North Carolina Periodicals Index," East Carolina University: "For those on the Outer Banks and Carteret County, conflict with the British Navy was continual between 1776 and 1782. Yocum describes the six-year struggle and the patriots who defended coastal Carolina."]

Caswell County [Hillsborough District]

[Note: For various state government documents relating to Caswell County during the Revolutionary period, search the MARS online catalog using the advanced search: http://mars.archives.ncdcr.gov/AdvancedSearch.aspx. Use the "Year" search box to restrict the searching to 1775-1783 and enter the county's name in the "Subjects" box, and hit the "Search" button near the top. This will retrieve any cataloged document for the county from that time period. These materials can vary considerably from personal or county petitions to the General Assembly, Loyalist matters, land disputes and claims, tax collection, exemptions from taxation, payments to county veterans, county divisions, personal collections, genealogical material, British claims against North Carolinians, etc. There is considerable information in these materials that could provide interesting documentation for persons living during the Revolution. The results will also include all of the wills and probates recorded in the county during the period set for the search. We had hoped to include many of these listings in this guide, but they are too voluminous. Citations to many of these search results for the eastern counties do, however, appear in the text.]

"1777 Tax List of Caswell County, North Carolina." *Eswau Huppeday: Bulletin of the Broad River Genealogical Society,* 2:4 (November 1982), 96-99; 3:1 (February 1983), 1-4.

"Artificers & Laborers at Mt. Tirzah in Caswell County, North Carolina, 1781-1782." *North Carolina Genealogical Society Journal,* 25:4 (November 1999), 411-417.

"Caswell County (N. C.) Papers, 1701-1905." Manuscript 144, Southern Historical Collection, Louis Round Wilson Library Special Collections, University of North Carolina, Chapel Hill; online finding aid available at http://www2.lib.unc.edu/mss/inv/c/Caswell_County.html. [Online catalog description: "Caswell County, N.C., was established in 1777. The collection includes unrelated business and legal papers and books of several generations of Caswell County, N. C., residents, including papers, 1701-1905, relating to pension claims, bonds, mortgages, real estate, and other legal matters; and volumes, 1807-1873, ..."]

Caswell County. "Caswell County Miscellaneous Records, 1775-1900: Justices of the Peace Commissions, 1779-1849." Manuscript C.R.020.928.4, State Archives of North Carolina, Raleigh.

Caswell County. "Caswell County Miscellaneous Records, 1775-1900: Revolutionary War Claims, 1786." Manuscript C.R.020.928.5, State Archives of North Carolina, Raleigh.

Caswell County. "Caswell County Miscellaneous Records, 1775-1900: Revolutionary War Veterans Who Settled in Caswell County." Manuscript C.R.020.928.5, State Archives of North Carolina, Raleigh.

Dunaway, Stewart E. *Caswell County, North Carolina, Ordinary (Tavern) Bonds, 1771-1815.* Hillsborough: North Carolina Historical Books, 2009. [Note: While not specifically concerning the Revolution, these sources can be used in tandem with land records and other documents to help locate places of residence, occupations, geographical features, and place names.]

Kendall, Katherine Kerr. *Caswell County 1777-1787, Historical Abstracts of Minutes of Caswell County, North Carolina.* Raleigh: K. K. Kendall, 1976. [Provides details mostly for civil and patriotic service with few military service references.]

Kendall, Katherine Kerr. "List of Officers and Soldiers of the Revolutionary War, Who Subsequently Resided in the County of Caswell." *Bulletin of the VA-NC Piedmont Genealogical Society*, 3:4 (November 1981), 143-144.

Powell, William S. *When the Past Refused to Die: A History of Caswell County.* Durham: Moore Pub. Co., 1977.

Turner, Grace. "The Robbery of Rebecca Watkins, 1780, Caswell Co., NC, Criminal Actions." *Bulletin of the Genealogical Society of Old Tryon County*, 21:3 (August 1993), 131.

Catawba County

Catawba County Historical Association, Inc.; Charles J. Preslar, Jr. *A History of Catawba County.* Salisbury: The Association, 1954.

Menzies, Robert. "Barringer House." *The State: A Weekly Survey of North Carolina*, 2:13 (August 1934), 11; http://digital.ncdcr.gov/cdm/ref/collection/p16062coll18/id/3540. [Online description from "North Carolina Periodicals Index," East Carolina University: "The Barringer House, located in Catawba County, is one of the oldest houses in North Carolina. Menzies discusses the interesting history attached to the house, which was built by Matthias Barringer in 1762."]

Chatham County

[Note: For various state government documents relating to Chatham County during the Revolutionary period, search the MARS online catalog using the advanced search: http://mars.archives.ncdcr.gov/AdvancedSearch.aspx. Use the "Year" search box to restrict the searching to 1775-1783 and enter the county's name in the "Subjects" box, and hit the "Search" button near the top. This will retrieve any cataloged document for the county from that time period. These materials can vary considerably from personal or county petitions to the General Assembly, Loyalist matters, land disputes and claims, tax collection, exemptions from taxation, payments to county veterans, county divisions, personal collections, genealogical material, British claims against North Carolinians, etc. There is considerable information in these materials that could provide interesting documentation for persons living during the Revolution. The results will also include all of the wills and probates recorded in the county during the period set for the search. We had hoped to include many of these listings in this guide, but they are too voluminous. Citations to many of these search results for the eastern counties do, however, appear in the text.]

Arthur, Billy. "Cornwallis' Chatham County Surrender?" *The State: Down Home in North Carolina*, 60:5 (October 1992), 10; online: http://digital.ncdcr.gov/cdm/ref/collection/p16062coll18/id/65703. [Online description from "North Carolina Periodicals Index," East Carolina University: "Speculation centers on the possibility that British general Cornwallis might have surrendered in Chatham County (March 1781) except for the detection of colonial troops that caused the British to flee south to Fayetteville."]

Chatham County. "Miscellaneous Records, 1772-1956." Manuscript, CR.022.928.5-CR.022.928.8 State Archives of North Carolina, Raleigh. [Online catalog description: Includes "affidavit stating that Conner Dowd had joined the British Army in the 'late war' to avoid a debt, 1788; affidavit of George Dudley concerning his Revolutionary War service, 1824…"]

"Chatham, Orange, Randolph, and Surry Counties: Men Who Enlisted in the Continental Line, 1780." *North Carolinian: Quarterly Journal of Genealogy & History*, 6:3 (September 1960), 728-729.

"Colonel Ambrose Ramsey for the Chatham Regiment on an Expedition to Cross Creek against the Insurgents." In Weynette Parks Haun, *North Carolina Revolutionary Army Accounts, Part I, Secretary of State Treasurer's & Comptroller's Papers Journal "A", (Public Accounts) 1775-1776* (Durham: W. P. Haun, 1988), 42-43.

Comer, James Vann. "Revolutionary War Soldiers of Chatham County, NC." *Central North Carolina Journal*, 4:1 (March 1993), 1-2.

Cooper, J. M. "Abstracts of Court Minutes (P Q & S) of Chatham Co., NC, May 1774-May 1778." *North Carolina Genealogical Society Journal*, 3:3 (August 1977), 195-204; 5:1 (February 1979), 31-36.

Dunaway, Stewart E. *Chatham County, North Carolina, Road and Bridge Records, Vol. 1 (1781-1899).* Hillsborough: North Carolina Historical Books, 2008. [Note: While not specifically concerning the Revolution, these sources can be used in tandem with land records and other documents to help locate places of residence, occupations, geographical features, and place names.]

Goerch, Doris. "Chatham County." *The State: A Weekly Survey of North Carolina*, 8:45 (April 1941), 1-4, 21-23; online: http://digital.ncdcr.gov/cdm/ref/collection/p16062coll18/id/39355. [Online description from "North Carolina Periodicals Index," East Carolina University: "Chatham County is a great county but it could have been the greatest county in the state if it hadn't missed three golden opportunities including losing locations of: the state capitol to Wake County; the University of North Carolina to Chapel Hill because Chatham County had too many saloons; and the first railroad in the state was to have been built in Chatham, but farmers objected. Despite of all the might-have-been, Chatham is still a county of rich history."]

Hadley, Wade; Doris Goech Horton; and Nell Craig Strowd. *Chatham County, 1771-1971.* Durham: Moore Pub. Co., 1976.

Lewis, J. D. "Patriot Leaders in North Carolina: Ambrose Ramsey: Colonel over the Chatham County Regiment of Militia - 1775-1783; Brigadier General (Pro Tempore) of the Salisbury District Brigade of Militia, (March 15, 1781)." Online: http://www.carolana.com/NC/Revolution/patriot_leaders_nc_ambrose_ramsey.html.

Lewis, J. D. "Patriot Leaders in North Carolina: John Luttrell: Lt. Colonel in the 9th NC Regiment - 1776-1778; Lt. Colonel in the Chatham County Regiment of Militia - 1779-1781; Colonel in the Chatham County Regiment of Militia – 1781." Online: http://www.carolana.com/NC/Revolution/patriot_leaders_nc_john_luttrell.html.

Lindley, Andrew Hoyt, "The Revolutionary History of Chatham County." Undergraduate thesis, Elon University, 1941.

London, Henry Armand. *An Address on the Revolutionary History of Chatham County, N. C., Delivered at the Centennial Celebration at Pittsborough, N. C., on the Fourth Day of July, 1876*. Sanford: Cole Print. Co., 1894.

North Carolina (State). General Assembly. "[Document dated:] April-May 1777: Joint Papers, Committee Papers, Resolutions, Senate Bills, House Bills, Papers Concerning Justices of the Peace and Militia Officer Appointments, 1777." Manuscript; General Assembly Record Group; Session Records, Apr-May 1777, Box 1 (MARS ID: 66.8.9.8), State Archives of North Carolina, Raleigh. [Online catalog description: "Documents concerning Governor Caswell's appointment of officers to the militia regiments of Cumberland and Chatham counties, and his appointments of Justices of the Peace for Onslow and Pasquotank counties."]

North Carolina Daughters of the American Revolution. "Chatham Co. NC – Revolutionary Soldiers." *North Carolina DAR Genealogical Records Committee Report, Series 1, Volume 75: Genealogical Records* (typescript, 1941), 16); digital surrogate, DAR Library, Washington, D. C.

Willcox, George W. *John Willcox, 1728-1793, of Chester County, Pennsylvania, Cumberland County, North Carolina, and Chatham County, North Carolina.* [S. l.]: Historical Research Co., 1988.

Chowan County and Edenton [Edenton District]

[Note: For various state government documents relating to Edenton during the Revolutionary period, search the MARS online catalog using the advanced search: http://mars.archives.ncdcr.gov/AdvancedSearch.aspx. Use the "Year" search box to restrict the searching to 1775-1783 and enter the town's name in the "Subjects" box, and hit the "Search" button near the top. This will retrieve any cataloged document for the county from that time period. These materials can vary considerably from personal or county petitions to the General Assembly, Loyalist matters, land disputes and claims, tax collection, exemptions from taxation, payments to county veterans, county divisions, personal collections, genealogical material, British claims against North Carolinians, etc. There is considerable information in these materials that could provide interesting documentation for persons living during the Revolution. The results will also include all of the wills and probates recorded in the county during the period set for the search. We had hoped to include many of these listings in this guide, but they are too voluminous. Citations to many of these search results for the eastern counties do, however, appear in the text.]

Barber, Ira Wilson, Jr. "The Ocean-Borne Commerce of Port Roanoke, 1771-1776." M. A. thesis, University of North Carolina at Chapel Hill, 1931.

Bell, Smith, and Company. "Records, 1782-1783." Manuscript AB.199, State Archives of North Carolina, Raleigh.

Bivins, John, Jr.; James Melchor; Marilyn Melchor, and Richard Parsons. "The Cupola House: An Anachronism of Style and Technology." *Journal of Early Southern Decorative Arts*, 15:1 (May 1989), 56-132; online: https://ia600300.us.archive.org/15/items/journalofearlyso1521989muse/journalofearlyso1521989muse.pdf. [Online description from "North Carolina Periodicals Index," East Carolina University: "This article analyses the Cupola

House in Edenton as a cultural object for chronology, style, and technology. Through examination of the house, a mixture of architecture and technology can be identified which assist in cementing the Cupola House as an important structure to the history of North Carolina."]

Blair, George. "George Blair Daybook, 1771-1772." Manuscript AB.325, State Archives of North Carolina, Raleigh.

Boeschenstein, Warren. *Historic American Towns along the Atlantic Coast.* Baltimore: Johns Hopkins University Press, 1999. [Includes Edenton.]

Brodsky, Marc D. *The Courthouse at Edenton.* Edenton: Chowan County, 1989.

Butchko, Thomas R. *Between the River and the Sound: The Architectural Heritage of Chowan County, North Carolina.* Edenton: Edenton Women's Club, 2012.

Butchko, Thomas R. *Edenton, an Architectural Portrait: The Historic Architecture of Edenton, North Carolina.* Edenton: Edenton Woman's Club, 1992.

Byrd, William L. *North Carolina Slaves and Free Persons of Color: Chowan County.* Bowie, Md.: Heritage Books, 2002-2004. [Publisher's description: "Interactions between Blacks and Whites are dramatically played out through crime and punishment. Records include: Civil Actions (1757-1819); Criminal Actions (1777-1817); and Miscellaneous Records containing gun permits, sales and hiring of slaves, and criminal actions."]

Chappell, Mack. "The Cupola House and Its Associations." *North Carolina Booklet*, 15:4 (April 1916), 203-217.

Cheeseman, Bruce S. "The History of the Cupola House, 1725-1777." *Journal of Early Southern Decorative Arts*, 15:1 (May 1989), 1-55; online: https://ia600300.us.archive.org/35/items/journalofearlyso1511989muse/journalofearlyso1511989muse.pdf. [Online description from "North Carolina Periodicals Index," East Carolina University: "This article discusses the early history and significance of the Cupola House in Edenton from 1724 to 1777. One of the most architecturally significant homes in North Carolina and built in the state's third oldest incorporated town, the Cupola House has a storied and colorful history that reflects the changing nature of North Carolina."]

Cheeseman, Bruce S. "The Survival of the Cupola House: A Venerable Old Mansion." *North Carolina Historical Review*, 63:1 (January 1986), 40-73. [Online description from "North Carolina Periodicals Index," East Carolina University: "This article examines the architecturally distinguished Cupola House of Edenton and the steps taken to preserve the house. Built by Richard Sanderson in the 1720s, the house was a blend of Jacobean and early Georgian styles. After the house came into the possession of Dr. Samuel Dickinson in 1777, it remained in his family until 1918. In 1918, then owner Tillie Bond sold the first floor woodwork to the Brooklyn Museum to the community's outrage. A grass roots movement was organized by local residents to purchase the house and preserve it as a historic site."]

Colihan, Jane. "At Home in Edenton: A Colonial Capital Remembered for its Women." *American Heritage,* 55:1 (February/March 2004), 33-35. [Topic: Edenton "Tea Party" of 1774.]

"Chowan County Enlistments, 1779." *Quarterly Review of the Eastern North Carolina Genealogical Society*, 14:1 (March 1987), 28.

Chowan County. "Chowan County Miscellaneous Records, 1719-1916: List of British Property Held by Dickinson." Manuscript C.R.024.928.37, Manuscript C.R.020.928.5, State Archives of North Carolina, Raleigh.

Chowan County. "Chowan County Miscellaneous Records, 1719-1916: List of Debts Due Payne by British." Manuscript C.R.024.928.37, Manuscript C.R.020.928.5, State Archives of North Carolina, Raleigh.

Chowan County. "Chowan County Miscellaneous Records, 1719-1916: List of Debts Due British by Johnson." Manuscript C.R.024.928.37, Manuscript C.R.020.928.5, State Archives of North Carolina, Raleigh.

Chowan County. "Chowan County Miscellaneous Records, 1719-1916: Loyalty Oaths, 1777-1868." Manuscript C.R.024.928.37, Manuscript C.R.020.928.5, State Archives of North Carolina, Raleigh.

Chowan County. "Chowan County Miscellaneous Records, 1719-1916: Military Records, 1762-1870." Manuscript C.R.024.928.37, Manuscript C.R.020.928.5, State Archives of North Carolina, Raleigh.

Chowan County. "Chowan County Miscellaneous Records, 1719-1916: Pension Records, 1823-1890." Manuscript C.R.024.928.37, Manuscript C.R.020.928.5, State Archives of North Carolina, Raleigh.

Chowan County. "Chowan County Miscellaneous Records, 1719-1916: Pardons, 1775-1870." Manuscript C.R.024.928.38, Manuscript C.R.020.928.5, State Archives of North Carolina, Raleigh.

Chowan County. "Election Returns and Lists of Voters, 1772-1796..." Manuscript, State Archives of North Carolina, Raleigh. [Consult the State Archives to determine the exact years that are available.]

Chowan County. "Ferriage Docket, 1781-1783." Microfilm, State Archives of North Carolina, Raleigh.

Chowan County. "Tax Lists, 1785." Manuscript GA 64.1, State Archives of North Carolina, Raleigh.

Cupola House, Edenton. "Cupola House Papers, 1758-1868." Manuscript CR.024.928.42, State Archives of North Carolina, Raleigh. [This collection includes miscellaneous Chowan County estate, guardian and probate records; and court records 1756-1856. Records include Election Records, 1813, 1836; Land Grant to Henry Lyles, 1764; Land Surveys, 1776, n.d.; Marriage bond for James Woodberry to Mary Benbury, June 10, 1811;

Militia lists, 1758, n.d.; Personal account for William Littlejohn, 1774; Scheme for organizing the town of Corbinton, n.d.; Ordinary bond for Elizabeth Hornblow, 1801; Records relating to public buildings--courthouse, 1769, 1816, 1825; Shipping records, 1802-1826 (Sloop Betsey, Schooner Zane, and Schooner Henry Whitenell); Treaty with Tuscarora Indians, n.d.; Tax lists, 1868, n.d.]

"Committee of Secrecy and Correspondence, March 17th, 1776 (Original in Court House at Edenton, N. C.)" *North Carolina Historical and Genealogical Register*, 2:2 (April 1901), 217-218.

Dillard, Richard. "A Declaration of Independence [by the Vestry of St. Paul's, Edenton, North Carolina, 19 June 1776]." *Magazine of American History*, 28:6 (December 1892?), 401-410. [Includes historical background on the church, the text of the statement *professing loyalty to the king of England* and opposition to taxation imposed by Parliament, and the signatures of the men.]

Dixon, Richard. "A Courthouse Talks." *Popular Government*, 2:2 (December 1934), 7, 19-20. [Online description from "North Carolina Periodicals Index," East Carolina University: "In 1934, Chowan County Courthouse was the oldest in the state, 167 years old. The Colonial-style structure stood in Edenton and Mr. Dixon explained its history through historical documentation and anecdotal evidence."]

Dixon, Richard. "Old Edenton." *The State: A Weekly Survey of North Carolina*, 1:10 (August 1933), 13; online: http://digital.ncdcr.gov/cdm/ref/collection/p16062coll18/id/2233. Online description from "North Carolina Periodicals Index," East Carolina University: "Dixon describes some of the customs, incidents, and episodes of Edenton's early days."]

Dillard, Richard. "St. Paul's Church, Edenton, N. C., and Its Associations." *North Carolina Booklet*, 5:1 (July 1905), 19-35.

Dunaway, Stewart E. *Chowan County, North Carolina, Mill Records (1731-1813) and Ferry Records.* Hillsborough: North Carolina Historical Books, 2010. [Note: While not specifically concerning the Revolution, these sources can be used in tandem with land records and other documents to help locate places of residence, occupations, geographical features, and place names.]

Dunaway, Stewart E. *Chowan County, North Carolina, Road Records (1717-1819) and Bridge Records (1744-1900.* Hillsborough: North Carolina Historical Books, 2013. [Note: While not specifically concerning the Revolution, these sources can be used in tandem with land records and other documents to help locate places of residence, occupations, geographical features, and place names.]

Dunaway, Stewart E. *Chowan County, North Carolina, Tavern (Ordinary) Bonds, 1738-1799.* Hillsborough: North Carolina Historical Books, 2013. [Note: While not specifically concerning the Revolution, these sources can be used in tandem with land records and other documents to help locate places of residence, occupations, geographical features, and place names.]

"Edenton (N. C.) Papers, 1717-1937." Manuscript 1910, Southern Historical Collection, Louis Round Wilson Special Collections Library, University of North Carolina, Chapel Hill; online finding aid and some digital surrogates available at http://www2.lib.unc.edu/mss/inv/e/Edenton%28N.C.%29Papers.html. [Online finding aid description: "The collection includes miscellaneous papers, chiefly bills, receipts, deeds, court proceedings, wills, estate settlements (including the division of slaves), and other legal and business papers of Edenton and Chowan County, N.C., citizens, mainly before 1820. There are few letters. Several items concern the awarding of prizes by the Admiralty Court during the Revolution."]

Egan, John. "Letter from John Egan to Col. James Blount, Col. of Chowan Militia." *North Carolina Historical and Genealogical Register*, 2:2 (April 1901), 195. [1779]

Foss, Robert W.; Patrick H. Garrow, and Silas D. Hurry. *Archaeological Investigations of the Edenton Snuff and Tobacco Manufacture.* (North Carolina Archaeological Council Publication no. 12) Raleigh: North Carolina Archaeological Council and the Office of State Archaeology, 1979; reprinted 1982; online: http://www.rla.unc.edu/NCAC/Publications/NCAC_12.pdf.

Fouts, Raymond Parker. *Following the Land: A Genealogical History of Some of the Parkers of Nansemond County, Virginia, and Chowan/Hertford/Gates Counties, North Carolina, 1604-2004*. Cocoa, Fla.: R. P. Fouts, 2005.

Funk, Thomas. "Archaeological Excavations at the Edenton Tea Party House Lot." Manuscript (1981), Historic Sites Section, Division of Archives and History, North Carolina Department of Cultural Resources, Raleigh.

Funk, Thomas; C. Terry Erlandson, and Jennifer Garlid. "Archaeological Excavations on the Edenton Teaparty House Lot." Manuscript (1979), Historic Sites Section, Division of Archives and History, North Carolina Department of Cultural Resources, Raleigh.

"A General Return of the Chowan Regiment of Militia, June 21, 1779, With Names of Commissioned Officers." *Quarterly Review of the Eastern North Carolina Genealogical Society*, 14:1 (March 1987), 28.

Goerch, Carl. "The County of Chowan." *The State: A Weekly Survey of North Carolina*, 10:8 (July 1942), 1-3, 16-18; online: http://digital.ncdcr.gov/cdm/ref/collection/p16062coll18/id/33008. [Online description from "North

Carolina Periodicals Index," East Carolina University: "Chowan is the smallest county in the state, but at the same time is filled with more history than any other county in North Carolina. Edenton, the county seat, has adopted the slogan, 'Cradle of the Colony.' Among its famous citizens were Governor Charles Eden, Joseph Hewes, a signer of the Declaration of Independence, Penelope Barker, leader of the Edenton Tea Party, and James Iredell Sr. and Jr. The county also has a number of historic buildings, including the famous Cupola House, Hayes, the home of Governor Samuel Johnston, and St. Paul's Church, the second oldest church building in North Carolina."]

Great Britain. Colonial Office. "N. C.: 'An Act Directing the Boundary Line between the Counties of Perquimons and Chowan…' [1773]." Mansucript Z.5.27 (MARS ID: 21.1.10.58; folder), State Archives of North Carolina, Raleigh.

Harrington, Thelma Bell. "Edenton." *The State: Down Home in North Carolina*, 25:20 (February 1958), 10-11, 33; online: http://digital.ncdcr.gov/cdm/ref/collection/p16062coll18/id/50936. [Online description from "North Carolina Periodicals Index," East Carolina University: "Queen Anne's Town, also known as the Port of Roanoke, Edenton, is the goober capital of North Carolina as well as the second largest peanut market in the world. Settled in 1658 by colonists from Jamestown, Edenton is a historic town located on the shores of Pamlico Sound."]

Hathaway, J. R. B. "Benedict Arnold in Edenton, N. C., March 2, 1774 as Master of the Brig *Harriet and John*. He Gave a Vessel-Bond as Follows (Original in the Court House at Edenton, N. C.)." *North Carolina Historical and Genealogical Register*, 3:1 (January 1903), 299.

Hathaway, J. R. B. "The Old Cannon in Edenton." *The North Carolina Historical and Genealogical Register*, 593-595.

Hathaway, J. R. B. "Thomas Barker of Edenton and the Oath of Allegiance in 1778." *North Carolina Historical and Genealogical Register*, 1:4 (October 1900), 515.

Idol, Coy Jacob. "Investigations into the Oldest Standing Structure in North Carolina." M. A. thesis, East Carolina University, 2015; online: http://thescholarship.ecu.edu/handle/10342/5108. [Lane House, Edenton, along with discussion of other eighteenth-century structures in the town and the history of the community]

Johnson, Daniel Snipes. *Descendants of Charles Johnson of Scotland and Chowan County, North Carolina.* [S. l.: D. S. Snipes, 2009. [Charles Johnson (1730-1802); Strawberry Hill Plantation, Edenton; Bandon Plantation, Chowan County]

Johnston Family and Wood Family. "Hayes Collection, 1694-1928." Manuscript 324 and microfilm 1-4485 (35 reels in the Davis Library), Southern Historical Collection, Louis Round Wilson Special Collections Library, University of North Carolina, Chapel Hill; online finding aid available at http://www2.lib.unc.edu/mss/inv/h/Hayes_Collection.html. [Online finding aid description: "Johnston and Wood family members owned and operated Hayes Plantation on the Albemarle Sound near Edenton, N.C. Members of the Johnston family include Gabriel Johnston (1699-1752), royal governor of the colony of North Carolina and planter; his brother Samuel Johnston (1702-1757), surveyor-general of the colony of North Carolina and planter; Samuel Johnston's son, Samuel Johnston (1733-1816), North Carolina governor, state and federal legislator, delegate to the Continental Congress, judge, lawyer, politician, and planter; and James Cathcart Johnston (1782-1865), son of Samuel Johnston (1733-1816), planter and businessman. Members of the Wood family include Edward Wood (1820-1872), planter and businessman; his wife Caroline Moore Gilliam Wood (1824-1886); and their sons, Edward Wood (1851-1898) and John Gilliam Wood (1853-1920). The Hayes Collection, named after Hayes Plantation, documents the lives of three generations of the Johnston family and two generations of the Wood family whose members owned and operated the plantation. The collection consists of correspondence, diaries, financial materials (account books, receipts, bonds), legal materials (wills, agreements, indentures, deeds of property and land, petitions, judgments, and suits), and photographs that reflect the varied interests and activities of Johnston and Wood family members. These included politics, particularly of the colonial era, the American Revolution, and the early United States; the development and management of several plantations, including Hayes in Chowan County, Caledonia in Halifax County, and Poplar Plains in Pasquotank County, as well as several fisheries, of which Greenfield in Chowan County was most prominent; … Pictures include photographs of portraits of Johnston and Wood family members and others, as well as images of the Hayes plantation house."] [Note: Some of the documents in the "Hayes Collection" for the years 1748 to 1803 were calendared and published in 1926.][39]

[39] In D. L. Corbitt, ed., *Calendar of Manuscript Collections, Vol. 1* (Raleigh: Edwards & Broughton [for the North Carolina Historical Commission], 1926), 11-27.

"Journal, 1775-1796." Manuscript AB.333, State Archives of North Carolina, Raleigh. [Business journal of an unidentified merchant in Edenton.]

Kickler, Troy. *The King's Trouble Makers: Edenton's Role in Creating a Nation and a State*. Edenton: Edenton Historical Commission, 2013.

Lowther, William. "William Lowther Paper, 1776." PC.716 (MARS ID: 1226; record group), State Archives of North Carolina, Raleigh. [Online catalog description: "Photocopy of letter written from New York City by Lowther, resident of Edenton, commenting on rumors in North Carolina, Clinton's going to Cape Fear, and defense of New York (Mar., 1776)."]

Luten, William. "William Luten Ledger, 1764-1787." Manuscript AB.214, State Archives of North Carolina, Raleigh.

McCall, Marguerite Butler, ed. *Business as Usual: Edenton Merchant Ledgers, 1759-1819*. Edenton: Chowan Herald for the County of Chowan, 1988. [Contents: Bk. 1. George Blair Private Ledger. Bk. 2. Edmund Hoskins Receipt Book.]

McCall, Marguerite. "The Unfired Cannons of Edenton." *The State: Down Home in North Carolina*, 51:10 (March 1984), 15-17; online: http://digital.ncdcr.gov/cdm/ref/collection/p16062coll18/id/60684. [Online description from "North Carolina Periodicals Index," East Carolina University: "The town of Edenton is guarded by several cannons which were shipped there in July 1778. The citizens, however, had not expected their arrival, and they did not have the funds to pay for them. Later, it was discovered that American agents in France had arranged the order and never notified Edenton's citizens. Fearing that Lord Cornwallis might seize them on his way to Virginia in 1781, townspeople dumped the cannons into the river. In 1785, the cannons were raised and are again stationed around the town. They were never fired in defense of the town."]

McCrea, William J. "History through Timber: Dendrochronology Dating of Early North Carolina Architecture." *Carolina Comments*, 43:3 (May 1995), 69-74. [Online description from "North Carolina Periodicals Index," East Carolina University: "Dendrochronology, a way to date trees, has been refined by Dr. Herman J. Heikkenen and is now a valuable research tool for state historians in accurately dating historic buildings, like Edenton's Cupola House."]

"Men From Chowan County Enlisted into the Continental Line, 1779." *Quarterly Review of the Eastern North Carolina Genealogical Society*, 14:1 (March 1987), 28.

Neidinger, Adriane Askins. "Archaeological and Historical Site investigation/Thesis of the John's Island Wreck." M. A. thesis, East Carolina University, 2000. [study of the site of the wrecked ship *Holy Heart of Jesus*, which sunk during the American Revolution near John's Island, in Pembroke Creek, close to Edenton, Chowan County]

"Northeastern Historic Sites Section: Pvt. Jonathan Overton (1752-1853)." *Carolina Comments: Published Quarterly by the North Carolina Office of Archives and History,* 51:3 (July 2003), 85. [African American Soldier in the 10th North Carolina Regiment]

Norris, Jeannie Faris. "Blast from the Past in Edenton." *Metro Magazine*, 5:5 (May 2004), 1-15; online: http://www.metronc.com/article/?id=667. [Online description from "North Carolina Periodicals Index," East Carolina University: "The picturesque cast-iron Revolutionary War-era cannons mounted throughout Edenton have an interested history."]

Norris, Jeannie Faris. "Chowan County Courthouse Awarded Federal Preservation Grant." *Carolina Comments: Published Quarterly by the North Carolina Office of Archives and History*, 51:1 (January 2003), 6-7; online: http://www.ncpublications.com/comments/ccjan03.pdf. [Online description from "North Carolina Periodicals Index," East Carolina University: "The Chowan County Courthouse is the oldest public building in North Carolina. Built in 1767, it is also one of the country's best-preserved colonial courthouses. Recently the National Park Service awarded a grant of $208,000 to the North Carolina Department of Cultural Resources to assist in restoration."]

Norris, Jeannie Faris. "Dendrochronology: A New Look at Old Wood." North Carolina Preservation, 83 (Fall 1991), 1. [Online description from "North Carolina Periodicals Index," East Carolina University: "Researchers are using the method of dendrochronology to determine the construction date of the historic Cupola House in Edenton."]

Norris, Jeannie Faris. "Picturesque Edenton." *The State: A Weekly Survey of North Carolina*, 4:42 (March 1937), 5, 7, 32; online: http://digital.ncdcr.gov/cdm/ref/collection/p16062coll18/id/102009. [Online description from "North Carolina Periodicals Index," East Carolina University: "There are few towns anywhere that possess the quiet dignity, peace, culture, and serenity that is Edenton's, the historic town located on Edenton Bay at the mouth of the Chowan River. The town was settled about 1658, and throughout the 18th-century was a place of considerable social and political importance."]

North Carolina (State). General Assembly. "[Document dated:] Jan. 23, 1779: Joint Papers, Committee Papers, Resolutions, Senate Bills, House Bills, Granting Citizenship to Thomas Britain (with Messages and Petition)." Manuscript, General Assembly Record Group, Session Records, January-February 1779, Box 1 (MARS ID: 66.8.15.11.8; item), General Assembly Record Group, Session Records, State Archives of North Carolina, Raleigh. [Online catalog description: "The resolution grants citizenship to Thomas Britain, of Edenton, without making him take the oath of allegiance, for in his petition he stated that he had taken a similar oath as a member of the Chowan County militia."]

North Carolina. Office of the Secretary of State. "Chowan-Perquimans, 1773, 1820." Manuscript SS.XX, Box 1, folder 6 (MARS ID: 12.110.1.6 (folder)), State Archives of North Carolina, Raleigh. [Online catalog description: "This folder contains a 1773 report of the commissioners appointed to consider the boundary line between Chowan and Perquimans counties and a map of the boundary between the two counties dated September 11, 1820."]

"Oath of Allegiance in 1777. *North Carolina Historical and Genealogical Register*, 2:2 (April 1901), 205-206. [signers of the Chowan County oath to North Carolina]

"Oath of Allegiance & Affirmation, 1778, Capt. John Beasley's District." Manuscript in: Chowan County. "Chowan County Miscellaneous Records, 1719-1916." Manuscript C.R.024.928.37, Manuscript C.R.020.928.5, State Archives of North Carolina, Raleigh.

Oldham, Thomas. "Thomas Oldham Records, 1771-1775." Manuscript AB.326, State Archives of North Carolina, Raleigh.

Parramore, Thomas C. *Cradle of the Colony: The History of Chowan County and Edenton, North Carolina*. Edenton: Chamber of Commerce, 1967; reprinted, 2005.

Powell, Diana Barbara. "Artisans in the Colonial South: Chowan County, North Carolina, 1714-1776, as a Case Study." M. A. thesis, University of North Carolina at Chapel Hill, 1983.

Righton, William. "William Righton Papers, 1776-1790." Manuscript AB.221, State Archives of North Carolina, Raleigh.

Sharpe, Bill. "Little Chowan, Big in Beauty, Big in Deeds." *The State: Down Home in North Carolina*, 25:20 (February 1958), 18-28; online: http://digital.ncdcr.gov/cdm/ref/collection/p16062coll18/id/50936. [Online description from "North Carolina Periodicals Index," East Carolina University: "Located on the shores of Albemarle Sound, Chowan County was settled during the 17th-century by colonists in Virginia. An official port of entry, equipped with two shipyards, Chowan had the most densely populated region Native Americans on Albemarle Sound."]

Smith, Pam. "Christmas in Edenton: A Revolutionary Holiday." *Coastwatch*, (Holiday 2001); online: https://ncseagrant.ncsu.edu/coastwatch/previous-issues/2001-2/holiday-2001-table-of-contents/christmas-in-edenton/. [Publisher's summary: "Edenton residents are proud of the town's historic past. They keep the holiday spirit alive with a traditional candlelight tour of historic homes, complete with candles glowing in the window and a church decorated with greenery."]

Smith, Robert. "Robert Smith to Governor Caswell." *Washington County Genealogical Society Journal*, 5:3 (December 1997), 87. [1777 letter from Edenton]

Spearman, R. Alan. "The Johnston Library at Hayes Plantation: The Character of the Eighteenth-Century Library and Its Evolution in the First Half of the Nineteenth Century." M. A. thesis, University of North Carolina, 1988.

"The State of North Carolina, Chowan County, The Oath of Allegiance or Affirmation to the Inhabitants in Capt. Jonathan Beasley's District, May 1778." Manuscript, [location not given], copy in the DAR Library Geographic Files, Washington, D. C. This item is most likely from the State Archives of North Carolina, Raleigh, but it cannot be located in its online MARS catalog.]

"Togetherness: The Family That Strays Together, Stays Together?" *Washington County Genealogical Society Journal*, 4:3 (December 1996), 84. [Absalom and Daniel Leggett accused of treason in 1777 in Edenton District Court]

Webb and Bateman. "Webb and Bateman Records, 1781-1786." Manuscript AB.211, 6 volumes, State Archives of North Carolina, Raleigh. [Description: "Commission merchants. Daybooks and ledgers."]

Webb Bryer and Company. "Webb Bryer and Company Records, 1781-May 1786." Manuscript AB.653, State Archives of North Carolina, Raleigh. [Stored offsite. Request in advance.]

Westbrook, Kathy Grant. "Edenton." *State: Down Home in North Carolina*, 73:2 (July 2005), 18-20, 22-23; online: http://digital.ncdcr.gov/cdm/ref/collection/p16062coll18/id/83809. [Online description from "North Carolina Periodicals Index," East Carolina University: "Edenton, in Chowan County, has historic buildings spanning three centuries and representing many styles of architecture. Named for Gov. Charles Eden, the town served as the colonial capital until the mid-1740s. It was home to Penelope Barker, organizer of Edenton Tea Party in

1774. The town's restoration began in the early 20th-century. Current preservation activities include an overhaul of the Edenton Cotton Mill. Of the 70 remaining mill houses, 57 have been purchased by families for restoration, and the 1899 mill building is being converted into 30 condominiums."]

Westmore, Joseph. "Joseph Westmore Ledger, 1780-1784, 1864-1865." Manuscript 5658, David M. Rubenstein Rare Book & Manuscript Library, Duke, University, Durham, N. C. [Online catalog description: "A greater portion of the ledger consists of the records of Joseph Westmore, trader and merchant, containing an inventory of the ships and cargoes at the dissolution of the firm of Joseph Westmore and William Savage in 1780; and records after 1784 of the coastwise trade from Edenton; Williamsburg and Petersburg, Virginia; and New York City, with names of brigs and schooners and mention of cargoes." Westmore lived in Edenton, N. C.]

Westmore, Joseph. "Journal, 1780-1784." Manuscript RUB Bay 0036:05 items 1, David M. Rubenstein Rare Book & Manuscript Library, Duke University, Durham. [Online catalog description: "Trader and merchant of Edenton (Chowan Co.), N. C. Journal of Edenton, N.C., merchant Joseph Westmore, who prospered during the Revolution by privateering and by investing in shipping along the Atlantic Coast and with the West Indies, the Canary islands, and France, and after the war with England and Scotland. During the war, Westmore sold goods to the North Carolina government for the use of the state troops. His journal records mercantile accounts and also accounts of various ships, including cargoes, maintenance and repairs, names and wages of captains and crew, etc. Mercantile accounts illustrate trade with Suffolk, Portsmouth, Petersburg, and Williamsburg, Va., as well as Philadelphia, Pa.; New York, N. Y.; Haiti; and Jamaica."]

Wiggins, Jasper L. "Historic Chowan." *The State: A Weekly Survey of North Carolina*, 16:41 (March 1949), 6-7, 15; online: http://digital.ncdcr.gov/cdm/ref/collection/p16062coll18/id/23606. [Online description from "North Carolina Periodicals Index," East Carolina University: "The author discusses the history of Chowan County from the colonial period through contemporary history. Historic landmarks described include: Cupola House, Bandon Plantation, and the Chowan County Courthouse."]

William Bozman and Company. "Daybook, 1781-1786." Manuscript AB.323, State Archives of North Carolina, Raleigh.

Zehmer, John G. *Hayes: The Plantation, Its People, and Their Papers*. Raleigh: North Carolina Office of Archives and History, 2007. [Publisher's description: "*Hayes: The Plantation, Its People, and Their Papers* is a fascinating portrayal of a handsome, timeless house in Chowan County near Edenton and of the people associated with it. Designed by British architect William Nichols and built for prominent planter James Cathcart Johnston, the home and its collections have remained intact for almost two hundred years. Many lavish color photographs by John O. Peters depict both the interior and exterior of the house. A large number of original documents are reproduced that chronicle Johnston's management of the plantation during the antebellum period. This new book will appeal to local and state historians, architectural historians, genealogists, and anyone interested in the Albemarle region of North Carolina during the nineteenth and twentieth centuries."]

Cleveland County

Dean, Earl. "Three Men of Kings Mountain." *The State: A Weekly Survey of North Carolina*, 17:37 (February 1950), 10, 20; online: http://digital.ncdcr.gov/cdm/ref/collection/p16062coll18/id/25020. [Online description from "North Carolina Periodicals Index," East Carolina University: "Many famous names have been associated with Cleveland County. Three men, whose names loom large in the pages of history, are closely identified with Cleveland County and its capital, Shelby. They are Colonel Benjamin Cleveland, the hero of the Battle of King's Mountain; Colonel Isaac Shelby, the first governor of Kentucky; and Major Patrick Ferguson, the inventor of the breech-loading rifle."]

Gardner, P. Cleveland. "Cleveland has been Divided Eight Times." *Eswau Huppeday: Bulletin of the Broad River Genealogical Society,* 29:3 (2009).

"Revolutionary War Soldiers Buried in Cleveland County, North Carolina." *Eswau Huppeday: Bulletin of the Broad River Genealogical Society,* 33:3 (August 2013), 153-155.

Star, Shelby Daily. *Our Heritage: A History of Cleveland County*. Shelby: Shelby Daily Star, 1976.

Columbus County

Little, Ann C. W. *Columbus County, North Carolina: Recollections and Records*. Whiteville: Columbus County Commissioners and Columbus County Public Library, 1980.

Norris, Jeannie Faris. "Duncan King." *The State: A Weekly Survey of North Carolina*, 8:33 (January 1941), 11, 22; online: http://digital.ncdcr.gov/cdm/ref/collection/p16062coll18/id/32694. [Online description from "North Carolina Periodicals Index," East Carolina University: Over two hundred years ago, Duncan King, one of North

Carolina's contributions to the then popular vocation of privateering, was roving the seas, sailing under the British flag and fighting for Great Britain. A native of Scotland, King chose North Carolina as his home and operated from there. Captain of a privateer, an officer under General Wolf at the Battle of Quebec, and a millionaire, King now lies buried in a forest in Columbus County."]

Sharpe, Bill. "Forest, Field, and Farm." *The State: Down Home in North Carolina*, 22:13 (November 1954), 14-22; online: http://digital.ncdcr.gov/cdm/ref/collection/p16062coll18/id/32694. [Online description from "North Carolina Periodicals Index," East Carolina University: "Originally, a tract of land between Whiteville and the South Carolina border, Columbus County is an expansive region, encompassing 939 square miles. Inhabited by Native Americans (pre-contact-1734), and serving as a refuge for non-combatants (1871), as well as a retreat for criminals and military renegades (1871-1808), Columbus County is historically known for the production of naval stores and the exploitation of lumber."]

Craven County and New Bern [New Bern District]

[Note: For various state government documents relating to New Bern during the Revolutionary period, search the MARS online catalog using the advanced search: http://mars.archives.ncdcr.gov/AdvancedSearch.aspx. Use the "Year" search box to restrict the searching to 1775-1783 and enter the town's name in the "Subjects" box, and hit the "Search" button near the top. This will retrieve any cataloged document for the county from that time period. These materials can vary considerably from personal or county petitions to the General Assembly, Loyalist matters, land disputes and claims, tax collection, exemptions from taxation, payments to county veterans, county divisions, personal collections, genealogical material, British claims against North Carolinians, etc. There is considerable information in these materials that could provide interesting documentation for persons living during the Revolution. The results will also include all of the wills and probates recorded in the county during the period set for the search. We had hoped to include many of these listings in this guide, but they are too voluminous. Citations to many of these search results for the eastern counties do, however, appear in the text.]

Alford, Michael B. "The Ferry from Trent – Researching Colonial River Ferries." *Tributaries*, 1:1 (October 1991), 10-16. [Online description from "North Carolina Periodicals Index," East Carolina University: "Discovery in 1989 of a flatboat in a Trent River meander near New Bern gave insight into the building and use of an important transportation mode, the ferry in colonial North Carolina."]

Beaman, Thomas E., Jr. "The Archaeology of Morley Jeffers Williams and the Restoration of Historic Landscapes at Stratford Hall, Mount Vernon, and Tryon Palace." *North Carolina Historical Review*, 79:3 (July 2002), 47-372.

Beaman, Thomas E., Jr. "New Bern Archaeology: Digging Up the Past." *Journal of the New Bern Historical Society*, 10:2 (November 1997), 12-19. [Online description from "North Carolina Periodicals Index," East Carolina University: "Excavations at a small construction site near the Harvey Mansion in New Bern reveal items used in the 1700s and early 1800s, including pearl ware porcelain, moca ware, and black glass. The artifacts also reveal dietary practices."]

Bishir, Catherine W. *Crafting Lives: African American Artisans in New Bern, North Carolina, 1770-1900.* Chapel Hill: University of North Carolina Press, 2013. [Publisher's description: "From the colonial period onward, black artisans in southern cities – thousands of free and enslaved carpenters, coopers, dressmakers, blacksmiths, saddlers, shoemakers, bricklayers, shipwrights, cabinetmakers, tailors, and others – played vital roles in their communities. Yet only a very few black craftspeople have gained popular and scholarly attention. Catherine W. Bishir remedies this oversight by offering an in-depth portrayal of urban African American artisans in the small but important port city of New Bern. In so doing, she highlights the community's often unrecognized importance in the history of nineteenth-century black life. Drawing upon myriad sources, Bishir brings to life men and women who employed their trade skills, sense of purpose, and community relationships to work for liberty and self-sufficiency, to establish and protect their families, and to assume leadership in churches and associations and in New Bern's dynamic political life during and after the Civil War. Focusing on their words and actions, *Crafting Lives* provides a new understanding of urban southern black artisans' unique place in the larger picture of American artisan identity."]

Brigham, Mary, and Lynda de Nijs. "Waterways of New Bern and Craven County." *Journal of the New Bern Historical Society*, 17:2 (November 2004), 17-25. [Online description from "North Carolina Periodicals Index," East Carolina University: "The authors discuss the importance of waterways for transportation in eastern North Carolina during the 17th- and 18th-centuries. At that time it was the only mode of travel to cover any distance in a reasonable amount of time and remained so until railroads replaced them in the early 19th-century. Bridges and ferries were necessities and were sources of income to their operators, and many farmers and manufacturers relied on water travel to get their products to market."]

Cogdell, R. *At a Meeting of the Committee for the County of Craven, and Town of Newbern, on the 4th Day of March, 1775: Resolved, That at This Critical Juncture it Becomes the Duty of This Committee to Remind Their Constituents, That Several Important Rules and Regulations, Established by the General Congress, Have Now Lately Taken* [Newbern]: Printed by James Davis, 1775; micropublished (Early American Imprints. First Series, no. 42909).

Craven County. "Craven County Miscellaneous Records, 1757-1929: Military Claims, 1772-1833." Manuscript C.R.028.928.14, State Archives of North Carolina, Raleigh.

Craven County. "Craven County Miscellaneous Records, 1757-1929: Militia Record, [177?]." Manuscript C.R.028.928.14, State Archives of North Carolina, Raleigh.

Craven County. "Craven County Miscellaneous Records, 1757-1929: North Carolina Pension Roll, 1814-1834." Manuscript C.R.028.928.14, State Archives of North Carolina, Raleigh.

Craven County. "Craven County Miscellaneous Records, 1757-1929: Petition to House of Commons by Ann Furguson, etc., 1775." Manuscript C.R.028.928.14, State Archives of North Carolina, Raleigh.

Craven County. "Craven County Miscellaneous Records, 1757-1929: Soldiers' Vouchers of the Continental Army." Manuscript C.R.028.928.14, State Archives of North Carolina, Raleigh.

Craven County. "Craven County Miscellaneous Records, 1757-1929: Petition for Freedom, 1782." Manuscript C.R.028.928.15, State Archives of North Carolina, Raleigh.

Craven County. "Craven County Miscellaneous Records, 1757-1929: Robert Taylor's Citizenship Petition and Oath of Allegiance." Manuscript C.R.028.928.15, State Archives of North Carolina, Raleigh.

Craven County. "Craven County Miscellaneous Records, 1757-1929: Tullock's Receipt for Cattle for Army." Manuscript C.R.028.928.15, State Archives of North Carolina, Raleigh.

Craven County. Committee of Safety. *At a Meeting of the Committee for the County of Craven, and Town of Newbern, on the 4th Day of March, 1775, Resolved That at This Critical Juncture It Becomes the Duty of this Committee to Remind Their Constituents, That Several Important Rules and Regulations, Established by the General Congress, Have Now Lately Taken Place...* Newbern: Printed by James Davis, 1775; micropublished (Early American Imprints. First Series No. 42909) New York: Readex Microprint, 1985. [Online cataog description: "Signed by R. Cogdell and twelve other members of the Craven County Committee of Safety, including James Davis."]

Daves, Graham. "Town and County Resolutions of 1774." *Magazine of American History with Notes and Queries*, 30:1-2 (July-August 1893), 88-90. [Wilmington; Rowan County; Anson County; New Bern and Craven County]

Dill, Alonzo Thomas, Jr. "Eighteenth Century New Bern: A History of the Town and Craven County, 1700-1800, Part VII, During the Revolution." *North Carolina Historical Review*, 23:3 (July 1946), 325-359; online: http://digital.ncdcr.gov/cdm/ref/collection/p16062coll9/id/4207. [Online description from "North Carolina Periodicals Index," East Carolina University: "Part seven in this series concerning New Bern and all of Craven County focuses specifically on New Bern during the American Revolutionary War. The author begins by looking at changing citizen opinions and political shifts leading up the war. Much of the article discusses the treatment of Tories and Tory sympathizers and the increasing animosity and actions taken against these groups."]

Dill, Alonzo Thomas, Jr. "Eighteenth Century New Bern: A History of the Town and Craven County, 1700-1800, Part VIII." *North Carolina Historical Review*, 23:4 (October 1946), 495-535; online: http://digital.ncdcr.gov/cdm/ref/collection/p16062coll9/id/4207. [Online description from "North Carolina Periodicals Index," East Carolina University: "Part eight in this series looks at post-Revolutionary War New Bern and how the revolution affected the town and its citizens. Specifically the author discusses the loss of early newspapers and also the declining educational system immediately following the war. An empty Tryon Palace was also further evidence of the town's declining stature following war and the loss of its title of state capital."]

Dill, Alonzo Thomas, Jr. "Public Buildings in Craven County, 1722-1835." *North Carolina Historical Review,* 20:4 (October 1943), 301-326.

Dunaway, Stewart E. *Craven County, North Carolina, Mill Records (1766-1885) & Ferry Petitions (1784-1883).* Hillsborough: North Carolina Historical Books, 2012. [Note: While not specifically concerning the Revolution, these sources can be used in tandem with land records and other documents to help locate places of residence, occupations, geographical features, and place names.]

Dunaway, Stewart E. *Craven County, North Carolina, Road Records (1767-1839).* Hillsborough: North Carolina Historical Books, 2012. [Note: While not specifically concerning the Revolution, these sources can be used in tandem with land records and other documents to help locate places of residence, occupations, geographical features, and place names.]

Ewen, Charles; Patricia M. Samford; and Perry Mathewes. "The Sauthier Maps and the Formal Gardens at Tryon Palace: Myth or Reality?" *North Carolina Historical Review*, 79:3 (July 2002), 326-346.

Goerch, Carl. "Craven County." *The State: A Weekly Survey of North Carolina*, 9:29 (December 1941), 1-20, 23. [Online description from "North Carolina Periodicals Index," East Carolina University: "Continuing his travels around the state, Goerch describes the things of interest he found in Craven County. He says 'from an historical standpoint, the county probably has more firsts, to its credit than any other county in the state,' and he includes a list of them at the end of the article. The article includes small descriptions of a number of historic homes in the town of New Bern."]

Great Britain. Exchequer and Audit Department. Claims, American Loyalists, Series II (AO 13, Selections). Claims, Virginia. H-M. (AO 13/31). "[Claim of] John Lowry. [13 Aug. 1782]." Copy of a document in the National Archives of the United Kingdom (formerly the Public Records Office), 77.1461.1-2 (MARS ID: 21.3.25.15; folder), "British Records Collection," State Archives of North Carolina, Raleigh. [Online catalog description: "Estimate of loyalist losses, including land in Craven and Dobbs counties, North Carolina."]

Gregg, Frederick. "Frederick Gregg Collection, 1721-1867," PC.1550 (MARS ID: 2060; Record Group), State Archives of North Carolina, Raleigh. [The online catalog description shows that this collection contains printed material that includes …; *The Pennsylvania Mercury and Universal Advertiser* (Philadelphia), Oct. 27, 1775, with news of munitions found in Tryon Palace gardens;…"]

Henderson, Archibald. *Revolution in North Carolina in 1775: Transylvania, Craven, Anson, and Mecklenburg*. [S. l.: s. n.], 1916.

Herzog, Lynda Vestal. "The Early Architecture of New Bern, North Carolina, 1750-1850." Ph. D. dissertation, University of California, Los Angeles, 1977.

Hollister, William. "William Bryan of Craven County, Brigadier General in the American Revolution." *North Carolina Booklet*, 18:2 (October 1918), 105-115. [Online description from "North Carolina Periodicals Index," East Carolina University: "William Bryan, son of Irish immigrants to America, was not killed at the Battle of Alamance as is commonly believed. Much respected in his community, Bryan was also a key figure in the Battle of Moore's Creek Bridge."]

"John Tillman of Craven County for his Services of part of the Craven Militia on an Expedition to Wilmington." In Weynette Parks Haun, *North Carolina Revolutionary Army Accounts, Part I, Secretary of State Treasurer's & Comptroller's Papers Journal "A", (Public Accounts) 1775-1776* (Durham: W. P. Haun, 1988), 140-142.

Jones, Victor T., Jr. "The Best Way to Get There: A History of New Bern in Maps." *Journal of the New Bern Historical Society*, 20:1 (May 2007), 34-44. [maps from 1710-1817]

Kammerer, Roger. "1779 Craven County Tax List (Two Districts)." *Pitt County Genealogical Quarterly*, 14:2 (May 2007), 1-3.

Kirwan, Virginia. "New Bern as Colonial and State Capital." *New Bern Historical Journal*, 1:2 (November 1988), 3-13.

"Major John Bryan of Craven County for the Services of His Regiment on an Expedition against the Insurgents." In Weynette Parks Haun, *North Carolina Revolutionary Army Accounts, Part I, Secretary of State Treasurer's & Comptroller's Papers Journal "A", (Public Accounts) 1775-1776* (Durham: W. P. Haun, 1988), 106-119.

Neale, Christopher. "Christopher Neale Paper, 1776." Manuscript, PC.791, State Archives of North Carolina, Raleigh. [Online catalog description: "Deposition by Neale about a dispute (May 20, 1776) at Craven Co. general muster concerning proposal by some in the New Bern Company to raise a bounty to encourage volunteers for 'the Service of the colonies' as alternative to drafting from the militia."]

New Bern. Committee of Inquiry and Correspondence. *The Proceedings of the Revolutionary Committee of the Town of New Bern, North Carolina, 1775: A Newly Discovered Printed Document of the American Revolution Brought to Light by the American Imprints Inventory of the Historical Records Survey, Division of Women's & Professional Projects of the Works Progress Administration. Provided with an Introduction and Privately Printed by Douglas C. McMurtrie ... as a Keepsake for Presentation to Friends Attending the Sixtieth Annual Conference of the American Library Association at Kansas City, Missouri, June 13-18, 1938*. Chicago: Chicago School of Printing, 1938. [Caption title of facsimile: "Proceedings of the Committee for the Town of Newbern and County of Craven, May 31, 1775."]

New Bern (Town) and Craven County. *Proceedings of the Committee for the Town of Newbern and County of Craven, May 31, 1775*. New Bern: Printed by James Davis, 1775; micropublished (Early American Imprints. First Series No. 42910) New York: Readex Microprint, 1985.

New Bern/Craven County American Bicentennial Commission; H. Braughn Taylor, ed. *Guide to Historic New Bern, North Carolina.* New Bern: The Commission, 1974.

Newbern, August 9, 1774. To the Freeholders of Craven County. Gentlemen, This day a considerable number of the Inhabitants of Newbern met at the Court-House, and Appointed Abner Nash and Isaac Edwards, Esqrs. Deputies, to Act for them in the General Meeting to be held here on the 25th Instant. New Bern: Printed by James Davis, 1774; micropublished (Early American Imprints. First Series No. 42657) New York: Readex Microprint, 1985.

North Carolina (State). General Assembly. "[Document dated:] February 3, 1781: In Favor of James Biggleston (Rejected)." Manuscript; General Assembly Record Group; Session Records, January-February 1781; Joint Papers, Committee Papers, Resolutions, Senate Joint Resolutions, Box 1 (MARS ID: 66.8.23.11.1; item), State Archives of North Carolina, Raleigh. [Online catalog description: "As the lease of Biggleston's Craven County farm has expired and he and his family have been ordered off the land, the resolution would have permitted him a broader parole. He had been confined as a result of his activities as former Governer Josiah Martin's secretary."]

North Carolina. Secretary of State. "Miscellaneous Papers, 1741-1921." Manuscript Records Series (RS) Number 15680 (MARS ID: 12.23). State Archives of North Carolina, Raleigh. [Online catalog description shows that this collection includes: "...a report of the 1777 sale of Governor Josiah Martin's private effects in Tryon Palace..."]

Ogden Family. "Ogden Family Papers, 1773-1891." Manuscript 5481, Southern Historical Collection, Louis Round Wilson Special Collections Library, University of North Carolina, Chapel Hill; online finding aid available at http://www2.lib.unc.edu/mss/inv/o/Ogden_Family.html. [Online finding aid description: "Members of the Ogden family, headed by James and Mary Odgen, lived in Manchester, England. Their children Thomas Ogden (d. 1787), Titus Ogden (d. 1793), and Isaac Ogden (d. 1785) emigrated from Manchester to North America circa 1770, where they settled in New Bern, N. C., and became successful landowners and merchants. Titus Odgen later moved to Philadelphia, Pa., and then to Tennessee, where he died in 1793. Titus Ogden was a paymaster to the troops and of Native American annuities; he was present at the 1791 signing of the Treaty of Holston with the Cherokees in Philadelphia. The collection contains letters, legal documents, and other papers related to the Ogden family of Manchester, England, and New Bern, N. C. Included are six letters, 1773-1783, written by brothers Thomas, Titus, and Isaac Ogden to their parents James and Mary Ogden following the brothers' emigration from Manchester to New Bern. Topics include trade operations, the brothers' acclimation to North America and North Carolina, and the political unrest leading to and the impacts of the Revolutionary War. Also included are several 19th-century documents, among them wills, certificates, and other agreements concerning members of the Ogden family, as well as two folders of genealogical materials."]

Rippy, J. Fred. "A View of the Carolinas in 1783." *North Carolina Historical Review,* 6:4 (October 1929), 362-370; online: http://digital.ncdcr.gov/cdm/ref/collection/p16062coll9/id/4207. [Online description from "North Carolina Periodicals Index," East Carolina University: "A summary of descriptions and accounts of visits to several towns in North and South Carolina in 1783 culled from the diary of Francisco de Miranda, known best as a leader and proponent of the independence movement in the Spanish-American Colonies. Includes details of the Ocracroke Inlet area, New Bern, Beaufort, and Wilmington."]

Robinson, Kenneth W. "Port Brunswick and the Colonial Naval Stores Industry: Historical and Archaeological Observations." *North Carolina Archaeology*, 46 (1997), 51-68; online: http://www.rla.unc.edu/ Publications/ NCArch/NCA_46.pdf.

Sandbeck, Peter B. *The Historic Architecture of New Bern and Craven County, North Carolina*. New Bern: Tryon Palace Commission, 1988.

Sharpe, Bill. "Carolina's Colonial Capital." *The State: Down Home in North Carolina*, 25:23 (April 1958) 16-32. [Online description from "North Carolina Periodicals Index," East Carolina University: "Encompassing 725 square miles, Craven County was first settled in 1710 by Baron de Graffenried and the German and Swiss colonists that pursued him. A region plagued by the Tuscarora War, Craven's image improved when the second oldest city in North Carolina, New Bern, was appointed the colonial state capital. Commerce throughout the region grew via the expansion of maritime industries, agriculture, and improvements in transportation. Cherry Point serves as the biggest modern contribution to Craven's economy, generating some 35% of all trade."]

Sitgreaves, John. 1757-1802. "John Sitgreaves (1757-1802) Papers." Manuscript PC.925, (MARS ID: 1435; record group), State Archives of North Carolina, Raleigh. [Online catalog description: "Drafts on his salary as judge, addressed to cashier of Bank of the United States, Philadelphia, by Sitgreaves of New Bern, Revolutionary War officer, congressman (1784-1785), and U. S. District Court judge for North Carolina (1790-1802)."]

Turnage, Sheila. "Three Towns on the Eve of Revolution." *Our State: Down Home in North Carolina*, 68:10 (March 2001), 56-59; online: http://digital.ncdcr.gov/cdm/ref/collection/p16062coll18/id/72796. [Online description from "North Carolina Periodicals Index," East Carolina University: "Turnage gives a brief look at what was happening in New Bern, Beaufort, and Bath on the eve of the American Revolution."]

Craven County and New Bern – Tryon Palace

Beaman, Thomas E., Jr. "Beyond the Restoration: Reconstructing a Pattern of Elite Lifestyle at Colonial Tyron Palace." *North Carolina Archaeology*, 50 (2001), 47-72; online: http://www.rla.unc.edu/Publications/NCArch/NCA_50%28e-book%29.pdf.

Beaman, Thomas E., Jr. "Fables of Reconstruction: Morely Jeffers Williams and the Excavation of Tryon Palace, 1952-1956." *North Carolina Archaeology*, 49 (October 2000), 1-22; online: http://www.rla.unc.edu/PublicationsNCArch/NCA_49%28e-book%29.pdf. [Online description from "North Carolina Periodicals Index," East Carolina University: "It has been argued that historical archaeology began in North Carolina with the work of Talcott Williams in the 19th century in search of the Roanoke settlements or with the work of James Sprunt at Russellborough near Brunswick Town. Beaman argues that historical archaeology did not flourish in the state until the mid 20th century, when Morely Jeffers Williams conducted the first archaeological investigation into the opulent pre-Revolutionary home of William Tryon in New Bern."]

Bellamy, Terry. "At the Palace." *Our State: Down Home in North Carolina*, 76:11 (April 2009), 74-76, 78; online: http://digital.ncdcr.gov/cdm/ref/collection/p16062coll18/id/91674. [Online description from "North Carolina Periodicals Index," East Carolina University: "New Bern's Tryon Palace is marking the 50th year since it was reconstructed. The 18th-century manor house of Royal Governor William Tryon burned in 1798. The building is an exact reproduction built from the original plans. Harrison describes the gardens designed by William Morley that surround the structure."]

Bowie, Phil. "The American Palace." *The State: Down Home in North Carolina*, 50:12 (May 1983), 8-9. [Online description from "North Carolina Periodicals Index," East Carolina University: "Emmy-award-winning CC-M Productions, managed by Clare Crawford Mason and her husband, recently came to New Bern's Tryon Palace to film reenactments of the Civil War. CC-M is making a documentary on the pivotal role Tryon Palace played in 18th-century North Carolina history. The film is sponsored by Pepsi-Cola, a company which originated in New Bern. Filmed over the span of one week, the documentary will play in the Tryon Palace auditorium and will be called 'The American Palace'."]

Brooks, Tiffany Yecke. "The Incomplete Story of John Hawks." *The Palace*, 9:2 (Winter 2009), 3. [Online description from "North Carolina Periodicals Index," East Carolina University: "Although there is much information on William Tryon and his family, there is little on Tryon Palace's architect, John Hawks. Researchers at Tryon Palace are attempting to piece together Hawks' history."]

Carraway, Gertrude. "To Restore Tryon's Palace." *The State: A Weekly Survey of North Carolina*, 12:11 (August 1944), 1, 18; online: http://digital.ncdcr.gov/cdm/ref/collection/p16062coll18/id/19397. [Online description from "North Carolina Periodicals Index," East Carolina University: "Tryon's Palace will be the first historical area to become a State Park. More than half a million dollars will be spent in restoring the building to its original status."]

Cecelski, David. "What the Governor Grew." *Coastwatch*, (Winter 1998), 18-21. [Online description from "North Carolina Periodicals Index," East Carolina University: "The kitchen garden at Tryon Palace measured 16,200 square feet and was enclosed by an eight-foot-high wall. It provided the governor foods of American, European, and African origin, including squash and okra. Some, like salsify, are not common today."]

DeLue, Willard. "Two Women." *The State: Down Home in North Carolina*, 23:11 (October 1955), 21-22; online: http://digital.ncdcr.gov/cdm/ref/collection/p16062coll18/id/82062. [Online description from "North Carolina Periodicals Index," East Carolina University: "DeLue recounts his visit to New Bern. He provides a short history of New Bern and the construction of Royal Governor William Tyron's great palace on the banks of the Trent River. After interest was sparked with the restoration of Williamsburg, Virginia; two New Bern natives, Gertrude S. Carraway and J. E. Latham, decided Tryon Palace deserved to be included in the historic preservation."]

Dill, Alonzo Thomas. *Governor Tryon and His Palace*. Chapel Hill: University of North Carolina Press, 1955.

Dill, Alonzo Thomas, Jr. "Tryon's Palace: A Neglected Niche of North Carolina History." *North Carolina Historical Review*, 19:2 (April 1942), 119-167.

Farmer, Vina Hutchinson. "Partners in Preservation: DOT and Tryon Palace." *The Palace*, 7:3 (Spring 2007), 5, 8, 15. [Online description from "North Carolina Periodicals Index," East Carolina University: "When the Tryon

Palace Commission formed in 1945 it had many allies, one of which was the forerunner of the North Carolina Department of Transportation. Farmer recounts the evolution of Tryon Palace's partnership with the DOT."]

Herko, Carl. "The Hay House Comes Alive." *The Palace*, 1:1 (Fall 2000), 4-5. [Online description from "North Carolina Periodicals Index," East Carolina University: "Nearly two centuries old, the Robert Hay House at Tryon Palace is seeing current activity. Historical characters and interpreters are bringing new life into the old New Bern home."]

Herko, Carl. "How Do Our Gardens Grow?" *The Palace,* 1:2 (Winter 2001), 4-5. [Online description from "North Carolina Periodicals Index," East Carolina University: "Herko discusses the gardens and landscape of Tryon Palace in New Bern. Five staff gardeners work with an eye toward history in maintaining the grounds and presenting them as accurately as possible."]

Hunter, Priscilla Speed. "Anything but Palatial." *The Palace,* 3:1 (Fall 2002), 4-5. [Online description from "North Carolina Periodicals Index," East Carolina University: "Although a regal residence, Tryon Palace could only function by the work of spinners, weavers, cooks, and the like in performing their daily chores."]

Liederbach, Clarence A. "Ransom in Lieu of Pillage." *The State: Down Home in North Carolina*, 43:9 (February 1976), 9-10; online: http://digital.ncdcr.gov/cdm/compoundobject/collection/p16062coll18/id/11518. [Online description from "North Carolina Periodicals Index," East Carolina University: "Sir William Draper was known as the 'Conqueror of Manila' because of his mounted attack against Manila in 1762. This article discusses what brought him to New Bern, North Carolina, and his lasting effect on the town and Tryon Place."]

Mansfield, Nancy. "Helping the Future Meet the Past." *The Palace,* 1:3 (Spring 2001), 4-5. [Online description from "North Carolina Periodicals Index," East Carolina University: "Staff at Tryon Palace in New Bern play a key role in preserving the state's history through education programs and the re-creation of traditions."]

Mansfield, Nancy. "Making Beautiful Music Together." *The Palace*, 4:3 (Spring 2004), 4-5. [Online description from "North Carolina Periodicals Index," East Carolina University: "William Tryon needed loans to carry out the completion of his North Carolina Palace. Two centuries later, the first great public history project in the state also required help from public and private partnerships."]

Martin, Laura. "History in Flower." *North Carolina Home*, 2:2 (April 1993), 63-67. [Online description from "North Carolina Periodicals Index," East Carolina University: "History surrounds the origin, development and maintenance of Tryon Palace and its gardens in New Bern."]

Norris, Jeannie Faris. "Thoroughly Modern Shirley." *The Palace*, 2:3 (Spring 2002), 3. [Online description from "North Carolina Periodicals Index," East Carolina University: "Shirley Willis spends her day immersed in the past as she takes charge of all the kitchen activities at Tryon Palace in New Bern. Steeped in colonial era foodways and practices, Willis is key in the interpretation of life at Tryon Palace."]

Norris, Jeannie Faris. "Tryon Palace." *The State: A Weekly Survey of North Carolina*, 4:35 (January 1937), 3, 20; online: http://digital.ncdcr.gov/cdm/ref/collection/p16062coll18/id/101762. [Online description from "North Carolina Periodicals Index," East Carolina University: "Rich in its historical associations, Tryon Palace at one time was regarded as the most magnificent structure in the western hemisphere. The history of North Carolina's only royal palace command the interest of many, and citizens of New Bern and North Carolina are determined to restore the palace to its former glory."]

Rabb, Miriam. "Soon You Can See Famous Tryon Palace." *The State: Down Home in North Carolina*, 26:22 (April 1959), 8-9; online: http://digital.ncdcr.gov/cdm/compoundobject/collection/p16062coll18/id/36344. [Online description from "North Carolina Periodicals Index," East Carolina University: "Tryon Palace in New Bern opens to the public April 2, 1959. The original building was commissioned in 1767 by Royal Governor William Tryon (1729-1788); John Hawks (ca. 1734-1790) served as the architect. This article discusses the building's history and the restorations leading up to its grand opening."]

Rabb, Miriam. "Tryon Palace." *The State: Down Home in North Carolina*, 29:3 (July 1961), 9-11; online: http://digital.ncdcr.gov/cdm/ref/collection/p16062coll18/id/8574. [Online description from "North Carolina Periodicals Index," East Carolina University: "Once the home of North Carolina's royal governors, and later the capital of North Carolina, New Bern's Tryon Palace has been reconstructed to its previous splendor. Built in 1770, Tryon Palace was named for the first royal governor to occupy the building, William Tryon. Destroyed by fire in 1798, the 32 room palace has been restored in costly detail, and is now filled with a collection of rare pre-1770 antiques."]

Rabb, Miriam. "Tryon Palace to Be Opened in 1959." *We the People of North Carolina*, 16:7 (December 1958), 12, 21. [Online description from "North Carolina Periodicals Index," East Carolina University: "Tryon Palace, the residence of the Royal Governor in New Bern, was destroyed by fire in 1798. The building has been reconstructed and is being restored in costly detail to the magnificence for which it was famous during colonial times. The building will open in the spring of 1959."]

Reimer, Rebecca. "Constructing Nature: The Eighteenth Century Garden and Tryon Palace." *The Palace*, 9:4 (Summer 2009), 4-5. [Online description from "North Carolina Periodicals Index," East Carolina University: "Reimer discusses the preservation of Tryon Palace's famous gardens, including labor intensive archaeological investigations, historical investigations into garden designs and horticulture."]

Ruckert, Gordon N. "Between the Palaces: The Burned Out and the Rebuilt." *Journal of the New Bern Historical Society*, 19:1 (May 2006), 21-32. [Online description from "North Carolina Periodicals Index," East Carolina University: "Tryon Palace was constructed in New Bern between 1767 and 1770. The stately mansion, the seat of Royal Governor William Tryon, was considered the most elegant government building in English America. In 1798, it burned to the ground and was rebuilt from the original plans in the 1950s. Ruckart describes how the land, on which the original Tryon Palace had stood, was used in the intervening years."]

Samford, Patricia. "The Great Tryon Palace Treasure Hunt." *The Palace*, 2:2 (Winter 2002), 4-5. [Online description from "North Carolina Periodicals Index," East Carolina University: "Archaeological excavations have been taking place at Tryon Palace in New Bern for nearly fifty years, but there is still more to examine, including building foundations and numerous artifacts."]

Shannon, George Ward, Jr. "225 Years and Counting." *The Palace*, 2:3 (Spring 2002), 4-5. [Online description from "North Carolina Periodicals Index," East Carolina University: "April 2002 marks the 225th anniversary of the first North Carolina General Assembly, which met at the Palace in New Bern where the state of North Carolina was born."]

Sharpe, Bill. "'Detective Scholars Gather in New Bern to Investigate Past." *Carolina Comments*, 40:4 (July 1992), 83-84. [Online description from "North Carolina Periodicals Index," East Carolina University: "Recently-discovered documents that describe the government house and gardens of Tryon Palace between 1767 and 1770 have scholars abuzz."]

Sharpe, Bill. "Most Magnificent Building in Colonial America to Be Rebuilt." *We the People of North Carolina*, 2:8 (December 1944), 13, 31. [Online description from "North Carolina Periodicals Index," East Carolina University: "Tryon's Palace, once called the most beautiful building in either North or South America, is to be rebuilt, using the original plans which were discovered in the New[-]York Historical Society after being closed for ninety years. A fire destroyed the main building and one wing in 1798. Estimated cost is between one-half and one million dollars."]

Sharpe, Bill. "Restoration of Hay House Completed at Tryon Palace." *Carolina Comments*, 46:6 (November 1998), 137-140. [Online description from "North Carolina Periodicals Index," East Carolina University: "The five-year restoration of the John Hay House, ca. 1805, at Tryon Palace Historic Site in New Bern is complete. The house stands on its original Eden Street location. Hay, a native of Scotland and a skilled artisan, came to New Bern around 1800. The house will be used to interpret his life."]

Sharpe, Bill. "Tryon Palace Identifies Undiscovered 18th Century Evidence." *Carolina Comments*, 40:2 (March 1992), 25-29. [Online description from "North Carolina Periodicals Index," East Carolina University: "A recently discovered plan of the Tryon Palace gardens in New Bern suggests that the grounds were considerably different in the 18th-century."]

Sickles, Dolly R. "Baroque'n Record." *Our State: Down Home in North Carolina*, 74:12 (May 2007), 164-166, 168, 170-171; online: http://digital.ncdcr.gov/cdm/ref/collection/p16062coll18/id/89271. [Online description from "North Carolina Periodicals Index," East Carolina University: "The Craven Historical Dancers and the New Bern Dancing Assembly re-create life in Tryon Palace in the days of the Royal Governor. Unlike modern day entertainment and entertainers, people in Colonial America provided entertainment for each other. The Baroque dance was a noble dance style and technique of the period. Sickles discusses the dance and the work of the two dance groups."]

Taylor, Donald R. "A Trip Back Two Centuries to Royal Governor's Time." *We the People of North Carolina*, 38:7 (July 1980), 84-85. [Online description from "North Carolina Periodicals Index," East Carolina University: "New Bern's Tryon Palace served as capitol of the Royal Colony of North Carolina and as residence of the royal governor. The restored palace and gardens reflect the state's colonial past in impressive fashion."]

Turnage, Sheila. "Mystery of the Palace Garden." *Our State: Down Home in North Carolina*, 67:11 (April 2000), 50-53; online: http://digital.ncdcr.gov/cdm/ref/collection/p16062coll18/id/70991. [Online description from "North Carolina Periodicals Index," East Carolina University: "There is a mystery on the Tryon Palace grounds. Where was the palace's original garden? There are three maps of it prepared by Claude Joseph Southier in the 18th-century, but they are contradictory. One, the Miranda Map of 1783, was lost and did not surface until 1991 in Venezuela. Using maps, historical documents, and dirt, an archaeological team from East Carolina University is working to solve the mystery. A 1999 north lawn dig eliminated that area as the possible site. The team will return in the summer of 2000 for a dig on the south lawn."]

Wharton, Rachael. "Making and Remaking the State's First Mansion." *Coastwatch*, (November/December 1996), 8-11. [Online description from "North Carolina Periodicals Index," East Carolina University: "In 1798, fire destroyed Tryon Palace in New Bern, only twenty-eight years after its completion. In the 1920s, citizens began to work for its reconstruction, and on April 9, 1959, the palace opened to the public."]

Wharton, Rachael, and Jeannie Faris Norris. "Tryon Palace Reconstructions of Christmases Past." *Coastwatch*, (November/December 1996), 2-7. [Online description from "North Carolina Periodicals Index," East Carolina University: "Christmas tours of New Bern's Tryon Palace and other historic sites, including the John Wright Stanley House, give visitors a feel for Christmas celebrations from the 1770s onward."]

Whitfield, Pam. "The Royal Treatment." *The State: Down Home in North Carolina*, 62:3 (August 1994), 26-29; online: http://digital.ncdcr.gov/cdm/compoundobject/collection/p16062coll18/id/66889. [Online description from "North Carolina Periodicals Index," East Carolina University: "New Bern's Tryon Palace attracts approximately 75,000 visitors each year. The restored palace and gardens reflect the state's colonial past in impressive fashion."]

Cumberland County [Wilmington District]

[Note: For various state government documents relating to Cumberland County during the Revolutionary period, search the MARS online catalog using the advanced search: http://mars.archives.ncdcr.gov/AdvancedSearch.aspx. Use the "Year" search box to restrict the searching to 1775-1783 and enter the county's name in the "Subjects" box, and hit the "Search" button near the top. This will retrieve any cataloged document for the county from that time period. These materials can vary considerably from personal or county petitions to the General Assembly, Loyalist matters, land disputes and claims, tax collection, exemptions from taxation, payments to county veterans, county divisions, personal collections, genealogical material, British claims against North Carolinians, etc. There is considerable information in these materials that could provide interesting documentation for persons living during the Revolution. The results will also include all of the wills and probates recorded in the county during the period set for the search. We had hoped to include many of these listings in this guide, but they are too voluminous. Citations to many of these search results for the eastern counties do, however, appear in the text.]

"American Independence – Fayetteville." Online: http://www.visitfayettevillenc.com/assets/files/driving_trails/AmericanIndependence.pdf.

Bennett, William. "1777 Tax List for Captain Thomas Dobbins' District, Cumberland County, North Carolina." *Argyll Colony Plus*, 3:4 (Fall 1988), 133-134.

"Company of Capt Ebenezer Folsom of Cumberland for the Services of His Company of Militia on an Expedition to Cross Creek against the Insurgents." In Weynette Parks Haun, *North Carolina Revolutionary Army Accounts, Part I, Secretary of State Treasurer's & Comptroller's Papers Journal "A", (Public Accounts) 1775-1776* (Durham: W. P. Haun, 1988), 130.

[Carmichael, Maurice]. "Correspondence, Accounts, Power of Attorney, 1775-1803 (broken series)." In Cumberland County Clerk of Superior Court; Clerk of Court of Pleas and Quarter Sessions; Register of Deeds. "Cumberland County Miscellaneous Records, 1758-1965, no date," Manuscript CR.029.928.3-CR.029.928.9 (MARS ID: 229.103.2; box), State Archives of North Carolina, Raleigh.

Comer, James Vann. "Revolutionary War Soldiers of Cumberland County, NC." *Central North Carolina Journal*, 4:2 (June 1993), 6.

Cumberland Association. "Cumberland Association Papers, 1775; 1830." Manuscript 2075-z, Southern Historical Collection, Louis Round Wilson Special Collections Library, University of North Carolina, Chapel Hill; online finding aid available at http://www2.lib.unc.edu/mss/inv/c/Cumberland_Association.html. [Online finding aid description: "The Cumberland Association was a declaration, 20 June 1775, signed by citizens of Cumberland County, N.C., associating to resist Britain. The Cumberland Association is also known as the Liberty Point Resolves. The collection contains the Cumberland Association and items related to the declaration, including a letter transmitting the document from Fayetteville, N. C., to Raleigh, N. C., 1830, and materials about the declaration including a photographic reproduction and transcripts."]

Cumberland County. "Cumberland County Miscellaneous Records, 1758-1965: Cumberland County Miscellaneous Records, 1758-1965: Memoranda as to the Liability of British Subjects to Perform Military Duty (no date)." Manuscript C.R.0298.928.7, State Archives of North Carolina, Raleigh.

Cumberland County. "Cumberland County Miscellaneous Records, 1758-1965: Cumberland County Miscellaneous Records, 1758-1965: Justices of the Peace, 1777-1918." Manuscript C.R.0298.928.7, State Archives of North Carolina, Raleigh.

Cumberland County. "Cumberland County Miscellaneous Records, 1758-1965: Cumberland County Miscellaneous Records, 1758-1965: Tax Records, no date, 1783-1893." Manuscript C.R.0298.928.9, State Archives of North Carolina, Raleigh.

Cumberland County. "Cumberland County Miscellaneous Records, 1758-1965: Slave Records, 1754-1897 and no date." Manuscript C.R.0298.928.9, State Archives of North Carolina, Raleigh.

"Cumberland List of Officers." In Walter Clark, ed., *State Records of North Carolina: Laws, 1715-1776, Volume 22: Misceallaneous* (Goldsboro: Nash Bros., Book and Job Printers, 1907; reprinted: Wilmington: Broadfoot Publishing Company, 1994), 473.

"Cumberland County/Wilmington District Militia under Captain Arthur Council on an Expedition against the Insurgents." In Weynette Parks Haun, *North Carolina Revolutionary Army Accounts, Part I, Secretary of State Treasurer's & Comptroller's Papers Journal "A", (Public Accounts) 1775-1776* (Durham: W. P. Haun, 1988), 6-7. [County determined by Arthur Council's appointment as captain in the Wilmington District on April 16, 1776, *Colonial Records of North Carolina*, Volume 10, p. 523 and "Cumberland List of Officers", *State Records of North Carolina,* Vol. 22, p. 473, as well as Micajah Terrell, Andrew Beard, Peter Mercer, Mark Russell, John Elwell, all members of this company and whose established residence by the DAR is Cumberland County).]

Curry, Calvin H. "1779 Tax Roll for Captain Neill McCrainie's District, Cumberland County, North Carolina." *Argyll Colony Plus*, 3:1 (Winter 1988), 20-23.

Curry, Calvin H. "1780 Tax Roll for Captain Neill McCrainie's District, Cumberland County, North Carolina." *Argyll Colony Plus*, 3:3 (Summer 1988), 87-91.

Fuller, Elijah. "Elijah Fuller Papers, 1786-1911." Manuscript 1573, Southern Historical Collection, Louis Round Wilson Special Collections Library, University of North Carolina, Chapel Hill; online finding aid available at http://www2.lib.unc.edu/mss/inv/f/Fuller,Elijah.html. [Online finding aid description: "Elijah Fuller was born in 1810 to Bartholomew Fuller of Franklin County, N. C., Revolutionary patriot and Baptist preacher, and Sarah Cooke Fuller… In addition to his activities as a merchant, he was a Revolutionary War pension agent and an assignee in bankruptcy court for Cumberland County… [Includes r]eceipts, bills of sale, account statements, shipping statements, notes, bankruptcy cases, invoices, Revolutionary War pension claims, insurance policies, promissory notes, and other material relating to William MacLennan's and Elijah Fuller's business activities in Fayetteville, N. C."]

Lewis, J. D. "Patriot Leaders in North Carolina: Alexander McAllister: Lt. Colonel in the Cumberland County Regiment of Militia - 1775-1776; Colonel/Commandant over the Cumberland County Regiment of Militia – 1776." Online: http://www.carolana.com/NC/Revolution/patriot_leaders_nc_alexander_mcallister.html.

Lewis, J. D. "Patriot Leaders in North Carolina: Philip Alston: Major in the Cumberland County Regiment of Militia - 1776-1778; Lt. Colonel in the Cumberland County Regiment of Militia – 1778; Colonel over the Cumberland County Regiment of Militia - 1778-1781." Online: http://www.carolana.com/NC/Revolution/patriot_leaders_nc_philip_alston.html.

Lewis, J. D. "Patriot Leaders in North Carolina: Thomas Rutherford: Colonel over the Cumberland County Regiment of Militia - 1775-1776." Online: http://www.carolana.com/NC/Revolution/patriot_leaders_nc_thomas_rutherford.html.

Lewis, J. D. "Patriot Leaders in North Carolina: Robert Rowan: Captain in the 1st NC Regiment (NC Continental Line) - 1775-1776; Captain in the Cumberland County Regiment of Militia - 1776-1778; Colonel in the Cumberland County Regiment of Militia - 1778 & 1780; Superintendent Commissary for the Wilmington District Brigade of Militia, with the rank of Colonel - 1780-1783 (sporadically); Clothier General for North Carolina with the rank of Colonel - 1780-1783." Online: http://www.carolana.com/NC/Revolution/patriot_leaders_nc_robert_rowan.html.

[McKay, John]. "John McKay [Letter] to His Mother from Camp Ashleyhill [S. C.?], Sept. 5, 1782." In Cumberland County Clerk of Superior Court; Clerk of Court of Pleas and Quarter Sessions; Register of Deeds. "Cumberland County Miscellaneous Records, 1758-1965, no date," Manuscript CR.029.928.3-CR.029.928.9 (MARS ID: 229.103.2; box), State Archives of North Carolina, Raleigh.

North Carolina (State). General Assembly. "[Document dated:] April-May 1777: Papers Concerning Justices of the Peace and Militia Officer Appointments, 1777." Manuscript; General Assembly Record Group; Session Records; Joint Papers, Committee Papers, Resolutions, Senate Bills, House Bills; Apr-May 1777, Box 1 (MARS ID: 66.8.9.8), State Archives of North Carolina, Raleigh. [Online catalog description: "Documents concerning Governor Caswell's appointment of officers to the militia regiments of Cumberland and Chatham counties, and his appointments of Justices of the Peace for Onslow and Pasquotank counties."]

North Carolina (State). General Assembly. "[Document dated:] February 1, 1779: Resolution Appoint David Smith Colonel of the Militia in Cumberland County (with Message)." General Assembly Record Group; Session Records, January-February 1779; Joint Papers, Committee Papers, Resolutions; Senate Joint Resolutions: January 21-February 1779, Box 1 (MARS ID: 66.8.15.10.17; item), State Archives of North Carolina, Raleigh.

North Carolina (State). General Assembly. "[Document dated]: July 4, 1781: Petition of Thomas Cabeen." Manuscript; General Assembly Record Group; Session Records, June-July 1781; Joint Papers, Committee Papers, Resolutions; Joint Papers (June-July 1781): Miscellaneous Petitions, Box 1 (MARS ID: 66.8.25.7.4; item), (MARS ID: 66.8.23.13.3; item), State Archives of North Carolina, Raleigh. [Online catalog description: "Cabeen, a tanner from Cross Creek but writing from Campbellton, asks the Assembly to make some provision for the protection of his life and property from the results of false charges of toryism."]

North Carolina. "Miscellaneous Papers, 1689-1912." Manuscript PC.21 (MARS ID: 530; record group), State Archives of North Carolina, Raleigh. [Online catalog description shows that this collection includes: "... reminiscences by William Polk on the Cumberland Association..."]

Oates, John A. *The Story of Fayetteville and the Upper Cape Fear.* Fayetteville: Fayetteville Woman's Club, 1981.

"Oaths of Allegiance." In William C. Fields, ed., Abstracts of Minutes of the Court of Pleas and Quarter Sessions of Cumberland County, October, 1755—January, 1779 (Fayetteville: Cumberland County Bicentennial Commission, 1977), 1:189a-189g, 270. [These same court records also include the names of a number of civil service appointees."]

Parker, Roy, Jr. *Cumberland County: A Brief History.* Raleigh: Division of Archives and History, North Carolina Department of Cultural Resources, 1990.

Shaw, Colin. "Colin Shaw Papers." Manuscript PC.20 (MARS ID: 529; Record Group), State Archives of North Carolina, Raleigh. [Online catalog description: "Papers of three generations of Colin Shaws in Cumberland Co. Papers of Colin Shaw I (d. ca. 1791) include letters from Scotland about family and immigration to North Carolina (1764, 1770, 1789); militia commissions and certificate of service under Donald McDonald until defeat at Moores Creek Bridge; letters from Shaw as loyalist refugee in New York; partnership agreement (1780) for trade in Georgia; fragment of a petition to remain in North Carolina (1782); and proposal for building two meetinghouses along the Cape Fear, 1785..."]

"Sketch of Cumberland County, 1782." Manuscript map MC.029.1782c (MARS ID: 3.1.27.1 and 3.1.27.2; folder), State Archives of North Carolina, Raleigh. [Online catalog description: "This 1782 map was prepared by an unidentified cartographer/surveyor, probably to accompany the 1784 petition to the General Assembly to create a new county from the northwest part of Cumberland County. The map portrays the boundaries of Cumberland County in 1782 and shows rivers and creeks, roads, residences of some individuals, and other landmarks. Four potential dividing lines are recorded on the map. The proposed line from Cole's Bridge on Drowning Creek to the Wake County line is the one adopted in the act creating Moore County in 1784. Portions of surrounding counties are also portrayed."]

Willcox, George W. *John Willcox, 1728-1793, of Chester County, Pennsylvania, Cumberland County, North Carolina, and Chatham County, North Carolina.* [S. l.]: Historical Research Co., 1988.

Currituck County [Edenton District]

[Note: For various state government documents relating to Currituck County during the Revolutionary period, search the MARS online catalog using the advanced search: http://mars.archives.ncdcr.gov/AdvancedSearch.aspx. Use the "Year" search box to restrict the searching to 1775-1783 and enter the county's name in the "Subjects" box, and hit the "Search" button near the top. This will retrieve any cataloged document for the county from that time period. These materials can vary considerably from personal or county petitions to the General Assembly, Loyalist matters, land disputes and claims, tax collection, exemptions from taxation, payments to county veterans, county divisions, personal collections, genealogical material, British claims against North Carolinians, etc. There is considerable information in these materials that could provide interesting documentation for persons living during the Revolution. The results will also include all of the wills and probates recorded in the county during the period set for the search. We had hoped to include many of these listings in this guide, but they are too voluminous. Citations to many of these search results for the eastern counties do, however, appear in the text.]

Baum Family. "Baum Family Papers, 1700-1984." Manuscript, Outer Banks History Center, State Archives of North Carolina, Manteo. [Online finding aid description: "The Baum family has a long history of living on the Outer Banks; it is likely it is one of the oldest families that settled there. The family can trace roots back to the early 1700s and owned extensive property in Currituck and surrounding counties. The materials in this collection primarily relate to the genealogy/family history of the Baum family of Currituck County. The collection includes correspondence, financial records, genealogical material, deeds, wills, publications and photographs. Many of the materials are photocopies and not original."]

Burgess, Carla B. "Looking Back at the Land of Fish and Fowl." *Coastwatch*, 17:10 (November/December 1990), 2-3. [Online description from "North Carolina Periodicals Index," East Carolina University: "Burgess discusses the history and culture of Currituck County, whose unique environment are home to numerous fish and waterfowl."]

Cockton, John. "[Daybook and Ledger, 1771-1794]." Manuscript AB.78 (MARS ID: 2978; record group), State Archives of North Carolina, Raleigh. [2 vols. Currituck County]

"Currituck County Militia under the Command of Gideon Lamb." In Weynette Parks Haun, *North Carolina Revolutionary Army Accounts, Part I, Secretary of State Treasurer's & Comptroller's Papers Journal "A", (Public Accounts) 1775-1776* (Durham: W. P. Haun, 1988), 12-14.

Great Britain. Exchequer and Audit Department. "[Claim of] Francis Williamson, 17 March 1784." Copy of a manuscript in the National Archives of the United Kingdom (formerly the Public Records Office), Kew, Richmond, Surrey, England; X77.1078.1-3 (MARS ID: 21.3.35.4; folder), "British Records Collection," State Archives of North Carolina, Raleigh. [Online catalog description: "Memorial of Thomas Macknight on behalf of the family of this deceased Currituck County loyalist."]

Great Britain. Exchequer and Audit Department. "[Claim of] Logan, Gilmour and Co. 8 June, 1784." Manuscript 77.1463.1-2 (MARS ID: 21,3.26.6; folder), State Archives of North Carolina, Raleigh. [Online catalog description: "Affidavit of Thomas Macknight late of Belville, Currituck County, North Carolina, in behalf of Isabella Logan, widow of a partner in the firm trading in Pasquotank County."]

Great Britain. Colonial Office. "N. C. Act to Appoint Trustees to Erect Chapel and Enclose Burial Ground at Indian Town in Currituck County." Manuscript (MARS ID: 21.2.25.28), State Archives of North Carolina, Raleigh.

Jones, Gordon C., comp. Abstracts of Land-Grants, Tax Lists, Orphans Dockets, Inventories and Other Records: Currituck and Dare Counties, North Carolina (1666-1831). 2nd ed. Elizabeth City: Family Research Society of Northeastern North Carolina, 2003. Includes:
"List of Taxables, Married Men Poll Tax, Single Men Poll Tax, Currituck County, 1779," 10-15.
"A List of Capt. Jacob Farrow's Company (Probably 1776)," 85-86.
"Payroll of Captain Alexander Whitehall's Company of the 1st North Carolina Regiment of Militia, Commanded by Col. Sam'l Jarvis – June 2, 1780," 87-88.
"Currituck County Revolutionary War Pensioners, March 4, 1831," 91.

Lewis, J. D. "Patriot Leaders in North Carolina: Samuel Jarvis: Colonel over the Currituck County Regiment of Militia - 1775-1783; Colonel over the 1st NC Regiment of Militia – 1780." Online: http://www.carolana.com/NC/Revolution/patriot_leaders_nc_samuel_jarvis.html.

Lewis, J. D. "Patriot Leaders in North Carolina: Solomon Perkins: Captain in the Currituck County Regiment of Militia – 1776; Lt. Colonel in the Currituck County Regiment of Militia - 1776-1777; Colonel in the Currituck County Regiment of Militia - 1777-1779." Online: http://www.carolana.com/NC/Revolution/patriot_leaders_nc_solomon_perkins.html.

Norris, Jeannie Faris. "The Cataclysm of Currituck." *The State: Down Home in North Carolina,* 22:3 (July 1954), 6-8. [Online description from "North Carolina Periodicals Index," East Carolina University: "Located near the Virginia-North Carolina state lines, Currituck has been explored and inhabited since the 18th-century. Experiencing topographical changes pertaining to the opening and closing of ocean inlets, the waters of Currituck sound have changed from salt to fresh numerous times."]

North Carolina (State). General Assembly. "[Document dated:] April 26, 1777: Report on Defense Necessary for Ocacock Inlet and the Ports of Beaufort and Roanoke (Messages Only)." Manuscript; General Assembly Session Records; Session of April-May 1777; Joint Papers, Committee Papers, Resolutions, Miscellaneous Bills, Box 1 (MARS ID: 66.8.9.10.10; item), State Archives of North Carolina, Raleigh. [Online catalog description: "Message concerning the report on defense measures to be taken for the security of Ocacock Inlet, Beaufort, and Roanoke; reference made to defense capability of the row galleys constructed by Virginia."]

North Carolina (State). General Assembly. "[Document dated:] December 3, 1777: John Humphries to Sell Boats Belonging to Public Purchased for Independent Company Stationed at Currituck Inlet and Take into Possession All Guns of Said Company." Manuscript; General Assembly Session Records; Session of April-May 1777; , Miscellaneous, Joint Papers, Committee Papers, Resolutions, Box 1 (MARS ID: 66.8.10.9.4; item), State Archives of North Carolina, Raleigh.

North Carolina (State). General Assembly. "[Document dated:] April 23, 1778): Bill for directing and appointing the place where the clerk of the court of Currituck Co. and the naval officers of port Currituck shall keep their offices." Manuscript, General Assembly Record Group, Session Records, April-May 1778; Joint Papers, Committee Papers, Resolutions, Senate Bills, House Bills, Senate Bills (April 23): Box 2 (MARS ID: 66.8.13.9), State Archives of North Carolina, Raleigh.

North Carolina (State). General Assembly. "[Document dated:] 1779: Miscellaneous." Manuscript; General Assembly Record Group; Session Records, May 1779; Joint Papers, Committee Papers, Resolutions, Senate Bills, House Bills, Box 1 (MARS ID: 66.8.17.8; folder), State Archives of North Carolina, Raleigh. Online catalog description: "Contains a letter from James Green, Jr., to the Speaker of the House of Commons concerning the lack of an officer to receive Continental taxes; a list of militia draftees who failed to appear when required; an inventory of accounts settled by committees from May, 1776 to January, 1779; and two letters to Thomas Younghusband, of Currituck County, describing attacks on that county by privateers."]

North Carolina (State). General Assembly. "May 14, 1779: Joint Papers, Committee Papers, Resolutions, Senate Bills, House Bills, Report Re[specting] Petition of Inhabitants of Currituck County (Messages and Petition – Partial Only)." Manuscript; General Assembly Record Group; Session Records, May 1779, Box 1 (MARS ID: 66.8.17.10.8; item), State Archives of North Carolina, Raleigh. [Online catalog description: "Only the top half of the petition is present, in which the petitioners explain that the draft is leaving their county defenseless. The messages give no indication of the content of the committee report."]

North Carolina (State). General Assembly. "June 2, 1779: Joint Papers, Committee Papers, Resolutions, Senate Bills, House Bills, Petition of James Beaton, John Johnston, and Alex MacLean." Manuscript; General Assembly Record Group; Session Records, October-November 1779, Box 1 (MARS ID: 66.8.18.6.1; item), State Archives of North Carolina, Raleigh. [Online catalog description: "The petitioners were on a British privateer that wrecked off the coast of the state; as a result, they lost all their clothes and were taken prisoner by John Humphrey of Currituck County. They request parole to Philadelphia to be exchanged."]

North Carolina (State). General Assembly. "October 22, 1779: Joint Papers, Committee Papers, Resolutions, Senate Bills, House Bills, Furnishing Currituck County with Arms (with Message)." Manuscript, General Assembly Record Group, Session Records October-November 1779, Box 1 (MARS ID: 66.8.18.12.9; item), State Archives of North Carolina, Raleigh. [Online catalog description: "The commissary of stores of Edenton is ordered to supply Col. Samuel Jarvis with arms and ammunition for the defense of Currituck County."]

North Carolina (State). General Assembly. "February 5, 1781: Letter from Colonel Gideon Lamb and Bonds Given by Tories." Manuscript; General Assembly Record Group; Session Records, January-February 1781, Box 1 (MARS ID: 66.8.23.3.3; item), State Archives of North Carolina, Raleigh. [Online catalog description: "Lamb informs the Assembly that in his opinion the only way to deal with the numerous loyalists in Currituck, Camden, Pasquotank, and Perquimans Counties is to forgive them on the condition that they sign bonds for their good behavior, which he has done. He includes several of the bonds."]

Seiling, Erin. "Carotank…Currituck: Land of the Wild Goose." *Coastwatch,* (High Season 2006), 6-11. [Online description from "North Carolina Periodicals Index," East Carolina University: "The Currituck Heritage Park, located in Corolla, provides visitors a unique look in the past, present, and future of the Currituck region, which was once known as Carotank. Seiling describes two familiar features of the thirty-nine-acre park, the Whalehead Club and the Currituck Beach Lighthouse, and introduces the newest addition, the Outerbanks Center for Wildlife Education."]

Sharpe, Bill. "Far Away Currituck." *The State: Down Home in North Carolina,* 27:18 (February 1960), 8-11, 25, 27. [Online description from "North Carolina Periodicals Index," East Carolina University: "Settled in 1663 and designated as a precinct in 1670, the rural and agricultural Currituck, located in the northeastern most section of North Carolina, is one of the state's oldest counties. Encompassing 273 square miles and located on a peninsula formed by the North River and Albemarle Sound, residents of Currituck have enjoyed an extensive maritime history. The site of one of the state's first conflicts, Gibb's Rebellion, Currituck has since remained a relatively peaceful area sustained through fishing, hunting, agriculture, and dog racing."]

Dare County

Delaney, Norman C. "The Outer Banks for North Carolina during the Revolutionary War." *North Carolina Historical Review*, 36:1 (January 1959), 1-16; online: http://digital.ncdcr.gov/cdm/ref/collection/p16062coll9/id/4207. [Online description from "North Carolina Periodicals Index," East Carolina University: "This article provides a history of the Outer Banks during the period of the Revolutionary War with a particular focus on Ocracoke Island and Ocracoke Inlet. Progressing chronologically, the author details troop positions, defenses, and naval maneuvers made on the barrier islands during the war years."]

Sharpe, Bill. "North Carolina's Favorite County." *The State: A Weekly Survey of North Carolina*, 21:7 (July 1953), 9, 11-15; online: http://digital.ncdcr.gov/cdm/ref/collection/p16062coll18/id/30672. [Online description from

"North Carolina Periodicals Index," East Carolina University: "Sharpe examines the history, geography, economic conditions, industries, and general society of Dare County."]

Stick, David. "The Revolution: Dare County: A History." *Carolina Trees & Branches*, 2:1 (January 1993), [4].

Stick, David. *The Outer Banks of North Carolina 1584-1958*. Chapel Hill: University of North Carolina Press, 1958.

Walser, Richard. "The Hatterasman." *The State: Down Home in North Carolina*, 26:4 (July 1958), 18. [Online description from "North Carolina Periodicals Index," East Carolina University: "The history and folklore of concerning Hatteras banks has been recounted in Ben Dixon MacNeill's *The Hatterasman*. Although not a native of North Carolina, MacNeill, a well-known newspaperman, spent his youth enjoying Hatteras. MacNeil's volume outlines the early settlement of Hatteras, through the World War II."]

Whedbee, Charles H. *Outer Banks Mysteries and Seaside Stories*. Winston-Salem: John F. Blair, 1978.

Davidson County

Goerch, Carl. "Davidson County." *The State: A Weekley Survey of North Carolina,* 8:50 (May 1941), 3-6, 25, 27-29; online: http://digital.ncdcr. gov/cdm/ref/collection/p16062coll18/id/39528. [Online description from "North Carolina Periodicals Index," East Carolina University: "Davidson County was named for General Davidson, but it has been made famous for other reasons as well. Davidson County was the home of the Boone family, Daniel Boone that is, where Boone park is now located. Davidson County also houses the monument at Trading Fork where General Greene crossed the Yadkin River in his retreat toward Guilford Courthouse. It is also the locate of Thomasville, known for not only the largest chair factory in the country but al knitting mills, silk and rayon mills, and other manufacturing."]

Haun, Weynette Parks. *Morgan District North Carolina Superior Court of Law & Equity*. 4 vols. Durham: W. P. Haun, 1987-[1995].

Johnson, William Perry. "Loyalists and Tories in the Rowan-Davidson Counties Area, 1778." *Journal of North Carolina Genealogy*, 14:4 (Winter 1968), 2239-2244.

"Loyalists and Tories in the Rowan-Davidson-Davie Counties Area – 1778." *Journal of the Genealogical Society of Rowan County, North Carolina*, 11:3 (September 1997), 104-108.

Reid, John. "John Reid, Richmond, [to] Governor." Manuscript letter, Library of Virginia, Richmond online: http://image.lva.virginia.gov/GLR/05036. [Online catalog description: "Part of a collection of letters and other documents received in the Governor's Office during the period June 29, 1776-Nov. 30, 1784. Presenting an account of his actions since January 1783 as they relate to bringing about a successful peace treaty with the Cherokees. (Enclosures – 'several letters' [one from James Robertson; others unidentified and therefore lacking].) Oct. 27, 1783, James Robertson, on behalf of a Committee of Davidson County, North Carolina, 'To Whom it May Concern,' presenting their opinion, as expressed to Reid, re holding the forthcoming peace talks with the Cherokees in their settlement."]

Sink, M. Jewell, and Mary Green Matthews. *Pathfinders, Past and Present: A History of Davidson County, North Carolina*. High Point, N. C., Hall Printing Co., 1972.

Whitley, Edythe Rucker. "Revolutionary Soldiers in Davidson County, Tennessee." *William and Mary Quarterly*, 2nd series, 11:1 (January 1931), 13-19.

Davie County

Davie County Heritage 1997. Waynesville, NC: Davie County Heritage Book Committee and Don Mills, Inc., 1997.

Fred Hughes, Mapmaker, *Davie County North Carolina Historical Documentation* (map). Jamestown: The Custom House, 1977

James W. Wall, *Davie County: A Brief History*. Raleigh: North Carolina Department of Cultural Resources, Division of Archives and History, 1976

James W. Wall, *History of Davie County in the Forks of the Yadkin*. Davie County: Historical Publishing Association, 1969.

"Loyalists and Tories in the Rowan-Davidson-Davie Counties Area – 1778." *Journal of the Genealogical Society of Rowan County, North Carolina*, 11:3 (September 1997), 104-108.

North Carolina (State). Land Office. "Davie County Land Grants, [1752-1822], 1976." Manuscript, MC.033.1976l, State Archives of North Carolina, Raleigh. [Online catalog description: "This map was prepared by Andrew Lagle in 1976. The deed research was performed by Pink Tatum and lettering by George Hairston. The map portrays Davie County and shows the plats giving the location of land grants in Davie County from 1752 to 1822. Rivers and creeks are also identified. A personal name index accompanies the map."]

Pruitt, Albert Bruce. *Index to North Carolina County Maps: Davie, Guilford, Montgomery, Randolph, Rockingham,*

Stokes, Surry, & Yadkin. Whitakers: A. B. Pruitt, 1988.

"Revolutionary War Marker Dedicated 22 March 2009 in Davie County." *NCGS News: Newsletter of the North Carolina Genealogical Society*, 33:3 (Summer 2009), 10. [marker on the grave of Richmond Pearson (1751-1819) near Cooleemee]

Wall, James W. *Davie County: A Brief History*. Raleigh: Division of Archives and History, North Carolina Department of Cultural Resources, 1976.

Wall, James W. *History of Davie County in the Forks of the Yadkin*. Mocksville: Davie County Historical Publications Association, 1969; reprinted: Spartanburg S. C.: Reprint Company, 1985.

Dobbs County [New Bern District]

[Note: For various state government documents relating to Dobbs County during the Revolutionary period, search the MARS online catalog using the advanced search: http://mars.archives.ncdcr.gov/AdvancedSearch.aspx. Use the "Year" search box to restrict the searching to 1775-1783 and enter the county's name in the "Subjects" box, and hit the "Search" button near the top. This will retrieve any cataloged document for the county from that time period. These materials can vary considerably from personal or county petitions to the General Assembly, Loyalist matters, land disputes and claims, tax collection, exemptions from taxation, payments to county veterans, county divisions, personal collections, genealogical material, British claims against North Carolinians, etc. There is considerable information in these materials that could provide interesting documentation for persons living during the Revolution. The results will also include all of the wills and probates recorded in the county during the period set for the search. We had hoped to include many of these listings in this guide, but they are too voluminous. Citations to many of these search results for the eastern counties do, however, appear in the text.]

Ainsworth, Fern. "Dobbs County Militia, 1777." *The Genie: Ark-La-Tex Genealogical Association, Inc.*, 13:2 (April 1979), 87. [Capt. John Sheppard's Company]

"Colonel Abraham Sheppard of Dobbs County for the Services of His Regiment of Militia on an Expedition against the Insurgents." In Weynette Parks Haun, *North Carolina Revolutionary Army Accounts, Part I, Secretary of State Treasurer's & Comptroller's Papers Journal "A", (Public Accounts) 1775-1776* (Durham: W. P. Haun, 1988), 84-96.

"A Descriptive List of the Men Raised in the Dobbs Regiment of Militia for Twelve Months Service in the Continental Service under an act of the General Assembly passed in February 1781." *North Carolinian: Quarterly Journal of Genealogy & History*, 6:3 (September 1960), 729-730. [This list includes ages, height, complexion, occupation, and the name of the militia captain under whom they served.]

"Dobbs County Militia: 1777." *The Genie*, 13:2 (April 1979), 87.

Great Britain. Exchequer and Audit Department. Claims, American Loyalists, Series I (AO 12, Selections). Documents Communicated by State Governments – North Carolina (with Report). (AO 12/91). "An Account of Debts Condemn'd to Confiscation in Dobbs County, ca. 1788." Manuscript (MARS ID: 21.2.14.18; folder), State Archives of North Carolina, Raleigh. [Online catalog description: "Columns showing garnishee, to whom due, amount of debt, to whom paid, form of payment."]

Great Britain. Exchequer and Audit Department. Claims, American Loyalists, Series I (AO 12, Selections). Documents Communicated by State Governments – North Carolina (with Report). (AO 12/91). "An Account of the Property Condemned by the Court and Sold by the Commissioners of Confiscation in the County of Dobbs." Manuscript (MARS ID: 21.2.14.19; folder), State Archives of North Carolina, Raleigh. [Online catalog description: "Columns showing former owner, article sold, to whom sold, amount, to whom paid."]

Great Britain. Exchequer and Audit Department. Claims, American Loyalists, Series I (AO 12, Selections). Various. (AO 12/99). "Examination and Decision on [Application for Immediate Relief as a Suffering Loyalist] of Mrs. George Miller, Dobbs Co., N. C., Mar. 26, 1783." Copy of a manuscript in the National Archives of the United Kingdom (formerly the Public Records Office), Kew, Richmond, Surrey, England; X77.181.1 (MARS ID: 21.2.16.15; folder), "British Records Collection, State Archives of North Carolina, Raleigh.

Great Britain. Exchequer and Audit Department. Claims, American Loyalists, Series II (AO 13, Selections). Claims, Virginia. H-M. (AO 13/31). "[Claim of] John Lowry. [13 Aug. 1782]." Copy of a manuscript in the National Archives of the United Kingdom (formerly the Public Records Office), Kew, Richmond, Surrey, England; 77.1461.1-2 (MARS ID: 21.3.25.15; folder), "British Records Collection," State Archives of North Carolina, Raleigh. [Online catalog description: "Estimate of loyalist losses, including land in Craven and Dobbs counties, North Carolina."]

Great Britain. Colonial Office. American and West Indies: North Carolina, Original Correspondence, Board of Trade. Secretary of State (CO 5/318). "Address from Inhabitants of Dobbs Co. Feb. 20, 1775." Manuscript

Copy of a manuscript in the National Archives of the United Kingdom (formerly the Public Records Office), Kew, Richmond, Surrey, England; (MARS ID: 21.1.27.19; folder), "British Records Collection," State Archives of North Carolina, Raleigh.

Guilford Battle Chapter, North Carolina Daughters of the American Revolution. "Dobbs County Militia." *North Carolina DAR Genealogical Records Committee Report, Series 1, Volume 270: [North Carolina Family, Cemetery, Marriage, and Service Records]* (typescript (1959), 98; digital surrogate, DAR Library, Washington, D. C.

Moore, Terry. "Researching in Dobbs County, North Carolina." *NCGS News: The Newsletter of the North Carolina Genealogical Society*, 38:6 (November 2014), 10-11; online: http://www.ncgenealogy.org/articles_tools/Researching_in_Dobbs_County.pdf.

North Carolina (State). General Assembly. "[Document dated:] May 8, 1779: "Report on the Election in Dobbs County (with Petition and List of Voters)." General Assembly Session Records; Session of May 1779; Joint Papers, Committee Papers, Resolutions, Senate Bills, House Bills; House Committee Reports (May 1779): Committee of Privileges and Elections, Box 1 (MARS ID: 66.8.17.11.2; item), State Archives of North Carolina, Raleigh. [Online catalog description: Etheldred Ruffin charges that the election to the Assembly in Dobbs County was in violation of the constitution, and the committee agrees with him."] [Voter lists are usually considered acceptable patriotic service because one would have to have taken an oath of allegiance before being eligible to vote (despite the absence of an oath list).]

Pridgen, Thomas. "Thomas Pridgen Papers, 1764-1817." Manuscript PC.1612 (MARS ID: 2122; record group), State Archives of North Carolina, Raleigh. [Online catalog description: "Grants, deeds, and plats (1764-1817) for land owned by Pridgen in Dobbs and Greene counties. Also tax receipt (1764); militia commission as captain, Dobbs Co. (1777); receipt for four militiamen drafted at Kingston (1779); and an undated division of slaves by heirs of Ezekiel Ward."]

Duplin County [Wilmington District]

[Note: For various state government documents relating to Duplin County during the Revolutionary period, search the MARS online catalog using the advanced search: http://mars.archives.ncdcr.gov/AdvancedSearch.aspx. Use the "Year" search box to restrict the searching to 1775-1783 and enter the county's name in the "Subjects" box, and hit the "Search" button near the top. This will retrieve any cataloged document for the county from that time period. These materials can vary considerably from personal or county petitions to the General Assembly, Loyalist matters, land disputes and claims, tax collection, exemptions from taxation, payments to county veterans, county divisions, personal collections, genealogical material, British claims against North Carolinians, etc. There is considerable information in these materials that could provide interesting documentation for persons living during the Revolution. The results will also include all of the wills and probates recorded in the county during the period set for the search. We had hoped to include many of these listings in this guide, but they are too voluminous. Citations to many of these search results for the eastern counties do, however, appear in the text.]

Angley, Wilson. "Colonial Phantom on the Northeast Cape Fear: A Brief History of the Exeter Site." *Tributaries*, 3 (October 1993), 26-31. [Online description from "North Carolina Periodicals Index," East Carolina University: "Exeter, a proposed town in colonial North Carolina's New Hanover County, never developed as its promoters had hoped. Two centuries later little is known of the Northeast Cape Fear River settlement or its ultimate fate."]

Bizzell, Virginia L., and Oscar M. Bizzell. *Revolutionary War Records, Duplin and Sampson Counties: Contributions to Genealogy*. Newton Grove, N. C.: Sampson County Historical Society, 1997.

Byrd, Tom. "Navigation on Goshen Swamp, Duplin County, NC, 1785." *North Carolina Genealogical Society Journal*, 8:1 (February 1982), 2. ["The names of 231 settlers who lived along Goshen, some of whom are not found on the 1783 tax list, the 1786 state census, or the 1790 US census are included in the following article."]

Carr, J. O. "The Battle of Rockfish Creek in Duplin County." *North Carolina Booklet*, 6:3 (January 1907), 177-184; online: http://digital.ncdcr.gov/cdm/ref/collection/p249901coll37/id/14180. [Online description from "North Carolina Periodicals Index," East Carolina University: "This article describes the Battle of Rockfish Creek, which took place on August 2, 1781 between a Whig militia of 330 troops and 500 British. The British defeated the militia and took over 30 prisoners. The British troops were marching through the counties surrounding Wilmington arresting Whigs and enlisting more Loyalist supporters."]

"Chronology of Events in the History of Duplin County, NC." Online: http://www.duplincountync.com/aboutDuplinCounty/chronologyOfEvents.html. ["1777 – Duplin County Oath of Allegiance and Abjuration – a testimony of support and faithfulness to the State of North Carolina and a renouncement of the authority of Great Britain, was signed by twenty-five of Duplin's early leaders."]

"Colonel James Kenan of Duplin for the Services of His Regiment of Militia on an Expedition against the Insurgents." In Weynette Parks Haun, *North Carolina Revolutionary Army Accounts, Part I, Secretary of State Treasurer's & Comptroller's Papers Journal "A", (Public Accounts) 1775-1776* (Durham: W. P. Haun, 1988), 124-129.

Davis, Julie Fussell. "'All Rigid Whigs': William Dickson and the American Revolution in Duplin County, North Carolina." M. A. thesis, University of North Carolina-Greensboro, 1993.

Dosher, Randall. "The Old Middle Cape Fear in the Colonial and Antebellum Eras: Manuscript: An Introduction." *Footnotes: Occasional Publication of the Research Committee of the Duplin County Historical Society*, no. 46 (1992), 42 pages.

Duplin County. "Duplin County Miscellaneous Records, 1754-1947: no date, Valuation of Slave Executed in 1761 for the Murder of William Peacock, 1774, 1779, 1783, 1789, 1893." Manuscript C.R.035.928.6, State Archives of North Carolina, Raleigh.

"Duplin County in the Revolutionary War." *Quarterly Review of the Eastern North Carolina Genealogical Society*, 14:4 (December 1987), 169-170. [reprinted from *The Wallace Enterprise*.]

"Duplin County Militia, 1779." *Quarterly Review of the Eastern North Carolina Genealogical Society*, 14:1 (March 1987), 29.

Grady Family. "Grady Family Papers, 1793-2002, undated." Manuscript Collection #898, Joyner Library, East Carolina University, Greeneville; online finding aid available at https://digital.lib.ecu.edu/special/ead/findingaids/0898. [Online finding aid description: "Papers (ca. 1793-2002, undated) of the history of the Grady family, of Duplin County, North Carolina including correspondence, legal papers, financial documents, clippings, and photographs relating to various members of the Grady family; also including biographical information on John Grady, who fought in the American Revolution and who is known as the first North Carolinian to die in the war; … Series 5: Consists of printed materials (undated) including two photocopied clippings entitled, 'John Grady of Duplin County, The First North Carolina Man to Die in the Revolutionary War,' by Patsy M. Boyette (undated) that was published by the *Old Kinston Gazette* which focuses on a John Grady who served in the American Revolution. The article gives information not only on this John Grady who was the first North Carolinian to die in the Revolutionary War but gives a detail account of the Battle of Moore's Creek and biographical information on Benjamin Franklin Grady."]

Haines, Jeffrey L. "Duplin County 1786 Tax Lists." *North Carolina Genealogical Society Journal*, 34:4 (November 2008), 331.

Haines, Jeffrey L. "Petition from the Adjoining Inhabitants of the Counties of New Hanover, Duplin, and Bladen, 23 October 1779." *North Carolina Genealogical Society Journal*, 33:3 (August 2007), 244.

"A History of Exeter, North Carolina." Online: http://www.carolana.com/NC/Towns/Exeter_NC.html.

Johnson, William Perry. "Duplin County: 1783 Tax List." *Journal of North Carolina Genealogy*, 18:2 (Fall/Winter 1972), 2778-2782; 19:1 (Spring/Summer 1973), 2313-2821.

Lawrence, R. C. "The Kenans of Duplin." *The State: A Weekly Survey of North Carolina*, 8:13 (August 1940), 5, 16; online: http://digital.ncdcr.gov/cdm/ref/collection/p16062coll18/id/5990. [Online description from "North Carolina Periodicals Index," East Carolina University: "The Kenan family was in Duplin County years before it became a county, and they have served the state and its people in numerous ways. Among them were James Kenan, a member of the Provisional Congress; Thomas S. Kenan, who was Colonel of the 43rd North Carolina Regiment during the Civil War; and William Rand Kenan, who donated the Stadium to the University of North Carolina at Chapel Hill." James Kenan (1740-1810).]

Lewis, J. D. "Patriot Leaders in North Carolina: James Kean: Colonel over the Duplin County Regiment of Militia - 1775-1783; Brigadier General (Pro Tempore) of the Wilmington District Brigade of Militia, (1781)." Online: http://www.carolana.com/NC/Revolution/patriot_leaders_nc_james_kenan.html.

"A List of 25 Men Who Took the Oath of Allegiance in Duplin County." In John H. Wheeler, *Historical Sketches of North Carolina from 1584 to 1851*. 2 vols. (Philadelphia: Lippincott, Grambo, and Company, 1851; reprinted: New York: Frederick H. Hitchcock, 1925), 2:138-139.

Maxwell Jennifer Martin. "Rosin, Rail Lines, and Rent Shares: The Historical and Architectural Development of Duplin County, North Carolina, 1726-1943." M. A. thesis, Middle Tennessee State University, 1994.

Moore, Terry. "Duplin County, North Carolina, Research." *NCGS News: The Newsletter of the North Carolina Genealogical Society*, 39:5 (September 2015), 10-11; online: http://www.ncgenealogy.org/articles_tools/Duplin_County_NC_Research.pdf.

North Carolina (State). General Assembly. "[Document dated:] April 20, 1778: Bill to Impower the Justices of Duplin Co. to Take into Their Possession the Records of Said County Now in Possession of James Sampson." Manuscript: General Assembly Record Group; Session Records, April-May 1778, Senate Bills, House Bills, House Resolutions (April 27-May 1, 1778), Box 2 (MARS ID: 66.8.13.20; folder), State Archives of North Carolina, Raleigh.

North Carolina (State). General Assembly. "[Document dated:] January 28, 1779: Petition of a number of Inhabitants of New Hanover, Duplin, and Bladen Counties for Erecting a Separate County from the Above Counties." Manuscript; General Assembly Record Group; Session Records, January-February 1779, Box 1 (MARS ID: 66.8.15.9.8; item), January-February 1779, State Archives of North Carolina, Raleigh. [Online catalog description: "The petitioners refer to the difficulties they face in attending general musters and jury service at the courthouses of their respective counties and request that a new county be erected within the boundaries suggested."]

North Carolina (State). General Assembly. [Document dated:] October 23, 1779: Petition from the Adjoining Inhabitants of the Counties of New Hanover, Duplin & Bladen." Manuscript; General Assembly Session Records; Session of October-November 1778; Joint Papers, Committee Papers, Resolutions, Box 1 (MARS ID: 66.8.18.7.11; item), State Archives of North Carolina, Raleigh. [The purpose of this petition was to form a New County in Order to Help Facilitate Attendance of General Muster."]

North Carolina (State). General Assembly. "[Document dated:] April 27, 1780: Re[specting] Petitions of William Houston and William Skinner." Manuscript; General Assembly Record Group; Session Records, April-May 1780, Box 1 (MARS ID: 66.8.20.8.11; item), State Archives of North Carolina, Raleigh. [Online catalog description: "Houston informs the Assembly that in 1742 he took possession of a tract of land in Duplin County from his uncle, Henry McCulloh, who left the state in 1747. Because he never acquired a title or deed, Houston is concerned that the land is subject to confiscation and asks the Assembly to vest him with a title to the land by law. Skinner informs the Assembly that the law prohibiting individuals who have not taken the affirmation of allegiance to the state has had the effect of disabling Quakers in Pasquotank and Perquimans Counties from maintaining possession of their own land and asks the Assembly to pass a law in their behalf. The committee recommends that both petitions be granted, and the Assembly concurs."]

North Carolina (State). General Assembly. "[Document dated:] May 1, 1782: In Favor of John Devane of New Hanover Co. (Message and Petition Only)." Manuscript; General Assembly Record Group; Session Records, April-May 1782, Box 2 (MARS ID: 66.8.28.5.7; item), State Archives of North Carolina, Raleigh. [Online catalog description: "Petition of John Devane requests that he be released from taxation in Duplin County because he is only a transient resident there while avoiding the British; messages from both houses concurring with resolution."]

Ransom, Douglas. "Highway Men, Robbers, & Murderers – Duplin and Wayne Cos., N. C., 1781-1784." *North Carolina Genealogical Society Journal*, 5:4 (November 1979), 246.

"A Return of all the Effective Men in the Duplin Regiment, June 12, 1779, with Names of the Commissioned Officers." *Quarterly Review of the Eastern North Carolina Genealogical Society*, 14:1 (March 1987), 29. [Dated: Duplin, June 12, 1779.]

Salyers, Frances R. Nelson. "The Wilkins Family of Muhlenburg County, Kentucky: Proving an Ancestral Line to a North Carolina Revolutionary War Patriot." Kentucky Ancestors: A Genealogical Quarterly, 48:3 (Spring 2013), 126-131. [William Wilkins, Duplin County]

Durham County and Durham

Anderson, Jean Bradley. *A History of Durham County, North Carolina*. Durham: Duke University Press, 1990.

Edgecombe County

[Note: For various state government documents relating to Edgecombe County during the Revolutionary period, search the MARS online catalog using the advanced search: http://mars.archives.ncdcr.gov/AdvancedSearch.aspx. Use the "Year" search box to restrict the searching to 1775-1783 and enter the county's name in the "Subjects" box, and hit the "Search" button near the top. This will retrieve any cataloged document for the county from that time period. These materials can vary considerably from personal or county petitions to the General Assembly, Loyalist matters, land disputes and claims, tax collection, exemptions from taxation, payments to county veterans, county divisions, personal collections, genealogical material, British claims against North Carolinians, etc. There is considerable information in these materials that could provide interesting documentation for persons living during the Revolution. The results will also include all of the wills and probates recorded in the county during the period set for the search. We had hoped to include many of these listings in this guide, but they are too voluminous. Citations to many of these search results for the eastern counties do, however, appear in the text.]

Dunaway, Stewart E. *Edgecombe County, North Carolina, Mill Records (1760-1868), Bridge Records (1787-1890).* Hillsborough: North Carolina Historical Books, 2010. [Note: While not specifically concerning the Revolution, these sources can be used in tandem with land records and other documents to help locate places of residence, occupations, geographical features, and place names.]

Dunaway, Stewart E. *Edgecombe County, North Carolina, Road Records (1761-1849).* Hillsborough: North Carolina Historical Books, 2011. [Note: While not specifically concerning the Revolution, these sources can be used in tandem with land records and other documents to help locate places of residence, occupations, geographical features, and place names.]

Great Britain. Exchequer and Audit Department. Audit Office. "[Claim of] William McClellan. [5] May 1785." Manuscript 77.2248.1-2 (MARS ID: 21.3.71.32; folder), State Archives of North Carolina, Raleigh. [Online catalog description: "True copy of proceedings from the Edgecombe County, North Carolina, Court of Pleas and Quarter Sessions concerning the Tarborough property of McClellan, a loyalist."]

Johnson, William Perry. "Descriptions of Soldiers from Militia Returns, 1778-1782." *North Carolinian: A Quarterly Journal of Genealogy and History*, 6:3 (September 1960), 725-730, 751-758. [Includes: "Edgecombe County, Drafts and Substitutes, 1782," 752.]

Johnston, Hugh Buckner. "Columns, 1982." Manuscript accession no. 31570, Personal Papers Collection, Library of Virginia, Richmond. [Online catalog description: "Columns, dated 16 and 30 March, 6, 14, and 20 April 1982 {*Wilson Daily Times*, Wilson, N. C.}, by Hugh Buckner Johnston, Jr. (1913-1990), of Wilson, North Carolina, regarding the movement of British troops under the command of Charles, Lord Cornwallis and Banastre Tarleton through that part of Edgecombe County, North Carolina, which later became Wilson County, North Carolina, during the American Revolution. Column dated 16 March is a fictional account of a young North Carolina soldier avoiding the dragoons under Tarleton's command."]

Johnston, Hugh Buckner. "Hugh Buckner Johnston Collection, 1755-1967." Manuscript PC.206, State Archives of North Carolina, Raleigh. [The collection includes: "…an oath of allegiance (1776) and correspondence (1777-1779) between Col. Jonas Johnston of Edgecombe Co. and Gov. Richard Caswell about deserters, bounty payments, and action in South Carolina;…"]

Johnston, Hugh Buckner. "Thomas Howell, Revolutionary War Patriot." *Georgia Genealogical Magazine: A Magazine of Genealogical Source Material Concerning Georgians,* no. 97 (Summer 1985), 223-224. [from Edgecombe County]

Lea, Diane. "Tarboro: The Little Town That Did." *Metro Magazine*, 5:6 (June 2004), 28-34; online: http://www.metronc.com/article/?id=678. [Online description from "North Carolina Periodicals Index," East Carolina University: "Tarboro was settled in 1732 and has been the county seat of Edgecombe County since 1741. It is a town rich in history. Tarboro and Boston are the country's only cities retaining town commons established by legislative act in 1760. The commons in Tarboro is surrounded by a forty-five block historic district. Lea discusses the history and architecture of the town and how Tarboro coped with the great flood produced by Hurricane Floyd in 1999."]

"List of Revolutionary War Era Militia Officers of Edgecombe County." In "Lewis Family Papers, 1730-1956, Edgecombe County, North Carolina; Also Alabama, Mississippi, and Tennessee." Manuscript, Southern Historical Collection, Manuscripts Department, Library of the University of North Carolina, Chapel Hill; also available on microfilm [reels 1-3242. Series J.; Pt. 12, reels 13 and 14] as part of: Kenneth M. Stampp, gen. ed. *Records of Ante-Bellum Southern Plantations form the Revolution through the Civil War, Series J, Part 12: Selections from Southern Historical Collection, University of North Carolina, Chapel Hill [1701-1990]* Frederick, Md.: University Publications of America, 1992.

North Carolina. General Assembly. "May 2, 1782: Resolutions in Favor of Thomas Tynes (Messages and Petition Only), and in Favor of John Stewart (with Sworn Statement) (Rejected)." Manuscript; General Assembly Record Group; Session Records, April-May 1782, Box 2 (MARS ID: 66.8.28.8.14; item), State Archives of North Carolina, Raleigh. [Online catalog description: "Resolution would allow John Stewart sums for goods impressed into service; messages from both houses about concurrence; and depositions from Stewart and Tynes about impressment of their goods."]

North Carolina. General Assembly. "May 25, 1784: Report on the Petition of Michael Hearn of Edgecombe County." Manuscript; General Assembly Record Group; Session Records, April-June 1784, Box 1 (MARS ID: 66.8.31.9.11), State Archives of North Carolina, Raleigh. [Online catalog description: "Petition awards compensation for a portion of pork lost at sea that Michael Hearn had sold to the commissary of the army. The committee awards compensation."]

Schackell, Aubrey. "Tarboro and Edgecombe County." *The State: A Weekly Survey of North Carolina*, 14:46 (April 1947), 20-27; online: http://digital.ncdcr.gov/cdm/ref/collection/p16062coll18/id/20478. [Online description from "North Carolina Periodicals Index," East Carolina University: "Edgecombe County, named after Richard first Baron of Edgecombe, once encompassed an area equal to 17 modern era counties drawn from Bertie Precinct in 1732. Initially the county seat was Enfield, and then moved to Halifax, before finally being established at Tarboro. Tarboro, then Tarborough, was incorporated September 23, 1760 and historically the spelling was not agreed upon until January 14, 1898 by the Post Office that recognized only the current spelling. In 1947, Tarboro represented a vibrant county seat with modern hospitals, public facilities, and industry."]

Simpson, Kenrick N. "Hurricane Floyd and the Court Records of Edgecombe County." *Carolina Comments*, 48:5 (September 2000), 124-128. [Online description from "North Carolina Periodicals Index," East Carolina University: "he devastating floods produced by Hurricane Floyd severely damaged county records in the Edgecombe County Courthouse. Simpson summarizes the efforts made to salvage these records and their results."]

Turnage, Sheila. "Past Perfect." *Our State: Down Home in North Carolina*, 65:3 (August 1997), 16-19; online: http://digital.ncdcr.gov/cdm/ref/collection/p16062coll18/id/69100. [Online description from "North Carolina Periodicals Index," East Carolina University: "Tarboro, in Edgecombe County, features a 45-block historic district-one of the state's largest - that includes Calvary Episcopal Church, the Blount-Bridgers House, the 1760 Town Common, and the restored town fountain."]

Turner, Joseph Kelly, and John Luther Bridges. *History of Edgecombe County, North Carolina*. Raleigh: Edwards & Broughton Printing Company, 1920.

Watson, Alan D. *Edgecombe County: A Brief History*. Raleigh: North Carolina. Dept. of Cultural Resource, Division of Archives and History, 1979.

Watson, Alan D. "Orphanage in Colonial North Carolina: Edgecombe County as a Case Study." *North Carolina Historical Review*, 52:2 (April 1975), 105-119.

Watson, Alan D. "Society and Economy in Colonial Edgecombe County." *North Carolina Historical Review*, 50:3 (July 1973), 231-255.

Watson, Helen R. "The Books They Left: Some 'Liberies' in Edgecombe County, 1733-1783." *North Carolina Historical Review*, 48:3 (July 1971), 245-257. [Online description from "North Carolina Periodicals Index," East Carolina University: "An examination of the estates records of Edgecombe County during its first fifty years, through October court, 1783, reveals the type and size of private libraries."]

Forsyth County, Winston-Salem, Old Salem, and the Wachovia Tract

[Note: For various state government documents relating to Salem during the Revolutionary period, search the MARS online catalog using the advanced search: http://mars.archives.ncdcr.gov/AdvancedSearch.aspx. Use the "Year" search box to restrict the searching to 1775-1783 and enter the town's name in the "Subjects" box, and hit the "Search" button near the top. This will retrieve any cataloged document for the county from that time period. These materials can vary considerably from personal or county petitions to the General Assembly, Loyalist matters, land disputes and claims, tax collection, exemptions from taxation, payments to county veterans, county divisions, personal collections, genealogical material, British claims against North Carolinians, etc. There is considerable information in these materials that could provide interesting documentation for persons living during the Revolution. The results will also include all of the wills and probates recorded in the county during the period set for the search. We had hoped to include many of these listings in this guide, but they are too voluminous. Citations to many of these search results for the eastern counties do, however, appear in the text.]

[Note: See also the section in Chapter Sixteen on the Moravians of North Carolina.]

Africa, Philip. "Slaveholding in the Salem Community, 1771-1851." *North Carolina Historical Review*, 45:3: (July 1977), 271-307.

Bynum, Flora Ann L. *The Christmas Heritage of Old Salem*. Williamsburg, Va.: Williamsburg Publishing Company, 1983.

Bynam, Flora Ann L. *Old Salem Garden Guide*. Winston-Salem: Old Salem, Inc., 1979.

Campbell, Betty. "The Buildings of Salem, North Carolina, 1766-1856." Ph. D. dissertation, Florida State University, 1975.

Capps, Gene. "A Town Called Salem." *Tar Heel Junior Historian*, 14:2 (December 1974), 2-3. [Online description from "North Carolina Periodicals Index," East Carolina University: "Salem, once a thriving craftsmen settlement, now exists as a living history museum. Moravian settlers moved south and established Salem in 1752. Today, tourists can walk through the historic settlement and enter various trade buildings such as the historic bakery or tobacco shop."]

Crews, Hall; photographs by Kenneth Clark. *Old Salem, Now a Part of Winston-Salem, North Carolina*. New York: R. F. Whithead, 1929.

Davis, Chester. *Hidden Seed and Harvest: A History of the Moravians*. Winston-Salem: Wachovia Historical Society, 1959.

Ellis, Marshall. "Between Heaven and Earth." *Our State: Down Home in North Carolina*, 67:7 (December 1999), 74-86; online: http://digital.ncdcr.gov/cdm/ref/collection/p16062coll18/id/68691. [Online description from "North Carolina Periodicals Index," East Carolina University: "On January 6, 1766, twelve men set forth from the villages of Bethania and Bethabara in the North Carolina Piedmont and walked ten miles to begin construction of a new settlement called Salem. The new town was founded to serve as the church's administrative and commercial center. Today Old Salem is a National Historic District and stands as one of the best colonial restoration projects in the nation.:]

Engel. Katherine Carté. "Moravians in the Eighteenth-Century Atlantic World." *Journal of Moravian History*, 12:1 (Spring 2012), 1-19.

Ferguson, Leland. *God's Fields: Landscape, Religion, and Race in Moravian Wachovia.* University: Pennsylvania State University Press, 2011.

Ferguson, Leland. "What Means 'Gottes Acker"? Leading and Misleading Translations of Salem Records." *Journal of Moravian History*, 5 (Falll 2008), 68-87.

Fox, Janet. "Gardens of Necessity." *The State: Down Home in North Carolina*, 56:12 (May 1989), 18-21; online: http://digital.ncdcr.gov/cdm/ref/collection/p16062coll18/id/63614. [Online description from "North Carolina Periodicals Index," East Carolina University: "The re-created gardens at the Moravian village of Old Salem in Winston-Salem remind visitors how much settlers depended on their fruits and vegetables, plants for medicines, and food for livestock."]

Fries, Adelaide L. *The Town Builders.* Raleigh: Edwards & Broughton Printing Company, 1915.

Gray, James A. "A Little Lump of Heaven." *The Torch*, 35:2 (April 1962), 35-42. [Description: "History of the Moravian Church, with an emphasis on Salem, N. C."]

Griffin, Frances. *Cooking in Old Salem*. Williamsburg: Williamsburg Publishing Company, 1981.

Griffin, Frances. *A Day of Thanksgiving, Salem, North Carolina, July 4, 1783: An Account of the First Fourth of July Observance by Legislative Enactment in America*. Winston-Salem: Old Salem, Inc., 1966.

Griffin, Frances. *Old Salem: An Adventure in Historic Preservation*. Winston-Salem: Old Salem, Inc., [1970].

Gutek, Gerald Lee. *Visiting Utopian Communities: A Guide to the Shakers, Moravians, and Others*. Columbia: University of South Carolina Press, 1998.

Holder, Edward M. "Cornwallis in Wachovia." *The State: A Weekly Survey of North Carolina*, 10:38 (February 1943), 6-7, 20; online: http://digital.ncdcr.gov/cdm/ref/collection/p16062coll18/id/16810. [Online description from "North Carolina Periodicals Index," East Carolina University: "Holder describes the invasion of the Moravian territory on the northwest corner of the Wachovian tract, by the British forces who were in pursuit of General Nathanael Greene. British soldiers spent two days in the vicinity of Bethania."]

Hunter, Rixie. "Hear an Easter Choir in Brass: Moravian Sect's Sunrise Service, Held for 188 Years, Attracts Thousands to Restored Old Salem Village in North Carolina." *Ford Times*, 55:4 (April 1962), 2-5.

James, Hunter. *Old Salem Official Guidebook*, Winston-Salem: Old Salem, Inc., 1977, 1982, 1987, 1994.

Lehman, Emma A. "Bethania: Salem in Revolutionary Days." In *Salem's Remembrancers: Seven Moravian Historians Who Presented Their Papers before the Wachovia Historical Society of Salem, North Carolina, 1898-1910* (Winston-Salem: Wachovia Historical Society, 1976).

Montgomery, G. T. *Ghosts of Old Salem, North Carolina*. Charleston, S. C.: Haunted American, 2014.

Nelson, Kay Shaw. "A Moravian Christmas: At Old Salem and Bethlehem, the Holidays Are Marked by the Warmth of the Hospitality and the Delectability of the Food." *Americana*, 7:5 (November/December 1979), 54-61, 92.

Norris, Jeannie Faris. "187-Year-Old Tobacco Shop Joins Old Salem Restoration." *We the People of North Carolina*, 18:2 (June 1960), 6-7. [Online description from "North Carolina Periodicals Index," East Carolina University: "In 1771, Johann Matthew Miksch opened a tobacco shop in the Moravian village of Salem along with a log-cabin tobacco manufactory. Both buildings have now been restored and authentically furnished as part of the Old Salem Restoration project. To date, eight village buildings have been restored to their original appearance."]

Old Salem Gleaner, Winston-Salem: Old Salem, Inc., 1962-. ["The newsletter is for the Friends of Old Salem, the

Museum of Early Southern Decorative Arts (MESDA), the Old Salem Toy Museum, and the Old Salem Children's Museum."] *Old Salem Friends*, 1-12:1 (1990- Summer 2002).

Old Salem in North Carolina: A Moravian Congregation Town, Settled in 1766, Now Being Preserved and Restored as an Historic Site. Winston-Salem: Old Salem, [196?]

Owen, Mary Barrow. *Old Salem, North Carolina.* [Winston-Salem]: Garden Club of North Carolina, 1946.

Patterson Family. "Patterson Papers, 1748-1925." Manuscript PC.104 (MARS ID: 613; record group), State Archives of North Carolina, Raleigh. [Online catalog description: "Papers of the family of Rufus Lenoir Patterson (1830-1879), agriculturist, banker, and manufacturer of Salem and Caldwell Co., and his second wife, Mary Fries Patterson. Early material (1765-1875) relates to her relatives the Voglers, gunsmiths and silversmiths of Salem, including business letters, papers, and account books, some in German; letters about the Moravian church; currency exchange books in German (1765);…"]

Pfohl, Bernard J. "The Early Music of Salem Congregation." In *Salem's Remembrancers: Seven Moravian Historians Who Presented Their Papers before the Wachovia Historical Society of Salem, North Carolina, 1898-1910* (Winston-Salem: Wachovia Historical Society, 1976).

Reavis, Scott Aaron. "Wachovia during the Revolutionary Era: Societal Transformation and Cultural Assimilation." M. A. thesis, Western Carolina University, 1998.

Reichel, Levin T. *The Moravians in North Carolina*. Salem, N. C.: O. A. Keehln, 1857. [Contents: First Settlers and Heads of Families; Churches and Other Public Buildings; Houses Built in Salem, 1766-1816; Additions and notes.]

Reichel, Levin T. *A History of Nazareth Hall, from 1755 to 1855, and the Reunions of the Former Pupils, in 1854 and 1855*. Philadelphia: J. B. Lippincott & Company, 1855; available online through the HathiTrust. ["Catalog of the Pupils of Nazareth Hall {1785-1855}," 49-98.]

Reif, George A. "Old Salem, North Carolina and the Preservation Movement: A Case Study in a Community's Decision to Preserve Its Historic Fabric." M. R. P. thesis, University of North Carolina at Chapel Hill, 1966.

Reines, Philip. "A Cultural History of the City of Winston-Salem, North Carolina, 1766-1966." Ph. D. dissertation, University of Denver, 1970.

Restoring Old Salem in North Carolina: The Preservation of a Unique Heritage. Winston-Salem: Old Salem, 1960.

Sommer, Elisabeth W. *Serving Two Masters: Moravian Brethren in German and North Carolina, 1727-1801*. Lexington: University Press of Kentucky, 2000.

South, Stanley A. "Searching for Clues to History through Historic Site Archaeology." *North Carolina Historical Review*, 43:2 (April 1966), 166-173.

Spencer, Darrell. *The Gardens of Salem: The Landscape History of a Moravian Town in North Carolina*. Winston-Salem: Old Salem, 1997.

Starbuck, Richard W.; artwork by Lu Newman. *Ghosts of Salem and Other Tales*. Winston-Salem: Moravian Archives, 2002.

Stone, Walter. *A Walk through Old Salem*. Winston-Salem: John F. Blair, 2000.

Surratt, Jerry L. "From Theocracy to Voluntary Church and Secularized Community: A Study of the Moravians in Salem, North Carolina, 1772-1860." Ph. D. dissertation, Emory University, 1968.

Wade, Wellman Manly. *The Founders*. Winston-Salem: Wachovia Historical Society, 1966.

Winston-Salem in History. Winston-Salem: published for the Wachovia Historical Society by H. F. Blair, 1966-1976. [13 Volume series including *The Founders*, by Manly Wade Wellman; *The War*, by Manly Wade Wellman; *Education*, by Manly Wade Wellman and Larry Edward Tise; *Transportation and Communication*, by Manly Wade Wellman; *A City's Culture: Painting, Music, Literature*, by Manly Wade Wellman and Larry Edward Tise; *Government*, by Larry Edward Tise; *Industry and Commerce 1766-1896*, by Manly Wade Wellman and Larry Edward Tise; *Industry and Commerce 1896-1975*, by James Howell Smith; *Building and Architecture*, by Larry Edward Tise; *The Churches*, by Larry Edward Tise; *Medicine*, by Robert W. Prichard; *Publications*, by Larry Edward Tise; *The Character of the Community*, by Chester S. Davis.]

Forsyth County, Winston-Salem, Old Salem, and the Wachovia Tract – Salem Female Academy/Salem College (1772-present)

Allen, Madeline May. "An Historical Sketch of Moravian Education in North Carolina: The Evolution and Practice of the Moravian Concept of Education as It Is Applied to Women." Ph. D. dissertation, Florida State University, 1971.

Fries, Adelaide L. *Historical Sketch of Salem Female Academy.* Salem, N. C.: Crist & Keehln, 1902; online through the HathiTrust and Google Books.

Griffin, Frances. *Less Time for Meddling: A History of Salem Academy and College, 1772-1866*. Winston-Salem: J. F. Blair, 1979.
Salem Academy and College through the Years. Winston-Salem: Salem College Alumnae Association, 1951.
Salem Academy and College, Winston-Salem, North Carolina. Winston-Salem: Salem Academy, [1915?].

Franklin County

[Note: For various state government documents relating to Franklin County during the Revolutionary period, search the MARS online catalog using the advanced search: http://mars.archives.ncdcr.gov/AdvancedSearch.aspx. Use the "Year" search box to restrict the searching to 1775-1783 and enter the county's name in the "Subjects" box, and hit the "Search" button near the top. This will retrieve any cataloged document for the county from that time period. These materials can vary considerably from personal or county petitions to the General Assembly, Loyalist matters, land disputes and claims, tax collection, exemptions from taxation, payments to county veterans, county divisions, personal collections, genealogical material, British claims against North Carolinians, etc. There is considerable information in these materials that could provide interesting documentation for persons living during the Revolution. The results will also include all of the wills and probates recorded in the county during the period set for the search. We had hoped to include many of these listings in this guide, but they are too voluminous. Citations to many of these search results for the eastern counties do, however, appear in the text.]

North Carolina. General Assembly. "February 9, 1781: In Favor of George Harper (Message Only, with Petition)." Manuscript; General Assembly Record Group; Session Records, January-February 1781, Box 1 (MARS ID: 66.8.23.13.5), State Archives of North Carolina, Raleigh. [Online cataog description: "Harper, of Franklin County, informs the Assembly that he volunteered for the militia and received a disabling wound at the Battle of Camden, thus preventing him from working."]
Pearce, T. H. "Cascine True to Two Centuries." *The State: Down Home in North Carolina*, 38:17 (February 1971), 12-14; online: http://digital.ncdcr.gov/cdm/ref/collection/p16062coll18/id/54128. [Online description from "North Carolina Periodicals Index," East Carolina University: "The Cascine plantation, built in 1750 and located three miles south of Louisburg in Franklin County, NC, was selected by the advisory committee of the Historic American Buildings Survey as possessing exceptional historic or architectural interest worthy of most careful preservation for the benefit of future generations. The 1500-acre plantation is owned today by Bennett H. Perry, a Henderson attorney and direct descendant of one of the seven Perry brothers who settled the land in 1746. The Perry brothers came from Virginia after receiving the land by grant from the Earl of Granville."]
Pearce, T. H. *Early Architecture of Franklin County*. [S. l.: s. n.], 1977.
Pearce, Thilbert H. *Franklin County, 1779-1979*. Freeman, [S. l.]: Pine Hill Press, 1979.

Gaston County

Byrd, William L., and John H Smith. *North Carolina Slaves and Free Persons of Color: Mecklenburg, Gaston, and Union Counties*. Bowie, Md.: Heritage Books, 2001.
Cope, Robert F., and Manly Wade Wellman. *The County of Gaston: Two Centuries of a North Carolina County*. [S. l.]: Gaston County Historical Society, 1961.
Hall, J. B. "South Folk Boys – Their Life & Times." *Gaston County Historical Bulletin*, 11 (1965).
"Homes of Revolutionary Soldiers of Gaston County, North Carolina - Pictures of Homes that are Still Standing Today [1954]." Manuscript MssColl 336 Box1 file2, DAR Library, NSDAR, Washington D. C.
Hope, James Madison. "The Fight at Butterfly Spring." Broad River Journal, 14:4 (December 2006), 3-4. [from a letter by Hope to Lyman C. Draper dated August 10, 1874, relating a story about Loyalist and Patriot children in modern Gaston County, N. C. and events in 1780]
Ramsey, Robert W. "Captain Samuel Cobrin's Company of Militia: The First Settlers of Gaston and Lincoln Counties." *Journal of North Carolina Genealogy*, 12:4 (Winter 1966), 1773-1779.
"Soldiers from Gaston County That Participated Oct. 7, 1780 [Battle of King's Mountain]." Online: http://ncrevwar.lostsoulsgenealogy.com/gastonsoldiers.htm.
Williams, Robert L. "Mystery of the 218-Year-Old Man." *The State: Down Home in North Carolina*, 48:7 (December 1980), 17-18; online: http://digital.ncdcr.gov/cdm/ref/collection/p16062coll18/id/59408. [Online description from "North Carolina Periodicals Index," East Carolina University: "Olney Presbyterian Church of Gastonia has a graveyard with one particularly interesting grave. The tombstone of William Barnes, who died in 1823, is inscribed with the phrase 'aged 218 years.' Although there is no acceptable explanation for why the marker reads this way, members of the church today do not think Barnes lived to be 218."]

William Gaston Chapter, North Carolina Daughters of the American Revolution. *North Carolina DAR Genealogical Records Committee Report, Series 1, Volume 167: Revolution Soldiers and Patriots* (typescript, 1954); digital surrogate, DAR Library, Washington, D. C. [Gaston County, N. C.]

Gates County

[Note: For various state government documents relating to Gates County during the Revolutionary period, search the MARS online catalog using the advanced search: http://mars.archives.ncdcr.gov/AdvancedSearch.aspx. Use the "Year" search box to restrict the searching to 1775-1783 and enter the county's name in the "Subjects" box, and hit the "Search" button near the top. This will retrieve any cataloged document for the county from that time period. These materials can vary considerably from personal or county petitions to the General Assembly, Loyalist matters, land disputes and claims, tax collection, exemptions from taxation, payments to county veterans, county divisions, personal collections, genealogical material, British claims against North Carolinians, etc. There is considerable information in these materials that could provide interesting documentation for persons living during the Revolution. The results will also include all of the wills and probates recorded in the county during the period set for the search. We had hoped to include many of these listings in this guide, but they are too voluminous. Citations to many of these search results for the eastern counties do, however, appear in the text.]

Butchko, Thomas R. *Forgotten Gates: The Historical Architecture of a Rural North Carolina County*. Gatesville: Gates County Historical Society, 1991.

Dunaway, Stewart E. *Gates County Road (1779-1849) and Bridge Records (1786-1900).* Hillsborough: North Carolina Historical Books, 2013. [Note: While not specifically concerning the Revolution, these sources can be used in tandem with land records and other documents to help locate places of residence, occupations, geographical features, and place names.]

Dunaway, Stewart E. *Gates County, North Carolina, Mill Records (1754-1890).* Hillsborough: North Carolina Historical Books, 2010. [Note: While not specifically concerning the Revolution, these sources can be used in tandem with land records and other documents to help locate places of residence, occupations, geographical features, and place names.]

Fouts, Raymond Parker. *Following the Land: A Genealogical History of Some of the Parkers of Nansemond County, Virginia, and Chowan/Hertford/Gates Counties, North Carolina, 1604-2004*. Cocoa, Fla.: R. P. Fouts, 2005.

Gates County. "Election Records, 1783-1882." Manuscript, State Archives of North Carolina, Raleigh. [Consult the State Archives to determine the exact years that are available.]

Gates County. "Gates County Miscellaneous Records, 1780-1912: Pension Records, 1821-1883, and no date." Manuscript C.R.041.928.8, State Archives of North Carolina, Raleigh.

Harrell, Isaac Samuel. *Gates County to 1860*. Gatesville: Gates County Arts Council Bicentennial Committee, [197?].

Hill, Michael. "Buckland Update." *The State: Down Home in North Carolina*, 52:1 (June 1984), 23; online: http://digital.ncdcr.gov/cdm/ref/collection/p16062coll18/id/60843. [Online description from "North Carolina Periodicals Index," East Carolina University: "Buckland Plantation played an important role in Gates County's early history. Dating from the early 1700s, Buckland Plantation grew to over 3,000 acres and had over 100 slaves working its fields. Following a succession of several owners, Buckland Plantation shrank in size. Today, the Buckland home is in disrepair. Plans are under way to begin restoration."]

McClenny, W. E. *The History of Gates County*. Gatesville: Gates County Arts Counticl Bicentennial Committee, [1976?]

Rankin, Richard, and Robin Brabham. *Gaston & Lincoln Sketches*. Gastonia: Pipes & Timbrels Press, 2006. [Includes a chapter titled: "Revolution, Violence, and Lawlessness in Old Tryon."]

Tucker, Harry Z. "Buckland." *The State: A Weekly Survey of North Carolina*, 6:15 (September 1938), 7; online: http://digital.ncdcr.gov/cdm/ref/collection/p16062coll18/id/38356. [Online description from "North Carolina Periodicals Index," East Carolina University: "In 1938, Buckland was considered to be the oldest home standing in the state. Believed to have been built as early as 1650, the home stood in Gates County. By the early 20th-century, the home's shell stood but much of the interior was removed and sent to a northern museum."]

Wester, Paulette Felton. *A Journey in Time: A History of Gates County*. [North Carolina?]: P. F. Wester, 1995.

Granville County

[Note: For various state government documents relating to Granville County during the Revolutionary period, search the MARS online catalog using the advanced search: http://mars.archives.ncdcr.gov/AdvancedSearch.aspx. Use the

"Year" search box to restrict the searching to 1775-1783 and enter the county's name in the "Subjects" box, and hit the "Search" button near the top. This will retrieve any cataloged document for the county from that time period. These materials can vary considerably from personal or county petitions to the General Assembly, Loyalist matters, land disputes and claims, tax collection, exemptions from taxation, payments to county veterans, county divisions, personal collections, genealogical material, British claims against North Carolinians, etc. There is considerable information in these materials that could provide interesting documentation for persons living during the Revolution. The results will also include all of the wills and probates recorded in the county during the period set for the search. We had hoped to include many of these listings in this guide, but they are too voluminous. Citations to many of these search results for the eastern counties do, however, appear in the text.]

"An Account of Persons who took the State Oath, 1778." In Walter Clark, ed., *State Records of North Carolina: Miscellaneous*, 22 (Goldsboro: Nash Bros., Book and Job Printers, 1907; reprinted: Wilmington: Broadfoot Publishing Company, 1994), 165-179.

"Accounts of Memucan Hunt for the Granville County Militia." In Weynette Parks Haun, *North Carolina Revolutionary Army Accounts, Part I, Secretary of State Treasurer's & Comptroller's Papers Journal "A", (Public Accounts) 1775-1776* (Durham: W. P. Haun, 1988), 160-161.

Caldwell, J. R., Jr. "Churches of Granville County, North Carolina in the Eighteenth Century." In Joseph Carlyle Sitterson, ed., *Studies in Southern History* (James Sprunt Historical Publications, v. 39) (Chapel Hill: University of North Carolina Press, 1957), 1-22.

"Colonel James Martin, Guilford County, for the Services of his Regiment of Militia on an Expedition to Cross Creek against the Insurgents." In Weynette Parks Haun, *North Carolina Revolutionary Army Accounts, Part I, Secretary of State Treasurer's & Comptroller's Papers Journal "A", (Public Accounts) 1775-1776* (Durham: W. P. Haun, 1988), 61-76.

Douthat, James L. *1771 Granville County, North Carolina, Militia Records*. Signal Mountain, Tenn.: Mountain Press, 1999. [pre-Revolution]

Dunaway, Stewart E. *Granville County, North Carolina, Bridge Records, 1748-1868.* Hillsborough: North Carolina Historical Books, 2009. [Note: While not specifically concerning the Revolution, these sources can be used in tandem with land records and other documents to help locate places of residence, occupations, geographical features, and place names.]

Dunaway, Stewart E. *Granville County, North Carolina, Road Records, Vol. 1 (1747-1799).* Hillsborough: North Carolina Historical Books, 2009. [Note: While not specifically concerning the Revolution, these sources can be used in tandem with land records and other documents to help locate places of residence, occupations, geographical features, and place names.]

Dunaway, Stewart E. *Granville County, North Carolina, Tavern (Ordinary) Bonds (1748-1838).* Hillsborough: North Carolina Historical Books, 2012. [Note: While not specifically concerning the Revolution, these sources can be used in tandem with land records and other documents to help locate places of residence, occupations, geographical features, and place names.]

Goerch, Carl. "Granville County." *The State: A Weekly Survey of North Carolina*, 9:37 (February 1942), 1-3-18-21; online: http://digital.ncdcr.gov/cdm/ref/collection/p16062coll18/id/43418. [Online description from "North Carolina Periodicals Index," East Carolina University: "Goerch started his visit to Granville County by stopping at an unusually fine place to eat, the Walters House in Oxford, then progressed on to a 48-room house. He also wrote of the former grave of one of the signers of the Declaration of Independence, a frustrated romance, and some interesting history and towns."]

Granville County: "Granville County Miscellaneous Records, 1722, 1747-1920: Deposition of John Kelley on Behalf of Asa Tyner, 1782." Manuscript C.R.044.928.23, State Archives of North Carolina, Raleigh.

Granville County: "Granville County Miscellaneous Records, 1722, 1747-1920: List of Persons Who Took State Oath." Manuscript C.R.044.928.25, State Archives of North Carolina, Raleigh.

Granville County: "Granville County Miscellaneous Records, 1722, 1747-1920: List of Names and Signatures, 1777, 1790, 1805, and no date." Manuscript C.R.044.928.25, State Archives of North Carolina, Raleigh.

Granville County. "Granville County Miscellaneous Records, 1722, 1747-1920: Military Records, 1766-1870." Manuscript C.R.044.928.25, State Archives of North Carolina, Raleigh.

Granville County. "Granville County Miscellaneous Records, 1722, 1747-1920: Money and Bonds Inventories in Speromarrow District, 1780." Manuscript C.R.044.928.25, State Archives of North Carolina, Raleigh.

Granville County. "Granville County Miscellaneous Records, 1722, 1747-1920: Oath of Allegiance, Joseph Hart Ordered to Take." Manuscript C.R.044.928.26, State Archives of North Carolina, Raleigh.

Granville County. "Granville County Miscellaneous Records, 1722, 1747-1920: Treason Trial, State vs. John Williams." Manuscript C.R.044.928.26, State Archives of North Carolina, Raleigh.

Granville County. "Granville County Miscellaneous Records, 1722, 1747-1920: Reports on Condition of Clerk's and Register's Offices, 1783, 1798, 1806, 1817, 1840, 1857, 1859. Manuscript C.R.044.928.26, State Archives of North Carolina, Raleigh.

"Granville County, North Carolina: A Descriptive List of Men Raised under the Present Act of Assembly – 1778 (Abstracted from the Original, NC Archives, Granville County Records, {Mil TR4-40})." *Granville Connections, Journal of the Granville County Genealogical Society*, 1:1 (Winter 1995), 10-15. [This list gives age, height, and occupation.]; also printed in *North Carolinian, Quarterly Journal of Genealogy & History*, 6:3 (September 1960), 726-727; Also printed in *The Roster of Soldiers from North Carolina in the American Revolution* (Baltimore: Geneal. Pub., 1972), 600. [This copy does not include ages.]

Great Britain. Exchequer and Audit Department. Claims, American Loyalists, Series II (AO 12, Selections), Various. (AO 12/107). "Letter from 'A Gentleman in Granville County' [i. e., George Alston], to [John Hamilton]. Jan. 18, 1785." Copy of a manuscript in the National Archives of the United Kingdom, formerly the Public Records Office, Kew, Richmond, Surrey, England), 77.42.2-3 (MARS ID: 21.2.21.20; folder), "British Records Collection," State Archives of North Carolina, Raleigh. [Online catalog description: "Complaining that he had been bound over to appear before the next session of Hillsborough District Superior Court despite a protection given him by the Governor of N.C. {apparently for having returned to the state despite an act banishing him as a loyalist}. For heading, see BR77.40.4."]

Great Britain. Exchequer and Audit Department. Claims, American Loyalists, Series II (AO 13, Selections). Various Claims. (AO 13/85). "Archibald and John Hamilton [n. d.], 1785." Copy of a manuscript in the National Archives of the United Kingdom, formerly the Public Records Office, Kew, Richmond, Surrey, England), 77.1632.1-4 (MARS ID: 21.3.40.4; folder), "British Records Collection," State Archives of North Carolina, Raleigh. [Online catalog description: "Extracts of letters from Willie Jones (1785 Mar. 15); John Sym (1785 Mar. 31); Tho{ma}s Mutter of Granville County, North Carolina (1785 Feb. 28); and one from Charleston, S. C. (1785 Apr. 4). Portraying 'a melancholy picture of Carolina Matters' and difficulties of collecting pre-Revolutionary War debts owing to Hamilton & Co."]

Great Britain. Exchequer and Audit Department. Claims, American Loyalists, Series II (AO 13, Selections). Various Claims. (AO 13/85). "[Claim of] George Alston, 10 Dec. 1784." Copy of a manuscript in the National Archives of the United Kingdom, formerly the Public Records Office, Kew, Richmond, Surrey, England), 77.1657.1 (MARS ID: 21.3.40.29; folder), "British Records Collection," State Archives of North Carolina, Raleigh. [Online catalog description: "Pass to Granville County, signed by Governor Alexander Martin. (A true copy)."]

Great Britain. Exchequer and Audit Department. Claims, American Loyalists, Series II (AO 13, Selections). Various Claims. (AO 13/85). "Granville County, North Carolina. [George Alston] to John Hamilton. 18 Jan. 1785." Copy of a manuscript in the National Archives of the United Kingdom, formerly the Public Records Office, Kew, Richmond, Surrey, England), 77.1658.1 (MARS ID: 21.3.40.30; folder), "British Records Collection," State Archives of North Carolina, Raleigh. [Online catalog description: "On his arrest despite a pass signed by Governor Alexander Martin."]

Great Britain. Exchequer and Audit Department. Claims, American Loyalists, Series II (AO 13, Selections). Various Claims. (AO 13/91). "[Claim of] James McCallum. 22 May 1783." Copy of a manuscript in the National Archives of the United Kingdom, formerly the Public Records Office, Kew, Richmond, Surrey, England), 77.1710.1-2 (MARS ID: 21.3.45.23; folder), "British Records Collection," State Archives of North Carolina, Raleigh. [Online catalog description: "Loyalist losses in Granville County, North Carolina, attested by self and by John Hamilton."]

Great Britain. Exchequer and Audit Department. Claims, American Loyalists, Series II (AO 13, Selections). Various Claims. (AO 13/91). "[Claim of] James McCallum. 25 May 1783." Copy of a manuscript in the National Archives of the United Kingdom, formerly the Public Records Office, Kew, Richmond, Surrey, England), 77.1712.1-2 (MARS ID: 21.3.45.25; folder), "British Records Collection," State Archives of North Carolina, Raleigh. [Online catalog description: "Memorial of loyalist losses in Granville County and Wilmington, North Carolina."]

Great Britain. Exchequer and Audit Department. Claims, American Loyalists, Series II (AO 13, Selections), Various Papers. (AO 13/100). "Hillsborough. William Johnston to Edmund Fanning, New York. 28 Aug. 1775." Copy of a manuscript in the National Archives of the United Kingdom, formerly the Public Records Office, Kew, Richmond, Surrey, England), 77.1929.1-4 (MARS ID: 21.3.54.42; folder), "British Records Collection," State Archives of North Carolina, Raleigh. [Online catalog description: "Puzzled by a labyrinthine financial manoeuvre by Henry Eustace McCulloh. 200,000 bricks for Fanning's house are in preparation by a workman in Granville County. Provincial Congress in Hillsborough has yet done nothing but proceedings are to be published. Includes a significant statement concerning the Transylvania Company, in which Fanning appears to have been involved."]

Guilford County: A Map Supplement. Jamestown: The Custom House, 1988. [This book includes military, civil, and patriotic service.]

"A Listing of Recruits for the Revolutionary War, May 25, 1778, Granville County." Photographic images of a manuscript, N.85.7.68 (MARS ID: 4.4.2.5), State Archives of North Carolina, Raleigh. [Online catalog description: "Photo of a listing of recruits for the Revolutionary War dated May 25, 1778. From the "Military Collection: Troop Returns," Box 4, Granville County."]

"Major Samuel Smith of Granville, by Expenses of the Guard & Prisoners on the Road from South Side Haw River to Halifax." In Weynette Parks Haun, *North Carolina Revolutionary Army Accounts, Part I, Secretary of State Treasurer's & Comptroller's Papers Journal "A", (Public Accounts) 1775-1776* (Durham: W. P. Haun, 1988), 27.

McDaniel, Jo Anna B "Granville County, North Carolina a Descriptive List of Men Raised under the Present Act of Assembly-1778." *Granville Connections: Journal of the Granville County Genealogical Society*, 1:1 (Winter 1995), 10-15.

North Carolina (State). General Assembly. "[Document Dated]: May 10, 1779: Resolution Establishing Academy in Granville County (Messages Only)." Manuscript; General Assembly Record Group; Session Records, May 1779; Joint Papers, Committee Papers, Resolutions, Senate Bills, House Bills; House Joint Resolutions: May 3-15, 1779, Box 1 (MARS ID: 66.8.17.13.13; item), State Archives of North Carolina, Raleigh.

North Carolina (State). General Assembly. "October 20, 1779: Exempting Certain Persons from Taxes (Granville County and Pasquotank County) (with Messages)." Manuscript; General Assembly Record Group; Session Records, October-November 1779, Box 1 (MARS ID: 66.8.18.12.4), State Archives of North Carolina, Raleigh. [Online catalog description: "John Duncan, James Stanly, and James Head, of Granville County, and Christopher Nicholson, of Pasquotank County, are exempted from poll taxes."]

North Carolina (State). General Assembly. "[Document Dated]: October 27, 1779: Bill for Establishing an Academy in Granville County, for Appointing Trustees, etc." Manuscript; General Assembly Record Group; Session Records, October-November 1779; Unidentified Amendments, Senate Bills, House Bills, Box 2 (MARS ID: 66.8.19.48; folder), State Archives of North Carolina, Raleigh. [Online catalog description: "The academy is to be called Granville Hall, and the trustees are also authorized to establish a town next to it."]

North Carolina (State). General Assembly. "[Document Dated]: 1780: Petition from the Inhabitants of Granville County." Manuscript; General Assembly Record Group; Session Records, August-September 1780; Joint Papers, Committee Papers, Resolutions, Senate Bills, House Bills, Miscellaneous Petitions and Accounts, Box 1 (MARS ID: 66.8.22.6; item), State Archives of North Carolina, Raleigh. [Online catalog description: "The petitioners, Thomas Person among them, ask the governor and council of state to show mercy to John Hampton, who, despite a brief period of activity against America, is nevertheless a good citizen."]

North Carolina (State). General Assembly. "[Document Dated]: May 1, 1782: Resolution Allowing a Sum to Benjamin Wade for Collecting Livestock." Manuscript; General Assembly Record Group; Session Records, April-May 1782; Committee Papers, Resolutions, Senate Bills, House Bills, House Joint Resolutions: April 17-May , 1782, Box 2 (MARS ID: 66.8.28.8.12; item), State Archives of North Carolina, Raleigh. [Online catalog description: "Resolution would allow Benjamin Wade of Granvile Co. a sum for collection of livestock for public use; with message sending resolution to Senate for concurrence."]

North Carolina (State). General Assembly. "[Document Dated]: May 10, 1782: Resolution in Favor of Dennis O'Bryan, George Duncan, and Joseph Pittman of Granville Co. (with Message)." Manuscript; General Assembly Record Group; Session Records, April-May 1782; Committee Papers, Resolutions, Senate Bills, House Bills, Senate Joint Resolutions: May 7-May 15, 1782, Box 2 (MARS ID: 66.8.28.6.3; item), State Archives of North Carolina, Raleigh. [Online catalog description: "Resolved that O'Bryan, Duncan, and Pitman were unlawfully turned over for military service; message sends resolution to House for concurrence."]

North Carolina Daughters of the American Revolution. "Granville Co. NC – Revolutionary Soldiers." *North Carolina DAR Genealogical Records Committee Report, Series 1, Volume 75: Genealogical Records* (typescript, 1941), 32-46; digital surrogate, DAR Library, Washington, D. C.

Owen, Thomas McAdory. *History and Genealogies of Old Granville County, North Carolina, 1746-1800.* Greenville, S. C.: Southern Historical Press, 1993.

"Rangers in Guilford County, Captain Arthur Forbes' Company (1775-1776)." In Weynette Parks Haun, *North Carolina Revolutionary Army Accounts, Part I, Secretary of State Treasurer's & Comptroller's Papers Journal "A", (Public Accounts) 1775-1776* (Durham: W. P. Haun, 1988), 68-69.

Ray, Worth S. *Colonial Granville County and Its People: Lost Tribes of North Carolina*. Austin, Texas: Ray, 1945; reprinted: Baltimore: Genealogical Publishing Company, 1965.

"Revolutionary Patriots, Bertie and Granville Counties, N. C." *Mississippi DAR Genealogical Records Committee Report, Series 1, Volume 141: Genealogical Records* (typescript, 1986), 38-44; digital surrogate, DAR Library, Washington, D. C.

Taylor, John, 1756-1837. "[Revolutionary War Memoir]." In John C. Dann, ed. *The Revolution Remembered: Eyewitness Accounts of the War for Independence* (Chicago: University of Chicago Press, 1980), Chapter 6: "War in the Carolinas," 204-211. [John Taylor, Granville County, North Carolina]

Tilley, Nannie M. "The Settlement of Granville County." *North Carolina Historical Review*, 11:1 (January 1934), 1-19.

Tilley, Nannie May. "Industries of Colonial Granville County." *North Carolina Historical Review*, 13:4 (October 1936), 273-289; online: http://digital.ncdcr.gov/cdm/ref/collection/p16062coll9/id/4207. [Online description from "North Carolina Periodicals Index," East Carolina University: "The natural bounty of Granville County nourished an agricultural industry but also supported hunting and trapping were important trades for colonists. The article reviews the men engaged in these activities, the items produced from hunting and trapping, and the values of these items in the colonial economy."]

Tilley, Nannie May. "Political Disturbances in Colonial Granville County." *North Carolina Historical Review*, 18:4 (October 1941), 339-359; online: http://digital.ncdcr.gov/cdm/ref/collection/p16062coll9/id/4207. [Online description from "North Carolina Periodicals Index," East Carolina University: "This article on legal and political history of Granville County examines the role of the colonial squire as a dominant figure in provincial and local government."]

Williams, John. "Papers, 1775-1824." Manuscript Sec. A Box 136 items 1-17, David M. Rubenstein Rare Book & Manuscript Library, Duke University, Durham. [Online catalog description: "North Carolina militia officer during the Revolution; from Granville County, N. C. Papers relating chiefly to land grants and land settlement, the Louisa and Transylvania land companies, supplies for the colonial army, Loyalists in North Carolina, and North Carolina politics and government during and after the Revolution. Correspondents and persons mentioned include Charles Bondfield, James Harrod, Nathaniel Henderson, Richard Henderson, James Hogg, William Hooper, William Johnston, James Luttrell, Abner Nash, John Penn, Bromfield Ridley, James Stephens, and John Williams, Jr."]

Greene County [Glasgow County, 1791-1798]

Koontz, Russell S. "A County Name Changes." *Tar Heel Junior Historian*, 44:2 (Spring 2005), 14-17; online: http://ncpedia.org/geography/greene/history. [Online description from "North Carolina Periodicals Index," East Carolina University: "Koonts discusses the interesting connection between Arthur Dobbs, the royal governor of North Carolina; James Glasgow, the first North Carolina secretary of state; and General Nathaniel Greene, the Revolutionary War hero. Present-day Greene County at one time bore the name of each man. Koonts discusses how the name changes occurred."]

Murphy, Mrs. W. B. "The Old Best House." *The State: A Weekly Survey of North Carolina*, 7:48 (April 1940), 6; online: http://digital.ncdcr.gov/cdm/ref/collection/p16062coll18/id/5451. [Online description from "North Carolina Periodicals Index," East Carolina University: "Mrs. Murphy describes the Best House, located near Snow Hill in Greene County, one of the oldest houses in the county, and perhaps in the state. Henry Best I built it in 1735 using workmen brought from England. In its day it was one of the most pretentious mansions in the eastern part of the state where guests were entertained royally. His grandson Henry Best III later remodeled the house."]

Murphy, William L. "North Carolina Architects and Builders: Murfree and Obediah Dixon." *North Carolina Preservation*, 69 (Fall 1987), 3-5. [Online description from "North Carolina Periodicals Index," East Carolina University: "Murfree Dixon, cabinet maker and carpenter, came to North Carolina in 1747, where he became established as an ornate carpenter and builder throughout Greene County. Obediah Dixon, the only one of Murfree's six sons to take up his trade, was also known for his carpentry skills, some of which still remain in Greene County today."]

Guilford County

[Note: For various state government documents relating to Guilford County during the Revolutionary period, search the MARS online catalog using the advanced search: http://mars.archives.ncdcr.gov/AdvancedSearch.aspx. Use the "Year" search box to restrict the searching to 1775-1783 and enter the county's name in the "Subjects" box, and hit the "Search" button near the top. This will retrieve any cataloged document for the county from that time period. These materials can vary considerably from personal or county petitions to the General Assembly, Loyalist matters, land disputes and claims, tax collection, exemptions from taxation, payments to county veterans, county divisions, personal collections, genealogical material, British claims against North Carolinians, etc. There is considerable information in these materials that could provide interesting documentation for persons living during the Revolution. The results will also include all of the wills and probates recorded in the county during the period set for the search. We had hoped to include many of these listings in this guide, but they are too voluminous. Citations to many of these search results for the eastern counties do, however, appear in the text.]

Abernathy, Jack. "Two Counties in Search of a Boundary." *Popular Government*, 14:2 (December 1948), 6, 8. [Online description from "North Carolina Periodicals Index," East Carolina University: "This summer the commissioners of Guilford and Randolph counties waded into a swampland of confusion over the exact location of their 28 mile common boundary line."]

Bandy, James M. "Cornwallis in Guilford County, 1781: Clapp's Mill and Wetzell's Mill." *College Magazine* [Greensboro Female College], 8:6 (1898), 252-265.

"A Cousin's War." *The Genealogical Journal by the Randolph County Genealogical Society*, 24:3 (Fall 2000), 6-16. [Burrow Family records, Guilford County]

Dunaway, Stewart E. *Summers Mill: A Historical Overview.* Hillsborough: North Carolina Historical Books, 2010. [Originally known as Weitzell's Mill. Reedy Fork, Guilford County, North Carolina.]

Fombery, Paul E. "Historic Preservation in Guilford County, North Carolina from the 1780s to the 1980s." M. A. thesis, Middle Tennessee State University, Murfreesboro, 1985.

Goerch, Carl. "Guilford County." *The State: A Weekly Survey of North Carolina*, 8:48 (April 1941), 3-6, 20-21, 23; online: http://digital.ncdcr.gov/cdm/ref/collection/p16062coll18/id/39454. [Online description from "North Carolina Periodicals Index," East Carolina University: "Guilford County is best known for Battle of Guilford Courthouse, but other places and events exist and have taken place within its boundaries. Beautiful Brandt Lake is considered one of the loveliest lakes in the Piedmont. Also of interest is the Bruce Plantation, the colonial homestead of Charles Bruce, a member of the committee that framed the North Carolina Constitution, and the Oak Ridge Military Institute, established in 1852. Guilford County is also the home of Guilford College, established by the Society of Friends in 1837."]

Guilford Battle Chapter, North Carolina Daughters of the American Revolution. "Soldiers of Revolution and War of 1812 from Granville County." *North Carolina DAR Genealogical Records Committee Report, Series 1, Volume 270: [North Carolina Family, Cemetery, Marriage, and Service Records]* (typescript, 1959), 112-126; digital surrogate, DAR Library, Washington, D. C.

Guilford Battle Chapter, North Carolina Daughters of the American Revolution. "Revolutionary Soldiers of Guilford Co. Area." *North Carolina DAR Genealogical Records Committee Report, Series 1, Volume 270: [North Carolina Family, Cemetery, Marriage, and Service Records]* (typescript, 1959), 127-136; digital surrogate; DAR Library, Washington, D. C.

Guilford County. Citizens. "June 28, [1781]: Re Petition from the Inhabitants of Guilford County (Petition Only)." Manuscript, General Assembly Record Group, Session Records June-July 1781, Box 1 (MARS ID: 66.8.25.8.3; item), State Archives of North Carolina, Raleigh. [Online catalog description: "The petitioners describe the county's losses at the hands of the British army, ask that a board of auditors be appointed to examine claims of the county, and also ask for stricter regulation of Tories."]

Guilford County. "Guilford County Miscellaneous Records, 1771-1934: Revolutionary War Pension Applications – Edward Jones (1822), William Riley (1826), Joseph Lovat (1827), and John Carmack (1831)." Manuscript C.R.046.928.7, State Archives of North Carolina, Raleigh.

Johnson, William Perry. "Guilford (and Rockingham) County Tories, 1782." *Journal of North Carolina Genealogy*, 13:2 (Summer 1967), 1870.

Lewis, J. D. "Patriot Leaders in North Carolina: James Martin: Lt. Colonel in the Guilford County Regiment of Militia - 1775-1776; Colonel over the Guilford County Regiment of Militia - 1776-1782." Online: http://www.carolana.com/NC/Revolution/patriot_leaders_nc_james_martin.html.

Lindsey, William D. "The Story of a Murdered Quaker." *Drumbeat with Flintlock & Powderhorn: News of the Sons of the Revolution,* 27:3 (Fall 2009), 12-13. [Brazelton family of Frederick County, Maryland, and Guilford County, North Carolina]

Parsons, Elsie Clews. "Tales from Guilford County, North Carolina." *Journal of American Folk-Lore*, 30:116 (April-June 1917), 168-200. [from page 169: "Between the Bahama Islands and the Carolinas there is an historical connection which may account in part for the number of tales they have, I find, in common. During the period of the Revolutionary War a number of Tories known as United Empire Loyalists migrated from the Carolinas to the Bahamas; and they took with them, of course, their household slaves. In connection with this migration, it was of interest to find that what is still current belief in the Bahamas serves as a tale in North Carolina. I refer to the magical beliefs embodied in Nos. 28, 34, 35."]

Poquette, Nancy. "History of the Guilford Militia: Whitesell's Mill and Battle of Guilford Courthouse." *The Guilford Genealogist*, 35:2 (Summer 2008), 26-60.

Pruitt, Albert Bruce. *Index to North Carolina County Maps: Davie, Guilford, Montgomery, Randolph, Rockingham, Stokes, Surry, & Yadkin*. Whitakers: A. B. Pruitt, 1988.

Rayl, Samuel. "Samuel Rayl, 1834." Manuscript MS 497, Friends Historical Collection, Hege Library, Guilford College, Greensboro. [Online catalog description: "Samuel Rayl's account of the Revolutionary War in Guilford County, and his nine months in the army between July 1777 and March 1778."]

Robinson, Blackwell P, and Alexander R. Stoesen. *The History of Guilford County, North Carolina, U. S. A. to 1980, A. D.* Greensboro: Guilford County Commissioners, [1981?].

Stockard, Sallie W. *The History of Guilford County, North Carolina*. Knoxville: Gaut-Ogden Book Printers and Book Binders, 1902.

Weatherly, A. Earl. *The First Hundred Years of Historic Guilford, 1771-1871*. Greensboro: A. Earl Weatherly: printed by Greensboro Print Co., 1972.

Halifax County

[Note: For various state government documents relating to Halifax County during the Revolutionary period, search the MARS online catalog using the advanced search: http://mars.archives.ncdcr.gov/AdvancedSearch.aspx. Use the "Year" search box to restrict the searching to 1775-1783 and enter the county's name in the "Subjects" box, and hit the "Search" button near the top. This will retrieve any cataloged document for the county from that time period. These materials can vary considerably from personal or county petitions to the General Assembly, Loyalist matters, land disputes and claims, tax collection, exemptions from taxation, payments to county veterans, county divisions, personal collections, genealogical material, British claims against North Carolinians, etc. There is considerable information in these materials that could provide interesting documentation for persons living during the Revolution. The results will also include all of the wills and probates recorded in the county during the period set for the search. We had hoped to include many of these listings in this guide, but they are too voluminous. Citations to many of these search results for the eastern counties do, however, appear in the text.]

"Account of Josiah Reddick, Commissary to the Militia of Halifax District on an Expedition against the Insurgents, February 1776." In Weynette Parks Haun, *North Carolina Revolutionary Army Accounts, Part I, Secretary of State Treasurer's & Comptroller's Papers Journal "A", (Public Accounts) 1775-1776* (Durham: W. P. Haun, 1988), 15-17.

Allen, William C. *History of Halifax County*. Boston: The Cornhill Company, 1918.

Babits, L. E. "Excavations of Halifax Town Lot 52." *Tar Heel Junior Historian*, 14:1 (September 1974), 4-5. [Online description from "North Carolina Periodicals Index," East Carolina University: "In 1974, archaeological digs began at Halifax which included professionals and students from Meredith College. The goal of excavation was to locate and examine a large unidentified building on a 1769 city map. Preliminary digs determined the location on the map to be correct and determined it was a household complete with tableware fragments and a large hearth used for cooking."]

Baldridge, Ede. "Historic Halifax." *Our State: Down Home in North Carolina*, 66:3 (August 1998), 47-50; online: http://digital.ncdcr.gov/cdm/ref/collection/p16062coll18/id/70118. [Online description from "North Carolina Periodicals Index," East Carolina University: "Halifax, founded in 1760 in Halifax County, was a force in the state's politics, economy, and culture between 1760 and 1820. When the new railroads bypassed the town, its influence diminished. Today, a quiet, 40-acre, non-commercial site with seven restored buildings attracts tourists."]

Cook, Norma M. "First for Freedom." *The State: Down Home in North Carolina*, 51:1 (June 1983), 27-28; online: http://digital.ncdcr.gov/cdm/ref/collection/p16062coll18/id/12300. [Online description from "North Carolina Periodicals Index," East Carolina University: "Since 1976, the Town of Halifax has performed the play 'First for Freedom.' The summer production includes both fact and fiction in telling the story of Halifax's role during the Revolutionary War. The Halifax Resolves, signed a few months before the United States Declaration of Independence, was the first official declaration of independence from Great Britain. The play, written by

Maxville Burt Williams, includes scenes from historic Halifax as well as scenes from the Fourth Provincial Congress that met at the Halifax courthouse on April 12, 1776."]

de Silva, Ian. "Halifax, N. C." *Carolina Country*, 30:4 (April 1998), 30-31. [Online description from "North Carolina Periodicals Index," East Carolina University: "Founded in 1760, Halifax was once a business, social, and political center. It is also the place where the first formal statement for independence was made on April 12, 1776. Today, the town of 400 attracts visitors with its restored historic site."]

Dean, Earl. "Making History in Halifax." *The State: A Weekly Survey of North Carolina*, 17:26 (November 1949), 10; online: http://digital.ncdcr.gov/cdm/ref/collection/p16062coll18/id/24701. [Online description from "North Carolina Periodicals Index," East Carolina University: "November marks the 173rd birthday of North Carolina's first state constitution. This and many other important events took place in Halifax County."]

Dudley, Guilford, 1756-1833. "[Revolutionary War Memoir]." In John C. Dann, ed. *The Revolution Remembered: Eyewitness Accounts of the War for Independence* (Chicago: University of Chicago Press, 1980), Chapter 6: "War in the Carolinas," 211-228. [The original is owned by the Huntington Library, San Marino, Calif. and is titled: "A Sketch of My Military Service, by Guilford Dudley, Then of the Town of Halifax, North Carolina in the Revolutionary War." It was originally published as: "The Carolinas during the Revolution." *Southern Literary Messenger*, 11:3 (March 1845), 144-149; 11:5 (May 1845), 281-278; and, 11:6 (June 1845), 370-375]

Dudley, Guilford, 1756-1833; Charles Campbell, ed. "A Sketch of the Military Services Performed by Guilford Dudley, Then of the Town of Halifax, North Carolina, during the Revolutionary War." *Southern Literary Messenger*, 11:3 (March 1845), 144-148; 11:4 (April 1845), 231-235; 11:5 (May 1845), 281-287; 11:6 (June 1845), 370-375; online at Making of America, University of Michigan: http://quod.lib.umich.edu/m/moajrnl/.

Faulkner, Janice Hardison. "The Restoration of Colonial Halifax." *New East*, 3:4 (September/October 1975), 6-9. [Online description from "North Carolina Periodicals Index," East Carolina University: "Halifax is the site of the first documented vote for American independence from England. It was cast by the Fourth Provincial Congress convened there on April 4, 1776. Faulkner discusses the history of the town and the buildings under restoration there."]

Gery, Michael E. C. "The Spirit of Independence: Halifax County and the Roanoke Valley." *Carolina Country*, 44:4 (April 2012), 54-55 and a map; online: http://www.carolinacountry.com/index.php/carolina-adventures/adventures/travel/halifax-county-and-the-roanoke-valley. [Online description from "North Carolina Periodicals Index," East Carolina University: "They say the spirit of independence was born in Halifax County, and when you visit, you are certainly free to take advantage of the many opportunities. These include heritage sites, outdoor recreation sites, and shopping areas."]

Goerch, Carl. "Halifax County." *The State: A Weekly Survey of North Carolina*, 9:5 (July 1941), 3-6, 23-25; online: http://digital.ncdcr.gov/cdm/ref/collection/p16062coll18/id/39814. [Online description from "North Carolina Periodicals Index," East Carolina University: "Continuing his travels around the state, Goerch describes the things of interest he found in Halifax County. Many important historical events have occurred there, and many of its citizens have been prominent internationally."]

Great Britain. Colonial Office. American and West Indies: North Carolina, Original Correspondence, Board of Trade: Secretary of State (CO 5/318). "Halifax Co. Proceedings of 'the Committee of the Said County'. Dec. 21, 1774." Copy of a manuscript in the National Archives of the United Kingdom (formerly the Public Records Office), Kew, Richmond, Surrey, England; (MARS ID: 21.1.27.11; folder), "British Records Collection," State Archives of North Carolina, Raleigh.

Great Britain. Exchequer and Audit Department. Audit Office. "Examination and Decision on [Application for Immediate Relief as a Suffering Loyalist] of Mr. James McNeal, of Halifax County, N. C., Mar. 8, 1783." Copy of a manuscript in the National Archives of the United Kingdom (formerly the Public Records Office), Kew, Richmond, Surrey, England; X77.179.1 (MARS ID: 21.2.16.13; folder), "British Records Collection," State Library of North Carolina, Raleigh.

Great Britain. Exchequer and Audit Department. Audit Office. "Hamilton Hill [Halifax County]. Archibald Hamilton and Co. to Benjamin McCulloch. 8 Oct. 1777." Copy of a manuscript in the National Archives of the United Kingdom (formerly the Public Records Office), Kew, Richmond, Surrey, England; 77.1790.1-3 (MARS ID: 21.3.49.23; folder), "British Records Collection," State Library of North Carolina, Raleigh. [Online catalog description: "Acknowledges receipt of bond, £5700, and terms of agreement concerning land the company's partners are obliged to leave in North Carolina."]

Halifax County. "Halifax County Miscellaneous Records, 1761-1927: Slave Records Including Cross-Reference to List of Invalids of Capt. Adam Sanders' Co." Manuscript C.R.047.928.8, State Archives of North Carolina, Raleigh.

"Historic Halifax: Halifax and the Revolution." Online: http://www.nchistoricsites.org/halifax/revolution.htm.

Jenkins, Jay. "History in the Making." *North Carolina's Eastern Living Magazine*, 6:2 (Winter 2014), 96-100. [Online description from "North Carolina Periodicals Index," East Carolina University: "Built in the 1730s, Person's Ordinary served as a tavern and a stagecoach station in Littleton, North Carolina. Local efforts by the Littleton Woman's Club led to the site's preservation and today visitors can visit this historic site."]

"John Bradford, Colonel of the Halifax Regiment of Militia Guards." In Weynette Parks Haun, *North Carolina Revolutionary Army Accounts, Part I, Secretary of State Treasurer's & Comptroller's Papers Journal "A", (Public Accounts) 1775-1776* (Durham: W. P. Haun, 1988), 98-100.

Johnson, Rufus, and Jerry Dickerson. *Treasures of the Roanoke Valley: Historical and Interesting Sites in Halifax and Northampton Counties*. Gaston: J. Dickerson; Roanoke Rapids: Printed by River Stone Graphics, 2000.

Knapp, Richard F. "Discovery on Lot 52." *The State: Down Home in North Carolina*, 52:6 (November 1984), 22-24; online: http://digital.ncdcr.gov/cdm/ref/collection/p16062coll18/id/61074. [Online description from "North Carolina Periodicals Index," East Carolina University: "Joseph Montfort was a prominent man in colonial North Carolina. He was a clerk of the Halifax County Court, a member of the North Carolina colonial Assembly, a colonel in the militia, and a treasurer of the northern counties of the colony. In 1771 he was named Provincial Grand Master of America by the English Masonic order, the highest office an American has held in the Masonic organization. Montfort built his home in the town of Halifax on lot 52. This fashionable home existed till 1872, when it burnt down. The site was then covered with dirt and used for cotton farming. In 1972, the lot was found again using C. J. Sauthier's 1769 map. Archaeological excavations on the site began in 1978 and continued in 1979. The original foundation was uncovered, along with 1,600 other artifacts. Today a museum sits over the archaeological site. Visitors can view the foundation and other artifacts as well as tour the thirty-two-acre historic Halifax district."]

Lawrence, R. C. "The Bar of Halifax." *The State: A Weekly Survey of North Carolina*, 12:38 (February 1945), 5, 16-17; online: http://digital.ncdcr.gov/cdm/ref/collection/p16062coll18/id/12783. [Online description from "North Carolina Periodicals Index," East Carolina University: "Willie Jones, William R. Davie, Abner Nash, John Branch, the Kitchins, and many other famous lawyers, jurists, and statesmen have come from Halifax County and rendered outstanding service to North Carolina and United States."]

Norris, Jeannie Faris. "Boundary Disputes." *Popular Government*, 20:6 (March 1954), 5. [Online description from "North Carolina Periodicals Index," East Carolina University: "Northampton and Halifax counties have recently appointed a commission to establish the dividing line between the two counties. Long a matter of controversy, the issue has recently become serious due to the impending construction by the Virginia Electric and Power Company of the Roanoke Rapids Dam."]

North Carolina (State). General Assembly. "[Documents dated:] April 24, 1778: Resolution Appoint Militia Officers, Halifax County (with Messages)." Manuscript; General Assembly Record Group; Session Records, April-May 1780; Joint Papers, Committee Papers, Senate Resolutions, House Resolutions; House Resolultions: April 16-24, 1778, Box 1 (MARS ID: 66.8.12.16.18; item), State Archives of North Carolina, Raleigh.

North Carolina (State). General Assembly. "[Documents dated:] May 2, 1783: Resolution on Petition of William Branch of Halifax County to Restore His Commission as Justice of the Peace (Rejected)." Manuscript; General Assembly Record Group; Session Records, Apri-May 1783; Joint Papers, Committee Papers, Resolutions, Box 1 (MARS ID: 66.8.29.12.11; item), State Archives of North Carolina, Raleigh. [Online catalog description: "Resolution in response to a petition that requests reinstatement for a justice of the peace who took a parole from the British and therefore was disqualified from office. Petition included."]

Orvedahl, Ginny. "Getting Historic in Halifax." *The State: Down Home in North Carolina*, 62:9 (February 1995), 22-23; online: http://digital.ncdcr.gov/cdm/ref/collection/p16062coll18/id/14332. [Online description from "North Carolina Periodicals Index," East Carolina University: "Visitors to historic Halifax, founded in Halifax County in 1760 and site of the Halifax Resolves signing, find quiet, informative tours with no lines or fees. Currently seven restored historic structures sit on the 40-acre town historic site."]

Pressley, Leigh. "Historic Halifax." *Our State: Down Home in North Carolina*, 70:5 (October 2002), 103-131, 133-134; online: http://digital.ncdcr.gov/cdm/ref/collection/p16062coll18/id/75933. [Online description from "North Carolina Periodicals Index," East Carolina University: "Halifax, county seat of Halifax County, was in the late 1700s, the center of power and influence in the state. Today this town on the Roanoke River is restored 'as a port, trading center, and cradle of revolutionary ideals.' Pressley describes how to spend a perfect weekend there."]

Rauschenberg, Bradford L. "Discovery: A Documented Bow Bowl Made for Halifax-Lodge, North Carolina." *Journal of Early Southern Decorative Arts*, 1:1 (May 1975), 3-13; online: https://archive.org/details/journalofearlyso11muse. [Online description from "North Carolina Periodicals Index," East Carolina University: "This article presents information on a Masonic punch bowl made by the Bow factory in London for 'Halifax-

Lodge/North-Carolina' that was part of a 1767 order for four Bow China bowls. This example is the first time a documented reference has been found specifying an order of Bow porcelain decorated especially for the American market. Archival and archaeological information on the bowl and its owners along with a diagnostic analysis of the bowl as an example of Bow porcelain are included."]

Sharpe, Bill. "Water, History, and Peanuts." *The State: A Weekly Survey of North Carolina*, 19:39 (February 1952), 3-5, 16-17; online: http://digital.ncdcr.gov/cdm/ref/collection/p16062coll18/id/28233. [Online description from "North Carolina Periodicals Index," East Carolina University: "Sharpe details the history, geography, and industries of Halifax County."]

Halifax County – Halifax Resolves

Corbitt, D. L. "Resolutions by the Citizens of Halifax." *North Carolina Historical Review*, 4:1 (January 1927), 105.

Gregory, Jane. *Celebrating the Halifax Resolves Bicentennial, 1776-1976*. Scotland Neck: Roanoke Valley Publishing Company, 1976.

"Halifax Resolves, Halifax, N. C., 1776." Photographs, 56.2.12 (MARS ID: 4.1.7.13), State Archives of North Carolina, Raleigh. [Online catalog description: "Real Photographic Copy of the Halifax Resolves, Drafted at Halifax, Halifax County, North Carolina, April, 1776."]

Mitchell, Memory F., ed. *North Carolina Documents, 1584-1868*. Raleigh: State Department of Archives and History, 1967. [Revolutionary War-era contents: Halifax Resolves, Apr. 12, 1776.]

North Carolina. [Provincial?] Congress. "Halifax Resolves, Halifax, North Carolina." Photographs of manuscript, N.54.2.12 (MARS ID: 4.1.4.131; folder), State Archives of North Carolina, Raleigh.

Harnett County

Byrd, Lois. "Harnett's Big Party." *The State: Down Home in North Carolina*, 23:9 (September 1955), 39; online: http://digital.ncdcr.gov/cdm/ref/collection/p16062coll18/id/81964. [Online description from "North Carolina Periodicals Index," East Carolina University: "Harnett County will present an elaborate celebration to its 100th birthday. Harnett County was formed from Cumberland County and named for Cornelius Harnett, a Revolutionary War patriot of the lower Cape Fear. The Centennial celebration is designed to unite the citizens in a common cause by participating in various activities that stimulate interest in Harnett County's historical development."]

Fowler, Malcolm. *They Passed This Way: A Personal Narrative of Harnett County History*. [S. l.]: Harnett County Centennial, Inc., 1955.

Goerch, Carl. "Harnett County." *The State: A Weekly Survey of North Carolina*, 9:6 (July 1941), 3-6, 20-22; online: http://digital.ncdcr.gov/cdm/ref/collection/p16062coll18/id/39847. [Online description from "North Carolina Periodicals Index," East Carolina University: "Continuing his travels around the state, Goerch describes the things of interest he found in Harnett County. Many important historical events have occurred there since the first settlers arrived."]

Roberts, Hilda J. "Tombstone Inscriptions of Two McLean Loyalists, Harnett Co., N. C." *North Carolina Genealogical Society Journal*, 11:2 (May 1985), 103.

Haywood County

"Deeds of Trust, Mortgage Deeds, and Land Grants, 1786-1948." Manuscript, Call Number CR.049. 401.23, Haywood County, Deeds, State Archives of North Carolina, Raleigh. [Online catalog description: Includes land grants for 1786, 1804, 1805, and 1812-1879.]

Lanman, Charles. "Cherokee Church." *The State: Down Home in North Carolina*, 22:14 (December 1954), 15-16, 24; online: http://digital.ncdcr.gov/cdm/ref/collection/p16062coll18/id/32739. [Online description from "North Carolina Periodicals Index," East Carolina University: "Qualla Town, located in Haywood County, is an area encompassing 72,000 acres of land inhabited by the Cherokee and Catawba Native Americans. Divided into seven clans, each of which is managed by a chief, the indigenous peoples of this area still function and practice beliefs despite the widespread Native American removal that devastated tribes and belief systems elsewhere in North America."]

"Marker on the Grounds of the Haywood County Court House." *Bulletin of the Genealogical Society of Old Tryon County*, 4:1 (February 1976), 21. [names of Revolutionary War soldiers from that county]

Henderson County

Helsley, Alexia Jones. *The 1840 Revolutionary Pensioners of Henderson County, North Carolina.* Columbia, S. C. AJH Historical Enterprises, 1996.

Jones, George Alexander, ed. *The Heritage of Henderson County, North Carolina.* Spartanburg: The Reprint Company, 2003.

Joseph McDowell Chapter, North Carolina Daughters of the American Revolution. "Unveiling of Tablets on Graves or Revolutionary Soldiers in [Henderson] County." *North Carolina DAR Genealogical Records Committee Report, Series 1, Volume 59: Work of the Historical and Genealogical Committees of the Joseph McDowell Chapter* (typescript, 1939), 25-38; digital surrogate, DAR Library, Washington, D. C. [Includes grave markers for Jesse Rickman, Andrew James Miller, John Peter Corn, James Johnson, Benjamin Davidson, Samuel Kin, Joseph Henry, and James Brittain.]

Lyda, Forrest Edgar. *The American Revolution: A Local Tradition.* (Henderson County Genealogical Workbooks, series 1, no. 2) Henderson County: F. E. Lyda, 1977.

Patton, Sadie Smathers. *The Story of Henderson County.* Ashville: Miller Printing Company, 1947.

Rucsin, Terry. *Glimpses of Henderson County, North Carolina.* Charleston, S. C.: History Press, 2014.

Hertford County [Edenton District]

[Note: For various state government documents relating to Hertford County during the Revolutionary period, search the MARS online catalog using the advanced search: http://mars.archives.ncdcr.gov/AdvancedSearch.aspx. Use the "Year" search box to restrict the searching to 1775-1783 and enter the county's name in the "Subjects" box, and hit the "Search" button near the top. This will retrieve any cataloged document for the county from that time period. These materials can vary considerably from personal or county petitions to the General Assembly, Loyalist matters, land disputes and claims, tax collection, exemptions from taxation, payments to county veterans, county divisions, personal collections, genealogical material, British claims against North Carolinians, etc. There is considerable information in these materials that could provide interesting documentation for persons living during the Revolution. The results will also include all of the wills and probates recorded in the county during the period set for the search. We had hoped to include many of these listings in this guide, but they are too voluminous. Citations to many of these search results for the eastern counties do, however, appear in the text.]

"5 November 1778, A True List of the Draft Made Out of the Regiment of Hertford County." Manuscript, State Archives of North Carolina, Raleigh.

"1778-1780, The Third Division of the Militia Draughted in the Regiment of Hertford County." Manuscript, State Archives of North Carolina, Raleigh.

Fouts, Raymond Parker. *Following the Land: A Genealogical History of Some of the Parkers of Nansemond County, Virginia, and Chowan/Hertford/Gates Counties, North Carolina, 1604-2004.* Cocoa, Fla.: R. P. Fouts, 2005.

McBride, Ransom. "Hertford County, 1784 Tax List." Manuscript, State Archives of North Carolina, Raleigh; published: *North Carolina Genealogical Society Journal*, 9:3 (August 1983), 130-136.

Moore, Terry. "Introducing Hertford County." *NCGS News: The Newsletter of the North Carolina Genealogical Society*, 39: 1 (January 2015), 10-11; online: http://www.ncgenealogy.org/articles_tools/Introducing_Hertford_County.pdf.

Murfree, William. "William Murfree Tax Receipt Book, 1768-1770." Manuscript PC.1801 (MARS ID: 2311; record group), State Archives of North Carolina, Raleigh. Published: Raymond Parker Fouts. *William Murfree Tax Receipt Book, Hertford County, North Carolina, 1768-1770.* Cocoa Beach, Fla.: GenRec Books, 1993. [Online catalog description: "This volume appears to be a private record kept by William Murfree, sheriff of Hertford County, as a result of an investigation into the public accounts by the General Assembly of 1768 which reported that many of the county sheriffs were in arrears in their settlements with the colonial treasury. Murfree seems to have kept this record to show precisely what had been collected in his name and from whom. He not only names the taxpayers of the county, but indicates which of the three years they were subject to pay tax in the county, the sum collected, and, frequently, to whom they had paid the tax and the medium of exchange."]

North Carolina (State). General Assembly. "[Document dated:] May 5, 1780: Resolution Permitting Resignations of James Ransom as Justice of the Peace and Stakey Sharpe as Militia Office (with Resignation of Sharp)." Manuscript; General Assembly Record Group; Session Records, April-May 1780; Joint Papers, Committee Papers, Resolutions: House Joint Resolutions, Box 1 (MARS ID: 66.8.20.17.10; item), State Archives of North Carolina, Raleigh. [Online catalog description: "Sharp resigns as second major of Hertford County; Ransom was a justice for Warren County."]

North Carolina (State). General Assembly. "[Document dated:] February 3, 1781: Resolution Appointing Field Officers for Hertford County Militia." Manuscript; General Assembly Record Group; Session Records; Joint Papers, Committee Papers, Resolutions; House Joint Resolutions: February 3-4, 1781; January-February 1781, Box 1 (MARS ID: 66.8.23.16.3; item), State Archives of North Carolina, Raleigh. [Online catalog description: "The resolution also directs the governor to commission the newly appointed officers."]

North Carolina (State). General Assembly. "[Document dated:] May 4, 1782: "Report on the Petition of Joseph Benthall, Jr., of Hertford Co. Suspending Joseph Wood from the Office of Justice of the Peace (with Petition, Messages, and Enclosures)." Manuscript; General Assembly Record Group; Session Records; Joint Papers, Committee Papers; Joint Select Committees; Reports and Papers (Petitions, Messages, etc.): April 29-…; April-May 1782, Box 1 (MARS ID: 66.8.27.9.8), State Archives of North Carolina, Raleigh. [Online catalog description: "Petition requests the removal of Joseph Wood from office because of Wood's misconduct in the seizure of slaves from the petitioner; includes depositions of witnesses; committee report recommending suspension of Woods; and messages from both houses appointing members to committee to consider petition and concurring with report."]

Powell, David. *Records and Remembrances of Hertford County, North Carolina: A Compendium: 1760, 1770, 1780, 1790, 1800, 1810, 1820, 1830, 1840*. Greenville: Liberty Shield Press, 1997.

Sharpe, Bill. "A New Geography of North Carolina." *The State: Down Home in North Carolina*, 24:2 (June 1956), 14-27; online: http://digital.ncdcr.gov/cdm/ref/collection/p16062coll18/id/7212. [Online description from North Carolina Periodicals Index," East Carolina University: "An agricultural county settled prior to 1707 and officially established in 1760, Hertford County, encompasses three rivers and over 130,000 acres of forests. Prior to the Civil War, the region was sustained primarily via the plantation system. Expansion into maritime and modern industries came in the late-19th-century in the form of port trade, fishing, hosiery mills, ice plants, and lumber."]

"Third Division of the Militia Drafted in the Regiment of Hertford County [1778]" Manuscript, [location not given], copy in the DAR Library Geographic Files, Washington, D. C. This item is most likely from the State Archives of North Carolina, Raleigh, but it cannot be located in its online MARS catalog.]

"A True List of the Draft Made Out of the Regiment of Hertford County in the State of North Carolina, November 5, 1778." Manuscript, [location not given], copy in the DAR Library Geographic Files, Washington, D. C. This item is most likely from the State Archives of North Carolina, Raleigh, but it cannot be located in its online MARS catalog.]

Tucker, Harry Z. "Historic Winton." *The State: A Weekly Survey of North Carolina*, 8:3 (June 1940), 11; online: http://digital.ncdcr.gov/cdm/ref/collection/p16062coll18/id/5686. [Online description from "North Carolina Periodicals Index," East Carolina University: "Nestled by the beautiful Chowan River in Hertford County is the quaint and historic old town of Winton, incorporated in 1766. Governor Lane, chief of Sir Walter Raleigh's first attempt at English colonization in America, explored and traveled the town. During the Revolutionary War, Winton was the assembly point for soldiers and supplies."]

Winborne, Benjamin Brodie. *The Colonial and State History of Hertford County*. Raleigh: Edwards & Broughton, 1906; reprinted: Baltimore: Genealogical Publishing Company, 1976.

Hoke County

Sharpe, Bill, and Susan S. Zarr. "Where Scotsmen Met the Sandhills." *The State: Down Home in North Carolina*, 31:18 (February 1964), 16-17, 24-27; online: http://digital.ncdcr.gov/cdm/ref/collection/p16062coll18/id/46448. [Online description from "North Carolina Periodicals Index," East Carolina University: "Established in 1911 as the 99th district in North Carolina, Hoke County was the second to last province founded in the state. Settled by Scotsmen and subjected to minor controversies during the Revolutionary War, Hoke County is currently known for the Army installation, Fort Bragg…"]

Hyde County and Ocracoke Island

[Note: For various state government documents relating to Hyde County during the Revolutionary period, search the MARS online catalog using the advanced search: http://mars.archives.ncdcr.gov/AdvancedSearch.aspx. Use the "Year" search box to restrict the searching to 1775-1783 and enter the county's name in the "Subjects" box, and hit the "Search" button near the top. This will retrieve any cataloged document for the county from that time period. These materials can vary considerably from personal or county petitions to the General Assembly, Loyalist matters, land disputes and claims, tax collection, exemptions from taxation, payments to county veterans, county divisions, personal collections, genealogical material, British claims against North Carolinians, etc. There is considerable information in these materials that could provide interesting documentation for persons living during the Revolution. The results will also include all of the wills and probates recorded in the county during the period set for the search. We had hoped to include many of these listings in this guide, but they are too voluminous. Citations to many of these search results for the eastern counties do, however, appear in the text.]

"Ballotted Men and Volunteers from Hyde County to Serve Nine Months as Continental Soldiers Beginning 1 March 1779." *North Carolinian: Quarterly Journal of Genealogy & History*, 6:3 (September 1960), 728. [Gives names, ages, and places of birth]

Byrd, William L., and John H Smith. *North Carolina Slaves and Free Persons of Color: Hyde and Beaufort Counties*. Bowie, Md.: Heritage Books, 2002.

"Depositions of and concerning James Rawlins of Martin County, Edenton District Court." *Bulletin of the Genealogical Society of Old Tryon County*, 25:4 (November 1997), 175-177. [relating to events in 1777 against the state of North Carolina]

Dunaway, Stewart E. *Hyde County, North Carolina, Bridge Records (1748-1890), Road Records (1742-1859)* Hillsborough: North Carolina Historical Books, 2012. [Note: While not specifically concerning the Revolution, these sources can be used in tandem with land records and other documents to help locate places of residence, occupations, geographical features, and place names.]

Gammon, David B. "Martin County Insolvents, 1779." *North Carolina Genealogical Society Journal*, 12:3 (August 1986), 172-187.

Goerch, Carl. "Land of Hoigh Toides." *The State: A Weekly Survey of North Carolina*, 7:43 (March 1940), 1-3, 20, 26; online: http://digital.ncdcr.gov/cdm/ref/collection/p16062coll18/id/5282. [Online description from "North Carolina Periodicals Index," East Carolina University: "In another of his travel articles to various places in the state, Goerch visits Ocracoke Island, part of the Outer Banks."]

Great Britain. Exchequer and Audit Department. Audit Office. "[Claim of] Thomas Dailey, 28 November 1785." Copy of a manuscript in the National Archives of the United Kingdom (formerly the Public Records Office), Kew, Richmond, Surrey, England; 77.1905.1 (MARS ID: 21.3.54.14; folder), Exchequer and Audit Department. Claims, American Loyalists, Series II (AO 13, Selections), Various Papers. (AO 13/100), "British Records Collection," State Archives of North Carolina, Raleigh. [Online catalog description: "Concerning refusal of Thomas Dailey to take the oath of allegiance to North Carolina."]

"Hide [sic] County Militia List, 1778". *The Quarterly Review of the Eastern North Carolina Genealogical Society*, 5:4 (Fall 1978), 167.

Hyde County. "Hyde County Miscellaneous Records, 1735-1952: Express Riders, 1778, 1779." Manuscript C.R.053.928.4, State Archives of North Carolina, Raleigh.

Hyde County. "Hyde County Miscellaneous Records, 1735-1952: Military Records, 1755-1853 and no date." Manuscript C.R.053.928.4, State Archives of North Carolina, Raleigh.

"Hyde County Field Return, 1774." *Quarterly Review of the Eastern North Carolina Genealogical Society*, 14:1 (March 1987), 33. [pre-Revolution]

"Hyde County Militia List, 29 May 1780." *Quarterly Review of the Eastern North Carolina Genealogical Society*, 14:1 (March 1987), 26.

"Hyde County Field Return, 1774." *Quarterly Review of the Eastern North Carolina Genealogical Society*, 14:2 (June 1987), 61-63.

Hyde County Bicentennial Committee. *Hyde County History*. Charlotte: Herb Easton, Inc.,1976.

Johnson, William Perry. "Martin County: 1779 Tax List." *Journal of North Carolina Genealogy*, 11:2 (Summer 1965), 1461-1468.

Jones, Abram. "Deposition, Mattamuskeet, Hyde Co. [N. C.] Signed Abram Jones." Manuscript MSS L1991.1.371, Society of the Cincinnati Library, Anderson House, Washington, D. C. [Online catalog description: "Concerns the capture of Loyalist James Rawlins, in the words of Abram Jones, who 'understood by report that a certain James Rawlins was one of the heads amongst the Tories and that he was expected to pass by the settlement of Mattamuskeet or to call there about the next day and I was resolved to apprehend him ...{.}' Apparently in the hand of James Davis, who signs at bottom: 'Sworn to before me this 9th Aug 1777.'"]

North Carolina (State). General Assembly. "[Document dated:] September 2, 1777: North Carolina. Hyde County. Order form the County Court of Pleas and Quarter Sessions to Arrest Thomas Dailey, Seth Hovey, Rotheas Latham, and Phineas Latham. 2 September 1777." Copy at 77.1906.1 (MARS ID: 21.3.54.15; folder), State Archives of North Carolina, Raleigh. [Online catalog description: "'. . . as their conduct has for some time been suspected of being inimical to their county & Liberty of America'."]

North Carolina (State). General Assembly. "[Document dated:] July 30, 1779: Petition from the Inhabitants of the Lower End of Hyde County at the Settlement of Mattamuskeet." Manuscript; General Assembly Record Group; Session Records, October-November 1779: Joint Papers, Committee Papers, Resolutions; Petitions Addressed to the Governor and Council; Box 1 (MARS ID: 66.8.18.6.3; item), State Archives of North Carolina, Raleigh. [Online catalog description: "The petitioners request that the draft be suspended in their area because its population is too low to provide men for both service to the state and defense of their land."]

"Oracoke, Yesterday and Today." 25:7 (August 24, 1957), 8-9; online: http://digital.ncdcr.gov/cdm/ref/collection/p16062coll18/id/41512. [Online description from "North Carolina Periodicals Index," East Carolina University: "A onetime free and independent nation situated twenty miles off the mainland, Ocracoke Island was incorporated into North Carolina in 1770 as a taxable portion of Carteret County. Famous for ponies, pirates, and shipwrecks, Ocracoke remains a popular attraction for locals and tourists alike."]

"Our Greatest Lake." *The State: A Weekly Survey of North Carolina*, 25:7 (August 24, 1957), 8-9; online: http://digital.ncdcr.gov/cdm/ref/collection/p16062coll18/id/41512. [Online description from "North Carolina

Padgett, Dora Adele. *William Howard: Last Colonial Owner of Ocracoke Island, North Carolina, His Family and Descendants*. Washington, D. C.: Padgett, 1974.

Rondthaler, Alice K. "The Story of Ocracoke." *The State: A Weekly Survey of North Carolina*, 7:12 (August 1939), 6-8, 29-30; online: http://digital.ncdcr.gov/cdm/ref/collection/p16062coll18/id/35407. [Online description from "North Carolina Periodicals Index," East Carolina University: "To the majority of North Carolinians, Ocracoke Island is merely a place for hunting and fishing, but the island provides so much more in history and culture. The purported home of the notorious Blackbeard, Ocracoke also provided the commercial key to North Carolina with Ocracoke Inlet. Ocracoke was also the scene of many stirring Revolutionary sea fights among vessels. Even after the hostilities ceased and the lighthouse was built, Ocracoke continued to thrive in trade."]

Sharpe, Bill. "Way Down Yonder in the Land of Hyde." 25:7 (August 24, 1957), 16-17; online: http://digital.ncdcr.gov/cdm/ref/collection/p16062coll18/id/41512.

Stedman, Benjamin. "*North Carolina Gazette*, New Bern, N. C., July 25, 1777, #386." "Hyde County Field Return, 1774." *Quarterly Review of the Eastern North Carolina Genealogical Society*, 14:2 (June 1987), 63. [advertisement for deserters by Capt. Benjamin Stedman]

Turnage, Sheila. "Swan Quarter." *Our State: Down Home in North Carolina*, 66:2 (July 1998), 12-16; online: http://digital.ncdcr.gov/cdm/ref/collection/p16062coll18/id/70033. [Online description from "North Carolina Periodicals Index," East Carolina University: "Swan Quarter, named for Samuel Swann, who settled in the 1700s, is a town most people pass through on their way to the ferry. If they stopped, they could enjoy the natural beauty; historic places, including one of the last ante-bellum courthouses still in use; and the Cutrell Inn."]

Watson, Alan D. "Pilotage and Pilots in Colonial North Carolina: The Case of Ocracoke Inlet." *Tributaries*, 3:1 (October 1993), 20-25. [Online description from "North Carolina Periodicals Index," East Carolina University: "Pilots directed ships through the often tricky inlet system separating state rivers from ocean-going commerce. Specifically, the history of Ocracoke pilots and legislation governing them is presented."]

Weslager, C. A. "Place Names on Ocracoke Island." *North Carolina Historical Review*, 31:1 (January 1954), 41-49; online: http://digital.ncdcr.gov/cdm/ref/collection/p16062coll9/id/4207. [Online description from "North Carolina Periodicals Index," East Carolina University: "Until recently, the fishing community of Ocracoke Island had little direct contact with the outside world. The present population speaks a language unlike anything else heard in Virginia or the Carolinas, maintaining early English influence in idioms and place names."]

Wolfram, Walt, and Natalie Schilling-Estes. *Hoi Toide on the Outer Banks: The Story of the Oracoke Brogue*. Chapel Hill: University of North Carolina Press, 1997. [Publisher's description: "As many visitors to Ocracoke will attest, the island's vibrant dialect is one of its most distinctive cultural features. In *Hoi Toide on the Outer Banks*, Walt Wolfram and Natalie Schilling-Estes present a fascinating account of the Ocracoke brogue. They trace its development, identify the elements of pronunciation, vocabulary, and syntax that make it unique, and even provide a glossary and quiz to enhance the reader's knowledge of 'Ocracokisms.' In the process, they offer an intriguing look at the role language plays in a culture's efforts to define and maintain itself. But *Hoi Toide on the Outer Banks* is more than a linguistic study. Based on extensive interviews with more than seventy Ocracoke residents of all ages and illustrated with captivating photographs by Ann Ehringhaus and Herman Lankford, the book offers valuable insight on what makes Ocracoke special. In short, by tracing the history of island speech, the authors succeed in opening a window on the history of the islanders themselves."]

Iredell County

Byrd, William L., and John H Smith. *North Carolina Slaves and Free Persons of Color: Iredell County*. Bowie, Md.: Heritage Books, 2002.

Clark, Rosamond. "A Sketch of Fort Dobbs." *North Carolina Booklet*, 19:4/20:1 (April-July 1920), 132-138.

Douglas, Scott. "Understanding Fort Dobbs." *Carolina Comments*, 60:2 (April 2012), 33-36; online: http://www.ncpublications.com/comments/Apr.%2012.pdf.

Eliason, Minnie Hampton. *Fort Dobbs: Historical Sketch*. Statesville: Fort Dobbs Chapter, North Carolina Daughters of the American Revolution, 1915.

Evans, Virginia Fraser. *Iredell County Landmarks: A Pictorial History of Iredell County*. [Statesville?]: Iredell County American Revolution Bicentennial Commission, 1976.

Hartung, A. Bruce. "Fort Dobbs – Guardian of the Frontier." *Journal of America's Military Past*, 14:2 (June 1986), 52-54. ["a history of this North Carolina fort built in 1764."]

Keever, Homer M, Iredell County American Revolution Bicentennial Commission. *Iredell, Piedmont County*. [Statesville?]: The Commission by Brady Print Co., 1976.

Tomlin, Jimmy. "Living in the Past." *Our State: Down Home in North Carolina*, 73:3 (August 2005), 124-127; online: http://digital.ncdcr.gov/cdm/ref/collection/p16062coll18/id/84024. [Online description from "North Carolina Periodicals Index," East Carolina University: "John McElwrath built the brick house on his Iredell County cotton plantation in 1753, and it is one of the oldest residences still standing in North Carolina. McElwrath died in 1785. Tomlin traces the ownership down to the present owners, Susan and Meredith Hall, who live on the plantation as they restore it. The Halls purchased the property thirty-six years ago and renamed it Darshana Hall Plantation. In 1973, the property was added to the National Register of Historic Places."]

Wooten, Hugh Hill. "The Land Valuations of Iredell County in 1800." *North Carolina Historical Review*, 29:4 (October 1952), 523-539; online: http://digital.ncdcr.gov/cdm/ref/collection/p16062coll9/id/4207. [Online description from "North Carolina Periodicals Index," East Carolina University: "Understanding land use and ownership in the Piedmont during the late 18th and early 19th century is a difficult topic of study due to lack of documentation. One glimpse into this world is a County Land Valuation Book for Iredell County 1800. This work includes not only land records but family papers, deeds, farming accounts, and surveyor's notes. The author examines this document to present a picture of early agricultural life in the Piedmont, specifically Iredell County, which includes not only a historical account but statistical data."]

Wooten, Hugh Hill. "Wesern Migration from Iredell County, 1800-1850." *North Carolina Historical Review*, 30:1 (January 1953), 61-71; online: http://digital.ncdcr.gov/cdm/ref/collection/p16062coll9/id/4207. [Online description from "North Carolina Periodicals Index," East Carolina University: "This article looks at the heavy migration from Iredell County between 1800 and 1850. An examination of land records and wills indicates that military bounty lands in Tennessee and land sales in Kentucky were early motivators for the exodus, however the popularity of westward migrations skyrocketed as people moved towards the waters of Ohio, Tennessee and Mobile, as well Missouri, Illinois and the western states seeking land employment opportunities as population pressures in counties in NC were increasing. Some reprints of letters written by migrants to family or friends back in Iredell country are included."]

Johnston County

[Note: For various state government documents relating to Johnston County during the Revolutionary period, search the MARS online catalog using the advanced search: http://mars.archives.ncdcr.gov/AdvancedSearch.aspx. Use the "Year" search box to restrict the searching to 1775-1783 and enter the county's name in the "Subjects" box, and hit the "Search" button near the top. This will retrieve any cataloged document for the county from that time period. These materials can vary considerably from personal or county petitions to the General Assembly, Loyalist matters, land disputes and claims, tax collection, exemptions from taxation, payments to county veterans, county divisions, personal collections, genealogical material, British claims against North Carolinians, etc. There is considerable information in these materials that could provide interesting documentation for persons living during the Revolution. The results will also include all of the wills and probates recorded in the county during the period set for the search. We had hoped to include many of these listings in this guide, but they are too voluminous. Citations to many of these search results for the eastern counties do, however, appear in the text.]

"Copies of the Original Record Book A #2." In Weynette Parks Haun, *Johnston County, North Carolina, Record Book A #2, 1810-1864* (Durham: W. P. Haun, 1983), 17-33. [Note from the Genealogy Office, Office of the Registrar General, National Society Daughters of the American Revolution, Washington, D. C.: "Not all names mentioned here have valid service, but many county militia officers are named as well as those individuals who were fined. Some mention is also made of individuals who were excused from service due to age or disability."]

Johnston County. "Court Martial Minutes, 1761-1779." Manuscript and 1 microfilm reel, State Archives of North Carolina, Raleigh; published in: "Johnston County North Carolina Court Martial Minutes, 1761-1779." In Wynette Parks Haun, *Johnston County North Carolina Record Book A#2, 1810-1864; Court Martial Minutes, 1761-1779*. Durham: W. P. Haun, [1983].

"Johnston County Militia under the Command of Colonel William Bryan." In Weynette Parks Haun, *North Carolina Revolutionary Army Accounts, Part I, Secretary of State Treasurer's & Comptroller's Papers Journal "A", (Public Accounts) 1775-1776* (Durham: W. P. Haun, 1988), 25-26.

Lewis, J. D. "Patriot Leaders in North Carolina: Samuel Smith, Jr.: Major in the Johnston County Regiment of Militia - 1775-1780; Lt. Colonel in the Johnston County Regiment of Militia - 1780-1783." Online: http://www.carolana.com/NC/Revolution/patriot_leaders_nc_samuel_smith_jr.html.

Lewis, J. D. "Patriot Leaders in North Carolina: William Bryan: Lt. Colonel in the Johnston County Regiment of Militia - 1775-1776; Colonel over the Johnston County Regiment of Militia - 1776-1777 & 1781; Brigadier General over the New Bern District Brigade of Militia - 1777-1779." Online: http://www.carolana.com/NC/Revolution/patriot_leaders_nc_william_bryan.html.

Sharpe, Bill. "A Sample Slice of Rural North Carolina." *The State: Down Home in North Carolina,* 24:8 (September 1956), 14-17, 34-38; online: http://digital.ncdcr.gov/cdm/ref/collection/p16062coll18/id/7522. [Online description from "North Carolina Periodicals Index," East Carolina University: "Ranging in altitude from 80 to 350 feet, Johnston County is a rural area settled by Ulster Scots and the English, in 1746. Comprising ten towns, Johnston County residents have survived through subsistence farming and the production of naval stores, tobacco, and lumbering."]

Jones County

[Note: For various state government documents relating to Jones County during the Revolutionary period, search the MARS online catalog using the advanced search: http://mars.archives.ncdcr.gov/AdvancedSearch.aspx. Use the "Year" search box to restrict the searching to 1775-1783 and enter the county's name in the "Subjects" box, and hit the "Search" button near the top. This will retrieve any cataloged document for the county from that time period. These materials can vary considerably from personal or county petitions to the General Assembly, Loyalist matters, land disputes and claims, tax collection, exemptions from taxation, payments to county veterans, county divisions, personal collections, genealogical material, British claims against North Carolinians, etc. There is considerable information in these materials that could provide interesting documentation for persons living during the Revolution. The results will also include all of the wills and probates recorded in the county during the period set for the search. We had hoped to include many of these listings in this guide, but they are too voluminous. Citations to many of these search results for the eastern counties do, however, appear in the text.]

North Carolina (State). General Assembly. "[Document dated:] April 21, 1780: Exempting from Poll Taxes Jacob Ipock, Sr. (with Jones County Recommendation)." Manuscript; General Assembly Record Group; Session Records, April-May 1780: Joint Papers, Committee Papers, Resolutions, Box 1 (MARS ID: 66.8.20.15.5; item), State Archives of North Carolina, Raleigh. [Online catalog description: "The court informs the Assembly that Ipock is aged and infirm and possesses very little property."]

North Carolina (State). General Assembly. "[Document dated:] September 3, 1780: Allowing John Bryan to Resign as Justice of the Peace, Jones County." Manuscript; General Assembly Record Group; Session Records, August-September 1780, Box 1 (MARS ID: 66.8.22.10.8), April-May 1782, State Archives of North Carolina, Raleigh.

North Carolina (State). General Assembly. "[Document dated:] May 2, 1782: In Favor of Hezekiah Marrett of Jones Co. (Messages and Affadavit Only)." Manuscript, General Assembly Record Group, Session Records, April-May 1782, Box 2 (MARS ID: 66.8.28.5.10; item), State Archives of North Carolina, Raleigh. [Online catalog description: "Affidavit stating that Hezekiah Marrett had a pay voucher but it was taken away by British; with messages from both houses concurring with resolution."]

North Carolina (State). General Assembly. "[Document dated:] May 2, 1782: Recommendation That Tabes Bumpas of Jones Co. Be Exempted from the Payment of Taxes (with Message and Petition)." Manuscript, General Assembly Record Group, Session Records April-May 1782, Box 2 (MARS ID: 66.8.28.5.8; item), State Archives of North Carolina, Raleigh. [Online catalog description: "Petition requests tax exemption due to age and infirmity; resolution exempts Bumpas from paying poll taxes only; with message from Senate concurring with resolve."]

North Carolina (State). General Assembly. "[Document dated:] May 13, 1782: Resolution in Favor of Nathan and Lewis Bryan (with Petitions and Committee Report (Rejected)." Manuscript; General Assembly Record Group; Session Records, April-May 1782, Box 2 (MARS ID: 66.8.28.10.3; item), State Archives of North Carolina, Raleigh. [Online catalog description: "Petition of Nathan and Lewis Bryan of Jones County requests aid in securing restitution from property of Tories who, aided by the British Army, plundered petitioners' property; committee report recommends that petitioners' right to restitution not be impinged on by any other act of assembly; resolution would bar any acts of confiscation being pleaded against their recovery of property; includes messages from both houses appointing members to committee to hear petition, and concurring with report and resolution."]

North Carolina (State). General Assembly. "[Document dated:] April 23, 1783: In Favor of Robert Jermain of Jones County." Manuscript; General Assembly Record Group; Session Records, April-May 1783, Box 1 (MARS ID: 66.8.28.13.10; item), State Archives of North Carolina, Raleigh. [Online catalog description: "Resolution gives compensation to Robert Jermain for a slave condemned to death."]

Lenoir County

Johnson, Talmage C., and Charles R. Holloman. *The Story of Kinston and Lenoir County*. Raleigh, Edwards & Broughton Co., 1954.

Lincoln County (formed April 14, 1779 from the division of old Tryon County)

[Note: For various state government documents relating to Lincoln County during the Revolutionary period, search the MARS online catalog using the advanced search: http://mars.archives.ncdcr.gov/AdvancedSearch.aspx. Use the "Year" search box to restrict the searching to 1775-1783 and enter the county's name in the "Subjects" box, and hit the "Search" button near the top. This will retrieve any cataloged document for the county from that time period. These materials can vary considerably from personal or county petitions to the General Assembly, Loyalist matters, land disputes and claims, tax collection, exemptions from taxation, payments to county veterans, county divisions, personal collections, genealogical material, British claims against North Carolinians, etc. There is considerable information in these materials that could provide interesting documentation for persons living during the Revolution. The results will also include all of the wills and probates recorded in the county during the period set for the search. We had hoped to include many of these listings in this guide, but they are too voluminous. Citations to many of these search results for the eastern counties do, however, appear in the text.]

Arthur, Billy. "Plundering Sam Brown." *The State: Down Home in North Carolina*, 61:12 (May 1994), 17, 19-20; online: http://digital.ncdcr.gov/cdm/ref/collection/p16062coll18/id/66742. [Online description from "North Carolina Periodicals Index," East Carolina University: "Lincoln County's Sam Brown was a notorious robber and opponent of the American Revolution who, with his sister Charity, terrorized counties along the Yadkin River and in South Carolina. He was killed in 1780 by an outraged citizen."]

Blythe, Dolores S. "Cornwallis at Forney's Farm." *The State: Down Home in North Carolina*, 47:8 (January 1980), 20-21; online: http://digital.ncdcr.gov/cdm/ref/collection/p16062coll18/id/58877. [Online description from "North Carolina Periodicals Index," East Carolina University: "After replenishing his troops as Ramsour's Mill, Lord Cornwallis marched them to the Catawba River on January 28, 1781. For three days and four nights, the army camped at Jacob Forney's plantation while waiting for the river's waters to subside so that they could cross it. The British soldiers searched for and found gold, silver, and jewelry buried in the distillery. Cornwallis' Table, a smooth-faced rock used by the British to dine on while at Forney's, stands in Lincolnton's town square."]

Brevard, Alexander, 1755-1829. "Alexander Brevard (ca. 1755-1829) Papers, 1751-1911." Manuscript PC.2, State Archives of North Carolina, Raleigh. [Online catalog description: "Papers of Alexander Brevard, Revolutionary officer and Lincoln Co. ironmaster, including appointments as quartermaster (1778- 1782), papers concerning reorganization of N. C. Continental Line (1782), lists of men raised in Morgan District, broadside defending Gen. Nathanael Greene, settlements of Revolutionary accounts, recollections by Gen. Joseph Graham (1824), and pension claims…"]

Brevard and McDowell Families. "Brevard and McDowell Family Papers, 1754-1953." Manuscript 86, Southern Historical Collection, The Wilson Library, University of North Carolina at Chapel Hill. [Partial online catalog description: "The Brevard family included brothers Alexander (1755-1829) of Lincoln County, N. C., and Joseph (1766-1821), lawyer of Camden, S. C." Includes: "Papers of Alexander Brevard include land grants, deeds, wills, and business papers relating to Mount Tirzah Forge in Lincoln County, including some relating to slaves working at the Forge; North Carolina Revolutionary War militia papers, including a muster roll, 1780-1781…"]

Dellinger, Paul. "Militia Lists and Tory Citations, Lincoln County." *Eswau Huppeday: Bulletin of the Broad River Genealogical Society,* 10:2 (May 1990), 131.

"Descriptive List of Men Raised from Morgan District to Serve Eighteen Months in the Continental Army. Received by Capt. Brevard at Ramsour's Mill between the 20th day of August & 12th October 1782." *Eswau Huppeday: Bulletin of the Broad River Genealogical Society*, 14:2 (May 1994), 132-133. [Lincoln County, North Carolina]

Dunaway, Stewart E. *Lincoln County Road Records (1781-1822), Bridge Records (1813-1868).* Hillsborough: North Carolina Historical Books, 2015. [Note: While not specifically concerning the Revolution, these sources can be used in tandem with land records and other documents to help locate places of residence, occupations, geographical features, and place names.]

Hunter, Cyrus Lee. *Sketches of Western North Carolina Historical and Biographical, Illustrating Principally the Revolutionary Period of Mecklenburg, Rowan, Lincoln and Adjoining Counties, Accompanied with Miscellaneous Information, Much of It Never Before Published.* Raleigh: Raleigh News Steam Job Print, 1877; reprinted: Raleigh: Edwards & Broughton, 1930; Baltimore: Regional Publishing Company, 1970.

Landrum, John Belton O'Neall. *Colonial and Revolutionary History of Upper South Carolina; Embracing for the Most Part the Primitive and Colonial History of the Territory Comprising the Original County of Spartanburg; with a General Review of the Entire Military Operations in the Upper Portion of South Carolina and Portions of North Carolina.* Greenville, S. C.: Shannon & Co., Printers, 1897; reprinted: (South Carolina Heritage Series, no. 1) Spartanburg: The Reprint Company, 1959; reprinted 1962, 1977.

Lincoln County. "Lincoln County Miscellaneous Records, 1764-1923: Payment for Acting as Attorney for the State, 1779-1804." Manuscript C.R.060.928.1, State Archives of North Carolina, Raleigh.

Lincoln County. "Lincoln County Miscellaneous Records, 1764-1923: Bounty Claims, 1764-1779." Manuscript C.R.060.928.1, State Archives of North Carolina, Raleigh. [Note: These may all relate to colonial wars and not the Revolution. Inspection of this material would be necessary before claiming any document in this file as proof of Revolutionary War service.]

Lincoln County. "Lincoln County Miscellaneous Records, 1764-1923: Condolences: Alfred Morrison, John Ellis; Confiscation of Property from Tory Sympathizers." Manuscript C.R.060.928.1, State Archives of North Carolina, Raleigh.

Lincoln County. "Lincoln County Miscellaneous Records, 1764-1923: Payment for Serving as Constable." Manuscript C.R.060.928.1, State Archives of North Carolina, Raleigh.

Lincoln County. "Lincoln County Miscellaneous Records, 1764-1923: Provisions for Military Troops, 1780-1781." Manuscript C.R.060.928.4, State Archives of North Carolina, Raleigh.

Lincoln County. "Lincoln County Miscellaneous Records, 1764-1923: Miscellaneous Tax Records, 1779-1868." Manuscript C.R.060.928.6, State Archives of North Carolina, Raleigh.

Lincoln County. "Lincoln County Miscellaneous Records, 1764-1923: Revolutionary War Records – Declarations of Service and Related Records, 1792-1838." Manuscript C.R.060.928.6, State Archives of North Carolina, Raleigh.

Lincoln County. "Lincoln County Miscellaneous Records, 1764-1923: List of Soldiers in Capt. Collans' Company Who Surrendered at Charleston, 1786." Manuscript C.R.060.928.6, State Archives of North Carolina, Raleigh.

Lincoln County. "Lincoln County Miscellaneous Records, 1764-1923: Troop Return of Capt. Wm. Moore's Company, ca. 1782." Manuscript C.R.060.928.6, State Archives of North Carolina, Raleigh.

"Lincoln County: Nominated to General Assembly as Field Officers." *Bulletin of the Genealogical Society of Old Tryon,* 2:2 (May 1974), 86-87.

"A 'Lost' List of Continental Soldiers from the Western Counties." *North Carolina Genealogical Society Journal,* 9:3 (August 1983), 142. [Lincoln, Burke, Wilkes, and Rutherford Counties]

MacLean, William, 1756-1825. "William MacLean Papers, 1787-1844." Manuscript 1579-z, Southern Historical Collection, Louis Round Wilson Special Collections Library, University of North Carolina, Chapel Hill; online finding aid available at http://www2.lib.unc.edu/mss/inv/m/MacLean,William.html. [Online finding aid description: "William MacLean (1756-1825) of Lincoln County (later Gaston County), N. C., was a surgeon and physician, Revolutionary soldier, and statesman. The collection contains miscellaneous papers of MacLean including a certificate of membership in the American Medical Society signed by William Shippen (Philadelphia, 1797); part of a memorial address at King's Mountain, 1814, by MacLean (typed transcription); a letter from MacLean to his wife, Mary Davidson MacLean, while he was travelling in Tennessee, 1811, telling of his travels and mentioning family members; and a letter to Mrs. MacLean from the Reverend A. L. Watts of Mecklenburg County, N. C., 1844, about a pension and some Davidson College business."]

McAllister, Anne Williams, and Kathy Gunter Sullivan. *Court of Pleas & Quarter Sessions, Lincoln County, North Carolina April 1779-January 1789* (Lenoir: McAllister-Sullivan, 1988), 1-61 [Contains some civil service appointments.]

Nixon, Joseph R. "German Settlers in Lincoln County and Western North Carolina." *James Sprunt Historical Publications*, 11:2 (1912), 25-62. [Contents: Chapter I: The German Migration; Chapter II: German Life in North Carolina; Chapter III: The Ramsour Family.]

North Carolina (State). General Assembly. Senate. "[Document dated:] April 24, 1780): Joint Papers, Committee Papers, Resolutions, Senate Bills, House Bills, Senate Bill to Attaint Samuel Brown, Junior, of High Treason (Rejected)." Manuscript; General Assembly Record Group; Session Records, April-May 1782, Box 2 (MARS ID: 66.8.21.9), State Archives of North Carolina, Raleigh. [Online catalog description: "The bill would have convicted Brown, of Lincoln County, of high treason, robbery, burglary, and larceny and sentenced him to death. On the day of the bill's introduction, the two chambers appoint a joint select committee to investigate the charges."]

Ramsey, Robert W. "Captain Samuel Cobrin's Company of Militia: The First Settlers of Gaston and Lincoln Counties." *Journal of North Carolina Genealogy*, 12:4 (Winter 1966), 1773-1779.

Rankin, Richard, and Robin Brabham. *Gaston & Lincoln Sketches*. Gastonia: Pipes & Timbrels Press, 2006. [Includes a chapter titled: "Revolution, Violence, and Lawlessness in Old Tryon."]

"A Return of Captain William Moore's Company under Brigadier General Rutherford, 1782." Manuscript, Lincoln County Clerk of Courts, Lincolnton, Lincoln County.

Sharpe, Bill. "Patriots, Iron and Spindles: Lincoln County Produced Famous Ironmasters and Commenced the South's Greatest Industry." *The State: Down Home in North Carolina*, 27:24 (April 1960), 8-10, 23-26, 28; online: http://digital.ncdcr.gov/cdm/ref/collection/p16062coll18/id/42356. [Online description from "North Carolina Periodicals Index," East Carolina University: "Encompassing 308 square miles and located in the Piedmont region of the state, Lincoln County is predominately an industrial community. Long sustained via enterprises such as paper mills, tanneries, coach assembly, cotton factories, iron harvesting and production, Lincoln was also the leading pine planting county in 1959."]

Sherrill, William L. (William Lander). *Annals of Lincoln County, North Carolina: Containing Interesting and Authentic Facts of Lincoln County History through the Years 1749 to 1937*. Baltimore: Regional Publishing Company, 1972.

Sullivan, Kathy Gunter. "Lincoln County Grand Jury Indictments, 1779-1789." *Bulletin of the Genealogical Society of Old Tryon County*, 41:1 (Spring 2013), 2-8.

Macon County

Morgan, Stacey. "American Revolutionary Soldier Wakefield's Grave Honored." *Macon County Times* (Elizabethtown), (October 22, 2014).

Martin County

[Note: For various state government documents relating to Martin County during the Revolutionary period, search the MARS online catalog using the advanced search: http://mars.archives.ncdcr.gov/AdvancedSearch.aspx. Use the "Year" search box to restrict the searching to 1775-1783 and enter the county's name in the "Subjects" box, and hit the "Search" button near the top. This will retrieve any cataloged document for the county from that time period. These materials can vary considerably from personal or county petitions to the General Assembly, Loyalist matters, land disputes and claims, tax collection, exemptions from taxation, payments to county veterans, county divisions, personal collections, genealogical material, British claims against North Carolinians, etc. There is considerable information in these materials that could provide interesting documentation for persons living during the Revolution. The results will also include all of the wills and probates recorded in the county during the period set for the search. We had hoped to include many of these listings in this guide, but they are too voluminous. Citations to many of these search results for the eastern counties do, however, appear in the text.]

Butchko, Thomas R., ed. *Martin Architectural Heritage: The Historic Structures of a Rural North Carolina County*. Williamston: Martin County Historical Society, 1998.

Hughes, Shelby Jean Nelson, ed. *Martin County Heritage*. Williamston: Martin County Historical Society, 1980.

"A List of Men of Martin County, N. C., after 1774." *North Carolina Genealogical Society Journal*, 13:2 (May 1987), 113 [date penciled in as "after 1774;" [This *may* be a militia list.]

"A List of Volunteers and Drafts Raised in Martin County for 'the Present Expedition,' June 4, 1780." In Walter Clark, ed., *State Records of North Carolina, Vol. 14, 1779-1780* (Winston: M. I. & J. C. Stewart, 1896; reprinted: Wilmington: Broadfoot Publishing Company, 1994).

Martin County. "Martin County Miscellaneous Records, 1774-1906: Property Tax for Robert Lenox, 1781." Manuscript C.R.063.928.1, State Archives of North Carolina, Raleigh.

"Martin County Militia, December 1, 1779." *Daughters of the American Revolution Magazine,* 83:6 (June 1949), 519.

North Carolina (State). General Assembly. "[Document dated:] April 24, 1778: Resolution Appointing Militia Officers, Martin and Wake Counties (with Messages)." Manuscript; General Assembly Record Group; Session Records, April-May 1778; Joint Papers, Committee Papers, Resolutions, Senate Bills, House Bills; House Joint Resolutions: April 16-24, 1778; Box 1 (MARS ID: 66.8.12.16.17), State Archives of North Carolina, Raleigh.

North Carolina (State). General Assembly. "[Document dated:] February 11, 1779: Resolution in Favor of Whitmell Hill (Messages Only)." Manuscript; General Assembly Record Group; Session Records, April-May 1778; Joint Papers, Committee Papers, Resolutions, Senate Bills, House Bills; Senate Joint Resolutions; April 16-24, 1778, Box 1 (MARS ID: 66.8.12.16.17), State Archives of North Carolina, Raleigh. [Online catalog description: "The resolution alluded to compensates Hill for mon{e}y he advanced to the militia of Martin County."]

Peele, Wendell. "Return to the River." *The State: Down Home in North Carolina*, 35:1 (June 1967), 8-9; online: http://digital.ncdcr.gov/cdm/ref/collection/p16062coll18/id/50206. [Online description from "North Carolina Periodicals Index," East Carolina University: "The history of the Roanoke River in Martin County dates back to the time of Sir Walter Raleigh. Crews of men from Raleigh's expedition oared their way up the Roanoke to the present day site of the Williamston bridge before being attacked and driven back to their boats by Tuscarora Indian warriors. Since that time, the Roanoke has served Martin County as a fishery, as a means of transportation, as a resource for manufacturing plants, and even as a military conduit during the Civil War. Because of this long-term interconnectivity, many Martin County residents feel that the river, despite flowing through two states and many counties, is their own."]

McDowell County

Byrd, William L., and John H Smith. *North Carolina Slaves and Free Persons of Color: McDowell County.* Westminster, Md.: Heritage Books, 2007.

Fossett, Mildred B. *History of McDowell County.* Durham: Seeman Printers, 1976.

Hicklin, J. B. "Old Fort's Arrowhead." *The State: A Weekly Survey of North Carolina*, 8:27 (November 1940), 5, 22; online: http://digital.ncdcr.gov/cdm/ref/collection/p16062coll18/id/6466. [Online description from "North Carolina Periodicals Index," East Carolina University: "The largest arrowhead in the world is one of the things which distinguishes Old Fort, in McDowell County from other western North Carolina communities. From 1756 to 1776 Old Fort was the westernmost outpost of the white settlers in the frontier. The arrowhead monument was dedicated to the memory of the gallant band of men who braved the dangers to establish this frontier outpost."]

McDowell County American Revolution Bicentennial Commission. Heritage Committee. *A Pictorial History of McDowell County, North Carolina, 1775-1975*. Marion: The Commission, 1975.

Padgett, Mary Jo. "Old Fort." *The State: Down Home in North Carolina*, 64:4 (September 1996), 10-11; online: http://digital.ncdcr.gov/cdm/ref/collection/p16062coll18/id/34131. [Online description from "North Carolina Periodicals Index," East Carolina University: "Old Fort, with a population under 1,000, is located off Interstate 40 in McDowell County. The town, which has a history dating back to colonial times and a strong industrial base, seeks to expand its tourist trade as well."]

Suther, Steve. "Cathey's Fort." In William S. Powell, ed.; Jay Mazzocchi, assoc. ed., *Encyclopedia of North Carolina* (Chapel Hill: University of North Carolina Press in association with the University of North Carolina Library, 2006), 194; online: http://ncpedia.org/catheys-fort.

Mecklenburg County and Charlotte

[Note: For various state government documents relating to Mecklenburg County and Charlotte during the Revolutionary period, search the MARS online catalog using the advanced search: http://mars.archives.ncdcr.gov/AdvancedSearch.aspx. Use the "Year" search box to restrict the searching to 1775-1783 and enter the county's name or the term "Charlotte" in the "Subjects" box, and hit the "Search" button near the top. This will retrieve any cataloged document for the county from that time period. These materials can vary considerably from personal or county petitions to the General Assembly, Loyalist matters, land disputes and claims, tax collection, exemptions from taxation, payments to county veterans, county divisions, personal collections, genealogical material, British claims against North Carolinians, etc. There is considerable information in these materials that could provide interesting documentation for persons living during the Revolution. The results will also include all of the wills and probates recorded in the county during the period set for the search. We had hoped to include many of these listings in this guide, but they are too voluminous. Citations to many of these search results for the eastern counties do, however, appear in the text.]

250 Years of Service: Mecklenburg County Sheriff's Office. Charlotte: Mecklenburg County Sheriff's Office, 2013.

Alexander, James. "James Alexander (active 1778) letter to Mark Alexander, 1778 June 10." Manuscript MS 2958.101, Patricia D. Klingenstein Library, New-York Historical Society, New York. [Description on ArchiveGrId: "Signed letter, dated Mecklenburg, N. C., June 10, 1778, to his uncle Mark Alexander, a prominent merchant in Baltimore. Respecting the internal affairs of the country during the American Revolution, including the trade between northern and southern states. Speaks very favorably of American independence and the mercantile class. personal matters."]

Alexander, John Brevard. *The History of Mecklenburg County from 1740 to 1900.* Charlotte: Observer Print House, 1902.

Alexander, John McKnitt, and William Polk. *Documents Shewing That Mecklenburg County, North Carolina, Declared Her Independence of Great-Britain, May 20, 1775.* Raleigh: Printed by J. Gales & Son, 1822.

Alexander, Violet G. "The Old Cemetery, Charlotte, N. C.: Some Unusual Notations Concerning This Ancient Burial Place, Which Holds the Dust of Many Patriots of Fame in North Carolina." *North Carolina Booklet*, 16:3 (1917), 145-153.

Ashe, Samuel A'Court. "Colonel Polk's Rebellion." *North Carolina Booklet*, 10:1 (July 1910), 43-47; online: http://digital.ncdcr.gov/cdm/ref/collection/p249901coll37/id/14180. [Online description from "North Carolina Periodicals Index," East Carolina University: "Mecklenburg County, North Carolina resident, Colonel Thomas Polk has been credited with a major role in the May 1775 declaration of independence from British rule. However, contemporary documentation of the event seems to be lacking."]

Blythe, Dolores S. "Hornets at Work." *The State: Down Home in North Carolina*, 64:6 (November 1978), 12; online: http://digital.ncdcr.gov/cdm/ ref/collection/p16062coll18/id/58157. [Online description from "North Carolina Periodicals Index," East Carolina University: "Lord Cornwallis and his British army had been in Charlotte for almost a week when Cornwallis dispatched a foraging party led by Major John Doyle on October 3, 1780. Captain James Thompson and thirteen other local residents surrounded the party and ambushed them, causing the British to believe they were under attack of a large force. Soon after, British forces retreated from Charlotte."]

Blythe, LeGette. *The Hornet's Nest: The Charlotte Bicentennial Play with Music, Song, Dancing, and Pantomine.* Charlotte: W. Loftin, 1968.

Blythe, LeGette. *Shout Freedom!: A Symphonic Drama in Two Acts.* Charlotte: [s. n., 1948?]

Byrd, William L., and John H Smith. *North Carolina Slaves and Free Persons of Color: Mecklenburg, Gaston, and Union Counties.* Bowie, Md.: Heritage Books, 2001.

Cabarrus Black Boys Chapter, North Carolina Daughters of the American Revolution. "Revolutionary Veterans Graves, Charlotte, Mecklenburg County." *North Carolina DAR Genealogical Records Committee Report, Series 2, Volume 29: Miscellaneous Records* (typescript, 1999), 63-116; digital surrogate, DAR Library, Washington, D. C.

"A Carolina Woman of the Revolution: Susannah Smart." *Godey's Ladies Book,* (February 1856); reprinted in: *Bulletin of the Chester District Genealogical Society*, 14:1 (March 1991), 2-9. [Mecklenburg County]

"Change of Command at Charlotte Town." *Southern Campaigns of the American Revolution*, 2:12 (December 2005), 1; online: http://southerncampaign.org/newsletter/v2n12.pdf. [Features a copy of Werner Willis' painting of the change-of-command ceremony when command of the southern Continental forces transferred from Major General Horatior Gates to Major General Nathaniel Greene on December 2, 1780.]

"Charlotte Town, North Carolina: North Carolina Campaign of 1780; 26 September 1780." *Southern Campaigns of the American Revolution*, 2:10.1 (October 2005), 1-3; online: http://southerncampaign.org/newsletter/v2n10.pdf.

Clarkson, Heriot. "The Hornet's Nest: Sketch of Revolutionary War at Charlotte and Vicinity." *North Carolina Booklet*, 1:6 (October 10, 1901), 3-24; online: http://digital.ncdcr.gov/cdm/ref/collection/p249901coll37/id/14180. [Online description from "North Carolina Periodicals Index," East Carolina University: "An essay on events in colonial and revolutionary North Carolina with a particular focus on Mecklenburg County and recurring religious and political themes."]

"Cornwallis' Attack on Charlotte Town." *Southern Campaigns of the American Revolution*, 2:10.1 (October 2005), 1-2; online: www.southerncampaign.org [September 1780]

Couch, Dale L. "Four Mecklenburg County, North Carolina Chairs: An Examination of Style and Technology." *Journal of Early Southern Decorative Arts*, 14:1 (May 1988), 14:1 (May 1988), 1-18; online: https://ia800502.us.archive.org/28/items/journalofearlyso1411988muse/journalofearlyso1411988muse.pdf. [Online description from "North Carolina Periodicals Index," East Carolina University: "This article examines the chair-making tradition of Mecklenburg County through the analysis of four chairs from the late 18th century. By analyzing the chairs, the tradition can be traced back to prior forms before the artisans migrated to North Carolina, which affected the style and technology of construction."]

Darr, John W. "New Role for the Old Rock House." *The State: Down Home in North Carolina*, 38:4 (July 1970), 13-14; online: http://digital.ncdcr.gov/cdm/ref/collection/p16062coll18/id/53652. [Online description from "North Carolina Periodicals Index," East Carolina University: "In 1774, Hezekiah Alexander built what generations of Charlotteans knew as the 'Old Rock House.' Alexander, who was a lawyer by trade, was a signer of the Mecklenburg Declaration of Independence in 1775, an elected member of North Carolina's provincial Congress in 1776, and one of the founders of Queen's College in Charlotte. In an effort to restore the Alexander Home and open it as a museum, a group of Charlotte's leading citizens have formed the Hezekiah Alexander Foundation."]

Davidson, Chalmers G. "Independent Mecklenburg." *North Carolina Historical Review*, 46:2 (April 1969), 122-129. [Online description from "North Carolina Periodicals Index," East Carolina University: "This article looks at historical acts indicative of a spirit of independence in Mecklenberg County and its county seat, Charlotte, that predate American independence and the Revolutionary War."]

Davidson, Chalmers G[aston]. *Major John Davidson of "Rural Hill," Mecklenburg County, N. C.* Charlotte: Lassiter Press, 1943. [John Davidson (1735-1832)]

"Death Notices for Mecklenburg Soldiers of American Revolution." *Olde Mecklenburg Genealogical Society Quarterly*, 23:1 (2005), 24-34.

Dunaway, Stewart E. *Mecklenburg County, North Carolina, Road, Bridge, and Ferry Records, 1783-1921.* Hillsborough: North Carolina Historical Books, 2009. [Note: While not specifically concerning the Revolution, these sources can be used in tandem with land records and other documents to help locate places of residence, occupations, geographical features, and place names.]

Flono, Fannie. *Thriving in the Shadows: Black Experience in Charlotte and Mecklenburg County*. Charlotte: Novello Festival Press, 2006.

Groome, Bailey Troy. *Mecklenburg in the Revolution, 1740-1783, Written in Honor of the Sons of the American Revolution upon the Occasion of Their 42nd Annual Congress, at Charlotte, Mecklenburg County, North Carolina, May 17-21, 1931*. Charlotte: Sons of the American Revolution, 1931. ["Discussion of the role of Mecklenburg County throughout the Revolution, with special attention to the Mecklenburg Declaration."]

Henderson, Archibald. *Revolution in North Carolina in 1775: Transylvania, Craven, Anson, and Mecklenburg.* [S. l.: s. n.], 1916.

Holcomb, Brent H. *Mecklenburg County, North Carolina, Abstracts of Early Wills, 1763-1790 (1749-1790).* Greenville: A Press, 1980.

Holcomb, Brent H. and Elmer O. Parker. *Mecklenburg County, North Carolina, Deed Abstracts, 1763-1779.* Easley, S. C.: Southern Historical Press, 1979.

Hunter, Cyrus Lee. *Sketches of Western North Carolina Historical and Biographical, Illustrating Principally the Revolutionary Period of Mecklenburg, Rowan, Lincoln and Adjoining Counties, Accompanied with Miscellaneous Information, Much of It Never Before Published.* Raleigh: Raleigh News Steam Job Print, 1877; reprinted: Raleigh: Edwards & Broughton, 1930; Baltimore: Regional Publishing Company, 1970.

Lewis, J. D. "Patriot Leaders in North Carolina: Robert Irwin: Captain in the Mecklenburg County Regiment of Militia - 1775, 1776-1777; Captain in the 2nd Salisbury District Minutemen - 1775-1776; Lt. Colonel in the Mecklenburg County Regiment of Militia - 1777-1778; Colonel in the Mecklenburg County Regiment of Militia - 1778-1783." Online: http://www.carolana.com/NC/Revolution/patriot_leaders_nc_robert_irwin.html.

"List of Public Officials of Mecklenburg County, North Carolina from 1775-1785, Taken from County Records (Includes the Names of some Militia Officers)." In Worth S. Ray, *The Mecklenburg Signers and their Neighbors* (Austin, Texas: Ray, 1946), 352-356.

McShane, Chuck. "A Fighting, Triffling Place." *Charlotte Magazine*, 19:6 (June 2014), 41-47; online: http://www.charlottemagazine.com/Charlotte-Magazine/June-2014/The-Story-of-Charlotte-Part-2-A-Fighting-Trifling-Place/. [Online description from "North Carolina Periodicals Index," East Carolina University: "Part 2 of the Story of Charlotte series, 'A Fighting, Trifling Place' describes the events in Mecklenburg County from

1770 through the early 1790s. Ideology from Orange and Rowan counties' Regulator Movement causes some riots, but county elites capitalize on the insurrection to reduce colonial taxes and establish Queen's College. Revolutionary thought contributes to the alleged signing of the Mecklenburg Declaration in 1775, while encounters with British troops come in 1780."]

McShane, Chuck. "Parcel of Blockheads." *Charlotte Magazine*, 19:5 (May 2014), 41-46; online: http://www.charlottemagazine.com/Charlotte-Magazine/May-2014/The-Story-of-Charlotte-Part-1-Parcel-of-Blockheads/. [Online description from "North Carolina Periodicals Index," East Carolina University: "Part 1 of the Story of Charlotte series, 'Parcel of Blockheads,' introduces the first settlers of Mecklenburg County, who were primarily Scots Irish Presbyterians migrating from Pennsylvania and Maryland. Settlement was sparse and riddled with disorder, for religion and land were points of contention. The arrival of the surveyor Henry Eustace McCulloh in 1765 sparked a riot and legal debate over who owned the land in Mecklenburg County, eventually leading to the construction of a courthouse in what became Charlotte."]

Mecklenburg Chapter, North Carolina Society, Sons of the American Revolution. *Mecklenburg in the Revolution, 1740-1783*. Charlotte: The Chapter, 1931.

"Mecklenburg Co., N. C. Revolutionary War Pensioners, 1841. *The Carolinas Genealogical Society Bulletin*, 11:1, 10.

"Mecklenburg County, North Carolina in the Revolutionary War." *American Monthly Magazine* [DAR], 31:4 (October 1907), 626-629.

Mecklenburg County. "Mecklenburg County Miscellaneous Records, 1759-1959: Tax Records, 1777-1900." Manuscript C.R.065.928.9, State Archives of North Carolina, Raleigh.

"[Mecklenburg County] Militia under Major John Fifer." In Weynette Parks Haun, *North Carolina Revolutionary Army Accounts, Part I, Secretary of State Treasurer's & Comptroller's Papers Journal "A", (Public Accounts) 1775-1776* (Durham: W. P. Haun, 1988), 52-54. [County designation determined by pension records such as those of Elias Mairs (Moirs) S2719, Robert Martin S2732, Moses Justice (Justus) S32351, John Purvians S32459 and William Akins W5600. The pension record of Robert Martin S2732, states that Colonel John Fifer and General Rutherford had command of the troops from Mecklenburg and Rowan Counties. {This analysis was performed by genealogists in the Genealogy Office, Office of the Registrar General, National Society Daughters of the American Revolution, Washington, D. C.}]

Misenheimer, John. "Mecklenburg Militia at Battle of Moores Creek Bridge." *Olde Mecklenburg Genealogical Society Quarterly*, 20:3 (2002), 31-34.

Misenheimer, John E. "American Revolution Pensioners with Ties to Mecklenburg County." *Olde Mecklenburg Genealogical Society Quarterly*, 22:2 (2004), 27-36.

Misenheimer, John E., Jr. "Brigadier General William Lee Davidson and First Major John Davidson: Leading Revolutionary Patriots in Mecklenburg County, North Carolina." *The Golden Nugget (Cabarrus Genealogical Society)*, 11:4 (December 2003), 184-189.

Morrill, Dan L. *Historic Charlotte: An Illustrated History of Charlotte & Mecklenburg County*. San Antonio, Tex.: Historical Publishing Network for Historic Charlotte, Inc., 2001.

"Muster Roll of Captain Charles Polk's Company of Militia." In Bell Merrill Draper, comp., *Pension Papers, Volume 20* (Washington, D. C.: NSDAR, 1912), 188-196 (unpublished typescript). [Note: The roll was found in the Revolutionary War pension record of Charles Polk, W5571, pages 182-196.]

Nixon, Brevard. "Revolutionary Records: The Mecklenburg County Militia, North Carolina." *American Monthly Magazine* [DAR], 31:1 (July 1907), 7-10; and, 31:2 (August 1907), 363-366. Reprinted: *Daughters of the American Revolution Magazine*, 61:7 (July 1927), 547-551. [Includes many civil service appointees.]

Norris, David A., and Daniel W. Barefoot. "Charlotte, Battle of." In William S. Powell, ed.; Jay Mazzocchi, assoc. ed., *Encyclopedia of North Carolina* (Chapel Hill: University of North Carolina Press in association with the University of North Carolina Library, 2006), 201-202. [1780]

Norris, Jeannie Faris. "Yesterday in Mecklenburg County." *The State: Down Home in North Carolina*, 30:23 (April 1963), 12-13, 31-37; online: http://digital.ncdcr.gov/cdm/ref/collection/p16062coll18/id/45439. [Online description from "North Carolina Periodicals Index," East Carolina University: "Settled around 1750, the residents of Mecklenburg County have enjoyed a lucrative and varied history. Sustained through a variety of agricultural and eventually, commercial ventures, residents of Mecklenburg initially relied heavily upon cotton. Joining in the American dream of finding gold, Mecklenburgers first discovered the rare mineral in 1799. Dubbed by Cornwallis as the 'hornet's nest of stubborn revolutionaries,' Mecklenburgers experienced the War of Sugar Creek, instigated a military campaign against a group of South Carolinian Tories, known as Scoffelites, and wrote their own Declaration of Independence. Mecklenburgers additionally participated in the Civil War, furnishing some 2,700 men to the cause, or one sixth of the county population."]

North Carolina (State). General Assembly. "[Document dated:] Aprill [*sic*] 18, 1778: Joint Papers, Committee Papers, Resolutions, Senate Bills, House Bills, Petition of the Inhabitants of Mecklenburg Co., 1778." Manuscript; General Assembly Record Group; Session Records, April-May, 1778, Box 1, State Archives of North Carolina, Raleigh. [Online catalog description: "Petition in which the inhabitants of Mecklenburg Co. express concern over an act which provides officers and soldiers with grants of land in return for military service. The petitioners fear that the act provides insufficient protection against greed and speculation."]

North Carolina Daughters of the American Revolution. "Mecklenburg Militia." *North Carolina DAR Genealogical Records Committee Report, Series 1, Volume 11: County Records* (typescript, 1930), 60-63; digital surrogate, DAR Library, Washington, D. C.

"Patriot Resistance in Rowan and Mecklenburg Cos., N. C., 1780-1781." *North Carolina Genealogical Society Journal*, 9:4 (November 1983), 9:4 (November 1983), 228.

Phifer, Cordelia White. *Revolutionary Historical Spots in Charlotte and Mecklenburg County; Also Some Confederate History of Charlotte & Mecklenburg County*. Charlotte: Chamber of Commerce, [193?].

Plumer, Richard P. *Charlotte and the American Revolution: Reverend Alexander Craighead, the Mecklenburg Declaration and the Foothills Fight for Independence*. Charleston, S. C.: History Press, 2014. [Contents: Mecklenburg's Fiery Preacher; Reverend Craighead's Ferocious Parishioners; The War of Sugar Creek; Reverend Alexander Craighead's Death; Rebellion in Mecklenburg County and the Foothills of North Carolina; The First Battle of the Revolutionary War; The Mecklenburg Declaration of Independence and Resolves; Mecklenburg's Role in the Revolutionary War; Appendix: List of Mecklenburg County Revolutionary War Soldiers. Publisher's description: "Charlotte was a hotbed of Revolutionary activity well before the fervency of revolt reached its boiling point in New England. Considered a wild frontier region at the time, Mecklenburg County welcomed the Reverend Alexander Craighead with ready hands for battle. Craighead's fiery rhetoric inspired the people of the region to action. What resulted was the creation of the Mecklenburg Declaration of Independence, the first such document in the nation, and although the county had less than 3 percent of the colony's population, its Patriots accounted for over one-quarter of North Carolina's Revolutionary troops. Join author Richard P. Plumer as he reveals how the Queen City played an integral role in the formation of a proud and free America."]

"Polk, Charles: Supplemental." In Bell Merrill Draper, Comp. *Pension Papers, Vol 20 [DAR]*, 182-196. Digital surrogate available at the DAR Library, Washington, D. C. [Includes Muster Roll of Captain Charles Polk's Company of Militia.]

Poteet, Ellen. "Banastre Tarleton's Description of Charlotte in 1780." *Olde Mecklenburg Genealogical Society Quarterly*, 24:2 (2006), 18-22.

Poteet, Ellen. "Locating the 1777-1778 Mecklenburg Tax List." *Olde Mecklenburg Genealogical Society Quarterly*, 20:1 (2002), 14-29. [Includes the lists themselves.]

Poteet, Ellen. "Mecklenburg Pensioners in 1840 Census." *Olde Mecklenburg Genealogical Society Quarterly*, 22:4 (2004), 23-27.

Price, Betty K. "The 1840 Mecklenburg County, North Carolina Census Contains the Following Pensioners of Revolutionary War or Military Service." *Olde Mecklenburg Genealogical Society Quarterly*, 5:1 (Spring-Summer 1987), 9.

"Princeton of the South: Rebelling against the King, the founders of Charlotte established Queen's College. Had the college survived the Revolutionary War, Charlotte – not Chapel Hill – would have claimed the nation's first public university." *Our State: Celebrating North Carolina*, (June 1, 2010); online: https://www.ourstate.com/queens-college/.

Ray, Worth S. *The Mecklenburg Signers and Their Neighbors*. Baltimore: Genealogical Publishing Co., 1962. Study of the people of Mecklenburg County in the colonial and Revolutionary periods. Some of the material is more relevant for genealogy but there are also many maps and lists of Mecklenburg County inhabitants that may help in finding of primary source material.

Rhyne, Nancy Garrison. "Queen Charlotte's Big 200th." *The State: Down Home in North Carolina*, 36:4 (July 1968), 8; online: http://digital.ncdcr.gov/cdm/ref/collection/p16062coll18/id/103963. [Online description from "North Carolina Periodicals Index," East Carolina University: "On May 20, 1968, the anniversary of the signing of the Mecklenburg Declaration of Independence, Charlotte will celebrate its bicentennial. A bill introduced by Senator Sam Ervin, Jr. and cosponsored by Senator B. Everett Jordan making May 20 'Charlotte Day' was signed into law by President Lyndon Johnson. Mrs. Johnson accepted Mayor Brookshire's invitation to come to Charlotte and dedicate the restored birthplace of the 11th president of the United States, James K. Polk, and the Hezekiah Alexander Home, built in 1774. The town of Charlotte was named for the wife of King George III of England, and the county, Mecklenburg, was named for Charlotte's royal house in Germany. Charlottetown, as it was then known, was built on 369 acres donated by Lord Proprietor George Augustus Selwyn and was chartered on December 7, 1768."]

Roebuck, Haywood. "Some Continental Line Deserters from Rowan, Surry, and Mecklenburg Counties, N. C. 1780-1782." *North Carolina Genealogical Society Journal*, 1:2 (April 1975), 102-104.

Saxon, John L. "Places You Can Visit." *The State: Down Home in North Carolina*, 46:6 (November 1978), 13; online: http://digital.ncdcr.gov/cdm/compoundobject/collection/p16062coll18/id/58157. [Online description from "North Carolina Periodicals Index," East Carolina University: "The McIntyre Historic Site was opened in October, 1976, just north of Charlotte. Visitors are invited to come and learn about the historical significance of the area as well as why Cornwallis dubbed Mecklenburg County 'The Hornet's Nest'."]

Sellers, Charles Grier, Jr. "Old Mecklenburg and the Meaning of the American Experience." *North Carolina Historical Review*, 46:2 (April 1969), 142-156.

Shields, E. Thomson, Jr. "'A Modern Poem,' by the Mecklenburg Censor: Politics and Satire in Revolutionary North Carolina." *Early American Literature*, 29:3 (1994), 205-232.

Shriner, Charles A. "Mecklenburg." *Americana (American Historical Magazine)*, 19:1 (January 1925), 1-19.

"Simon Hager." *Olde Mecklenburg Genealogical Society Quarterly*, 10:4 (October-December 1992), 17-18.

"Steel Creek Grave-Yard, North Carolina." *Daughters of the American Revolution Magazine*, 44:4 (April 1914), 239. [Steel Creek Presbyterian Church, Mecklenburg County, N. C. Contains the grave of Captain Henry Neel of the 1st North Carolina Regiment.]

Torrance Family and Banks Family. "Torrance-Banks Family Papers, 1769-1932." Manuscript 087, J. Murray Atkins Library, University of North Carolina at Charlotte. [Online catalog description: "Papers of Hugh Torance (1743-1816) and his descendants, including especially his son, James Galbraith Torrance [*sic*] (1784-1847), and his grandson Richard Allison Torrance (1833-1927), concerning their extensive mercantile, planting, and milling operations at Cedar Grove plantation in northern Mecklenburg County, N. C. Includes account books, Revolutionary War service records, family correspondence, land and estate records, information on slaves, contracts with overseers, two acrostics by George Moses Horton ('the slave poet of Chapel Hill'), and poems and notes by area schoolmaster Peter Stuart Ney, whom some believe to have been Marshall Michael Ney, one of Napoleon's generals."]

Watson, Alan D. "Colonial Constables." *Olde Mecklenburg Genealogical Society Quarterly*, 20:3 (2002), 35-37. [Mecklenburg County, 1774-1780.]

Mecklenburg County and Charlotte – The Mecklenburg Resolves, May 31, 1775

Corbitt, D. L. "Resolutions of Mecklenburg County. *North Carolina Historical Review,* 7:3 (July 1930), 404-406.

"Resolves Passed at Mecklenburg, N. C., 30th May 1775." *Proceedings of the Massachusetts Historical Society*, 12 (1871-1873), 158.

Weeks, Stephen Beauregard. *Truth and Justice for the History of North Carolina: The Mecklenburg Resolves of May 31, 1775 vs. the Mecklenburg Declaration of May 20, 1775.* Greensboro: C. L. Van Noppen, 1908?.

Mecklenburg County and Charlotte – Queen's Museum/Liberty Hall Academy

"Cemeteries of Mecklenburg County: Liberty Hall/Queens Museum/British Cemetery." Online: http://www.cm story.org/content/liberty-hallqueens-museumbritish-cemetery.

Haywood, Marshall De Lancey. "The Story of Queen's College or Liberty Hall in the Province of North Carolina." *North Carolina Booklet*, 11:3 (January 1912), 169-175.

"Queen's Museum in the American Revolution History Facts." Online: http://www.ashevillelist.com/history/queens-museum.htm.

Mitchell County

Bailey, Lloyd Richard, Sr., ed. *The Heritage of the Toe River Valley*. 12 vols. Durham: L. R. Bailey, 1994-2007. [Avery, Mitchell, and Yancey Counties]

Montgomery County

[Note: For various state government documents relating to Montgomery County during the Revolutionary period, search the MARS online catalog using the advanced search: http://mars.archives.ncdcr.gov/AdvancedSearch.aspx. Use the "Year" search box to restrict the searching to 1775-1783 and enter the county's name in the "Subjects" box, and hit the "Search" button near the top. This will retrieve any cataloged document for the county from that time period. These materials can vary considerably from personal or county petitions to the General Assembly, Loyalist matters, land disputes and claims, tax collection, exemptions from taxation, payments to county veterans, county divisions, personal collections, genealogical material, British claims against North Carolinians, etc. There is considerable information in these materials that could provide interesting documentation for persons living during the Revolution. The results will also include all of the wills and probates recorded in the county during the period set for the search. We had hoped to include many of these listings in this guide, but they are too voluminous. Citations to many of these search results for the eastern counties do, however, appear in the text.]

"The Burned Courthouse Records of Montgomery County, NC." *North Carolina Genealogical Society Journal*, 17:4 (November 1991), 223.

Goodpasture, Albert V. "Beginnings of Montgomery County." *American Historical Magazine*, 8:3 (July 1903), 193-215.

McBride, Ransom. "Montgomery County, N. C.: A New Look at Its 'Wandering' Courthouse, 1779-1844." *North Carolina Genealogical Society Journal*, 18:3 (August 1992), 217-227.

"Montgomery County Voter List for 1779." *North Carolina Genealogical Society Journal,* 10:1 (February 1984), 44-46.

Moore, Terry. "A Birdseye View of Montgomery County Records before 1840." *North Carolina Genealogical Society Journal*, 39:2 (March 2015), 10-11; online: http://www.ncgenealogy.org/articles_tools/Birdseye_View_of_Montgomery_County_Records.pdf.

Pruitt, Albert Bruce. *Index to North Carolina County Maps: Davie, Guilford, Montgomery, Randolph, Rockingham, Stokes, Surry, & Yadkin*. Whitakers: A. B. Pruitt, 1988.

Stanback, J. F. "The DeBerrys of Montgomery Co.," *Charlotte Observer*, 10 November 1950.

Moore County

Comer, James Vann. "Revolutionary War Soldiers of Moore County, NC." *Central North Carolina Journal*, 4:1 (March 1993), 6-7.

North Carolina Daughters of the American Revolution. "Moore Co., NC Revolutionary Soldiers." *North Carolina DAR Genealogical Records Committee Report, Series 1, Volume 2: Records* (typescript, 1926), 28; digital surrogate, DAR Library, Washington, D. C.

Owen, Ray, with Keitt Akin, *et al. Plain Style: The Work of 18th and 19th Century Craftsmen in Moore County, North Carolina: A Catalog*. Southern Pines: Moore County Historical Association, 1993.

Robinson, Blackwell P. *A History of Moore County North Carolina 1747-1847*. Southern Pines: Moore County Historical Association, 1956.

Wellman, Manly Wade. "The Lady and the House-Burner." *The State: A Weekly Survey of North Carolina*, 21:9 (August 1953), 6, 13; online: http://digital.ncdcr.gov/cdm/ref/collection/p16062coll18/id/30730. [Online description from "North Carolina Periodicals Index," The Philip Alston house, standing in Deep River's Horseshoe Bend in upper Moore County may soon become one of North Carolina's historical shrines. The house is one of the finest surviving examples of colonial architecture in the state and has a thrilling history of blood and battle. But it came very close to vanishing by fire in 1781, when Tory David Fanning, a notorious house-burner during the Revolutionary War, tried to destroy it. However, the site was saved by a lady, Miss Elizabeth Chancy Alston."]

Wicker, Rassie Everton. *Map of the Region of Moore County, 1747 to 1847: Showing Stream Names and Road Locations*. [North Carolina: R. E. Wicker, 1956?] [A copy is in the Genealogy Map Collection, State Library of North Carolina, Raleigh. "Includes Key: Military Movements, 1776-1781."]

Nash County

[Note: For various state government documents relating to Nash County during the Revolutionary period, search the MARS online catalog using the advanced search: http://mars.archives.ncdcr.gov/AdvancedSearch.aspx. Use the "Year" search box to restrict the searching to 1775-1783 and enter the county's name in the "Subjects" box, and hit the "Search" button near the top. This will retrieve any cataloged document for the county from that time period. These materials can vary considerably from personal or county petitions to the General Assembly, Loyalist matters, land disputes and claims, tax collection, exemptions from taxation, payments to county veterans, county divisions, personal collections, genealogical material, British claims against North Carolinians, etc. There is considerable information in these materials that could provide interesting documentation for persons living during the Revolution. The results will also include all of the wills and probates recorded in the county during the period set for the search. We had hoped to include many of these listings in this guide, but they are too voluminous. Citations to many of these search results for the eastern counties do, however, appear in the text.]

"Captain Edward Clinch's Company of the Nash County Regiment (December 1778-February 1779)." *North Carolina Genealogical Society Journal,* 10:4 (November 1984), 248-249.

Dunaway, Stewart E. *Nash County, North Carolina, Bridge Records (1779-1834).* Hillsborough: North Carolina Historical Books, 2011. [Note: While not specifically concerning the Revolution, these sources can be used in tandem with land records and other documents to help locate places of residence, occupations, geographical features, and place names.]

Dunaway, Stewart E. *Nash County, North Carolina, Mill Records (1782-1875).* Hillsborough: North Carolina Historical Books, 2010. [Note: While not specifically concerning the Revolution, these sources can be used in tandem with land records and other documents to help locate places of residence, occupations, geographical features, and place names.]

Dunaway, Stewart E. *Nash County, North Carolina, Road Records (1768-1833).* Hillsborough: North Carolina Historical Books, 2013. [Note: While not specifically concerning the Revolution, these sources can be used in tandem with land records and other documents to help locate places of residence, occupations, geographical features, and place names.]

Johnson, William Perry. "Nash County: 1782 Tax List." *Journal of North Carolina Genealogy*, 10:1 (Spring 1964), 1249-1250; 10:3 (Fall 1964), 1322-1327

Lea, Diane. "An Amazing Story of Family and Fortitude." *Metro Magazine*, 12:5 (August/September 2011), 46-53; online: http://www.metronc.com/article/?id=2290. [Online description from "North Carolina Periodicals Index," East Carolina University: "METRO design editor Diane Lea discusses the Boddie family and the Rose Hill Plantation located in Nash County. The family moved to North Carolina from Virginia in 1734. The original home does not stand, but part of the one built in 1792, survived and is the back wing of the present, restored Rose Hill Plantation."]

McBride, Ransom. "Capt. Edward Clinch's Company of the Nash County Regiment (Dec. 1778-Feb. 1779)." *North Carolina Genealogical Society Journal*, 10:4 (November 1984), 248-249.

McBride, Ransom. "A List of Men from Nash County, NC, Probably Militia, 1780." *North Carolina Genealogical Society Journal*, 12:4 (November 1986), 233.

Micajah Petway Chapter, North Carolina Daughters of the American Revolution. "Nash Co., NC Revolutionary Soldiers Exempt from Service 1780-1782." *North Carolina DAR Genealogical Records Committee Report, Series 1, Volume 344: Genealogical Records* (typescript, 1969), 1-8; digital surrogate, DAR Library, Washington, D. C.

Nash County. "Nash County Miscellaneous Records, 1778-1909: Loyalty Oaths, no date and 1778-1873." Manuscript C.R.069.928.1, State Archives of North Carolina, Raleigh.

North Carolina. General Assembly. "[Document dated:] April 29, 1780: Resolution Exempting from Poll Taxes James Deen, James Atkins, and Thomas Tucker of Nash County." Manuscript; General Assembly Record Group; Session Records, April-May, 1780: Joint Papers, Committee Papers, Resolutions; House Joint Resolutions: April 28-May 1, 1780, Box 1 (MARS ID: 66.8.20.16.3; item), State Archives of North Carolina, Raleigh.

North Carolina. General Assembly. "[Document dated:] June 1781: Petition of John Evans of Nash County (Laid Over)." Manuscript; General Assembly Record Group; Session Records, June-July 1781; Joint Papers, Committee Papers, Resolutions, Senate Bills, House Bills, Box 1 (MARS ID: 66.8.25.7.2), State Archives of North Carolina, Raleigh. [Online catalog description: "Evans asks the Assembly to discharge him from the militia, as he feels he was threatened into enlisting."]

North Carolina. General Assembly. "[Document dated:] May 4, 1782: Report on Petition of Edward Nicholson of Nash County (Messages and Petition Only)." Manuscript; General Assembly Record Group; Session Records, April-May, 1782: Joint Papers, Committee Papers: Joint Select Committees: Reports and Papers (Petitions, Messages, etc.): April 29-May 1782, Box 1 (MARS ID: 66.8.27.9.10; item), State Archives of North Carolina, Raleigh. [Online catalog description: "Petition requests reinstatement as Justice of the Peace of Nash County after Edward Nicholson's parole by the British; messages from both houses refer petition to committee."]

North Carolina. General Assembly. "[Document dated:] April 22, 1783: Petition of John Evans of Nash County (Laid Over)." Manuscript; General Assembly Record Group; Session Records,June-July 1781; Joint Papers, Committee Papers, Resolution; House Joint Resolutions: April 21-30, 1783, Box 1 (MARS ID: 66.8.29.13.3), State Archives of North Carolina, Raleigh. [Online catalog description: "Bunn was wounded in a skirmish with a loyalist. He seeks compensation for the cost of healing. The document is a recommendation of the case from the court of Nash County to the General Assembly."]

"Oath of Allegiance and Jurors." In Walter Clark, ed., *State Records of North Carolina: Laws, 1715-1776*, 22 (Goldsboro: Nash Bros., Book and Job Printers, 1904; reprinted: Wilmington: Broadfoot Publishing Company, 1994), 168-179.

Ricks, T. E. *Nash County Historical Notes: A Bicentennial Tribute*. Rocky Mount: Nash County Bicentennial Commission, 1976.

Vester, Benjamin H. "Papers, 1772-1877." Manuscript RUB Bay 0035:09 items 1-134, David M. Rubenstein Rare Book & Manuscript Library, Duke University, Durham. [Online catalog description: "Resident of Nash County, N. C. The collection contains receipts, promissory notes, deeds, and letters relating to Benjamin H. Vester and his family including an order, 1780, to Solomon Vester, a Revolutionary soldier, instructing him to assist in the capture of deserters and delinquents in Nash County, N.C.; ..."]

New Hanover County and Wilmington

[Note: For various state government documents relating to Wilmington during the Revolutionary period, search the MARS online catalog using the advanced search: http://mars.archives.ncdcr.gov/AdvancedSearch.aspx. Use the "Year" search box to restrict the searching to 1775-1783 and enter the town's name in the "Subjects" box, and hit the "Search" button near the top. This will retrieve any cataloged document for the county from that time period. These materials can vary considerably from personal or county petitions to the General Assembly, Loyalist matters, land disputes and claims, tax collection, exemptions from taxation, payments to county veterans, county divisions, personal collections, genealogical material, British claims against North Carolinians, etc. There is considerable information in these materials that could provide interesting documentation for persons living during the Revolution. The results will also include all of the wills and probates recorded in the county during the period set for the search. We had hoped to include many of these listings in this guide, but they are too voluminous. Citations to many of these search results for the eastern counties do, however, appear in the text.]

Anders Family. "Mrs. I. F. Lee Collection, 1751-1875." Manuscript, PC.130, State Archives of North Carolina, Raleigh. [Online catalog description: "Papers of the Anders family of Bladen and New Hanover counties, including grants, deeds, plats and other land papers; copy of will of William Anders (1813); estate papers of John and Steven Anders; militia commissions of James M. Anders (1820, 1821); maintenance bond for Enoch H. Anders (1865); and draft power of attorney from Penelope Lewis to William Anders for collecting pay of soldier in the N. C. Continental Line (1791), bearing names and addresses of several widows and former soldiers in the New Hanover (Pender) Co. area."]

Bellamy, John Dillard. *Speech of Hon. John D. Bellamy, of North Carolina, in the House of Representatives, February 14, 1903, on H. R. 17356, to Erect an Equestrian Statue at Wilmington, N. C., to the Memory of Major Gen. Robert Howe, of the American Revolution*. Washington, D. C.: [Government Printing Office?], 1903.

Brewer, James Howard. "An Account of Negro Slavery in the Cape Fear Region prior to 1860." Ph. D. dissertation, University of Pittsburgh, 1949.

Burr, James G[reen]. "Historic Homes: The Hermitage, Burguin's Seat." *Magazine of History*, 16:5 (November 1886), 433-442.

Burr, James G[reen]. *Old Mansions of Cape Fear: The Hermitage*. Wilmington: [s. n.], 1885.

Clifford, Mary Louise. *From Slavery to Freetown: Black Loyalists after the American Revolution*. Jefferson: McFarland, 1999. [Include a section on: "Thomas Peters of Wilmington, North Carolina."]

Cometti, Elizabeth. "Morals and the American Revolution." *South Atlantic Quarterly*, 46:1 (January 1947), 62-71. [Mrs. Austin was warned by the North Carolina's Safety Committee of Wilmington not to give a public ball at her house.]

Cooke, Robert Bruce. "Robert Bruce Cooke Papers, 1757-1786, 1962." Manuscript PC.1256, State Archives of North Carolina, Raleigh. [Online catalog description: "Letter (1962) from Cooke describing his efforts to separate the identities of two prominent colonials, Thomas Lloyd of Orange Co. and Thomas Lloyd of New Hanover Co., with abstracts from Colonial and State Records of North Carolina and New Hanover Co. court minutes."]

Cooper, A. W. "Smith Island." *Wildlife in North Carolina*, 30:1 (January 1966), 16-19. [Online description from "North Carolina Periodicals Index," East Carolina University: "North Carolina possesses one of the last remaining wilderness areas along the Atlantic Coast. It's called Smith Island, more popularly known as Bald Head. The island is home to a number of wildlife species and contains numerous salt marsh areas which produce food for resident fish and sea mammals. Cooper writes, 'It is the last vestige in North Carolina of a primitive coast line. Unfortunately, plans are being made for its development, and, if steps are not taken to preserve its natural features, this last North Carolina coastal wilderness will disappear, transformed into a jungle of concrete, beach houses, and hotels'."]

Crow, Terrell Armistead. "'The Task That Is Ours': Planning the North Carolina Women's History Project." *Carolina Comments*, 35:4 (July 1987), 97-106. [Includes mention of a 1773 petition of freeholders in Wilmington, N. C. to the governor that included the names of four women: Mary DeRosset, Rebecca Mortimer, Rebecca Lloyd, and Jean DuBois.]

De Van Massey, Gregory. "The British Expedition to Wilmington, January-November, 1781." *North Carolina Historical Review*, 66:4 (October 1989), 387-411. [Online description from "North Carolina Periodicals Index," East Carolina University: "A look at the role that the British garrison in Wilmington played in the loyalist uprisings during the spring and summer of 1781. Information on the impact of British Major James Henry Craig's use of Wilmington, North Carolina, as a base of operations and protection of Tory supporters, and his organized of military units against the Patriot militia resulting in civil war within the state is provided." James Henry Craig (1748-1812).]

Davis and Walker Families. "Davis and Walker Family Papers, 1755-1962." Mansucript 4172, Southern Historical Collection, Louis Round Wilson Special Collections Library, University of North Carolina at Chapel Hill. [Online catalog description shows that this collection includes: "...a contemporary set of caricatures of locally prominent Revolutionary War-era figures;..."]

Frech, Laura Page. "The Wilmington Committee of Public Safety and the Loyalist Rising of February 1776." *North Carolina Historical Review*, 41:1 (January 1964), 1-20. [Online description from "North Carolina Periodicals Index," East Carolina University: "The article reviews the role of Committee of Public Safety in the Wilmington-New Hanover area during the Revolutionary War. Committee members were entrusted to contain British Governor Martin and squelch Highlander loyalties to the British Crown. The author documents the connection between the Committee's decisions and outcomes of two important events: The Battle of Moore's Creek (1776) and the Highland rising at Cross Creek (1776)."]

Godfrey, Michael A. "A Day on Smith Island." *Wildlife in North Carolina*, 38:2 (February 1974), 8-11. [Online description from "North Carolina Periodicals Index," East Carolina University: "Smith Island is the state's most isolated coastal area and one of the last remaining wilderness areas along the Atlantic Coast. Actually, it is made up of three sub-islands, Bluff, Middle, and Bald Head. Godfrey does not dwell on the island's rich and fascinating history nor its uncertain and controversial future with proposed development on Bald Head Island. Instead he describes the incredible natural beauty of the landscape."]

Goerch, Carl. "Wilmington." *The State: A Weekly Survey of North Carolina*, 8:29 (October 1940), 1-6; online: http://digital.ncdcr.gov/cdm/ref/collection/p16062coll18/id/6229. [Online description from "North Carolina Periodicals Index," East Carolina University: "With a history of over two centuries, it is only natural that Wilmington should have many unusual, historic, and odd things of interest. For example, in the St. James Episcopal Church there hangs a famous painting of Christ which was taken from a capture Spanish pirate ship that attempted to seize the town of Brunswick in 1748. Among other things, there is also the Bellamy Mansion, an example of Greek Revival architecture, which was occupied by Union forces during the American Civil War."]

Haines, Jeffrey L. "Petition from the Adjoining Inhabitants of the Counties of New Hanover, Duplin, and Bladen, 23 October 1779." *North Carolina Genealogical Society Journal*, 33:3 (August 2007), 244-249. [for a new county]

Hall, Margaret Tannanhill. "The Restored Cornwallis House." *The State: A Weekly Survey of North Carolina*, 19:12 (August 1951), 4-5; online: http://digital.ncdcr.gov/cdm/ref/collection/p16062coll18/id/27402. [Online description from "North Carolina Periodicals Index," East Carolina University: "The Cornwallis House at the corner of Third and Market Streets in Wilmington has been restored by the Colonial Dames and opened to the public."]

Hewlett, Crockette William. *Between the Creeks: A History of Masonboro Sound, 1735-1970*. Wilmington: Printed by Wilmington Print. Co., 1971.

Hewlett, Crockette W.; foreword by Claude Howell. *Two Centuries of Art in New Hanover County*. Durham: Moore Publishing Company, 1976.

Hill, William; A. S. Salley, Jr., ed. *Col. William Hill's Memoirs of the Revolution*. Columbia: Historical Commission of South Carolina, 1921.

Hill, William; Griffith J. McRee, ed. "Extracts from the Letter-Book of William Hill, of Cape Fear, N. C." *New England Historical and Genealogical Register*, 13:4 (October 1859), 329-330. [Brunswick, N. C., 1774-1775]

Hirchak, John. *Legends of Old Wilmington & Cape Fear*. Charleston: History Press, 2014.

Hooper, William. *At a General Meeting of the Inhabitants of the District of Wilmington in the Province of North-Carolina, Held at the Town of Wilmington, July 21st, 1774. William Hooper, Esq. Chairman*. Wilmington:

Printed by Adam Boyd, 1774; micropublished: (Early American Imprints. First Series. No. 42755) New York: Readex Microprint, 1985. [Note: "Resolutions appointing a Committee of Correspondence and recommending other measures concerning 'the present alarming state of British America'."]

Howell, Andrew J. *The Book of Wilmington*. Wilmington: The Compiler, 1930.

Howell, Andrew J. "The Rouse House Massacre of 1781." *Wilmington Star-News*, (27 September 1931).

"J." "'The Old Mulberry Tree at the Rouse House:' A Revolutionary Reminiscence." *Our Living and Our Dead* (North Carolina Branch, Southern Historical Society), 3 (October 1875), 456-457.

Kellam, Ida Brooks. *Historic Wilmington, New Hanover County, North Carolina*. [Wilmington]: Stamp Defiance Chapter, North Carolina Daughters of the American Revolution, 1958.

Kellam, Ida Brooks. *Members of Safety Committee, 1774, 1775, 1776, Wilmington, North Carolina.* Wilmington: I. B. Kellam, 1959. [Description: "These names are taken from the Minutes of the Safety Committee, and their proceedings, on file in the Public Library in Wilmington, North Carolina."]

La Vere, David. "Walking Preservationist." *Our State: Down Home in North Carolina*, 73:3 (August 2005), 134-138; online: http://digital.ncdcr.gov/cdm/ref/collection/p16062coll18/id/84024. [Online description from "North Carolina Periodicals Index," East Carolina University: "Bob Jenkins, a native of Sneads Ferry, spent much of his early life in Wilmington, before going off to study interior design. When he returned to Wilmington in the late 1960s, he found the downtown area had become seedy and catered to a coarse trade. Families had moved out, and many of the old historic homes were decaying or being torn down. Jenkins became a pioneer when he opened a design shop near the riverfront and purchased one of the historic homes nearby. Fortunately, he found other like-minded individuals who cared about revitalizing downtown and preserving historic buildings. Today more than three hundred blocks of downtown Wilmington are on the National Register of Historic Places, and the town is mentioned in the same breath as Savannah and Charleston. Jenkins retired in 1989, and is the owner and sole employee of Wilmington's Adventure and Walking Tours."]

Lawrence, R. C. "Patriots of New Hanover." *The State: A Weekly Survey of North Carolina*, 13:42 (March 1946), 20; online: http://digital.ncdcr.gov/cdm/ref/collection/p16062coll18/id/15230. [Online description from "North Carolina Periodicals Index," East Carolina University: "Quite a number of outstanding citizens in the Cape Fear area were rebelling against British tyranny long before the signing of the Mecklenburg Declaration."]

Lea, Diane. "Colonial Dames Restore Trio of Historic Houses." *Metro Magazine*, 5:12 (December 2004), 37-44; online: http://www.metronc.com/article/?id=874. [Online description from "North Carolina Periodicals Index," East Carolina University: "*Metro* design editor Diane Lea discusses the role of The National Society of Colonial Dames of America in the State of North Carolina in saving, restoring, and maintaining three of the most significant residences associated with the role of the state and the capital city in the Revolutionary War. The residences are the Joel Lane House (Raleigh) ca. 1770; Haywood Hall at New Bern Place (Raleigh) 1799; and the Burgwin-Wright House (Wilmington) 1770."]

Lee, Lawrence. *New Hanover County: A Brief History*. Raleigh: Division of Archives and History, 1977.

Lewis, J. D. "Patriot Leaders in North Carolina: William Purviance: Colonel over the New Hanover County Regiment of Militia - 1775-1776." Online: http://www.carolana.com/NC/Revolution/patriotleaders_nc_william_purviance.html.

MacMillan, Emma Woodward. *Wilmington's Vanished Homes and Buildings*. Raleigh: [s. n.], 1966.

Martin, Laura. "Plantation Punch." *North Carolina Home*. 2:4 (August 1993), 63-67. [Online description from "North Carolina Periodicals Index," East Carolina University: "Orton Plantation, built in the 1730s on the lower Cape Fear, has witnessed 250 years of North Carolina history and is a standing reminder of North Carolina's heritage. The gardens are open to the public from March to November."]

Massey, Gregory De Van. "The British Expedition to Wilmington, January-November 1781." *North Carolina Historical Review*, 66:4 (October 1989), 387-411.

Massey, Gregory De Van. "The British Expedition to Wilmington, North Carolina, January-November, 1781." M. A. thesis, East Carolina University, 1987.

McEachern, Leora H., and Isabel M. Williams, eds.; introduction by Lawrence Lee. *Wilmington-New Hanover Safety Committee Minutes, 1774-1776*. Wilmington: Wilmington-New Hanover County American Revolution Bi-centennial Association, 1974.

McKellar, Wiley. "Smith Island." *Wildlife in North Carolina*, 33:10 (October 1969), 26-27. [Online description from "North Carolina Periodicals Index," East Carolina University: "Smith Island, more popularly known as Bald Head, is the state's most isolated coastal area and one of the last remaining wilderness areas along the Atlantic Coast. A familiar island landmark is the Coast Guard Lighthouse, built in 1817. The island is home to a number of wildlife species and contains numerous salt marsh areas. Visitors to the island are occasional, and the place can be reached only by boat. How long the island will remain untouched before it disappears under a conglomeration of concrete, beach houses, and hotels is unknown."]

"Memorial of Merchants, Traders and Others Residing at Cape Fear." Manuscript, "Miscellaneous Petitions, General Assembly Records, April-May 1780," Box 1, State Archives of North Carolina, Raleigh.

Moore, Louis T. "The House of Three Wars." *The State: A Weekly Survey of North Carolina*, 11:28 (December 1943), 6-7, 11; online: http://digital.ncdcr.gov/cdm/ref/collection/p16062coll18/id/18238. [Online description from "North Carolina Periodicals Index," East Carolina University: "The Cornwallis House built around 1770 in Wilmington functioned as a meeting house for military men in three different historic conflicts. During the Revolutionary War, Lord Cornwallis and his British officers established headquarters there after Wilmington's capture. Federal officers frequented the place for entertainment during the Civil War, especially after Wilmington's capture in 1865. Lastly, World War II brought American Army servicemen from Camp Davis, Fort Fisher, and Camp LeJeune as an officers' meeting place."]

Moore, Louis T. "How a Slave Preserved the Records of New Hanover County." *The State: A Weekly Survey of North Carolina*, 12:46 (April 1945), 7; online: http://digital.ncdcr.gov/cdm/ref/collection/p16062coll18/id/13027. [Online description from "North Carolina Periodicals Index," East Carolina University: "Moore recounts how Jeff Norment, a slave owned by Michael Cronly, saved and preserved New Hanover County's records from Gen. William T. Sherman's approaching Union army."]

Moore, Louis T. "Louis T. Moore Collection, 1766-1950." Manuscript PC.777 (MARS ID: 1287; record group), State Archives of North Carolina, Raleigh. [Online catalog description shows that this collection includes: "Items collected by Moore, chairman of New Hanover Historical Commission, including original of the London Chronicle, No. 1443 (Mar. 18-20, 1766), with news of Wilmington's resistance to the Stamp Act; newspaper clipping containing extracts (1774-1775) from letter book of William Hill, Brunswick merchant;...; Also typed copy of Griffith J. McRee's *Imperfect Sketch* (1846) of Wilmington history, 1730-1779; ..."]

Moore, Louis T. *Stories Old and New of the Cape Fear Region*. Wilmington: [s. n.], 1956.

New Hanover County. "New Hanover County Miscellaneous Records, 1756-1945: Miscellaneous Records Concerning the Revolution, 1776, 1789." Manuscript C.R.070.928.6, State Archives of North Carolina, Raleigh.

Norris, Jeannie Faris. "Restoring a Colorful Past Pays Off in the Present." *We the People of North Carolina*, 38:6 (June 1980), 24-26, 52-54. [Online description from "North Carolina Periodicals Index," East Carolina University: "Wilmington's traditions, history, and heritage is preserved in its historic district. Covering an area of thirty-five blocks, it is the largest in the country."]

North Carolina (State). General Assembly. "[Document dated:] January 20, 1779: Joint Papers, Committee Papers, Resolutions, Senate Bills, House Bills, Petition of John London." Manuscript; General Assembly Record Group; Session Records, January-February 1779, Box 1 (MARS ID: 66.8.15.9.2; item), State Archives of North Carolina, Raleigh. [Online catalog description: "London petitions Governor Caswell to permit him to stay in the state until he can petition the Assembly for citizenship; several Justices of the Peace in New Hanover County recommend London for citizenship."]

North Carolina (State). General Assembly. "[Document dated:] January 20, 1779: Joint Papers, Committee Papers, Resolutions, Senate Bills, House Bills, Petition of John London." Manuscript; General Assembly Record Group; Session Records, January-February 1779, Box 1 (MARS ID: 66.8.15.9.2; item), State Archives of North Carolina, Raleigh. [Online catalog description: "London petitions Governor Caswell to permit him to stay in the state until he can petition the Assembly for citizenship; several Justices of the Peace in New Hanover County recommend London for citizenship."]

North Carolina (State). General Assembly. "[Document dated:] January 23, 1779: Joint Papers, Committee Papers, Resolutions, Senate Bills, House Bills, Report of Committee on Citizenship on Petitions of Thomas Barker, Samuel Marshall, Robert Hogg, and Others (with Petitions and Messages)." Manuscript; General Assembly Record Group; Session Records, January-February 1779, Box 1 (MARS ID: 66.8.15.8.3), State Archives of North Carolina, Raleigh. [Online catalog description: "Includes testimony of Jonas Dunbibin and Thomas Walker, Justices of the Peace of New Hanover County." Names that appear are: Thomas Barker, John Burgwin, Jonas Dunbibin, Robert Hogg, Thomas Hooper, John London, Samuel Marshall, Samuel Peele, and Thomas Walker.]

North Carolina (State). General Assembly. "[Document dated:] January 28, 1779: Petition of a number of Inhabitants of New Hanover, Duplin, and Bladen Counties for Erecting a Separate County from the Above Counties." Manuscript; General Assembly Record Group; Session Records, January-February 1779, Box 1 (MARS ID: 66.8.15.9.8; item), January-February 1779, State Archives of North Carolina, Raleigh. [Online catalog description: "The petitioners refer to the difficulties they face in attending general musters and jury service at the courthouses of their respective counties and request that a new county be erected within the boundaries suggested."]

North Carolina (State). General Assembly. "[Document dated:] May 10, 1779: Joint Papers, Committee Papers, Resolutions, Senate Bills, House Bills, Petition of a Number of Inhabitants of New Hanover Co. for a Guard over the Salt Works (rejected)." Manuscript; General Assembly Record Group; Session Records, May 1779, Box 1 (MARS ID: 66.8.17.6.4; item), State Archives of North Carolina, Raleigh.

North Carolina (State). General Assembly. [Document dated:] October 23, 1779: Petition from the Adjoining Inhabitants of the Counties of New Hanover, Duplin & Bladen." Manuscript; General Assembly Session Records; Session of October-November 1778; Joint Papers, Committee Papers, Resolutions, Box 1 (MARS ID: 66.8.18.7.11; item), State Archives of North Carolina, Raleigh. [The purpose of this petition was to form a New County in Order to Help Facilitate Attendance of General Muster."]

North Carolina (State). General Assembly. "[Document dated:] October 25, 1779: Joint Papers, Committee Papers, Resolutions, Senate Bills, House Bills, Petition of Elizabeth Heron, Minor and Orphan Daughter of Benjamin Heron." Manuscript; General Assembly Record Group; Session Records, October-November 1779, Box 1 (MARS ID: 66.8.18.7.13; item), State Archives of North Carolina, Raleigh. [Online catalog description: "Heron, of New Hanover County, asks that the toll be raised for a bridge over the Cape Fear River which her father built at the request of the colonial assembly and bequeathed to her as her chief source of income. Given the depreciation of the currency and the bridge's need for repairs, the previous toll allowed by law is insufficient."]

North Carolina (State). General Assembly. "[Document dated:] January-February 1781: Joint Papers, Committee Papers, Resolutions, Senate Bills, House Bills, Joint Papers: Miscellaneous Accounts, Certificates, Bonds, and Letters." Manuscript; General Assembly Record Group; Session Records, January-February 1781, Box 1 (MARS ID: 66.8.23.6), State Archives of North Carolina, Raleigh. [Online catalog description shows that this collection includes: "…a letter to the speakers from Samuel Ashe describing the situation in the Wilmington area."]

North Carolina (State0. General Assembly. "[Document dated:] April 20, 1778: Joint Papers, Committee Papers, Resolutions, Senate Bills, House Bills, Resignation of Timothy Bloodworth as Justice of the Peace in New Hanover Co. (with Messages)." Manuscript; General Assembly Record Group; Session Records, Apr-May 1778, Box 1 (MARS ID: 66.8.12.16.9), State Archives of North Carolina, Raleigh.

North Carolina (State). General Assembly. "[Document dated:] April 17-24, 1780: Joint Papers, Committee Papers, Resolutions, Senate Bills, House Bills, Re[specting] the Election of William Hill of New Hanover County (with Petition, Letter of William Hill, and Poll List.)." Manuscript; General Assembly Record Group; Session Records, Apr-May 1780, Box 1 (MARS ID; 66.8.20.11.1; item), State Archives of North Carolina, Raleigh. [Online catalog description: "Fifteen inhabitants of Wilmington charge in a petition to the House that Hill's election was illegal because several voters were ineligible and because Hill already holds the positions of county trustee and customs official. By order of the committee, Thomas Person, chairman, issues a summons to Hill and to the sheriff of New Hanover County for the election returns. Upon receipt of the summons, Hill writes to Person, explaining the election, enclosing his certification of appointment as trustee, and resigning the seat. Also includes the poll list of the county."]

North Carolina (State). General Assembly. "[Document dated:] April-May 1780: Joint Papers, Committee Papers, Resolutions, Senate Bills, House Bills, Petition from the Inhabitants of Hanover (New Hanover) County." Manuscript; General Assembly Record Group; Session Records, Apr-May 1780, Box 1 (MARS ID: 66.8.20.7.3; item), State Archives of North Carolina, Raleigh. [Online catalog description: "The petitioners of Black River ask that Thomas Rogers be allowed to sell the horses and wagons he can take from a Tory neighborhood in order to recover the damages caused to him by Tories."]

North Carolina (State). General Assembly. "[Document dated:] April-May 1780: Joint Papers, Committee Papers, Resolutions, Senate Bills, House Bills, Election Certificates." Manuscript; General Assembly Record Group; Session Records, Apr-May 1780, Apr-May 1780, Box 1 (MARS ID: 66.8.20.5; folder), State Archives of North Carolina, Raleigh. [Online catalog description: "Includes election certificate from Onslow County and the election returns for New Hanover County and Wilmington."]

North Carolina (State). General Assembly. "[Document dated:] May 5, 1780: Joint Papers, Committee Papers, Resolutions, Senate Bills, House Bills, Report on the Election of John Ashe of New Hanover County." Manuscript; General Assembly Record Group; Session Records, Apr-May 1780, Box 1 (MARS ID: 66.8.20.10.3), State Archives of North Carolina, Raleigh. [Online catalog description: "The committee reports that Ashe's election appears to be illegal because he is a resident of New Bern, not New Hanover County, and that his seat should be vacated."]

North Carolina (State). General Assembly. "[Document dated:] April 19, 1782: Joint Papers, Committee Papers, Resolutions, Senate Bills, House Bills, Regarding the Elections in New Hanover Co. and the Town of Wilmington." Manuscript; General Assembly Record Group; Session Records, Apr-May 1780, Apr-May 1782, Box 2 (MARS ID: 66.8.28.3.1), Archives of North Carolina, Raleigh. [Online catalog description: "Committee report states that the elections for New Hanover Co. and Wilmington were illegally conducted and suggests that the seats be vacated; message from House to Senate refers petition of inhabitants of New Hanover County to committee."]

North Carolina (State). General Assembly. "[Document dated:] June 1, 1784: Joint Papers, Committee Papers, Resolutions, Senate Bills, House Bills, Resolution to Restore to Office Magistrates and Officers Who Had Sought Voluntary Capture by the British in New Hanover County (Rejected)." Manuscript; General Assembly Record Group; Session Records, Apr-May 1780, Apr-June 1784, Box 2 (MARS ID: 66.8.32.5.38; item), State Archives of North Carolina, Raleigh. [Online catalog description: "Memorial maintains that the men in question took arms against the British but were afraid that their families were in danger so sought paroles from the British in New Hanover County. Resolution restores them to office but is rejected."]

O'Brien, Frank. "Happy 250th Birthday, Orton!" *The State: Down Home in North Carolina*, 42:10 (March 1975), 16-17, 37; online: http://digital.ncdcr.gov/cdm/ref/collection/p16062coll18/id/9293. [Online description from "North Carolina Periodicals Index," East Carolina University: "Orton Plantation Gardens turned 250 in 1975. The columned mansion built in classic antebellum architectural style provides the focal point for the historic site, first owned by 'King' Roger Moore in pre-Revolutionary War days."]

Powell, John W. "George Reed." *Clarendon Courier*, 7 (Winter 1995), 79-81.

Pleasant, Paul. "History in Anecdotes." *The State: A Weekly Survey of North Carolina*, 19:43 (March 22, 1952), 20-21, 27; online: http://digital.ncdcr.gov/cdm/compoundobject/collection/p16062coll18/id/28357. [Online description from "North Carolina Periodicals Index," East Carolina University: "For 200 years, there has always been something fascinating happening in New Hanover County."]

Proceedings of the Safety Committee, for the Town of Wilmington, N. C.: From 1774 to 1776. Raleigh: T. Loring, 1844.

Pruitt, Albert Bruce. *Index to People & Places in New Hanover Co., NC, Deed Books A-AA (1726-1845)*. Whitakers: A. B. Pruitt, 2014.

Rankin, Richard, ed. "'Musquetoe' Bites: Caricatures of Lower Cape Fear Whigs and Tories on the Eve of the American Revolution." *North Carolina Historical Review*, 65:2 (April 1988), 173-207.

Rayburn, Richard H. "Infallible Power: The 'Musquetoe,' The Wilmington-New Hanover County Safety Committee, and the Coming of the Revolution in the Lower Cape Fear, 1775-1776." *North Carolina Historical Review*, 92:4 (October 2015), 387-425. [The "Musquetoe" was the pseudonym of Dr. James Fallon.]

Reaves, Bill. "Balance of the Books of Hogg & Campbell, Late of Wilmington, North Carolina, So Taken in February, 1778." *Clarendon Courier: Journal of the Old New Hanover Genealogical Society*, 6:4 (December 1994), 14-18.

Reaves, Bill. "Historic Wilmington: The Rouse House Massacre." *Coastal Carolinian*, 25 (August 1983).

Reaves, William M. "The Bill Reaves Collection." Manuscript, North Carolina Room, Main Library, New Hanover County Public Library, Wilmington. [The collection includes subject files on the Revolutionary War in North Carolina, the South, and New Hanover County and Wilmington in particular.]

Reilly, J. S. *Wilmington: Past, Present & Future, Embracing Historical Sketches of Its Growth and Progress from Its Establishment to the Present Time*. Wilmington: J.S. Reilly, 1884.

Rippy, J. Fred. "A View of the Carolinas in 1783." *North Carolina Historical Review,* 6:4 (October 1929), 362-370; online: http://digital.ncdcr.gov/cdm/ref/collection/p16062coll9/id/4207. [Online description from "North Carolina Periodicals Index," East Carolina University: "A summary of descriptions and accounts of visits to several towns in North and South Carolina in 1783 culled from the diary of Francisco de Miranda, known best as a leader and proponent of the independence movement in the Spanish-American Colonies. Includes details of the Ocracroke Inlet area, New Bern, Beaufort, and Wilmington."]

Seapker, Janet K. "St. John's Masonic Lodge: Part 1: Orange Street Lodge." *Lower Cape Fear Historical Society Bulletin*, 50:1 (January 2006), 1-8. [Online description from "North Carolina Periodicals Index," East Carolina University: "St. John's Masonic Lodge in Wilmington, the oldest Masonic lodge building in the state, celebrated its 250th anniversary in 2005. Few urban buildings have survived from this period because of fires and subsequent urban rebuilding, making St. John's a rare survivor."]

Sprunt, James. *A Colonial Plantation: Notes on Cape Fear History*. [S. l.: s. n., 1893-1895?] [Orton Plantation]

Sprunt, James Laurence. *The Story of Orton Plantation, As Gathered from Various Histories and Documents*. [Wilmington: S. L. Sprunt], 1958.

Stamp Defiance Chapter, North Carolina Daughters of the American Revolution. *Wilmington, Historic Colonial City*. [S. l.] F. W. Cox, 1952.

Strudwick Family. "Strudwick Family Papers, 1728-1831." Manuscript, Collection Number: 00701, Southern Historical Collection, Louis Round Wilson Special Collections Library, University of North Carolina at Chapel Hill; microfilmed: *Records of Ante-Bellum Southern Plantations from the Revolution through the Civil War. Series J, Selections from the Southern Historical Collection, Manuscript Department, Library of the University of North Carolina at Chapel Hill. Part 12, Tidewater and Coastal Plains North Carolina*. Bethesda, Md.: University Publications of America, 1992; reel 1.

Trawick, Gary E. "Attack from the Cypress Fort." *The State: Down Home in North Carolina*, 36 (August 1, 1968), 7-8; online: http://digital.ncdcr.gov/cdm/compoundobject/collection/p16062coll18/id/104008. [Online description from "North Carolina Periodicals Index," East Carolina University: "Colonel Thomas Bloodworth discovered a hollowed out Cyprus tree that he then used to harass the British who had occupied Wilmington during the American Revolutionary War."]

Tripp, Gladys Best. "The Old Cornwallis House." *The State: A Weekly Survey of North Carolina*, 7:8 (July 1939), 5, 22. [Online description from "North Carolina Periodicals Index," East Carolina University: "Located in Wilmington, the Cornwallis House is one of the finest examples of Colonial architecture to be found anywhere. It was built by John Burgwin, secretary to the Royal Governor in 1754. During the Revolutionary War it was used by General Cornwallis. Tripp lists individuals who have owned it since then. Recently the North Carolina Society of Colonial Dames purchased the house to restore it to serve as their state headquarters."]

Tucker, Harry Z. "In Old Wilmington." *The State: A Weekly Survey of North Carolina*, 11:20 (October 1943), 4, 25; online: http://digital.ncdcr.gov/cdm/ref/collection/p16062coll18/id/17972. [Online description from "North Carolina Periodicals Index," East Carolina University: "Immigrants settled Wilmington in 1730 and called it New Liverpool or Newton. In 1739 the city was incorporated and officially named Wilmington. Situated on a fresh-water harbor and near the Cape Fear River, Wilmington's maritime industry was always at the forefront. Shipbuilding and maritime trade accounted for the city's historic prosperity. Historically, ships from Wilmington engaged in naval encounters and privateering during the Revolutionary War, War of 1812 and Civil War."]

Waddell, Alfred Moore. *A History of New Hanover County and the Lower Cape Fear Region*. Wilmington: The Compiler, 1909.

Walker, John, 1741-1813. "Papers, 1735-1909." Manuscript PC.254, State Archives of North Carolina, Raleigh. ["Papers of Major Walker, merchant, planter, and Revolutionary War officer. Deeds and grants relate to his lands in New Hanover Co." Online catalog description shows that this collection also includes: "Letters (1780) from Michael Levy in Edenton and New Bern concern trade and news of British in Virginia. Other items include list of slave births and deaths (1781-1810);…"]

Watson, Alan D. *Wilmington: Port of North Carolina*. Columbia: University of South Carolina Press, 1992.

Willcox, George W. "Profile of an Irish Lady: Bridget Day Beatty." *Lower Cape Fear Historical Society Bulletin*, 37:3 (May 1993), 1-8. [Online description from "North Carolina Periodicals Index," East Carolina University: "Bridgett Day Beatty was an interesting and prominent woman in 18th- and 19th-century Wilmington." Bridgett Day Beatty (1748-1804)]

Wilmington. Committee of Correspondence. *Gentlemen, At this conjuncture of British politics when the liberty and property of North-American subjects are at stake ... To avoid such imputations to this part of the province, we, the subscribers appointed a Committee of Correspondence for the town and district of Wilmington, at a most respectable meeting of the freeholders of this district.* Wilmington: Printed by Adam Boyd, 1774; micropublished: (Early American Imprints. First Series. No. 42754) New York: Readex Microprint, 1985.

Wilmington. Committee of Safety. *Proceedings of the Safety Committee for the Town of Wilmington, N. C., from 1774 to 1776.* Raleigh: T. Loring, 1844.

Wilmington, North Carolina: Past, Present and Future: A History of Its Harbor, with Detailed Reports of the Work for Improving and Restoring the Same, Now Being Conducted by the U. S. Government: Resources and Advantages as an Entrepot for Western Cities: Harbor of Refuge, and Coaling Depot for the Navy and Merchant Marine. Wilmington: Chamber of Commerce, 1872; reprinted: Chapel Hill: Academic Affairs Library, University of North Carolina at Chapel Hill, 2002; online: http://docsouth.unc.edu/nc/wilming72/wilming72.html.

[Women of Wilmington, N. C.]. "Petition of the Whig Women of Wilmington, North Carolina." In Cynthia A. Kierner, ed., *Revolutionary America, 1750-1815: Sources and Interpretation* (Upper Saddle River, N. J.: Prentice Hall, 2003), 191-193.

Women of Wilmington, North Carolina. "[Petition] To His Excellency Gov. Alex Martin and the Members of the Honorable Council," Early American Women Writers. Online at: http://www.eaww.uconn.edu/writings/women_of_wilmington.html. [Signed by the following women: Anne Hooper, Ann Towkes, Mary Allen, M. Hand, Sarah Nash, S. Wilkings, Mary Nash, M. Lord, Mary Moore, Isabella Read, E. Nash, Sally Read, Sarah Moore, Mary Granger, M. Loyd, Jane Ward, Catharine Young, Hannah Ward, J. M. Drayton, Kitty Ward, E. Wilkings.]

Wood, Tom. "Contributions to North Carolina Colonial History by the Roger and James Moore Family: Address Given by Tom Wood at the November 11, 2000, Meeting of the North Carolina Society of the Cincinnati in Washington, D. C." Typescript, North Carolina Room, New Hanover County Public Library, Wilmington.

Wrenn, Tony P. *Wilmington, North Carolina: An Architectural and Historical Portrait.* 2 vols. Wilmington: The Junior League of Wilmington, 1977; reprinted: Charlottesville: University Press of Virginia for the Junior League of Wilmington, N. C., Inc., 1984.

Wyche, Blonnie Bunn. *An Abbreviate Sketch: Colonial Brunswick and Wilmington.* [Wilmington?]: Lower Cape Fear Historical Society, [2000?].

Northampton County

[Note: For various state government documents relating to Northampton County during the Revolutionary period, search the MARS online catalog using the advanced search: http://mars.archives.ncdcr.gov/AdvancedSearch.aspx. Use the "Year" search box to restrict the searching to 1775-1783 and enter the county's name in the "Subjects" box, and hit the "Search" button near the top. This will retrieve any cataloged document for the county from that time period. These materials can vary considerably from personal or county petitions to the General Assembly, Loyalist matters, land disputes and claims, tax collection, exemptions from taxation, payments to county veterans, county divisions, personal collections, genealogical material, British claims against North Carolinians, etc. There is considerable information in these materials that could provide interesting documentation for persons living during the Revolution. The results will also include all of the wills and probates recorded in the county during the period set for the search. We had hoped to include many of these listings in this guide, but they are too voluminous. Citations to many of these search results for the eastern counties do, however, appear in the text.]

"Colonel Allen Jones." In Weynette Parks Haun, *North Carolina Revolutionary Army Accounts Secretary of State Treasurer's and Comptroller's Papers Journal "A" (Public Accounts), 1775-1776* (Durham: W. P. Haun, 1988), 20-22. [Company roll or muster roll?]

Council Family. "Council Family Papers, 1733-1892." Manuscript PC.525 (MARS ID: 1035; record group), State Archives of North Carolina, Raleigh. [Online catalog description: "Unbound fragmentary account book belonging to the Counsell/Council family of Northampton Co. Retail sales of rum and sugar are recorded (1733-1734), and there are isolated notations about debts and estates, several (1759-1793) concerning Charles Council. Also recorded are birth dates of family members and a few slaves (1727-1892)."]

Great Britain. Treasury. "[Claim of] Cuming, Warwick and Co., North Carolina and Virginia, 1 Aug. 1775 Copy of a manuscript in the National Archives of the United Kingdom (formerly the Public Records Office), Kew, Richmond, Surrey, England; 77.2393.1-2 (MARS ID: 21.111.29.20; folder), "British Records Collection," State Archives of North Carolina, Raleigh. [Online catalog description: "An abstract of a 'List of debts due . . . Northampton Store, No. Carolina, August, 1st 1775.' [Prepared, 1798?]."]

Johnson, Rufus, and Jerry Dickerson. *Treasures of the Roanoke Valley: Historical and Interesting Sites in Halifax and Northampton Counties*. Gaston: J. Dickerson; Roanoke Rapids: Printed by River Stone Graphics, 2000.

Norris, Jeannie Faris. "Boundary Disputes." *Popular Government*, 20:6 (March 1954), 5. [Online description from "North Carolina Periodicals Index," East Carolina University: "Northampton and Halifax counties have recently appointed a commission to establish the dividing line between the two counties. Long a matter of controversy, the issue has recently become serious due to the impending construction by the Virginia Electric and Power Company of the Roanoke Rapids Dam."]

North Carolina (State). General Assembly. "[Document dated:] April 30, 1783." Manuscript; General Assembly Record Group; Session Records; Joint Papers, Committee Papers, Resolutions; Joint Senate Committees: Reports and Papers, April 19-May 2, 1783; April-May 1783, Box 1 (MARS ID: 66.8.29.8.12); State Archives of North Carolina, Raleigh. [Online catalog description: "Petition is an attempt to reinstate Joseph Wood to post of justice of the peace in Northampton County."]

Northampton County. "Miscellaneous Records, 1774-1936." Manuscript, CR.071.928.13-CR.071.928.18, State Archives of North Carolina, Raleigh. [Online catalog description: Includes … "notice by Thomas Green offering services to claimants for Revolutionary War services, 1843."]

Northampton County. "Northampton County Miscellaneous Records, 1774-1936: Certificate of Revolutionary War Service of Edmond Jordan [1833]." Manuscript C.R.071.928.13, State Archives of North Carolina, Raleigh.

"Northampton County Militia under the Command of Colonel Allin Jones." In Weynette Parks Haun, *North Carolina Revolutionary Army Accounts, Part I, Secretary of State Treasurer's & Comptroller's Papers Journal "A", (Public Accounts) 1775-1776* (Durham: W. P. Haun, 1988), 20-22.

Society for the Propagation of the Gospel in Foreign Parts. "St. George's Parish, Northampton Co., Letter from Rev. C. E. Taylor to [Sec. SPG]. May 17, 1774." Manuscript Z.5.223 (MARS ID: 21.5.5.48; folder), State Archives of North Carolina, Raleigh. [Online catalog description: "Wants books; lawless state of the province; dissenters very troublesome; Rev. Devereux Jarrat; his parish flourishes; recommends Hezekiah Ford of Va. for holy orders."]

Society for the Propagation of the Gospel in Foreign Parts. "London. Extract from Minutes of the General Meeting of the Society for the Propagation of the Gospel. Oct. 21, 1774." Manuscript and microfilm 237-238 (MARS ID: 21.9.20.6; folder), State Archives of North Carolina, Raleigh. [Online catalog description: Letter read from Rev. Charles Taylor, Northampton Co., dated 17 May 1774."]

Society for the Propagation of the Gospel in Foreign Parts. "Bertie Co. Letter from Rev. C. E. Taylor to [Sec., SPG], Oct. 13, 1783." Manuscript Z.5.294 (MARS ID: 21.6.3.21; folder), State Archives of of North Carolina, Raleigh. [Online catalog description: "Report on his activities during the war. Was before 1776 'happy in St. George's Parish,' Northampton Co., with 'two new and elegant Churches built for me, and two others enlarged and beautified,' but all was changed by war; resigned his parish on declaration of independence, when establishment ceased; 'I could not labour, and to beg was ashamed," therefore was reduced to selling his land and houses to support his wife and five children; during war officiated on the coast and elsewhere, baptising many; serves Halifax Town since July, because a sum was raised for him there; no more than five clergy in province, and Methodists make great inroads; 'The Gentleman who presides at present in No. Carolina' has told him that he would encourage an orthodox clergy, but the assembly refuses any establishment; wishes to be recalled to England, but in any event wants assistance from the Society since he has received no salary for seven years and is in danger of confinement for debt'."]

Onslow County [Wilmington District]

[Note: For various state government documents relating to Onslow County during the Revolutionary period, search the MARS online catalog using the advanced search: http://mars.archives.ncdcr.gov/AdvancedSearch.aspx. Use the "Year" search box to restrict the searching to 1775-1783 and enter the county's name in the "Subjects" box, and hit the "Search" button near the top. This will retrieve any cataloged document for the county from that time period. These materials can vary considerably from personal or county petitions to the General Assembly, Loyalist matters, land disputes and claims, tax collection, exemptions from taxation, payments to county veterans, county divisions, personal collections, genealogical material, British claims against North Carolinians, etc. There is considerable information in these materials that could provide interesting documentation for persons living during the Revolution. The results will also include all of the wills and probates recorded in the county during the period set for the search. We had hoped to include many of these listings in this guide, but they are too voluminous. Citations to many of these search results for the eastern counties do, however, appear in the text.]

"1777 Onslow Field Return." *Quarterly Review of the Eastern North Carolina Genealogical Society*, 14:1 (March 1987), 27.

"Ballotted Men and Volunteers from Onslow County to Serve Nine Months as Continental Soldiers Beginning 1 March 1779." *North Carolinian, Quarterly Journal of Genealogy & History*, 6:3 (September 1960), 728. [Names, ages, places of birth]

Bellamy, Donnie D. "Slavery in Microcosm: Onslow County, North Carolina." *Journal of Negro History*, 62:4 (October 1977), 339-350.

Brown, Joseph Parsons. *The Commonwealth of Onslow: A History*. New Bern: Owen G. Dunn Company, 1960.

"Captain John King's Company of Militia from Onslow County on an Expedition against the Insurgents." In Weynette Parks Haun, *North Carolina Revolutionary Army Accounts, Part I, Secretary of State Treasurer's & Comptroller's Papers Journal "A", (Public Accounts) 1775-1776* (Durham: W. P. Haun, 1988), 30.

Dean, Earl. "Onslow County's Six Courthouses." *The State: A Weekly Survey of North Carolina*, 17:10 (August 1949), 10. [Online description from "North Carolina Periodicals Index," East Carolina University: "Of all North Carolina's one hundred courthouses, few have had as exciting a history as Onslow County's second seat of justice. Six courthouses were built before one would stay put."]

Dulin, Sugar, 1763-1845. "Sugar Dulin Autobiographical Sketch, ca. 1833." Manuscript 5339-z, Southern Historical Collection, Louis Round Wilson Special Collections Library, University of North Carolina at Chapel Hill. [Online catalog description: "Sugar Dulin was born in Onslow County, N.C. He moved to Mecklenburg County, N.C., in 1791, where he bought a large tract of land east of Charlotte and lived until his death in 1845. Dulin fought as a soldier in the Revolutionary War. The collection consists of an autobiographical sketch, written by Dulin circa 1833. Most of the information relates to his time as a soldier during the Revolutionary War. Dulin detailed troop movements, locations, and orders. He described his surroundings and mentioned the names of fellow soldiers and officers. At one point, Dulin repeated a friend's story of being shot by the Whigs while at home. Also included is a short overview of his life, giving his place and date of birth and describing his joining the army and later moving to Mecklenberg County. The only date mentioned in the sketches is 1781."]

Dunaway, Stewart E. *Onslow County Road Records (1775-1889), Bridge Records (1779-1875).* Hillsborough: North Carolina Historical Books, 2013. [Note: While not specifically concerning the Revolution, these sources can be used in tandem with land records and other documents to help locate places of residence, occupations, geographical features, and place names.]

Dunaway, Stewart E. *Onslow County, North Carolina, Mill Records (1765-1861), Ferry Records (1774-1906).* Hillsborough: North Carolina Historical Books, 2010. [Note: While not specifically concerning the Revolution, these sources can be used in tandem with land records and other documents to help locate places of residence, occupations, geographical features, and place names.]

"Field Return of the Onslow County Militia, 1777, with the Names of Commissioned Officers." *Quarterly Review of the Eastern North Carolina Genealogical Society*, 14:2 (March 1987), 30.

Green, Ann. "Swansboro, Quaint Village Is Former Port." *Coastwatch*, (Spring 2000), 28-29, [Online description from "North Carolina Periodicals Index," East Carolina University: "Settled around 1730, Swansboro, in Onslow County, was a busy Revolutionary War port with a major shipbuilding industry. After the Civil War, the shipping industry declined and was replaced by lumber and fishing interests. Today Swansboro is a picturesque town filled with shops, restaurants, and historic homes, a place many tourists miss in their haste to reach their beach rentals."]

Hairr, John. "The Eye of the Storm." *Our State: Down Home in North Carolina*, 64:6 (November 1996), 36-37; online: http://digital.ncdcr.gov/cdm/ref/collection/p16062coll18/id/34245. [Online description from "North Carolina Periodicals Index," East Carolina University: "Hurricanes have been a threat to the state for centuries. In 1752, a powerful storm destroyed the town of Johnston, then the county seat of Onslow County, taking lives and property, and bringing government to a halt by scattering deeds and other documents."]

Ijames, Earl. "Hurricane Warning! The Storm of 1752." *Tar Heel Junior Historian*, 48:2 (Spring 2009), 28; online: http://ncpedia.org/climate/hurricanes/18th-century-hurricanes. [Online description from "North Carolina Periodicals Index," East Carolina University: "The 1752 hurricane hit Onslow County's barrier islands and destroyed the New River Inlet, crops, timber and livestock. Equally devastating was complete destruction of the courthouse and all public records. The General Assembly approved construction of a new courthouse further inland than Johnston at Wantland's Ferry, later known as Snead's Ferry."]

Lewis, J. D. "Patriot Leaders in North Carolina: George Mitchell: Captain in the Salisbury District Minutemen - 1775-1776; Captain in the 6th NC Regiment - 1776-1777; Captain in the Onslow County Regiment of Militia - 1777-1780; Major in the Onslow County Regiment of Militia – 1780; Colonel in the Onslow County Regiment of Militia - 1780-1783." Online: http://www.carolana.com/NC/Revolution/patriot_leaders_nc_george_mitchell.html.

"Men from Onslow County Volunteering for Duty in the North Carolina Continental Line, September 3, 1778." *Quarterly Review of the Eastern North Carolina Genealogical Society*, 14:1 (March 1987), 30. [Includes residence, place of birth, age, physical description.]

Morton, Ted. "My Patriot: Conducting a Search for an Elusive Ancestor." Palmetto Patriot: South Carolina Society Sons of the American Revolution, Palmetto Patriot: South Carolina Society Sons of the American Revolution, 2008:2 (Summer 2008), 7; online: http://www.scssar.org . [Caleb Smith, ca. 1755-1811 (Onslow County, N. C.]

North Carolina (State). General Assembly. "[Document Dated]: February 13, 1781: That Militia Company Be Reaised for Defense of Sea Coast of Onslow County." Manuscript; General Assembly Record Group; Session Records, January-February 1781; Joint Papers, Committee Papers, Resolutions, House Joint Resolutions: February 12-14, Box 1 (MARS ID: 66.8.23.19.11; item), State Archives of North Carolina, Raleigh. [Online catalog description: "The resolution directs that the company be stationed at the mouth of the White Oak River."]

North Carolina (State). General Assembly. "[Document dated:] April-May 1777: Joint Papers, Committee Papers, Resolutions, Senate Bills, House Bills, Papers Concerning Justices of the Peace and Militia Officer

Appointments, 1777." Manuscript; General Assembly Record Group; Session Records, Apr-May 1777, Box 1 (MARS ID: 66.8.9.8), State Archives of North Carolina, Raleigh. [Online catalog description: "Documents concerning Governor Caswell's appointment of officers to the militia regiments of Cumberland and Chatham counties, and his appointments of Justices of the Peace for Onslow and Pasquotank counties."]

North Carolina (State). General Assembly. "[Document Dated]: June 29, 1781: For Raising Company of Light Horse in Onslow County (Messages Only)." Manuscript; General Assembly Record Group; Session Records; Joint Papers, Committee Papers, Resolutions, June-July 1781, Box 1 (MARS ID: 66.8.25.13.4), State Archives of North Carolina, Raleigh.

North Carolina (State). General Assembly. "[Document Dated]: June-July 1781: Justices of the Peace and Militia Officers – Recommendations and Resignations." Manuscript; General Assembly Record Group; Session Records, June-July 1781; Joint Papers, Committee Papers, Resolutions, Box 1 (MARS ID: 66.8.25.5; folder), State Archives of North Carolina, Raleigh. [Online catalog description: "Contains several recommendations, resignations, and appointments for justices of the peace and the militia, as well as one commission from the governor for the justices of the peace for Onslow County."]

Onslow County. "Onslow County Miscellaneous Records, 1732-1950: Bounty Claims, 1777-1806." Manuscript C.R.072.928.1, State Archives of North Carolina, Raleigh.

Onslow County. "Onslow County Miscellaneous Records, 1732-1950: Jury Lists, 1756-1839." Manuscript C.R.072.928.4, State Archives of North Carolina, Raleigh.

Onslow County. "Onslow County Miscellaneous Records, 1732-1950: Military Records, 1778-1865." Manuscript C.R.072.928.6, State Archives of North Carolina, Raleigh.

Onslow County. "Onslow County Miscellaneous Records, 1732-1950: Oath to Support the Constitution, 1777." Manuscript C.R.072.928.6, State Archives of North Carolina, Raleigh.

Onslow County. "Onslow County Miscellaneous Records, 1732-1950: petition to Clear John Simpson of Responsibility in the Loss of Funds Due the Assembly." Manuscript C.R.072.928.6, State Archives of North Carolina, Raleigh.

Onslow County. "Onslow County Miscellaneous Records, 1732-1950: Salt Works, 1782." Manuscript C.R.072.928.8. State Archives of North Carolina, Raleigh.

Onslow County. "Onslow County Miscellaneous Records, 1732-1950: Slave Records (Bills of Sale), 1763-1869." Manuscript C.R.072.928.9, State Archives of North Carolina, Raleigh.

Onslow County. "Onslow County Miscellaneous Records, 1732-1950: Slave Records (Civil Actions-Runaways), 1763-1868." Manuscript C.R.072.928.6, State Archives of North Carolina, Raleigh.

"Onslow County Conscripts, 1778." *Quarterly Review of the Eastern North Carolina Genealogical Society*, 14:1 (March 1987), 30. [This includes residence, place of birth, age, and physical description.]

"Onslow County Militia List, 1778." *The Quarterly Review of the Eastern North Carolina Genealogical Society*, 5:4 (Fall 1978), 168-169.

"Onslow County Recruiting Officer Report, 1777." *Quarterly Review of the Eastern North Carolina Genealogical Society*, 14:1 (March 1987), 29.

"Onslow County, March 10th, 1779, a Return of Volunteers and Drafted Men." *Quarterly Review of the Eastern North Carolina Genealogical Society,* 14:1 (March 1987), 31. [While it does not specifically state these men are being drafted into the Continental Line, if you read the top paragraph on the opposite page, it becomes clear that was what was happening. As the need for the Continental Line troops increased, militiamen were drafted or enlisted into the Continental Line. (This analysis is by the Genealogy Office, Office of the Registrar General, National Society Daugthers of the American Revolution, Washington, D. C.]

"Onslow Militia Volunteers and Draftees, 1779." *Quarterly Review of the Eastern North Carolina Genealogical Society*, 14:1 (March 1987), 31.

Owens, Dave. "How Snead's Ferry Got Its Name." *The State: Down Home in North Carolina*, 42:1 (June 1974), 14, 20; online: http://digital.ncdcr.gov/cdm/ref/collection/p16062coll18/id/56658. [Online description from "North Carolina Periodicals Index," East Carolina University: "The present-day village of Sneads Ferry gets its name from the ferry crossing first used before the Revolutionary War. In 1760, Robert Snead operated a tavern on the south shore of the New River. Presently, the entire southern shore of the New River, from the old ferry crossing to the mouth of the river, is known as Sneads Ferry."]

North Carolina (State). General Assembly. "Joint Papers (April-May 1780): Election Certificates." Manuscript; General Assembly Record Group; Session Records, Apr-May 1780, Box 1 (MARS ID: 66.8.20.5; folder), State Archives of North Carolina, Raleigh. [Online catalog description: "Includes election certificate from Onslow County and the election returns for New Hanover County and Wilmington."]

Powell, John W. "George Reed." *Clarendon Courier*, 7:4 (Winter 1995), 79-81. [Revolutionary War pension application of Reed who was originally from Onslow County, North Carolina, but moved to Warrick County, Indiana]

"A Return of the Captured Deserters from the 6th & 8th North Carolina Regiments Delivered to Captain Daniel Williams, 6th Regiment, October 30, 1777." *Quarterly Review of the Eastern North Carolina Genealogical Society*, 14:1 (March 1987), 29.

Still, William N., Jr. "Shipbuilding and Boatbuilders in Swansboro, 1800-1950." *Tributaries*, 5:1 (October 1995), 7-14. [Online description from "North Carolina Periodicals Index," East Carolina University: "Shipbuilding was a tradition in Onslow County even before its boundaries were officially drawn in 1734. This shipbuilding tradition was not limited to small riverine craft and dugouts but included large vessels and steamboats. Swansboro was the main location for these boatbuilding endeavors constituting over half of the vessels built within the county."]

Stone-Wilson, Georgie. *New River: The Jewel of Onslow County*. Akron, Ohio: 48Hr Books, 2012.

Stone-Wilson, Georgie. *New River: The Jewel of Onslow County, A Sequel*. Akron, Ohio: 48Hr Books, 2012.

Orange County and Hillsborough

[Note: For various state government documents relating to Orange County and Hillsborough during the Revolutionary period, search the MARS online catalog using the advanced search: http://mars.archives.ncdcr.gov/AdvancedSearch.aspx. Use the "Year" search box to restrict the searching to 1775-1783 and enter the county's or the town's name in the "Subjects" box, and hit the "Search" button near the top. This will retrieve any cataloged document for the county from that time period. These materials can vary considerably from personal or county petitions to the General Assembly, Loyalist matters, land disputes and claims, tax collection, exemptions from taxation, payments to county veterans, county divisions, personal collections, genealogical material, British claims against North Carolinians, etc. There is considerable information in these materials that could provide interesting documentation for persons living during the Revolution. The results will also include all of the wills and probates recorded in the county during the period set for the search. We had hoped to include many of these listings in this guide, but they are too voluminous. Citations to many of these search results for the eastern counties do, however, appear in the text.]

Benton, Jesse. *Jesse Benton Letters (1780-1790), Hartford, Hillsborough, N. C.* [North Carolina: S. E. Dunaway; Morrisville: Lulu.com, 2009. [Publisher's description: "The Jesse Benton papers are a collection of letters written by Jesse Benton to Thomas Hart. Thomas Hart was the owner of a mill complex, which he named Hartford .... Jesse Benton ... was a lawyer in ... [the] county seat of Orange County. All of these original letters reside in the Library of Congress."]

Butler, Lindley S. "200 Years Ago and Lindley's Mill." *The State: Down Home in North Carolina*, 49:5 (October 1981), 12-13; online: http://digital.ncdcr.gov/cdm/ref/collection/p16062coll18/id/60425. [Online description from "North Carolina Periodicals Index," East Carolina University: "On September 12, 1781, Loyalist partisan Colonel David Fanning and his militia surrounded the temporary state capital, Hillsborough. The one-thousand-man force successfully captured state officers, army officials, and Governor Thomas Burke. While Fanning marched his men to loyalist stronghold Wilmington, Whig general John Butler quickly assembled 400 militia at the mill of Quaker Thomas Lindley to block Fanning. The Whigs were overpowered, however, and the Loyalists were able to deliver their prisoners to Major James H. Craig in Wilmington."]

Cates, Larry W. "A Bitter Legacy: The Revolution's Effect on the Summers Estate." *North Carolina Genealogical Society Journal*, 40:1 (February 2014), 51-67. [John Summers/Somers of Orange County]

"Chatham, Orange, Randolph, and Surry Counties: Men who Enlisted in the Continental Line, 1780." *North Carolinian, Quarterly Journal of Genealogy & History*, 6:3 (September 1960), 728-729.

Colton, Henry E. "Towns of the Revolution – Hillsborough, N. C." *Southern Literary Messenger* [Richmond, Va.], 23:3 (September 1856), 161-176; online at Memory of America, University of Michigan, website.

Cooke, Robert Bruce. "Robert Bruce Cooke Papers, 1757-1786, 1962." Manuscript PC.1256, State Archives of North Carolina, Raleigh. [Online catalog description: "Letter (1962) from Cooke describing his efforts to separate the identities of two prominent colonials, Thomas Lloyd of Orange Co. and Thomas Lloyd of New Hanover Co., with abstracts from Colonial and State Records of North Carolina and New Hanover Co. court minutes."]

Davie Poplar Chapter, North Carolina Daughters of the American Revolution. "Orange Co. N.C. Revolutionary Soldiers." *North Carolina DAR Genealogical Records Committee Report, Series 1, Volume 214: Orange*

County, NC Wills, [and Other Records] (typescript, 1957), 115; digital surrogate, DAR Library, Washington, D.C.

Dixon, Simon. "Recollections of Lord Cornwallis' Encampment at Dixon's Mill, Orange County, 1781." Typescript Cp398 D62r, North Carolina Collection, Louis Round Wilson Special Collections Library, University of North Carolina at Chapel Hill. [Online catalog description: "Copied by Eleanor L. Fox from original in possession of Mrs. W.A. White, of Guilford College. Simon Dixon, son of Benjamin, who was the youngest son of the first Simon Dixon, wrote the above recollections ... Eleanor L. Fox, July 1935. Poetry.]

Dula, Lucile Noell. "Ancient Inn Is Restored." *The State: A Weekly Survey of North Carolina*, 15:10 (August 1947), 10; online: http://digital.ncdcr.gov/cdm/ref/collection/p16062coll18/id/21037. [Online description from "North Carolina Periodicals Index," East Carolina University: "You can now dine and sleep in the same old building, The Colonial Inn, in Hillsboro, where Lord Cornwallis once held forth."]

Dunaway, Stewart E. *Orange County, North Carolina, Mill Records (1782-1859).* Hillsborough: North Carolina Historical Books, 2010. [Note: While not specifically concerning the Revolution, these sources can be used in tandem with land records and other documents to help locate places of residence, occupations, geographical features, and place names.]

Engstrom, Mary C. "The Hartford Mill Complex during the Revolution." *Eno Journal*, 7 (July 1978); online: http://www.enoriver.org/store/journals/volume-7-special-issue/hartford-mill/.

Fraser, James. "James Fraser Papers, 1779-1789." Manuscript, David M. Rubenstein Rare Book & Manuscript Library, Duke University, Durham. [Description: "Copies of deeds, affidavits, a bill of sale for Negroes, inventories of real and personal property, and a catalog of books of the property of a Presbyterian clergyman of Hillsborough, North Carolina, who fled as a Loyalist to New Brunswick and later to Halifax during the American Revolution. Fraser's Hillsborough estate, 'Hartford,' was used by Cornwallis as British headquarters in Hillsborough and later occupied and, according to Fraser, damaged by American troops."]

Goerch, Carl. "Orange County." *The State: A Weekly Survey of North Carolina*, 9:40 (March 1942), 1-3, 16-18; online: http://digital.ncdcr.gov/cdm/ref/collection/p16062coll18/id/43517. [Online description from "North Carolina Periodicals Index," East Carolina University: "Goerch continues his travels to the state's counties, this time reaching Orange County, a place he describes as 'so full of history that it's hard to decide where to start.' He highlights some of the history, burial sites of famous North Carolinians, and historic homes."]

Haun, Weynette Parks. *Orange County, North Carolina Court Minutes, 1777-1786, Book 3.* Durham: W. P. Haun, 1991. [This volume contains many civil service appointments and some oaths of allegiance.]

Jacobs, Barry. "Sitting Pretty." *Tar Heel,* 6:3 (May/June 1978), 26-29. [Online description from "North Carolina Periodicals Index," East Carolina University: "Founded in 1754, Hillsborough, the county seat of Orange County, is a historic spot of serenity in the midst of the bustling, urban Piedmont. Jacobs takes the reader on a guided tour, discussing places and memorable events."]

Johnson, William Perry. "Orange County, 1779 Tax List (Early Settlers in Alamance, Orange, and Durham Counties)." *Journal of North Carolina Genealogy*, 15:2 (Summer 1969), 2349-2365.

Jones, H. B., with David Southern. *Miss Mary's Money: Fortune and Misfortune in a Carolina Plantation Family, 1760-1924*. Jefferson: McFarland and Company, 2015. [Francis Jones (1760-1844) and his descendants through his daughter Delia Jones Smith. Orange and Chatham Counties. Publisher's description: "The Smith fortune was made by Mary's grandfather, Revolutionary War veteran Francis Jones, and survived the profligacy of his son-in-law, Dr. James Smith, before being willed to the university and the North Carolina Episcopal diocese. Hundreds of descendants have been virtually ignored. This book, the result of eight years of research, is for them."]

Leffler, Hugh T., and Paul Wager, editors. *Orange County –1752-1952*. Chapel Hill: Orange Printshop, 1953.

Lewis, J. D. "Patriot Leaders in North Carolina: William Moore: Major in the Orange County Regiment of Militia - 1775-1776; Lt. Colonel in the Northern Orange County Regiment of Militia - 1776-1777; Colonel in the Caswell County Regiment of Militia - 1777-1782." Online: http://www.carolana.com/NC/Revolution/patriot_leaders_nc_william_moore.html.

Nash, Francis. "Historic Hillsboro." *North Carolina Booklet*, 3:4 (August 1903), 5-18; online: http://digital.ncdcr.gov/cdm/ref/collection/p249901coll37/id/14180. [Online description from "North Carolina Periodicals Index," East Carolina University: "An account of the history and establishment of Hillsboro in Orange County, North Carolina."]

Nash, Francis. "The History of Orange County – Part I." *North Carolina Booklet*, 10:2 (October 1910), 55-113; online: http://digital.ncdcr.gov/cdm/ref/collection/p249901coll37/id/14180. [Online description from "North Carolina Periodicals Index," East Carolina University: "The history of Orange County, North Carolina began the 1752 creation of the county by an act of the Assembly. This survey of county history covers from settlement through to the establishment of an academic academy during the 1780s."]

Nash, Frank, and John J. Parker. *Hillsboro: Colonial and Revolutionary*. Raleigh: Edwards & Broughton, printers, 1903; reprinted: Chapel Hill: Orange Printshop, 1953.

North Carolina (State). General Assembly. "[Document dated:] October 19, 1779: Resolution Exempting Certain Persons from Taxes (Orange County and Wilkes County) (with Messages)." Manuscript; General Assembly Record Group; Session Records, October-November 1779, Joint Papers, Committee Papers, Resolutions, Senate Bills, House Bills, House Joint Resolutions, Box 1 (MARS ID: 66.8.18.13.2), State Archives of North Carolina, Raleigh. [Online catalog description: "The Wilkes County Court of Pleas and Quarter Sessions recommends that John Murphy, John Fugit, and Robert Jones, being poor, old, and infirm, be exempted from paying taxes; the Orange County Court recommends likewise on behalf of John May. The Assembly concurs with both courts."]

Orange County. "Insolvents, 1773-1887." Manuscript, State Archives of North Carolina, Raleigh. [Consult the State Archives to determine the exact years that are available.]

Orange County. "Jury Records, 1772-1878." Manuscript, State Archives of North Carolina, Raleigh. [Consult the State Archives to determine the exact years that are available.]

Orange County. "Orange County Miscellaneous Record, 1768-1942: Commissioners of Confiscated Property, 1780, 1783, 1803." Manuscript C.R.073.928.10, State Archives of North Carolina, Raleigh.

Orange County. "Orange County Miscellaneous Record, 1768-1942: Revolutionary War Claims, 1818-1836 [for Pensions]." Manuscript C.R.073.928.13, State Archives of North Carolina, Raleigh.

Orange County. "Orange County Miscellaneous Record, 1768-1942: Tax Records, 1781-1881 and no date." Manuscript C.R.073.928.14, State Archives of North Carolina, Raleigh.

Orange County. "Slave Records, 1783-1865." Manuscript, State Archives of North Carolina, Raleigh. [Consult the State Archives to determine the exact years that are available.]

"Orange County Militia under the Command of Colonel Ambrose Ramsey, August 1776." In William L Saunders, Ed., *Colonial Records of North Carolina, Vol 10* (Wilmington: Broadfoot, 1993), 753-754.

"Revolutionary War Soldiers, North Carolina: From Monument at New Hope Presbyterian Church in Orange County, N. C.: In Memory of Known Revolutionary War Soldiers of New Hope Community, 1775-1783." *Southern Genealogist's Exchange Quarterly*, 11:whole no. 55 (Fall 1970), 7.

"Roll of Officers and Private Soldiers Detached from the first or Southern Battalion of the Militia of the County of Orange to March against the Hostile Indians under the Command of Colonel Ambrose Ramsey." In William L. Saunders, col. and ed. *The Colonial Records of North Carolina, Vol. 10: 1775-1776*. Raleigh: Josephus Daniels, 1890), 753-754.

Sharpe, Bill. "Orange Finishes 200 Years." The State: A Weekly Survey of North Carolina, 21:18 (October 1953), 1-3, 14-18; online: http://digital.ncdcr.gov/cdm/ref/collection/p16062coll18/id/31019. [Online description from "North Carolina Periodicals Index," East Carolina University: "Sharpe details the geography, history, development, industry, and society of Orange County."]

Stokes, Durward T. "Thomas Hart in North Carolina." *North Carolina Historical Review*, 41:3 (July 1964), 324-337; online: http://digital.ncdcr.gov/cdm/ref/collection/p16062coll9/id/4207. [Online description from "North Carolina Periodicals Index," East Carolina University: "Thomas Hart was a prominent businessman in 18th century Orange County. He served both Hillsboro and Orange County in a number of ways from political, to business, religion, and through military service. The author recounts Hart's service to the community from his move from Virginia to his service as Sheriff and later as the Captain of the Orange County Militia."]

Vidmar, Elizabeth. "A General Meeting of Delegates in Hillsborough, 1775." *Quarterly Review of the Eastern North Carolina Genealogical Society*, 14:4 (December 1987), 171-172.

Warren, Mary Bondurant. "A List of the Taxable Persons in the County of Orange with the Amt. of Their Taxable Property, vizt., for the Year 1779 [tax amount omitted in transcription]." *The Carolina Genealogist*, no. 17 (Winter 1974), County Records/Orange County Tax List 1779, 1-12.

Williams, Otho Holland. "[A Signed Letter of Otho Holland Williams Salisbury, N.C., 8 Nov. 1780, to Major General Wm. Smallwood, Col. Fords Camp]." Manuscript MSS L1998G84, Society of the Cincinnati Library, Anderson House, Washington, D. C. [Online catalog description: "After the battle of Camden, Williams was put in command of a corps of light troops. This letter was written just prior to the beginning of Greene's southern campaign, Dec. 1780. 'The Brigade of Delaware, Maryland and Virginia Troops, and Captain Singletons Company of Artillery marched from Hillsborough ... where I am to await the arrival of General Gates....' 'The Board of War in Hillsborough induced us to believe, Magazines at the Post were abundantly {chargd?} with Provisions. The truth is not so....Col. Ford will inform you of particulars.'"]

Orange County and Hillsborough – Hillsborough Academy

Anderson, Jean B. "Hillsborough Academy." *NCPedia*, 1 January 2006, http://ncpedia.org/hillsborough-academy.

Hillsborough Academy. "Hillsborough Academy Papers, 1776, 1783-1790." Manuscript PC.596 (MARS ID: 1106; record group), State Archives of North Carolina, Raleigh. [Online catalog description: "Papers relating to the academy, including list of 73 subscribers (1783); and partial minutes (1784-1788) of the board of trustees (James Hogg, William Hooper, William Johnston, James Iredell, Alfred Moore, Alexander Martin, and others) concerning board elections, teachers, repairs, land purchase, curriculum, schedule, examinations, fees, and collection of subscriptions. Also included are an account book of receipts and expenditures (1784-1789); list of 65 defaulting subscribers (1788), some taken to court; receipts for salaries and tuition; and settlement with estate of schoolmaster Zadoc Squire (1787-1790)."]

Ross, Stephen A. "To Prepare Our Sons for all the Duties That May Lie before Them: The Hillsborough Military Academy and Military Education in Antebellum North Carolina." *North Carolina Historical Review*, 79:1 (January 2002), 1-27.

Pamlico County

Sharpe, Bill. "Anecdotes & Incidents about Pamlico County." *The State: Down Home in North Carolina*, 29:7 (September 1961), 27-28; online: http://digital.ncdcr.gov/cdm/ref/collection/p16062coll18/id/8758. [Online description from "North Carolina Periodicals Index," East Carolina University: "Pamlico County has three large rivers forming borders at its top and bottom, the Pamlico and Neuse Rivers, with one river in the middle known as the Bay River. Statistics of these rivers list their drainage areas, depth, and tributaries. Further statistics list resources abounding in these rivers, as well as population estimates back to 1880."]

Pasquotank County

[Note: For various state government documents relating to Pasquotank County during the Revolutionary period, search the MARS online catalog using the advanced search: http://mars.archives.ncdcr.gov/AdvancedSearch.aspx. Use the "Year" search box to restrict the searching to 1775-1783 and enter the county's name in the "Subjects" box, and hit the "Search" button near the top. This will retrieve any cataloged document for the county from that time period. These materials can vary considerably from personal or county petitions to the General Assembly, Loyalist matters, land disputes and claims, tax collection, exemptions from taxation, payments to county veterans, county divisions, personal collections, genealogical material, British claims against North Carolinians, etc. There is considerable information in these materials that could provide interesting documentation for persons living during the Revolution. The results will also include all of the wills and probates recorded in the county during the period set for the search. We had hoped to include many of these listings in this guide, but they are too voluminous. Citations to many of these search results for the eastern counties do, however, appear in the text.]

Albertson, Catherine. "John Koen – Soldier of the Revolution." In Catherine Albertson, *In Ancient Albemarle* (Raleigh: Commercial Printing Company for the North Carolina Society Daughters of the American Revolution, 1914); reprinted in: *Pasquotank History Society Yearbook*, 2 (1956-1957); reprinted in *Carolina Trees & Branches*, 8:1 (January 1999), 7-9.

Butchko, Thomas R. *On the Shores of the Pasquotank: The Architectural Heritage of Elizabeth City and Pasquotank County, North Carolina.* Elizabeth City: Museum of the Albemarle, 1989.

Byrd, William L. *North Carolina Slaves and Free Persons of Color: Pasquotank County.* Bowie, Md.: Heritage Books, 2006.

Dean, Earl. "Plantations on the Pasquotank." *The State: A Weekly Survey of North Carolina*, 18:7 (July 1950), 10; online: http://digital.ncdcr.gov/cdm/ref/collection/p16062coll18/id/25645. [Online description from "North Carolina Periodicals Index," East Carolina University: "Nowhere else in North Carolina did early settlers live on a grander scale than those who first settled on large plantations along the Pasquotank River."]

Dean, G. E. "The Old Brick House." *The State: A Weekly Survey of North Carolina*, 3:47 (April 1936), 3; online: http://digital.ncdcr.gov/cdm/ref/collection/p16062coll18/id/10224. [Online description from "North Carolina Periodicals Index," East Carolina University: "The Old Brick House, located in Pasquotank County three miles from Elizabeth City, is one of the oldest buildings in the state. It was built sometime between 1725 and 1750 and will soon be restored to its original appearance."]

Dunaway, Stewart E. *Pasquotank County, North Carolina, Mill Records (1731-1813) and Goat Island Ferry Records.* Hillsborough: North Carolina Historical Books, 2009. [Note: While not specifically concerning the

Revolution, these sources can be used in tandem with land records and other documents to help locate places of residence, occupations, geographical features, and place names.]

Dunaway, Stewart E. *Pasquotank County, North Carolina, Road Records (1734-1799).* Hillsborough: North Carolina Historical Books, 2010. [Note: While not specifically concerning the Revolution, these sources can be used in tandem with land records and other documents to help locate places of residence, occupations, geographical features, and place names.]

Goerch, Carl. "Pasquotank." *The State: A Weekly Survey of North Carolina*, 9:24 (November 1941), 1-3, 18-22; online: http://digital.ncdcr.gov/cdm/ref/collection/p16062coll18/id/40457. [Online description from "North Carolina Periodicals Index," East Carolina University: "Continuing his travels around the state, Goerch describes the things of interest he found in Pasquotank County. The county is where the first session of a North Carolina legislature was held, where the state's first schoolhouse was built, and where the first revolt against British rule took place."]

Great Britain. Exchequer and Audit Department. Audit Office. "[Claim of] Logan, Gilmour and Co. 8 June, 1784." Copy of a manuscript in the National Archives of the United Kingdom (formerly the Public Records Office), Kew, Richmond, Surrey, England; 77.1463.1-2 (MARS ID: 21.3.26.6; folder), State Archives of North Carolina, Raleigh. [Online catalog description: "Affidavit of Thomas Macknight late of Belville, Currituck County, North Carolina, in behalf of Isabella Logan, widow of a partner in the firm trading in Pasquotank County."]

Hart, Dave. "Waterways of Pasquotank." *Our State: Down Home in North Carolina*, 65:11 (April 1998), 38-43; online: http://digital.ncdcr.gov/cdm/ref/collection/p16062coll18/id/69742. [Online description from "North Carolina Periodicals Index," East Carolina University: "Far from being isolated in the northeastern part of the state, Pasquotank County and county seat Elizabeth City blend old and new through promoting historic preservation, supporting arts, culture and education; and beckoning to tourists and retirees."]

Haun, Weynette Parks. *Old Albemarle County, North Carolina: Pasquotank Precinct (County) Births, Marriages, Deaths, Brands and Flesh Marks, & County Claims, 1691-1833.* Durham: W. P. Haun, 1981.

"Minute Men and Militia: Congresses, Provincial and Continental." In Lou N. Overman and Edna M. Shannonhouse, eds., *Year Book, Pasquotank Historical Society, Elizabeth City, North Carolina, Volume 3* (Baltimore: Gateway Press, 1975), 28-31.

North Carolina (State). General Assembly. "[Document dated:] April-May 1777: Joint Papers, Committee Papers, Resolutions, Senate Bills, House Bills, Papers Concerning Justices of the Peace and Militia Officer Appointments, 1777." Manuscript; General Assembly Record Group; Session Records, Apr-May 1777, Box 1 (MARS ID: 66.8.9.8), State Archives of North Carolina, Raleigh. [Online catalog description: "Documents concerning Governor Caswell's appointment of officers to the militia regiments of Cumberland and Chatham counties, and his appointments of Justices of the Peace for Onslow and Pasquotank counties."]

North Carolina (State). General Assembly. "[Document dated:] October 20, 1779: Joint Papers, Committee Papers, Resolutions, Senate Bills, House Bills, Exempting Certain Persons from Taxes (Granville County and Pasquotank County) (with Messages)." Manuscript; General Assembly Record Group; Session Records, Oct-Nov 1779, Box 1 (MARS ID: 66.8.18.12.4), State Archives of North Carolina, Raleigh. [Online catalog description: "John Duncan, James Stanly, and James Head, of Granville County, and Christopher Nicholson, of Pasquotank County, are exempted from poll taxes."]

North Carolina (State). General Assembly. "[Document dated:] May 9, 1780: Joint Papers, Committee Papers, Resolutions, Senate Bills, House Bills, Directing Payment to the Miles Gale Estate by Commissioners for Selling Confiscated Property in Pasquotank County (Messages Only)." Manuscript; General Assembly Record Group; Session Records, April-May 1780, Box 1 (MARS ID: 66.8.20.17.13), State Archives of North Carolina, Raleigh.

North Carolina (State). General Assembly. "[Document dated:] February 5, 1781: Joint Papers, Committee Papers, Resolutions, Senate Bills, House Bills, Letter from Colonel Gideon Lamb and Bonds Given by Tories." Manuscript; General Assembly Record Group; Session Records, Jan-Feb 1781, Box 1 (MARS ID: 66.8.23.3.3; item), State Archives of North Carolina, Raleigh. [Online catalog description: "Lamb informs the Assembly that in his opinion the only way to deal with the numerous loyalists in Currituck, Camden, Pasquotank, and Perquimans Counties is to forgive them on the condition that they sign bonds for their good behavior, which he has done. He includes several of the bonds."]

North Carolina (State). General Assembly. "[Document dated:] May 10, 1784: Joint Papers, Committee Papers, Resolutions, Senate Bills, House Bills, House Bill to Authorize Issac Gregory, Former Sheriff of Pasquotank County, to Collect Arrears of Taxes." Manuscript; General Assembly Record Group; Session Records, Apr-June 1784, Box 4 (MARS ID: 66.8.34.1; folder), State Archives of North Carolina, Raleigh. [Online catalog description: "Bill empowers Issac Gregory to collect arrears on taxes due from 1769-1774 and to collect them as they would have been collected then, and to collect from all except those who have a receipt that proves that they paid."]

Overman, Lou Newsome. "The Liberty Pole House." In Lou N. Overman and Edna M. Shannonhouse, eds., *Year Book, Pasquotank Historical Society, Elizabeth City, North Carolina, Volume 3* (Baltimore: Gateway Press, 1975), 24-25.

Paden, John. "A Study in Southern Loyalism: The Politics of Thomas Macknight." *Southern Historian*, 15 (Spring 1994), 78-89. [Pasquotank and Currituck Counties]

Pasquotank County. "Insolvent Debtors, 1744-1877." Manuscript, State Archives of North Carolina, Raleigh. [Consult the State Archives to determine the exact years that are available.]

Pasquotank County. "Justice of the Peace, Records of, 1720-1896." Manuscript, State Archives of North Carolina, Raleigh. [Consult the State Archives to determine the exact years that are available.]

Pasquotank County. "Miscellaneous Land Records, 1694-1946." Manuscript, CR.075.408.6-CR.075.408.8, State Archives of North Carolina, Raleigh. [Online catalog description: Includes a "Revolutionary War land grant to Selby Harney and Anthony Bledsoe, assignees of Robert Jackson, 1793."]

Pasquotank County. "Pasquotank County Miscellaneous Records, 1703-1940: Appointment of Officials, 1732-1923 and no date." Manuscript C.R.075.928.11, State Archives of North Carolina, Raleigh.

Pasquotank County. "Pasquotank County Miscellaneous Records, 1703-1940: Jury Lists and Records, 1730-1924 and no date." Manuscript C.R.075.928.14, State Archives of North Carolina, Raleigh.

Pasquotank County. "Pasquotank County Miscellaneous Records, 1703-1940: Oaths, 1776, 1779, 1876, and ..." Manuscript C.R.075.928.16, State Archives of North Carolina, Raleigh.

Pasquotank County. "Pasquotank County Miscellaneous Records, 1703-1940: Shipping Records, 1735-1910." Manuscript C.R.075.928.17, State Archives of North Carolina, Raleigh.

Pasquotank County. "Pasquotank County Miscellaneous Records, 1703-1940: Wharf Records, 1771-1801." Manuscript C.R.075.928.17, State Archives of North Carolina, Raleigh.

Pasquotank County. "Slaves and Free Persons of Color, Records of, 1733-1892." Manuscript, State Archives of North Carolina, Raleigh. [Consult the State Archives to determine the exact years that are available.]

Portoukalian, Shelah. "William Boswell, Revolutionary War Patriot." *Carolina Trees & Branches: Family Research Society of Northeastern North Carolina*, 21:3 (July 2012), 64-67. [Pasquotank County; descendant of George Durant through the Waller and Boswell Families]

Sharpe, Bill. "Queen of the Albemarle." *The State: A Weekly Survey of North Carolina*, 19:25 (November 1951), 3-5, 28-29; online: http://digital.ncdcr.gov/cdm/ref/collection/p16062coll18/id/27795. [Online description from "North Carolina Periodicals Index," East Carolina University: "Assured by history, confident of her future, Pasquotank is a small but thriving principality."]

White, Julia S. "The Quakers of Perquimans." *North Carolina Booklet*, 7:4 (April 1908), 278-289; online: http://digital.ncdcr.gov/cdm/ref/collection/p249901coll37/id/14180. [Online description from "North Carolina Periodicals Index," East Carolina University: "Quakers were the first to bring organized Christianity to North Carolina, and counted among them a number of intelligent and well-disposed members, particularly in Perquimans and Pasquotank."]

Year Book, Pasquotank Historical Society, Elizabeth City, North Carolina, Volume 3. Baltimore: Gateway Press, 1975.

Pender County

Angley, Wilson S. "New Topsail Inlet: A Brief History." *Tributaries*, 5 (October 1995), 15-21. [Online description from "North Carolina Periodicals Index," East Carolina University: "Since people began settling near it in the early 1700s, New Topsail Inlet has witnessed commerce passing, ships sinking, wars, and now extensive recreational development."]

Lee, Mrs. I. F., and the Anders Family. "Mrs. I. F. Lee Collection." Manuscript PC.130 (MARS ID: 639; Record Group), State Archives of North Carolina, Raleigh. [Online catalog description: "Papers of the Anders family of Bladen and New Hanover counties, including grants, deeds, plats and other land papers;... ; draft power of attorney from Penelope Lewis to William Anders for collecting pay of soldier in the N. C. Continental Line (1791), bearing names and addresses of several widows and former soldiers in the New Hanover (Pender) Co. area."]

Sharpe, Bill. "Land of Blueberries, Bays and Battlefields." *The State: Down Home in North Carolina*, 26:8 (September 1958), 14-16, 26-29; online: http://digital.ncdcr.gov/cdm/ref/collection/p16062coll18/id/51771.

[Online description from "North Carolina Periodicals Index," East Carolina University: "Pender County is a hybrid, both rural and resort, its vast plain wild and yet well cultivated. Pender, witness to the first battle of the revolution, is hemmed against the water by a slender ridge, near both U.S. 17 and the Atlantic Coast Line rails. Its landscape features bays, botanical gardens with meat-eating plants, and an abundance of blueberries that were first planted by Harrold Huntington of New Jersey."]

Whitfield, Pam. "This Old House." *The State: Down Home in North Carolina*, 63:7 (December 1995), 25-27, 29; online: http://digital.ncdcr.gov/cdm/ref/collection/p16062coll18/id/37533. [Online description from "North Carolina Periodicals Index," East Carolina University: "When Mae Blake and J. Walton Graves bought and restored the Sloop Point Plantation in Pender County, they had no idea the North Carolina Division of Archives and History would declare it, at 269 years, the state's oldest standing structure."]

Perquimans County

[Note: For various state government documents relating to Perquimans County during the Revolutionary period, search the MARS online catalog using the advanced search: http://mars.archives.ncdcr.gov/AdvancedSearch.aspx. Use the "Year" search box to restrict the searching to 1775-1783 and enter the county's name in the "Subjects" box, and hit the "Search" button near the top. This will retrieve any cataloged document for the county from that time period. These materials can vary considerably from personal or county petitions to the General Assembly, Loyalist matters, land disputes and claims, tax collection, exemptions from taxation, payments to county veterans, county divisions, personal collections, genealogical material, British claims against North Carolinians, etc. There is considerable information in these materials that could provide interesting documentation for persons living during the Revolution. The results will also include all of the wills and probates recorded in the county during the period set for the search. We had hoped to include many of these listings in this guide, but they are too voluminous. Citations to many of these search results for the eastern counties do, however, appear in the text.]

Conner, B. H. "Bridges, Old and New." *The State: A Weekly Survey of North Carolina*, 5:38 (February 1938), 1, 16; online: http://digital.ncdcr.gov/cdm/ref/collection/p16062coll18/id/37533. [Online description from "North Carolina Periodicals Index," East Carolina University: "One of the state's earliest bridges was constructed near Hertford in the 1780s. Citizens of the town wished to cross the Perquimans River to visit Elizabeth City and Virginia destinations. The man hired for the job was Mr. Perry who traversed the river that was 20 feet deep and 600 feet wide with old whiskey barrels lashed together. A more modern bridge replaced the whiskey barrels in 1885 and finally a steel and concrete bridge was erected in 1928."]

Dunaway, Stewart E. *Perquimans County, North Carolina, Mill Records (1744-1885) & Ferry Petitions (1740-1866).* Hillsborough: North Carolina Historical Books, 2009. [Note: While not specifically concerning the Revolution, these sources can be used in tandem with land records and other documents to help locate places of residence, occupations, geographical features, and place names.]

Dunaway, Stewart E. *Perquimans County, North Carolina, Road and Bridge Records, Vol. 1: 1711-1799.* Hillsborough: North Carolina Historical Books, 2009. [Note: While not specifically concerning the Revolution, these sources can be used in tandem with land records and other documents to help locate places of residence, occupations, geographical features, and place names.]

Dungy, Katherine. "A Friend in Deed: Quakers and Manumission in Perquimans County, North Carolina, 1775-1800." *The Southern Friend: Journal of the North Carolina Friends Historical Society*, 24:1 (Spring 2002), 5-36.

Dungy, Kathryn Renee. "Life on a Tightrope: The Problems of Becoming Free in Perquimans County, North Carolina, 1775-1800." M. A. thesis, Duke University, 1993.

Goerch, Carl. "Perquimans." *The State: A Weekly Survey of North Carolina*, 10:9 (August 1942), 1-2, 16-18; online: http://digital.ncdcr.gov/cdm/ref/collection/p16062coll18/id/33037. [Online description from "North Carolina Periodicals Index," East Carolina University: "Continuing his travels to the state's counties, Goerch explores Perquimans County, a Native American name that reportedly means, 'Land of Beautiful Women.' Some of the earliest settlements in the state are located there. The courthouse was built in 1732. It is predominately an agricultural county; over seventy percent of its families live on farms. The nearby waters supply both commercial and sport fishing. The town of Hertford is a combination of the old and new with many houses over a century old."]

Great Britain. Colonial Office. "N. C.: 'An Act Directing the Boundary Line between the Counties of Perquimons and Chowan…' [1773]." Copy of a manuscript in the National Archives of the United Kingdom (formerly the

Public Records Office), Kew, Richmond, Surrey, England; Z.5.27 (MARS ID: 21.1.10.58; folder), "British Records Collection," State Archives of North Carolina, Raleigh.

Haley, Dru Gatewood, and Raymond A. Winslow. *The Historic Architecture of Perquimans County, North Carolina.* Hertford: Town of Hertford, 1982.

Harvey, John, 1725?-1775. *Advertisement: Perquimans County, Feb. 11, 1775. The Respective Counties and Towns in This Colony Are Requested to Elect Delegates to Represent Them in Convention, Who Are Desired to Meet at the Town of Newbern on Monday the 3d Day of April Next.* Newbern: Printed by James Davis, 1775; micropublished: (Early American Imprints. First Series. No. 42761) New York: Readex Microprint, 1985.

LaVere, David. "Unhurried in Hertford." *Our State: Down Home in North Carolina*, 71:8 (January 2004), 106-108; online: http://digital.ncdcr.gov/cdm/ref/collection/p16062coll18/id/78730. [Online description from "North Carolina Periodicals Index," East Carolina University: "Chartered in 1758, the Perquimans County town of Hertford is one of the state's oldest towns. It survived both the Revolutionary War and Civil War. LaVere discusses the town's history and things to see and do on a visit."]

Leloudis, James, II. "Tokens of Death: Tales from Perquimans County." *North Carolina Folklore Journal*, 25:2 (November 1977), 47-60. [Online description from "North Carolina Periodicals Index," East Carolina University: "A common form of folk tales in eastern Perquimans, a county located near the coast in northeastern North Carolina, is that of 'tokens of death.' They are tales and statements of belief concerning both natural and supernatural phenomena which were considered to have been omens, or tokens, of various deaths. These tales are intimately related to the history of Perquimans County and to the course of its economic and cultural development."]

Lewis, J. D. "Patriot Leaders in North Carolina: Miles Harvey: Colonel over the Perquimans County Regiment of Militia - 1775-1776." Online: http://www.carolana.com/NC/Revolution/patriot_leaders_nc_miles_harvey.html.

[Newby, Thomas, ca. 1725-1793]. "Papers, 1750-1784, 1893, 1896." Manuscript PC.1519 (MARS ID: 2029; record group), State Archives of North Carolina, Raleigh. [Online catalog description: "Account books (1750-1755, 1761-1775; portions missing) kept by Newby, Quaker merchant and planter in Perquimans Co., recording purchases and payments, usually in kind, at his general store at Newby's Bridge on Perquimans River, with occasional information on occupation or parentage of customer. Also recorded are expenses and returns of voyages to West Indies by several vessels (1763-1773), with details of cargo, captains, crew (part slave), wages, and pilotage and duties paid."]

Newby, W. G. *Town of Hertford Bicentennial, 1758-1958.* [Hertford?: The Town?, 1958].

North Carolina (State). General Assembly. "[Document dated:] January 23, 1779: Joint Papers, Committee Papers, Resolutions, Senate Bills, House Bills, Report Re[specting] Petitions of People Called Moravians and Quakers (with Petition and Messages)." Manuscript; General Assembly Record Group; Session Records, Jan-Feb 1779, Box 1 (MARS ID: 66.8.15.8.2; item), State Archives of North Carolina, Raleigh. [Online catalog description: "The petition of the Quakers from their yearly meeting committee in Perquimans County asks the Assembly not to consider them enemies of the state because they will not swear the oath of allegiance. The committee recommends that Moravians and Quakers be allowed to take an affirmation instead of the oath, with which the Assembly concurs."]

North Carolina (State). General Assembly. "[Document dated:] April 27, 1780: Joint Papers, Committee Papers, Resolutions, Senate Bills, House Bills, Report Re[specting] Petitions of William Houston and William Skinner." Manuscript; General Assembly Record Group; Session Records, Apr-May 1780, Box 1 (MARS ID: 66.8.20.8.11; item), State Archives of North Carolina, Raleigh. [Online catalog description: "Houston informs the Assembly that in 1742 he took possession of a tract of land in Duplin County from his uncle, Henry McCulloh, who left the state in 1747. Because he never acquired a title or deed, Houston is concerned that the land is subject to confiscation and asks the Assembly to vest him with a title to the land by law. Skinner informs the Assembly that the law prohibiting individuals who have not taken the affirmation of allegiance to the state has had the effect of disabling Quakers in Pasquotank and Perquimans Counties from maintaining possession of their own land and asks the Assembly to pass a law in their behalf. The committee recommends that both petitions be granted, and the Assembly concurs."]

North Carolina (State). General Assembly. "[Document dated:] n. d. [1781]: Joint Papers, Committee Papers, Resolutions, Senate Bills, House Bills, Petition of Edward Hall of Perquimans County (Rejected) (with Letter from Thomas Harvey)." Manuscript; General Assembly Record Group; Session Records, June-July 1781, Box 1 (MARS ID: 66.8.25.7.1; item), State Archives of North Carolina, Raleigh. [Online catalog description: "Hall, Captain John Harvey's lieutenant, explains why he is not guilty of any charge of desertion or misconduct with regard to his actions prior to the South Carolina campaign; Thomas Harvey, colonel of the county, explains why he is."]

North Carolina (State). General Assembly. "[Document dated:] February 5, 1781:]: Joint Papers, Committee Papers, Resolutions, Senate Bills, House Bills, Letter from Colonel Gideon Lamb and Bonds Given by Tories." Manuscript; General Assembly Record Group; Session Records, Jan-Feb 1781, Box 1 (MARS ID: 66.8.23.3.3; item), State Archives of North Carolina, Raleigh. [Online catalog description: "Lamb informs the Assembly that in his opinion the only way to deal with the numerous loyalists in Currituck, Camden, Pasquotank, and Perquimans Counties is to forgive them on the condition that they sign bonds for their good behavior, which he has done. He includes several of the bonds."]

North Carolina (State). General Assembly. "[Document dated:] May 1779: Joint Papers, Committee Papers, Resolutions, Senate Bills, House Bills, Joint Papers: Justice of the Peace Appointments." Manuscript; General Assembly Record Group; Session Records, May 1779, Box 1 (MARS ID: 66.8.17.4; folder), State Archives of North Carolina, Raleigh. [Online catalog description: "Includes messages debating the appointment of Ephraim Barns, of Edgecombe County, and recommendations from the Court of Perquimans County." Personal names that appear in this document are: Ephraim Barnes/Barns; Charles Moore; Frederick Norcom; William Reed; Robert Riddick, Jr.; Joshua Skinner; John Whedbee, Jr.; and, John Wyatt.]

North Carolina (State). General Assembly. "[Document dated:] June 24, 1781: Joint Papers, Committee Papers, Resolutions, Senate Bills, House Bills, Ordering Draft of Perquimans County Militia as Required by Law and Court Martial of Colonel Thomas Harvey (Rejected)." Manuscript; General Assembly Record Group; Session Records, June-July 1781, Box 1 (MARS ID: 66.8.25.10.5), State Archives of North Carolina, Raleigh. [Online catalog description: "The draft would have provided men to serve in the state's Continental battalions."]

North Carolina (State). Office of the Secretary of State. "Chowan-Perquimans, 1773, 1820." Manuscript SS.XX, Box 1, folder 6 (MARS ID: 12.110.1.6; folder), State Archives of North Carolina, Raleigh. [Online catalog description: "This folder contains a 1773 report of the commissioners appointed to consider the boundary line between Chowan and Perquimans counties and a map of the boundary between the two counties dated September 11, 1820."]

[Perquimans County. Clerk of Superior Court; Clerk of Court of Pleas and Quarter Sessions, Register of Deeds]. "Miscellaneous Records, 1710-1933, no date." Manuscript, CR.077.928.3-CR.077.928.8, (MARS ID: 277.103.3), State Archives of North Carolina, Raleigh. [This collection includes: "...appointments of justice of peace, 1727-1867; appointments- miscellaneous, no date, 1777-1899; appointment of sheriff, 1770-1774;...; commission to justices of peace, 1781;...; list of inhabitants, 1753-1786;...; oaths, no date, 1712-1852 [the type of oaths is not specified in the description];...; vessels, 1722-1876; wardens of the poor, 1774-1866."]

Perquimans County. "Jury Lists, 1709-1868." Manuscript, State Archives of North Carolina, Raleigh. [Consult the State Archives to determine the exact years that are available.]

Perquimans County. "Miscellaneous Records, 1762-1891." Manuscript, CRX Records, State Archives of North Carolina, Raleigh. [Consult the State Archives to determine the exact years that are available.]

Perquimans County. "Perquimans County Miscellaneous Records, 1710-1933: Appointment of Justices of Peace, 1727-1867." Manuscript C.R.077.928.3, State Archives of North Carolina, Raleigh.

Perquimans County. "Perquimans County Miscellaneous Records, 1710-1933: Appointment – Miscellaneous, no date and 1777-1899." Manuscript C.R.077.928.3, State Archives of North Carolina, Raleigh.

Perquimans County. "Perquimans County Miscellaneous Records, 1710-1933: Commission to Justices of Peace, 1781." Manuscript C.R.077.928.4, State Archives of North Carolina, Raleigh.

Perquimans County. "Perquimans County Miscellaneous Records, 1710-1933: List of Inhabitants, 1753-1786." Manuscript C.R.077.928.6, State Archives of North Carolina, Raleigh.

Perquimans County. "Perquimans County Miscellaneous Records, 1710-1933: Oaths, no date and 1712-1852." Manuscript C.R.077.928.6, State Archives of North Carolina, Raleigh.

Perquimans County. "Perquimans County Miscellaneous Records, 1710-1933: Petition—Allowance for Extra Services for Clerk and Sheriff, 1782." Manuscript C.R.077.928.7, State Archives of North Carolina, Raleigh.

Perquimans County. "Perquimans County Miscellaneous Records, 1710-1933: Vessels, 1722-1876." Manuscript C.R.077.928.8, State Archives of North Carolina, Raleigh.

Perquimans County. "Slave Records, 1759-1864." Manuscript, State Archives of North Carolina, Raleigh. [Consult the State Archives to determine the exact years that are available.]

"Perquimans County Muster Roll [undated]." *Quarterly Review of the Eastern North Carolina Genealogical Society*, 14:2 (June 1987), 61-63. [Includes many Quakers.]

Perquimans County, N. C. "Tax List, 1775." Manuscript (Record series G. A. 11.1, Perquimans County, List of Taxables, 1773-1776), North Carolina Archives, Raleigh. [Online: http://perqtax.homestead.com.]

"Perquimans County, N. C. "Tax List, 1779." Manuscript (Perquimans County, List of Taxables, Record Group CR.077.701.1), North Carolina Archives, Raleigh. [Online: http://perqtax.homestead.com.]

Roberts, Frank M. "You'll Visit the Oldest House." *The State: Down Home in North Carolina*, 41:6 (November 1973), 17-18, 33; online: http://digital.ncdcr.gov/cdm/ref/collection/p16062coll18/id/56279. [Online description from "North Carolina Periodicals Index," East Carolina University: "The Newbold-White House, north of Hertford was restored by the Perquimans County Restoration Association. The brick house is said to be the North Carolina's oldest, built somewhere between 1685 and 1725. The house-now-tourist attraction includes a museum containing several thousand artifacts from the 1700s found by archaeologists during the restoration."]

Sharpe, Bill, and Susan Sharpe Zarr. "Peaceful Perquimans." *The State: Down Home in North Carolina*, 30:7 (September 1962), 12-14, 20-22; online: http://digital.ncdcr.gov/cdm/ref/collection/p16062coll18/id/44719. [Online description from "North Carolina Periodicals Index," East Carolina University: "Comprised of land purchased by George Durant from Chief Kilcocanean of the Yeopim Native American Tribe in 1661, Perquimans County is comprised of two peninsulas that extend into Albemarle Sound. Containing three rivers, the Perquimans, Yeopim, and the Little, Perquimans County, encompassing some 167,040 acres, reportedly means, 'Land of beautiful women.' A region exposed to a myriad of conflicts, religion, and history, the residents of Perquimans created their livelihoods based on the processing and exportation of corn, wheat, oats, cotton, wool, and fish."]

Tucker, Harry Z. "Harvey's Point." *The State: A Weekly Survey of North Carolina*, 11:18 (October 1943), 6, 34; online: http://digital.ncdcr.gov/cdm/ref/collection/p16062coll18/id/17906. [Online description from "North Carolina Periodicals Index," East Carolina University: "Harvey's Point denotes an area between the Perquimans and Yeopim Rivers in Perquimans County. Harvey derives from the distinguished Harvey family who settled there in 1658. In 1663, the Harvey's built and incorporated the Belgrade Plantation. Remnants of the Belgrade Plantation could be seen in 1943, specifically the Ashland a Revolutionary War era two-story home."]

White, Julia S. "The Quakers of Perquimans." *North Carolina Booklet*, 7:4 (April 1908), 278-289; online: http://digital.ncdcr.gov/cdm/ref/collection/p249901coll37/id/14180. [Online description from "North Carolina Periodicals Index," East Carolina University: "Quakers were the first to bring organized Christianity to North Carolina, and counted among them a number of intelligent and well-disposed members, particularly in Perquimans and Pasquotank."]

Winslow, Ellen Goode Rawlings. *History of Perquimans County as Compiled from Records Found There and Elsewhere; Abstracts of Deeds from 1681 through the Revolution - Petitions, Divisions, and Marriages Found in Perquimans and Adjacent Counties - A Brief Summary of the Settling of Perquimans, with the Kind and Manner of Settlers - Two Maps, One of the Old Order, and One a Present Day Map - Illustrations of a Few Old Residences and Several More Modern Ones.* Raleigh: Edwards & Broughton Company, 1931. [Description: "This county history is extraordinarily rich in primary source materials, including abstracts of deeds from 1681 through the Revolutionary War period and, moreover, petitions, divisions of estates, wills, and marriages found in the records of Perquimans and adjacent North Carolina counties. Numbering in the tens of thousands, the records provide the names of all principal parties and related family members, places of residence and migration, descriptions of real and personal property, dates, boundary surveys, names of executors, witnesses, and appraisers, and dates of recording."]

Winslow, Raymond A. *Perquimans County 300th Anniversary, 1670-1970*. Elizabeth City: Family Research Society of Northeastern North Carolina, 2003.

Person County

Frost, David. "Polynomous Succession of Militia-Tax Districts in Person County, North Carolina, 1791-1823." *Piedmont Lineages: Quarterly Journal of the VA-NC Piedmont Genealogical Society*, 23:2 (May 2001), 52-56. [Includes a map/chart of the "1777 Caswell County, NC Tax Districts" for the area that became Person County in 1791.]

Moore, Stephen, 1734-1799. "Stephen Moore Papers, 1767-1867, Orange and Person Counties, North Carolina; Also Maryland, New York, and Quebec (Canada)." Manuscript 2205, Southern Historical Collection, Louis Round Wilson Special Collections Library, University of North Carolina, Chapel Hill; online finding aid available at http://www2.lib.unc.edu/mss/inv/m/Moore,Stephen.html. Also available on microfilm: 2 microfilm reels. *Records of Antebellum Southern Plantations from the Revolution through the Civil War, Series J, Selections from the Southern Historical Collection, Manuscript Department, Library of the University of North Carolina at Chapel Hill, Part 13, Piedmont North Carolina, reels 8-10.* Bethesda, Md.: University Publications of America, 1993. [Online finding aid description for the manuscript collection at SHC: "The collection includes accounts and business papers of Stephen Moore of New York, who moved to North Carolina during the Revolution, and of his son, Phillips (b. 1771), and grandsons Stephen and William, merchants in

Hillsborough, N. C. Included are occasional letters from Stephen (1734-1799) to his father, Phillips, a New York City merchant, documenting their business affairs. Volumes include one shipping account book, New York City, 1767-1770; eighteen account books, 1781-1827, for farming operations, sales, and miscellany, at Mount Tirzah plantation in Person County, N. C.; thirteen account books, 1831-1867, of a general merchant at Hillsborough; and letters from William Moore to his father." Online description for the microfilm version: "This collection consists chiefly of scattered letters, 1805-1851, most of which are addressed to Phillips Moore, and concern family finances and related matters; miscellaneous bills, receipts, tax records, 1769-1869, some of which concern slaves, chiefly of Phillips Moore and Stephen Moore; Moore family farm and household account books, 1782-1816; and account books, 1831-1867, of Stephen Moore's general store and a shoe shop in Hillsborough, N. C. Other items include a shipping and general merchandise ledger, 1767-1770, Quebec City, Can., probably from an enterprise of Stephen Moore (1734-1799); some items relating to Moore's property at West Point, N. Y.; records of Moore's estate; shipping accounts, 1807-1809, from Chestertown, Md.; and early 19th century instructions for constructing grist mills. Stephen Moore (1734-1799), born in New York City, was a merchant in Quebec, Can., in the 1760s, owned property at West Point, N. Y., bought an estate, Mt. Tirzah, on the Flat River in Person County, N. C., in 1777, and was a U. S. congressman from North Carolina in 1793. His son, Phillips Moore, was a surveyor and farmer in Person County. Phillips Moore's son, Stephen Moore (b. 1801), was a general merchant and shoe shop operator in Hillsborough, N. C."]

Norris, Jeannie Faris. "The Indians of Person County." *The State: A Weekly Survey of North Carolina*, 16:37 (February 1949), 3-4, 20; online: http://digital.ncdcr.gov/cdm/ref/collection/p16062coll18/id/23490. [Online description from "North Carolina Periodicals Index," East Carolina University: "The article describes Person County Native Americans and their activities including church and school attendance."]

Person County. "Person County Miscellaneous Records, 1771-1954: Revolutionary War Pension Applications, 1811, 1820, 1828." Manuscript C.R.078.928.4, State Archives of North Carolina, Raleigh.

Wright, Stuart T. *Historical Sketch of Person County*. Danville: The Womack Press, 1974.

Pitt County

[Note: For various state government documents relating to Pitt County during the Revolutionary period, search the MARS online catalog using the advanced search: http://mars.archives.ncdcr.gov/AdvancedSearch.aspx. Use the "Year" search box to restrict the searching to 1775-1783 and enter the county's name in the "Subjects" box, and hit the "Search" button near the top. This will retrieve any cataloged document for the county from that time period. These materials can vary considerably from personal or county petitions to the General Assembly, Loyalist matters, land disputes and claims, tax collection, exemptions from taxation, payments to county veterans, county divisions, personal collections, genealogical material, British claims against North Carolinians, etc. There is considerable information in these materials that could provide interesting documentation for persons living during the Revolution. The results will also include all of the wills and probates recorded in the county during the period set for the search. We had hoped to include many of these listings in this guide, but they are too voluminous. Citations to many of these search results for the eastern counties do, however, appear in the text.]

Anderson, Jean. "The Census of 1775 as Seen in Pitt County, N. C." *North Carolina Genealogical Society Journal*, 7:4 (November 1991), 186-196.

Buck, Samuel. "Buck Family History." *Pitt County Genealogical Quarterly*, 14:3 (August 2007), 1-2. [Includes Revolutionary War service references.]

Cline, Ned. "Old-Wall Overhaul." *Our State: Down Home in North Carolina*, 79:6 (November 2011), 58-60, 62-63; online: http://digital.ncdcr.gov/cdm/ref/collection/p16062coll18/id/98003. [Online description from "North Carolina Periodicals Index," East Carolina University: "To prepare two historic buildings for exhibition, the North Carolina Museum of History hired architectural restorer Dean Ruedrich, sole-proprietor of Reudrich Restorations in Louisburg. The Pitt County farmhouse dates to 1742 and is believed to be the state's third oldest, surviving and documented one in the state. The second building is a 19th century slave cabin from Martin County."]

Copeland, Elizabeth H., ed. *Chronicles of Pitt County, North Carolina*. 2 vols. Greenville: Pitt County Historical Society, Inc., 1982.

"Field Return of the Regiment of Militia for Pitt County at a General Muster the 12th Day of October 1775." *Quarterly Review of the Eastern North Carolina Genealogical Society*, 14:1 (March 1987), 32.

"General Musters, Pitt Co. Militia." *Pitt County Genealogical Quarterly*, 6:1 (February 1999), 7-8.

Goodwin, Katherine T. "Emanuel Teel, Rev. War Soldier." *Pitt County Genealogical Quarterly*, 14:1 (February 2007), 17-18.

Gravelle, Candace. "James Ross, Rev. Soldier." *Pitt County Genealogical Quarterly*, 14:1 (February 2007), 14-16.

Kammerer, Roger. "Benjamin Hodges Blount, Soldiers Bond, 1794." *Pitt County Genealogical Quarterly*, 16:2 (May 2009), 8-9.

Kammerer, Roger. "Captain John Hodges Company Militia, 1780." *Pitt County Genealogical Quarterly*, 12:4 (November 2005), 1.

Kammerer, Roger. "First Courthouse Marker." *Greenville Times/Pitt's Past*, (August 25-September 7, 1999), 10. [Online description from "North Carolina Periodicals Index," East Carolina University: "Pitt County's first courthouse was a house serving from 1760 until 1774 and located on Highway 33 East, across from the entrance to the Brook Valley subdivision. In 1924, a campaign began to preserve the old house, which failed. In October 1930, the Daughters of the American Revolution successfully erected a marker at the site, commemorating the historic structure."]

Kammerer, Roger. "General Assembly Papers." *Pitt County Genealogical Quarterly*, 11:3 (August 2004), 1-2. [documents relating to Pitt County residents in 1782-1783.]

Kammerer, Roger. "Giles Bowers, Rev. War Settlement." *Pitt County Genealogical Quarterly*, 16:2 (May 2009), 7.

Kammerer, Roger. "Harry Harris, Revolutionary War Soldier." *Pitt County Genealogical Quarterly*, 8:2 (May 2001), 17.

Kammerer, Roger. "In Search of Charles Read." *Greenville Times/Pitt's Past*, (January 5-18, 2005), 5. [Online description from "North Carolina Periodicals Index," East Carolina University: "Charles Read was a leading politician in colonial days. In the spring of 1773 he fled his native state of New Jersey, where he faced a long jail sentence for bankruptcy. Read moved to Martinborough, North Carolina, where he died in 1774. Martinborough was renamed Greenesville in 1786. Today, it is believed that Reade Street in Greenville is named for him."]

Kammerer, Roger. "John and Benjamin Garris, Counterfeiters, 1780." *Pitt County Genealogical Quarterly*, 12:2 (May 2005), 26.

Kammerer, Roger. "Pitt County Celebrates 250 Years." *Greenville Times/Pitt's Past*, (September 16-30, 2009), 5. [Online description from "North Carolina Periodicals Index," East Carolina University: "Pitt County's land formed from Bath County in 1696, before that county divided into Beaufort County in 1712. It formed into Pitt County, named in honor of William Pitt, the elder, Earl of Chatham, and then Prime Minister of England, in 1760."]

Kammerer, Roger. "Pitt County's First Courthouse." *Greenville Times/Pitt's Past*, (October 14-27, 1987), 8-9. [Online description from "North Carolina Periodicals Index," East Carolina University: "In November 1760, John Simpson presented a bill to form another county from the upper region of Beaufort County to the legislature. It passed January 1, 1761, forming Pitt County. Colonel John Hardee's home served as Pitt County's first courthouse and records office in 1761 to 1774, and also served as the local parish house for the Church of England. After the construction of a permanent courthouse, Hardee's land and historic house changed owners several times. In 1924, James E. W. Cook encouraged the county to restore the first historic courthouse; later destroyed in 1926. In 1930, a marker, erected on Highway 33 East across from the entrance to the Brook Valley Country Club, commemorates the site of the courthouse."]

Kammerer, Roger. "Pitt County's Five Courthouses." *Greenville Times/Pitt's Past*, (September 18-October 1, 1985), 10-11. [Online description from "North Carolina Periodicals Index," East Carolina University: "The first courthouse (picture available) was a house built in 1761 on Highway 33 East, in adjacent to the entrance of the Brook Valley subdivision. The second courthouse, built by 1775, was on the corner of Evans and Third streets. The third, completed in 1834, was located on Evans Street. A man named Croom, trying to destroy a will, burned the courthouse in 1858. The fourth courthouse, completed in 1877, and destroyed by fire on February 24, 1910. The fifth courthouse (picture available) is located downtown, has a 1,300-pound cornerstone laid on January 26, 1911."]

Kammerer, Roger. "Pitt County's Six Courthouses." *Greenville Times/Pitt's Past*, (March 1-14, 2006), 5, 10. [Online description from "North Carolina Periodicals Index," East Carolina University: "The Act that created Pitt County on January 1, 1761 also called for the creation of a courthouse, prison, and stocks on John Hardee's land who also donated his house as the first courthouse of Pitt County. An Act of the State Assembly in 1775 appointed George Evans, Charles Forbes, Henry Ellis, Benjamin May, and William Roberson to oversee the building of a new courthouse, completed in Martinsborough around 1776. Following a petition by Pitt County to implement an annual tax to build a third courthouse in 1789, the government appointed James Armstrong, Shadrach Allen, John Moye, Arthur Forbes, Samuel Simpson, Benjamin Bell, and William Blount to oversee the process. The builders completed the third courthouse about 1792 on the courthouse square at the corner of Evans and Third Street. George Eason, James Blow, Bryan Grimes, Goold Hoyt and John Norcott commissioned Goold Hoyt to build the fourth courthouse, completed in 1834. A man named Croom burned this courthouse down on January 7, 1858 in order to destroy a will. A Pitt County committee awarded the contract to Dabney Cosbey to build the fifth courthouse in August 1858, though the courthouse was not completed until 1877. This courthouse burned down on February 24, 1910. The architectural firm of Milburn and Heister of Baltimore Maryland designed the sixth and final courthouse, built in 1911."]

Kammerer, Roger. "Revolutionary War Militia List, ca. 1781." *Pitt County Genealogical Quarterly*, 12:2 (May 2005), 1.

Kammerer, Roger. "Soldiers' Petitions: Gen. Assembly, 1804." *Pitt County Genealogical Quarterly*, 6:1 (February 1999), 18. [Christopher Morning and Solomon Carr, both of Pitt County]

King, Henry T. *Sketches of Pitt County*. Raleigh: Edwards & Broughton Printing Company, 1909.

Meeks, Jeffrey. "Loderick Teel, Aged 113." *Pitt County Genealogical Quarterly*, 5:2 (May 1998), 6. [veteran of the Revolution]

Meeks, Jeffrey. "William Spain." *Pitt County Genealogical Quarterly*, 5:2 (May 1998), 7. [veteran of the Revolution]

North Carolina (State). General Assembly. [Document dated:] April 18, 1778: "Allowance to Pitt Co. Sheriff for Insolvent Taxables (with List and Messages)." Manuscript; General Assembly Record Group; Session Records, April-May 1778; Miscellaneous, Joint Papers, Committee Papers, Senate Resolutions, …, Box 1 (MARS ID: 66.8.12.16.6; item), State Archives of North Carolina, Raleigh.

North Carolina (State). General Assembly. "[Documents dated:] April 20, 1780: Resolution Exempting from Poll Taxes William Whitfield of Pitt County and James Smith of Anson County (with Anson County Court Recommendation and Whitfield's Petition." Manuscript; General Assembly Record Group; Session Records, April-May 1780; Joint Papers, Committee Papers, Resolutions; House Joint Resolutions: April 17-27, 1780; Box 1 (MARS ID: 66.8.20.15.4; item), State Archives of North Carolina, Raleigh. [Online catalog description: "The Anson County Court recommends exemption for James Smith, as he is poor, aged, and infirm. Whitfield informs the Assembly in his petition that he is disabled and must care for small children."]

North Carolina (State). General Assembly. "[Documents dated:] January 31, 1781: Resolution allowance to William Kilpatrick, Pitt County (with Recommendations from County Court) (Rejected)." Manuscript; General Assembly Record Group; Session Records, January-February 1781; Joint Papers, Committee Papers, Resolutions; Senate Joint Resolutions: January 29-31, 1781; Box 1 (MARS ID: 66.8.23.9.9; item), State Archives of North Carolina, Raleigh. [Online catalog description: "The Pitt County court recommends that Kilpatrick be exempted from paying taxes as he was wounded in defense of his country, but the resolution would have allowed him twenty barrels of corn."]

North Carolina (State). General Assembly. "[Documents dated:] January 31, 1781: Resolution Exempting from Poll Taxes William Kilpatrick, Pitt County." Manuscript; General Assembly Record Group; Session Records, January-February 1781; Joint Papers, Committee Papers, Resolutions; House Joint Resolutions: January 29-February 1, 1781; Box 1 (MARS ID: 66.8.23.15.6; item), State Archives of North Carolina, Raleigh. [Online catalog description: "The resolution alluded to is a substitute for a Senate resolution concerning Kilpatrick."]

North Carolina (State). General Assembly. "[Documents dated:] April 30, 1783: Resolution for John Simpson of Pitt County (Rejected)." Manuscript; General Assembly Record Group; Session Records, April-May 1783; Joint Papers, Committee Papers, Resolutions; Senate Joint Resolutions: April 20-May 17, 1783; Box 1 (MARS ID: 66.8.29.12.9; item), State Archives of North Carolina, Raleigh. [Online catalog description: "Resolution would give allowances to John Simpson for time served as a member of the General Assembly."]

"Petition for Land of Abraham Tison; Secretary of State, Revolutionary Military Papers, North Carolina Archives." *Pitt County Genealogical Quarterly*, 3:1 (February 1996), 3-4.

"Petition for Land of Elisha Mills; Secretary of State, Revolutionary Military Papers, North Carolina Archives." *Pitt County Genealogical Quarterly*, 3:2 (May 1996), 6-7.

"Pitt County Militia, 1775. *Quarterly Review of the Eastern North Carolina Genealogical Society*, 14:1 (March 1987), 32.

[Pitt County. Committee of Safety]. "Record of the Proceedings of the Committee in Pitt County, North Carolina, in the Years 1774 and 1775." Manuscript CC970.32 P68, North Carolina Collection, Louis Round Wilson Special Collections Library, University of North Carolina at Chapel Hill. [Alternate title: "Partial Record of the Proceedings of the Patriots of Pitt County in the Years 1774, 1775 & 1776." Online catalog note: "This was copied from a copy in the Office of the Register of Deeds, at Greenville, N. C., the said being a copy from the original by James H. McCleur, May, 1851. Henry T. King, Greenville, N. C., Jan. 31st 1893."]

Pitt County. "Pitt County Miscellaneous Records, 1763-1924: Account of Expenditures for North Carolina by John Simpson, Colonel of Pitt Regiment of Militia." Manuscript C.R.079.928.16, State Archives of North Carolina, Raleigh.
Pitt County. "Pitt County Miscellaneous Records, 1763-1924: Copy of Letter to John Simpson, 1780." Manuscript C.R.079.928.16, State Archives of North Carolina, Raleigh.
Pitt County. "Pitt County Miscellaneous Records, 1763-1924: Correspondence, Richard Moye to Major Mountflo(u)rence Concerning Provisions, 1782." Manuscript C.R.079.928.16, State Archives of North Carolina, Raleigh.
Pitt County. "Pitt County Miscellaneous Records, 1763-1924: Pitt Committee to Paul White Concerning Seizure of Sloop *Temperance*." Manuscript C.R.079.928.17, State Archives of North Carolina, Raleigh.
Pitt County. "Pitt County Miscellaneous Records, 1763-1924: Return of Continental Soldiers Raised in Pitt, 1779." Manuscript C.R.079.928.17, State Archives of North Carolina, Raleigh.
Simpson, John. "John Simpson (1728-1788) Papers, 1766-1781, n.d." Manuscript, PC.920, State Archives of North Carolina, Raleigh. [Online catalog description: "Papers relating to Simpson of Pitt Co., brigadier general of militia in the Revolutionary War, including lighterage account, 1774-1777; photocopy of letter from Simpson to Governor Nash about the 'Pitt Volunteers' (1780); and letter to Simpson from William Brown of Bath, unable to attend the General Assembly (1781). Also an opinion as to Massachusetts law governing descent of real estate to John Simpson's heirs, signed 'D. Webster' (ca. 1820). See also P.C. 1533{Simpson and Biddle Family Papers, 1721-1928 (MARS ID: 2043)}."]

Polk County

Allhands, William A. "Polk County Was Formed Twice." *The State: A Weekly Survey of North Carolina*, 15:5 (July 1947), 5; online: http://digital.ncdcr.gov/cdm/ref/collection/p16062coll18/id/20874. [Online description from "North Carolina Periodicals Index," East Carolina University: "The mountain county of Polk has a rather odd distinction - it has existed as a county twice, having been formed twice from the same territory, once for a brief period in 1846 and again for good in 1849."]
Mosseller, Lillian Mills. "Landed Gentry of the Blue Ridge." *The State: Down Home in North Carolina*, 42:6 (November 1974), 18-20, 38; online: http://digital.ncdcr.gov/cdm/ref/collection/p16062coll18/id/56923. [Online description from "North Carolina Periodicals Index," East Carolina University: "The landed gentry colonized a part of the Appalachian Mountains. The first white settlers in the area were Ambrose and son, William Mills. The Mills family faced multiple attacks, some due in part to their Royalist persuasion, but mostly from Native Americans who pillaged and burned their homes on several occasions."]
Patton, Sadie Smathers. *Sketches of Polk County History*. Hendersonville, N.C.: Patton, 1950; reprinted: Spartanburg: The Reprint Company, 1976.
Polk County Historical Association. *Polk County, North Carolina, History*. Spartanburg, S. C.: The Reprint Company, 2006.
Sharpe, Bill. "A Persuasive Picture of Picturesque Polk." *The State: Down Home in North Carolina*, 27:21 (March 1960), 11-12, 24-26; online: http://digital.ncdcr.gov/cdm/ref/collection/p16062coll18/id/42221. [Online description from "North Carolina Periodicals Index," East Carolina University: "Located on the southern slopes of the Blue Ridge Mountains, Polk County, is a distinctive region. Originally a part of Mecklenburg County, Polk was also known as Tryon from 1768 through 1779. Aside from difficulties presented by Tories, Cherokees, and the Civil War, residents have sustained by utilizing profits derived from land holdings, the Gold Rush, tourism, agricultural endeavors, the railroad, and modern industry."]

Randolph County [Salisbury District]

[Note: For various state government documents relating to Randolph County during the Revolutionary period, search the MARS online catalog using the advanced search: http://mars.archives.ncdcr.gov/AdvancedSearch.aspx. Use the "Year" search box to restrict the searching to 1775-1783 and enter the county's name in the "Subjects" box, and hit the "Search" button near the top. This will retrieve any cataloged document for the county from that time period. These materials can vary considerably from personal or county petitions to the General Assembly, Loyalist matters, land disputes and claims, tax collection, exemptions from taxation, payments to county veterans, county divisions, personal collections, genealogical material, British claims against North Carolinians, etc. There is considerable information in these materials that could provide interesting documentation for persons living during the Revolution. The results will also include all of the wills and probates recorded in the county during the period set for the search. We had hoped to include many of these listings in this guide, but they are too voluminous. Citations to many of these search results for the eastern counties do, however, appear in the text.]

Abernathy, Jack. "Two Counties in Search of a Boundary." *Popular Government*, 14:2 (December 1948), 6, 8. [Online description from "North Carolina Periodicals Index," East Carolina University: "This summer the commissioners of Guilford and Randolph counties waded into a swampland of confusion over the exact location of their 28 mile common boundary line."]

"Aged, Impoverished, and Infirm: Two Pension Petitions in Randolph County Court Minutes." *The Genealogical Journal by the Randolph County Genealogical Society*, 26:1 (Spring 2002), 23-25. [John Slack and Jesse Gatlin]

Beck, Donald E. "Jeffrey Beck's Revolutionary War Record." *The Genealogical Journal by the Randolph County Genealogical Society*, 15:3 (Summer 1991), 16.

Blair, J. A. *Reminiscences of Randolph County*. Greensboro: Reece & Elam, Book and Job Printers, 1890.

Bowman, Becky. "Lt. Joseph Johnson's Revolutionary War Service." *The Genealogical Journal by the Randolph County Genealogical Society*, 33:3 (Fall 2009), 14-16.

Brower, (Mr. and Mrs.) W. L. "Roderick Craig's Revolutionary Papers." *The Genealogical Journal by the Randolph County Genealogical Society*, 7:4 (Fall 1983), 24-27.

Cates, Larry W. "'A Patriot in Obscurity': Teasing Out the Revolutionary War Connection of the Routh Family." *The Genealogical Journal by the Randolph County Genealogical Society*, 26:4 (Winter 2004), 3-16.

"Chatham, Orange, Randolph, and Surry Counties: Men Who Enlisted in the Continental Line, 1780." *North Carolinian: Quarterly Journal of Genealogy & History*, 6:3 (September 1960), 728-729.

Dunaway, Stewart E. *Randolph County, North Carolina, Bridge Records (1803-1864) and Mill Records, (1782-1879)*. Hillsborough: North Carolina Historical Books, 2009.

Farlow, Isaac. "Isaac Farlow Paper, 1852." Manuscript MS 437, Friends Historical Collection, Hege Library, Guilford College, Greensboro. [Online finding aid description: "'Isaac Farlow's Statement of Revolutionary Events' recounts events in and around Randolph County, NC (typescript)."]

Galbreath, Carol J. "Revolutionary Soldiers of Randolph County: Anthony Rains." *The Genealogical Journal by the Randolph County Genealogical Society*, 16:3 (Summer 1992), 24.

Galbreath, Carol J. "The Steeds, Part One: Nathaniel Steed." *The Genealogical Journal by the Randolph County Genealogical Society*, 15:2 (Spring 1991), 4-8. [Includes his Revolutionary War service.]

"The Infamous Colonel Fanning Tells All." *Genealogical Journal by the Randolph County Genealogical Society*, 25:2 (Summer 2001), 54-59. [Includes listings of militia officers from Randolph County during the Revolution.]

"Jeduthan Harper's Revolutionary War Records. *The Genealogical Journal by the Randolph County Genealogical Society*, 15:4 (Fall 1991), 6-7.

Johnson, William Perry. "1779 Tax List of Randolph County." *The North Carolinian: A Quarterly Journal of Genealogy and History*, 2:2 (June 1956), 179-186.

Johnson, William Perry. "Revolutionary Soldiers of Randolph Co., N. C." *Journal of North Carolina Genealogy*, 10:4 (Winter 1964), 1387-1388.

Lacy, Maxine. "William Marley – Revolutionary Ancestor." *The Genealogical Journal by the Randolph County Genealogical Society*, 16:2 (Spring 1992), 49.

Mills, L. Barron, Jr. *Randolph County: A Brief History*. Raleigh: Office of Archives and History, North Carolina Department of Cultural Resources, 2008.

Morgan, Tom. "Revolutionary War Pensioners of Randolph County: Henry Morgan and James Morgan." *The Genealogical Journal by the Randolph County Genealogical Society*, 16:4 (Fall 1992), 35.

Norris, Jeannie Faris. "Old Dan Tucker." *The State: Down Home in North Carolina*, 29:14 (December 1961), 11, 20; online: http://digital.ncdcr.gov/cdm/ref/collection/p16062coll18/id/9057. [Online description from "North Carolina Periodicals Index," East Carolina University: "Old Dan Tucker, subject of the song sung through the middle of the 18th-century, was no myth. Dan Tucker was a hearty man, beloved by his neighbors in Randolph County. Born in London in 1720, Tucker came to America at six years old with his parents who settled in Bath, eventually becoming a farmer and hunter."]

"Pay Roll of Capt. Samuel Reid Company in Col. Alexander's Regiment and General [Griffith] Rutherford's Brigade, Aug. 9th, 1780." *Georgia Genealogical Society Quarterly*, 5:4 (December 1969), 304-305. [Salisbury District]

"Payroll of Captain Samuel Reid, August 9th, 1780 – Name and Rank." In *Roster of Soldiers from North Carolina in the American Revolution with an Appendix Containing a Collection of Miscellaneous Records*. Baltimore, Md.: Genealogical Publishing Co., 1972), 601.

Pruitt, Albert Bruce. *Index to North Carolina County Maps: Davie, Guilford, Montgomery, Randolph, Rockingham,*

Stokes, Surry, & Yadkin. Whitakers: A. B. Pruitt, 1988.
Randolph County. "Jury Lists and Excuses, 1779-1869." Manuscript, State Archives of North Carolina, Raleigh. [Consult the State Archives to determine the exact years that are available.]
Randolph County. "Randolph County Miscellaneous Records, 1781-1922: Confiscation Act (Lists of Plunder and Several Suits, 1781-1783." Manuscript C.R.080.928.4, State Archives of North Carolina, Raleigh.
Randolph County. "Randolph County Miscellaneous Records, 1781-1922: Pension Records, 1785-1866, 1899, 1903." Manuscript C.R.080.928.8, State Archives of North Carolina, Raleigh.
"Randolph County's First Tax List." *The Genealogical Journal by the Randolph County Genealogical Society*, 24:1 (Spring 2000), 15-25; 24:2 (Summer 2000), 5-12, [1779].
"Randolph County Militiamen under the Command of John Hinds, 1780-1781." *Journal of North Carolina Genealogy*, 10:4 (Winter 1964), 1388.
"Randolph Tories Revealed." *The Genealogical Journal by the Randolph County Genealogical Society*, 30:4 (Winter 2006), 43-44.
Wicker, Jim. "The Escape at Faith Rock." *The State: Down Home in North Carolina*, 42:6 (November 1974), 27-28; online: http://digital.ncdcr.gov/cdm/ref/collection/p16062coll18/id/56923. [Online description from "North Carolina Periodicals Index," East Carolina University: "Faith Rock marks the site of Andrew Hunter's daring escape from the infamous Tory bandit David Fanning and his band of killers. The out-jutting boulder sloping into Franklinville's Deep River afforded a nearly impossible escape route for Hunter and the mare he had stolen from Fanning."]
"Willey Burrow's Declaration of Military Service." *The Genealogical Journal by the Randolph County Genealogical Society*, 8:3 (Summer 1984), 44.

Richmond County

[Note: For various state government documents relating Richmond County to during the Revolutionary period, search the MARS online catalog using the advanced search: http://mars.archives.ncdcr.gov/AdvancedSearch.aspx. Use the "Year" search box to restrict the searching to 1775-1783 and enter the county's name in the "Subjects" box, and hit the "Search" button near the top. This will retrieve any cataloged document for the county from that time period. These materials can vary considerably from personal or county petitions to the General Assembly, Loyalist matters, land disputes and claims, tax collection, exemptions from taxation, payments to county veterans, county divisions, personal collections, genealogical material, British claims against North Carolinians, etc. There is considerable information in these materials that could provide interesting documentation for persons living during the Revolution. The results will also include all of the wills and probates recorded in the county during the period set for the search. We had hoped to include many of these listings in this guide, but they are too voluminous. Citations to many of these search results for the eastern counties do, however, appear in the text.]

Bridges, Myrtle N. *Our Native Heath: Richmond County, North Carolina, 1779-1899*. Franklin: Genealogy Publishing Service, 1997.
Dunaway, Stewart E. *Richmond County Road Records (1778-1826), Bridge Records (1790-1897), Ferry Records, 1784-1857), Mill Records (1790-1875).* Hillsborough: North Carolina Historical Books, 2013.
Goesch, Carl. "Richmond County." *The State: A Weekly Survey of North Carolina*, 8:31 (December 1940), 1-4, 20-22; online: http://digital.ncdcr.gov/cdm/ref/collection/p16062coll18/id/6594. [Online description from "North Carolina Periodicals Index," East Carolina University: "Richmond comes closer to any other county to having all four of North Carolina's regional characteristics, and it is one of the state's most diversified counties physically and economically. Sharpe explores Richmond County's history, geography, industry, and people."]
Haines, Jeffrey L. "Richmond County Levies on Land, 1779." *North Carolina Genealogical Society Journal*, 33:2 (May 2007), 169-175.
Harrington, Henry William. "Henry William Harrington Papers." Manuscript 314, Southern Historical Collection, Louis Round Wilson Library, University of North Carolina at Chapel Hill; online finding aid available at http://www2.lib.unc.edu/mss/inv/h/Harrington,Henry_William.html. [Partial online catalog description: "Henry William Harrington (1748-1809) was a brigadier general in the American Revolution, a legislator in both North Carolina and South Carolina, and a planter. His son, Henry William Harrington Jr. (1793-1868) was a successful planter, businessman, and landowner of Richmond County, N. C., who served in the United States Navy during the War of 1812 and as a representative in the North Carolina House of Commons and to Constitutional Convention. The collection is chiefly political, military, and family correspondence of Revolutionary General Henry William Harrington and Henry William Harrington Jr. Early papers concern

military actions of the Revolution in the Carolinas and political and legal affairs in its aftermath. Correspondents include John Auld, Horatio Gates, Charles W. Goldsborough, William Barry Grove, Paul Hamilton, John Henry, A. M. Hopper, Charles Cotesworth Pinckney, and Benjamin W. Williams, among others."]

Honeycutt, James E., and Ida C. Honeycutt. *A History of Richmond County.* Rockingham: [s. n.], 1976.

Hutchinson, John. *No Ordinary Lives: A History of Richmond County, North Carolina, 1750-1900.* Virginia Beach: Donning Company Publishers, 1998.

North Carolina (State). General Assembly. "[Document dated:] January 29, 1781: Joint Papers, Committee Papers, Resolutions, Senate Bills, House Bills, In Favor of John Wooten (with Petition)." Manuscript; General Assembly Record Group; Session Records, Jan-Feb 1781, Box 1 (MARS ID: 66.8.23.9.2; item), State Archives of North Carolina, Raleigh. [Online catalog description: "John Wotton, of Richmond County, informs the Assembly that he volunteered to help defend the state and was wounded so badly at the Battle of Camden that he can no longer work; he asks for assistance, as he is poor. Benjamin Seawell, commanding officer of Wotton's regiment, attests to the truth of the petition. The Assembly allows him twenty barrels of corn annually. Includes two copies of the resolution."]

North Carolina (State). General Assembly. Senate. "Depositions Filed in Richmond County on 15 Nov. in Reference to John Gilchrist, 1797." Manuscript; General Assembly Record Group; Session Records, November-December 1797 (MARS Id: 66.8.83.1.9, State Archives of North Carolina, Raleigh. [Online catalog description: "Several depositions from neighbors of John Gilchrist attesting he did not aid or assist the British Army during war times."]

North Carolina (State). General Assembly. Senate. "Depositions in Reference to John Gilchrist 20 Oct., 1797." Manuscript; General Assembly Record Group; Session Records, November-December 1797, Senate Committee Reports (MARS Id: 66.8.83.1.16), State Archives of North Carolina, Raleigh. [Online catalog description: "On the 20th day of October 1797 being this present day and date firmly appeared John Willis Esquire before me George Moore a Justice of the Peace for said county, who then and there did impeach John Gilchrist Esquire of his being disqualified from holding any public office in this state, owing to his having attached himself to the enemies of the United States in time of the late war, John Gilchrist being here present when sundry witnesses were sworn and examined. To wit William Brown deposeth and saith that in time of the late war when the British troops were in Wilmington camped by Major Craig, that he this deponent in company with his brothers Neil Brown, Mr. John Gilchrist with another man returned home from Wilmington as he understood and that he said he has been to Wilmington to see Major Craig or the British to know of him or them, if the people or himself must join the British and that he plenty knew they must do so and bear arms and that the said John was then armed with a gun and that he heard after that, that he had joined the tory party, by report but does not know by whom upon being asked by Mr. Gilchrist if he did not hear that the torries were disappointed at his not joining them he answered that he did but that he did not know by whom or when. Mr. Brown further saith that all this happened some time not many months before General Rutherford came through this county and before the British left Wilmington. Upon Mr. Gilchrist asking Mr. Brown if he knew that he advised any person to join the enemy. He answered that he might or might not he lived about ten miles from him and that he did not see him after upon being asked if he ever saw him in the tory camp, he answered no."]

Richmond County. "Miscellaneous Records, 1779-1939." Manuscript, CR.081.928.3-CR.082.928.7, State Archives of North Carolina, Raleigh. [Online catalog description: Includes "Thomas Adcock and William Mullen from 1778-1779, 1792; Revolutionary War pension applications, 1832-1840, no date (broken series)"]

Richmond County. "Slave Records, 1778-1866." Manuscript, State Archives of North Carolina, Raleigh. [Consult the State Archives to determine the exact years that are available.]

Sharpe, Bill. "Mountains, Piedmont, Sandhills." *The State: Down Home in North Carolina*, 21:21 (October 1953), 3-5, 22-24; online: http://digital.ncdcr.gov/cdm/ref/collection/p16062coll18/id/31397. [Online description from "North Carolina Periodicals Index," East Carolina University: "Richmond comes closer to any other county to having all four of North Carolina's regional characteristics, and it is one of the state's most diversified counties physically and economically. Sharpe explores Richmond County's history, geography, industry, and people."]

Robeson County

"Bladen (Robeson) Patriots Council's Militia Expedition." *Robeson County Register*, 9:4 (November 1994), 154-155.

"Claims against Bladen (Robeson) Residents by British Merchants after the Revolutionary War." *The Robeson County Register*, 6:3 (August 1991), 123.

McKinnon, Henry A. "A North Carolina Scot and the Confiscation Acts." *The Robeson County Register*, 1:3 (August 1986), 105-106. [Archibald McEacharn]

McKinnon, Henry A., Jr. *Historical Sketches of Robeson County.* [Robeson County, N. C.]: Historic Robeson, Inc., [and] Friends of the Robeson County Public Library, 2001.

McKinnon, Henry A., Jr. "Revolution in Robeson." *The Robeson County Register*, 4:4 (November 1989), 132-136.

Moss, Bobby. "The Other Side: [Loyalists in the Revolution]." *The Robeson County Register*, 11:1 (February 1996), 16-23.

"Revolutionary Soldiers from Robeson County: Fredrick Johnston." *The Robeson County Register*, 9:3 (August 1994), 103.

Shoop, Michael I. "Your Obedient Humble Servant – William Tatham." *The Robeson County Register*, 1:4 (November 1986), 122-132.

Smith, Margie C. "George Willis' Revolutionary War Application." *The Robeson County Register*, 4:2 (May 1989), 75-76.

"Thomas Wilkins: Revolutionary Soldier from Robeson." *The Robeson County Register*, 11:3 (August 1996), 117.

Rockingham County

Boisseau, Mary Leigh. "Virginia Revolutionary Veterans in Rockingham and Stokes Counties, North Carolina." *Piedmont Lineages: Bulletin of the VA-NC Piedmont Genealogical Society*, 14:3 (August 1991), 95-99.

Butler, Lindley S. "The Tides of War at Troublesome Creek." *The State: Down Home in North Carolina*, 40:3 (December 1972), 8-10; online: http://digital.ncdcr.gov/cdm/ref/collection/p16062coll18/id/55639. [Online description from "North Carolina Periodicals Index," East Carolina University: "On August 13, 1972, a monument was rededicated at Speedwell Furnace, the colonial ironworks on Troublesome Creek in Rockingham County. Speedwell Furnace was an important county location for nearly 150 years, serving as a crossroad store, polling place and grist mill. Its statewide historical significance stems from its use as a bivouac during General Nathaniel Greene's southern campaign, which led to the final defeat of the British at Yorktown."]

Butler, Lindley S. "Troublesome Creek Ironworks." In William S. Powell, ed.; Jay Mazzocchi, assoc. ed., *Encyclopedia of North Carolina* (Chapel Hill: University of North Carolina Press in association with the University of North Carolina Library, 2006), 1135-1136. [modern Rockingham County; active during the Revolution]

"[Correspondence, Reports, and Maps Concerning a Proposed State Park to Commemorate Events of the American Revolution and Located on Rockingham County Land Offered by James G. W. MacLamroc]." Manuscript Folio FCp971.79 M16c, North Carolina Collection, Louis Round Wilson Special Collections Library, University of North Carolina at Chapel Hill.

Hughes, Fred. *Rockingham County, North Carolina: Historical Documentation*. Jamestown: Custom House, 1979. [map]. [Description from the University of North Carolina's online library catalog: "Includes ill., outline map of Leaksville, and 8 short essays: Campaign of 1781 in Rockingham County, by Kenneth R. Haynes, Jr.; Leaksville early lot owners; Land of Eden; Carolina-Virginia boundary; Indians in Rockingham; Governor Alexander Martin, 1740-1807; Speedwell iron works; How a water-powered overshot grist mill worked. Shows original landowners and land grants, colonial roads, military routes, historical sites, and natural features."]

Pruitt, Albert Bruce. *Index to North Carolina County Maps: Davie, Guilford, Montgomery, Randolph, Rockingham, Stokes, Surry, & Yadkin*. Whitakers: A. B. Pruitt, 1988.

"Rockingham County, North Carolina, Historical Documentation." Manuscript, MC.084.1977h, State Archives of North Carolina, Raleigh. [Online catalog description: "Map shows locations of historic events, mills, landowners, military routes for the Revolutionary War, churches, land grants (along with the dates issued), ferries, mines, Indian sites and trails, iron works. The margins contain descriptions of the Campaign of 1781, "Land of Eden" for William Byrd II, the Carolina-Virginia boundary, Indians, Governor Alexander Martin, (1740-1807), Speedwell Iron Works, and a drawing and description of 'how a water-powered overshot grist mill worked'."

"A Rockingham County, N. C. Militia List (Capt. Richard Vernon's Company N. C. Militia)." *North Carolina Genealogical Society Journal*, 2:2 (April 1976), 102.

Webster, Mrs. S. F. "A Rockingham County, North Carolina, Militia List." *North Carolina Genealogical Society Journal*, 2:2 (April 1976), 102.

Rowan County and Salisbury

[Note: For various state government documents relating to Salisbury during the Revolutionary period, search the MARS online catalog using the advanced search: http://mars.archives.ncdcr.gov/AdvancedSearch.aspx. Use the "Year" search box to restrict the searching to 1775-1783 and enter the town's name in the "Subjects" box, and hit the "Search" button near the top. This will retrieve any cataloged document for the county from that time period. These materials can vary considerably from personal or county petitions to the General Assembly, Loyalist matters, land disputes and claims, tax collection, exemptions from taxation, payments to county veterans, county divisions, personal collections, genealogical material, British claims against North Carolinians, etc. There is considerable information in these materials that could provide interesting documentation for persons living during the Revolution. The results will also include all of the wills and probates recorded in the county during the period set for the search. We had hoped to include many of these listings in this guide, but they are too voluminous. Citations to many of these search results for the eastern counties do, however, appear in the text.]

"Address from Rowan Militia Officers for Consideration [1778; to the North Carolina General Assembly]." *The State Records of North Carolina, Vol. 13: 1778-79*. (Winston: M. I. & J. C. Stewart, 1895; reprinted: Wilmington: Broadfoot Publishing Company, 1993), 389-390; reprinted in: *Rowan County Register*, 10:3 (August 1995), 2299-2300.

Barekman, June B. "Bible Record of Revolutionary Soldier, John Lanning." *Southern Genealogist's Exchange Quarterly*, 23:3 (Fall 1982), 118. [Lanning was from Bordentown, Burlington County, N. J., and moved to Rowan County, N. C. and served in the Revolution from there.]

Beck, John V. "1782 Legislative Petition." *Rowan County Register*, 3:1 (February 1988), 516-521.

Brawley, James S. *Rowan County: A Brief History*. Raleigh: North Carolina Division of Archives and History, 1974.

Brawley, James S. "The Rowan Resolves [1774]." *Rowan County Register*, 3:2 (May 1988), 580-581.

Brawley, James S. *The Rowan Story, 1753-1953: A Narrative History of Rowan County, North Carolina*. Salisbury, N. C.: Rowan Print Co., 1953.

Buerbaum, Theo. "A Revolutionary Benefactor." *Journal of the Genealogical Society of Rowan County, North Carolina*, 19:3 (2005), 82. [Originally published in the *Salisbury Evening Post*, April 23, 1912, this article relates stories by J. L. Hedrick concerning the passage of General Greene's army through the area.]

"Captains' Tax Districts [Rowan County and vicinity]." *Journal of the Genealogical Society of Rowan County, North Carolina*, 21:1 (2007), 10-11. [Many are for 1778.]

Crane, Madilyn L. "Revolutionary War Record of William Hickman." *Rowan County Register*, 4:1 (February 1989), 766.

Crawford, Sybil F. "John Crawford, a Migration Story." *Rowan County Register*, 4:3 (August 1989), 884-886. [Followed by "Revolutionary War Pension Record of John Crawford," 887-888.]

Daves, Graham. "Town and County Resolutions of 1774." *Magazine of American History with Notes and Queries*, 30:1-2 (July-August 1893), 88-90. [Wilmington; Rowan County; Anson County; New Bern and Craven County]

Dunaway, Stewart E. *Rowan County, North Carolina, Ferry Records (1793-1848), Mill Records (1769-1895)*. Hillsborough: North Carolina Historical Books, 2010. [Note: While not specifically concerning the Revolution, these sources can be used in tandem with land records and other documents to help locate places of residence, occupations, geographical features, and place names.]

Dunaway, Stewart E. *Rowan County, North Carolina, Road and Bridge Records (1758-1882)*. Hillsborough: North Carolina Historical Books, 2010. [Note: While not specifically concerning the Revolution, these sources can be used in tandem with land records and other documents to help locate places of residence, occupations, geographical features, and place names.]

Ervin, Sam J. *A Colonial History of Rowan County, North Carolina*. Chapel Hill: University of North Carolina Press, 1917.

Ferguson, H. W. "Map of Rowan County, North Carolina, 1780." *Rowan County Register*, 11:1 (February 1996), 2440-2441.

Freeze, Gary R. "Reading 'the Writing on the Walls' of Backcountry Rowan County's Stone Sanctuaries, 1774-1795." *Journal of Backcountry Studies*, 1:1 (Spring 2006); online: http://libjournal.uncg.edu/jbc/article/view/64/49 and http://libjournal.uncg.edu/jbc/article/view/65/48. [2 parts]

Green, Virginia S. "1782 Legislative Petition." *Rowan County Register*, 2:3 (August 1987), 397-399.

Hall, Moses, 1760-after 1835. "[Revolutionary War Memoir]." In John C. Dann, ed. *The Revolution Remembered: Eyewitness Accounts of the War for Independence* (Chicago: University of Chicago Press, 1980), Chapter 6: "War in the Carolinas," 196-204. [Moses Hall, Rowan County, North Carolina]

Heraldson, Irene Everman, for the Taneycomo Chapter, Missouri DAR. *Missouri DAR Genealogical Records Committee Report, Series 1, Volume 316: The Six Militia Companies of Rowan County, North Carolina, 1778* (typescript, 1971?); digital surrogate, DAR Library, Washington, D. C.

Hood, Davyd Foard. *The Architecture of Rowan County, North Carolina: A Catalogue and History of Surviving 18th, 19th, and Early 20th Century Structures*. Salisbury: Rowan County Historic Properties Commission, 1983; reprinted: Salisbury: Historic Salisbury Foundation, 2000.

Hood, Davyd Foard. "Log Construction in Rowan County." *North Carolina Preservationist*, 9 (October 1977), 4-6. [Online description from "North Carolina Periodicals Index," East Carolina University: "This article details the log buildings found in Rowan County in terms of both architectural and cultural history, and preservation."]

Howard, Joseph H. "Captain John Dickey, Patriot." *Rowan County Register*, 11:1 (February 1996), 2443-2450.

Hunter, Cyrus Lee. *Sketches of Western North Carolina Historical and Biographical, Illustrating Principally the Revolutionary Period of Mecklenburg, Rowan, Lincoln and Adjoining Counties, Accompanied with Miscellaneous Information, Much of It Never Before Published.* Raleigh: Raleigh News Steam Job Print, 1877; reprinted: Raleigh: Edwards & Broughton, 1930; Baltimore: Regional Publishing Company, 1970.

Irwin, Lyndon N. "Revolutionary War Lieutenant John Graham: Patriot or Horse Thief." *Rowan County Register*, 10:1 (February 1995), 2182-2186.

James Hunter Chapter, North Carolina Daughters of the American Revolution *North Carolina DAR Genealogical Records Committee Report, Series 1, Volumes 427, 431: Early Families of the North Carolina Counties of Rockingham and Stokes with Revolutionary Service* (typescripts, 1978, 1981); digital surrogates, DAR Library, Washington, D. C.; Reprinted: Easley, S. C.: Southern Historical Press, 1990.

Johnson, William Perry. "Loyalists and Tories in the Rowan-Davidson Counties Area, 1778." *Journal of North Carolina Genealogy*, 14:4 (Winter 1968), 2239-2244.

Kluttz, James W. "Early Landowners of Rowan County, North Carolina, Period 1753-1810." Maps MC.085.1995k, Search Room, State Archives of North Carolina, Raleigh. [Online catalog description: "Large portions of these maps are based on research and drawings done around 1950 by David A. Rendleman of Salisbury, N.C. They have been remapped and extended by James W. Kluttz of Landis, N.C. 1200 early landowners are shown and appear in the index. Most of the land records are dated between 1753 and 1810. Some measurements have been altered slightly in order to properly show the intent of the deeds. Each sheet represents a separate area of Rowan county: Northwest, West, North Central, Southwest, South Central, and Southeast. Roads, waterways, and county boundaries are given. A key map and match lines show the relationship of each sheet to the other."]

Lewis, J. D. "Patriot Leaders in North Carolina: Charles McDowell: Captain in the 2nd Rowan County Regiment of Militia - 1775-1776; Lt. Colonel in the 2nd Rowan County Regiment of Militia - 1776-1777; Colonel over the Burke County Regiment of Militia - 1777-1782; Brigadier General of the Morgan District Brigade of Militia - 1782-1783." Online: http://www.carolana.com/NC/Revolution/patriot_leaders_nc_charles_mcdowell.html.

Lewis, J. D. "Patriot Leaders in North Carolina: James Brandon: 2nd Major in the Rowan County Regiment of Militia – 1775; Major in the 1st Rowan County Regiment of Militia - 1775-1777; Major in the Rowan County Regiment of Militia - 1777-1780; Lt. Colonel in the Rowan County Regiment of Militia - 1780-1782; Colonel over the 2nd Rowan County Regiment of Militia - 1782-1783." Online: http://www.carolana.com/NC/Revolution/patriot_leaders_nc_james_brandon.html.

Lewis, Johanna Miller. "Women Artisans in Backcountry North Carolina, 1753-1790." *North Carolina Historical Review,* 68 (July 1991), 214-236. [Online description from "North Carolina Periodicals Index," East Carolina University: "An examination of women artisans in Rowan County, which in the late 18th century encompassed the entire northwestern quadrant of the modern state. While the actual number of women artisans will never be known because the business activities of some married women were run by their husbands, but the count of women artisans evidenced in county records grew in the last half of the 18th century with spinning and weaving being the most popular craft."]

Linn, Jo White. "1778 & 1779 Guards at the Salisbury District Gaol." In Jo White Linn, *Rowan County, North Carolina Tax Lists, 1757-1800* (Salisbury: J. W. Linn, 1995), 159-167.

Linn, Jo White. "1779 Pay Roll to Goal Guards in Salisbury." *Rowan County Register*, 14:4 (November 1999), 3326-3328.

Linn, Jo White. "1779 Rowan County Militia List." In Jo White Linn, *Rowan County, North Carolina Tax Lists, 1757-1800* (Salisbury: J. W. Linn, 1995), 171.

[Linn, Jo White]. "1779 Rowan County Petition." *Rowan County Register*, 12:2 (May 1997), 2754.

Linn, Jo White. "1781 Rowan County Petition." *Rowan County Register*, 14:2 (May 1999), 3244-3245.

Linn, Jo White. "1782 Remonstrance & Petition from Inhabitants of Salisbury District." *Rowan County Register*, 12:1 (February 1997), 2657-2666; 12:2 (May 1997), 2735-2742.

Linn, Jo White. "1791 Memorial of Joseph Was(s)on, Formerly of Rowan County, Now in Iredell County." *Rowan County Register*, 12:2 (May 1997), 2757-2760. [regarding his injuries during the war]

Linn, Jo White. "1791 Revolutionary War Petition of John Lopp." *Journal of the Genealogical Society of Rowan County, North Carolina*, 17:3 (August 2003), 105-107.

Linn, Jo White. *Abstracts of the Minutes of the Court of Pleas and Quarter Sessions: Rowan County, North Carolina, Vol. III*. Salisbury: J. W. Linn, 1982. [There are some civil service appointments and patriotic service on various pages. Includes the names of a number of non-jurors.]

Linn, Jo White. "Bounty Land Warrants Recorded in Rowan County." *Rowan County Register*, 8:3 (August 1993), 1834-1835.

Linn, Jo White. "George Godbey of Rowan, Revolutionary War Soldier under George Washington." *Rowan County Register*, 14:2 (May 1999), 3222.

Linn, Jo White. "Salisbury District State Docket, Superior Court." *Rowan County Register*, 7:2 (May 1992), [September Court 1778] 1519-1526; 8:1 (February 1993), [March Court 1779] 1713-1717; 8:2 (May 1993), [March Court 1782] 1771-1778; 8:4 (November 1993), [September Court 1782] 1881-1887; 9:3 (August 1994), [March Court 1783] 2080-2090; 10:2 (May 1995), [September Court 1783] 2243-2252.

Linn, Jo White. "Virginia-North Carolina Migrations As Identified in the First Ten Deed Books of Rowan County, North Carolina." *Magazine of Virginia Genealogy*, 23:2 (May 1985), 30-35. [This article compiles abstracts of Rowan County deeds, including information on many who had immigrated to Rowan County from the Shenandoah Valley in Virginia. Immigrant names and Virginia place names are provided.]

Linn, Jo White. "William Lorance, Revolutionary War Soldier: Migration from Rowan Co., NC to Owen County, KY." *Rowan County Register*, 16:2 (May 2001), 3657.

Linn, Jo White. "William Steelman of Rowan: Revolutionary War Soldier." *Rowan County Register*, 16:2 (May 2001), 3644.

Livengood, Bradley. "The Hand Diligent: A Revolutionary History of Rowan County, 1753-1791." M. A. thesis, University of North Carolina at Greensboro, 1991.

"Loyalists and Tories in the Rowan-Davidson-Davie Counties Area – 1778." *Journal of the Genealogical Society of Rowan County, North Carolina*, 11:3 (September 1997), 104-108.

MacDonald, James M. "Politics of the Personal in the Old North State: Griffith Rutherford in Revolutionary North Carolina" Ph. D. dissertation, Louisiana State University and Agricultural & Mechanical College, 2006. [Rowan Co.; militia officer and elected official].

McCorkle, George. "Sketch of Colonel Francis Locke." *North Carolina Booklet*, 10:1 (July 1910), 12-21; online: http://digital.ncdcr.gov/cdm/ref/collection/p249901coll37/id/14180. [Online description from "North Carolina Periodicals Index," East Carolina University: "Colonel Francis Locke of Rowan County was a North Carolina native and Patriot leader during the Revolutionary War. The article highlights the military service during the Revolution as well as his legislative service during the early days of the United States."]

McCubbins, "Mame" Mary Louise Gaskill. "[List of Men Whose Property was Threatened with Confiscation. 1782.]" *Rowan County Register*, 3:3 (August 1988), 620.

Meroney, Thomas Theresa. "This Old Stone House." *The State: A Weekly Survey of North Carolina*, 4:15 (September 1936), 7, 16; online: http://digital.ncdcr.gov/cdm/ref/collection/p16062coll18/id/11218. [Online description from "North Carolina Periodicals Index," East Carolina University: "The Old Stone House, built in 1766, is located about three miles from Salisbury. Thomas describes the house and some of the interesting events that happened there during the Colonial period."]

Nolan, John B. "The Revolutionary Era in Rowan County, North Carolina: From Colony to Statehood." *Rowan County Register*, 12:4 (November 1997), 2837-2845.

North Carolina (State). General Assembly. "[Document dated]: 1778: Petition of the Militia Officers of Rowan Co. (no date)." Manuscript; General Assembly Record Group; Session Records, April-May 1778; Miscellaneous; Joint Papers, Committee Papers, Senate Resolutions, House Resolutions: Joint Papers: Petitions (April 18-May 1, 1778), Box 1 (MARS ID: 66.8.12.11.1; item), State Archives of North Carolina, Raleigh. [Online catalog description: "Petition requesting the use of regular soldiers in the militia, rather than yeoman volunteers."]

North Carolina (State). General Assembly. "[Document Dated]: August 17, 1778: Report on the Petitions of Col. Philip Alston, John Hinton, and Inhabitants of Rowan Co. (with Messages and Petitions)." Manuscript; General Assembly Record Group; Session Records, August 1778; Joint Papers, Committee Papers, Senate Resolutions, House Resolutions; Joint Select Committee Reports, Box 1 (MARS ID: 66.8.14.7.7; item), State Archives of North Carolina, Raleigh. [Online catalog description: "The petitioners are officers in the militia and claim that upon the resignation of superior officers, they are entitled to a promotion to the rank of the discharged officer.

The Assembly disagrees, holding that it has the authority to appoint men to the vacated positions and that there is no such thing as a 'right to promotion'."]

North Carolina (State). General Assembly. "[Document dated]: August 15, 1778: Bill for Making Two Medicinal Springs and the Lands Adjacent thereto in Rowan and Burke Counties Public Property." Manuscript; General Assembly Record Group; Session Records; Joint Papers, Committee Papers, Senate Resolutions, House Resolutions, Box 1 (MARS ID: 66.8.14.11; folder), State Archives of North Carolina, Raleigh.

North Carolina (State). General Assembly. "[Document dated]: January 13, 1779: Petitions of Hardy Jones and Thomas Saint (Sent by Governor Jan. 13, 1779)." Manuscript; General Assembly Record Group; Session Records, January-February 1779; Joint Papers, Committee Papers; Joint Papers (January-February 1779): Petitions, Box 1 (MARS ID: 66.8.15.9.1), State Archives of North Carolina, Raleigh. [Online catalog description: "Hardy Jones petitions Gov. Caswell concerning alleged land fraud perpetrated by John Jacks in Rowan County; Thomas Saint, a Quaker, petitions the General Assembly to permit him to register his land without having to make a sworn declaration of fidelity to the state."]

North Carolina (State). General Assembly. "[Document dated]: January 26, 1779: Petition of the Militia Officers in the Western End of Rowan County." Manuscript; General Assembly Record Group; Session Records, January-February 1779: Joint Papers, Committee Papers, Resolutions; Joint Papers (Janurary-February 1779): Petitions, Box 1 (MARS ID: 66.8.15.9.7; item), State Archives of North Carolina, Raleigh. [Online catalog description: "The petitioners request that a new administrative department be created in the western part of Rowan County due to their distance from the courthouse in Salisbury."]

North Carolina (State). General Assembly. "[Document dated]: November 2, 1779: Resolution in Favor of Colonel Walter Lindsay." Manuscript; General Assembly Record Group; Session Records, October-November 1779; Joint Papers, Committee Papers, Resolutions; Senate Joint Resolutions: October 19-November 10, 1779, Box 1 (MARS ID:66.8.18.12.17; item), State Archives of North Carolina, Raleigh. [Online catalog description: "In response to the memorial of Lindsay, of Rowan County, in which he describes his history of military service to the state, the Assembly authorizes an annual pension of fifty pounds."]

North Carolina (State). General Assembly. "[Document Dated]: May 3, 1780: Resolution Granting Replacement Certificate to Moses Leinster (with Deposition)." Manuscript; General Assembly Record Group; Session Records, April-May 1780; Joint Papers, Committee Papers, Resolutions; Joint Senate Resolutions: April 27-May 4, 1780, Box 1 (MARS ID: 66.8.20.13.11; item), State Archives of North Carolina, Raleigh. [Online catalog description: "The certificate which Leinster, of Rowan County, lost had been granted for flour."]

North Carolina (State). General Assembly. "[Document dated]: May 3, 1780: Resolution Granting Replacement Certificate to William Brandon (with Petition and Deposition). "Manuscript; General Assembly Record Group; Session Records, April-May 1780; Joint Papers, Committee Papers, Resolutions; Joint Senate Resolutions: April 27-May 4, 1780, Box 1 (MARS ID: 66.8.20.13.12; item), State Archives of North Carolina, Raleigh. [Online catalog description: "The certificate which Brandon, of Rowan County, lost had been granted for wagons."]

North Carolina (State). General Assembly. "[Document dated]: September 13, 1780: Resolution Requesting Governor to Issue Warrants in Favor of Commanding Officer of Rowan County (Messages Only)." Manuscript; General Assembly Record Group; Session Records, August-September 1780; Joint Papers, Committee Papers, Resolutions; House Joint Resolutions: September 8-13, 1780, Box 1 (MARS ID: 66.8.22.11.9; item), State Archives of North Carolina, Raleigh.

North Carolina (State). General Assembly. "[Document dated]: July 14, 1781: "Resolution in Favor of Joseph Kerr of Rowan County (Messages Only)." Manuscript; General Assembly Record Group; Session Records, June-July 1781; Joint Papers, Committee Papers, Resolutions; Senate Joint Resolutions: July 6-14, 1781, Box 1 (MARS ID: 66.8.25.11.13; item), State Archives of North Carolina, Raleigh.

North Carolina (State). General Assembly. "[Document dated]: May 2, 1782: Remonstrance and Petition from a Number of Inhabitants of the District of Salisbury." Manuscript; General Assembly Record Group; Session Records, April-May 1782; Joint Papers, Committee Papers; Propositions and Grievances – Report and Papers, Box 1 (MARS ID: 66.8.27.7.9; item), State Archives of North Carolina, Raleigh. [Online catalog description: "Petition on behalf of Rowan Co. residents complaining about unfair militia drafts, crimes committed by militia officers, and the British army marching through Salisbury; includes messages from both about referral to committee."]

North Carolina (State). General Assembly. "[Document dated]: May 8, 1782: Report on Memorial of James Houston of Rowan County. (Messages Only)." Manuscript; General Assembly Record Group; Session Records, April-May 1782; Manuscript; General Assembly Record Group; Session Records, April-May 1782; Joint Papers, Committee Papers; Joint Select Committees: Reports and Papers, May 8-May 18, 1782, Box 1 (MARS ID:

66.8.27.11.3; item), State Archives of North Carolina, Raleigh. [Online catalog description: "Messages from both houses referring petition to committee."]

North Carolina (State). General Assembly. "[Document dated]: April 23, 1783: Resolution in Favor of William Mclaine of Rowan County." Manuscript; General Assembly Record Group; Session Records, April-May 1783; Joint Papers, Committee Papers, Resolutions; House Joint Resolutions: April 21-30, 1783, Box 1 (MARS ID: 66.8.29.13.9; item), State Archives of North Carolina, Raleigh. [Online catalog description: "Resolution provides yearly allowance for William Mclaine who was wounded in battle and is unable to provide his own subsistance."]

North Carolina (State). General Assembly. "[Document dated]: May 16, 1783: Resolution to Empower the Governor to Grant a Cavaet to John Swink of Rowan County." Manuscript; General Assembly Record Group; Session Records, April-May 1783; Joint Papers, Committee Papers, Resolutions; House Joint Resolutions: May 1-17, 1783, Box 1 (MARS ID: 66.8.29.14.25; item), State Archives of North Carolina, Raleigh. [Online catalog description: "Resolution regards the petition of John Swink, who maintains that he purchased land from John Leafe and allowed Hugh Montgomery to enter the claim to land when the land office opened. Montgomery neglected to make the claim and Benjamin Howard received the claim to his land. Swink is applying for a caveat until the proper title can be established. Resolution grants the caveat and applies this circumstance for any Quaker, Moravian, or Mennonist (Mennonite). Includes petition, deposition, and resolution."]

North Carolina (State). General Assembly. "[Document dated]: May 17, 1783: Resolution in Favor of John Archibald of Rowan County." Manuscript; General Assembly Record Group; Session Records April-May 1783; Joint Papers, Committee Papers, Resolutions; House Joint Resolutions: May 1-17, 1783, Box 1 (MARS ID: 66.8.29.14.19; item), State Archives of North Carolina, Raleigh. [Online catalog description: "Resolution gives compensation to John Archibald of Rowan County for an indentured servant who was drafted into the militia and who afterwards deserted. Includes petition, depositions, committee report, and resolution."]

North Carolina (State). General Assembly. "[Document Dated]: May 20, 1784: Report on Memorials of James Kerr, Commissioner of Rowan County." Manuscript; General Assembly Record Group; Session Records, April-June 1784; Committee Papers, Resolutions: Joint Select Committees: Reports and Papers: May 20-June 3, 1784, Box 2 (MARS ID:66.8.32.2.1; item), State Archives of North Carolina, Raleigh. [Online catalog description: "Report is on two memorials of James Kerr, Commissioner of Rowan County: The first memorial concerns the borrowing of salt by Kerr to fill a military requisition and asks for compensation to pay the donors. The second memorial concerns the collections of the specific tax in the county, where Kerr collected receipts instead of the money he was directed to collect in an act of the Assembly. Committee awards compensation for salt, but finds Kerr's conduct irregular in the collection of taxes."]

"Oaths of Allegiance-Rowan County, North Carolina, 1778." *Daughters of the American Revolution Magazine,* 82:2 (February 1948), 208-209.

Patrick, Edward F. "[Revolutionary War Memoir]." In John C. Dann, ed. *The Revolution Remembered: Eyewitness Accounts of the War for Independence* (Chicago: University of Chicago Press, 1980), Chapter 11: "Logistics," 374-376. [Edward F. Patrick, Salisbury, North Carolina]

"Patriot Resistance in Rowan and Mecklenburg Cos., N. C., 1780-1781." *North Carolina Genealogical Society Journal*, 9:4 (November 1983), 9:4 (November 1983), 228.

"Patriots Oath of Allegiance." *Journal of the Genealogical Society of Rowan County, North Carolina*, 3:2 (March 1989), 55.

Raynor, George. *Piedmont Passages II: Patriots and Tories in Piedmont Carolina.* Salisbury: Salisbury Post, 1990.

"Regiment of Rowan County Militia under the command of Colonel Griffith Rutherford on an Expedition to Cross Creek against the Insurgents." In Weynette Parks Haun, *North Carolina Revolutionary Army Accounts, Part I, Secretary of State Treasurer's & Comptroller's Papers Journal "A", (Public Accounts) 1775-1776* (Durham: W. P. Haun, 1988), 30-40. [County designation determined by a number of officers whose commissions in the Rowan militia are documented in *NC State Records*, Rowan County (N.C.). Committee of Safety November 10, 1775 - November 11, 1775, Volume 10, Pages 319-320. Also, pension records such as those of John Woodside (Woodsides) W6585, Henry Winkler W3061 and Frederick Miller W8460. The pension record of Robert Martin S2732, states that Colonel John Fifer and General Rutherford had command of the troops from Mecklenburg and Rowan Counties. {This analysis was performed by genealogists in the Genealogy Office, Office of the Registrar General, National Society Daughters of the American Revolution, Washington, D. C.}]

Rockwell, E[lijah] F[rink]. "Rowan County, North Carolina, in 1774." *Historical Magazine*, 2d series, 5:2 (February 1869), 118-123.

Roebuck, Haywood. "Some Continental Line Deserters from Rowan, Surry, and Mecklenburg Counties, N. C. 1780-1782." *North Carolina Genealogical Society Journal*, 1:2 (April 1975), 102-104.

Rosenthal, Patricia, and Jean K. Ramsey. "Bounty Land [for Joseph Eller, Davidson County, Tennessee]." *Journal of the Genealogical Society of Rowan County, North Carolina*, 8:2 (June 1994), 57.

"Roster of North Carolina Soldiers in the American Revolution: Rowan County." *Journal of the Genealogical Society of Rowan County, North Carolina*, 8:2 (June-July 1985), 77. [This is actually a listing from the pension rolls.]

Rouse, J. K. *Another Revolutionary Hero Dies*. Kannapolis, N. C.: J. K. Rouse, 1978. [Includes North Carolina veterans.] [Excerpts from this publication featuring veterans from Rowan County appear in *Journal of the Genealogical Society of Rowan County, North Carolina*, 7:3 (September 1993), 99-101; 7:3 (December 1993), 165.

Rowan County. "Jury Lists, 1779-1913." Manuscript, State Archives of North Carolina, Raleigh. [Consult the State Archives to determine the exact years that are available.]

Rowan County. "Justice of the Peace, Records of, 1778-1924." Manuscript, State Archives of North Carolina, Raleigh. [Consult the State Archives to determine the exact years that are available.]

Rowan County. "Military Records, 1781-1919." Manuscript, CR.084.920.1-CR.085.920.2, Rowan County, Military Records, State Archives of North Carolina, Raleigh. [Box 1 contains: "Confiscation of Tory Lands, 1781-1782" Box 2 contains: "Substitutes and Replacements for the Revolution."]

Rowan County. "Rowan County Miscellaneous Records, 1740-1940: Slaves and Persons of Color, 1767-1870." Manuscript C.R.085.928.4, State Archives of North Carolina, Raleigh.

Rowan County. "Miscellaneous Records, 1763-1940." Manuscript, CRX Records, State Archives of North Carolina, Raleigh. [Consult the State Archives to determine the exact years that are available.]

Rowan County. "Slave Records, 1779-1866." Manuscript, CRX Records, State Archives of North Carolina, Raleigh. [Consult the State Archives to determine the exact years that are available.]

Rumple, Jethro. *A History of Rowan County, North Carolina, Containing Sketches of Prominent Families and Distinguished Men, with an Appendix*. Salisbury, N. C.: J. J. Bruner, 1881; reprinted: Salisbury: Elizabeth Maxwell Steele Chapter, North Carolina Daughters of the American Revolution, [1916]; Raleigh: Edwards and Broughton Company, 1929; Baltimore: Regional Publishing Company, 1974.

Scarborough, Franklin. "Rediscovery of the King George Picture." *The State: Down Home in North Carolina*, 49:10 (March 1979), 18-19; online: http://digital.ncdcr.gov/cdm/ref/collection/p16062coll18/id/59551. [Online description from "North Carolina Periodicals Index," East Carolina University: "Pictures of King George III and Queen Charlotte were returned to their home in the Salisbury Tavern in 1977. During the Revolutionary War, American General Nathaniel Greene stopped by the tavern, owned by the Steele family, and wrote 'King George, hide they face and mourn' on the back of his portrait. After Mrs. Steele's death, the portraits passed to David L. Swain, president of the University of North Carolina. The pictures were later auctioned to William J. Andrews in 1883, who kept the pictures in his family in California until 1977, when the Neel family, descendants of the Steeles, bought the portraits and returned them to the tavern wall."]

"Second Regiment of Rowan Militia on an Expedition against the Insurgents." In Weynette Parks Haun, *North Carolina Revolutionary Army Accounts Secretary of State Treasurer's and Comptroller's Papers Journal "A" (Public Accounts), 1775-1776* (Durham: W. P. Haun, 1988), 4-5.

"Second Regiment of Rowan County Militia under Colonel Christopher Beckman on an Expedition against the Insurgents." In Weynette Parks Haun, North Carolina Revolutionary Army Accounts, Part I, Secretary of State Treasurer's & Comptroller's Papers Journal "A", (Public Accounts) 1775-1776 (Durham: W. P. Haun, 1988), 4-5.

Sharpe, Bill. "Industrious, Gallant Nation." *Friend of Wildlife*, 20:45 (April 1953), 1-3, 16-19. [Online description from "North Carolina Periodicals Index," East Carolina University: "Home of the Old Catawba and Cherokee Trading Fort on the Yadkin River, Rowan County was settled by Scotch-Irish and German immigrants in the 1740s. Rowan is famous for being the birthplace or home of Griffith Rutherford, Andrew Jackson, General William Davidson, John Brevard, William R. Davie, Daniel Boone, and Alexander Martin."]

Sloan, Henry. "Sloan-Osborne Ciphering Book, 1753; 1778-1779; 1782." Manuscript PC.1955, State Archives of North Carolina, Raleigh. [Adlai Osborne (1744-1814), lawyer and political and educational leader, was born in either New Jersey or Delaware, son of Alexander and Agnes McWhorter Osborne. At the age of five he was brought by his parents to what is now southeastern Iredell County. Henry Sloan (1769-1783), was the son of John and Agnes Sloan of Rowan (subsequently Davidson) County.]

Smith, Renee Jackson. "Revolutionary War Record of James McCollum." *Rowan County Register*, 4:1 (February 1989), 767-768. [with editorial notes by the editor]

Steele, Ephraim, active 1778-1787. "Ephraim Steele Papers, 1755-1877 (bulk 1773-1823)." Manuscript 3876-z, Southern Historical Collection, Louis Round Wilson Special Collections Library, University of North Carolina at Chapel Hill. [The collection includes letters from "his brother's family in Rowan County, N.C. (parents of Federalist leader John Steele)."]

Stutesman, John Hale. "An Old Soldier's Memories? Or Imaginings?" *North Carolina Genealogical Society Journal*, 18:4 (November 1992), 227. [John Snoddy, Rowan County, N. C.]

Thomas, Heath. "The Old Stone House Preserved." *The State: Down Home in North Carolina*, 33:2 (November 1965), 11-12; online: http://digital.ncdcr.gov/cdm/ref/collection/p16062coll18/id/48551. [Online description from "North Carolina Periodicals Index," East Carolina University: "Three miles east of Salisbury stands the oldest house in western North Carolina. Called the Old Stone House, it was built by Michael Braun in 1766. The Rowan County Museum is sponsoring its restoration."]

Thorp, Daniel B. "Taverns and Communities: The Case of Rowan County, North Carolina." In David Colin Crass, Steven D. Smith, Martha A. Zierden, and Richard D. Brooks, *The Southern Colonial Backcountry: Interdisciplinary Perspectives on Frontier Communities* (Knoxville: University of Tennessee Press, 1998), 76-86.

Thorp, Daniel B. "Taverns and Tavern Culture on the Southern Colonial Frontier: Rowan County, North Carolina, 1753-1776." *Journal of Southern History*, 62:4 (November 1996), 661-688.

"Three Revolutionary Soldiers Gone!" *Journal of the Genealogical Society of Rowan County, North Carolina*, 8:4 (December 1994), 162. [William Mason, Edward Stewart, John Myers]

Warren, Mary Bondurant. "Evidence of Military Service Found in Loose Papers [Rowan County, N. C.; Revolutionary War and War of 1812]." *The Carolina Genealogist*, no. 48 (Fall 1982), 1-6.

Rutherford County [Salisburg District before 1782. Morgan District after 1782]

[Formed April 14, 1779 from the division of old Tryon County.]

[Note: For various state government documents relating to Rutherford County during the Revolutionary period, search the MARS online catalog using the advanced search: http://mars.archives.ncdcr.gov/AdvancedSearch.aspx. Use the "Year" search box to restrict the searching to 1775-1783 and enter the county's name in the "Subjects" box, and hit the "Search" button near the top. This will retrieve any cataloged document for the county from that time period. These materials can vary considerably from personal or county petitions to the General Assembly, Loyalist matters, land disputes and claims, tax collection, exemptions from taxation, payments to county veterans, county divisions, personal collections, genealogical material, British claims against North Carolinians, etc. There is considerable information in these materials that could provide interesting documentation for persons living during the Revolution. The results will also include all of the wills and probates recorded in the county during the period set for the search. We had hoped to include many of these listings in this guide, but they are too voluminous. Citations to many of these search results for the eastern counties do, however, appear in the text.]

"Another Revolutionary Hero Gone." *American Monthly Magazine* [DAR], 42:3 (March 1913), 141. [Colonel Benjamin Hardin, from Rutherford County, North Carolina; fought at the Battle of King's Mountain.]

"Confiscated Property Sales, Rutherford County, N. C." *Eswau Huppeday: Bulletin of the Broad River Genealogical Society,* 11:2 (May 1991), 118-119.

"A Descriptive List of the 18 Months Men Raised in Rutherford County, N. C. for the Revolutionary War." *Eswau Huppeday: Bulletin of the Broad River Genealogical Society*, 19:3 (August 1999), 176.

"Descriptions of Soldiers from Militia Returns, 1778-1782." *North Carolinian: A Quarterly Journal of Genealogy and History*, 6:4 (December 1960), 751. [Includes: List of 18 month's men drafted to fill the Continental Battalion of North Carolina from Rutherford County.]

Ferguson, Nancy Ellen. "Gilbert Town: Its Place in North Carolina and Revolutionary War History, with Information on Andrew Hampton, Griffith Rutherford, William Gilbert, and the Death of James Dunlap." Online: http://www.overmountainvictory.org/Gtown.htm. [The site includes section titled: "Formation;" "The County Government;" "The Courthouse at Gilbert Town;" "Early Court Cases;" "William Gilbert;" "The Village at Gilbert Town;" "The Early Forts of Rutherford;" "Patrick Ferguson at Gilbert Town and Vicinity;" "Overmountain Men & the Overmountain Victory National Historic Trail;" "Colonel Andrew Hampton;" "General Griffith Rutherford;" "The Hated Major James Dunlap;" "Gilbert Town: The Key Points;" "Suggested Reading."]

Griffin, Clarence W. *Essays on North Carolina History*. Forest City: Forest City Courier, 1951. [Originally published as a series titled "Dropped Stitches in Rutherford History," *Forest City Courier*, beginning in April 1947.

"How George Lewis Lost His Eyesight; NC General Assembly Sessions Records, April-May 1782." *Bulletin of the*

Genealogical Society of Old Tryon County, 22:3 (August 1994), 137. [Lewis, of Rutherford County, contracted smallpox at the Siege of Augusta and lost his sight as a result.]

Johnson, William Perry. "Rutherford Co.: 1782 Tax List." *Journal of North Carolina Genealogy*, 13:3 (Fall 1967), 1919-1923.

Johnson, William Perry. "Tryon (Rutherford) Co: An Early Tax List." *Journal of North Carolina Genealogy*, 14:2 (Summer 1968), 2104-2105. [Apparently, the tax list is from sometime between 1776 and 1780.]

Landrum, John Belton O'Neall. *Colonial and Revolutionary History of Upper South Carolina; Embracing for the Most Part the Primitive and Colonial History of the Territory Comprising the Original County of Spartanburg; with a General Review of the Entire Military Operations in the Upper Portion of South Carolina and Portions of North Carolina.* Greenville, S. C.: Shannon & Co., Printers, 1897; reprinted: (South Carolina Heritage Series, no. 1) Spartanburg: The Reprint Company, 1959; reprinted 1962, 1977.

"A 'Lost' List of Continental Soldiers from the Western Counties." *North Carolina Genealogical Society Journal*, 9:3 (August 1983), 142. [Lincoln, Burke, Wilkes, and Rutherford Counties]

Newton, Hedy Hughes. *Rutherford County, North Carolina, Abstracts of Minutes, Court of Pleas and Quarterly Sessions, 1779-1787.* Forest City: H. H. Newton, 1974.

North Carolina (State). General Assembly. "[Document dated:] January 31, 1781: Appointing Field Officers of Rutherford County." Manuscript; General Assembly Record Group; Session Records, January-February, 1781: Joint Papers, Committee Papers, Joint Papers, Committee Papers, Resolutions, Senate Bills, House Bills; Resolutions House Joint Resolutions: January 29- February 1, Box 1, [MARS Id: 66.8.23.15.7; item), State Archives of North Carolina, Raleigh. [Online catalog description: "The resolution also directs the governor to issue commissions to the newly appointed officers. Includes a letter from Andrew Hampton, of Rutherford County, informing the Assembly of his resignation as colonel and the local elections to suggest replacements to the vacant officer positions."]

"Petition from Rutherford County Regarding Field Officers, N. C. General Assembly, Session Records, 1783." *Bulletin of the Genealogical Society of Old Tryon County*, 25:1 (February 1997), 34-35.

"Presentment to Confiscate Property of Tories, Morgan District, NC, Court Records." *Bulletin of the Genealogical Society of Old Tryon County*, 21:3 (August 1993), 129. [Rutherford County]

Rollins, Harold W. "Eighteen Months Men Raised in Rutherford County, 1782." *Bulletin of the Genealogical Society of Old Tryon County*, 11:1 (February 1983), 23, 8.

Rollins, Harold W. "The First Civil War: A Series of Articles." *Bulletin of the Genealogical Society of Old Tryon County*, 3:3 (August 1975), 120-125; 3:4 (November 1975), 154-160; 4:1 (February 1976), 4-11 [includes "A Partial List of Persons from Old Rutherford County, Who Served, or Were Accused of Having Served, in Loyalist Units, 1778-1782," 8-10]; 4:2 (May 1976), 88-96 [with corrections to Part Three in previous issue].

Rutherford County. Citizens. "Nov 24, [1796]: Petition from the County of Rutherford." Manuscript, General Assembly Record Group, Session Records, Nov 1796-Dec1796; Petitions, Amendments, Miscellaneous Correspondence, Box 3 (MARS ID: 66.8.89.7.2; item), State Archives of North Carolina, Raleigh. [Online catalog description: "Certain persons of the said county propose that a law forbidding those persons who helped the British during the war from electing or holding an office in the General Assembly of this state, be redrawn due to the peaceful nature between this country and Great Britain at the present time."]

Rutherford County. "Rutherford County Miscellaneous Records, 1784-1950: Lists of Public Officials of Rutherford County." Manuscript C.R.086.928.2, State Archives of North Carolina, Raleigh.

"Rutherford County Continental Line Replacements." *Eswau Huppeday: Bulletin of the Broad River Genealogical Society*, 4:3 (August 1984), 229-230.

"Rutherford County Petition to Governor Richard Caswell, 29 September 1779." *Bulletin of the Genealogical Society of Old Tryon County*, 15:2 (May 1987), 52-53. [Numerous citizens of Rutherford County begging the governor to spare the life of "the said youth John Osborn" who was judged guilty of high treason against the state of North Carolina. The petition includes language in support of the patriot cause as well however.]

Sims, Carlton, ed. *A History of Rutherford County.* Murfreesboro, Tenn.: C. Sims, 1947.

Sampson County

Bizzell, Oscar M. *The Heritage of Sampson County, North Carolina.* [S. l.]: Sampson County Historical Society, 1983.

Bizzell, Oscar M., and Virginia L. Bizzell. *A Portrait of Eighteenth Century Sampson County as Revealed by Sampson County Court Minutes, 1784-1800.* Clinton: Sampson County Historical Society, [s. d.].

Bizzell, Virginia L., and Oscar M. Bizzell. *Revolutionary War Records, Duplin and Sampson Counties:*

Contributions to Genealogy. Newton Grove, N. C.: Sampson County Historical Society, 1997.

Butchko, Thomas R. *An Inventory of Historic Architecture, Sampson County, North Carolina*. Clinton: City of Clinton, [1981?].

Hintz, Fred M. "Three Johns(t)on Men from Sampson County Who Served in the American Revolution War." Typescript (2001), North Carolina Room, New Hanover County Public Library, Wilmington. [Online catalog description: "Three John(t)son brothers (Ephrim, Solomon, and Soasby) from Sampson County, N. C. served in the 2nd North Carolina Continental Army under Capt. Benjamin Coleman."]

Stanly County

Gantt, Wanda Mechling, *et al*. *Stanly County Revolutionary Soldiers and Patriots*. Albemarle: Yadkin River Patriots Chapter of the Daughters of the American Revolution, 2009.

Stanly County Heritage, North Carolina. Waynesville: Stanly County Historical Book Committee and County Heritage, Inc., 2002.

Stokes County

Absher, Mrs. W. O. "Some Stokes County Revolutionary War Pensioners Deaths." *North Carolina Genealogical Society Journal*, 3:1 (February 1977), 40-42.

Absher, Mrs. W. O. "Stokes County, N. C. Revolutionary War Pension Abstracts." *North Carolina Genealogical Society Journal*, 1:4 (October 1975), 174-178.

Boisseau, Mary Leigh. "Virginia Revolutionary Veterans in Rockingham and Stokes Counties, North Carolina." *Piedmont Lineages: Bulletin of the VA-NC Piedmont Genealogical Society*, 14:3 (August 1991), 95-99.

Byrd, William L., and John H Smith. *North Carolina Slaves and Free Persons of Color: Stokes and Yadkin Counties*. Bowie, Md.: Heritage Books, 2001.

James Hunter Chapter, North Carolina Daughters of the American Revolution *North Carolina DAR Genealogical Records Committee Report, Series 1, Volumes 427, 431: Early Families of the North Carolina Counties of Rockingham and Stokes with Revolutionary Service* (typescripts, 1978, 1981); digital surrogates, DAR Library, Washington, D. C.; Reprinted: Easley, S. C.: Southern Historical Press, 1990.

Pruitt, Albert Bruce. *Index to North Carolina County Maps: Davie, Guilford, Montgomery, Randolph, Rockingham, Stokes, Surry, & Yadkin*. Whitakers: A. B. Pruitt, 1988.

Stokes County. Clerk of Superior Court; Clerk of Court of Pleas and Quarter Sessions; Register of Deeds. "Military and Pension Records, 1779-1913." Manuscript CR.090.920.1 (MARS ID: 290.95.1; box), State Archives of North Carolina, Raleigh. [Online catalog description: "Arranged chronologically. Includes: 1779 military discharge, financial records, correspondence, pension records, provisions for families of soldiers, etc."]

Thomas, Sam, active 1786-1802. "Sam Thomas Papers, 1786-1835." Manuscript 5067-z, Southern Historical Collection, Louis Round Wilson Special Collections Library, University of North Carolina at Chapel Hill. [Online catalog description: "Sam Thomas was a free black man in Stokes County, N.C., in 1786. It appears that he was able to free his wife Amy in 1802. It also appears that members of the Thomas family moved to Ohio in the early 1800s, settling in Zanesville and Chillicothe. Their relationship to Sam Thomas is unknown. At some point, a Sam Thomas was accused of several crimes in Salem, N.C., including poisoning his wife…"]

Thore, J. E. "Restoration of 'Rock House' (Near Vade Mecum, Stokes County, Home Place of Col. Jack Mathis, Used as a Headquarters by Officers Formulating Plans for a Campaign during the American Revolution; Placed by George Reynolds Chapter, DAR." Manuscript (1932) 548, "William Roy Wallace Architectural Papers, c. 1913-2000," Manuscript, MC 00517, Box 4, folder 8, Special Collections Research Center, North Carolina State University, Raleigh.

Surry County [Salisbury District before 1782. Morgan District after 1782]

[Note: For various state government documents relating to Surry County during the Revolutionary period, search the MARS online catalog using the advanced search: http://mars.archives.ncdcr.gov/AdvancedSearch.aspx. Use the "Year" search box to restrict the searching to 1775-1783 and enter the county's name in the "Subjects" box, and hit the "Search" button near the top. This will retrieve any cataloged document for the county from that time period. These materials can vary considerably from personal or county petitions to the General Assembly, Loyalist matters, land disputes and claims, tax collection, exemptions from taxation, payments to county veterans, county divisions, personal collections, genealogical material, British claims against North Carolinians, etc. There is considerable information in these materials that could provide interesting documentation for persons living during the Revolution. The results will also include all of the wills and probates recorded in the county during the period set for the search.

We had hoped to include many of these listings in this guide, but they are too voluminous. Citations to many of these search results for the eastern counties do, however, appear in the text.]

"Chatham, Orange, Randolph, and Surry Counties: Men Who Enlisted in the Continental Line, 1780." *North Carolinian: Quarterly Journal of Genealogy & History*, 6:3 (September 1960), 728-729.

"Colonel Joseph Williams of Surry County by his Services as Lieutenant Colonel of the Surry Militia in the Cross Creek Expedition." In Weynette Parks Haun, *North Carolina Revolutionary Army Accounts, Part I, Secretary of State Treasurer's & Comptroller's Papers Journal "A", (Public Accounts) 1775-1776* (Durham: W. P. Haun, 1988), 27-28.

Davis, Mrs. Hayne. "Panther Creek." *North Carolina Booklet*, 3:6 (October 1903), 18-31; online: http://digital.ncdcr.gov/cdm/ref/collection/p249901coll37/id/14180. [Online description from "North Carolina Periodicals Index," East Carolina University: "A description of Revolutionary war Colonel Joseph Williams and his wife Rebecca (nee Lanier), their family, and their homestead in Surry County, NC."]

Downey, Jerry Craig. "Soldier of the Revolution: Joseph Winston in the Surry Backcountry of North Carolina." M. A. thesis, Wake Forest University, 1989.

Dunaway, Stewart E. *Surry County, North Carolina, County Records: Road, Bridge, Ferry, Mill Petitions and Tavern Bonds (1772-1839).* Hillsborough: North Carolina Historical Books, 2011. [Contents: County records; Ordinary record: Surry County, 1774; Road records, 1772-1799 (broken series); Bridge repair records, 1777-1839 (broken series); Bridge records, 1822; Mill records, 1823; Ordinary bond, 1774; Reference maps.] [Note: While not specifically concerning the Revolution, these sources can be used in tandem with land records and other documents to help locate places of residence, occupations, geographical features, and place names.]

Hollingsworth, J. G. *History of Surry County, or Annals of Northwest North Carolina.* Greensboro: Fisher Publishers, 1935. [Contains: "Various Types of Revolutionary Service from Surry County, including Minutes from the Committee of Safety." (Greensboro: W. H. Fisher Company, 1935; reprinted: Greenville, S. C.: Southern Historical Press, 2005), 71-106.

Lewis, J. D. "Patriot Leaders in North Carolina: Elijah Isaacs: Captain in the Surry County Regiment of Militia - 1776-1777; Captain in the Wilkes County Regiment of Militia - 1777-1778; Major in the Wilkes County Regiment of Militia - 1778-1779; Colonel in the Wilkes County Regiment of Militia - 1779-1783." Online: http://www.carolana.com/NC/Revolution/patriot_leaders_nc_elijah_isaacs.html.

Lewis, J. D. "Patriot Leaders in North Carolina: Joel Lewis: Ensign in the NC Continental Line - 1776-1779; Lieutenant in the 2nd NC Regiment – 1779; Captain in the Surry County Regiment of Militia - 1780-1781; Captain in the NC Light Horse Regiment – 1781; 1st Major in the NC State Regiment (State Troops) – 1781; Lt. Colonel/Colonel over the NC State Regiment (State Troops) - 1781-1783." Online: http://www.carolana.com/NC/Revolution/patriot_leaders_nc_joel_lewis.html.

Lewis, J. D. "Patriot Leaders in North Carolina: Joseph Williams: Lt. Colonel in the Surry County Regiment of Militia - 1775-1776; Colonel in the Surry County Regiment of Militia - 1776-1783." Online: http://www.carolana.com/NC/Revolution/patriot_leaders_nc_joseph_williams.html.

Lewis, J. D. "Patriot Leaders in North Carolina: Martin Armstrong: Colonel over the Surry County Regiment of Militia - 1775-1783." Online: http://www.carolana.com/NC/Revolution/patriot_leaders_nc_martin_armstrong.html.

Pruitt, Albert Bruce. *Index to North Carolina County Maps: Davie, Guilford, Montgomery, Randolph, Rockingham, Stokes, Surry, & Yadkin.* Whitakers: A. B. Pruitt, 1988.

Riggs, Samuel, 1760-after 1833. "[Revolutionary War Memoir]." In John C. Dann, ed. *The Revolution Remembered: Eyewitness Accounts of the War for Independence* (Chicago: University of Chicago Press, 1980), Chapter 8: "The Indian Frontier," 306-309. [Samuel Riggs, Surry County, North Carolina]

Roebuck, Haywood. "Some Continental Line Deserters from Rowan, Surry, and Mecklenburg Counties, N. C. 1780-1782." *North Carolina Genealogical Society Journal*, 1:2 (April 1975), 102-104.

Snow, Carol Leonard. *Revolutionary War Soldiers from Surry County, N. C.* Toast, N. C.: C & L Historical Publications, 2011. [Vol. 1, A-C]

Surry County Historical Society and Surry County American Revolution Bicentennial Commission. *Historic Sites of Surry County* [Surry County: The Society and the Commission], 1976.

Surry County. Committee of Safety. "Journal, August 25-September 21, 1775, from Secretary of State Records." Photographic images of manuscript N.2006.8.69-80- (MARS ID: 4.1.33.59; folder), State Archives of North Carolina, Raleigh. [Online catalog description: "Copy of the Surry County Committee of Safety Journal, August 25-September 21, 1775, from North Carolina Secretary of State Records, SS.XX, Box 1, Committees of Safety, 1774-1776."]

Surry County. "Miscellaneous Records, 1774-1869." One microfilm reel, State Archives of North Carolina, Raleigh. [Consult the State Archives to determine the exact years that are available.]

Surry County. "Surry County Miscellaneous Records, 1771-1928: Election Records, 1776-1804." Manuscript C.R.092.928.2, State Archives of North Carolina, Raleigh.

Surry County. "Surry County Miscellaneous Records, 1771-1928: Jury Lists and Records, 1772-1904." Manuscript C.R.092.928.3, State Archives of North Carolina, Raleigh.

Surry County. "Surry County Miscellaneous Records, 1771-1928: Memorandum for Search of Records, 1774, 1775." Manuscript C.R.092.928.4, State Archives of North Carolina, Raleigh.

Surry County. "Surry County Miscellaneous Records, 1771-1928: Slave Records, 1781-1839." Manuscript C.R.092.928.5, State Archives of North Carolina, Raleigh.

Surry County Bicentennial Commission Book Committee. *The Surry County Book: Recollections of the Life, History & Culture of Old Surry County in Northwestern North Carolina.* [Elkin?]: Surry County Historical Society, 1981.

"Surry County Militia Involved in Campaign against the Tories, Which Ended with the Battle of Moore's Creek Bridge, 27 February 1776." *Records of the Moravians in North Carolina, Vol. 3, 1776-1779* (Raleigh: State Department of Archives and History, 1968), 1121-1126.

"Various Companies, Surry County Militia, 1776." In Weynette Parks Haun, *North Carolina Revolutionary Army Accounts, Part I, Secretary of State Treasurer's & Comptroller's Papers Journal "A", (Public Accounts) 1775-1776* (Durham: W. P. Haun, 1988), 162-166.

Warren, Mary Bondurant. "Surry Superior Court Minutes, 1779-1802." *The Carolina Genealogist*, no. 47 (Summer 1982), County Records/Surry County Court Minutes, 1-4; no. 48 (Fall 1982), County Records/Surry County Court Minutes, 5-8; no. 49 (Winter 1983-1984), County Records/Surry County Court Minutes, 9-24; no. 50 (Spring 1984), County Records/Surry County Court Minutes, 25-34.

Watts, Garret, 1756-1838. "[Revolutionary War Memoir]." In John C. Dann, ed. *The Revolution Remembered: Eyewitness Accounts of the War for Independence* (Chicago: University of Chicago Press, 1980), Chapter 6: "War in the Carolinas," 192-196. [Garret Watts, Surry County, North Carolina]

Wells, Agnes M.; Virginia G. Phillips, and Carol J. Leonard. *Joseph Winston: His Entry Book Surry County, North Carolina Land Entries 1778-1781.* Mount Airy: A. M. Wells, 1987.

Transylvania County

Henderson, Archibald. *Revolution in North Carolina in 1775: Transylvania, Craven, Anson, and Mecklenburg.* [S. l.: s. n.], 1916.

Tryon County [Abolished in 1779 with Its Division into Lincoln and Rutherford Counties]

During its existence (1768/1769-1779), Tryon County, North Carolina straddled the modern North Carolina-South Carolina border and included the territory of Burke, Cleveland, Gaston, Henderson, Lincoln, McDowell, and Rutherford Counties, North Carolina, and claimed the territory in all or parts of modern Cherokee, Chester, Greenville, Lancaster, Laurens, Spartanburg, Union, and York Counties, and the Catawba Indian Reservation, South Carolina. Consequently, any studies of people and events in the northern part of South Carolina in the Revolutionary period must involve Tryon County sources and vice versa.

[Note: For various state government documents relating to Tryon County during the Revolutionary period, search the MARS online catalog using the advanced search: http://mars.archives.ncdcr.gov/AdvancedSearch.aspx. Use the "Year" search box to restrict the searching to 1775-1783 and enter the county's name in the "Subjects" box, and hit the "Search" button near the top. This will retrieve any cataloged document for the county from that time period. These materials can vary considerably from personal or county petitions to the General Assembly, Loyalist matters, land disputes and claims, tax collection, exemptions from taxation, payments to county veterans, county divisions, personal collections, genealogical material, British claims against North Carolinians, etc. There is considerable information in these materials that could provide interesting documentation for persons living during the Revolution. The results will also include all of the wills and probates recorded in the county during the period set for the search. We had hoped to include many of these listings in this guide, but they are too voluminous. Citations to many of these search results for the eastern counties do, however, appear in the text.]

Abernethy, Edgar. "Tryon County." *The State: Down Home in North Carolina*, 11:31 (January 1944), 7, 27; online: http://digital.ncdcr.gov/cdm/ref/collection/p16062coll18/id/18339. [Online description from "North Carolina

Periodicals Index," East Carolina University: "Tryon County, at one time one of the leading counties in the state, was formed in 1769, yet vanished ten years later when it was divided between Lincoln and Rutherford counties. Abernethy recounts some of the events in its lively existence."]

Backstrom, Carolyn Murphree. "Pilgrim Ancestors of Revolution Soldiers: Mercy Raymond Bedford of North Carolina, Patriot." *Mayflower Quarterly*, 44:3 (August 1978), 80-84. [descendants of Peter Browne of the *Mayflower*. Born in Middleborough in 1740, she moved with her family to New Jersey, married Jonas Bedford, and moved to Pennsylvania and later to Old Tryon County, North Carolina.]

Black, A. K. "Edward Vann, Revolutionary War Soldier." *Bulletin of the Genealogical Society of Old Tryon County*, 15:1 (February 1987), 25-28.

Brooks, Roy. "Abstracts of the Minutes of the Court of Pleas and Quarter Sessions of Tryon County, North Carolina." *Bulletin of the Genealogical Society of Old Tryon County*, 6:2 (May 1978), 74-79 [This long-running series of abstracts in this publication now reaches 1775 and continues to the last minutes in 1778]; 6:3 (August 1978), 120-127, 130; 7:1 (February 1979), 3-5, 8; 7:2 (May 1979), 84-89; 7:3 (August 1979), 118-127; 8:2 (May 1980), 62-67; 9:1 (February 1981), 2-11; 9:2 (May 1981), 52-59; 9:3 (August 1981), 106-117, 129.

Bulletin of the Genealogical Society of Old Tryon County, North Carolina. Forest City, N. C., vol. 1 (1973)-present (2013). [This journal contains many articles on the history and records of Tryon County. See: "Topical Guide to Volumes 1-29," in the *Bulletin*, 30:1 (February 2002), 2-24 for an overview of the contents.]

"Captain Robert Porter's Company, Tryon County, 1777." *Bulletin of the Genealogical Society of Old Tryon County*, 22:1 (February 1994), 23-25.

Carmichael, Erma. "William Cogdill – Revolutionary Soldier." *Bulletin of the Genealogical Society of Old Tryon County*, 5:2 (May 1977), 76-80, 99.

Crow, Jeri, and Judson. "Tryon County, NC, Crown Docket, January 1775 – April 1776." *Bulletin of the Genealogical Society of Old Tryon County*, 20:4 (November 1992), 173-181.

Crow, Jeri, and Judson. "Tryon County, NC, State Docket, October 1777 – January 1779." *Bulletin of the Genealogical Society of Old Tryon County*, 21:1 (February 1993), 3-10.

Culbreth, Blanch Waldrop. "Revolutionary War Record of Benjamin Hyder." *Bulletin of the Genealogical Society of Old Tryon County*, 4:1 (February 1976), 20-21.

Griffin, Clarence. "Some Signers of the Tryon 'Association'." *North Carolina Historical and Genealogical Record: A Quarterly Magazine of North Carolina Genealogy, Biography and Local History*, 2:4 (October 1933), 32-48. [1775]

Griffin, Clarence W. *History of Old Tryon and Rutherford Counties, North Carolina, 1730-1936*. Ashville, N. C.: Miller Printing Company, 1937.

Holcomb, Brent H. *Anson County, North Carolina Deed Abstracts, 1749-1766; Abstracts of Wills & Estates, 1749-1795*. Baltimore: Genealogical Publishing Company, 1980.

Holcomb, Brent H. *Deed Abstracts of Tryon, Lincoln and Rutherford, Counties, North Carolina, 1769-1786; Tryon County Wills and Estates*. Easley, S. C.: Southern Historical Press, 1977.

Holcomb, Brent H. *Mecklenburg County, North Carolina, Abstracts of Early Wills, 1763-1790 (1749-1790)*. Greenville: A Press, 1980.

Holcomb, Brent H. *North Carolina Land Grants in South Carolina*. Baltimore: Genealogical Publishing Company, 1980.

Holcomb, Brent H. *Tryon County, North Carolina, Minutes of the Court of Pleas and Quarter Sessions, 1769-1779*. Columbia: SCMAR, 1994.

Holcomb, Brent H., and Elmer O. Parker. *Mecklenburg County, North Carolina, Deed Abstracts, 1763-1779*. Easley, S. C.: Southern Historical Press, 1979.

Holland, Jim. "Col. Gallert's Historical Writing." *Bulletin of the Genealogical Society of Old Tryon County*, 19:3 (August 1991), 107-110.

"John McKinney." *Broad River Journal*, 14:3 (August 2006), 5-6. [1740 (Pa.) - 1804; Tryon County resident, member of the Committee of Safety, militia captain in 1775 and 1776, justice of the peace in 1777 and 1778.]

Johnson, William Perry. "Tryon (Rutherford) Co: An Early Tax List." *Journal of North Carolina Genealogy*, 14:2 (Summer 1968), 2104-2105. [Apparently, the tax list is from sometime between 1776 and 1780.]

Landrum, John Belton O'Neall. *Colonial and Revolutionary History of Upper South Carolina; Embracing for the Most Part the Primitive and Colonial History of the Territory Comprising the Original County of Spartanburg; with a General Review of the Entire Military Operations in the Upper Portion of South Carolina and Portions of North Carolina*. Greenville, S. C.: Shannon & Co., Printers, 1897; reprinted: (South Carolina Heritage Series, no. 1) Spartanburg: The Reprint Company, 1959; reprinted 1962, 1977.

Mills, Mary N. "Abraham Hembree, Revolutionary Service, S-929." *Bulletin of the Genealogical Society of Old*

Tryon County, 15:3 (August 1987), 117-120.
Mitchell, Memory F., ed. *North Carolina Documents, 1584-1868*. Raleigh: State Department of Archives and History, 1967. [Revolutionary War-era contents: Minutes of Committee of Safety, Tryon County, 1775-1776; Halifax Resolves, Apr. 12, 1776.]
Nanny, Morris R. "The Fort at Montford's Cove." *Bulletin of the Genealogical Society of Old Tryon County*, 3:4 (November 1975), 173.
North Carolina (State). General Assembly. "[Document Dated]: August 15, 1778: Report on Accounts of William Gilbert, Commissary of Tryon Co. (with Messages)." Manuscript; General Assembly Record Group; Session Records, August 1778; Joint Papers, Committee Papers, Resolutions, Senate Bills, House Bills; Joint Select Committee Reports, Box 1 (MARS ID: 66.8.14.7.5; item), State Archives of North Carolina, Raleigh.
North Carolina (State). General Assembly. "[Document Dated]: February 6, 1779: Report Re[specting] Accounts of William Gilbert (with Messages)." Manuscript; General Assembly Record Group; Session Records, January-February 1779; Joint Papers, Committee Papers, Resolutions: Joint Select Committees, Box 1 (MARS ID: 66.8.15.8.14; item), State Archives of North Carolina, Raleigh. [Online catalog description: "Report on the accounts of William Gilbert and William Alston, commissaries for Tryon County, and a resolution that Gilbert shall comply with the report."]
North Carolina (State). General Assembly. "[Document Dated]: February 9, 1779: Resolution Allowing William Gilbert to Resign (with Message)." Manuscript; General Assembly Record Group; Session Records, January-February 1779; Joint Papers, Committee Papers, Resolutions; House Joint Resolutions: February 6-13, 1779, Box 1 (MARS ID: 66.8.15.12.4; item), State Archives of North Carolina, Raleigh. [Online catalog description: "The resolution gives Gilbert leave to resign as a Justice of the Peace in Tryon County."]
North Carolina (State). General Assembly. "[Document Dated]: February 12, 1779: Report Re[specting] Insurrection in Tryon County (with Amendment and Messages)." Manuscript; General Assembly Record Group; Session Records, January-February 1779; Joint Papers, Committee Papers, Resolutions: Joint Select Committees, Box 1 (MARS ID: 66.8.15.8.21), State Archives of North Carolina, Raleigh. [Online catalog description: "The committee recommends detailed mobilization of the militia, including appointing Matthew Locke Brigadier General pro tempore of the District of Salisbury."]
North Carolina (State). General Assembly. "[Document Dated]: February 12, 1779: "Resolution to Send to Governor and to Governor of Virginia Information about Insurrection in Tryon County (with Message)." Manuscript; General Assembly Record Group; Session Records, January-February 1779; Joint Papers, Committee Papers, Resolutions; House Joint Resolutions: February 6-13, 1779, Box 1 (MARS ID: 66.8.15.12.15; item), State Archives of North Carolina, Raleigh.
North Carolina (State). General Assembly. "[Document Dated]: May 13, 1779: Re[specting] Petition of George Lamkin, Late Sheriff of Tryon County (Rejected) (Message Only)." Manuscript; General Assembly Record Group; Session Records, May 1779; Joint Papers, Committee Papers, Resolutions, Senate Bills, House Bills; Joint Select Committees, Box 1 (MARS ID: 66.8.17.10.4), State Archives of North Carolina, Raleigh. [Online catalog description: "Lamkin describes his difficulties when sheriff regarding tax collection and asks to be discharged. Although the House of Commons appointed a committee to consider the petition, the Senate did not."]
Owen, Jane. "Chasing Ancestors in Tryon County." *The State: Down Home in North Carolina*, 48:11 (April 1981), 11-12, 30; online: http://digital.ncdcr.gov/cdm/ref/collection/p16062coll18/id/60124. [Online description from "North Carolina Periodicals Index," East Carolina University: "Named after Royal Governor William Tryon, Tryon County was created in 1769 and disbanded in 1778. Because of a boundary dispute, a land survey was done and half the county was found to lie in South Carolina and the county was divided. Although it is not easy to locate ancestors in Tryon County, efforts made by genealogists over the last century have proven fruitful."]
Parker, Elmer Oris. "Site of Old Tryon County, North Carolina, Courthouse." *Bulletin of the Chester County Genealogical Society*, 3:3 (September 1980), 47-48. [with map of the site in present York County; 1769-1771]
Parker, Hershel. "The Tryon County Patriots of 1775 and Their 'Association'." *Journal of the American Revolution: Annual Volume 2015*, 2 (2015), 63-72; online: online: https://allthingsliberty.com/2014/08/the-tryon-county-patriots-of-1775-and-their-association/.
"Partial Tax List of Tryon County, c. 1777-78." *Bulletin of the Genealogical Society of Old Tryon County, North Carolina*, 2:3 (August 1974), 106-107.
"Petitioners from 'South Carolina,' Formerly Tryon County, 1775." *Bulletin of the Genealogical Society of Old Tryon County*, 38:2 (Mary 2010), 82-99.
Pettus, Louise. "Old North Corner." Online: http://www.rootsweb.ancestry.com/~sclancas/history/history_oldnorthcorner.htm.

Pettus, Louise. "North Carolina – South Carolina Boundary Line." (2001). Online: http://www.rootsweb.ancestry.com/~sclancas/history/boundary.htm.

Pettus, Louise. "Tryon (N. C.) Courthouse in York County." *The Charlotte* Observer, (May 30, 1986); reprinted: The *Quarterly: A Publication of the York County Genealogical and Historical Society*, 5:3 (December 1993), 26.

Philbeck, Miles S. *Tryon County, North Carolina, Index to Land Surveys*. Chapel Hill: M. S. Philbeck, 1987. [from the beginning of the index: "Although usually considered to have been formed in 1769 and to have been abolished in 1779 in favor of Rutherford and Lincoln Counties, Tryon County land grants begin in 1768 and continued into 1784 with one being granted as late as 1789."]

Philbeck, Miles S. *Tryon County, North Carolina Land Warrants, 1768-1774*. Chapel Hill: M. S. Philbeck, 1987. [from the introduction: "These records are in the Secretary of State collection with current stack numbers S.S. 946, S.S. 946.3, and S.S. 588 and consist of lists of the warrants by number, name, acreage, and brief description."]

"Pioneer Families of Old Tryon County." *Broad River Notebook: A Publication of the Broad River Basin Historical Society*, 3:4 (December 1994), 85-87.

Pruitt, A. B. [Albert Bruce]. *Abstracts of Land Entrys, Tryon and Lincoln Counties, North Carolina, 1778-1780; Lincoln County, North Carolina, 1780 and 1783-1834; and Lincolnton, North Carolina, 1785-1868*. 4 vols. [Whitakers, N. C.]: A. B. Pruitt, 1987. [Contents: Vol. 1: Tryon and Lincoln Counties, 1778-1780; Vol. 2: Lincoln County, 1783-1795; Vol. 3: Lincoln County, 1798-1825; Vol. 4: Abstracts of Lincoln County, North Carolina: Land Entries 1780 and 1795-1797; Land Processions 1789-1834; and Lincolnton, North Carolina, Deeds 1785-1868.]

Rollins, Harold W. "Cap McFadden Company sit out to plunder…" *Bulletin of the Genealogical Society of Old Tryon County*, 23:2 (May 1995), 51-53. [1782]

Rollins, Harold W. "The Wars of Tryon: Part One: The Snow Campaign of 1775." *Bulletin of the Genealogical Society of Old Tryon County*, 8:1 (February 1980), 25-27.

Salley, A. S. "The Boundary Line between North and South Carolina." *South Carolina Historical Commission Bulletin 10*. Columbia: The State Company, 1929.

Skaggs, Marvin Lucian. *North Carolina Boundary Disputes Involving Her Southern Line*. Chapel Hill: University of North Carolina Press, 1941.

Sullivan, Kathy Gunter. "The Court Martial of Colonel Charles McDowell, March 1782." *Bulletin of the Genealogical Society of Old Tryon County*, 18:3 (August 1990), 102-111; 18:4 (November 1990), 165-171. [Contains the names of many men involved in the Revolution.]

Sullivan, Kathy Gunter. *Tryon County Documents, 1769-1779: A North Carolina County*. Forest City: The Genealogical Society of Old Tryon County, 2000.

Temple, Robert D. "Troublesome Boundaries: Royal Proclamations, Indian Treaties, Lawsuits, Political Deals, and Other Errors Defining Our Strange State Lines." *Carologue: A Bulletin of South Carolina History*, 27:1 (Summer 2011), 12-19.

Tryon County. Committee of Safety. "Minutes of Committees of Safety, Tryon County, 1775-1776." Manuscript 33MSS-17-7 (MARS ID: 5000.6.822.7; item), State Archives of North Carolina, Raleigh.

"Tryon County Militia under the Command of Colonel William Graham." In Weynette Parks Haun, North Carolina Revolutionary Army Accounts, Part I, Secretary of State Treasurer's & Comptroller's Papers Journal "A", (Public Accounts) 1775-1776 (Durham: W. P. Haun, 1988), 9-10. [County designation determined from *North Carolina State Records*, Volume 10, pp. 423-424, "Minutes of the Tryon County Committee of Safety Tryon County, January 23, 1776 - January 24, 1776." {This analysis was performed by genealogists in the Genealogy Office, Office of the Registrar General, National Society Daughters of the American Revolution, Washington, D. C.}]

Tryon County. "Miscellaneous Records, 1765-1788." Manuscript and one microfilm reel, State Archives of North Carolina, Raleigh.

Tryon County, North Carolina. *Tryon County, North Carolina Crown Docket, July 1769-April 1776; Tryon County, North Carolina, State Docket, October 1777-January 1779; Lincoln County, North Carolina, State Docket, April 1779-April 1780*. Forest City: The Genealogical Society of Old Tryon County, [1994?]

Tryon County, North Carolina. Inferior Court of Pleas and Quarter Sessions. "Court Minutes of Tryon and Lincoln Counties, North Carolina, 1769-1782." State Archives of North Carolina, Raleigh; also available on LDS Family History Library microfilm 833297.

Tryon County, North Carolina. Inferior Court of Pleas and Quarter Sessions. Tryon County; Virginia Greene DePriest and Lucille Hendrick Gardner, [eds]. *Minutes of the Inferior Court of Please and Quarter Sessions for*

Tryon County, North Carolina. Shelby: V. G. DePriest and L. H. Gardner, 1985. [Vol. 1: 1769-1772; Vol. 2: 1773-1779.

"Tryon County Association." In Walter Clark, ed., *State Records of North Carolina, Vol. 10 (1775-1776)*, (Raleigh Josephus Daniels, 1890; reprinted: Wilmington: Broadfoot Publishing Company, 1993), 161-164.

Turner, Grace. "Accusations by John Walker." *Bulletin of the Genealogical Society of Old Tryon County*, 19:2 (May 1991), 77-78. [Salisbury District Criminal Actions, 1778; Loyalists and Patriots on the frontier]

Turner, Grace. "Action on the Tryon Insurrection." *Bulletin of the Genealogical Society of Old Tryon County*, 18:4 (November 1990), 179-180.

Turner, Grace. "Petition of Charles McLean." *Bulletin of the Genealogical Society of Old Tryon County*, 18:4 (November 1990), 180. [1780; to the North Carolina General Assembly; for reward for fighting local Loyalists]

Turner, Grace. "Report of Charles McLean, 1779." *Bulletin of the Genealogical Society of Old Tryon County*, 19:2 (May 1991), 78. [from North Carolina General Assembly Session Records, 1779 relating to military actions in the area]

Wallace, Robert E. "The North-South Carolina Lines and Counties, 1669-1897." *The Quarterly: A Publication of the York County Genealogical and Historical Society*, 5:2 (September 1993), 12-14.

Warmack, Joann A. "The Book of Leaves of Memory, No. 2." *Bulletin of the Genealogical Society of Old Tryon County*, 18:1 (February 1990), 59-60. [Dickey and Gray information from the Lyman Draper Papers].

"The Whiskey Wagon and the State Line." *Bulletin of the Chester District Genealogical Society*, 11:2 (June 1988), 38-39.

Whiteside, Don. *Whiteside(s) Names Abstracted from 1) Tryon County, North Carolina, Court Minutes, 1772-1779; 2) Rutherford County, North Carolina, Court Minutes, 1779-1799*. Ottawa, Ont.: D. Whiteside, 1983.

Tyrrell County

[Note: For various state government documents relating to Tyrrell County during the Revolutionary period, search the MARS online catalog using the advanced search: http://mars.archives.ncdcr.gov/AdvancedSearch.aspx. Use the "Year" search box to restrict the searching to 1775-1783 and enter the county's name in the "Subjects" box, and hit the "Search" button near the top. This will retrieve any cataloged document for the county from that time period. These materials can vary considerably from personal or county petitions to the General Assembly, Loyalist matters, land disputes and claims, tax collection, exemptions from taxation, payments to county veterans, county divisions, personal collections, genealogical material, British claims against North Carolinians, etc. There is considerable information in these materials that could provide interesting documentation for persons living during the Revolution. The results will also include all of the wills and probates recorded in the county during the period set for the search. We had hoped to include many of these listings in this guide, but they are too voluminous. Citations to many of these search results for the eastern counties do, however, appear in the text.]

Basnight, Gordon L., and Tyrrell County Genealogical and Historical Society. *Tyrrell County, North Carolina, 1784-87, State Census, 1790 Federal Census, 1800 Federal Census*. Columbia: Tyrrell County Genealogical and Historical Society, 1997.

Davis, David. *History of Tyrrell County*. Norfolk, Va.: Printed offset by J. Christopher Printing, 1963.

Davis, David E. "Conspiracy in Old Tyrrell." *Washington County Genealogical Society Journal*, 6:3 (December 1998), 72-73.

Everett, Vernon L., and Chester A. Lawton. "Tyrrell County Everetts in the Revolutionary War." *Washington County Genealogical Society Journal*, 5:3 (December 1997), 75-77.

"Five Years Later." *Washington County Genealogical Society Journal*, 5:3 (December 1997), 81. [list from 1782 of Tyrrell County Tories]

"General Howe: Great Red-Coated Hope of the Tyrrell Tories. Stubbs, Thomas, Sr. "...A World of Blood Shed." *Washington County Genealogical Society Journal*, 4:3 (December 1996), 81.

McBride, Ransom. "List of Taxables, Tyrrell Co., N. C. – 1782." *North Carolina Genealogical Society Journal*, 10:4 (November 1984), 242-247; 11:4 (November 1985), 227-238.

"Menonists." *Washington County Genealogical Society Journal*, 5:3 (December 1997), 92. [listed in the Tyrrell County tax list of 1772]

Norman, Edwin A. "The Tyrrell Ordinary: A Bit of Cheer for the War-Time Traveler." *Washington County Genealogical Society Journal*, 4:3 (December 1996), 69.

North Carolina (State). General Assembly. "Dec. 8: Report on Petition of Isaac Davenport, Jonathan Phelps, and John Davenport (With Petition) (Rejected)." Manuscript; General Assembly Record Group; Session Records,

November 1786-January 1787, Box 2 (MARS ID: 66.8.42.2.4; item), State Archives of North Carolina, Raleigh. [Online catalog description: "Petitioners protest the sale of their land in Tyrrell County under the Confiscation Act. Report rejects petition on the grounds that should petitioners' land grants be legal, their case requires no interference from the legislature."]

Stubbs, Thomas, Sr. "...A World of Blood Shed." *Washington County Genealogical Society Journal*, 4:3 (December 1996), 79. [statement by Thomas Stubbs, Sr., of Tyrrell County, July 11, 1777, relating to Thomas Harrison (son of John) and Tory activities]

Tyrrell County. "Tyrrell County Miscellaneous Records, 1735, 1756-1975: Receipt for Confiscated Property, 1783." Manuscript C.R.096.928.6, State Archives of North Carolina, Raleigh.

Tyrrell County. "Miscellaneous Records, 1764-1937." Manuscript, CRX Records, State Archives of North Carolina, Raleigh. [Consult the State Archives to determine the exact years that are available.]

"Tyrrell County Tax List, 1782." *Tyrrell Branches*, 4:1 (April 1999), 1-7; 4:2 (October 1999), 22-29; 5:2 (October 2000), 2-16.

"Tyrrell Delegates to the Provincial Congresses at the Time of the Revolutionary War." *The Quarterly Review of the Eastern North Carolina Genealogical Society*, 7:4 (Fall 1980), 159.

"Tyrrell County Troops in Continental Army." *Tyrrell Branches*, 7:1 (April 2002), 11.

"Tyrrell County's Wartime Court." *Washington County Genealogical Society Journal*, 5:3 (December 1997), 80.

"Tyrrell's Legislators, 1777-1783." *Washington County Genealogical Society Journal*, 4:3 (December 1996), 76.

"Tyrrell's Militia Officers." *Washington County Genealogical Society Journal*, 5:3 (December 1997), 73. [1776]

"Tyrrell's Tories: Our Home-Grown Plotters of Dark Deeds." *Washington County Genealogical Society Journal*, 4:3 (December 1996), 78-79.

Venters, Vic. "The Scuppernong Runs through It." *Wildlife in North Carolina*, 58:6 (June 1994), 8-13. [Online description from "North Carolina Periodicals Index," East Carolina University: "The Scuppernong River is the centerpiece of an ambitious plan, the Walter B. Jones Center for the Sounds project, that could save the river, protect vast areas of wetland habitat, and bring economic prosperity to Tyrrell County through increased tourism."]

"Veterans Speak from the Deed Books." *Washington County Genealogical Society Journal*, 6:3 (December 1998), 74-75. [Provides information on Revolutionary War service for various men who made powers of attorney in the 1790s in Tyrrell County.]

Wall, Bennett H. "The Founding of the Pettigrew Plantations." *North Carolina Historical Review*, 27:4 (October 1950), 395-418; online: http://digital.ncdcr.gov/cdm/ref/collection/p16062coll9/id/4207. [Online description from "North Carolina Periodicals Index," East Carolina University: "Following the Revolutionary War, Charles Pettigrew turned to agriculture to supplement his family's income. The reverend owned no property until his marriage to Mary Blount on October 29, 1778. From this nuptial he gained both property and slaves in Tennessee and North Carolina. Pettigrew established the Pettigrew Plantation in North Carolina acquiring lands in Tyrell and Washington Counties. The article summarizes the Pettigrew's development of the plantation and general history of the area."]

Watson, Alan D. *Tyrrell County: A Brief History*. Raleigh: Office of Archives and History, North Carolina Department of Cultural Resources, 2010. [Publisher's description: "Created in 1729, Tyrrell County is one of North Carolina's oldest counties; yet, geographically isolated and always sparsely populated, it never played a significant role in statewide affairs. In this thorough and detailed history, Alan Watson chronicles Tyrrell County over almost three centuries. The development of county government and courts from the proprietary period through the end of the twentieth century is the author's central theme. The narrative expands to include discussion topics such as the local economy, agriculture, internal improvements, and the lifestyles of the residents. More than sixty illustrations enhance the reader's experience."]

Union County

Bjorlin, Virginia. "Union County Revolutionary Ancestors." *Carolinas Genealogical Society Bulletin*, 52:2 (Fall 2015-2016), 50.

Byrd, William L., and John H Smith. *North Carolina Slaves and Free Persons of Color: Mecklenburg, Gaston, and Union Counties*. Bowie, Md.: Heritage Books, 2001.

Laney, Clara. "Revolutionary Soldiers." *North Carolina DAR Genealogical Records Committee Report, Series 1, Volume 259: Union County Cemeteries, 1710-1914 and Roster of Confederate and Revolutionary Soldiers* (typescript, 1959), 183; digital surrogate, DAR Library, Washington, D. C.

McNeely, Robert Ney. "Union County and the Old Waxhaw Settlement." *North Carolina Booklet*, 12:1 (July 1912),

6-20. [Includes a list of Revolutionary War soldiers.]

Moore, Benjamin. "Revolutionary Patriots of Union County." *Carolinas Genealogical Society Bulletin*, 52:2 (Fall 2015-2016), 51.

North Carolina Daughters of the American Revolution. "Tombstones of Revolutionary Soldiers, Union Co., N. C." *North Carolina DAR Genealogical Records Committee Report, Series 1, Volume 221: Miscellaneous Records from North Carolina* (typescript, 1957), 252-262; digital surrogate, DAR Library, Washington, D. C.

"Revolutionary War Patriots from Union County." *Carolinas Genealogical Society Bulletin*, 36:3 (Winter 1999-2000), 57.

Vance County

Tucker, Harry Z. "Nine Oaks." *The State: A Weekly Survey of North Carolina*, 6:14 (September 1938), 3; online: http://digital.ncdcr.gov/cdm/ref/collection/p16062coll18/id/38327. [Online description from "North Carolina Periodicals Index," East Carolina University: "Located in Vance County between Petersburg and Fayetteville, Major Bromfield Ridley built Nine Oaks before the Revolutionary War. The exterior presented a plain façade but inside the interior was once decorated with frescoes and intricately carved woodworking."]

Wake County and Raleigh [Hillsborough District]

[Note: For various state government documents relating to Wake County and Raleigh during the Revolutionary period, search the MARS online catalog using the advanced search: http://mars.archives.ncdcr.gov/AdvancedSearch.aspx. Use the "Year" search box to restrict the searching to 1775-1783 and enter the county's name or the term "Raleigh" in the "Subjects" box, and hit the "Search" button near the top. This will retrieve any cataloged document for the county from that time period. These materials can vary considerably from personal or county petitions to the General Assembly, Loyalist matters, land disputes and claims, tax collection, exemptions from taxation, payments to county veterans, county divisions, personal collections, genealogical material, British claims against North Carolinians, etc. There is considerable information in these materials that could provide interesting documentation for persons living during the Revolution. The results will also include all of the wills and probates recorded in the county during the period set for the search. We had hoped to include many of these listings in this guide, but they are too voluminous. Citations to many of these search results for the eastern counties do, however, appear in the text.]

Babits, L. E. "Report of Investigations of Suspected Revolutionary War Entrenchment, Holly Springs [Wake County], North Carolina." Manuscript, Archaeology Branch, North Carolina Office of Archives and History, Raleigh.

Barnes, Julia. "Gravesite of Grandfather of S. C. Governor James Orr." *Palmetto Patriot: South Carolina Society Sons of the American Revolution*, 2009:1 (Spring 2009), 8; online: http://www.scssar.org. [Jehu Orr (1763-1827) from Wake County, N. C.; buried in modern Anderson County, S. C.]

Battle, Kemp P. "Raleigh and the Old Town of Bloomsbury." *North Carolina Booklet*, 2:7 (November 1902), 1-20; online: http://digital.ncdcr.gov/cdm/ref/collection/p249901coll37/id/14180. [Online description from "North Carolina Periodicals Index," East Carolina University: "This article discusses the founding of the colony, that would one day become the State of North Carolina, by land grants from Charles II and the establishing of a capital founded in Raleigh."]

Belvin, Lynne W., and E. W. May. "Wake County Taxes, 1771-1780." *Wake Treasures*, 3:3 (Fall 1993), 3-7.

"Colonel John Hinton of Wake County for the Services of his Regiment of Militia on an Expedition to Moore's Creek against the Insurgents." In Weynette Parks Haun, *North Carolina Revolutionary Army Accounts, Part I, Secretary of State Treasurer's & Comptroller's Papers Journal "A", (Public Accounts) 1775-1776* (Durham: W. P. Haun, 1988), 77-80. [County designation backed by the Revolutionary War pension records of Thomas Hutchins, W7836; Charles Upchurch S16562. {This analysis was performed by genealogists in the Genealogy Office, Office of the Registrar General, National Society Daughters of the American Revolution, Washington, D. C.}]

Colyer, Rick, Madlyn Jamison, and E. W. May. "Wake County Taxes, 1781." *Wake Treasures*, 3:3 (Fall 1993), 8-12.

Dees, Elizabeth, and E. W. May. "Wake County Taxes, 1782-1783." *Wake Treasures*, 3:3 (Fall 1993), 13-18.

Dunaway, Stewart E. *Wake County, North Carolina, Mill Records, 1772-1872.* Hillsborough: North Carolina Historical Books, 2009. [Note: While not specifically concerning the Revolution, these sources can be used in tandem with land records and other documents to help locate places of residence, occupations, geographical features, and place names.]

Dunaway, Stewart E. *Wilkes County Road Records (1776-1853).* Hillsborough: North Carolina Historical Books, 2013. [Note: While not specifically concerning the Revolution, these sources can be used in tandem with land records and other documents to help locate places of residence, occupations, geographical features, and place names.]

Haywood, Marshall DeLancey. "The Genesis of Wake County." *North Carolina Booklet*, 5:1 (July 1905), 2-17; online: http://digital.ncdcr.gov/cdm/ref/collection/p249901coll37/id/14180.

Haywood, Marshall DeLancey. "Joel Lane: A Pioneer and Patriot of Wake County, North Carolina." *North Carolina Booklet*, 20:2-4 (October 1920-April 1921), 191-206. [Online description from "North Carolina Periodicals Index," East Carolina University: "A look at the origin, colonial history, Revolutionary War History, and general history of Wake County through the year of 1783."]

Haywood, Martha Helen. "Wakefield." *North Carolina Booklet*, 2:9 (January 1903), 23-25; online: http://digital.ncdcr.gov/cdm/ref/collection/p249901coll37/id/14180. [Online description from "North Carolina Periodicals Index," East Carolina University: "This article discusses the history and importance of Wakefield estate, located outside of Raleigh. Wakefield was a patriot meeting location and the site of the election of Thomas Burke as the state's first governor in June 1781."]

Hinton, Mary Hillard. "Clay Hill-on-the-Neuse." *North Carolina Booklet*, 3:6 (October 1903), 24-37; online: http://digital.ncdcr.gov/cdm/ref/collection/p249901coll37/id/14180. [Online description from "North Carolina Periodicals Index," East Carolina University: "A description of 'Clay Hill,' the home of Revolutionary Major John Hinton in Wake County, N. C."]

Hinton, Mary Hilliard. "Colonel John Hinton." *North Carolina Booklet*, 14:4 (April 1915), 225-236.

Hinton, Mary Hilliard. "Presentation of Joel Lane Tablet to the City of Raleigh." *North Carolina Booklet*, 13:1 (July 1913), 47-59. ["Includes addresses by Mary Hilliard Hinton, Joseph G. Brown and 'Deed of Joel Lane for site of City of Raleigh'."]

Huler, Scott. "City Portrait: Raleigh." *Our State: Down Home in North Carolina*, 83:7 (December 2015), 58, 60, 62, 64, 66-67; online: https://www.ourstate.com/city-portrait-raleigh/. [Online description from "North Carolina Periodicals Index," East Carolina University: "The city of Raleigh dates back to the late eighteenth century and it has undergone a number of structural changes ever since. Author Scott Huler examines Raleigh through the history of its streets and parks, reflecting on how the early grid system influenced Raleigh's growth over the years."]

Lally, Kelly A. *The Historic Architecture of Wake County, North Carolina.* Raleigh: Wake County, 1994.

Lawrence, R. C. "Down through the Years." *The State: A Weekly Survey of North Carolina*, 10:37 (February 1943), 4-5, 26; online: http://digital.ncdcr.gov/cdm/ref/collection/p16062coll18/id/16777. [Online description from "North Carolina Periodicals Index," East Carolina University: "Lawrence lists chronologically important events that have happened in Raleigh since the arrival of John Lawson, the first white man to visit the area in 1708."]

Lea, Diane. "Colonial Dames Restore Trio of Historic Houses." *Metro Magazine*, 5:12 (December 2004), 37-44; online: http://www.metronc.com/article/?id=874. [Online description from "North Carolina Periodicals Index," East Carolina University: "*Metro* design editor Diane Lea discusses the role of The National Society of Colonial Dames of America in the State of North Carolina in saving, restoring, and maintaining three of the most significant residences associated with the role of the state and the capital city in the Revolutionary War. The residences are the Joel Lane House (Raleigh) ca. 1770; Haywood Hall at New Bern Place (Raleigh) 1799; and the Burgwin-Wright House (Wilmington) 1770."]

May, Elizabeth W. "Introduction to the Wake County Tax List Project." *Wake Treasures*, 3:3 (Fall 1993), 2.

May, Elizabeth W. "Wake County Military Districts, 1771-1805." *Wake Treasures*, 3:1 (Spring 1993), 3-10.

McCarty, DeWayne. "Abstracts of Wake County Militia Officers for 1771, 1773, & 1777." *Wake Treasures*, 1:2 (Summer 1991), 31-33.

Murray, Elizabeth Reid. *Wake: Capital County of North Carolina.* Raleigh: Captial County Publishing Company, 1983.

Norris, Jeannie Faris. "Wake County's 10 Towns." *The State: Down Home in North Carolina*, 32:23 (April 1965), 21-22, 38-39, 42-47; online: http://digital.ncdcr.gov/cdm/ref/collection/p16062coll18/id/47879. [Online description from "North Carolina Periodicals Index," East Carolina University: "Providing history and information relative to the towns in Wake County facts pertaining to: Apex, Cary, Fuquay-Varina, Garner, Knightdale, Morrisville, Holly Springs, Wake Forest, Wendell, Zebulon, and Rolesville, can be found within this article."]

North Carolina Society of the Daughters of the Revolution. Bloomsbury Chapter. "Marking the Site of the Old Town of Bloomsbury, or Wake Court House: Presentation of Tablet to the City of Raleigh." *North Carolina Booklet*, 11:1 (July 1911), 45-53.

Potts, Guy. "Revolutionary War Pension for Frederick Rigsby [Rigsbee], Wake County, North Carolina." *Wake Treasures*, 18:1 (Winter/Spring 2007), 10-13.

Sharpe, Bill. "Wake County Yesterday." *The State: Down Home in North Carolina*, 32:23 (April 1965), 10-11, 65-70; online: http://digital.ncdcr.gov/cdm/ref/collection/p16062coll18/id/47879. [Online description from "North Carolina Periodicals Index," East Carolina University: "Named for Governor William Tryon's wife, Margaret Wake, Wake County was first settled in the 1740s. Designated the temporary seat of government in 1781 during the American Revolution, Wake County continues in this role today."]

Wake County. "Miscellaneous Records, 1772-1952." Manuscript, State Archives of North Carolina, Raleigh. [Consult the State Archives to determine the exact years that are available.]

Waugh, Elizabeth Culbertson, and Ralph Mills. *North Carolina's Capital: Raleigh*. Raleigh: Junior League of Raleigh, 1967.

Young, Eva M. "The Cottage That Roamed for a Century." *The State: Down Home in North Carolina*, 34:23 (May 1967), 15-16; online: http://digital.ncdcr.gov/cdm/ref/collection/p16062coll18/id/50114. [Online description from "North Carolina Periodicals Index," East Carolina University: "The former president Andrew Jackson's birthplace has been restored. The cottage was once home to Jackson's parents, employees of Peter Casso's Inn in Raleigh. The inn was torn down in 1937, but the cottage was saved and sent on a tour of the state before resting at Pullen Park in the 1950s. The home has been preserved at State College Campus in Raleigh during the 1960s and much of the original furniture remains."]

Warren County [Halifax District]

[Note: For various state government documents relating to Warren County during the Revolutionary period, search the MARS online catalog using the advanced search: http://mars.archives.ncdcr.gov/AdvancedSearch.aspx. Use the "Year" search box to restrict the searching to 1775-1783 and enter the county's name in the "Subjects" box, and hit the "Search" button near the top. This will retrieve any cataloged document for the county from that time period. These materials can vary considerably from personal or county petitions to the General Assembly, Loyalist matters, land disputes and claims, tax collection, exemptions from taxation, payments to county veterans, county divisions, personal collections, genealogical material, British claims against North Carolinians, etc. There is considerable information in these materials that could provide interesting documentation for persons living during the Revolution. The results will also include all of the wills and probates recorded in the county during the period set for the search. We had hoped to include many of these listings in this guide, but they are too voluminous. Citations to many of these search results for the eastern counties do, however, appear in the text.]

North Carolina (State). General Assembly. "[Document dated:] May 5, 1780: Resolution Permitting Resignations of James Ransom as Justice of the Peace and Stakey Sharpe as Militia Office (with Resignation of Sharp)." Manuscript; General Assembly Record Group; Session Records, April-May 1780; Joint Papers, Committee Papers, Resolutions: House Joint Resolutions, Box 1 (MARS ID: 66.8.20.17.10; item), State Archives of North Carolina, Raleigh. [Online catalog description: "Sharp resigns as second major of Hertford County; Ransom was a justice for Warren County."]

North Carolina (State). General Assembly. "[Document dated:] July 13, 1781: Resolution Appointing Joseph Hawkins Lieutenant Colonel of Warren County Pro Tempore (Message Only)." Manuscript; General Assembly Record Group; Session Records, June-July 1781; Joint Papers, Committee Papers, Resolutions: House Joint Resolutions, Box 1 (MARS ID: 66.8.25.15.13; item), State Archives of North Carolina, Raleigh.

Sumner, Jethro. "A Signed Letter of Jethro Sumner, Warren [County, North Carolina], 20th July, 1780: to General Horatio Gates." Manuscript MSS L2006G7 M, Society of the Cincinnati Library, Anderson House, Washington, D. C. [Online catalog description: " In this letter, Continental Brigadier General Sumner reported to his new southern commander, General Gates on difficulties of recruiting Continental Army. Following the surrender of Charleston by General Benjamin Lincoln in early May, the South was assigned to General Gates. One month later Gates was back at Hillsboro after his infamous retreat from the Camden battlefield and Congress soon looked for another Southern commander."]

Warren County. "Miscellaneous Records, 1769-1963." Manuscript, State Archives of North Carolina, Raleigh. [Consult the State Archives to determine the exact years that are available.]

Warren County. "Slaves and Free Persons of Color, Records of, 1779-1870." Manuscript, State Archives of North Carolina, Raleigh. [Consult the State Archives to determine the exact years that are available.]

Wellman, Manly Wade. *The County of Warren, North Carolina, 1586-1917.* Chapel Hill: University of North Carolina Press, 1959.

Washington County (modern county in North Carolina)

Bonner, R. T. "Col. James Bonner, Patriot, Founder of Washington, N. C." *Pamtico Tracings*, 13:1 (June 1997), 12-15. [Originally published in *The Washington Progress*, Thursday, May 23, 1912.]

"Gideon Lamb: The Colonel Buys Land." *Washington County Genealogical Society Journal*, 4:3 (December 1996), 82.

Jones, Abram. "Every Man for Himself: The Abrupt End of the [Lewellen] Conspiracy." Stubbs, Thomas, Sr. "…A World of Blood Shed." *Washington County Genealogical Society Journal*, 4:3 (December 1996), 80.

"Levi Norman: He Didn't Come Home. *Washington County Genealogical Society Journal*, 4:3 (December 1996), 72.

Long, James. "Col. James Long to Gov. Caswell [from Executive Letter Book]." *Washington County Genealogical Society Journal*, 5:3 (December 1997), 86. [1780 letter]

Manning, Francis M., and W. H. Booker. "Lewellen/Lewelling Conspiracy." *Washington County Genealogical Society Journal*, 4:3 (December 1996), 71.

Rankin, Hugh F. "'Brier Creek': Not Our Finest Hour." *Washington County Genealogical Society Journal*, 5:3 (December 1997).

Simpson, Bland. "The Bull Neck of Heart's Delight." *Wildlife in North Carolina*, 61:2 (December 1997). [Online description from "North Carolina Periodicals Index," East Carolina University: "Bull Neck Swamp, a 5,000-acre swamp forest bordering the Albemarle Sound and Scuppernong River in Washington County, is unique in that it remains as it was when the first Europeans came. Purchase by the state in 1995 has preserved it."]

Watauga County

Wadsworth, E. W. "Daniel Boone Stopped Here." *The State: Down Home in North Carolina*, 42:5 (October 1974), 26-28; online: http://digital.ncdcr.gov/cdm/ref/collection/p16062coll18/id/56874. [Online description from "North Carolina Periodicals Index," East Carolina University: "The Wilkinson Cabin, thought to have been built by a man named Reese in 1760, is the oldest home in Watauga County. Today, is it located on Highway 421, which was formerly part of the Daniel Boone Trail. Through the years buffaloes, Native Americans, settlers, soldiers, pioneers heading west, and Daniel Boone passed by this historic structure."]

Wayne County

[Note: For various state government documents relating to Wayne County during the Revolutionary period, search the MARS online catalog using the advanced search: http://mars.archives.ncdcr.gov/AdvancedSearch.aspx. Use the "Year" search box to restrict the searching to 1775-1783 and enter the county's name in the "Subjects" box, and hit the "Search" button near the top. This will retrieve any cataloged document for the county from that time period. These materials can vary considerably from personal or county petitions to the General Assembly, Loyalist matters, land disputes and claims, tax collection, exemptions from taxation, payments to county veterans, county divisions, personal collections, genealogical material, British claims against North Carolinians, etc. There is considerable information in these materials that could provide interesting documentation for persons living during the Revolution. The results will also include all of the wills and probates recorded in the county during the period set for the search. We had hoped to include many of these listings in this guide, but they are too voluminous. Citations to many of these search results for the eastern counties do, however, appear in the text.]

Goerch, Carl. "Wayne County." *The State: A Weekly Survey of North Carolina*, 8:14 (August 1940), 1-5, 21-22; online: http://digital.ncdcr.gov/cdm/ref/collection/p16062coll18/id/6019. [Online description from "North Carolina Periodicals Index," East Carolina University: "Wayne County was formed from Dobbs County in 1779 and was named for General 'Mad Anthony' Wayne of Revolutionary fame. The county seat lies in Goldsboro and there are also many other interesting places in and interesting facts about Wayne County, such as Saponey Cliffs and the invasion of General Sherman."]

Great Britain. Exchequer and Audit Department, Claims, American Loyalists, Series I (AO 12, Selections). Documents Communicated by State Governments – North Carolina (with Report) (AO 12/91). "Copy of Judgment in John Fleetwood v. John Hamilton, Wayne County Court, October 1782." Copy of a manuscript in

the National Archives of the United Kingdom (formerly the Public Records Office), Kew, Richmond, Surrey, England; (MARS ID: 21.2.14.36), "British Records Collection," State Library of North Carolina, Raleigh.
Johnstone, Mary Daniels. *The Heritage of Wayne County, North Carolina.* Goldsboro: Wayne County Historical Association, 2010.
Monnette, Orra Eugene. "Franklin, the Unrecognized Commonwealth." *Americana Illustrated*, 29:3 (July 1935), 321-330.
Shriner, Charles A. "The State of Franklin." *Americana (American Historical Magazine)*, 19:2 (April 1925), 148-173.
Slack, E. Munsey. "The Loss of the State of Franklin to the Union." Bulletin of the Historical Society of Washington County, Virginia, no. 2 (1937) - no. 6 (July 1941).

Wilkes County [Salisbury District before 1782; Morgan District after 1782]

[Note: For various state government documents relating to Wilkes County during the Revolutionary period, search the MARS online catalog using the advanced search: http://mars.archives.ncdcr.gov/AdvancedSearch.aspx. Use the "Year" search box to restrict the searching to 1775-1783 and enter the county's name in the "Subjects" box, and hit the "Search" button near the top. This will retrieve any cataloged document for the county from that time period. These materials can vary considerably from personal or county petitions to the General Assembly, Loyalist matters, land disputes and claims, tax collection, exemptions from taxation, payments to county veterans, county divisions, personal collections, genealogical material, British claims against North Carolinians, etc. There is considerable information in these materials that could provide interesting documentation for persons living during the Revolution. The results will also include all of the wills and probates recorded in the county during the period set for the search. We had hoped to include many of these listings in this guide, but they are too voluminous. Citations to many of these search results for the eastern counties do, however, appear in the text.]

"Abstract of William Lenoir's Payroll for the Expedition to Kings Mountain, September 7, 1780 to __." In Paul W. Gregory, *Early Settlers of Reddies River* (Wilkes Co.: Wilkes Genealogical Society, 1976), 43.
Baity, Joan R. "Tory Oak." In William S. Powell, ed., Jay Mazzocchi, assoc. ed., *Encyclopedia of North Carolina* (Chapel Hill: University of North Carolina Press in association with the University of North Carolina Library, 2006), 1127. [tree in Wilkesboro; aka "Cleveland Oak."]
"Captain William Lenoir's Company and the Battle of King's Mountain." *North Carolina Genealogical Society Journal*, 9:4 (November 1983), 234-235.
"Catawba River Expedition, August 30, 1780." In Paul W. Gregory, *Early Settlers of Reddies River* (Wilkes Co.: Wilkes Genealogical Society, 1976), 48.
"Expedition to Hillsboro, February 14, 1781." In Paul W. Gregory, *Early Settlers of Reddies River* (Wilkes Co.: Wilkes Genealogical Society, 1976), 46.
"Expedition to Moravian Town, February 1, 1781." In Paul W. Gregory, *Early Settlers of Reddies River* (Wilkes Co.: Wilkes Genealogical Society, 1976), 47.
"Expedition to New River, November 22, 1780." In Paul W. Gregory, *Early Settlers of Reddies River* (Wilkes Co.: Wilkes Genealogical Society, 1976), 46.
Harris, Joe. "Memorial Service & Grave Marking Ceremony for a Revolutionary War Hero." *Recall*, 7:2 (Fall 2001), 9-10. [Online description from "North Carolina Periodicals Index," East Carolina University: "Harris, a descendant of a Revolutionary War soldier, Samuel Johnson of Wilkes County, recounts his war experiences and the battle at King's Mountain. He entered the war as a private 1776 and eventually promoted and received an officer's commission as Captain. Harris conducted a memorial service for his ancestor in August 2001 at the Little Stone Mountain Baptist Church in Traphill, N. C. Later at the graveyard, a new marble headstone which was supplied by the US Veterans Administration was unveiled."]
Hayes, Johnson J. *The Land of Wilkes*. Wilkesboro: Wilkes County Historical Society, 1962.
Hayes, Laurie B., ed. *Heroes of Red, White and Blue: Wilkes County Veterans, Volume 1.* [S. l.]: Wilkes Heritage Museum, 2007.
"King's Mountain Expedition, September 7-November 7, 1780." In Paul W. Gregory, *Early Settlers of Reddies River* (Wilkes Co.: Wilkes Genealogical Society, 1976), 48.
"1.) A List of Volunteers Who Marched North, 19 May 1778, under the Command of Colonel Charles Gordon, *Wilkes Genealogical Society*, 13:1 (Spring 1979), 17.
"A 'Lost' List of Continental Soldiers from the Western Counties." *North Carolina Genealogical Society Journal*, 9:3 (August 1983), 142. [Lincoln, Burke, Wilkes, and Rutherford Counties]

"Mustered at Aquilla Greer's Home, January 26, 1781." In Paul W. Gregory, *Early Settlers of Reddies River* (Wilkes Co.: Wilkes Genealogical Society, 1976), 47.

North Carolina (State). General Assembly. "[Document dated:] October-November 1779: Joint Papers, Committee Papers, Resolutions, Senate Bills, House Bills, Senate Joint Resolutions: November 6: Requesting Governor to Pardon Benjamin Cleveland and Others for Killing Traitors (with Messages)." Manuscript; General Assembly Record Group; Session Records, October-November 1779, Box 1 (MARS ID: 66.8.18.12.21), State Archives of North Carolina, Raleigh. [Online catalog description: "Cleveland had been joined by Benjamin Herndon, of Wilkes County, and others in killing Lemuel Jones and William Coyle and beating James Harvil."]

North Carolina (State). General Assembly. "[Document dated:] October-November 1779: Unidentified Amendments, Senate Bills, House Bills, Senate Bills (October 20): Bill to indemnify certain persons therein named for putting to death William Coyl and Lemuel Jones, etc. (rejected)." Manuscript; General Assembly Record Group; Session Records, October-November 1779, Box 2 (MARS ID: 66.8.19.3), State Archives of North Carolina, Raleigh. [Online catalog description: "The bill sought to protect from prosecution Benjamin Cleveland, Benjamin Herndon, William Carrol, and about twenty others for killing Lemuel Jones and William Coyl and for beating James Harvill, all three of whom were alleged to be bandits and traitors."]

North Carolina (State). General Assembly. "[Document dated:] October-November 1779: Joint Papers, Committee Papers, Resolutions, Senate Bills, House Bills, House Joint Resolutions: October 19, 1779: Exempting Certain Persons from Taxes (Orange County and Wilkes County) (with Messages)." Manuscript; General Assembly Record Group; Session Records, October-November 1779, Box 1 (MARS ID: 66.8.18.13.2), State Archives of North Carolina, Raleigh. [Online catalog description: "The Wilkes County Court of Pleas and Quarter Sessions recommends that John Murphy, John Fugit, and Robert Jones, being poor, old, and infirm, be exempted from paying taxes; the Orange County Court recommends likewise on behalf of John May. The Assembly concurs with both courts."]

"Roster of Soldiers in Expedition against the Indians, May 31, 1776." In Paul W. Gregory, *Early Settlers of Reddies River* (Wilkes Co.: Wilkes Genealogical Society, 1976), 45.

"Roster of William Lenoir's Company, March 30, 1776." In Paul W. Gregory, *Early Settlers of Reddies River* (Wilkes Co.: Wilkes Genealogical Society, 1976), 44.

"Soldiers Discharged at Wilkes County Court House, January 1781." In Paul W. Gregory, *Early Settlers of Reddies River* (Wilkes Co.: Wilkes Genealogical Society, 1976), 46.

Turrentine, Joseph Dempsey. "Why Neighbor Fought Neighbor." B. A. thesis, University of Georgia, 2009. [Thesis description: "During the Revolutionary War, western North Carolina maintained one of the highest loyalist populations of any region in the thirteen colonies. Nearly one hundred years later, this same region contained widespread unionist sentiment during the Civil War. In a region just tame enough to settle yet too wild to firmly control, the ruling class chose repression to maintain their grip on the region. In both centuries, conditions were ripe for internal conflict, but for different reasons. Eventually, in both conflicts neighbor executed neighbor and western North Carolina populations descended into anarchy. In Wilkes Country during the Revolutionary War, Benjamin Cleveland personified the western ruling class, their overall impact on the outcome of the American Revolution, and Cleveland's story represents a good starting point for comparison. By comparing and contrasting these two internal conflicts, I hope to more fully expose the societal parallels that led to total breakdown, and to detect what impacts, if any, that the first struggle had on the second."]

Wilkes County. "Insolvents Records, 1780-1896." Manuscript, State Archives of North Carolina, Raleigh. [Consult the State Archives to determine the exact years that are available.]

Wilkes County. "Miscellaneous Records, 1775-1946." Manuscript, State Archives of North Carolina, Raleigh. [Consult the State Archives to determine the exact years that are available.]

Wilkes County. "Wilkes County Miscellaneous Records, 1771-1928: Justices of the Peace, 1781." Manuscript C.R.104.928.3, State Archives of North Carolina, Raleigh.

Wilkes County. "Wilkes County Miscellaneous Records, 1771-1928: Military, 1778-1897." Manuscript C.R.104.928.4, State Archives of North Carolina, Raleigh.

Wilkes County. "Wilkes County Miscellaneous Records, 1771-1928: Slave Papers, undated and 1779-1811." Manuscript C.R.104.928.6, State Archives of North Carolina, Raleigh.

Yancey County

Abernethy, Edgar. "The Cane River Valley." *The State: Down Home in North Carolina*, 12:18 (September 1944), 8-9; online: http://digital.ncdcr.gov/cdm/ref/collection/p16062coll18/id/19620. [Online description from "North Carolina Periodicals Index," East Carolina University: "Cane River is Yancey County's own private rivers. Not a single stream flows into the county or out of it, and there are many interesting and beautiful places to be found in the valley."]

Bailey, Lloyd Richard, Sr., ed. *The Heritage of the Toe River Valley*. 12 vols. Durham: L. R. Bailey, 1994-2007. [Avery, Mitchell, and Yancey Counties]

Sharpe, Bill. "Yancey – Rooftop of the South." *The State: Down Home in North Carolina*, 28:9 (October 1960), 10-12, 23-27; online: http://digital.ncdcr.gov/cdm/ref/collection/p16062coll18/id/42915. [Online description from "North Carolina Periodicals Index," East Carolina University: "Known for its highest elevation of any county in North Carolina, Yancey, encompasses 311 square miles and contains the tallest peak in eastern America, Mt. Mitchell. Although established in December 1833, records indicate that settlers inhabited the region as far back as 1778. The first road built in the region was in 1840 and the railroad arrived in 1901. Yancey, primarily a lumber region, survived off agricultural endeavors as well, specifically apples and dairy products."]

Counties of Modern Tennessee in the Revolutionary Era

[Note: For various state government documents relating to Tennessee during the Revolutionary period, search the MARS online catalog using the advanced search: http://mars.archives.ncdcr.gov/AdvancedSearch.aspx. Use the "Year" search box to restrict the searching to 1775-1783 and enter the state's name in the "Subjects" box, and hit the "Search" button near the top. This will retrieve any cataloged document for the county from that time period. These materials can vary considerably from personal or county petitions to the General Assembly, Loyalist matters, land disputes and claims, tax collection, exemptions from taxation, payments to county veterans, county divisions, personal collections, genealogical material, etc. There is considerable information in these materials that could provide interesting documentation for persons living during the Revolution. The results will also include all of the wills and probates recorded in the county during the period set for the search. We had hoped to include many of these listings in this guide, but they are too voluminous. Citations to many of these search results for the eastern counties do, however, appear in the text.]

"Tennesse Counties Originally in North Carolina." Online: http://statelibrary.ncdcr.gov/ghl/resources/genealogy/tncounties.html.

Washington County, North Carolina (First) (Modern State of Tennessee) [Salisbury District before 1782; Morgan District after 1782]

[Note: Washington County was created in 1777 from Washington District and all of modern Tennessee.]

[Note: During the Revolution, the area now known as Tennessee was claimed and loosely administered by North Carolina. The settlers in northeastern Tennessee, in the area around the Watauga River, drew up a compact of government called the Watauga Association. This association petitioned the North Carolina Legislature in August 1776 requesting annexation to North Carolina. In May 1780, persons from a settlement on the Cumberland River in Middle Tennessee drafted the Cumberland Compact. Signers of both documents are considered to have patriotic service as a signer of a petition. Men from the area that isnow Tennessee served in North Carolina units.][40]

[Note: For various state government documents relating to Washington County during the Revolutionary period, search the MARS online catalog using the advanced search: http://mars.archives.ncdcr.gov/AdvancedSearch.aspx. Use the "Year" search box to restrict the searching to 1775-1783 and enter the county's name in the "Subjects" box, and hit the "Search" button near the top. This will retrieve any cataloged document for the county from that time period. These materials can vary considerably from personal or county petitions to the General Assembly, Loyalist matters, land disputes and claims, tax collection, exemptions from taxation, payments to county veterans, county divisions, personal collections, genealogical material, British claims against North Carolinians, etc. There is considerable information in these materials that could provide interesting documentation for persons living during the Revolution. The results will also include all of the wills and probates recorded in the county during the period set for the search. We had hoped to include many of these listings in this guide, but they are too voluminous. Citations to many of these search results for the eastern counties do, however, appear in the text.]

---

[40] *Is That Service Right?* (Washington, D. C.: NSDAR, 2005), 44.

Abernathy, Thomas P. *From Frontier to Plantation in Tennessee: A Study in Frontier Democracy*. University: University of Alabama Press, 1932.

Agee, Michael. " 'Restrained from Necessity': The Development of the Station Mode of Settlement and Its Impact on the Cumberland Valley." M. A. thesis, Middle Tennessee State University, 2005.

Albright, Edward. *Early History of Middle Tennessee*. Nashville: Brandon Printing, 1909.

Alden, John Richard. *John Stuart and the Southern Colonial Frontier: A Study of Indian Relations, War, Trade, and Land Problem in the Southern Wilderness, 1754-1775*. Ann Arbor: University of Michigan Press, 1944.

Alderman, Pat. *The Overmountain Men; Early Tennessee History, 1760-1795*. Johnson City, Tenn.: Overmountain Press, 1970.

Alderman, Pat, Lee B. Andrews, and Verna Alderman. *Overmountain Men; Early Tennessee History, 1760-1780. The Exploration, Settlement and Founding of the First Free Government in America; Its Struggles for Survival, Culminating in the Battle of King's Mountain*. [Erwin?, Tenn.]: Privately printed, 1958; Reprinted Erwin, Tenn.: Wintergreen Print Co., 1968.

Alderson, William T., and Robert M. McBride. *Landmarks of Tennessee History*. Nashville: Tennessee Historical Society, 1965.

Alderson, William T[homas], and Robert Hiram White. *A Guide to the Study and Reading of Tennessee History*. Nashville: Tennessee Historical Commission, 1959.

Allen, Penelope Johnson. *Tennessee Soldiers in the Revolution: A Roster of Soldiers Living during the Revolutionary War in the Counties of Washington and Sullivan, Taken From the Revolutionary Army Accounts of North Carolina*. Bristol, Tenn.: The King Printing Company, 1935. [Contents: Introduction; Index to Revolutionary Soldiers; Revolutionary Pensioners of Tennessee, Act of 1828; Index to Wills of Washington County, Tennessee; Abstracts of Wills of Washington County; Marriage Records of Blount County; Marriage Records of Davidson County; Revolutionary Grants of Davidson County.]

Allison, John. *Dropped Stitches in Tennessee History*. Nashville: Marshall & Bruce Company, 1897.

Alvey, Richard L. "Consumerism on the Tennessee Frontier." M. A. thesis, Texas Tech University; 1997.

"Ann Robertson Cockrill Honored." *Tennessee Historical Quarterly*, 5:4 (December 1946), 313-314.

Bergeron, Paul H. *Paths of the Past: Tennessee, 1770-1970*. Knoxville: Published in cooperation with the Tennessee Historical Commission [by] University of Tennessee Press, 1979.

Blackmon, Richard D. *Dark and Bloody Ground: The American Revolution along the Southern Frontier*. Yardley, Pa.: Westholme Publishing, 2012. [Publisher's description: "The Battles along the Rivers, Mountains, and in the Deep Woods of the South that Changed the Fate of Nations. The American Revolution marked a dramatic change in the struggle for land along the southern frontier. In the colonial era, American Indian leaders and British officials attempted to accommodate the westward expansion of Anglo-Americans through land cessions designed to have the least impact on Indian societies. The region remained generally peaceful, but with the onset of the Revolution, the British no longer exercised sole authority to curb the settlements appearing within territory claimed by the Creeks, Shawnee, and most importantly, the Cherokee. Whether it was to escape the economic uncertainty of the east, the rigors of the conflict, or the depredations of troops and militias on both sides, settlers flooded west. Under these conditions, the war in the south took on a savage character as Indians, Loyalists, and Whigs all desperately fought to defend their communities and maintain control of their own destinies. Taking advantage of the political turmoil in the east, the Cherokee Nation launched a coordinated offensive in 1776 against illegal frontier settlements. The Whigs responded with a series of expeditions from each of the Southern colonies that razed Cherokee towns and their food supplies. All the while, both British and Whig leaders walked a fine line: If the Indians attacked settlers without distinguishing between Loyalists and Whigs, those groups could unite and thwart both British and Indian interests; if the Indians attacked the western frontier with Loyalist and British support, the Whigs would face a two-front war – an event that ended up happening. Blackmon uses a wealth of primary source material to recount the conflict between American Indians and Anglo-Americans in the colonial South during one of the most turbulent periods of North American history. He explains the complex points of contact in Georgia, Kentucky, North Carolina, South Carolina, Tennessee, and Virginia between native groups and settlers, while revealing the political gamesmanship between rival British and Whig traders and officials to secure Indian loyalty. The author also explains the critical role of the southern frontier to the American victory, a victory achieved long after the decision at Yorktown. Before the war, clashes between Cherokee and Shawnee hunters in Kentucky had become so commonplace that it was known as a 'dark and bloody ground.' With the rise in Anglo-American settlements there, led by Daniel Boone and others, the dark and bloody ground became a metaphor for the entire struggle for the Southern frontier."]

Boniol, John Dawson, Jr. "The Walton Road." *Tennessee Historical Quarterly*, 30:4 (Winter 1971), 402-412.

Bowes, John P. "Shawnee Geography and the Tennessee Corridor in the Seventeenth and Eighteenth Centuries." In Kristofer Ray, ed., *Before the Volunteer State: New Thoughts on Early Tennessee, 1540-1800* (Knoxville: University of Tennessee Press, 2014), 83-105.

Breazeale, J. W. M. *Life as It Is, or, Matters and Things in General: Containing amongst Other Things, Historical Sketches of the Exploration and First Settlement of the State of Tennessee* [from 1760s–1803]. Appalachian Echoes series. Knoxville: University of Tennessee Press, 2009; Originally published: Knoxville: Printed by J. Williams, 1842.

Britton, David. "Desperate Enterprizes and Men of Broken Fortunes: Loyalty and Identity on the Tennessee Frontier, 1793-1794" [Middle Tenn.]. *Tennessee Historical Quarterly*, 70:4 (Winter 2012), 288-299.

Britton, David. "John Montgomery and the Perils of American Identity in the Mero District, 1780-1795." In Kristofer Ray, ed., *Before the Volunteer State: New Thoughts on Early Tennessee, 1540-1800* (Knoxville: University of Tennessee Press, 2014), 185-200.

Brown, John P. *Old Frontiers: The Story of the Cherokee Indians from Earliest Times to the Date of Their Removal to the West, 1838*. Kingsport, Tenn.: Southern Publishers, 1938.

Browning, Howard M. "The Washington County Court, 1778-1789: A Study in Frontier Administration." *Tennessee Historical Quarterly*, 1:4 (December 1942), 328-343.

Calloway, Brenda. *America's First Western Frontier: East Tennessee*. Johnston City: Overmountain Press, 1989.

Cappon, Lester J., editor-in-chief ; Barbara Bartz Petchenik, cartographic editor ; John Hamilton Long, assistant editor; William B. Bedford, *et al.*, research associates; Nancy K. Morbeck, cartographic assistant; Gretchen M. Oberfranc, editorial assistant. *Atlas of Early American History: The Revolutionary Era, 1760-1790*. Princeton: Published for the Newberry Library and the Institute of Early American History and Culture by Princeton University Press, 1976.

Caruso, John A.; maps by Francis J. Mitchell. *The Appalachian Frontier: America's First Surge Westward.* Indianapolis: Bobbs-Merrill, 1959; reprinted with a new introduction by John C. Inscoe. Knoxville: University of Tennessee Press, 2003.

Champagne, Duane. *Social Order and Political Change: Constitutional Governments among the Cherokee, the Choctaw, the Chickasaw, and the Creek*. Stanford, Calif.: Stanford University Press, 1992.

Clack, Miss Tommie. "Dr. James Cozby." *Echoes from the East Tennessee Historical Society*, 2:3 (July 1956), 3-4; reprinted as "Tennessee's Little Known Pioneers – Part 1." *Tennessee Ancestors: A Tri-Annual Publication of the East Tennessee Historical Society*, 27:1 (April 2011), 28-33.

Clayton, LaReine Warden, Jane Gray Buchanan, ed. *Stories of Early Inns and Taverns of the East Tennessee Country* [endpapers map: "Routes of Migration in the Old East Tennessee Country, 1760-1860"]. Nashville: National Society of the Colonial Dames of America in the State of Tennessee, 1995.

Clements, Paul. "Tennessee Notes: An Analysis of 'The Original' Donelson Journal and Associated Accounts of the Donelson Party Voyage" [1779-1780; Col. John Donelson; Cumberland River to Nashville]. *Tennessee Historical Quarterly* 64:4 (Winter 2005): 338-349.

Coggins, Jack. *Ships and Seamen of the American Revolution: Vessels, Crews, Weapons, Gear, Naval Tactics, and Actions of the War for Independence.* Harrisburg, Pa.: Stackpole Books, 1969.

Connelly, Thomas J. "Indian Warfare on the Tennessee Frontier." *East Tennessee Historical Society Publications,* 36 (1964), 3-22.

Conner, Martha. *A Contribution towards a Bibliography of Tennessee History*. [S. l.: s. n.], 1920.

Coker, Charles Frederick William, and George Stevenson, eds. *Records relating to Tennessee in the North Carolina State Archives* (Archives Information Circular no. 3). Raleigh: North Carolina Department of Archives and History, 1980.

Connelly, Thomas Lawrence. "Indian Warfare on the Tennessee Frontier, 1776-1794: Strategy and Tactics." *Publications of the East Tennessee Historical Society,* no. 36 (1964), 3-22.

Corkran, David H. *The Creek Frontier, 1540-1783*. (Civilization of the American Indian Series, no. 86). Norman: University of Oklahoma Press, 1967.

Corlew, Robert E. *Tennessee: A Short History*. 2nd ed. Knoxville: University of Tennessee Press, 1993.

Cox, Joyce, and W. Eugene Cox. *History of Washington County, Tennessee, 1988*. [Johnson City, Tenn.]: Overmountain Press, 2001.

Creekmore, Pollyanna. "Early East Tennessee Taxpayers: Washington County, Tennessee, 1778 Taxpayers List." *East Tennessee Historical Society Special Publication,* no. 34 (1962), 118-131.

Creekmore, Pollyanna. "Greene County, Tennessee, 1783 Taxpayers List." *East Tennessee Historical Society Special Publication,* 39 (1937), 118-130.

Creekmore, Pollyanna. "A Note on the Family of Colonel John Carter (d. 1781): Proof that there was a John Carter, Jr." *Tennessee Ancestors*, 5:2 (August 1989), 108-113.
Davis, Louise Littleton. *Frontier Tales of Tennessee*. Gretna, La.: Pelican Publishing Company, 1978.
Dickinson, W. Calvin, and Eloise R. Hitchcock. *A Bibliography of Tennessee History, 1973-1996*. Knoxville: University of Tennessee Press, 1999.
Dorsey, Jean Muir. "Captain Benjamin Gist." *Echoes from the East Tennessee Historical Society*, 2:4 (October 1956), 51-52; reprinted as "Tennessee's Little Known Pioneers – Part 2." *Tennessee Ancestors: A Tri-Annual Publication of the East Tennessee Historical Society*, 27:2 (August 2011), 137-138.
Dorsey, Jean Muir. "Joshua Grist." *Echoes from the East Tennessee Historical Society*, 2:4 (October 1956), 50-51; reprinted as "Tennessee's Little Known Pioneers – Part 2." *Tennessee Ancestors: A Tri-Annual Publication of the East Tennessee Historical Society*, 27:2 (August 2011), 137-138.
Downes, Randolph C. "Cherokee-American Relations in the Upper Tennessee Valley 1776-1791." *East Tennessee Historical Society Publications*, 8 (1936), 35-53.
Durham, Walter T. "The Southwest Territory: Progression to Statehood." *Journal of East Tennessee History*, 62 (1990), 3-17.
Dykeman, Wilma. *Tennessee: A Bicentennial History*. New York: W. W. Norton & Company, Inc., 1975.
Epps, Katie. "Early Religious Developments in Middle Tennessee." M. A. thesis, Middle Tennessee State University, 1954.
Ewing, James. *It Happened in Tennessee*. Nashville: Rutledge Hill Press, 1986.
Ewing, James. *A Treasury of Tennessee Tales*. Nashville: Rutledge Hill Press, 1985.
Faulkner, Charles H. "Here Are Frame Houses and Brick Chimneys: Knoxville, Tennessee in the Late Eighteenth Century." In David Colin Crass, Steven D. Smith, Martha A. Zierden, and Richard D. Brooks, eds., *The Southern Colonial Backcountry: Interdisciplinary Perspectives on Frontier Communities* (Knoxville: University of Tennessee Press, 1998), 136-161.
Fels, Elizabeth Meek. "The Battle of Point Pleasant: Its Relation to the American Revolution and to Tennessee." *Tennessee Historical Quarterly*, 33:2 (Winter 1974), 367-378.
Finger, John R. *Tennessee Frontiers: Three Regions in Transition*. Bloomington: Indiana University Press, 2001.
Fischer, David Hackett. *Albion's Seed: Four British Folkways in America*. New York: Oxford University Press, 1989.
Fischer, Marjorie Hood. *Tennesseans before 1800: Washington County*. Galveston, Texas: Frontier Press, 1996.
Folmsbee, Stanley J. "The Journal of John Cotten, the 'Reluctant Pioneer' – Evidences of its Unreliability." *Tennessee Historical Quarterly*, 28:1 (Spring 1969), 84-94.
Folmsbee, Stanley J.; Robert E. Corlew; and Enoch L. Mitchell. *Tennessee: A Short History*. Knoxville: University of Tennessee Press, 1969; 2nd ed. Knoxville: University of Tennessee Press, 1981.
Fox, George, and Juanita Fox. *History of East Tennessee, 1740-1800*. [Tennessee?]: G. & J. Fox, 2009.
Franklin, Ann York. *Clues for Tennessee Revolutionary Patriots from Birth to Burial*. [S. l.]: John Marshall Chapter, NSDAR, 2011. [This compilation is based on the 2000 "SAR Revolutionary Graves Register" and the printed 2003 *DAR Patriot Index*.]
Free, George D. *History of Tennessee from Its Earliest Discoveries and Settlements*. Nashville: G. D. Free, 1895l.
Gentry, Susie. "Graves of Revolutionary Soldiers in Tennessee." *American Monthly Magazine* [DAR], 35:6 (December 1909), 1188-1191. [burials in Bedford, Davidson, Franklin, Jefferson, Lincoln, Madison, Maury, Robertson, Rutherford, Smith, Weakley, and Williamson Counties]
Gildrie, Richard. "Tennessee in the American Revolution: A Reconsideration." In Kristofer Ray, ed., *Before the Volunteer State: New Thoughts on Early Tennessee, 1540-1800* (Knoxville: University of Tennessee Press, 2014), 109-130.
Gilmore, James R., pseud. Edmund Kirke. *The Rear Guard of the Revolution*. New York: Appleton, 1986.
Goodpasture, Albert V. "Indian Wars and Warriors of the Old Southwest, 1730-1807." *Tennessee Historical Magazine*, 4:1 (March 1918), 3-49; 4:2 (June 1918), 106-145; 4:3 (September 1918), 161-210; 4:4 (December 1918), 252-289.
Great Britain. Colonial Office. American and West Indies, Original Correspondence, Board of Trade and Secretary of State: Indian Affairs, Surveys, etc. (CO 5/77). {[Document dated: 7 May 1776. "Toqueh, [Tennessee]. [Copy of] Alex[ander] Cameron, [Dep. Supt. for Indian Affairs, Southern District] to John Stuart [Supt. for Indian Affairs, Southern District]." Copy of a manuscript in the National Archives of the United Kingdom, Kew, London (formerly the Public Record Office), Z.5.16N (MARS ID: 21.20.64.35; folder), "British Records Collection," State Archives of North Carolina, Raleigh. [Online catalog description: "Topics include arrival of

Henry Stuart with ammunition; attempts of rebels to win over Cherokee; Taitt is prepared to bring Creeks to frontier. Enclosed in John Stuart to [Lord George] Germain, 23 August 1776 (21.20.64.1.33).”]

Great Britain. Colonial Office. American and West Indies, Original Correspondence, Board of Trade and Secretary of State: Indian Affairs, Surveys, etc. (CO 5/77). “[Document dated: 7 May 1776. Toqua, [Tennessee]. [Copy of] Henry Stuart and Alex[ande]r Cameron [Dep. Supt. for Indian Affairs, Southern District] to ‘The Inhabitants of Watauga and Nonatluchky....’.” Copy of a manuscript in the National Archives of the United Kingdom, Kew, London (formerly the Public Record Office), Z.5.16N (MARS ID: 21.20.64.36; folder), “British Records Collection,” State Archives of North Carolina, Raleigh. [Online catalog description: “Letter warns of the danger from Indians, who ‘expect that you will remove in twenty days’; suggest removal to West Florida, where they may expect immediate grants of land ‘in a Climate and Situation much better suited to industrious white people than where you now live and where you may hope to rise in the world by your own industry. Enclosed in John Stuart to [Lord George] Germain, 23 August 1776 (21.20.64.1.33)’.”]

Great Britain. Colonial Office. American and West Indies, Original Correspondence, Board of Trade and Secretary of State: Indian Affairs, Surveys, etc. (CO 5/77). “[Document dated: 7 May 1776: Toquah, [Tennessee], in the Overhill Cherokee Nation. [Copy of] Henry Stuart to John Stuart, [Supt. for Indian Affairs, Southern District].” Copy of a manuscript in the National Archives of the United Kingdom, Kew, London (formerly the Public Record Office), Z.5.16N (MARS ID: 21.20.64.37; folder), “British Records Collection,” State Archives of North Carolina, Raleigh. [Online catalog description: “Topics include Henry Stuart’s arrival in Toquah after a journey of 55 days from the Chickasaw; dispensing of the ammunition; meeting with headmen, who professed loyalty; Cherokee feel ‘hemmed in’ by settlements at Holstens River and ‘Watoga’, and the younger Indians are for decisive action against settlers there. Enclosed in John Stuart to [Lord George] Germain, 23 August 1776 (21.20.64.1.33).”]

Great Britain. Colonial Office. American and West Indies, Original Correspondence, Board of Trade and Secretary of State: Indian Affairs, Surveys, etc. (CO 5/77). “[Document dated: 12 May 1776: Toqua, [Tennessee]. Extract of H[enry] Stuart and Alex[ander] Cameron [Dep. Supt. for Indian Affairs, Southern District] to John Carter ‘and The other Inhabitants of Watauga’.” Copy of a manuscript in the National Archives of the United Kingdom, Kew, London (formerly the Public Record Office), Z.5.16N (MARS ID: 21.20.64.40; folder), “British Records Collection,” State Archives of North Carolina, Raleigh. [Online catalog description: “Extract reiterates that Indians are determined to recover their lands. Enclosed in John Stuart to [Lord George] Germain, 23 August 1776 (21.20.64.1.33).”]

Great Britain. Colonial Office. American and West Indies, Original Correspondence, Board of Trade and Secretary of State: Indian Affairs, Surveys, etc. (CO 5/77). “[Document dated: 28 June 1776: Taqua [Tennessee]. [Copy of] Henry Stuart to Edward Wilkinson.” Copy of a manuscript in the National Archives of the United Kingdom, Kew, London (formerly the Public Record Office), Z.5.16N (MARS ID: 21.20.64.42; folder), “British Records Collection,” State Archives of North Carolina, Raleigh. [Online catalog description: “Letter encloses certain correspondence, and hopes he can ‘bring to justice those Villains that Can be Capable of Forgery in Order to involve the Settlements of Virginia & North Carolina in an unjust war with the Indians’; details of the affair. Enclosed in John Stuart to [Lord George] Germain, 23 August 1776 (21.20.64.1.33).”]

Great Britain. Colonial Office. American and West Indies, Original Correspondence, Board of Trade and Secretary of State: Indian Affairs, Surveys, etc. (CO 5/78). “[Document dated: 19 January 1777: Fort Patrick Henry, [Tennessee].” [Copy of] talk from William Christian to the Raven [Cherokee chief].” Copy of a manuscript in the National Archives of the United Kingdom, Kew, London (formerly the Public Record Office), Z.5.17N (MARS ID: 21.20.64.41; folder), “British Records Collection,” State Archives of North Carolina, Raleigh. [Online catalog description: “Talk relates Christian’s regret of the necessity of having had to wage war against Cherokee; British have told them many lies; invites Cherokee to a meeting at Williamsburgh. Enclosed in John Stuart to Lord George Germain, 14 June 1777 (21.20.65.1.40).”]

Great Britain. Colonial Office. American and West Indies, Original Correspondence, Board of Trade and Secretary of State: Indian Affairs, Surveys, etc. (CO 5/77). “[Document dated: 4 July 1776: Cane Creek, [Tennessee]. [Copy of] Hugh Hamilton to [Alexander Cameron, Dep. Supt. for Indian Affairs, Southern District].” Copy of a manuscript in the National Archives of the United Kingdom, Kew, London (formerly the Public Record Office), Z.5.17N (MARS ID: 21.20.64.43; folder), “British Records Collection,” State Archives of North Carolina, Raleigh. [Online catalog description: “Letter includes news of Indian attacks; news from Charles Town and Savannah. Enclosed in John Stuart to [Lord George] Germain, 23 August 1776 (21.20.64.1.33).”]

Great Britain. Colonial Office. American and West Indies, Original Correspondence, Board of Trade and Secretary of State: Indian Affairs, Surveys, etc. (CO 5/77). “[Document dated: 5 July 1776: Cane Creek Camp, [Tennessee]. [Copy of] Hugh Hamilton to [Alexander Cameron, Dep. Supt. for Indian Affairs, Southern

District]. Copy of a manuscript in the National Archives of the United Kingdom, Kew, London (formerly the Public Record Office), Z.5.16N (MARS ID: 21.20.64.44; folder), "British Records Collection," State Archives of North Carolina, Raleigh. [Online catalog description: "Letter states that Hamilton has seen his friend the Turkey; Cameron's clothes; the Turkey desires news from Cameron's area, and instructions concerning action against the rebels. Enclosed in John Stuart to [Lord George] Germain, 23 August 1776 (21.20.64.1.33)."]

Great Britain. Colonial Office. American and West Indies, Original Correspondence, Board of Trade and Secretary of State: Indian Affairs, Surveys, etc. (CO 5/77). "[Document dated: 9 July 1776: Toquah, [Tennessee]. [Copy of] Alex[ander] Cameron, [dep. supt. for Indian affairs] to John Stuart, [supt. for Indian affairs]." Copy of a manuscript in the National Archives of the United Kingdom, Kew, London (formerly the Public Record Office), Z.5.16N (MARS ID: 21.20.64.46; folder), "British Records Collection," State Archives of North Carolina, Raleigh. [Online catalog description: "Topics include the danger to settlers at 'Wataga' and Nonatluchky; northern Indians solicit help from Cherokee against whites; his financial accounts; Capt. W[illia]m Guest from Virginia wishes to raise a regiment to fight rebels. Enclosed in John Stuart to [Lord George] Germain, 23 August 1776 (21.20.64.1.33)."]

Great Britain. Colonial Office. American and West Indies, Original Correspondence, Board of Trade and Secretary of State: Indian Affairs, Surveys, etc. (CO 5/77). "[Document dated: 31 August 1776: Toqueh, [Tennessee]. [Copy of] Alex[ande]r Cameron [Deputy Superintendent for Indian Affairs, Southern District] to John Stuart [Supt. for Indian Affairs, Southern District]." Copy of a manuscript in the National Archives of the United Kingdom, Kew, London (formerly the Public Record Office), Z.5.16N (MARS ID: 21.20.65.5; folder), "British Records Collection," State Archives of North Carolina, Raleigh. [Online catalog description: "Letter describes Cherokee setbacks, but states that with proper support from government, Cherokee will 'distress the Rebels in Georgia, both the Carolinas and Virginia so much this Fall and winter' that the rebels will sue for peace; Capt. Gest assists him among Cherokee; various concerning affairs in Cherokee country. Enclosed in John Stuart to Lord George Germain, 25 Oct. 1776 (21.20.65.1.3)."]

Great Britain. Colonial Office. American and West Indies, Original Correspondence, Board of Trade and Secretary of State: Indian Affairs, Surveys, etc. (CO 5/77). "[Document dated: 23 September 1776: Toqueh, [Tennessee]. [Copy of] Alex[ander] Cameron [dep. supt. for Indian affairs] to John Stuart [supt. for Indian affairs, southern district]." Copy of a manuscript in the National Archives of the United Kingdom, Kew, London (formerly the Public Record Office), Z.5.16N (MARS ID: 21.20.65.14; folder), "British Records Collection," State Archives of North Carolina, Raleigh. [Online catalog description: "Letter states that Cameron has not heard from Stuart recently, a 'delay [that] may be dangerous'; army from North Carolina and Virginia have destroyed the Middle Settlement; Cherokee diminished in numbers; Creek refuse to help; Catawba with Americans; Cameron fears for his own safety among Cherokee; supplies very much needed. Enclosed in John Stuart to Lord George Germain, 25 Oct. 1776 (21.20.65.1.3)."]

Great Britain. Colonial Office. American and West Indies, Original Correspondence, Board of Trade and Secretary of State: Indian Affairs, Surveys, etc. (CO 5/78). "[Document dated: 19 January 1777: Fort Patrick Henry, [Tennessee]. [Copy of] talk from William Christian to the Raven [Cherokee chief]." Copy of a manuscript in the National Archives of the United Kingdom, Kew, London (formerly the Public Record Office), Z.5.16N (MARS ID: 21.20.65.41; folder), "British Records Collection," State Archives of North Carolina, Raleigh. [Online catalog description: "Talk relates Christian's regret of the necessity of having had to wage war against Cherokee; British have told them many lies; invites Cherokee to a meeting at Williamsburgh. Enclosed in John Stuart to Lord George Germain, 14 June 1777 (21.20.65.1.40)."]

Greene, Evarts, and Virginia Harrington. *American Population before the Federal Census of 1790.* New York: Columbia University Press, 1932: Gloucester, Mass., P. Smith, 1966; reprinted: Baltimore: Genealogical Publishing Company, 1993.

Gump, Lucy K. "Possessions & Patterns of Living in Washington County: The 20 Years before Statehood, 1777-1796." M. A. thesis, East Tennessee State University, 1989.

Hamer, Philip M. "The Wataugans and the Cherokee Indians in 1776." *East Tennessee Historical Publications,* 3 (1931), 108-126.

Hamer, Philip M., ed. "Correspondence of Henry, Stuart, and Alexander Cameron with the Wataugans." *Mississippi Valley Historical Review*, 17:3 (December 1930), 451-459.

Hamer, Philip M., ed. *Tennessee: A History 1673-1932*. New York: The American Historical Society, 1933.

Hamlett, James C. "Long-Lots in Washington County, Tennessee." *Southeastern Geographer*, 3 (1963), 34-45.

Hatley, Thomas. "The Three Lives of Keowee: Loss and Recovery in Eighteenth-Century Cherokee Villages." In Peter H. Wood, Gregory A. Waselkov, and M. Thomas Hatley, eds., *Powhatan's Mantle: Indians in the Colonial Southeast* (Lincoln: University of Nebraska Press, 1980), 223-248.

Haun, Weynette Parks. *Morgan District North Carolina Superior Court of Law & Equity*. 4 vols. Durham: W. P. Haun, 1987-[1995].

Haywood, John. *The Civil and Political History of the State of Tennessee, from Its Earliest Settlement up to the Year 1796, Including the Boundaries of the State*. Knoxville: Heiskell and Brown, 1823; reprinted: 1969; Johnson City: The Overmountain Press, 1999.

Hesseltine, William B. "Lyman Draper and the South." *Journal of Southern History*, 19:1 (February 1953), 20-31.

Hoffman, Paul Taylor, and Carroll Van West. "The Old West Passage: Exploring the First Road into Middle Tennessee." M. A. thesis, Middle Tennessee State University, 2012.

Holmes, Jack D. L. "Spanish-American Rivalry over the Chickasaw Bluffs, 1780-1795." *East Tennessee Historical Society Publications*, 34 (1962), 26-57.

Holt, Albert C. "The Economic and Social Beginnings of Tennessee." *Tennessee Historical Magazine*, 7:3 (October 1921), 194-230; 7:4 (January 1922), 251-313; 8:1 (April 1923), 24-86. [This article includes a few very useful maps: "Map 1. 'Taken from Schoolcraft, Vol. 1 page 312," [Shows the general Indian boundaries in Tennessee in the late eighteenth century {on page 208 of the article}. "Map 2. "Main Land Cessions by Indians (after Garret & Goodpasture, page 128)." {on page 228 of the article} {Map 3}."State of Franklin, 1784-1788." {Map 4}. "Early Forts and Stations." {Map 5}. "Roads of Tennessee {Taken from Daniel Smith Ramsey and Goodspeed." {Map 6} "Land Reservations {in Tennessee showing the North Carolina Military Tract of 1783; Greene's Tract of 1783; and Congressional Lands of 1806."]

Hsiung, David C. "Seeing Early Appalachian Communities through the Lenses of History, Geography, and Sociology." In David Colin Crass, Steven D. Smith, Martha A. Zierden, and Richard D. Brooks, eds., *The Southern Colonial Backcountry: Interdisciplinary Perspectives on Frontier Communities* (Knoxville: University of Tennessee Press, 1998), 162-181.

Hsiung, David C. *Two Worlds in the Tennessee Mountains: Exploring the Origins of Appalachian Stereotypes*. Lexington: University Press of Kentucky, 1997.

Hubbard, Philip M. *Itinerary of George Washington during the War of the American Revolution*. Dayton, Ohio: [P. M. Hubbard?], ca. 2000-2002[?].

Hyder, John, 1762-1826. *The Natural and Aboriginal History of Tennessee Up to the First Settlements Therein by the White People in the Year 1768: Including Archaeological, Geological, and Historical Annotations Bringing the Ancient Account into Focus with Present Day Knowledge, and an Introductory Sketch of the Author John Hayward*. Kingsport: F. M. Hill-Books, 1973.

Inman, Natalie. "Military Families: Kinship in the American Revolution." In Kristofer Ray, ed., *Before the Volunteer State: New Thoughts on Early Tennessee, 1540-1800* (Knoxville: University of Tennessee Press, 2014), 131-154.

Invidiato, Ramona. "'Trust the Lord, but keep your powder dry!" A Tale of Black Powder Makers in the Revolutionary Era." *Drumbeat, with Flintlock & Powderhorn: News of the Sons of Revolution*, 29:4 (Winter 2011), 19-20. [Mary McKeehan Patton (1751-1836) of Cumberland County, Pennsylvania, and frontier Tennessee during the Revolution.]

Irwin, Ned L. "Voice in the Wilderness: John Haywood and the Preservation of Early Tennessee History." *Tennessee Historical Quarterly*, 58:4 (Winter 1999), 239-252.

Jackson, George B. "John Stuart: Superintendent of Indian Affairs for the Southern District." *Tennessee Historical Magazine*, 3:3 (September 1917), 165-191.

Jones, William Nathan. *By the River and Beyond: History and Humor from the Mountains of East Tennessee*. Newport, Tenn.: Printed and Distributed by Newport Printing Company, 1996.

Jordan, René. "The Evolution of Early Tennessee County Boundaries: Washington County." *Tennessee Ancestors: A Tri-Annual Publication of the East Tennessee Historical Society*, 10:1 (April 1994), 4-10.

Kanon, Tom. "The Kidnapping of Martha Crawley and Settler-Indian Relations Prior to the War of 1812." *Tennessee Historical Quarterly*, 64:1 (Spring 2005), 2-23.

Keefe, Stuart. "The Dixon's [*sic*] 1778-82, Washington County, NC (Tennessee)." *North Carolina Genealogical Society Journal*, 3:2 (May 1977), 115.

Kirke, Edmund [pseud.] (James R. Gilmore). *The Rear-Guard of the Revolution*. New York: D. Appleton & Co., 1886; reprinted 1891; online: http://catalog.hathitrust.org/Record/006539349.

Klebenow, Anne. *200 Years through 200 Stories: A Tennessee Bicentennial Collection*. Knoxville: University of Tennessee Press, 1996.

Lester, Anne J. "Settlement Patterns in the Upper Counties of East Tennessee to 1796." M. A. thesis, University of Virginia, 1981.

Lightfoot, Marise Parrish. *Let the Drums Roll: Veterans and Patriots of the Revolutionary War Who Settled in Maury County, Tennessee*. Columbia, Tenn.: Maury County Historical Society, 1976.

Lynch, Michael. "Creating Regional Heroes: Traditional Interpretations of the Battle of King's Mountain." *Tennessee Historical Quarterly*, 68:3 (Fall 2009), 224-249.

Marsh, Carole. *Tennessee Bandits, Bushwackers, Outlaws, Crooks, Devils, Ghosts, Desperadoes, Rogues, Heroes, & Assorted & Sundry Characters*. Decatur, Ga.: Gallopade Publishing Group, 1997.

Matlock, J. W. L., ed. "The Battle of the Bluffs, from the Journal of John Cotten," *Tennessee Historical Quarterly*, 18:3 (September 1959), 252-265.

McBridge, Robert M. *More Landmarks of Tennessee History*. Nashville: Tennessee Historical Society, Tennessee Historical Commission, 1969.

McBride, Robert M. "Tennessee: Lost Counties." *East Tennessee Historical Society Special Publication*, no. 38 (1966), 3-15.

McGhee, Lucy Kate. *Tennessee Historical Records from Indian & Revolutionary Times up to 1883, Consisting of History of Indians, Revolutionary Soldiers, War of 1812 Soldiers, Indian War Soldiers, Mexican War Soldiers*. Washington, D. C.: L. K. McGhee, 1956.

McGill, J. T. "Andrew Greer." *Tennessee Historical Magazine*, 2 (1916): 204-207.

McNamara, Billie R. "An Introduction to the History of Tennessee's Confusing Land Laws." *Tennessee Ancestors: A Tri-Annual Publication of the East Tennessee Historical Society*, 12:1 (April 1996), 11-24. [Covers legislation put in place by North Carolina during the Revolution and after]

Mitchell, Robert D., ed. *Appalachian Frontiers: Settlement, Society & Development in the Preindustrial Era* Lexington: University Press of Kentucky, 1991. [Originated with papers presented at the Conference on the Appalachian Frontier, held in May 1985 at James Madison University and Mary Baldwin College, and sponsored by the Shenandoah Valley Historical Institute and the American Frontier Culture Foundation.]

Montgomery, James R. "The Nomenclature of the Upper Tennessee Valley." *East Tennessee Historical Society Publications,* 38 (1965), 46-57.

North Carolina (State). General Assembly. "[Document dated:] December 6, 1777: Bill for appointing commissioners to lay off and mark a road from the courthouse in the county of Washington through the mountains into the country of Burke." Manuscript; General Assembly Session Records; Session of November-December 1777; House Bills, Box 2 (MARS ID: 66.8.11.27), State Archives of North Carolina, Raleigh.

North Carolina (State). General Assembly. "[Document dated:] October 25, 1779: Bill for Securing the Right of Such Persons in the County of Washington as Lie between the River Holstein and the Line Lately Run by Commissioners of North Carolina and Virginia." Manuscript; General Assembly Session Records; Session of October-November 1779; Unidentified Amendments, Senate Bills, House Bills; Senate Bills, Box 2 (MARS ID: 66.8.19.8; folder), State Archives of North Carolina, Raleigh. [Online catalog description: "The bill also divides Washington County into the counties of Washington and Sullivan, appoints commissioners to oversee the establishment of the new county, sets up its basic court regulations, and levies taxes for various purposes."]

North Carolina (State). General Assembly. "[Document dated:] May 6, 1780: Bill for vesting in Hannah Reed, widow of Reverend James Reed, his estate [and for suspending law concerning land grants near Virginia]." Manuscript; General Assembly Session Records; Session of April-May 1780; Miscellaneous Bills, Senate Bills, House Bills; Senate Bills, Box 2 (MARS ID: 66.8.21.19; folder), State Archives of North Carolina, Raleigh. [Online catalog description: "The bill also suspends the operation of the intestate law until the next session in the region recently discovered to be in the state due to the extension of the boundary line with Virginia. Also includes a draft of the bill."]

North Carolina (State). General Assembly. "[Document dated:] February 3, 1781: Resolution that the Assembly at next session hear claims of patentees and settlers under the State of Virginia." Manuscript; General Assembly Session Records; Session of January-February 1781; Joint Papers, Committee Papers, Resolutions; House Joint Resolutions: February 3-4, 1781, Box 1 (MARS ID: 66.8.23.16.2; item), State Archives of North Carolina, Raleigh.

North Carolina (State). Office of Secretary of State. Office of the Secretary. Land Office. "Land Warrents, Plats of Survey, and Related Records. Tennessee, Eastern District, 1779-1802." Manuscript S.108.361-S.108.363, 3 microfilm reels (MARS ID: 12.14.3; folder), State Archives of North Carolina, Raleigh.

North Carolina (State). Office of Secretary of State. Office of the Secretary. Land Office. "Land Warrents, Plats of Survey, and Related Records. Tennessee, Middle District, 1783-1797." Manuscript S.108.363-S.108.365, 3 microfilm reels (MARS ID: 12.14.4; folder), State Archives of North Carolina, Raleigh.

North Carolina (State). Office of Secretary of State. Office of the Secretary. Land Office. "Land Warrents, Plats of Survey, and Related Records. Tennessee, Washington County, 1770-1803." Manuscript S.108.390-S.108.395, 6 microfilm reels (MARS ID: 12.14.20; folder), State Archives of North Carolina, Raleigh. [Online catalog description: "Washington County, Tennessee began as the District of Washington (a part of North Carolina) in 1776. The county designation was granted in 1777. A portion of the district along with a portion of Surry County, NC were formed into Wilkes County, NC in 1777. Washington County encompassed the territory west of Wilkes County (between Wilkes, the Virginia line, the hunting grounds of the Cherokee Indians, and the Mississippi River). It was named in honor of George Washington. The county seat of Jonesboro was named after Willie Jones and was established in 1779. A portion of Washington County became Sullivan County in 1779, and portions of Washington County became Davidson and Greene counties in 1783. Other areas of Washington were annexed to Sullivan County in 1788 and Wilkes County, NC in 1792. Carter County was formed from Washington County in 1796."]

North Carolina (State). Office of Secretary of State. Office of the Secretary. Land Office. "Land Warrents, Plats of Survey, and Related Records. Tennessee, No County Given." Manuscript S.108.395, 1 microfilm reel (MARS ID: 12.14.23; folder), State Archives of North Carolina, Raleigh.

North Carolina (State). Office of Secretary of State. Office of the Secretary. Land Office. "Land Warrents, Plats of Survey, and Related Records. Tennessee, Western, 1783-1802." Manuscript S.108.366-S.108.367, 3 microfilm reels (MARS ID: 12.14.3; folder), State Archives of North Carolina, Raleigh.

O'Donnell, James H. *Southern Indians and the American Revolution*. Knoxville: University of Tennessee Press, 1973.

Oldham, Bethenia McLemore. *Tennessee and Tennesseans*. Clarksville: W. P. Titus, 1903.

Pate, James Paul. "The Chickamauga: A Forgotten Segment of Indian Resistance on the Southern Frontier." Ph. D. dissertation, Mississippi State University, 1969.

Phelan, James. *History of Tennessee: The Making of a State*. Boston: Houghton, Mifflin and Company, 1888.

Price, Prentiss. "A Further Note on Doctor James Cozby." *Echoes from the East Tennessee Historical Society*, 3:1 (January 1957), 60; reprinted as "Tennessee's Little Known Pioneers – Part 2." *Tennessee Ancestors: A Tri-Annual Publication of the East Tennessee Historical Society*, 27:2 (August 2011), 141.

Price, Prentiss. "John Haile, Esq. (And Joab Mitchell)." *Echoes from the East Tennessee Historical Society*, 2:3 (July 1956), 4-5; reprinted as "Tennessee's Little Known Pioneers – Part 1." *Tennessee Ancestors: A Tri-Annual Publication of the East Tennessee Historical Society*, 27:1 (April 2011), 28-33.

Price, Prentiss, ed. "Two Petitions to Virginia of the North of Holston Men 1776, 1777." *East Tennessee Historical Society's Publications*, 21 (1949), 95-110; Reprinted in *Tennessee Ancestors: A Tri-Annual Publication of the East Tennessee Historical Society*, 16:3 (December 2000), 207-220. [From the introduction of the article in *Tennessee Ancestors*: "The significance of these petitions is that they illustrate the exercise of jurisdiction, Virginia as a colony and as a state, over a considerable portion of what is now upper Tennessee from the beginning of settlement until 1779."]

Putnam, Albigence W. *History of Middle Tennessee*. Knoxville: University of Tennessee Press, 1971.

Raimo, John W. *Biographical Directory of American Colonial and Revolutionary Governors, 1607-1789*. Westport, Conn.: Meckler Books, 1980.

Ramsey, J. G. M. *The Annals of Tennessee to the End of the Eighteenth Century; Comprising Its Settlement, as the Watauga Association, from 1769 to 1777; a Part of North-Carolina, from 1777 to 1784; a Part of North-Carolina, from 1788 to 1790; the Territory of the U. States, South of the Ohio, from 1790 to 1796; the State of Tennessee, from 1796 to 1800*. Charleston: John Russell, 1853; reprinted: Kingsport: Kingsport Press, 1926.

Ray, Kristofer. *Before the Volunteer State: New Thoughts on Early Tennessee, 1540-1800*. Knoxville: University of Tennessee Press, 2015.

Ray, Kristofer. *Middle Tennessee, 1775-1825: Progress and Popular Democracy on the Southwestern Frontier*. Knoxville: University of Tennessee Press, 2007.

"The Records of Washington County (1778-1782)." *American Historical Magazine,* 5:4 (October 1900), 326-381; 6:1 (January 1901), 51-93; 6:2 (April 1901), 191-192; 6:3 (July 1901), 283-288. [Includes some civil service appointments. May be helpful for determining an individuals residence.]

Reeves, Charles A. *Early Roads to the Tennessee Country (Before 1796)*. Knoxville: First Families of Tennessee; East Tennessee Historical Society, 2000.

Roebuck, Hayward. "Washington and Sullivan Counties, (Tennessee) Revolutionary War Stub Indent Books." *North Carolina Genealogical Society Journal,* 1:2 (April 1975), 91-96.

Rogers, William Flinn. "Life on the Kentucky-Tennessee Frontier near the End of the Eighteenth Century." M. A. thesis, University of Tennessee, 1925.

Roper, James E. "The Revolutionary War on the Fourth Chickasaw Bluff." *West Tennessee Historical Society Papers*, 95-118; online: http://register.shelby.tn.us/wths/?acc=Y.

Smith, Sam B. *Tennessee History: A Bibliography*. Knoxville: University of Tennessee Press, 1974.
Tannehill, Wilkins, 1787-1858. *Tales of the Revolution, by a Young Gentleman of Tennessee*. Nashville: Hunt, Tardiff, 1833.
Three Pioneer Tennessee Documents: Donelson's Journal, Cumberland Compact, Minutes of Cumberland Court. Nashville: Tennessee Historical Commission, 1964.
Timmons, William E. "The Conundrum of the Two Charles Robertsons of Watauga and Washington County, North Carolina/Tennessee." *Tennessee Ancestors: A Tri-Annual Publication of the East Tennessee Historical Society*, 20:2 (August 2004), 119-132. [Two separate, prominent early settlers of the Watauga settlement.]
Watauga Association of Genealogists. *History of Washington County, Tennessee, 1988*. [Johnson City, Tenn.]: The Association, 1988.
West, Carol Van. *The Tennessee Encyclopedia of History & Culture*. Nashville: Tennessee Historical Society; Rutledge Hill Press, 1998; online edition: Knoxville: University of Tennessee Press, 2002.; online: https://tennesseeencyclopedia.net/index.php.
Whitley, Edythe Rucker. "Revolutionary Soldiers in Davidson County, Tennessee." *William and Mary Quarterly*, 2nd series, 11:1 (January 1931), 13-19.
Williams, Samuel Cole. *Beginnings of West Tennessee: In the Land of the Chickasaws, 1541-1841*. Johnson City: Watauga Press, 1930.
Williams, Samuel Cole. "Colonel Elijah Clarke in the Tennessee Country." *Georgia Historical Quarterly*, 25:2 (June 1941), 151-158.
Williams, Samuel Cole. *Early Travels in the Tennessee Country, 1540-1800*. Johnson City: Watauga Press, 1928.
Williams, Samuel Cole. "The First Court West of the Alleghanies." *Green Bag*, (November 1893), 505-505.
Williams, Samuel Cole. "First Territorial Division Named for Washington." *Tennessee Historical Magazine*, 2nd series, 2:2 (January 1932), 153-164. [Washington County, Tennessee, created by North Carolina in 1777.]
Williams, Samuel Cole. "The First Volunteers from the 'Volunteer State'." *Tennessee Historical Magazine*, 8:2 (July 1924), 132-139. [Dunmore's War, 1774]
Williams, Samuel Cole. "Henderson and Company's Purchase with in the Limits of Tennessee." *Tennessee Historical Magazine*, 1:1 (April 1919), 5-23.
Williams, Samuel Cole. "Shelby's Fort." *East Tennessee Historical Society Publications*, 7 (1935), 28-37.
Williams, Samuel Cole. *Tennessee during the Revolutionary War*. Nashville: Tennessee Historical Commission, 1944; reprinted: Knoxville: University of Tennessee Press, 1974.
Williams, Samuel Cole. "Western Representation in North Carolina Assemblies, 1776-1790." *East Tennessee Historical Society's Publications*, 14 (1942), 106-112.
Wilson, Marshall A. "Joseph Willson: Magistrate – Captain," *Echoes from the East Tennessee Historical Society* 2:2 (April 1956), 5-6; reprinted as "Tennessee's Little Known Pioneers – Part 1." *Tennessee Ancestors: A Tri-Annual Publication of the East Tennessee Historical Society*, 27:1 (April 2011), 28-33.
Young, Carol Furlong. "A Study of Some Developing Interpretations of the History of Revolutionary Tennessee." *Publications of the East Tennessee Historical Society*, 25 (1953), [24]-36.

Washington County, North Carolina (First) (Modern State of Tennessee) – Jonesborough

Eberling, May D. "History in Towns: Jonesboro, Tennessee's Oldest Town." *Antiques*, (September 1971), 420-424.
Fink, Miriam L. "Some Phases of the Social & Economic History of Jonesboro, Tenn., prior to the Civil War." M. A. thesis, University of Tennessee at Knoxville, 1934.
Fink, Paul M. "The Early Press of Jonesboro." *East Tennessee Historical Society Publications,* 10 (1938), 57-70.
Fink, Paul M. *Jonesboro: The First Century of Tennessee's First Town, 1776-1876*. Johnson City, Overmountain Press, 1972; 2nd ed. 1989.
Fink, Paul M. "Methodism in Jonesboro, Tennessee." *East Tennessee Historical Society's Publications*, 22 (1950), 45-59.
Robinson, Blackwell P. "Willie Jones of Halifax." *North Carolina Historical Review,* 18:1 (January 1941), 1-26; 18:2 (April 1941), 133-170. [Jonesboro was named for Willie Jones.]
A Visitor's Guide to Historic Jonesborough, Tennessee's Oldest Town: Close Encounters with History on The Old Great Stage Road. Jonesboro: Stage Road Interiors, 1986.
Williams, Samuel Cole. "The Founder of Tennessee's First Town: Major Jesse Walton." *East Tennessee Historical Society's Publications*, 3 (1930), 70-80. [Jessee Walton (d. ca. 1792)]

Washington County, North Carolina (First) (Modern State of Tennessee) – Proposed State of Franklin

Alden, George H. "The State of Franklin." *American Historical Review*, 8 (1902-1903), 271-289.

Ashe, S. A. "The State of Franklin." *North Carolina Booklet*, 14:1 (July 1914), 28-49; online: http://digital.ncdcr.gov/cdm/ref/collection/p249901coll37/id/14180. [Online description from "North Carolina Periodicals Index," East Carolina University: "The state of Franklin flourished from 1784 to 1787. Promoted by many inhabitants from the western most settlements of North Carolina, it led the creation of modern day Tennessee."]

Barksdale, Kevin. "The State of Franklin: Separatism, Competition, and the Legacy of Tennessee's First State, 1783-1789." In Kristofer Ray, ed., *Before the Volunteer State: New Thoughts on Early Tennessee, 1540-1800* (Knoxville: University of Tennessee Press, 2014), 155-184.

Barksdale, Kevin T. *The Lost State of Franklin: America's First Secession*. Lexington: University Press of Kentucky, 2008.

Black, Henry C. "Some Forgotten Constitutions: Franklin." *Constitutional Review*, 10 (1926), 115-119.

Cannon, Walter F. "Four Interpretations of the History of the State of Franklin." *East Tennessee Historical Society Publications*, 22 (1950), 3-18.

Clemens, Will M. "Lost State of Franklin." *New England Magazine*, (February 1903), 772-774.

Corbitt, D. L. "New State of Frankland." *North Carolina Historial Review*, 2:3 (July 1925), 395-396.

Corbitt, D. L. "Washington, Sullivan and Greene Declare Independence." *North Carolina Historial Review*, 2:3 (July 1925), 393-394.

Cotham, Steve. "The Flags of the State of Franklin." *Tennessee Ancestors*, 1:3 (December 1985), 119-120.

Dale, Reed. *John Tipton, John Sevier, and the State of Franklin*. [United States: Tipton Family of American Association, 1998]. [A copy is located at Special Collections Library (Rare Books: F.436.R44 1998), University of Tennessee, Knoxville.]

Drake, Doug; Jack Masters; and Bill Puryear. *Founding of the Cumberland Settlements: The First Atlas, 1779-1804*. Gallatin, Tenn.: Warioto Press, 2009.

Drake, Doug; Jack Masters; and Bill Puryear. *Founding of the Cumberland Settlements: Data Supplements 1 & 2, The First Atlas, 1779-1804*. 2 vols. Gallatin, Tenn.: Warioto Press, 2009.

Fink, Paul M. "Some Phases of the History of the State of Franklin." *Tennessee Historical Quarterly*, 16:3 (September 1957), 195-213.

Fitch, William E. *The Origin, Rise & Downfall of the State of Franklin under Her First & Only Governor, John Sevier*. New York: Society of the Order of Founders & Patriots of America, 1910.

Foster, Dave. Franklin: The Stillborn State and the Sevier/Tipton Political Feud. Pigeon Forge, Tenn.: Top Ten Press, 1994.

Garrett, William R. "The Provisional Constitution of Frankland." *American Historical Magazine*, 1 (1896), 48-63.

Gentry, Susie. "Susie Gentry Papers, 1861-1934." Manuscript III-F-6 and mss. drawer 1 ac. nos. 292, 652 67-005 mf. 1193 mf. 418, Tennessee State Library and Archives, Nashville; also available on microfilm. [Contains: "…a scrapbook on Revolutionary War soldiers of Tennessee."]

Gerson, Noel B. *Franklin: America's "Lost State."* New York: Crowell-Collier Press, 1968.

Goodpasture, Albert V., ed. "Constitution of the State of Franklin." *American Historical Magazine*, 9 (1904), 399-408.

Hagy, James W., and Stanley J. Folmsbee. "Arthur Campbell & the Separate State Movements in VA & NC." *East Tennessee Historical Society Papers*, 42 (1970), 20-46.

Hagy, James W., and Stanley J. Folmsbee. "Democracy Defeated: The Frankland Constitution of 1785." *Tennessee Historical Quarterly*, 40:3 (Fall 1981), 239-256.

Hart, Dave. "The State of Franklin." *Our State: Down Home in North Carolina*, 76:8 (January 2009), 28-3, 32; online: http://digital.ncdcr.gov/cdm/ref/collection/p16062coll18/id/91165. [Online description from "North Carolina Periodicals Index," East Carolina University: "Hart recounts an unusual and little-remembered incident in the early history of North Carolina. In 1784, residents in the western part of the state felt isolated from the eastern section because of the Appalachian Mountains and formed their own state called Franklin."]

Hicklin, J. B. "The Lost State of Franklin." *The State: A Weekly Survey of North Carolina*, 6:25 (November 1938), 11; online: http://digital.ncdcr.gov/cdm/ref/collection/p16062coll18/id/38690. [Online description from "North Carolina Periodicals Index," East Carolina University: "Hicklin recounts a little-remembered incident in Western North Carolina in the period following the Revolutionary War. In 1784, citizens there felt isolated from the eastern section because of the Appalachian Mountains and formed, along with citizens in Eastern Tennessee, their own state called Franklin. It didn't last."]

Humphrey, Richard Alan. "The State of Franklin: Clergy, Controversy, and Constitution," *Appalachian Heritage: A Magazine of Southern Appalachian Life and Culture*, 7 (Fall 1979), 35-36.

Irwin, Neal. "The Lost Papers of the 'Lost State of Franklin.'" *Journal of East Tennessee History*, no. 69 (1997), 84-96.

Kastor, Peter J. "'Equitable Rights and Privileges': The Divided Loyalties in Washington County, Virginia, during the Franklin Separatist Crisis." *Virginia Magazine of History and Biography*, 105:2 (Spring 1997), 193-226.

Lacy, Eric R. "The Persistent State of Franklin." *Tennessee Historical Quarterly,* 23:4 (December 1964), 321-332.

Lewis, J. D. "The State of Franklin: A History of the State of Franklin." Online: http://www.carolana.com/NC/Early_Statehood/nc_state_of_franklin.html.

Lewis, J. D. "North Carolina – From Statehood to 1800: A Petition for the State of Franklin, December 1787." Online: http://www.carolana.com/NC/Early_Statehood/nc_statehood_1800_state_of_franklin_petition.html.

Lewis, J. D. "North Carolina – From Statehood to 1800: The State of Franklin." Online: http://www.carolana.com/NC/Early_Statehood/nc_statehood_1800_state_of_franklin.html.

Martin, Georgia Worth. "North Carolina after the Revolution." *North Carolina Booklet*, 12:4 (April 1913), 216-223; online: http://digital.ncdcr.gov/cdm/ref/collection/p249901coll37/id/14180. [Online description from "North Carolina Periodicals Index," East Carolina University: "In 1784 after the end of the Revolutionary War, attempts to establish normalcy were plagued by civil unrest and violence. Western settlers attempted to secede from North Carolina and form the state of Franklin. This movement was marked by violence from both sides before being resolved in 1787."]

Masters, Jack, and Bill Puryear. *Thoroughfare for Freedom: The Second Atlas of the Cumberland Settlements, 1779-1804*. Gallatin, Tenn.: Wariot Press, 2011.

Masters, Jack, and Bill Puryear. *Land Grant Genealogy: North Carolina Warrants, Surveys & Surveyor Plats, 1779-1804*. Gallatin, Tenn.: Warioto Press, 2011. [Variant title: *Land Grant Genealogy: The Second Atlas, 1779-1804, Data Supplement 3, North Carolina Warrants, Surveys & Surveyor Plats*.]

Masters, Jack, and Bill Puryear. *Land Grant Genealogy: North Carolina Warrants, Surveys & Surveyor Plats, 1779-1804: The Third Atlas, Data Supplement*. Gallatin, Tenn.: Warioto Press, 2012.

Masters, Jack, and Bill Puryear. *The First Southwest: The Third Atlas, the Cummberland and Duck River Settlements, Tennesseans Expand Out Nation South and West.* Gallatin: Warioto Press, 2012.

McGhee, Lucy Kate. *Partial Census of 1787 to 1791 of Tennessee as Taken from North Carolina Land Grants*. 3 vols. Washington, D. C.: L. K. McGhee, 1955.

McGill, J. T. "Franklin & Frankland: Names & Boundaries." *Tennessee Historical Magazine,* 8:4 (January 1925), 248-257.

Miles, Suzannah Smith. "Affairs of State." *WNC Magazine*, 2:4 (June 2008), 60-65. [Online description from "North Carolina Periodicals Index," East Carolina University: "Following the Revolutionary War, a group of far western North Carolina counties attempted to create their own State of Franklin. It had its own governor, legislature, and state capitol but failed to survive statehood."]

Moore, Louis T. "The State of Franklin." *The State: A Weekly Survey of North Carolina*, 13:42 (March 1946), 10, 18; online: http://digital.ncdcr.gov/cdm/ref/collection/p16062coll18/id/15230.

Quarles, Robert T., Jr. *State of Franklin.* [S. l.: s. n.], 1917. [Description: "Consists of data published in the Colonial records of North Carolina."]

Ray, Kristofer. "Leadership, Loyalty, and Sovereignty in the Revolutionary American Southwest: The State of Franklin as a Test Case." *North Carolina Historical Review*, 92:2 (April 2015), 123-144. [Online description from "North Carolina Periodicals Index," East Carolina University: "In 1784, the state of North Carolina offered to cede the land from the North Carolina-Virginia border to Georgia, and from the Appalachian mountains to the Mississippi River and form a new state called 'Franklin.' The article examines the intentions of those urging for Franklin's establishment and the nature of government and politics in post-Revolutionary North America."]

"A Scheam to Chose Deputies for Counties on Westruning Waters…" Manuscript, Library of Virginia, Richmond; online: http://image.lva.virginia.gov/GLR/03073. [Online catalog description: "To meet in convention for consideration of recent resolutions of Congress respecting their country; counties involved are Montgomery, Washington, Lincoln, Jefferson, Fayette; and in North Carolina, Sullivan and Washington."]

Sevier, John. "Governor's Proclamation from the State of Franklin [1785 May 15]." Manuscript 42074, Manuscript File Box M-8, Tennessee State Library and Archives, Nashville; digital image online: http://teva.contentdm.oclc.org/cdm/ref/collection/p15138coll18/id/611. [Online catalog description: "One-page handwritten proclamation issued by John Sevier as Governor of the State of Franklin requiring all citizens to ignore a manifesto currently circulating in the state that incites insurrection. The manifesto referenced was issued by the Governor of North Carolina, Alexander Martin, on April 25, 1785, reacting to Franklin's proclaiming its independence as a separate state. Governor Martin threatened the Franklin citizenry if they did not abandon this path and accused Sevier of being a traitor. Sevier countered with this proclamation that encouraged the Franklinites to obey their new laws and chastised North Carolina for providing the reasons for separation. Notably, Sevier evoked the Revolutionary War, dated the proclamation with the reference "in first year of our Independence" and ended with 'God Save the State.' North Carolina never recognized the independence of the State of Franklin, and it ceased to exist in 1788."]

Sevier, John. "Letter from John Sevier to Governor Patrick Henry Announcing the Formation of the State of Franklin [1785, July 9]." Manuscript 42078, VI-C-1, Box 1, Folder 25 in the "Penelope Johnson Allen Cherokee Collection," Tennessee State Library and Archives, Nashville; digital image online: http://teva.contentdm.oclc.org/cdm/ref/collection/p15138coll18/id/617. [Online catalog description: "Negative photostat (possibly from the Virginia state papers) of a two-page handwritten letter John Sevier wrote to the governor of Virginia, Patrick Henry, announcing the formation of the State of Franklin and Sevier's appointment as governor. This notification followed the first official meeting of the Franklin Assembly in March of 1785 and the subsequent election of John Sevier by delegates as governor of the State of Franklin. The letter represents Sevier filling his role as head of this newly formed state, communicating with another state leader, and informing Henry of trade negotiations with the Chickasaw undertaken by the State of Franklin. At the same time, Sevier, recognizing the volatile climate in the area, reassured Governor Henry that Franklin intended to incite no unrest in Virginia, nor encourage encroachment on Native American lands. Notably, Sevier mentions that he expects no official correspondence with Governor Henry until the State of Franklin is recognized by Congress, an acknowledgement that never materialized."]

State of Franklin. *A Declaration of Rights, Also the Constitution, or Form of Government, Agreed to, & Resolved upon, by the Representatives of the Freemen of the State of Franklin, Elected & Chosen for That Particular Purpose, in Convention Assembled, at Greeneville, the 14th of Nov. 1785*. Philadelphia, PA, Francis Bailey, 1786; reprinted: *American Historical Magazine,* 1 (1896), 50-63.

Swint, Henry L. "Ezekiel Birdseye & the FREE STATE of Frankland." *Tennessee Historical Quarterly*, 3:3 (September 1944), 226-236.

Williams, Samuel Cole. *History of the Lost State of Franklin*. Johnson City: Watauga, 1924; rev. ed. New York: Press of the Pioneers, 1933.

Washington County (First) – Watauga Association and Settlement; Fort Watauga

Alderman, Patricia. *The Overmountain Men.* Johnson City: Overmountain Press, 1970; reprinted: 1986.

Allen, Ben, and Dennis T. Lawson. "The Wataugans & the 'Dangerous Example'." *Tennessee Historical Quarterly*, 26:2 (Summer 1967), 137-147.

Burnett, Swan M. "The Over-Mountain Men: Some Passages from a Page of Neglected History." *American Historical Register*, no. 4 (December 1894), 313-324; no. 5 (January 1895), 421-431. [Essay read before the Literary Society of Washington, Feb. 24, 1894.]

Caldwell, Joshua W. "The Watauga Association." *American Historical Magazine*, 3:4 (October 1898), 312-315.

Caldwell, Mary French. *Tennessee: The Dangerous Example; Watauga to 1849*. Nashville: Aurora Publishers, 1974.

Dickinson, W. Calvin. "Watauga Association." Online (2009): http://tennesseeencyclopedia.net/entry.php?rec=1475.

Dixon, Max. *The Wataugans*. Nashville: Tennessee American Revolution Bicentennial Commission, 1976; reprinted: Nashville: ARBC, 1989.

Fitch, William Edward. "The Battle of Alamance: The First Battle of the American Revolution." *Burlington Times-News* [n. d.]; reprinted: Burlington: Burlington, North Carolina, Alamance Battle Ground Commission, 1939. [Battle of Alamance, 1771. Contains information on the Regulator Movement, the Watauga Association, and the proposed State of Franklin.]

Hamer, Philip M. "The Wataugans and the Cherokee Indians in 1776." *East Tennessee Historical Publications,* 3 (1931), 108-126.

Hamer, Philip M., ed. "Correspondence of Henry Stuart and Alexander Cameron with the Wataugans." *Mississippi Valley Historical Review*, 17:3 (December 1930), 451-459.

Hyder, N. E. "Watauga Old Fields." *American Historical Magazine*, 8 (1903): 253-255.

Krause, Bob. "Sycamore Shoals: Major Role in 18th Century History." *Palmetto Patriot: South Carolina Sons of the American Revolution*, 2012:4 (Winter 2012), 10. [assembly area in the Watauga for that Overmountain men in 1780.]

Kuttruff, Carl. "Fort Watauga." Nashville: Tennessee Division of Archaeology, 1979. Unpublished.

McCown, Mary Hardin, and Irma Bowman Kitzmiller. *The Wataugah Purchase, March 19, 1775, at Sycamore Shoals of Wataugah River: The Cherokee Indians to Charles Robertson, Trustee for the Wataugah Settlers: An Index of the Wataugah Purchase, the North Carolina Land Grants, and Deeds through 1792: A Bicentennial Contribution*. Johnson City, Tenn.: M. H. McCown, 1976.

Nance, Benjamin C. "Fort Watauga." Online (2009): http://tennesseeencyclopedia.net/entry.php?rec=498.

North Carolina (State). General Assembly. "[Document dated:] November 1776: Watauga Petition." Manuscript; General Assembly Session Records; Session of November 1776; Session Records – Oversized; Colonial and State (Upper and Lower Houses), Oversize Box 3 (MARS ID: 66.9.3.8; folder), State Archives of North Carolina, Raleigh. [Online catalog description: "Requesting that the inhabitants of Washington District be recognized as residents of North Carolina, that a court system be organized in the district, and that their chosen representatives be allowed to vote in the General Assembly."] [DAR notes on this petition and its use for patriotic service for membership purposes follow: "Watauga Petition, July 5, 1776 Received August 22, 1776 from the inhabitants of Washington District, including the River Wataugah, Nonachuckie This petition can be found in multiple sources, such as Patricia Alderman's *The Overmountain Men*, pp. 56-57. It is also in William L. Saunders, ed., *Colonial Records of North Carolina, Volume X,* pages 708-711. The text also found in J. G. M. Ramsey's *Annals of Tennessee*, pages 134-138. However, this source states the document is undated, but that has endorsed upon it, 'Received August 22, 1776'." For those citing a residence for in individual using that person for a DAR membership application, this detail should be: Watauga Settlement, Washington District, North Carolina.]

Parris, John A., Jr. "Tom Collins, Feudal Lord." *The State: A Weekly Survey of North Carolina*, 4:17 (September 1936), 2, 22. [Online description from "North Carolina Periodicals Index," East Carolina University: "Tom Collins was the chieftain of one of the most aggressive clans in western North Carolina, as well as a pioneer, and feudal lord of the Great Smokies. Originally from Scotland, the Collins clan swore the English as their enemies, and this continued with Tom, a member of the Watauga Association. He is now memorialized in a ballad and alcoholic drink." Tom Collins (ca. 1710-1770)]

Pittman, Betsy Dodd. "Petition of Inhabitants of the Watauga Settlement, 1775." *North Carolina Genealogical Society Journal*, 28:4 (November 2002), 413-419.

Ramsey, J. G. M. *The Annals of Tennessee to the End of the Eighteenth Century; Comprising Its Settlement, as the Watauga Association, from 1769 to 1777; a Part of North-Carolina, from 1777 to 1784; a Part of North-Carolina, from 1788 to 1790; the Territory of the U. States, South of the Ohio, from 1790 to 1796; the State of Tennessee, from 1796 to 1800*. Charleston: John Russell, 1853; reprinted: Kingsport: Kingsport Press, 1926.

Redmon, Lois Kivett. "The Watauga Story of the American Revolution." *Daughters of the American Revolution Magazine*, 108:2 (February 1974), 112-116.

Stinson, Byron. "The Watauga Association." *American History Illustrated*, 8:1 (April 1973), 20-32.

The Wataugans: Their History & Their Influence on Southern Appalachia & the Nation: An American Revolution Roundtable. Boone: Appalachian Consortium Press, [1976?] [Description, State Library of North Carolina online catalog: "Edited transcript of the taped proceedings of a roundtable held June 22, 1976, at Elizabethton, Tenn., to celebrate the issuance of *The Wataugans*, by Max Dixon."]

Williams, Cratis. "The Mountain Folk of Western North Carolina." *Tar Heel Junior Historian*, 17:1 (Fall 1977), 2-6. [Online description from "North Carolina Periodicals Index," East Carolina University: "Settlers in the western portion of the state were far removed from both their state and national government. In an effort to organize, this group created the Watauga Association in 1772. The Watauga Settlements encompassed an area in western North Carolina and eastern Tennessee and was populated primarily by Scotch-Irish and German settlers."]

Williams, Samuel C. "Ann Robertson: An Unsung Tennessee Heroine." *Tennessee Historical Magazine*, 3:2 (June 1944), 150-155. [Led women to throw boiling water on attacking American Indians at Fort Caswell in July of 1776.]

Washington County (First) – Cumberland Compact, May 1, 1780

"Articles of Agreement, or Compact of Government, Entered into by the Settles on the Cumberland River, 1st May, 1780." In A. W. Putnam, *History of Middle Tennessee of Life and Times of Gen. James Robertson* (Knoxville: University of Tennessee Press, 1971), 94-102.

"Cumberland Compact." Online: http://www.ajlambert.com/history/hst_cc.pdf.

"Cumberland Compact." Online: https://tennesseeencyclopedia.net/entry.php?rec=335.

"Cumberland Compact & Cumberland Compact Signers." Online: http://www.cumberlandpioneers.com/cumberlandcompact.html.

Hale, Will T., and Dixon L. Merritt. *A History of Tennessee and Tennesseans: The Leaders and Representative men in Commerce, Industry and Modern Activities* (Chicago and New York: The Lewis Publishing Co. 1913), 94-97.

Henderson, Richard, 1753-1785. "Cumberland Compact." Manuscript THS 155, Tennessee State Library and Archives, Nashville. [Online catalog description: "Original manuscript of the Cumberland Compact of Government, or Articles of Agreement, entered into by settlers on the Cumberland River, May 1, 1780, at what is now Nashville, and signed May 13, 1780 by 255 inhabitants of five stations on the river. First page missing; some following pages damaged, some quite significantly. Handwritten in ink on paper. One of the most important documents pertaining to the early history of the state of Tennessee is the Cumberland Compact. Richard Henderson, the representative for North Carolina on the western Virginia/North Carolina survey team, drew up the Cumberland Compact in May 1780 along with 250 other signatories. The Cumberland Compact called for a representative form of civil government by which the basis for courts, governance, and taxation were established. Each of the seven stations, or forts, of the Cumberland settlement was allowed a certain number of elected representatives to form a 'Tribunal of Notables,' which included a total of twelve men. No voting qualifications were specified, but the Compact was open to all free white men who were willing to sign. This tribunal settled land claims and regulated the land office, in addition to receiving and dispersing funds and acting as a judicial body. At the same time, and perhaps more important, the document also created a favorable legal setting for Richard Henderson's business in land speculation. In fact, only a small part of the document was devoted to governance; it was in large measure a contract dictating a legal framework for land transfers. Although Henderson did not remain in Tennessee like many of the other signatories, the document created a legal means for land transactions to occur, including the transfer of land from Native Americans to the early settlers. By 1784, about one third of the men who had signed the compact had been killed in battles with Native Americans. Additionally, many of their forts had been destroyed during Native American attacks. Despite these setbacks, the Cumberland Compact still represents one of the earliest declarations of self-governance for the state of Tennesseee."]

"The Notables, 1783." In Pat Alderman, *The Overmountain Men* (Johnson City, Tenn.: Overmountain Press, 1970), 159-160. [Includes a transcript of the first assembly of the elected Notables, January 7, 1783, including the twelve men elected]

Later Tennessee Counties

McBride, Robert M. "Tennessee: Lost Counties." *East Tennessee Historical Society Special Publication,* no. 38 (1966), 3-15.

North Carolina (State). General Assembly. House of Commons. "[Document dated:] May 5, [1782]: House Bill for Establishing a County by the Name of ___ on the Cumberland River (Petition and Committee Report Only)." Manuscript, General Assembly Record Group, Session Records April-May 1782; Joint Papers, Committee Papers, Resolutions, Senate Bills, House Bills, (MARS ID: 66.8.28.25; folder), State Archives of North Carolina, Raleigh. [Online catalog description: "Petition of inhabitants of land near Cumberland River requesting protection from Indians; committee report considering possibility of forming a county in the area; second report offering objections to proposed county by soldiers of the Continental Line who were to be given land grants in the area; and messages from both houses appointing members to committee to review petition."] [Was this precursor legislation for the creation of Davidson County?]

Bedford County

Marsh, Helen Crawford, and Timothy R. Marsh. *Soldiers of the Revolution in Bedford County, Tennessee.* Easley, S. C.: Southern Historical Press, 1989.

Bledsoe County

Campbell Chapter, Tennessee Daughters of the American Revolution. *Tennessee DAR Genealogical Records Committee Report, Series 1, Volume 41: Applications for Pensions, Made under Acts of 1832 and Later by Revolutionary War Soldiers of Bledsoe County, Tenn.* (typescript, 1947); digital surrogate, DAR Library, Washington, D. C.

Blount County

Allen, Penelope Johnson. *Tennessee Soldiers in the Revolution: A Roster of Soldiers Living during the Revolutionary War in the Counties of Washington and Sullivan, Taken From the Revolutionary Army Accounts of North Carolina*. Bristol, Tenn.: The King Printing Company, 1935; reprinted: Baltimore: Genealogical Publishing Company, 1996. [Contents: Introduction; Index to Revolutionary Soldiers; Revolutionary Pensioners of Tennessee, Act of 1828; Index to Wills of Washington County, Tennessee; Abstracts of Wills of Washington County; Marriage Records of Blount County; Marriage Records of Davidson County; Revolutionary Grants of Davidson County.]

Jordan, Rene. "The Evolution of Early Tennessee County Boundaries: Sevier County and Blount County." *Tennessee Ancestors: A Tri-Annual Publication of the East Tennessee Historical Society*, 11:3 (December 1995), 206-210.

Tennessee Daughters of the American Revolution. "Blount Co. TN Soldiers Revolution; War of 1812." *Tennessee DAR Genealogical Records Committee Report, Series 1, Volume 52: Miscellaneous Records* (typescript, 1952), 1-7; digital surrogate, DAR Library, Washington, D. C.

Carter County and Sycamore Shoals

Anthony, Mark C. "SC Compatriots Attend Gathering at Sycamore Shoals." *Palmetto Patriot: South Carolina Society Sons of the American Revolution,* 201:4 (Winter 2010), 13.

Compton, Brian P. "Revised History of Fort Watauga." M. A. thesis, East Tennessee State University, 2005; online: http://dc.etsu.edu/cgi/viewcontent.cgi?article=2260&context=etd.

Creekmore, Pollyanna. "Historical Research: Syacamore Shoals State Park and Colonel John Carter House." Manuscript (1974), Headquarters, Sycamore Shoals State Park, Elizabethton, Tenn.

Dickinson, W. Calvin. "Frontier Splendor: The Carter Mansion at Sycamore Shoals." *Tennessee Historical Quarterly*, 41:4 (Winter 1982), 317-325. [John Carter Sr. was one of the first settlers in Tennessee; this article also talks about Landon Carter, who fought in North Carolina during the Revolution.]

Jordan, Rene. "The Evolution of Early East Tennessee County Boundaries: Carter County and Grainger County." *Tennessee Ancestors: A Tri-Annual Publication of the East Tennessee Historical Society*, 12:2 (August 1996), 139-144.

Krause, Bob. "Sycamore Shoals: Major Role in 18th Century History." *Palmetto Patriot: South Carolina Sons of the American Revolution*, 2012:4 (Winter 2012), 10. [assembly area in the Watauga for the Overmountain men in 1780.]

McCown, Mary Hardin, and Irma Bowman Kitzmiller. *The Wataugah Purchase, March 19, 1775, at Sycamore Shoals of Wataugah River: The Cherokee Indians to Charles Robertson, Trustee for the Wataugah Settlers: An Index of the Wataugah Purchase, the North Carolina Land Grants, and Deeds through 1792: A Bicentennial Contribution*. Johnson City, Tenn.: M. H. McCown, 1976.

Merritt, Frank. *Early History of Carter County, 1760-1861*. Knoxville: East Tennessee Historical Society, 1950.

Spoden, Hal T., and Muriel C. Spoden. "Sycamore Shoals State Historic Area." *Tennessee Historical Quarterly*, 36:1 (Spring 1977), 3-18.

"Sycamore Shoals." Online: http://www.tnhistoryforkids.org/places/sycamore_shoals.

"The Treaty of Sycamore Shoals." Online: http://www.foresthistory.org/ASPNET/Publications/region/8/daniel_boone/chap8.htm.

Van West, Carroll. "Sycamore Shoals State Historic Area." Online (2009): http://tennesseeencyclopedia.net/entry.php?rec=1289.

Claiborne County

Burns, Annie Walker. *Abstract of Pensions of the Revolution, War of 1812 and All Wars Prior to 1883 of Claiborne County, Tennessee*. Washington, D. C.: A. W. Burns, 1952.

Young, Frances Curtis. "Carter County, Tennessee Historical Notes." *Tennessee Ancestors: A Tri-Annual Publication of the East Tennessee Historical Society*, 12:1 (April 1996), 25-30. [Describes Carter County's founding, annexation by North Carolina, and its admission to the Union as part of Tennessee.]

Coffee County

Brown, David J. "The Construction, Occupation, and Abandonment of Fort Nash." M. A. thesis, Middle Tennessee State University, Murfreesboro, 1977.

Jernigan, V. H. " Fort Nash – Outpost of the 1790's." *Tennessee Historical Quarterly*, 29:2 (Summer 1970), 130-138. [from page 130: "Fred Doak, late publisher and editor of the Manchester *Times* and a student to early Tennessee history, wrote in the Centennial edition of that paper in May 1936: 'A garrison of soldiers had been stationed near Beech Grove during the Revolution. They gave the name 'Garrison' to the creek that ran from the spring where their camp was located."]

Cumberland County

Robinson, Dan M. "Robert Hays, Unsung Pioneer of the Cumberland Country." *Tennessee Historical Quarterly*, 26:3 (Fall 1967), 263-278. [Hays was in the 4th North Carolina Regiment. He received 36,762 acres from land grants in Tennessee]

Davidson County and Nashville

Allen, Penelope Johnson. *Tennessee Soldiers in the Revolution: A Roster of Soldiers Living during the Revolutionary War in the Counties of Washington and Sullivan, Taken From the Revolutionary Army Accounts of North Carolina*. Bristol, Tenn.: The King Printing Company, 1935; reprinted: Baltimore: Genealogical Publishing Company, 1996. [Contents: Introduction; Index to Revolutionary Soldiers; Revolutionary Pensioners of Tennessee, Act of 1828; Index to Wills of Washington County, Tennessee; Abstracts of Wills of Washington County; Marriage Records of Blount County; Marriage Records of Davidson County; Revolutionary Grants of Davidson County.]

Burns, Frank. *Davidson County*. Memphis: Memphis State University Press, 1989.

Clayton, W. W. *History of Davidson County, Tennessee*. Philadelphia: J. W. Lewis, 1880.

Elliott, Lizzie P. *Early History of Nashville*. Nashville: Board of Education, 1911.

Fischer, Marjorie Hood. *Tennesseans before 1800: Davidson County*. Galveston, Texas: Frontier Press, 1997.

Fulcher, Richard Carlton. *1770-1790 Census of the Cumberland Settlements of Davidson, Sumner, and Tennessee Counties*. Baltimore: Genealogical Publishing Company, 1987.

Goodstein, Anita S. "Black History on the Nashville Frontier, 1780-1810." *Tennessee Historical Quarterly*, 38:4 (Winter 1979), 401-420.

Goodstein, Anita S. "Leadership on the Nashville Frontier, 1780-1800." *Tennessee Historical Quarterly*, 35:2 (Summer 1976), 175-198.

Goodstein, Anita Shafer. *Nashville, 1780-1860: From Frontier to City*. Gainesville: University of Florida Press, 1989.

Jordan, René. "The Evolution of Early Tennessee County Boundaries: Greene County and Davidson County." *Tennessee Ancestors: A Tri-Annual Publication of the East Tennessee Historical Society*, 10:3 (December 1994), 196-201.

Lewis, J. D. "Davidson County – Ceded to Tennessee: A History of Davidson County." Online: http://www.carolana.com/NC/Counties/davidson1_county_nc.html.

Lewis, J. D. "Davidson County NC (TN): Evolution of Boundaries – with Known Towns & Villages." Online: http://www.carolana.com/NC/Counties/davidson_county_tn_evolution_with_towns.html.

North Carolina (State). General Assembly. "[Document dated:] May 14, 1784: Senate Bill for Relief of Sundry Inhabitants of Davidson County (Petition and Committee Report Only)." Manuscript; General Assembly Record Group; Session of April-June 1784; Senate Bills, House Bills (April 24-May 6, 1784), Box 3 (MARS ID: 66.8.33.18; folder), State Archives of North Carolina, Raleigh. [Online catalog description: "Petition of inhabitants of Davidson County requests that the state take into account the fact that they have been settlers in a dangerous and unhospitable area. They request relief from normal state prices on land as well as from taxes."]

North Carolina (State). General Assembly. Acts, 1784. "An Act for the Relief of Sundry Petitioners Inhabitants of Davidson County Whose Names Are Therein Mentioned." [not dated, though listed among legislative acts of 1784]. "This petition includes the names of a number of individuals 'who were killed in the defence and settlement of the said county of Davidson…shall be entitled to receive…a grant for six hundred and forty acres,' *The State Records of North Carolina, Volume XXIV, Laws 1777-1788*, pages 629-630. The DAR has decided that in order to accept this as a service source, it should be accompanied by the preemption warrant that was granted for the land. Sources for many of these individuals include Irene M. Griffey's *The Preemptors: Middle Tennessee's First Settlers*, Volume 1, and B. G. C. Cartwright and L. J. Gardiner's *North Carolina Land Grants in Tennessee 1778-1791,* Section II, pages 70-81 (Rank, Patriotic Service). A service description example is: 'Killed in the Defense of Davidson County (or Washington County, as Davidson County was created from Washington County on 18 April 1783), Heirs Received Preemption Warrant.' Cite both the North Carolina State Records giving the act as well as the source that includes the land warrant."]

North Carolina (State). General Assembly. "[Document dated:] May 6, 1783: House Bill to Create Davidson County in What Is Now Tennessee." Manuscript; General Assembly Session Records; Session of April-May, 1783: Unidentified Amendments, Senate Bills, House Bills, …, Box 2 (MARS ID: 66.8.30.72; folder), State Archives of North Carolina, Raleigh. [Online catalog description: "Bill follows a petition from settlers along the Cumberland River along the Virginia line that requests that North Carolina recognize their area as a distinct county. The bill creates a boundary for the county, names it Davidson, and sets up provisions for a county court and land office for the county. Includes petition and legislative messages concerning amendments."]

North Carolina (State). General Assembly. House of Commons. "[Document dated:] May 5, [1782]: House Bill for Establishing a County by the Name of __ on the Cumberland River (Petition and Committee Report Only)." Manuscript, General Assembly Record Group, Session Records April-May 1782; Joint Papers, Committee Papers, Resolutions, Senate Bills, House Bills, (MARS ID: 66.8.28.25; folder), State Archives of North Carolina, Raleigh. [Online catalog description: "Petition of inhabitants of land near Cumberland River requesting protection from Indians; committee report considering possibility of forming a county in the area; second report offering objections to proposed county by soldiers of the Continental Line who were to be given land grants in the area; and messages from both houses appointing members to committee to review petition."] [Was this precursor legislation for the creation of Davidson County?]

North Carolina (State). Office of Secretary of State. Office of the Secretary. Land Office. "Land Warrents, Plats of Survey, and Related Records. Tennessee, Davidson County, 1783-1824." Manuscript S.108.350-S.108.361, 12 microfilm reels (MARS ID: 12.14.2; folder), State Archives of North Carolina, Raleigh. [Online catalog description: "Davidson County (formed in 1783 from Washington County, Tennessee) was named after General William Lee Davidson. The county seat was named Nashville after General Francis Nash. A portion of Davidson became Sumner County in 1787, and another portion of Davidson became Tennessee County in 1799. Part of Davidson became Williamson County in 1799."]

Tennessee Daughters of the American Revolution. "Davidson Co. TN – Soldiers – Revolution." *Tennessee DAR Genealogical Records Committee Report, Series 1, Volume 1: Miscellaneous Records* (typescript, 1929), 1-4; digital surrogate, DAR Library, Washington, D. C.

West, Carroll Van. "Fort Nashborough." *Tennessee Encyclopedia of History and Culture* (version 2.0), online (2009): http://tennesseeencyclopedia.net/entry.php?rec=491.

Whitley, Edith Rucker. *Davidson County Pioneers, Revolutionary and War of 1812*. Nashville: [E. R. Whitley], 1965; reprinted with the title *Pioneers of Davidson County, Tennessee* (Baltimore: Clearfield Company, 2002.

Whitley, Edith Rucker. "Revolutionary Soldiers in Davidson County, Tennessee." *William and Mary Quarterly*, 2nd series, 11:1 (January 1931), 13-19; reprinted in: Elizabeth Petty Bentley, ed. *Virginia Military Records from the Virginia Magazine of History and Biography, the William and Mary College Quarterly, and Tyler's Quarterly* (Baltimore: Genealogical Publishing Company, 1983), 926-932.

Wooldridge, John. *History of Nashville, Tenn.* Nashville: H. W. Crew by the Publishing House of the Methodist Episcopal Church, South, 1970.

Franklin County

Sherrill, Charles A. *Revolutionary War Pension Applications from Franklin County, Tennessee*. Cleveland Heights, Ohio: C. A. Sherrill, 1982.

Giles County

North Carolina (State). Office of Secretary of State. Office of the Secretary. Land Office. "Land Warrents, Plats of Survey, and Related Records. Tennessee, Giles County, 1778-1820." Manuscript S.108.373.1 microfilm reel (MARS ID: 12.14.8; folder), State Archives of North Carolina, Raleigh. [Online catalog description: "Giles County (formed in 1809 from Maury County, Tennessee) was named after Virginia Governor William B. Giles, upon the suggestion of Andrew Jackson. The county seat of Pulaski was named after Casimir Pulaski, a Polish patriot who served as a Revolutionary War cavalry leader. The site of the county seat was below the Congressional Indian Reservation line and land titles in that area were not clear until 1812 when restrictions on settlement in the Indian lands were removed."]

Grainger County

Grainger County, Tennessee and Its People, 1796-1998. Waynesville: Don Mills, 1998.

Jordan, Rene. “The Evolution of Early East Tennessee County Boundaries: Carter County and Grainger County.” *Tennessee Ancestors: A Tri-Annual Publication of the East Tennessee Historical Society*, 12:2 (August 1996), 139-144.

North Carolina (State). Office of Secretary of State. Office of the Secretary. Land Office. “Land Warrents, Plats of Survey, and Related Records. Tennessee, Grainger County, 1783-1807.” Manuscript S.108.367-S.108.373, 7 microfilm reels (MARS ID: 12.14.7; folder), State Archives of North Carolina, Raleigh. [Online catalog description: “Grainger County (formed in 1796 from Hawkins and Knox counties, Tennessee) was named in honor of William Blount’s wife, Mary Grainger Blount. The county seat of Rutledge was named after George Rutledge. The courthouse was erected in 1801.”]

Greene County

[Note: For various state government documents relating to Greene County during the Revolutionary period, search the MARS online catalog using the advanced search: http://mars.archives.ncdcr.gov/AdvancedSearch.aspx. Use the “Year” search box to restrict the searching to 1775-1783 and enter the county’s name in the “Subjects” box, and hit the “Search” button near the top. This will retrieve any cataloged document for the county from that time period. These materials can vary considerably from personal or county petitions to the General Assembly, Loyalist matters, land disputes and claims, tax collection, exemptions from taxation, payments to county veterans, county divisions, personal collections, genealogical material, British claims against North Carolinians, etc. There is considerable information in these materials that could provide interesting documentation for persons living during the Revolution. The results will also include all of the wills and probates recorded in the county during the period set for the search. We had hoped to include many of these listings in this guide, but they are too voluminous. Citations to many of these search results for the eastern counties do, however, appear in the text.]

Creekmore, Pollyanna. “Greene County, Tennessee, 1783 Taxpayers List.” *East Tennessee Historical Society Special Publication,* 39 (1937), 118-130.

Jordan, René. “The Evolution of Early Tennessee County Boundaries: Greene County and Davidson County. *Tennessee Ancestors: A Tri-Annual Publication of the East Tennessee Historical Society*, 10:3 (December 1994), 196-201.

North Carolina (State). Office of Secretary of State. Office of the Secretary. Land Office. “Land Warrents, Plats of Survey, and Related Records. Tennessee, Greene County, 1778-1803.” Manuscript S.108.367-S.108.373, 7 microfilm reels (MARS ID: 12.14.3; folder), State Archives of North Carolina, Raleigh. [Online catalog description: “Greene County (formed in 1783 from Washington County, Tennessee) was named for General Nathaniel Greene, as was Greeneville, the county seat. Portions of Greene County became Jefferson and Knox counties in 1792.”]

Hawkins County

Jordan, Rene. “The Evolution of Early East Tennessee County Boundaries: Hawkins County and Sumner County.” *Tennessee Ancestors: A Tri-Annual Publication of the East Tennessee Historical Society*, 11:1 (April 1995), 4-11.

North Carolina (State). Office of Secretary of State. Office of the Secretary. Land Office. “Land Warrents, Plats of Survey, and Related Records. Tennessee, Hawkins County, 1778-1804.” Manuscript S.108.373-S.108.378, 5 microfilm reels (MARS ID: 12.14.9; folder), State Archives of North Carolina, Raleigh. [Online catalog description: “Hawkins County (formed in 1787 from Sullivan County, Tennessee) was named for Benjamin Hawkins. The county seat of Rogersville was founded in 1789 on the land of Joseph Rogers and James Hogan. Portions of Hawkins County became Jefferson and Knox counties in 1792, and another portion became Grainger County in 1796.”]

Jefferson County

Jordan, Rene. “The Evolution of Early Tennessee County Boundaries: Tennessee County, Knox County, and Jefferson County.” *Tennessee Ancestors: A Tri-Annual Publication of the East Tennessee Historical Society*, 11:2 (August 1995), 83-90.

North Carolina (State). Office of Secretary of State. Office of the Secretary. Land Office. “Land Warrents, Plats of Survey, and Related Records. Tennessee, Jefferson County, 1779-1803.” Manuscript S.108.378, 1 microfilm reel (MARS ID: 12.14.10; folder), State Archives of North Carolina, Raleigh. [Online catalog description: “Jefferson County (formed in 1792 from Greene and Hawkins counties, Tennessee) was named in honor of

Thomas Jefferson. The county seat of Dandridge was established in 1793. A portion of Jefferson County became Sevier County in 1794."]

Knox County

Jordan, Rene. "The Evolution of Early Tennessee County Boundaries: Tennessee County, Knox County, and Jefferson County." *Tennessee Ancestors: A Tri-Annual Publication of the East Tennessee Historical Society*, 11:2 (August 1995), 83-90.

North Carolina (State). Office of Secretary of State. Office of the Secretary. Land Office. "Land Warrents, Plats of Survey, and Related Records. Tennessee, Knox County, 1778-1796." Manuscript S.108.378, 1 microfilm reel (MARS ID: 12.14.11; folder), State Archives of North Carolina, Raleigh. [Online catalog description: "Knox County (formed in 1792 from Greene and Hawkins counties, Tennessee) was named in honor of General Henry Knox. Knoxville, the county seat, was established in 1791-1792. Prior to that, the location was known as White's Fort. In 1792 Governor William Blount made Knoxville the territorial capital, and the town continued as the Tennessee state capital from 1796 to 1813, when Nashville became the capital. A portion of Knox County became Grainger County in 1796."]

Lincoln County

Anderson, William Lee. "Lincoln County Men at Kings Mountain." Online: http://www.elehistory.com/amrev/LincolnCountyMenAtKingsMountain.pdf.

Carpenter, William L. *Lincoln County Sketchbook*. [Raleigh?: W. L. Carpenter], 1976. [Description: "A series of 27 articles appearing in the *Lincoln Times-News* from May 2, 1975 to May 3, 1976 as a contribution to the bicentennial ; presented to this library by the author, June 1976."]

Payseur, Stephen. *Lincoln County during the Revolutionary War.* (We the People Series, v. 1) Lincolnton: CreekSide Publishing Company, 2009.

Tennessee Daughters of the American Revolution. "Lincoln Co., TN Soldiers Revolution." *Tennessee DAR Genealogical Records Committee Report, Series 1, Volume 112: Miscellaneous Records* (typescript, 1968), 43-44; digital surrogate, DAR Library, Washington, D. C.

Marshall County

Alford, Jane Wallace. *Revolutionary War Patriots of Marshall County, Tennessee*. Lewisburg, Tenn.: Robert Lewis Chapter, Tennessee Society Daughters of the American Revolution, 1976.

Maury County

Embry, Hermione D., Tennessee Daughters of the American Revolution. "Eighty-Eight Revolutionary Soldiers, Buried in Maury Co., Tenn., and Their Places of Burial." *Tennessee DAR Genealogical Records Committee Report, Series 1, Volume 108: Family Histories and Miscellaneous Data, Vol. V* (typescript, 1966), 1-5; digital surrogate, DAR Library, Washington, D. C.

Lightfoot, Marise Parish. "Let The Drums Roll: Veterans and Patriots of the Revolutionary War Who Settled in Maury County, Tennessee." M.A. thesis, Middle Tennessee State University, 1974; published: Nashville: Parthenon Press for the Maury County Historical Society, 1976.

North Carolina (State). Office of Secretary of State. Office of the Secretary. Land Office. "Land Warrents, Plats of Survey, and Related Records. Tennessee, Maury County, 1778-1815." Manuscript S.108.378, 1 microfilm reel (MARS ID: 12.14.12; folder), State Archives of North Carolina, Raleigh. [Online catalog description: "Maury County (formed in 1807 from Williamson County, Tennessee) was named after Major Abram P. Maury. Columbia was selected as the county seat in 1808 and was incorporated in 1817. A portion of Maury County became Giles County in 1809."]

Turner, William Bruce. *History of Maury County, Tennessee*. Nashville: Pantheon Press, 1855.

Monroe County and Fort Loudoun

Kelly, James C. "Fort Loudoun: British Stronghold in the Tennessee Country." *East Tennessee Historical Society's Publications,* 50 (1978), 72-91.

Kuttruff, Carl; Beverly Bastian; Jenna Tedrick Kuttruff; and Stuart Stumpf. "Fort Loudoun in Tennessee, 1756-1760: History, Archaeology, Replication, Exhibits, and Interpretation." *Report of the Tennessee Wars Commission and Tennessee Division of Archaeology* (Research Series, no. 17) Walden, Tenn.: Waldenhouse

Publishers, 2010; online: https://www.tn.gov/assets/entities/environment/attachments/arch_rs17_fort_loudoun_2010.pdf.

Montgomery County

North Carolina (State). Office of Secretary of State. Office of the Secretary. Land Office. "Land Warrents, Plats of Survey, and Related Records. Tennessee, Montgomery County, 1785-1802." Manuscript S.108.378, 1 microfilm reel (MARS ID: 12.14.13; folder), State Archives of North Carolina, Raleigh. [Online catalog description: "Montgomery County (along with Robertson County) was formed in 1796 when Tennessee County was split to form two new counties. The county was named after John Montgomery. In 1784 John Montgomery and Martin Armstrong laid off the town of Clarksville on a parcel of land for which they had entered a claim. They named the town after George Rogers Clark. It became Montgomery County's seat after serving as county seat for Tennessee County."]

Robertson County

North Carolina (State). Office of Secretary of State. Office of the Secretary. Land Office. "Land Warrents, Plats of Survey, and Related Records. Tennessee, Robertson County, 1785-1804." Manuscript S.108.378, 1 microfilm reels (MARS ID: 12.14.14; folder), State Archives of North Carolina, Raleigh. [Online catalog description: "Robertson County (along with Montgomery County) was formed in 1796 when Tennessee County was split to form two new counties. It was named after James Robertson. The county seat of Springfield was established in 1798."]

Sevier County

Henderson, Cherel Bolin. "James Hubbert: The Tennessee Years, Part I." *Tennessee Ancestors: A Bi-Annual Publication of the East Tennessee Historical Society*, 30:1 (June 2014), 23-46.

Jordan, Rene. "The Evolution of Early Tennessee County Boundaries: Sevier County and Blount County." *Tennessee Ancestors: A Tri-Annual Publication of the East Tennessee Historical Society*, 11:3 (December 1995), 206-210.

North Carolina (State). Office of Secretary of State. Office of the Secretary. Land Office. "Land Warrents, Plats of Survey, and Related Records. Tennessee, Sevier County, 1799." Manuscript S.108.378, 1 microfilm reel (MARS ID: 12.14.15; folder), State Archives of North Carolina, Raleigh. [Online catalog description: "Sevier County (formed in 1794 from Jefferson County) was named after John Sevier. The county seat of Sevierville was laid off in 1795. [The area was once known as the 'State of Franklin,' formed extra legally 1785-1788."]

Rose, D. Morton J. "Early Land Grants in Sevier County, NC-TN." *Tennessee Ancestors: A Tri-Annual Publication of the East Tennessee Historical Society*, 9:2 (August 1993), 83-92.

Shelby County and Memphis

Stigall, Mrs. Terry for the Watauga Chapter, Tennessee Daughters of the American Revolution. "Roster of Soldiers of the American Revolution Buried in Shelby County." *Tennessee DAR Genealogical Records Committee Report, Series 2, Volume 4: Miscellaneous Tennessee Records* (typescript, 1990), 80-87; digital surrogate, DAR Library, Washington, D. C.

Smith County

North Carolina (State). Office of Secretary of State. Office of the Secretary. "Land Office: Land Warrents, Plats of Survey, and Related Records. Tennessee, Smith County, 1783-1804." Manuscript S.108.378, 1 microfilm reel (MARS ID: 12.14.16; folder), State Archives of North Carolina, Raleigh. [Online catalog description: "Smith County (formed in 1799 from Sumner County, Tennessee) was named for General Daniel Smith. In 1804 the county seat was established at the location of the present-day town of Carthage. The courthouse was erected in 1805."]

Sullivan County [Salisbury District before 1781. Morgan District after 1782]

[Note: For various state government documents relating to Sullivan County during the Revolutionary period, search the MARS online catalog using the advanced search: http://mars.archives.ncdcr.gov/AdvancedSearch.aspx. Use the "Year" search box to restrict the searching to 1775-1783 and enter the county's name in the "Subjects" box, and hit the "Search" button near the top. This will retrieve any cataloged document for the county from that time period.

These materials can vary considerably from personal or county petitions to the General Assembly, Loyalist matters, land disputes and claims, tax collection, exemptions from taxation, payments to county veterans, county divisions, personal collections, genealogical material, British claims against North Carolinians, etc. There is considerable information in these materials that could provide interesting documentation for persons living during the Revolution. The results will also include all of the wills and probates recorded in the county during the period set for the search. We had hoped to include many of these listings in this guide, but they are too voluminous. Citations to many of these search results for the eastern counties do, however, appear in the text.]

Barnes, Thelma G. *Adventures in Education, Sullivan County, 1773-1983*. [S. l.], Sullivan County Retired Teachers Association, 1985.

Jordan, René. "The Evolution of Early Tennessee County Boundaries: Sullivan County." *Tennessee Ancestors: A Tri-Annual Publication of the East Tennessee Historical Society*, 10:2 (August 1994), 94-103.

Lewis, J. D. "Patriot Leaders in North Carolina: Anthony Bledsoe: Major in a VA unit – 1776; Major in the Washington County Regiment of Militia - 1777-1779; Major in the Sullivan County Regiment of Militia - 1779-1781 ; Lt. Colonel in the Sullivan County Regiment of Militia - 1781-1783; Colonel over the Davidson County Regiment of Militia – 1783." Online: http://www.carolana.com/NC/Revolution/patriot_leaders_nc_anthony_bledsoe.html.

Lewis, J. D. "Patriot Leaders in North Carolina: Isaac Shelby: First in VA Militia; Captain in the Washington District/County Regiment of Militia - 1776-1779; Major in the Washington County Regiment of Militia – 1779; Colonel over the Sullivan County Regiment of Militia - 1779-1783." Online: http://www.carolana.com/NC/Revolution/patriot_leaders_nc_isaac_shelby.html.

North Carolina (State). Office of Secretary of State. Office of the Secretary. Land Office. "Land Warrents, Plats of Survey, and Related Records. Tennessee, Sullivan County, 1770-1798." Manuscript S.108.378-S.108.382, 5 microfilm reel (MARS ID: 12.14.17; folder), State Archives of North Carolina, Raleigh. [Online catalog description: "Sullivan County (formed in 1779 from Washington County, Tennessee) was named for John Sullivan. Blountsville was made the county seat. A portion of Sullivan County became Hawkins County in 1787, and a portion of Washington County was annexed to Sullivan County in 1788."]

Price, Prentiss, ed. "Two Petitions to Virginia of the North of Holston Men 1776, 1777." *East Tennessee Historical Society's Publications*, 21 (1949), 95-110; Reprinted in *Tennessee Ancestors: A Tri-Annual Publication of the East Tennessee Historical Society*, 16:3 (December 2000), 207-220. [From the introduction of the article in *Tennessee Ancestors*: "The significance of these petitions is that they illustrate the exercise of jurisdiction, Virginia as a colony and as a state, over a considerable portion of what is now upper Tennessee from the beginning of settlement until 1779."]

Roebuck, Hayward. "Washington and Sullivan Counties, (Tennessee) Revolutionary War Stub Indent Books." *North Carolina Genealogical Society Journal,* 1:2 (April 1975), 91-96.

Sullivan County, Tennessee, 1779-1979. Blountville, Sullivan County Board of Commissioners, 1979.

Sullivan County Historical Society. *Foundations of Faith in Sullivan, 1777-1935*. Blountville: The Society, 1986.

Taylor, Oliver. *Historic Sullivan: A History of Sullivan County, Tennessee with Brief Biographies of the Makers of History*. Bristol, King, 1909.

Tennessee Daughters of the American Revolution. "Some Revolutionary Soldiers Buried in the Kingsport Area." *Tennessee DAR Genealogical Records Committee Report, Series 1, Volume 132: Tennessee Genealogical Records Committee NSDAR [bk.8]* (typescript, 1974), 1-2; digital surrogate, DAR Library, Washington, D. C.

Williams, Samuel C. "Fort Robinson on the Holston." *East Tennessee Historical Society Publications.* 4 (1932), 22-31.

Williams, Samuel C. "Shelby's Fort." *East Tennessee Historical Society Publications*. 7 (1935), 28-37.

Sumner County

Fulcher, Richard Carlton. *1770-1790 Census of the Cumberland Settlements of Davidson, Sumner, and Tennessee Counties.* Baltimore: Genealogical Publishing Company, 1987.

Jordan, Rene. "The Evolution of Early East Tennessee County Boundaries: Hawkins County and Sumner County." *Tennessee Ancestors: A Tri-Annual Publication of the East Tennessee Historical Society*, 11:1 (April 1995), 4-11.

North Carolina (State). Office of Secretary of State. Office of the Secretary. Land Office. "Land Warrents, Plats of Survey, and Related Records. Tennessee, Sumner County, 1780-1803." Manuscript S.108.382-S.108.387, 6 microfilm reels (MARS ID: 12.14.9; folder), State Archives of North Carolina, Raleigh. [Online catalog description: "Sumner County (formed in 1787 from Davidson County, Tennessee) was named for General Jethro Sumner. The county seat of Gallatin, named for Albert Gallatin, was established in 1804. A portion of

Sumner County became Davidson County in 1787, and other portions became Smith County and Wilson County in 1799."]

Smith, Kevin E. "Bledsoe Station: Archaeology, History, and the Interpretation of the Middle Tennessee Frontier, 1770-1820." *Tennessee Historical Quarterly*, 59:3 (Fall 2000), 174-187.

Wilson, Alma Lackey. *Veterans of the American Revolutionary War of Sumner County*. [S. l.]: A. L. Wilson, 1962.

Tennessee County

Fulcher, Richard Carlton. *1770-1790 Census of the Cumberland Settlements of Davidson, Sumner, and Tennessee Counties*. Baltimore: Genealogical Publishing Company, 1987.

Jordan, Rene. "The Evolution of Early Tennessee County Boundaries: Tennessee County, Knox County, and Jefferson County." *Tennessee Ancestors: A Tri-Annual Publication of the East Tennessee Historical Society*, 11:2 (August 1995), 83-90.

North Carolina (State). Office of Secretary of State. Office of the Secretary. Land Office. "Land Warrents, Plats of Survey, and Related Records. Tennessee, Tennessee County, 1780-1819." Manuscript S.108.387-S.108.390, 4 microfilm reel (MARS ID: 12.14.19; folder), State Archives of North Carolina, Raleigh. [Online catalog description: "Tennessee County (formed in 1788 from Davidson County, Tennessee) was named after the ancient capital of the Cherokee Indians. The county seat was Clarksville. The town was laid off in 1784 by John Montgomery and Martin Armstrong on a parcel of land for which they had entered a claim. The town was named after George Rogers Clark. Clarksville later served as the county seat of Montgomery County. Upon the admission of the state of Tennessee into the Union in 1796, the county of Tennessee was split to form Montgomery and Robertson counties."]

"Tennesse Counties Originally in North Carolina." Online: http://statelibrary.ncdcr.gov/ghl/resources/genealogy/tncounties.html.

Willis, Laura. *Tennessee County, N. C., Early Deeds, 1784-1797*. Melber, Ky.: Simmons Historical Publications, 1994. [Contents: Vol. 1: 1784-1793; Vol. 2: 1794-1797]

Williamson County

Kindard, Margaret. "Frontier Development of Williamson County." *Tennessee Historical Quarterly*, 8:1 (March 1949), 3-33; 8:2 (June 1949), 127-153. [the first article of this set covers the Revolution]

Lynch, Louise Gillespie. *Our Valiant Men: Soldiers and Patriots of the Revolutionary War Who Lived in Williamson County, Tennessee*. Franklin, Tenn.: L. G. Lynch, 1976.

North Carolina (State). Office of Secretary of State. Office of the Secretary. Land Office. "Land Warrents, Plats of Survey, and Related Records. Tennessee, Williamson County, 1800-1801." Manuscript S.108.373-S.108.378, 5 microfilm reels (MARS ID: 12.14.22; folder), State Archives of North Carolina, Raleigh. [Online catalog description: "Williamson County (formed in 1799 from Davidson County, Tennessee) was named for General Williamson of North Carolina or Dr. Hugh Williamson (also from North Carolina) and the county seat was supposed to have been named for Dr. Williamson's good friend, Benjamin Franklin. Part of Williamson County became Maury County in 1807."]

Wilson County

North Carolina (State). Office of Secretary of State. Office of the Secretary. Land Office. "Land Warrents, Plats of Survey, and Related Records. Tennessee, Wilson County, 1783-1802." Manuscript S.108.395, 1 microfilm reel (MARS ID: 12.14.9; folder), State Archives of North Carolina, Raleigh. [Online catalog description: "Wilson County (formed in 1799 from Sumner County, Tennessee) was named for Major David Wilson. Lebanon was chosen as the county seat in 1802."]

Partlow, Thomas E. "Revolutionary Soldiers in Wilson County, Tennessee." Typescript, Tennessee State Library and Archives, Nashville. Puckett, Tommy Rose. *Lower Black Creek Church Deaths and Military Service*. [North Carolina?]: T. R. Puckett, 2000. [Description: "Includes a name index of deaths recorded in church records from 1810 to 1978, and an index of soldiers from the American Revolution, War of 1812, {and the} War between the States."]

Chapter Sixteen: Distinctive Groups in North Carolina and Tennessee during the American Revolution

North Carolina and Tennessee Society in General

Ashe, Samuel A'Court. "Social Conditions in North Carolina in 1783." *North Carolina Booklet*, 10:4 (April 1911), 200-222.

Breen, T. H. *Shaping Southern Society: The Colonial Experience.* New York: Oxford University Press, 1976.

Bridenbaugh, Carl. *Myths and Realities: Societies of the Colonial South.* Baton Rouge: Louisiana State University Press, 1952.

Cary, Lorin Lee. "Class, Mobility, and Conflict in North Carolina on the Eve of the Revolution." In Jeffrey J. Crow and Larry E. Tise, eds., *The Southern Experience in the American Revolution.* (Chapel Hill: University of North Carolina Press, 1978), 109-151.

Cecil-Fronsman, Bill. *Common Whites: Class and Culture in Antebellum North Carolina.* Lexington: University Press of Kentucky, 1992.

Escott, Paul D., and Jeffrey J. Crown. "The Social Order and Violent Disorder: An Analysis of North Carolina in the Revolution and the Civil War." *Journal of Southern History*, 52:3 (August 1986), 373-402.

Kay, Marvin L. Michael, and Lorin Lee Cary. "Class, Mobility, and Conflict in North Carolina on the Eve of the American Revolution." In Jeffrey J. Crow and Larry E. Tise, eds., *The Southern Experience in the American Revolution* (Chapel Hill: University of North Carolina Press, 1978), 109-151.

Mathews, Alice Elaine. *Society in Revolutionary North Carolina.* (Bicentennial Pamphlet Series, no. 8) Raleigh: North Carolina Department of Archives and History, 1976.

Raper, Charles Lee. "Social Life in Colonial North Carolina." *North Carolina Booklet*, 3:5 (September 1903), 5-21; online: http://digital.ncdcr.gov/cdm/ref/collection/p249901coll37/id/14180. [Online description from "North Carolina Periodicals Index," East Carolina University: "An attempt to lay the groundwork for the study of the social history of Colonial North Carolina, including the identification of topics and areas of study that are in need of further scholarship."]

Read, Wingate. "Hereditary Nobility in North Carolina." *The State: Down Home in North Carolina*, 28:26 (May 27, 1961), 15-16. Online: http://digital.ncdcr.gov/cdm/compoundobject/collection/p16062coll18/id/8401. [Online description from "North Carolina Periodicals Index," East Carolina University: "290 years ago, the true and absolute Lords Proprietors of Carolina conceived and attempted to spawn a government of landed aristocracy in the sparsely populated wilderness of Carolina."]

Sachs, William, and Ari Hoogenboom. *The Enterprising Colonials: Society on the Eve of the Revolution.* Chicago: Argonaut, 1965.

Sarson, Steven. "Similarities and Continuities: Free Society in the Tobacco South before and after the American Revolution." In Eliga H. Gould and Peter S. Onuf, eds., *Empire and Nation: the American Revolution in the Atlantic World* (Anglo-America in the Transatlantic World series) Baltimore: Johns Hopkins University Press, 2005, 136-158.

Waldrup, J. Charles. "'Uneasy Lies the Head that Wears a Crown': Ruling Elites in North Carolina, 1776-1789." M. A. thesis, University of North Carolina at Chapel Hill, 1977.

Watson, Alan D. *Society in Colonial North Carolina.* Raleigh: North Carolina Office of Archives and History, 1996.

Watson, Alan D. *Society in Early North Carolina: A Documentary History.* Raleigh: North Carolina Division of Archives and History, 2000.

Williams, Jack K. *Dueling in the Old South: Vignettes of Social History.* College Station: Texas A & M University Press, 1980.

Wilson, Charles Reagan, gen. ed. *The New Encyclopedia of Southern Culture* 24 vols. Chapel Hill: University of North Carolina Press, 2006-2013.

Samuel S. Hill, ed.; Charles Reagan Wilson, gen. ed. *Volume 1: Religion.* Chapel Hill: University of North Carolina Press, 2006. [Publisher's description: "Evangelical Protestant groups have dominated religious life in the South since the early nineteenth century. Even as the conservative Protestantism typically associated with the South has risen in social and political prominence throughout the United States in recent decades, however, religious culture in the South itself has grown increasingly diverse. The region has seen a surge of immigration from other parts of the United States as well as from Latin America, Asia, and the Middle East, bringing increased visibility to Catholicism, Islam, and Asian religions in the once solidly Protestant

Christian South. In this volume of *The New Encyclopedia of Southern Culture*, contributors have revised entries from the original *Encyclopedia* on topics ranging from religious broadcasting to snake handling and added new entries on such topics as Asian religions, Latino religion, New Age religion, Islam, Native American religion, and social activism. With the contributions of more than 60 authorities in the field – including Paul Harvey, Loyal Jones, Wayne Flynt, and Samuel F. Weber – this volume is an accessibly written, up-to-date reference to religious culture in the American South."]

Richard Pillsbury, ed.; Charles Reagan Wilson, gen. ed. *Volume 2: Geography.* Chapel Hill: University of North Carolina Press, 2006. [Publisher's description: "The location of "the South" is hardly a settled or static geographic concept. Culturally speaking, are Florida and Arkansas really part of the same region? Is Texas considered part of the South or the West? This volume of *The New Encyclopedia of Southern Culture* grapples with the contestable issue of where the cultural South is located, both on maps and in the minds of Americans. Richard Pillsbury's introductory essay explores the evolution of geographic patterns of life within the region – agricultural practices, urban patterns, residential buildings, religious preferences, foodways, and language. The entries that follow address general topics of cultural geographic interest, such as Appalachia, exiles and expatriates, Latino and Jewish populations, migration patterns, and the profound Disneyfication of central Florida. Entries with a more concentrated focus examine major cities, such as Atlanta, New Orleans, and Memphis; the influence of black and white southern migrants on northern cities; and individual subregions, such as the Piedmont, Piney Woods, Tidewater, and Delta. Putting together the disparate pieces that make up the place called 'the South,' this volume sets the scene for the discussions in all the other volumes of *The New Encyclopedia of Southern Culture*."]

Charles Reagan Wilson, ed.; Charles Reagan Wilson, gen. ed. *Volume 3: History.* Chapel Hill: University of North Carolina Press, 2006. [Publisher's description: "Providing a chronological and interpretive spine to the twenty-four volumes of The New Encyclopedia of Southern Culture, this volume broadly surveys history in the American South from the Paleoindian period (approximately 8000 B.C.E.) to the present. In 118 essays, contributors cover the turbulent past of the region that has witnessed frequent racial conflict, a bloody Civil War fought and lost on its soil, massive in- and out-migration, major economic transformations, and a civil rights movement that brought fundamental change to the social order. Charles Reagan Wilson's overview essay examines the evolution of southern history and the way our understanding of southern culture has unfolded over time and in response to a variety of events and social forces – not just as the opposite of the North but also in the larger context of the Atlantic World. Longer thematic essays cover major eras and events, such as early settlement, slave culture, Reconstruction, the New Deal, and the rise of the New South. Brief topical entries cover individuals--including figures from the Civil War, the civil rights movement, and twentieth-century politics--and organizations such as the Southern Christian Leadership Conference, Daughters of the Confederacy, and Citizens' Councils, among others. Together, these essays offer a sweeping reference to the rich history of the region."]

Charles Reagan Wilson, ed.; Charles Reagan Wilson, gen. ed. *Volume 4: Myth, Manners, and Memory.* Chapel Hill: University of North Carolina Press, 2006. [Publisher's description: "This volume of The New Encyclopedia of Southern Culture addresses the cultural, social, and intellectual terrain of myth, manners, and historical memory in the American South. Evaluating how a distinct southern identity has been created, recreated, and performed through memories that blur the line between fact and fiction, this volume paints a broad, multihued picture of the region seen through the lenses of belief and cultural practice. The 95 entries here represent a substantial revision and expansion of the material on historical memory and manners in the original edition. They address such matters as myths and memories surrounding the Old South and the Civil War; stereotypes and traditions related to the body, sexuality, gender, and family (such as debutante balls and beauty pageants); institutions and places associated with historical memory (such as cemeteries, monuments, and museums); and specific subjects and objects of myths, including the Confederate flag and Graceland. Together, they offer a compelling portrait of the "southern way of life" as it has been imagined, lived, and contested."]

Michael Montgomery and Ellen Johnson, eds.; Charles Reagan Wilson, gen. ed. *Volume 5: Language.* Chapel Hill: University of North Carolina Press, 2007. [Publisher's description: "The fifth volume of The New Encyclopedia of Southern Culture explores language and dialect in the South, including English and its numerous regional variants, Native American languages, and other non-English languages spoken over time by the region's immigrant communities. Among the more than sixty entries are eleven on indigenous languages and major essays on French, Spanish, and German. Each of these provides both historical and contemporary perspectives, identifying the language's location, number of speakers, vitality, and sample distinctive features. The book acknowledges the role of immigration in spreading features of Southern

English to other regions and countries and in bringing linguistic influences from Europe and Africa to Southern English. The fascinating patchwork of English dialects is also fully presented, from African American English, Gullah, and Cajun English to the English spoken in Appalachia, the Ozarks, the Outer Banks, the Chesapeake Bay Islands, Charleston, and elsewhere. Topical entries discuss ongoing changes in the pronunciation, vocabulary, and grammar of English in the increasingly mobile South, as well as naming patterns, storytelling, preaching styles, and politeness, all of which deal with ways language is woven into southern culture."]

Celeste Ray, ed.; Charles Reagan Wilson, gen. ed. *Volume 6: Ethnicity.* Chapel Hill: University of North Carolina Press, 2007. [Publisher's description: "Transcending familiar categories of 'black' and 'white,' this volume of The New Encyclopedia of Southern Culture complicates and enriches our understanding of "southernness" by identifying the array of cultures that combined to shape the South. This exploration of southern ethnicities examines the ways people perform and maintain cultural identities through folklore, religious faith, dress, music, speech, cooking, and transgenerational tradition. Accessibly written and informed by the most recent research that recovers the ethnic diversity of the early South and documents the more recent arrival of new cultural groups, this volume greatly expands upon the modest Ethnic Life section of the original *Encyclopedia.* Contributors describe 88 ethnic groups that have lived in the South from the Mississippian Period (1000-1600) to the present. They include 34 American Indian groups, as well as the many communities with European, African, and Asian cultural ties that came to the region after 1600. Southerners from all backgrounds are likely to find themselves represented here."]

John T. Edge, ed.; Charles Reagan Wilson, gen. ed. *Volume 7: Foodways.* Chapel Hill: University of North Carolina Press, 2007. [Publisher's description: "When the original Encyclopedia of Southern Culture was published in 1989, the topic of foodways was relatively new as a field of scholarly inquiry. Food has always been central to southern culture, but the past twenty years have brought an explosion in interest in foodways, particularly in the South. This volume marks the first encyclopedia of the food culture of the American South, surveying the vast diversity of foodways within the region and the collective qualities that make them distinctively southern. Articles in this volume explore the richness of southern foodways, examining not only what southerners eat but also why they eat it. The volume contains 149 articles, almost all of them new to this edition of the *Encyclopedia.* Longer essays address the historical development of southern cuisine and ethnic contributions to the region's foodways. Topical essays explore iconic southern foods such as MoonPies and fried catfish, prominent restaurants and personalities, and the food cultures of subregions and individual cities. The volume is destined to earn a spot on kitchen shelves as well as in libraries."]

Martin Melosi, ed.; Charles Reagan Wilson, gen. ed. *Volume 8: Environment.* Chapel Hill: University of North Carolina Press, 2007. [Publisher's description: "From semitropical coastal areas to high mountain terrain, from swampy lowlands to modern cities, the environment holds a fundamental importance in shaping the character of the American South. This volume of *The New Encyclopedia of Southern Culture* surveys the dynamic environmental forces that have shaped human culture in the region – and the ways humans have shaped their environment. Articles examine how the South's ecology, physiography, and climate have influenced southerners – not only as a daily fact of life but also as a metaphor for understanding culture and identity. This volume includes ninety-eight essays that explore – both broadly and specifically – elements of the southern environment. Thematic overviews address subjects such as plants, animals, energy use and development, and natural disasters. Shorter topical entries feature familiar species such as the alligator, the ivory-billed woodpecker, kudzu, and the mockingbird. Also covered are important individuals in southern environmental history and prominent places in the landscape, such as the South's national parks and seashores. New articles cover contemporary issues in land use and conservation, environmental protection, and the current status of the flora and fauna widely associated with the South."]

M. Thomas Inge, ed.; Charles Reagan Wilson, gen. ed. *Volume 9: Literature.* Chapel Hill: University of North Carolina Press, 2008. [Publisher's description: "Offering a comprehensive view of the South's literary landscape, past and present, this volume of *The New Encyclopedia of Southern Culture* celebrates the region's ever-flourishing literary culture and recognizes the ongoing evolution of the southern literary canon. As new writers draw upon and reshape previous traditions, southern literature has broadened and deepened its connections not just to the American literary mainstream but also to world literatures – a development thoughtfully explored in the essays here. Greatly expanding the content of the literature section in the original *Encyclopedia*, this volume includes 31 thematic essays addressing major genres of literature; theoretical categories, such as regionalism, the southern gothic, and agrarianism; and themes in southern writing, such as food, religion, and sexuality. Most striking is the fivefold increase in the number of biographical entries, which introduce southern novelists, playwrights, poets, and critics. Special attention is given to contemporary writers and other individuals who have not been widely covered in previous scholarship."]

James W. Ely, Jr. and Bradley G. Bond, eds.; Charles Reagan Wilson, gen. ed. *Volume 10: Law and Politics.* Chapel Hill: University of North Carolina Press, 2008. [Publisher's description: "Volume 10 of The New Encyclopedia of Southern Culture combines two of the sections from the original edition, adding extensive updates and 53 entirely new articles. In the law section of this volume, 16 longer essays address broad concepts ranging from law schools to family law, from labor relations to school prayer. The 43 topical entries focus on specific legal cases and individuals, including historical legal professionals, parties from landmark cases, and even the fictional character Atticus Finch, highlighting the roles these individuals have played in shaping the identity of the region. The politics section includes 34 essays on matters such as Reconstruction, social class and politics, and immigration policy. New essays reflect the changing nature of southern politics, away from the one-party system long known as the 'solid South' to the lively two-party politics now in play in the region. Seventy shorter topical entries cover individual politicians, political thinkers, and activists who have made significant contributions to the shaping of southern politics."]

Melissa Walker and James C. Cobb, eds.; Charles Reagan Wilson, gen. ed. *Volume 11: Agriculture and Industry.* Chapel Hill: University of North Carolina Press, 2008. [Publisher's description: "Volume 11 of The New Encyclopedia of Southern Culture examines the economic culture of the South by pairing two categories that account for the ways many southerners have made their living. In the antebellum period, the wealth of southern whites came largely from agriculture that relied on the forced labor of enslaved blacks. After Reconstruction, the South became attractive to new industries lured by the region's ongoing commitment to low-wage labor and management-friendly economic policies. Throughout the volume, articles reflect the breadth and variety of southern life, paying particular attention to the region's profound economic transformation in recent decades. The agricultural section consists of 25 thematic entries that explore issues such as Native American agricultural practices, plantations, and sustainable agriculture. Thirty-eight shorter pieces cover key crops of the region – from tobacco to Christmas trees – as well as issues of historic and emerging interest – from insects and insecticides to migrant labor. The section on industry and commerce contains 13 thematic entries in which contributors address topics such as the economic impact of military bases, resistance to industrialization, and black business. Thirty-six topical entries explore particular industries, such as textiles, timber, automobiles, and banking, as well as individuals – including Henry W. Grady and Sam M. Walton--whose ideas and enterprises have helped shape the modern South."]

Bill C. Malone, ed.; Charles Reagan Wilson, gen. ed. *Volume 12: Music.* Chapel Hill: University of North Carolina Press, 2009. [Publisher's description: "Southern music has flourished as a meeting ground for the traditions of West African and European peoples in the region, leading to the evolution of various traditional folk genres, bluegrass, country, jazz, gospel, rock, blues, and southern hip-hop. This much-anticipated volume in *The New Encyclopedia of Southern Culture* celebrates an essential element of southern life and makes available for the first time a stand-alone reference to the music and music makers of the American South. With nearly double the number of entries devoted to music in the original *Encyclopedia*, this volume includes 30 thematic essays, covering topics such as ragtime, zydeco, folk music festivals, minstrelsy, rockabilly, white and black gospel traditions, and southern rock. And it features 174 topical and biographical entries, focusing on artists and musical outlets. From Mahalia Jackson to R.E.M., from Doc Watson to OutKast, this volume considers a diverse array of topics, drawing on the best historical and contemporary scholarship on southern music. It is a book for all southerners and for all serious music lovers, wherever they live."]

Nancy Bercaw and Ted Ownsby, eds.; Charles Reagan Wilson, gen. ed. *Volume 13: Gender.* Chapel Hill: University of North Carolina Press, 2009. [Publisher's description: "This volume of The New Encyclopedia of Southern Culture reflects the dramatic increase in research on the topic of gender over the past thirty years, revealing that even the most familiar subjects take on new significance when viewed through the lens of gender. The wide range of entries explores how people have experienced, understood, and used concepts of womanhood and manhood in all sorts of obvious and subtle ways. The volume features 113 articles, 65 of which are entirely new for this edition. Thematic articles address subjects such as sexuality, respectability, and paternalism and investigate the role of gender in broader subjects, including the civil rights movement, country music, and sports. Topical entries highlight individuals such as Oprah Winfrey, the Grimké sisters, and Dale Earnhardt, as well as historical events such as the capture of Jefferson Davis in a woman's dress, the Supreme Court's decision in *Loving v. Virginia*, and the Memphis sanitation workers' strike, with its slogan, 'I *AM* A MAN.' Bringing together scholarship on gender and the body, sexuality, labor, race, and politics, this volume offers new ways to view big questions in southern history and culture."]

Hinson, Glenn, and William Ferris, eds.; Charles Reagan Wilson, gen. ed. *Volume 14: Folklife.* Chapel Hill: University of North Carolina Press, 2009. [Publisher's description: "Southern folklife is the heart of southern culture. Looking at traditional practices still carried on today as well as at aspects of folklife that are dynamic and emergent, contributors to this volume of *The New Encyclopedia of Southern Culture* examine a broad range of folk traditions. Moving beyond the traditional view of folklore that situates it in historical practice and narrowly defined genres, entries in this volume demonstrate how folklife remains a vital part of communities' self-definitions. Fifty thematic entries address subjects such as car culture, funerals, hip-hop, and powwows. In 56 topical entries, contributors focus on more specific elements of folklife, such as roadside memorials, collegiate stepping, *quinceañera* celebrations, New Orleans marching bands, and hunting dogs. Together, the entries demonstrate that southern folklife is dynamically alive and everywhere around us, giving meaning to the everyday unfolding of community life."]

Wanda Rushing, ed.; Charles Reagan Wilson, gen. ed. *Volume 15: Urbanization.* Chapel Hill: University of North Carolina Press, 2010. [Publisher's description: "This volume of The New Encyclopedia of Southern Culture offers a current and authoritative reference to urbanization in the American South from the eighteenth century to the twenty-first, surveying important southern cities individually and examining the various issues that shape patterns of urbanization from a broad regional perspective. Looking beyond the post-World War II era and the emergence of the Sunbelt economy to examine recent and contemporary developments, the 48 thematic essays consider the ongoing remarkable growth of southern urban centers, new immigration patterns (such as the influx of Latinos and the return-migration of many African Americans), booming regional entrepreneurial activities with global reach (such as the rise of the southern banking industry and companies such as CNN in Atlanta and FedEx in Memphis), and mounting challenges that result from these patterns (including population pressure and urban sprawl, aging and deteriorating infrastructure, gentrification, and state and local budget shortfalls). The 31 topical entries focus on individual cities and urban cultural elements, including Mardi Gras, Dollywood, and the 1996 Atlanta Olympics."]

Harvey H. Jackson, III, ed.; Charles Reagan Wilson, gen. ed. *Volume 16:Sports and Recreation*. Chapel Hill: University of North Carolina Press, 2011. [Publisher's description: "What southerners do, where they go, and what they expect to accomplish in their spare time, their 'leisure,' reveals much about their cultural values, class and racial similarities and differences, and historical perspectives. This volume of *The New Encyclopedia of Southern Culture* offers an authoritative and readable reference to the culture of sports and recreation in the American South, surveying the various activities in which southerners engage in their nonwork hours, as well as attitudes surrounding those activities. Seventy-four thematic essays explore activities from the familiar (porch sitting and fairs) to the essential (football and stock car racing) to the unusual (pool checkers and a sport called 'fireballing'). In seventy-seven topical entries, contributors profile major sites associated with recreational activities (such as Dollywood, drive-ins, and the Appalachian Trail) and prominent sports figures (including Althea Gibson, Michael Jordan, Mia Hamm, and Hank Aaron). Taken together, the entries provide an engaging look at the ways southerners relax, pass time, celebrate, let loose, and have fun."]

Clarence L. Mohr, ed.; Charles Reagan Wilson, gen. ed. *Volume 17: Education.* Chapel Hill: University of North Carolina Press, 2011. [Publisher's description: "Offering a broad, up-to-date reference to the long history and cultural legacy of education in the American South, this timely volume of The New Encyclopedia of Southern Culture surveys educational developments, practices, institutions, and politics from the colonial era to the present. With over 130 articles, this book covers key topics in education, including academic freedom; the effects of urbanization on segregation, desegregation, and resegregation; African American and women's education; and illiteracy. These entries, as well as articles on prominent educators, such as Booker T. Washington and C. Vann Woodward, and major southern universities, colleges, and trade schools, provide an essential context for understanding the debates and battles that remain deeply imbedded in southern education. Framed by Clarence Mohr's historically rich introductory overview, the essays in this volume comprise a greatly expanded and thoroughly updated survey of the shifting southern education landscape and its development over the span of four centuries."]

Allison Graham and Sharon Montieth, eds.; Charles Reagan Wilson, gen. ed. *Volume 18: Media*. Chapel Hill: University of North Carolina Press, 2011. [Publisher's description: "This volume of The New Encyclopedia of Southern Culture examines how mass media have shaped popular perceptions of the South – and how the South has shaped the history of mass media. An introductory overview by Allison Graham and Sharon Monteith is followed by 40 thematic essays and 132 topical articles that examine major trends and seminal moments in film, television, radio, press, and Internet history. Among topics explored are the southern media boom, beginning with the Christian Broadcast Network and CNN; popular movies, television shows, and periodicals that have shaped ideas about the region, including *Gone with the Wind*, *The Beverly Hillbillies*, *Roots*, and *Southern Living*; and southern media celebrities such as Oprah Winfrey, Truman Capote, and Stephen Colbert. The volume details the media's involvement in southern history, from depictions of race in the movies to news coverage of the civil rights movement and Hurricane Katrina. Taken together, these entries reveal and comment on the ways in which mass media have influenced, maintained, and changed the idea of a culturally unique South."]

Amy Loise Wood, ed.; Charles Reagan Wilson, gen. ed. *Volume 19: Violence*. Chapel Hill: University of North Carolina Press, 2011. [Publisher's description: "Much of the violence that has been associated with the United States has had particular salience for the South, from its high homicide rates, or its bloody history of racial conflict, to southerners' popular attachment to guns and traditional support for capital punishment. With over 95 entries, this volume of *The New Encyclopedia of Southern Culture* explores the most significant forms and many of the most harrowing incidences of violence that have plagued southern society over the past 300 years. Following a detailed overview by editor Amy Wood, the volume explores a wide range of topics, such as violence against and among American Indians, labor violence, arson, violence and memory, suicide, and anti-abortion violence. Taken together, these entries broaden our understanding of what has driven southerners of various classes and various ethnicities to commit acts of violence, while addressing the ways in which southerners have conceptualized that violence, responded to it, or resisted it. This volume enriches our understanding of the culture of violence and its impact on ideas about law and crime, about historical tradition and social change, and about race and gender--not only in the South but in the nation as a whole."]

Larry J. Griffin and Peggy G. Hargis, eds.; Charles Reagan Wilson, gen. ed. *Volume 20: Social Class*. Chapel Hill: University of North Carolina Press, 2012. [Publisher's description: "This volume of The New Encyclopedia of Southern Culture offers a timely, authoritative, and interdisciplinary exploration of issues related to social class in the South from the colonial era to the present. With introductory essays by J. Wayne Flynt and by editors Larry J. Griffin and Peggy G. Hargis, the volume is a comprehensive, stand-alone reference to this complex subject, which underpins the history of the region and shapes its future. In 58 thematic essays and 103 topical entries, the contributors explore the effects of class on all aspects of life in the South – its role in Indian removal, the Civil War, the New Deal, and the civil rights movement, for example, and how it has been manifested in religion, sports, country and gospel music, and matters of gender. Artisans and the working class, indentured workers and steelworkers, the Freedmen's Bureau and the Knights of Labor are all examined. This volume provides a full investigation of social class in the region and situates class concerns at the center of our understanding of Southern culture."]

Judith H. Bonner and Estil Curtis Pennington, eds.; Charles Reagan Wilson, gen. ed. *Volume 21: Art and Architecture*. Chapel Hill: University of North Carolina Press, 2013. [Publisher's description: "From the Potomac to the Gulf, artists were creating in the South even before it was recognized as a region. The South has contributed to America's cultural heritage with works as diverse as Benjamin Henry Latrobe's architectural plans for the nation's Capitol, the wares of the Newcomb Pottery, and Richard Clague's tonalist Louisiana bayou scenes. This comprehensive volume shows how, through the decades and centuries, the art of the South expanded from mimetic portraiture to sophisticated responses to national and international movements. The essays treat historic and current trends in the visual arts and architecture, major collections and institutions, and biographies of artists themselves. As leading experts on the region's artists and their work, editors Judith H. Bonner and Estill Curtis Pennington frame the volume's contributions with insightful overview essays on the visual arts and architecture in the American South."]

James G. Thomas, Jr., and Charles Reagan Wilson, eds.; Charles Reagan Wilson, gen. ed. *Volume 22: Science and Medicine*. Chapel Hill: University of North Carolina Press, 2013. [Publisher's description: "Science and medicine have been critical to southern history and the formation of southern culture. For three centuries, scientists in the South have documented the lush natural world around them and set a lasting tradition of inquiry. The medical history of the region, however, has been at times tragic. Disease, death, and generations of poor health have been the legacy of slavery, the plantation economy, rural life, and poorly planned cities. The essays in this volume explore this legacy as well as recent developments in technology, research, and medicine in the South. Subjects include natural history, slave health, medicine in the Civil War, public health, eugenics, HIV/AIDS, environmental health, and the rise of research institutions and hospitals, to name but a few. With 38 thematic essays, 44 topical entries, and a comprehensive overview essay, this volume offers an authoritative reference to science and medicine in the American South.

Carol Crown and Cheryl Rivers, eds. *Volume 23: Folk Art*. Chapel Hill: University of North Carolina Press, 2013. [Publisher's description: "Folk art is one of the American South's most significant areas of creative achievement, and this comprehensive yet accessible reference details that achievement from the sixteenth century through the present. This volume of *The New Encyclopedia of Southern Culture* explores the many forms of aesthetic expression that have characterized southern folk art, including the work of self-taught artists, as well as the South's complex relationship to national patterns of folk art collecting. Fifty-two thematic essays examine subjects ranging from colonial portraiture, Moravian material culture, and southern folk pottery to the South's rich quilt-making traditions, memory painting, and African American vernacular art, and 211 topical essays include profiles of major folk and self-taught artists in the region."]

Thomas C. Holt and Laurie B. Green; Charles Reagan Wilson, gen. ed. *Volume 24: Race*. Chapel Hill: University of North Carolina Press, 2013. [Publisher's description: "There is no denying that race is a critical issue in understanding the South. However, this concluding volume of *The New Encyclopedia of Southern Culture* challenges previous understandings, revealing the region's rich, ever-expanding diversity and providing new explorations of race relations. In 36 thematic and 29 topical essays, contributors examine such subjects as the Tuskegee Syphilis Study, Japanese American incarceration in the South, relations between African Americans and Native Americans, Chinese men adopting Mexican identities, Latino religious practices, and Vietnamese life in the region. Together the essays paint a nuanced portrait of how concepts of race in the South have influenced its history, art, politics, and culture beyond the familiar binary of black and white."]

African Americans of North Carolina and Tennessee and Slavery

Adams, Natalie P. "A Pattern of Living: A View of the American Slave Experience in the Pine Forests of the Lower Cape Fear." In J. W. Joseph and Martha Zierden, eds., *Another's Country: Archaeological and Historical Perspectives on Cultural Interaction in the Southern Colonies* (Tuscaloosa: University of Alabama Press, 2002), 65-78.

Africa, Philip. "Slaveholding in the Salem Community, 1771-1851." *North Carolina Historical Review*, 45:3: (July 1977), 271-307. [Online description from "North Carolina Periodicals Index," East Carolina University: "Between the founding of Salem in 1771 as a Moravian community and the outbreak of Civil War, community attitudes went through a transition. The communal sense of *gemeinschaft* slowly changed during the 19th century to a more business-like attitude of *gesellschaft*. Secular pressures eroded opposition to slavery on religious and moral grounds, and by the 1850s Moravians came to regard slaves not as persons but as property."]

African Impact on the Material Culture of the Americas: A Conference Presented at Diggs Gallery at Winston-Salem State University, Old Salem, the Museum of Early Southern Decorative Arts, May 30-June 2, 1996. Winston-Salem: Museum of Early Southern Decorative Arts, 1998. [Contents include: "Tools of the Spirit: Reflections on the Enduring Meaning of African American Culture"; "African Influences on the Decorative Arts of Tidewater Virginia and Maryland, and the Carolinas before 1800"; "African American Material Culture in North Carolina."]

Bellamy, Donnie D. "Slavery in Microcosm: Onslow County, North Carolina." *Journal of Negro History*, 62:4 (October 1977), 339-350.

Bishir, Catherine W. *Crafting Lives: African American Artisans in New Bern, North Carolina, 1770-1900.* Chapel Hill: University of North Carolina Press, 2013.

Bontemps, Arna Alexander. "A Social History of Black Culture in Colonial North Carolina." Ph. D. dissertation, University of Illinois – Urbana-Champaign, 1989. [Abstract: "By surveying the full range of existing contemporary documents available for the study of slavery in colonial North Carolina, this study has attempted to provide a social history of black culture in colonial North Carolina against which it has sought to outline the aesthetic dimension of black life in that colony. The organization of the study--beginning with chapters on the historical background to the subject and including sections on life at sea; the slave trade and its mythology; the lore and reality of the coastal environment; the art and craft of agricultural production; measured experience (time, space and distance); the law and lawlessness; the lore of race relations; health, spirituality and romance – reflects its effort to focus analysis primarily on aesthetic considerations as opposed to acculturative concerns. A concluding section, 'Jonkonnu and the Art of Liminality', argues that the expressive behavior of blacks in colonial North Carolina generally mirrored the acculturative patterns of other aspects of colonial life among black Carolinians in its outward forms and institutional functions. However, on an emotional and intellectual level, especially as it was reflected in the folklore and ritual life of the black slave, it reflected a persistent sense of cultural estrangement that inhibited cultural reconciliation. In the tenacity of African influences and atavistic perspectives on their art and lore; in their spontaneity and liminal exuberance as artists; and in their imaginative use of unconventional strategies of expressive indirection, black Carolinians both celebrated and lamented their liminality as a reflection of slavery's tragic inner contradictions and as a defense against psychological domination."]

Brewer, James Howard. "An Account of Negro Slavery in the Cape Fear Region Prior to 1860." Ph. D. dissertation, University of Pittsburgh, 1949.

Brewer, James Howard. "Legislation Designed to Control Slavery in Wilmington and Fayetteville." *North Carolina Historical Review*, 30:2 (April 1953), 155-166; online: http://digital.ncdcr.gov/cdm/ref/collection/p16062coll9/id/4207. [Online description from "North Carolina Periodicals Index," East Carolina University: "This article looks at a laxity and indifference toward the enforcement of slave controls in the towns of Wilmington and Fayetteville in the colonial and antebellum periods. Geographic and economic factors are deemed to be largely responsible for the different views of legislators on slave controls, as the industrial and commercial concerns of both towns lead to high slave populations where slave owners allowed slaves certain freedoms like owning their own homes in town apart from their masters and no supervision or controls on the leisure activities of slaves. Legislators feared the potential outcomes of this behavior and attempted to pass laws to pass tougher slave codes with little to no success."]

Brown, Douglas. "A Preliminary Slave Name Database for the North Carolina State Archives." *NCGS News: The Newsletter of the North Carolina Genealogical Society*, 28:1 (Winter 2004), 8-11.

Brown, Hugh Victor. *A History of Education of Negroes in North Carolina*. Raleigh: Irving Swain Press, 1961.

Bryan, Sarah; Beverly Patterson; and Michelle Lanier. *African American Music Tales of Eastern North Carolina*. Chapel Hill: University of North Carolina Press, 2013. [Publisher's description: "Thelonius Monk, Billy Taylor, and Maceo Parker – famous jazz artists who have shared the unique sounds of North Carolina with the world – are but a few of the dynamic African American artists from eastern North Carolina featured in The African American Music Trails of Eastern North Carolina. This first-of-its-kind travel guide will take you on a fascinating journey to music venues, events, and museums that illuminate the lives of the musicians and reveal the deep ties between music and community. Interviews with more than 90 artists open doors to a world of music, especially jazz, rhythm and blues, funk, gospel and church music, blues, rap, marching band music, and beach music. New and historical photographs enliven the narrative, and maps and travel information help you plan your trip. Included is a CD with 17 recordings performed by some of the region's outstanding artists."]

Byrd, William L. *In Full Force and Virtue: North Carolina Emancipation Records, 1713-1860*. Bowie, Md.: Heritage Books, Inc., 2000.

Byrd, William L. *North Carolina Assembly Sessions Records: Slaves and Free Persons of Color, 1709-1789*. Bowie, Md.: Heritage Books, 2001.

Byrd, William L. *North Carolina Slaves and Free Persons of Color: Pasquotank County*. Bowie, Md.: Heritage Books, 2006.

Byrd, William L., and John H Smith. *North Carolina Slaves and Free Persons of Color: Hyde and Beaufort Counties*. Bowie, Md.: Heritage Books, 2002.

Byrd, William L., and John H Smith. *North Carolina Slaves and Free Persons of Color: Iredell County*. Bowie, Md.: Heritage Books, 2002.

Byrd, William L., and John H Smith. *North Carolina Slaves and Free Persons of Color: McDowell County*. Westminster, Md.: Heritage Books, 2007.

Byrd, William L., and John H Smith. *North Carolina Slaves and Free Persons of Color: Mecklenburg, Gaston, and Union Counties*. Bowie, Md.: Heritage Books, 2001.

Byrd, William L., and John H Smith. *North Carolina Slaves and Free Persons of Color: Stokes and Yadkin Counties*. Bowie, Md.: Heritage Books, 2001.

Calhoon, Robert. *Religion and the American Revolution in North Carolina*. Raleigh: North Carolina Department of Cultural Resources, Division of Archives and History, 1976.

Cecelski, David S. *The Waterman's Song: Slavery and Freedom in Maritime North Carolina.* Chapel Hill: University of North Carolina Press, 2001.

Clark, Ernest James, Jr. "Aspects of the North Carolina Slave Code, 1715-1860." *North Carolina Historical Review*, 39:2 (April 1962), 148-164; online: http://digital.ncdcr.gov/cdm/ref/collection/p16062coll9/id/4207. [Online description from "North Carolina Periodicals Index," East Carolina University: "The North Carolina slave code was not a product of legal theory or thought, but developed gradually based on the needs of the population. The code was intended to police the slave population and establish and maintain a unique social standard in the community. Later on the code, also developed the purpose of extending to slaves the basic civil privileges and personal security."]

Clark, Walter. "Negro Soldiers." *North Carolina Booklet*, 18:1 (July 1918), 57-62.

Clifford, Mary Louise. *From Slavery to Freetown: Black Loyalists after the American Revolution*. Jefferson: McFarland, 1999. [Include a section on: "Thomas Peters of Wilmington, North Carolina."]

Countryman, Edward. *Enjoy the Same Liberty: Black Americans and the Revolutionary Era.* Lanham, Md.: Rowman & Littlefield, 2012.

Crawford, Michael J. "The Pace of Manumission among Quakers in Revolutionary-Era North Carolina." *Quaker History: The Bulletin of Friends Historical Association*, 102:1 (Spring 2013), 1-16.

Crawford, Michael J. "'The Small Black Boy at My Right Hand is Christ': George Walton and Friends' Manumission of Slaves in Revolutionary-Era North Carolina." *The Southern Friend*, 28:2 (2006), 3-17.

Crawford, Michael J., ed. *The Having of Negroes Is Becoming a Burden: The Quaker Struggle to Free Slaves in Revolutionary North Carolina*. Gainesville: University Press of Florida, 2010.

Crow, Jeffrey. "Liberty to Slaves: The Black Response." *Tar Heel Junior Historian*, 32:1 (Fall 1992), 18-22; online: http://ncpedia.org/history/usrevolution/african-americans. [Online description from "North Carolina Periodicals Index," East Carolina University: "The American Revolution divided the state's African American population because both Loyalists and Patriots promised freedom for slaves. At the time of revolution, African American totaled 25 percent of the state's overall population and of that only 5 percent were free. British enticed groups of slaves to revolt, yet some African Americans independently fought for the colonist; the most famous soldier was John Chavis."]

Crow, Jeffrey J. *The Black Experience in Revolutionary North Carolina*. (North Carolina Bicentennial Pamphlet Series, no. 16) Raleigh: North Carolina Deparment of Cultural Resources, Division of Archives and History, 1977; reprinted: 1996.

Crow, Jeffrey J. "Equal Justice: Afro-American Perceptions of the Revolution in North Carolina, 1775-1802." Manuscript of a lecture, Cp326.1 C95e, North Carolina Collection, University of North Carolina Library, Chapel Hill.

Crow, Jeffrey J. *A History of African Americans in North Carolina*. Raleigh: North Carolina Division of Archives and History, Department of Cultural Resources, 1992.

Crow, Jeffrey J. "Slave Rebelliousness and Social Conflict in North Carolina, 1775-1802." *William and Mary Quarterly,* 3rd series, 37:1 (January 1980), 79-102.

Crow, Jeffrey J., and Flora J. Hatley, eds. *Black Americans in North Carolina and the South: Papers Presented at a Symposium, Sponsored by the North Carolina Division of Archives and History in February 1981.* Chapel Hill: University of North Carolina Press, 1984.

Dungy, Kathryn Renee. "Life on a Tightrope: The Problems of Becoming Free in Perquimans County, North Carolina, 1775-1800." M. A. thesis, Duke University, 1993.

Edwards, Laura F. "Enslaved Women and the Law: Paradoxes of Subordination in the Post-Revolutionary Carolinas." *Slavery and Abolition* 26:2 (August 2005), 305-323. [focusing on court cases in North and South Carolina from 1787 to 1840]

Edwards, Laura F. *The People and Their Peace: Legal Culture and the Transformation of Inequality in the Post-Revolutionary South*. Chapel Hill: University of North Carolina Press, 2009. [Description: "This study discusses changes in the legal logic of slavery, race, and gender. Drawing on extensive archival research in North and South Carolina, Laura F. Edwards illuminates those changes by revealing the importance of localized legal practice." Contents: All Was Chaos in Our Legal World: Excavating Localized Law from Beneath the Layers of Southern History; Keeping the Peace: People's Proximity to Law; Bread from Chaff: Defining Offenses against the Peace; Possession and the Personality of Property: The Material Basis of Authority; Wasted Substance: The Operation and Regulation of Patriarchy; Subjects vs. Rights-Holding Individuals; New States: Freemen as Consistent Units of Measure.]

Farley, Jennifer. "A Forced Migration." *Tar Heel Junior Historian*, 45:2 (Spring 2006), 15-17. [Online description from "North Carolina Periodicals Index," East Carolina University: "The state adopted its first slave code in 1715. This document defined the social, economic, and physical places of enslaved people. Most of the slaves purchased in the colony came from Virginia and South Carolina, and most lived on large plantations in the eastern section. The largest plantation was Stagville, established in 1787, and located in parts of what is now Orange and three other counties. More than 900 slaves worked on the 30,000-acre plantation."]

Franklin, John Hope. *The Free Negro in North Carolina, 1790-1860.* Chapel Hill: University of North Carolina Press, 1995. [References to 18th century African American women are interspersed throughout the chapters.]

Fraser, Rebecca J. *Courtship and Love among the Enslaved in North Carolina.* Jackson: University Press of Mississippi, 2007. [See Chapter 1: "Love Seems with Them More to be an Eager Desire" Racialized Stereotypes in the Slaveholding South," 22-31, posits that slaveholders fashioned stereotypes regarding the sexuality and fecundity of Black women to justify their treatment of female slaves; offers passages from Thomas Jefferson's *Notes on the State of Virginia*, as being representative of slaveholder views of Black women and their capacity for affection.]

Gaillard, Frye, Richard Maschal, and Ed Williams; epilogue by Vanessa Gallman and Jerry Shinn. *Becoming Truly Free: 300 Years of Black History in the Carolinas.* Charlotte: Charlotte Observer, 1985.

Galle, Jillian E., and Amy L. Young, eds. *Engendering African American Archaeology: A Southern Perspective.* Knoxville: University of Tennessee Press, 2004. [Chapter 6: Patricia Samford, "Engendering Enslaved Communities on Virginia's and North Carolina's Eighteenth-and Nineteenth-Century Plantations," 151-175.]

Gehrke, William Herman. "Negro Slavery among the Germans of North Carolina." *North Carolina Historical Review*, 14:4 (October 1937), 307-324; online: http://digital.ncdcr.gov/cdm/ref/collection/p16062coll9/id/4207. [The article discusses the once very "industrious" Germans in the 18th century who worked all their own labor till the turn of the century when they broke away from tradition and the majority of them became slaveholders.]

Gilbert, Alan. *Black Patriots and Loyalists: Fighting for Emancipation in the War for Independence*. Chicago and London: University of Chicago Press, 2012.

Grundset, Eric G., Briana L. Diaz, Hollis L. Gentry, and Jean D. Strahan. *Forgotten Patriots: African American and American Indian Patriots in the Revolutionary War* (2008). Free online at: http://www.dar.org/library/fp.cfm.

Gutman, Herbert G. *The Black Family in Slavery and Freedom, 1750-1925.* New York: Pantheon Books, 1976. [Description: "Discusses the slaves of Richard Bennehan and the Cameron family of Orange County, N. C."]

Hall, Robert L. "Africa and the American South: Culinary Connections." *Southern Quarterly*, 44:2 (Winter 2007), 19-52.

Haller, Charlotte A. "'And Made Us to Be a Kingdom:' Race, Antislavery, and Black Evangelicals in North Carolina's Early Republic." *North Carolina Historical Review*, 80:2 (April 2003), 125-152.

Haller, Charlotte Ann. "Taking Liberties: Households, Race, and Black Freedom in Revolutionary North Carolina." Ph. D. dissertation, University of Wisconsin, Madison, 2000.

Heinegg, Paul. *Free African Americans of North Carolina, Including the History of More Than 80% of Those Counted as "All Other Free Persons" in the 1790 and 1800 Census.* Abqaiq, Saudi Arabia: P. Heinegg, 1990; 2 vols. 2nd ed. Baltimore: Genealogical Publishing Company, 1994; 3rd ed.: Baltimore: Genealogical Publishing Company, 1997; rev. 4th ed.: Baltimore: Clearfield Company, 2001; 5th ed.: Baltimore: Clearfield Company, 2005. Online at: http://www.freeAfrican americans.com/

Higgins, W. Robert. "The Ambivalence of Freedom: Whites, Blacks, and the Coming of the American Revolution on the South." In W. Robert Higgins, ed., *The Revolutionary War in the South: Power, Conflict, and Leadership; Essays in Honor of John Richard Allen* (Durham: Duke University Press, 1979), 43-64.

Huddle, Mark Andrew. "Quaker Abolitionists: The Large Slaveholders in the State?" *Tar Heel Junior Historian*, 36:1 (Fall 1996), 16-18. [Online description from "North Carolina Periodicals Index," East Carolina University: "Quakers felt the need to free their slaves but were prohibited by a 1741 law that stated only the state could grant freedom. To get around this, Quakers deeded slaves to the Yearly Meeting, which by 1814 had around 800. They were later moved out of state."]

Huggins, Nathan Irvin. *Black Odyssey: The Afro-American Ordeal in Slavery*. New York: Pantheon Books, 1977.

Inscoe, John C. "An Adaptable Institution: Slavery in Western North Carolina." *Tar Heel Junior Historian*, 35:1 (Fall 1995), 8-11. [Online description from "North Carolina Periodicals Index," East Carolina University: "Slavery in the state's mountains differed from that supported by the cash-crop economy of the east. In the west, slave owners were mostly professional men who used the slaves in their businesses or hired them out to others."]

Inscoe, John C. "Mountain Masters: Slaveholding in Western North Carolina." *North Carolina Historical Review*, 61:2 (April 1984), 143-173.

Inscoe, John C. "Carolina Slave Names: An Index to Acculturation." *Journal of Southern History,* 49:4 (November 1983), 527-554.

Kay, Marvin L., and Lorin Lee Cary. "A Demographic Analysis of Colonial North Carolina with Special Emphasis upon the Slave and Black Populations." In Jeffrey J. Crow and Flora J. Hatley, eds., *Black Americans in North Carolina and the South* (Chapel Hill: University of North Carolina Press, 1984), 71-121.

Kay, Marvin L. Michael, and Lorin Lee Cary. "'The Planters Suffer Little or Nothing': North Carolina Compensations for Executed Slaves, 1748-1772." *Science and Society*, 40:3 (1976), 288-306.

Kay, Marvin L. Michael, and Lorin Lee Cary. "Slave Runaways in Colonial North Carolina, 1748-1775." *North Carolina Historical Review*, 63:1 (January 1986), 1-39. [Online description from "North Carolina Periodicals Index," East Carolina University: "This article examines the 30 years prior to the American Revolution for patterns regarding runaway slaves attempts and their success. Historical records indicated several interesting trends including the smaller number of escape attempts when compared to surrounding colonies, the increase in attempts when African-born slaves were involved, and the increased success rate when American-born slaves attempted escape."]

Kay, Marvin L. Michael, and Lorin Lee Cary. *Slavery in North Carolina, 1748-1775.* Chapel Hill: University of North Carolina Press, 1995.

Kay, Marvin L. Michael, and Lorin Lee Cary. "'They Are Indeed the Constant Plague of Their Tyrants': Slave Defence of a Moral Economy in Colonial North Carolina, 1748-1772." *Slavery and Abolition*, 6:3 (1985), 37-56.

Leaming, Hugo Prosper. *Hidden Americans: Maroons of Virginia and the Carolinas.* New York: Garland Publishing, Inc., 1995.

Lofton, John. "Enslavement of the Southern Mind, 1775-1825." *Journal of Negro History*, 43:2 (April 1958), 132-139.

Lucas, Jill Warren. "Foods of Servitude." *Indy Week*, 30:34 (August 2013), 32; online: http://www.indyweek.com/indyweek/chef-michael-twitty-explores-the-culinary-traditions-of-slavesby-jill-warren-lucas/Content?oid=3700562. [Online description from "North Carolina Periodicals Index," East Carolina University: "Historian and chef Michael Twitty has devoted his life's work to exploring the culinary traditions of slaves and how their foodways spread from Southeastern plantations and farms. His work has been recognized by the Smithsonian Institution, Colonial Williamsburg, Monticello, and others."]

Mallinson, Christine, and Becky Childs. "The Intersection of Regional and Ethnic Identity: African American English in Appalachia." *Journal of Appalachian Studies*, 129-142.

Minchinton, Walter E. "The Seaborne Slave Trade of North Carolina." *North Carolina Historical Review*, 71:1 (January 1994), 1-61. [Online description from "North Carolina Periodicals Index," East Carolina University: "This article examines and calculates the number of slaves imported into North Carolina before slave trade restrictions were imposed in the mid-1790s. Overall slave trade in North Carolina was limited in scope as the state was not part of the triangular trade. Specialized slave merchants in the region were rare as the slave trade was incidental to the activities of the vessels engaging in it. Available records indicate the import of 3,236 slaves through sea routes, almost half from the West Indies."]

Mooney, Chase C. *Slavery in Tennessee.* Bloomington, Indiana University Press 1957.

Moore, Louis T. "Servants and Slaves in Colonial Carolina." *The State: A Weekly Survey of North Carolina*, 13:32 (January 1946), 6, 18; online: http://digital.ncdcr.gov/cdm/ref/collection/p16062coll18/id/14908. [Online description from "North Carolina Periodicals Index," East Carolina University: "In addition to Africans, there were also Indian and white slaves, and there were many rules and regulations in force with respect to their treatment."]

Moss, Bobby Gilmer, and Michael Scoggins. *African-American Patriots in the Southern Campaign of the American Revolution*. Blacksburg, S. C.: Scotia-Hibernia Press, 2004. [Description: "Provides biographical and military service information on African-Americans who participated with American forces patriots in the southern campaign of the American Revolution. The coverage area includes Maryland, Virginia, North Carolina, South Carolina, Georgia, and Florida."]

Newton, James E. and Ronald L. Lewis. *The Other Slaves: Mechanics, Artisans, and Craftsmen.* Boston: G. K. Hall, 1978.

North Carolina (State). General Assembly. "[Document dated:] January 27, 1779: Joint Papers, Committee Papers, Resolutions, Senate Bills, House Bills, Report on the Petition of the People of Pasquotank County Relative to the Slaves Liberated by the Quakers (with Messages)." Manuscript; General Assembly Record Group; Session Records, Jan-Feb 1779, Box 1 (MARS ID: 66.8.15.8.6; item), State Archives of North Carolina, Raleigh. [Online catalog description: "The petitioners complain to the Assembly that Quakers are freeing slaves. The committee recommends that a bill be drafted pertaining to slaves, for independence has nullified portions of the relative colonial law."]

Padgett, James A. "The Status of Slaves in Colonial North Carolina." *Journal of Negro History*, 14:3 (July 1929), 300-327.

Parker, Freddie Lee. "Runaway Slaves in North Carolina, 1775-1835." Ph. D. dissertation, University of North Carolina at Chapel Hill, 1987.
Parker, Freddie L. *Running for Freedom: Slave Runaways in North Carolina, 1775-1840.* New York: Garland, 1993.
Parker, Freddie Lee. "Slave Protest in North Carolina – 1775-1835." M. A. thesis, North Carolina Central University, 1976.
Phifer, Edward W., Jr. "Slavery in Microcosm: Burke County, North Carolina." *Journal of Southern History*, 28:2 (May 1962), 137-165.
Philips, Ulrich Bonnell, and Eugene D. Genovese. *The Slave Economy of the Old South: Selected Essays in Economic and Social History.* Baton Rouge: Louisiana State University Press [1968].
Poe, Clarence H. "Indians, Slaves, and Tories: Our 18th Century Legislation Regarding Them." *North Carolina Booklet*, 9 (1909), 3-15.
"Quaker Petition for Manumission of Slaves-1778." Manuscript MS 251, Friends Historical Collection, Hege Library, Guilford College, Greensboro.
Quarles, Benjamin. *The Negro in the American Revolution.* Chapel Hill: University of North Carolina Press for the Institute of Early American History and Culture, 1961.
Schweninger, Loren, ed.; Robert Shelton, asst. ed. *Race, Slavery, and Free Blacks. Series I and II: Petitions to Southern Legislatures, 1777-1867.* Bethesda, Md.: University Publications of America, 1999; 2002-2005; and, Charles E. Smith. *Guide to the Microfilm Edition of Race, Slavery, and Free Blacks.* 2 vols. [Microfilm publication. Description: "Reproduces a collection of nearly 3,000 petitions assembled over a period of ten years by the Race and Slavery Petitions Project, University of North Carolina at Greensboro from state archives in Alabama, Delaware, Florida, Mississippi, Missouri, North Carolina, South Carolina, Tennessee, Texas, and Virginia."]
Sensbach, Jon. *African Americans in Salem: Brother Abraham: An African Moravian in Salem; Peter Oliver: Life of a Black Moravian Craftsman.* Winston-Salem: Old Salem, Inc., [s. d.] [Briefly mentions a few African American women living in Salem during the late eighteenth century.]
Sensbach, Jon F. "Brothers in Bondage: The Moravians Struggle with the Institution of Slavery." *Tar Heel Junior Historian*, 51:2 (Spring 2012), 31-33. [Online description from "North Carolina Periodicals Index," East Carolina University: "The German religious immigrants known as the Moravians, settled in North Carolina in and around what is now the city of Winston-Salem. Although some groups struggled with the institution of slavery, the Moravians took enslaved Africans and baptized them into the church, allowing them to work, live, and worship together in close quarters."]
Sensbach, Jon F. "Interracial Sects: Religion, Race, and Gender among Early North Carolina Moravians." In Catherine Clinton and Michele Gillespie, eds., *The Devil's Lane: Sex and Race in the Early South* (New York and London: Oxford University Press, 1997), 155-167, Part III, Chapter 11.
Sensbach, Jon F. *A Separate Canaan: The Making of an Afro-Moravian World in North Carolina, 1763-1840.* Chapel Hill: University of North Carolina Press for the Omohundro Institute of Early American History and Culture, 1998; based on his "A Separate Canaan: The Making of an Afro-Moravian World in North Carolina, 1763-1856." Ph. D. dissertation, Duke University, 1991.
Sensbach, Jon. "Sister Anna: An African Woman in Early North Carolina." In Michele Gillespie and Sally G. McMillen, eds. *North Carolina Women: Their Lives and Times.* 2 vols. (Athens: University of Georgia Press, 2014), 1: 34-53. 1760?-1829.
Sharpe, Bill. "Notes on Slavery." *The State: Down Home in North Carolina*, 22:19 (February 12, 1955), 8-9, 16; online: http://digital.ncdcr.gov/cdm/compoundobject/collection/p16062coll18/id/81156. [Online description from "North Carolina Periodicals Index," East Carolina University: "Most slaves in North Carolina came second-hand from other states since there was no deep-sea fleet for the state. Regardless, North Carolina accepted the institution of slavery; the author provides a brief history of slavery in the state."]
Sharpe, Bill. "Slave History through Advertisements." *Endeavors*, 10:2 (April 1993), 20-21. [Online description from "North Carolina Periodicals Index," East Carolina University: "Freddie Parker, a history student in the Carolina Minority Postdoctoral Fellowship Program, is attempting to uncover information about the days of slavery by analyzing advertisements for runaway slaves."]
Shriner, Kevin Nelson. "African-Americans in the Militias of Virginia, Georgia, and the Carolinas, 1639-1792." M. A. thesis, University of Arkansas, Fayetteville, 1994.
Silcox-Jarrett, Diane. "Freedom Bound." *Our State: Down Home in North Carolina*, 66:9 (February 1999), 38, 40, 42-43; online: http://digital.ncdcr.gov/cdm/ref/collection/p16062coll18/id/67435. [Online description from "North Carolina Periodicals Index," East Carolina University: "Quakers in the Piedmont originated the first national Underground Railroad in the 1700s. This was a secret network of people and places set up to help

slaves escaping to the North. It was not without danger for the Quakers, for anyone caught helping runaways could be punished."]

Sowle, Patrick. "The North Carolina Manumission Society," *The North Carolina Historical Review*, 42 (1965), 48.

Stanford, Karin L., ed. *If We Must Die: African American Voices on War and Peace.* Lanham, Md.: Rowman & Littlefield Publishers, Inc., 2008.

Surratt, Jo Ann Freeman. "Blacks in the American Revolution." *Eswau Huppeday: Bulletin of the Broad River Genealogical Society*, 14:2 (May 2004), 113.

Taylor, R. H. "Humanizing the Slave Code in North Carolina." *North Carolina Historical Review*, 2:3 (July 1925), 323-331; online: http://digital.ncdcr.gov/cdm/ref/collection/p16062coll9/id/4207. [Online description from "North Carolina Periodicals Index," East Carolina University: "Slavery in North Carolina was not addressed or recognized legally or by a governing body until it was given legal status by the General Assembly in 1715. From that point and continuing throughout the 18th- and 19th-centuries, laws were passed that gradually shaped the treatment and rights of slaves and an examination of these changes and of other efforts to effect changes in the law illustrate the attitudes of the people of North Carolina towards slaves' rights in this period."]

Taylor, R. H. "Slave Conspiracies in North Carolina." *North Carolina Historical Review*, 5:1 (January 1928), 20-34; online: http://digital.ncdcr.gov/cdm/ref/collection/p16062coll9/id/420. [Online description from "North Carolina Periodicals Index," East Carolina University: "The South's white population often lived in a state of fear of slave uprisings, especially where runaway slave communities existed such as the Dismal Swamp. This article presents the historic legislative measures taken by the state's General Assembly to prevent slave violence against whites."]

Waggoner, Martha. "1st Black Joins NC's Sons of American Revolution." *Associated Press; AP Regional State Report: Massachusetts,* February 20, 2012. [Publisher's summary: "Raleigh, N. C. (AP) A chapter of the Sons of the American Revolution in North Carolina is inducting its first black member, a firefighter who only recently learned his ancestor was freed from slavery after fighting for American independence. Thirty-year-old Chaz Moore is a descendant of Toby Gilmore, the son of a chieftain in coastal West Africa who was kidnapped at the age of 16 and sold into slavery in Massachusetts. He gained his freedom by joining the fight for what would become the United States."]

Watson, Alan D. *African American in Early North Carolina: A Documentary History.* Raleigh: Office of archives and History North Carolina Department of Cultural Resources, 2005.

Watson, Alan D. "Impulse toward Independence: Resistance and Rebellion among North Carolina Slaves, 1750-1775." *The Journal of Negro History*, 63:4 (October 1978), 317-328.

Watson, Alan D. "North Carolina Slave Courts, 1715-1785," *North Carolina Historical Review,* 60:1 (January 1983), 24-36. [Online description from "North Carolina Periodicals Index," East Carolina University: "A look at the origins and functionality of the slave courts in North Carolina between 1715 and 1785, an institution that reflected the desired slave behaviors as set by white slave owners, provides evidence of white society's fears of a disobedient slave population, and reveals the fears of the slaves themselves. Like in other British colonies, these courts were created to handle slave criminality beyond the scope of ordinary police regulations. They were designed to assure slaves a judicial hearing, to curtail the cost of a regular trial, and to expedite justice and reduce the loss of slave labor time."]

Wheaton, Thomas R. "Colonial African American Plantation Villages." In J. W. Joseph and Martha Zierden, eds., *Another's Country: Archaeological and Historical Perspectives on Cultural Interaction in the Southern Colonies* (Tuscaloosa: University of Alabama Press, 2002), 30-44.

Wiecek, William M. "The Statutory Law of Slavery and Race in the Thirteen Mainland Colonies of British America." *William and Mary Quarterly*, 3rd series, 34:2 (April 1977), 258-280.

Wiggins, David K. "Sports and Recreation in the Slave Community." *Tar Heel Junior Historian*, 34:1 (Fall 1994), 6-8. [Online description from "North Carolina Periodicals Index," East Carolina University: "Such recreational activities as marbles, cards, dancing, swimming, and fishing enabled slaves in North Carolina to mitigate the difficulties and harshness of their lives in ways that were neither violent nor competitive."]

Williams, Robert. *Clear Views in 1782, Concerning the Effects of Slavery, Expressed by Robert Willliams, of Carteret County, North Carolina.* Cincinnati, Wrightson & Co., 1867.

Wood, Peter H. "'The Dream Deferred:' Black Freedom Struggles on the Eve of White Independence." In Gary Y. Okihiro, ed., *In Resistance: Studies in African, Caribbean, and Afro-American History* (Amherst: University of Massachusetts Press, 1986), 167-187.

Wood, Peter H. "Impatient of Oppression: Black Freedom Struggles on the Eve of White Independence." *Southern Exposure*, 12 (November/December 1984), 10-16.

Woodson, Carter G. "Freedom and Slavery in Appalachian America." *Journal of Negro History*, 1:2 (April 1916), 132-150.

American Indians of North Carolina and Tennessee

Ashe, Samuel A'Court. "Rutherford's Expedition against the Indians, 1776." *North Carolina Booklet*, 4:8 (December 1904), 3-28; online: http://digital.ncdcr.gov/cdm/ref/collection/p249901coll37/id/14180. [Online description from "North Carolina Periodicals Index," East Carolina University: "This article details General Rutherford's 1776 expedition into western North Carolina to combat hostile Indian forces, led by the Cherokee Indian tribe."]

Ashe, Samuel A'Court. *Rutherford's Expedition against the Indians, 1776, by Captain S. A. Ashe*. Raleigh: E. M. Uzzell & Co., 1904.

Boyce, Douglas W. "Iroquoian Tribes of the Virginia-North Carolina Coastal Plain." In Bruce G. Trigger, vol. ed. *Handbook o f North American Indians, Volume 15: Northeast* (Washington, D. C.: Smithsonian Institution, 1978), 282-289.

Byrd, William L. *For So Long as the Sun and Moon Endure: Indian Records from the North Carolina General Assembly Sessions and Other Sources*. Westminster, Md.: Heritage Books, 2006.

Claggett, Stephen. "First Immigrants: Native American Settlement of North Carolina." *Tar Heel Junior Historian*, 34:2 (Spring 1995), 3-7. [Online description from "North Carolina Periodicals Index," East Carolina University: "Before English colonists arrived, Native Americans had lived in the state 12,000 years. Thirty tribes totaling 100,000 occupied the state in the late 1500s, but colonial wars and diseases rapidly decreased that number to 20,000 in 1800."]

Coe, Joffre L. "The Indian in North Carolina." *North Carolina Historical Review*, 56:2 (April 1979), 158-161.

Crane, David. "Colonial Identifications for Native Americans in the Carolinas, 1540-1790." M. A. thesis, University of North Carolina Wilmington, 2006.

Day, Jean. *Carolina Indians*. Newport: Golden Age Press, 1998.

De Vorsey, Louis, Jr. *The Indian Boundary in the Southern Colonies, 1763-1775*. Chapel Hill: University of North Carolina Press, 1961.

Dennis, Jeff W. "Native Americans and the Southern Revolution." *Southern Campaigns of the American Revolution*, 3:6-7-8 (June-July-August 2006), 27-31; online: http://southerncampaign.org/newsletter/v3n678.pdf; "Part II: Independence and the 1776 Cherokee War" 4:3 (July-August-September 2007), 21-27; online: http://southern campaign.org/newsletter/v4n789.pdf.

Dillard, Richard. "The Indian Tribes of Eastern North Carolina." *North Carolina Booklet*, 6:1 (July 1906), 4-26; online: http://digital.ncdcr.gov/cdm/ref/collection/p249901coll37/id/14180. [Online description from "North Carolina Periodicals Index," East Carolina University: "This article examines the various Indian tribes of Eastern North Carolina and their interactions with each other and early English colonists. The article also provides additional information regarding the Tuscarora War and how the Indian tribes were affected by its outcome."]

Ellis, Clyde. "First North Carolinians." *Our State: Down Home in North Carolina*, 68:6 (November 2000), 50-53; online: http://digital.ncdcr.gov/cdm/ref/collection/p16062coll18/id/72174. [Online description from "North Carolina Periodicals Index," East Carolina University: "Besides the Eastern Cherokees, who are a federally recognized tribe living in North Carolina, the state also recognizes six other tribes. They are the Coharie, Haliwa-Saponi, Lumbees, Waccamaw-Siouan, Meherrin, and Indians of Person County. Currently six other groups are seeking recognition as Indian tribes."]

Feest, Christian F. "North Carolina Algonquians." In Bruce G. Trigger, vol. ed. *Handbook of North American Indians, Volume 15: Northeast* (Washington, D. C.: Smithsonian Institution, 1978), 271-281.

Finger, John R. "Tennessee Indian History: Creativity and Power." *Tennessee Historical Quarterly*, 54:4 (Winter 1995), 286-305.

Fundaburk, Emma Lila. *Southeastern Indians, Life Portraits: A Catalogue of Pictures, 1764-1860*. Tuscaloosa: University of Alabama Press, 2000.

Grundset, Eric G., Briana L. Diaz, Hollis L. Gentry, and Jean D. Strahan. *Forgotten Patriots: African American and American Indian Patriots in the Revolutionary War* (2008). Free online at: http://www.dar.org/library/fp.cfm.

Haas, Mary R. "Southeastern Indian Folklore." *Journal of American Folkore*, 60:238 (October-December 1947), 403-406.

Haithcock, Richard L. *Indian Surnames of the Piedmont, Smokies, Blue Ridge, Coastal Plains, and the Ohio Valley*. Beavercreek, Ohio: Red-Trail Publications, 2009.

Hamar, Philip M. "John Stuart's Indian Policy during the Early Months of the Revolution." *Mississippi Valley Historical Review*, 17 (1930), 351-366.

Henley, David, 1749-1823. "Papers, 1791-1800." Manuscript RUB Bay 0034:04 items 1-50, David M. Rubenstein Rare Book & Manuscript Library, Duke University, Durham. [Online catalog description: "Continental Army officer; commissioner of Indian Affairs in Tennessee; and clerk in the War Dept., Washington, D. C. Correspondence and papers dealing with treaties, agreements, and relations between the whites and the Choctaw and Creek Indians, including the exchange of prisoners, reparations for murders, inroads by whites and Indians, and compensation for stolen horses; establishment of post roads from Tennessee to the South Carolina border and to Natchez, Miss.; establishment of a trading post at Muscle Shoals, Ala.; and the establishment of the Indian Treaty Line from the Kentucky Trace to the Gaps of the Cumberland and along Campbell's line to the Clinch River, and the difficulties of the commissioners in deciding on this line. Among the correspondents are William Blount, Benjamin Hawkins, William McCleish, James McHenry, Samuel Mitchell, and James Robertson."]

Higginbotham, Don, and William S. Price, Jr. "Notes and Documents: Was It Murder for a White Man to Kill a Slave? Chief Justice Martin Howard Condemns the Peculiar Institution in North Carolina." *William and Mary Quarterly*, 3rd series, 36:4 (October 1979), 593-601. [1771]

Holton, Woody. *Black Americans in the Revolutionary Era: A Brief History with Documents*. Boston: Bedford/St. Martin's, 2009. [Publisher's description: "In this fresh look at liberty and freedom in the Revolutionary era from the perspective of black Americans, Woody Holton recounts the experiences of slaves who seized freedom by joining the British as well as those – slave and free – who served in Patriot military forces. Holton's introduction examines the conditions of black American life on the eve of colonial independence and the ways in which Revolutionary rhetoric about liberty provided African Americans with the language and inspiration for advancing their cause. Despite the rhetoric, however, most black Americans remained enslaved after the Revolution. The introduction outlines ways African Americans influenced the course of the Revolution and continued to be affected by its aftermath. Amplifying these themes are nearly forty documents – including personal narratives, petitions, letters, poems, advertisements, pension applications, and images – that testify to the diverse goals and actions of African Americans during the Revolutionary era. Document headnotes and annotations, a chronology, questions for consideration, a selected bibliography, and index offer additional pedagogical support."]

Hudson, Charles M. *Four Centuries of Southern Indians*. Athens: University of Georgia Press, 1975.

Hudson, Charles M. *The Southeastern Indians*. Knoxville: University of Tennessee Press, 1976.

Jacobs, Janet Y. "Indians in North Carolina." *Tar Heel Junior Historian*, 19:2 (Winter 1980), 18-21. [Online description from "North Carolina Periodicals Index," East Carolina University: "By 1980, the state was home to the nation's fifth largest Native American population and the greatest east of the Mississippi. Five tribes made up the state's total population of approximately 50,000 Native Americans and included; Eastern Band of Cherokees, Lumbee, Coharie, Haliwa, and the Waccamaw-Siouan."]

Jacobs, Wilbur R. *Indians of the Southern Colonial Frontier: The Edmond Atkin Report and Plan of 1775*. Columbia: University of South Carolina Press, 1954.

Lee, Lawrence E. *Indians Wars in North Carolina, 1663-1763*. Raleigh: Division of Archives and History, 1997.

LeMaster, Michelle. "In the 'Scolding Houses:' Indians and the Law in Eastern North Carolina, 1684-1760." *North Carolina Historical Review*, 83:2 (April 2006), 193-232.

McNally, Michael D. "The Practice of Native American Christianity." *Church History*, 69:4 (2000), 834-859.

Milling, Chapman J. *Red Carolinians*. Columbia: University of South Carolina Press, 1969.

Norris, Jeannie Faris. "The Indians of Person County." *The State: A Weekly Survey of North Carolina*, 16:37 (February 1949), 3-4, 20; online: http://digital.ncdcr.gov/cdm/ref/collection/p16062coll18/id/23490. [Online description from "North Carolina Periodicals Index," East Carolina University: "The article describes Person County Native Americans and their activities including church and school attendance."]

North Carolina Commission of Indian Affairs. "A Historical Perspective about the Indians of North Carolina and an Overview of the Commission of Indian Affairs." *North Carolina Historical Review*, 56:2 (April 1979), 162-176.

North Carolina (Colony and State). Office of State Treasurer. "Indian Affairs and Lands, 1712, 1739-1957)." Manuscript Box 1-Box 17 (MARS ID: 13.21; series), State Archives of North Carolina, Raleigh. [Online catalog description: "An artificial and diverse collection of accounts, certificates, warrants, survey plats, reports, receipt books, depositions, court papers, deeds, and correspondence relating to the Cherokee and Tuscarora Indians, 1739-1900, 1911, 1923, 1956-1957. For the former, most of the records are of the antebellum period and concern lands sold and leased by the state and by the Cherokee, and also the 'life reservations' created for them by the state. Public claims and payrolls (1759-1760, 1771, 1791) concern expeditions against the Cherokee. Other records concern treaties, and the furnishing of provisions and supplies. Miscellaneous items include copies of Col. George Washington's orders for escorting Cherokees from Virginia to the Nation; a typed copy of a journal of a visit to the Cherokee by Thomas Griffin, 1767; an 1846 history of the *Cherokee in North Carolina since 1809*; a census of the Eastern Cherokee in 1923; and photographs of the Qualla Reservation. Records relating to the Tuscarora mainly concern leases and sales of land in Bertie County. Most of them date from the antebellum period, but there is also a Tuscarora petition (1956-1957) before the Indian Claims Commission for rights to lands in North Carolina. There is also a copy of a treaty of 1712. Other material concerns the service of Tuscaroras in the French and Indian War, and supplies furnished them by the state."]

North Carolina (State). General Assembly. "[Document dated:] August 13, 1778: Report on Indian Affairs (Message Only)." Manuscript; General Assembly Session Records; Session of August 1778; Joint Papers, Committee Papers, Resolutions, Senate Bills, House Bills, Box 1 (MARS ID: 66.8.14.7.2; item), State Archives of North Carolina, Raleigh.

North Carolina (State). General Assembly. "[Document dated:] January 29, 1779: Resolution Re[specting] James Robertson, Superintendent of Indian Affairs (Messages Only)." Manuscript; General Assembly Session Records; Session of January-February 1779; Joint Papers, Committee Papers, Resolutions; Senate Joint Resolutions: January 21-February 13, 1779, Box 1 (MARS ID: 66.8.15.10.11; item), State Archives of North Carolina, Raleigh.

North Carolina (State). General Assembly. "[Document dated:] January 25, 1779: Resolution Appointing Ellis Harling Superintendent of Indian Affairs (with Message)." Manuscript; General Assembly Session Records; Session of January-February 1779; Joint Papers, Committee Papers, Resolutions; House Joint Resolutions: January 19-February 4, 1779, Box 1 (MARS ID: 66.8.15.11.11; item), State Archives of North Carolina, Raleigh.

North Carolina (State). General Assembly. "[Document dated:] January 29, 1779: Resolution Appointing Ellis Harling Superintendent of Indian Affairs (with Message)." Manuscript; General Assembly Session Records; Session of January-February 1779; Joint Papers, Committee Papers, Resolutions; Senate Joint Resolutions: January 21-February 13, 1779, Box 1 (MARS ID: 66.8.15.10.12; item), State Archives of North Carolina, Raleigh. [Online catalog description: "The resolution appoints Harling Superintendent and requests that the Governor answer the Raven of Chota."]

North Carolina (State). General Assembly. "[Document dated:] May 2, 1780: Resolution Requesting Governor to Require Persons Settled in Indian Lands to Move Off (Message Only)." Manuscript; General Assembly Session Records; Session of April-May 1780; Joint Papers, Committee Papers, Resolutions; House Joint Resolutions: May 2-10, 1780, Box 1 (MARS ID: 66.8.20.17.1; item), State Archives of North Carolina, Raleigh.

North Carolina (State). General Assembly. "[Document dated:] May 5, 1780: Resolution Concerning Letters about Indian Affairs (with Messages and Committee Report)." Manuscript; General Assembly Session Records; Session of April-May 1780; Joint Papers, Committee Papers, Resolutions; Senate Joint Resolutions: May 5-10, 1780, Box 1 (MARS ID: 66.8.20.14.1; item), State Archives of North Carolina, Raleigh. [Online catalog description: "Contains the appointments to the committee to which the letters were referred; the committee report, which discusses the situation and recommends the raising of more troops to aid South Carolina and to guard the west; and messages alluding to a resolution regarding the committee report."]

North Carolina (State). General Assembly. "[Document dated:] May 2, 1780: Resolution Requesting Governor to Require Persons Settled in Indian Lands to Move Off (Message Only)." Manuscript; General Assembly Session Records; Session of April-May 1780; Joint Papers, Committee Papers, Resolutions; House Joint Resolutions: May 2-10, 1780, Box 1 (MARS ID: 66.8.20.17.1; item), State Archives of North Carolina, Raleigh.

North Carolina (State). General Assembly. "[Document dated:] August 18, 1778: Bill to Prevent Trading with the Cherokee Indians without License." Manuscript; General Assembly Session Records; Session of August 1778; Joint Papers, Committee Papers, Resolutions, Senate Bills, House Bills, Box 1 (MARS ID: 66.8.14,18; folder), State Archives of North Carolina, Raleigh.

O'Donnell, James H., III. *Southern Indians in the American Revolution*. Knoxville: University of Tennessee Press, 1972.

O'Donnell, James H. "Southern Indians in the War for American Independence, 1775-1783." In Charles M. Hudson, ed., *Four Centuries of Southern Indians* (Athens: University of Georgia Press, 1975), 46-64.

O'Donnell, James Howlett. "The Southern Indians in the War of Independence, 1775-1783." Ph. D Thesis, Duke University, 1963. [Cherokees, Chickasaws, Choctaws, Creeks]

O'Donnell, James H. " The South on the Eve of the Revolution: The Native Americans." In W. Robert Higgins, ed., *The Revolutionary War in the South: Power, Conflict, and Leadership; Essays in Honor of John Richard Allen* (Durham: Duke University Press, 1979), 64-78.

Perdue, Theda. *"Mixed Blood" Indians; Racial Construction of the Early South.* Athens: University of Georgia Press, 2003.

Perdue, Theda. *Native Carolinians: The Indians of North Carolina.* Raleigh: Division of Archives and Hitory, North Carolina Department of Cultural Resources, 1985.

Phelps, David S. "The Carolina Algonquians: Archaeology and History." *Tar Heel Junior Historian*, 24:2 (Winter 1985), 16-19. [Online description from "North Carolina Periodicals Index," East Carolina University: "The state's Algonquian population stretched along the tidewater zone and especially along the Neuse River. The tribe was an agricultural based society and lived a sedentary life with a complex social structure. English colonization decimated the Algonquian population and what remains are historic accounts and archaeological data."]

Poe, Clarence H. "Indians, Slaves, and Tories: Our 18th Century Legislation Regarding Them." *North Carolina Booklet*, 9 (1909), 3-15. [Online description from "North Carolina Periodicals Index," East Carolina University: "North Carolina has the largest American Indian population east of the Mississippi River. The 2000 U.S. Census counts 99,551 individuals who listed as American Indians. The state recognizes eight tribes: Eastern Band of the Cherokee; Coharie; Lumbee; Haliwa-Saponi; Sappony; Meherrin; Occaneechi Band of Saponi Nation; and Waccamaw-Siouan. The federal government officially recognizes one tribe – the Cherokee."]

Rand, James H. *The North Carolina Indians and Their Relations with the Settlers.* Chapel Hill: University of North Carolina Press, 1913.

Ray, Jonathan. "Andrew Jackson and the Indians, 1767-1815." Ph. D. dissertation, University of Alabama, 2014.

Richardson, Gregory A. "NC Commission of Indian Affairs." *Tar Heel Junior Historian*, 45:1 (Fall 2005), ; online: http://ncpedia.org/government/nc-commission-indian.

Richardson, Gregory A. "The State and Its Tribes." *Tar Heel Junior Historian*, 45:1 (Fall 2005), 22-24; online with the title "American Indian Tribes in North Carolina: http://ncpedia.org/tribes. [Online description: "North Carolina has the largest American Indian population east of the Mississippi River and the eighth-largest Indian population in the United States. As noted by the 2000 U.S. Census, 99,551 American Indians lived in North Carolina, making up 1.24 percent of the population. This total is for people identifying themselves as American Indian alone. The number is more than 130,000 when including American Indian in combination with other races."]

Rights, Douglas. "Indians of Cabarrus County." *The State: A Weekly Survey of North Carolina*, 19:27 (December 1951), 16-17; online: http://digital.ncdcr.gov/cdm/ref/collection/p16062coll18/id/27853. [Online description from "North Carolina Periodicals Index," East Carolina University: "Before the first settlers arrived in colonial days to find a home in what is now Cabarrus County, Siouan Indians claimed the land."]

Rights, Douglas L. "Traces of the Indians in Piedmont North Carolina." *North Carolina Historical Review*, 1:3 (July 1924), 277-288. [Online description from "North Carolina Periodicals Index," East Carolina University: "Rev. Rights attempts to reconstruct the state's Native American history through sparse historical records. Specifically, the article records tribes' history within the Piedmont region in Orange, Chatham, Wilkes, Cabarrus counties. He studies material culture to better understand the Native American population that once inhabited the Piedmont."]

Rights, Douglas LeTell. *The American Indian in North Carolina.* Durham: Duke University Press, 1947; reprinted: Winston-Salem: John F. Blair, 1957.

Ross, Thomas E. *American Indians in North Carolina: Geographic Interpretations.* Southern Pines: Karo Hollow Press, 1999.

Ross, Thomas E.; Wesley D. Taukchiray; and Nathan Phillipi. "Map Errors and Indians of the Carolinas." *North Carolina Geographer*, 17 (2009), 54-59.

Rutherford, Griffith, 1721-1805. "Griffith Rutherford Letter, 1776." Manuscript 2188-z, Southern Historical Collection, Louis Round Wilson Special Collections Library, University of North Carolina, Chapel Hill; online finding aid available at http://www2.lib.unc.edu/mss/inv/r/Rutherford,Griffith.html. [Online finding aid description: "Griffith Rutherford (1721-1805) was a colonial and Revolutionary official, military officer, and land speculator. He was born in Ireland, but by the early 1750s, had settled in Rowan County, N. C. The collection is a letter, 18 November 1776, to Brigadier General Griffith Rutherford from Captain William Moore concerning an expedition against Indians in western North Carolina."]

Samford, Patricia M. "Discovering What Native North Carolinians Ate." *Tar Heel Junior Historian*, (Spring 2007); online with the title "American Indian Food:" http://ncpedia.org/culture/food/american-indian-food.

Satz, Ronald N. *Tennessee's Indian Peoples: From White Contact to Removal, 1540-1840.* Knoxville: University of Tennessee Press, 1979.

Shaw, Helen Louise. "British Administration of the Southern Indians, 1756-1783." Ph. D. dissertation, Bryn Mawr College, 1931; published: Lancaster, Pa.: Lancaster Press, 1931.

Shrader, Richard A. "Joseph Martin, Indian Agent, 1777-1789." M. A. thesis, University of North Carolina at Chapel Hill, 1973.

South, Stanley A. *Indians in North Carolina.* Raleigh: North Carolina Department of Cultural Resources, Division of Archives and History, 1959.

Spivey, Michael. *Native Americans in the Carolina Borderlands: A Critical Ethnography.* Southern Pines: Carolinas Press, 2000.

Stevenson, George, Jr. "Indian Reservations in North Carolina." *Carolina Comments,* 57:1 (January 2009), 26-31; online: http://www.ncpublications.com/comments/Jan09.pdf. [Online description from "North Carolina Periodicals Index," East Carolina University: "In North Carolina, Native Americans were considered occupants of the land, not owners, but they were allowed to hold their lands more securely by defensible fee simple estate rather than by sufferance. The state has had seven such tracts, all but one held by Native Americans in fee simple. Stevenson describes each tract and the tribe that held it."]

Stotik, Jeffrey Phillips. "Incorporation and Resistance: The Native Southeast and the World Economy, 1670s-1830s." Ph. D. dissertation, 1994.

Taukchiray, Wes. "Wes Taukchiray Collection." Manuscript, Special Collections and Archives, Mary Livermore Library, University of North Carolina Pembroke, Pembroke. [This collection is the result of the compilers research on Native Americans in the United States with significant focus on those in North Carolina including the Catawba."]

Tenney, Brooks. "From Hatteras to Hiawassee." *Wildlife in North Carolina*, 57:12 (December 1993), 24-27. [Online description from "North Carolina Periodicals Index," East Carolina University: "All across North Carolina, native Americans have left a permanent legacy in the names of many towns, rivers, and other places."]

Vaughan, Alden T., and Deborah A. Rosen, eds., *Early American Indian Documents: Treaties and Laws, 1607-1789: Volume XVI: Carolina and Georgia Laws.* Bethesda, Md.; University Publications of America, 1998.

Ward, H. Trawick, and R. P. Stephen Davis, Jr. *Time before History: The Archaeology of North Carolina.* Chapel Hill: University of North Carolina Press, 1999. [Publisher's description: "North Carolina's written history begins in the sixteenth century with the voyages of Sir Walter Raleigh and the founding of the ill-fated Lost Colony on Roanoke Island. But there is a deeper, unwritten past that predates the state's recorded history. The region we now know as North Carolina was settled more than 10,000 years ago, but because early inhabitants left no written record, their story must be painstakingly reconstructed from the fragmentary and fragile archaeological record they left behind. *Time before History* is the first comprehensive account of the archaeology of North Carolina. Weaving together a wealth of information gleaned from archaeological excavations and surveys carried out across the state – from the mountains to the coast--it presents a fascinating, readable narrative of the state's native past across a vast sweep of time, from the Paleo-Indian period, when the first immigrants to North America crossed a land bridge that spanned the Bering Strait, through the arrival of European traders and settlers in the sixteenth and seventeenth centuries."]

Well, Warner. "Indian Medicine in North Carolina." *The State: Down Home in North Carolina*, 25:21 (March 22, 1958), 11-12, 20; online: http://digital.ncdcr.gov/cdm/ref/collection/p16062coll18/id/50973. [Online description from "North Carolina Periodicals Index," East Carolina University: "Utilizing empiricism as well as methods passed down from previous generations of Native American 'doctors,' used a variety of techniques to cure illnesses. Sweathouses (bagnios), flagellation with rattlesnake teeth, moxabustion, inunctions with bear grease, deer tendons as sutures, use of ground up shells, and ingesting local plant life, are a few methods."]

Winston, Sanford. "Indian Slavery in the Carolina Region." *Journal of Negro History*, 19:4 (October 1934), 431-440.

Wetmore, Ruth Y. *First on the Land: The North Carolina Indians*. Winston-Salem: J. F. Blair, 1975.

Wetmore, Ruth Y. "The Role of Indians in North Carolina History." *North Carolina Historical Review*, 56:2 (April 1979), 158-161. [Online description from "North Carolina Periodicals Index," East Carolina University: "This article examines the ways in which Native Americans have directly shaped North Carolina history focusing on four distinct roles that they have played: Native Americans as independent nations, as defeated adversaries, as invisible men, and as emerging communities."]

Ziegler, Wilbur, and Ben S. Grosscup. "Our First Mountaineers." *The State: Down Home in North Carolina*, 23:25 (May 5, 1956), 19-20; online: http://digital.ncdcr.gov/cdm/ref/collection/p16062coll18/id/7031. [Online description from "North Carolina Periodicals Index," East Carolina University: "This article is taken from the 1881 travel book. This excerpt details the background of the Alleghany Mountains from the view of the Indian population."]

American Indians of North Carolina and Tennessee – Catawba

Andrews, N. J. "Cherokees and Catawbas." *The State: A Weekly Survey of North Carolina*, 6:44 (April 1939), 9, 20; online: http://digital.ncdcr.gov/cdm/ref/collection/p16062coll18/id/34727. [Online description from "North Carolina Periodicals Index," East Carolina University: "A distinct difference between the Cherokee and Catawba tribes was their treatment of European settlers. The Cherokees rebelled and fought against encroachment while the Catawba embraced and aided the newcomers. However, allegiance did not save the Catawba tribe. In 1939, their reservation near Rock Hill, South Carolina consisted of 652 acres and a $9,000 state allotment to cover education, health care, and a small stipend to those who lived on the reservation."]

Battle, Kemp Plummer. "The Catawba and Yadkin and Their Associations." *University Magazine,* old series, 18; new series 5:6 (April 1886), 219-222.

Brown, Douglas Summers. *The Catawba Indians: The People of the River*. Columbia: University of South Carolina Press, 1966.

Byrd, William L. *Villainy Often Goes Unpunished: Indian Records from the North Carolina General Assembly Sessions, 1675-1789.* Bowie, Md.: Heritage Books, 2002.

Calloway, Colin G. *The American Revolution in Indian Country: Crisis and Diversity in Native American Communities*. Cambridge: Cambridge University Press, 1995.

Davis, R. P. Stephen, Jr., and Brett H. Riggs. "An Introduction to the Catawba Project." *North Carolina Archaeology*, 53 (October 2004), 1-41; online: http://www.rla.unc.edu/Publications/NCArch/NCA_53.pdf. [Online description from "North Carolina Periodicals Index," East Carolina University: "In 2001, the UNC Research Laboratories of Archaeology began the Catawba Project, an extension of the 20-year Siouan Project that seeks to trace the evolution of native societies of the Carolina Piedmont through the 18th and early 19th centuries. Documentary and archaeological research have exposed a series of settlements now known to have given rise to the modern Catawba Nation."]

Fitts, Mary Elizabeth. "Mapping Catawba Coalecence." *North Carolina Archaeology*, 55 (2006), 1-59; online: http://www.rla.unc.edu/Publications/NCArch/NCA_55%28e-book%29.pdf.

Freeze, Gary R. *The Catawbans: Crafters of a North Carolina County, 1747-1900.* Newton: Catawba County Historical Association, 1995.

Haithcock, Richard L. *The Catawba Confederacy: Tutelo, Saponi, Nahyssan and Monacan Tribal History.* Beavercreek, Ohio: R. L. Haithcock, 2009.

Haithcock, Richard L. *The Mosopelea Ofo Ganatchi and Occaneechi: The Ohio River Valley Sioux and the Siouan Monacan, Mannahoac and the Siouan Piedmont Catawba of Virginia, Carolina Piedmont.* [Beavercreek, Ohio]: R. L. Haithcock, 1999.

Haithcock, Richard L. *Tutelo, Saponi, Nahyssan, Monacan aka Piedmont Catawba Diaspora.* 6 vols. [Beavercreek, Ohio]: R. L. Haithcock, 2006-2007.

Haithcock, Richard L., and Vicki L. Haithcock. *Occaneechie Saponi and Tutelo of the Saponi Nation, aka Piedmont Catawba: Southeastern Indian Refugees from Virginia, the Carolinas, and Tennessee in Ohio, Indiana and Michigan.* 3 vols. [Beavercreek, Ohio]: R. L. Haithcock, 1996.

Harrington, M. R. "Catawba Potters and Their Work." *North Carolina Archaeology*, 55 (2006), 89-102; online: http://www.rla.unc.edu/Publications/NCArch/NCA_55%28e-book%29.pdf.

Heath, Charles L. "Catawba Militarism: An Ethnohistorical and Archaeological Overview." *North Carolina Archaeology*, 53 (October 2004), 80-121.

Hudson, Charles M. *The Catawba Nation* (University of Georgia Monographs, vol. 18). Athens: University of Georgia Press, 1970.

McReynolds, Theresa E. "Catawba Population Dynamics during the Eighteenth and Nineteenth Centuries." *North Carolina Archaeoogy*, 53 (October 2004), 42-59; online: http://www.rla.unc.edu/Publications/NCArch/NCA_53.pdf.

Merrell, James H. *The Indians' New World: Catawbas and Their Neighbors from Contact through the Age of Removal*. New York: W. W. Norton, 1989.

Misenheimer, John E., Jr. "Catawba Indian Patriots in the American Revolution." *Olde Mecklenburg Genealogical Society Quarterly*, 24:4 (2006), 3-9.

Norris, Jeannie Faris. "A Nation Liquidates." *The State: Down Home in North Carolina*, 28:21 (March 18, 1961), 12; online: http://digital.ncdcr.gov/cdm/ref/collection/p16062coll18/id/8160. [Online description from "North Carolina Periodicals Index," East Carolina University: "Amassing a population of nearly 5,000 members by the turn of the 18th-century, the Catawba Native Americans, named for the river region they inhabited, have disbanded. The tribal reservation, valued at nearly $250,000 will be sold and the proceeds divided amongst the remaining 650 Catawba."]

Plaine, Mark R. "Catawba Ethnicity: Identity and Adaptation on the English Colonial Landscape." *North Carolina Archaeology*, 53 (October 2004), 41-59; online: http://www.rla.unc.edu/Publications/NCArch/NCA_53.pdf.

Rudes, Blair A., Thomas J. Blumer, and J. Alan May. "Catawba and Neighboring Groups." In Raymond D. Fogelson, vol. ed. *Handbook of North American Indians, Volume 14: Southeast* (Washington, D. C.: Smithsonian Institution, 2004), 301-318.

Speck, Frank G. "The Catawba Nation and Its Neighbors." *North Carolina Historical Review*, 16:4 (October 1939), 404-417; online: http://digital.ncdcr.gov/cdm/ref/collection/p16062coll9/id/4207. [Online description from "North Carolina Periodicals Index," East Carolina University: "This article presents data pertaining to the name identity of the Catawba tribe and neighboring groups which was collected from the few remaining speakers of the language during the last days of the tribe's cultural life."]

American Indians of North Carolina and Tennessee – Cherokee

[Note: A large literature exists on the history of the Cherokees. The entries that follow focus mostly on records and events in modern North Carolina and Tennessee during the period of the American Revolution. They are a significant sampling but are by no means a complete list.]

Abram, Susan. "'Souls in the Treetops': Cherokee War, Masculinity, and Community, 1760-1820." Ph. D. dissertation, Auburn University, 2009.

Alden, John R. "The Eighteenth Century Cherokee Archives." *American Archivist*, 5 (1942), 240-244.

Allhands, William A. "Some Noted Cherokees." *The State: A Weekly Survey of North Carolina*, 13:33 (January 1946), 11, 30; online: http://digital.ncdcr.gov/cdm/ref/collection/p16062coll18/id/14945. [Online description from "North Carolina Periodicals Index," East Carolina University: "Among the Cherokees whose memory is still being kept alive are Chuttahsotee, Yonaguska, Cornsilk, and Junaluska. Each was a great leader among their people."]

Anderson, William L., and James A. Lewis. *A Guide to Cherokee Documents in Foreign Archives.* Metuchen, N. J. and London: Scarecrow Press, 1983.

Anderson, William L., and Ruth Y. Wetmore. "Cherokee Indians." In William S. Powell, ed.; Jay Mazzocchi, assoc. ed., *Encyclopedia of North Carolina* (Chapel Hill: University of North Carolina Press in association with the University of North Carolina Library, 2006), 207-212. [Includes: "The Revolutionary War, Cherokee Defeat, and Additional Land Cessions," 209-210.]

Andrews, N. J. "Cherokees and Catawbas." *The State: A Weekly Survey of North Carolina*, 6:44 (April 1939), 9, 20; online: http://digital.ncdcr.gov/cdm/ref/collection/p16062coll18/id/34727. [Online description from "North Carolina Periodicals Index," East Carolina University: "A distinct difference between the Cherokee and Catawba tribes was their treatment of European settlers. The Cherokees rebelled and fought against encroachment while the Catawba embraced and aided the newcomers. However, allegiance did not save the Catawba tribe. In 1939, their reservation near Rock Hill, South Carolina consisted of 652 acres and a $9,000 state allotment to cover education, health care, and a small stipend to those who lived on the reservation."]

Ashe, Samuel A'Court. "Rutherford's Expedition against the Indians, 1776." *North Carolina Booklet*, 4:8 (December 1904), 3-28; online: http://digital.ncdcr.gov/cdm/ref/collection/p249901coll37/id/14180. [Online description from "North Carolina Periodicals Index," East Carolina University: "This article details General Rutherford's 1776 expedition into western North Carolina to combat hostile Indian forces, led by the Cherokee Indian tribe."]

Bartram, William. "Bartram's Travels VI." *The State: Down Home in North Carolina*, 27:13 (November 28, 1959), 10, 16; online: http://digital.ncdcr.gov/cdm/ref/collection/p16062coll18/id/37151. [Online description from "North Carolina Periodicals Index," East Carolina University: "The visit of William Bartram in 1776 to western North Carolina was recorded in his book, Travels. In the sixth installment of his diary offered by The State, Bartram discusses his encounter with Little Carpenter, emperor or grand chief of the Cherokees."]

Blackmon, Richard D. *Dark and Bloody Ground: The American Revolution along the Southern Frontier.* Yardley, Pa.: Westholme Publishing, 2012. [Publisher's description: "The Battles along the Rivers, Mountains, and in the Deep Woods of the South that Changed the Fate of Nations. The American Revolution marked a dramatic change in the struggle for land along the southern frontier. In the colonial era, American Indian leaders and British officials attempted to accommodate the westward expansion of Anglo-Americans through land cessions designed to have the least impact on Indian societies. The region remained generally peaceful, but with the onset of the Revolution, the British no longer exercised sole authority to curb the settlements appearing within territory claimed by the Creeks, Shawnee, and most importantly, the Cherokee. Whether it was to escape the economic uncertainty of the east, the rigors of the conflict, or the depredations of troops and militias on both sides, settlers flooded west. Under these conditions, the war in the south took on a savage character as Indians, Loyalists, and Whigs all desperately fought to defend their communities and maintain control of their own destinies. Taking advantage of the political turmoil in the east, the Cherokee Nation launched a coordinated offensive in 1776 against illegal frontier settlements. The Whigs responded with a series of expeditions from each of the Southern colonies that razed Cherokee towns and their food supplies. All the while, both British and Whig leaders walked a fine line: If the Indians attacked settlers without distinguishing between Loyalists and Whigs, those groups could unite and thwart both British and Indian interests; if the Indians attacked the western frontier with Loyalist and British support, the Whigs would face a two-front war – an event that ended up happening. Blackmon uses a wealth of primary source material to recount the conflict between American Indians and Anglo-Americans in the colonial South during one of the most turbulent periods of North American history. He explains the complex points of contact in Georgia, Kentucky, North Carolina, South Carolina, Tennessee, and Virginia between native groups and settlers, while revealing the political gamesmanship between rival British and Whig traders and officials to secure Indian loyalty. The author also explains the critical role of the southern frontier to the American victory, a victory achieved long after the decision at Yorktown. Before the war, clashes between Cherokee and Shawnee hunters in Kentucky had become so commonplace that it was known as a 'dark and bloody ground.' With the rise in Anglo-American settlements there, led by Daniel Boone and others, the dark and bloody ground became a metaphor for the entire struggle for the Southern frontier."]

Blethen, Tyler. "Museum of the Cherokee Indian Qualla Boundary." *North Carolina Folklore Journal*, 49:1 (Spring/Summer 2002), 43-44. [Online description from "North Carolina Periodicals Index," East Carolina University: "The Museum of the Cherokee Indian opened in 1948 on the Qualla Boundary in Western North Carolina. Over 125,000 people visit it annually. The museum received the North Carolina Folklore Society 2001 Community Traditions Award for outstanding contributions to preservation, continuation, and appreciation of Cherokee traditional culture."]

Bloom, Leonard. "The Acculturation of the Eastern Cherokee: Historical Aspects." *North Carolina Historical Review*, 19:4 (October 1942), 323-358.

Boosinger, Elby A. "The Cherokee Indians in the Revolutionary War." M. A. thesis, University of Nebraska – Lincoln, 1951.

Brown, John P. *Old Frontiers: The Story of the Cherokee Indians from Earliest Times to the Date of Their Removal to the West, 1838*. Kingsport, Tenn.: Southern Publishers, 1938.

Brown, Patrick Cavan. "Saving Cherokee." *Our State: Down Home in North Carolina*, 82:12 (May 2015), 53-54; online: https://www.ourstate.com/cheerokee-language-atse-kituwah-academy/. [Online description from "North Carolina Periodicals Index," East Carolina University: "The Cherokee language is slowly dying out as the younger generations are taught English rather than Cherokee. An immersion program at the Atse Kituwah Academy in Cherokee, North Carolina teaches students the language to avoid its extinction."]

Burrell, Jean. "Wedgwood and the Cherokees." *The State: A Weekly Survey of North Carolina*, 18:31 (December 1950), 3, 22; online: http://digital.ncdcr.gov/cdm/ref/collection/p16062coll18/id/26381. [Online description from "North Carolina Periodicals Index," East Carolina University: "The basic material in antique Wedgwood plates may have come from the land of the Cherokees more than 200 years ago."] [Josiah Wedgwood & Co.]

Casanova, Richard L. "Richard L. Casanova Papers." Manuscript, Call Number PC.1191, State Archives of North Carolina, Raleigh. [Online catalog description: "Seventy-two page typescript of 'Patriots in Buckskin,' a history by Casanova of the Cherokee Indians during the period of the American Revolution (1763-1785); with bibliography, and appendix concerning frontiersman's uniform during Revolution."]

Cashion, Jerry C. "North Carolina and the Cherokee: The Quest for Land on the Eve of the American Revolution, 1754-1776." Ph. D. Dissertation, University of North Carolina at Chapel Hill, 1979.

Champagne, Duane. *Social Order and Political Change: Constitutional Governments among the Cherokee, the Choctaw, the Chickasaw, and the Creek*. Stanford, Calif.: Stanford University Press, 1992.

"Cherokee Documents in Foreign Archives, 1632-1909." Accession no. MSS 83-3; 821 microfilm reels, Special Collections, Hunter Library, Western Carolina University, Cullowhee. [Online catalog description: "Cherokee Documents in Foreign Archives includes materials relating to the Cherokee Indians housed in archives of Canada, France, Great Britain, Mexico, and Spain. The collection consists of 821 reels of microfilm and includes sources which directly mention the Cherokee Indians or Cherokee territory, or which refer to Southern Indians in general. Most of the documents were written during the colonial era of the 17th and 18th centuries, when European nations courted the support of southeastern Indian nations. Documents include letters, diplomatic reports, journals, diaries, census records, and narratives of Indian captives. William L. Anderson and James A. Lewis' book, *A Guide to Cherokee Documents in Foreign Archives* (Metuchen, N. J. and

London: The Scarecrow Press, 1983), is the finding aid for the collection, and is a descriptive list of all Cherokee-related materials. The Guide has a subject/name index that provides senders and recipients of letters, the geographical origin of correspondence sent from Cherokee territory, and all proper nouns found in the documents. Indexed under the heading 'Cherokee' are topics such as agriculture, boundaries, character traits, customs, education, hostilities, land cessions, language, population statistics, relations with whites, towns, trade and treaties…"]

"Cherokee Maps, 1580-1863." Accession MSS 85-14, Special Collections, Hunter Library, Western Carolina University, Cullowhee. [Online catalog description: "The collection consists of reproductions of 108 maps from archives in Canada, Great Britain and Spain. The maps feature Cherokee towns and place names or refer to Cherokee territory."]

"The Cherokee War of 1776." Online: http://sc_tories.tripod.com/cherokee_war.htm.

Claggett, Stephen. "First Immigrants: Native American Settlement of North Carolina." *Tar Heel Junior Historian*, 34:2 (Spring 1995), 3-7. [Online description from "North Carolina Periodicals Index," East Carolina University: "Before English colonists arrived, Native Americans had lived in the state 12,000 years. Thirty tribes totaling 100,000 occupied the state in the late 1500s, but colonial wars and diseases rapidly decreased that number to 20,000 in 1800."]

Cockran, David K. *The Cherokee Frontier: Conflict and Survival, 1740-1762*. Norman: University of Oklahoma Press, 1962.

Cooper, Patricia Irwin. "Cabins and Deerskins: Log Building and the Charles Town Indian Trade" [now Charleston, Bradley Co., Tenn.]. *Tennessee Historical Quarterly* 71:1 (Spring 2012): 2-15. ["How can we account for Cherokee log building so early..." {early 1700s}.]

Corbitt, D. L. "Dividing Line between North Carolina and the Cherokees." *North Carolina Historial Review*, 2:3 (July 1925), 390.

Corn Tassel; translated by William Tatum. "Cherokee Reply to the Commissioners of North Carolina and Virginia, 1777." *Journal of Cherokee Studies*, 1 (Fall 1976), 128-129.

Cotterill, Robert S. *The Southern Indians: The Story of the Civilized Tribes before Removal*. Norman: University of Oklahoma Press, 1954.

Cumfer, Cynthia. *Separate Peoples, One Land: The Minds of Cherokees, Blacks, and Whites on the Tennessee Frontier.* Chapel Hill: University of North Carolina Press, 2007.

De Vorsey, Louis, Jr. "The Virginia-Cherokee Boundary of 1771" *East Tennessee Historical Society's Publications*, no. 33 (1961), 17-31.

Dickens, Roy S., Jr. "A Note on Cherokee House Construction of 1776." *Southern Indian Studies*, 19 (1967), 35.

Dickens, Roy S., Jr. "The Route of Rutherford's Expedition against the North Carolina Cherokees." *Southern Indian Studies*, 19 (1967), 3-24; online: http://www.rla.unc.edu/Publications/NCArch/SIS_19%28e-book%29.pdf.

Downes, Randolph C. "Cherokee-American Relations in the Upper Tennessee Valley 1776-1791." *East Tennessee Historical Society's Publications*, 8 (January 1936), 35-53.

Duncan, Barbara R., and Brett H. Riggs. *Cherokee Heritage Trails Guidebook*. Chapel Hill: University of North Carolina Press, 2003. [Publisher's description: "Enriched by Cherokee voices, this guidebook offers a unique journey into the lands and culture of the Eastern Band of Cherokee Indians in the mountains of North Carolina, Tennessee, and Georgia. Every year millions of tourists visit these mountains, drawn by the region's great natural beauty and diverse cultural traditions. Many popular aspects of Cherokee culture are readily apparent; beneath the surface, however, lies a deeper Cherokee heritage – rooted in sacred places, community ties, storytelling, folk arts, and centuries of history. *Cherokee Heritage Trails Guidebook* is your introduction to this vibrant world. The book is organized around seven geographical hubs or communities within the original Cherokee homeland. Each chapter covers sites, side trips, scenic drives, and events. Cherokee stories, history, poems, and philosophy enrich the text and reveal the imagination of Cherokees past and present. The Museum of the Cherokee Indian in Cherokee, North Carolina, is the main interpretive center for the Cherokee Heritage Trails. Among the many other featured sites are Kituhwa Mound, origin of the mother town of the Cherokees; Junaluska Memorial and Museum, with a preserved gravesite and medicine plant trail; and Unicoi Turnpike Trail, part of the Trail of Tears and one of sixteen national millennium trails in the United States."]

Fields, Elizabeth Arnett. "Between Two Cultures: Judge John Martin and the Struggle for Cherokee Sovereignty." In David Colin Crass, Steven D. Smith, Martha A. Zierden, and Richard D. Brooks, eds., *The Southern Colonial Backcountry: Interdisciplinary Perspectives on Frontier Communities* (Knoxville: University of Tennessee Press, 1998), 182-199.

Franklin, W. Neil. "Virginia and the Cherokee Indian Trade, 1753-1775." *East Tennessee Historical Society's Publications,* no. 5 (1933), 22-38.

Frost, Ralph Walter. "A History of the Cherokee Indians of the Tennessee Region from 1783 to 1794." M. A. thesis, University of Tennessee, 1925. [Author's summary from the preface: "The purpose of this thesis is to narrate the relationships that existed between the settlers and the Cherokee Indians occupying particularly what is now the State of Tennessee, with special attention to the character of both powers as brought forth by their contact with each other, and to the policies of each toward the other. The years 1783 to 1794 form an important period in the history of the United States and also the history of the Tennessee region. The Nation was in a state of confusion. The Continental Congress constituted the National power during most of these years and the states refused to abide by the acts of that body and consequently many conflicts in authority arose which caused much antagonism and also much blood-shed."]

Ganyard, Robert L. "Threat from the West: North Carolina and the Cherokeee, 1776-1778." *North Carolina Historical Review*, 45:1 (January 1968), 47-66.

Goodwin, Gary C. *Cherokees in Transition: A Study of Changing Culture and Environment prior to 1775*. Chicago: University of Chicago, Department of Geography, Research Paper 181), 1977.

Great Britain. Colonial Office. "Toqueh, [Tennessee]. [Copy of] Alex[ande]r Cameron [Deputy Superintendent for Indian Affairs, Southern District] to John Stuart [Supt. For Indian Affairs, Southern District]. 31 Aug., 1776." Copy of a manuscript in the National Archives of the United Kingdom (formerly the Public Records Office), Kew, Richmond, Surrey, England; Z.5.16N, State Archives of North Carolina, Raleigh. [Online catalog description: "Letter describes Cherokee setbacks, but states that with proper support from government, Cherokee will 'distress the Rebels in Georgia, both the Carolinas and Virginia so much this fall and winter' that the rebels will sue for peace; Capt. Gest assists him among Cherokee; various concerning affairs in Cherokee country. Enclosed in John Stuart to Lord George Germain, 25 Oct. 1776 (21.20.65.1.3)."]

Great Britain. Colonial Office. "Toqueh, [Tennessee]. [Copy of] Alex[ander] Cameron [Dep. Supt. For Indian Affairs] to John Stuart [Supt. For Indian Affairs, Southern District]. 23 Sep., 1776." Copy of a manuscript in the National Archives of the United Kingdom (formerly the Public Records Office), Kew, Richmond, Surrey, England; Z.5.16N, State Archives of North Carolina, Raleigh. [Online catalog description: "Letter states that Cameron has not heard from Stuart recently, a "delay [that] may be dangerous"; army from North Carolina and Virginia have destroyed the Middle Settlement; Cherokee diminished in numbers; Creek refuse to help; Catawba with Americans; Cameron fears for his own safety among Cherokee; supplies very much needed. Enclosed in John Stuart to Lord George Germain, 25 Oct. 1776 (21.20.65.1.3)."]

Hagy, James W., and Stanley J. Folmsbee. "The Lost Archives of the Cherokee Nation." *East Tennessee Historical Society's Publications*, "Part 1, 1763-1772" no. 43 (1971), 112-122; "Part 2, 1772-1775" no. 44 (1972), 114-125, "Part 3, 1777" no. 45 (1973), 88-98.

Hamer, Philip M. "The Wataugans and the Cherokee Indians in 1776." *Publications of the Tennessee Historical Society,* no. 3 (1931), 108-126.

Hatley, Thomas M. *The Dividing Paths: Cherokees and South Carolinians through the Era of Revolution*. New York: Oxford University Press, 1993.

Hill, Sarah H. "Made by the Hands of Indians: Cherokee Women and Trade." In Susanna Delfino and Michele Gillespie, eds., *Neither Lady nor Slave: Working Women in the Old South* (Chapel Hill: University of North Carolina Press, 2002), 34-54.

Hughes, N. C., Jr. "The Naming of Chocowinity." *The State: A Weekly Survey of North Carolina*, 17:33 (January 1950), 11; online: http://digital.ncdcr.gov/cdm/ref/collection/p16062coll18/id/24904. [Online description from "North Carolina Periodicals Index," East Carolina University: "For many years people have been saying that nobody knows the meaning of the word Chocowinity, but Hughes did some research and found its Indian origin."]

Kelton, Paul. *Cherokee Medicine, Colonial Germs: An Indigenous Nation's Fight against Smallpox, 1518-1824*. Norman: University of Oklahoma Press, 2015.

King, Duane H. "The Cherokees: This Land Is Our Land." *Tar Heel Junior Historian*, 30:2 (Spring 1991), 9-13. [Online description from "North Carolina Periodicals Index," East Carolina University: "At one time the Cherokees occupied territory covering 40,000 square miles, but after their first contact with the Europeans in the 1500s, life became a struggle to keep the white man from taking their land. Treaties were made and broken, and wars were fought until 1794. Finally in 1838-39, the United States forcibly removed the Cherokees to the Oklahoma Territory. Around a thousand escaped to the North Carolina mountains, and their descendants live on the 56,000- acre Qualla Boundary, a fraction of their once vast territory."]

King, Duane H. "Long Island of the Holston: Sacred Cherokee Ground." *Journal of Cherokee Studies*, 1:2 (Fall 1976), 113-127.

Lanman, Charles. "Cherokee Church." *The State: Down Home in North Carolina*, 22:14 (December 4, 1954), 15-16, 24; online: http://digital.ncdcr.gov/cdm/ref/collection/p16062coll18/id/32739. [Online description from "North Carolina Periodicals Index," East Carolina University: "Qualla Town, located in Haywood County, is an area encompassing 72,000 acres of land inhabited by the Cherokee and Catawba Native Americans. Divided into seven clans, each of which is managed by a chief, the indigenous peoples of this area still function and practice beliefs despite the widespread Native American removal that devastated tribes and belief systems elsewhere in North America."]

Lee, Wayne E. "Fortify, Fight, or Flee: Tuscarora and Cherokee Defensive Warfare and Military Culture Adaptation." *Journal of Military History*, 68:3 (July 2004), 713-770.

Malone, Henry T. *Cherokees of the Old South*. Athens: University of Georgia Press, 1956.

North Carolina. Office of the State Treasurer. State Comptroller. "Indian Affairs and Lands, 1712, 1739-1957." Manuscript (MARS ID: 13.21; series), 4 vols., State Archives of North Carolina, Raleigh. [Online catalog description: "An artificial and diverse collection of accounts, certificates, warrants, survey plats, reports, receipt books, depositions, court papers, deeds, and correspondence relating to the Cherokee and Tuscarora Indians, 1739-1900, 1911, 1923, 1956-1957. For the former, most of the records are of the antebellum period and concern lands sold and leased by the state and by the Cherokee, and also the 'life reservations' created for them by the state. Public claims and payrolls (1759-1760, 1771, 1791) concern expeditions against the Cherokee. Other records concern treaties, and the furnishing of provisions and supplies. Miscellaneous items include copies of Col. George Washington's orders for escorting Cherokees from Virginia to the Nation; a typed copy of a journal of a visit to the Cherokee by Thomas Griffin, 1767; an 1846 history of the Cherokee in North Carolina since 1809; a census of the Eastern Cherokee in 1923; and photographs of the Qualla Reservation. Records relating to the Tuscarora mainly concern leases and sales of land in Bertie County. Most of them date from the antebellum period, but there is also a Tuscarora petition (1956-1957) before the Indian Claims Commission for rights to lands in North Carolina. There is also a copy of a treaty of 1712. Other material concerns the service of Tuscaroras in the French and Indian War, and supplies furnished them by the state."]

North Carolina (State). General Assembly. "[Document Dated]: December 2, 1777: Resolution Ordering James Miller of Tryon County to Keep an Indian Boy in His Possession." Manuscript; General Assembly Record Group; Session Records, November-December 1777; Miscellaneous; Joint Papers, Committee Papers, Resolutions; Senate Joint Resolutions: November 19-December 24, 1777, Box 1 (MARS ID: 66.8.10.9.3; item), State Archives of North Carolina, Raleigh. [Online catalog description: Cherokee child.]

North Carolina (State). General Assembly. "[Document dated:] August 18, 1778: Bill to Prevent Trading with the Cherokee Indians without License." Manuscript; General Assembly Session Records; Session of August 1778; Joint Papers, Committee Papers, Resolutions, Senate Bills, House Bills, Box 1 (MARS ID: 66.8.14,18; folder), State Archives of North Carolina, Raleigh.

North Carolina (State). General Assembly. "[Document dated:] April 27, 1782: House Bill for Extending Boundary Line between This State and the Cherokee (Petition Only)." Manuscript; General Assembly Session Records; Session of April-May 1782; Joint Papers, Committee Papers, Resolutions, Box 2 (MARS ID: 66.8.20.14.1; item), State Archives of North Carolina, Raleigh. [Online catalog description: "Petition requests that western boundary be extended because of Indian hostilities."]

North Carolina (State). General Assembly. "[Document dated:] May 8, 1783: Senate Bill to Vest the Title of Lands Purchased from the Cherokee Indians in Richard Henderson and Others." Manuscript; General Assembly Session Records; Session of April-May 1783; Unidentified Amendments, Senate Bills, House Bills, Box 2 (MARS ID: 66.8.30.25; folder), State Archives of North Carolina, Raleigh. [Online catalog description: "The memorial of Richard Henderson and Company requests some portion of the land they had purchased from the Cherokee Indian tribe in 1775. The original purchase encompassed tens of millions of acres roughly bounded by the Ohio, Kentucky, and Cumberland Rivers. In the memorial, they give all claim to such land that fell in the state of North Carolina to North Carolina and request some sort of compensation in return for their trouble and risk. The bill vests in the company the title to about 200,000 acres around the Clinch and Powell rivers in what are now Hancock and Claiborne Counties, Tenn. Includes true copies of the deed and contract between the Cherokee and the Transylvania Company, as well as the bill, memorial, and bonds." Richard Henderson and Company; Transylvania Company; Claiborne and Hancock Counties, Tennessee; Clinch, Cumberland, New, Ohio, Powell, and Tennessee Rivers]

North Carolina (State). General Assembly. "[Document dated:] May 13, 1783: House Bill for Extending Boundary Line between This State and the Cherokee (Petition Only)." Manuscript; General Assembly Session Records; Session of April-May 1783; Unidentified Amendments, Senate Bills, House Bills, Box 2 (MARS ID: 66.8.30.82; folder), State Archives of North Carolina, Raleigh. [Online catalog description: "Bill requests the governor to appoint an agent or agents to be the contact between the state and the Cherokee Indians and to negotiate in all matters with them."]

O'Donnell, James H. III. *Cherokees of North Carolina in the American Revolution.* (Bicentennial Pamphlet Series, no. 9) Raleigh: North Carolina Department of Archives and History, 1976.

O'Donnell, James H. *Southern Indians and the American Revolution.* Knoxville: University of Tennessee Press, 1973.

O'Donnell, James H. "Southern Indians in the War for American Independence, 1775-1783." In Charles M. Hudson, ed., *Four Centuries of Southern Indians* (Athens: University of Georgia Press, 1975), 46-64.

O'Donnell, James H., III. "The Virginia Expedition against the Overhill Cherokees, 1776." *Publications of the East Tennessee Historical Society*, 39 (1967), 13-25.

Page, John. "John Page Letters, 1776." Manuscript Accession 24721, Library of Virginia, Richmond; online finding aid available at http://ead.lib.virginia.edu/vivaxtf/view?docId=lva/vi00722.xml. [Online finding aid description: "Letters, 1776, from John Page (1743-1808) to Charles Lee (1731-1782) consisting of: letter, 12 July 1776, describing the defense of Gwynn{'s} Island against the fleet of Lord Dunmore; and letter, 13 August 1776, discussing Lee's military maneuvers, campaigns against the Cherokee by the militias of Virginia and North Carolina, the arrival of the Chevalier de St. Aubin, and mail difficulties. These letters are printed in *Lee Papers* volume II, volume 5 of the New York Historical Society, pp. 131-136 and 214-216."]

Perdue, Theda. *Slavery and the Evolution of Cherokee Society, 1540-1866.* Knoxville: University of Tennessee Press, 1979.

Reid, John. "John Reid, Richmond, [to] Governor." Manuscript letter, online: http://image.lva.virginia.gov/GLR/05036, Library of Virginia, Richmond. [Online catalog description: "Part of a collection of letters and other documents received in the Governor's Office during the period June 29, 1776-Nov. 30, 1784. Presenting an account of his actions since January 1783 as they relate to bringing about a successful peace treaty with the Cherokees. (Enclosures – 'several letters' [one from James Robertson; others unidentified and therefore lacking].) Oct. 27, 1783, James Robertson, on behalf of a Committee of Davidson County, North Carolina, 'To Whom it May Concern,' presenting their opinion, as expressed to Reid, re holding the forthcoming peace talks with the Cherokees in their settlement."]

Reid, John Phillip. *A Law of Blood: The Primitive Law of the Cherokee Nation.* New York: New York University Press, 1970.

Rockwell, Elijah Frink. "Parallel and Combined Expeditions against the Cherokee Indians in South and in North Carolina, in 1776." *Historical Magazine with Notes and Queries*, 1 (October 1867), 212-220.

Rockwell, E[lijah] F[rink]., ed. "Parallel and Combined Expeditions against the Cherokee Indians in South and North Carolina in 1776." *Historical Magazine*, 2nd series, 2 (October 1867), 212-220.

Rozema, Vicki. *Footsteps of the Cherokees: A Guide to the Eastern Homelands of the Cherokee Nation.* Winston-Salem: John F. Blair, 1995.

Schroedl, Gerald F. "Cherokee Ethnohistory and Archaeology from 1540 to 1838." In Bonnie McEwan, ed., *Indians of the Greater Southeast during the Historic Period.* Gainesville: University Press of Florida, 2000, 204-241.

Scott, Bob. "Secrets Dug from a Cornfield." *The State: Down Home in North Carolina*, 37:4 (July 1969), 14-15; online: http://digital.ncdcr.gov/cdm/ref/collection/p16062coll18/id/52742. [Online description from "North Carolina Periodicals Index," East Carolina University: "Archaeological excavations are currently being carried out in a mountain cornfield located near the east fork of the Tuckasegee River in Jackson County. The cornfield is thought to be the site of a Cherokee Village that once may have contained over 300 houses and that was destroyed in a raid in 1780 by John Sevier. Pottery, stone tools and weapons are among the artifacts that have been recovered. Additionally, several home sites have been excavated, revealing circular fireplaces in excellent condition, with ashes still intact."]

Sharp, Bill. "Cherokees in Cherokee." *The State: Down Home in North Carolina*, 23:1 (June 1955), 13-14; online: http://digital.ncdcr.gov/cdm/ref/collection/p16062coll18/id/81572. [Online description from "North Carolina Periodicals Index," East Carolina University: "In response to a claim that there were no Cherokees in Cherokee County, the author provides the location and numbers of all registered Cherokees in North Carolina counties. New definitions of what an Indian may be are examined, as well the challenges faced when registering peoples of Indian inter-marriage as one tribe or the other. Often the government does not recognize the origins of certain groups of people, and therefore may overlook the Cherokees hidden in the mix."]

Sharpe, Bill. "How Much Indian Blood Makes an Indian an Indian?" *The State: Down Home in North Carolina*, 34:8 (September 1996), 9-11, 35-36; online: http://digital.ncdcr.gov/cdm/ref/collection/p16062coll18/id/49473. [Online description from "North Carolina Periodicals Index," East Carolina University: "Native Americans of Cherokee decent are undergoing profound changes within North Carolina. An increase in employment off the reservation, coupled with the strengthening of industry on the reservation, is resulting in the decline of Native Americans being able to speak in their native tongue or write using the traditional alphabet. Modernization and exposure to life outside of the reservation is leading to an intensification of interracial marriages, or rather, individuals claiming to have Cherokee blood, thus entitling them to a share in the ownership of the reservation. In an attempt to curb the risiLng number of individuals professing Cherokee heritage, it is now required that individuals be at least 1/16th true Cherokee prior to acceptance into the Eastern Band."]

Smith, Katy Simpson. "'I Look on You … As My Children:' Persistence and Change in Cherokee Motherhood, 1750-1835." *North Carolina Historical Review*, 87:4 (October 2010), 403-430. [Online description from "North Carolina Periodicals Index," East Carolina University: "This article examines how the Cherokee Nation, especially its mothers, tried to adapt to the cultural changes forced on them by white Americans during the late 18th and early 19th century while also maintaining their own traditional culture. The efforts by Christian missionaries to 'civilize' the Cherokee people are also discussed and the matrilineal structure and child raising practices of Cherokee society."]

Tatum, William, tr. Corn Tassel. "Cherokee Reply to the Commissioners of North Carolina and Virginia, 1777." *Journal of Cherokee Studies*, 1:2 (Fall 1976), 128-129.

Whitaker, A. P. "Spain and the Cherokee Indians, 1783-1798." *North Carolina Historical Review,* 4:3 (July 1927), 252-269.

Wilburn, H. C. "A River and a Name: Both Beautiful." *The State: A Weekly Survey of North Carolina*, 19:43 (March 1952), 8. [Online description from "North Carolina Periodicals Index," East Carolina University: "Oconaluftee was the original name of a village destroyed by Colonel Moore on the banks of the river also named Oconaluftee."]

Wilson, Eddie W. "Some Tales about Snakes." *The State: A Weekly Survey of North Carolina*, 16:2 (June 1948), 9, 22; online: http://digital.ncdcr.gov/cdm/ref/collection/p16062coll18/id/22449. [Online description from "North Carolina Periodicals Index," East Carolina University: "The author outlines both Native American and contemporary lore about snakes, including religious and medicinal qualities. Cherokee religion believed rattlesnakes to be men in a different form. Dr. John Brickell's writing included snake folklore in *Natural History of North Carolina*. There is also a discussion about North Carolina snake lore, with folktales and medicinal/therapeutic qualities of native snake species."]

American Indians of North Carolina and Tennessee – Chickamauga

North Carolina (State). General Assembly. "[Document dated:] January 20, 1779: Report on Letter from Governor of Virginia Re[specting] Expedition against Chickamauga (with Messages)." Manuscript; General Assembly Record Group; Session Records, January-February 1779, Joint Papers, Committee Papers, Resolutions, Box 1 (MARS ID: 66.8.15.8.1; folder), State Archives of North Carolina, Raleigh. [Online catalog description: "The committee recommends mobilization of certain militia elements to Washington County to move against the Chickamauga Indians."]

North Carolina (State). General Assembly. "[Document dated:] January 21, 1779: Resolutions (2) Re[specting] Indian Expedition (Chickamauga) (with Messages)." Manuscript; General Assembly Record Group; Session Records, January-February 1779; Joint Papers, Committee Papers, Resolutions, Box 1 (MARS ID: 66.8.15.10.1; folder), State Archives of North Carolina, Raleigh. [Online catalog description: "Resolutions to request that Col. Long transport ammunition for the expedition against the Chickamauga and to appoint Jesse Walton as commissary to the troops on the expedition commanded by Col. Robertson."]

Pate, James Paul. "The Chickamauga: A Forgotten Segment of Indian Resistance on the Southern Frontier." Ph. D. dissertation, Mississippi State University, 1969.

Parmenter, Jon W. "Dragging Canoe (Tsi'yu-g~nsi'ni): Chickamauga Cherokee Patriot." In Nancy L. Rhoden and Ian K. Steele, eds., The Human Tradition in the American Revolution (The Human Tradition in America series, no. 2) (Wilmington, Del.: Scholarly Resources, Inc., 2000), V.1, 117-137.

American Indians of North Carolina – Chickasaw

Champagne, Duane. *Social Order and Political Change: Constitutional Governments among the Cherokee, the Choctaw, the Chickasaw, and the Creek.* Stanford, Calif.: Stanford University Press, 1992.

Great Britain. Colonial Office. "Mobile, [Alabama]. [Copy of] Talk from John Stuart [Supt. For Indian Affairs, Southern District] to Chickasaw and Choctaw. 14 May, 1777." Copy of a manuscript in the National Archives of the United Kingdom (formerly the Public Records Office), Kew, Richmond, Surrey, England; Z.5.17.N, State Archives of North Carolina, Raleigh. [Online catalog description: "Talk reviews of progress of the war, etc.; is 'certain' that rebel plans to proceed by boat from backcountry of North Carolina and Virginia down Cherokee River; asks that they not be allowed to pass through their lands. Enclosed in John Stuart to Lord George Germain, 14 June 1777 (21.20.65.1.40)."]

Williams, Samuel Cole. *Beginnings of West Tennessee: In the Land of the Chickasaws, 1541-1841*. Johnson City: Watauga Press, 1930.

American Indians of North Carolina – Chowan

Hazel, Forest. "Looking for Indian Town: The Dispersal of the Chowan Indian Tribe in Eastern North Carolina, 1780-1915." *North Carolina Archaeology*, 63 (2014), 34-64.

Milteer, Warren E., Jr. "From Indians to Colored People: The Problem of Racial Categories and the Persistence of the Chowans in North Carolina." *North Carolina Historical Review*, 93:1 (January 2016), 28-57.

American Indians of North Carolina – Coharie

Burns-Ramsey, Wanda. "The Coharie Indians." *Tar Heel Junior Historian*, 22:2 (Winer 1983), 16-17. [Online description from "North Carolina Periodicals Index," East Carolina University: "The Coharie tribes lived in Sampson and Harnett Counties and according to census data approximately 1,200 live between these two counties. In 1981, the tribe was given the East Carolina Indian School, one of the few in the state specifically focused on preserving Native American heritage."]

American Indians of North Carolina – Coree

Pate, Albert F. *The Coree Are Not Extinct: Discussion of Some Indian, White, and Black Relationships in Early America*. Pikeville: A. F. Pate, 1993.

American Indians of North Carolina – Creek

Champagne, Duane. *Social Order and Political Change: Constitutional Governments among the Cherokee, the Choctaw, the Chickasaw, and the Creek*. Stanford, Calif.: Stanford University Press, 1992.

Cockran, David K. *The Creek Frontier, 1540-1783*. Norman: University of Oklahoma Press, 1967.

American Indians of North Carolina and Tennessee – Lumbee

Blu, Karen I. "Lumbee." In Raymond D. Fogelson, vol. ed. *Handbook of North American Indians, Volume 14: Southeast* (Washington, D. C.: Smithsonian Institution, 2004), 319-328.

Blu, Karen I. *The Lumbee Problem: The Making of an American Indian People*. New York: (Cambridge studies in cultural systems, no. 5) Cambridge University Press, 1980; reprinted with a new afterword by the author: Lincoln: University of Nebraska Press, 2001.

Carter, Gazelia. "Lumbee English." Online at LearnNC: http://www.learnnc.org/lp/editions/nc-american-indians/5569.

DeMarce, Virginia Easley. "Looking at Legends-Lumbee and Melungeon: Applied Genealogy and the Origins of the Tri-Racial Isolate Settlements." *National Genealogical Society Quarterly*, 81:1(March 1993), 24-45.

Dial, Adolph L., and David K. Eliades. *The Only Land I Know: A History of the Lumbee Indians*. San Francisco: Indian Historian Press, 1975.

Gray, Penn. "30,000 North Carolinians Vote Themselves a Name." *The State: A Weekly Survey of North Carolina*, 19:35 (January 1952), 6-7, 14; online: http://digital.ncdcr.gov/cdm/ref/collection/p16062coll18/id/28109. [Online description from "North Carolina Periodicals Index," East Carolina University: "Thirty thousand people in Robeson County will soon decide what their official name should be. Of course, they do have a name, but a large group of the people considers it misleading, inappropriate, and inaccurate. Are the Indians of Robeson County Cherokees, Siouan, Croatans, or Lumbee?"]

"Lumbee Collection." Manuscript, Special Collections and Archives, Mary Livermore Library, University of North Carolina at Pembroke, Pembroke. [Online catalog description: "The Lumbee Collection is a compilation of newspaper clippings, books, and journal articles written by and about the Lumbee Indians of Robeson County including the story of Henry Berry Lowry and his wife, Rhoda. The Lumbee Tribe is the largest group of Indians east of the Mississippi River. The Lumbee live primarily in Robeson, Scotland and Hoke counties; however, for economic reasons many relocated over the years to larger cities such as Charlotte, Greensboro and Raleigh, North Carolina and Detroit, Michigan and Baltimore, Maryland. Pembroke is recognized as the home of the Lumbee. In 1885 the State of North Carolina recognized the Lumbee as the Croatan Indians of Robeson

County. At the same time it allowed for the establishment of a separate school system for Indian children. In 1887 the state established the Croatan Indian Normal School which is known today as The University of North Carolina at Pembroke."]

McMillan, Alex Few. "Lost Cause." *Business North Carolina*, 15:10 (October 1995), 40-44, 46, 48-49. [Online description from "North Carolina Periodicals Index," East Carolina University: "Although the Lumbee Indians are the state's largest Indian tribe, the federal government does not recognize them as such and grants them little funding. A bill to grant recognition was stalled in the U. S. Congress in 1994."]

Norris, Jeannie Faris. "The Indians of Robeson County." *The State: A Weekly Survey of North Carolina*, 18:47 (April 1951), 3, 22; online: http://digital.ncdcr.gov/cdm/ref/collection/p16062coll18/id/26906. [Online description from "North Carolina Periodicals Index," East Carolina University: "The request for a change in the tribal name of these Indians is a reminder that their origin is still as much of a mystery as it has been throughout the years."]

Sider, Gerald M. *Living Indian Histories: Lumbee and Tuscarora People in North Carolina*. Chapel Hill: University of North Carolina Press, 2003.

Sider, Gerald M. *Lumbee Indian Histories: Race, Ethnicity, and Indian Identify in the Southern United States*. New York: Cambridge University Press, 1993.

American Indians of North Carolina and Tennessee – Mattamuskeet

Garrow, Patrick H. "The Mattamuskeet Indians and Their Descendants." *Carolina Comments*, 25:2 (March 1977), 41-46. [Online description from "North Carolina Periodicals Index," East Carolina University: "Mattamuskeet refers to a group of Native Americans who, after losing in the Tuscarora War (1711-1715), were given land around the Mattamuskeet Lake in Hyde County. The group sold land to white developers and the population of the Mattamuskeet dwindles. The Mackeys Family, of Fairfield, was the only family in the late 1970s able to trace its lineage back to the first Mattamuskeet lands."]

American Indians of North Carolina and Tennessee – Meherrin

Dawdy, Shannon Lee. "The Meherrin's Secret History of the Dividing Line." *North Carolina Historical Review*, 72:4 (October 1995), 386-415. [Online description from "North Carolina Periodicals Index," East Carolina University: "This article looks at the history of the Meherrin Indians to uncover their pivotal role in the colonial era Virginia-North Carolina Boundary Dispute. Examination of the dispute enlarges the understanding of the Meherrin's relations with white colonists and their survival strategies under European colonialism, explains how this small group of Indians was able to maintain its identity and political autonomy for the greater part of the colonial period, and provides a look at the complexity of Anglo-Indian relations."]

American Indians of North Carolina and Tennessee – Occaneechi Saponi

Beaman, Thomas E., Jr. "Fables of Reconstruction: Morely Jeffers Williams and the Excavation of Tryon Palace, 1952-1956." *North Carolina Archaeology*, 49 (October 2000), 1-22; online: http://www.rla.unc.edu/Publications/NCArch/NCA_49%28e-book%29.pdf. [Online description from "North Carolina Periodicals Index," East Carolina University: "It has been argued that historical archaeology began in North Carolina with the work of Talcott Williams in the 19th century in search of the Roanoke settlements or with the work of James Sprunt at Russellborough near Brunswick Town. Beaman argues that historical archaeology did not flourish in the state until the mid 20th century, when Morely Jeffers Williams conducted the first archaeological investigation into the opulent pre-Revolutionary home of William Tryon in New Bern."]

Chavis, Talena. "North Carolina Recognizes Occaneechi as an Official Indian Tribe." *Carolina Comments*, 34:5 (May 2002), 24. [Online description from "North Carolina Periodicals Index," East Carolina University: "The Occaneechi Band of the Saponi Nation, an Indian community living in Alamance County, has received official state recognition as a tribe living in North Carolina. The Occaneechi Band had sought recognition for seventeen years. To achieve recognition, a tribe must meet five of eight criteria, including tracing lineage in North Carolina back at least 200 years, as specified by the North Carolina Commission on Indians Affairs."]

Church, L. Teresa. "The Occaneechi Band of Saponi Nation: Archival Documentation in a Native American Community." *Journal of the Society of North Carolina Archivists,* 4:1 (Summer 2005).

Davis, R. P. Stephen, Jr.; I. Randolph Daniel; Mary Ann Holm; H. Trawick Ward; Linda F. Carnes; and Kristen Johnson Gremillion. "Archaeology of the Historic Occaneechi Indians." *Southern Indian Studies*, 36-37 (October 1988), 1-128; online: http://www.rla.unc.edu/Publications/NCArch/SIS_36&37.pdf. [Online description from "North Carolina Periodicals Index," East Carolina University: "This volume discusses archaeological investigations surrounding the historic Occaneechi settlement visited by John Lawson in 1701, near Hillsborough. Researches examine pottery, historic artifacts, faunal remains, plant remains, burials, and structures."]

Hazel, Forest. "Occaneechi-Saponi Descendants in the North Carolina Piedmont: The Texas Community." *Southern Indian Studies*, 40 (1991), 3-29; online: http://www.rla.unc.edu/Publications/NCArch/SIS_40%28e-book%29.pdf. [Online description from "North Carolina Periodicals Index," East Carolina University: "There is still uncertainty about many of the tribal origins of many of the Native American groups in North Carolina. However, recent archaeological work near the Occaneechi village on the banks of the Eno River near Hillsborough exposed the community as descendants of the Saponi and Occaneechi, thought to have been completely gone years ago."]

Thomas, Theresa M. "Historic Places in the Piedmont." *The State: A Weekly Survey of North Carolina*, 4:32 (January 1937), 26; online: http://digital.ncdcr.gov/cdm/ref/collection/p16062coll18/id/101659. [Online description from "North Carolina Periodicals Index," East Carolina University: "Piedmont, North Carolina is rich in historic landmarks. Among these are Trading Ford, Boone's Cave, the Old Stone Wall, and Sapona. Trading Ford was located where the old trading path crossed the Yadkin River; there the Sapona Indians had an important trading post where traders stopped to trade and recruit. Sapona is located on the Davidson County side of the Yadkin River and was the headquarters and principle town of the Sapona Tribe. Tradition tells us that Boone's Cave is where Daniel Boone hid upon being pursued by Indians."]

American Indians of North Carolina and Tennessee – Tuscarora

Boyce, Douglas W. "Tuscarora Political Organization, Ethnic Identity, and Socio-Historical Demography, 1711-1825." Ph. D. dissertation, University of North Carolina at Chapel Hill, 1973.

Covington, James W. *The Tuscaroras: Mythology-Medicine-Culture, Vol. 1.* Murfreesboro: Johnson Publishing Company, [1967-1968?]

Covington, James W. *The Tuscaroras: History-Traditions-Culture, Vol.2.* Murfreesboro: Johnson Publishing Company, 1968.

Greene, Elton. *The Tuscarora Language.* Murfreesboro: Johnson, 1969.

Haas, Marilyn L. *The Seneca and Tuscarora Indians: An Annotated Bibliography.* Metuchen, N. J.: Scarecrow Press, 1994.

Holloman, Charles R. "Charles R. Holloman Collection, 1759-1833." Manuscript PC.606 (MARS ID: 1116; record group), State Archives of North Carolina, Raleigh. [The online catalog description of this collection shows that it contains articles that Holloman wrote about the Tuscaroras.]

La Vere, David. *The Tuscarora War: Indians, Settlers, and the Fight for the Carolina Colonies.* Chapel Hill: University of North Carolina Press, 2013.

Lee, Wayne E. "Fortify, Fight, or Flee: Tuscarora and Cherokee Defensive Warfare and Military Culture Adaptation." *Journal of Military History*, 68:3 (July 2004), 713-770.

McDonald, Forrest, and Ellen Shapiro McDonald. "The Ethnic Origins of the American People, 1790." *William and Mary Quarterly*, 3rd series, 37:2 (April 1980), 179-199.

North Carolina. General Assembly. "[Document dated:] December 22, 1777: Joint Papers, Committee Papers, Resolutions, Senate Bills, House Bills, Appointing Commissioners to Superintend Affairs of the Tuscarora Indians in Bertie Co. (Message Only)." Manuscript; General Assembly Record Group; Session Records, Nov-Dec 1777, Box 1 (MARS ID: 66.8.10.8.15; item), General Assembly Record Group, Session Records, State Archives of North Carolina, Raleigh.

North Carolina. General Assembly. "[Document dated:] December 22, 1777: Resolution Appointing Commissioners to Superinted Affairs of the Tuscarora Indians in Bertie Co. (Message Only)." Manuscript; General Assembly Record Group; Session Records, Miscellaneous; Joint Papers, Committee Papers, Resolutions; House Joint Resolutions: November 20-December 22, 1777; November-December 1777, Box 1 (MARS ID: 66.8.20.7.4), State Archives of North Carolina, Raleigh.

North Carolina. General Assembly. "[Document dated:] April-May, 1780: Petition of the Tuscarora Indians of Bertie County." Manuscript; General Assembly Record Group; Session Records; Joint Papers, Committee Papers, Resolutions, Senate Bills, House Bills; April-May 1780, Box 1 (MARS ID: 66.8.20.7.4), State Archives of North Carolina, Raleigh. [Online catalog description: "The petitioners inform the Assembly that an act appointing commissioners to settle disputes between the Tuscaroras and the whites is not serving its purpose due to the fact that jurors often fail to attend when summoned; they ask for assistance."]

North Carolina. General Assembly. House. "[Document dated:] April 28, 1780: House Bill to Amend Act for Quieting and Securing the Tuscarora Indians." Manuscript; General Assembly Record Group; Session Records; Joint Papers, Committee Papers, Resolutions, Senate Bills, House Bills; Apr-May 1780, Box 2 (MARS ID: 66.8.21.30), State Archives of North Carolina, Raleigh. [Online catalog description: "Correcting an oversight in the original act, the bill imposes a penalty on jurors and witnesses, duly summoned, who fail to attend. The fines are to be levied by the commissioners appointed to hold a court for the Tuscarora claims and are to be applied to the charges of Bertie County. Clauses relating to overseers of the poor were deleted."]

North Carolina. Office of the State Treasurer and Office of State Comptroller. "Indian Affairs and Lands, 1712, 1739-1957." Manuscript (MARS ID: 13.21; series), 4 vols., State Archives of North Carolina, Raleigh. [Online catalog description: "An artificial and diverse collection of accounts, certificates, warrants, survey plats, reports, receipt books, depositions, court papers, deeds, and correspondence relating to the Cherokee and Tuscarora Indians, 1739-1900, 1911, 1923, 1956-1957. For the former, most of the records are of the antebellum period and concern lands sold and leased by the state and by the Cherokee, and also the 'life reservations' created for them by the state. Public claims and payrolls (1759-1760, 1771, 1791) concern expeditions against the Cherokee. Other records concern treaties, and the furnishing of provisions and supplies. Miscellaneous items include copies of Col. George Washington's orders for escorting Cherokees from Virginia to the Nation; a typed copy of a journal of a visit to the Cherokee by Thomas Griffin, 1767; an 1846 history of the Cherokee in North Carolina since 1809; a census of the Eastern Cherokee in 1923; and photographs of the Qualla Reservation. Records relating to the Tuscarora mainly concern leases and sales of land in Bertie County. Most of them date from the antebellum period, but there is also a Tuscarora petition (1956-1957) before the Indian Claims Commission for rights to lands in North Carolina. There is also a copy of a treaty of 1712. Other material concerns the service of Tuscaroras in the French and Indian War, and supplies furnished them by the state."]

Parramore, Thomas C. "The Tuscarora Ascendancy." *North Carolina Historical Review*, 59:4 (October 1982), 307-326.

Paschal, Herbert Richard. "The Tuscarora Indians in North Carolina." M. A. thesis, University of North Carolina, Chapel Hill, 1953.

Sider, Gerald M. *Living Indian Histories: Lumbee and Tuscarora People in North Carolina.* Chapel Hill: University of North Carolina Press, 1993; reprinted with a new preface by the author in 2003.

Wallace, Anthony F. C. *Tuscarora: A History*. Albany: State University of New York Press, 2012.

American Indians of North Carolina and Tennessee – Tutelo

DeMallie, Raymond J. "Tutelo and Neighboring Groups." In Raymond D. Fogelson, vol. ed. *Handbook of North American Indians, Volume 14: Southeast* (Washington, D. C.: Smithsonian Institution, 2004), 286-300.

Haithcock, Richard L. *The Catawba Confederacy: Tutelo, Saponi, Nahyssan and Monacan Tribal History.* Beavercreek, Ohio: R. L. Haithcock, 2009.

Haithcock, Richard L. *Tutelo, Saponi, Nahyssan, Monacan aka Piedmont Catawba Diaspora*. 6 vols. [Beavercreek, Ohio]: R. L. Haithcock, 2006-2007.

Haithcock, Richard L., and Vicki L. Haithcock. *Occaneechie Saponi and Tutelo of the Saponi Nation, aka Piedmont Catawba: Southeastern Indian Refugees from Virginia, the Carolinas, and Tennessee in Ohio, Indiana and Michigan.* 3 vols. [Beavercreek, Ohio]: R. L. Haithcock, 1996.

Hale, Horatio. *The Tutelo Language*. Bristol, Pa.: Evolution Publishing, 2001.

Speck, Frank G. "Siouan Tribes of the Carolinas Known from Catawba, Tutelo, and Documentary Sources." *American Anthropologist,* new series, 37:2:pt 1 (April-June 1935), 201-225.

American Indians of North Carolina – Waccamaw-Siouan

Alexander, James Ervin. "The Waccamaw Indians." *The State: A Weekly Survey of North Carolina*, 17:51 (May 1950), 3-4, 17-18; online: http://digital.ncdcr.gov/cdm/ref/collection/p16062coll18/id/25413. [Online description from "North Carolina Periodicals Index," East Carolina University: "The story of the Waccamaw Indians has been tragic. For years they have been trying to improve their status and gain recognition but their efforts have been unsuccessful."]

Lerch, Patricia B. "Longtime Chief of the Waccamaw-Siouan: Priscella Freeman Jacobs." *Tar Heel Junior Historian*, 45:1 (Fall 2005), 30-31. [Online description from "North Carolina Periodicals Index," East Carolina University: "Priscilla Freeman Jacobs led the Waccamaw-Siouan, a state recognized American Indian tribe, from 1986 to 2005. She is the first woman to hold the position of chief in her tribe in the 20th-century and is the first tribal woman to become a minister. Lerch discusses Jacobs' role as tribal chief. Deciding not to seek reelection as chief in 2005, Jacobs now serves as pastor of the Life Changing Community Church in Riegelwood."]

Peters, Sarah Friday. "A Community Reaches Back to Its Ancestors." *Coastwatch*, (September/October 1992), 16-19. [Online description from "North Carolina Periodicals Index," East Carolina University: "Some present-day NC Indian tribes, especially the Waccamaws, take great pains to preserve their past."]

American Indians of North Carolina – Weapemeoc

Mook, Maurice A. "Algonkian Ethnohistory of the Carolina Sound." *Journal of the Washington Academy of Sciences,* 34:6 (15 June 1944), 181-190; 34:7 (15 July 1944), 213-227.

Petrey, Whitney R. "Weapemeoc Shores: The Loss of Traditional Maritime Culture among the Weapemeoc Indians." M. A. thesis, East Carolina University, 2014.

"The Weapemeoc Indians." Online: http://www.carolana.com/Carolina/Native_Americans/native_americans_weapemeoc.html.

American Indians of North Carolina – Yadkin

Battle, Kemp Plummer. "The Catawba and Yadkin and Their Associations." *University Magazine,* old series, 18; new series 5:6 (April 1886), 219-222.

American Indians of North Carolina – Women

Rodning, Christopher B. "Mortuary Ritual and Gender Ideology in Protohistoric Southwestern North Carolina." In Jane M. Eastman and Christopher Rodning, eds. *Archaeological Studies of Gender in the Southeastern United States* (Gainesville: University Press of Florida, 2001), 77-100.

Sparks, Elizabeth Hedgecock. *North Carolina and Old Salem Cookery.* Kernersville, N. C.: E. H. Sparks, 1955. [Includes American Indian women's cooking and the history of Moravian families' cooking.]

English Immigrants to North Carolina, 1774-1775

Newsome, A. R. "Records of Emigrants from England and Scotland to North Carolina, 1774-1775." *North Carolina Historical Review*, 11:1 (January 1934), 39-54; online: http://digital.ncdcr.gov/cdm/ref/collection/p16062coll9/id/4207; 11:2 (April 1934), 129-143; online: http://digital.ncdcr.gov/cdm/ref/collection/p16062coll9/id/4207. [Online description from "North Carolina Periodicals Index," East Carolina University: "Reprinted here is a compilation of records for Scottish emigrants to North Carolina gathered from Public Record Office of Great Britain in the Treasury Department and organized by the North Carolina Historical Commission. These records include names or emigrants, age, occupation, departure dates, port of departure, and reason for visiting the state. Dates of records in this installment are from January 1774 through May 1775."]

Freemasons/Masons in North Carolina and Tennessee

Bridges, Early Winfred. *The Masonic Governors of North Carolina*; *Their Masonic Records and Orations; Newspaper Articles of Events Pertaining to the Craft, and Other Information of Interest to Masonry about the Governors of North Carolina*. Greensboro: E. M. Bridges, 1937.

Haywood, Marshall DeLancey. "The Masonic Revolutionary Patriots of North Carolina." *North Carolina Booklet*, 12:1 (July 1912), 21-40.

Kammerer, Roger. "A History of Masonic Lodges." *Greenville Times/Pitt's Past*, (July 9-22, 1986), 7. [Online description from "North Carolina Periodicals Index," East Carolina University: "Thomas Cooper at Crown Point established the first Masonic lodge in Pitt County and in the state in 1766. Sharon Lodge established in 1822 and the Woodson Lodge Number 16 Knights of Pythias organized in 1874. By 1888, Greenville had five lodges with many more by 1900."]

Parramore, Thomas C. *Launching the Craft: The First Half-Century of Freemasonry in North Carolina*. [Raleigh?]: Grand Lodge of North Carolina, 1975.

Rauschenberg, Bradford L. "Discovery: A Documented Bow Bowl Made for Halifax-Lodge, North Carolina." *Journal of Early Southern Decorative Arts*, 1:1 (May 1975), 3-13; online: https://archive.org/details/journalofearlyso11muse. [Online description from "North Carolina Periodicals Index," East Carolina University: "This article presents information on a Masonic punch bowl made by the Bow factory in London for 'Halifax-Lodge/North-Carolina' that was part of a 1767 order for four Bow China bowls. This example is the first time a documented reference has been found specifying an order of Bow porcelain decorated especially for the American market. Archival and archaeological information on the bowl and its owners along with a diagnostic analysis of the bowl as an example of Bow porcelain are included."]

Sasche, Julius F. "Freemasonry in the Continental Army." *American Historical Register*, 2:1 (March 1895), 621-631.

Seapker, Janet K. "St. John's Masonic Lodge: Part 1: Orange Street Lodge." *Lower Cape Fear Historical Society Bulletin*, 50:1 (January 2006), 1-8. [Online description from "North Carolina Periodicals Index," East Carolina University: "St. John's Masonic Lodge in Wilmington, the oldest Masonic lodge building in the state, celebrated its 250th anniversary in 2005. Few urban buildings have survived from this period because of fires and subsequent urban rebuilding, making St. John's a rare survivor."]

Speidel, Frederick C. *North Carolina Masons in the American Revolution*. Oxford: Press of Oxford Orphanage, 1975.

Speidel, Frederick G. "North Carolina Masons in the American Revolution." *Carolina Trees & Branches*, 5:8 (August 1996), 72-73; 5:9 (September 1996), 86.

"St. John's Masonic Lodge Archives on Loan to Tryon Palace." *Carolina Comments,* 59:2 (April 2011), 8-9.

French in North Carolina and the French Alliance

De Roulhac and Company. "De Roulhac Collection, 1778-1780." Manuscript PC.449 (MARS ID: 959; record group), State Archives of North Carolina, Raleigh. [Online catalog description: "Account book of shipping firm De Roulhac and Company of Edenton, and five letters of a commercial nature, all in French, one addressed to the French consul at Philadelphia. Account book contains credits and debits for various voyages of nine French vessels."] [Edenton and Philadelphia]

Graham, Anne S. "Anne S. Graham Collection, 1733-1892." Manuscript MfP.127 (MARS ID: 2637; record group), State Archives of North Carolina, Raleigh. [This collection includes "two items in French relating to Thomas Barker's travels in Europe as an agent in 1778."]

"Jolidon Revolutionary Collection, 1778-1783." Manuscript Library Service Center Box 1, David M. Rubenstein Rare Book & Manuscript Library, Duke University, Durham. [Online catalog description: "Military and official correspondence passing between French agents and French naval officers during the closing years of the Revolution. They relate to such matters as the obtaining of supplies for the French forces off the Carolina coast. Chiefly in French, some English."]

North Carolina (State). General Assembly. "[Document dated:] June 24, 1781: Appointing the Marquis de Britaigny [Bretigny] Agent for the State to the French Islands; Directing Sheriff of Craven County to Procure a Quantity of Tobacco (Messages Only)." Manuscript; General Assembly Record Group; Session Records, June-July 1781; Joint Papers, Committee Papers, Resolutions, Box 1 (MARS ID: 66.8.25.10.2; item), State Archives of North Carolina, Raleigh. [Online catalog description: "A committee is appointed to consider a letter from the Marquis de Britaigny, and its report is concurred with, along with the two resolutions."]

North Carolina (State). General Assembly. "[Document dated:] November 21, 1785: "Papers (1784): Report Concerning the Payment of French Military Officers for Their Services in the War." Manuscript; General Assembly Record Group; Session Records, November-December 1785; Joint Papers, Committee Papers, Grand Committee to Consider the Message from the Governor and Resolves of Congress, Box 1 (MARS ID: 66.8.37.11.2; item), State Archives of North Carolina, Raleigh. [Online catalog description: "Included is a letter from the French Chargé des Affairs in America, Monsieur de Marbois [François Barbé-Marbois], who states that French officers and their agents are encountering difficulty in the settling of their accounts due to the slowness or reluctance of Americans in paying them. De Marbois would like Congress to recommend to the states that they pass laws to expedite the payment of officers. Also included is the resolve of Congress on the matter, which asks that copies of de Marbois letter should be immediately sent to the states with a recommendation that they pass such laws."]

Ratchford, B. U. "An International Debt Settlement: The North Carolina Debt to France." *American Historical Review*, 40:1 (October 1934), 63-69.

Stover, John F. "French-American Trade during the Confederation, 1781-1789." *North Carolina Historical Review*, 35:4 (October 1958), 399-414; online: http://digital.ncdcr.gov/cdm/ref/collection/p16062coll9/id/4207. [Online description from "North Carolina Periodicals Index," East Carolina University: "French commerce and military aid to the colonies helped to fill the trade vacuum left by British commerce loss. French exports to America reached a high level in the 1780s. Trade directed toward North Carolina was extensive because larger American ports were blockaded or occupied by the British during the Revolution. Additionally, naval stores, North Carolina's major export, figured into the French-American trade, although only slightly."]

Germans in North Carolina and Tennessee

Ash, William J. "Remembering Our Swiss and German Beginnings." *The Palace*, 10:2 (Winter 2010), 13. [Online description from "North Carolina Periodicals Index," East Carolina University: "As New Bern celebrates its 300th anniversary, it remembers its Swiss and German settlers who agreed to put down roots where the Trent and Neuse rivers converged."]

Bernhaim, G. D. *History of the German Settlements and of the Lutheran Church in North and South Carolina.* Philadelphia: Lutheran Book Store, 1872.

Elliott, Rita Folse, and Daniel T. Elliott. "Guten Tag Bubba: Germans in the Colonial South." In J. W. Joseph and Martha Zierden, eds., *Another's Country: Archaeological and Historical Perspectives on Cultural Interaction in the Southern Colonies* (Tuscaloosa: University of Alabama Press, 2002), 79-92.

Gehrke, William Herman. "The German Element in Rowan and Cabarrus Counties, North Carolina." M. A. thesis, University of North Carolina at Chapel Hill, 1934.

Gehrke, William Herman. "Negro Slavery among the Germans of North Carolina." *North Carolina Historical Review*, 14 (1937), 307-324; online: http://digital.ncdcr.gov/cdm/ref/collection/p16062coll9/id/4207. [The article discusses the once very "industrious" Germans in the 18th century who worked all their own labor till the turn of the century when they broke away from tradition and the majority of them became slaveholders.]

Gehrke, William Herman. "The Transition from the German to the English Language in North Carolina." *North Carolina Historical Review*, 12:1 (January 1935), 1-19; online: http://digital.ncdcr.gov/cdm/ref/collection/ p16062coll9/id/4207. [Online description from "North Carolina Periodicals Index," East Carolina University: "This article traces the development of English language skills among the Pennsylvania-German in North Carolina. It is divided into sections that look at the German Period, 1747-1790, the original dialect, the mixed dialect, the bi-lingual period 1790-1825, the efforts to preserve the German language, the arguments for German, English marching on, and the English period, 1825—."]

Hammer, Carl. *Rhinelanders on the Yadkin: The Story of the Pennsylvania Germans in Rowan and Cabarrus Counties, North Carolina.* [Salisbury?: s. n., 1965].

Leonard, Jacob Calvin. *The Germans in North Carolina.* Lititz, Pa.: Express Printing Company, 1909.

Nixon, Joseph R. "German Settlers in Lincoln County and Western North Carolina." *James Sprunt Historical Publications*, 11:2 (1912), 25-62. [Contents: Chapter I: The German Migration; Chapter II: German Life in North Carolina; Chapter III: The Ramsour Family.]

Rolland, Susanne Mosteller. "From the Rhine to the Catawba: A Study of Eighteenth-Century Germanic Migration and Adaptation." Ph. D. dissertation, Emory University, 1991.

Schreiben des Evangelisch-Lutherischen und Reformirten Kirchen-Raths, wie auch der Beamten der Teutschen Gesellschaft in der Stadt Philadelphia, an die teutschen Einwohner der Provinzen von Neuyork und Nord-Carolina. Philadelphia: Gedruckt bey Henrich Miller, in der Rees-Strasse, 1775; micropublished (Early American Imprints. First Series No. 14394) New York: Readex Microprint, 1985. [Online description from Evans: "The object of this letter, which was authorized by the official boards of the German churches and the German Society in Philadelphia, was to furnish the Germans in New York, and in North Carolina, with information which would lead them to join with the Germans of Pennsylvania, in supporting the measures of Congress, and to ally themselves with the supporters of the American Revolution."]

Seidler, Ute-Ingrid. "A List of Children of Settlers of German Descent in Central North Carolina, 1775-1791." *North Carolina Genealogical Society Journal*, 8:4 (November 1982), 194-198

Slonina, Maria. "German-Speaking Peoples in Tennessee from Colonial Times to World War I: An Introduction and Bibliography." M. A. thesis, University of Tennessee Knoxville, 1973.

Irish in North Carolina and Tennessee

Dickson, William; compiled and edited by James Osborn Carr, ed. "The Dickson Letters, [1784-1794]." Manuscripts P (Dickson, William), Manuscripts Division, South Caroliniana Library, University of South Carolina, Columbia. [Online catalog description: "Compilation of records and letters written by William Dickson in North Carolina to Rev. Robert Dickson and other relatives in Ireland, 1784-1794, re the Revolutionary War; family, local and national news; politics and government; and other matters during the Early National Period."]

Duncan, Gwyneth. "Irish Customs and Beliefs in North Carolina." *North Carolina Folklore Journal*, 18:3 (November 1970), 148-153. [Online description from "North Carolina Periodicals Index," East Carolina University: "Much of the folklore in North Carolina has its roots in British and European folklore, brought over by the original settlers. This article deals with material collected from Mrs. Bridget Van Steen, an Irishwoman now living in Winston-Salem. Mrs. Van Steen was born and raised in County Mayo and takes great interest in the folklore of Ireland."]

Ferris, William R. "'A Lengthening Chain in the Shape of Memories:' The Irish and Southern Culture." *Southern Cultures*, 17:1 (Spring 2011), 9-29.
Giemza, Bryan. "Turned Inside Out: Black, White, and Irish in the South." *Southern Cultures*, 18:1 (Spring 2012), 34-57.
Haltigan, James. *The Irish in the American Revolution and Their Early Influence in the Colonies*. Washington, D. C.: Patrick J. Haltigan, 1908; online at https://books.google.com.
Seymour, William, Sergeant Major. "A Sergeant Loves the Irish." *Southern Campaigns of the American Revolution*, 2:3 (March 2005), 14; online: http://southerncampaign.org/newsletter/v2n3.pdf. [Taken from Seymour's *A Journal of the Southern Expedition* and dated March 14, 1781. Seymour served in the 2nd Maryland Regiment. The observation describes the population in the area around Guilford Court House.]
Smith, Christopher J. "Blacks and Irish in the Riverine Frontiers: The Roots of American Popular Music." *Southern Cultures*, 17:1 (Spring 2011), 75-102.

Jews of North Carolina

Dinnerstein, Leonard, and Mary Dale Palsson. *Jews in the South*. Baton Rouge: Louisiana State University Press, [1973].
Evans, Eli N., and Willie Morris. *The Provincials: A Personal History of Jews in the South*. Chapel Hill: University of North Carolina Press, 2005. [Publisher's description: "In this classic portrait of Jews in the South, Eli N. Evans takes readers inside the nexus of southern and Jewish histories, from the earliest immigrants to the present day. Evoking the rhythms and heartbeat of Jewish life in the Bible belt, Evans weaves together chapters of recollections from his youth and early years in North Carolina with chapters that explore the experiences of Jews in many cities and small towns across the South. He presents the stories of communities, individuals, and events in this quintessential American landscape that reveal the deeply intertwined strands of what he calls a unique 'Southern Jewish consciousness.' First published in 1973 and updated in 1997, *The Provincials* was the first book to take readers on a journey into the soul of the Jewish South, using autobiography, storytelling, and interpretive history to create a complete portrait of Jewish contributions to the history of the region. No other book on this subject combines elements of memoir and history in such a compelling way. This new edition includes a gallery of more than two dozen family and historical photographs as well as a new introduction by the author."]
Golden, Harry L. "The Jewish People of North Carolina." *North Carolina Historical Review*, 32:2 (April 1955), 194-216.
Rogoff, Leonard. *Down Home: Jewish Life in North Carolina*. Chapel Hill: University of North Carolina Press, 2010. [Publisher's description: "A sweeping chronicle of Jewish life in the Tar Heel State from colonial times to the present, this beautifully illustrated volume incorporates oral histories, original historical documents, and profiles of fascinating individuals. The first comprehensive social history of its kind, *Down Home* demonstrates that the story of North Carolina Jews is attuned to the national story of immigrant acculturation but has a southern twist. Keeping in mind the larger southern, American, and Jewish contexts, Leonard Rogoff considers how the North Carolina Jewish experience differs from that of Jews in other southern states. He explores how Jews very often settled in North Carolina's small towns, rather than in its large cities, and he documents the reach and vitality of Jewish North Carolinians' participation in building the New South and the Sunbelt. Many North Carolina Jews were among those at the forefront of a changing South, Rogoff argues, and their experiences challenge stereotypes of a society that was agrarian and Protestant. More than 125 historic and contemporary photographs complement Rogoff's engaging epic, providing a visual panorama of Jewish social, cultural, economic, and religious life in North Carolina. This volume is a treasure to share and to keep. Published in association with the Jewish Heritage Foundation of North Carolina, *Down Home* is part of a larger documentary project of the same name that will include a film and a traveling museum exhibition, to be launched in June 2010."]

Lawyers/Attorneys of North Carolina

Alderman, Ernest H. "The North Carolina Colonial Bar." *James Sprunt Historical Publications*, 13:1 (1913), 5-21.
de Roulhac Hamilton, J. G. "Southern Members of the Inns of Court." *North Carolina Historical Review*, 10:4 (October 1933), 273-286; online: http://digital.ncdcr.gov/cdm/ref/collection/p16062coll9/id/4207. [Online description from "North Carolina Periodicals Index," East Carolina University: "This article looks at the involvement of 255 Southern men (11 from or associated with North Carolina) in the English legal intellectual institution known as the Inns of Court, and its associated groups, The Inner Temple, The Middle Temple,

Gray's Inn and Lincoln's Inn. The article provides background information for each associated group, and then lists the American Southern men admitted to the institution by state and including their year of admission and the group to which they belonged. The North Carolina inductees mentioned are William Brimage {d. 1793}, Gabriel {Johnston} Cathcart, Thomas Child, Sir Richard Everard, Enoch Hall, Henry Eustace McCulloh {d. 1778}, Thomas McGuire, Josiah Martin {1737-1786}, Sir Walter Raleigh, Benjamin Smith {1756-1826}, and Alexander White. Some biographical information on certain members from Southern states follows this list."]

Golumbic, Lars. "Dueling Legal Visions: Lawyers, the Backcountry, and the Law in Revolutionary Era North Carolina." M. A. thesis, University of North Carolina-Chapel Hill, 1994.

Golumbic, Lars C. "Who Shall Dictate the Law?: Political Wrangling Between 'Whig' Lawyers and Backcountry Farms in Revolutionary Era North Carolina." *North Carolina Historical Review* 73:1 (January 1996), 56-82.

Lawrence, R. C. "The Bar of Halifax." *The State: A Weekly Survey of North Carolina*, 12:38 (February 1945), 5, 16-17; online: http://digital.ncdcr.gov/cdm/ref/collection/p16062coll18/id/12783. [Online description from "North Carolina Periodicals Index," East Carolina University: "Willie Jones, William R. Davie, Abner Nash, John Branch, the Kitchins, and many other famous lawyers, jurists, and statesmen have come from Halifax County and rendered outstanding service to North Carolina and United States."]

North Carolina (State). General Assembly. "October 1782-May 1783: Committee of the Whole House: Papers Relating to the Charges against Archibald Maclaine, Member of the House and Attorney-at-Law, for Bladen and New Hanover Counties." Manuscript; General Assembly Record Group; Session Records, Apr-May 1783, Box 1 (MARS ID: 66.8.29.11; folder), State Archives of North Carolina, Raleigh. [Online catalog description: "Documents are relevant to the May 7, 1783 hearing against Archibald Maclaine in the Committee of the Whole House. The hearing arises from a petition from the justices and citizens of Bladen County that charges Maclaine with being an enemy to the peace and government of the state. He is accused of disregarding the law and siding with the British. Included are depositions from various justices of Bladen and New Hanover counties as well as letters from Maclaine."]

Loyalists/Tories of North Carolina

"1784 List of Men Banished from North Carolina." *Southern Genealogist's Exchange Quarterly,* 38:whole no.163 James Iredell and the Revolutionary Politics of North Carolina (September 1997), 20, 40.

Allen, W. C. "Whigs and Tories." *North Carolina Booklet*, 2:5 (September 10, 1902), 1-24; online: http://digital.ncdcr.gov/cdm/ref/collection/p249901coll37/id/14180. [Online description from "North Carolina Periodicals Index," East Carolina University: "This article examines the origin of Whig and Tory political parties and its spread to the North American colonies, including North Carolina. It also examines the actions of both parties in the colonies during the American Revolution and what happened after the end of hostilities."]

American Loyalist Claims AO 12 Series 1 1776-1831. 30 microfilm reels. Nendeln, Lichtenstein: Kraus-Thomson Organization, 1972. [Images of documents in the Auditor's Office collections at the National Archives of the United Kingdom, Kew, London.]

American Loyalist Claims AO 13 Series 1 1780-1831. 145 microfilm reels. Nendeln, Lichtenstein: Kraus-Thomson Organization, 1975. [Images of documents in the Auditor's Office collections at the National Archives of the United Kingdom, Kew, London.]

Arthur, Billy. "Plundering Sam Brown." *The State: Down Home in North Carolina*, 61:12 (May 1994), 17, 19-20; online: http://digital.ncdcr.gov/ cdm/ref/collection/p16062coll18/id/66742. [Online description from "North Carolina Periodicals Index," East Carolina University: "Lincoln County's Sam Brown was a notorious robber and opponent of the American Revolution who, with his sister Charity, terrorized counties along the Yadkin River and in South Carolina. He was killed in 1780 by an outraged citizen."]

Baker, Joanna A. "Lt. Moses Whitley, Loyalist." *Bulletin of the Genealogical Society of Old Tryon County*, 18:3 (August 1990), 127-129.

Bellamy, Marsden. "The North Carolina Tory in the Revolution." B. A. thesis, University of North Carolina at Chapel Hill, 1899.

Bennett, William Doub. "Tories in Southwestern North Carolina." *Burke Genealogical Society Journal*, 6:4 (December 1988), 95-100.

Bidlack, Russell. "James Smiley – Tory." *The North Carolinian: A Quarterly Journal of Genealogy and History*, 2:2 (June 1956), 178.

Blount, Thomas W. "Daniel Leggett: Lee's Mills Tory Leader." *Washington County Genealogical Society Journal*, 4:3 (December 1996), 73.

Braistad, Todd. "The King's Carolina Rangers." *The Loyalist Gazette*, 29:2 (Fall 1991), 63. [Florida, Georgia and Carolina troops]

Britt, Kent; photographs by Ted Spiegel. "The Loyalists." *National Geographic Magazine*, 147:4 (April 1975), 510-539. [The online catalog of the University of North Carolina Libraries shows that this article "Includes map showing North Carolina troops at the Battle of Camden and picture of button worn by a North Carolina Loyalist soldier."]

Brown, Alan S. "James Simpson's Reports on the Carolina Loyalists, 1779-1780." *Journal of Southern History*, 21:4 (November 1955), 513-519.

Brown, Wallace. *King's Friends: The Composition and Motives of the American Loyalist Claimants.* Providence: Brown University Press, 1951. [Loyalists in all 13 colonies. North Carolina, 195-213.]

Bull, Stewart. "The Loyalist Who Saved the Colour!" *The Loyalist Gazette*, 33:2 (Fall 1995), 19-22. [Solomon Austin of Maryland and North Carolina]

Butler, Lindley S. "David Fanning's Militia: A Roving Partisan Community." In Robert M. Calhoon, *et al.*, eds, *Loyalists and Community in North Carolina* (Westport, Conn.: Greenwood Press, 1994), 147-161.

Butler, Lindley S. "Raft Swamp, Engagement at." In William S. Powell, ed.; Jay Mazzocchi, assoc. ed., *Encyclopedia of North Carolina* (Chapel Hill: University of North Carolina Press in association with the University of North Carolina Library, 2006), 936. [1781; Loyalist refuge]

Butler, Lindley S., ed. *The Narrative of Colonel David Fanning*, Davidson: Briarpatch Press, 1981.

Cain, Robert J. "Loyalist Widow Pension Document of Rebecca McDugald of Moore County, North Carolina." *Argyll Colony Plus*, 4:4 (Fall 1989), 140-141.

Calhoon, Robert M. "Loyalism and Neutrality." In Jack P. Greene and J. R. Pole, eds., *A Companion to the American Revolution* (Malden, Mass.: Blackwell Publishers, 2000), 235-247.

Calhoon, Robert M. *Loyalists in Revolutionary America, 1760-1781.* New York: Harcourt Brace Jovanovich, 1973. [North Carolina 439-447]

Calhoon, Robert M. "The Reintegration of the Loyalists and the Disaffected." In Jack P. Greene, ed., *The American Revolution: Its Character and Limits* (New York: New York University Press, 1987), 51-74.

Callahan, North. *Royal Raiders: The Tories of the American Revolution.* Indianapolis: Bobbs-Merrill, 1963.

Carpenter, Charles F. "The Southern Loyalists in British Strategic Military Planning for the American War of Independence." Honors essay, University of North Carolina at Chapel Hill, 1979.

Cary, James. "James Cary Papers (1776-1807)." In the "Thomas Merritt Pittman (1857-1932) Collection, 1747-1934)." Manuscript PC.123, State Archives of North Carolina, Raleigh. [Online catalog description: "James Cary papers (1776-1807) include letter book (1782-1789) recording letters to former North Carolina agent Alexander Elmsley and British officials regarding his claims for losses as a loyalist and for pay as loyalist militia officer; papers relating to his property in South Carolina, Jamaica, and Virginia; and papers of his wife Mary Cary."]

"The Cary Will." *North Carolina Booklet*, 14:2 (October 1914), 102-106; online: http://digital.ncdcr.gov/cdm/ref/collection/p249901coll37/id/14180. [Online description from "North Carolina Periodicals Index," East Carolina University: "Mary Kearney of Virginia, married first William Bennett of Northampton County, North Carolina. She later married Major James Cary, a Tory whose property was confiscated. The 1801 will of Mary Cary of Surry County, Virginia demonstrates that Mary nonetheless possessed considerable property in North Carolina that she bequeathed to relations."]

Chesney, Louisa Fletcher; Stanley Lane-Poole, ed. *The Life of the Late General F. R. Chesney, Colonel Commandant Royal Artillery, D.C.L., F.R.S., F.R.G.S., etc.* 2nd. London and Sydney: Eden, Remington & Co., 1893. [Online catalog note: "Chapter 1 deals with Alexander Chesney, a Carolina loyalist in the War of Independence."]

Clark, Murtie June. *Loyalists in the Southern Campaign of the Revolutionary War: Official Rolls of Loyalists Recruited from North and South Carolina, Georgia, Florida, Mississippi, and Louisiana.* Baltimore: Genealogical Publishing Company, 1981. [Contents: v. 1. Official rolls of Loyalists recruited from North and South Carolina, Georgia, Florida, Mississippi, and Louisiana; v. 2. Official rolls of Loyalists recruited from Maryland, Pennsylvania, Virginia, and those recruited from other colonies for the British Legion, Guides and Pioneers, Loyal Foresters, and Queens Rangers; v. 3. Official rolls of Loyalists recruited from the Middle Atlantic colonies, with lists of refugees from other colonies.]

Clifford, Mary Louise. *From Slavery to Freetown: Black Loyalists after the American Revolution.* Jefferson: McFarland, 1999. [Include a section on: "Thomas Peters of Wilmington, North Carolina."]

Crary, Katherine S., ed. *The Price of Loyalty: Tory Writings from the Revolutionary Era.* New York: McGraw-Hill, 1973.

Crow, Jeffrey J. "Liberty Men and Loyalists: Disorder and Disaffection in the North Carolina Backcountry." In Ronald Hoffman, Thad W. Tate, and Peter J. Albert, eds., *An Uncivil War: The Southern Backcountry during the American Revolution* (Charlottesville: University Press of Virginia for the U. S. Capitol Historical Society, 1985), 125-178.

Crow, Jeffrey J. "Tory Plots and Anglican Loyalty: The Llewelyn Conspiracy of 1777." *North Carolina Historical Review*, 55:1 (January 1978), 1-17. [Online description from "North Carolina Periodicals Index," East Carolina University: "During the American Revolution, John Llewelyn led a group of loyalists against the North Carolina state government, both spiritually and militarily. This Tory group opposed a series of laws passed by the North Carolina congress and fought to dis-establish the Anglican Church, against the oath of allegiance to the new state government and the military draft. Several members were caught and tried but most were released."]

Crow, Jeffrey J. "What Price Loyalism? The Case of John Cruden, Commissioner of Sequestered Estates." *North Carolina Historical Review*, 58:3 (July 1981), 215-233. [Online description from "North Carolina Periodicals Index," East Carolina University: "An examination of the two week occupation and plundering of Beaufort by British troops that began on April 5, 1782, a full six months after Lord Cornwallis' surrender at Yorktown, to identify why the battle took place, what the purpose of the invasion was, and why coastal North Carolina was targeted so late in the Revolutionary War. Particular attention is given to the career of the mastermind of the attack, North Carolina loyalist John Cruden, the commissioner of sequestered estates for Lord Cornwallis, and his motives for attachment to the British cause."]

Culpepper, Linda Parramore. "Blood, the Tie That Binds: The Role of Scottish Clans in North Carolina Loyalism during the Revolutionary Era." M. A. thesis, Western Carolina University, 1998.

Dauphinee, Andrew D. "Lord Cornwallis and the Loyalists: A Study in British Pacification during the American Revolution." Ph. D. dissertation, Temple University, 2011.

Davis, Robert S. "Biography: Colonel John Hamilton of the Royal North Carolina Regiment." *Southern Campaigns of the American Revolution*, 3:5 (May 2006), 32-34; online: www.southerncampaign.org.

Dellinger, Paul. "Militia Lists and Tory Citations, Lincoln County." *Eswau Huppeday: Bulletin of the Broad River Genealogical Society,* 10:2 (May 1990), 131.

DeMond, Robert O. "The Loyalists in North Carolina during the Revolution." Ph. D. dissertation, Duke University, 1938; published: Durham: Duke University Press, 1940; reprinted: Hamden, Conn.: Archon Books, 1964.

DeMond, Robert O. *The Loyalists in North Carolina during the Revolution*. Durham: Duke University Press, 1940; reprinted: Hamden, Conn.: Archon Books, 1964; reprinted: Baltimore: Genealogical Publishing Company, 1979. [Examines military action, legislation, and social factors.]

DePriest, Virginia Greene. "A Tory Draft." *Eswau Huppeday: Bulletin of the Broad River Genealogical Society*, 28:4 (November 2008), 209. [John Sartin]

Dudley, Harold J. *Toryism in North Carolina: Paper Presented before the Combined Raleigh and Chapel Hill-Durham Torch Clubs, March 26, 1964, in Raleigh*. [Raleigh?: s. n., 1964?]

Dunaway, Stewart E. *Henry McCulloh and Son Henry Eustace McCulloh: 18th Century Entrepreneurs, Land Speculators of North Carolina.* Hillsborough: North Carolina Historical Books, 2011. [Henry McCulloh (1700-1779); Henry Eustace McCulloh (?-ca. 1810); Loyalists]

Fanning, David. *Col. David Fanning's Narrative of His Exploits and Adventures as a Loyalist of North Carolina in the American Revolution*. Toronto: Reprinted from the Canadian magazine, 1908.

Fanning, David. *The Narrative of Colonel Fanning (A Tory in the Revolutionary War with Great Britain) Giving an Account of His Adventures in North Carolina from 1775 to 1783, As Written by Himself.* Richmond: printed for private distribution only, in the first year of the independnence [*sic*] of the Confederate States of America, 1861; reprinted: New York: Joseph Sabin, 1865; micropublished: (Historical Documents Relating to the Old North Stae, no. 1) Louisville: Lost Cause Press, 1959.

Fanning, David; Lindley S. Butler, ed. *The Narrative of David Fanning.* Davidson, N. C.: Briarpatch Press; Charleston, S. C.: Tradd Street Press, 1981.

Fanning, Edmund. "Edmund Fanning Paper, 1775." Manuscript, PC.490, State Archives of North Carolina, Raleigh. [Online catalog description: "Will of Edmund Fanning, North Carolina loyalist, 'being about to embark for New York,' June 3, 1775."]

Ferguson, Clyde R. "Carolina and Georgia Patriots and Loyalist Militia in Action, 1778-1783." In Jeffrey J. Crow and Larry E. Tise, eds., *The Southern Experience in the American Revolution, 1778-1783* (Chapel Hill: University of North Carolina Press, 1978), 174-199.

Fingerhut, Eugene R. "Uses and Abuses of the American Loyalists' Claims: A Critique of Quantitative Analyses." *William and Mary Quarterly,* 3rd series, 25:2 (April 1968), 245-258.

Fraser, James. "Papers, 1779-1789." Manuscript RUB Bay 0036:10, David M. Rubenstein Rare Book & Manuscript Library, Duke University, Durham. [Online catalog description: "Presbyterian minister of Hillsborough, N.C., who fled to Halifax, Nova Scotia, during the Revolution. Copies of deeds, affidavits, a bill of sale for slaves, inventories of real and personal property, and a catalog of books. Fraser's Hillsborough estate, 'Hartford,' was used by Cornwallis as British headquarters and later occupied and, according to Fraser, damaged by American troops."]

Frech, Laura Page. "The Wilmington Committee of Public Safety and the Loyalist Rising of February 1776." *North Carolina Historical Review*, 41:1 (January 1964), 1-20. [Online description from "North Carolina Periodicals Index," East Carolina University: "The article reviews the role of Committee of Public Safety in the Wilmington-New Hanover area during the Revolutionary War. Committee members were entrusted to contain British Governor Martin and squelch Highlander loyalties to the British Crown. The author documents the connection between the Committee's decisions and outcomes of two important events: The Battle of Moore's Creek (1776) and the Highland rising at Cross Creek (1776)."]

Graves, Donald E. *Guide to Canadian Sources Related to Southern Revolutionary War National Parks*. (Research Project for Southern Revolutionary War National Parks, National Parks Service Solicitation Number 500010388). Carleton Place, Ont.; Ensign Heritage Consulting; Leesburg, Va.: REEP Inc., [2001?]; online: http://www.nps.gov/revwar/educational_resources/southern_campaigns_research/sc_revwar_phasei.pdf. [Provides an extensive listing of Loyalist sources in Canadian repositories for individuals and their claims, British and Loyalist military units, and various groups of Loyalists such as women, African Americans, and others. Loyalist military units are not limited to the Southern States and include some from New York and Pennsylvania. The Battles of Cowpens, King's Mountain and Guilford Courthouse are featured prominently in many of the cited sources.]

Great Britain. Colonial Office. "Headquarters, Camden, S. C. Duplicate of Josiah Martin, [Former Gov. of N. C.], to Lord George Germain, [Sec. of State]. 10 Jun., 1780." Copy of a manuscript in the National Archives of the United Kingdom (formerly the Public Records Office), Kew, Richmond, Surrey, England; 71.334.1-6, "British Records Collection," State Archives of North Carolina, Raleigh. [Online catalog description: "Requests assistance for the widow and family of Archibald McArthur, a N. C. Loyalist killed in that province at the beginning of the revolution."]

Great Britain. Colonial Office. "James Island, S. C. 'State of the Provincial Troops in South Carolina and Georgia under the Command of … Sir Henry Clinton.' 8 Mar., 1780." Copy of a manuscript in the National Archives of the United Kingdom (formerly the Public Records Office), Kew, Richmond, Surrey, England; 70.419.1-4, "British Records Collection," State Archives of North Carolina, Raleigh. [Online catalog description: "Includes the Royal North Carolina Volunteers."]

Great Britain. Colonial Office. "London. The Memorial and Petition of Anthony Warwick, Former Merchant and Loyalist Refugee from Va., to Lord George Germain, Sec. of State. 5 July 1780." Copy of a manuscript in the National Archives of the United Kingdom (formerly the Public Records Office), Kew, Richmond, Surrey, England; 71.181.1, "British Records Collection," State Archives of North Carolina, Raleigh. [Online catalog description: "He must return to Charleston for an extended period and requests that the Treasury continue to pay his 100 pound annuity during his absence. Also, he volunteers his knowledge of N. C. and his connections in that colony for the Crown's efforts against the rebels."]

Great Britain. Colonial Office. "New York. Address to the King from 'Loyal Refugees.' 23 Dec., 1779." Copy of a manuscript in the National Archives of the United Kingdom (formerly the Public Records Office), Kew, Richmond, Surrey, England; Z.5.19N (MARS ID: 21.20.67.69; folder), "British Records Collection," State Archives of North Carolina, Raleigh. [Online catalog description: "Address is from 'loyal Refugees' of various provinces, including North Carolina. The 'Refugees' pledge support to the king. Signed by Danl. Coxe, president, 'by order and appointment of the board chosen to represent the American Refugees.'."]

Great Britain. Colonial Office. "New York. Letter from Gov. Josiah Martin to Ld. George Germain, Sec. of State. 15 Sept, 1777." Copy of a manuscript in the National Archives of the United Kingdom (formerly the Public Records Office), Kew, Richmond, Surrey, England; (MARS ID: 21.1.27.101; folder), "British Records Collection," State Archives of North Carolina, Raleigh. [Online catalog description: "Arrival of loyalist from N. C.; discusses various of them, incl. Martin Howard and William Knight; payment to those serving in the military; has not yet been afforded a chance to serve; introduces Mr. Stuart, customs collector at New London; recommends James Cotton; transmits copy of law passed by rebels."]

Great Britain. Colonial Office. "New York, [N. Y.]. Josiah Martin, [Former Gov. of N. C.], to Lord George Germain, [Sec. of State]. 18 Dec., 1778." Copy of a manuscript in the National Archives of the United Kingdom (formerly the Public Records Office), Kew, Richmond, Surrey, England; (MARS ID: 71.329.1-3), "British

Records Collection," State Archives of North Carolina, Raleigh. [Online catalog description: "Letter of introduction for John Lancaster and William McCormick, N. C. Loyalist refugees."]

Great Britain. Colonial Office. "New York, [N. Y.]. Josiah Martin, [Former Gov. of N.C.], to Lord George Germain, [Sec. of State]. 17 June 1779." Copy of a manuscript in the National Archives of the United Kingdom (formerly the Public Records Office), Kew, Richmond, Surrey, England; (MARS ID: 71.331.1-2), "British Records Collection," State Archives of North Carolina, Raleigh. [Online catalog description: "Requests assistance for the widow and family of Archibald McArthur, a N. C. Loyalist killed in that province at the beginning of the revolution."]

Great Britain. Colonial Office. "New York, [N. Y.]. Nov. 10. Josiah Martin, [Former Gov. of N. C.], to Lord George Germain, [Sec. of State]. 23 Jan., 1778." Copy of a manuscript in the National Archives of the United Kingdom (formerly the Public Records Office), Kew, Richmond, Surrey, England; (MARS ID: 71.324.1-6), "British Records Collection," State Archives of North Carolina, Raleigh. [Online catalog description: "Report of affairs in N. C., obtained by Samuel Cornell, a prominent N. C. merchant newly arrived in N. Y. General topics: former N. C. colonial officials swearing rebel oath of allegiance; difficulty in raising sufficient rebel troops necessary for the 1778 campaign; strong rebel sentiments; Port Ocracoke the prime inlet for rebel supplies; N.C. Loyalist refugees in N. Y. including Highlanders."]

Great Britain. Colonial Office. "No. 36 Snow Hill, London. Robert Nelson, Former N. C. Merchant, to Lord George Germain. 9 Jun., 1781." Copy of a manuscript in the National Archives of the United Kingdom (formerly the Public Records Office), Kew, Richmond, Surrey, England; (MARS ID: 71.302.1-4), State Archives of North Carolina, Raleigh. [Online catalog description: "Detailed narrative of his Loyalist service; the seizure of his ship, the Polly, and her cargo near R.I. by Sir Peter Parker in accordance with an act of Parliament; and his request for the return of the ship and cargo or payment of compensation for the seizure. Encloses a letter of introduction by Josiah Martin, 14 March 1777 (21.20.133.1.6)."]

Great Britain. Commission Appointed to Enquire into the Losses of American Loyalists, 1783-1789. "American Loyalists Transcript of the Manuscript Books and papers of the Commission of Enquiry into the Losses and Aervices of the American Loyalists Held under Acts of Parliament of 23, 25, 26, 28 and 29 of George III., Preserved amongst the Audit Office Records in the Public Record Office of England, 1783-1790 ... Transcribed for the New York Public Library." 60 vols. of transcripts, 6 volumes of a calendar, and 8 volumes of memorials; also on 25 rolls of microfilm titled: "American Loyalists Collection, 1777-1790." Manuscript (MssCol 83), Manuscript and Archives Division, Stephen A. Schwarzman Building, New York Public Library, New York City.

Great Britain. Exchequer and Audit Department. Audit Office. "American Loyalists Collection: "Collection consists of transcripts and digests from the Audit Office records in the Public Record Office in London and from the Royal Institution of Great Britain of the books and papers of the Commission of Enquiry into the losses and services of American loyalists between 1783 and 1790. Volumes contain information conveyed to the commissioners to prevent imposition and fraud; examinations and decisions on temporary support claims; calendars of original memorials, vouchers, etc.; and minutes of the commissioners in London and in Nova Scotia. Also, the Commission's reports; claims liquidated; acts of Parliament establishing and regulating the Commission; examinations and determinations of claimants in Nova Scotia and London; and Royal Institution transcripts of memorials, correspondence, accounts, returns, paylists, etc., 1778-1783. The transcripts were made between 1898 and 1903 for the New York Public Library. [Online finding ald: http://www.nypl.org/sites/default/files/archivalcollections/pdf/americanloyalists.pdf. [See specifically the sections on N. C. claimants.]

Great Britain. Exchequer and Audit Department. Audit Office. "Exchequer and Audit Department. Claims, American Loyalists, Series I (AO 12, Selections), 1785-1790." Copy of a manuscript in the National Archives of the United Kingdom (formerly the Public Records Office), Kew, Richmond, Surrey, England; (MARS Id: 21.2; series), "British Records Collection." State Archives of North Carolina, Raleigh. [Online catalog description: "Mainly entry book copies of documents (memorials, petitions, accounts, vouchers, correspondence, inventories of estates, etc.) relating to claims for compensation for losses by British subjects (Loyalists and others) during and after the Revolutionary War. Subjects include individual service during the war; trade; landholding; finance; administration of relief to Loyalists, and various American and British laws concerning them; supplies furnished the British army and navy during the war."]

Great Britain. Exchequer and Audit Department. Audit Office. "Exchequer and Audit Department. Claims, American Loyalists, Series II (AO 13, Selections), 1785-1790." Copy of a manuscript in the National Archives of the United Kingdom (formerly the Public Records Office), Kew, Richmond, Surrey, England; (MARS Id: 21.3; series), "British Records Collection," State Archives of North Carolina, Raleigh. [Online catalog description: "Records (memorials, petitions, accounts, vouchers, correspondence, inventories of estates, etc.)

relating to claims for compensation for losses by British subjects (Loyalists and others) during and after the Revolutionary War. Subjects include individual service during the war; trade; landholding; finance; administration of relief to Loyalists; and various American and British laws concerning them; supplies furnished the British army and navy during the war."]

Great Britain. Exchequer and Audit Department. Audit Office. Claims, American Loyalists, Series I (AO 13, Selections), Claims, Virginia, H-M (AO 13/31)."Claim of James Lowry [13 August 1782]." Copy of a manuscript in the National Archives of the United Kingdom (formerly the Public Records Office), Kew, Richmond, Surrey, England; (MARS ID: 21.3.25.13; folder), "British Records Collection," State Archives of North Carolina, Raleigh. [Online catalog description: "Estimate of loyalist losses, including land in Craven and Dobbs counties, North Carolina."]

Great Britain. Exchequer and Audit Department. Audit Office. "[Papers in the Loyalist Claim of] Alexander Telfair (Formerly Merchant of Halifax). [n. d.]." Copy of a manuscript in the National Archives of the United Kingdom (formerly the Public Records Office), Kew, Richmond, Surrey, England; (MARS ID: 21.3.7.3), "British Records Collection," State Archives of North Carolina, Raleigh. [Online catalog description: "Memorial concerning his losses; schedule of same; minutes of testimony concerning his case; printed 'Resolves of the Inhabitants of the Town of Newbern,' 28 July 1783, to prevent return of Loyalist refugees; descriptions of lands granted in 1730 and 1745."]

Groner, Richard. "'Tory' Hager." *The Golden Nugget (Cabarrus Genealogical Society)*, 9:2 (June 2001), 45. [Frederick Hager, brother of John Hager, a Loyalist in Cabarrus County]

Hairr, John. *Colonel David Fanning: The Adventures of a Carolina Loyalist.* Erwin, N. C.: Averasboro Press, 2000.

Hamilton, John. "Royal North Carolina Regiment." Manuscript RCB 19863, file C301792, Georgia Parks and Historic Sites, Historic Preservation Section, Research Report Files, 1963-1978, A thru F," Georgia Archives, Morrow.

Harrell, Isaac S. "North Carolina Loyalists." *North Carolina Historical Review*, 3:4 (October 1926), 575-590; online: http://digital.ncdcr.gov/cdm/ref/collection/p16062coll9/id/4207. [Online description from "North Carolina Periodicals Index," East Carolina University: "Through historical research the author attempts to quantify the number of loyalists in North Carolina during the American Revolution. From this, the author also tries to ascertain how many were convicted and types of punishment charged to loyalists."]

Hodges, Betty Mae. "Betty Mae Hodges Bibliography of North Carolina Loyalists during the American Revolution." Manuscript AC.840, Belk Library, Appalachian State University, Boone; online finding aid available at http://collections.library.appstate.edu/findingaids/ac854. [Online finding aid description: "This collection consists of Betty Mae Hodges' bibliography of the Loyalists of North Carolina during the American Revolution, whether for a paper or book is not known. She had handwritten each reference on each card, about 150 index cards and papers."]

Hoffman, Ronald. "The 'Disaffected' in the Revolutionary South." In Alfred F. Young, ed., *The American Revolution: Explorations in the History of American Radicalism* (DeKalb: University of Northern Illinois Press, 1976), 273-316.

Hunt, Marvin w. "The Carolinians of Cherokee Sounds: Cultural and Linguistic Connections between North Carolina and the Bahamas." *North Carolina Literary Review*, 7 (1998), 82-95. [Online description from "North Carolina Periodicals Index," East Carolina University: "Following the American Revolution, defeated Loyalists fled to the remote corner of Abaco in The Bahamas. Since then, the descendants of those Loyalists have maintained a population that is racially, culturally, and politically distinct from the other twenty-nine populated islands that make up The Bahamas. The Abaco population more closely resembles isolated communities on Ocracoke and Harkers Island, where the population still speaks with a brogue, resembling the tongue spoken by the earliest Scot-Irish settlers."]

Jasanoff, Maya. *Liberty's Exiles: American Loyalists in the Revolutionary World.* New York: Alfred A. Knopf, 2011.

Johnson, William. "William Johnson Paper, 1783." Photocopy of a manuscript, PC.644 (MARS ID: 1154; record group), State Archives of North Carolina, Raleigh. [Online catalog description: "Photocopy of letter (Dec. 2, 1783) from William Johnston, Orange Co. legislator and agent of loyalist Edmund Fanning, to Adlai Osborn of Rowan Co., concerning sale of Fanning's lands there for execution of judgment, and commenting on death of former governor, Dr. [Thomas] Burke."]

Johnson, William Perry. "Loyalists and Tories in the Rowan-Davidson Counties Area, 1778." *Journal of North Carolina Genealogy*, 14:4 (Winter 1968), 2239-2244.

Johnson, William Perry. "Tories in Jail, 1776." *Journal of North Carolina Genealogy*, 20:1 (Spring/Summer 1974), 2921.

Jones, Abram. "Every Man for Himself: The Abrupt End of the [Lewellen] Conspiracy." Stubbs, Thomas, Sr. "...A World of Blood Shed." *Washington County Genealogical Society Journal*, 4:3 (December 1996), 80.

Katcher, Philip R. N. *Encyclopedia of British, Provincial, and German Army Units, 1775-1783*. Harrisburg, Pa.: Stackpole, 1973. [Describes various Loyalist units.]

Koyle, Susan Lewis, and Patricia Lewis Cramer. "British Tories or Revolutionary Whigs in Colonial North Carolina." *A Lot of Bunkum*, 18:2 (May 1997), 27-33.

Landin, Anne. "Carolina Loyalists in Nova Scotia." *The Argyll Colony Plus: The Journal of the North Carolina Scottish Heritage Society*, 21:1 (Spring 2007), 38-45.

"Law Case, Tried and Determined, at a Supreme Court of Law and Equity, for the District of Newbern, North Carolina, on the 30th of November 1787." *American Museum*, (April 1789), 371-372. [Online catalog description: "Case of Bayard vs. Singleton for property of Samuel Cornell, Tory."]

Lawrence, R. C. "Toryism in Carolina." *The State: A Weekly Survey of North Carolina*, 13:12 (August 1945), 9, 23-24; online: http://digital.ncdcr.gov/cdm/ref/collection/p16062coll18/id/13567. [Online description from "North Carolina Periodicals Index," East Carolina University: "The safety of North Carolina was threatened on several fronts prior to the start of the Revolutionary War. Toryism among the colonists was one of the principal agencies."]

"Loyalists in North Carolina during the Revolution." Reference Vertical File, State Library of North Carolina, Raleigh.

Lucas, J. P. "Cooling by Degrees: Reintegration of Loyalists in North Carolina, 1776-1790." M. A. thesis, Department of History, North Carolina State University, 2007. http://www.lib.ncsu.edu/theses/available/etd-03262007-104125/unrestricted/etd.pdf.

MacDonald, Donald. "Donald MacDonald Paper, 1776." Manuscript PC. 721 (MARS ID: 1231; record group), State Archives of North Carolina, Raleigh. ["Communication of MacDonald, in command of Loyalist forces near Fayetteville, N. C., requesting an American General [James Moore] and his soldiers to lay down their arms and swear allegiance to the king and stating that if the Americans failed in this, he would consider them traitors to the constitution and would "take necessary steps to conquer and subdue" them; letter written Feb. 26, 1776."[41]]

Miller, Randall M. "A Backcountry Loyalist Plan to Retake Georgia and the Carolinas, 1778." *South Carolina Historical Magazine*, 75 (1974), 207-214.

Misenheimer, John E., Jr. "Mary Brevard Davidson and Others after the American Revolution." *The Golden Nugget (Cabarrus Genealogical Society)*, 13:3 (Autumn 2005), 82-84. [Mary Davidson, Ann Christenbury, Sarah Rounsevall, and Nancy Horah of Western North Carolina. The latter's husband was a Loyalist.]

Moss, Bobby Gilmer. *Roster of the Loyalists at the Battle of Moores Creek Bridge*. Blacksburg, S. C.: Scotia-Hibernia Press, 1992.

Murray, James, 1713-1781; Nine Moore Tiffany, ed.; assisted by Susan I. Lesley. *Letters of James Murray, Loyalist*. Boston: [s. n.], 1901.

Norris, David A. "Tory." In William S. Powell, ed.; Jay Mazzocchi, assoc. ed., *Encyclopedia of North Carolina* (Chapel Hill: University of North Carolina Press in association with the University of North Carolina Library, 2006), 1126-1127.

North Carolina (State). General Assembly. "[Document dated:] January 27, 1779: Joint Papers, Committee Papers, Resolutions, Senate Bills, House Bills, Report on the Petition of the People of Pasquotank County Relative to the Slaves Liberated by the Quakers (with Messages)." Manuscript; General Assembly Record Group; Session Records, Jan-Feb 1779, Box 1 (MARS ID: 66.8.15.8.6; item), State Archives of North Carolina, Raleigh. [Online catalog description: "The petitioners complain to the Assembly that Quakers are freeing slaves. The committee recommends that a bill be drafted pertaining to slaves, for independence has nullified portions of the relative colonial law."]

North Carolina (State). General Assembly. "Sesson of Feb. 12, [1779]: Joint Papers, Committee Papers, Resolutions, Senate Bills, House Bills, For Disarming Tories (With Message)." Manuscript; General Assembly Record Group; Session Records, Jan-Feb 1779, Box 1, State Archives of North Carolina, Raleigh. [Online catalog description: "The resolution requests that the governor order the commanding officers in the counties to disarm disaffected persons and turn over the weapons to the state's soldiers."]

North Carolina (State). General Assembly. "[Document dated:] February 5, [1781]: Joint Papers, Committee Papers, Resolutions, Senate Bills, House Bills, Letter from Colonel Gideon Lamb and Bonds Given by Tories." Manuscript; General Assembly Record Group; Session Records, January-February 1781, Jan-Feb 1781, Box 1,

[41] North Carolina Historical Records Survey Project. *Guide to the Manuscript Collections in the Archives of the North Carolina Historical Commission* (Raleigh: North Carolina Historical Commission, 1942), 88.

State Archives of North Carolina, Raleigh. [Online catalog description: "Lamb informs the Assembly that in his opinion the only way to deal with the numerous loyalists in Currituck, Camden, Pasquotank, and Perquimans Counties is to forgive them on the condition that they sign bonds for their good behavior, which he has done. He includes several of the bonds."]

North Carolina (State). General Assembly. "[Document dated:] February 5, 1781: Joint Papers, Committee Papers, Resolutions, Senate Bills, House Bills, Letter from Colonel Gideon Lamb and Bonds Given by Tories." Manuscript; General Assembly Record Group; Session Records, January-February 1781, Box 1 (MARS ID: 66.8.23.3.3; item), State Archives of North Carolina, Raleigh. [Online catalog description: "Lamb informs the Assembly that in his opinion the only way to deal with the numerous loyalists in Currituck, Camden, Pasquotank, and Perquimans Counties is to forgive them on the condition that they sign bonds for their good behavior, which he has done. He includes several of the bonds."]

North Carolina (State). General Assembly. House of Delegates. "[Document dated:] June 29, [1781]. "House Bill to Indemnify and Absolve from Criminal Prosecution… Persons who… Have Put [Tories] to Death (Failed)." Manuscript, General Assembly Record Group, Session Records, June-July 1781; Joint Papers, Committee Papers, Resolutions, Senate Bills, House Bills, Box 2, (MARS ID: 66.8.26.19; folder), State Archives of North Carolina, Raleigh.

"Papers Relating to Samuel Cornell, North Carolina Loyalist." *Bulletin of the New York Public Library*, 17:6 (June 1913), 443-484; online: http://babel.hathitrust.org/cgi/pt?id=loc.ark:/13960/t1gh9xn2n;view=1up;seq=9.

Parsons, Elsie Clews. "Tales from Guilford County, North Carolina." *Journal of American Folk-Lore*, 30:116 (April-June 1917), 168-200. [from page 169: "Between the Bahama Islands and the Carolinas there is an historical connection which may account in part for the number of tales they have, I find, in common. During the period of the Revolutionary War a number of Tories known as United Empire Loyalists migrated from the Carolinas to the Bahamas; and they took with them, of course, their household slaves. In connection with this migration, it was of interest to find that what is still current belief in the Bahamas serves as a tale in North Carolina. I refer to the magical beliefs embodied in Nos. 28, 34, 35."]

Piecuch, James. *Three Peoples, One King: Loyalists, Indians, and Slaves in the American Revolutionary South, 1775-1782*. Columbia: University of South Carolina Press, 2008.

Poe, Clarence H. "Indians, Slaves, and Tories: Our 18th Century Legislation Regarding Them." *North Carolina Booklet*, 9 (1909), 3-15.

Polen, Debi. *North Carolina Loyalists in the American Revolution.* Durham: Duke University Press, 2008.

Rindfleisch, Bryan. "'The World Turned Upside Down': The Impact of the American Revolution on the Patterns of Inheritance, Marriage, and Kinship among Southern Planter Loyalist Families." *Southern Historian*, 31 (Spring 2010), 48-65.

Rollins, Harold W. "The First Civil War: A Series of Articles." *Bulletin of the Genealogical Society of Old Tryon County*, 3:3 (August 1975), 120-125; 3:4 (November 1975), 154-160; 4:1 (February 1976), 4-11 [includes "A Partial List of Persons from Old Rutherford County, Who Served, or Were Accused of Having Served, in Loyalist Units, 1778-1782," 8-10]; 4:2 (May 1976), 88-96 [with corrections to Part Three in previous issue].

Sammons, Helen. "Loyalists or Helpless Prisoners?" *Clarendon Courier*, 6:3 (September 1994), 9. [residents of Wilmington and vicinity; 1781]

"The Secretary of Loyalist Descendants Seeks Information on NC's 'Truce Lands' during the Revolutionary War." *North Carolina Genealogical and Historical News*, 4:1 (January-February 1988), 6-8. [Discusses this area mostly in South Carolina to the northeast of the Pee Dee River and supposedly crossing over into portions of North Carolina's modern Robeson and Columbus Counties. It includes a map of the region where Loyalists led by "Colonel David Fanning attempted to have the Cumberland County area of North Carolina 'neutralized' into a truce area during 1781 and 1782. Strong opposition, however, prevented the realization of this attempt'." While there is more information on the "Truce Lands," the term coming from a truce agreement between General Francis Marion and Loyalist Colonel Micajah Ganey/Gainey, there is not a lot on this general subject in print.]

Simpson, James; Alan Scouter Brown, ed. *James Simpson's Reports on the Carolina Loyalists, 1779-1780.* Lexington, Ky.: s. n., 1955.

Smith, Mary Larratt. "The Canadian Bethunes." *The Loyalist Gazette*, 28:2 (Fall 1990), 30-32. [with North Carolina connections before the Revolution]

Smith, Paul Hubert. *Loyalists and Redcoats: A Study in British Revolutionary Policy*. Chapel Hill: University of North Carolina Press for the Institute of Early American History and Culture, 1964.

"Sticks, Signs, and Senior Wardens." *Washington County Genealogical Society Journal*, 4:3 (December 1996), 77-78. [Tory forms of indentifying each other]

"Thomas Blair, A Tory Captain." *North Carolina Genealogical Society Journal*, 3:3 (August 1977), 165.

"Tories Held in Halifax Jail, 1776." *North Carolina Genealogy*, 20:1 (Spring-Summer, 1974), 2921.

"The Tory Conspiracy." *Washington County Genealogical Society Journal*, 4:3 (December 1996), 77. [1776-1777]

Troxler, Carole Watterson. "'The Great Man of the Settlement': North Carolina's John Legett at Country Harbour, Nova Scotia, 1783-1812." *North Carolina Historical Review,* 67:3 (July 1990), 285-314. [Online description from "North Carolina Periodicals Index," East Carolina University: "This article looks at the life of Bladen County resident John Legett, as a loyalist in exile in Nova Scotia between 1783 and 1812. During the Revolutionary War, Legett led one of the few loyalist brigades in the South. After the war, some loyalists were given free land grants in Nova Scotia by the British government. Legett and his followers were given County Harbour in Nova Scotia, where Legett persevered over the many hardships that occurred to him in an effort to build a new life and properly discharge his duties as magistrate."]

Troxler, Carole Watterson. *The Loyalist Experience in North Carolina.* Raleigh: North Carolina Department of Archives and History, 1976. [See the section, "Loss by Debt: The Trials of Mary Dowd," 32-35, about a family's legal claims to confiscated land and Mary Dowd's attempts to sue for her loyalist husband's debts.]

Troxler, Carole Watterson. "The Migration of Carolina and Georgia Loyalists to Nova Scotia and New Brunswick." Ph. D. dissertation, University of North Carolina at Chapel Hill, 1974.

Troxler, Carole Watterson. "Royal North Carolina Regiment." In William S. Powell, ed.; Jay Mazzocchi, assoc. ed., *Encyclopedia of North Carolina* (Chapel Hill: University of North Carolina Press in association with the University of North Carolina Library, 2006), 991-992.

Troxler, Carole Watterson. "'To Git Out of a Troublesome Neighborhood:' David Fanning in New Brunswick." *North Carolina Historical Review*, 56:4 (October 1979), 343-365.

Troxler, Carole Watterson. "Refuge, Resistance, and Reward: The Southern Loyalists' Claim on East Florida." *Journal of Southern History*, 55:4 (November 1989), 563-596.

Troxler, Carole Watterson, and David A. Norris. "Llewelyn Conspiracy." In William S. Powell, ed.; Jay Mazzocchi, assoc. ed., *Encyclopedia of North Carolina* (Chapel Hill: University of North Carolina Press in association with the University of North Carolina Library, 2006), 688. [1776; aka "Tory Plot"]

Troxler, Carole Watterson, and Laura Morgan. "Loyalists." In William S. Powell, ed.; Jay Mazzocchi, assoc. ed., *Encyclopedia of North Carolina* (Chapel Hill: University of North Carolina Press in association with the University of North Carolina Library, 2006), 697-699.

Turner, Grace. "Accusations by John Walker." *Bulletin of the Genealogical Society of Old Tryon County*, 19:2 (May 1991), 77-78." [Salisbury District Criminal Actions, 1778; Loyalists and Patriots on the frontier]

Turner, Grace W. "A Bill to Bring Traitors to Trial, 1782." *North Carolina Genealogical Society Journal*, 28:4 (November 2002), 420-427.

Turrentine, Joseph Dempsey. "Why Neighbor Fought Neighbor." B. A. thesis, University of Georgia, 2009. [Thesis description: "During the Revolutionary War, western North Carolina maintained one of the highest loyalist populations of any region in the thirteen colonies. Nearly one hundred years later, this same region contained widespread unionist sentiment during the Civil War. In a region just tame enough to settle yet too wild to firmly control, the ruling class chose repression to maintain their grip on the region. In both centuries, conditions were ripe for internal conflict, but for different reasons. Eventually, in both conflicts neighbor executed neighbor and western North Carolina populations descended into anarchy. In Wilkes Country during the Revolutionary War, Benjamin Cleveland personified the western ruling class, their overall impact on the outcome of the American Revolution, and Cleveland's story represents a good starting point for comparison. By comparing and contrasting these two internal conflicts, I hope to more fully expose the societal parallels that led to total breakdown, and to detect what impacts, if any, that the first struggle had on the second."]

Tyson, George F., Jr. "The Carolina Black Corps: Legacy of the Revolution, 1783-1798." *Revista/Review Interamericana*, 4:4 (Winter 1975), 648-664.

"Warrants to Survey for King's Carolina Rangers, South Carolina Regiment [sic], Royal North Carolina Regiment, February, 1, February 18, April 23, 1784." Manuscript, Public Archives of Nova Scotia, Halifax.

White, James Samuel. "The Tories in North Carolina." Senior thesis, University of North Carolina at Chapel Hill, 1896.

Winslow, Raymond A., Jr. "Two Lists of North Carolinians and Others Serving in British Armies during the American Revolution." *North Carolina Genealogical Society Journal*, 16:3 (August 199), 142-146; (part 2), 20:2 (May 1994), 96-117; (part 3), 20:4 (November 1994), 242-276.

Wyche, Mary Clayton. "The Tory War in North Carolina." Graduate thesis. Chapel Hill: University of North Carolina, 1941. [Examination of the conflict between the loyalist Tories and the Patriotic Whigs from 1776-

1782, with special emphasis on the loyalists' role in the British invasion of 1780 and the lasting effects of the war.]

Loyalists/Tories in North Carolina – Confiscation, Forfeiture, Attainder, etc.

Bell, John L. "Confiscation Acts." In William S. Powell, ed.; Jay Mazzocchi, assoc. ed., *Encyclopedia of North Carolina* (Chapel Hill: University of North Carolina Press in association with the University of North Carolina Library, 2006), 274.

Bennett, William D., and Jo White Linn. "North Carolina Confiscated Property, 1777-1786." *Rowan County Register*, 3:3 (August 1988), 618-619.

"Confiscated Property Sales, Rutherford County, N. C." *Eswau Huppeday: Bulletin of the Broad River Genealogical Society,* 11:2 (May 1991), 118-119.

Dunaway, Stewart E. *Confiscation Act & Pardon and Oblivion Act: A Complete History (1776-1812).* Hillsborough, N. C.: S. E. Dunaway, 2015. [Publisher's description: "During the formation of an independent government, the legislature of North Carolina designed several laws –Treason Act and Confiscation Act which defined limitations on the citizens of the state. These laws supported the effort towards independence, and legislated penalties for those who remain loyal to the crown. In addition, land owners outside North Carolina (either in other states, or in Europe etc.) had to declare their allegiance to the state, or subject their estates to confiscation ... North Carolina will create the Pardon and Oblivion Act in an attempt to reconcile local anguish between differing views and rolls [i.e. roles] during the war. This book covers all of this information in great detail, illustrating both sides of the issues. All of the information contained in this book originates from primary sources ... Lastly, this book will review the Treaty of Peace (1783) as well as the Jay Treaty (1798) in order to understand the contention of state's rights versus the new federal government."]

Dunaway, Stewart E. *North Carolina Confiscation Records*. 3 vols. Hillsborough: S. E. Dunaway, 2010-[2013?]. [Publisher's description: "This book contains images of the original records, as preserved by the State Archives (Raleigh). These records are transcribed and cataloged (including detailed indexing) to assist researchers as they delve into the difficult area of Land Confiscation. In NC, land was confiscated by Act of Assembly, for those people who remained loyal to the King during the American Revolution." Contents:

- Vol. 1: 1782-1788 {1779-1800}: covering the counties of Orange, Randolph, Chatham, Guilford, Granville, Wake, and Montgomery. [These records are primarily documenting Henry E. McCulloh's land, although, Fanning, Tryon, Josiah Martin, and Milner are included. In this volume are the records for Chatham, Guilford, Montgomery, Orange, Randolph, and Wake County. This book includes data tables and some maps to assist researchers. Orange County has the largest quantity of records, and data tables were included with numerous sorts to assist researching this collection."]
- Vol. 2: 1779-1800: Anson, Beaufort, Bertie, Bladen, Brunswick, Camden, Chowan, Craven, and Currituck Counties.
- Vol. 3: 1779-1803: Dobbs, Duplin, Edgecombe, Halifax, Hertford, Hyde, Lenoir, Lincoln, Martin, Mecklenburg, Moore, Nash, New Hanover, Northampton, Pasquotank, Pitt, Richmond, Rowan, Sampson, Surry and Tyrell Counties.]

Great Britain. Exchequer and Audit Department. "'Extracts of all Such Grants of Confiscated Property as are Recorded in the Office of the Secretary of State of North Carolina.' April 29." Copy of a manuscript in the National Archives of the United Kingdom (formerly the Public Records Office), Kew, Richmond, Surrey, England; (MARS Id: 21.2.14.16; folder), "British Records Collection," State Archives of North Carolina, Raleigh. [Online catalog description: "Columns showing date of sale, name of former owner, name of purchaser, county, number of acres, description of land, sum paid."]

Great Britain. Exchequer and Audit Department. "[Papers in the Loyalist Claim of] Archibald Taylor (formerly of Bladen Co.) [n. d.]." Copy of a manuscript in the National Archives of the United Kingdom (formerly the Public Records Office), Kew, Richmond, Surrey, England; (MARS ID: 21.3.7.15; Folder), "British Records Collection," State Archives of North Carolina, Raleigh. [Online catalog description: "Memorials concerning his losses; schedules of same; affidavit of John Syeds concerning same; letter of attorney; copy of order to take part in attack on New Providence; depositions of John Kerr and others; abstracts of two land grants in N.C. made to Taylor in 1774; certificates by J. H. Craig and others."]

Great Britain. Exchequer and Audit Department. "[Papers in the Loyalist Claim of] Henry Eustace McCulloh. [n.d.]." Copy of a manuscript in the National Archives of the United Kingdom (formerly the Public Records Office), Kew, Richmond, Surrey, England;MARS Id: 21.3.1.14 (Folder), "British Records Project," State Archives of North Carolina, Raleigh. [Online catalog description: "Memorials concerning losses in N. C.;

schedule "of the Particulars of Mr. McCulloh's Landed Property in North Carolina, with the Valuations thereof"; schedule of his personal property there…"] Henry Eustace McCulloh."]

Great Britain. Exchequer and Audit Department. "[Papers in the Loyalist Claim of] Lord Granville. [n. d.]." Copy of a manuscript in the National Archives of the United Kingdom (formerly the Public Records Office), Kew, Richmond, Surrey, England; Z.5.110N, "British Records Collection," State Archives of North Carolina, Raleigh. [Online catalog description: "Memorials concerning losses in N. C.; summary of number of grants made in N.C., with discussion of same; abstract of title of Rt. Hon. Henry Frederick, Ld. Carteret, to one eighth of N.C., incl. engraved map of grant."]

Great Britain. Exchequer and Audit Department. "[Papers in the Loyalist Cliam [*sic*] of] Angus Campbell (Capt., N.C. Highlanders; Cumberland Co.) [n. d.]." Copy of a manuscript in the National Archives of the United Kingdom (formerly the Public Records Office), Kew, Richmond, Surrey, England; Z.5.110N, "British Records Collection," State Archives of North Carolina, Raleigh. [Online catalog description: "Memorials concerning losses in N. C.; schedules of same; certificates by Josiah Martin, Neil McArthur, Alexander McKay; land grants (original) to William West and Richard Creech, 22 July 1774, with plats; deeds of sale of land in Cumberland Co., John Phillips to Angus Campbell, 29 Dec 1775, and Richard Creech to same, 12 Jan 1776; letter, Andrew Lawrie, York Bldgs., to Commissioners for Loyalist Claims, 23 June 1787; minutes of examination of Campbell."]

Great Britain. Colonial Office. America and the West Indies, Original Correspondence, Board of Trade and Secretary of State, Miscellaneous Correspondence. (CO 5/43). "A General Statement of the Status of American Loyalists' Property Confiscated under the Laws of the United States. July 1783." Copy of a manuscript in the National Archives of the United Kingdom (formerly the Public Records Office), Kew, Richmond, Surrey, England; 70.109.1-4 (MARS ID: 21.20.34.6; folder), "British Records Collection," State Archives of North Carolina, Raleigh. [Online catalog description: "Prepared by agents for the American Loyalists and presented to Charles Fox, sec. of state, this statement lists, state by state, including N.C., the disposition of American Loyalist property."] [Note: Crown copyright. These copies are supplied for information and research only. No reproduction may be made for publication without the assent of the Public Record Office, London."]

Great Britain. Colonial Office. "New York, [N. Y.]. Commissioners for Quieting the Disorders in N. Am., to Lord George Germain, [Sec. of State]. 5 Sep, 1778." Copy of a manuscript in the National Archives of the United Kingdom (formerly the Public Records Office), Kew, Richmond, Surrey, England; 71.362.1-3 (MARS ID: 21.20.142.3; folder), "British Records Collection," State Archives of North Carolina, Raleigh. [Online catalog description: "Acknowledges receipt of Germain to Commissioners, 29 May 1778 (21.20.142.1.2), requesting assistance for Henry Eustace McCulloh and John Burgwin who are returning to N. C. in an effort to protect their property from confiscation by the rebels. The commissioners – Frederick Howard (Earl of Carlisle), William Eden, and George Johnstone – pledge to do all within their powers to help McCulloh and Burgwin."]

Great Britain. Colonial Office. "Whitehall, [London]. Draft of Lord George Germain, [Sec. of State], to the Commissioners for Quieting the Disorders in N. Am. May 29, 1778." Copy of a manuscript in the National Archives of the United Kingdom (formerly the Public Records Office), Kew, Richmond, Surrey, England; 71.361.1-3 (MARS ID: 21.20.142.1; folder), "British Records Collection," State Archives of North Carolina, Raleigh. [Online catalog description: "Requests commissioners' protection and assistance for Henry Eustace McCulloh and John Burgwin who are returning to N. C. in an attempt to protect their property from confiscation by the rebels."]

Linn, Jo White. "Burke County, NC, Confiscation Proceeding, 1780: Bond of John Bowman." *Journal of the Burke County Genealogical Society*, 17:1 (February 1999), 4.

McColloh Family. "Lawrence James Collection, 1762-1871." Manuscript call number PC.1704.1, State Archives of North Carolina, Raleigh. [Online catalog description: "Papers from four generations of the McCulloh family from whom Lawrence James descended: Henry McCulloh of Cullo, Henry Eustace McCulloh, George McCulloh and W. D. McCulloh. Twenty-two of the folders contain materials relating to the McCulloh lands in North Carolina and relate directly to Henry Eustace McCulloh and to his natural son, George, who was his agent to recover lands in North Carolina following the Revolutionary War (the lands of Henry Eustace McCulloh being specifically confiscated by name in the confiscation act)."]

McCubbins, "Mame" Mary Louise Gaskill. "[List of Men Whose Property was Threatened with Confiscation. 1782.]" *Rowan County Register*, 3:3 (August 1988), 620.

McKinnon, Henry A. "A North Carolina Scot and the Confiscation Acts." *The Robeson County Register*, 1:3 (August 1986), 105-106. [Archibald McEacharn]

North Carolina General Assembly. *An Act for Confiscating the Property of All Such Persons, As Are Inimical to the United States* ... Newbern, N. C.: Printed by James Davis, 1778; micropublished: (Early American Imprints. First Series, no. 43520).

North Carolina (State). General Assembly. "[Document dated]: October 26, 1779: Bill to Vest the Title of Certain Lands therein Mentioned to Abner Nash." Manuscript; General Assembly Record Group; Session Records, October-November 1779; Unidentified Amendments, Senate Bills, House Bills, Box 2 (MARS ID: 66.8.19.14), State Archives of North Carolina, Raleigh. [Online catalog description: "The bill carries into effect the recommendations of the committee that investigated the petitions of Abner Nash, Thomas Burke, and Thomas Person." Other names mentioned: Edmund Fanning (1739-1818), William Field, Thomas Hart, Richard Augustus Lathbury, Andrew Miller, and James Milner.]

North Carolina (State). General Assembly. "[Document dated:] 1780: "Petition of William Collson (Rejected)." Manuscript; General Assembly Record Group; Session Records, August-September 1780; Joint Papers, Committee Papers, Resolutions, Senate Bills, House Bills, Box 1, (MARS ID: 66.8.22.6.2; item), State Archives of North Carolina, Raleigh. [Online catalog description: "Collson informs the Assembly that he realizes he was wrong to have withdrawn his allegiance to the state, that as reparation he has entered the military of the United States, and that he hopes to have his estate restored and to be considered a citizen."]

North Carolina (State). General Assembly. "[Document dated:] April 27, 1780: Joint Papers, Committee Papers, Resolutions, Senate Bills, House Bills, Re[specting] Petitions of William Houston and William Skinner." Manuscript; General Assembly Record Group; Session Records, Apr-May 1780, Box 1 (MARS ID: 66.8.20.8.11; item), State Archives of North Carolina, Raleigh. [Online catalog description: "Houston informs the Assembly that in 1742 he took possession of a tract of land in Duplin County from his uncle, Henry McCulloh, who left the state in 1747. Because he never acquired a title or deed, Houston is concerned that the land is subject to confiscation and asks the Assembly to vest him with a title to the land by law. Skinner informs the Assembly that the law prohibiting individuals who have not taken the affirmation of allegiance to the state has had the effect of disabling Quakers in Pasquotank and Perquimans Counties from maintaining possession of their own land and asks the Assembly to pass a law in their behalf. The committee recommends that both petitions be granted, and the Assembly concurs."]

North Carolina (State). General Assembly. "[Document dated:] May 9, 1780: Joint Papers, Committee Papers, Resolutions, Senate Bills, House Bills, Directing Payment to the Miles Gale Estate by Commissioners for Selling Confiscated Proprety in Pasquotank County (Messages Only)." Manuscript; General Assembly Record Group; Session Records, Apr-May 1780, Box 1 (MARS ID: 66.8.20.17.13), State Archives of North Carolina, Raleigh.

North Carolina (State). General Assembly. "[Document dated:] September 4, [1780]: House Bills: Re the French Fleet and Thomas Buckle." Manuscript, General Assembly Record Group, Session Records, August-September 1780; Joint Papers, Committee Papers, Resolutions, Senate Bills, Box 1 (MARS ID: 66.8.22.3.5), State Archives of North Carolina, Raleigh. [Online catalog description: "Governor Nash informs the Assembly of the probable arrival of the French fleet despite a lack of official confirmation by the Continental Congress. He also refers to a letter concerning the confiscated property of Thomas Buckle, whom Nash considers a loyalist for signing a letter to General Henry Clinton at Charleston."]

North Carolina (State). General Assembly. "[Document dated]: July 13, 1781: Resolution in Favor of ___Aldridge, Father of William Aldridge of Rowan County (with Petition) (Rejected)." Manuscript; General Assembly Record Group; Session Records, June-July 1781; Joint Papers, Committee Papers, Resolutions; Senate Joint Resolutions: July 6-14, 1781, Box 1 (MARS ID: 66.8.25.11.6; item), State Archives of North Carolina, Raleigh. [Online catalog description: "William Aldredge informs the Assembly that David Caldwell, a Rowan County commissioner of confiscated property, has confiscated his father's lands based on an unproven suspicion of toryism. The resolution would have ordered Caldwell to return the land."]

North Carolina (State). General Assembly. "[Document dated]: May 4, 1782: Resolution in Favor of William Eldridge [Alldredge]. (Messages and Petition Only)." Manuscript; General Assembly Record Group; Session Records, April-May 1782; Committee Papers, Resolutions, Senate Bills, House Bills; House Joint Resolutions, May 3-May 9, 1782, Box 2 (MARS ID:), State Archives of North Carolina, Raleigh. [Online catalog description: "Petition of William Aldridge requests return of land in Rowan Co. which was confiscated after his father was accused of harboring petitioner's brother, who had joined the British; with messages from both houses concurring with resolution."]

North Carolina (State). General Assembly. "[Document dated]: May 12, 1784: Resolution in Favor of John Braley, Register of Rowan County." Manuscript; General Assembly Record Group; Session Records, April-June 1784; Committee Papers, Resolutions; Senate Joint Resolutions, Box 2 (MARS ID: 66.8.32.4.11; item), State

Archives of North Carolina, Raleigh. [Online catalog description: "Resolution awards compensation for John Braley's furnishing of copies of deeds of confiscated lands to the commissioner of the District of Salisbury."]

North Carolina (State). General Assembly. Senate. "[Document dated:] Nov. 8, [1784]: Senate Bill to Ascertain Titles to Certain Lands." Manuscript, General Assembly Session Records, October-November 1784, Oct-Nov 1784; Joint Papers, Committee Papers, Resolutions, Senate Bills, House Bills, Box 1 (MARS ID: 66.8.35.40; folder), State Archives of North Carolina, Raleigh. [Online catalog description: "Bill would require county sheriffs to obtain a list of the property of those persons who took the British side and fled or were killed in the war. Those lands that were granted to loyalists will be drawn up and collected by the Secretary of State, then the owners will have a period of time in which to claim them, after which the lands will revert to the state. The bill also describes methods of trying the cases."]

North Carolina (State). General Assembly. "[Document Dated]: November 28, 1785: Report on the Petition of William Field (with Petition) (Rejected)." Manuscript; General Assembly Record Group; Session Records, November-December 1785; Joint Papers, Committee Papers; Committee of Propositions and Grievances; Reports and Papers, Box 1 (MARS ID: 66.8.37.9.3; item), State Archives of North Carolina, Raleigh. [Online catalog description: "Report rejects the petition for the reason that it doesn't fall under the jurisdiction of the Assembly because it concerns the Confiscation Act. Petition is from William Fields, who took an Oath of Allegiance to the King and a commission as an officer in the British Army. He now seeks to regain his citizenship. Included are court reports from Randolph County."]

North Carolina (State). General Assembly. "[Document dated:] December 8, 1787: Report on Petition of Isaac Davenport, Jonathan Phelps, and John Davenport (With Petition) (Rejected)." Manuscript; General Assembly Record Group; Session Records, November1786-January 1787; Joint Papers, Committee Papers, Resolutions, Senate Bills, House Bills, Box 2 (MARS ID: 66.8.42.2.4), State Archives of North Carolina, Raleigh. [Online catalog description: "Petitioners protest the sale of their land in Tyrrell County under the Confiscation Act. Report rejects petition on the grounds that should petitioners' land grants be legal, their case requires no interference from the legislature."]

North Carolina (State). General Assembly. "[Document dated:] December 5, 1789: Report on Petition of Colonel Nicholas Long, as Agent of 26 Officers of North Carolina Continental Line (Petition only). December 5." Manuscript; General Assembly Record Group; Session Records, November-December, 1789; Joint Papers, Committee Papers, Resolutions, Senate Bills, House Bills, Box 2 (MARS ID: 66.8.53.4.5; item), State Archives of North Carolina, Raleigh. [Online catalog description: "Petition of Colonel Nicholas Long, agent for officers of the Continental Line, requests that he be allowed to pay for slaves he bought at a confiscation sale with certificates rather than money. He was paid by the officers, for whom he purchased the slaves, with certificates. Includes testimony of the officers involved and verification of Long's debt as decided by the Superior Court of Hillsboro District."]

"Presentment to Confiscate Property of Tories, Morgan District, NC, Court Records." *Bulletin of the Genealogical Society of Old Tryon County*, 21:3 (August 1993), 129. [Rutherford County]

Pruitt, Albert Bruce. *Abstracts of Sales of Confiscated Loyalists' Land and Property in North Carolina*. Whitakers: A. B. Pruitt, 1989.

Steinle, Bessie Maxine. "Confiscation of Royalist Property during and after the Revolution in North Carolina." M. A. thesis, University of Texas, 1935.

Loyalists/Tories in North Carolina – Llewelyn Conspiracy/Gourd Patch Affair/Tory Plot, 1777

Crow, Jeffrey J. "Tory Plots and Anglican Loyalty: The Llewelyn Conspiracy of 1777." *North Carolina Historical Review*, 55:1 (January 1978), 1-17.

Edenton District Superior Court. "Depositions Relative to Llewelyn Conspiracy, 1777." Manuscript in "Rowan County Miscellaneous Records, 1699-1865," Box 4, folder 1, State Archives of North Carolina, Raleigh.

"'The Gourd Patch Affair' or 'The Llewellyn Conspiracy'." Online: http://www.rawlins.org/origins/hearsay/thegourdpatch.html.

"Our Tylers – Loyalists in the Llewellyn Conspiracy in the Revolutionary War?" Online: http://andreamusgroveperisho.com/?p=258.

"Taylor-Best-Wallace Part in the John Llewellyn Conspiracy of 1777." Online: https://familysearch.org/photos/stories/1196459.

"Tories in Bertie County." Online: http://www.rootsweb.ancestry.com/~ncbertie/conspiracy.htm.

Troxler, Carole Watterson. *The Loyalist Experience in North Carolina*. Raleigh: North Carolina Department of Archives and History, 1976.

Troxler, Carole Watterson, and David A. Norris. "Llewelyn Conspiracy." Online at NCpedia website: http://ncpedia.org/llewelyn-conspiracy.

Melungeons of North Carolina and Tennessee

Ball, Donald B. *A Bibliography of Tennessee Anthropology, Including Cherokee, Chickasaw, and Melungeon Studies*. Knoxville: Tennessee Anthropological Association, 1977.

Estes, Robert J., *et al*. "Melungeons, a Multiethnic Population." *Journal of Genetic Genealogy*, 7 (Fall 2011), 1-91.

Hashaw, Tim. *Children of Perdition: Melungeons and the Struggle of Mixed America*. Macon, Ga.: Mercer University Press, 2006.

Hirschman, Elizabeth C. *Melungeons: The Last Lost Tribe in America*. Macon, Ga.: Mercer University Press, 2005.

Langdon, Barbara Tracy. *The Melungeons: An Annotated Bibliography*. Woodville, Tex.: Dogwood Press, 1998.

"[Melungeons in North Carolina]." Reference Vertical File, State Library of North Carolina, Raleigh.

Schrift, Melissa. *Becoming Melungeon: Making an Ethnic Identify in the Appalachian South*. Lincoln: University of Nebraska Press, 2013.

Winkler, Wayne. *Walking toward the Sunset: The Melungeons of Appalachia*. Macon, Ga.: Mercer University Press, 2004.

Neutral North Carolinians

Great Britain. Colonial Office. America and West Indies: North Carolina, Original Correspondence, Board of Trade, Secretary of State. (CO 5/318). "Order of N. C. Council of Safety. July 4, 1776." Copy of a manuscript in the National Archives of the United Kingdom (formerly the Public Records Office), Kew, Richmond, Surrey, England; (MARS ID: 21.1.27.92; folder), "British Records Collections," State Archives of North Carolina, Raleigh. [Online catalog description: "Persons claiming neutrality in the conflict must render an inventory of their property."]

Religious History, Groups, and Individuals in Revolutionary North Carolina

Calhoon, Robert McCluer. *Evangelicals and Conservatives in the Early South*. Columbia: University of South Carolina Press, 1988.

Calhoon, Robert M. *Religion and the American Revolution in North Carolina*. (North Carolina Bicentennial Pamphlet Series, no. 11) Raleigh: North Carolina Dept. of Cultural Resources, Division of Archives and History, 1976. [Collection of primary materials relating to the experiences of various religious groups in North Carolina during the Revolution.]

Conkin, Paul. "The Church Establishment in North Carolina, 1765-1776." *North Carolina Historical Review*, 32:1 (January 1955), 1-30; online: http://digital.ncdcr.gov/cdm/ref/collection/p16062coll9/id/4207. [Online description from "North Carolina Periodicals Index," East Carolina University: "This article looks at the establishment of various religious groups and their infrastructure in colonial North Carolina, most notably with the establishment of the Anglican Church and its place as the official church of the state. Attention is given to other religious groups whose congregations gained a foothold in the state during this period including Anabaptists, German Reformed, Lutheran, Moravian, Quakers, Baptists, and Presbyterians, as well as laws passed related to religion or to clergy."]

Conser, Walter H., Jr. *A Coat of Many Colors: Religion and Society along the Cape Fear River of North Carolina*. Lexington: The University Press of Kentucky, 2006. [Publisher's description: "While religious diversity is often considered a recent phenomenon in America, the Cape Fear region of southeastern North Carolina has been a diverse community since the area was first settled. Early on, the region and the port city of Wilmington were more urban than the rest of the state and thus provided people with opportunities seldom found in other parts of North Carolina. This area drew residents from many ethnic backgrounds, and the men and women who settled there became an integral part of the region's culture. Set against the backdrop of national and southern religious experience, *A Coat of Many Colors* examines issues of religious diversity and regional identity in the Cape Fear area. Author Walter H. Conser Jr. draws on a broad range of sources, including congregational records, sermon texts, liturgy, newspaper accounts, family memoirs, and technological developments to explore the evolution of religious life in this area. Beginning with the story of prehistoric Native Americans and continuing through an examination of life at the end of twentieth century, Conser tracks the development of the various religions, denominations, and ethnic groups that call the Cape Fear region home. From early Native American traditions to the establishment of the first churches, cathedrals, synagogues, mosques, and temples, *A Coat of Many Colors* offers a comprehensive view of the religious and ethnic diversity that have characterized Cape Fear throughout its history. Through the lens of regional history, Conser explores how this area's rich religious and racial diversity can be seen as a microcosm for the South, and he examines the ways in which religion can affect such diverse aspects of life as architecture and race relations."]

Davis, Vernon Perdue. *The Colonial Churches of Virginia, Maryland, and North Carolina: Their Interiors and Worship*. Richmond: Dietz Press, 1985.

Epps, Katie. "Early Religious Developments in Middle Tennessee." M. A. thesis, Middle Tennessee State University, 1954.

Gobble, Luther L. *Church-State Relationships in Education in North Carolina since 1776*. Durham: Duke University Press, 1938.

Graham-Voelker, Graham. "Four Denominations of the Colonial Era: Anglicans, Quakers, Presbyterians, and Moravians." *Tar Heel Junior Historian*, 37:2 (Spring 1998), 7, 10-11. [Online description from "North Carolina Periodicals Index," East Carolina University: "Although the Church of England, or Anglican Church, was the colony's official religion, it grew slowly. Colonists were spread out, and churches were few. Because of the colony's religious tolerance, three dissenting groups developed: Quakers, Presbyterians, and Moravians."]

Hall, Cline Edwin. "The Southern Dissenting Clergy and the American Revolution." Ph. D. dissertation, University of Tennessee, 1975.

Haller, Charlotte A. "'And Made Us to Be a Kingdom:' Race, Antislavery, and Black Evangelicals in North Carolina's Early Republic." *North Carolina Historical Review*, 80:2 (April 2003), 125-152.

Hill, Samuel S. *Encyclopedia of Religion in the South.* Macon, Ga.: Mercer University Press, 1984.

Latham, Bea. "Backward in Religious Matters: The Church in Colonial North Carolina." *Tar Heel Junior Historian*, 51:2 (Spring 2012), 15-17. [Online description from "North Carolina Periodicals Index," East Carolina University: "Religion played an important role from the beginning of European exploration and settlement in the New World. Early North Carolina experienced constant tension, though, over religion. In the 1700s the colony developed as an independent place, mostly tolerant of different faiths but ministers and missionaries to the North Carolina colony found spreading religion difficult."]

Lawrence, R. D. "Early Churches of Carolina." *The State: A Weekly Survey of North Carolina*, 8:8 (July 1940), 9, 22; online: http://digital.ncdcr.gov/cdm/ref/collection/p16062coll18/id/5839. [Online description from "North Carolina Periodicals Index," East Carolina University: "Lawrence details the interesting story of how the Baptists, Methodists, and Presbyterians established themselves within the boundaries of North Carolina during its early history."]

McCauley, Deborah Vansau. *Appalachian Mountain Religion: A History*. Urbana: University of Illinois Press, 1995.

Pauley, William Everett, Jr. "Religion and the American Revolution in the South, 1760-1781." Ph. D. dissertation, Emory University, 1974.

Posey, Walter Brownlow. *Frontier Mission: A History of Religion West of the Southern Appalachians to 1861.* Lexington: University of Kentucky Press, 1966.

Rouse, J. K. *Some Interesting Colonial Churches in North Carolina*. Kannapolis: Rouse, 1961.

Weeks, Stephen Beauregard. *Church and State in North Carolina* (Johns Hopkins University Studies in Historical and Political Science series) Baltimore: Johns Hopkins Press,1893; Reprinted: [New York: Johnson Reprint Corp], 1973.

Weis, Frederick Lewis. *The Colonial Churches and the Colonial Clergy of the Middle and Southern Colonies, 1607-1776.* Lancaster, Mass.: Society of the Descendants of the Colonial Clergy, 1938.

Weis, Frederick Lewis. *The Colonial Clergy of Virginia, North Carolina, and South Carolina*. Boston: Society of the Descendants of Colonial Clergy, 1955; reprinted: Baltimore: Genealogical Publishing Company, 1976.

Anglicans/Church of England/Episcopalians

Conkin, Paul. "The Church Establishment in North Carolina, 1765-1776." *North Carolina Historical Review*, 32:1 (January 1955), 1-30; online: http://digital.ncdcr.gov/cdm/ref/collection/p16062coll9/id/4207. [Online description from "North Carolina Periodicals Index," East Carolina University: "This article looks at the establishment of various religious groups and their infrastructure in colonial North Carolina, most notably with the establishment of the Anglican Church and its place as the official church of the state. Attention is given to other religious groups whose congregations gained a foothold in the state during this period including Anabaptists, German Reformed, Lutheran, Moravian, Quakers, Baptists, and Presbyterians, as well as laws passed related to religion or to clergy."]

Crow, Jeffrey J. "Tory Plots and Anglican Loyalty: The Llewelyn Conspiracy of 1777." *North Carolina Historical Review*, 55:1 (January 1978), 1-17.

Caruthers, Eli Washington. *A Sketch of the Life and Character of the Rev. David Caldwell, D. D.: Near Sixty Years Pastor of the Churches of Buffalo and Alamance: Including Two of His Sermons, Some Account of the Regulation, Together with the Revolutionary... Incidents in Which He was Concerned, and a Very Brief Notice of the Ecclesiastical and Moral Condition of North Carolina while in its Colonial State.* Greensborough: Swaim and Sherwood, 1842.

Dorsey, Stephen Palmer. *Early English Churches in America, 1607-1807.* New York: Oxford University Press, 1952.

Ervin, Spencer. "The Anglican Church in North Carolina." *Historical Magazine of the Protestant Episcopal Church,* 25:3 (June 1956, 158-161.

Garland, John M. "The Nonecclesiastical Activities of An England and a North Carolina Parish: A Comparative Study." *North Carolina Historical Review*, 50:1 (January 1973), 32-51.

Great Britain. Exchequer and Audit Department. Claims, American Loyalist, Series II (AO 13, Selections), Claims, Miscellaneous. (AO 13/137). "Certificate Addressed to Governor Richard Caswell from John Johnson, Clerk of Bertie County Court, 14 Aug. 1777." Copy of a manuscript in the National Archives of the United Kingdom (formerly the Public Records Office), Kew, Richmond, Surrey, England; 77.2203.1 (MARS ID: 21.3.70.19), "British Records Collec-tion," State Archives of North Carolina, Raleigh. [Online catalog description: "Stating that Reverend Francis Johnston has given bond that he will depart the state within 60 days, having been banished for refusing to take an oath of allegiance to the state."]

Hardesty, Fred. "The Church Courts." *The State: Down Home in North Carolina*, 37:5 (August 1969), 11-12; online: http://digital.ncdcr.gov/cdm/ref/collection/p16062coll18/id/52787. [Online description from "North Carolina Periodicals Index," East Carolina University: "Bath's St. Thomas Episcopal Church, North Carolina's oldest church in its oldest town, was not merely the center of religious study in the community. Like most early American denominations, it was also the local community's primary center of discipline and legal recourse. Most churches forbade its members from taking a fellow member to court before 'gospel steps' had been taken. As the antebellum period progressed and the church began to gradually lose control of its members, church courts became less and less effective."]

Haywood, Marshall DeLancey. "Thomas and Henry John Burges: Church of England Missionaries in the Provinces of Virginia and North Carolina during the Eighteenth Century." *North Carolina Booklet,* 23:1-4 (1926), 63-75.

Lawrence, Alfred S[tratton]. "George Micklejohn." *Carolina Churchman*, 12:11 (December 1921), 9-12. [George Micklejohn (?-1811)]

Lemmon, Sarah McCulloh. "The Genesis of the Protestant Episcopal Diocese of North Carolina, 1701-1823." *North Carolina Historical Review*, 28:4 (October 1951), 426-462; online: http://digital.ncdcr.gov/cdm/ref/collection/p16062coll9/id/4207. [Online description from "North Carolina Periodicals Index," East Carolina University: "This article looks at the genesis of the Protestant Episcopal Diocese of North Carolina including the settlement of the colony and the establishment of the Church of England in the region, church politics and vestry elections, problems with clergy, establishment of new parishes, education, and changes within the church during and after the American Revolution."]

McKoy, William B. "Activities of the S[ociety for the] P[ropagation of the] G[ospel]." In Addresses Delivered under the Auspices of the North Carolina Society of the Colonial Dames of American, 1900-1926. [S. l.]: Jackson & Bell, [1927?].

Morgan, David Taft. "North Carolina Clergy and the American Revolution." M. A. thesis, University of North Carolina, 1963.

Morrison, A. J. "James Macartney." *William and Mary Quarterly,* 2rd series, 19:1 (January 1939), 116-119

Rohrer, S. Scott. *Hope's Promise: Religion and Acculturation in the Southern Backcountry*. Tuscaloosa: University of Alabama Press, 2005.

Sheppard, Joseph. "Revisiting SPG Missionaries in the Lower Cape Fear and Some Sources for Anglican Research in Colonial North Carolina." *Lower Cape Fear Historical Society Bulletin*, 46:1 (February 2002), 1-8. [Online description from "North Carolina Periodicals Index," East Carolina University: "The Society for the Propagation of the Gospel in Foreign Parts played an important role in the early religious life of colonial North Carolina. The SPG, chartered on June 16, 1701, sent Christian missionaries to the colony until the Revolutionary War. Between 1701 and 1783, about forty-six Anglican clergymen served in North Carolina. Sheppard discusses the role they played, the difficulties of procuring missionaries for the colony, and some notable missionaries from this period, including Richard Marsden. Sources for Anglican research are provided at the end of the article."]

Society for the Propagation of the Gospel in Foreign Parts. "Bertie Co. Letter from Rev. C. E. Taylor to [Sec., SPG], Oct. 13, 1783." Manuscript Z.5.294 (MARS ID: 21.6.3.21; folder), State Archives of of North Carolina,

Raleigh. [Online catalog description: "Report on his activities during the war. Was before 1776 'happy in St. George's Parish,' Northampton Co., with 'two new and elegant Churches built for me, and two others enlarged and beautified,' but all was changed by war; resigned his parish on declaration of independence, when establishment ceased; "I could not labour, and to beg was ashamed," therefore was reduced to selling his land and houses to support his wife and five children; during war officiated on the coast and elsewhere, baptising many; serves Halifax Town since July, because a sum was raised for him there; no more than five clergy in province, and Methodists make great inroads; 'The Gentleman who presides at present in No. Carolina' has told him that he would encourage an orthodox clergy, but the assembly refuses any establishment; wishes to be recalled to England, but in any event wants assistance from the Society since he has received no salary for seven years and is in danger of confinement for debt'."]

Society for the Propagation of the Gospel in Foreign Parts. "London. Extract from Minutes of the General Meeting of the Society for the Propagation of the Gospel. March 19, 1784." Manuscript (MARS ID: 21.9.23.5; microfilm volume), State Archives of of North Carolina, Raleigh. [Online catalog description: "Letter read from Mr. Charles Edward Taylor dated Bertie Co., N. C., 13 Oct 1783. Agreed that Taylor be informed that his connection with the Society ceased in 1772."]

Society for the Propagation of the Gospel in Foreign Parts. "St. Anne's. (London) Dr. Hind to the Rev. Mr. Christian, Brunswick, North Carolina. (2 Jan 1775)." Manuscript (MARS ID: 21.8.1.4), State Archives of of North Carolina, Raleigh. [Online catalog description: "Concerns an application for increase of salary and gives a clarification of the nature of his appointment, which under the new rules, is for two years only as a missionary of the Society."]

Society for the Propagation of the Gospel in Foreign Parts. "St. Anne's. (London) Dr. Hind to the Rev. Reed, Craven County, North Carolina. (6 May.), 1775." Manuscript, MARS Id: 21.8.1.6 (Folder), State Archives of North Carolina, Raleigh. [Online catalog description: "Concerns Mr. Reed's situation in regard to the growing conflict of the American Revolution and the Society's inability to offer him any relief."]

Stokes, Durward T. "Different Concepts of Government Expressed in the Sermons of Two Eighteenth Century Clergyman." *Historical Magazine of the Protestant Episcopal Church*, 40:1 (March 1971), 81-94. [George Micklejohn (?-1811) and Adam Boyd (1738-1803)]

Stokes, Durward Turrentine. "The Clergy of the Carolinas and the American Revolution." Ph. D. dissertation, University of North Carolina, 1968.

Baptists

Albritton, Tom. "The Baptist Collection." *The State: Down Home in North Carolina*, 57:4 (September 1989), 10-14; online: http://digital.ncdcr.gov/cdm/ref/collection/p16062coll18/id/63814. [Online description from "North Carolina Periodicals Index," East Carolina University: "The Ethel Taylor Crittendon Collection of Baptist History at Wake Forest University includes 12,000 books and 420 collections of personal papers that reflect not only denominational history, but also history of the state."]

Bennett, William Doub. "Troubles of Baptist Minister – 1776." *The Carolinas Genealogical Society Bulletin*, 20:4 (Spring 1984), 71-73. [James Terry, Jr., of Anson County]

Blanks, James Bailey. "Social Control by the Baptist Churches in North Carolina and Virginia, 1775-1928." M. A. thesis, Wake Forest University, 1929.

Courtney, Clifton, Jr. "Question of Participation in the Lord's Supper among Baptists of North Carolina and Virginia, 1742-1845." Th. M. Southern Baptist Theological Seminary, 1963.

Deweese, Charles W. *Women Deacons and Deaconesses: 400 Years of Baptist Service.* Brentwood, Tenn.: Baptist History and Heritage Society; Macon, Ga.: Mercer University Press, 2005. [On pages 58-59 is a discussion of the roles of women in Baptist churches in North Carolina and Virginia.]

Hammon, Stratton Owen. "Another Bicentennial – The Baptist Exodus from Virginia through North Carolina to Kentucky." *Kentucky Ancestors: A Genealogical Quarterly*, 18:4 (April 1983), 220-226.

Morgan, David T., Jr. "The Great Awakening in North Carolina, 1740-1775: The Baptist Phase." *North Carolina Historical Review*, 45:3 (July 1968), 264-283.

Hayslette, Sandra. "Faithful Individuals, Loving Communities: The Methodists and Baptists." *Tar Heel Junior Historian*, 37:2 (Spring 1998), 18-19. [Online description from "North Carolina Periodicals Index," East Carolina University: "Because of their emphasis on heartfelt faith, Baptist and Methodist churches appealed to people more than the Anglican church's emphasis on wealth and liturgy. The first Baptist church was founded in Camden County in 1727, while Methodists became a denomination in December, 1784."]

Huggins, M. A. *A History of North Carolina Baptists, 1727-1932*. Raleigh: General Board, State Baptist State Convention of North Carolina, 1967.

Lawrence, R. C. "Early Churches of Carolina." *The State: A Weekly Survey of North Carolina*, 8:8 (July 1940), 9, 22. [Online description from "North Carolina Periodicals Index," East Carolina University: "Lawrence details the interesting story of how the Baptists, Methodists, and Presbyterians established themselves within the boundaries of North Carolina during its early history."]

Marshall, David Weston. "Southern Baptist Patriots: Religion, Revolution and Nationalism, 1776-1876." Ph. D. dissertation, Texas Tech University, 1989.

Morgan, David T. "The Great Awakening in North Carolina, 1740-1775: The Baptist Phase." *North Carolina Historical Review*, 45:3 (July 1968), 264-283. [Online description from "North Carolina Periodicals Index," East Carolina University: "During the Great Awakening in Britain and its colonies, George Whitefield had little success in North Carolina in spreading his doctrine. While Whitefield failed, the Separate Baptists from New England had greater success after 1755 led by Shubal Stearns and Daniel Marshall. Numerous Baptists joined the Separates who founded many churches before the American Revolution."]

Pandoff, Ryan Dene. "The Law of Canaan in North Carolina: An Analysis of Discipline and Social Control in the Yadkin and Sandy Creek Baptist Associations, 1755-1860." M. A. thesis, Appalachian State University, 2010.

Paschal, George Washington. *History of North Carolina Baptists*. 2 vols. Raleigh, General board, North Carolina Baptist State convention, 1930-1955; reprinted Gallatin, Tenn.: Church History Research and Archives, 1990. [V. 1 1663-1805. -V. 2 1805-]

Paschal, George Washington. "Morgan Edwards' Materials toward a History of the Baptists in the Province of North Carolina." *North Carolina Historical Review*, 7:3 (July 1930), 365-399; online: http://digital.ncdcr.gov/cdm/ref/collection/p16062coll9/id/4207. [Online description from "North Carolina Periodicals Index," East Carolina University: "Reverend Morgan Edwards was a prolific American Baptist Preacher in Colonial America. He toured the country writing his notes and impressions of Baptists across the different provinces. Reprinted here is Tour of Morgan Edwards, of Pennsylvania, to the American Baptists in North Carolina in 1772-73 which is heavily footnoted by Mr. Pashcal to highlight errors in Edwards' work."]

Stroupe, Henry S. "'Cite Them Both to Attend the Next Church Conference:' Social Control by North Carolina Baptist Churches, 1772-1908." *North Carolina Historical Review*, 52:2 (April 1975), 156-170.

Wardin, Albert W. Jr. *Tennessee Baptists: A Comprehensive History, 1779-1999*. Brentwood: Executive Board of the Tennessee Baptist Convention, 1999.

Baptists, Free Will

Davidson, William Franklin. *An Early History of Free Will-Baptists: The Original Free Will Baptists in America, a Continuing Witness from Infancy to Identity (1727-1830)*. Th. D. thesis, New Orleans Baptist Theological Seminary. Nashville: Randall House Publications [1974].

Brethren/Dunkers

Sappington, Roger E. *The Brethren in the Carolinas: The History of the Church of the Brethren in the District of North and South Carolina*. Kingsport, Tenn.: Southeastern District, 1971.

Sappington, Roger E. "Dunker Beginnings in North Carolina in the Eighteenth Century." *North Carolina Historical Review*, 46:3 (July 1969), 214-238.

Lutherans

Boyd, William K., and Charles A. Krummel. "German Tracts Concerning the Lutheran Church in North Carolina during the Eighteenth Century." *North Carolina Historical Review*, 7:1 (January 1930), 79-147; 7:2 (April 1930), 225-282; online: http://digital.ncdcr.gov/cdm/ref/collection/p16062coll9/id/4207. [Online description from "North Carolina Periodicals Index," East Carolina University: "…a reprint of reports by Velthusen which includes a series of letters of Lutheran officials. The authors provided the translation of these texts."]

Lawrence, R. C. "Pioneer Lutheran." *The State: A Weekly Survey of North Carolina*, 7:36 (February 1940), 12-13; online: http://digital.ncdcr.gov/cdm/ref/collection/p16062coll18/id/5039. [Online description from "North Carolina Periodicals Index," East Carolina University: "Reverend Adolphus Nussman emigrated to the United States in 1773 and became a valiant religious and educational leader in his lifetime. Nussman was the first Lutheran minister to reach North Carolina and held pastorates in Rowan and Cabarrus Counties, as well as in Mecklenburg. In 1786, Nussman was appointed as one of the Commissioners for erecting an Academy in Salisbury."]

Mennonites/Mennonists

Haller, Charles R. *Across the Atlantic and Beyond: The Migration of German and Swiss Immigrants to America.* Westminster, Md.: Heritage Books, 1993; reprinted 2003.

Landis, Ira D. "The 1797 North Carolina Land Swindle." *Mennonite Historical Bulletin*, 7:1 (March 1946), 1-3.

Mast, C[hristian] Z. "Brief Notes on Carolina Mennonites." *Mennonite Historical Bulletin*, 1:2 (October 1940), 1, 3.

North Carolina (State). General Assembly. "[Document dated]: May 16, 1783: Resolution to Empower the Governor to Grant a Cavaet to John Swink of Rowan County." Manuscript; General Assembly Record Group; Session Records, April-May 1783; Joint Papers, Committee Papers, Resolutions; House Joint Resolutions: May 1-17, 1783, Box 1 (MARS ID: 66.8.29.14.25; item), State Archives of North Carolina, Raleigh. [Online catalog description: "Resolution regards the petition of John Swink, who maintains that he purchased land from John Leafe and allowed Hugh Montgomery to enter the claim to land when the land office opened. Montgomery neglected to make the claim and Benjamin Howard received the claim to his land. Swink is applying for a caveat until the proper title can be established. Resolution grants the caveat and applies this circumstance for any Quaker, Moravian, or Mennonist (Mennonite). Includes petition, deposition, and resolution."]

Methodists

Asbury, Francis, 1745-1816. "Letter, 1780 Sept." Accession 20324, Personal Papers Collection, Library of Virginia, Richmond. [Online catalog description: "Letter, September 1780, from the Methodist minister Francis Asbury (1745-1816), to the Reverend John Wesley (1703-1791) detailing his travels and activities to spread the Methodist Church in Virginia and North Carolina. Asbury wishes for peace between America and Britain, sends love to his parents, and requests permission to print Wesley's books. This is the earliest extant letter from Asbury to Wesley."]

Ashby, C. A. "The Diary of Bishop Coke." *The State: A Weekly Survey of North Carolina*, 16:3 (June 1948), 11; online: http://digital.ncdcr.gov/cdm/ref/collection/p16062coll18/id/22478. [Online description from "North Carolina Periodicals Index," East Carolina University: "Methodist bishop Thomas Coke traveled through North Carolina in 1785, and documented his experiences in a diary. Parts of these observations appeared in *Arminian Magazine*, Vol. 1, 1789, and are reprinted here."]

Boyd, William Kenneth. "Methodist Expansion in North Carolina during the Revolution." *Trinity College Historical Society Papers*, 12 (1916), 37-55.

Chreitzberg, Abel M. *Early Methodism in the Carolinas.* Nashville: Publishing House of the Methodist Episcopal Church, South, 1897.

Hayslette, Sandra. "Faithful Individuals, Loving Communities: The Methodists and Baptists." *Tar Heel Junior Historian*, 37:2 (Spring 1998), 18-19. [Online description from "North Carolina Periodicals Index," East Carolina University: "Because of their emphasis on heartfelt faith, Baptist and Methodist churches appealed to people more than the Anglican church's emphasis on wealth and liturgy. The first Baptist church was founded in Camden County in 1727, while Methodists became a denomination in December, 1784."]

Ingram, O. Kelly. *Methodism Alive in North Carolina: A Commemorative Volume for the Bicentennial of the First Carolina Circuit.* Durham: Divinity School of Duke University/North Carolina Conference and the Western North Carolina Conference, United Methodist Church, 1976.

Jordan, N. Fred. "Into the Wilderness: Circuit Riders Take Religion to the People." *Tar Heel Junior Historian*, 37:2 (Spring 1998), 12-13. [Online description from "North Carolina Periodicals Index," East Carolina University: "When the Revolutionary War broke the ties with the Anglican Church, the Methodist societies within it became the Methodist Episcopal Church in America. Methodist circuit riders, or preachers, assigned to a particular territory, rode far and wide to bring religion to the people."]

Lawrence, R. C. "Early Churches of Carolina." *The State: A Weekly Survey of North Carolina*, 8:8 (July 1940), 9, 22. [Online description from "North Carolina Periodicals Index," East Carolina University: "Lawrence details the interesting story of how the Baptists, Methodists, and Presbyterians established themselves within the boundaries of North Carolina during its early history."]

Mathews, Donald G. *Slavery and Methodism: A Chapter in American Morality, 1780-1845.* Princeton, N. J.: Princeton University Press, 1965.

Taylor, James A. "Where Methodism Obtained Is Start." *The State: A Weekly Survey of North Carolina*, 2:26 (November 1934), 8; online: http://digital.ncdcr.gov/cdm/ref/collection/p16062coll18/id/3957. [Online description from "North Carolina Periodicals Index," East Carolina University: "Pilmoor Memorial Methodist Church, founded in 1928, at Currituck Courthouse was erected as a memorial to Reverend Joseph Pilmore. He was the first minister of the Methodist Church to preach in North Carolina. Sent to America in 1769 by the

Conference of England, Pilmore preached his first sermon three hundred yards from the church site on September 28, 1772."]

Moravians

[Note: See also the section in Chapter Fifteen: "Forsyth County, Winston-Salem, Old Salem, and the Wachovia Tract."]

Africa, Philip. "Slaveholding in the Salem Community, 1771-1851." *North Carolina Historical Review*, 45:3: (July 1977), 271-307. [Online description from "North Carolina Periodicals Index," East Carolina University: "Between the founding of Salem in 1771 as a Moravian community and the outbreak of Civil War, community attitudes went through a transition. The communal sense of *gemeinschaft* slowly changed during the 19th century to a more business-like attitude of *gesellschaft*. Secular pressures eroded opposition to slavery on religious and moral grounds, and by the 1850s Moravians came to regard slaves not as persons but as property."]

Beaver, Emily Conrad. "Piety and Profit: Moravians in the North Carolina Backcountry, 1770-1810." In Michele Gillespie and Robert Beachy, eds., *Pious Pursuits: German Moravians in the Atlantic World* (European Expansion & Global Interaction series, vol. 7) (New York: Berghahn Books, 2007), 127-141.

Blackwelder, Ruth. "Attitude of the North Carolina Moravians toward the American Revolution." *North Carolina Historical Review,* 9:1 (January 1932), 1-21. [Online description from "North Carolina Periodicals Index," East Carolina University: "Moravian doctrine discourages members of the community from fighting in wars. During the American Revolution the state's Moravians, especially older individuals, avoided war either by pardons from the English Parliament or by paying somebody else to serve in their place. Though some citizens viewed the Moravian brethren as cowardly, this group of people served troops throughout the war by feeding and caring for wounded soldiers."]

Campbell, Betty. "The Buildings of Salem, North Carolina, 1766-1856." Ph. D. dissertation, Florida State University, 1975.

Capps, Gene. "References to Women at Work in Salem, 1774-1833." Paper (1989) available at the library of Old Salem Museums and Gardens, Winston-Salem, N. C.

Carr, Genie. "House of Passage." *Our State: Down Home in North Carolina*, 67:7 (December 1999), 114-116; online: http://digital.ncdcr.gov/cdm/ref/collection/p16062coll18/id/68691. [Online description from "North Carolina Periodicals Index," East Carolina University: "In the winter of 1753, the Moravian church in Pennsylvania sent twelve young men to the Piedmont section of North Carolina to start a settlement which they called Bethabara. This village gave way in the 1760s to the newer town of Salem. Several of Bethabara's original buildings and stone foundations remain. Today the state's first Moravian settlement is a historic site and city park."]

Crews, C. Daniel. *Through Fiery Trials: The Revolutionary War and the Moravians*. Winston-Salem, N. C.: Moravian Archives, 1996. ["Discussion of the Moravian experience during the Revolutionary War, with close analysis of their controversial position in terms of loyalty, geography, and religious values."]

Davis, Chester. "Story of the Moravians No. 6: Peaceful Settlers Turn to Muskets." *The State: Down Home in North Carolina*, 29:2 (June 1961), 11-12; online: http://digital.ncdcr.gov/cdm/ref/collection/p16062coll18/id/8523. [Online description from "North Carolina Periodicals Index," East Carolina University: "The North Carolina Moravians had to temper their pacifism with some dependence on force concerning the native Indians in the western part of the state. The worst of the troubles came during the French and Indian Wars as the Cherokees 'sold' their land in the Treaty of Sycamore Shoals from 1754-1770. Fighting in the Northern colonies drove many Moravians into the Carolinas, particularly Bethabara, and after 1779, Bethania. Despite their scruples against bearing arms, the Moravians established a militia headed by Brother Jacob Loesch."]

Davis, Chester. "Story of the Moravians No. 11: Moravians and the Revolution." *The State: Down Home in North Carolina*, 29:8 (September 1961), 10; online: http://digital.ncdcr.gov/cdm/ref/collection/p16062coll 18/id/8795. [Online description from "North Carolina Periodicals Index," East Carolina University: "As the American Revolution drew near, the Moravians were in an impossible position, refusing to take an oath of allegiance and bear arms. Further problems arose from the Moravians' reluctance to accept paper currency, an offense that would make them enemies of the state. Tensions eased with the editing of the oath of allegiance, allowing Moravians to make an affirmation of their loyalty."]

Davis, Chester S. *Moravians in Europe and America, 1415-1865: Hidden Seed and Harvest*. Winston-Salem: Wachovia Historical Society, 2000.

Duncan, Wanda. "There's Kremser!" *The State: Down Home in North Carolina*, 76:5 (October 2008), 126-128, 130; online: http://digital.ncdcr.gov/cdm/ref/collection/p16062coll18/id/100420. [Online description from "North Carolina Periodicals Index," East Carolina University: "Andreas Kremser, a Moravian who lived in the Single Brothers House in Salem, was killed when an excavation at the house collapsed on him. Duncan recounts sightings of him up till 1950, when a visiting minister determined that he should "slay the ghost."]

Fries, Adelaide. "Der North Carolina Land und Colonie Etablissement." *North Carolina Booklet*, 9:4 (April 1910), 199-214.

Fries, Adelaide L. "The Moravian Contribution to Colonial North Carolina." *North Carolina Historical Review*, 7:1 (January 1930), 1-14; online: http://digital.ncdcr.gov/cdm/ref/collection/p16062coll9/id/4207. [Online description from "North Carolina Periodicals Index," East Carolina University: "The Moravian settlement in Wachovia brought many advancements to the then 'untamed' western portion of North Carolina during the colonial period. The first group of Moravian Brethren, fifteen men between the ages of 28-40, arrived in Wachovia on November 17, 1753. From this humble beginning, a larger Moravian community thrived - bringing schools, medicine, and churches to this otherwise unsettled part of the state."]

Fries, Adelaide L; Douglas LeTell Rights; Minnie J. Smith; and Kenneth G. Hamilton, trans. and eds. *The Records of the Moravians of North Carolina.* 13 Vols. Raleigh: North Carolina Historical Commission, 1922-2006.

Gibson, George H. "Twenty-Seven Tickets." *North Carolina Historical Review*, 37:4 (October 1960), 477-487. [Online description from "North Carolina Periodicals Index," East Carolina University: "During the American Revolution, the British came to North Carolina when the Colonial armies crossed the Catawba River and began the retreat to the Dan River. During this time, the arrival of British troops to the Moravian settlements at Bethania, Bethabara, and Salem caused anxiety and heavy losses in livestock, forage, and provisions. To provide for the losses, the acting Commissary A. Knect wrote reimbursement tickets to those residents who supplied the British with supplies."]

Gray, James A. "A Little Lump of Heaven." *The Torch*, 35:2 (April 1962), 35-42. [Description: "History of the Moravian Church, with an emphasis on Salem, N. C."]

Gray, James A[lexander]. "Moravians and the Revolutionary War: A Paper Given by James A. Gray, Winston-Salem Torch Club, November 13, 1969." Typescript Cp284.6 G77m, North Carolina Collection, Louis Round Wilson Special Collections Library, University of North Carolina at Chapel Hill.]

Grigg, Jessie S. "Old Salem Lives Again." *Early American Life*, 5:1 (February 1974), 30-35.

Gutek, Gerald Lee. *Visiting Utopian Communities: A Guide to the Shakers, Moravians, and Others*. Columbia: University of South Carolina Press, 1998.

Hamilton, J. Taylor, and Kenneth G. Hamilton. *History of the Moravian Church: The Renewed Unitas Fratrum, 1722-1957.* Bethlehem, Pa.: Interprovincial Board of Christian Education, Moravian Church in America, 1967.

Hamilton, Kenneth G. "The Moravians and Wachovia." *North Carolina Historical Review,* 44:2 (April 1967), 144-153; online: http://digital.ncdcr.gov/cdm/ref/collection/p16062coll9/id/4207. [Online description from "North Carolina Periodicals Index," East Carolina University: "This article looks at the history of Winston-Salem and the Moravian Community's contribution to the state since its establishment."]

Hamilton, Kenneth Gardiner. "John Ettwein and the Moravian Church during the Revolutionary Period." Ph. D. dissertation, Columbia University, 1941.

Holder, Edward M. "Community Life in Wachovia, 1752-1780." M. A. thesis, University of North Carolina, Chapel Hill, 1929.

Holder, Edward M. "Social Life of the Early Moravians in North Carolina." *North Carolina Historical Review*, 11:3 (July 1934), 167-184; online: http://digital.ncdcr.gov/cdm/ref/collection/p16062coll9/id/4207. [Online description from "North Carolina Periodicals Index," East Carolina University: "Moravian director Count Zinzendorf envisioned a colony 'on a large tract of land on which the Moravians might live undisturbed, having the liberty of excluding all strangers from their settlements.' This idea of a colony was distinct from other Piedmont settlers like the Scotch-Irish and Germans whom chose to settle on independent and isolated farms. From this colony a number of distinct social and religious behaviors evolved and are reviewed in this article."]

James, Hunter. *The Quiet People of the Land: A Story of the North Carolina Moravians in Revolutionary Times.* (Old Salem Series) Chapel Hill: University of North Carolina Press for Old Salem, Inc., 1976.

Kapp, Michael Keith. "The North Carolina Moravians in the American Revolution: A Study of Pacificism in a Christian Communal Society." Honors essay, University of North Carolina, 1976. [Includes bibliographic essay.]

Fries, Adelaide L., et al. *Records of the Moravians in North Carolina, 1780-1783. 13 Vol.* Raleigh: Edwards and Broughton, 1930. [V. 1. 1752-1771; v. 2. 1752-1775; v. 3. 1776-1779; v. 4. 1780-1783; v. 5. 1784-1792; v. 6. 1793-1808; v. 7. 1809-1822; v. 8. 1823-1837vv. 9. 1838-1847; v. 10. 1841-1851; v. 11. 1852-1879; v. 12. 1856-

1866; v. 13. 1867-1876.]

Kirkland, Winifred. "A Christmas City of the Old South." *North American Review*, 218:6 (December 1923), 790-804.

North Carolina (State). General Assembly. "[Document dated:] January 23, 1779: Joint Papers, Committee Papers, Resolutions, Senate Bills, House Bills, Report Re[specting] Petitions of People Called Moravians and Quakers (with Petition and Messages)." Manuscript, General Assembly Record Group, Session Records, January-Februay 1779, Box 1 (MARS ID: 66.8.15.8.2; item), State Archives of North Carolina, Raleigh. [Online catalog description: "The petition of the Quakers from their yearly meeting committee in Perquimans County asks the Assembly not to consider them enemies of the state because they will not swear the oath of allegiance. The committee recommends that Moravians and Quakers be allowed to take an affirmation instead of the oath, with which the Assembly concurs."]

North Carolina (State). General Assembly. "[Document dated]: May 16, 1783: Resolution to Empower the Governor to Grant a Cavaet to John Swink of Rowan County." Manuscript; General Assembly Record Group; Session Records, April-May 1783; Joint Papers, Committee Papers, Resolutions; House Joint Resolutions: May 1-17, 1783, Box 1 (MARS ID: 66.8.29.14.25; item), State Archives of North Carolina, Raleigh. [Online catalog description: "Resolution regards the petition of John Swink, who maintains that he purchased land from John Leafe and allowed Hugh Montgomery to enter the claim to land when the land office opened. Montgomery neglected to make the claim and Benjamin Howard received the claim to his land. Swink is applying for a caveat until the proper title can be established. Resolution grants the caveat and applies this circumstance for any Quaker, Moravian, or Mennonist (Mennonite). Includes petition, deposition, and resolution."]

Reichel, Levin T. *The Moravians in North Carolina*. Salem, N. C.: O. A. Keehln, 1857. [Contents: First Settlers and Heads of Families; Churches and Other Public Buildings; Houses Built in Salem, 1766-1816; Additions and notes.]

Reichel, Levin T. *A History of Nazareth Hall, from 1755 to 1855, and the Reunions of the Former Pupils, in 1854 and 1855*. Philadelphia: J. B. Lippincott & Company, 1855; available online through the HathiTrust. ["Catalog of the Pupils of Nazareth Hall {1785-1855}," 49-98.]

Restoring Old Salem in North Carolina: The Preservation of a Unique Heritage. Winston-Salem: Old Salem, 1960.

Rights, Douglas LeTell. "Adelaide Lisetta Fries." *North Carolina Historical Review*, 29:1 (January 1952), 1-7; online: http://digital.ncdcr.gov/cdm/ref/collection/p16062coll9/id/4207. [Online description from "North Carolina Periodicals Index," East Carolina University: "Adelaide Fries was born in Salem on November 12, 1871 and did on November 29, 1949. The author writes a brief memorial to her life and especially focuses on her career as a historian and writer. The final two pages of the article outline the various publications she wrote, edited, and collaborated on, most dealing with North Carolina, Salem, and the Moravians."]

Rohrer, S. Scott. "Searching for Land and God: The Pietist Migration to North Carolina in the Late Colonial Period." *North Carolina Historical Review*, 79:4 (October 2002), 409-439. [Online description from "North Carolina Periodicals Index," East Carolina University: "This article examines the migration of Moravian families from the northeast United States, into Wachovia settlements in North Carolina during the mid-18th century. This movement stemmed from a desire for more land but also from the importance of religion and common places of worship. Settlement in North Carolina was accompanied by settlement from European immigrants and other Moravian settlements in America."]

Sensbach, Jon F. "Brothers in Bondage: The Moravians Struggle with the Institution of Slavery." *Tar Heel Junior Historian*, 51:2 (Spring 2012), 31-33. [Online description from "North Carolina Periodicals Index," East Carolina University: "The German religious immigrants known as the Moravians, settled in North Carolina in and around what is now the city of Winston-Salem. Although some groups struggled with the institution of slavery, the Moravians took enslaved Africans and baptized them into the church, allowing them to work, live, and worship together in close quarters."]

Sensbach, Jon F. "Interracial Sects: Religion, Race, and Gender among Early North Carolina Moravians." In Catherine Clinton and Michele Gillespie, eds., *The Devil's Lane: Sex and Race in the Early South* (New York and London: Oxford University Press, 1997), 155-167, Part III, Chapter 11.

Sensbach, Jon F. *A Separate Canaan: The Making of an Afro-Moravian World in North Carolina, 1763-1840*. Chapel Hill: University of North Carolina Press for the Omohundro Institute of Early American History and Culture, 1998; based on his "A Separate Canaan: The Making of an Afro-Moravian World in North Carolina, 1763-1856." Ph. D. dissertation, Duke University, 1991.

Sherman, William Thomas. "Staying at Peace in Wartime." *Southern Campaigns of the American Revolution*, 2:6 (June 2005), 25-26; online: www.southerncampaign.org ["from the minutes of the Salem Congregation" and "from the minutes of the Bethabara Congregation;" Moravians]

Sommer, Elisabeth W. *Serving Two Masters: Moravian Brethren in Germany and North Carolina, 1727-1801.* Lexington: University Press of Kentucky, 2000.

Surratt, Jerry L. "From Theocracy to Voluntary Church and Secularized Community: A Study of the Moravians in Salem, North Carolina, 1772-1860." Ph. D. dissertation, Emory University, 1968.

Surratt, Jerry L. "The Moravian as Businessman: Gottlieb Schober of Salem." *North Carolina Historical Review*, 60:1 (January 1983), 1-23. [Online description from "North Carolina Periodicals Index," East Carolina University: "An examination of the founding of the Moravian towns of Salem and Bethabara and the development of their businesses and economic systems. A particular focus is placed on the life and career of Gottlieb Schober, a Moravian who personified the successful community small businessman."]

Surratt, Jerry L. "The Role of Dissent in Community Evolution among Moravians in Salem, 1772-1860." *North Carolina Historical Review,* 52:3 (July 1975), 235-255. [Online description from "North Carolina Periodicals Index," East Carolina University: "Changes in the nature of the Salem Moravian ruling theology, from 'gemeinschaft' to 'gesellschaft', can be viewed in the context of rising dissent on military involvement, relationships between the sexes, and the rise of economic individualism. Between 1820 and 1850, Moravians in Salem were forced to permit residents to join the militia, ease the strict rules regarding courting and marriage, abandon the community landholding system, and allow residents to engage in the slave trade."]

Taylor, Jessica Lauren. "To Learn the Trade of a Potter: Apprenticeship, Conflict, and Deviance in the Wachovian Tradition." *North Carolina Historical Review*, 89:2 (April 2012), 127-154. [Online description from "North Carolina Periodicals Index," East Carolina University: "This article examines the late North Carolina potter Jacob Meyer with particular focus on his apprenticeship and the apprenticeship system created by the colony of North Carolina with regards to its similarities to the Moravian system of mutual responsibility. While discussing Meyer's apprenticeship experience, the deficiencies of the master-apprentice relationship of second-generation Moravian settlers in North Carolina are revealed."]

Thomas, Brian W. "Inclusion and Exclusion in the Moravian Settlements in North Carolina, 1770-1790." Historical Archaeology, 28:3 (1994), 15-30.

Thorp, Daniel B. "Assimilation in North Carolina's Moravian Community." *Journal of Southern History*, 52:1 (February 1986), 19-42.

Thorp, Daniel B. "Moravian Colonization of Wachovia, 1753-1772: The Maintenance of Community in Late Colonial North Carolina." Ph. D. dissertation, Johns Hopkins University, 1982.

Thorp, Daniel B. *The Moravian Community in Colonial North Carolina: Pluralism on the Southern Frontier.* Knoxville: University of Tennessee Press, 1989.

Troyer, James R. "Early American Moravian Botanists in North Carolina and Elsewhere." *Journal of the North Carolina Academy of Science*, 125:1 (Spring 2009), 1-6; online: http://dc.lib.unc.edu/cdm/singleitem/collection/jncas/id/3930/rec/1. [Online description from "North Carolina Periodicals Index," East Carolina University: "In the 18th- and 19th-centuries a number of Moravians pursued botanical activities in the eastern part of the country. Troyer provides biographical information and summarizes their contributions."]

Wiley, Mary C. "Medicine in Old Wachovia." *The State: Down Home in North Carolina*, 22:4 (July 1954), 10-12; online: http://digital.ncdcr.gov/cdm/ref/collection/p16062coll18/id/32241. [Online description from "North Carolina Periodicals Index," East Carolina University: "When pioneer Moravian physicians came to the Salem community, they brought the skills they learned in the Old World with them. To this they added the healing qualities of native herbs in their cures. Many of these items, such as dental surgery equipment, brass mortar and pestle, small wooden pill bottles, and apothecary scales, may be viewed at the Moravian Museum, which is located in the old Boys' School in the heart of Old Salem."]

Nicholites

Carroll, Kenneth L. *Joseph Nichols and the NIcholites: A Look at the "New Quakers" of Maryland, Delaware, North and South Carolina*. Easton, Md.: Easton Publishing Company, 1962.

Carroll, Kenneth L. "The Nicholites of North Carolina." *North Carolina Historical Review*, 31:4 (October 1954), 453-462; online: http://digital.ncdcr.gov/cdm/ref/collection/p16062coll9/id/4207. [Online description from "North Carolina Periodicals Index," East Carolina University: "In the last quarter of the 18th century a group of people in Guilford County were known as the Nicholites, taking their name from the founder of a religious society, Joseph Nichols. This group abstained from war, swearing, profanity, and oath making."]

Turner, Grace W. "Petition of the Nicholites, 1778." *North Carolina Genealogical Society Journal*, 25:1 (February 1999), 36-37.

Presbyterians

An Address of the Presbyterian Ministers, of the City of Philadelphia, to the Ministers and Presbyterian Congregations, in the County of [blank] *in North-Carolina*. Philadelphia: [s. n.], 1775; micropublished: (Early American Imprints. First Series, no. 14411).

Baldwin, Alice M. "Sowers of Sedition: The Political Theories of Some of the New Light Presbyterian Clergy of Virginia and North Carolina." *William and Mary Quarterly*, 3rd series, 5:1 (January 1948), 52-76.

Breed, William Pratt. *Presbyterians and the Revolution*. Philadelphia: Presbyterian Board of Publication, 1876.

Conser, Walter H., Jr., and Robert J. Cain. *Presbyterians in North Carolina: Race, Politics, and Religious Identity in Historical Perspective*. Knoxville: University of Tennessee Press, 2011.

Dussek, Hugh. "Pre-Revolutionary History: Socio-Religious Perspectives on the Scots-Irish and Highland Scots in the Backcountry of North Carolina." Thesis (Ph. D.) Union Institute and University, 2002. [Online catalog description: "The study examines the history of the pre-revolutionary developments in the backcountry of North Carolina through an analysis and comparison of the influence of Presbyterianism on the cultures of two communities: the Scots-Irish of Mecklenburg County and the Highland Scots of Cumberland County. Using historical and interdisciplinary perspectives, the study traces the histories of the settlement of these two communities and the effect of social influences stemming from their earlier histories in Britain and America, the history of the Presbyterian Church in America, the local Presbyterian clergy and churches, the revivals of the Great Awakening, the relationship of these communities to the British crown and the development of a 'revolutionary syndrome' in North Carolina. The study analyzes the role of Presbyterianism in supporting and legitimizing both loyalty and rebellion to the British crown among the Scots-Irish, who were mostly second and third generation settlers from the northern colonies, and the Highland Scots, who largely came directly from Scotland. The study examines the role of the Presbyterian clergy and other local social leaders, many of whom were educated at the College of New Jersey, in developments in Mecklenburg County leading from support of the British crown to support of the Revolution. The study also examines the role of the Presbyterian clergy in the development of a division in Cumberland County between the earlier Highlander settlers, who largely became revolutionary, and the later settlers, who mainly remained loyal to the British crown."]

Hall, Nell K. "The Reverend James Hall." *The State: A Weekly Survey of North Carolina*, 11:38 (February 1944), 6, 22; online: http://digital.ncdcr.gov/cdm/ref/collection/p16062coll18/id/18572. [Online description from "North Carolina Periodicals Index," East Carolina University: "Hall was born in Pennsylvania in 1744 and came with his parents to North Carolina in 1751. He decided on a ministerial career and studied at Princeton. He was preaching in Rowan County when he entered the Revolutionary War, serving as a valiant soldier. He was a fine preacher, a good schoolteacher, and a great leader of men."]

Lawrence, R. C. "Early Churches of Carolina." *The State: A Weekly Survey of North Carolina*, 8:8 (July 1940), 9, 22. [Online description from "North Carolina Periodicals Index," East Carolina University: "Lawrence details the interesting story of how the Baptists, Methodists, and Presbyterians established themselves within the boundaries of North Carolina during its early history."]

McCall, Alfred Clarence, J. "Serving God and Country: Presbyterian Leadership in Civic Affairs in North Carolina, 1750-1800." Ph. D. dissertation, Union Theological Seminary in Virginia, 1996. [Online abstract: "Presbyterian settlement in piedmont North Carolina began to be significant in the late 1740's, and within twenty years, Presbyterian pastors and lay leaders were playing important roles in local and provincial matters. Their involvement in civic affairs soon extended to such momentous events as the American Revolution and the writing and ratification of the United States Constitution. Presbyterians were largely responsible for the founding and early guidance of the University of North Carolina, an institution intended to provide pastors and other leaders of society with a classical education within a context of Christian piety. Presbyterian pastors thought religious belief and practice to be the true foundation of public welfare and sought to defend them against the assaults of rationalism and the influence of the French Revolution. They extolled George Washington as the finest example of an educated and religious man who had dedicated himself to the service of his country. Education and religious piety, properly begun in early childhood within the family and congregation, produced citizens who would maintain America as a land of freedom and opportunity. This study examines both the involvement of Presbyterians in civic affairs and their sermons and other public writings in an attempt to understand what they hoped to achieve. Attention is also given to important influences on Presbyterians: their religious and cultural heritage, their educational experiences, the communities in which they lived, and their visions for American society. Scotch-Irish Presbyterian settlers brought to North Carolina a rich heritage as a faith community that shaped their lives in the backcountry. They remembered economic and religious oppression in Northern Ireland, they were adherents or opponents of the Great Awakening, and they had come from Pennsylvania, Maryland, Virginia, and South Carolina in search of better opportunity. Largely frustrated in their hopes by weakness and corruption in local government in North Carolina, many joined the Regulator movement to secure redress and democratic reform. Presbyterian leaders and people joined the struggle to shape American society and expressed the vitality and diversity of the North Carolina backcountry communities."]

Moore, Joseph S. "Irish Radicals, Southern Conservatives: Slavery, Religious Liberty and the Presbyterian Fringe in the Atlantic World, 1637-1877." Ph. D. dissertation, University of North Carolina at Greensboro, 2011.

Sendgikoski, Anne Medlin, and Wilma Linder. "Alexander Craighead: Revolutionary Minister of Sugaw Creek Presbyterian Church." *Olde Mecklenburg Genealogical Society Quarterly*, 25:1 (2007), 11-14.

Society for the Propagation of the Gospel in Foreign Parts. "New York. N. Y. Clergy's Discussion of the Plight of the Orthodox Clergy Since the Start of the Revolution. 28 Oct., 1780." Manuscript, (MARS Id: 21.15.8.17; folder), State Archives of North Carolina, Raleigh. [Online catalog description: "Accuses Presbyterians and dissenters of helping to lead the country to war; describes the Presbyterian synods' colonial network of organization and work, including that of N. C."]

Stevens, Robert J., Sr., ed.; Linda Stevens Crissinger, assoc. ed.; Bettye Smith Renfro, asso. Researcher. *The Legacy of Father James H. Saye (1808-1892), a Presbyterian Divine: A Record of His Historical and Genealogical Writings of Union, Spartanburg, Chester, and Many Other Counties of South Carolina, with Parts of Georgia and North Carolina, Encompassing the Years 1755-1892*. Spartanburg: The Reprint Company, 2007.

Stokes, Durward T. "Henry Pattillo in North Carolina." *North Carolina Historical Review*, 44:4 (October 1967), 373-391; online: http://digital.ncdcr.gov/cdm/ref/collection/p16062coll9/id/4207. [Online description from "North Carolina Periodicals Index," East Carolina University: "This biographical essay looks at the life of 18 century North Carolina Presbyterian minister Henry Pattillo. Particular attention is given Pattillo's journal as well as his published writings and from period records." Henry Pattillo (1726-1801)]

Stone, Robert Hamlin. *A History of Orange Presbytery, 1770-1970*. Greensboro, N. C.: Orange Presbytery, 1970.

Taylor, William Harrison. "'One Body and One Spirit': Presbyterians, Interdenominationalism, and the American Revolution." Ph. D. dissertation, Mississippi State University, 2009.

Thompson, Ernest Trice. *Presbyterians in the South, 1607-1865*. 2 vols. Richmond: John Knox Press, 1963.

Tucker, Harry Z. "Old Longstreet." *The State: Down Home in North Carolina*, 6:9 (July 1938), 3, 22; online: http://digital.ncdcr.gov/cdm/ref/collection/p16062coll18/id/38174. [Online description from "North Carolina Periodicals Index," East Carolina University: "Longstreet fortunately stood within the confines of Fort Bragg and became a landmark that aviators trained their eyes to spot during practice operations. The Presbyterian Church was built sometime during the mid-18th-century and the first sermon delivered by Reverend Hugh McAden on January 28, 1756. In the church's cemetery are tombs of the first church elders and soldiers from the colonial period to Confederate boys who defended Cape Fear against General Sherman's march." Hugh McAden (ca. 1730-1781)]

Quakers/Friends

Calhoon, Robert. *Religion and the American Revolution in North Carolina*. Raleigh, N. C.: North Carolina Department of Cultural Resources, Division of Archives and History, 1976. ["A Quaker Asks for Permission to Free a Slave," 46, Thomas Newby requests the freedom of his elderly slave, Hannah, who is too feeble to work and once was an excellent midwife.]

Cecelski, David. "The Lamb's Army." *Coastwatch*, (Autumn 2000), 26-29. [Online description from "North Carolina Periodicals Index," East Carolina University: "Englishwoman Catharine Phillips, a Quaker missionary, evangelized in the North Carolina coastal regions and as far west as Alamance County, beginning in 1753. Phillips wrote an account of her travels and work in Memories of the Life of Catharine Phillips, which was published in London in 1797."]

Crawford, Michael J. "The Pace of Manumission among Quakers in Revolutionary-Era North Carolina." *Quaker History: The Bulletin of Friends Historical Association*, 102:1 (Spring 2013), 1-16.

Crawford, Michael J. "'The Small Black Boy at My Right Hand is Christ': George Walton and Friends' Manumission of Slaves in Revolutionary-Era North Carolina." *The Southern Friend*, 28:2 (2006), 3-17.

Crawford, Michael J., ed. *The Having of Negroes Is Becoming a Burden: The Quaker Struggle to Free Slaves in Revolutionary North Carolina*. Gainesville: University Press of Florida, 2010.

Hilty, Hiram H. *Toward Freedom for All: North Carolina Quakers and Slavery*. Richmond, Ind.: Friends United Press, 1984.

Hinshaw, Seth B., and Mary Edith Hinshaw. *Carolina Quakers: Our Heritage, Our Hope: Tercentenary, 1672-1972*. Greensboro, N. C.: North Carolina Yearly Meeting, 1972.

Hinshaw, William Wade. *Encyclopedia of American Quaker Genealogy. Volume 1: Records and Minutes of the*

Thirty-Three Oldest Monthly Meetings Which Belong, or Ever Belonged, to the North Carolina Yearly Meeting of Friends. Ann Arbor, Mich.: Edwards Brothers, Inc., 1936.

James, Sydney V. "The Impact of the Amerian Revolution on Quakers' Ideas about Their Sect." *William and Mary Quarterly*, 3rd series, 19:3 (July 1962), 360-382.

Lindsey, William D. "William Brazelton: A Patriotic Quaker and Veteran of War." *Drumbeat, with Flintlock & Powerhorn: News of the Sons of the Revolution*, 27:2 (Summer 2009), 18-19.

McKiever, Charles Fitzgerald. *Slavery and the Emigration of North Carolina Friends*. Murfreesboro: Johnson Pub. Co., [1970].

North Carolina (State). General Assembly. "[Document dated:] January 23, 1779: Joint Papers, Committee Papers, Resolutions, Senate Bills, House Bills, Report Re[specting] Petitions of People Called Moravians and Quakers (with Petition and Messages)." Manuscript, General Assembly Record Group, Session Records, January-February 1779, Box 1 (MARS ID: 66.8.15.8.2; item), State Archives of North Carolina, Raleigh. [Online catalog description: "The petition of the Quakers from their yearly meeting committee in Perquimans County asks the Assembly not to consider them enemies of the state because they will not swear the oath of allegiance. The committee recommends that Moravians and Quakers be allowed to take an affirmation instead of the oath, with which the Assembly concurs."]

North Carolina (State). General Assembly. "[Document dated:] January 27, 1779: Joint Papers, Committee Papers, Resolutions, Senate Bills, House Bills, Report on the Petition of the People of Pasquotank County Relative to the Slaves Liberated by the Quakers (with Messages)." Manuscript; General Assembly Record Group; Session Records, January-February 1779, Box 1 (MARS ID: 66.8.15.8.6; item), State Archives of North Carolina, Raleigh. [Online catalog description: "The petitioners complain to the Assembly that Quakers are freeing slaves. The committee recommends that a bill be drafted pertaining to slaves, for independence has nullified portions of the relative colonial law."]

North Carolina (State). General Assembly. "[Document dated:] April 27, 1780: Joint Papers, Committee Papers, Resolutions, Senate Bills, House Bills, Re[specting] Petitions of William Houston and William Skinner." Manuscript; General Assembly Record Group; Session Records, April-May 1780, Box 1 (MARS ID: 66.8.20.8.11; item), State Archives of North Carolina, Raleigh. [Online catalog description: "Houston informs the Assembly that in 1742 he took possession of a tract of land in Duplin County from his uncle, Henry McCulloh, who left the state in 1747. Because he never acquired a title or deed, Houston is concerned that the land is subject to confiscation and asks the Assembly to vest him with a title to the land by law. Skinner informs the Assembly that the law prohibiting individuals who have not taken the affirmation of allegiance to the state has had the effect of disabling Quakers in Pasquotank and Perquimans Counties from maintaining possession of their own land and asks the Assembly to pass a law in their behalf. The committee recommends that both petitions be granted, and the Assembly concurs."]

North Carolina (State). General Assembly. "[Document dated]: May 16, 1783: Resolution to Empower the Governor to Grant a Cavaet to John Swink of Rowan County." Manuscript; General Assembly Record Group; Session Records, April-May 1783; Joint Papers, Committee Papers, Resolutions; House Joint Resolutions: May 1-17, 1783, Box 1 (MARS ID: 66.8.29.14.25; item), State Archives of North Carolina, Raleigh. [Online catalog description: "Resolution regards the petition of John Swink, who maintains that he purchased land from John Leafe and allowed Hugh Montgomery to enter the claim to land when the land office opened. Montgomery neglected to make the claim and Benjamin Howard received the claim to his land. Swink is applying for a caveat until the proper title can be established. Resolution grants the caveat and applies this circumstance for any Quaker, Moravian, or Mennonist (Mennonite). Includes petition, deposition, and resolution."]

Opper, Peter Kent. "North Carolina Quakers: Reluctant Slaveholders." *North Carolina Historical Review,* 52:1 (January 1975), 37-58. [Online description from "North Carolina Periodicals Index," East Carolina University: "North Carolina Quakers, openly opposed to slavery, were put in the position of caring for many former slaves over whom they had assumed guardianship between 1775 and 1856. Because state law barred freeing slaves, Quakers attempted to remove African Americans from the state, sending them to northern states or to Haiti and Liberia. Despite slave resistance against resettlement, Northern and Haitian resentment to black immigration, and a shortage of resettlement funds, almost all former Quaker slaves had been resettled by 1856."]

"Quaker Petition for Manumission of Slaves-1778." Manuscript MS 251, Friends Historical Collection, Hege Library, Guilford College, Greensboro.

Sappington, Roger E. "North Carolina and the Non-Resistant Sects during the American War of Independence." *Quaker History*, 60:1 (Spring 1971), 29-47.

Silcox-Jarrett, Diane. "Freedom Bound." *Our State: Down Home in North Carolina*, 66:9 (February 1999), 38, 40, 42-43; online: http://digital.ncdcr.gov/cdm/ref/collection/p16062coll18/id/67435. [Online description from

"North Carolina Periodicals Index," East Carolina University: "Quakers in the Piedmont originated the first national Underground Railroad in the 1700s. This was a secret network of people and places set up to help slaves escaping to the North. It was not without danger for the Quakers, for anyone caught helping runaways could be punished."]

Thorne, Dorothy Gilbert. "Dorothy Gilbert Thorne Papers, 1947-1950." Manuscript MS 74, Friends Historical Collection, Hege Library, Guilford College, Greensboro. [Online finding aid description: "Historical papers: NC Quakers and the Revolution; early Quakerism in NC, etc."]

Thorne, Dorothy Gilbert. "North Carolina Friends and the Revolution." *North Carolina Historical Review*, 38:3 (July 1961), 323-340; online: http://digital.ncdcr.gov/cdm/ref/collection/p16062coll9/id/4207. [Online description from "North Carolina Periodicals Index," East Carolina University: "This article examines the antiwar stance and general perspectives on the American Revolution held by the North Carolina Friends (Quakers). All nature of Friends life and culture related to this period is examined including analysis of minutes from Friends monthly, yearly, and council meetings, discussion of the disowning of members who took up arms as well a look at those who joined the Friends during this period, the taxing of Friends members, Friends involvement in the care of war wounded, and Friends' burial traditions."]

White, Julia S. "The Quakers of Perquimans." *North Carolina Booklet*, 7:4 (April 1908), 278-289; online: http://digital.ncdcr.gov/cdm/ref/collection/p249901coll37/id/14180. [Online description from "North Carolina Periodicals Index," East Carolina University: "Quakers were the first to bring organized Christianity to North Carolina, and counted among them a number of intelligent and well-disposed members, particularly in Perquimans and Pasquotank."]

White, Steven Jay. "Friends and the Coming of the Revolution." *The Southern Friend: Journal of the North Carolina Friends Historical Society*, 4:1 (Spring 1982), 16-27.

White, Steven Jay. "North Carolina Quakers in the Era of the American Revolution." M. A. thesis, University of Tennessee – Knoxville, 1981. ["Traces the role of the Quakers throughout the Revolutionary period in North Carolina, with special attention to peace movements and abolitionism."]

Roman Catholics

Griffin, Martin I[gnatius] J[oseph]. *Catholics and the American Revolution*. 3 vols. Ridley Park, Pa.: M. I. J. Griffin, 1907-1911.

Powers, William F. *Tar Heel Catholics: A History of Catholicism in North Carolina*. Lanham, Md.: University Press of America, 2003.

Woods, James M. *A History of the Catholic Church in the American South, 1513-1900*. Gainesville: University Press of Florida, 2011.

Scots in North Carolina

Beach, Kathryn. "From Caledonia to Carolina: The Highland Scots." *Tar Heel Junior Historian*, 45:2 (Spring 2006), 6-8; online: http://ncpedia.org/highland-scots. [Online description from "North Carolina Periodicals Index," East Carolina University: "Beach recounts Highland Scots immigration to North Carolina and how they dealt with the differences they encountered. The first organized immigration came in 1739, when 350 people from Scotland sailed to Wilmington and latter settled in what would become Cumberland County. New arrivals priorities included selecting land, surveying it, and planting crops. By the late 18th-century, the largest population of Scots outside Scotland lived in the state."]

Black, Ronald. "The Nine: A Scottish Gaelic Charm in the North Carolina State Archives." *North Carolina Historical Review*, 84:1 (January 2007), 37-58. [Online description from "North Carolina Periodicals Index," East Carolina University: "This article examines a Gaelic charm found in the North Carolina State Archives as the only known 18th century example found in the New World. Written in poorly spelled Scottish Gaelic, the charm was to ward off evil and originated from an 18th century Gaelic community in Cumberland County."]

Campbell, John C. *The Southern Highlander and His Home Land*. New York: Russell Sage Foundation, 1921.

Carter, Laura G. "Great Scot!" *Our State: Down Home in North Carolina*, 68:3 (August 2000), 72-77, 79; online: http://digital.ncdcr.gov/cdm/ref/collection/p16062coll18/id/71551. [Online description from "North Carolina Periodicals Index," East Carolina University: "Conditions in Scotland in the 1700s, including the start of sheep raising, changes in the hierarchy of clans, and uniting England and Scotland, encouraged many to seek a new life in North Carolina. By the late 18th-century, the largest population of Scots outside Scotland lived in the state. Their history is remembered yearly in the Grandfather Mountain Highland Games and Gathering of the

Scottish Clans. Ancestry can be traced through libraries, courthouses, and the Scottish Heritage Center at St. Andrews Presbyterian College."]

Culpepper, Linda Parramore. "Blood, the Tie That Binds: The Role of Scottish Clans in North Carolina Loyalism during the Revolutionary Era." M. A. thesis, Western Carolina University, 1998.

Dobson, David. *Directory of Scots in the Carolinas, 1680-1830.* Baltimore: Genealogical Publishing Company, 1986.

Dobson, David D. *Scottish Emigration to Colonial America, 1607-1785.* Athens: University of George Press, 1994.

Dussek, Hugh. "Pre-Revolutionary History: Socio-Religious Perspectives on the Scots-Irish and Highland Scots in the Backcountry of North Carolina." Ph. D. thesis, Union Institute and University, 2002. [Online catalog description: "The study examines the history of the pre-Revolutionary developments in the backcountry of North Carolina through an analysis and comparison of the influence of Presbyterianism on the cultures of two communities: the Scots-Irish of Mecklenburg County and the Highland Scots of Cumberland County. Using historical and interdisciplinary perspectives, the study traces the histories of the settlement of these two communities and the effect of social influences stemming from their earlier histories in Britain and America, the history of the Presbyterian Church in America, the local Presbyterian clergy and churches, the revivals of the Great Awakening, the relationship of these communities to the British crown and the development of a 'revolutionary syndrome' in North Carolina. The study analyzes the role of Presbyterianism in supporting and legitimizing both loyalty and rebellion to the British crown among the Scots-Irish, who were mostly second and third generation settlers from the northern colonies, and the Highland Scots, who largely came directly from Scotland. The study examines the role of the Presbyterian clergy and other local social leaders, many of whom were educated at the College of New Jersey, in developments in Mecklenburg County leading from support of the British crown to support of the Revolution. The study also examines the role of the Presbyterian clergy in the development of a division in Cumberland County between the earlier Highlander settlers, who largely became revolutionary, and the later settlers, who mainly remained loyal to the British crown."]

Fowler, Malcolm. *Valley of the Scots: A History of the First Scottish Settlers in North Carolina.* Raleigh: Edwards & Broughton, 1986.

Garrison, Roy Charles. "Migration, Settlement and Revolution: The Highland Scots in the Cape Fear Region of Colonial North Carolina." M. A. thesis, University of North Carolina at Charlotte, 1998. [Online catalog description: "Cultural traditions and new environment have generally been opposing influences on the behavior of immigrants. Under some circumstances these forces can fragment a community of newcomers. Such was the case of the Highland Scots in colonial North Carolina. Choosing to migrate as a result of economic hardship in Scotland and opportunity in the Cape Fear region, they established a distinct community that initially preserved many of their cultural traditions. However, in their efforts to establish themselves successfully in their new home, many adopted new behaviors such as the production of naval stores and lumber, as well as the purchase and development of land throughout the Upper Cape Fear region. When the American Revolution broke out, many Scots fought to maintain their ties to Britain, but many others chose neutrality or embraced insurrection as a method of preserving their newly established economic security."]

Great Britain. Colonial Office. America and West Indies. Original Correspondence, Board of Trade and Secretary of State. Despatches and Miscellaneous (Military). (CO 5/8). "Whitehall, [London]. Extract of a Letter from the Earl of Dartmouth to Lt. Gen. [Thomas] Gage. 15 Apr., 1775." Copy of a manuscript in the National Archives of the United Kingdom (formerly the Public Records Office), Kew, Richmond, Surrey, England; 70.417.1-3 (MARS ID: 21.20.6.3), "British Records Collection," State Archives of North Carolina, Raleigh. [Online catalog description: "Discusses the proposals of Lt. Col. Allan Maclean and Lt. Col. Gorham to form armed 'associations' of emigrant Scots living in New York and North Carolina 'to support the Authority of the Kingdom.' Grants Gage the authority to execute these proposals if he should deem it necessary. See also Maclean's 'Form of Association' (MARS ID: 21.20.6.1.2)."]

Grimble, Ian. "Emigration in the Time of Rob Dunn, 1714-1778." *Scottish Studies*, 7:9 (1963), 129-153.

Hanson, Timothy. "Cultural Commerce: Scottish Immigrants, Trade and Politics in 18th Century North Carolina." Manuscript paper, January 17, 1997. "Shenandoah Valley Regional Studies Seminar Collection, 1995-2009." Manuscript SC#5027, Manuscript paper, Box 2 (Papers-1995-1997), folder 9, Special Collections, Carrier Library, James Madison University, Harrisonburg.

Kelly, Douglas F., with Caroline Switzer Kelly. *Carolina Scotts: An Historical and Genealogical Study of Over 100 Years of Emigration.* Dillon, S. C.: 1739 Publications, 1998.

Mackenzie, James. "Odyssey of John MacRae." *The State: Down Home in North Carolina*, 39:13 (December 1971), 8-11; online: http://digital.ncdcr.gov/cdm/compoundobject/collection/p16062coll18/id/54828. [Online description from "North Carolina Periodicals Index," East Carolina University: "John MacRae (1774-1780) was a Scot who wrote poems and songs and convinced many of his fellow countrymen to immigrate to North Carolina. This article presents his legacy and impact on North Carolina."]

Mackenzie, James. "Over the Isles to America." *The State: Down Home in North Carolina*, 40:3 (July 1972), 12-14. [Online description from "North Carolina Periodicals Index," East Carolina University: "In 1773, thousands of Scottish citizens from the Isle of Skye immigrated to North Carolina's Cape Fear Valley region to escape unaffordable rent increases. To celebrate their new lives, the immigrants created a new dance called *America*, which was performed to a brisk reel. The accompanying song, *Over the Isles to America*, is still a popular folk song in Scotland, according to Scottish folk song authority James E. Scott."]

Macrae, James C. "The Highland-Scotch Settlement in North Carolina." *North Carolina Booklet*, 4:10 (February 1905), 3-24; online: http://digital.ncdcr.gov/cdm/ref/collection/p249901coll37/id/14180. [Online description from "North Carolina Periodicals Index," East Carolina University: "This article details the culture, practices, and colonial history of the Highland Scots who eventually created several settlements in the Cape Fear region of North Carolina. It also discusses the history of those settlements from the mid 18th century up to the late 19th century in North Carolina."]

Malone, E. T., Jr. "Remembering Malcolm Fowler." *North Carolina Folkore Journal*, 59:1 (Spring-Summer 2012), 4-10; online: http://paws.wcu.edu/ncfj/. [Online description from "North Carolina Periodicals Index," East Carolina University: "Although not particularly successful in the ways the world measures success, Malcolm Fowler, a businessman and amateur historian, made his life's work to tell the story of the Scottish Highlanders in the upper Cape Fear region of North Carolina, and in this he was the most successful."]

McDonald, Patrick H. *Between the Creeks: A History of the Highland Scots Immigration into Moore County, North Carolina*. Raleigh, NC: P.H. McDonald, 1999.

McKinnon, Henry A. "A North Carolina Scot and the Confiscation Acts." *Robeson County Register*, 1:3 (August 1986), 105-106. [Archibald McEacharn]

McLean, Hamilton; John Edwin Purcell; John Edwin Purcell [2nd]; Archibald Gilchrist Singletary. *The Lumber River Scots and Their Descendants: The McLeans, the Torreys, the Purcells, the McIntyres, the Gilchrists.* Richmond: William Byrd Press, 1942; reprinted: 1986.

Meyer, Duane Gilbert. *The Highland Scots of North Carolina, 1732-1776*. Chapel Hill: University of North Carolina Press, [1961].

Moss, Bobby Gilmer. "The Role of the Scots and the Scotch-Irish in the Southern Campaigns of the War of American Independence, 1780-83." Ph. D. dissertation, University of St. Andrews, Scotland, 1979.

Murdoch, Alexander. "A Scottish Document Concerning Emigration to North Carolina in 1772." *North Carolina Historical Review*, 67:4 (October 1990), 438-449. [Online description from "North Carolina Periodicals Index," East Carolina University: "This article examines a pamphlet circulated in the western highlands of Scotland that glowingly describes the opportunities in North Carolina during the 1770s. The pamphlet also describes the process by which a large number of Scots from Argyll, Skye, and Sutherland moved to North America during this time period."]

"North Carolina and the Scottish Highlanders." *Argyll Colony Plus*, 2:4 (Fall 1987), 122-128. [Includes a section: "Role in the American Revolution," 127-128.]

Newsome, A. R. "Records of Emigrants from England and Scotland to North Carolina, 1774-1775." *North Carolina Historical Review*, 11:1 (January 1934), 39-54; online: http://digital.ncdcr.gov/cdm/ref/collection/p16062coll9/id/4207; 11:2 (April 1934), 129-143; online: http://digital.ncdcr.gov/cdm/ref/collection/p16062coll9/id/4207. [Online description from "North Carolina Periodicals Index," East Carolina University: "Reprinted here is a compilation of records for Scottish emigrants to North Carolina gathered from Public Record Office of Great Britain in the Treasury Department and organized by the North Carolina Historical Commission. These records include names or emigrants, age, occupation, departure dates, port of departure, and reason for visiting the state. Dates of records in this installment are from January 1774 through May 1775."]

Parker, James. "Papers of James Parker. (LPL Parker, Selections)." Manuscript, (MARS Id: 21.263; series), State Archives of North Carolina, Raleigh. [Online catalog description: "The numerous North Carolina items in this collection consist mainly of correspondence and related papers of James Parker, a Scottish merchant resident in Virginia but with extensive interests in North Carolina. Topics include, among others, his property and business affairs in North Carolina, the Revolutionary War, the Dismal Swamp reclamation scheme, family matters, the siege and capture of Charleston in 1780, his loyalist claim."]

Ray, Celeste. *Highland Heritage: Scottish Americans in the American South*. Chapel Hill: University of North Carolina Press, 2001. [Publisher's description: "Each year, tens of thousands of people flock to Grandfather Mountain, North Carolina, and to more than two hundred other locations across the country to attend Scottish Highland Games and Gatherings. There, kilt-wearing participants compete in athletics, Highland dancing, and bagpiping, while others join clan societies in celebration of a Scottish heritage. As Celeste Ray notes, however, the Scottish affiliation that Americans claim today is a Highland Gaelic identity that did not come to characterize that nation until long after the ancestors of many Scottish Americans had left Scotland. Ray explores how Highland Scottish themes and lore merge with southern regional myths and identities to produce a unique style of commemoration and a complex sense of identity for Scottish Americans in the South. Blending the objectivity of the anthropologist with respect for the people she studies, she asks how and why we use memories of our ancestral pasts to provide a sense of identity and community in the present. In so doing, she offers an original and insightful examination of what it means to be Scottish in America."]

Reigh, Croftan. "Washington's Scotch Comrades." *Argyll Colony Plus*, 19:2 (July 2005), 16-17.

Smith, Jonathan. "The Scotch Presbyterian in the American Revolution." *Granite Monthly*, (January-March 1918), 37-44.

Scots Irish in North Carolina

Blethen, H. Tyler, and Curtis W. Wood, Jr. "Scotch-Irish Frontier Society in Southwestern North Carolina, 1780-1840." In H. Tyler Blethen and Curtis W. Wood, Jr., ed., *Ulster and North America: Transatlantic Perspectives on the Scotch-Irish* (Tuscaloosa: University of Alabama Press, 1997), 213-226.

Blethen, H. Tyler, and Curtis W. Wood, Jr. *From Ulster to Carolina: The Migration of the Scotch-Irish to Southwestern North Carolina*. Raleigh: North Carolina Deparment of Cultural Resources, 1998.

Brown, William L. *Revolutionary Spirit: A View of the Scotch-Irish Influence in America.* Rocheport, Mo.: Pebble Publishing, 2007. [Scots in North Carolina; Mecklenburg Declaration of Independence.]

Dussek, Hugh. "Pre-Revolutionary History: Socio-Religious Perspectives on the Scots-Irish and Highland Scots in the Backcountry of North Carolina." Ph. D. dissertation, Union Institute and University, 2002. [Online catalog description: "The study examines the history of the pre-revolutionary developments in the backcountry of North Carolina through an analysis and comparison of the influence of Presbyterianism on the cultures of two communities: the Scots-Irish of Mecklenburg County and the Highland Scots of Cumberland County. Using historical and interdisciplinary perspectives, the study traces the histories of the settlement of these two communities and the effect of social influences stemming from their earlier histories in Britain and America, the history of the Presbyterian Church in America, the local Presbyterian clergy and churches, the revivals of the Great Awakening, the relationship of these communities to the British crown and the development of a 'revolutionary syndrome' in North Carolina. The study analyzes the role of Presbyterianism in supporting and legitimizing both loyalty and rebellion to the British crown among the Scots-Irish, who were mostly second and third generation settlers from the northern colonies, and the Highland Scots, who largely came directly from Scotland. The study examines the role of the Presbyterian clergy and other local social leaders, many of whom were educated at the College of New Jersey, in developments in Mecklenburg County leading from support of the British crown to support of the Revolution. The study also examines the role of the Presbyterian clergy in the development of a division in Cumberland County between the earlier Highlander settlers, who largely became revolutionary, and the later settlers, who mainly remained loyal to the British crown."]

Green, E. R. R. [Edward Rodney Richey]. "The Scotch-Irish and the Coming of the Revolution in North Carolina." *Irish Historical Studies*, 7:26 (1950), 77-86.

Hofstra, Warren R. *Ulster to America: The Scots-Irish Migration Experience, 1680-1830.* Knoxville: University of Tennessee Press, 2012.

Leyburn, James G. *The Scotch-Irish: A Social History*. Chapel Hill: University of North Carolina Press, 1961.

McKelway, A. J. "The Scotch-Irish of North Carolina." *North Carolina Booklet*, 4:1 (March 1905), 3-24; online: http://digital.ncdcr.gov/cdm/ref/collection/p249901coll37/id/14180. [Online description from "North Carolina Periodicals Index," East Carolina University: "This article details the European history and Colonial settlement patterns of the Scotch-Irish community, culminating with settlements in North Carolina. The first settlement in North Carolina was founded in 1736 in Duplin County."]

Moss, Bobby Gilmer. "The Role of the Scots and the Scotch-Irish in the Southern Campaigns of the War of American Independence, 1780-83." Ph. D. dissertation, University of St. Andrews, Scotland, 1979.

Swiss in North Carolina

Ash, William J. "Remembering Our Swiss and German Beginnings." *The Palace*, 10:2 (Winter 2010), 13. [Online description from "North Carolina Periodicals Index," East Carolina University: "As New Bern celebrates its 300th anniversary, it remembers its Swiss and German settlers who agreed to put down roots where the Trent and Neuse rivers converged."]

Schütz, Géza. "Additions to the History of Swiss Colonization Projects in Carolina." *North Carolina Historical Review*, 10:2 (April 1933), 133-141.

Women and Girls of North Carolina and Tennessee

Abernethy, Edgar. "Heroines of the Past." *The State: A Weekly Survey of North Carolina*, 11:31 (January 1944), 3-4; online: http://digital.ncdcr.gov/cdm/ref/collection/p16062coll18/id/18339. [Online description from "North Carolina Periodicals Index," East Carolina University: "Women played an important part in the Revolutionary War. Abernethy recounts a few outstanding incidents, including Susan Twitty, Mary Slocumb, and Elizabeth Steele."]

Alexander Martin Chapter, DAR. *North Carolina Heroines of the American Revolution.* High Point, N. C.: The Chapter, 1971.

American Association of University Women. *Making a Difference: Women of Mecklenburg.* Charlotte: Charlotte Branch, American Association of University Women, 1980.

Arthur, Billy. "Acts of Defiance." *The State: Down Home in North Carolina*, 59:1 (June 1991), 12-13; online: http://digital.ncdcr.gov/cdm/compoundobject/collection/p16062coll18/id/64875. [Online description from "North Carolina Periodicals Index," East Carolina University: "The author presents women from North Carolina during the Revolutionary and Civil Wars and how they participated in protecting their state and property. For example, some women spied on British troops for American soldiers during the Revolutionary War."]

Barefoot, Daniel W. *Touring North Carolina's Revolutionary War Sites.* Winston-Salem: John F. Blair, 1998. [Includes references to many women throughout.]

Belton, Tom. "Legendary Women." *Tar Heel Junior Historian*, 32:1 (Fall 1992), 13-17. [Online description from "North Carolina Periodicals Index," East Carolina University: "Women served both the loyalists and the patriots during the American Revolution. Some of the famous women on the Loyalists side were native-Scotswoman Flora McDonald and Elizabeth Cornell Bayard. Margaret Sharpe, Betsy Dowdy, Mary Slocumb, and Elizabeth Maxwell Steele served the Patriots during the Revolution."]

Brown, Roy M. *Public Poor Relief in North Carolina*. Chapel Hill: University of North Carolina Press, 1928; reprinted: New York: Arno Press, 1976. ["Under the Wardens of the Poor, 1776-1868," 26-68.]

Butler, Lindley S., and Alan D. Watson, eds. *The North Carolina Experience: An Interpretive and Documentary History.* Chapel Hill: University of North Carolina Press, 1984. [Chapter 6: Don Higginbotham, "Decision for Revolution," 125-146, includes Document 6.2: "Association Signed by Ladies of Edenton, North Carolina, 25 October 1774" pages 136-137; Chapter 19: Jane De Hart Mathews, "The Status of Women in North Carolina," 427-451.]

Caruthers, E[li] W[ashington]. *Revolutionary Incidents and Sketches of Character, Chiefly in the "Old North State."* Philadelphia: Hayes & Zell, 1854; 2nd series printed with the title: *Interesting Revolutionary Incidents: and Sketches of Character, Chiefly in the "Old North State."* Philadelphia: Hayes & Zell, 1856; first series reprinted: typed, and indexed by Ruth F. Thompson with the original title. Greensboro, N. C.: Guilford County Genealogical Society, 1985; online: http://hdl.loc.gov/loc.gdc/scd0001.0000516025A. [Information on women appears dotted throughout the book. The book includes the following map: Hayes & Zell. *Map Showing the Routes of Lord Cornwallis and Genl. Greene in North Carolina.* 2nd ed. Philadelphia: Hayes & Zell, 1856.]

Ceremonies at the Unveiling of the Monument upon Moore's Creek Battle Ground to the Women of the Revolution, August 1907. [S. l.]: Moore's Creek Monumental Association, 1907?

Claiborne, Jack and William Price, eds. *Discovering North Carolina: A Tar Heel Reader.* Chapel Hill: University of North Carolina Press, 1991. [Michael G. Martin, Jr., "Rejecting a Pernicious Custom," 115-117, discusses Penelope Barker.]

Clinton, Catherine. "Women on the Land (I)." In Charles Reagan Wilson and William Ferris, coeditors, *Encyclopedia of Southern Culture* (Chapel Hill: University of North Carolina Press, 1989), 1550-1551.

Crow, Terrell A., with Ansley Herring Wagner. "Women." In William S. Powell, ed.; Jay Mazzocchi, assoc. ed., *Encyclopedia of North Carolina* (Chapel Hill: University of North Carolina Press in association with the University of North Carolina Library, 2006), 1219-1224. [Includes a section: "Women in the Revolutionary Era and Early Statehood," 1220.]

Dillard, Richard. "Some North Carolina Heroines of the Revolution." *North Carolina Booklet*, 8:4 (April 1909), 325-333; online: http://digital.ncdcr.gov/cdm/ref/collection/p249901coll37/id/14180. [Online description from "North Carolina Periodicals Index," East Carolina University: "Several North Carolina women who played parts in various phases of the Revolutionary War including Betsy Dowdy, Mary Slocumb, and Flora MacDonald."]

Dunkerly, Robert M. *Women of the Revolution: Bravery and Sacrifice on the Southern Battlefields*. Charleston, S. C.: History Press, 2007. [Publisher's description: "Each of the Southern Revolutionary battlefields holds the history of soldiers and legends of women. From the wooded slopes of Kings Mountain to the fields of Cowpens, to the lesser-known sites like Fishing Creek and Hanging Rock, author Robert M. Dunkerly uncovers the stories and legends surrounding the women who were caught up in the struggle. This book serves not only as a study of the battles, but also as a chronicle of the experiences of women in the eighteenth century. Some were camp followers attached to the armies, while others were civilians caught in the line of fire. Women were present on nearly every battlefield, and their stories are told here for the first time." Contents: The Values of the Eighteenth-Century World; The Eighteenth-Century Woman; Moores Creek, North Carolina, February 27, 1776 Savannah, Georgia, September 16-October 19, 1779; Spring and Summer 1780; Charleston, South Carolina, April 2-May 12, 1780; Brattonsville, South Carolina (Williamson's Plantation), July 12, 1780; Hanging Rock, South Carolina, August 6, 1780; Camden, South Carolina, August 16, 1780; Fishing Creek, South Carolina, August 18, 1780; Stallions, South Carolina, Summer 1780; Fall 1780; Kings Mountain, South Carolina, October 7, 1780; Winter 1780-81; Cowpens, South Carolina, January 17, 1781; Guilford Courthouse, North Carolina, March 15, 1781; Spring and Summer 1781; Fort Motte, South Carolina, May 8-May 12, 1781; Ninety Six, South Carolina, May 22-June 19, 17891; Alston House, North Carolina (House In the Horseshoe), July 29, 1781 Eutaw Springs, South Carolina, September 8, 1781; Lindley's Mill, North Carolina, September 13, 1781; Southeastern North Carolina, Spring 1781; Bacon's Bridge, South Carolina, Summer 1782.]

Eberlein, Tori Ann. "To Be Amiable and Accomplished: Fitting Young Women for Upper-Class Virginia Society, 1760-1810." M. A. thesis, College of William and Mary, 1982. [Description: Ervin, William Carson. "Grace Greenlee: A Revolutionary Heroine." Typescript c. 1954 (Mss7:1 G8465:1), Virginia Historical Society, Richmond. [Online catalog description: "Concerns Grace Greenlee's early life in Virginia and her experiences in western North Carolina during the American Revolution.]

Escott, Paul D., and Jeffrey J. Crow. "The Social Order and Violent Disorder: An Analysis of North Carolina in the Revolution and the Civil War." *Journal of Southern History,* 52 (August 1986), 373-402. [Briefly mentions mistreatment of women during the Revolution.]

Fischer, Kirsten. "'False, Feigned, and Scandalous Words': Sexual Slander and Racial Ideology Among Whites in Colonial North Carolina." In Catherine Clinton and Michele Gillespie, eds., *The Devil's Lane: Sex and Race in the Early South* (New York and London: Oxford University Press, 1997), Part III, Chapter 10, 140-153.

Fountain, Mrs. Alvin M. "Women of North Carolina." *The State: A Weekly Survey of North Carolina*, 10:14 (September 1942), 8-9, 25-26; online:. [Online description from "North Carolina Periodicals Index," East Carolina University: "From the Colonial period to modern times, the women of North Carolina have played important roles in many lines of work such as education, politics, and business, and have assisted materially in its progress and developments."]

Grundset, Eric G., Briana L. Diaz, and Hollis L. Gentry. *America's Women in the Revolutionary Era: A History through Bibliography*. 3 vols. Washington, D. C.: National Society Daughters of the American Revolution, 2011.

Gillespie, Michele, and Sally G. McMillen, eds. *North Carolina Women: Their Lives and Times*. Athens: University of Georgia Press, 2014.

Gundersen, Joan R. *To Be Useful to the World: Women in Revolutionary America, 1740-1790*. Chapel Hill: University of North Carolina Press, 2006.

Hinton, Mary Hilliard. "Other North Carolina Heroines." *North Carolina Bulletin,* 18:1 (July 1918), 64-75. [Discusses Elizabeth Forbis, Mary Morgan, Rachel Denny, Sarah Logan, Elizabeth McGraw, Ann Fergus, Margaret Caruthers, and Margaret McBride.]

Hinton, Mary Hilliard. "The Spirit of the Revolution." *North Carolina Booklet*, 20:2-4 (October 1920-April 1921), 207-212. [Includes women's role.]

Jones, H. G. *Scoundrels, Rogues and Heroes of the Old North State*. Charleston, S. C.: History Press, 2004. ["North Carolina Governor Married Fifteen-Year-Old Girl," 31-32, Justina Davis Dobbs Nash (actually married two governors! She lived from 1747 to 1773); "Postmaster Had Shady Reputation," 61-62, Sarah DeCrow; and "Martha McFarlane McGee Bell, Heroine," 73-74.]

Jordan, Paula Stahls, and Kathy Warden Manning. *Women of Guilford County, North Carolina: A Study of Women's Contributions, 1740-1979.* Greensboro, N. C.: Women of Guilford, 1979. [Chapter I: "Women in the Early Colonies," 1-8; Chapter II: "The Revolution," 9-20, includes "The War in Guilford County," "Martha

McFarlain McGee Bell," "Rachel Craighead," and "Women under the Constitution." Chapter III: "The New Nation and the Era of Reform," 21-44.

Kerber, Linda K. *Women of the Republic: Intellect and Ideology in Revolutionary America.* Chapel Hill: University of North Carolina Press, 1980.

Kierner, Cynthia. *Southern Women in the Revolution, 1776-1800: Personal and Political Narratives.* Columbia: University of South Carolina Press, 1998. [Contents: Families at War; The Cost of Liberty; The Loyalist Legacy; Women, Allegiance, and Citizenship; The Limits of Revolution; Women's Legislative Petitions by Subject; North Carolina, 1775-1800; Women's Legislative Petitions by Subject: South Carolina, 1776-1800.]

King, Henry. *Hooray for Heroines: Tar Heel Women Who Faced the Enemy and Made The Enemy Blink.* Franklinton, N. C.: Possum Press, 2003. [The section "Oh, Those Revolutionary Ladies" includes numerous accounts of North Carolina women during the War for Independence.]

King, Martha Joanne. "Making an Impression: Women Printers in the Southern Colonies in the Revolutionary Era." Ph. D. dissertation, College of William and Mary, 1992.

Klepp, Susan E. *Revolutionary Conceptions: Women, Fertility, and Family Limitation in America, 1760-1820.* Chapel Hill: University of North Carolina Press. 2009.

Leary, Helen F. M. and Maurice R. Stirewalt, ed. *North Carolina Research: Genealogy and Local History.* Raleigh, N. C.: North Carolina Genealogical Society, 1980. [This book is useful to show strategies on how to research marriage records, divorce records, vital records, state census: 1785-1787, wills, court records, and tax records in the state of North Carolina.]

Lee, Lawrence. *The Lower Cape Fear in Colonial Days.* Chapel Hill: University of North Carolina Press, 1965. [Chapter 14: "The People and the Way They Lived," 182-204.]

Lee, Wayne E.; foreword by Stanley Harrold and Randall J. Miller. *Crowds and Soldiers in Revolutionary North Carolina: The Culture of Violence in Riot and War.* Gainesville: University Press of Florida, 2001. [Chapter 4: "Colonial Ways of War: Tradition and Development," 104-136, contrasts the treatment of women captives by Native American warriors and European/colonial soldiers, noting that the former generally did not rape their captives, whereas the latter did.]

Lefler, Hugh T., and William S. Powell. *Colonial North Carolina: A History.* New York: Charles Scribner, 1973. [See Chapter 8: "The People at Home," 175-190.]

Mathews, Alice Elaine. *Society in Revolutionary North Carolina.* Raleigh: North Carolina Department of Archives and History, 1976. [Chapter 3: "North Carolinians at Home, 48-73.]

Matthews, Alice Elaine. "Women in Late-Eighteenth-Century North Carolina: Politics and Private Lives." Durham, N. C.: Office of Continuing Education, Duke University, 1985.

Misenheimer, John E., Jr. "Misenheimer Ladies of the American Revolution." *The Golden Nugget (Cabarrus Genealogical Society)*, 13:2 (Summer 2005), 42-45.

Moore, Mrs. James C. [Grady R.] *North Carolina Heroines of the American Revolution.* High Point: Alexander Martin Chapter, DAR, 1972. [Includes Elizabeth Montford Ashe, Penelope Barker, Elizabeth Vail, Martha Bell, Hannah Millikan Blair, Rachael Caldwell, Mary Dunlap, Ruth Davidson, Betsy Dowdy, Dorcas Bell Love, Jane Parks McDowell, Martha (Witherspoon) Pettigrew, Mary Hooks Slocumb, Elizabeth Maxwell Steele, Caroline Close Stuart, Jane Thomas, Sally Thomas, Susan Twitty, and Dolley Payne Madison.]

Mozingo, Kimberly. "Amid Hostilities and Destruction: North Carolina Women and Their Impact on the American Revolution." Online paper, University of North Carolina at Greensboro: https://libres.uncg.edu/ir/uncg/f/K_Mozingo_Amid_2013.pdf.

North Carolina Women: Reclaiming Their Place in History. Raleigh: North Carolina Division of Archives and History, North Carolina Museum of History, North Carolina Women's History Project, [1990?].

"North Carolina Women during the Revolutionary War." Reference Vertical File, State Library of North Carolina, Raleigh.

Pendleton, Hazel E. "Patriotic Women of North Carolina for Whom DAR Chapters are Named." *Daughters of the American Revolution Magazine*, 96:11 (November 1962), 683-685, 715. [Dorcas Beel, Ruth Davidson, Rachel Caldwell, Elizabeth Montford Ashe, Mary Slocumb, Elizabeth Maxwell Steele, and Betsy Dowdy.]

Pickens, [Blance Armfield]. "Women of N. C. in the Revolution." Typescript in the "Women in the American Revolution Collection," DAR Library, Washington, D. C.; Highpoint, N. C.: B. A. Pickens, pre-1938.

Powell, William S., ed. *Dictionary of North Carolina Biography.* 6 vols. Chapel Hill: University of North Carolina Press, 1979-1996. [Vol. 1: "A-C," includes Michael E. Martin Jr., "Penelope Barker (1728-96)," 95-96, Barker was involved in the Edenton Tea Party; Eva Burbank Murphy, "Elizabeth Cornell Bayard (1761/1762-17 Jan. 1854)," 121-122, Elizabeth Cornell Bayard unsuccessfully attempted to get back the confiscated land that her loyalist father had given her in a 1787 lawsuit; Joseph R. Suggs, "Martha McFarlane McGee Bell (1735-9 Sept.

1820)," 132; Paula S. Jordan, "Hannah Millikan Blair (1756-14 Jan. 1852)," 171; Vol. 2: "D-G," includes, Jaquelin Drane Nash, "Justina Davis (1745-Dec. 1771)," 38, the second wife Governor Arthur Dobbs; Mary Hinton Duke Kerr, "Sarah DeRippe Falkener (1755-24 Feb. 1819)," 178-179, came from England to American in 1787 and later became "Lady Principal" of the Falkener Seminary for Young Ladies; Vol. 3: "H-K," includes Treva W. Mathis, "Ann Matthews Jessup (10 Oct. 1738-26 Sept. 1822)," 281, Quaker minister and horticulturist; Vol. 4: "L-O," includes Maud Thomas Smith, "Flora MacDonald (1722-Mar. 1790)," 138-139; Nancy V. Smith, "Janet Smith MacNeill (Jennie Bahn) (1720-1791)," 181, during the Revolutionary war Jennie Bahn is rumored to have split her six sons so that half served the British and half the fight for independence, while she "remained neutral in order to sell cattle to both sides"; Vol. 5: "P-S," includes Hugh F. Rankin, "Janet Schaw (b.ca.1740)," 294, loyalist and diarist; William S. West, "Elizabeth Maxwell Steel (1733-22 Nov. 1790)," 432, innkeeper.]

Rodman, Lida Tunstall. "Patriotic Women of North Carolina in the Revolution." *Daughters of the American Revolution Magazine*, 45:2/3 (August/September 1914), 145-152.

Sharpless, Rebecca. "Southern Women and the Land." *Agricultural History*, 67:2 (Spring 1993), 30-42.

Smith, Margaret Supplee, and Emily Herring Wilson; foreword by Doris Betts. *North Carolina Women: Making History.* Chapel Hill: University of North Carolina Press, 1999. [This excellent, illustrated state survey includes Part I: "Prehistory through the Eighteenth Century" with general text and biographical sections on Nancy Ward (Nanye-hi), Rebecca Bryan Boone, Ann Matthews Floyd Jessup, "Moravian Women," and "The Bondswomen of Somerset Place, 1786-1860."]

Smith, T. Marshall. *Legends of the War of Independence and of the Earlier Settlements in the West.* Louisville, Ky.: J. F. Brennan, Publishers, 1855. [Includes "The Whig Women of North Carolina – A Few Touching Biographical Sketches of them during the War," includes Esther Simpson, Aunt Molly, Mrs. Polly Rust, and Elizabeth Smith.]

"Some of North Carolina's Notable Women." *North Carolina Booklet*, 19:4/20:1 (April-July 1920), 148-149. [Includes as listing of "Revolutionary Heroines."]

Spruill, Julia Cherry. *Women's Life and Work in the Southern Colonies*. Chapel Hill: University of North Carolina Press, 1938.

Spruill, Julia Cherry. "Southern Housewives before the Revolution." *North Carolina Historical Review*, 13:1 (January 1936), 25-46.

Swann, Lee Ann Caldwell. "Land of Their Own: Land Grants to Women in the Lower Colonial South." Ph. D. dissertation, University of Georgia, 1986. [North Carolina, South Carolina, Georgia]

Thompson, Catherine E. *A Selective Guide to Women-Related Records in the North Carolina State Archives.* Raleigh: North Carolina Division of Archives and History, 1977.

Troxler, George Wesley. "The Homefront in Revolutionary North Carolina." Ph. D. dissertation, University of North Carolina, Chapel Hill, 1970.

Watson, Alan D., comp. and ed. *Society in Early North Carolina: A Documentary History*. Raleigh: North Carolina Division of Archives and History, Department of Cultural Resources, 2000. [Contains various texts (newspaper articles, manuscripts, excerpts, letter sections, etc.) relating to women in North Carolina and in America during the Revolutionary era under such subject headings in the index as: "Family," "Homes and Possessions," and "Education." Examples: "The Duty of a Wife." *North Carolina Gazette* (New Bern), July 14, 1775; and "Gentlewoman of Prudence" and "Choice of a Husband." *Wilmington Centennial, and General Advertiser*, June 25, 1788.]

Watson, Alan Douglas. "Women in Colonial North Carolina: Overlooked and Underestimated." *North Carolina Historical Review,* 58:1 (Winter 1981), 1-22. [Online description from "North Carolina Periodicals Index," East Carolina University: "This article examines the ideology of subordination that has allowed the role of women in North Carolina history to be overlooked, as well as the roles and achievements of women in the colonial settlement period."]

Watson, Harry L.; research and marginalia by Jean B. Anderson; Sydney Nathans, ed. *An Independent People: The Way We Lived in North Carolina, 1770-1820.* Chapel Hill: University of North Carolina Press, 1983. [Includes a little information on women's daily duties and lives.]

Weatherford, Doris. "North Carolina." 3:155-168, with a sidebar on the Edenton Tea Party, and a subsection, "American Revolution to Civil War (1776-1861)," includes Rachel Craighead Caldwell was repeatedly harassed by local Loyalists, Margaret Sharpe Gaston saw her husband shot by Loyalists, Elizabeth Maxwell Steele gave her savings to American soldiers, Martha Polk Brevard traveled far to nurse prisoners of war at Charleston, Betsy Dowdy warned Gen. William Skinner of an impending British attack, Cherokee had a less governance role, and Mary Bledsoe lost her husband and two sons to violence with the Cherokee.

"Women Active in Revolution; Miss Mary Wyche, of Chapel Hill, Digs up Forgotten History." *News and Observer*, 192? [date missing from copy in the file at the North Carolina State Library: "N. C. – History – Revolution – Women's Work."]

Wood, Betty. "Southern Women of Color and the American Revolution, 1775-1783." In S. Jay Kleinberg, Eileen Boris, and Vicki L. Ruiz, eds., *The Practice of U. S. Women's History: Narratives, Intersections, and Dialogues* (New Brunswick, N. J.: Rutgers University Press, 2007), 67-82.

Women and Girls of North Carolina – Legal Status

Fraser, Lynne Howard. "Nobody's Children: The Treatment of Illegitimate Children in Three North Carolina Counties, 1760-1790." M. A. thesis, College of William and Mary, 1987.

Leary, Helen F. M. "Marriage, Divorce, and Widowhood: A Study of North Carolina Law Governing the Property and Person of Married Women, 1663-1869." *North Carolina Genealogical Society Journal*, 16 (August 1990), 130-136.

Mathews, Jane De Hart. "The Status of Women in North Carolina." In Lindley S. Butler and Alan D. Watson, eds., *The North Carolina Experience: An Interpretive and Documentary History* (Chapel Hill: University of North Carolina Press, 1984), 427-451.

Morgan, Lynda J. "Status of Women in New Hanover County, North Carolina, 1750-1800." M. A. thesis, Western Carolina University, 1978.

Semonche, John E. "Common Law Marriage in North Carolina: A Study in Legal History." *American Journal of Legal History*, 9:4 (October 1965), 320-349. [The history of common law marriage, illegal marriages of white men with African American or American Indian women, and invalid marriages in North Carolina during the mid-seventeenth century to the mid-nineteenth century.]

Women and Girls of North Carolina – Widows

"J. H. Kirkham, Land and Pension Agent, Raleigh, North Carolina, Has Valuable Information for the Following Named Widows of Revolutionary Soldiers…" Broadside, No date J:3 Broadsides, Virginia Historical Society, Richmond.

Wood, Kirsten E. *Masterful Women: Slaveholding Widows from the American Revolution through the Civil War*. Chapel Hill: University of North Carolina Press, 2004.

Chapter Seventeen:
Lineage Societies in North Carolina Related to the American Revolution

North Carolina Daughters of the American Revolution

Bjorlin, Virginia; Elizabeth Gibson; Robert Hart; Frances Vick; Peggy Otterbourg; Kathlee Hick; Ellen Hinson; and Sarah Leathers. *The North Carolina Society Daughters of the American Revolution, Inc.: The First One Hundred Years, 1898-1998*. Monroe: The Society, 1998.

Carraway, Gertrude S., ed. National Society Daughters of the American Revolution of North Carolina. *N.C.D.A.R. Genealogical Register: Members and Revolutionary Ancestors, 1890 through 1947*. New Bern: Owen G. Dunn Co., 1948.

Hay, Gertrude Sloan. *Chapter Histories of the North Carolina Daughters of the American Revolution: A Partial List, and a Brief Compilation of a Number of Chapter Histories with Tabulations and Achievements*. [North Carolina]: The Society, 1930.

MacLeod, Mrs. John Blount, *et al. Seventy-Five Years of Service: History of the National Society Daughters of the American Revolution of North Carolina*. New Bern: Printed by O. G. Dunn Co., 1975.

National Society Daughters of the American Revolution of North Carolina. *Genealogical Register of Members and Revolutionary Ancestors, 1890-1981*. Charlotte: Delmar Company, 1981.

North Carolina Society Children of the American Revolution

North Carolina Society, Children of the American Revolution. *Tarheel Tattler*, 1 (1980)-?

North Carolina Society Daughters of the Revolution of 1776

"Daughters of the Revolution of 1776." See this explanation of the history and demise of the national organization in 1983 and research their records that reside at the library of the Suffolk County Historical Society, Riverhead, N.Y. The index to the lineage records of this organization have been indexed by the German Genealogical Group, hence its presence on their website: http://www.germangenealogygroup.com/records-search/daughters-of-the-revolution.php.

Moffitt, Mrs. E. E. "The N. C. Society Daughters of the Revolution and Its Objects." *North Carolina Booklet*, 6:2 (October 1906), 146-150; online: http://digital.ncdcr.gov/cdm/ref/collection/p249901coll37/id/14180. [Online description from "North Carolina Periodicals Index," East Carolina University: "This article examines the history of the North Carolina Society of the Daughters of the Revolution from its founding in 1890 by Mrs. Flora Adams Darling up to 1906. It also looks at the requirements for membership into the Society as well as some of the various projects members undertook."]

North Carolina Society of the Sons of the American Revolution

Dunaway, Stewart E. *The Old North State Newsletters, North Carolina Society, Sons of the American Revolution: A Historical Review (1993-2010)*. [North Carolina: S. E. Dunaway], 2011.

Parker, William A.; James G. W. MacClamrock; and Fitzhugh L. Morris. *Lineage Book of Past and Present Members of the North Carolina Society of Sons of the American Revolution*. [Raleigh, N. C.]: North Carolina Society of Sons of the American Revolution, 1951.

Sons of the American Revolution. North Carolina Society. *Charter Roll, North Carolina Society, Sons of the American Revolution*. [North Carolina: The Society, 1928?].

Waggoner, Martha. "1st Black Joins NC's Sons of American Revolution." *Associated Press; AP Regional State Report: Massachusetts*, February 20, 2012. [Publisher's summary: "Raleigh, N. C. (AP) A chapter of the Sons of the American Revolution in North Carolina is inducting its first black member, a firefighter who only recently learned his ancestor was freed from slavery after fighting for American independence. Thirty-year-old Chaz Moore is a descendant of Toby Gilmore, the son of a chieftain in coastal West Africa who was kidnapped at the age of 16 and sold into slavery in Massachusetts. He gained his freedom by joining the fight for what would become the United States."]

Sons of the Revolution in the State of North Carolina

Comer, James V. *Sons of the Revolution in the State of North Carolina, Inc., and Its Predecessor, North Carolina Society of the Sons of the Revolution.* Southern Pines: Cyril Gray Cogswell, 1990.

Haywood, Marshall DeLancey. *The North Carolina Society of the Sons of the Revolution and Its Past Patriotic Activities.* [Raleigh: The Society], 1928.

Haywood, Marshall DeLancey. *Sons of the Revolution in the State of North Carolina. The Membership and Ancestral Register, By-Laws and Charter of the North Carolina Society of the Sons of the Revolution, Including Also the Constitution of the General Society, etc.* Raleigh: The Society, 1898.

Kilbourne, John Dwight. *Sons of the Revolution: A History, 1875-2001.* New York: The Society, 2002.

North Carolina Society of the Sons of the Revolution. *Prospectus.* Raleigh: Edwards & Broughton, Printers and Binders, for the Society, 1894. [From the cover: "In making application for membership observe carefully directions on page 5.' 'Temporarily instituted Oct. 24, 1893. Permanently organized Nov. 21, 1893. Legally incorporated Jan. 8, 1894."]

North Carolina Society of the Sons of the Revolution. *Lineage Book of Past and Present Members of the North Carolina Society of Sons of the American Revolution.* Raleigh: The Society, 1951.

Society of the Cincinnati in North Carolina

Bellas, Henry Hobart. "The North Carolina Society of the Cincinnati." *American Historical Register*, 2 (July 1895), 1207-1217.

Davis, Curtis Carroll. *Revolution's Godchild: The Birth, Death, and Regeneration of the Society of the Cincinnati in North Carolina.* Chapel Hill: University of North Carolina Press for the North Carolina Society of the Cincinnati, 1976.

Davis, Charles Lukens. *The Society of the Cincinnati in the Southern States.* Washington, D. C.: Southern Historical Association, 1898.

Davis, Charles Lukens, and Henry Hobart Bellas. *A Brief History of the North Carolina Troops on the Continental Establishment in the War of the Revolution, With a Register of Officers of the Same; Also a Sketch of the North Carolina Society of the Cincinnati from Its Organization in 1783, to Its So-Called Dissolution after 1790.* Philadelphia: [s. n.], 1896. [Includes: Henry Hobart Bellas' "A Sketch of the North Carolina Society of the Cincinnati from Its Organization in 1783, to Its So-Called Dissolution after 1790," 75-106.]

Myers, Mnor, Jr. *Liberty without Anarchy: A History of the Society of the Cincinnati.* Charlottesville: University Press of Virginia 1983.

North Carolina Society of the Cincinnati. *North Carolina Society of the Cincinnati: Past and Present Members.* [Raleigh: The Society], 1961.

Tennessee Society Daughters of the American Revolution

Cummings, Martha Fuquay, and Ida Garrett Herod Smothers. *Historical Markers Placed by the Tennessee Daughters of the American Revolution.* Knoxville: Tennessee Valley Publishing, 2007.

Jones, Mrs. J. Sutton. *Roster of Membership, Tennessee Society, Daughters of the American Revolution.* Brownsville, Tenn.: The States Graphic, 1940.

Tennessee Society Daughters of the American Revolution. *Legacies of Our Great Grandmothers: Early Tennessee Women.* 2 vols. Monteagle, Tenn.: The Society, 2015.

White, Kate K., for the Tennessee Daughters of the American Revolution. *Tennessee State History of the Daughters of the American Revolution.* Knoxville: S. B. Newman, 1930.

Willis, Mrs. Thomas William. *History of the Tennessee Society Daughters of the American Revolution, 1892-1990: Celebrating the Centennial of the National Society Daughters of the American Revolution.* [Knoxville?]: The Society, 1991.

Tennessee Society Sons of the American Revolution

Tennessee Society Sons of the American Revolution. "Applications, 1899-1980." Manuscript THS 879, "Tennessee Historical Society Collection," Tennessee State Library and Archives, Nashville; online finding aId: http://share.tn.gov/tsla/history/manuscripts/findingaids/ths879.pdf.

Tennessee Society Sons of the American Revolution. *Membership and Directory, 1889-1959.* [S. l.: The Society], 1959.

Tice, Robert D. *Tennessee Society Sons of the American Revolution, 1889-1989: A Centennial History.* Chattanooga: Chattanooga New-Free Press, 1989.

"What's the Difference between Sons of the Revolution and Sons of the American Revolution?" Online: http://tnsor.org/revolutionary_documents.html.

Tennessee Society Sons of the Revolution

The Tennessee Rifleman: The Official Record of the Sons of the Revolution in the State of Tennessee (Knoxville: The Society, 1— (1960-present). There are indexes for volumes 1-25, 26-35, and 36-45.

"What's the Difference between Sons of the Revolution and Sons of the American Revolution?" Online: http://tnsor.org/revolutionary_documents.html.

Tennessee State Society of the Children of the American Revolution

Sloan, Susan Giddens. *A Chronological History of the Tennessee State Society of the Children of the American Revolution and Some of the Local Societies of Tennessee*. [Springhill, Tenn.: The Society], 1960.

Chapter Eighteen:
Prominent North Carolinians and Others Active in the State during the American Revolution

North Carolina and Tennessee Collected Biographies

[Note: The titles in this section contain information on North Carolinians famous and obscure. Researchers should consult these for basic information on an individual and for further studies about them that may not appear in this publication.]

Ashe, Samuel A'Court, ed. *Biographical History of North Carolina from Colonial Times to the Present.* 8 vols. Greensboro: Charles L. Van Nopper, 1905-1917.

Biographical Directory of the United States Congress, 1774-Present. Online: http://bioguide.congress.gov/biosearch/biosearch.asp

Connor, Robert D. W. *Makers of North Carolina History.* Raleigh: Thompson Publishing Co., 1911.

Connor, R. D. W. *Revolutionary Leaders of North Carolina.* (Archives Information Circular no. 13) Raleigh: Department of Archives & History, 1923.

Connor, Robert D. W. *Revolutionary Leaders of North Carolina.* [Greensboro]: The College, 1916; reprinted: Greensboro, North Carolina College for Women, 1930; reprinted: Spartanburg, S. C., Reprint Co. [1971]. [Lectures delivered at North Carolina State Normal & Industrial College, now UNC Greensboro, during the spring of 1913.] [Detailed biographies of major leaders of the Revolution in North Carolina: John Harvey (1725?-1775), Cornelius Harnett (1723-1781), Richard Caswell (1729-1789), and Samuel Johnston (1733-1816)]

Garraty, John A., and Mark C. Carnes, gen. eds. *American National Biography.* 26 vols. New York: Oxford University Press, 1999.

Gates, Henry Louis, Jr., and Evelyn Brooks Higginbotham, eds. *African American National Biography.* 8 vols. New York: Oxford University Press, 2008.

Hartley, Cecil B.; with engravings from original designs by G. G. White. *Heroes and Patriots of the South: Comprising Lives of General Francis Marion, General William Moultrie, General Andrew Pickens, and Governor John Rutledge, with Sketches of Other Distinguished Heroes and Patriots Who Served in the Revolutionary War in the Southern States.* Philadelphia: G. G. Evans, 1860.

Johnson, Allen, and Dumas Malone, eds. *Dictionary of American Biography.* 16 vols. New York: Scribner's, 1928-1958.

The National Cyclopedia of American Biography. 63 vols. New York: J. T. White, 1891-1984.

Powell, William S., ed. *Dictionary of North Carolina Biography.* 6 vols. Chapel Hill: University of North Carolina Press, 1979-1996; online as part of NCPedia: http://ncpedia.org/category/entry-source/dictionary-no. [Provides short entries on prominent North Carolinians throughout the state's history. Most entries include bibliographies.]

Powell, William S.; Jay Mazzocchi, assoc. ed. *Encyclopedia of North Carolina.* Chapel Hill: University of North Carolina Press, 2006.

Raimo, John W. *Biographical Directory of American Colonial and Revolutionary Governors, 1607-1789.* Westport, CT: Meckler Books, 1980.

North Carolina and Tennessee Biographies

Abbot, John, 1751-ca. 1840

Simpson, Marcus B., Jr. "The Artist-Naturalist John Abbot (1751-ca. 1840): Contributions to the Ornithology of the Southeastern United States." *North Carolina Historical Review*, 61:3 (July 1984), 347-390. [Online description from "North Carolina Periodicals Index," East Carolina University: "John Abbot was an American naturalist and biological illustrator of the 18th century through whose work the ornithology and entomology of the southeastern coastal plain were examined in minute detail. First visiting Virginia in 1773, Abbott spent the next decades cataloging and studying the birds and insects of the Southeastern United States. In 1797 he published a book of his findings including wonderful watercolors of his specimens in *The Natural History of the Rarer Lepidopterous Insects of Georgia*."]

Alves, Walter, 1768-1819

Alves, Walter. "Walter Alves Papers, 1771-1858." Manuscript 3792, Southern Historical Collection, Louis Round Wilson Special Collections Library, University of North Carolina, Chapel Hill; online finding aid available at http://www2.lib.unc.edu/mss/inv/a/Alves,Walter.html. [Online finding aid description: "Walter Alves of Orange County, N.C., was the son of James Hogg (1730-1804) and Ann McDowal (Alves) Hogg (1732-1801) of Scotland. The family emigrated to America in 1774, settling in North Carolina. His father legally changed his sons' last names from Hogg to Alves in honor of their mother. Walter Alves married Mary Amelia Johnston, daughter of William Johnston (d. 1785) and had with her nine children. Alves, a staunch Federalist, served in the North Carolina General Assembly, 1793- 1795; was a trustee of the University of North Carolina, 1795-1813; and speculated heavily in North Carolina and Tennessee lands. The collection is primarily business papers of Walter Alves. The bulk consists of correspondence, surveys, rental accounts, and other papers pertaining to Alves's extensive land holdings in North Carolina and in the Clinch and Powell rivers areas of east Tennessee. Also included are family correspondence, letters from Federalist politicians, and papers pertaining to Alves's move to Henderson, Ky. Correspondents include Gavin Alves, Richard Bennehan, William Boylan, Duncan Cameron, Walter Evans, William Gaston, William B. Grove, Archibald Henderson, James Hogg, Alex Mebane, James Norwood, and Henry Tazewell. Many items pertain to the estate of Alves's father-in-law, William Johnston (d. 1785), mainly concerning the efforts of Edmund Fanning (1739-1818), North Carolina colonial official and Loyalist for whom Johnston had been agent, to recover properties confiscated during the Revolution. These estate papers include correspondence, 1805-1812, between Alves and John Wickham (1763-1839), noted Virginia lawyer, and relevant earlier papers."]

Ashe, John, ca. 1720-1781

"Ashe, John." Reference Vertical File, State Library of North Carolina, Raleigh.

Davis, Robert S. "General John Ashe, NC Patriot Militia." *Southern Campaigns of the American Revolution*, 3:10-11 (October-November 2006), 28; online: http://southerncampaign.org/newsletter/v3n1011.pdf.

Hooper, Archibald Maclaine. "John Ashe." Manuscript, Southern Historical Collection, University of North Carolina at Chapel Hill. [John Ashe (1720?-1781) was a Major General in the Revolutionary War. The collection contains a draft of a biography of Ashe written by Archibald Maclaine Hooper (1775-1853). The biography includes an account of Ashe's court martial over the Battle of Briar Creek, Ga., and appendices include transcriptions of letters to General Benjamin Lincoln (1733-1810).]

Hooper, Archibald MacLaine, and Griffith John McRae. "Memoir of Gen. John Ashe of the Revolution." *University of North Carolina Magazine*, 3 (October 1854), 366-376.

Piecuch, Jim. "John Ashe (1720?-1781)." In Gregory Fremont-Barnes and Richard Alan Ryerson, eds., *The Encyclopedia of the American Revolutionary War: A Political, Social and Military History* (Santa Barbara, Calif.: ABC Clio, 2006), 1:65.

Ashe, Samuel, 1725-1813

Lawrence, R. C. "Soldiers Who Became Judges." *The State: A Weekly Survey of North Carolina*, 8:7 (July 1940), 10, 25; online: http://digital.ncdcr.gov/cdm/ref/collection/p16062coll18/id/5810. [Online description from "North Carolina Periodicals Index," East Carolina University: "Lawrence has compiled a list of soldiers in the Revolutionary War, Civil War, and World War who later became members of the judiciary of North Carolina. Among them are Colonel John Stokes and Samuel Ashe of New Hanover County."]

Avery, Waightstill, 1741-1821

Avery, Waightstill. "Papers." Manuscript in the Draper Mss KK MAD 4/13/D2, the Draper Manuscripts: North Carolina Papers, 1756, 1768-1818, Wisconsin Historical Society, Madison. [Includes Isaac T. Avery's "A Sketch of the Life of Waightstill Avery."]

Eaton, Clement. "A Mirror of the Southern Colonial Lawyer: The Fee Books of Patrick Henry, Thomas Jefferson and Waightstill Avery." *William and Mary Quarterly*, 3rd series, 8:4 (October 1951), 520-534.

Balfour, Elizabeth Dayton, ca. 1755-1818

Hennessee, W. E. "The First Postmistress." *The State: A Weekly Survey of North Carolina*, 7:38 (February 1940), 3; online: http://digital.ncdcr.gov/cdm/ref/collection/p16062coll18/id/5105. [Online description from "North Carolina Periodicals Index," East Carolina University: "Rowan County has the distinction of having had the first postmistress in the United States. Her name was Mrs. Elizabeth Balfour, and she was appointed to the Salisbury office by President George Washington."]

Bartram, John, 1699-1777, and William Bartram, 1738-1823

Bolen, Eric G. "The Bartrams in North Carolina." *Wildlife in North Carolina*, 60:5 (May 1996), 16-21. [Online description from "North Carolina Periodicals Index," East Carolina University: "John Bartram, botanist to King George III, and his son William, were eminent naturalists who traveled the Carolinas and the Southeast collecting botanical specimens. William's 1791 book, *Travels*, is considered a landmark of early botanical study."]

Earnest, Ernst. *John and William Bartram: Botanists and Explorers, 1699-1777, 1739-1823*. Philadelphia: University of Pennsylvania Press, 1940.

Nickens, T. Edward. "William Bartram's Big Adventure." *Friend of Wildlife*, 46:1 (Winter 1999), 8-9. [Online description from "North Carolina Periodicals Index," East Carolina University: "William Bartram, son of the famous royal botanist, John Bartram, left Philadelphia in 1773, on a four-year botanizing expedition across the Southeast. When he returned in 1777, he had categorized over 100 plants and 215 birds and had written an incomparable travel epic."]

Bayard, Elizabeth Cornell, 1761 or 1762-1854

Murphy, Eva Burbank. "Elizabeth Cornell Bayard (1761/1762-17 Jan. 1854)." In William S. Powell, ed., *Dictionary of North Carolina Biography, vol. 1: A-C* (Chapel Hill: University of North Carolina Press, 1979-1996), 121-122.

Bell, Martha McFarlane McGee, 1735-1820

Hinton, Mary Hilliard. "Martha McFarlane Bell." *North Carolina Booklet*, 16:2 (October 1916), 88-96.

Jones, H. G. *Scoundrels, Rogues and Heroes of the Old North State*. Charleston, S. C.: History Press, 2004. ["North Carolina Governor Married Fifteen-Year-Old Girl," 31-32, Justina Davis Dobbs Nash (actually married two governors! She lived from 1747 to 1773); "Postmaster Had Shady Reputation," 61-62, Sarah DeCrow; and "Martha McFarlane McGee Bell, Heroine," 73-74.]

"[Martha MacFarlane Bell]." Reference Vertical File, State Library of North Carolina, Raleigh.

Suggs, Joseph R. "Martha McFarlane McGee Bell (1735-9 Sept. 1820)." In William S. Powell, ed., *Dictionary of North Carolina Biography, vol. 1: A-C* (Chapel Hill: University of North Carolina Press, 1979-1996), 132.

Wellborn, Jennifer M. *Martha MacFarlane McGee Bell, Heroine, Patriot, and Spy; and, The Case for Caruthers*. Rock Hill, S. C.: J. M. Wellborn, 2002. [Description: "The story of Mattie Bell and the justification for believing in Eli W. Caruthers accounts of her life."]

Benbury, Thomas, 1736-1793

Haywood, Emily Ryan Benbury. "Thomas Benbury – A Brigadier General of the American Revolution." *North Carolina Booklet*, 18:3 (January 1919), 134-142; online: https://books.google.com/books?id=kzAUAAAAYAAJ&pg=PA134&lpg=PA134&dq=Thomas+Benbury&source=bl&ots=cNbDpPwzXj&sig=7PdUzSMnPR4UX_SMFcGt61kYJ3w&hl=en&sa=X&ved=0ahUKEwiG74j5_ujKAhVDVj4KHYNKA7sQ6AEIJDAB#v=onepage&q=Thomas%20Benbury&f=false.

Johnson, Elmer D. "Thomas Benbury." Online: http://ncpedia.org/biography/benbury-thomas.

"Thomas Benbury." Online: http://www.carolana.com/NC/Revolution/patriot_leaders_nc_thomas_benbury.html.

Bennehan, Richard, 1743-1825

Bullock, J. Marshall. "A Portrait of Richard Bennehan." *Bookmark* [Chapel Hill], no. 53 (1961), 35-37.

Cameron Family. "Cameron Family Papers, 1757-1978 (bulk 1770-1894)." Manuscript 133 and microfilm M-133, Southern Historical Collection, Louis Round Wilson Special Collections Library, University of North Carolina at Chapel Hill. [Online catalog description: "Cameron family of Orange and Durham counties and Raleigh, N.C. Among antebellum North Carolina's largest landholders and slave holders, the Camerons also owned substantial plantations in Alabama and Mississippi. Prominent family members included Richard Bennehan (1743-1825), merchant; Duncan Cameron (1777-1853), lawyer, judge, banker, and legislator; and Paul C. Cameron (1808-1891), planter, agricultural reformer, and railroad builder. The bulk of the collection consists of correspondence, financial and legal documents, and account books. In addition, there are speeches, writings, printed material, pictures, and miscellaneous other types of personal papers. Included is extensive information about Richard Bennehan's store at Stagville, N. C., and the Stagville and Fairntosh plantations, including crop and slave records. Family correspondence details the familial relationships and social behavior of a wealthy planter family, particularly the women. In addition to documentation about Duncan Cameron's legal career, there is also information about the State Bank of North Carolina and the banking industry, the education of the Cameron children at various schools, the development of the University of North Carolina, the state militia, the Episcopal Church, railroads, and state government." Includes in Box 1, folder 1: "Correspondence of Richard Bennehan and his family, 1757-1796."]

Gutman, Herbert G. *The Black Family in Slavery and Freedom, 1750-1925*. New York: Pantheon Books, 1976. [Description: "Discusses the slaves of Richard Bennehan and the Cameron family of Orange County, N. C."]

Sanders, Charles Richard. *The Cameron Plantation in Central North Carolina (1776-1973) and Its Founder Richard Bennehan*. Durham: C. R. Sanders, 1974.

Benton, Thomas Hart, 1752-1858

Chambers, William N. "As The Twig is Bent: The Family and North Carolina Years of Thomas Hart Benton, 1752-1801." *North Carolina Historical Review*, 26:4 (October 1949), 385-416.

Meigs, William Montgomery. *Life of Thomas Hart Benton*. New York: Da Capo Press, 1970.

Rogers, Joseph Morgan. *Thomas H. Benton*. Philadelphia: G. W. Jacobs & Company, 1905.

Roosevelt, Theodore. *Thomas Hart Benton*. Boston: Houghton, Mifflin, 1895; online through the HathiTrust.

Smith, Elbert B. *Magnificent Missourian: The Life of Thomas Hart Benton*. Philadelphia: Lippincott, 1958.

Bingham, William, 1752-1804

Alberts, Robert C. *The Golden Voyage: The Life and Times of William Bingham, 1752-1804*. Boston: Houghton-Mifflin, 1969.

Curtis, Robert L. "The Bingham School and Classical Education in North Carolina, 1793-1873." *North Carolina Historical Review*, 73:3 (July 1996), 328-377. [Online description from "North Carolina Periodicals Index," East Carolina University: "This article examines the history of North Carolina's Bingham School, a private classical academy that ran from 1793 to 1928. During the school's first 80 years, it focused on a classical education while fending off claims that a more practical curriculum was needed. It was claimed by headmasters up to 1873 that classical study remained central to the training of a Southern gentleman and expressed the conservative nature of South both politically and socially."]

Lawrence, R. C. "Leaders in Education." *The State: A Weekly Survey of North Carolina*, 12:48 (April 1945), 6, 20-22; online: http://digital.ncdcr.gov/cdm/ref/collection/p16062coll18/id/13089. [Online description from "North Carolina Periodicals Index," East Carolina University: "Lawrence presents ten outstanding educators in the history of North Carolina, such as David Caldwell of Guilford College, William Bingham of Orange County, and Kemp Battle of the University of North Carolina at Chapel Hill."]

Blair, Hannah Millakin, 1756-1852

Jordan, Paula S. "Hannah Millikan Blair (1756-14 Jan. 1852)." In William S. Powell, ed., *Dictionary of North Carolina Biography, vol. 1: A-C* (Chapel Hill: University of North Carolina Press, 1979), 171.

Blake, Isham, 1766-1836

"[Isham Blake]." Reference Vertical File, State Library of North Carolina, Raleigh.

Wehlitz, Lou Rogers. "The Fifer Who Stole the Show." *The State: Down Home in North Carolina*, 43:5 (October 1975),15-16; online: http://digital.ncdcr.gov/cdm/ref/collection/p16062coll18/id/9638. [Online description from "North Carolina Periodicals Index," East Carolina University: "Isham Blake of Fayetteville was born June 21, 1766. He served as General Marquis de Lafayette's fifer in 1779, and witnessed Cornwallis's surrender at Yorktown in 1781. After the war, Blake married, fathered eight children, and was a successful mason. As a member of the Fayetteville Independent Light Infantry, he served as a body guard when Lafayette returned to the area in 1825. Blake died in 1836."]

Bloodworth, Timothy, 1736-1814

Lawrence, R. C. "From Cobbler to Senator." *The State: A Weekly Survey of North Carolina*, 8:33 (January 1941), 5, 16; online: http://digital.ncdcr.gov/cdm/ref/collection/p16062coll18/id/38963. [Online description from "North Carolina Periodicals Index," East Carolina University: "Timothy Bloodworth was born in New Hanover County in 1736. In his early life he was a cobbler by trade. He educated himself, and later in life became a schoolmaster and such an influential figure in the public life of New Hanover that he was a member of the second House of Commons which met after the establishment of the State. In 1789, Bloodworth found himself as a member of the State Senate, and his prominence held that he became a United States Senator."]

Lawrence, R. C. "Senator Timothy Bloodworth." *The State: A Weekly Survey of North Carolina*, 12:24 (November 1944), 9, 20, 22; online: http://digital.ncdcr.gov/cdm/ref/collection/p16062coll18/id/19806. [Online description from "North Carolina Periodicals Index," East Carolina University: "Timothy Bloodworth was one of the founders of the commonwealth and the only mechanic ever to be elected to the lofty position of United States Senator from North Carolina."]

Blount, John Gray, 1752-1833, Jacob Blount, and the Blount Family

Blount, John Gray. "John Gray Blount (1752-1833) Papers, 1706-1900." Manuscript PC.193 (MARS ID: 703; record group), State Archives of North Carolina, Raleigh. [Online catalog description: "Papers of John Gray Blount of Washington, N.C., planter, merchant, shipper, land speculator, and politician, including many letters from his partner-brothers Thomas (1759-1812) of Tarboro and William (1749-1800) of Greenville and later Tennessee. Correspondence of John Gray is concentrated in the period 1783-1800. Plantation operations are reflected in correspondence with brothers and letters from overseers and farmers, as well as in tax listings, slave lists and bills of sale, and receipts. Mercantile papers include correspondence with Thomas and William, letters from another partner, John Wallace, at Shell Castle, Ocracoke Inlet; bills of lading, receipts, lists; correspondence from commission merchants, ship captains, and agents aboard Blount vessels in American, European, and West Indian ports; and letters from Thomas Blount in England on the firm's business, 1785-1788. Many papers are concerned with land speculations in Beaufort, Bladen, Brunswick, Carteret, Craven, Cumberland, Columbus, Duplin, Hyde, Jones, Martin, Montgomery, Moore, New Hanover, Onslow, Robeson, Tyrrell, and Wake counties, as well as western lands (Buncombe and Burke counties) and Tennessee, especially the military bounty lands. In addition to surveys, plats, grants, deeds, courses, and maps, there is correspondence from or about Blount associates among the surveyors, entry takers, speculators, title searchers, and other agents, including John Allen, David Allison, John and James Armstrong, Stockley Donelson, Francis B. Fogg, Micajah Thomas, and Blount's sons Thomas Harvey and John Gray, Jr. All three brothers were state legislators in the period from 1780 to 1796 and Thomas was congressman for twelve years between 1793 and 1812. Their letters often refer to state and national politics, and political news is also in letters from Hugh Williamson, Abishai Thomas, Richard Dobbs Spaight, Sr., and later William Blackledge and Joseph B. Hinton. Letters from William Blount and Benjamin Hawkins concern relationships with Indians from the Treaty of Hopewell in 1785 until after William moved to Tennessee in 1790. Personal correspondence is chiefly from women in the family..." "Miscellaneous items include Jacob Blount's pocket notebooks (1764- 1767, 1771-1774); draft of speech to militia (ca. 1775); minutes of the Court of Vice Admiralty for the port of Beaufort, held at New Bern (1766-1771); accounts and commissions reflecting service of Jacob Blount and son as paymasters during Revolution...;]

Blount, John Gray; Alice Barnwell Keith and William H. Masterson, eds. *John Gray Blount Papers*. 3 vols. Raleigh: State Department of Archives and History, 1952-1965. [Online catalog description: "The papers cover the years 1764-1802."]

Goerch, Carl. "The Oldest Family in North Carolina." *The State; Down Home in North Carolina*, 19:25 (November 1951), 7, 10; online: http://digital.ncdcr.gov/cdm/ref/collection/p16062coll18/id/27795. [Online description from "North Carolina Periodicals Index," East Carolina University: "There are many well-known family names dating back 200 years or more, but there is one name that it seems to be generally agreed in the oldest in North Carolina - Blount."]

"[John Gray Blount]." Reference Vertical File, State Library of North Carolina, Raleigh.

North Carolina (State). General Assembly. "[Document dated:] 1780: Accounts of Jacob Blount and Benjamin Hawkins." Manuscript; General Assembly Record Group; Session Records, August-September 1780; Joint Papers, Committee Papers, Resolutions, Senate Bills, House Bills, Box 1 (MARS ID: 66.8.22.6.9; item), State

Archives of North Carolina, Raleigh. [Online catalog description: "Blount was paymaster of the North Carolina Continental Line; Hawkins' account involves John W. Stanly."]

Rodman, Lida Tunstall. "Residence of John Gray Blount, Esq., Built in 1778 – Taken Down – 1923, Washington, N. C." *North Carolina Booklet*, 22:1-4 (July 1922-April 1923), 46-52.

Blount, Nathaniel, 1748-1816

Lemmon, Sarah McCulloh. "Nathaniel Blount: Last Clergyman of the 'Old Church'." *North Carolina Historical Review*, 50:4 (October 1973), 351-364. [Online description from "North Carolina Periodicals Index," East Carolina University: "This biographical essay looks at the life and career of clergyman Nathaniel Blount, the longest-lived Anglican clergyman to survive the American Revolution."]

Blount, William, 1749-1800

Blount, William. "William Blount Papers, 1784-1797." Manuscript MS.0965, Special Collections Library, University of Tennessee, Knoxville. [Online catalog description: "This collection houses photocopies of three items documenting early Tennessee statesman William Blount. These materials include two letters that Blount wrote in 1784 and one letter from the Secretary of the Senate to the Governor of Tennessee (John Sevier) discussing Blount's expulsion from the Senate."]

Keith, Alice B. "William Blount in North Carolina Politics, 1781-1789." In Joseph Carlyle Sitterson, ed., Studies in Southern History (James Sprunt Historical Publications, v. 39) (Chapel Hill: University of North Carolina Press, 1957), 47-61.

Lawrence, R. C. "Senator William Blount." *The State A Weekly Survey of North Carolina*, 9:20 (October 1941), 5, 31; online: http://digital.ncdcr.gov/cdm/ref/collection/p16062coll18/id/40317. [Online description from "North Carolina Periodicals Index," East Carolina University: "William Blount was a member of the distinguished Blount family and served well during the Revolutionary period. He later served in the Continental Congress and in the convention of 1787 that drafted the Constitution. He was also Governor of North Carolina and later a Senator."]

Lawrence, R. C. "Signers of the Constitution." *The State: A Weekly Survey of North Carolina*, 10:14 (September 1942) 26; online: http://digital.ncdcr.gov/cdm/ref/collection/p16062coll18/id/33190. [Online description from "North Carolina Periodicals Index," East Carolina University: "North Carolina can proudly claim three men who signed the Constitution – Hugh Williamson of Chowan, Richard Dobbs Spaight and William Blount of Craven County. Lawrence provides biographical information on them."]

Masterson, William. *William Blount*. Baton Rouge: Louisiana State University Press, 1954.

North Carolina (State). General Assembly. House of Delegates. "[Document dated:] April 23, [1778]: Allowance to William Blount (With Messages)." Manuscript; General Assembly Record Group; Session Records, April-May 1778; Joint Papers, Committee Papers, Resolutions, Senate Bills, House Bills, Box 1 (MARS ID: 66.8.12.16.15; item), State Archives of North Carolina, Raleigh. [Online catalog description: "William Blount to be reimbursed for money advanced to Continental Army."]

Stewart, Alva. "Wm. Blount Was a Practical Man." *The State: Down Home in North Carolina*, 54:8 (January 1987), 7, 26; online: http://digital.ncdcr.gov/cdm/ref/collection/p16062coll18/id/62260. [Online description from "North Carolina Periodicals Index," East Carolina University: "William Blount was one of the thirty-nine United States delegates to sign the Constitution, but he did so reluctantly because of he was uncertain of North Carolina's support. His greatest contribution to the young nation might have been his administration of the region south of the Ohio River. In 1796 he was elected one of Tennessee's first two United States senators. He died suddenly in 1800."]

"[William Blount]." Reference Vertical File, State Library of North Carolina, Raleigh.

William Blount: The Man and His Mansion. Knoxville: Blount Mansion Association, 1977.

Wright, Marcus Joseph. *Some Account of the Life and Services of William Blount, an Officer of the Revolutionary Army, Member of the Continental Congress, and of the Convention Which Framed the Constitution of the United States, Also Governor of the Territory South of the Ohio River, and Senator in Congress U. S. 1783-1797. Together with a Full Account of His Impeachment and Trial in Congress, and His Expulsion from the U.S. Senate.* Washington, D. C.: E. J. Gray, 1884.

Boone, Daniel, 1734-1820

Cahill, Carl. "What's Ahead for Boone's Cave?" *The State: Down Home in North Carolina*, 53:7 (December 1985), 18-20; online: http://digital.ncdcr.gov/cdm/ref/collection/p16062coll18/id/61663. [Online description from

"North Carolina Periodicals Index," East Carolina University: "Legend has it that Daniel Boone lived in a log cabin near the Yadkin River in Davidson County and took refuge from Indians in a nearby cave. Now called Boone's Cave State Park, this 110-acres park falls short of the 400-acre minimum for a state park. The state says there is no real evidence that Daniel Boone ever occupied the territory and is ready to stop funding of the park. A local dentist named Dr. Wade Sowers has been collecting historical material to prove Boone did actually live there. A second replica of Boone's cabin was built by the Daniel Boone Memorial Association after the first was burned by vandals. A park office was added, as well as restrooms, a picnic area, and wooden steps leading down to the cave. But the state's interest in the park is waning and it stopped counting visitors in 1983. Both the state and surrounding counties agree that the territory is part of North Carolina's heritage and should be preserved."]

Clark, Walter. "The Colony of Transylvania." *North Carolina Booklet*, 3:9 (January 1904), 5-39; online: http://digital.ncdcr.gov/cdm/ref/collection/p249901coll37/id/14180. [Online description from "North Carolina Periodicals Index," East Carolina University: "This article describes a 1775 scheme to acquire, settle, and hold a large piece of land, called 'Transylvania County,' lying between the Kentucky and Cumberland rivers, in what is now Tennessee and Kentucky. Details include Boonesborough's establishment by a group of men led by North Carolina Judge Richard Henderson and frontiersman Daniel Boone. A reprint of Henderson's journal documenting his journey into this territory is included."]

Dean, Jim. "Daniel Boone in North Carolina." *Wildlife in North Carolina*, 43:6 (June 1979). [Online description from "North Carolina Periodicals Index," East Carolina University: "Although his name is more often linked with the state of Kentucky, Daniel Boone and his family lived in the western part of the state from 1751 to 1775."] [Online description from "North Carolina Periodicals Index," East Carolina University: "

Faragher, John Mack. *Daniel Boone: The Life and Legend of an American Pioneer*. New York: Henry Holt, 1992.

Faragher, John Mack. "White People That Live Like Savages: Daniel Boone in North Carolina." *Carolina Comments*, 45:3 (May 1997), 63-71. [Online description from "North Carolina Periodicals Index," East Carolina University: "Although his name is more often linked with the state of Kentucky, Daniel Boone and his family lived in the western part of the state from 1751 to 1775. He was well known for his marksmanship and hunting skills."]

Henderson, Archibald. "The Creative Forces of Westward Expansion: Henderson and Boone." *North Carolina Booklet*, 14:3 (January 1915), 111-139. [Online description from "North Carolina Periodicals Index," East Carolina University: "The the westward expansion of America was aided by two one-time residents of North Carolina: Daniel Boone and Richard Henderson. Though they differed in background and origins, the two became acquainted as early settlers of Rowan County. Their combined and related efforts helped open areas west of the mountains to settlement."]

Hodgkins, Hope. "Reading Boone's Writing: Issues in Backcountry Literacy." *Journal of Backcountry Studies*, 6:2 (Fall/Winter 2011); online: http://libjournal.uncg.edu/jbc/article/view/376/193.

Jones, K. Randell. *Trailing Daniel Boone*. Winston-Salem: Daniel Boone Footsteps, 2012.

Lawrence, R. C. "The Trail of Daniel Boone." *The State: A Weekly Survey of North Carolina*, 14:23 (November 1946), 7, 22; online: http://digital.ncdcr.gov/cdm/ref/collection/p16062coll18/id/16319. [Online description from "North Carolina Periodicals Index," East Carolina University: "Historian Major J. Hampton Rich researched Daniel Boone's activity specific to North Carolina. Boone's family moved to North Carolina from Pennsylvania after Boone's birth in 1734. Rich's research focuses on Boone's exploration of the state, and various encounters, both violent and peaceful, with the Native American population in the state.

Markovich, Jeremy. "Wagons Ho!" *Our State: Down Home in North Carolina*, 83:1 (June 2015), 45-46 48. [Online description from "North Carolina Periodicals Index," East Carolina University: "In 1963, North Carolinians searched for a way to celebrate the 300th anniversary of the charter that created North Carolina. They settled on reenacting Daniel Boone's trek through the Blue Ridge Mountains with a wagon train traveling from a farm in Wilkes County to Boone. The reenactment became an annual event until 1974 when locals lost interest as national social and political issues took their toll on these communities."]

Miles, Suzannah Smith. "The Real Daniel Boone." *WNC Magazine*, 4:7 (September 2010), 28-31. [Online description from "North Carolina Periodicals Index," East Carolina University: "Long before opening Kentucky, the pioneer, Daniel Boone, was active in western North Carolina. His explorations opened the way for settling lands west of the mountains.

Morgan, Robert. *Boone: A Biography*. Chapel Hill: Algonquin Books of Chapel Hill, 2007. [Contents: Contents: Brief chronology of Daniel Boone's life; Introduction; The mother world of the forest : People of the forest; The hills beyond the Yadkin; The Yadkin was the Wild West; Domestic arts : In search of the real west; Visions of Eden; Regulators: Return to the Bluegrass island; Where there was no forbidden fruit; Kentucky was the key;

The trace and the river; Freemasonry: Light and shadow; Sheltowee, Son of Blackfish; Farthest outpost of rebellion; With chain and compass; Father, I won't leave you; Filson, fame, and failure; A deale of sine is seen; Boating in the west: Going east to go west; To the farther west; Done all the good that I can; Across the river into legend. Publisher's summary from the dust jacket: "Born in 1734 in Pennsylvania to English Quaker colonists, Daniel Boone led hundreds of settlers west into Virginia and North Carolina, over the Cumberland Gap into Kentucky and the Ohio Valley, and, finally, to Missouri, where he died penniless at the age of eighty-six, having lost his holdings to lawyers and politicians and better businessmen. Morgan reminds us that Boone was more than a trailblazer: he fought in the French and Indian War and in the American Revolution; he served in the Virginia legislature; he was a Freemason; he was a settler, landowner, and sometime surveyor; and his reverence for life in the wilderness inspired Romantic writers like Wordsworth, Bartram, Byron, Whitman - inspired Romanticism itself. Boone was the first great American naturalist - he cherished the land, and while he wanted to settle it, he also longed to conserve its wildness. Almost alone among his fellow settlers, Daniel Boone revered, studied, and emulated the Native American way of life, especially in the preservation of land resources. But his own claim for himself was much simpler: 'I am a woodsman'."]

Norris, Jeannie Faris. "Daniel Boone." *The State: A Weekly Survey of North Carolina*, 17:38 (February 1950), 6, 20; online: http://digital.ncdcr.gov/cdm/ref/collection/p16062coll18/id/25049. [Online description from "North Carolina Periodicals Index," East Carolina University: "Although born in Pennsylvania and spending many years in the wilderness of Kentucky, Daniel Boone never forgot where he spent most of his boyhood days."]

Pleasant, Paul. "Gum King, Dan Boone, Buffalo Bill." *The State: Down Home in North Carolina*, 29:19 (February 1962), 11-12, 31. [Online description from "North Carolina Periodicals Index," East Carolina University: "...Dan Boone came to North Carolina in 1750, building a prototype of what became a perpetual cabin building program."]

Sharpe, Bill. "Dan'l Boone Still at Work." *The State: A Weekly Survey of North Carolina*, 12:16 (September 1944), 5; online: http://digital.ncdcr.gov/cdm/ref/collection/p16062coll18/id/19558. [Online description from "North Carolina Periodicals Index," East Carolina University: "Daniel Boone VII lives in the Burnsville area in western North Carolina. He is a blacksmith. Sharpe describes his activities as civilian repairman, war-worker, and knife maker."]

Taylor, Mark. "Long Hunter of the Yadkin." *Wildlife in North Carolina*, 52:1 (January 1988), 4-11. [Online description from "North Carolina Periodicals Index," East Carolina University: "Nearly everyone knows Daniel Boone helped settle Kentucky, but few know that this famous frontiersman lived much of his life in North Carolina."]

Tucker, Harry Z. "Daniel Boone." *The State: A Weekly Survey of North Carolina*, 6:20 (October 1938), 5, 20, 22; online: http://digital.ncdcr.gov/cdm/ref/collection/p16062coll18/id/38513. [Online description from "North Carolina Periodicals Index," East Carolina University: "Many people associate the name Daniel Boone with Kentucky; however, the Boone family came from Pennsylvania to North Carolina in 1750. Tucker recounts the years this intrepid and far-traveling explorer spent in the state."]

Wright, Renee. "Following the Footsteps of Daniel Boone." *North Carolina*, 64:7 (July 2006), 56. . [Online description from "North Carolina Periodicals Index," East Carolina University: "Daniel Boone came to western North Carolina in 1752 at the age of eighteen and remained there for twenty-one years. On August 14, 1756, he married Rebecca Bryan, a marriage that would last fifty-seven years. In 2006, each of the sites in the state associated with him are holding special events in his honor. Living history reenactments, family festivals, exhibits, and trade fairs are planned for Salisbury, Boone, Wilkesboro, Statesville, Bethabara, and Boone's Cave Park."]

Boone, Rebecca, 1739-1813

Roger, Lou. "Rebecca Boone: Pioneer Wife." *We the People of North Carolina*, 2:1 (May 1944), 19-22. [Online description from "North Carolina Periodicals Index," East Carolina University: "Rogers recounts the life of Rebecca Boone, the wife of the famous frontiersman, Daniel Boone."]

Brown, Thomas, 1744-1811

Brown, Thomas. "[Letters to John Alexander Lillington and to Thomas Robeson and Thomas Burke, 1781 and 1782]." Online at "Documenting the American South: http://docsouth.unc.edu/csr/index.html/creators/csr11340.

Pool, William C. "An Economic Interpretation of the Ratification of the Federal Constitution in North Carolina." *North Carolina Historical Review*, 27:2 (April 1950), 119-141; 27:3 (July 1950), 289-313; 27:4 (October 1950), 437-461.

Snow, Claude H., Jr. "Thomas Brown, 17 Jan.1744-24 Nov. 1811." Online: http://ncpedia.org/biography/brown-thomas.

Bryan, William, 1724-1781

Hollister, Mary Bryan. "Mary Bryan Hollister Collection, 1796-1960." Manuscript #86, Special Collections, Joyner Library, East Carolina University, Greenville. ["Section IV is devoted to the life of Revolutionary War Brigadier General William Bryan. Included is a biographical sketch, notes, and correspondence recounting various aspects of his life."]

Hollister, William. "William Bryan of Craven County, Brigadier General in the American Revolution." *North Carolina Booklet*, 18:2 (October 1918), 105-115. [Online description from "North Carolina Periodicals Index," East Carolina University: "William Bryan, son of Irish immigrants to America, was not killed at the Battle of Alamance as is commonly believed. Much respected in his community, Bryan was also a key figure in the Battle of Moore's Creek Bridge."]

Lewis, J. D. "Patriot Leaders in North Carolina: William Bryan: Lt. Colonel in the Johnston County Regiment of Militia - 1775-1776; Colonel over the Johnston County Regiment of Militia - 1776-1777 & 1781; Brigadier General over the New Bern District Brigade of Militia - 1777-1779." Online: http://www.carolana.com/NC/Revolution/patriot_leaders_nc_william_bryan.html.

North Carolina (State). General Assembly. "[Document dated:] April 23, 1783: Resolution in Favor of William Bryan of Craven County." Manuscript; General Assembly Record Group; Session Records, April-May 1783: Joint Papers, Committee Papers, Resolutions; House Joint Resolutions, April 21-30, 1780; Box 1 (MARS ID: 66.8.29.13.75; item), State Archives of North Carolina, Raleigh. [Online catalog description: "Resolution gives allowance to William Bryan of Craven County for the death of his slave during a slave rebellion. Memorial included."]

"[William Bryan]." Reference Vertical File, State Library of North Carolina, Raleigh.

Buncombe, Edward, 1742-1778

Blount, Thomas. "Buncombe Hall." *North Carolina Booklet*, 2:8 (December 1902), 14-31; online: http://digital.ncdcr.gov/cdm/ref/collection/p249901coll37/id/14180. [Online description from "North Carolina Periodicals Index," East Carolina University: "This article discusses Colonel Edward Buncombe, his family and their estate, Buncombe Hall. The article outlines the Buncombe family in the colonies, the establishment of the Buncombe Hall, and Colonel Buncombe's service during the Revolutionary War as an officer in the Continental Army."]

Blount, Thomas. "Buncombe Hall." *The State: Down Home in North Carolina*, 23:8 (September 1955), 16, 18, 26; online: http://digital.ncdcr.gov/cdm/ref/collection/p16062coll18/id/81911. [Online description from "North Carolina Periodicals Index," East Carolina University: "The history of Buncombe Hall is described with reference to its construction for Colonel Edward Buncombe, the life and times of Colonel Buncombe, and the passing of the Hall during marriages and deaths."]

Blount, Thomas W. "Buncombe Hall." *North Carolina Booklet*, 2:8 (December 1902), 14-31.

"Buncombe Hall." *Washington County Genealogical Society Journal*, 4:3 (December 1996), 68-69.

Edward Buncombe and Buncombe County: A British-Born American Patriot Lost His Family, His Wealth, and His Life in Helping Establish Independence for the Thirteen Colonies. Ashville: Buncombe County Bicentennial Commission, 1976.

Everett, Vernon L. "Colonel Edward Buncombe." *Washington County Genealogical Society Journal*, 4:3 (December 1996), 67.

Haywood, Marshall De Lancey. *Colonel Edward Buncombe, Fifth North Carolina Continental Regiment: His life, Military Career, and Death While a Wounded Prisoner in Philadelphia during the War of the Revolution. Address Delivered before the North Carolina Society of the Cincinnati at Its Meeting Held in Hillsborough, July 4, 1901*. North Carolina Society of the Cincinnati. Raleigh [N. C.]: Alford, Bynum & Christophers, printers, 1901.

Lawrence, R. C. "From Each War Two Warriors." *The State: A Weekly Survey of North Carolina*, 13:32 (January 1946), 7, 20-21; online: http://digital.ncdcr.gov/cdm/ref/collection/p16062coll18/id/14908. [Online description from "North Carolina Periodicals Index," East Carolina University: "From the Revolutionary War through the Spanish-American War, Lawrence has selected two North Carolinians whom he has considered to be particularly outstanding. From the Revolutionary War, Lawrence describes General Nash and Colonel

Buncombe; from the Mexican War Louis Wilson and General Bragg; from the Civil War, William Pender and James Pettigrew; and from the Spanish-American War Ensign Bagley, and Lieutenant William Shipp."]

"Washington Co. Hero of Rev. War Resting [in] Unknown Philadelphia Grave." *Roanoke Beacon*, (March 29, 1929); reprinted in: *Carolina Trees & Branches: Family Research Society of Northeastern North Carolina*, 5:12 (December 1996), 117-118. [Colonel Edward Buncombe, 1742-1778.]

Burgwin, John, 1731-1803

"Museum Received Copley Portrait." *Preview*, (July/August 2006), 9. [Online description from "North Carolina Periodicals Index," East Carolina University: "John Singleton Copley's portrait of Wilmington merchant and planter John Burgwin, which was painted in 1783, is one of only a few portraits of North Carolinians by America's first great artist. The painting remained in the family for 222 years, and in 2005, it was donated to the North Carolina Museum of Art."]

Norris, Jeannie Faris. "Art Museum Presented Portrait of Burgwyn." *Metro Magazine*, 7:6 (June 2006), 18; online: http://www.metronc.com/article/?id=1092. [Online description from "North Carolina Periodicals Index," East Carolina University: "

Burke, Thomas, 1744-1783

Burke, Thomas. "Letters, 1776, 1782." Manuscript, Sec. A Box 19 items 1-2, David M. Rubenstein Rare Book and Manuscript Library, Duke University, Durham. [Online catalog description: "Letters from Burke, to Richard Henry Lee concerning the movement of Virginia Tories (June 1776); and probably to Edmund Pendleton, complaining of the neglect Burke has suffered at the hands of the governor of North Carolina (April 1782). Resident of Hillsborough (Orange Co.), N. C., and governor of North Carolina, 1781-1782."]

Burke, Thomas. "Thomas Burke Papers, 1763-1852." Manuscript 104, Southern Historical Collection, Louis Round Wilson Special Collections Library, University of North Carolina, Chapel Hill; online finding aid and some digital surrogates available at http://www2.lib.unc.edu/mss/inv/b/Burke,Thomas.html. [Online finding aid description: "Thomas Burke was a native of Ireland who emigrated first to Virginia where he practiced medicine, then to North Carolina (1771) where he was a lawyer. He served in the provincial congress; was a delegate to the Continental Congress; and was governor, 1781-1782. The collection is the papers of Thomas Burke. Burke's early papers deal with personal and business affairs. Later papers pertain to public affairs while he was governor and include both civil and military materials of the Revolutionary period. Also included are papers relating to the settlement of Burke's estate." "Burke's early papers deal with personal and business affairs. Later papers pertain to public affairs while he was governor and include both civil and military materials of the Revolutionary period. Also included are papers relating to the settlement of Burke's estate. Microfilm contents: Reel 1. Correspondence: 1763-1781; reel 2. Correspondence, Undated Material: 1782-1852, undated; reel 3. Governor's Letter Books Volumes III and IV and Governor's Papers Volume VII (1774-1782; reel 4. Governor's Papers Volumes VIII and IX (1781-1782); reel 5. Correspondence (Addition to collection) (1765-1798; 1845; undated); reel 6. Thomas Burke letterbooks and ledger, transcripts of Emmet collection, and Miscellaneous papers Volume 1 (1769-1782)."]

deRoulhac Hamilton, J. G. "Governor Thomas Burke." *North Carolina Booklet*, 6:2 (October 1906), 103-122; online: http://digital.ncdcr.gov/cdm/ref/collection/p249901coll37/id/14180. [Online description from "North Carolina Periodicals Index," East Carolina University: "This article examines the life and family history of Thomas Burke, North Carolina's third governor and delegate to the Continental Congress."]

Douglas, Elisha P. "Thomas Burke, Disillusioned Democrat." *North Carolina Historical Review*, 26:2 (April 1949), 150-186; online: http://digital.ncdcr.gov/cdm/ref/collection/p16062coll9/id/4207. [Online description from "North Carolina Periodicals Index," East Carolina University: "This article looks at the tumultuous, short and tragic political career of Thomas Burke, the revolutionary patriot, representative to the Continental Congress, and third Governor of North Carolina."]

Dunaway, Stewart E. *The Complete History of Thomas Burke: Poet, Doctor, 3rd Governor of North Carolina*. Hillsborough: S. E. Dunaway, 2009.

"Governor Thomas Burke, 1781, G. P. 7, pp. 1-131, Calendar." Online at the State Archives of North Carolina website: http://archives.ncdcr.gov/Portals/3/PDF/findingaids/governors/Burke_Thomas_Calendar_GP7.pdf.

"Governor Thomas Burke, 1781, G. P. 8, pp. 1-135, Calendar." Online at the State Archives of North Carolina website: http://archives.ncdcr.gov/Portals/3/PDF/findingaids/governors/Burke_Thomas_Calendar_GP8.pdf.

"Governor Thomas Burke, 1781-1782, G. P. 9, pp. 1-131, Calendar." Online at the State Archives of North Carolina website: http://archives.ncdcr.gov/Portals/3/PDF/findingaids/governors/Burke_Thomas_Calendar_GP9.pdf.

Haywood, Martha Helen. "Wakefield." *North Carolina Booklet*, 2:9 (June 1903), 23-25; online: http://digital.ncdcr.gov/cdm/ref/collection/p249901coll37/id/14180. [Online description from "North Carolina Periodicals Index," East Carolina University: "This article discusses the history and importance of Wakefield estate, located outside of Raleigh. Wakefield was a patriot meeting location and the site of the election of Thomas Burke as the state's first governor in June 1781."]

Henderson, Archibald. "Thomas Burke, Revolutionary Governor and Champion of State Rights; Extension of Remarks of Hon. Carl T. Durham of North Carolina in the House of Representative, Tuesday, November 21, 1944." *Congressional Record,* (November 30, 1944), A4915-A4918.

Langston, Scott Michael. "Negotiating the Boundaries of Power: Governor Thomas Burke as Mediator in Revolutionary North Carolina." M. A. thesis, University of Texas-Arlington, 2000.

Lasley, Jim. "To Honor an Unsung Hero." *The State: Down Home in North Carolina*, 41:2 (July 1973), 17; online: http://digital.ncdcr.gov/cdm/ref/collection/p16062coll18/id/56071. [Online description from "North Carolina Periodicals Index," East Carolina University: "A graveside service and memorial plaque commemorated the life of Dr. Thomas Burke on May 27, 1973 at the Old Tyaquin Plantation, near Hillsborough. Burke was governor of North Carolina during the Revolutionary War, a lawyer, doctor, poet, and delegate to the Continental Congress at Philadelphia. He was one of the eight drafters of the Halifax Resolve. Burke County is named for him."]

Lawrence R. C. "Thomas Burke." *The State: Down Home in North Carolina*, 9:11 (August 1941), 5, 26; online: http://digital.ncdcr.gov/cdm/ref/collection/p16062coll18/id/40018. [Online description from "North Carolina Periodicals Index," East Carolina University: "Thomas Burke was a native of Ireland, a Catholic physician, lawyer, and soldier. He came to the colonies around 1760 and eventually moved to North Carolina in 1772. He held several high positions in the state, including that of Governor."]

Sanders, Jennings B. "Thomas Burke in the Continental Congress." *North Carolina Historical Review*, 9:1 (January 1932), 22-37; online: http://digital.ncdcr.gov/cdm/ref/collection/p16062coll9/id/4207. [Online description from "North Carolina Periodicals Index," East Carolina University: "Native Irishman Thomas Burke served first as a North Carolina delegate to the Continental Congress and later as state governor. The article is brief history of his political career with the state, and more specifically his efforts to limit government, separate church and state, and also striving for religious tolerance. He died in 1783."]

Smith, James E. "Thomas Burke: Governor of North Carolina." *Journal of the American Irish Historical Society*, 28 (1929-1930), 61-64.

Talbott, William. "North Carolina: Governor Thomas Burke and the Origins of Judicial Review." In William Talbot, *A Distinctive Judicial Power: The Origins of an Independent Judiciary, 1606-1787* (New York: Oxford University Press, 2011), Part 2, Chapter 9.

Valsame, James Mark. "Governor Thomas Burke Papers Finding Aid, 1774-1782, n. d." Online at the State Archives of North Carolina website: http://archives.ncdcr.gov/Portals/3/PDF/findingaids/governors/Burke_Thomas_finding_aid.pdf.

Walser, Richard. *The Poems of Governor Thomas Burke of North Carolina.* Raleigh: State Department of Archives and History, 1961.

Warren, Mary Bondurant. "The Thomas Burke Papers." *The Carolina Genealogist,* no. 2 (Winter 1970), 1-2; no. 11 (Summer 1972), 3-4.

Watterson, John. "Thomas Burke." Online at NCpedia's website: http://ncpedia.org/biography/burke-thomas.

Watterson, John S. "Thomas Burke, Paradoxical Patriot." *The Historian*, (August 1, 1979), 664-681.

Watterson, John S., III. "The Ordeal of Governor Burke." *North Carolina Historical Review*, 48:2 (April 1971), 95-117. [Online description from "North Carolina Periodicals Index," East Carolina University: "In 1781, North Carolina was a year into an extensive civil war, lacking resources and unified government. On June 25th Dr. Thomas Burke was elected as the state's third governor after having served for four years as one of North Carolina's delegates to the Continental Congress. Unable to contend with the problems of civil war within the state, he resigned after only 10 months of service."]

Watterson, John Sayle. *Thomas Burke, Restless Revolutionary.* Washington, D.C.: University Press of America, 1980.

Watterson, John Sayle. "Revolutionary Nonconformist: Thomas Burke of North Carolina." *South Dakota History*, 6:3 (Summer 1976), 334-352.

Watterson, John Sayle, III. "Dr. Thomas Burke, a Revolutionary Career." Ph. D. dissertation, Northwestern University, 1970.

Burton, Robert, 1747-1825

Burton, Robert. "Robert Burton Papers, 1775-1866." Manuscript 3973-z, Southern Historical Collection, Louis Round Wilson Special Collections Library, University of North Carolina, Chapel Hill; online finding aid and some digital surrogates available at http://www2.lib.unc.edu/mss/inv/b/Burton,Robert.html. [Online finding aid description: "Robert Burton, Revolutionary War officer, delegate to the Continental Congress, lawyer, and politician, owned a large plantation near Williamsboro in Granville County (now Vance County), N.C., as well as much land in what eventually became Tennessee. The collection includes correspondence; deeds, receipts, ledgers, and other financial and legal materials; and miscellaneous items of Robert Burton and his son, Horace A. Burton. Letters to Robert Burton include a letter, 1775, from Benjamin Hawkins (1754-1816) concerning the American cause; eight letters from John Williams (1731-1799), five of them, August-October 1778, from Philadelphia, where he was serving a delegate to the Continental Congress, with military news and other war-related information, and one February 1776, from Harrodsburg, Transylvania (now Kentucky), about his situation there and other matters; and two letters, 1779-1780, from Richard Henderson (1735-1785) in Holston, Tenn., and Boonesborough, Ky., about the Transylvania Colony and other matters. Letters to Horace A. Burton include one from Elisha Mitchell (1793-1857) concerning Mitchell's testing of mineral water that Burton had sent him. Many of the legal papers are late eighteenth- and early nineteenth-century items relating to land in Kentucky and the Powell River valley in Tennessee. Two ledgers of Robert Burton consist of general accounts, 1777-1785, including a record, 1780, of a sale of a horse to Daniel Boone and tables of depreciation and coinage for North Carolina and Virginia; and accounts of whiskey distilled, 1784-1789."]

Buysson, Charles-François, Chevalier du, des Aix/des Hays, 1752-1786

Dubuysson,___. *Descendants of le Chevalier Dubuysson and of Anthony Brisson of Bladen Co., NC.* [S. l.: s. n.], 2003; online: http://www.ncgenweb.us/bladen/reports/pait/dubuysson.lechevalier.pdf.

Du Buysson, Charles-François, Chevalier du. "Letters from De Buysson des Hays, Charles-Francois, Le Chevalier, Lt. Col. Aide-de-Camp of Gen. DeKalb." In Robert M. Kennedy and Thomas J. Kirkland, *Historic Camden.* 2 Vol. (Camden, SC: Kershaw County Historical Society, 1963, 1965), 189-191; online: http://www.battleofcamden.org/dubuysson.htm.

Peters, Richard, 1744-1828. "A Signed Letter of Richard Peters, War Office Sept. 7 1781 to Marqyus de Ségur, Minister of State for the War Dept. of France." Manuscript MSS:2011F91 MB, Society of the Cincinnati Library, Anderson House, Washington, D. C. [Online catalog description: " Letter of Commendation for the Chevalier Du Buysson, to Marquis de Ségur: 'The chevalier Du Buyson [sic], a Lieutenant Colonel in the armies of the United States & Brigadier General in the service of the State of North Carolina, to which latter promotion he was appointed by that state in consideration of his gallantry at the Battle of Cambden [*sic*], having obtained leave of absence to return to France ... the distinguished merit & conduct of the gentleman in the service of the United States & particularly of his bravery displayed in the action of the 16th of August near Cambden [sic] in South Carolina.'"]

Caldwell, David, 1725-1824

Brooks, Aubrey Lee. "Dr. Caldwell and His Log University." *North Carolina Historical Review*, 28:4 (October 1951), 399-407; online: http://digital.ncdcr.gov/cdm/ref/collection/p16062coll9/id/4207; a shorter version published in *The State: A Weekly Survey of North Carolina*, 19:38 (February 1952), 3-5; online: http://digital.ncdcr.gov/cdm/ref/collection/p16062coll9/id/4207. [Online description from "North Carolina Periodicals Index," East Carolina University: "Dr. David Caldwell started his own education late at 25 and taught dozens of state leaders and filled the Presbyterian pulpits of North Carolina."]

Lawrence, R. C. "David Caldwell." *The State: A Weekly Survey of North Carolina*, 9:32 (January 1942), 6, 20; online: http://digital.ncdcr.gov/cdm/ref/collection/p16062coll18/id/43269. [Online description from "North Carolina Periodicals Index," East Carolina University: "Many famous men in North Carolina's early history came from other states. David Caldwell was one, having been born in Pennsylvania and educated at Princeton. He was a Presbyterian minister, educator, and physician. In 1794 he was offered the first presidency of the University of North Carolina, but declined, preferring to teach at his Log College, one of the most outstanding schools in the South."]

Lawrence, R. C. "Leaders in Education." *The State: A Weekly Survey of North Carolina*, 12:48 (April 1945), 6, 20-22; online: http://digital.ncdcr.gov/cdm/ref/collection/p16062coll18/id/13089. [Online description from "North Carolina Periodicals Index," East Carolina University: "Lawrence presents ten outstanding educators in the history of North Carolina, such as David Caldwell of Guilford College, William Bingham of Orange County, and Kemp Battle of the University of North Carolina at Chapel Hill."]

Caldwell, Rachel Craighead, 1742-1825

Forgartie, Jimmie. "Rachel Craighead Caldwell." *Daughters of the American Revolution Magazine*, 103:8 (October 1969), 271, 273. [North Carolina]

Caswell, Richard, 1729-1789

Alexander, Clayton B.; W. Keats Sparrow, ed. *"First of Patriots and Best of Men:" Richard Caswell in Public Life*. Kinston, N. C.: Lenoir County Colonial Commission, 2007. [Written in 1930.]

Alexander, Clayton Brown. "The Public Career of Richard Caswell." Ph. D. dissertation, University of North Carolina at Chapel Hill, 1930.

Alexander, Clayton Brown. "Richard Caswell: Versatile Leader of the Revolution." *North Carolina Historical Review*, 23:2 (April 1946), 119-141. [Online description from "North Carolina Periodicals Index," East Carolina University: "On August 25, 1774 the first Provincial Congress met in New Bern and one item of business completed was choosing qualified men to represent the state in Philadelphia at the first Continental Congress. Richard Caswell was one of the men chosen and the author examines Caswell's leadership in this role and later as commander of a regiment in New Bern. The author examines the historical record and personal correspondence to and about Caswell to portray his various roles during the American Revolution."]

Alexander, Clayton Brown. "Richard Caswell's Military and Later Public Services." *North Carolina Historical Review*, 23:3 (July 1946), 287-312; online: http://digital.ncdcr.gov/cdm/ref/collection/p16062coll9/id/4207. [Online description from "North Carolina Periodicals Index," East Carolina University: "Caswell served the state as a military leader during the Revolution and his record has received criticism because of his defeat at the Battle of Camden. Caswell's more impressive feats occurred in the political realm following the war. The author splits this period into two three year time frames, 1782-1785 and 1785-1788, because of Caswell's differing roles in state government. From 1782-1785 he was the controller general before becoming and serving as governor from 1785-1788. The author details the responsibilities of each office and Caswell's performance as both."]

Alexander, Clayton Brown. "The Training of Richard Caswell." *North Carolina Historical Review*, 23:1 (January 1946), 13-31; online: http://digital.ncdcr.gov/cdm/ref/collection/p16062coll9/id/4207. [Online description from "North Carolina Periodicals Index," East Carolina University: "Richard Caswell is an important figure in the state's history serving as both the first and fifth governor and as a representative in the Continental Congress of 1774 and 1775. The article covers Caswell's early life from his legal training under William Herritage to his surveying work for Lord Granville during the French and Indian War. In 1770 Caswell was appointed Speaker of the House and the author summarizes Caswell's legislative career into four categories; trade and industry, court system reforms, financing public defense, and humanitarian efforts."]

Balko, Sheri L. "Richard Caswell, Lost Governor: Memory in Historical Archaeology." M. A. thesis, East Carolina University, 2009.

Brooks, Aubrey Lee. "Aubrey Lee Brooks Collection, 1758-1875." Manuscript, PC.359, State Archives of North Carolina, Raleigh. [Online catalog description: "Miscellaneous letters and documents collected for their autographs. Correspondence of interest includes Alexander Martin about his brother's estate in Virginia (1770); Gov. Richard Caswell to justices of Craven Co. on profiteering, suggesting seizure of clothing needed for troops (1778)…"]

Caswell, Richard. "Gov. Caswell to President Rutledge of S. C. (From Letter Book of Governor, Executive Office, Raleigh, N. C.; New Bern, 19th April 1777)." *North Carolina Historical and Genealogical Register*, 2:3 (July 1901), 379.

Caswell, Richard. "Richard Caswell (1729-1789) Papers, 1733-1790." Manuscript, PC.242, State Archives of North Carolina, Raleigh. [Online catalog description: "Papers of Caswell of Kinston, delegate to Continental Congress (1774-1776), major general of the state militia (1780-1781), and governor (1776-1780, 1785-1787), including journal of trip by Caswell to Philadelphia for first Continental Congress (Sept.-Nov., 1774); letter to son William describing journey to Philadelphia in May, 1775, and military preparations in Virginia, Maryland, and Philadelphia; letters to Caswell from Francis Locke, William R. Davie, and Abner Nash, and from Caswell to Nathanael Greene about campaign in the Carolinas (1780-1781)"]

Caswell, Richard. "Richard Caswell Collection, 1930-2007." Manscript collection no. 1117, "East Carolina Manuscript Collection," Special Collections and University Archives Department, J. Y. Joyner Library, East Carolina University, Greenville; online finding aId: https://digital.lib.ecu.edu/special/ead/findingaids/1117/.

Caswell, Richard, "Richard Caswell Papers, 1776-1914 (bulk 1776-1785)." Manuscript 145-z, Southern Historical Collection, Louis Round Wilson Library Special Collections, University of North Carolina, Chapel Hill; online finding aid available at http://www2.lib.unc.edu/mss/inv/c/Caswell,Richard.html. [Online finding aid description: "Richard Caswell was governor of North Carolina, 1776-1779 and 1785-1787, general in the state forces during the Revolutionary War, state comptroller, and speaker of the state senate. The collection is primarily correspondence relating to North Carolina and United States military and political issues of the Revolutionary and post-Revolutionary periods."]

Caswell, Richard. "Richard Henderson Letter." Manuscript, PC.584, State Archives of North Carolina, Raleigh. [Online catalog description: "Letter to Colonel Henderson from Richard Caswell in Kinston, Aug. 13, 1779, concerning shortage of money, problems of commissary, and possible need for more troops."]

Cooper, Richard. *Richard Caswell: A Leader for a New State*. Raleigh: Creative Productions, 1985.

Crabtree, Beth. "The First State Governor." *Tar Heel Junior Historian*, 12:2 (December 19792), 3. [Online description from "North Carolina Periodicals Index," East Carolina University: "Richard Caswell was the first governor despite no campaigning and not being directly elected by the state's citizens. He moved from Maryland in the mid-1700s to Lenoir County to be a surveyor and later county clerk. From 1776-1780 and again from 1784-1787, he served as governor and later as state Senator until his death on November 10, 1789."]

Crabtree, Beth G. *North Carolina Governors, 1585-1958: Brief Sketches*. Raleigh: State Dept. of Archives and History, 1958.

"Governor Richard Caswell, 1777, G. P. 1, pp. 1-145, Calendar." Online at the State Archives of North Carolina website: http://archives.ncdcr.gov/Portals/3/PDF/findingaids/governors/Caswell_Richard_1st_Calendar_GP1.pdf.

"Governor Richard Caswell, 1777-1778, G. P. 2, pp. 1-152, Calendar." Online at the State Archives of North Carolina website: http://archives.ncdcr.gov/Portals/3/PDF/findingaids/governors/Caswell_Richard_1st_Calendar_GP2.pdf.

"Governor Richard Caswell, 1778, G. P. 3, pp. 1-163." Online at the State Archives of North Carolina website: http://archives.ncdcr.gov/Portals/3/PDF/findingaids/governors/Caswell_Richard_1st_Calendar_GP3.pdf.

"Governor Richard Caswell, 1778-1779, G. P. 4, pp. 1-159, Calendar." Online at the State Archives of North Carolina website: http://archives.ncdcr.gov/Portals/3/PDF/findingaids/governors/Caswell_Richard_1st_Calendar_GP4.pdf.

"Governor Richard Caswell, 1779-1780, n. d., G. P. 5, pp. 1-149, Calendar." Online at the State Archives of North Carolina website: http://archives.ncdcr.gov/Portals/3/PDF/findingaids/governors/Caswell_Richard_1st_Calendar_GP5.pdf

Henry, Patrick, 1736-1799. "Papers, 1777-1786." Manuscript 19779, Library of Virginia, Richmond. [Online catalog description: "[Includes] one letter to Governor Richard Caswell (1729-1789) of North Carolina discussing possible action by the British along the Eastern Shore and recommending opening a front there if necessary and commenting on General John Burgoyne's troops in New York."]

Holloman, Charles R. "Richard Caswell." Online at the NCpedia website: http://ncpedia.org/biography/caswell-richard-0.

Jakubowski, Glenda. "Lost in History." *Our State: Down Home in North Carolina*, 68:10 (March 2001), 62-66. [Online description from "North Carolina Periodicals Index," East Carolina University: "Where is Richard Caswell buried? Caswell, Revolutionary War hero and first governor of North Carolina, died in 1789. The funeral was held in Fayetteville, but no one can prove whether he was buried in Fayetteville or in Kinston, as some claim. It is a grave, historical mystery."]

Lawrence, R. C. "Richard Caswell." *The State: A Weekly Survey of North Carolina*, 13:1 (June 1945), 1, 20; online: http://digital.ncdcr.gov/cdm/ref/collection/p16062coll18/id/13238. [Online description from "North Carolina Periodicals Index," East Carolina University: "Richard Caswell was one of the most loyal patriots during the early history of North Carolina and rendered outstanding services as both a statesman and a solider."]

Lewis, J. D. "Patriot Leaders in North Carolina: Richard Caswell: Colonel over the New Bern District Minutemen - 1775-1776; Brigadier General over the New Bern District Brigade of Militia - 1776-1777; Major General over all NC Militia - 1780 & 1781-1783; 1st Governor of North Carolina - 1777-1780 & 1784-1786." Online: http://www.carolana.com/NC/Revolution/patriot_leaders_nc_richard_caswell.html.

Norris, Jeannie Faris. "Caswell's Ordeal." *The State: Down Home in North Carolina*, 27:11 (October 1959), 32-33; online: http://digital.ncdcr.gov/cdm/ref/collection/p16062coll18/id/37065. [Online description from "North

Carolina Periodicals Index," East Carolina University: "Born in Maryland in 1729, Richard Caswell served North Carolina as governor in 1776, 1777, 1778, 1785, 1786, and 1787. Surveyor, lawyer, legislator, and soldier, Caswell also served as delegate to the Constitutional Convention, held in Philadelphia. A Federalist, Caswell died on 5 November 1789, at a convention in Fayetteville."]

North Carolina (State). General Assembly. "[Document dated:] 1777. Papers Concerning Justices of the Peace and Militia Officers Appointments, 1777." Manuscript; General Assembly Record Group; Session Records, April-May 1777; Joint Papers, Committee Papers, Resolutions, Senate Bills, House Bills, Box 1 (MARS ID: 66.8.9.8; folder), State Archives of North Carolina, Raleigh. [Online catalog description: "Documents concerning Governor Caswell's appointment of officers to the militia regiments of Cumberland and Chatham counties, and his appointments of Justices of the Peace for Onslow and Pasquotank counties."]

Sadler, W. J. "Governors of North Carolina." *The State: A Weekly Survey of North Carolina*, 3:12 (August 1935), 6; online: http://digital.ncdcr.gov/cdm/ref/collection/p16062coll18/id/4319. [Online description from "North Carolina Periodicals Index," East Carolina University: "Richard Caswell was a militia officer and the first Governor of North Carolina to be elected by an independent legislature. He served during the Revolutionary period, and during his term many reforms in government were inaugurated, among them being the drafting of the state constitution on December 18, 1776 and the establishment of county and Superior courts."]

Strother, Jake. "A Historic Gem is Preserved." *The State: Down Home in North Carolina*, 51:3 (August 1983), 13-16; online: http://digital.ncdcr.gov/cdm/ref/collection/p16062coll18/id/12388. [Online description from "North Carolina Periodicals Index," East Carolina University: "Harmony Hall was the home of Richard Caswell from 1777 till 1782. During this time, the Kinston home served as North Carolina's unofficial capital. Because New Bern was susceptible to British attack, Caswell, North Carolina's first Governor, moved the state's records to his home. Caswell gave Harmony Hall to his son, Richard, in 1782, where it remained in the family till 1824. Since then the home has served as a hospital, a church, a public library, and a Women's Club. In 1830, two one-story additions were built on each side. The Preservation for Harmony Hall Committee has recently completed its restoration of the home, and it now serves as a museum and social hall. Rooms, such as the second-story master bedroom, are restored to 18th-century condition, while the kitchen is furnished with modern appliances so that it can serve the Kinston Noon Rotary Club. Harmony Hall is Kinston's only 18th-century structure still standing."]

Valsame, James Mark. "Governor Richard Caswell, 1777-1780, n. d., Finding Aid." Online at the State Archives of North Carolina's website: http://archives.ncdcr.gov/Portals/3/PDF/findingaids/governors/Caswell_Richard_1st_Admin_finding_aid.pdf.

Caswell, William, 1755-1785

Caswell, William. "Papers 1778-1784." Manuscript PC.412 (MARS ID: 922), State Archives of North Carolina, Raleigh. [Online catalog description: "Papers of Caswell, son of Gov. Richard Caswell and brigadier general of New Bern District. Subjects of correspondence include his execution of loyalists and threat of British retaliation on Maj. Samuel Ashe and others (1781); military action at Bryan's Mill (1781); ball given in Halifax, and Gen. Thomas Eaton's daughter; runaway slaves; seizure in 1781 of French row galley the Fortunee in Currituck Co., with copy of Gov. Thomas Burke's letter to Gen. Isaac Gregory (1782); parole of Lord Charles Montagu at New Bern; proclamation ending hostilities; and the assembly of 1784. Among the correspondents are James Armstrong, Samuel Ashe, William Brown, Richard Caswell, John Easton, James Gorham, J. West Green, Alexander Martin, and Samuel Smith."]

Chavis, John, c. 1763-1838

Chavis, John, and Lunsford Lane; W. Sherman Savage, ed. "The Influence of John Chavis and Lunsford Lane on the History of North Carolina." *Journal of Negro History*, 25:1 (January 1940), 14-24.

Deschamps, Margaret Burr. "John Chavis as a Preacher to Whites." *North Carolina Historical Review*, 32:2 (April 1955), 165-172.

Hudson, Gossie Harold. "John Chavis, 1763-1838: A Social-Phychological Study." *Journal of Negro History*, 64:2 (Spring 1979), 142-156.

Knight, Edgar W. "Notes on John Chavis." *North Carolina Historical Review*, 7:3 (July 1930), 326-345. [Provides a biography of Chavis and mentions his Revolutionary War service on page 327.]

Cleveland, Benjamin, 1738-1806

Arthur, Billy. "Wild Thing." *Our State: Down Home in North Carolina*, 66:10 (March 1999), 22-25; online: http://digital.ncdcr.gov/cdm/ref/collection/p16062coll18/id/67536. [Online description from "North Carolina Periodicals Index," East Carolina University: "Benjamin Cleveland was born in Virginia in 1738 and moved, in 1769, to Rowan County. He was a prominent figure in the early history of the area. However, it was as the leader of soldiers from Wilkes and Surry Counties at the Battle of King's Mountain that he won lasting fame. After the war, he moved to South Carolina and became a county judge." Benjamin Cleveland (1738-1806)]

Boyden, Lucile K. "Colonel Benjamin Cleveland." *The State: A Weekly Survey of North Carolina*, 13:31 (December 1945); online: http://digital.ncdcr.gov/cdm/ref/collection/p16062coll18/id/14234. [Online description from "North Carolina Periodicals Index," East Carolina University: "Benjamin Cleveland was one of the outstanding characters during the Revolutionary War period, and his exploits in and around Wilkes County, were of a varied nature."]

Dean, Earl. "Three Men of Kings Mountain." *The State: A Weekly Survey of North Carolina*, 17:37 (February 1950), 10, 20; online: http://digital.ncdcr.gov/cdm/ref/collection/p16062coll18/id/25020. [Online description from "North Carolina Periodicals Index," East Carolina University: "Many famous names have been associated with Cleveland County. Three men, whose names loom large in the pages of history, are closely identified with Cleveland County and its capital, Shelby. They are Colonel Benjamin Cleveland, the hero of the Battle of King's Mountain; Colonel Isaac Shelby, the first governor of Kentucky; and Major Patrick Ferguson, the inventor of the breech-loading rifle."]

Norris, Jeannie Faris. "History's Hangman." *The State: Down Home in North Carolina*, 23:18 (January 1956), 13, 15; online: http://digital.ncdcr.gov/cdm/ref/collection/p16062coll18/id/6692. [Online description from "North Carolina Periodicals Index," East Carolina University: "The lives of four history-makers of Wilkes County are recounted in this article. Ben Cleveland, founder of the county, was a justice of the peace, rose to a colonelcy in the militia because of service against the Cherokees, and commanded the left wing against King's Mountain. For 57 years, Montfort Stokes held public offices in the state of North Carolina. He was named Indian commissioner in 1832 by President Andrew Jackson. James Wellborn and William Lenoir served under Ben Cleveland."]

Sprague, Lynn Tew. "The Terror of the Tories: Colonel Benjamin Cleavland, Old Roundabout." *Outing Magazine*, (October 1908), 59-67.

Cogdell, Richard, 1724-1787

Cogdell, Richard. "Richard Cogdell (1724-1787) Papers, 1761-1784." Manuscript, PC.414, State Archives of North Carolina, Raleigh. [Online catalog description: "Correspondence of Cogdell, chairman of New Bern Committee of Safety (1775) and admiralty court judge, concerning seat of government (1761); slave insurrection (1775); Cogdell's loyalty to patriot cause (1776); lack of provisions on board Royal Navy vessels at Wilmington [1776]; and problem (1784) securing law license for Marmaduke Jones, who had been in England during Revolution. Letters are from Jones, Cogdell, John Campbell, John Simpson, and Gideon Lamb. A letter from South Carolina Sons of Liberty concerns partial repeal of Townshend duties and need for continued unity and nonimportation (1770). Also photocopy of letter from Cogdell to Richard Caswell in Philadelphia (June 8, 1775), commenting on Mecklenburg Resolves, activities of committee of safety, Gov. Josiah Martin and loyalists, elections, militia, and Congress."]

Collet, John Abraham, active 1756-1789

Cumming, William P. "John Abraham Collet (Collett), fl. 1756-89." Online: http://ncpedia.org/biography/collet-collett-john.

Merrens, Roy H., and Herbert R. Paschal. "A Map-Maker's View of Anson County in 1769." *North Carolina Historical Review*, 59:4 (October 1982), 271-278. [Online description from "North Carolina Periodicals Index," East Carolina University: "In 1769, map-maker John Abraham Collet provided a short description of Anson County, North Carolina to promote the interior of the state. Collet wrote quite positively about the area on everything from agriculture to roads, even if the information was at sometimes inaccurate."]

Collins, Josiah, 1735-1819, and Somerset Place (Creswell)

Ellis, Marshall. "A Place Called Somerset." *Our State: Down Home in North Carolina*, 67:3 (August 1999), 96-102. [Online description from "North Carolina Periodicals Index," East Carolina University: "Built by Josiah Collins in the late 1700s, Somerset Place was one of the state's most prosperous plantations in pre-Civil War days. Debt and the Civil War began its downward spiral. In 1889, it was sold out of the family, passing through numerous owners until acquired by the state in 1939. Now almost restored, it is a State Historic Site."]

Davidson, Elizabeth Mary Brevard, 1748-1823 or 1824

Misenheimer, John E. "Mary Brevard Davidson: Widow of the Revolution." *Olde Mecklenburg Genealogical Society Quarterly*, 24:1 (2006), 16-19.

Misenheimer, John E., Jr. "Mary Brevard Davidson and Others after the American Revolution." *The Golden Nugget (Cabarrus Genealogical Society)*, 13:3 (Autumn 2005), 82-84. [Mary Davidson, Ann Christenbury, Sarah Rounsevall, and Nancy Horah of Western North Carolina. The latter's husband was a Loyalist.]

Davidson, Samuel, 1737-1784

Norris, Jeannie Faris. "First across the Blue Ridge." *The State: A Weekly Survey of North Carolina*, 16:32 (January 1949), 8. [Online description from "North Carolina Periodicals Index," East Carolina University: "Western North Carolina proved a rough country in the late 18th Century. In this article, the story of Samuel Davidson is told. He attempted to settle the area beyond the Blue Ridge in 1784. Unfortunately he met his demise after he encountered a band of Cherokee Indians. A year later the first permanent settlements would take hold in that area."]

Seay, Majel Ivey. "First across the Blue Ridge." *The State: A Weekly Survey of North Carolina*, 3:7 (July 1935), 2; online: http://digital.ncdcr.gov/cdm/ref/collection/p16062coll18/id/4170. [Online description from "North Carolina Periodicals Index," East Carolina University: "Colonel Samuel Davidson bravely explored western North Carolina and was a trailblazer for future settlers. Davidson with his wife, daughter, and servant settled at the base of Jones Mountain in July, 1784. He would be murdered by members of the Cherokee tribe and his wife, child, and servant fled fifteen miles back to the safety of Old Fort."]

Davidson, William Lee, 1746-1781

Davidson, Chalmers. *Piedmont Partisan: The Life and Times of Brigadier-General William Lee Davidson*. Davidson, N. C.: Davidson College, 1951.

Davidson, Chalmers G[aston]. "Papers of a Piedmont Partisan: Few Papers Remain from a Little-Known Revolutionary General." *Autograph Collectors' Journal*, 4:1 (Fall 1951), 37-38.

Davidson, William Lee, 1746-1781. "Papers, 1792-1794." Manuscript (OCLC no. 20736902), Sec A. Box 33 items 1-3, David M. Rubenstein Rare Book & Manuscript Library, Duke University, Durham. [Online catalog description: "Papers dealing with claims of the heirs of William Lee Davidson, brigadier general of the militia of the Salisbury District of North Carolina, against the U.S. Treasury and the State of North Carolina for compensation after his death during the Revolutionary War."]

"General William Lee Davidson." *Olde Mecklenburg Genealogical Society Quarterly*, 10:4 (October-December 1992), 18.

Graham, William Alexander. "General William Lee Davidson." *North Carolina Booklet*, 13:1 (July 1913), 11-39.

Graham, William Alexander. *General William Lee Davidson: An Address Delivered at the Unveiling of a Monument to General Davidson, Voted by Congress, at the Guilford Battle Ground, July 4, 1906*. Greensboro: Guilford Battle Ground Co., 1906.

Graham, William Oscar. "William Graham, The Signer." *Olde Mecklenburg Genealogical Society Quarterly*, 17:3 (1999), 26-29.

Lawrence, R. C. "Gen. William Lee Davidson." *The State: A Weekly Survey of North Carolina*, 14:7 (July 1946), 9, 18; online: http://digital.ncdcr.gov/cdm/ref/collection/p16062coll18/id/15813. [Online description from "North Carolina Periodicals Index," East Carolina University: "Davidson was an outstanding soldier/patriot during the Revolutionary War. He was killed at the Battle of Cowan's Ford, February 1, 1781, at age 35."]

Misenheimer, John E., Jr. "Brigadier General William Lee Davidson and First Major John Davidson: Leading Revolutionary Patriots in Mecklenburg County, North Carolina." *The Golden Nugget (Cabarrus Genealogical Society)*, 11:4 (December 2003), 184-189.

Mitchell, Tucker. "Lost and Found." *Our State: Down Home in North Carolina*, 69:4 (September 2001), 26, 28, 30; online: http://digital.ncdcr.gov/cdm/ref/collection/p16062coll18/id/73742. [Online description from "North Carolina Periodicals Index," East Carolina University: "When General William Lee Davidson was killed in February 1781 in Mecklenburg County during the American Revolution, British soldiers stole his wallet. Years later it turned up in Great Britain's Public Records Office. In 2000, North Carolina 'colonials' prevailed upon the British for its return. In July 2001, the wallet was placed in the General Davidson exhibit in the museum at the Guilford Courthouse National Park in Greensboro.

"NC Patriot Militia Gen. William Lee Davidson." *Southern Campaigns of the American Revolution*, 3:2.3 (February 2006), 2-3; online: http://southerncampaign.org/newsletter/v3n2.pdf.

Siry, Steven F. *Liberty's Fallen Generals: Leadership and Sacrifice in the American War of Independence.* Washington, D. C.: Potomac Books, 2012. [Includes: William Lee Davidson (August 1780-February 1781).]

Tallent, Fran. "Gen. Davidson's Wallet." *The Golden Nugget (Cabarrus Genealogical Society)*, 9:3 (September 2001), 87.

Williams, Samuel Cole. *Generals Francis Nash and William Lee Davidson.* Nashville: Tennessee Historical Commission, 1942.

"Who Shot General Davidson?" *Olde Mecklenburg Genealogical Society Quarterly*, 10:4 (October-December 1992), 14-17.

Davie, William Richardson, 1756-1820

Clark, Walter. "General William Richardson Davie 1756-1820." *Magazine of American History*, 28 (December 1892), 415-430; reprinted in: W. J. Peele, ed., *Lives of Distinguished North Carolinians with Illustrations and Speeches* (Raleigh: North Carolina Publishing Society, 1897), 59-80.

Davie, James C. "William Richardson Davie, Commissary General of the Amry of the South during the War for American Independence." *Quartermaster Review,* 23:4 (January/February 1944), 67-68, 110.

Davie, William Richardson. "William Richardson Davie Papers, 1758-1819." Manuscript 1793, Southern Historical Collection, Louis Round Wilson Special Collections Library, University of North Carolina, Chapel Hill; online finding aid available at http://www2.lib.unc.edu/mss/inv/d/Davie,William_Richardson.html. [Online finding aid description: "William Richardson Davie was a lawyer, state legislator, Revolutionary officer, member of the United States Constitutional Convention, Federalist governor of North Carolina, and peace commissioner to France, and was influential in the founding of the University of North Carolina. He moved from Halifax County, N. C., to Lancaster District, S.C., in 1805. These papers include letters to, from, and about Davie and his family. Two long narratives pertain to Davie's Revolutionary War experiences as a cavalry officer in North and South Carolina and as commissary general to Nathanael Greene. Other papers, of scattered dates, relate to Davie's varied activities and to his family and the related Crockett family, with only a few items later than 1805. Also present is a copy of a report of William Richardson, Presbyterian minister, on his mission to the Cherokee Indians, 1758. Collection is, in part, photostatic and typed transcript copies. The Addition of March 2009 consists of a land survey and a land grant signed by Davie. The Addition of November 2012 consists of a 14 June 1787 letter from Davie to Mary Edwards concerning the case of 'Bayard versus Singleton,' which helped establish the principle of judicial review."]

Davie, William Richardson; Blackwell P. Robinson, ed. *The Revolutionary War Sketches of William R. Davie.* (North Carolina Bicentennial Pamphlet series, no. 4) Raleigh: North Carolina Dept. of Cultural Resources, Division of Archives and History, 1976.

Fulghum, R. Neil. *William Richard Davie, Soldier, Statesman, and Founder of the University of North Carolina: 1756-2006, Semiquincentennial.* Chapel Hill: The North Carolina Collection, The University Library, The University of North Carolina at Chapel Hill, 2006.

Manning, John. "General William R. Davie." *North Carolina University Magazine* (1884), new series, 23:3 = old series 12:3 (January 1893), 98-105.

Murphy, Walter. "Davie, McCorkle, and Avery." *The State: A Weekly Survey of North Carolina*, 10:29 (December 1942), 9, 28; online: http://digital.ncdcr.gov/cdm/ref/collection/p16062coll18/id/33628. [Online description from "North Carolina Periodicals Index," East Carolina University: "William Richardson Davie, Waightstill Avery, and Samuel Eusebius McCorkle were responsible for man any {*sic*} others for the establishment of the University of North Carolina at Chapel Hill, which celebrates its 150th anniversary next year."]

Robinson, Blackwell, ed. *The Revolutionary War Sketches of William R. Davie.* Raleigh: North Carolina Department of Cultural Resources, Division of Archives and History, 1976.

Robinson, Blackwell P. *William R. Davie.* Chapel Hill: University of North Carolina Press, 1957.

Watson, Harry L. "William Richardson Davie and the University of the People: Ironies and Paradoxes." *Carolina Comments*, 55:2 (April 2007), 65-73; online: http://www.ncpublications.com/comments/Apr07.pdf.

Yankle, Bob. "William Richardson Davie (1756-1820): A Great Man in a Time of Great Men." *Southern Campaigns of the American Revolution*, 3:9 (September 2006), 16-18; online: http://southerncampaign.org/newsletter/v3n9.pdf.

Davis, James, 1721-1785

Breytspraak, Charlotte, and Jack Breytspraak. "Historical Profile: James Davis." *Journal of the New Bern Historical Society*, 1:1 (May 1988), 27-30. [Online description from "North Carolina Periodicals Index," East Carolina University: "James Davis became public printer in 1749 by appointment of the General Assembly. He also began the state's first newspaper, *The North Carolina Gazette*, in 1751, and held many local offices, including postmaster of New Bern and Carteret County sheriff."]

Carraway, Gertrude. "James Davis: First Printer." *The State: A Weekly Survey of North Carolina*, 5:25 (November 1937), 6; online: http://digital.ncdcr.gov/cdm/ref/collection/p16062coll18/id/102939. [Online description from "North Carolina Periodicals Index," East Carolina University: "James Davis ran the state's first printing press in New Bern, 1749. The General Assembly hired Davis as the official state printer. He was charged with printing money, journals about the assembly's activities, and the state's first newspaper called the *North Carolina Gazette* in 1751."]

Corbitt, D. L. "Historical Notes: *The North Carolina Gazette*." *North Carolina Historical Review*, 2;1 (January 1925), 83-89. [Online description from "North Carolina Periodicals Index," East Carolina University: "The North Carolina Gazette was the first newspaper published in North Carolina. The oldest found edition was published on November 15, 1751 by James Davis and was number 15.The paper was printed in New Bern, and included information on a range of topics including period laws for tavern and ordinary keepers."]

Elliott, Robert N., Jr. "James Davis and the Beginning of the Newspaper in North Carolina." *North Carolina Historical Review*, 42:1 (January 1965), 1-20; online: http://digital.ncdcr.gov/cdm/ref/collection/p16062coll9/id/4207. [Online description from "North Carolina Periodicals Index," East Carolina University: "This article examines the beginnings of newspapers in the American colonies starting with papers in Boston in the late 17th century and continuing to the Baltimore province in Maryland, to Charleston, and then to Williamsburg in Virginia. The latter became the first newspaper to be read in North Carolina due to the two colonies' commercial and cultural ties. Further information on the spread of printing to North Carolina and the development of papers there as well as information on period printing and printing offices are included."]

McMurtrie, Douglas Crawford. "The First Twelve Years of Printing in North Carolina, 1749-1760." *North Carolina Historical Review*, 10:3 (July 1933), 214-234.

North Carolina History Museum Staff. "James Davis – Printer, Postmaster, and Politician." *Tar Heel Junior Historian*, 21:3 (Spring 1982), 2-4, 28. [Online description from "North Carolina Periodicals Index," East Carolina University: "The life of James Davis, North Carolina's first public printer, is recounted. Davis was appointed to the printer's position in 1749 by the North Carolina House of Burgess. He later started the state's first newspaper, *The North Carolina Gazette*, in New Bern in 1751. He held many local offices, including New Bern postmaster."]

Roger, Lou. "James Davis: Printer." *We the People of North Carolina*. 7: 8 (December 1949), 18-19. [Online description from "North Carolina Periodicals Index," East Carolina University: "James Davis came to North Carolina about two hundred years ago to become the state's first printer and to print the laws of the colony. He remained thirty-six years. He was the first man to establish a newspaper, print a magazine, and print a book."]

Decrow, Sarah, ca. 1750-1795

Evans, Esther. "Sarah Moore Delano Decrow (ca. 1750-1795)," in William S. Powell, ed., *Dictionary of North Carolina Biography, Vol. 2: D-G* (Chapel Hill: University of North Carolina Press, 1986), 48-49.

"Postmaster Had Shady Reputation." In H. G. Jones, *Scoundrels, Rogues and Heroes of the Old North State* (Charleston, S. C.: History Press, 2004), 61-62.

Dickson, William, 1740-1820

Dickson, William. "The Dickson Letters, 1783-1818." Manuscript MASC (Cage 4615), Holland Library, Washington State University, Pullman. [Online catalog description: "Typescript transcriptions of letters to relatives concerning the war in North Carolina, the United States Constitution, and North Carolina."]

Dickson, William. "William Dickson Papers, 1772-1804, 1921." Manuscript, PC.1088, State Archives of North Carolina, Raleigh. [Online catalog description: "Four letters (1784-1790) from planter William Dickson of Duplin Co., colonial and state legislator to cousin, Rev. Robert Dickson, Presbyterian minister in northern Ireland, about family including his uncle, Maturine Colvill, a Bladen Co. loyalist; and the Revolutionary War in North Carolina since the Battle of Guilford Court House, chiefly in Duplin and Bladen counties, describing forays by Major Craig's men into countryside around Wilmington, the fight at 'Great Bridge' on the Northeast Cape Fear River between the British and local militia (including Dickson), foraging and looting by loyalists and their women, prisoners on prison ships, and organization of and fighting between patriot and loyalist militia. Other comments concern Irish struggles for freedom; prospects for Presbyterian clergy in North Carolina; Grove Academy in Duplin Co. and other schools; problems of some Scotch-Irish settlers; settlements in Kentucky, Tennessee, and Georgia; the state of Franklin; and the new federal Constitution."]

Donelson, John, c. 1718-c. 1780

Donelson, John. "[Journal] Dec. 22, 1779, Fort Patrick Henry, Holston River." Manuscript, Document ID: s1375, Special Collections Library, University of Tennessee, Knoxville; Tennessee State Library and Archives, Nashville; online transcription: http://diglib.lib.utk.edu/cgi/t/text/text-idx?c=tdh;view=text;rgn=main;idno=sl375. [Online cata-log description: This is the Journal kept by John Donelson on his trip from Fort Patrick Henry to French Salt Springs which he also refers to as the Big Salt Lick. He travels down the Holston, French Broad, Clinch, Tennessee, and Cumberland Rivers. The trip starts on December 22, 1779 and is completed on April 24, 1780. Donelson's boat is joined early in the voyage by several others going along the same route. Donelson writes about an accident they have on the French Broad River in February. One of the other vessels sinks. A slave dies on the Clinch river in March from severe frost bite. Later that month the travellers have trouble with the Chickamaugas, who have villages down the south side of the Tennessee River. Captain Blackemore's boat, which had been quarantined from the others due to small pox, is attacked by these natives, and many people are killed or captured. Donelson writes about the flotilla trying to navigate the Whirl, a particularly dangerous place on the Tennessee River near Chattanooga. There, they are attacked again by the Chickamaugas. One family named Jennings is left behind when their boat becomes trapped in the Whirl, but they are able to eventually catch up to the others. Donelson writes about trouble they have going through the Muscle Shoals in mid-March. On the Cumberland River they begin to have food shortages and are forced to hunt buffalo to survive. When they arrive in Big Salt Lick, they meet Captain Robertson and company. The group decides to stay temporarily in some log cabins they find."]

Spence, Richard Douglas. "John Donelson and the Opening of the Old Southwest." *Tennessee Historical Quarterly*, 50:3 (Fall 1991), 157-172.

Dowdy, Betsy, active 1770s

Creecy, Richard Benbury. "Legend of Betsy Dowdy: An Historical Tradition of the Battle of Great Bridge." *North Carolina Booklet,* 1:5 (10 September 1901), 3-7. [In 1775, Betsy Dowdy from the coast of North Carolina warned General William Skinner that the Lord Dunmore's army was heading towards North Carolina. Online description from "North Carolina Periodicals Index," East Carolina University: "The recounting of the Revolutionary War legend of a young girl who, facing fear that the British may steal Outer Banks' ponies, rode on a perilous journey to alert the militia and thus aided in the victory at Great Bridge."]

Griffin, Kitty; Marjorie Priceman, illus. *The Ride: The Legend of Betsy Dowdy*. New York: Atheneum, 2010. [a book for young readers about the story of this North Carolinian during the Revolution]

Hall, Leslie. "The All Night Ride of Betsy Dowdy." reprinted in Edna M. Shannonhouse, ed., *Year Book, Pasquotank Historical Society* (Baltimore: Gateway Press, Inc., 1983), 51-53. [Poem written about Betsy Dowdy's sixty mile night ride to warn American forces of British threats to coastal North Carolina.]

Houck, C. B. "Ride of Betsy Dowdy for Help Rivals the Jaunt of the Famous Paul Revere." *Greensville Daily News*, October 25, 1925. [a copy of this article is available in the file collection of the North Carolina State Library, Raleigh in the file headed: "N. C. – History – Revolution – Women's Work" and in the DAR Library's collection on women during the American Revolution. Currituck County; Battle of Great Bridge in Virginia.]

Moore, Carole. "Betsy's Wild Ride." *Our State: Down Home in North Carolina,* 74:5 (October 2007), 76-78, 80; online: http://digital.ncdcr.gov/cdm/ref/collection/p16062coll18/id/87516. [Online description from "North Carolina Periodicals Index," East Carolina University: "In November 1775, Lord Dunmore, Virginia's last Royal Governor, planned to invade North Carolina. After capturing Portsmouth and Norfolk, he barricaded Great Bridge on the Carolina side, blocking all shipments to the Norfolk port. A small force of Americans marched on Great Bridge. Seeking reinforcements for the outnumbered American troops, Betsy Dowdy from Currituck Banks rode her horse, Black Bess, fifty miles on the night of December 10, 1775, to alert General William Skinner and his men at Hertford. Skinner's force reached Great Bridge in time to help defeat Dunmore on December 11, 1775, and end the invasion threat. Moore discusses how people from colonial times down to the present have reacted to the ride. Some feel it actually happened; some, that the account does not jibe with the facts; and some, that it was a combination of a little truth and a little myth."]

Seay, Majel Ivey. "Betsy Dowdy's Ride." *The State: A Weekly Survey of North Carolina,* 4:47 (April 1937), 5.

Smith, Donna. "Betsy Dowdy's Ride." *Our State: Down Home in North Carolina,* 67:2 (May 2000), 25-27; online: http://digital.ncdcr.gov/cdm/ref/collection/p16062coll18/id/71146.

Smith, Donna Campbell. *An Independent Spirit: The Tale of Betsy Dowdy and Black Bess*. (Legends of the Carolinas series) Wilmington, N. C.: Coastal Carolina Press, 2002; 2nd ed. Buford, Ga.: Faithful Publishing, 2006. [The fictionalized tale of a fourteen-year old Quakeress who made an all-night ride to warn American forces in an impending attack from Lord Dunmore royal governor of Virginia is the subject of this book for young readers. A study guide is included.]

Downs, Henry, 1728-1798

King, Victor C. *Lives and Times of the 27 Signers of the Mecklenburg Declaration of Independence of May 20, 1775.* Charlotte: Anderson Press, 1956.

Sharpe, E. M. "Henry Downs: Signer of the Mecklenburg Declaration of Independence." *Olde Mecklenburg Genealogical Society Quarterly*, 11:3 (1993), 10-13.

Ernst, Anna Catharina, active 1770s

Fries, Adelaide L. *The Road to Salem.* Chapel Hill: University of North Carolina Press, 1944. [Includes the story of Anna Catharina Ernst, a North Carolina Moravian during the Revolution.]

Evans, Henry, c. 1760-1810

Barfield, Rodney. "The Black Experience." *Tar Heel Junior Historian*, 16:1 (Fall 1976), 6-14. [Online description from "North Carolina Periodicals Index," East Carolina University: "From emancipation to the Civil Rights, the African American movement for equality was led by exceptional individuals. Highlighted are the lives of some of the most influential including; George Moses Horton, John Chavis, Henry Evans, and Lunsford Lane."]

Fallon, James, active 1770s-1780s

Rankin, Richard, ed. "'Musquetoe' Bites: Caricatures of Lower Cape Fear Whigs and Tories on the Eve of the American Revolution." *North Carolina Historical Review*, 6:2 (April 1988), 173-207.

Rayburn, Richard H. "Infallible Power: The 'Musquetoe,' The Wilmington-New Hanover County Safety Committee, and the Coming of the Revolution in the Lower Cape Fear, 1775-1776." *North Carolina Historical Review*, 92:4 (October 2015), 387-425. [The "Musquetoe" was the pseudonym of Dr. James Fallon.]

Virginius [pseud. of Charles Lee]. "To Those Whom It May Concern." *Freeman's Journal; or, The North American Intelligencer*, (September 25, 1782).

Fanning, David, 1756?-1825

Butler, Lindley S., ed. *The Narrative of Colonel David Fanning*, Davidson: Briarpatch Press, 1981.

Caruthers, E[li] W[ashington]. *A Brief History of Col. David Fanning; Also, Naomi Wise, or the Wrongs of a Beautiful Girl; and Randolph's Manufacturing*. Weldon: Harrell's Printing House, 1888; online: https://archive.org/details/briefhistoryofco00caru. [Naomi Wise (1789-1807 or 1808)]

Fanning, David. *Col. David Fanning's Narrative of His Exploits and Adventures as a Loyalist of North Carolina in the American Revolution*. Toronto: Reprinted from the Canadian magazine, 1908.

Fanning, David. *The Narrative of Colonel Fanning (A Tory in the Revolutionary War with Great Britain) Giving an Account of His Adventures in North Carolina from 1775 to 1783, As Written by Himself.* Richmond: 1861; reprinted: New York: Joseph Sabin, 1865.

Fanning, David; Lindley S. Butler, ed. *The Narrative of David Fanning.* Davidson, N. C.: Briarpatch Press; Charleston, S. C.: Tradd Street Press, 1981.

Hairr, John. *Colonel David Fanning: The Adventures of a Carolina Loyalist*. Erwin, N. C.: Averasboro Press, 2000.

"The Infamous Colonel Fanning Tells All." *The Genealogical Journal by the Randolph County Genealogical Society*, 25:2 (Summer 2001), 54-59. [Includes listings of militia officers from Randolph County during the Revolution.]

Parker, Hershel. "The Memorial of David Fanning." *Southern Campaigns of the American Revolution*, 10:4.1 (August 2015), 1-6; online: http://www.southerncampaign.org/wordpress/wp-content/uploads/2015/08/SCAR-Vol-10-No-4.1.pdf.

S__, H. F. "[Article from the *Carthage Blade* newspaper about Col. David Fanning, 'the great N. C. Tory'.]" In Manuscript MS172, "Dr. Thomas Fanning Wood Family Papers," Archives and Special Collections, William M. Randall Library, University of North Carolina Wilmington.

Troxler, Carole Watterson. "'To git out of a troublesome neighborhood': David Fanning in New Brunswick." *North Carolina Historical Review*, 56:4 (October 1979), 343-365.

Fanning, Edmund, 1739-1818

Dunaway, Stewart E. *The Life and Times of Edmund Fanning, 1739-1818: Hillsborough, N. C.* Hillsborough: North Carolina Historical Books, 2015.

Fanning, Edmund. "Edmund Fanning Paper, 1775." Manuscript, PC.490, State Archives of North Carolina, Raleigh. [Online catalog description: "Will of Edmund Fanning, North Carolina loyalist, 'being about to embark for New York,' June 3, 1775."]

Johnson, William. "William Johnson Paper, 1783." Photocopy of a manuscript, PC.644 (MARS ID: 1154; record group), State Archives of North Carolina, Raleigh. [Online catalog description: "Photocopy of letter (Dec. 2, 1783) from William Johnston, Orange Co. legislator and agent of loyalist Edmund Fanning, to Adlai Osborn of Rowan Co., concerning sale of Fanning's lands there for execution of judgment, and commenting on death of former governor, Dr. [Thomas] Burke."]

Franklin, Jesse, 1760-1823

Alderman, J. T. "Governor Jesse Franklin." *North Carolina Booklet*, 6:3 (January 1907), 185-203; online: http://digital.ncdcr.gov/cdm/ref/collection/p249901coll37/id/14180. [Online description from "North Carolina Periodicals Index," East Carolina University: "This article examines the life and service of Jesse Franklin of Surry County. Franklin was commissioned a Lieutenant in George Washington's army and took part in numerous military engagements. After the Revolutionary War, Franklin was a member of the state legislature and was eventually elected to Congress as a Senator. After he retired from Congress, Franklin was appointed to treat with the Chickasaw Indians and was elected governor of North Carolina in 1820."]

Gaston, Alexander, c. 1735-1781

Davidson, Chalmers G. "Alexander Gaston, ca. 1735-20 Aug. 1781." Online: http://ncpedia.org/biography/gaston-alexander.

Norris, Jeannie Faris. "State Song." *The State: A Weekly Survey of North Carolina*, 20:31 (January 1953), 76-77; online: http://digital.ncdcr.gov/cdm/ref/collection/p16062coll18/id/29768. [Online description from "North Carolina Periodicals Index," East Carolina University: "Written in honor of Dr. Alexander Gaston, an Irish doctor who was murdered by Tories, the North Carolina state song is titled, 'The Old North State Forever'."]

Gates, Horatio, 1727-1806, in North Carolina

Dean, Earl. "General Horatio Gates." *The State: A Weekly Survey of North Carolina*, 17:26 (November 1949), 4; online: http://digital.ncdcr.gov/cdm/ref/collection/p16062coll18/id/24701. [Online description from "North Carolina Periodicals Index," East Carolina University: "Historians haven't been kind to Horatio Gates, the Revolutionary War hero for whom Gates County was named 168 years ago."]

Nelson, Paul David. *General Horatio Gates: A Biography.* Baton Rouge: Louisiana State University Press, 1976.

Nelson, Paul David. "Horatio Gates in the Southern Department, 1780: Serious Errors and a Costly Defeat." *North Carolina Historical Review,* 50:3 (July 1973), 256-272.

George III, King of the United Kingdom, 1738-1820

Humphrey, Carol Sue. "Validating the Declaration of Independence: Events in North Carolina and the Charges against George III." M. A. thesis, Wake Forest University, 1979.

Scarborough, Franklin. "Rediscovery of the King George Picture." *The State: Down Home in North Carolina*, 49:10 (March 1979), 18-19; online: http://digital.ncdcr.gov/cdm/ref/collection/p16062coll 18/id/59551. [Online description from "North Carolina Periodicals Index," East Carolina University: "Pictures of King George III and Queen Charlotte were returned to their home in the Salisbury Tavern in 1977. During the Revolutionary War, American General Nathaniel Greene stopped by the tavern, owned by the Steele family, and wrote "King George, hide they face and mourn" on the back of his portrait. After Mrs. Steele's death, the portraits passed to David L. Swain, president of the University of North Carolina. The pictures were later auctioned to William J.

Andrews in 1883, who kept the pictures in his family in California until 1977, when the Neel family, descendants of the Steeles, bought the portraits and returned them to the tavern wall."]

Gerrard, Charles, 1750-1797

Campbell, Wesley Judkins. "Charles Gerrard: Early Benefactor of the University of North Carolina." *North Carolina Historical Review*, 83:3 (July 2006), 293-321. [Online description from "North Carolina Periodicals Index," East Carolina University: "This article examines the life and career of Charles Gerrard, a leading citizen of North Carolina who served in the Continental Army and became a successful businessman in Tarboro after the war. Gerrard was also a delegate to the 1789 North Carolina Constitutional Convention and an early supporter of the University of North Carolina. His donation of land to the University was eventually sold off to build a chapel on campus which has since been renamed Gerrard Hall."]

Glasgow, James, c. 1735-1819

Abernethy, Mrs. Max. "Why We Lost Glasgow County." *The State: A Weekly Survey of North Carolina*, 18:34 (January 1951), 8; online: http://digital.ncdcr.gov/cdm/ref/collection/p16062coll18/id/26505. [Online description from "North Carolina Periodicals Index," East Carolina University: "The change in name of Glasgow County to Greene County involved a betrayal of trust on the part of a prominent state official and also an attempt to burn the state capitol in Raleigh."]

Arthur, Billy. "Fallen Patriot." *The State: Down Home in North Carolina*, 57:12 (May 1990), 13-14; online: http://digital.ncdcr.gov/cdm/ref/collection/p16062coll18/id/64218. [Online description from "North Carolina Periodicals Index," East Carolina University: "James Glasgow was the state's first secretary of state (1776 to 1779).When people learned that the perceived model citizen had used the office for corrupt land dealings, he was fined and disgraced. A county named for him was changed to Greene County."]

Battle, Kemp P. "The Trial of James Glasgow, and the Supreme Court of North Carolina." *North Carolina Booklet*, 3:1 (May 1903), 5-11; online: http://digital.ncdcr.gov/cdm/ref/collection/p249901coll37/id/14180. [Online description from "North Carolina Periodicals Index," East Carolina University: "An account of the trial of North Carolina's first secretary of state, James Glasgow, for the issuing of fraudulent land grants in Tennessee and western North Carolina."]

Koonts, Russell Scott. "'An Angel has Fallen!:' The Glasgow Land Frauds and the Establishment of the North Carolina Supreme Court." M. A. thesis, North Carolina State University, 1995; available online at http://www.danielhaston.com/history/rev-war/glasgow-frauds.htm.

Grady, John, 1738-1776

Grady Family. "Grady Family Papers, 1793-2002, undated." Manuscript Collection #898, Joyner Library, East Carolina University, Greeneville; online finding aid available at https://digital.lib.ecu.edu/special/ead/findingaids/0898. [Online finding aid description: "Papers (ca. 1793-2002, undated) of the history of the Grady family, of Duplin County, North Carolina including correspondence, legal papers, financial documents, clippings, and photographs relating to various members of the Grady family; also including biographical information on John Grady, who fought in the American Revolution and who is known as the first North Carolinian to die in the war; … Series 5: Consists of printed materials (undated) including two photocopied clippings entitled, 'John Grady of Duplin County, The First North Carolina Man to Die in the Revolutionary War,' by Patsy M. Boyette (undated) that was published by the *Old Kinston Gazette* which focuses on a John Grady who served in the American Revolution. The article gives information not only on this John Grady, who was the first North Carolinian to die in the Revolutionary War, but gives a detail account of the Battle of Moore's Creek and biographical information on Benjamin Franklin Grady."]

Haines, Jeffrey L. "Petition from the Adjoining Inhabitants of the Counties of New Hanover, Duplin, and Bladen, 23 October 1779." *North Carolina Genealogical Society Journal*, 33:3 (August 2007), 244-249. [for a new county]

Graham, Joseph, 1759-1836

Clark, (Mrs.) Walter. "General Joseph Graham." *North Carolina Booklet*, 9:2 (October 1909), 62-78.

Graham, Joseph. *Battle of Ramsour's Mill*. Lincolnton: J. R. Nixon, 1955. [Alternate title: *General Benjamin Lincoln.*]

Graham, Joseph. "Joseph Graham (1759-1836) Papers, 1782, 1813-1836." Manuscript, PC.60, State Archives of North Carolina, Raleigh. [Online catalog description: "Papers of Gen. Joseph Graham, Revolutionary officer, state senator, Lincoln Co. iron manufacturer, and commander of militia in Creek Indian War (1814). Material on the Revolution includes his pension application and drafts of four articles and a letter written by Graham (1820-1821, 1827) concerning action in western North Carolina from June, 1780, to Mar., 1781, with sketches of positions at Cowan's Ford and Clapp's Mill."]

Graham, Joseph. "Celebration of the Anniversary of May 20, 1775." *North Carolina Booklet*, 5:3 (January 1906), 209-216; online: http://digital.ncdcr.gov/cdm/ref/collection/p249901coll37/id/14180. [Online description from "North Carolina Periodicals Index," East Carolina University: "A reprint of an address given by Revolutionary War General Joseph Graham on the first anniversary of the Mecklenburg Declaration of Independence at celebrations in Charlotte, North Carolina on May 20, 1835."]

Graham, Joseph, ed. "General Joseph Graham's 'Narrative of the Revolutionary War in North Carolina in 1780 and 1781'." *North Carolina University Magazine,* 4 (1855), 338-352; 5 (1856), 2-16; 6 (1857), 203; 7 (1858), 203; and in William Henry Hoyt, ed., *The Papers of Archibald D. Murphey*. 2 vols. (Raleigh: North Carolina Historical Commission), 2:300-306.

Graham, Joseph. "Revolutionary Services of General Joseph Graham: Letters and Memorial of Judge Murphey." *North Carolina University Magazine*, 3:10 (December 1854), 433-449.

Graham, William A[lexander]. *General Joseph Graham and His Papers on North Carolina Revolutionary History, with Appendix: An Epitome of North Carolina's Military Services in the Revolutionary War and of the Laws Enacted for Raising Troops*. Raleigh: Edwards & Broughton, 1904.

Graham, William A. "Some Autography Writings of General Joseph Graham." *North Carolina Booklet*, 19:3 (January 1920), 89-91.

Graham, William, active 1770s-1780s

Simpson, Elizabeth. "The Hero of Graham's Fort." *The State: Down Home in North Carolina*, 40:7 (September 1972), 8-9; online: http://digital.ncdcr.gov/cdm/ref/collection/p16062coll18/id/55470. [Online description from "North Carolina Periodicals Index," East Carolina University: "Colonel William Graham, Cleveland County delegate to the Third and Fifth Provincial Congresses in 1775 and 1776, ran afoul of public opinion during his tenure as Commander of the South Fork militia during the Battle of King's Mountain in 1780. After leaving the area with permission to attend to his ailing wife, his successor in command, Major Chronicle, as well as eight of Graham's men, was killed in the battle. Additionally, Chronicle's replacement, Lt. Col. Frederick Hambright and eight enlisted men were seriously wounded. Graham emerged unscathed physically but was branded by some as a cowardly deserter, despite conflicting reports that he participated vigorously in the battle."]

Greene, Nathanael, 1742-1786, in North Carolina

Brooking, Greg. "'I am an independent spirit, and confide in my own resources': Nathanael Greene and His Continental Subordinates, 1780-1781." In Gregory D. Massey and Jim Piecuch, eds., *General Nathanael Greene and the American Revolution in the South* (Columbia, S. C.: University of South Carolina Press, 2012), 85-118.

Capps, Velma Pool. "Velma Pool Capps Collection, 1781-1964." Manuscript, Dolph Briscoe Center for American History, The University of Texas at Austin. [The collection includes materials on: "Nathanael Greene's involvement in the American Revolution."]

Carbone, Gerald M. *Nathanael Greene: A Biography of the American Revolution*. Basingstoke, Eng.: Palgrave Macmillan, 2008; New York: Palgrave, 2008.

"Change in Command at Charlotte Town." *Southern Campaigns of the American Revolution*, 2:12 (December 2005), 1; online: www.southerncampaign.org. [December 2, 1780; Painting of Major General Horatio Gates transfering command of the Southern Army to Major General Nathanael Greene.]

Clodfelter, Mark A. "Between Virtue and Necessity: Nathanael Greene and the Conduct of Civil-Military Relations in the South, 1780-1782." *Military Affairs,* 52:4 (October 1988), 169-175.

Coleman, Charles Washington. "Southern Campaign of General Greene, 1781-2." *Magazine of American History with Notes and Queries*, 7:6 (December 1881), 431-445.

Conrad, Dennis M. "General Nathanael Greene: An Appraisal." In Gregory D. Massey and Jim Piecuch, eds., *General Nathanael Greene and the American Revolution in the South* (Columbia, S. C.: University of South Carolina Press, 2012), 7-28.

Conrad, Dennis M. "Nathanael Greene and the Southern Campaigns, 1780-1783." Ph. D. dissertation, Duke University, 1979.

Corbitt, D. L. "General Green Avoids Encounter with Lord Cornwallis; Great Numbers Join Royal Army." *North Carolina Historical Review*, 3:1 (January 1926), 130-131.

Dederer, John M. "Making Bricks without Straw: Nathanael Greene's Southern Campaigns and Mao Tse-Tung's Mobile War" *Military Affairs*, 47 (October 1983), 115-121.

Edmonds, Thomas J. *The Tactical Retreat of General Nathanael Greene.* Greensboro: J. Graham, 2007.

Erection of Monument to Commemorate the Battle of Guilford Courthouse, N. C., and in Memory of Maj. Gen. Nathanael Greene and the Officers and Soldiers of the Continental Army Who Participated with Him in the Battle of Guilford Courthouse. Washington: G. P. O., 1912.

Ferling, John. "100 Days that Shook the World: The All-But-Forgotten Story of the Unlikely Hero Who Ensured Victory in the American Revolution." *Smithsonian,* (July 2007), 44-54. [Nathanael Greene]

Foote, Anna Elizabeth, and Avery Warner Skinner. *Makers and Defenders of America.* New York: American Book Company, 1910; online through the HathiTrust or Google Books.

Gels, Douglas J. "Finding the Trail to Troublesome Creek: An Application of GIS to Identify Nathanael Greene's Withdrawal Route and Position after the Battle of Guilford Courthouse, 15-16 March 1781." M. A. thesis, University of North Carolina-Greensboro, 2005.

Golway, Terry. *Washington's General: Nathanael Greene and the Triumph of the American Revolution.* New York: Henry Holt, 2005.

Graham, William A. *The Life and Character of Gen. Nathaniel* [*sic*] *Greene, with an Epitome of North Carolina's Services in the Revolutionary War: An Address Delivered at Greensboro, N. C., December, 1860.* Lincolnton: Journal Printing Company, 1901.

Greene, Francis Vinton. *General Greene.* (Great Commanders series) New York: D. Appleton and Company, 1893; reprinted: New York: Research Reprintes, 1970; Bowie, Md.: Heritage Books, 2002.

Greene, Nathanael, 1742-1786. "Nathanael Greene (1742-1786) Papers, 1781, 1782." Manuscript, PC.534, State Archives of North Carolina, Raleigh. [Online catalog description: "Manuscript copy of General Greene's orders of the day, Mar. 16, 1781, including assessment of previous day's action at Guilford Court House and commendation of certain commanders and units. Also copy of statement by Gen. Anthony Wayne and others on rearrangement of officers in reorganized units."]

Greene, Nathanael. "Nathanael Greene Letters, 1778-1783." Manuscript 290-z, Southern Historical Collection, The Louis Round Wilson Special Collections Library, University of North Carolina at Chapel Hill. [Online catalog description: "Nathanael Greene was a Revolutionary War major general in the Continental Army. The collection includes typescript copies of personal, family, military, and political correspondence of Greene to his cousin, Griffin Greene, written from various fields of battle during the Revolution, including Fredericksburg, Va., Philadelphia, West Point, Morristown, and in South Carolina, and containing keen observations on events and personages."]

Greene, Nathanael. "Nathanael Greene Collection of Correspondence, 1775-1786." Manuscript mssGreene correspondence, Huntington Library, San Marino, Calif.; online finding aid available through http://www.oac.cdlib.org/findaid/ark:/13030/tf5z09n7t8/. [Online catalog description: "The collection of Nathanael Greene's correspondence was assembled at the Huntington Library from pieces acquired at different occasions prior to 1927. The collection consists of the original correspondence of Nathanael Greene, largely with Robert Morris and Henry Lee, and more than 2600 copies of the military correspondence gathered by George Washington Greene."]

Greene, Nathanael, "Nathanael Greene Letters, 1781." Manuscript 4/Mss001, Martha Blakeney Hodges Special Collections and University Archives, University of North Carolina, Greensboro. [Online catalog description: "The letters were written in January and February of 1781, in the months immediately preceding the Battle of Guilford Court House on March 15. It is obvious from many of these letters that Greene was appalled by the state of the army in the South. In a long letter to North Carolina Governor Abner Nash dated January 7, 1781, Greene details the present condition of the army and its needs: 'Unless the men are clothed, armed and properly equipped, numbers do but add to the distress of an army. And never was there a more convincing proof of the truth of this proposition, than can be exhibited from the state of our troops at this time; more than one half of whom, are unfit for any kind of duty; hundreds being without shirts, shoes, stockings, or any other clothing, either to render them decent in their appearance, or to secure them from the weather'. One of the main problems Greene faced during these months was equipping the soldiers properly and obtaining food supplies. Greene speaks frankly in his January 13, 1781 letter to General Washington: 'It is true, I came to the Southward in expectation of meeting with difficulties, but they far exceed, what I had any idea of. This Country is so extensive and supplies are so difficult to obtain, that it is impossible to carry on the war, any great length of time with the militia. The waste of Stores and consumption of provisions and forage, must ruin any nation in the

Universe, whose resource is not greater than ours.'" For a fuller description of this collection see the online finding aId: http://libapps.uncg.edu/archon/index.php?p=collections/controlcard&id=16.]

Greene, Nathanael. "Orderly Book of Nathanael Greene, 1781, Apr. 1-July 25." Manuscript mssHM 683, Huntington Library, San Marino, Calif. [Online catalog description: "Orderly book of the Southern Department under the command of Nathanael Greene kept during his operations against Rawdon in the spring and summer of 1781."] – Not sure if these two are relevant specifically to North Carolina.

Greene, Nathanael. "Nathanael Greene Papers, 1775-1785." Manuscript MSS24026, Library of Congress Manuscript Division, Madison Building, Washington, D. C.; online finding aid available at http://hdl.loc.gov/loc.mss/eadmss.ms009092. [Online finding aid description: "The papers document Greene's military career, especially his involvement in the Continental Army's Southern Campaign. There are reconnaissance reports, accounts of battles and skirmishes, reports and instructions from Congress, lists of militia, and returns on casualties, supplies, and reinforcements. Included is Marquis Charles Cornwallis's plan for creating a loyalist militia in South Carolina, dated June 4, 1780; Daniel Morgan's report, January 19, 1781, on the victory at Cowpens, South Carolina, two days earlier; reports of the casualties at Guilford Court House near Greensboro, North Carolina, on March 15, 1781; and correspondence with British officers in Charleston on the treatment of prisoners, 1780-1783."]

Greene, Nathanael. "Nathanael Greene Papers, 1778-1786 [manuscript]." Manuscript Library Service Center Box 1, David M. Rubenstein Rare Book & Manuscript Library, Duke University, Durham. [Online catalog description: "Reports, requisitions, and correspondence pertaining to the quartermaster department of the Continental Army while Greene was quartermaster general, 1778-1780; papers concerning the war in South Carolina and Georgia during Greene's term as commander of the troops in the southern states, 1780-1783; and papers, 1783-1786, pertaining to Greene's business affairs. Correspondents include John Habersham, Wade Hampton, John Houston, Henry Lee, Andrew Pickens, Charles Cotesworth Pinckney, Thomas Posey, and Anthony Wayne."]

Greene, Nathanael, 1742-1786, and Catherine (Caty), Littlefield Greene, 1755-1814. "Nathanael Greene Collection, 1780-1785." Manuscript (artificial collection gathered by the Manuscript Division, William L. Clements Library; 1928-2010. M-337 et al.), Manuscript Division, William L. Clements Library, University of Michigan, Ann Arbor; online finding aId: http://quod.lib.umich.edu/cgi/f/findaid/findaid-idx?c=clementsmss;idno=umich-wcl-M-337gre. [Online catalog description: "The Nathanael Greene papers contain Greene's military and personal correspondence during American Revolution, with the bulk of the collection documenting his command in the Southern Department (1780-1783). The collection includes Greene's communications with George Washington, the Continental Congress, the War Board, state governors, and Continental Army officers and subordinates. Also present are military documents, such as returns, memoranda, and expense reports, and personal letters to and from his wife Catherine." The finding aid for this collection is accessible through the online catalog record.]

Greene, Nathanael; Richard K. Showman, ed. (vols. 1-7); Margaret Cobb and Robert E. McCarthy, assist. eds.; assisted by Joyce Boulind, Noel P. Conlon, and Nathaniel N. Shipton; and Dennis M. Conrad, ed. (vols. 8-12); Roger N. Parks, ed. (vol. 13). *The Papers of General Nathanael Greene*. 13 vols. Chapel Hill: University of North Carolina Press, 1976-2005. [Contents: v. 1. December 1766-December 1776; v. 2. 1 January 1777-16 October 1778; v. 3. 18 October 1778-10 May 1779; v. 4. 11 May 1779-31 October 1779; v. 5. 1 November 1779-31 May 1780; v. 6. 1 June 1780-25 December 1780; v. 7. 26 December 1780-29 March 1781; v. 8. 30 March-10 July 1781; v. 9. 11 July 1781-2 December 1781; v. 10. 3 December 1781-6 April 1782; v. 11. 7 April-30 September 1782; v. 12. 1 October 1782-21 May 1783; v. 13. 22 May 1783-13 June 1786.] [Greene's papers are also available on 4 microfilm reels: Wilmington, Del.: Scholarly Resources, 1989.]

Greene, George Washington. *The Life of Nathanael Greene, Major-General in the Army of the Revolution*. 3 vols. New York: Hurd and Houghton, 1871.

Hairr, John. *Guilford Courthouse: Nathanael Greene's Victory in Defeat, March 15, 1781*. (Battleground America series) Cambridge, Mass.: Da Capo Press, 2002. [Examination of the battle with information about touring the site; includes pictures of the site as it appears today.]

Hall, John W. "*Petite Guerre* in Retreat." *Patriots of the American Revolution*, 4:5 (September/October 2011), 14-19. [the Southern Campaigns, Nathanael Greene, and the path to Yorktown]

Haw, James. "'Every Thing Here Depends upon Opinion': Nathanael Greene and Public Support in the Southern Campaigns of the American Revolution." *South Carolina Historical Magazine,* 109:3 (July 2008), 212-231.

Hill, Daniel Harvey. "Greene's Retreat." *North Carolina Booklet*, 1:7 (November 10, 1901), 3-26; online: http://digital.ncdcr.gov/cdm/ref/collection/p249901coll37/id/14180. [Online description from "North Carolina Periodicals Index," East Carolina University: "A look at General Cornwallis' campaign against North Carolina during the Revolutionary War beginning in Charlotte, where he was opposed by Continental General Nathaniel

Greene. Cornwallis' and Green's maneuvers, as well as positions of the other British and Continental Army forces over the course of a year are discussed."]

Johnson, Joseph. *Sketches of the Life and Correspondence of Nathanael Greene, Major General of the Armies of the United States, in the War of the Revolution Compiled Chiefly from Original Materials*. 2 vols. Charleston, S. C.: A. E. Miller, 1822; reprinted: 2 vols. New York: De Capo Press, 1973.

Kennedy, Michael David. "Major General Nathanael Greene's Role in the Southern Campaign of the American Revolution, December 1780 to December 1781." M. A. Thesis, Jacksonville State University, 1997.

Kyte, George W. "Victory in the South: An Appraisal of General Greene's Strategy in the Carolinas." *North Carolina Historical Review*, 37:3 (July 1960), 321-347. [Online description from "North Carolina Periodicals Index," East Carolina University: "North Carolina militia men proved themselves to be tough soldiers during the War for American Independence, and success in the Carolinas rested on them under the command of General Nathanael Greene."]

Latham, Frank Brown. *The Fighting Quaker: The Southern Campaigns of General Nathanael Greene*. New York: Aladdin Books, 1953.

Lee, Henry, Jr. *The Campaign of 1781 in the Carolinas: with Remarks Historical and Critical on Johnson's Life of Greene; to Which Is Added an Appendix of Original Documents, Relating to the History of the Revolution.* Philadelphia: E. Little, 1824; reprinted: Chicago: Quadrangle Books, 1962; Spartanburg, S. C.: The Reprint Co., 1975; Cranbury, N. J.: Scholar's Bookshelf, 2006.

Lee, Henry, 1787-1873. *Observations on the Writings of Thomas Jefferson, with Particular Reference to the Attack They Contain on the Memory of the Late Gen. Henry Lee.* New York: C. De Behr, 1832.

Liles, Justin S. "The Reluctant Partisan: Nathanael Greene's Southern Campaign, 1780-1783." M. A. thesis, University of North Texas, 2005.

Lodge, Henry Cabot. "The Story of the Revolution: Green's [sic] Campaign in the South." *Scribner's Magazine*, 24 (September 1898), 333-348.

Maass, John R. "'With Humanity, Justice and Moderation': Nathanael Greene and the Reconciliation of the Disaffected in the South, 1780-1783." In Gregory D. Massey and Jim Piecuch, eds., *General Nathanael Greene and the American Revolution in the South* (Columbia, S. C.: University of South Carolina Press, 2012), 191-213.

Massey, Gregory D. "Independence and Slavery: The Transformation of Nathanael Greene, 1781-1786." In Gregory D. Massey and Jim Piecuch, eds., *General Nathanael Greene and the American Revolution in the South* (Columbia, S. C.: University of South Carolina Press, 2012), 238-262.

Massey, Gregory D., and Jim Piecuch, eds., *General Nathanael Greene and the American Revolution in the South.* Columbia, S. C.: University of South Carolina Press, 2012.

McIntyre, James R. "Nathanael Greene: Soldier-Statesman of the War of Independence in South Carolina." In Gregory D. Massey and Jim Piecuch, eds., *General Nathanael Greene and the American Revolution in the South* (Columbia, S. C.: University of South Carolina Press, 2012), 167-190.

Morehead, Joseph Motley. *Appeal to the Descendants of General Nathanael Greene for His Remains, and to Congress for a Monument Over These, at Guilford Battle Ground, N. C.* Greensboro: [s. n.], 1902.

Morgan, Curtis F. Jr. "A Merchandise of Small Wares": Nathanael Greene's Northern Apprenticeship, 1775-1780." In Gregory D. Massey and Jim Piecuch, eds., *General Nathanael Greene and the American Revolution in the South* (Columbia, S. C.: University of South Carolina Press, 2012), 29-55.

Moseley, John M., and Robert M. Calhoon. "Nathanael Greene and Republican Ethics." In Gregory D. Massey and Jim Piecuch, eds., *General Nathanael Greene and the American Revolution in the South* (Columbia, S. C.: University of South Carolina Press, 2012), 147-166.

Rankin, Hugh F. "Greene and Cornwallis: The Campaign in the Carolinas, 1780-1781." M. A. thesis, University of North Carolina at Chapel Hill, 1950; published with the same title: Raleigh: N. C. Divison of Archives & History, 1976.

Roe, Clara Goldsmith. "Major General Nathanael Greene and the Southern Campaign of the American Revolution, 1780-83." Ph. D. Dissertation, University of Michigan, 1947.

Simms, William Gilmore, ed. *The Life of Nathanael Greene, Major-General in the Army of the Revolution.* New York: Derby & Jackson, 1856.

Thane, Elswyth. *The Fighting Quaker: Nathanael Greene.* New York: Hawthorn Books, 1972.

Thayer, Theodore. *Nathanael Green: Strategist of the American Revolution.* New York: Twayne Publishers, 1960.

Treacy, Mildred Freeman. "Nathaniel [sic] Greene and the Southern Campaign: August, 1780-April 1781." Ph. D. dissertation, University of Utah, 1962.

Treacy, Mildred Freeman. *Prelude to Yorktown: The Southern Campaign of Nathaniel* [sic] *Greene, 1780-1781.* Chapel Hill: University of North Carolina Press, 1963.

Tretler, David Allan. "The Making of a Revolutionary General: Nathanael Greene, 1742-1779." Ph. D. dissertation, Rice University, 1986.

Wilson, David K. "'Against the Tide of Misfortune:' Civil-Military Relations, Provincialism, and the Southern Command in the Revolution." In Gregory D. Massey and Jim Piecuch, eds., *General Nathanael Greene and the American Revolution in the South* (Columbia, S. C.: University of South Carolina Press, 2012), 56-84.

Greenlee, Grace, 1750-1823

Ervin, W. C. "Grace Greenlee – A Revolutionary Heroine." *Journal of the Burke County Genealogical Society*, 18:3 (August 2000), 11-17.

Ervin, William Carson. "Grace Greenlee, a Revolutionary Heroine." *North Carolina Booklet,* 15:1 (July 1915), 12-27.

Ervin, William Carson. "Grace Greenlee: A Revolutionary Heroine." Manuscript Mss7:1 G8456:1, Virginia Historical society, Richmond. [Online catalog description: Concerns Grace Greenlee's early life in Virginia and her experiences in western North Carolina during the American Revolution. Also, includes genealogical data concerning the Greenlee, McDowell, and Tate families."]

Gregory, Isaac, c. 1737-1800

Banastre Tarleton, *History of the Campaigns of Seventeen Eighty and Seventeen Eighty-One in the Southern Province of North America.* Ayer Company Publishers, Inc., 1975 (orig. pub. 1787)

Bennett, Charles E., and Donald R. Lennon. *A Quest for Glory: Major General Robert Howe and the American Revolution.* Chapel Hill: University of North Carolina Press, 1991. [Publisher's description: "Born into a wealthy and prominent Cape Fear River plantation family, Howe became a militia officer, justice of the peace, and legislator. In 1775 he was appointed colonel of the Second North Carolina Regiment and became commanding general of the Southern Department and the highest ranking officer in the states south of Virginia. He also served as a division commander with General Washington's main army in the New York Highlands, commanded the crucial West Point post, and put down mutinies in the American army."]

Daniel E. Harmon, *Lord Cornwallis.* Chelsea House Publishers, 2001.

Hoffman, Ronald, Thad W. Tate, and Peter J. Albert, eds. *An Uncivil War: The Southern Backcountry during the American Revolution.* Charlottesville: The University Press of Virginia, for the United States Capitol Historical Society, 1985.

Lewis, J. D. "The Patriot Leaders in North Carolina: Isaac Gregory: Lt. Colonel in the Pasquotank County Regiment of Militia – 1775; Colonel over the 2nd Pasquotank County Regiment of Militia - 1775-1777; Colonel over the Camden County Regiment of Militia - 1777-1779; Brigadier General over the Edenton District Brigade of Militia - 1779-1783." Online: http://www.carolana.com/NC/Revolution/patriot_leaders_nc_isaac_gregory.html.

Willard, Linda. "General Isaac Gregory." *Carolina Trees & Branches*, 22:2 (April 2013), 33-34.

Hannah, active 1770s

Calhoon, Robert. *Religion and the American Revolution in North Carolina.* Raleigh, N. C.: North Carolina Department of Cultural Resources, Division of Archives and History, 1976. ["A Quaker Asks for Permission to Free a Slave," 46. Thomas Newby requests the freedom of his elderly slave, Hannah, who is too feeble to work and once was an excellent midwife.]

Haralson, Paul, ca. 1720-1805, and Herndon Haralson, 1757-1847

Haralson, Herndon; Jonathan Kennon Thompson Smith, ed. *Selected Gleanings form the Diaries of Captain Herndon Haralson.* Jackson, Tenn.: J. K. T. Smith, 2006.

Harrelson, Ronald. "Herndon Haralson." Online at NCpedia.

Haralson, Herndon. "Herndon Haralson Papers, 1791, 1842," Typescript PC.556, State Archives of North Carolina, Raleigh. [Online catalog description: "Typed copies of Haralson's Caswell Co. marriage bond and of his autobiographical sketch about his ancestors, Revolutionary War service, and later life."]

Lewis, J. D. "The American Revolution in North Carolina: Capt. Herndon Haralson's Regiment." Online: http://www.carolana.com/NC/Revolution/patriots_nc_capt_herndon_haralson.html.

Styles, Marshall L. *Captain Herndon Haralson, a Revolutionary War Soldier from Caswell County, North Carolina*. Asheville: Old Buncombe County Genealogical Society, 2010. [Copy available at University of North Carolina at Chapel Hill.]

Harnett, Cornelius, 1723-1781

Connor, R. D. W. *Cornelius Harnett: An Essay in North Carolina History*. Raleigh: Edwards and Broughton Printing Company, 1909; reprinted: Freeport, N. Y.: Books for Libraries Press, [1971].

Connor, Robert Digges Wimberly. "Cornelius Harnett: The Pride of the Cape Fear." *North Carolina Booklet*, 5:3 (January 1906), 171-201. [Online description from "North Carolina Periodicals Index," East Carolina University: "An enthusiastic biographical sketch of Wilmington merchant, planter, and Revolutionary War statesman Cornelius Harnett, Jr."]

Harnett, Cornelius. "Cornelius Harnett Letters, 1777-1778." Manuscript 311-z, Southern Historical Collection, Louis Round Wilson Special Collections Library, University of North Carolina, Chapel Hill; online finding aid available at http://www2.lib.unc.edu/mss/inv/h/Harnett,Cornelius.html. [Online finding aid description: "Cornelius Harnett (1723-1781) of Wilmington, N. C., was a leader of revolutionary activity in North Carolina and a delegate to the Continental Congress. The collection contains letters from Harnett in Philadelphia, Pa. and York, Pa., to his friend and neighbor, William Wilkinson, of Wilmington, N. C., containing messages for Mrs. Harnett, information on provisions and prices in the North, political and military news, and occasional comment on the work of the Continental Congress."]

Harnett, Cornelius. "Cornelius Harnett Papers, 1742-1746, 1775, 1928." Manuscript PC.559 (MARS ID: 1069; record group), State Archives of North Carolina, Raleigh. [Online catalog description: "Letter of May 8, 1775, from Cornelius Harnett, Jr., Wilmington Committee of Safety, to Richard Quince in Brunswick, forwarding southward the dispatch bearing news of the Battle of Lexington; with copy of letter from historian W. H. Hoyt concerning letter's purchase, and the papers of Archibald D. Murphy in which it was found (1928). Also typed copies of inventory and sale of estate, including slaves, of Cornelius Harnett, Sr., of New Hanover Co.; and of a Bladen Co. deed from Mary Harnett (1742)."]

Howell, Andrew Jackson. *Cornelius Harnett, A Revolutionary Patriot*. Wilmington: Wm. L. de Rosset, Jr., 1896.

Morgan, David T. "Cornelius Harnett: Revolutionary Leader and Delegate to the Continental Congress." *North Carolina Historical Review*, 49:3 (July 1972), 229-241. [Online description from "North Carolina Periodicals Index," East Carolina University: "Known as 'the Samuel Adams of North Carolina' for his anti-British sentiment and activities, Cornelius Harnett was also a delegate to the Continental Congress during the Revolutionary War. His contributions to the American cause have given him minor fame in American history as an early statesman."]

Smith, C. Alphonso. *Our Debt to Cornelius Harnett: An Address*. [Chapel Hill, N. C.: The University, 1907.

Smith, C. Alphonso. "Our Debt to Cornelius Harnett." In *Addresses Delivered under the Auspices of the North Carolina Society of the Colonial Dames of American, 1900-1926*. [S. l.]: Jackson & Bell, [1927?].

Watson, Alan D., Dennis R. Lawson, and Donald R. Lennon. *Harnett, Hooper & Howe: Revolutionary Leaders of the Lower Cape Fear*. Wilmington, N. C.: L. T. Moore Memorial Commission and the Lower Cape Fear Historical Society, 1949. [Cornelius Harnett (1723-1781); William Hooper (1742-1790); Robert Howe (1732-1785)]

Winstead, Thomas P. "Cornelius Harnett, a North Carolina Patriot." *Recall: The North Carolina Military History Society's Newsletter*, 19:1 (Spring 2013), 14-17. [Online description from "North Carolina Periodicals Index," East Carolina University: "The group known as the 'founding fathers' of the United States came from all thirteen colonies. Winstead recounts the life of one of them – Cornelius Harnett, Jr. – who is all but unknown to North Carolinians today but who deserves to be counted among them. 'He was neither a signer of the Declaration of Independence or a framer of the Constitution, but instead was one of those who aided the cause to resist the efforts of the British Government'."]

Harrington, Agnes Hill, 1730-c. 1797

Dennison, Bob. "Grandmother Agnes Hill Harrington … A Patriot." *The Middle Tennessee Journal of Genealogy & History*, 22:4 (Spring 2009), 147-148. [Chatham County, North Carolina]

Harrington, William Henry, 1748-1809

Harrington, Henry William, 1748-1809. "Henry William Harrington Papers, 1775-1890." Manuscript 314, Southern Historical Collection, Louis Round Wilson Special Collections Library, University of North Carolina, Chapel

Hill; online finding aid available at http://www2.lib.unc.edu/mss/inv/h/Harrington,Henry_William.html. [Online finding aid description: "Henry William Harrington (1748-1809) was a brigadier general in the American Revolution, a legislator in both North Carolina and South Carolina, and a planter. His son, Henry William Harrington Jr. (1793-1868) was a successful planter, businessman, and landowner of Richmond County, N. C., who served in the United States Navy during the War of 1812 and as a representative in the North Carolina House of Commons and to Constitutional Convention. The collection is chiefly political, military, and family correspondence of Revolutionary General Henry William Harrington and Henry William Harrington Jr. Early papers concern military actions of the Revolution in the Carolinas and political and legal affairs in its aftermath. Correspondents include John Auld, Horatio Gates, Charles W. Goldsborough, William Barry Grove, Paul Hamilton, John Henry, A. M. Hopper, Charles Cotesworth Pinckney, and Benjamin W. Williams, among others."]

Harvey, John, 1724-1775 or 1776?

Connor, R. D. W. "John Harvey." *North Carolina Booklet*, 8:1 (July 1908), 3-42; online: http://digital.ncdcr.gov/cdm/ref/collection/p249901coll37/id/14180. [Online description from "North Carolina Periodicals Index," East Carolina University: "This article chronicles family and personal deeds of John Harvey who was integral to the colonial government in North Carolina prior to the Revolutionary War and who was also an important cog in the push for independence from England leading up to the Revolution."]

Harvey, John, 1725?-1775. *Advertisement: Perquimans County, Feb. 11, 1775. The Respective Counties and Towns in This Colony Are Requested to Elect Delegates to Represent Them in Convention, Who Are Desired to Meet at the Town of Newbern on Monday the 3^d Day of April Next.* Newbern: Printed by James Davis, 1775; micropublished: (Early American Imprints. First Series. No. 42761) New York: Readex Microprint, 1985.

Lawrence, R. C. "John Harvey: Colonial Leader." *The State: A Weekly Survey of North Carolina*, 15:22 (November 1947), 9, 19-20; online: http://digital.ncdcr.gov/cdm/ref/collection/p16062coll18/id/21415. [Online description from "North Carolina Periodicals Index," East Carolina University: "John Harvey did more than any other man to bring on the Revolution in North Carolina; and had he not died in 1776, there is no question but that he, and not Richard Caswell, would have been the first Governor of North Carolina after its organization as an independent commonwealth."]

Roger, Lou. "John Harvey: Colonial Leader." *We the People of North Carolina*, 6:2 (June 1948), 14-15. [Online description from "North Carolina Periodicals Index," East Carolina University: "Born in Perquimans County, John Harvey was a colonial and Revolutionary leader. His bold work in behalf of freedom from England was one of the leading causes for the North Carolina colony's early stand for independence. Harvey died before independence for all the colonies was achieved."]

Troxel, George. "John Harvey." *North Carolina Bicentennial Newsletter*, (special edition, 4 July 1976).

Hawkins, Benjamin, 1754-1816

Grant, C. L., and Gerald H. Davis. "The Wedding of Col. Benjamin Hawkins." *North Carolina Historical Review*, 54:3 (July 1977), 308-314. [Online description from "North Carolina Periodicals Index," East Carolina University: "This article looks at the deathbed preparations undertaken in January of 1812 by Benjamin Hawkins, principal agent to the Indians south of Ohio, as he suffered from 'a severe fit of pleurisy,' with no expectation of recovery. One of those last actions was to legally marry his common-law wife of more than a decade, Lavinia Downs. The episode passed, however, and Hawkins' health was much improved four days later. Shortly after, a letter was written by the Moravian missionary who performed the marriage, Karsten Petersen, detailing the events that had transpired. A reprint of the letter is included."]

Harmon, George D. "Benjamin Hawkins and the Federal Factory System." *North Carolina Historical Review*, 9:2 (April 1932), 138-152; online: http://digital.ncdcr.gov/cdm/ref/collection/p16062coll9/id/4207. [Online description from "North Carolina Periodicals Index," East Carolina University: "Benjamin Hawkins was born in Warren County on August 15, 1754 served as George Washington's interpreter during the Revolutionary War before returning to his native state. From 1787-1795 he served as a state legislator before being appointed to Superintendent to all Native American tribes south of the Ohio River. In this role, he was influential in establishing favorable trading practice between American and Native American tribes throughout the south."]

Hawkins, Benjamin. "Letter from Benjamin Hawkins to Governor Caswell [Bath, 1780]." *Magazine of History,* 1:4 (April 1905), 248-250.

North Carolina (State). General Assembly. "[Document dated:] 1780: Accounts of Jacob Blount and Benjamin Hawkins." Manuscript; General Assembly Record Group; Session Records, August-September 1780; Joint

Papers, Committee Papers, Resolutions, Senate Bills, House Bills, Box 1 (MARS ID: 66.8.22.6.9; item), State Archives of North Carolina, Raleigh. [Online catalog description: "Blount was paymaster of the North Carolina Continental Line; Hawkins' account involves John W. Stanly."]

Pound, Merritt Boodworth. "Colonel Benjamin Hawkins, North Carolina Benefactor of the Southern Indians." *North Carolina Historical Review*, 19:1 (January 1942); 1-21; online: http://digital.ncdcr.gov/cdm/ref/collection/p16062coll9/id/4207; 19:2 (April 1942), 168-186.]

Henderson, Richard, 1735-1785

Clark, Walter. "The Colony of Transylvania." *North Carolina Booklet*, 3:9 (January 1904), 5-39; online: http://digital.ncdcr.gov/cdm/ref/collection/p249901coll37/id/14180. [Online description from "North Carolina Periodicals Index," East Carolina University: "This article describes a 1775 scheme to acquire, settle, and hold a large piece of land, called 'Transylvania County,' lying between the Kentucky and Cumberland rivers, in what is now Tennessee and Kentucky. Details include Boonesborough's establishment by a group of men led by North Carolina Judge Richard Henderson and frontiersman Daniel Boone. A reprint of Henderson's journal documenting his journey into this territory is included."]

Henderson, Archibald. "The Creative Forces in Westward Expansion: Henderson and Boone." *North Carolina Booklet*, 14:3 (January 1915), 111-139; online: http://digital.ncdcr.gov/cdm/ref/collection/p249901coll 37/id/14180. [Online description from "North Carolina Periodicals Index," East Carolina University: "The the westward expansion of America was aided by two one-time residents of North Carolina: Daniel Boone and Richard Henderson. Though they differed in background and origins, the two became acquainted as early settlers of Rowan County. Their combined and related efforts helped open areas west of the mountains to settlement."]

Henderson, Archibald. "Richard Henderson: The Authorship of the Cumberland Compact and the Founding of Nashville." *Tennessee Historical Quarterly*, 2:3 (September 1916) 155-174; reprinted in: *North Carolina Booklet*, 21:1-4 (July 1921-April 1922), 28-50.

Henderson, Archibald. "Richard Henderson and the Occupation of Kentucky." *Mississippi Valley Historical Review,* 1:3 (December 1914), 341-363.

Howell, Edward Vernon. "E. V. Howell Papers, 1725-1929." Manuscript 1060, Southern Historical Collection, Louis Round Wilson Special Collections Library, University of North Carolina, Chapel Hill; online finding aid available at http://www2.lib.unc.edu/mss/inv/h/Howell,E.V.html. [Online finding aid description: "E. V. (Edward Vernon) Howell (1872-1931) was the founder of the University of North Carolina's School of Pharmacy and its dean for 33 years. The collection includes Howell's personal and professional correspondence, 1900-1929, …, together with historical materials, 1725-1871 (originals and copies), largely connected with North Carolina. The latter includes items relating to Richard Henderson (1735-1785), and the Transylvania (Ky.) Land Company; the Revolutionary War in North Carolina…"]

Hewes, Joseph, 1730-1779

Abernethy, Mrs. Max. "Signers of the Declaration." *The State: A Weekly Survey of North Carolina*, 19:6 (July 1951), 3, 17; online: http://digital.ncdcr.gov/cdm/ref/collection/p16062coll18/id/27249. [Online description from "North Carolina Periodicals Index," East Carolina University: "There were three men from North Carolina who signed the Declaration of Independence, but none of the three was a native-born son of the Old North State."]

Connor, Robert Digges Wimberly. "Joseph Hewes and the Declaration of Independence." *North Carolina Booklet*, 10:3 (January 1911), 155-164; online: http://digital.ncdcr.gov/cdm/ref/collection/p249901coll37/id/14180. [Online description from "North Carolina Periodicals Index," East Carolina University: "Colonial North Carolina politician Joseph Hewes enjoyed an undeserved reputation for being slow to embrace the cause independence."]

Hewes, Joseph. "Joseph Hewes Papers, 1736-1936." Manuscript PC.591 (MARS ID: 1101; record group), State Archives of North Carolina, Raleigh. [Online catalog description: "Papers of Hewes, member of General Assembly for Edenton, delegate to Continental Congress (1774-1776), and signer of Declaration of Independence. Included are … letter (May 26, 1776) from Hewes at Philadelphia to Samuel Johnston about prisoners arriving from North Carolina with Colonel Haynes, medicines sent, British shipload of arms captured, and events in town. Photograph of draft letter from John Paul Jones to Hewes (Oct., 1776) concerns problems of infant navy, with discussion of expedition to Canadian waters, privateers, and need for a department to regulate the navy. Also legislative settlement of accounts with Col. Nicholas Long, deputy quartermaster general (1779).

Later material (1919-1936) about Hewes concerns his burial place; Pennsylvania Supreme Court case involving him in 1762; remains of his shipyard near Edenton (1936); and a statue of him."]

Hewes, Joseph. "Joseph Hewes Papers, 1765-1776." Manuscript 1381-z, Southern Historical Collection, Louis Round Wilson Special Collections Library, University of North Carolina, Chapel Hill; online finding aid available at http://www2.lib.unc.edu/mss/inv/h/Hewes,Joseph.html. [Online catalog description: "Joseph Hewes (1730-1779) was a signer of the Declaration of Independence from North Carolina and member of the Continental Congress. The collection includes miscellaneous papers, consisting of copies of letters and originals of two letters and a postscript to a third letter from Hewes. The two letters were written from Philadelphia, 6 February and 27 March 1776, to Robert Smith, Williamsburg, Va.; they concern the brig 'Fanny,' lying in the York River, and arrangements for chartering vessels to go to Europe to procure articles needed by the army and navy and to sell tobacco and other American exports. The postscript, 7 January 1776 {misdated 1775}, is to a letter from Hewes to Samuel Johnston; it reports the arrival of vessels with powder and saltpetre."]

Hooper, William, and Joseph Hewes. *To the Committees of the Several Towns and Counties of the Province of North-Carolina: Appointed for the Purpose of Carrying into Execution the Resolves of the Continental Congress*. [New Bern, N. C.?: Printed by James Davis?], 1775. [William Hooper, 1742-1790; Joseph Hewes, 1730-1779; Richard Caswell, 1729-1789. Description from the online Hollis Catalog, Harvard University: "Circular letter, exhorting the people of North Carolina to awake to their present danger, and to train and equip a militia; signed and dated on p. [2]: William Hooper, Joseph Hewes, Richard Caswell. Philadelphia, June 19, 1775. Hooper, Hewes and Caswell were the delegates to the Continental Congress from North Carolina."]

Lawrence, R. C. "Signers of the Declaration." *The State: A Weekly Survey of North Carolina*, 8:42 (March 1941), 5, 21; online: http://digital.ncdcr.gov/cdm/ref/collection/p16062coll18/id/39248. [Online description from "North Carolina Periodicals Index," East Carolina University: "It is a singular fact that none of the three North Carolina signers of the Declaration of Independence was a native of North Carolina. William Hooper was from Massachusetts, Joseph Hewes from New Jersey, and John Penn from Virginia, but all rendered distinguished service to North Carolina and the nation as a whole."]

Marks, Jan Allen. "Leadership and Deference in North Carolina: A Study of Four Revolutionary Leaders." Honors Essay, University of North Carolina, Chapel Hill, 1979. [Joseph Hewes, William Hooper, James Iredell, and Samuel Johnston]

Martin, Michael Glover, Jr. "Joseph Hewes, 'Reluctant Revolutionary?': a Study of a North Carolina Whig and the War for American Independence (1730-1779)." M. A. thesis, University of North Carolina at Chapel Hill, 1969.

McCurry, Allan J. "Joseph Hewes and Independence: A Suggestion." *North Carolina Historical Review*, 40:4 (October 1963), 455-464; online: http://digital.ncdcr.gov/cdm/ref/collection/p16062coll9/id/4207. [Online description from "North Carolina Periodicals Index," East Carolina University: "This article discusses historical assumptions made based on John Adams' account of Continental Congress proceedings. The account states that success of the final vote on and in favor of independence depended on the sudden decision of Joseph Hewes of North Carolina, and examines whether he was in the 'cold party' or if he was a moderate."]

Park, Mrs. Robert E. "Homes of the Signers of the Declaration of Independence." *American Monthly Magazine*, 20:4 (April 1902), 325-328. [Includes North Carolina signers: William Hooper, Joseph Hewes, John Penn]

Sikes, Walter. "Joseph Hewes." *North Carolina Booklet*, 4:5 (September 1904), 24-36; online: http://digital.ncdcr.gov/cdm/ref/collection/p249901coll37/id/14180. [Online description from "North Carolina Periodicals Index," East Carolina University: "This article examines 18th century Edenton resident, colonial leader, and Continental Congress delegate Joseph Hewes. A Quaker merchant, Hewes was one of the original signers of the Declaration of Independence who died in Philadelphia in 1779 at the age of fifty."]

Hill, Whitmill, 1743-1797

Swain, David L[owry]. "Life and Letters of Whitmill Hill." *North Carolina University Magazine, 10:7* (March 1861), 385-398. [Whitmill was a member of the Provincial Congress in 1775, and a delegate to the Continental Congress in 1780. This article describes his involvement in the American Revolution and includes transcriptions of some letters he sent about Revolutionary activities.]

Hogun, James, 17??-1781

Clark, Walter. "Career of General James Hogun, One of North Carolina's Revolutionary Officers." *Magazine of American History with Notes and Queries*, 28:4 (October 1892), 285-287.

Clark, Walter. "Career of General James Hogun, One of North Carolina's Revolutionary Officers." *North Carolina Booklet*, 11:2 (October 1911), 105-110.

Hooper, William, 1742-1790

Abernethy, Mrs. Max. "Signers of the Declaration." *The State: A Weekly Survey of North Carolina*, 19:6 (July 1951), 3, 17; online: http://digital.ncdcr.gov/cdm/ref/collection/p16062coll18/id/27249. [Online description from "North Carolina Periodicals Index," East Carolina University: "There were three men from North Carolina who signed the Declaration of Independence, but none of the three was a native-born son of the Old North State."]

Alderman, Edwin Anderson. *Address by Edwin A. Alderman, Professor of the University of North Carolina on the Life of William Hooper, "The Prophet of American Independence:" Guilford Battleground, July 4, 1894*. Chapel Hill: University Press, 1894.

Hooper, Archibald MacLaine. "Life of William Hooper, Signer of the Declaration of Independence." *The North Carolina Booklet*, 5:1 (July 1905), 37-71; online: http://digital.ncdcr.gov/cdm/ref/collection/p249901coll37/id/14180. [Online description from "North Carolina Periodicals Index," East Carolina University: "This is a re-print of a biographical sketch of William Hooper, signer of the Declaration of Independence, that first appeared in the *Hillsboro Recorder* in November-December of 1822, published in four parts. The sketch was written by Hooper's nephew, Archibald Maclaine Hooper, and the preface to the sketch was written by his great-great-grand-daughter Mrs. Spier Whitaker, nee Fannie De Berniere Hooper."]

Hooper, William. *At a General Meeting of the Inhabitants of the District of Wilmington in the Province of North-Carolina, Held at the Town of Wilmington, July 21st, 1774. William Hooper, Esq. Chairman*. Wilmington: Printed by Adam Boyd, 1774; micropublished: (Early American Imprints. First Series. No. 42755) New York: Readex Microprint, 1985. [Note: "Resolutions appointing a Committee of Correspondence and recommending other measures concerning 'the present alarming state of British America'."]

Hooper, William. "Memorandum Book, 1780-1783." Microfilm of the original in the New-York Historical Society, New York City, MfP.50 (MARS ID: 2560; record group), State Archives of North Carolina, Raleigh. [Online catalog description: "Memorandum book of Hooper, attorney, signer of the Declaration of Independence, member of the Continental Congress, 1775-1777. Many of the entries are accounts of fees received for legal services in criminal and civil cases in superior courts, with clients including John Alston, Richard Blackledge, Richard Dobbs Spaight, Thomas Harvey, and Samuel Swann. Other entries record traveling expenses, wardrobe, purchase of land, money borrowed and lent, bonds and notes held, and Negro laborers sent to a saltworks. The original is in the collections of the New-York Historical Society."]

Hooper, William. *To the Committees of the Several Towns and Counties of the Province of North-Carolina, Appointed for the Purpose of Carrying into Execution the Resolves of the Continental Congress*. Newbern: [Printed by James Davis?], 1775; micropublished: (Early American Imprints. First Series. No. 42946) New York: Readex Microprint, 1985. [Online description: "Circular letter, exhorting the people of North Carolina to awake to their present danger, and to train and equip a militia; signed and dated on p. {2}: William Hooper, Joseph Hewes, Richard Caswell. Philadelphia, June 19, 1775. Hooper, Hewes and Caswell were the delegates to the Continental Congress from North Carolina."]

Hooper, William. "Unpublished Letters by William Hooper." *Historical Magazine,* 4:1 (August 1868), 87-90.

Hooper, William. "William Hooper (1742-1790) Papers, 1773-1810." Manuscript, PC.1141 (MARS ID: 1651; record group), State Archives of North Carolina, Raleigh. [Online catalog description: "Papers relating to Hooper, lawyer, legislator from New Hanover and Orange counties, and delegate to Continental Congress (1774-1777), including letter from Commissary General Joseph Trumbull describing the siege of Boston (Mar., 1776); one concerning medicines ordered; and one from loyalist Mary Middleton about vessel taken as prize (n. d.). Letters from Hooper include photocopies of two undated letters (Nov.-Dec., 1775?) about politics in Pennsylvania, American vessels and prizes, need for imported powder, and war news; and three postwar letters, one a copy, from Hooper in Hillsborough to his brother in Wilmington about a lawsuit, his sons, the constitutional ratification conventions, Willie Jones, and Orange Co. and Wilmington politics (1788). Miscellaneous items include a manuscript biographical sketch of Hooper, written about 1825 and containing comments on Cape Fear society before the Revolution and quotations from Hooper's contemporaries; copies of letters from John Penn and Cornelius Harnett to Governor Caswell about militia, pay of a major general and staff, provisions for army, and prisoners of war (Feb. 18, 1776), and from Joseph Hewes to James Iredell about his ill health, Congress, and Hessians (May 17, 1776); copy of proclamation by Gen. Jethro Sumner pardoning deserters and 'delinquents' who join the troops (Jan. 25, 1781); and copies of obituary (1810) and biographical sketch of Judge Alfred Moore."]

Hooper, William. "William Hooper Papers, 1770-1822." Manuscript 352-z, Southern Historical Collection, Louis Round Wilson Special Collections Library, University of North Carolina, Chapel Hill; online finding aid available at http://www2.lib.unc.edu/mss/inv/h/Hooper,William.html. [Online finding aid description: "William

Hooper of North Carolina was a leader in the American Revolution and a signer of the Declaration of Independence. The collection contains a biographical sketch of William Hooper by his nephew Archibald Maclaine Hooper that appeared in the *Hillsboro Recorder* in 1822; a letter from John H. Craig, British commander at Wilmington, N. C., to Hooper, 1781, concerning business of the North Carolina revolutionary government; and a writ signed by Hooper in the 1770 Chatham County, N.C., case of Peter O'Neal versus Charles Harrington."]

Hooper, William, and Joseph Hewes. *To the Committees of the Several Towns and Counties of the Province of North-Carolina: Appointed for the Purpose of Carrying into Execution the Resolves of the Continental Congress*. [New Bern, N. C.?: Printed by James Davis?], 1775. [William Hooper, 1742-1790; Joseph Hewes, 1730-1779; Richard Caswell, 1729-1789. Description from the online Hollis Catalog, Harvard University: "Circular letter, exhorting the people of North Carolina to awake to their present danger, and to train and equip a militia; signed and dated on p. [2]: William Hooper, Joseph Hewes, Richard Caswell. Philadelphia, June 19, 1775. Hooper, Hewes and Caswell were the delegates to the Continental Congress from North Carolina."]

Kneip, Robert Charles. "William Hooper, 1742-1790: Misunderstood Patriot." Ph. D. dissertation, Tulane University, 1980.

Lawrence, R. C. "Signers of the Declaration." *The State: A Weekly Survey of North Carolina*, 8:42 (March 1941), 5, 21; online: http://digital.ncdcr.gov/cdm/ref/collection/p16062coll18/id/39248. [Online description from "North Carolina Periodicals Index," East Carolina University: "It is a singular fact that none of the three North Carolina signers of the Declaration of Independence was a native of North Carolina. William Hooper was from Massachusetts, Joseph Hewes from New Jersey, and John Penn from Virginia, but all rendered distinguished service to North Carolina and the nation as a whole."]

Lawrence, R. C. "William Hooper, Patriot." *The State: A Weekly Survey of North Carolina*, 13:16 (September 1945), 7, 18. [Online description from "North Carolina Periodicals Index," East Carolina University: "William Hooper was one of North Carolina's three signers of the Declaration of Independence; he was also an outstanding lawyer and a leader in the political life of the State."]

Marks, Jan Allen. "Leadership and Deference in North Carolina: A Study of Four Revolutionary Leaders." Honors Essay, University of North Carolina, Chapel Hill, 1979. [Joseph Hewes, William Hooper, James Iredell, and Samuel Johnston]

Park, Mrs. Robert E. "Homes of the Signers of the Declaration of Independence." *American Monthly Magazine*, 20:4 (April 1902), 325-328. [Includes North Carolina signers: William Hooper, Joseph Hewes, John Penn]

Roger, Lou. "William Hooper." *We the People of North Carolina*, 5:3 (July 1947), 14-15, 19 [Online description from "North Carolina Periodicals Index," East Carolina University: "William Hooper was a native of Massachusetts. He came to North Carolina as a young lawyer in 1764 and later married Anne Clark of Wilmington. He became an ardent supporter of independence from England and is one of three North Carolinians who signed the Declaration of Independence. His support of independence was not without cost, and his home, his fortune, and his health were lost in the interest of the new nation."]

Watson, Alan D., Dennis R. Lawson, and Donald R. Lennon. *Harnett, Hooper & Howe: Revolutionary Leaders of the Lower Cape Fear*. Wilmington, N. C.: L. T. Moore Memorial Commission and the Lower Cape Fear Historical Society, 1949. [Cornelius Harnett (1723-1781); William Hooper (1742-1790); Robert Howe (1732-1785)]

Howe, Robert, Major General, 1732-1785

Bellamy, John D. "General Robert Howe." *North Carolina Booklet*, 7:3 (January 1908), 165-192; online: http://digital.ncdcr.gov/cdm/ref/collection/p249901coll37/id/14180. [Online description from "North Carolina Periodicals Index," East Carolina University: "A reprint of an address given by North Carolina Congressman John D. Bellamy to the 57th Congress of the United States about H. R. 17356, a bill to erect an equestrian statue of Revolutionary War Major General Robert Howe in Wilmington, NC. Biographical, career, and military information on Howe is provided."]

Bellamy, John D., Jr. *Sketch of Maj. Gen. Robert Howe, of the American Revolution: Delivered March 16th, [1882]*. Wilmington: S. G. Hall for the Historical & Scientific Society, 1882

Bellamy, John Dillard. *Speech of Hon. John D. Bellamy, of North Carolina, in the House of Representatives, February 14, 1903: On H. R. 17356, to Erect an Equestrian Statue at Wilmington, N. C., to the Memory of Maj. Gen. Robert Howe, of the American Revolution*. Washington: [s. n], 1903.

Bennett, C. E., and D. R. Lennon. *A Quest for Glory: Major General Robert Howe and the American Revolution*. University of North Carolina Press, Chapel Hill, North Carolina, 1991.

Howe, Robert. "General Robert Howe Letter, 1779." Manuscript MS 2514, Hargrett Rare Book and Manuscript Library, University of Georgia Libraries, Athens. [Online catalog description: "The collection consists of one ALS written by Major-General Robert Howe in Charleston, South Carolina to General Benjamin Lincoln, his successor in command of the Department of the South. The letter is five pages, quarto, and is dated January 23, 1779. An address leaf is included. The letter concerns the transfer of command of the army of the Department of the South in Savannah from Howe to Lincoln."]

Howe, Robert. *Proceedings of a General Court Martial, Held at Philadelphia, In the State of Pennsylvania, By Order of His Excellency General Washington, Commander in Chief of the Army of the United States of America For the Trial of Major General Howe, December 7, 1781. Major General Baron Steuben, President.* New-York Historical Society Collections for 1879, 215-311.

Howe, Robert. "Robert Howe (1732-1786) Papers, 1777, 1780." Manuscript, PC.612, State Archives of North Carolina, Raleigh. [Online catalog description: "Letters from Major General Howe of Brunswick Co., including note to Gov. Richard Caswell about Cosmo de Medici, appointed captain of light horse; one to New York Gov. George Clinton about relocation of two families near Stony Point, N.Y., with draft of Clinton's reply (Apr., 1780); and one to Gen. Nathanael Greene about a staff appointment (June, 1780)."]

Howe, Robert, 1732-1786. "Robert Howe Papers, 1776-1853." Manuscript 358, Southern Historical Collection, Louis Round Wilson Special Collections Library, University of North Carolina, Chapel Hill; online finding aid available at http://www2.lib.unc.edu/mss/inv/h/Howe,Robert.html. [Online finding aid description: "Robert Howe (1732-1786) was a major-general in the Continental Army during the American Revolution. The collection includes papers of and about Howe, some of which are handwritten transcriptions and photostatic copies, including three letters from him concerning military affairs; papers pertaining to his court martial for evacuating Savannah, Ga.; and materials compiled about Howe and writings about him by Archibald Maclaine Hooper (1775-1853)."]

Howe, Robert. "Robert Howe Letters, 1778-1779." Manuscript MS 400, Georgia Historical Society, Savannah. [Online catalog description: "This collection consists of negative photocopies of General Howe's letters from Papers of the Continental Congress: Letters in the Library of Congress, No. 158, p. 189-192 and No. 160, p. 418-507, passim. The letters are to John Houston, Governor of Georgia; Col. Samuel Elbert, Gen. Benjamin Lincoln and Henry Laurens, written from Savannah, Camp on Great Satilla, 'Camp on the road 4 miles from Zubly's Ferry,' in Georgia and Charleston, South Carolina. Included is one letter of John White to General Howe, November 21, 1778. All deal with the military situation. The letter of December 30, 1778, describes the capture of Savannah by the British. There is also a typed copy of this last letter." Note: "Original letters located in Papers of the Continental Congress: Letters in the Library of Congress, No. 158, p. 189-192 and No. 160, p. 418-507, passim."]

Lawrence E. Babits & Joshua B. Howard, *Long, Obstinate, and Bloody - The Battle of Guilford Courthouse*. Chapel Hill: UNC Press, 2009

Lennon, Donald R. "Cape Fear's General Robert Howe: A Man of the World, the Sword, the Senate, and the Buck." *New East*, 4:3 (June 1976), 33-34, 55. [Online description from "North Carolina Periodicals Index," East Carolina University: "Planter, soldier, and politician, General Robert Howe probably was the most dashing and most controversial Revolutionary War leader from North Carolina. Howe was a supporter of anti-British resistance from the very beginning."]

Naisawald, L. Van Loan. "Major General Robert Howe's Activities in South Carolina and Georgia, 1776-1779." *Georgia Historical Quarterly,* 35:1 (March 1951), 23-30.

Naisawald, Louis Van Loan. "The Military Career of Robert Howe." M. A. thesis, University of North Carolina at Chapel Hill, 1948.

Naisawald, L[ouis] VanLoan. "Robert Howe's Operations in Virginia, 1775-1776." *Virginia Magazine of History and Biography*, 60:3 (July 1952), 437-443.

Proceedings of a General Court Martial, Held at Philadelphia, in the State of Pennsylvania, by Order of His Excellency General Washington, Commander in Chief of the Army of the United States of America, for the Trial of Major General Howe, December 7, 1781. Major General Baron Steuben, President. Philadelphia: Printed by Hall and Sellers, 1782.

Rankin, Hugh F., *Greene and Cornwallis: The Campaign in the Carolinas*. Raleigh: North Carolina Divison of Archives & History, 1976

Ranlet, Philip. "Loyalty in the Revolutionary War: General Robert Howe of North Carolina." *The Historian*, 53:4 (1991), 721-742.

Watson, Alan D., Dennis R. Lawson, and Donald R. Lennon. *Harnett, Hooper & Howe: Revolutionary Leaders of the Lower Cape Fear*. Wilmington, N. C.: L. T. Moore Memorial Commission and the Lower Cape Fear

Historical Society, 1949. [Cornelius Harnett (1723-1781); William Hooper (1742-1790); Robert Howe (1732-1785)]

Huber, Andreas/Andrew Hoover, ?-1794

Tucker, Harry Z. "The Hoover Family." *The State: A Weekly Survey of North Carolina*, 16:49 (May 1949), 6; online: http://digital.ncdcr.gov/cdm/ref/collection/p16062coll18/id/23854. [Online description from "North Carolina Periodicals Index," East Carolina University: "President Herbert Hoover's original ancestor in this country is buried in Randolph County, where he and many of his family resided. Andreas Huber came to Pennsylvania in 1738, made a career for himself and married. The Hubers later moved to Maryland, but because they were Quakers, they were not popular in the Catholic colony. Around 1772, they came to North Carolina where he was known as Andrew Hoover. He died in 1794, and President Hoover was responsible for the monument that marks his grave – the first member of the family to settle in the state."]

Hunter, Andrew, active 1770s-1780s

Norris, Jeannie Faris. "The Tracks on Faith Rock." *The State: A Weekly Survey of North Carolina*, 16:49 (May 1949), 6; online: http://digital.ncdcr.gov/cdm/ref/collection/p16062coll18/id/23854. [Online description from "North Carolina Periodicals Index," East Carolina University: "The author retells a story that includes mix of historic fact and folklore of Andrew Hunter's daring escape that took place at Faith Rock, near Franklinville, during the Revolutionary War. Hunter, an outspoken patriot was hunted by Colonel David Fanning, commander of all Tories in the state. The evidence of his escape, now obliterated, was once seen on the river banks at Faith Rock."]

Hunter, Humphrey, 1755-1827

Abernethy, Edgar. "Dr. Humphrey Hunter." *The State: A Weekly Survey of North Carolina*, 11:3 (January 1944), 9, 21-22; online: http://digital.ncdcr.gov/cdm/ref/collection/p16062coll18/id/18405. [Online description from "North Carolina Periodicals Index," East Carolina University: "Hunter was born in Ireland and came to America at age four with his widowed mother. They settled on a farm near Charlotte. At the outbreak of the Revolutionary War, he joined the army and during the war was recognized as one of the state's outstanding soldiers. He was ordained a Presbyterian minister after the war in 1789 and in the same year married Jane Ross, the daughter of a physician. For the next thirty-eight years he established Presbyterian churches in the North Carolina Piedmont and also practiced his needed medical skills in the backcountry."]

Iredell, Hannah Johnston, 1747-1826

Iredell, James; Don Higginbotham, ed., Donna Kelly and Lang Baradell, eds. *The Papers of James Iredell*. 3 vols. Raleigh: Division of Archives and History, 1976, 2003. [Focuses a great deal on the relationship between James Iredell and his future wife, Hannah Johnston Iredell.]

Iredell, James, 1751-1799

Barber, Ira Wilson, Jr. "The Ocean-Borne Commerce of Port Roanoke, 1771-1776." M. A. thesis, University of North Carolina at Chapel Hill, 1931.

Connor, Henry G. "James Iredell: Lawyer, Statesman, Judge, 1751-1799." *University of Pennsylvania Law Review and American Law Register*, 60:4 (January 1912), 225-253.

Connor, Henry Groves. "James Iredell, 1751-1799." *North Carolina Booklet*, 11:4 (April 1912), 201-250.

Craige, Burton. *The Federal Convention of 1789: North Carolina in the Great Crisis.* Kewick, Va.: Archibald Craige; Richmond: Expert Graphics, 1987.

Dabney, Virginius; introduction by Henry Steele Commager. *The Patriots: The American Revolution Generation of Genius*. New York: Atheneum, 1975. [Features: Nathanael Greene, John Paul Jones, Richard Henderson, James Iredell, and Willie Jones.]

Davis, Junius. *Alfred Moore and James Iredell, Revolutionary Patriots, and Associate Justices of the Supreme Court of the United States: An Address Delivered in Presenting Their Portraits to the Supreme Court of the North Carolina on Behalf of the North Carolina Sons of the Revolution.* Raleigh: The Society, 1899.

Fordham, Jefferson B. "Political Ideas of James Iredell." M. A. thesis, University of North Carolina at Chapel Hill, 1929.

Griffin, Lloyd. "Iredell – Forgotten Patriot." *We the People of North Carolina*, 25:1 (May 1967), 17-18, 30-31.

[Online description from "North Carolina Periodicals Index," East Carolina University: "Griffin recounts the life of James Iredell, Sr. – patriot of the Revolution, state judge, state attorney general, and United States Supreme Court justice."]

Herndon, Nettie S. "James Iredell." Ph. D. dissertation, Duke University, 1944.

Higginbotham, Don. "James Iredell and the Revolutionary Politics of North Carolina." In W. Robert Higgins, ed., *Revolutionary War in the South: Power, Conflict and Leadership* (Durham: Duke University Press, 1979), 79-97.

Higginbotham, Don. "James Iredell's Efforts to Preserve the First British Empire." *North Carolina Historical Review*, 49:2 (April 1972), 127-145. [Online description from "North Carolina Periodicals Index," East Carolina University: "This paper examines essays written by James Iredell of Edenton, North Carolina during the American Revolution. The essays in question analyzed the origins of the conflict between England and its colonies and included his recommendations for restoring a peaceful coexistence between the two parties."[

Higginbotham, Don. *War and Society in Revolutionary America: The Wider Dimensions of Conflict*. Columbia: University of South Carolina Press, 1988.

Iredell, James. "James Iredell Papers." In the "Charles E. Johnson Collection, 1685-1875." Manuscript PC.67 (MARS ID: 576; Record Group), State Archives of North Carolina, Raleigh. [Online catalog description: "Papers of James Iredell, Sr. (1751-1799), of Edenton, state attorney general and U. S Supreme Court justice (1790-1799); …; Letters (1772- 1790) from James Iredell, Sr., to wife Hannah Johnston Iredell were written on travels to eastern and piedmont courts, describing towns, legal and political figures, court cases, actions of the legislature, Onslow Co. property, and celebrations at New Bern and Wilmington for the French alliance and the peace. His correspondence with family in England and Jamaica concerns his friends and fiancee; trade; politics in Britain, America, and France (including mention of the Edenton Tea Party); English society in London and Bath; and Carolinians abroad. Letters to Iredell during the Revolution are from brother-in-law Samuel Johnston, Thomas Jones, Richard Caswell, Abner Nash, Alfred Moore, John Johnston, Robert Smith, John Williams, and William Hooper, concerning provincial congresses (1775-1776), agreement on independence, the state constitution, defense plans, the land and naval war, Iredell's appointment as attorney general (1779), charges being made against judges (1780), prisoner exchange, and unfair taxation. Among the postwar correspondents are Henry E. McCullough, Nathaniel Duckenfield, Archibald Nielson, Archibald MacClaine, Charles Johnson, Hugh Williamson, Pierce Butler, James Hogg, John Burgwin, Baron Poellnitz, Richard D. Spaight, William Cumming, Samuel Spencer, and Samuel Ashe, as well as Samuel Johnston. Subjects include loyalists and confiscation laws; conflict with Cherokee Indians; western lands; the state court system; judges' salaries; location of state capital; incorporation of towns; ratification of the U. S. Constitution; assumption of state debts; conflict between North and South; fraudulent Revolutionary certificates; …Iredell's miscellaneous papers include Jones, Chowan, and Onslow county deeds (1722-1756); Port Roanoke customs records (1767- 1799); Edenton Post Office records (1770); lists of his taxable property (1777-1796); estate papers of Robert Smith and minutes of Smith's Academy, Edenton (1782-1789); a Chowan Co. confiscation paper (1780); lists of North Carolina court cases (1779-1789); resolutions from citizens of Edenton to their representatives about current issues (1783); … Many of the papers of James Iredell, Sr., have been published by the North Carolina Division/Office of Archives and History in three volumes. The Papers of James Iredell, Sr. and Jr., and Samuel Johnston are in the Southern Historical Collection, UNC, and the Manuscript Dept., Duke University Library."]

Iredell, James. "James Iredell Papers, 1771-1799." Manuscript 365, Southern Historical Collection, Louis Round Wilson Special Collections Library, University of North Carolina, Chapel Hill; online finding aid available at http://www2.lib.unc.edu/mss/inv/i/Iredell,James%281751-1799%29.html. [Online finding aid description: "James Iredell was a lawyer, colonial customs collector, state official, and United States Supreme Court justice, of Edenton, N. C. The collection includes Port of Roanoke (N.C.) customs records, 1771-1776; legal fee books, 1774-1799, and case book, 1786-1790; case books, 1793-1799, of Federal circuit courts in New Jersey, Pennsylvania, Rhode Island, South Carolina, and Virginia; and personal accounts, law notes, and legal writings, and an essay on the causes of the American Revolution (on microfilm)."]

Iredell, James, Sr., and James Iredell, Jr. "James Iredell Sr. and James Iredell Jr. Papers, 1724-1890 and Undated." Manuscript RL.10053, Library Service Center, Boxes 2-6 and others [see online catalog], David M. Rubenstein Rare Book & Manuscript Library, Duke University, Durham; online finding aid available at http://library.duke.edu/rubenstein/findingaids/iredelljames/. [Online finding aid description: "The papers of the elder Iredell concern colonial life and Revolutionary sentiment in North Carolina; the Revolution and North Carolina's ratification of the Constitution; and North Carolina and national politics (1780s and 1790s); and include early letters from friends and relatives in England and Ireland, including the Macartney family. Most of the correspondence between 1799 and the War of 1812 concerns family and business matters. Papers of James

Iredell, Jr., pertain mostly to his legal career. Other topics include his student activities at Yale, national and North Carolina politics, naval appointments, patronage matters, the nullification crisis, and family affairs. Correspondents in the collection include John Branch, John C. Calhoun, Henry Clay, Samuel Chase, William R. Davie, Oliver Ellsworth, Robert Y. Hayne, Joseph Hewes, William Hooper, John Jay, Charles Lee, Henry Lee, H. E. McCulloh, John Marshall, A. Nielson, William Paterson, Timothy Pickering, Richard Dobbs Spaight, Sr., Zachary Taylor, and John Tyler."]

Iredell, James; Don Higginbotham, ed. *The Papers of James Iredell.* 3 vols. Raleigh: Division of Archives and History, Department of Cultural Resources, 1976- . [Contents: v. 1. 1767-1777; v. 2. 1778-1783; v. 3. 1784-1789.]

Iredell, James; Griffith J. McRee, ed. *Life and Correspondence of James Iredell.* 2 vols. New York: Peter Smith, 1949.

Lawrence, R. C. "Governor James Iredell, Jr." *The State: A Weekly Survey of North Carolina*, 9:33 (January 1942), 5; online: http://digital.ncdcr.gov/cdm/ref/collection/p16062coll18/id/43298. [Online description from "North Carolina Periodicals Index," East Carolina University: "Although some feel that his name has been eclipsed by his distinguished father, James Iredell, Jr. has earned an important place in the state's history. He was a U.S. Senator, Governor, general of the state militia, and Superior Court judge."]

Marks, Jan Allen. "Leadership and Deference in North Carolina: A Study of Four Revolutionary Leaders." Honors Essay, University of North Carolina, Chapel Hill, 1979. [Joseph Hewes, William Hooper, James Iredell, and Samuel Johnston]

McRee, Griffith J. Life and Correspondence of James Iredell, One of the Associate Justices of the Supreme Court of the United States. New York: Peter Smith, 1949.

Stewart, Al. "Judicial Climb." *The State: Down Home in North Carolina*, 63:9 (February 1996), 33; online: http://digital.ncdcr.gov/cdm/ref/collection/p16062coll18/id/33784. [Online description from "North Carolina Periodicals Index," East Carolina University: "James Iredell, Sr., jurist, statesman, and Revolutionary War patriot, is one of only two North Carolinians ever appointed to the United States Supreme Court."]

Sykes, John. "'A Public and Private Calamity:' The Death of Justice James Iredell and Funeral Customs in the Eighteenth-Century Albemarle." *Carolina Comments*, 48:2 (March 2000), 45-56. [Online description from "North Carolina Periodicals Index," East Carolina University: "State and National citizens mourned the death of Justice James Iredell on October 20, 1799. In August the ill Iredell returned to his Edenton home. No contemporary accounts of his funereal exist but it is believed events were typical of eastern North Carolina with burial within a family cemetery, funeral oration Sunday following burial, and an extravagant funeral feast."]

Waldrup, John Charles. "James Iredell and the Practice of Law in Revolutionary Era North Carolina." Ph. D. dissertation, University of North Carolina, 1985.

Whichard, Willis P. "James Iredell: A Look at the Private Man." *Carolina Comments*, 48:1 (January 2000), 20-27. [Online description from "North Carolina Periodicals Index," East Carolina University: "The year 2000 marked the 200th anniversary of James Iredell's death. Some historians argue Iredell was the most prominent man in the state and a nationally respected gentleman during the 18th-century. However, the article focuses on his personal qualities which made him a grand man to friends and family."]

Whichard, Willis P. "James Iredell: Revolutionist, Constitutionalist, Jurist." In Scott Douglas Gerber, ed., *Seriatim: The Supreme Court before John Marshall* (New York: New York University Press, 1998, 198-230.

Whichard, Willis P. "Justice James Iredell." *Carolina Comments*, 45:4 (July 1997), 92-99. [Online description from "North Carolina Periodicals Index," East Carolina University: "James Iredell, Sr., is one of only two North Carolinians ever appointed to the United States Supreme Court. His dissenting opinion in the case of Chisholm v. Georgia was the basis for the Eleventh Amendment."]

Whichard, Willis P. "The Sixth Justice: A Life of James Iredell." Ph. D. dissertation, University of Virginia, 1994; revised and published with the same title: Durham: Carolina Academic Press, 2000.

Winborne, John Wallace, 1884-1966. "James Iredell." B. A. thesis, University of North Carolina at Chapel Hill, 1906.

Jack, James, 1739-1823

Allhands, William A. "The Ride of Captain Jack." *The State: A Weekly Survey of North Carolina*, 14:32 (January 1947), 6-7; online: http://digital.ncdcr.gov/cdm/ref/collection/p16062coll18/id/20032. [Online description from "North Carolina Periodicals Index," East Carolina University: "Captain James Jack was responsible for delivering Mecklenburg County's declaration of independence from British rule. On the morning of May 20th, 1775, a group of prominent male citizens unanimously adopted the Declaration of Independence and called upon Captain James Jack to deliver it to Congress meeting in Philadelphia. He rode from Charlotte to

Philadelphia, a trip reported to take 18-20 days by horseback. The declaration was given to North Carolina delegates, an act ahead of even Congress' decision to declare independence from Britain." James Jack (1739-1823)]

McNinch, Mary Groome. "The Ride of Captain Jack – 1775." *North Carolina Booklet*, 18:4 (April 1918), 187-188. [Jack Gilpin]

Northrup, Mary. "Paul Revere of the South." *The State: A Weekly Survey of North Carolina*, 18:32 (January 1951), 10; online: http://digital.ncdcr.gov/cdm/ref/collection/p16062coll18/id/26439. [Online description from "North Carolina Periodicals Index," East Carolina University: "His name was Captain James Jack, and the folks of Mecklenburg County regard him as one of the most outstanding patriots that ever lived in that part of North Carolina."]

Jackson, Andrew, 1767-1845, and North Carolina

Brands, H. W. *Andrew Jackson: His Life and Times*. New York: Doubleday, 2005.

Buchanan, John. *Jackson's Way: Andrew Jackson and the People of the Western Waters*. New York: Wiley, 2001.

Burstein, Andrew. *The Passions of Andrew Jackson*. New York: Random House, 2003.

Henderson, Archibald. "Andrew Jackson's Birthplace." *The State: A Weekly Survey of North Carolina*, 17:19 (October 1949), 6-7, 18; online: http://digital.ncdcr.gov/cdm/ref/collection/p16062coll18/id/24498. [Online description from "North Carolina Periodicals Index," East Carolina University: "The controversy between North Carolina and South Carolina probably will continue for a long time to come, but Dr. Henderson presents a strong case for North Carolina as the birthplace of Andrew Jackson."]

Hunsicker, Jennifer. *Young Andrew Jackson in the Carolinas: A Revolutionary Boy*. Charleston, S. C.: History Press, 2014.

Jackson, Andrew. "Letter from Andrew Jackson to Governor Samuel Ashe" Manuscript, Call Number N.95.3.2, Photographic Collections, State Archives of North Carolina, Raleigh. [Online catalog description: "Letter from Andrew Jackson to Governor Samuel Ashe Referring to the Military Land Fraud in Tennessee, 6 December 1797."]

John Foster Chapter, North Carolina Daughters of the American Revolution. "Affidavits Proving the Birthplace of Andrew Jackson: From Records in the Archives in the North Carolina State Department of Archives & History, Raleigh, N. C." Typescript (1959), State Library of North Carolina, Raleigh.

"The Mecklenburg Declaration of Independence and Andrew Jackson's Birthplace." *Mississippi Valley Historical Review*, 29:1 (January 1942), 79-90.

Misenheimer, John E., Jr. "Andrew Jackson and His Life in North Carolina before He Became the Seventh President of the United States." *The Golden Nugget (Cabarrus Genealogical Society)*, 13:2 (Summer 2005), 54-55. [Includes his experiences in the American Revolution.]

Ray, Jonathan. "Andrew Jackson and the Indians, 1767-1815." Ph. D. dissertation, University of Alabama, 2014.

Young, Eva M. "No One Will Ever Know." *The State: Down Home in North Carolina*, 34:19 (March 1967), 11-12; online: http://digital.ncdcr.gov/cdm/ref/collection/p16062coll18/id/49950. [Online description from "North Carolina Periodicals Index," East Carolina University: "The birthplace of Andrew Jackson has been claimed by both Carolinas. In 1957, South Carolina created the Andrew Jackson Historic Park that honors his birthplace, though North Carolina also claimed Jackson, since his mother birthed him when she went to a funeral inside the state. The historical argument is based on differing primary sources that have him born at Waxhaw, South Carolina or Twelve Miles Creek, North Carolina."]

Jackson, Elizabeth Hutchinson, 1740-1781

Roger, Lou. "Elizabeth Hutchinson Jackson, Mother of a President." *We the People of North Carolina*, 1:7 (November 1943), 21, 31-32. [Online description from "North Carolina Periodicals Index," East Carolina University: "Elizabeth Hutchinson was born in Ireland and came to America with her husband Andrew Jackson a decade before the Revolutionary War. They settled in North Carolina. She was widowed when her children were young and was largely responsible for the development of the character of her son Andrew, who would later become President of the United States. While caring for wounded American Revolutionary War soldiers in Charleston, South Carolina, she contracted a fever, died, and was buried in an unmarked grave."]

Jessup, Ann Mathews, 1738-1822

Mathis, Treva W. "Ann Matthews Jessup (10 Oct. 1738-26 Sept. 1822)." In William S. Powell, ed., *Dictionary of North Carolina Biography, vol. 3: H-K* (Chapel Hill: University of North Carolina Press, 1979-1996), 281. [Quaker minister and horticulturist]

Johnston, Samuel, 1733-1816

Connor, Robert Digges Wimberly. "Governor Samuel Johnston of North Carolina." *North Carolina Booklet*, 11:4 (April 1912), 259-285.

Dillard, Richard. "Hayes and Its Builder." *North Carolina Booklet*, 2:8 (December 1902), 32-39; online: http://digital.ncdcr.gov/cdm/ref/collection/p249901coll37/id/14180. [Online description from "North Carolina Periodicals Index," East Carolina University: "This article examines the construction of Hayes Plantation in Edenton by Governor Samuel Johnston in 1801, with attention placed on Johnston's history, background, and the steps he took in building the city."]

Johnston, Samuel, 1733-1816. "Samuel Johnston (1733-1816) Papers, 1731, 1763-1803." Manuscript PC. 68 (MARS ID: 577; record group), State Archives of North Carolina, Raleigh. [Online catalog description: "Papers of Johnston, Edenton lawyer, state legislator (1759-1784) and member of the Continental Congress (1780-1782), governor (1787- 1789) and U.S. senator (1789-1793), including a letter from John Rutherfurd about Henry McCullough's land (1763); correspondence (1769-1774) between Johnston and colonial agent Alexander Elmsley in London, letters from Joseph Hewes and William Hooper at the Continental Congress in Philadelphia (1775-1776) and from loyalist Thomas Macknight (1775); and Johnston's copies of his letter to the Wilmington Committee of Safety and his circular to sheriffs concerning elections for provincial congress at Hillsborough (1775). Other letters are to Johnston from the Wilmington Committee of Safety (photocopy, 1775) and from Lemuel Riddick (1776); and from Johnston (1778-1803) to Thomas Barker, Mrs. Penelope Barker, Henry Laurens, James Iredell, and Robert Carter about the General Assembly of 1788 and the estates of Gov. Gabriel Johnston, Thomas Barker, and Richard Lemmon. A letter from the North Carolina delegation to the Continental Congress to John Laurens, envoy extraordinary to France (1781), concerns British attacks on the interior of North Carolina (1781). Also included are three printed Acts of Parliament (1731) concerning debts, silk, and hops in America. Other Johnston papers are in the Hayes Collection, Southern Historical Collection, UNC."]

Marks, Jan Allen. "Leadership and Deference in North Carolina: A Study of Four Revolutionary Leaders." Honors Essay, University of North Carolina, Chapel Hill, 1979. [Joseph Hewes, William Hooper, James Iredell, and Samuel Johnston]

Lawrence, R. C. "Samuel Johnston." *The State: A Weekly Survey of North Carolina,* 10:40 (March 1943), 1, 16-17; online: http://digital.ncdcr.gov/cdm/ref/collection/p16062coll18/id/16876. [Online description from "North Carolina Periodicals Index," East Carolina University: "Many consider Samuel Johnston Carolina's greatest statesman. He was a patriot and champion of independence from English oppression, as well as a member of the General Assembly, Clerk of Court for the Edenton District, Deputy Naval Officer for the Province, a member of the committee on Continental Correspondence, and a delegate to Congress."]

Norris, Jeannie Faris. "Was He the First President?" *The State: Down Home in North Carolina,* 25:20 (February 1958), 12; online: http://digital.ncdcr.gov/cdm/ref/collection/p16062coll18/id/50936. [Online description from "North Carolina Periodicals Index," East Carolina University: "Samuel Johnston, native of Hayes, North Carolina, was the first person elected to the Presidency of the United States after the ratification of the Constitution. Johnston refused the position. Ballots were recast under the Articles of Confederation. Thomas McKean won, serving from 10 July 1781 through 5 November 1781."]

Jones, Allen, 1739-1798

Blackwell, R. T. "The Famous Jones Brothers." *The State: A Weekly Survey of North Carolina*, 9:2 (June 1941), 29; online: http://digital.ncdcr.gov/cdm/ref/collection/p16062coll18/id/39705. [Online description from "North Carolina Periodicals Index," East Carolina University: "Willie Jones was a strong, fearless Republican and his brother Allen was a strong, fearless Federalist. As such they often opposed each other on public questions. Yet each in his own way rendered valuable service to the state during the Revolutionary Period."]

Jones, Allen. "Allen Jones Papers, 1752-1806." Manuscript PC.645 (MARS ID: 1155; record group), State Archives of North Carolina, Raleigh. [Online catalog description: "Papers of General Jones of Northampton Co., member of the General Assembly, provincial congress (1773-1776), and the Continental Congress (1779-1780), including slave deeds, promissory notes, agreements, bills, and receipts. A few papers refer to John Sitgreaves and James Brownlow, as well as to Jones."]

Jones, Allen. "Allen Jones Papers, 1781." Manuscript 2043-z, Southern Historical Collection, Louis Wilson Library Special Collections, University of North Carolina, Chapel Hill; online finding aid available at http://www 2.lib.unc.edu/mss/inv/j/Jones,Allen.html. [Online finding aid description: "Allen Jones was brigadier general of the North Carolina Militia. The collection contains letters concerning military affairs addressed to Brigadier General Jones. Two letters, 10 July and 27 August 1781, are from the Marquis de Lafayette concerning Cornwallis's actions in Virginia and the impending invasion of North Carolina; one letter, 10 July 1781, is from Colonel Josiah Parker; one is from Colonel John Wills; and one, a contemporary handwritten copy, 18 July 1781, is probably from Thomas Burke."]

Jones, Allen. "Letter to Patrick Henry from General Allen Jones, May 17, 1779." Photographs N.86.11.19 (MARS ID: 4.1.13.340; folder), State Archives of North Carolina, Raleigh. [Online catalog description: "Letter addressed to Patrick Henry from General Allen Jones of North Carolina. The letter contains Allen Jones' signature, and is dated May 17, 1779. Taken from P.C. 21.2, Miscellaneous Papers, Volume I, Series I, p. 58."]

Jones, John Paul, 1747-1792, and North Carolina

Cotton, Elizabeth H. *The John Paul Jones-Willie Jones Tradition: A Defense of the North Carolina Position.* Chapel Hill: Cotton, 1966.

Norris, Jeannie Faris. "Founder of Our Navy." *The State: Down Home in North Carolina*, 37:11 (November 1969), 15, 23; online: http://digital.ncdcr.gov/cdm/ref/collection/p16062coll18/id/52980. [Online description from "North Carolina Periodicals Index," East Carolina University: "John Paul, born in 1747 in Scotland, would later add Jones to his last name in honor of the Jones family of Halifax, NC. After coming to the United States in 1773, Paul made his way to North Carolina where he met Wiley Jones, who invited him to stay at his home, known as The Grove. Here, Paul met influential members of society, including Mr. Hewes, of Edenton, who served on the Committee on Marine Affairs and helped to secure Paul's commission as Senior First Lieutenant of the Continental Navy. John Paul added Jones, thus becoming John Paul Jones, in appreciation for all that the family of Wiley Jones had done for him."]

Rogers, Lou. "John Paul Jones." *We the People of North Carolina*, 7:6 (October 1949), 22-25. [Online description from "North Carolina Periodicals Index," East Carolina University: "Although John Paul Jones was not a native North Carolinian, he enjoyed the friendship of a number of prominent individuals in the state. Willie Jones of Halifax provided a home for him when he was down and out, and he secured his first commission in the first United States Navy through the influence of Joseph Hewes of Edenton."]

Willcox, Mrs. W. A. "John Paul Jones." *The State: A Weekly Survey of North Carolina*, 7:28 (December 1939), 11; online: http://digital.ncdcr.gov/cdm/ref/collection/p16062coll18/id/35945. [Online description from "North Carolina Periodicals Index," East Carolina University: "John Paul, a young Scotsman born in 1747 went to sea as apprentice at the age of 12 and later became involved in the slave trade. He made his way to North Carolina where he met Wiley Jones of Halifax County, and took up the name of Jones. Jones became the Senior First Lieutenant of the Continental Navy and the United States' first well-known naval fighter of the Revolutionary War."]

Jones, William/Willie, 1740-1801

Burgwyn, ___, Col. "The Groves – The Home of Willie Jones." *North Carolina Booklet*, 2:9 (January 1903), 3-15; online: http://digital.ncdcr.gov/cdm/ref/collection/p249901coll37/id/14180. [Online description from "North Carolina Periodicals Index," East Carolina University: "This article examines the political history of Willie Jones and describes in great detail his family estate, the Groves near Halifax."]

Jones, Joe. "From Royalist to Revolutionary." *The State: Down Home in North Carolina*, 41:9 (February 1974), 7-8; online: http://digital.ncdcr.gov/cdm/ref/collection/p16062coll18/id/56442. [Online description from "North Carolina Periodicals Index," East Carolina University: "Willie Jones, a wealthy pre-Revolution aristocrat began his political career as a Royalist but deferred summons from His Majesty's Council of the Province to join radicals in support of the Revolution. Jones was known for his leadership abilities and acted as a virtual governor as president of the Council of Safety during the war. Jones was also instrumental in founding Raleigh, North Carolina."]

Jones, William/Willie. "Willie Jones Papers, 1781, 1852, 1959." Manuscript PC.656 (MARS ID: 1166; record group), State Archives of North Carolina, Raleigh. [Online catalog description: "Letter to Gov. Thomas Burke from Jones, Halifax Co. legislator, president of N. C. Council of Safety (1776), and member of Continental Congress (1780-1781), relaying rumors of a British cavalry raid toward Halifax from Virginia (July, 1781). Material relating to Jones includes a biographical sketch by Fred A. Olds; appeals for preservation of

'Constitution House' and Jones's home 'The Grove' in Halifax; statement by descendant of Allen Jones concerning John Paul Jones's adoption of that surname; and a photocopy of 'The Willie Jones-John Paul Jones Tradition' by Samuel Eliot Morison (*William and Mary Quarterly*, 3rd Series, April 1959)…"]

Lawrence, R. C. "The Bar of Halifax." *The State: A Weekly Survey of North Carolina*, 12:38 (February 1945), 5, 16-17; online: http://digital.ncdcr.gov/cdm/ref/collection/p16062coll18/id/12783. [Online description from "North Carolina Periodicals Index," East Carolina University: "Willie Jones, William R. Davie, Abner Nash, John Branch, the Kitchins, and many other famous lawyers, jurists, and statesmen have come from Halifax County and rendered outstanding service to North Carolina and United States."]

Morison, Samuel Eliot. "The Willie Jones-John Paul Jones Tradition." *William and Mary Quarterly*, 3rd series, 16:2 (April 1959), 198-206.

Robinson, Blackwell Pierce. "Willie Jones of Halifax." *North Carolina Historical Review*, 18:1 (January 1941), 1-26; online: http://digital.ncdcr.gov/cdm/ref/collection/p16062coll9/id/4207; 18:2 (April 1941), 133-170; online: http://digital.ncdcr.gov/cdm/ref/collection/p16062coll9/id/4207. [Online description from "North Carolina Periodicals Index," East Carolina University: "This article is … a biographical essay on the life of Willie Jones, a plantation owner, politician, and advocate of Jeffersonian states rights during the Revolutionary War and Federalist periods. This installment covers his life from his birth and family background to age 35."]

Lane, Joel, ca. 1740-1795

Cheshire, Elizabeth Silver. "Joel Lane's House." *The State: Down Home in North Carolina*, 51:6 (November 1983), 23-24: online: http://digital.ncdcr.gov/cdm/ref/collection/p16062coll18/id/12533. [Online description from "North Carolina Periodicals Index," East Carolina University: "The Joel Lane house, located in Raleigh, was where the decision as to where to locate the state's capitol building was made. The home, built in 1760, was home to Joel Lane's family. Lane was born in Halifax County to parents who had emigrated from England. He served in the General Assembly and in 1770 introduced a bill that created Wake County. Following independence, the state legislature decided to locate the state's capital in Wake County. Lane hosted the nine-member committee whose job was to decide where in Wake County to place the capital. After an amusing night of entertainment in the Lane house, the committee decided to buy 1,000 acres of property that belonged to Joel Lane. This property became the site of North Carolina's capital. The home was bought by the Wake County of Colonial Dames in 1927. They began a major renovation project on the home in 1968 and the house was opened to the public in 1976."]

Lawrence, R. C. "Joel Lane's Plantation." *The State: A Weekly Survey of North Carolina*, 13:18 (September 1945), 13, 22; online: http://digital.ncdcr.gov/cdm/ref/collection/p16062coll18/id/13745. [Online description from "North Carolina Periodicals Index," East Carolina University: "It was on Colonel Joel Lane's land that the capital city of North Carolina was built. Lane himself, was one of the most prominent citizens of his time and was outstanding in several lines of service."]

Lenoir, Thomas, Jr., 1741-1816, and Martha Lenoir

Tucker, Harry Z. "Martha Lenoir's Earrings." *The State: A Weekly Survey of North Carolina*, 9:25 (November 1941), 12, 30; online: http://digital.ncdcr.gov/cdm/ref/collection/p16062coll18/id/40494. [Online description from "North Carolina Periodicals Index," East Carolina University: "When Colonel Thomas Lenoir was captured at the Battle of Camden he was imprisoned in Lord Cornwallis' camp. Prisoners there were underfed and suffered greatly. Lenoir's oldest daughter Martha, twelve at the time, heard of the misery and rode off to the camp with a basket of food for her father. Her stout bravery impressed Cornwallis and he set her father free. Upon returning to the plantation, Thomas Lenoir forged a pair of gold earrings for his daughter, which became the subject of a well-known North Carolinian tale."]

Lenoir, William, 1751-1839

Application for Pension by Gen'l Wm. Lenoir. [S. l.: s. n.]: [1888]. [Online catalog description: "Describes William Lenoir's experiences in the Revolutionary War; information taken from Lenoir's application for a pension." Copy available at the University of North Carolina at Chapel Hill.]

Coffey, R. Kelley. "Fort Defiance." *Our State: Down Home in North Carolina*, 69:10 (March 2002), 25-26, 28; online: http://digital.ncdcr.gov/cdm/ref/collection/p16062coll18/id/74734. [Online description from "North Carolina Periodicals Index," East Carolina University: "Fort Defiance, the Caldwell County home of Revolutionary War General William Lenoir, takes its name from a local frontier fort. The state purchased the structure from the Lenoir family in the mid-1960s. Now a historic site, Fort Defiance has been restored to its

1792 appearance, complete with over 300 articles, ranging from books to furniture, originally owned by Lenoir."]

Hamilton, J. G. De Roulhac, ed. "Revolutionary Diary of William Lenoir." *Journal of Southern History*, 6:2 (May 1940), 247-259.

Harper, Margaret. "House of History." *The State: Down Home in North Carolina*, 32:24 (May 1965), 12-13, 20; online: http://digital.ncdcr.gov/cdm/compoundobject/collection/p16062coll18/id/47916. [Online description from "North Carolina Periodicals Index," East Carolina University: "This article presents the history and significance of a historical home called Fort Defiance in the Yadkin Valley. It was owned by General William Lenoir (1751-1839), a Captain of Militia during the American Revolutionary War."]

Lawrence, R. C. "General William Lenoir." *The State: A Weekly Survey of North Carolina*, 15:44 (April 1948), 9; online: http://digital.ncdcr.gov/cdm/ref/collection/p16062coll18/id/22101. [Online description from "North Carolina Periodicals Index," East Carolina University: "Not only was William Lenoir an outstanding soldier during the American Revolutionary War, but he also served the state as Speaker of the North Carolina Senate and a member of the state Legislature."]

Lenoir, [Clyde Lyndon] Mrs. Rufus Theodore. "Fort Defiance." *North Carolina Booklet,* 3:6 (October 1903), 4-17; online: http://digital.ncdcr.gov/cdm/ref/collection/p249901coll37/id/14180. [Online description from "North Carolina Periodicals Index," East Carolina University: "A description of 'Fort Defiance,' also known as 'The Fort,' the home built by Revolutionary War General William Lenoir between 1784 and 1785 in what is now Lenoir, NC in Caldwell County.

Lenoir, William. "Application for Pension by Gen'l Wm. Lenoir." Typescript CpB L574b1, North Carolina Collection, Louis Round Wilson Special Collections Library, University of North Carolina at Chapel Hill.

Lenoir Family. "Lenoir Family Papers, 1763-1940, 1969-1975." Manuscript 426 and microfilm reel M-1793, Southern Historical Collection, Louis Round Wilson Special Collections Library, University of North Carolina, Chapel Hill; online finding aid and some digital surrogates available at http://www2.lib.unc.edu/mss/inv/l/Lenoir_Family.html. [Online finding aid description: "Topics include Revolutionary War pensions; banking and international trade issues; the containment of slavery; Thomas Jefferson and his political opponents; Israel Pickens's career as a member of Congress during the War of 1812 and as Alabama governor; and distaste for Andrew Jackson. Abstract 1.1.b: Business letters relate chiefly to plantation management, including buying, selling, and supervising slaves; land speculation chiefly in North Carolina and Tennessee; and William Lenoir's unsuccessful attempt to retain lands confiscated from Moravians after the Revolutionary War. Family letters express the hopes and aspirations of family members relating to mates, children, careers, and living conditions. Much correspondence relates to the lives of the women of the family. Letters discuss births, marriages, and deaths; the education of male and female family members, chiefly at the Bingham School, Salem Academy, and the University of North Carolina; health issues, especially relating to Waightstill Avery, lawyer, legislator, and signer of the Mecklenburg Declaration; feelings towards slavery; and William Lenoir's exploits at the Battle of King's Mountain."]

Shrader, Richard Alexander. "William Lenoir, 1751-1839." Ph. D. dissertation, University of North Carolina at Chapel Hill, 1978.

Thompson, Peter. "Peter Thompson (d. 1832) Papers, 1745-1960." Manuscript PC.1377, State Archives of North Carolina, Raleigh. [Online catalog description shows that this collection includes: "…oath of allegiance (1778); undated list of Capt. William Lenoir's company;…"]

Lillington, John Alexander, 1720s-1786, and the Lillington Family

Bellamy, John D[illard]. *Address by John D. Bellamy on the Life and Services of General Alexander Lillington: Semi-Centennial Celebration of the Establishment of Harnett County and the Town of Lillington*. Washington, D. C.: Press of Judd & Detweiler, Inc., 1905.

Lillington, John A. "John A. Lillington Letters, 1780-1782." Manuscript 2050-z, Southern Historical Collection, Louis Round Wilson Special Collections Library, University of North Carolina, Chapel Hill; online finding aid available at http://www2.lib.unc.edu/mss/inv/l/Lillington,John_A.html. [Online finding aid description: "John Alexander Lillington (1725-1786) was a Patriot general from North Carolina who served in the Revolutionary War. The collection includes letters to and from General Lillington, 1780-1782, concerning drafting of militia, movements of the enemy, care of the sick, and other Revolutionary War military affairs in North Carolina. Correspondents are M. L. Brown, Governor Samuel Ashe, General Isaac Huger, Major [?] Molton, and Henry Young."]

Lillington Family. "Lillington Family Papers, 1741-1839." Manuscript, PC.1815, State Archives of North Carolina, Raleigh. [Online catalog description: "The papers include letters, indentures, receipts, an inventory, a will, agreements, and a slave list. Within the papers are several documents relating to Revolutionary War activities. Of special interest (because the original apparently does not exist) is Lillington's copy of an extract of orders from Governor Thomas Burke to General William Caswell, 13 July 1781. The record of the births of sixty Lillington slaves, 1802-1839, includes individual names and year of birth."]

Macdonald, Flora, 1722-1790

Ayer, Mrs. S. G. "Sketch of Flora McDonald [sic]." *North Carolina Booklet,* 9:1 (July 1909), 36-51.

Banks, James. "Life and Character of Flora McDonald." *North Carolina University Magazine*, 5 (December 1856), 433-446.

Banks. James. *Life and Character of Flora McDonald.* Fayetteville, N. C.: Printed by E. J. Hale & Son, 1857.

Bennion, Linda F. "Flora MacDonald College for Women, Red Springs." *Argyll Colony Plus*, 17:3 (Fall/Winter 2003-04), 25-28; originally published in *The Fayetteville Observer*, January 29, 1914.

Bowler, R. Arthur. "Flora MacDonald." In Jack P. Greene and J. R. Pole, eds., *The Blackwell Encyclopedia of the American Revolution* (Cambridge, Mass.: Basil Blackwell, Inc., 1991, 1994), 750.

Carruth, J. A. *Flora MacDonald, the Highland Heroine*. Norwich, Eng.: Jarrold and Sons, 1973.

Caudill, William S. "Flora MacDonald Homesite." In William S. Powell, ed., and Jay Mazzocchi, assoc. ed. *Encyclopedia of North Carolina*. Chapel Hill: University of North Carolina Press in association with the University of North Carolina at Chapel Hill Library, 2006), 439-440.

Chidsey, Donald Barr. *The War in the South: The Carolinas and Georgia in the American Revolution, an Informal History.* New York: Crown Publishers, 1969. [The book briefly mentions Flora MacDonald, the heroine of the Bonnie Prince Charlie escape legend. During the American Revolution her husband served in the British army while they were living in North Carolina, 25, 29, 32.]

Creznic, J. "Flora McDonald: The Story of a Scottish Heroine who emigrated to North Carolina in 1774, only to find herself allied with the crown during the American Revolution." *American History*, 32:2 (May-June 1997), 22-25.

De La Torre, Lillian. *The White Rose of Stuart: The Story of Flora Macdonald.* New York: T. Nelson, 1954.

Douglas, Hugh. *Flora MacDonald: The Most Loyal Rebel.* Phoenix Mill, Eng.: Alan Sutton Publishing Limited, 1993; Phoenix Mill, Gloucestershire, U. K.: Sutton Publishing, 2003.

Drummond, J. *The Female Rebels, Being Some Remarkable Incidents in the Lives, Characters and Families of the Titular Duke and Duchess of Perth, the Lord and Lady Ogilvy and of Miss Flora MacDonald.* London: Edinburgh printed: London reprinted; and sold by L. Gilliver, in the Oxford Arms Passage, Warwick-lane; Mrs. Dodd, without Temple-Bar; and G. Woodfall, at Charing-Cross, 1747.

Fryar, Jack E., Jr. "Flora MacDonald." In Jack E. Fryar, Jr., ed., *The Coastal Chronicles: Volume II: Popular History Stories of the Coastal Carolinas as Seen in* Coastal Chronicles Magazine (Wilmington, N. C.: Dram Tree Books, 2004), 28-32.

Gesner, C. E. "Loyalty and Devotion: The Story of Flora Macdonald." In Donald Wetmore and Lester B. Sellick, eds., *Loyalists in Nova Scotia* (Hantsport, Nova Scotia: Lancelot Press, 1983), 28-37.

Grant, William Lawson. "'The Heroine of the Forty-Five': Flora MacDonald's Part in the American Rebellion, 1776." *Chambers's Journal*, 8th series, 15 (1946), 182-184.

Green, Paul. "Flora MacDonald's Home in North Carolina." *Argyll Colony Plus*, 13:3 (November 1999), 229-233.

Jones, Joseph Seawell. *Memorials of North Carolina*. New York: Scatcherd & Adams, 1838. [Contains: Miss Flora Macdonald. The chapters were previously published in "the literary Gazettes of the day."—Preface.]

Kerrigan, Deanna. "The Bright and Particular Star." *Tar Heel Junior Historian*, 39:2 (Spring 2000), 9-11; online: http://ncpedia.org/biography/macdonald-flora. [Flora MacDonald lived through the glory days and hard times. In 1745, she became a legend in her native Scotland by helping the pretender to the Scottish throne, Prince Charles, escape after he was defeated at the Battle of Culloden. Later she and her husband came to North Carolina, hoping for a better life. Their decision to remain loyal to England during the Revolution angered many and forced their return to Scotland, where they lived the reminder of their lives.]

Lossing, Benson J., ed. "Flora McDonald." *American Historical Record*, 1:3 (March 1872), 109-111.

MacDonald, Allan Reginald; Donald MacKinnon, ed. *The Truth about Flora MacDonald.* Inverness, Scotland: Northern Chronicle Office, 1938.

MacDonald, Flora. *Autobiography of Flora M'Donald: Being the Home Life of a Heroine; Edited by Her Granddaughter.* 2 vols. Edinburgh, Scotland: W. P. Nimmo, 1870. [This account is considered to be highly suspect in its authenticity.]

MacDonald, James Alexander. *Flora MacDonald: A History and a Message from James A. MacDonald.* Washington: James William Bryan Press, 1916.

MacGregor, Alexander. *The Life of Flora Macdonald.* Inverness, Scotland: A. & W. MacKenzie, 1896; reprinted: Sterling, Scotland: Mackay, 1901.

MacLean, J[ohn] P[atterson]. *Flora Macdonald in America: With a Brief Sketch of Her Life and Adventures.* Lumberton, N. C.: A. W. MacLean, 1909; 1925.

MacLeod, Ruairidh H. *Flora MacDonald: The Jacobite Heroine in Scotland and North America.* London: Shepheard-Walwyn, 1995.

MacQueen, Edith E. "Highland Tragedy: The Story of Flora Macdonald in North Carolina." *Scots Magazine* (Scotland), 17:4 (July 1932), 257-266; 17:5 (August 1932), 351-359.

Magee, Joan; with contributions by John S. Dietrich and Mary Beacock Fryer and a foreword by Charles J. Humber. *Loyalist Mosaic: A Multi-Ethnic Heritage.* Toronto: Dundurn Press, 1984. [Chapter 8: "Flora Macdonald [1722-1790]: A Loyalist from the Scottish Highlands," 137-154]

Merritt, Susan E. *Her Story: Women From Canada's Past.* St. Catharines, Ont.: Vanwell Pub., 1993. [Includes Flora Macdonald (1722-1790), a loyalist in North Carolina.]

Quynn, Dorothy Mackay. "Flora MacDonald in History." *North Carolina Historical Review*, 18:3 (July 1941), 236-258.

Ramage, B. J. "Flora MacDonald." *Sewanee Review,* 2:2 (February 1894), 212-226.

Ravi, Jennifer. *Notable North Carolina Women.* Winston-Salem, N. C.: Bandit Books, 1992. [Includes Flora MacDonald (1722-1790).]

Robertson, Beth Whatley. "Mentioned with Honor: The Story of Flora MacDonald." *Dalhousie Review*, 45:2 (Summer 1965), 165-181.

Rose, Duncan. *Flora MacDonald and the Scottish Highlanders in America.* Boston: American Historical Register, 1897.

Schafer, Elizabeth D. "Flora MacDonald." In Richard L. Blanco, ed.; Paul J. Sanborn, contrib. ed., *The American Revolution, 1775-1783: An Encyclopedia, vol. II: M-Z* (New York: Garland, 1993), 989-990.

Shepherd, Henry E. "Flora McDonald." In Samuel A. Ashe, ed. *Biographical History of North Carolina.* 8 vols. (Greensboro: Charles L. Van Noppen, Publisher, 1908), 7:292-296.

Smith, Elva S., ed. *Heroines of History and Legend: Stories and Poems.* Boston: Lothrop, Lee & Shepard Co., 1921. [Includes "Flora MacDonald, The Heroine of the 'Forty-Five'," and, "The Lament of Flora MacDonald."]

Smith, Maud Thomas. "Flora MacDonald (1722-Mar. 1790)." In William S. Powell, ed., *Dictionary of North Carolina Biography, vol. 4: L-O* (Chapel Hill: University of North Carolina Press, 1979-1996), 138-139.

Symonds, James. "Surveying the Remains of a Highland Myth: Investigations at the Birthplace of Flora MacDonald, Airigh-mhuilinn, South Uist." In Marjory Harper and Michael E. Vance, eds., *Myth, Migration, and the Making of Memory: Scotia and Nova Scotia, c. 1700-1990* (Halifax, N. S.: Fernwood Publishing and John Donald Publishers Limited for the Gorsebrook Research Institute for Atlantic Canada Studies, 1999), 73-88.

Toffey, John J. *A Woman Nobly Planned: Fact and Myth in the Legacy of Flora MacDonald.* Durham, N. C.: Carolina Academic Press, 1997. [Summary from the online Hollis Catalog, Harvard University: "Flora MacDonald is one of Scotland's leading ladies of legend. Her ten-day adventure with charismatic Bonnie Prince Charlie in June 1746 and her consequent confinement at Leith and in London brought her instant and lasting fame. Fame did not bring fortune, however. At fifty-two, Flora, with her husband and some of her family, left Scotland for better times in North Carolina. Instead, she and her family were caught up on the losing side of the American Revolution and suffered separation and hardship. In the two and a half centuries since her precipitating adventure, Flora has been mentioned in history and celebrated in legend. In the eighteenth century, Johnson praised her, London society flocked to her, and the principal portraitists of the day painted her. In the nineteenth century, Sir Walter Scott, King George IV, and Queen Victoria paid tributes to her, and her descendants built and dedicated memorials in her honor. In the twentieth century, Flora has continued to be celebrated in portrait, play, poem, song, and story; her name was given to a college, and her image has adorned marmalade jars and shortbread tins."]

Vining, Elizabeth Gray. *Flora: A Biography.* Philadelphia: J. B. Lippincott Company, 1996.

Vining, Elizabeth Gray. *Flora MacDonald: Her Life in the Highlands and America.* Philadelphia and New York: J.B. Lippincott Company, 1966. [biography of Flora Macdonald]

Wetmore, Donald, and Lester B. Sellick, eds. *Loyalists in Nova Scotia.* Hantsport, Nova Scotia: Lancelot Press, 1983. [C. E. Gesner, "Loyalty and Devotion: The Story of Flora Macdonald," 28-37.]

Wicker, Rassie E. "The Anson County Highland Settlement, Allan and Flora Macdonald." *Argyll Colony Plus*, 16:1 (March 2002), 29-41.

Wylde, Flora Frances MacDonald. *The Autobiography of Flora M'Donald: Being the Home Life of a Heroine.* 2 volumes. Edinburgh: W.P. Nimmo, 1870. [Accepted as a book of historical fiction/biography written by her granddaughter rather than an autobiography.]

MacNeill, Janet Smith (Jennie Bahn), 1720-1791

Smith, Nancy V. "Janet Smith MacNeill (Jennie Bahn) (1720-1791)." In William S. Powell, ed., *Dictionary of North Carolina Biography, vol. 4: L-O* (Chapel Hill: University of North Carolina Press, 1979-1996), 181. [During the Revolutionary war Jennie Bahn is rumored to have split her six sons so that half served the British and half the fight for independence, while she "remained neutral in order to sell cattle to both sides."]

Macon, Nathaniel, 1758-1837

Arthur, Billy. "The Legacy of Nathaniel Macon." *The State: Down Home in North Carolina*, 61:8 (January 1994), 12-13; online: http://digital.ncdcr.gov/cdm/ref/collection/p16062coll18/id/66512.

Barry, Stephen J. "Nathaniel Macon: The Prophet of Pure Republicanism, 1758-1837." Ph. D. dissertation, State University of New York at Buffalo, 1996.

Benton, Thomas H. "Nathaniel Macon." In W. J. Peele, ed., Lives of Distinguished North Carolinians with Illustrations and Speeches (Raleigh: North Carolina Publishing Society, 1897),81-110.

Bonath, Shawn. *Buck Spring Plantation: Archaeology of an Old South Plantation in Warren County, North Carolina.* [Raleigh]: Archeology Branch, Division of Archives and History, N. C. Dept. of Cultural Resources, 1978.

Buck Spring Plantation, Home of Nathaniel Macon: Historic Site, Warren County, North Carolina. Warrenton: Warren County Historical Association, [1974?].

Cathey, Boyd. "Nathaniel Macon and Buck Spring." Typescript and microfilm (Historical Research Reports, Series 1, no. 39), Research Branch, State Archives of North Carolina, Raleigh.

Dodd, William E[dward]. *The Life of Nathaniel Macon.* Raleigh: Edwards & Broughton, Printers and Binders, 1903; reprinted: [Whitefish, Mont.]: Kessinger Publishing Company, 2007.

Dodd, William E[ward]. "The Place of Nathaniel Macon in Southern History." *American Historical Review,* 8:4 (July 1902), 663-675.

Edwards, Weldon Nathanael. *Memoir of Nathaniel Macon, of North Carolina.* Raleigh: Raleigh Register Steam Power Press, 1962.

Macon, Nathaniel. "Papers, 1798-1854." Manuscript Sec. A Box 90 items 1-37, David M. Rubenstein Rare Book & Manuscript Library, Duke University, Durham. [Online catalog description: "Revolutionary War figure and member of the U. S. Congress; from Monroe (Warren Co.), N. C. Papers concerning the settlement of claims from the Revolution…"]

Macon, Nathaniel. "Papers of Nathaniel Macon [Manuscript] 1798-1874." Manuscript MSS 2618, Special Collections, University of Virginia, Charlottesville. [Online catalog description: "Papers consist of typed transcriptions of miscellaneous correspondence, 1798-1837, of Nathaniel Macon regarding a Revolutionary War claim, the tobacco market, tax legislation, the election of Thomas Jefferson as president, Macon's tours of duty during the Revolution, the election of 1836, and U. S. politics… a letter, 14 November 1828, from Macon, simultaneously resigns his positions as U. S. Senator from North Carolina, trustee of the University of North Carolina, and justice of the peace for Warren County, N.C"]

Macon, Nathaniel; Elizabeth Gregory McPherson, ed. "Letters from Nathaniel Macon to John Randolph of Roanoke." *North Carolina Historical Review*, 39:2 (April 1962), 195-211.

Palmer, John B. "Nathaniel Macon – the Last of the Romans." *The State: A Weekly Survey of North Carolina*, 1:36 (February 1934), 27-28; online: http://digital.ncdcr.gov/cdm/ref/collection/p16062coll18/id/2643. [Online description from "North Carolina Periodicals Index," East Carolina University: "Palmer recounts notable events in the life of Nathaniel Macon, one of the foremost public men in the state. Among them were Revolutionary War soldier; serving in Congress for thirty-five years; and president of the Constitutional Convention of 1835."]

Price, William S[olomon], Jr. "Nathaniel Macon, Antifederalist." *North Carolina Historical Review*, 81:3 (July 2004), 288-312.

Price, William S[olomon], Jr. "Nathaniel Macon, Planter." *North Carolina Historical Review*, 78:2 (April 2001),

187-214. [Online description from "North Carolina Periodicals Index," East Carolina University: "This biographical essay examines the life and career of Nathaniel Macon, a Warren County planter who was elected three times as speaker of the House of Representatives, served as US senator from North Carolina for 13 years, and presided over the 1835 North Carolina state constitutional convention. In spite of his political success, Macon's role as a planter was the one that gave him the most satisfaction."]

Price, William S[olomon], Jr. *Nathaniel Macon of North Carolina: Three Views of His Character and Creed.* Raleigh: North Carolina Office of Archives and History in association with the North Caroliniana Society of Chapel Hill, 2008.

Roule, R. Charles, III. "Nathaniel Macon." *Tar Heel Junior Historian*, (Falll 1996), ; online: http://ncpedia.org/biography/macon-nathaniel.

Madison, Dorothy "Dolley" Payne Todd, 1768-1849

Allgor, Catherine. *A Perfect Union: Dolley Madison and the Creation of the American Nation.* New York: Henry Holt, 2006.

Anthony, Carl Sferrazza. "Skirting the Issue: First Ladies and African Americans." *American Visions,* 7:5 (October/November 1992), 28-32. [Explores First Ladies perspectives towards and interactions with African Americans and how they influenced their husbands' policies towards African Americans. The discussion covers First Ladies up to Barbara Bush, mentions Martha Washington, Abigail Adams, Dolly Madison, and Louisa Adams.]

Anthony, Katharine. *Dolly Madison: Her Life and Times.* Garden City, N. Y.: Doubleday, 1949. [Includes discussion of her childhood during the Revolutionary period.]

Arnett, Ethel Stephens. *Mrs. James Madison: The Incomparable Dolley.* Greensboro: Piedmont Press, 1972. [Includes material on her childhood during the Revolution in Guilford County, North Carolina.]

Ashby, Ruth. *James and Dolley Madison.* (Presidents and First Ladies series) New York: World Almanac Library, 2005. [a book for young readers]

Barnard, Ella Kent. *Dorothy Payne, Quakeress.* Philadelphia: Ferris & Leach Co., 1909; micropublished in *History of Women.* (New Haven: Research Publications, Inc., 1975), reel 705, no. 5650. [Dorothy Payne became "Dolly" Madison, wife of James Madison.]

Boller, Paul F. *Presidential Wives: An Anectodal History.* New York: Oxford University Press, 1998. [a book for young readers; Chapter 1: "Martha Washington (1731-1802)," 3-12; Chapter 2: "Abigail Adams (1744-1818)," 13-30; Chapter 3: "Martha Jefferson (1749-1782)," 31-35; Chapter 4: "Dolley Madison (1768-1849), 36-48; Chapter 7: "Rachel Jackson (1767-1830), 49-72.]

Brant, Irving. "Dolley Payne Todd Madison [1768-1849]." In Edward T. James, ed., *Notable American Women, 1607-1950: A Biographical Dictionary, vol. II: G-O* (Cambridge: Belknap Press of Harvard University Press, 1971), 483-485. [Discusses her early life in North Carolina and Virginia.]

Brant, Irving. *James Madison: The Virginia Revolutionist.* Indianapolis: Bobbs-Merrill Company, 1941.

Caroli, Betty Boyd. *America's First Ladies.* Garden City, N. Y.: Doubleday Direct, Inc., 1996. [Includes Dorothea "Dolly" Payne Todd Madison, 72-73, 84-86, 90-91, 102, 106-107, 119, 123, 140, 181-182, 203, 211.]

Caroli, Betty Boyd. *First Ladies: From Martha Washington to Laura Bush.* New York: Oxford University Press, 1987; reprinted: Garden City, N. Y.: Doubleday Book & Music Clubs, 1989; 2nd ed. Garden City, N. Y.: Doubleday Book & Music Clubs, 1993; expanded ed. New York: Oxford University Press, 1995; expanded and updated ed. Oxford and New York: Oxford University Press, 2003. [Chapter 1: "Setting Precedents: The First Presidents' Wives (1789-1829)," 3-32. Includes Dolley Madison.]

Caroli, Betty Boyd. *Inside the White House: America's Most Famous Home, the First 200 Years.* New York: Canopy Books, 1992. [Includes information about the First Ladies who have lived in the White House.]

Clark, Allen C[ulling]. *Life and Letters of Dolly Madison.* Washington, D. C.: Press of W. F. Roberts Co., 1914.

Coalwell, Christine. "Dolley Payne Todd Madison (1768-1849), First Lady." In Paul A. Gilje, ed., Gary B. Nash, gen. ed. *Encyclopedia of American History, Volume III: Revolution and New Nation, 1761 to 1812.* Revised ed. (New York: Facts on File, 2010), 280-281.

Cote, Richard N. *Strength and Honor: The Life of Dolley Madison.* Mt. Pleasant, S. C.: Corinthian Books, 2005.

Cutts, Lucia B. *Memoirs and Letters of Dolly Madison.* Boston: Houghton Mifflin, 1886; new edition edited by her grand-neice, Lucia Beverly Cutts, and with subtitle: *Wife of James Madison, President of the United States.* Boston: Houghton Mifflin, 1911; reprinted: Port Washington, N. Y.: Kennikat Press, 1971.

Daugherty, Sonia Medvedeva; with drawings by James Daugherty. *Ten Brave Women: Anne Hutchinson, Abigail Adams, Dolly Madison, Narcissa Whitman, Julia Ward Howe, Susan B. Anthony, Dorothea Lynde Dix, Mary Lyon, Ida M. Tarbell, [and] Eleanor Roosevelt.* Philadelphia: Lippincott, 1953.

Dean, Elizabeth Lippincott. *Dolly Madison, The Nation's Hostess.* Boston: Lothrope, Lee, and Shepard Company, 1928.

Doyle, Rebecca Smith. "Dolley Madison: An American Queen." M. A. thesis, University of Central Arkansas, 1997

Ewing, Mrs. Sallie M. "The Wives of Three Great Men," *American Monthly Magazine*, 3:1 (July 1893), 145-146. [Includes Martha Washington and Dolley Madison.]

"First Lady Biography: Dolley Madison." Online: National First Ladies' Library: http://www.firstladies.org/biographies/firstladies.aspx?biography=4.

Fleming, Thomas. *The Intimate Lives of the Founding Fathers.* New York: HarperCollins, 2009. [Includes chapters that focus on Washington, Franklin, Adams, Hamilton, Jefferson, Madison, their respective wives and daughters, and other women in their lives such as Sally Fairfax, Sally Hemings, and Mercy Otis Warren.]

Fursee, Corinne. *The Forgotten Women of History.* Portland, Maine: J. W. Walch, 1963. [Chapter 15: "Dolley Madison-The National Hostess (1772-1848), 71-75; and, Chapter 26: "Martha Washington-First First Lady (1732-1802), 131-137]

Gerson, Noel B. *The Velvet Glove: A Life of Dolley Madison.* Nashville, Tenn.: Thomas Nelson & Sons, 1975.

Gibson, Emma Ghering. *Pioneer Women of Historic Haddonfield.* West Collingswood, N. J., Varacomp, 1973. [Julia Gill, "Leaden Sacrifice," 49-57; Julia B. Gill, "The Indian King Tavern and Dolly Madison," 75-79; Emma G. Gibson, "Dolly Payne Madison," 82-95; and Julia B. Gill, "The Garden at Greenfield Hall," 96-98.]

Goodwin, Maud Wilder. *Dolly Madison.* (Women of Colonial and Revolutionary Times series, v. 2) New York: Scribner, 1896; reprinted: New York: C. Scribner's Sons, 1911; reprinted (Virginia Heritage Series, v. 5) New York: Scribner's Sons, 1916.

Gormley, Beatrice. *First Ladies: Women Who Called the White House Home.* New York: Scholastic, 1997. [a book for young readers; Martha Dandridge Custis Washington (1731-1802) {who never lived in the White House}, 6-7; Abigail Smith Adams (1744-1818), 8-9; Martha Wayles Skelton Jefferson (1748-1782), 10-11; and Dolly Payne Todd Madison (1768-1849), 12-13.]

Grant, Matthew G, and Nancy Inderieden. *Dolley Madison: First Lady of the Land.* Mankato, Minn.: Childrens Press, for Creative Education, 1974.

Hunt, Gaillard, ed. *The Life of James Madison*. New York: Doubleday, Page and Company, 1902.

Hunt-Jones, Conover. *Dolley and the "Great Little Madison."* Washington, D.C.: American Institute of Architects, 1977.

Klingel, Cynthia Fitterer, and Robert B. Noyed. *Dolley Madison: First Lady.* Chanhassen, Minn.: Child's World, 2003.

Leininger, Tracy M., Kelly Pulley, and Lisa Reed. *Unfading Beauty: The Story of Dolley Madison.* San Antonio, Tex.: His Seasons, 2000.

Mader, Jan. *Dolley Madison.* Mankato, Minn.: Pebble Books, 2007.

Madison, Dolly Payne Todd; David B. Mattern and Holly Cowan Shulman, eds. *The Selected Letters of Dolley Payne Madison*. Charlottesville: University of Virginia Press, 2003. [Chapter 1: "Quaker Beginnings, 1768-1801," 9-37.]

Madison, Dorothy Payne Todd; Lucia Beverley Cutts, ed. *Memoirs and Letters of Dolley Madison, Wife of James Madison, President of the United States*. Boston: Houghton Mifflin Company, 1886.

Malone, Dumas. "Dolly Payne Madison." In Dumas Malone, ed., *Dictionary of American Biography, vol. 6, part 1: McCrady-Millington* (New York: Charles Scribner's Sons, 1964), 180-181.

Martin, Patricia Miles. *Dolley Madison*. New York: Putnam, 1967.

Mattern, David B. "Dolley Madison Has the Last Word: The Famous Letter." *White House History*, 4 (Fall 1998), 228-233.

Mattern, Joanne. *Dolley Madison*. Edina, Minn.: ABDO Pub. Co., 2007. [biography for young readers]

Mayer, Jane R. *Dolley Madison*. New York: Random House, 1954.

Minnigerode, Meade. "Dolley Madison: Informal Biography." *Saturday Evening Post*, 197:22 (November 29, 1924), 3-4.

Moore, Virginia. *The Madisons: A Biography*. New York: McGraw-Hill Book Company, 1979.

Morgan, Helen L. *Mistress of the White House: The Story of Dolley Madison*. Philadelphia: Westminister Press, 1946.

Nolan, Jeannette Covert. *Dolley Madison*. New York: Messner, 1958.

Patrick, Jean L. S. *Dolley Madison.* Minneapolis: Lerner Publications, 2002.

Pflueger, Lynda. *Dolley Madison: Courageous First Lady.* Springfield, N. J.: Enslow Publishers, 1999.

Quackenbush, Robert M. *James Madison and Dolley Madison and Their Times.* New York: Pippin Press, 1992.

Quiri, Patricia Ryon. *Dolley Madison*. New York: F. Watts, 1993.

Remarkable American Women, 1776-1976. (Life special report) Chicago: Life Magazine/Time, Inc., 1976. ["Washington's First and Long-Reigning Hostess-with-the-Mostest," Dolley Madison," 78.]

Rosenfelt, Willard E., general ed.; Howard Lindberg, illustrator. *The Spirit of '76: A Compilation of Exemplary Acts of Conduct by American Men and Women Throughout the First Two Hundred Years of the United States History*. Minneapolis: Denison, 1976. [Dolley Madison, 355.]

Sandak, Cass R. *The Madisons.* (First Families series) New York: Crestwood House, 1992. [a book for young readers]

Shulman, Holly Cowan. "Dolley Madison." In John A. Garraty and Mark C. Carnes, general editors, *American National Biography, vol. 14: Lovejoy-McCurdy* (New York and Oxford: Oxford University Press; Published under the Auspices of the American Council of Learned Societies, 1999), 302-304.

Shulman, Holly Cowan. "Dolley Payne Todd Madison." In Louis L. Gould, ed., American First Ladies: Their Lives and Their Legacy. 2nd ed. (New York: Routledge, 2001), 21-36.

Shulman, Holly Cowan, and David B. Mattern. *Dolley Madison: Her Life, Letters, and Legacy.* New York: PowerPlus Books. 2003.

Sifton, Paul G., "'What A Dread Prospect…": Dolley Madison's Plague Year," *Pennsylvania Magazine of History and Biography*, 87:2 (April 1963), 182-188. [Dolley Madison's struggle to receive her inheritance from her husband's estate based on letters written by her and other members of the family.]

Snodgrass, Mary Ellen. "Prominent Women [Washington, D. C.]." In Doris Weatherford, general ed., *A History of Women in the United States: State-by-State Reference.* 4 vols. Danbury, Conn.: Grolier Academic Reference 2004), In Doris Weatherford, general ed., *A History of Women in the United States: State-by-State Reference.* 4 vols. Danbury, Conn.: Grolier Academic Reference 2004), 4:183-193. [Includes biographical sketch of Dolley Madison (1768-1849.]

Waldrop, Ruth W.; illustrated by Hurston Holland Hendrix. *Dolley Madison.* Tuscaloosa, Ala.: RuSK, 1989.

Walker, Edgar Martin. *Twenty Women Who Helped Make America Great.* New York: Carleton Press, 1995. [Dolly Payne Todd Madison," 1-6.]

Weatherly, Myra. *Dolley Madison: America's First Lady*. Greensboro: Morgan Reynolds, 2003.

Wilson, Dorothy Clarke. *Queen Dolley: The Life and Times of Dolley Madison.* Garden City, N. Y.: Doubleday and Company, 1987.

Witteman, Barbara. *Dolley Madison: First Lady.* Mankato, Minn.: Bridgestone Books, 2003. [a book for young readers]

Zall, Paul M. *Dolley Madison.* Huntington, N. Y.: Nova History Publications, 2001.

Mare, John, 1739-1803

Smith, Helen Burr, and Elizabeth V. Moore. "John Mare: A Composite Portrait." *North Carolina Historical Review*, 44:1 (January 1967), 18-52. [Edenton merchant, politician and artist.]

Martin, Alexander, 1740-1807

Angley, Wilson. "Alexander Martin." Online at the NCpedia website: http://ncpedia.org/biography/governors/martin-alexander.

Douglas, Robert M. *Address upon the Life and Character of Governor Alexander Martin, Delivered at the Annual Celebration of the Battle of Guilford Court House, July 4, 1898.* [Greensboro?: s. n., 1898]; online through the HathiTrust.

"Governor Alexander Martin, 1781-1785, G. P. 10, pp. 1-66, Calendar." Online at the State Archives of North Carolina website: http://archives.ncdcr.gov/Portals/3/PDF/findingaids/governors/Martin_Alexander_Calendar_GP10.pdf.

Lawrence, R. C. "Senator Alexander Martin." *The State: A Weekly Survey of North Carolina*, 13:45 (April 1946), 11, 24; online: http://digital.ncdcr.gov/cdm/ref/collection/p16062coll18/id/15341. [Online description from "North Carolina Periodicals Index," East Carolina University: "Alexander Martin was a Colonel during the Revolution, Speaker of the Senate, thrice Governor of North Carolina and held numerous other positions of considerable importance."]

Martin, Alexander, 1740-1807. "Alexander Martin (1740-1807) Papers, 1780-1790. Manuscript, PC.752, State Archives of North Carolina, Raleigh. [Online catalog description: "Correspondence of Colonel Martin, member of the board of war and governor of North Carolina (1782-1784, 1789-1792), including authorization for payment of expenses of Joseph Kidd (1782); letter to Comptroller Francis Child (1788) about settlement of

Revolutionary army accounts with certain individuals and merchants who furnished supplies; and copy of letter from Patrick Henry introducing lawyer Edward Johnston."]

Rodenbough, Charles D.; foreword by Lindley S. Butler. *Governor Alexander Martin: Biography of a North Carolina Revolutionary War Statesman.* Jefferson, N. C.: McFarland, 2004.

Troxler, Carole Watterson. "Governor Alexander Martin: Biography of a North Carolina Revolutionary War Statesman." *Journal of Southern History*, 71:2 (May 2005), 431-432.

Valsame, James Mark. "Governor Alexander Martin (First Administration), 1781-1785, n. d., Finding Aid." Online at the State Archives of North Carolina website: http://archives.ncdcr.gov/Portals/3/PDF/findingaids/governors/Martin_Alexander_1st_Admin_finding_aid.pdf.

Martin, François-Xavier, 1762-1846

Lawrence, R. C. "François-Xavier Martin." *The State: A Weekly Survey of North Carolina*, 9:42 (March 1942), 9, 24; online: http://digital.ncdcr.gov/cdm/ref/collection/p16062coll18/id/43579. [Online description from "North Carolina Periodicals Index," East Carolina University: "Martin was born in Marseilles, France, in 1762, and arrived in New Bern near the end of the Revolutionary War. He sought employment, beginning as a French tutor, but few were interested in learning the language. He then learned the printer's trade, and advanced rapidly from printer to newspaper editor, legislator, and one of the first to publish a history of North Carolina. He was also a lawyer and outstanding jurist. His was a full life indeed."]

Martin, François X. *The History of North Carolina, From the Earliest Period. New-Orleans: Printed by A.T. Penniman & Co., 1829.*

Yearns, Wilfred B., Jr. "François X. Martin and His *History of North Carolina.*" *North Carolina Historical Review*, 36:2 (April 1959), 17-27; online: http://digital.ncdcr.gov/cdm/ref/collection/p16062coll9/id/4207. [Online description from "North Carolina Periodicals Index," East Carolina University: "This article looks at the life of Francois X. Martin and his writing of *The History of North Carolina, From the Earliest Period.* Biographical information on his early years, details of his writing of *The History of North Carolina*, as well as analysis of the quality of his writing, the text's content and historical value, and Martin's style are included."]

Martin, Howard, active 1770s

Higginbotham, Don, and William S. Price, Jr. "Notes and Documents: Was It Murder for a White Man to Kill a Slave? Chief Justice Martin Howard Condemns the Peculiar Institution in North Carolina." *William and Mary Quarterly*, 3rd series, 36:4 (October 1979), 593-601. [1771]

Martin, Josiah, 1737-1786

[Note: There are many documents relating to Josiah Martin in the "British Records Collection" of the North

Corbitt, D. L. "Governor Martin's Supply of Ammunition Discovered." *North Carolina Historical Review*, 4:1 (January 1927), 104-105.

Great Britain. Colonial Office. "Draft of Additional Instructions to William Tryon, Governor of New York, and Josiah Martin, Governor of North Carolina. 3 Apr, 1775." Copy of a manuscript in the National Archives of the United Kingdom (formerly the Public Records Office), Kew, Richmond, Surrey, England; Z.5.16M, State Archives of North Carolina, Raleigh. [Online catalog description: "Secret instructions concern grant of lands to emigrants from 'the North West parts of North Britain'; such emigrants as subscribe to annexed 'Association' are to be granted lands in fee simple, free of quitrents for 20 years, such lands to be held in trust by Lt. Col. Allan Maclean; if 'the whole or any part of' such emigrants subsequently serve in a military capacity, they are to receive further grants of land; including (pp. 71-72) the 'Form of Association' – an engagement to 'demean Ourselves as good & loyal Subjects of His Majesty,' to 'oppose all illegal Combinations or Insurrections,' and to 'assemble and embody..., and to serve on the same terms...as in His Majesty's other military Service and Establishment' if required to do so."]

Great Britain. Colonial Office. "Ft. Johnson. Letter from Gov. Josiah Martin to Ld. Dartmouth, Sec. of State, #34, June 20, 1775." Copy of a manuscript in the National Archives of the United Kingdom (formerly the Public Records Office), Kew, Richmond, Surrey, England; (MARS ID: 21.1.27.48; folder), "British Records Collection," State Archives of North Carolina, Raleigh. [Online catalog description: "Has fled to this place and sent his family to New York; expects arms from Gen. Gage; still sure that highlanders and western counties could be relied on, and requests arms and restoration of his rank as lt. colonel; Mecklenburg Resolves; Wilmington; John Ashe; S. C. congress attempting to recruit in N. C.; assembly prorogued to Sept 12; thinks better of council than he previously did, with the exception of Mr. Dry."]

Great Britain. Colonial Office. "Proclamation by Gov. Josiah Martin. June 16, 1775." Copy of a manuscript in the National Archives of the United Kingdom (formerly the Public Records Office), Kew, Richmond, Surrey, England; (MARS ID: 21.1.27.47; folder), "British Records Collection," State Archives of North Carolina, Raleigh. [

Great Britain. Colonial Office. "Ft. Johnson. Letter from Gov. Josiah Martin to Ld. Dartmouth, Sec. of State, #35, July 6, 1775." Copy of a manuscript in the National Archives of the United Kingdom (formerly the Public Records Office), Kew, Richmond, Surrey, England; (MARS ID: 21.1.27.49; folder), "British Records Collection," State Archives of North Carolina, Raleigh. [Online catalog description: "Acknowledges despatches; has at last been able to communicate with Gen. Gage; Dartmouth's despatches to Martin were opened by 'the Mob at Charles Town'; this despatch being delivered by Alexander Schaw, who can furnish news of potential support for government of N. C. and neighboring colonies; bridles at instruction that generals' orders to be supreme in military matters in colonies."]

Great Britain. Colonial Office. "Ft. Johnson. Minutes of the Executive Council. June 25, 1775." Copy of a manuscript in the National Archives of the United Kingdom (formerly the Public Records Office), Kew, Richmond, Surrey, England; (MARS ID: 21.1.27.51), "British Records Collection," State Archives of North Carolina, Raleigh. [

Great Britain. Colonial Office. "Marshalwick, St. Albans, [England]. Samuel Martin to Lord George Germain, [Sec. of State]. 12 Oct., 1780." Copy of a manuscript in the National Archives of the United Kingdom (formerly the Public Records Office), Kew, Richmond, Surrey, England; 71.296.1-3 (MARS ID: 21.20.132.1; folder), "British Records Collection," State Archives of North Carolina, Raleigh. [Online catalog description: "Requests compensation – in behalf of his brother, former N. C. Gov. Josiah Martin – for losses incurred by rebel actions in N. C."]

Great Britain. Colonial Office. "Marshalwick, St. Albans, [England]. Samuel Martin to Lord George Germain, [Sec. of State]. 20 Oct., 1780." Copy of a manuscript in the National Archives of the United Kingdom (formerly the Public Records Office), Kew, Richmond, Surrey, England; 71.296.1-3, "British Records Collection," State Archives of North Carolina, Raleigh. [Online catalog description: "Acknowledges Germain's approbation of compensation for N. C. losses sustained by Martin's brother Josiah (former N.C. Gov.) as a result of rebel actions in N. C."]

Great Britain. Colonial Office. "New Bern. Copy of Letter from Gov. Josiah Martin to Gen. Gage. March 16, 1775." Copy of a manuscript in the National Archives of the United Kingdom (formerly the Public Records Office), Kew, Richmond, Surrey, England; (MARS ID: 21.1.27.33; folder), "British Records Collection," State Archives of North Carolina, Raleigh. [Online catalog description: "Requests arms and ammunition for arming highlanders and inhabitants of western counties; Ft. Johnston in need of powder."]

Great Britain. Colonial Office. "New Bern. Letter from Gov. Josiah Martin to Ld. Dartmouth, Sec. of State, #24, May 5, 1774." M Copy of a manuscript in the National Archives of the United Kingdom (formerly the Public Records Office), Kew, Richmond, Surrey, England; Z.5.33 [and Z.5.216?] (MARS ID: 21.1.26.49; folder), "British Records Collection," State Archives of North Carolina, Raleigh. [Online catalog description: "Acknowledges despatches and instructions about grants of land; discusses land grants in N. C.; submits additional clauses for quitrent bill; urges royal ratification of 1754 quitrent act; Chief Justice Howard's remuneration; Fort Johnston and Capt. Collet; royal clemency for Ronald McDugal; suspension of collector at Port Curritück."]

Great Britain. Colonial Office. "New York, [N. Y.]. J[osiah] Martin, [Former Gov. of N. C.], to Lord George Germain, [Sec. of State]. 22 Mar., 1778," Copy of a manuscript in the National Archives of the United Kingdom (formerly the Public Records Office), Kew, Richmond, Surrey, England; 71.327.1-4 (MARS ID: 21.20.140.4; folder), "British Records Collection," State Archives of North Carolina, Raleigh. [Online catalog description: "Letter of recommendation for an Ensign Maclean who served Martin early in the revolution and has travelled to England seeking a position in the British army."]

Great Britain. Colonial Office. "Sovereign, New York. Letter from Gov. Josiah Martin to Ld. George Germain, Sec. of State, #3. Aug 7, 1776." Copy of a manuscript in the National Archives of the United Kingdom (formerly the Public Records Office), Kew, Richmond, Surrey, England; (MARS ID: 21.1.27.87; folder), "British Records Collection," State Archives of North Carolina, Raleigh. [Online catalog description: "Has arrived at New York with Gen. Clinton; Martin's establishment of vice admiralty court at Cape Fear River; hiring of transport for reception of loyalists at Cape Fear; thinks debacle in North Carolina could have been prevented by prudent behavior of loyalists; his family 'in a sort of Captivity' only twenty miles from here; Martin has 'spent nearly fourteen months on board divers ships under every possible disadvantage and inconvenience.'"]

Great Britain. Colonial Office. "Whitehall. Letter from [Ld.] George Germain to Gov. Josiah Martin, #3. Jan 14, 1777, Copy of a manuscript in the National Archives of the United Kingdom (formerly the Public Records Office), Kew, Richmond, Surrey, England; (MARS ID: 21.1.27.93; folder), "British Records Collection," State Archives of North Carolina, Raleigh. [Online catalog description: "Acknowledges dispatch; no prospect of re-establishing government in N. C. until forces can be spared to send there; grants leave to return to England."]

Great Britain. Colonial Office. "Whitehall, [London]. Draft of Lord George Germain, [Sec. of State], to [Josiah] Martin, [Former Gov. of N. C.]. 9 Nov., 1780." Copy of a manuscript in the National Archives of the United Kingdom (formerly the Public Records Office), Kew, Richmond, Surrey, England; 71.336.1-8 (MARS ID: 21.20.140.13; folder), State Archives of North Carolina, Raleigh. [Online catalog description: "General topics: acknowledges receipt of Martin's letters of 10 June (21.20.140.1.11) and 18 August (21.20.140.1.12); acknowledges Martin's efforts in behalf of British interests; Crown approbation of Martin's recommendation of Lewis Henry DeRosset to be provincial secretary of N. C.; Crown confirmation of Martin to be restored to governorship of N. C.; explains status of compensation for the personal losses of former Crown officials; commentary on the Battle of Camden."]

Hartsoe, Kenneth David. "Governor Josiah Martin and His 1772 Journey to the North Carolina Backcountry." M. A. thesis, San Jose State University, 2001. [Online abstract: "During the summer of 1772, North Carolina Governor Josiah Martin visited the backcountry region of his colony. His objective was to acquaint himself with settlers of the frontier counties who were socially and politically isolated from the established provincial leadership on the colony's eastern seaboard. Many of these settlers were Regulators defeated by Governor William Tryon at the Battle of Alamance in May 1771. As a result, Martin inherited a colony smoldering from several years of backcountry violence and disregard for government authority. Martin's trip to the backcountry was the first attempt by North Carolina's royal government to reach out to a bitter and defeated populace. This thesis examines the many challenges Martin faced while in the backcountry and how his response to these challenges secured the trust and respect of a defeated populace."]

Martin, Josiah. "Josiah Martin Proclamation, 1775?" Manuscript 3044-z, Southern Historical Collection, Louis Wilson Library Special Collections, University of North Carolina, Chapel Hill; online finding aid available at http://www2.lib.unc.edu/mss/inv/m/Martin,Josiah.html. [Online finding aid description: "Josiah Martin was the last royal governor of North Carolina, 1771-1775. The collection is a proclamation made by Martin, calling on the King's subjects to support the law and resist the rebels."]

Martin, Josiah. "[Correspondence to and from Governor Josiah Martin, 1773-1775." Manuscript, [numerous documents found in online catalog], State Archives of North Carolina, Raleigh. [These letters relate to many events and activities during the end of Martin's term as the last Royal governor of North Carolina.]

Martin, Josiah. "Governor Josiah Martin's Proclamation." *North Carolina Historical and Genealogical Register*, 2:4 (October 1901), 586-588. [1776]

Martin, Josiah. *North-Carolina. By His Excellency Josiah Martin, Esq. ... A Proclamation. Whereas I have received certain information, that sundry ill-disposed persons have been, and are still going about ... industriously propagating false, seditious, and scandalous reports, derogatory to the honour and justice of the King and his government ... Given ... at Fort Johnston, this sixteenth day of June, 1775 ...* Newbern: Printed by James Davis, 1775; micropublished: (Early American Imprints. First Series. No. 42915) New York: Readex Microprint, 1985. [Note: "Signed: By his excellency's command, Josiah Martin. Alexander Maclean pro James Biggleston, d. secretary."]

North Carolina (State). General Assembly. "[Document dated:] May 6, 1782: Resolution regarding petition of William Borden (messages only, with petition and a letter from William Tisdale regarding Gov. Josiah Martin's papers)." Manuscript; General Assembly Record Group; Session Records, April-May 1782, Committee Papers, Resolutions, Senate Bills, House Bills, Box 2 (MARS ID: 66.8.28; box), State Archives of North Carolina, Raleigh.

Sheridan, Richard B. "The West Indian Antecedents of Josiah Martin, Last Royal Governor of North Carolina." *North Carolina Historical Review*, 54:3 (July 1977), 253-270. [Online description from "North Carolina Periodicals Index," East Carolina University: "This is a biographical essay on the ancestors of Josiah Martin, North Carolina's last royal governor. Some information Josiah Martin's gubernatorial career is provided, but the predominant focus are the Martin family members who immigrated to Antigua in the 17th century, and Josiah's childhood years spent there."]

Stumpf, Vernon O. "Josiah Martin and His Search for Success." *North Carolina Historical Review*, 53:1 (January 1976), 55-79. [Online description from "North Carolina Periodicals Index," East Carolina University: "This article follows the career of Josiah Martin, the last royal governor of North Carolina. Plagued by financial insecurity for much of his life, Martin bought his way into public service in the colonies with assistance from influential friends. His governorship provided him the financial security he always craved."]

Stumpf, Vernon O. *Josiah Martin: The Last Royal Governor of North Carolina.* Durham: Carolina Academic Press for the Kellenberger Historical Foundation, 1986.

McCorkle, Samuel Eusebius, 1746-1811

Enger, William R. "Samuel Eusebius McCorkle: North Carolina Educator." Ed. D. dissertation, Oklahoma State University, 1973.

Murphy, Walter. "Davie, McCorkle, and Avery." *The State: A Weekly Survey of North Carolina*, 10:29 (December 1942), 9, 28; online: http://digital.ncdcr.gov/cdm/ref/collection/p16062coll18/id/33628. [Online description from "North Carolina Periodicals Index," East Carolina University: "William Richardson Davie, Waightstill Avery, and Samuel Eusebius McCorkle were responsible for man any {*sic*} others for the establishment of the University of North Carolina at Chapel Hill, which celebrates its 150th anniversary next year."]

Taylor, Thomas T. "Essays on the Career and Thoughts of Samuel Eusebius McCorkle." M. A. thesis, University of North Carolina at Greensboro, 1978.

McDowell, Charles, 1743-1815

McDowell, Charles. "Charles McDowell Papers, 1782." Manuscript, PC.29, State Archives of North Carolina, Raleigh. [Online catalog description: "Proceedings of court-martial in Burke Co. of McDowell, accused of 'countenancing Tories,' and a letter from Gen. Griffith Rutherford transmitting proceedings to the General Assembly with recommendation that McDowell's commission be restored."]

"A True List to Charles McDowell, B. Genl – District of Morgan." *Eswau Huppeday: Bulletin of the Broad River Genealogical Society*, 19:3 (August 1999), 177. [The date is not given, but it is probably ca. 1780-1782.]

McDugald, Rebecca

Cain, Robert J. "Loyalist Widow Pension Document of Rebecca McDugald of Moore County, North Carolina." *Argyll Colony Plus*, 4:4 (Fall 1989), 140-141.

McGee, Martha MacFarlane, 1735-1783

Arthur, Billy. "Mighty Martha." *The State: Down Home in North Carolina*, 62:3 (August 1994), 13-14; online: http://digital.ncdcr.gov/cdm/ref/ collection/p16062coll18/id/66889. [Online description from "North Carolina Periodicals Index," East Carolina University: "Randolph County's Martha Bell has been hailed as North Carolina's most courageous Revolutionary War heroine." Martha MacFarlane McGee (1735-1820)]

Duncan, Wanda. "Revolutionary Heroine." *Our State: Down Home in North Carolina*, 75:3 (August 2007), 25-26; online: http://digital.ncdcr.gov/cdm/ref/collection/p16062coll18/id/89990. [Online description from "North Carolina Periodicals Index," East Carolina University: "Duncan recounts events in the life of Martha MacFarlane McGee Bell during the Revolutionary War."]

McKeehan, Mary, aka "Gunpowder Mary," active 1770s-1780

Berg, Gordon, and Bruce Adams. *Laboring for Independence: Workers in the Revolution.* Washington, D. C.: U. S. Department of Labor, [1976?]. [Includes "Gunpowder Made by a Woman Helped Colonists Win Crucial Battle" (Kings Mountain, N. C.), 20].

Eakin, Stephen Robert. "'Gunpowder Mary' McKeehan, A Tennessee Heroine of the Revolution." *Flintlock & Powderhorn: Magazine of the Sons of the Revolution*, 9:1 (April 1991), 21-23. [Discusses McKeehan's involvement in the Battle of King's Mountain.]

McKissick, Jane Wilson, 1759-1844

Bolar, Mary. "Jane Wilson McKissick: Patriot of the American Revolution." *Daughters of the American Revolution Magazine*, 114:2 (February 1980), 152-155. [North Carolina]

McRee, John, 1758-1801

"[Notebook Containing the Biography of …Griffith John McRee (1758-1801), Revolutionary War Officer and Rice Planter on the Cape Fear River of North Carolina." In the Griffith J. McRee Papers, 1772-1908." Manuscript

479 and microfilm M-479, Southern Historical Collection, Louis Round Wilson Library, University of North Carolina at Chapel Hill.

Mebane, Alexander, 1744-1795

Arthur, Billy. "The Midnight Ride of Alexander Mebane." *Our State: Down Home in North Carolina*, 67:3 (August 1999), 18-20; online: http:// digital.ncdcr.gov/cdm/ref/collection/p16062coll18/id/68131. [Online description from "North Carolina Periodicals Index," East Carolina University: "North Carolina's Paul Revere was Col. Alexander Mebane. Captured by Tory Colonel David Fanning, Mebane escaped the night of September 12, 1781, and rode through Orange and Alamance Counties to warn the patriots of the Tories' approach. On September 13, Tories and Patriots fought at Lindley's Mill, with neither side achieving victory. After the war Mebane's activities included serving in the U. S. Congress, as a member of the Constitutional Convention, and as an original trustee of the University of North Carolina."]

Mebane, Robert, 1748-1781

Anderson, William Lee, III. "Lieutenant Colonel Robert Mebane: Revolutionary War Continental Army Officer, Commander of North Carolina's Third Regiment: Military Timeline Notes." Online: http://elehistory.com/amrev/RobertMebane.pdf. [Robert Mebane (1745-1781); Orange County]

Misenheimer Family Women

Misenheimer, John E., Jr. "Misenheimer Ladies of the American Revolution." *Golden Nugget (Cabarrus Genealogical Society)*, 13:2 (Summer 2005), 42-45.

Mitchell, Sarah, 1750-?

Hoxie, Elizabeth F. "Sarah Wilson [b.1750]." In Edward T. James, ed., *Notable American Women, 1607-1950: A Biographical Dictionary, vol. III: P-Z* (Cambridge: Belknap Press of Harvard University Press, 1971), 628. [con artist in Maryland, Virginia, and North Carolina in the 1770s. Passed herself off as Princess Sophia Carolina Matilda, the queen's younger sister.]

Lyman, Eliza B. *Reminiscences of Newport before and during the Revolutionary War.* [S. l.: s. n.], 1869; reprinted with the title: *A Reminiscence of Newport before and during the Revolutionary War.* Newport, R. I.: Milne Printery, 1906. [Chapter 17: "Sarah Wilson," 144-148 (an English convict women sent to Frederick County, Maryland in 1771 as a servant. She escaped and set up a scam operation in South Carolina and elsewhere using the name Princess Susanna Caroline Matilda, sister of Queen Charlotte, before being returned to her master in Maryland).]

Moore, Alfred, 1755-1810

Davis, Junius. *Alfred Moore and James Iredell, Revolutionary Patriots, and Associate Justices of the Supreme Court of the United States: An Address Delivered in Presenting Their Portraits to the Supreme Court of North Carolina on Behalf of the North Carolina Sons of the Revolution.* Raleigh: The Society, 1899.

Lawrence, R. C. "Chief Justice Moore." *The State: A Weekly Survey of North Carolina*, 16:5 (July 1948), 3, 17; online: http://digital.ncdcr.gov/cdm/ref/collection/p16062coll18/id/22536. [Online description from "North Carolina Periodicals Index," East Carolina University: "By 1948, only two North Carolinians had served as members of the Supreme Court. James Iredell was the first appointed followed by Alfred Moore, the focus of this article. The author supplies a brief familial history, charting the Moores back to the mid-18th-century in the lower Cape Fear region. The account of Alfred Moore's life touches on his previous military experience during the American Revolution and judicial career beginning as a lawyer, to Attorney General of the state, until then finally a Supreme Court Justice."]

Moore, Alfred. "Alfred Moore Papers, 1779-1802, n. d." Manuscript PC.774 (MARS ID: 1284), State Archives of North Carolina, Raleigh. [Online catalog description: "Memorandum book of Alfred Moore, Brunswick Co. lawyer and U.S. Supreme Court justice (1799-1804), containing illustrations of indicments (1779-1802) brought in various North Carolina superior court districts by Attorneys General James Iredell, John Haywood, Jr., Alfred Moore, and Blake Baker and by attorney for the state John Hay, including indictment of James Glasgow for land fraud (1799), and copy of Governor Benjamin Williams's commission for the court of conference to try Glasgow and others. Book also contains summaries of arguments on points that interested Moore, made by lawyers, attorneys general, and judges in a number of superior court cases (1784-1796). Also brief biography of Moore."]

Murfree, Hardy, 1752-1809

Murfree, Fanny Noailles Dickinson. *Hardy Murfree, 1752-1809*. [S. l.: s. n., 19??].

Murfree, W. L. "Colonel Hardy Murfree, of the North Carolina Continental Line." *North Carolina Booklet*, 17:3 (January 1918), 160-164. Online description from "North Carolina Periodicals Index," East Carolina University: "Colonel Hardy Murfree of Hertford County fought in the American Revolution and lived both near Murfreesboro, NC and Murfreesboro, TN, the latter having been named for him. He was buried with full Masonic honors."]

Nash, Abner, ca. 1740-1786

Dean, Earl. "Our Borrowed Governors." *The State: A Weekly Survey of North Carolina*, 18:41 (March 1951), 3, 17-18; online: http://digital.ncdcr.gov/cdm/ref/collection/p16062coll18/id/26708. [Online description from "North Carolina Periodicals Index," East Carolina University: "Born in Virginia, but bred in North Carolina, these three early governors, John Motley Morehead, James Turner, and Abner Nash, were successful politicians."]

"Governor Abner Nash, 1780-1781, n. d., G. P. 6, pp. 1-136, Calendar." Online at the State Archives of North Carolina website: http://archives.ncdcr.gov/Portals/3/PDF/findingaids/governors/Nash_Abner_Calendar_GP6.pdf.

Hamilton, Joseph Gregoire de Roulhac. *Presentation of Portrait of Governor Abner Nash to the State of North Carolina in the Hall of the House of Representatives, at Raleigh, November 15, 1909, by the North Carolina Society of the Sons of the Revolution; Address by J. G. de Roulhac Hamilton*. Raleigh: [s. n.], 1909.

Lawrence, R. C. "The Bar of Halifax." *The State: A Weekly Survey of North Carolina*, 12:38 (February 1945), 5, 16-17; online: http://digital.ncdcr.gov/cdm/ref/collection/p16062coll18/id/12783. [Online description from "North Carolina Periodicals Index," East Carolina University: "Willie Jones, William R. Davie, Abner Nash, John Branch, the Kitchins, and many other famous lawyers, jurists, and statesmen have come from Halifax County and rendered outstanding service to North Carolina and United States."]

Nash, Abner. "Abner Nash Correspondence, 1778-1781." Manuscript MSS3386 (Miscellaneous Manuscript Collection), Manuscript Division, James Madison Building, Library of Congress, Washington, D. C.

Nash, Abner. "Abner Nash Letters, 1777-1783." Manuscript 1223-z, Southern Historical Collection, Louis Round Wilson Special Collections Library, University of North Carolina, Chapel Hill; online finding aid available at http://www2.lib.unc.edu/mss/inv/n/Nash,Abner.html. [Online finding aid description: "Abner Nash (circa 1740-1786) was a Revolutionary governor of North Carolina, 1780-1781, and member of the Continental Congress. The collection includes letters to and from Nash, mostly concerned with state business in regard to military affairs."]

Nash, Frank. "Governor Abner Nash." *North Carolina Booklet*, 22:1-4 (July 1922-April 1923), 3-11.

Nash, Hugo O. *Patriot Sons, Patriot Brothers*. Nashville, Tenn.: Westview Publishing Company, 2006. [Description: "The story of a Prince Edward County, Virginia family and two sons who became North Carolina heroes of the American Revolution: Francis Nash (1742-1777), who gave his life for his country and his name to Nashville, Tenn.; Nashville, Ga.; and Nashville/Nash County, N. C. Abner Nash (1740-1786), Revolutionary leader; wartime governor of North Carolina, and member of the Second Continental Congress." Nash and Witherspoon Families]

North Carolina (State). General Assembly. "[Document dated:] January 28, [1781]: Address of Governor Nash." Manuscript; General Assembly Record Group; Session Records, January-February 1781; Joint Papers, Committee Papers, Resolutions, Senate Bills, House Bills, Box 1 (MARS ID: 66.8.23.3.1; item), State Archives of North Carolina, Raleigh. [Online catalog description: "Nash discusses recent events of the war and complains that the newly established board of war infringes on his powers as governor."]

Valsame, James Mark. "Governor Abner Nash Papers, n. d., 1780-1781, Finding Aid." Online at the State Archives of North Carolina website: http://archives.ncdcr.gov/Portals/3/PDF/findingaids/governors/Nash_Abner_finding_aid.pdf.

Nash, Francis, 1720-1777

Berry, Connely Burgin. "A Miscellaneous Collection of Letters and Papers from the Records of Connelly Burgin Berry, ca. 1972-2000." Manuscripts P, Manuscripts Division, South Caroliniana Library, University of South Carolina, Columbia. [The collection contains information on the death and burial of General Nash.]

"The Grave of General Francis Nash." *North Carolina Booklet*, 22:1-4 (July 1922-April 1923), 109-110." [Kulpsville, Montgomery County, Pennsylvania]

Lawrence, R. C. "From Each War Two Warriors." *The State: A Weekly Survey of North Carolina*, 13:32 (January 1946), 7, 20-21; online: http://digital.ncdcr.gov/cdm/ref/collection/p16062coll18/id/14908. [Online description from "North Carolina Periodicals Index," East Carolina University: "From the Revolutionary War through the Spanish-American War, Lawrence has selected two North Carolinians whom he has considered to be particularly outstanding. From the Revolutionary War, Lawrence describes General Nash and Colonel Buncombe; from the Mexican War Louis Wilson and General Bragg; from the Civil War, William Pender and James Pettigrew; and from the Spanish-American War Ensign Bagley, and Lieutenant William Shipp."]

Lawrence, R. C. "Some Military Heroes." *The State: A Weekly Survey of North Carolina*, 12:36 (February 1945), 7, 21; online: http://digital.ncdcr.gov/cdm/ref/collection/p16062coll18/id/12723.

Moffitt, Mrs. E. E. "Francis Nash." *North Carolina Booklet*, 6:2 (October 1906), 153-154; online: http://digital.ncdcr.gov/cdm/ref/collection/p249901coll37/id/14180. [Online description from "North Carolina Periodicals Index," East Carolina University: "This biography provides a short accounting of the life and family history of Francis Nash of Edgecombe County. Mr. Nash comes from a family of significant contributors to the state of North Carolina and he has continued this trend in public service to the state as a law clerk, lawyer, mayor, commissioner and contributor to North Carolina focused journals."]

Nash, Hugo O. *Patriot Sons, Patriot Brothers.* Nashville, Tenn.: Westview Publishing Company, 2006. [Description: "The story of a Prince Edward County, Virginia family and two sons who became North Carolina heroes of the American Revolution: Francis Nash (1742-1777), who gave his life for his country and his name to Nashville, Tenn.; Nashville, Ga.; and Nashville/Nash County, N. C. Abner Nash (1740-1786), Revolutionary leader; wartime governor of North Carolina, and member of the Second Continental Congress."]

"North Carolina Society of Pennsylvania. *Where General Nash of North Carolina Is Buried.* Philadelphia: North Carolina Society of Pennsylvania, [1923?].

Reed, John Ford. *Tragic Sword: Biography of Brigadier General Francis Nash of North Carolina, 1742-1777.* Valley Forge, Pa., Valley Forge Historical Society, [1973].

Siry, Steven F. *Liberty's Fallen Generals: Leadership and Sacrifice in the American War of Independence.* Washington, D. C.: Potomac Books, 2012. [Includes: Francis Nash (August-October 1777).]

Waddell, Alfred M[oore]. *Gen. Francis Nash: An Address by A. M. Waddell, Delivered at the Unveiling of a Monument to General Nash, Voted by Congress, at the Guilford Battle Ground, July 4, 1906.* Greensboro, N. C.: Guilford Battle Ground Company, 1906; reprinted: *North Carolina Booklet*, 14:2 (October 1914), 74-90; online: http://digital.ncdcr.gov/cdm/ref/collection/p249901coll37/id/14180. [Online description from "North Carolina Periodicals Index," East Carolina University: "The dedication on July 4, 1906 of a monument to General Francis Nash at the Guilford Courthouse National Military Park, served as an occasion to review his contributions to the Revolutionary movement in North Carolina and specific military service during the conflict."]

Waddell, A. M. "General Francis Nash." *North Carolina Booklet*, 14:2 (October 1914), 74-90.

Watson, Helen R. "The Tar Heel Hero of Germantown." *The State: Down Home in North Carolina*, 42:6 (November 1974), 10-11, 41; online: http://digital.ncdcr.gov/cdm/ref/collection/p16062coll18/id/ 569 23. [Online description from "North Carolina Periodicals Index," East Carolina University: "Revolutionary General and North Carolina native, Francis Nash, led troops under Washington in the battle at Germantown, Pennsylvania where Nash was mortally wounded. The Continental Congress voted funds for a monument in the General's memory. Nash is buried in Kulpsville, Pennsylvania."]

Williams, Samuel Cole. *Generals Francis Nash and William Lee Davidson.* Nashville: Tennessee Historical Commission, 1942.

O'Fallon, James, active 1770s-1780s

Parish, John Carl. "The Intrigues of Dr. James O'Fallon." *Mississippi Valley Historical Review*, 17:3 (September 1930), 230-263.

Osterlein, Elisabeth, active 1770s

Lewis, Johanna Miller. "A Social and Architectural History of the Girls' Boarding School Building at Salem, North Carolina." *North Carolina Historical Review*, 66:2 (April 1989), 126-148. [the school for little girls opened by 1772 by Sister Elisabeth Osterlein]

Paine, Elizabeth Miller,

Laird, Zelva Compton. "Elizabeth Miller Paine." In Zelva Compton Laird and the Historical Activities Committee, National Society of the Colonial Dames of America in the State of Texas. *Women Colonial and Pioneer.* ([Dallas]: The Society, [1982]), 13.

Patton, Mary McKeehan, 1751-1836

Eakin, Stephen Robert. "'Gunpowder Mary' McKeehan, a Tennessee Heroine of the Revolution." *Flintlock & Powderhorn: Magazine of the Sons of the Revolution*, 9:1 (April 1991), 21-23. [Mary McKeehan Patton]

Goodsell, Susan M. "Mary McKeehan Patton." Online: https://tennesseeencyclopedia.net/entry.php?rec=1043.

Howard, Robert A. *Mary Patton: Powder Maker of the Revolution.* Rocky Mount: Rocky Mount Historical Association, 1980.

Penn, John, 1740-1788

Abernethy, Mrs. Max. "Signers of the Declaration." *The State: A Weekly Survey of North Carolina*, 19:6 (July 1951), 3, 17; online: http://digital.ncdcr.gov/cdm/ref/collection/p16062coll18/id/27249. [Online description from "North Carolina Periodicals Index," East Carolina University: "There were three men from North Carolina who signed the Declaration of Independence, but none of the three was a native-born son of the Old North State."]

Lawrence, R. C. "Signers of the Declaration." *The State: A Weekly Survey of North Carolina*, 8:42 (March 1941), 5, 21; online: http://digital.ncdcr.gov/cdm/ref/collection/p16062coll18/id/39248. [Online description from "North Carolina Periodicals Index," East Carolina University: "It is a singular fact that none of the three North Carolina signers of the Declaration of Independence was a native of North Carolina. William Hooper was from Massachusetts, Joseph Hewes from New Jersey, and John Penn from Virginia, but all rendered distinguished service to North Carolina and the nation as a whole."]

Park, Mrs. Robert E. "Homes of the Signers of the Declaration of Independence." *American Monthly Magazine*, 20:4 (April 1902), 325-328. [Includes North Carolina signers: William Hooper, Joseph Hewes, John Penn]

Penn, John, 1741-1788. "John Penn (1741-1788) Papers, 1769-1788." Manuscript, PC.835, State Archives of North Carolina, Raleigh. [Online catalog description: "Papers of Penn, Granville Co. lawyer, member of the N. C. Board of War, delegate to the Continental Congress (1775-1779) and signer of the Declaration of Independence, including letter (Feb., 1776) from Penn in Philadelphia to Thomas Person about British plans, need to raise battalions in North Carolina, foreign trade, and the need for alliances and perhaps independence. Photocopies include guardian's permission for marriage of Frances Penn to John Hunt (Granville Co., 1771), list of goods sent North Carolina prisoners of war in South Carolina (1780), Penn's will and codicils (1784), memorandums to Granville Co. Clerk of Court Reuben Searcy about various lawsuits (1784-1787), a Granville Co. ordinary bond (1785), and a deed of gift (1788) from Penn to son William for land in Granville Co. Also an unidentified lawyer's account book (previously ascribed to John Penn) recording travels to courts in Rowan, Mecklenburg, Tryon, Anson, and Orange counties (1769-1770) and accounts with clients and with Col. Edmund Fanning."]

Pittman, Thomas Merritt. "John Penn." *North Carolina Booklet*, 4:5 (September 1904), 4-23; online: http://digital.ncdcr.gov/cdm/ref/collection/p249901coll37/id/14180. [Online description from "North Carolina Periodicals Index," East Carolina University: "This article discusses the life and times of 18th century North Carolinian John Penn. A lawyer from a well to do family, Penn was a political leader in Revolutionary North Carolina and a signer of the Declaration of Independence."]

Roger, Lou. "John Penn." *We the People of North Carolina*, 6:8 (December 1948), 22-23, 27. [Online description from "North Carolina Periodicals Index," East Carolina University: "John Penn was born in Caroline County, Virginia, and later relocated to Granville County, North Carolina. In a short time he was one of the colonial leaders of his country and state and was one of three North Carolinians who signed the Declaration of Independence."]

Taylor, John, 1753-1823. "Biographical Notes on John Penn." Manuscript accession no. 21999, Library of Virginia, Richmond. [Online catalog description: "Biographical Notes on John Penn (1740-1788) of North Carolina, written by John Taylor (1753-1824) of Caroline County, Virginia. Penn was the son of a neighbor and a relative of Edmund Pendleton (1721-1803) of Caroline County, who helped with his education. Penn served as a member of the Continental Congress from North Carolina from 1775 to 1780, signing the Declaration of Independence."]

Person, Thomas, 1733-1800

Norris, Jeannie Faris. "Whatever Happened to: Mosby Hall." *North Carolina Preservation.* 46 (January 1984), 9. [Online description from "North Carolina Periodicals Index," East Carolina University: "This seminal article discusses Mosby Hall, in Warren County, the home of General Thomas Person, a prominent Revolutionary War patriot."]

Person, Thomas, 1733-1800. "Thomas Person (1733-1800) Papers, 1769-1783." Manuscript, PC.839, State Archives of North Carolina, Raleigh. [Online catalog description: "Papers relating to Gen. Thomas Person, Regulator, legislator, and Revolutionary leader. A letter from Ben Person to brother William concerns Thomas's indictment for perjury in Granville Co. (1769). A letter from Thomas Person in Hillsborough to William concerns a Bute Co. estate settlement, Scottish loyalists in Cumberland Co., and planned movement of patriot forces toward Cross Creek (Feb. 12, 1776). Also letter from Person to Gen. Mordecai Gist about a shipment of iron and the military situation (Jan., 1781); fragment of letter from former resident of Orange Co. (1783); and brief note from John Penn, n. d."]

Person Family. "Person Family Papers, 1728-1907." Manuscript 590, Southern Historical Collection, Louis Round Wilson Special Collections Library, University of North Carolina, Chapel Hill; online finding aid and some digital surrogates available at http://www2.lib.unc.edu/mss/inv/p/Person_Family.html. [Online finding aid description: "Person family members included Thomas Person (1733-1800), North Carolina Revolutionary leader, born in Brunswick County, Va., but resident from infancy in Granville County, N. C. He became a surveyor for Lord Granville, and, over the years, he acquired a large estate in North Carolina and Tennessee. He became a justice of the peace in 1756, sheriff in 1762, and was representative in the Assembly in 1764 and frequently thereafter. When the Revolution began, he was elected a general of militia and again made a justice of the peace in 1776. He was a member of the House of Commons from 1777 to 1786, 1788 to 1791, 1793 to 1795, and in 1797 and a member of the Senate in 1787 and 1791. In 1760, Thomas Person married Johanna Thomas of Granville County. They had no children. Thomas Person's brother was William Person Jr. ... The collection includes letters, bills, receipts, deeds, and other papers, chiefly 1800-1825, of the Person family, large landowners and political leaders of Granville County, N. C., and nearby counties. Included are land grants, deeds, and other papers, 1739-1800, of William Person and his son, Thomas Person, pertaining to the surveying and sale of land in North Carolina and Tennessee; papers, 1801-1807, concerning Thomas Person's estate; letters, 1801-1804, from Thomas Dillon to William Person, regarding the administration of lands in Tennessee; deeds and indentures, 1798-1827, of William and Benjamin Eaton Person; and accounts, 1821-1824, of William Person with the general merchandise firm of Mitchell and White. ..."]

Weeks, Stephen B. "Thomas Person." *The North Carolina Booklet*, 9:1 (July 1909), 16-35.

Pettigrew, Charles, 1744-1807, and Pettigrew Family

Osborne, Mary Winder. "The Pettigrew Family." *The State: A Weekly Survey of North Carolina*, 5:6 (July 1937), 1, 24; online: http://digital.ncdcr.gov/cdm/ref/collection/p16062coll18/id/103220. [Online description from "North Carolina Periodicals Index," East Carolina University: "The Pettigrew family was one of the state's more historic names. Their ancestors moved to America from France, Ireland, and Scotland and settled in the state in 1740. Two more distinguished members included Reverend Charles Pettigrew and General Johnston Pettigrew. Reverend Charles Pettigrew was a noted orator and advocate of peace. His descendant Johnston became a worthy Civil War general who led troops in the Battle of Gettysburg where he was mortally wounded."]

Tucker, Henry Z. "St. David's Church." The State: A Weekly Survey of North Carolina, 6:50 (May 1939), 10, 20; online: http://digital.ncdcr.gov/cdm/ref/collection/p16062coll18/id/34909. [Online description from "North Carolina Periodicals Index," East Carolina University: "Formerly known as Pettigrew's Chapel, St. David's Episcopal Church, located in Creswell in Washington County, is one of the outstanding historical churches in the state. The church dates back to 1797 and serves as a memorial to Charles Pettigrew who was the first Bishop of the Episcopal Church in North Carolina."]

Wall, Bennett H. "Charles Pettigrew, First Bishop-Elect of the North Carolina Episcopal Church." *North Carolina Historical Review*, 28:1 (January 1951), 15-46; online: http://digital.ncdcr.gov/cdm/ref/collection/p16062coll9/id/4207. [Online description from "North Carolina Periodicals Index," East Carolina University: "This biographical essay looks at the life and career of Charles 'Old Parson' Pettigrew, with a detailed look at his youth, education, actions during the Revolutionary War, career in the North Carolina Episcopal Church and eventual election to Bishop. Excerpts from his writings and correspondence are included."]

Wall, Bennett H. "The Founding of the Pettigrew Plantations." *North Carolina Historical Review*, 27:4 (October 1950), 395-418; reprinted: Elinor Miller, ed. *Plantation, Town, and County: Essays on the Local History of*

American Slave Society (Urbana: University of Illinois Press, 1974); online: http://digital.ncdcr.govcdm/ref/collection/p16062coll9/id/4207. [Online description from "North Carolina Periodicals Index," East Carolina University: "Following the Revolutionary War, Charles Pettigrew turned to agriculture to supplement his family's income. The reverend owned no property until his marriage to Mary Blount on October 29, 1778. From this nuptial he gained both property and slaves in Tennessee and North Carolina. Pettigrew established the Pettigrew Plantation in North Carolina acquiring lands in Tyrell and Washington Counties. The article summarizes the Pettigrew's development of the plantation and general history of the area."]

Pike, Abigail, 1709-1781

Teague, Bobbie. "Quaker Profiles: Abigail Pike, A Woman Ahead of Her Time." *North Carolina Friends Historical Society Newsletter*, no. 24 (June 2006), [p. 4]. [Abigail Overman Pike of Cane Creek, North Carolina, was a Quaker minister and mother of nine children.]

Polk, Ezekiel, 1747-1824

Rogers, Wilmot P. "Ezekiel Polk and His Descendants." Typescript [San Francisco, 1939], Library of Congress, Washington, D. C

Sellers, Charles Grier. "Colonel Ezekiel Polk: Pioneer and Patriarch." *William and Mary Quarterly*, 3rd series, 10:1 (January 1953), 80-98.

Polk, Thomas, 1732-1794

Ashe, S. A. "Colonel Polk's Rebellion." *North Carolina Booklet*, 10:1 (July 1910), 43-47; online: http://digital.ncdcr.gov/cdm/ref/collection/p249901coll37/id/14180. [Online description from "North Carolina Periodicals Index," East Carolina University: "Mecklenburg County, North Carolina resident, Colonel Thomas Polk has been credited with a major role in the May 1775 declaration of independence from British rule. However, contemporary documentation of the event seems to be lacking."]

Lewis, J. D. "Patriot Leaders in North Carolina: Thomas Polk: Colonel over the Mecklenburg County Regiment of Militia – 1775; Colonel over the 2nd Battalion of Salisbury District Minutemen - 1775-1776; Colonel over the 4th NC Regiment - 1776-1778; Commissary General for the NC Continental Line – 1780." Online: http://www.carolana.com/NC/Revolution/patriot_leaders_nc_thomas_polk.html.

Misenheimer, John E. "Thomas Polk and the Liberty Bell." *Olde Mecklenburg Genealogical Society Quarterly*, 24:1 (2006), 12-15.

Polk, William, 1758-1834

Angellotti, Frank M. "The Polks of North Carolina and Tennessee." *New England Historical and Genealogical Register*, 77:2 (April 1923), 133-145; 77:3 (July 1923), 213-227; 77:4 (October 1923), 250-270; 78:1 (January 1924), 33-53; 77:2 (April 1924), 159-177; 77:3 (July 1924), 318-330; reprinted: Greenville, S. C.: Southern Historical Press, 1984.

Lawrence, R. C. "Colonel William Polk." *The State: A Weekly Survey of North Carolina*, 14:5 (June 1946), 23-24; online: http://digital.ncdcr.gov/cdm/ref/collection/p16062coll18/id/15755. [Online description from "North Carolina Periodicals Index," East Carolina University: "Colonel William Polk is a noteworthy American historical figure who was born and raised in North Carolina. The article contains an outline of Polk's life from birth in Mecklenburg 1758 to political appointments following his post-Revolutionary War career. Polk's exploits during the Revolutionary War are the main focus of this piece."]

Mac Donald, James M. "Politics of the Personal in the Old North State: Griffith Rutherford in Revolutionary North Carolina." Ph. D. dissertation, Louisiana State University, 2006; online: http://etd.lsu.edu/docs/available/etd-03022006-111555/unrestricted/Mac_Donald_dis.pdf.

North Carolina (State). General Assembly. "[Document dated:] August 15, [1778]: In Favor of Maj. William Polk (With Messages)." Manuscript, General Assembly Record Group, Session Records, August 1778; Joint Papers, Committee Papers, Resolutions, Senate Bills, House Bills, Box 1 (MARS ID: 66.8.14.8.9; item), State Archives of North Carolina, Raleigh. [Online catalog description: "William Polk is to fill the first vacancy made available in any Continental battalion for the office of major."]

Polk, William. "Autobiography of Colonel William Polk." In William Henry Hoyt, ed. *The Papers of Archibald D. Murphy* (Raleigh: North Carolina Historical Commission, 1914), 400-410.

Polk, William. "Colonel Polk's Account of the First Revolutionary Movements in North Carolina." Published in Archibald D. Murphey; William Henry Hoyt, ed. *Papers of Archibald D. Murphey* (: E. M. Uzell & Company, State Printers, 1914), 196-202.

Polk, William. "William Polk (1758-1834) Papers, 1721-1829." Manuscript, PC.47, State Archives of North Carolina, Raleigh. [Online catalog description: "Papers of William Polk, Revolutionary officer, legislator, and Raleigh lawyer, including letter from Polk to Gen. Nathanael Greene (1781), a power of attorney, and letters (1796-1798) to Tench Coxe of Philadelphia concerning sale by Polk of 20,445 acres in Mecklenburg Co. Also transcripts of letters in the Library of Congress, written to Polk about land in Tennessee belonging either to him or to UNC for which he was attorney, litigation over the lands, and attempts by Tennessee to gain control over unclaimed lands (1802-1823). Other transcribed letters refer to the 1824 presidential election and sentiments about Andrew Jackson and William H. Crawford; Archibald D. Murphey's finances and proposed history; Revolutionary activities of William and Thomas Polk; Lafayette's visit to the United States; the John Quincy Adams administration; and the election of 1828."]

Read, Charles, 17??-1774

Kammerer, Roger. "In Search of Charles Read." *Greenville Times/Pitt's Past*, (January 5-18, 2005), 5. [Online description from "North Carolina Periodicals Index," East Carolina University: "Charles Read was a leading politician in colonial days. In the spring of 1773 he fled his native state of New Jersey, where he faced a long jail sentence for bankruptcy. Read moved to Martinborough, North Carolina, where he died in 1774. Martinborough was renamed Greenesville in 1786. Today, it is believed that Reade Street in Greenville is named for him."]

Reiter, Anna Margaretha, active 1770s

Misenheimer, John. "Johann Jacob Meisenheimer, and Anna Margaretha Reiter, and Other German Patriots during the American Revolution." *Mecklenburg Genealogical Society Quarterly*, 15:1 (1997), 4-14.

Robertson, James Randolph, 1742-1814

Barnes, Katherine R. "James Robertson's Journey to Nashville: Tracing the Route of Fall 1779." *Tennessee Historical Quarterly*, 35:2 (Summer 1976), 145-161.

Brown, Lavinia Robertson Hill. "The Family of Gen. James Robertson." *American Historical Magazine* [DAR], 1:2 (April 1896), 174-188; 1:3 (July 1896), 271-279; 1:4 (October 1896), 357-389; 2:1 (January 1897), 45-59. [James Robertson (1742-1814); a founder of Tennessee]

Matthews, Thomas Edwin. *General James Robertson, Father of Tennessee*. Nashville: The Parthenon Press, 1934.

Pennywitt, Neil C. "James Robertson." Online at: NCPedia: http://ncpedia.org/biography/robertson-james.

Robertson, James. "The Correspondence of Gen. James Robertson." *American Historical Magazine*, 5:1 (January 1900), 67-96; 5:2 (April 1900), 162-190; 5:3 (July 1900), 252-286.

Robeson, Thomas, 1740-1785

Robeson, John Alexander. "John Alexander Robeson Collection, 1734-1941." Manuscript, PC.888, State Archives of North Carolina, Raleigh. [Online catalog description: "Papers concerning Col. Thomas Robeson (1740-1785), revolutionary leader, including Bladen Co. land grants to William Bartram (1734-1735) and Robeson (1782); promissory notes to Colonel Robeson for value received (1781); copy of revolutionary pension records of Col. Thomas Brown; and notes, extracts from records, and letters (1934-1941) from Congressman J. Bayard Clark and others concerning the Battle of Elizabethtown (1781) and whether Robeson or Brown was in command."]

Smith, Maud Thomas. "Thomas Robeson, Jr." Online at NCPedia: http://ncpedia.org/biography/robeson-thomas-jr.

Rochester, Nathaniel, 1752-1831

Arthur, Billy. "Nathaniel Rochester." *The State: Down Home in North Carolina*, 63:3 (August 1995), 10, 13; online: http://digital.ncdcr.gov/cdm/ ref/collection/p16062coll18/id/14642. [Online description from "North Carolina Periodicals Index," East Carolina University: "Born in Virginia, Nathaniel Rochester moved to Oxford in Granville County at age eleven. Active in the Revolutionary War, this multi-talented patriot was also a legislator, banker, manufacturer, and founder of the city of Rochester, New York."]

Stokes, Durward T. "Nathaniel Rochester in North Carolina." *North Carolina Historical Review*, 38:4 (October

1961), 467-481; online: http://digital.ncdcr.gov/cdm/ref/collection/p16062coll9/id/4207. [Online description from "North Carolina Periodicals Index," East Carolina University: "This biographical essay looks at the life of historical figure and founder of the city of Rochester, N. Y., Nathaniel Rochester with an emphasis on the early years of his life spent in North Carolina."]

Rowan, Robert, c. 1738-1798

"Col. Robert Rowan – American Revolutionary War Veteran Graves on Waymarking.com." Online: http://www.waymarking.com/waymarks/WMEF2_Col_Robert_Rowan

Lewis, J. D. "The American Revolution in North Carolina: Robert Rowan." Online: http://www.carolana.com/NC/Revolution/patriot_leaders_nc_robert_rowan.html.

Rutherford, Griffith, ca.1721-1805

Andrews, Edwin R. "A Revolutionary 'of Grit Renowned'." *The State: Down Home in North Carolina*, 44:9 (February 1977), 29-31, 39; online: http://digital.ncdcr.gov/cdm/ref/collection/p16062coll18/id/ 57082. [Online description from "North Carolina Periodicals Index," East Carolina University: "Brigadier General Griffith Rutherford led 2,500 militia men over a buffalo trail over twenty days in September of 1776, destroying Cherokee town, barns and crops, and driving the Indians into the hills. Today, the trail is called Rutherford's Trace and historical highway markers line its path from Old Fort to Murphy. In 1946, a monument was erected in Murfreesboro in Rutherford's honor."]

Ashe, Samuel A'Court. "Rutherford's Expedition against the Indians, 1776." *North Carolina Booklet*, 4:8 (December 1904), 3-28.

Ashe, Samuel A'Court. *Rutherford's Expedition against the Indians, 1776*. Raleigh: E. M. Uzzel, 1904.

Carpenter, Robert Claude. "Griffith Rutherford: Frontier Military and Political Leader." M. A. thesis, Wake Forest University, 1974.

Dickins, Roy S., Jr. "The Route of Rutherford's Expedition against the North Carolina Cherokee." *Southern Indian Studies*, 19 (October 1967), 3-24.

Long, Minnie R. H. *General Griffith Rutherford and Allied Families.* Milwaukee, Wisc.: Cuneo Press, 1942.

MacDonald, James M. "Politics of the Personal in the Old North State: Griffith Rutherford in Revolutionary North Carolina." Ph. D. dissertation, Louisiana State University, 2006.

Rutherford, Griffith, 1731-1800. "Griffith Rutherford (1731-1800) Paper, 1783." Manuscript, PC.1097, State Archives of North Carolina, Raleigh. [Online catalog description: "Typed copy of letter from General Rutherford to loyalist James Karr (Kerr) in Wilmington, referring to Kerr's kindness when Rutherford was a prisoner and Rutherford's friendship for Kerr's family, but refusing to intervene in confiscation of Kerr's lands. Copied from original in the British Public Record Office, London, with notes and comments by E. Alfred Jones on loyalist papers there."]

Salter, Salley/Sallie, active 1770s-1780s

Trawick, Gary E. "The Egg Peddler." *The State: Down Home in North Carolina*, 37:10 (October 1969), 10, 20; online: http://digital.ncdcr.gov/cdm/ref/collection/p16062coll18/id/52935. [Online description from "North Carolina Periodicals Index," East Carolina University: "On August 29, 1781, a small group of Patriots launched a surprise attack against Tories encamped at Elizabethtown. The Patriots believed that they were outnumbered but were unsure of the Tories exact numbers and who, specifically, was in command of their forces. A young woman named Sally (Sallie) Salter volunteered to infiltrate the Tory camp under the guise of a loyalist egg seller, seeking only to help feed the troops while garnering a small amount of business for herself. She identified the joint commanders as Colonels Slingby and Godden and placed the number of troops at approximately three to four hundred. Patriot commander, Col. Thomas Robeson, led the ensuing attack based on Salter's information, leading to a Patriot rout of the Tory forces in which both Colonels Slingby and Godden, as well as most of their troops were killed."]

Schaw, Janet, 1735-1801

Rankin, Hugh F. "Janet Schaw (b. ca. 1740)." In William S. Powell, ed., *Dictionary of North Carolina Biography, Volume 5: P-S* (Chapel Hill and London: University of North Carolina Press, 1994), 294. [Details Schaw's trip from Scotland to the West Indies, North Carolina and Portugal in 1774.]

[Schaw, Janet]. "Janet Schaw on the Mistreatment of North Carolina Loyalists (1775)." In Cynthia A. Kierner, ed., *Revolutionary America, 1750-1815: Sources and Interpretation* (Upper Saddle River, N. J.: Prentice Hall, 2003), 110-113. [an excerpt from her journal]

Schaw, Janet; Evangeline Walker Andrews and Charles McLean Andrews, eds. *Journal of a Lady of Quality: Being the Narrative of a Journey from Scotland to the West Indies, North Carolina, and Portugal, in the Years 1774-1776.* New Haven, Conn.: Yale University Press, 1923; reprinted: London: Oxford University Press, 1934; New Haven: Yale University Press, 1939.

Wood, Bradford J. *This Remote Part of the World: Regional Formation in Lower Cape Fear, North Carolina, 1725-1775.* Columbia, S. C.: University of South Carolina, 2004. [Chapter 3: "Families," 82-109; Chapter 6: "Lower Cape Fear Plantations," 174-216, Janet Schaw's visit and domestic tasks of a female slave]

Sevier, John, 1745-1815

[Note: There are many studies on Sevier and his life during the Revolution and as Governor of Tennessee. His name appears throughout Tennessee histories and journals. Only a few of these are included below.]

Belt, Gordon T. *John Sevier: Tennessee's First Hero*. Charleston, S. C.: History Press, 2014. [Contents: Part I. Pioneer; Pioneer Boy and Son of Tennessee; The Forgotten Heroine; A Dangerous Example; Part II. Soldier; That Memorable Victory; Old Tales Retold; A Suitable Monument to Commemorate Their Deeds; Thirty-Five Battles, Thirty-Five Victories; Part III. Statesman; God Save the State!; His Excellency Governor John Sevier; Your Most Obedient Humble Servant; A Cenotaph Worthy of Him; Postscript: 'Chucky Jack's a-comin'.]

Belt, Gordon T. "John Sevier: Tennessee's First Hero – A Remembrance." *Smoky Mountain Historical Society Journal*, 41:3 (Winter 2015), 3-7.

Corbitt, D. L. "Sevier, Seduced by the Devil to Do Mischief, Is Repelled." *North Carolina Historical Review,* 3:2 (April 1926), 373-374.

Dale, Reed. *John Tipton, John Sevier, and the State of Franklin.* [United States: Tipton Family of American Association, 1998]. [A copy is located at Special Collections Library (Rare Books: F.436.R44 1998), University of Tennessee, Knoxville.]

Davis, Ruth. "John Sevier: Chucky Jack." *Smoky Mountain Historical Society Journal*, 41:3 (Winter 2015), 8-14.

DeWitt, John H. "History of the Lost State of Franklin." *Tennessee Historical Magazine,* 8 (1924), 167-170; printed separately: Johnson City: Watauga Press, 1924.

Driver, Carl S. *John Sevier: Pioneer of the Old Southwest.* Chapel Hill: University of North Carolina Press, 1932.

Essington, Meghan. "Memory, Manhood, and Military Service: Gentlemen and Common Planters in the Battle of King's Mountain." *Journal of East Tennessee History*, no. 86 (2014), 2-17.

Faris, John T. *Nolichucky Jack:* Philadelphia: Lippincott, 1927.

Fitch, William E. *The Origin, Rise & Downfall of the State of Franklin under Her First & Only Governor, John Sevier*. New York: Society of the Order of Founders & Patriots of America, 1910.

Gilmore, James Roberts. *John Sevier as a Commonwealth-Builder: A Sequel to the Rear-Guard of the Revolution.* New York: D. Appleton and Company, 1887.

Henderson, Archibald. "John Sevier and the Evolution of American Democracy." Neale's Montly, (May 1913), 597-602.

Rose, Norvell Sevier. "John Sevier and Marble Springs." *Tennessee Historical Quarterly*, 29:3 (Fall 1970), 205-226Sevier, G. W. "Sevier, G. W. Correspondence to Isaac Shelby." ID # 36389, Tennessee Historical Society, Knoxville; digital surrogate available through the Revolutionary War Collection, Tennessee Virtual Archive at http://cdm15138.contentdm.oclc.org/cdm/singleitem/collection/p15138coll16/id/40/rec/64. [Description from TeVA: "Sevier, G. W. correspondence to Isaac Shelby with a certificate of John Sevier relative to the Battle of King's Mountain, 1823"]

"Sevier, George W. Presenting the Sword of Gov. John Sevier." ID # 36390, Tennessee Historical Society, Knoxville; [digital surrogate available through the Revolutionary War Collection Tennessee Virtual Archive at http://cdm15138.contentdm.oclc.org/cdm/singleitem/collection/p15138coll16/id/41/rec/65. [Description from TeVA: "Sevier, George W. Presenting the sword of Gov. John Sevier to the State of Tenn. This sword was presented to John Sevier by the State of North Carolina in recognition of his gallant conduct at the Battle of King's Mountain, Oct. 6, 1780."]

Sevier, James, 1765-1847. "James Sevier Letter, 1839." Manuscript MS.1565, Special Collections Library, University of Tennessee, Knoxville. [Online catalog description: "This document is a typed copy of a letter that James Sevier wrote to L. C. Draper on August 19, 1839. In it, Sevier discusses his and his father's service on the Appalachian frontier during the Revolutionary War, where they fought in the Battle of Kings Mountain and in several smaller campaigns against the Cherokee. He also briefly recounts conflicts between Native Americans and whites in the decade following the American victory."]

Sevier, John. "Governor's Proclamation from the State of Franklin [1785 May 15]." Manuscript 42074, Manuscript File Box M-8, Tennessee State Library and Archives, Nashville; digital image online: http://teva.contentdm.oclc.org/cdm/ref/collection/p15138coll18/id/611. [Online catalog description: "One-page handwritten proclamation issued by John Sevier as Governor of the State of Franklin requiring all citizens to ignore a manifesto currently circulating in the state that incites insurrection. The manifesto referenced was issued by the Governor of North Carolina, Alexander Martin, on April 25, 1785, reacting to Franklin's proclaiming its independence as a separate state. Governor Martin threatened the Franklin citizenry if they did not abandon this path and accused Sevier of being a traitor. Sevier countered with this proclamation that encouraged the Franklinites to obey their new laws and chastised North Carolina for providing the reasons for separation. Notably, Sevier evoked the Revolutionary War, dated the proclamation with the reference "in first year of our Independence" and ended with 'God Save the State.' North Carolina never recognized the independence of the State of Franklin, and it ceased to exist in 1788."]

Sevier, John. "John Sevier Diary, 1790-1815." Manuscript MS.1782, Special Collections Library, University of Tennessee, Knoxville. [Online catalog description: "This collection consists of a typescript of a diary of John Sevier, spanning from 1790-1815."]

Sevier, John. "Letter from John Sevier to Governor Patrick Henry Announcing the Formation of the State of Franklin [1785, July 9]." Manuscript 42078, VI-C-1, Box 1, Folder 25 in the "Penelope Johnson Allen Cherokee Collection," Tennessee State Library and Archives, Nashville; digital image online: http://teva.contentdm.oclc.org/cdm/ref/collection/p15138coll18/id/617. [Online catalog description: "Negative photostat (possibly from the Virginia state papers) of a two-page handwritten letter John Sevier wrote to the governor of Virginia, Patrick Henry, announcing the formation of the State of Franklin and Sevier's appointment as governor. This notification followed the first official meeting of the Franklin Assembly in March of 1785 and the subsequent election of John Sevier by delegates as governor of the State of Franklin. The letter represents Sevier filling his role as head of this newly formed state, communicating with another state leader, and informing Henry of trade negotiations with the Chickasaw undertaken by the State of Franklin. At the same time, Sevier, recognizing the volatile climate in the area, reassured Governor Henry that Franklin intended to incite no unrest in Virginia, nor encourage encroachment on Native American lands. Notably, Sevier mentions that he expects no official correspondence with Governor Henry until the State of Franklin is recognized by Congress, an acknowledgement that never materialized."]

Sevier, John. "John Sevier Letters, 1778-1809." Manuscript MS.0363, Special Collections, Library, University of Tennessee, Knoxvill; also: *Finding Aid for the John Sevier Letters MS.0368.* Knoxville: University of Tennessee Libraries, [s. d.]. [Online catalog description: "This collection includes letters from John Sevier to Colonels Henley and Meigs dated from 1778-1809."]

Sevier, John. "John Sevier Papers, 1778-1812." Manuscript, David M. Rubenstein Rare Book & Manuscript Library Duke University, Durham. [Description: "Papers of John Sevier (1745-1815), officer during the American Revolution and first governor of Tennessee, including a letter, 1787, from Richard Caswell, governor of North Carolina, concerning their land speculation in Tennessee, trials for fraud in the purchase of army supplies, a copy of a memorial sent in 1812 to the North Carolina legislature by Sevier and Isaac Shelby, first governor of Kentucky, requesting that the Assembly honor its commitment to grant the two men the sword and pistols that it had voted them for their services in the battle of King's Mountain, and the reply from John Steele; and routine papers concerning legal matters."]

Temple, Oliver Perry. *John Sevier: Citizen, Soldier, Legislator, Governor, Statesman, 1744-1815.* Knoxville: Zi-Po Press, Printers, 1910; online at Google Books.

Tennessee Society Daughters of the American Revolution. *Two Famous Tennesseans: John Sevier, Andrew Jackson. Tennessee Citizens' Week, December 2 to 7, 1923, Inaugurated by the Tennessee Daughters of the American Revolution.* [S. l.]: The Society, [1923?].

Turner, Francis Marion. *Life of General John Sevier*. New York: Neal Publishing Company, 1910.

Shelby, Isaac, 1750-1826

Beasley, Paul W. "The Life and Times of Isaac Shelby 1750-1826." Ph. D. Dissertation, University of Kentucky, 1968.

Dean, Earl. "Three Men of Kings Mountain." *The State: A Weekly Survey of North Carolina*, 17:37 (February 1950), 10, 20; online: http://digital.ncdcr.gov/cdm/ref/collection/p16062coll18/id/25020. [Online description from

"North Carolina Periodicals Index," East Carolina University: "Many famous names have been associated with Cleveland County. Three men, whose names loom large in the pages of history, are closely identified with Cleveland County and its capital, Shelby. They are Colonel Benjamin Cleveland, the hero of the Battle of King's Mountain; Colonel Isaac Shelby, the first governor of Kentucky; and Major Patrick Ferguson, the inventor of the breech-loading rifle."]

Henderson, Archibald. "Isaac Shelby: Revolutionary Patriot and Border Hero." *North Carolina Booklet*, (Part 1) 16:2 (October 1916), 109-144; (Part 2) 18:1 (July 1918), 3-56.

Keller, S. Roger. *Isaac Shelby: A Driving Force in America's Struggle for Independence*. Shippensburg, Penn.: Burd Street Press, 2000. [Online description from "North Carolina Periodicals Index," East Carolina University: "According to several contemporary sources, Colonel Isaac Shelby and his backcountry soldiers helped turn the tide in favor of the patriots at the Battle of King's Mountain during the American Revolution."]

Lawrence, R. C. "Colonel Isaac Shelby." *The State: A Weekly Survey of North Carolina*, 8:6 (July 1940), 6; online: http://digital.ncdcr.gov/cdm/ref/collection/p16062coll18/id/5777. [Online description from "North Carolina Periodicals Index," East Carolina University: "The county seat of the governor-produced county of Cleveland, North Carolina was named in honor of Colonel Isaas Shelby, tri-state pioneer - legislator in Virginia, solider in North Carolina, and first Governor of Kentucky. He also served in the War of 1812, and declined appointment as Secretary of War."]

Shelby, Isaac. "The Battle of King's Mountain." *Recall*, 3:2 (October 1997), 7-9. [Online description from "North Carolina Periodicals Index," East Carolina University: "General Martin D. Hardin of Kentucky spoke with Isaac Shelby in 1815 and again in 1819 about the Battle of King's Mountain. The notes he took were later communicated to the American Review in 1848 by his son John J. Hardin and are included in this article."]

Shelby, Isaac. "Letter from Isaac Shelby to John Sevier." ID # 36384, Tennessee State Historical Society, Nashville; digital surrogate available through the Revolutionary War Collection, Tennessee Virtual Archive at http://cdm15138.contentdm.oclc.org/cdm/compoundobject/collection/p15138coll16/id/70/rec/41. [Description from TeVA: "Letter from Isaac Shelby to John Sevier regarding misrepresentations of the part Colonel William Campbell took in the Battle of King's Mountain, October 7, 1780."]

Shelby, Isaac. "Letter from Isaac Shelby to John Sevier." ID # 36386, Tennessee State Historical Society, Nashville; digital surrogate available through the Revolutionary War Collection, Tennessee Virtual Archive at http://cdm15138.contentdm.oclc.org/cdm/compoundobject/collection/p15138coll16/id/78/rec/43. [Description from TeVA: "Letter from Isaac Shelby to John Sevier regarding Shelby's recent re-election as governor of Kentucky. Shelby notes that among his opponents in the race were Baptists and 'old Tories' who demeaned his military service."]

Shelby, Isaac. "Letter from Isaac Shelby to John Sevier, February 24, 1810." ID # 36387, Tennessee State Historical Society, Nashville; digital surrogate available through the Revolutionary War Collection, Tennessee Virtual Archive at http://cdm15138.contentdm.oclc.org/cdm/compoundobject/collection/p15138coll16/id/82/rec/44. [Description from TeVA: "Letter from Isaac Shelby to John Sevier regarding the pistols and swords voted to them by the North Carolina Legislature in honor of their services at the Battle of King's Mountain."]

Shelby, Isaac. "Letter from Isaac Shelby to John Sevier." ID # 36388, Tennessee State Historical Society, Nashville; digital surrogate available through the Revolutionary War Collection, Tennessee Virtual Archive at http://cdm15138.contentdm.oclc.org/cdm/compoundobject/collection/p15138coll16/id/86/rec/40. [Description from TeVA: "Letter from Isaac Shelby to John Sevier asking for corroborative testimony as to Shelby's services in the Battle of King's Mountain, South Carolina. Letter written on August 12, 1812."]

Shelby and Hart Families. "Shelby and Hart Family Papers, 1775-1814; 1899-1900." Manuscript 659-z, Southern Historical Collection, University of North Carolina at Chapel Hill. University of North Carolina at Chapel [Online catalog descrption: "In the Biographical sketches are reminiscences, letters, and business papers involving Evan Shelby, Isaac Shelby, Nathaniel Hart (1734-1782), and their kin and associates, and clippings 1899-1900. Many items concern lands claims and titles of members of the Hart family in Kentucky. Also included is a ten-page manuscript description by Isaac Shelby of the Battle of King's Mountain and other events of the Revolution in the South after 1780, and two related letters to him. Shelby and Hart families of Kentucky. Prominent family members include Isaac Shelby (1750-1826), Revolutionary officer and the first governor of Kentucky, 1792-1796 and 1812-1816. Some Shelby papers published in *Journal of Southern History*, 4:3 (August 1938), 367-377. This collection covers: Nathaniel Hart, 1734-1782; Hart family; Evan Shelby; Isaac Shelby, Isaac 1750-1826."]

Wrobel, Sylvia, and George Grider. *Issac Shelby, Kentucky's First Governor and Hero of Three Wars*. Danville, Ky.: Cumberland Press, 1974. [Served as a militia leader in the Carolinas during the Revolution.]

Sharpe, William, 1742-1818

Sharpe, William. "William Sharpe Correspondence and Expense Account, 1780-1781." Manuscript MSS1723, Manuscript Division, James Madison Building, Library of Congress Washington, D. C. [Online catalog description: "Expense account (1780 February 8) kept by Sharpe for his services as delegate to the U. S. Continental Congress from North Carolina and typewritten transcript of a letter (1781 April 7) from Sharpe to Gen. Nathanael Greene commenting on hardships faced by the Continental Army."]

Slocumb, Mary/Polly, active 1770s

Comstock, Charles. "The Midnight Ride of Mary Slocum." *The Orphans' Friend and Masonic Journal* [Oxford, N. C.], October 17, 1924. [Copy in the file at the North Carolina State Library: "N. C. – History – Revolution – Women's Work."]

Connor, R. D. W. "The Ride of Mary Slocumb." *American Monthly Magazine* [DAR], 29:6 (December 1906), 753-759.

Davis, Curtis Carroll. "Housewife vs. the Invader." *The State: Down Home in North Carolina*, 52:7 (December 1984), 16-18; online: http://digital.ncdcr.gov/cdm/ref/collection/p16062coll18/id/61111. [Online description from "North Carolina Periodicals Index," East Carolina University: "Elizabeth L. F. Ellet recently published *The Women of the American Revolution*. In this book, Ellet describes the lives of several extraordinary women. This article focuses on one of these women, Polly Slocumb, wife of colonial army captain Ezekiel Slocumb. Polly remained at their plantation outside of Wilmington, North Carolina, while Ezekiel served in the military. Following the battle of Guilford Courthouse in 1781, Mrs. Slocumb encountered the notorious Lieutenant Colonel Banastre Tarleton, who made camp on her property and quartered in the Slocumb home. Tarleton commanded three troops of British dragoons and was known for his cruelty toward both soldiers and civilians. Mrs. Slocumb withstood Tarleton's tirades against the American rebels with her terse banter. Contrary to his reputation, Tarleton did not burn and destroy the property but left the home intact."]

Flowers, John Baxton, III. "Did Polly Slocumb Ride to the Battle of Moore's Creek Bridge?" *Bulletin of the Lower Cape Fear Historical Society*, 19:2 (February 1976), [Historians for years have questioned the validity of the story of Mary "Polly" Hooks Slocumb. After having a frightening vision of her husband dying on the battlefield; Polly traveled 30 miles away from home to a battlefield and dressed the wounds of about twenty injured men.]

Hayden, Karen L. "Bringing up the Rear: Mary Slocum." *Continental Line*, 11:4 (Fall/Winter 1998). Online: http://www.continentalline.org/articles/article.php?date=9803&article=980302.

Hubbell, S. Michael. *Mary Slocumb's Ride to the Battle of Moore's Creek Bridge.* Washington, D. C.: National Park Service, United States Department of the Interior, 1962.

Kent, Scotti. *More Than Petticoats: Remarkable North Carolina Women.* Helena, Mont.: A Twodot Book, Falcon Publishing, Inc., 2000. [Includes "Mary Hooks 'Polly' Slocumb: Heroine of Moore's Creek Bridge."]

"Mary Slocumb Papers, 1937-1976." Manuscript, PC.929, State Archives of North Carolina, Raleigh. [Online catalog description: "Correspondence (1961-1962) between National Park Service and the N. C. Dept. of Archives and History concerning authenticity of Mary Slocumb's legendary ride to Moores Creek Bridge at the height of the battle in 1776. Also typed studies of the legend by Park Service historians Clyde B. King (1937) and S. Michael Hubbell (1961), and photocopied article by John B. Flowers III (1976)."]

Moore, Louis T. "Mary Slocumb's Famous Ride." *The State: A Weekly Survey of North Carolina*, 16:1 (June 1948), 41-42; online: http://digital.ncdcr.gov/cdm/ref/collection/p16062coll18/id/22420. [Online des-cription: "Mary Slocumb ran to her husband in battle after believing she dreamed he cried out for her. At the Battle of Moore's Creek Bridge during the Revolutionary War, Colonel Slocumb was engaged with British troops. His wife Mary believed she heard him call to her while she slept and decided to make a daring run to Moore's Creek from Goldsboro a sixty mile journey. Most of the article is a reprint of Mary Slocumb's own description of events, ending with the author mentioning the internment of Colonel Slocumb and his wife at Moore's Creek National Park."]

Norris, Jeannie Faris. "The Mary Slocumb Gourd." *The State: Down Home in North Carolina*, 40:6 (August 1972), 16; online: http://digital.ncdcr.gov/cdm/ref/collection/p16062coll18/id/55441. [Online description from "North Carolina Periodicals Index," East Carolina University: "In an effort to drum up publicity for their yearly gourd festival, the Cary Gourd Club is focusing attention on the display of the Mary Slocumb gourd at the Museum of History in Raleigh. The story of the gourd, which was allegedly used by Mrs. Slocumb as she ministered to the wounded soldiers at the Battle of Moores Creek Bridge during the Revolutionary War, has been recorded in

John H. Wheeler's *Historical Sketches of North Carolina* and Mrs. Eddie W. Wilson's *The Gourd in Folk Literature*."]

Seawell, Jos. Lacey. "The All-Night Ride of Mary Slocumb." *The State: A Weekly Survey of North Carolina*, 2:22 (October 1934), 24; online: http://digital.ncdcr.gov/cdm/ref/collection/p16062coll18/id/3817. [Online description from "North Carolina Periodicals Index," East Carolina University: "Many people know of the ride of Paul Revere, but few know of Mary Slocumb's thirty-mile, night-time ride from Wayne County to find her husband at the Battle of Moore's Creek Bridge. Seawell compares the two, concluding that Mary Slocumb's ride was the more dangerous one."]

Sherrod, Thomas, c. 1730 -1818

Sherrod Family. "Sherrod Family Papers, 1802-1967 (bulk 1802-1856)." Manuscript 05206, Southern Historical Collection, Lous Round Wilson Special Collections Library, University of North Carolina at Chapel Hill. [Online catalog description: " The Sherrod family resided in Franklin County, N.C., in the 19th century. Thomas Sherrod was a member of North Carolina's Fourth Provincial Congress, which met in Halifax on 4 April 1776, and he fought in the American Revolution, reaching the rank of colonel. He died in 1818, leaving Jordan R. Sherrod as one of the executors of his will. Jordan R. Sherrod's children included John, Henry, Lucian, Alphonzo, and Martha. John M. Sherrod and Henry H. Sherrod served in Company E, 15th Regiment North Carolina Infantry during the Civil War. The collection consists primarily of receipts, warrants, business correspondence, and other financial papers, 1802-1865. These papers provide a record of rent and tax payments, sales of cotton, and purchases of goods and services as well as transactions conducted to settle the estates of family members. Many of the receipts and warrants from the 1820s through the 1850s concern Jordan R. Sherrod, while most papers from the late 1850s and early 1860s relate to the business of Sherrod and Green of Franklinton, N.C., a partnership that included Henry H. Sherrod and Andrew Green. The collection also contains Confederate documents authorizing a disability discharge for John M. Sherrod and leaves of absence for Henry H. Sherrod. Other items include an 1802 marriage license, the text of Thomas Sherrod's 1818 will, an 1879 school report concerning Charlie Sherrod, and a 1967 letter about family genealogy."]

Smart, Susannah Barnett, 1761-?

"A Carolina Woman of the Revolution: Susannah Smart." *Godey's Lady's Book*, (March 1856), 213-217.

Gentry, Susan. "Susannah Barnett Smart." *American Monthly Magazine* [DAR], 25:4 (April 1905), 286-289. [In Mecklenburg Co., North Carolina, Susannah assisted her mother with serving and making meals for the refugees of South Carolina.]

Smith, Benjamin, 1756-1826

Arthur, Billy. "The Tragedy of Benjamin Smith." *The State: Down Home in North Carolina*, 65:9 (February 1998), 15-16; online: http://digital.ncdcr.gov/cdm/ref/collection/p16062coll18/id/69594. [Online description from "North Carolina Periodicals Index," East Carolina University: "Benjamin Smith of Brunswick County led a memorable life - Revolutionary War soldier, fifteen-term state senator, and benefactor of the University of North Carolina - yet he died a pauper and was buried in an unmarked grave."]

Moore, Louis T. "Governor Benjamin Smith." *The State: A Weekly Survey of North Carolina*, 15:46 (April 1948), 11, 20; online: http://digital.ncdcr.gov/cdm/ref/collection/p16062coll18/id/22159. [Online description from "North Carolina Periodicals Index," East Carolina University: "Many interesting and dramatic events occurred during the lifetime of Governor Benjamin Smith, and even after his death his body was not permitted to rest in peace."]

Watson, Alan D. "Benjamin Smith: Brunswick County General and North Carolina Governor, 1810-1811." *North Carolina Historical Review*, 87:1 (January 2010), 28-56. [Online description from "North Carolina Periodicals Index," East Carolina University: "Benjamin Smith was governor of North Carolina from 1810 to 1811. A prominent resident of the Lower Cape Fear region, Smith owned several plantations in Brunswick County. Little attention has been paid to Smith by historians as his short gubernatorial has been viewed as powerless. When examined, his tenure in office exposes the difficulties that governors are under during the early 19th century."]

Watson, Alan D. "Benjamin Smith: Remembrance and Rehabilitation." *Lower Cape Fear Historical Society Bulletin*, 53:1 (October 2009), 1-7. [Online description from "North Carolina Periodicals Index," East Carolina University: "Watson discusses the life and death of former North Carolina governor Benjamin Smith. Although despised by many, Smith's generosity provided over 20,000 acres to the University of North Carolina at Chapel Hill."]

Spaight, Richard Dobbs, 1758-1802

Andrews, Alexander B. "Richard Dobbs Spaight." *North Carolina Historical Review*, 1:2 (April 1924), 95-120; online: http://digital.ncdcr.gov/cdm/ref/collection/p16062coll9/id/4207. [Online description from "North Carolina Periodicals Index," East Carolina University: "Richard Dobbs Spaight was born in New Bern on March 25th, 1758 to Richard Spaight, a grand nephew of colonial Governor Arthur Dobbs. The article offers a biographical sketch of Spaight's life and his successful career as a state politician."]

Bowie, Phil. "The De-Weeding of Richard Spaight." *The State: Down Home in North Carolina*, 44:1 (June 1976), 20-21; online: http://digital.ncdcr.gov/cdm/ref/collection/p16062coll18/id/11738. [Online description from "North Carolina Periodicals Index," East Carolina University: "Recently, the gravesite of Richard Dobbs Spaight, Sr., was discovered. Spaight signed the U. S. Constitution and served as the first native-born North Carolina governor. He died in 1802, and his son, Richard, Jr., also served as governor and is buried in the same small cemetery as his father. The graveyard is located on Brice's Creek Road in New Bern, and the overgrowth has been cleared by a local Boy Scout Troop."]

Jones, Joe. "One the Field of Honor." *The State: Down Home in North Carolina*, 56:6 (November 1988), 16-17; online: http://digital.ncdcr.gov/cdm/ref/collection/p16062coll18/id/63292. [Online description from "North Carolina Periodicals Index," East Carolina University: "A political campaign dispute between Richard Dobbs Spaight, Sr., and John Stanly culminated in the summer of 1802, when the men fought the state's most famous duel in New Bern. Spaight was mortally wounded."]

Lawrence, R. C. "Signers of the Constitution." *The State: A Weekly Survey of North Carolina*, 10:14 (September 1942) 26; online: http://digital.ncdcr.gov/cdm/ref/collection/p16062coll18/id/33190. [Online description from "North Carolina Periodicals Index," East Carolina University: "North Carolina can proudly claim three men who signed the Constitution – Hugh Williamson of Chowan, Richard Dobbs Spaight and William Blount of Craven County. Lawrence provides biographical information on them."]

Lawrence, R. C. "Spaight: The Elder and Younger." *The State: A Weekly Survey of North Carolina*, 16:48 (April 1949), 3-4, 22; online: http://digital.ncdcr.gov/cdm/ref/collection/p16062coll18/id/23825. [Online description from "North Carolina Periodicals Index," East Carolina University: "Richard Dobbs Spaight and his son by the same name were influential political figures with both serving as governors. This article outlines the family's early history and public service careers beginning when the elder Spaight became governor in the late 18th-century followed by the younger Spaight in the mid-19th-century."]

Lawrence, R. C. "The Unique Career of Richard Dobbs Spaight." *The State: A Weekly Survey of North Carolina*, 12:32 (January 1945), 7, 16-17; online: http://digital.ncdcr.gov/cdm/ref/collection/p16062coll18/id/12599. [Online description from "North Carolina Periodicals Index," East Carolina University: "The case of Richard Dobbs Spaight is without parallel in North Carolina history: he was a grand-nephew of a Governor; he became a Governor himself, and his son was elected as Governor, among many other interesting features of his life."]

Norris, Jeannie Faris. "Spaight: Elder and Younger." *The State: Down Home in North Carolina*, 37:11 (November 1969), 25-26; online: http://digital.ncdcr.gov/cdm/ref/collection/p16062coll18/id/52980. [Online description from "North Carolina Periodicals Index," East Carolina University: "Richard Dobbs Spaight and his son, Richard Dobbs Spaight, Jr., represented the only instance of a father and son both serving as Governor of North Carolina, until the election of Bob Scott, son of former Governor Kerr Scott."]

Sadler, W. J. "Governors of North Carolina: Richard Dobbs Spaight." *The State: A Weekly Survey of North Carolina*, 3:18 (September 1935), 6; online: http://digital.ncdcr.gov/cdm/ref/collection/p16062coll18/id/4493. [Online description from "North Carolina Periodicals Index," East Carolina University: "Richard Dobbs Spaight, a man of wealth, education, and a signer of the federal Constitution, served North Carolina well during his three one-year terms as Governor. A political campaign dispute between Richard Dobbs Spaight, Sr., and John Stanly culminated in the summer of 1802, when the men fought the state's most famous duel in New Bern. Spaight was mortally wounded."]

Spaight, Richard Dobbs, Sr. "Papers, 1783-1801,1912." Manuscript PC.946 (MARS ID: 1456; record group), State Archives of North Carolina, Raleigh. [Online catalog description: "Papers of Spaight of Craven Co., delegate to Continental Congress (1782-1785), governor (1792-1795), and member of Congress (1798-1801), including account of his expenses as delegate to Continental Congress (1783);…"]

Spencer, Samuel, 1734-1793

Copeland, J. Isaac, and Jerry C. Cashion. "Samuel Spencer." Online at NCPedia (1994): http://ncpedia.org/biography/spencer-samuel.

Lewis, J. D. "Patriot Leaders in North Carolina: Samuel Spencer: Colonel over the Anson County Regiment of Militia - 1775-1776." Online: http://www.carolana.com/NC/Revolution/patriot_leaders_nc_samuel_spencer.html.

Spencer, Samuel. "Samuel Spencer Papers, 1781-1789." Manuscript, PC.948, State Archives of North Carolina, Raleigh. [Online catalog description: "Letters from Spencer of Anson Co., member of provincial congress and council (1774-1776), delegate to state constitutional conventions (1788, 1789), and superior court judge (1777-1794), to his brother Capt. Calvin Spencer. Topics include the captain's privateering and the judge's skirmish with tories (1781); family in the north; and the captain's hopes of being paid for revolutionary services."]

Springer, John, 1744-1789

Simpson, Addison W. *Life of Rev. John Springer*. Washington: Georgia Presbyterian Church, 1941?

Willingham, Robert M., Jr. "John Springer." In Kenneth Coleman and Charles Stephen Gurr, eds., *Dictionary of Georgia Biography*. 2 vols. (Athens: University of Georgia Press, 1983), 2:916-917. [1744-1789; born Wilmington, Del. In the Swedish community; baptized at Old Swedes Church; son of John and Mary Springer; Princeton graduate; Presbyterian minister; to NC before Revolution and served as a soldier; later to Georgia.]

Stanly, John Wright, 1742-1789

Hessel, Mary Stanley; Ann Ward Little, ed. *Profile of a Patriot: The Story of John Wright Stanly, Revolutionary War Privateer*. New Bern: Tryon Palace Commission, 1983.

Lawrence, R. C. "The Fighting Stanlys." *The State: A Weekly Survey of North Carolina*, 9:43 (March 1942), 7, 21; online:. [Online description from "North Carolina Periodicals Index," East Carolina University: "Three members of the Stanly family of New Bern – grandfather, son, and grandson – had interesting and turbulent careers and were outstanding figures during their respective generations. They were John Wright Stanly, John Stanly, and Edward Stanly."]

Steele, Elizabeth Maxwell, 1733-1790

Haines, Frank, and Elizabeth Haines. *Early American Brides: A Study of Costume and Tradition, 1594-1820*. Cumberland, Md.: Hobby House Press, Inc., 1982. [Most of the examples are from the early colonial period, but this volume of includes examples of two brides from the Revolutionary period: Mary MacTavish of Pennsylvania, and Elizabeth Maxwell Steele of North Carolina. The book features dolls of each bride, text about their lives and clothing, and photographs.]

Henderson, Archibald. "Elizabeth Maxwell: Patriot." *North Carolina Booklet*, 12:2 (October 1912), 67-103.

Norris, Jeannie Faris. "She Gave Her Savings." *We the People of North Carolina*, 1:1 (May 1943), 21, 38. [Online description from "North Carolina Periodicals Index," East Carolina University: "This is the first in a series of articles about women who have played dramatic and interesting roles in the history of North Carolina. The author describes an incident in the Revolutionary War when Gen. Nathanial Greene, weary, despondent, and lacking money for his troops, arrives at the Salisbury inn of Mrs. Elizabeth Maxwell Steele. Mrs. Steele, an ardent patriot, gave the general two bags of gold and silver, her entire life savings, so that he and his men could continue the fight for independence."]

Russell, Christopher L. "The Courage and Contributions of Elizabeth Maxwell Steele." *Patriots of the American Revolution*, 4:2 (March/April 2011), 6-9. [Tradition holds that tavern-owner Steele, of Salisbury, North Carolina, provided General Nathanael Greene with funds for supplies.]

Stewart, Cory Joe. "Elizabeth Maxwell Steele: 'A Great Politician' and the Revolution in the Southern Backcountry." In Michele Gillespie and Sally G. McMillen, eds. *North Carolina Women: Their Lives and Times*. 2 vols. (Athens: University of Georgia Press, 2014), 1: 54-72.

West, William S. "Elizabeth Maxwell Steel, (1733-22 Nov. 1790)." In William S. Powell, ed., *Dictionary of North Carolina Biography, vol. 5: P-S* (Chapel Hill: University of North Carolina Press, 1979-1996), 432. [innkeeper]

Steele, John, 1765-1815

Henderson, Archibald. "John Steele." *North Carolina Booklet*, 18:3 (January 1919), 123-133; 18:4 (April 1919), 159-177.

Lawrence, R. C. "General John Steele." *The State: A Weekly Survey of North Carolina*, 8:46 (April 1941), 8; online: http://digital.ncdcr.gov/cdm/ref/collection/p16062coll18/id/39388. [Online description from "North Carolina Periodicals Index," East Carolina University: "General John Steel was born at Salisbury, North Carolina in 1764. He became a general of militia, but his services to the State were upon fields of peace rather than in the theatre of war. He started life as a merchant, but his natural gift for public leadership and his power as a debater helped him to election to the House of Commons. He was also a delegate to the Convention in 1788 to consider the ratification of the Federal Constitution. In 1790, he was one of the first members of Congress."]

Steele, John. "Papers, 1777-1831." Manuscript PC.5 (MARS ID: 514; record group), State Archives of North Carolina, Raleigh. [Online catalog description: "Papers of John Steele, Rowan Co. Federalist, legislator, and congressman (1790-1792), including letters from his mother, especially about the British in Salisbury, Feb., 1781…"]

Steele, John; H. M. Wagstaff, ed. *The Papers of John Steele*. 2 vols. Raleigh: Edwards & Broughton Printing, 1924.

Stokes, John, 1756-1790, and Montfort Stokes, 1762-1842

Arthur, Billy. "The Man Who Refused to Be Senator." *The State: Down Home in North Carolina*, 52:8 (January 1985), 23-24; online: http://digital.ncdcr.gov/cdm/ref/collection/p16062coll18/id/61156. [Online description from "North Carolina Periodicals Index," East Carolina University: "Montfort Stokes once gave up an opportunity to fill a vacant U.S. Senate seat in 1805, citing family obligations. Stokes was later elected to the senate seat in 1816, and he held that position till 1823. Stokes was a Virginia native but lived in Salisbury and Wilkes County. Stokes assisted in the settlement of the North Carolina-South Carolina and the North Carolina-Tennessee boundaries while serving as boundary commissioner. Stokes remained active in state politics as a member of the state senate, the state house of commons, and as North Carolina governor from 1830-1832. Stokes died in 1842 while serving President Andrew Jackson in the Bureau of Indian Affairs."]

Foreman, Grant. "The Life of Montfort Stokes in the Indian Territory." *North Carolina Historical Review*, 16:4 (October 1939), 373-403; online: http://digital.ncdcr.gov/cdm/ref/collection/p16062coll9/id/4207. [Online description from "North Carolina Periodicals Index," East Carolina University: "This article looks at Governor Montfort Stokes' execution of President Andrew Jackson's Indian Removal Bill of 1830 and his negotiations with various tribes."]

Foster, William Omer. "The Career of Montfort Stokes in North Carolina." *North Carolina Historical Review*, 16:3 (July 1939), 237-272. [Online description from "North Carolina Periodicals Index," East Carolina University: "This article is a biography of War of 1812 veteran, U.S. Senator and North Carolina Governor Montfort Stokes."]

Lawrence, R. C. "The Famous Stokes Brothers." *The State: A Weekly Survey of North Carolina*, 17:7 (July 1949), 10, 22; online: http://digital.ncdcr.gov/cdm/ref/collection/p16062coll18/id/24152. [Online description from "North Carolina Periodicals Index," East Carolina University: "John and Montfort Stokes were Revolutionary Era North Carolinians who had an exciting life, and both received a number of signal honors. "]

Lawrence, R. C. "Soldiers Who Became Judges." *The State: A Weekly Survey of North Carolina*, 8:7 (July 1940), 10, 25; online: http://digital.ncdcr.gov/cdm/ref/collection/p16062coll18/id/5810. [Online description from "North Carolina Periodicals Index," East Carolina University: "Lawrence has compiled a list of soldiers in the Revolutionary War, Civil War, and World War who later became members of the judiciary of North Carolina. Among them are Colonel John Stokes and Samuel Ashe of New Hanover County."]

Norris, Jeannie Faris. "History's Hangman." *The State: Down Home in North Carolina*, 23:18 (January 1956), 13, 15; online: http://digital.ncdcr.gov/cdm/ref/collection/p16062coll18/id/6692. [Online description from "North Carolina Periodicals Index," East Carolina University: "The lives of four history-makers of Wilkes County are recounted in this article. Ben Cleveland, founder of the county, was a justice of the peace, rose to a colonelcy in the militia because of service against the Cherokees, and commanded the left wing against King's Mountain. For 57 years, Montfort Stokes held public offices in the state of North Carolina. He was named Indian commissioner in 1832 by President Andrew Jackson. James Wellborn and William Lenoir served under Ben Cleveland."]

Sumner, Jethro, c. 1733-1785

Battle, Kemp P. *Address on the Life and Services of Brigadier General Jethro Sumner: At the Battle Ground of Guilford Court House, July 4th, 1891*. Greensboro: Reese & Elam, Printers, 1891; online: https://archive.org/details/addressonlifeser00batt.

Battle, Kemp P. "The Life and Services of Brigadier General Jethro Sumner." *North Carolina Booklet*, 8:0 [*sic*] (October 1908), 111-140; online: http://digital.ncdcr.gov/cdm/ref/collection/p249901coll37/id/14180. [Online description from "North Carolina Periodicals Index," East Carolina University: "This article details the personal life, family history, and military service of Revolutionary War general Jethro Sumner. It highlights his service during the French and Indian War where he rose to the rank of lieutenant while commanding a fort, his service to Warren County as a justice of the peace, and his appointment as brigadier general by the Continental Congress in 1779."]

Battle, Kemp Plummer. "Career of Brigadier-General Jethro Sumner One of North Carolina's Revolutionary Officers." *Magazine of American History,* 26 (December 1891), 415-433.

Rankin, Hugh F. "Jethro Sumner." In William S. Powell, ed., *Dictionary of North Carolina Biography, Volume 5: P-S.* Chapel Hill: University of North Carolina Press, 1988), 476.

Sumner, Jethro, 1733-1785. "Jethro Sumner (1733-1785) Papers, 1760-1784." Manuscript, PC.83, State Archives of North Carolina, Raleigh. [Online catalog description: "Military papers of Brigadier General Sumner, Virginia native, resident of Warren Co., including orders during the French and Indian War from Col. William Byrd and Henry Bouquet. Correspondence from the Revolutionary period includes letters from Charles Lee, Abner Nash, Nicholas Long (deputy quartermaster), John Baptista Ashe, Benjamin Seawell, and Alexander Brevard; copies of letters from John Ashe to Benjamin Lincoln and from Horatio Gates and William Lee Davidson to Sumner; and drafts of Sumner to Nathanael Greene and others. Topics include desertions (1776), draft and reenlistments (1778-1783), provisions and arms, transportation, plans and orders, relationships between the Continental Line and the militia (1781), reorganization of officers (1782), and inflation (1783). Also included are notes on courts of enquiry into disputes over rank and over discharge eligibility claimed by soldiers of the 3rd N.C Battalion (1777); a report on meeting of North Carolina Virginia officers in Surry Co. (Oct., 1780) calling for surrender of insurgents after battle at Shallowford; and photograph of Sumner's certification of delegates to the general convention of the Society of the Cincinnati (1784)."]

Sumner, Jethro, 1733?-1785. "Jethro Sumner Papers, 1775-1791 (bulk 1781-1782). Manuscript 705, Southern Historical Collection, Louis Round Wilson Special Collections Library, University of North Carolina, Chapel Hill; online finding aid and digital surrogates available at http://www2.lib.unc.edu/mss/inv/s/Sumner,Jethro.html. [Online finding aid description: "Jethro Sumner (1733?-1785) was a brigadier general in the Continental Army. Sumner served in the Virginia militia, 1755-1761; was justice of the peace, 1768, and sheriff, 1772-1777, of Bute (now Warren) County, N.C.; and was colonel of the 3rd Battalion, North Carolina Continentals, 1776-1778, and brigadier-general 1779-1780. The collection contains Revolutionary War military correspondence of Continental Brigadier General Jethro Sumner. The bulk of the collection relates to the period 1781-1782, when Sumner was raising troops for General Nathanael Greene, whom he reinforced at the Battle of Eutaw Springs, and while he was in charge of forces in North Carolina. Letters are chiefly concerned with strategic matters including reports on engagements and the movement of British forces, procurement of arms and supplies, and issues of manpower including drafting of men and desertion. A few items pertain to his earlier service in the North. Among the correspondents are Martin Armstrong, Reading Blount, Thomas Burke, John B. Ashe, Baron Steuben, Alexander Martin, Benjamin Lincoln, Nathanael Greene, John Alexander Lillington, William Christmas, William R. Davie, Thomas Eaton, Joseph Hewes, Willie Jones, Nicholas Long, James Cole Mountflorence, Benjamin Seawell, H. Tatum, and Hugh Williamson."]

Sumner, Jethro, 1733-1785. "Jethro Sumner Papers, 1780-1781." Manuscript (1937. M-343.), Manuscript Division, William L. Clements Library, University of Michigan, Ann Arbor. [Online catalog description: "The Jethro Sumner papers contain incoming and outgoing letters relating to the progress of the Southern Campaign of the Revolutionary War, including the battles of Charlotte and King's Mountain, logistical and personnel concerns, and Sumner's resignation." The finding aid for this collection is accessible through the online catalog record.]

Tryon, William, 1729-1788

Dill, Alonzo Thomas. *Governor Tryon and His Palace*. Chapel Hill: University of North Carolina Press, 1955.

Farnham, Thomas J. "William Tryon, an Advocate of Desolation Warfare?" *New Bern Historical Journal*, 7:1 ( ), 25-35.

Harrold, Frances Long. "Governor William Tryon of North Carolina, 1765-1771." M. A. thesis, University of Wisconsin, Madison, 1954.

Haywood, Marshall De Lancey. *Governor William Tryon and His Administration in the Province of North Carolina, 1765-1771: Services in a Civil Capacity and Military Career as Commander-in-Chief of Colonial Forces which Suppressed the Insurrection of the Regulators*. Raleigh: Reproduced by Edwards & Broughton Co., 1958.

Kimball, Fiske, and Gertrude S. Carraway. "Tryon's Palace." New-York Historical Society Quarterly, 24:1 (January 1940), 13-22.

Nelson, Paul Davis. *William Tryon and the Course of Empire: A Life in British Imperial Service*. Chapel Hill: University of North Carolina Press, 1990.

North Carolina (State). Office of the Governor. "Memorial of Governor William Tryon for the Recovery of Losses of Personal and Real Property Incurred during the American Revolution, States of North Carolina and New York." Manuscript, CGP 6, CGP 9, (MARS ID: 308.8.98; box), State Archives of North Carolina, Raleigh. [Online catalog description: "Evidence supporting memorial, including list of real estate owned in North Carolina with estimate of value; sworn testimony to memorial."]

Sadler, W. J. "Governors of North Carolina: William Tryon." *The State: A Weekly Survey of North Carolina*, 3:9 (July 1935), 8; online: http://digital.ncdcr.gov/cdm/ref/collection/p16062coll18/id/4228. [Online description from "North Carolina Periodicals Index," East Carolina University: "William Tryon was a professional soldier and governor of the North Carolina colony on the eve of the American Revolution. Almost immediately following his arrival, he had to deal with resistance to the Stamp Act, which was finally repealed to head off bloodshed. Later, citizens, known as Regulators, banded together in armed resistance to excessive taxation. Tryon led the troops that put them down in 1771. After six years of strife and turmoil, the King named him Governor of New York. Although citizens were glad to see him go, Tryon's lasting monument in the state was the magnificent Palace in New Bern, which served as a state house as well as a home for governors."]

Stone, Richard Gabriel. "Governor William Tryon of North Carolina, 1765-1771." M. A. thesis, University of North Carolina at Chapel Hill, 1962.

Tryon, William; William S. Powell, ed. *The Correspondence of William Tryon and Other Selected Papers*. 2 vols. Raleigh: North Carolina Division of Archives and History, 1981.

Tryon, William; William S. Powell, ed. "Tryon's "Book" on North Carolina." *North Carolina Historical Review*, 34:3 (July 1957), 406-415.

Turner, Kerenhappuch Norman, c. 1715-1804

Bradshaw, G[eorge] S[amuel]. *Mrs. Kerenhappuch Turner, A Heroine of 1776: An Address by* G.S. *Bradshaw, Esq., on Occasion of the Unveiling of a Monument to Her Memory, at the Guilford Battle Ground, July 4th, 1902.* Greensboro, N. C.: Guilford Battle Ground Company, 1902. [The Maryland mother of Revolutionary War soldiers, her travel to North Carolina to nurse the wounded after the Battle of Guilford Courthouse, and the statue erected to her at this even in 1902.]

Davis, Curtis Carroll. "The Tribulations of Mrs. Turner: An Episode after Guilford Court House." *Maryland Historical Magazine*, 76:4 (Winter 1981), 376-379. [Kerenhappuch Norman Turner mother of Revolutionary soldiers from Maryland, her trip to nurse the wounded following the Battle of Guilford Courthouse in North Carolina, and the statue erected to her in 1902.]

Seymour, Mary E. "Revolutionary Heroines." *Daughters of the American Revolution Magazine*, 70:9 (September 1936), 933-934. [Includes Mrs. Kerenhappuch Turner, who rode all the way on horseback from her home in Maryland to Guilford Court House, North Carolina, and was able to nurse her son back to health after the battle there.]

Whitfield, Theodore M. "Kerenhappuch Turner." *Baltimore Sunday Sun Magazine*, (July 18, 1976), 32.

"Women Honored at Guilford Courthouse." Online: http://www.nps.gov/guco/planyourvisit/upload/Women%20Honored.doc [Features the stories of Kerenhappuch Turner and Martha McFarland McGee Bell and the wording on monuments to them at the battlefield park.]

Twitty, Susan, active 1770s-1780

Kent, Scotti. *More Than Petticoats: Remarkable North Carolina Women.* Helena, Mont.: A Twodot Book, Falcon Publishing, Inc., 2000. [Includes "Susan Twitty: Defender of Graham's Fort."]

Waddel, Moses, 1770-1840

Boney, F. N. *A Pictorial History of the University of Georgia*. Athens, University of Georgia Press, 2000.

Lyon, Ralph M. "Moses Waddel and the Willington Academy." *North Carolina Historical Review*, 8:3 (July 1931), 284-299; online: http://digital.ncdcr.gov/cdm/ref/collection/p16062coll9/id/4207. [Online description from "North Carolina Periodicals Index," East Carolina University: "This article looks at the development and typical characteristics of the antebellum southern educational institution known as the academy via a focus on the

Willington Academy in Abbeville District, S. C., regarded as the most characteristic institution of the type. It includes biographical information on headmaster and North Carolina native Moses Waddel."]

McLeod, James Lewis. *The Great Doctor Waddel (Pronounced Waddle)*. Spartanburg, S. C.: Southern Historical Press, 1985. [Publisher's description: "Moses Waddell (1770-1840), brother-in-law and teacher of John C. Calhoun, is considered one of the most famous and successful educators in Southern History. He was fifth President of the University of Georgia and was credited with saving the college during a crucial period in its history. Earlier in his career, he also formed the Willington Academy in South Carolina where an unusual number of leaders were produced. (Biographies of these are in the back of the book.)."]

"Moses Waddel." In *From Ahmedunggar to Lavonia: Presidents of the University of Georgia, 1785-1997*. Athens: University of Georgia Press, 2001; online: http://www.libs.uga.edu/hargrett/pexhibit/presiden/mwaddel.html.

Waddell, John Newton. *Memorials of Academic Life, Being an Historical Sketch of the Waddel Family*. Richmond: Presbyterian Committee of Publication, 1891.

Wake, Esther, active 1770s

Connor, R. D. W. "Was Esther Wake a Myth?" *North Carolina Booklet*, 14:4 (April 1915), 220-224.

Walker, Felix, 1753-1828

Arthur, Billy. "Word of Mouth." *Our State: Down Home in North Carolina*, 67:5 (October 1999), 18-20; online: http://digital.ncdcr.gov/cdm/ref/collection/p16062coll18/id/68379. [Online description from "North Carolina Periodicals Index," East Carolina University: "Revolutionary War soldier, frontiersman, U. S. Congressman, and skilled orator, Felix Walker claims fame not for the foregoing positions but for the meaning he gave to a word in Webster's Dictionary. During the Missouri Compromise debate in the Sixteenth Congress, Walker felt compelled to give a speech and talk for Buncombe County. Soon afterwards 'buncombe' came to mean speech-making to please constituents, or just plain bunk."]

Walker, Felix; Samuel R. Walker, ed. *Memoirs of the Late Hon. Felix Walker, of North Carolina,...from His Original Mansucript of Autobiography*. New Orleans: A. Taylor, Printer, 1877.

Walker Family

Griffin, Clarence W. *Revolutionary Service of Col. John Walker and Family; and, Memoirs of Hon. Felix Walker*. Forest City: The Forest City Courier, 1930. [John Walker (1728-1796); Felix Hampton Walker (1753-1828)]

Ward, Nancy,

[Note: For more on Nancy Ward, see the listings in our source guides on Georgia and South Carolina.]

Wilson, Emily Herring. "Nancy Ward: 'War Woman' of the Cherokees." *Tar Heel Junior Historian*, 33:2 (Spring 1994), 33:2 (Spring 1994), 2-4. [Online description from "North Carolina Periodicals Index," East Carolina University: "Nanye'hi, known to European settlers as Nancy Ward, was a 16th-century {*sic*; i. e. 18th-century} Cherokee woman known for her indomitable spirit and her good will toward the colonists. Nanye'hi, from the Cherokee town of Chota, was present at the Treaty of Hopewell in 1785."]

Washington, George, 1732-1799, and North Carolina

Claghorn, Charles Eugene. *Washington's Travels in the Carolinas & Georgia*. Cape Canaveral, Fla.: Pioneer Printing & Graphics, 1997.

Hoskins, Joseph A. "George Washington in Guilford." *North Carolina Booklet*, 19:3 (April 1920), 107-115.

Hubbard, Philip M. *Itinerary of George Washington during the War of the American Revolution*. Dayton, Ohio: [P. M. Hubbard?], ca. 2000-2002[?].

McPherson, Elizabeth Gregory. "Unpublished Letters from North Carolinians to Washington." *North Carolina Historical Review*, 12:2 (April 1935), 149-172. [Includes letters of Thomas Clark and Benjamin Hawkins.]

Stevens, John A. "Itinerary of General Washington, Commander-in-Chief of the Armies of the United States, 15 June 1775 to 23 December 1783." *Magazine of American History*, 3 (1879), 152-157.

Washington, George. "Gen. George Washington to Gov. Alex. Martin." *North Carolina Historical and Genealogical Register*, 2:4 (October 1901), 594-602. [June 14th, 1783]

Williams, Benjamin, 1751-1814

Lawrence, R. C. "Benjamin Williams, Soldier, Statesman." *The State: A Weekly Survey of North Carolina*, 13:19 (October 1945), 9, 23-24; online: http://digital.ncdcr.gov/cdm/ref/collection/p16062coll18/id/13782. [Online description from "North Carolina Periodicals Index," East Carolina University: "Benjamin Williams was four times Governor of North Carolina. He represented three counties in the Legislature, and he rendered valiant service as a solider during the Revolutionary War."]

Sadler, W. J. "Governors of North Carolina." *The State: A Weekly Survey of North Carolina*, 3:20 (October 1935), 6; online: http://digital.ncdcr.gov/cdm/ref/collection/p16062coll18/id/4551. [Online description from "North Carolina Periodicals Index," East Carolina University: "Benjamin Williams, who succeeded Governor William R. Davie, was Governor of North Carolina for three years. During his term the State Supreme Court and State Medical Society were established. He also gave considerable attention to agriculture and public education."]

Williams, John, 1731-1799

Williams, John. "John Williams Papers, 1772-1784." Manuscript PC.176 (MARS ID: 685; record group), State Archives of North Carolina, Raleigh. [Online catalog description: "Correspondence of Col. John Williams, Granville Co. lawyer, legislator, delegate to Continental Congress (1778-1779), judge, Revolutionary officer, and proprietor of the Transylvania Company. Letters concern family and business matters such as lawsuits and horse racing; suspension of the courts (1773); need for paymaster of troops (1777); the 1778 General Assembly; Tryon Co. loyalists; Transylvania Company's claim before the Virginia Assembly (1778); Williams's resignation from Congress; need to provide the Virginia-North Carolina Boundary Commission with militia protection against the Cherokee (1779); and the illegitimate daughter of Gen. Francis Nash. Among the correspondents are Robert Burton, Isaac Edwards, Richard Henderson, Robert Morris, Francis Nash, and William B. Smith."]

Williams, John. "Papers, 1775-1824." Manuscript, Small Manuscript Collections, Onsite, Sec. A Box 136 items 1-17, David M. Rubenstein Rare Book & Manuscript Library, Duke University, Durham. [Online catalog description: "North Carolina militia officer during the Revolution; from Granville County, N. C. Papers relating chiefly to land grants and land settlement, the Louisa and Transylvania land companies, supplies for the colonial army, Loyalists in North Carolina, and North Carolina politics and government during and after the Revolution. Correspondents and persons mentioned include Charles Bondfield, James Harrod, Nathaniel Henderson, Richard Henderson, James Hogg, William Hooper, William Johnston, James Luttrell, Abner Nash, John Penn, Bromfield Ridley, James Stephens, and John Williams, Jr."]

Williamson, Hugh, 1735-1819

Gilpatrick, Delbert Harold. "Comtemporary Opinion of Hugh Williamson." *North Carolina Historical Review*, 17:1 (January 1940), 26-36.

Hosack, David. *A Biographical Memoir of Hugh Williamson*. New York: E. Bliss and E. White, 1821.

"Hugh Williamson, 1735-1819." Reference Vertical File, State Library of North Carolina, Raleigh.

Lawrence, R. C. "Signers of the Constitution." *The State: A Weekly Survey of North Carolina*, 10:14 (September 1942) 26; online: http://digital.ncdcr.gov/cdm/ref/collection/p16062coll18/id/33190. [Online description from "North Carolina Periodicals Index," East Carolina University: "North Carolina can proudly claim three men who signed the Constitution – Hugh Williamson of Chowan, Richard Dobbs Spaight and William Blount of Craven County. Lawrence provides biographical information on them."]

Lawrence, R. C. "Some Colonial Physicians." The State: A Weekly Survey of North Carolina, 10:11 (August 1942), 3; online: http://digital.ncdcr.gov/cdm/ref/collection/p16062coll18/id/33095. [Online description from "North Carolina Periodicals Index," East Carolina University: "Physicians were in the North Carolina colony almost as early as there were preachers. John King practiced in Chowan as early as 1694, and Godfrey Spruill was practicing at Edenton as early as 1702. Lawrence lists other outstanding doctors, including one he considers the most famous, Dr. Hugh Williamson of Chowan, who was appointed Surgeon-General of the North Carolina troops by Governor Richard Caswell."]

Neal, John Washington. "Life and Public Services of Hugh Williamson." *Trinity College Historical Society Papers,* 13 (1919), 62-115.

Potts, Louis W. "Hugh Williamson: The Poor Man's Franklin and the National Domain." *North Carolina Historical Review*, 64:4 (October 1987), 371-393.

Sheldon, George F., and William C. Friday. *Hugh Williamson: Physician, Patriot, and Founding Father*. Amherst, N. Y.: Humanity Books, 2010. [1735-1819; signer of the Declaration of Independence; North Carolina]

Williamson, Hugh. "Hugh Williamson (1735-1819) Letters, 1778-1815." Manuscript, MfP.32, State Archives of North Carolina, Raleigh. [Online catalog description: "Letters to various correspondents from Williamson, physician, merchant, North Carolina delegate to the Continental Congress (1782-1785, 1787-1789) and Constitutional Convention (1787), and member of Congress (1789-1793). From Edenton Williamson wrote about trade and shipbuilding (1778); about Revolutionary pensions, commerce regulation, a money bill in Congress, and methods of conducting local elections (1786); and to Gov. Richard Caswell about cession of western lands by North Carolina (1785)."]

Williamson, Hugh. *The History of North Carolina.* 2 vols. Philadelphia: Thomas Dobson, 1812.

Wilson, Sarah, 1750-?

Hoxie, Elizabeth F. "Sarah Wilson [b.1750]." In Edward T. James, ed., *Notable American Women, 1607-1950: A Biographical Dictionary, vol. III: P-Z* (Cambridge: Belknap Press of Harvard University Press, 1971), 628. [con artist in Maryland, Virginia and North Carolina in the 1770s. Passed herself off as Princess Sophia Carolina Matilda, the queen's younger sister.]

Winston, Joseph, 1746-1815

Hendricks, J. Edwin. "Joseph Winston: North Carolina Jeffersonian." *North Carolina Historical Review*, 45:3 (July 1968), 284-297. [Online description from "North Carolina Periodicals Index," East Carolina University: "North Carolina native Joseph Winston, for whom Winston-Salem is named, was an important leader of the Revolutionary war and politician of early America. Thrice elected to Congress, Winston was a liberal humanitarian and a well-respected Jeffersonian who was against a standing military and for a limited government."]

Woodmason, Charles, c. 1720-1789

Osborne, Anne. "Charles Woodmason: Peripatetic Prelate of the Backwoods." *Newberry County Historical Society Bulletin*, 7:1 (December 1975), 19-29.

Woodmason, Charles; Richard J. Hooker, ed. *The Carolina Backcountry on the Eve of the Revolution: The Journal and Other Writings of Charles Woodmason, Anglican Itinerant.* Chapel Hill: University of North Carolina Press, 1953. [Contains Woodmason's observations on the residents of frontier areas of the Carolinas briefly mentioning business women, lewd women, American Indian women, widows, wives, and daughters.]

Yonaguska, ca. 1759-1839

Allhands, William A. "Some Noted Cherokees." *The State: A Weekly Survey of North Carolina*, 13:33 (January 1946), 11, 30; online: http://digital.ncdcr.gov/cdm/ref/collection/p16062coll18/id/14945. [Online description from "North Carolina Periodicals Index," East Carolina University: "Among the Cherokees whose memory is still being kept alive are Chuttahsotee, Yonaguska, Cornsilk, and Junaluska. Each was a great leader among their people."]

Parris, John A., Jr. "Big Chief Yonaguskah." *The State: A Weekly Survey of North Carolina*, 17:23 (November 1949), 10, 17; online: http://digital.ncdcr.gov/cdm/ref/collection/p16062coll18/id/24614. [Online description from "North Carolina Periodicals Index," East Carolina University: "Cherokee Chief Yonaguskah was responsible for what probably was the first prohibition pact ever to be signed in the United States."]

Walser, Richard. "Yonaguska, a Great Chieftan." *The State: A Weekly Survey of North Carolina*, 15:50 (May 1948), 6-7; online: http://digital.ncdcr.gov/cdm/ref/collection/p16062coll18/id/22277. [Online description from "North Carolina Periodicals Index," East Carolina University: "For many years the leader of the Eastern Cherokee tribe of Indians, Yonaguska was highly honored and widely acclaimed during his lifetime."]

Index

Please note that not every term that could be indexed has been. Users of this publication in the pdf version will be able to search the text within the pdf. Some purchasers may wish to have both versions to facilitate deeper searching of the contents. Terms such as "pension," "militia," "navy," etc., produce hundeds of results in an electronic search and their prolific appearance throughout the text precludes their full appearance in the index. The names of North Carolina and British government agencies appear throughout the text are are too numerous to index. They concentrate in the sections relating to governmental functions, land records, legislative petitions, military activities, and financial matters.

The table of contents leads to the major subject areas of the publication, and the index covers all personal and place names that appear throughout the book along with many subject terms. Remember than an index term can appear more than once on any given page.

D

G

M

O

T